HOOVER INSTITUTION PUBLICATIONS

# NATIONAL SECURITY

## Political, Military, and Economic Strategies in the Decade Ahead

# NATIONAL SECURITY
## Political, Military, and Economic Strategies in the Decade Ahead

*Edited by*

David M. Abshire *and* Richard V. Allen

*Introduction by*

Admiral Arleigh Burke, *Director*

THE CENTER FOR STRATEGIC STUDIES
GEORGETOWN UNIVERSITY

*Published for the*
HOOVER INSTITUTION ON WAR, REVOLUTION
AND PEACE
*by*
FREDERICK A. PRAEGER, *Publisher*
New York · London

Published in the United States of America in 1963 by

FREDERICK A. PRAEGER, *Publisher*

64 University Place, New York 3, N.Y., U.S.A.
49 Great Ormond Street, London W.C. 1, England

Library of Congress Catalog Card Number: 63-17834

Printed in the United States of America

# 66444

# Contents

## *Part I*
### SINO-SOVIET STRATEGY

## *Part II*
### POLITICAL REQUIREMENTS FOR U.S. STRATEGY

viii

## *Part III*
### U.S. MILITARY STRATEGIES

## *Part IV*
### U.S. ECONOMIC STRATEGIES

## *Part V*
### MEETING STRATEGY REQUIREMENTS
### IN THE FREE ECONOMY

# Introduction

The United States is the most powerful nation on earth. Strategy involves the use of that power in its full array, economic, military, political, cultural, social, moral, spiritual and psychological, to accomplish national objectives in the world. A strategy that neglects any element of national power, or declines to consider any reasonable opinion concerning it, is no strategy at all. It is, at best, a tactical exercise and, at worst, a patchwork of expediency which will quickly unravel under pressure. Nor is a stategy without objectives a real strategy. It is at best a holding action.

Thus, national power and national objectives are the irreducible elements of strategy. To understand and wisely marshal the one, and arrive at consensus on the other, is the purpose of strategic discussions. Having the power, we have the grave responsibility to pursue that purpose. We could not, if we wished, ignore the responsibility. Our position has imposed it upon us. We can fail the responsibility, of course. We cannot avoid it. This does not mean a call for some sort of American empire. It does mean a clear call for American leadership.

The people of the United States have demonstrated, more than any other nation in history, that we do not wish to impose control on any other peoples of the world. After World War II, the United States poured money, materials, ideas and equipment into countries which had been devastated by war—countries which had been our enemies as well as countries which had been our allies. Europe and free Asia, the countries of the Middle East, Latin America and Africa have more freedom, more prosperity, better health, because of the generosity of the United States. Even the USSR, whose avowed goal has been our destruction, has been benefitted greatly by the United States.

But no matter how generous the impulses of a nation, there is a limit on how much a nation can give of its substance, as the United States is learning now with its rapidly growing national debt, with its imbalance of payments, and with the ever growing competition facing our exports. Strategy demands a realistic view of these factors as part of the overall consideration. They cannot be put into a compartment labelled "economics" and isolated from the larger discussion. The welfare of the goose, in short, is of strategic concern to the man whose golden eggs are sustaining the neighborhood. It should be of as great concern to the neighbors, as a matter of fact.

In addition to its responsibility to assist other nations, the United States has the responsibility to protect its own freedom, and the freedom of other peoples, from the efforts of the Communists to destroy all freedom. Southeast Asia, Latin America, the Middle East are areas where now there is continuous danger of more people, more nations, being forced to submit to absolute Communist dictatorship as in Cuba.

There are differences of opinion among the various Communists in the world, but they do have a common overriding objective: to destroy all that we stand for. The USSR and Red China may be at each other's throats, but the grand strategic objective of each remains the same.

Change is the essence of history. But the trend of future events will not change in the direction we desire unless we do something about it. Time alone will not bring about a change in the methods and goals of international communism. We have within our power the capability of eroding communism, but it will not erode of itself. We must carefully avoid the assumption that trends we desire will take place without our influencing those trends. Communism has not yet reached a high water mark, and it will take more than one or two reverses for the Communists to renounce their stated goals and become non-Communists. At the present moment the Communists—both Soviet and Chinese—exude confidence in the historically inevitable triumph of their system and the downfall of ours. *Their* objectives are clear.

What, then, can be done? What are the objectives which the Free World, and the United States in particular, should try to achieve?

Most essential is a fundamental re-evaluation of our desired goals. It appears that there are three basic policy choices open to us:

First, we could retreat before Communist blackmail, making avoidance of confrontation our objective and leaving the Communists to rule the world. That alternative is unworthy of consideration.

A second choice is to attempt to "co-exist" with the Communists, declaring that our basic goal is to live in harmony with our fellow man. Although this is a laudable and worthy goal, it has a serious flaw: the Communists use the doctrine of "peaceful co-existence" as an offensive weapon to be utilized in the destruction of the West. "Peaceful coexistence" is to the Communists a strategem which has already begun to pay dividends.

A third policy choice is this: to take initiative toward the elimination of Communists from positions of power, thus causing the erosion of the Communist system. This would involve recognition that the existence of the Communist Party precludes the attainment of real peace, and recognition that, until the means of power have been taken out of the hands of the Communist Party, there will be no chance for a just and lasting peace.

It is well to be reminded that the third alternative does not call for the physical annihilation of the opponent; rather, it seeks to undermine, erode, and deteriorate his position of power—his whole system. It aims at having in power in Russia and China governments with legitimate, limited aims.

The strategy which the United States follows may be the most important element in determining the events of the future. In developing strategy, all aspects of the problems which confront a nation must be thoroughly examined. This requires that the best advocates of the various possible courses of action be heard. It is not enough to select one of just several theoretical courses of action. And, of course, the strategy cannot be formed at all until the objectives are decided.

A thorough understanding of the relationships among people is needed for any strategy to be implemented effectively. Relationships among nations must be clear, simple and uncomplicated. People in our own nation and those in other nations must have an unblurred understanding of what the United States stands for and what the United States wants to happen.

By our actions they will know us. A nation does not gain the confidence of another nation on demand. Nor does one nation have faith in the competence of another because the other loudly proclaims it.

A strong and cohesive Free World alliance depends on the demonstrated brainpower, manpower, machine power, and spiritual power of its individual signatories, and upon their willingness to commit those resources to the goals of the alliance.

The United States must take the lead in forming a strategic objective. From that point, the choices which will confront this nation also are enormous. Decisions which will affect all mankind and the future existence of the world will be made in our Capital. Wise choices involve the collation of the opinions of the best minds of the nation. It was to participate in that process that the Center for Strategic Studies held the Conference contained in this volume.

Arleigh Burke

# Acknowledgements

Any work of this size and scope requires the coordinated efforts of many people, and the editors would like to acknowledge their obligation not only to the contributors, who, through their wholehearted cooperation in reviewing their papers in the weeks following the Conference, permitted the early publication of the proceedings, but also to those who worked long and hard to make the actual production of this volume possible.

We would like to thank the staff of the Hoover Institution on War, Revolution, and Peace, and particularly Karl Hess, Consultant to the Institution's Publications Department, for invaluable advice and assistance.

Evelyn Pennebaker was helpful in assisting in many of the technical aspects of the Conference and the printing of the book. Mary Catherine McCarthy and Elizabeth Whitney were very helpful in giving their time to the project.

Diane Young, undergraduate assistant at the Center, and Betty Benswanger and Frances McGavin read the entire manuscript and offered helpful stylistic suggestions.

James H. McBride, Research Fellow at the Center, spent many hours in compiling the index. Assisting him in this undertaking was Dwight M. Keating, undergraduate assistant.

For criticism and suggestions we are particularly indebted to our colleagues, Henry W. Briefs, Karl H. Cerny, and Robert D. Crane, who read various parts of the manuscript and aided us with numerous and judicious comments.

We would like to extend a special acknowledgement to Jane Moretz and Susan Zimmerman, our Research Assistants at the Center for Strategic Studies, who gave unstintingly of their time, and without whose extraordinary labors at the time of the Conference and in the subsequent months this project would have been long delayed.

Our debt to John A. Patten III, Chief Editorial Assistant in this project, is great. Mr. Patten took upon himself the enormous burden of directing the printing of the volume and supervising all aspects of the assembly of the final manuscript.

D.M.A.
R.V.A.

# Preface To The Issues

## The Conference: Scope and Method

The Center for Strategic Studies was established in 1962 to study research on strategic problems confronting free societies. Clearly, there had been a serious lack of communication between those researching strategic and economic problems. To help provide a remedy, the Center sponsored the Conference, *National Security: The Demands of Strategy and Economics in the Decade Ahead*, from January 23-25, 1963.

While this Conference was basically an inquiry into the relation of strategic and economic issues, it also brought to the conference table specialists in international politics and science. As a result, the debate covered ground beyond the limits of strategy and economics as ordinarily conceived. The title of this book, therefore, is broader than that of the Conference.

Participants were assigned topics for study papers to be written and circulated among fellow participants prior to the Conference. Professional members of the Center staff analyzed these papers and drew from them key issues for the five panel discussions. Since the papers had been circulated in advance, the entire three days could be devoted to the discussion of key issues.

After the Conference, many participants updated or revised their papers, and these, along with the panel discussions, are contained in this volume.

The Conference was not intended to produce final judgments on the key strategy issues in the coming decade; rather, it was designed to generate a continuation of debate and research, a willingness to face unpleasant problems, and a clarification of the fundamental issues. This preface will attempt to focus the reader's attention on some 20 key issues of the Conference as reflected both in the papers and the panel discussions published in this volume.

## Part I: Sino-Soviet Strategy

Over the next ten years, the direction of Sino-Soviet strategy will be affected by four issues: polycentrism, economic constraints, erosion, and Sino-Soviet attitudes and capabilities regarding war as a policy instrument. The interplay of these issues, and the nature of our responses, could determine whether the developments of the Cold War will lead to: a) a showdown; b) a shift in favor of the East; c) a shift in favor of the West; d) protracted struggle; or e) settlement. Of significance is the consensus that the Communist goal or expectation of world domination is unchanged, and that the Communists are, as one participant put it, arguing as rival morticians over the best ways to bury us.

It should be noted that polycentrism and erosion are not synonymous, nor do they pose similar problems for US strategy-makers. A multi-centered communism does not necessarily reduce ideological vigor, while, by definition, erosion does.

*Polycentrism:* The most debated aspects of polycentrism are the nature, extent, and meaning of the "Sino-Soviet split." In fact, some participants argue that "bicentrism" is the real issue. Debate about the causes of the "split" includes varying interpretations: that the argument is over allocation of resources, with Peking objecting to the Soviet investment in Cuba and Indonesia instead of in Red China; that the "split" in some sense may reflect competing nationalistic aspirations; that it is really organizational, concerned with who will lead whom; and that the antagonism is actually "non-antagonistic," with one partner playing a peaceful, the other a war-like, role.

The fact that the Communists are debating real choices of resource allocation and of present versus future power indicates increasing strategic realism. It might portend a strategic flexibility, thereby opening for them more options and, as a result, complicating our own strategy problems in the next ten years. Local Communist Parties, for example, may come to be in a position to choose from among several policy courses as local or national political situations dictate.

*Economic Constraints on Strategy:* There is a basic conflict between short-run and long-run power needs on the one hand, and between consumer demands and power needs on the other. Whether such complications may constrain Soviet or Red Chinese aggressive strategy introduces questions concerning the possibilities of economic growth releasing any such constraint.

The relationship of the Red Chinese economic crisis to her aggressive strategy appears to be especially significant, for opinions are divided over whether such crises might increase or de-

crease her aggressiveness. A further complication may be introduced by the possibility that, even under conditions of temporary
nuclear stalemate between the two superpowers, Red China
would have greater freedom to pursue aggressive policies without fear of direct nuclear confrontation with the United States.

Red China's absolute inferiority, according to some of the contributors to this volume, may lead to overtures for a temporary
*détente* with the West, combined with a short-term estrangement
from the Bloc. Such a maneuver might be aimed at enticing
the West to aid China in overcoming pressing domestic economic
and social problems. In the long run, this could amount to Western reinforcement of a still aggressive Chinese regime.

*Erosion:* The issue involves two interpretations: one, that the
forces which cause erosion will be internal; the other that, for
modern totalitarian dictatorships, these forces initially must be
external.

Erosion is measured by a lessening of ideological vigor and
the gradual abandonment of aggressive objectives. Recognizing
that the Communist tide, after receding, has often returned with
greater intensity, how would we know *if* and *when* we were winning? Is there any real chance of winning through internal collapse of the Communist system, rather than through our own
initiative? What would produce an erosion of their objective to
destroy the West, and hence change their aggressive behavior?
Would the Communists conclude that they could no longer keep
pace with the West if confronted with an accomplished integration of US-European economic resources, or if militarily confronted with US technological supremacy?

Other significant aspects of the issue include succession in the
Communist camp, and the relationship of the armed forces to
the Communist Party.

*War Capabilities and Attitudes*\*: This issue involves primarily
the degree of risk of general nuclear war. The Soviet calculation
of this risk relates to their calculation of our resolve. If they

---

\* A subsequent publication by the Center for Strategic Studies presents
some of the arguments and conclusions of the leading American analysts
of Soviet strategy on the nature and extent of the strategy debate in the
Soviet Union and on the relation of Soviet strategy to Soviet military
capabilities. This volume is the result of panel discussions held during
the spring of 1963 by the Center's study group on Soviet military strategy,
and will be published in September, 1963, by Duell, Sloan and Pearce under
the title *Nuclear War and Soviet Strategy: A Critique of Recent Soviet
Doctrine,* edited by Robert Dickson Crane and W. Onacewicz.

calculate that that resolve is low, and if it is in fact low in a given crisis, they face low actual risk, although the risk may appear to be high.

Assume that communism begins to lose its ideological vigor, its expansionist *élan*, or its capability to deal with emerging problems, i.e., erosion sets in. Would this increase the likelihood of reckless gambles, and, hence, the possibility of war? Or have the Communists concluded that the consequences of war, at least nuclear war, would be disastrous for them?

Or assume that NATO power continues to expand, and that the unification of European and US strategic resources becomes a reality. Might the Soviet Union attempt either: (a) some sort of peace offensive or temporary accommodation with the West; (b) a psychological warfare campaign with a new space weapon; or (c) military action against the West? Would they, for example, test American resolve by threatening a disarming nuclear strike at Western Europe or by making a sudden conventional move against Berlin? For our NATO allies, what would be the consequences of any American indication of accommodation or *détente*?

Another aspect of this issue embraces the Soviet evaluation of technological breakthroughs in such areas as anti-missile development and biological warfare, and how dependent are those more aggressive aims upon rapid and significant progress in a particular aspect of weaponry.

## Part II: Political Requirements for US Strategy

Strategy must serve the political requirements of national policy. The United States has experienced two World Wars in which long range policy was not thought through, and the seeds were sown for more severe world conflicts. It is essential in the current protracted conflict that past mistakes not be repeated.

Although the subject of political objectives and the policy requirements for US strategy is virtually inexhaustible—with new "requirements" possible for every new contingency—three basic and recurrent issues have been selected: Over-all Cold-War Policy Objectives; Strategy Options in Areas of Indirect Confrontation; and Western Unity.

***Over-all Cold War Policy Objectives:*** Cold War objectives must be related to national purpose, a much-discussed but ever-important subject. Is our purpose to defend and extend our values throughout the world? If so, how do we decide on the techniques to achieve that goal? Do we in fact know what kind of world we want? And what kind of world we can get? What would constitute a termination of the Cold War—whether that termination be called "settlement" or "victory"?

The nature of our ultimate objectives vis-à-vis the Communist Bloc constitutes the paramount question of our national strategy. If, as some argue, the basic objective is described as the attainment of equilibrium with the Sino-Soviet powers, would such equilibrium simply be military, or political as well? Do those who hold equilibrium to be our goal believe it to be desirable, or just the best we can get under the circumstances?

Others hold that, were the United States to follow such a limited policy objective, particular dangers would be introduced in a confrontation with opponents possessing unlimited objectives. One position is that our objective should be to deprive the Communists of the means of power and to take the initiative to erode their system. Should they fall behind in the global confrontation because of vulnerabilities and mistakes, we should exploit these shortcomings rather than let them regain lost balance.

Pertinent policy questions include these: Is it possible to eject Communists from power, or to change their objectives and behavior? How can our strategy be designed to effect changes in political power in countries now under communism? How can one determine when and if the strategies of Soviet Russia and Red China have moved from unlimited to limited aims? What might be the consequences of a wrong assessment?

**Strategy Options in Areas of Indirect Confrontation:** To implement US goals, strategy options vary with each geographical area, with the particular character of the Communist power, and with elements of instability. In regard to Southeast Asia, three basic policy options are described—disengagement, containment, and roll-back. It is argued that containment, specifically in Southeast Asia, cannot be successful without a forward strategy of initiative strikes at sanctuary areas.

Relevant questions include: Would we or our Allies be the vehicle of such a strategy; would there be a real or imaginary risk of nuclear or general war; and would the basic strategic alternatives in Southeast Asia have applicability to other geographical areas, for example, in this Hemisphere?

Problems identified with the penetration of Latin American nations suggest a range of considerations. These include what the United States intends to do about communism in Latin America; what US actions would be necessitated by Communists fomenting "national revolution" in one or in several countries at once; whether the United States should employ air and sea supremacy to prohibit arms deliveries to Communists in Latin American countries; and what the strategic implication would be of depriving ourselves of the right of unilateral action in this Hemisphere.

In the Middle East, another area of indirect confrontation, there has emerged since 1955 the problem of a localized arms race which, if allowed to continue, could affect the behavior of the two major powers.

In Africa, developments may intensify the East-West confrontation and produce a general breakdown of public order in many newly independent states. The abandonment of the traditional criteria of recognition, it is argued by some, has increased this possibility. How would the Soviets capitalize on such political disintegration? What might be the consequence of a possible pan-African coalition against the Union of South Africa or Angola?

A satisfactory formula for using aid in support of, and not contrary to, our national interests is vital. Some hold that, unless aid is tied to a comprehensive strategy, it cannot truly be effective. There are, also, key political and economic interrelationships. What types of aid promote economies which destroy initiative, degrade individual dignity, and build values alien to our national purpose?

*Western Unity:* This issue attempts to separate appearances from realities. The key question is: Do we actually treat the European countries as true partners, or as satellites; and if as partners, just in economic matters where we need their support, or in nuclear matters where they need our support? This question has added relevance in such areas as our capability to produce a pooling of alliance R&D resources; in the achievement and maintenance of technological superiority; in our need for favorable trade arrangements with the Common Market; and in the management of our own balance-of-payments deficit. Obviously, it is perilous to treat such problems in isolation from other aspects of strategy.

Still another serious dilemma lies in possible conflicting interests between the European Community and the Atlantic Community. Might our efforts to push Atlantic Community wreck integration and splinter Europe? Is there a dangerous unwillingness to accept Europe as a full ally, thereby pushing her into a third force position? Are there problems which a United Europe might create for the United States? Or can the dilemma of European Community versus Atlantic Community be solved by the use of proper emphasis and timing? These and related issues receive considerable attention in a number of papers and in the discussion section of Part II.

## Part III: Military Strategy

Military strategy is concerned with deterring wars of all kinds, and with successfully fighting wars not deterred. But the role of military capabilities in the present conflict is not thus limited. In addition, military capability carries over into the area of political warfare, as the Soviets have demonstrated with nuclear blackmail tactics—even though their capabilities were inferior. Military capabilities also open options, especially in areas of advanced weaponry, for deception and stratagems. Superior military capability can offer a control over escalation, an advantage tantamount to holding the initiative. Finally, in the area of technology, the decisive battle may be won by attaining supreme offensive-defensive power-in-being, and by dominating the opponent's will without recourse to military action.

*Nuclear Weapons and the NATO Alliance:* Many participants feel that solution of the nuclear weapons question within the Alliance is fundamental to the solution of other political, economic, and scientific problems of the Alliance. Sharpened by the conflict between the US strategy of a centrally-controlled response and certain European national aspirations, this issue relates to estimates of: (a) the true state of the nuclear art; (b) European national capabilities of securing these weapons anyway; (c) the possibility that our efforts to prevent nuclear proliferation among our Allies will damage our relations with them and ultimately push them into "blocs."

Furthermore, the question is raised as to whether the need for central control of nuclear weapons in war necessitates central control in peace, to the extent of denying to an individual ally the capability of nuclear deterrence or limited retaliation. In short, within NATO, problems of deterring a war may not be the same as problems of fighting a war. To some extent this argument relates to another one: that the sea-based deterrent, even if workable, might still leave a gap in the deterrent spectrum by failing to insure an adequate response to a surprise Soviet land thrust in Europe.

The other side of the argument is the view that our present policies can succeed, that the present disarray in the Alliance is really the product of receding Soviet pressure on NATO, that mixed crews are workable, and that the present multilateral-force concept can satisfy European political needs and national aspirations.

***Future US Nuclear Strategies:*** This issue pivots on whether the future offers nuclear stalemate or decisive technological breakthroughs giving one side a true and maintainable supremacy. Questions are raised about the adequacy of our current efforts towards active and passive defense, especially since the most decisive breakthrough undoubtedly would be in the area of active defense.

Of concern are our future options on nuclear test bans, as well as comparisons of the nuclear technology of the United States with that of the USSR. Are we sufficiently ahead? Or are we in fact ahead? What effect would certain test-ban agreements have on the development of US missile defenses in the future? The present controlled response doctrine relies heavily on a counterforce capability. Will such capabilities deteriorate as missile forces become increasingly invulnerable? On the other hand, the question of invulnerability is raised, since it rests upon untested theories.

Theoretically, our future nuclear options can be categorized into emphasis on: (a) striking at what the enemy values, such as cities and industrial areas; (b) striking at the enemy forces; (c) limited strategic responses such as show of force, reprisals, constrained disarming attacks for purposes of bargaining, controlled responses with futuristic weapons; (d) or combinations of the three. At various levels of escalation, various options are possible either in deterrence or in defense. With increased control come increased options in both escalation and de-escalation.

Do we increase our options, our control, and our initiative by improving nuclear weapons and producing advanced and larger weapons? Will further development of advanced nuclear weapons help or hinder stability? And, lastly, how do we maintain the proper strategic mix in the decade ahead? These are core problems.

*Limited-War Strategies:* Central to this issue are the alternatives of dealing with the limited war problem through a strategy of attempted local superiority or through a strategy of calculated risks (including striking at sanctuary areas and limited strategic retaliation). One participant argues that the first alternative might concede the initiative to the Soviets.

This issue, discussed in several sections of this volume, also involves: alternatives of planning and organizing for limited nuclear war; the role of tactical nuclear weapons; the future possibilities of conventional limited wars; and the strategic decision of whether to limit war geographically, by choice of weapons, or by both.

Another unsettled problem relates to the way in which trends towards greater invulnerability or retaliatory capabilities might affect conventional force needs in the next ten years. Might there be a future strategic requirement for conventional or paramilitary forces to take the initiative in situations similar to the Hungarian uprising, or for counter-insurgency in Latin America, or for hitting at privileged sanctuaries?

*New Frontiers of Warfare:* Listed as an issue, this topic actually is an attempt to explore various non-traditional possibilities along such lines as paramilitary operations, space strategy, and arms bargaining. Questions that arise include: What are the possibilities of a military strategy in space, coupled with a communications-control network? Have we fully explored the psychological and political advantages accruing to a nation with superiority in space? Have we fully explored the potentialities of a maritime strategy and the uses of the oceans in the space age? What is the nature and what are the effects of the interaction between Soviet and US strategies and force postures? Are there possibilities of influencing Soviet behavior through the use of a large margin of technological superiority, even to the extent of persuading them that they cannot win, or that the costs and risks of any aggressive adventure outweigh the gain?

## Part IV: Economic Strategies

The United States possesses the greatest economic base for the pursuit of her strategies. Together, the United States and Western Europe can achieve enormous economic superiority over the Communist world. Yet history is filled with examples of superior nations and alliances succumbing to inferior ones because the latter were able to develop effective strategies to dis-

rupt the coordinated application of the superior resources. Unity
of effort is the first principle of strategy.

Two basic attitudes are taken regarding our economic power:
(a) that its development and application to our Cold War policy
objectives are now inevitable, because the forces of freedom are
so strong at this point in history; or (b) that such development
and application is dependent upon a strategy to marshal and
allocate those economic resources, in combination with other
aspects of power, to produce a favorable outcome of the Cold
War.

***Economics of Alliance:*** Fundamentally, this issue concerns
US partnership in, and leadership of, the marshalling of Allied
resources for the Cold War. The problem is not merely one of
the level of resource allocation to security and the distribution of
the burden among allies; it also is one of evaluating costs
relative to benefits.

These problems arise not only in regard to the over-all magnitude of the effort to provide for the contingencies of national
security; they also come up in regard to very specific questions
of resource utilization. Specific problems of allocation concern
both scientific and political aspects. Is cooperation lacking in
pooling European scientific talent? Assuming a strategy of technological superiority, how do we forge an alliance in Research
and Development? Is secrecy inhibiting the flow of strategic
information among the Allies? What is a "fair" distribution of
burdens?

Among Free World allies other than NATO, there are knotty
problems not only of evaluating costs in terms of benefits, but of
avoiding counter-productive programs. Have development-oriented aid programs, in contrast to alliance-oriented programs,
undercut alliance strategy by rewarding a policy of non- alliance?

***Aid, Trade, and Counter-Pressures vis-à-vis Communist Na-
tions:*** The topics considered under this issue include the utiliza-
of aid, trade, and embargoes as weapons in the conflict with
Communist nations. One argument is that we should trade with
satellite nations in order to influence them. The implication is
that the elimination of aid or trade would force them to integrate with, and adhere more completely to, the Soviet Union.
The opposing argument is that, historically, trade does not necessarily encourage peaceful relations, and that forcing the Satellites to disassociate from the Soviet Union could better be

accomplished by compelling them to suffer all the disadvantages of life under Soviet hegemony.

The position that economic warfare is ineffective, since it is not in itself a decisive Cold War instrument, is countered by the view that, in combination with other forms of power, economic warfare can exploit the inherent vulnerabilities of the Soviet Union, can be even more effective vis-à-vis underdeveloped nations, and could have prevented, for instance, the Cuban takeover. It is suggested that incentives and guidance might be offered to private efforts to assume a more active role in participating in a Cold War economic strategy, such as countering the Soviet oil offensive.*

***Aid and Trade with Underdeveloped Nations:*** Basically, the issue concerns ways to achieve stability, progress, and the development of a market economy in underdeveloped nations. It is argued that our fundamental economic strategy toward underdeveloped nations should aim at the improvement of real income, working conditions, and the dignity of the individual for the greatest number of people, and that policies which promote coercive forms of social and economic organization violate this objective. Concurrently, our strategy should encourage stable, responsible, non-Communist governments. The concrete problems that arise in this connection are serious and vexing. It is asserted, for example, that to introduce confiscation and to carve up productive land will make the country insecure for local and foreign private investment. The ultimate outcome may thus be political instability, with its concomitant opportunities for communism.

Two alternatives of aid strategy are: state-to-state transfer of capital, and private investment and loans. The participants who debate these alternatives strongly emphasize the latter in any strategic mix of the two. Questions are raised, however. One participant argues that, in the Middle East and North Africa, government investment of monies under public auspices has produced an improved infrastructure in terms of highways, public utilities, and educated manpower; and that these in turn have led to the emergence of a better climate for private investment.

---

* Economic warfare receives more detailed attention in sections other than that of the Part IV discussion formally devoted to it. The Center currently has in progress a special study on economic countermeasures.

*The Common Market: Ally or Third Force?* There is a divergence of economic interests that comes sharply into focus in Common Market relations not only with the United States, but also with the Outer Seven. The task of economic strategy is to maximize the community of interests. This issue involves a strategy: (a) to insure that the Free World does not shift from a free exchange of goods and services to the pitfalls of regionalism and protectionism; and (b) to insure continued progress towards integration and unity. In part, the success of our strategy depends upon the vigorous use of the Trade Expansion Act.

Interpretations differ over whether the remarkable economic progress in the Common Market area has been due primarily to the Market or to the sound economic policies pursued by France and Germany, for example. No one questions that the Market can have a most beneficial future effect. Some believe that the United States pushed too hard and too soon to get Britain into the EEC, and that the initial rebuff could produce strategic disunity, with French policies pushing the Market in the direction of protectionism.

Other questions are raised: Will there be a collision between the agricultural policies and interests of the United States and those of the Market? What should be done to foster the exchange of capital and patents, to induce the right kind of cooperation among corporations, and to promote the sharing of scientific know-how? What dangers are posed by cartel arrangements?

### Part V: Meeting Strategy Requirements in the Free Economy

In the decade ahead, strategic economic planning plainly demands allowances for a range of unexpected contingencies and a strong search for action to avoid adverse ones. Obviously, most important are requirements that the US economy be kept strong and viable, that allied confidence in our dollar be unshaken, that we not lose our freedom of strategic action through economic constraints, and that the economic potentials of the United States and the Free World be brought to bear on our Cold War objectives.

Strategy requirements pose questions of financing the cost, and insuring that the costs of strategy complexes on individual systems reflect maximum efficiency and savings. It goes without saying that the ability of industry to meet forward requirements will depend upon proper incentive and effective competition.

*Strategy Contingencies and Budget Requirements:* Specialists in the field of public finance have made budgetary forecasts for the next ten years, have identified possible competing demands between national security and non-national security spending, and have evaluated limited war contingencies. These specialists used somewhat different definitions of national security expenditures; they also disagreed as to the years selected for comparing defense and non-defense expenditures. A strong argument is made to show that, contrary to popular belief, non-defense expenditures tend to grow much more rapidly than outlays for defense. The contrary view is also presented.

Opinion is divided between those who feel that total effort is inadequate, and those who feel that total effort, while possibly adequate, needs reallocation within the national security area. A specific difficulty is in determining when investment in a given system or program has reached the point of diminishing returns, or is obsolete and should be terminated for that reason.

Opinions vary as to measures for financing additional contingencies. These may arise from a different strategic emphasis within a strategy complex, including a greater mix, greater efforts toward active and passive defense, and increased space expenditures. The character and extent of any such emphasis is, of course, determined not only by the over-all strategic objectives, but also by technology and cost-versus-effectiveness. Pro and con arguments over the financing of civil defense are presented, and attention is given to private initiative as well as tax incentives. Citing possible budgetary constraints or unnecessary increases in US defense expenditures, a strong case is made for a true pooling of Alliance resources to ease the burden on our budget.

Questions are raised as to whether state and local governments could bear a greater share of non-defense needs in the next decade and thus possibly help insure that an absolute priority is given to security requirements at the national level. No one doubts this country's basic ability to finance defense increases, or to meet unforeseen developments or additional requirements for cold- or limited-war contingencies.

*Economic and Budgetary Constraints on Strategy Contingencies:* This issue involves two considerations: (a) the total resources available over the future period under discussion (and this is, of course, influenced by economic growth) and the share of this total allocated to national security by means of the budgetary process; (b) the share allocated to national security and the

ability to change the input to meet any new strategy requirements.

If the aggregate of resources available is inadequate, we have
an economic constraint on strategy of the most fundamental kind.
If the share budgeted for national security cannot be changed so
as to satisfy new strategic requirements, there is an additional
economic constraint. Another type of economic constraint is
that of the balance of payments difficulties, which poses a constraint on our forward strategy today.

In regard to budgetary constraints, the totalitarian society
clearly has a marked advantage in its ability to compress the
share of total resources allocated to the non-defense area, and
to give absolute priority to resource allocation to meet strategy
requirements. Opinions are divided over the identification of
possible economic and budgetary constraints our strategists will
face. Other questions occur: Do the more politically appealing
non-defense programs actually place a budgetary constraint
upon defense programs? How do we insure adequate priority
being given a strategy to accomplish policy objectives in a free
society? What policies can insure that increased defense
spending is properly financed?

Quite apart from these over-all limitations, economic scarcity
may also exercise a very specific restriction on our strategic
capabilities. Obviously, certain strategy complexes presuppose
the availability of highly specialized resources, both human and
material. By definition, these cannot be increased on short
notice. A more precise delineation of defense strategy complexes
could be extended to the problem of changing the quantities of
these very special resources, taking into account the demands of
timing.

*Strategy Contingencies and Over-All Economic Policy:* One
position taken on this issue is that the over-all objectives of economic policy should be a high rate of growth, a high level of
employment, and price stability—and it is argued that these three
goals can be achieved simultaneously. In this way, the contribution which our economy can make toward increasing the nation's
strategic capabilities would be maximized. Pro and con positions
emerge over the question as to whether or not some slack in the
economy would tend to favor a US capability to meet emergency
strategy needs.

The issue involves other contingencies: What will be the consequences for defense programs and for our foreign trade if
wages rise faster than the annual increase of labor produc-

# Part I

# Sino-Soviet Strategy

# Soviet Strategy—1962-1970

—*ROBERT STRAUSZ-HUPÉ*

## Summary

There is no reason to assume that the Communists will discard the strategies and implementing techniques which, during the last decades, have proven so rewarding. The Communists have suffered many reverses. Perhaps the most spectacular defeat of a Communist power gambit has been administered by the United States in Cuba. Characteristically, every Communist power gambit is governed, in the last resort, by a military calculation. In Cuba the Communists were quick to recognize the military error, and, as they have always done, covered their military retreat by a prompt shift to diplomatic negotiations and psychological diversion. No doubt, the Communist withdrawal from Cuba was fraught with implication pleasing for the United States and displeasing for the Soviets. A Soviet move was checked; the image of Soviet might has shrunk; and many widely held apprehensions about the true strength of the United States and the mettle of its people have been allayed. Yet, it is far too early to claim, as did some of our most widely known commentators, that the Soviet withdrawal from Cuba marks a "watershed" in the history of US-Soviet relations. Ever since Brest-Litovsk the Soviets have withdrawn from many an exposed position— only to regroup and to advance again. Mao Tse-tung, in his On Protracted War, had interesting things to say on the strategy of withdrawal. His observations are as pertinent today as they were when he composed his tract on how to turn weakness into strength and wrest victory from defeat.

The Communists seek to attain decisive military superiority over the Western Powers and, until they have achieved this

*overarching purpose, to weaken the West by political-psycho-
logical warfare operations. The intermediate purpose of Communist strategy is to exacerbate divisions among the Western
countries in order to forestall the consolidation of the West's
superior resources. Although the Communists, as long as they
have not assured their military superiority, will rely chiefly on
political-psychological strategies, they aim ultimately at imposing their will by military means—preferably by the mere threat
to use them, but if the West refuses to surrender, by using them
in combat.*

*The West's determination to achieve unity introduces the
most important single imponderable into Soviet strategic calculations. In the past, divergencies within the Western Alliance
enhanced the leverage of Soviet strategy. As a matter of fact,
the quintessence of Soviet strategy has been to exacerbate Western divisions and to break up NATO and, more recently, the
European Common Market. Soviet insistence on the scrapping
of the US base system and the withdrawal of US nuclear weapons from Western Europe and Turkey is designed not only to
bring about an alteration of the military balance of power but
also to abort the closer integration of the NATO Alliance. This
has been all along the meaning of the Soviets' Berlin gambit.
This purpose, among others, no doubt, also prompted the Soviet
challenge in Cuba. To the extent that the Western Powers continue and accelerate the development of common political institutions and strengthen their common defenses, to that extent
Soviet strategy will meet with increasingly formidable and,
ultimately, insurmountable obstacles.*

---

In this age of rapid historic acceleration, ten years is a long
time. A forecast of the direction of Sino-Soviet strategy thus is
a perilous undertaking. Though in international politics the
only constant factor has always been the unexpected, the certainty of uncertainty is now being heightened by the rapidity of
technological change. Yet to govern is to foresee, and the making
of foreign policy implies necessarily a gamble on probabilities.
The direction which Soviet strategy will take can be discerned
from what the Communists have said and done in the past and
from an estimate of the general world situation—the general
historical environment, so to speak, within which the Communists as well as the rest of us must live.

The Communists rightly stress that correct theory is the prerequisite of correct action. In practice, proficiency in theory is the prerequisite of membership in the Communist Party, and it is the dictum of party leadership, not free inquiry, which determines what is correct theory. In the Communist Party, dogma and discipline are inseparable from one another. The Communists, like all doctrinaires, insist upon ideological conformity. Since ideological conformity is indispensable to the operation of a far-flung and complicated political apparatus, Communist leadership, must, willy-nilly, supply concise ideological directives. Secrecy is the first requirement of a conspiratorial apparatus. Yet, it is the fullest disclosure of doctrinal directives that insures the coordination of conspiratorial operations. This circumstance suggests a profound dilemma. The Communists, try as they may, cannot resolve this contradiction. They are caught in the pincers of the two opposing needs for operational secrecy on the one hand, and doctrinal disclosure on the other. The obtuseness of their opponents has been a great comfort to Communist leadership. It seems as though, for the last forty-odd years, the leaders of the Western democracies have done their level best to ignore Communist doctrine and to take their cue solely from the latest twists and turns of Soviet diplomacy, if not from their own wishful preconceptions.

**Communist Doctrine**

Again and again, the West, searching for a meaning of Communist conduct has fallen into a trap of its own making, namely the rationalist interpretation of stated Communist doctrine. The Communists' belief in their inevitable victory over capitalism is irrational. It is a quasi-religious belief notwithstanding the fact that it is couched in the rational form of Marxist-Leninist theory. Incidentally, it is the irrational, messianic core of Communist doctrine which endows it with far greater attraction, especially for backward peoples, than the allegedly scientific theories of historical materialism. Premier Khrushchev, speaking in May 1961 in Tiflis, said: "Victory is ours, for it is the meaning of history that we shall be victorious and that other peoples will follow the road we traced." When Khrushchev speaks of inevitable victory, he does so neither on the basis of economic analysis, nor for propaganda purposes. Like every trained Marxist, he is convinced of the inexorableness of the historical process. The West can make no graver error than to assume that Communist leaders speaking *ex cathedra* do not mean what they say, and, like Western leaders, are willing to accept a "reasonable" compromise between ideal and reality. Nor does psychological analysis help us to probe the inwardness of Communist purposes. Communist purpose is exactly what Communist avow it is. Today there is no better way for discerning Soviet strategic purpose than to take Premier Khrushchev at his word.

Premier Khrushchev's speech of January 6, 1961, delivered to a meeting of the Party organizations in the Higher Party School, the Academy of Social Sciences, and the Institute of Marxism-Leninism of the Central Committee of the Communist Party of the Soviet Union, belongs to that species of policy documents in which Communist leadership discloses from time to time its interpretation of Marxist-Leninist dogma and sets forth the long-range objectives of Communist policy. First, Premier Khrushchev referred specifically to the proletarian revolution and the dictatorship of the proletariat, thus reaffirming the central dogmas of Marxist orthodoxy. Then, he assigned specific objectives first, to the working class, namely to carry out revolution and rebuff imperialist reaction; secondly, to the nationalist independence movements (which, for all practical purposes, the Communists consider as part of the world Communist system), namely to overthrow Western and Western-oriented regimes in the underdeveloped countries and to draw these new countries into the Soviet system; and thirdly, to international pacifism, namely to support the strategy of "peaceful coexistence" and thus to blunt the West's resolution to stand up to Soviet pressures. These objectives are joined together in world-wide political warfare. Premier Khrushchev said: "We can be proud of the fact that the peoples' notions of peace and communism are all the more being identified as a single unit." Stefan Possony, in his analysis of the Khrushchev speech submitted to the United States Senate, concludes: "In fact, in Communist parlance, total peace is a synonym for communism. But the peace slogan and disarmament policies are being used as part of Soviet strategy to win the struggle against the United States and its allies."

Premier Khrushchev then proceeded to enumerate the basic undertakings of Soviet strategy, namely the advancement of the economic power of the Soviet Bloc, especially the increasing growth of industry in the Bloc countries and the perfection of Soviet technology. Premier Khrushchev said ". . . the primary task of Socialist countries is to exploit possibilities inherent in socialism to outstrip, as soon as possible, the world capitalist system in absolute volume of industrial and agricultural production and then to overtake the most developed capitalist countries in per capita production and living standards. . . . To win time in the economic contest with capitalism is now the main thing. The quicker we increase economic construction, the stronger we are economically and politically, the greater will be the influence of the Socialist camp on historical development, on the destiny of the world." Premier Khrushchev confided to his hearers that he relied upon Western disunity as one of the factors easing the accomplishment of the Communist strategic tasks. He said: ". . . the capitalist world is not divided into two imperialist camps, as it was on the eve of both world wars. Nevertheless, it is far from united and is divided by a cruel internal struggle."

Perhaps the most revealing passages in Premier Khrushchev's speech are those devoted to the redefinition of war as an instrument of the Communist revolution. Premier Khrushchev pointed out that war is not a necessary condition for Communist successes; for the class struggle issues in proletarian revolutions, and proletarian revolutions suffice to overthrow capitalism. On the face of it, this is a modification of classic Communist doctrine. Didactically, Premier Khrushchev admonished his readers to distinguish between various kinds of war: "In modern conditions the following categories of wars should be distinguished: world wars, local wars, liberation wars, and popular uprisings. This is necessary to work out the correct tactics with regard to these wars." The capitalist states cannot hope to win a general war since "capitalism would be wiped out." The might of the "Socialist camp" will deter the capitalist states from unleashing a general war—a general war which they would be doomed to lose. Premier Khrushchev concluded: "The present balance of power in the world arena enables the Socialist camp and other peace-loving forces to pursue the completely realistic task of compelling the imperialists, under the threat of the downfall of their system, not to unleash a world war." Local wars, too, can be thwarted and controlled by Communist powers, "for a small imperialist war, regardless of which imperialist begins it, may grow into a world thermonuclear rocket war." If the Communists are strong enough to deter the "imperialists" from general and local wars, i.e., can immobilize Western power through nuclear blackmail and pacifist propaganda, they feel also strong enough to wage all kinds of conflicts which weaken the West without endangering the security of their own base. Premier Khrushchev said: "A liberation war of a people for its independence is a sacred war. We recognize such wars, we help and will help the peoples striving for their independence." Further on in his speech, Premier Khrushchev expanded on this theme: "Liberation wars will continue to exist as long as imperialism exists, as long as colonialism exists. There are revolutionary wars. Such wars are not only admissible but inevitable, since the colonialists do not grant independence voluntarily. Therefore, the peoples can attain their freedom and independence only by struggle, including armed struggle."

Premier Khrushchev's speech touched on many topics, and no brief summary can do full justice to his wide ranging statement. Yet, the above quotations contain the gist of Communist strategy for the foreseeable future. The theme which provides the red thread of continuity of Premier Khrushchev's digressions is the blunt affirmation of Communist superiority in military power. The balance of power has changed and now favors the "Socialist camp." This fact endows Communist strategy with unprecedented maneuverability. The Communists can now choose freely the most suitable conflict techniques and the most favorable battlegrounds. Wars of "national liberation" constitute a most elastic category of conflict. This category of war includes virtually every kind of military and paramilitary conflict below the threshold of general war, such as guerrilla warfare, terrorism, sabotage, and mob violence.

Premier Khrushchev left neither his hearers nor the world-in-general in doubt that the Soviet Union feels free to intervene in any and all conflicts of this kind. Last, but not least, it is the Communists themselves who arrogate to themselves the right to define what is and is not a "national liberation war." It goes without saying that a rising *within* the Communist Bloc would not be dignified with the label "national liberation war," but would be denounced as "capitalist imperialist intervention." The Communists will not settle for anything short of a defense-less West, helpless to stem the tide of "national liberation wars." Premier Khrushchev stated bluntly: "We set ourselves the task of exposing the aggressive essence of all military-political alignments of the imperialists like NATO, SEATO, and CENTO, of seeking their isolation and ultimate liquidation." These are absolute goals. Their avowal does clarify the meaning of "peaceful coexistence."

If Premier Khrushchev provided the panoramic view of Soviet strategy, it was left to Marshal Malinovsky to supply the technical specifics. Marshal Malinovsky, addressing the 22nd Congress of the Soviet Communist Party, said: "Our country is big and vast. It is less vulnerable than the capitalist countries, but we are fully aware that it would be an exceptionally difficult war for us. We are firmly convinced that in such a war, should the imperialists thrust it on us, the socialist camp would prove victorious, whereas capitalism would be destroyed forever." Marshal Malinovsky's speech, like that of his master, needs to be read line by line to savor the full flavor of that sense of power which permeates all recent Soviet statements of high policy. To be sure, these statements are marred by a brutish boastfulness to which no democratic statesman would care to descend. Yet Communist self-confidence is genuine. It is based upon the remarkable Soviet achievements in the last fifteen years' military-technological race and the apparent inability of the Free World as a whole to join its resources in a resolute bid for military-technological supremacy.

## Underlying Assumptions

We can now assemble the assumptions which underlie Soviet strategy for the next ten years. Western power—specifically, United States power—is immobilized by the threat of nuclear war on the one hand and by internal divisions on the other hand. The gradual erosion of the Western Alliance systems must issue in the military and political isolation of the United States. The Alliance systems will be brought to fall in part by their inherent military inadequacies which are due to lagging technological progress and insufficient military budgets, and by an all-pervasive erosion of Western morale by defeatism, unilateralism, and a general crisis of confidence in the effectiveness of collective defense. The process of dissolution within the Western Alliance systems will be hastened by ubiquitous disturbances throughout the Free World such as uprisings throughout Latin America, Africa, and Asia; the loss of the West's investments in the so-called uncommitted world; and the shrinkage of the Free World market. The principal target is the United States which, so the Communists anticipate, will lose its allies, its sources of raw materials, its investments, and its markets. On the face of it, there is nothing novel in this view.

These have always been the Communist objectives and, as regards basic principles and transcendent aims, Premier Khrushchev has not deviated significantly from his predecessors. The
principal difference lies in a heightened confidence and acceleration of pace. Whereas Stalin talked in terms of forty, fifty, or
sixty years when he exhorted his followers to catch up with
and outdo the United States, Premier Khrushchev now envisages
his strategic tasks with unprecedented immediacy: the Western
Powers are cowed; the battle is all but won. More likely than
not, Premier Khrushchev, in order to impress his audience and
world opinion, affected a far more sanguine stance than real
power relations warrant. Yet his words glow with happy anticipation. His sense of power is shared by the entire Soviet elite,
civilian and military, and by all the leaders of the Communist
World Party. In this respect, the tenor of Soviet discussions
differs significantly from that of the Western controversy on
war and peace.

Marxists, like all didacts and ideologues, are compulsive
talkers. Premier Khrushchev and Marshal Malinovsky set forth
in minute detail the strategic design. How does the Soviet
long-range strategy stack up in the light of Soviet performance?

Ever since the Korean military confrontation, Soviet conduct
has been characterized by challenges below those that might
trigger a general nuclear war and, for that matter, below thresholds of limited war that might escalate into general war. The
basic characteristic of this strategy has been supplied by General
David Sarnoff who called it the "nibbling process." Soviet
strategy has been supported by a mix of politico-psychological,
paramilitary, and proxy conflict techniques. It is by virtue of
the adroit application of these techniques that, throughout the
last fifteen years, the Communists have retained the initiative.
Despite many verbal reaffirmations of the determination to
abjure "reactive" policies and seize the initiative, emanating
from our highest political quarters, the Communists have gained
ground whereas the Free World has become the "war zone"
in which the Communist-Free World conflict is being fought out.

Since the end of the Korean War, the Western territorial
holdings have shrunk; the Communists launched a series of
forays into the Free World; and the West failed to mount one
single successful incursion into the Communist Bloc. The best
that can be said about the Korean War is that it resulted in a
military draw. Subsequently, most of Southeast Asia has fallen
under the domination of the Communists or their proxies. East

Berlin has been sealed off, and thus the inter-Allied agreement on Berlin has been breached unilaterally by the Communists. Not the position of the Communists in East Berlin but the access rights to West Berlin of the Western Allies became the subject of East-West negotiations. The Soviets have become a party to the affairs of the Western Hemisphere and, at the moment of this writing, stand in Cuba. In 1952, the Communists did not participate overtly in the affairs of Africa; they do so now. Communist military and economic assistance now reaches deep into Africa, Indonesia, and Afghanistan. In spite of their fluctuating relations with individual Arab regimes, the Communists exercise today far greater influence in the Middle East than they did ten years ago. During the last ten years, the Communists have made tremendous strides in the military-technological race. Although the Western Powers may still hold a margin of superiority over Soviet military-technological power, that margin is a good deal narrower than it was ten years ago. On balance, the Communist World Party has gained in strength. Although its following in certain Western countries may have decreased, the membership of the various Communist Parties and related organizations throughout Africa, Asia, and Latin America has grown considerably. Perhaps more important still, the losses sustained by the Communist Parties throughout the West have been made up by the growth of diverse pacifist, unilateralist, and "third force" movements, with or without overt affiliation with the Communist movement.

Of course, the Western Powers have not stood still in their development of military-technological capabilities. The economic resurgence of Western Europe provides the basis upon which additional military-technological capabilities could be created. In the field of nucleonics, American inventiveness and enterprise have scored advances which preserved, if they have not enhanced, the credibility of American deterrent power. Power, however, is not an absolute. The power of one state or group of states can be assessed meaningfully only in relation to the power of another state or group of states. Furthermore, the balance sheet cannot be drawn up by juxtaposing capabilities on hand. Actual gains and losses of strategic positions must be entered. In the last analysis, Soviet capabilities must be assessed in the light not only of concrete power resources but also of the gains that have accrued to the Soviets by virtue of the political and psychological exploitation of their military-technological and economic assets. If the Soviets dispose of smaller military-technological and economic capabilities than we do, but derive a much higher political return than do we, then the Soviets are likely to attain both absolute and relative superiority. The world balance sheet does not, to say the least, reflect an improvement of the Western position.

The advances made by the Soviets have been achieved with a remarkable economy of means. The Soviet share in world trade—less than four per cent in 1961—and Soviet allocations to foreign military and economic assistance are mere fractions of the United States' outlay for the same purposes. Yet the enormous expenditures of the United States notwithstanding, the relatively paltry but highly selective effort of the Soviets in several segments of the global contest have paid off in the shape of several neutralist governments committed, more or less forthrightly, to anti-Western policies. More important still, Communist trade strategies have been successful in disrupting Free World commodity markets, particularly the market in petroleum products, and in obtaining, despite Allied agreements to restrict strategic exports to the Communist Bloc, all kinds of highly sophisticated Western technological goods.

True enough, throughout the world, many adverse forces other than those marshalled by Communist conflict strategy impinge upon the Western position. The Western strategy has been to contain Communist aggression and to smother the many conflicts that cleave the Free World. The strategy of the Communists has been to break through the lines of Western containment, to foment conflict throughout the Free World, and to aggravate those conflicts, especially conflicts between the Western Powers and the so-called emerging nations, that originated in the pre-Communist past. In a revolutionary age, the odds always favor the revolutionary power over the status-quo power—at least as long as the status-quo power does not itself organize the revolutionary forces on the loose throughout the world and goes over to the offensive.

There is no reason to assume that the Communists will discard the strategies and implementing conflict techniques which, during the last ten years, have proven so rewarding. It is probable that the Communists, during the next ten years, will employ exactly the same strategies and conflict techniques which they tested so successfully in the past. Premier Khrushchev's January 6, 1961, speech is thus a variation on an old theme: below the threshold of general war, the Communists have found the response of the West to a variety of their challenges either uncertain or altogether absent. The West has still to come up with a coherent and comprehensive answer to the Communist nibbling process. Although the Communists must be expected to adhere to their tried and tested strategies, they will, in all likelihood, develop new ones that will be commensurate with their increased capabilities. Specifically, their penetration into space opens new vistas: an intercontinental nuclear stalemate heightens the attractiveness of a war of attrition in space. Conceivably, victory in such a spatial contest could either break the intercontinental nuclear stalemate or nullify psychologically, if not materially, its strategic significance.

In brief, the Communists seek to attain decisive military superiority over the Western Powers and, until they have achieved this overarching purpose, to weaken the West by political-psychological warfare operations. The intermediate purpose of Communist strategy is to exacerbate divisions among the Western countries in order to forestall the consolidation of the West's superior resources. Although the Communists, as long as they have not assured their military superiority, will rely chiefly on political-psychological strategies, they aim ultimately at imposing their will by military means—preferably by the mere threat to use them, but if the West refused to surrender, by using them in combat.

Even the best-laid plans are but a rough gamble on future and mostly unforeseeable historical developments. On the whole, the record of the Communists' prescience is impressive. For a long time, the Communists have navigated skillfully the currents of historical change. Aware of the revolutionary nature of the age, they have managed to bend the revolutionary forces on the loose everywhere to their purpose. There is, however, reason to believe that they will encounter mounting obstacles on the path towards their avowed goals. For one, their fabulous success has alerted their opponents. Secondly, it is easier to conquer a large empire than to hold it together for any length of time. Thirdly, not a few of the causes which the Communists supported for opportunistic rather than for ideological reasons have won out—and stand no longer in need of Communist support.

Historically, democracies have been slow to respond to external threats. Yet, once aroused, democracies have shown themselves capable of far greater efforts than their totalitarian enemies, bemused by their own ideological preconceptions, thought possible. The Communists themselves instructed, in part by their actions and in part by the voluble disclosure of their intentions, the Western publics in the lore of Communist strategy. Communist expansion in Eastern Europe, culminating in the subversion of Czechoslovak democracy, triggered a vigorous Western response, namely the creation of NATO. The attack on South Korea reversed the calamitous decline of United States preparedness and provoked the United States into a rapid expansion of defense budgets. The Communist conquest of China and the Red Chinese bellicosity, far from cowing the United States into jettisoning its Far Eastern commitments and bestowing diplomatic recognition upon Red China, induced the United States to strengthen its positions and its allies along the rim of East Asia. Perhaps the greatest single obstacle, next to the US nuclear deterrent, to Communist expansion is the rising economic power of Western Europe as a whole and, especially, the ever closer economic integration of the major European industrial countries.

The very prosperity of Western Europe exposes the fallacy of Marxist dogma. The European refutation of Marxist economics is all the more grievous for the Communists because the Communist system, for all its military-technological achievements, has failed spectacularly to improve average standards of living within its own borders. While the peoples of Western Europe are rapidly approximating their standards of living to those of the United States, the Communist Bloc is plagued by chronic food shortages. There is good reason to believe that, despite tight censorship, the masses throughout the Communist Bloc are becoming increasingly aware of how drab is their existence compared with life in the so-called capitalist countries. Furthermore, it is not unlikely that Communist peace propaganda, beamed principally at the Western publics, has boomeranged at the Communists themselves and strengthened the latent pacifism of the war-weary and overtaxed Russian peoples. Perhaps more important still, the very success of Communist imperialism has created a number of vested interests that are at odds with one another. To be sure, the rulers of the Satellite empire, being Communists, are agreed upon an ultimate end, namely the world-wide victory of communism. Yet their views on tactical procedure vary, and each Satellite regime is, by necessity, divided between its stake in the world-wide Communist movement and its local interests. The old story of the conflict between the supreme ruler and his satraps, familiar to the students of the Alexandrine and the Roman Empires, has come to life again in the Communist Bloc.

The Communist alliance with various nationalist movements,

though a brazen deviation from Marxist teachings, has paid off handsomely. Communist-supported nationalist movements in Asia and Africa have culminated in the virtual ejection of Western power from most of Southeast and South Asia as well as the Middle East, all of Africa north of the Sahara and most of Africa south of the Sahara. Yet not a few of the rulers of the so-called emergent nations, having squeezed the last ounce of advantage from Communist support are now reappraising their own position as well as the world balance of power as a whole. Though one or two swallows should not be mistaken for heralding the coming of spring, the peregrinations in a westerly direction of Nehru and several African leaders point to novel trends in Asian and African political thought. The firming up of the Western position in general and the US posture in particular is likely to reinforce tendencies which, though they should not be taken for sudden conversions to the Western view, diminish Communist influence among the "uncommitted" and thus are conducive to political stability. In the last resort, the Western Powers must rely upon their own strength to combat communism. The so-called emergent nations have little to contribute *positively* to the Western Alliance. Yet their political stability and the subsidence of the revolutionary ferment throughout the underdeveloped world accrue to the benefit of the Western Alliance. To that extent, the danger of a two-front conflict, namely, one conflict with Soviet imperialism and another conflict with Afro-Asian nationalism, is receding. Of course, that danger will be with us for a long time, but, at present, the rapid devolution of Western colonialism, the brute assertion of Chinese power, and the growing unity of the Western peoples seem to have had a sobering effect upon Afro-Asian leadership. In brief, the centrifugal forces that threatened to tear the West apart, especially as regards the issue of colonialism, and to set Afro-Asian nationalists against the West as a whole, are now impinging upon the Communist system itself.

**Western Unity**

At the heart of the struggle between the Western Powers and the Communist Bloc is still the military-technological race. Yet the remarkable achievements of the Communists appear to have engendered a dialectic reaction which tends to cancel out whatever lead the Communists may have gained. The progressive integration of Western Europe and the drawing together of Western Europe and North America into a wider Atlantic Community are likely to issue into the consolidation of the immense scientific, technological resources of the Atlantic Community. There is no reason to assume that a united Europe cannot create far larger military-technological resources than individual West European states now make available separately to the Atlantic Alliance. Certainly, a United States-West European partnership could develop, without stinting the consumer sector, the technologies of nucleonics and space at a more rapid rate than can the Soviets—provided the partners are really willing to pool their knowledge and hardware rather than adhere, especially in the field of nuclear weaponry, to an outdated code of secrecy or pursue the will-of-the-wisp of total disarmament.

Thus, the West's determination to achieve unity introduces the most important single imponderable into Soviet strategic calculations. In the past, divergencies within the Western Alliance enhanced the leverage of Soviet strategy. As a matter of fact, the quintessence of Soviet strategy has been to exacerbate Western divisions and to break up NATO and, more recently, the European Common Market. Soviet insistence on the scrapping of the US base system and the withdrawal of US nuclear weapons from Western Europe and Turkey is designed not only to bring about an alteration of the military balance of power but also to abort the closer integration of the NATO Alliance. This has been all along the meaning of the Soviets' Berlin gambit. This purpose, among others, no doubt, also prompted the Soviet challenge in Cuba. To the extent that the Western Powers continue to accelerate the development of common political institutions and strengthen their common defenses, to that extent Soviet strategy will meet with increasingly formidable and, ultimately, insurmountable obstacles.

The divergencies within the NATO Alliance on nuclear strategy and nuclear sharing, which erupted in the controversy over the Skybolt and the French *force de frappe*, as well as the suspension in January 1963 of the negotiations over Britain's application to the Common Market, seem to put in doubt the cohesiveness of the Western Alliance and the potentiality of its federative growth. Only the Soviet Union can profit from the quarrels of the NATO partners with one another. So obvious are the advantages which accrue to Soviet policy from conflicts within the Alliance and, especially, from the vacillations of its leading member, that a serious rupture of the Alliance seems inconceivable and hence the reaffirmation of American leadership mandatory. Therefore, we must expect that NATO will surmount the crisis into which it had been plunged by the obsolescence of its strategies conceived when the US still held the monopoly of nuclear weapons. It is likely that the NATO Allies will arrive at an agreement on nuclear sharing and a common nuclear strategy. Similarly, the gains from a broadening Atlantic market outweigh the short-range economic stake of individual Western states in protective and restrictive policies. Perhaps the most perilous shortcoming of Western defense is the absence of an adequate organization for the conduct of political warfare —a political warfare general staff and high command. The greater grows the military and economic strength of the Western Alliance, the more must the Communists depend for the implementation of their strategy upon techniques of political and psychological warfare. It should be the purpose of Western statesmanship to seal off the gap which renders the West vulnerable to Communist political-psychological warfare, and to develop the strategy and means for turning the tables on the Communist conflict managers.

Although the Communists have scored vast successes, they have suffered many reverses. Yet, again and again, they have given ground only to redeploy their forces and to resume the offensive. The mole-like patience of the Communists has not been matched by the commensurate perseverance of their opponents. The attention span of Western statesmen and publics has been short. Rebuffed by Western strength, the Communists have nearly always managed to regain the initiative by shifting from one theater of action to another, and from one conflict technique to another. More likely than not, during the next ten years the danger of war will increase rather than decrease. Totalitarian regimes are most dangerous when they have passed the peak of their ideological vigor and expansionist *élan* and meet with growing external resistance. It will be precisely when the effectiveness of Communist psychological-political strategies decreases and the economic bankruptcy of the Communist system becomes apparent, that Communist leadership will be most tempted to forestall the slow erosion of its power by a quick military gamble. Paradoxically, this danger increases in direct ratio to the growth of Western strength. This circumstance enhances the importance of the West's organization for political and psychological warfare. The task is to persuade, by word and deed, the nations under Communist rule to compel their rulers to loosen their bonds and permit them to join a world order under freedom and justice. No one can now say whether Western policy can achieve this end while avoiding a military contest. The best hope for defeating communism without resort to arms lies in the making of an Atlantic Community, its military and economic power demonstrably superior to that of the Communists.

# Future Soviet Foreign Policy*

—*HERBERT S. DINERSTEIN*

## Summary

*The paper is in three parts. The first reviews the period of greatest Communist expansion from 1944 to 1949 with the particular purpose of isolating the principles guiding Soviet and Chinese policies in those years; the second analyzes the changes in the military balance since that time in order to establish how the principles of Communist advance have been accommodated to the new military environment; and the third part attempts to assess whether the present-day balance of political, economic, and military factors will spur Communist efforts at expansion or deter them.*

*Although between 1944 and 1949 the Western world had great economic and military superiority, these advantages were not employed to prevent the passage of most of Eastern Europe and the mainland of China to Communist control.*

*The reasons for the failure of the West to use its power were connected with failure to appreciate Soviet purposes in Eastern Europe. Once Soviet troops were ensconced in Eastern Europe after the war, the West would not face employing the ultimate sanction of dislodging Soviet troops by force. Moreover, rapid demobilization made such a course an impossibility.*

*For the Soviet Union the problem was to extend its control without provoking a rearmament of the West. This tactic was successful until the Greek Communist Rebellion and until the*

---

* The author of this paper is a member of The RAND Corporation, but the views expressed are his own and do not necessarily represent those of the Corporation.

19

*withdrawal of British responsibility for Greece provoked the Truman Doctrine and the Marshall Plan. From that moment forward the Soviet Union had to face overt hostility to its expansionist moves. The Western inability to respond promptly with military means, however, made Soviet advance in Czechoslovakia, for instance, irritating to the West but not a matter of military danger to the Soviet Union.*

*In discovering the limits of Western passivity in Europe in 1947 and 1948, the Soviet Union did not provoke a response so violent that it had to relinquish earlier gains. Only opportunities were abandoned.*

*The same pattern of passivity and related response explains, in part, the loss of China. Once China was lost, the Communist leaders felt that the relatively minor capture of South Korea would not provoke any response. Here they miscalculated with fateful changes in the military balance of forces.*

*The Korean War caused a steep increase in the level of the American military expenditure, much of it going to the improvement of strategic nuclear forces. This change meant that the United States, at least by the end of the Korean War, was capable of instantaneous and massive reaction to any Soviet probe. Now there was no longer a time cushion within which it was possible to retreat from a Soviet offensive which had provoked an unexpected response. Now probes had to be more tentative. Thus the 1944-49 period can be described as one of Communist advance and the period 1949-61 can be characterized as a period of geographical stability. The entry of Soviet forces into the Caribbean in 1962 probably marks the beginning of a new period. While observing caution in expansion after 1953 for a variety of reasons of which the military superiority of the United States was only one, the Soviet Union improved its military forces so that it could present a direct nuclear threat to the United States. Consequently, the theoretical possibility arose that Communist advance could proceed on "a pounce and snatch" principle. The Communists could seize a position and then say, "this is surely not worth a nuclear war!" Aggression has not become riskless, thereby, for the Soviet Union, but the present balance represents an improvement over the post-Korean situation.*

*Although the Soviet Union is changing in many areas, it has not yet abandoned the expectation that communism will advance as capitalism declines. However, the desire for advance must be put into the framework of other Communist political necessities. A short review will demonstrate the problems of choice for the Soviet Union.*

*Although the Soviet military program in absolute terms is not expensive by comparison with the United States, in the Soviet Union it represents a large charge on the total resources available. The maintenance of superiority in Europe and the attempt to get parity if not superiority with the United States in intercontinental weapons represent a very heavy cost for the Soviet Union. Because of the difficulty of out-producing the United States, the Soviet Union is driven to a strategy of "end runs," both technological and geographical. The Cuban venture is a good example of the latter. Technological outflanking depends on the Research and Development effort (of which the pursuit of anti-missile missiles is one example).*

*Soviet expectations of political gains depend on Soviet military posture, and the corollary is accepted that only minimal gains can be expected from minimal posture. One must expect a continued effort to improve the Soviet military establishment.*

*However, this effort competes with the desire to improve living standards in the Soviet Union. The rate of increase of the latter has recently been reduced but not without political problems.*

*Soviet policy in Europe and the military and political aid to underdeveloped countries also cannot be abandoned since they are believed to offer opportunities for Soviet expansion.*

*The paper concludes that policy choices are difficult in the Soviet Union because so many competing objectives have to be served. How tenaciously will the Soviet leaders pursue the effort to expand? Obviously they will hardly abandon ambitious goals as long as they continue to succeed. Therefore, it must be the object of our policy to make Soviet choices difficult rather than easy. Since the purpose of the policy of making Soviet choices difficult is to modify Soviet objectives, we must be alert to Soviet initiatives which may indicate that our policy has borne fruit and that Soviet leaders are modifying one objective or another.*

## The Most Successful Period of Communist Expansion, 1944-1949

Three principles guiding political expansion were confirmed or developed in this period. The first two retain their validity; the third has required modification. The principles are:

1) Passivity cannot produce gains for communism.
2) An active policy must eventually provoke a capitalist response. This realization is no excuse for inaction, but it influences the timing and intensity of a forward policy.
3) When capitalist response to Communist advance occurs, there is time to retreat, cut losses, and avoid major disaster. We shall examine later how this last conclusion has had to be modified.

Let us first examine the course of events which has produced these conclusions.

Between 1944 and 1949 most of Eastern Europe and the mainland of China passed under Communist control. The economic superiority of the Western world, and its much greater military potential, were not employed to prevent this enormous change in the balance of power, and communism was able to advance.

A major Soviet aim during and after the Second World War was to push its western borders into Central Europe with the ultimate object of making these Communist states. The plan was to advance in stages, the rate of transformation varying with circumstances. The Soviet Union had first obtained these territories in 1939 as the price for neutrality in the German war against France and Great Britain. After being forced into the war by German attack, the Soviet Union claimed these territories as a matter of right and used its military weakness as a lever to press its claim. Western leaders, impelled by the all-too-well-founded fear of a military collapse and, disturbed by rumors of a negotiated Russo-German peace, habitually postponed the determination of the political future of Eastern Europe. By the time they were prepared to negotiate, Soviet troops occupied the area, and, unless Western leaders were ready to face the task of dislodging these troops, a political solution acceptable to the Soviet Union was inescapable. Since the Soviet Union had absorbed these areas in stages, many Western leaders deceived themselves into believing that the latest Soviet advance in Eastern Europe was the last.

The verbal objections interposed by the Western members of the wartime alliance were deprived of any genuine force by the rapid demobilization of their military forces and the rapid removal of American forces from the Continent. When the United States demobilized even more efficiently and rapidly than it had mobilized, Stalin did not fail to seize the opportunity thus provided.

The Soviet problem was largely one of timing and dosage. Stalin had to calculate: (1) which moves would produce only verbal responses; (2) which might provoke the West to resist; and (3) which might stimulate Western remobilization and redeployment of forces on the Continent. If the Soviet Union had not been willing to risk Western displeasure, it would have had to settle, as it did not, for the *status quo ante bellum*. Stalin employed a probing tactic. When he thought he detected only *pro forma* objections, he continued; when he sensed determination to resist, he desisted. Thus he was deterred in Iran but not in Eastern Europe.

Western opposition finally crystallized around the Greek Communist threat which was the occasion for the enunciation of the Truman Doctrine. The Greek Communist Revolution, we know now, was supported by the Yugoslavs and discouraged by Stalin. Greece had been placed in the British sphere of influence as part of an informal arrangement between Churchill and Stalin. Tito wanted to deprive that informal agreement of any force, because among other things he very much wanted Greek Macedonia transferred to Yugoslavia. Stalin feared, correctly as events proved, that the loss of Greece to the Communists might make for a sharp change in Western policy. Paradoxically, the immediate cause of the crisis was British economic exhaustion which left no alternative but to dump the Greek problem into American hands on very short notice. In assuming the burden, Truman committed the United States to a policy of the containment of communism. Although the immediate stimulus for the promulgation of the policy was the fear that Comrade Markos might become the ruler of Greece, the Truman Doctrine was a response to all Communist gains in Eastern Europe since 1944.

The Truman Doctrine was essentially a statement of the intention to employ military force to contain Communist advance, if necessary. The actual improvements in military posture following upon the enunciation of the Truman Doctrine were very modest.

Very soon after the Truman Doctrine was promulgated, the Marshall Plan was put forward. Its aim was to improve economic and political life in Western Europe and thereby make it poor soil for the growth of communism. Although Italian and French communism were then powerful, the plan enjoyed very great success.

Stalin recognized the danger of the new policy immediately. He feared, probably correctly, that if Poland and Czechoslovakia were permitted to participate in the economic reconstruction of Western Europe, as they were eager to, they would be drawn into its political life. He therefore forbade Poland and Czechoslovakia to receive Marshall Aid, and proceeded to batten down the hatches in Eastern Europe. The pretence of multi-party Peoples Democracies was abandoned, non-Communists parties liquidated, and their leaders done to death, if they did not succeed in escaping.

The Greek Communist action might be considered a mistake since it galvanized the West without achieving its purpose. But "nothing ventured, nothing gained" is frequently a guide to Communist foreign policy. Often, as in this case, the local Communist Party lightly accepted the risk of the world-wide intensification of capitalist hostility. The prize was victory in their own country. From the Communist point of view, baseless fear of capitalist response means missing opportunities, and risks must be accepted.

But once Moscow, which was generally more cautious than the Communist leaders who yet had a country to win, decided that the Truman Doctrine marked a significant change in the direction of American policy, the question of provoking the West could be viewed in a different light. The price of provocation had already been paid since the West had crystallized its intention to oppose the spread of communism. But as the West was incapable of a *prompt military response*, it seemed to make little difference if its determination to resist became more intense. The *coup d'état* in Czechoslovakia followed. Increased Western hostility was probably considered a small price to pay for Czechoslovakia. Next, the Soviet Union tried to extract the right to a role in West German affairs by blockading Berlin, but the brilliant improvisation of the airlift frustrated that attempt. Moreover, it brought American bombing aircraft back to Great Britain—an important symbol of American political and military involvment in Western Europe.

In discovering the limits of Western passivity in Europe in 1947 and 1948, the Soviet Union did not provoke a response so violent that it had to relinquish earlier gains. Only opportunities were abandoned.

The same pattern of passivity and belated response can be discerned in Far Eastern developments, but the consequences were, if anything, more fateful. The Asian events of the 1940's which preceded the Chinese Communist Revolution are very similar to the events preceding the Communist Revolution of 1917. China had formed only the bare framework of a modern industrialized state and the shocks of war badly loosened the structure. The much more advanced Imperial Russian Government, a quarter of a century earlier, had suffered similar political and economic exhaustion. In both cases the allies of these battered states made demands, in the name of winning the war, which contributed to their speedy collapse. The democratic Provisional Russian Government, which had succeeded the Tsars, accepted the task imposed by her allies of continuing the war against Germany. Since the population was almost completely opposed to such a course, no democratic government which purported to represent the will of the people could stay in power and continue the war. In the hopeless effort to accomplish both tasks, the Provisional Government failed in both and made way for the Communist October Revolution.

In China, Chiang Kai-shek felt he was fighting a war on two fronts: against the Japanese and against the Chinese Communists. As events proved, the second front was decisive for the future of China, since it was the United States which beat Japan. The United States, however, believed, incorrectly as was learned later, that the Chinese Communists were making an important military effort against the Japanese and could make an even larger one if they had more arms. The Chinese Communists essentially shared Chiang's estimate that the Japanese would be beaten by non-Chinese forces and that the internal struggle was decisive.

During the war Chiang's efforts to reduce the strength of the Chinese Communists were hobbled by Allied disapproval. After the defeat of Japan, the Chinese Communists were able to improve their military capacities in a very short time because of the way in which the war had ended. At Yalta in 1944 the United States, in the belief that a long, hard war with Japan lay ahead, urged the Soviet Union to participate in the campaign against Japan by attacking the Kwantung Army in Manchuria.

Although it turned out that Soviet participation in the war against Japan was unnecessary, the Soviet Union collected what had been promised at Yalta. Incidentally, the Soviet Union occupied Manchuria for a time and made Japanese arms available to Chinese Communists who employed them to extend the area of their control and take up positions preparatory for a struggle with Chiang.

In these immediate postwar years, Stalin and the Chinese Communists differed on the best course to follow. The Chinese wanted to press the civil war vigorously, and they were willing to risk US military involvement on the mainland of China. The Russians were more fearful of provoking an American reaction, but by 1949 when Chiang's forces were driven from the mainland, it was obvious that the Chinese Communists had been right. In Greece, local Communist action against Moscow's advice had produced a significant Western reaction. In China, the boldness of the native Communists won for world communism the greatest prize since the Russian Revolution of 1917. Since the non-Communist world had accepted an enormous shift in the balance of power rather quietly, the conclusion was drawn that the mainland of Asia had been abandoned. If the United States, the Communists probably reasoned, could be effectively indifferent to the loss of all of China, why should they stick at the loss of the southern half of the Korean peninsula? Thus the US defense of South Korea came as an unpleasant surprise to the Communists. But in Asia, as in Europe, when Communist advance was stopped, only the latest forward thrust was parried. The Communists kept what they had gained earlier. Again the Communists demonstrated that only testing and probing could determine the limits the non-Communist world would put upon Communist expansion. Even the most sophisticated analyst of American policy, with all available information at his disposal, could not have confidently predicted the American response to the North Korean attack. Unless Communists were willing to risk such responses, they could not hope to advance their cause.

Risk of American response was, then, an inescapable part of any Communist forward policy. The problem for that policy was to keep risks in proportion to gains. During the Korean War at times it seemed as if the war might be extended to the Soviet Union and to China itself, but these dangers passed, and the West concluded peace on the basis of the restoration of the *status quo ante.*

Just as the lifting of the blockade in Berlin marked the end of a Soviet expansionist phase in Europe, so the Korean War marked the end of a similar phase in Asia. But during the course of the Korean War, important changes in the military balance were set into motion which significantly altered the environment in which communism would try to expand in the next phase.

## Changes in the Military Balance

The Korean War caused a very steep increase in the level of US military expenditures, much of it going for the improvement of strategic nuclear forces. This improvement introduced a new factor into the balance of forces. Now the United States could respond to Communist advance with very large forces at the very outset of the war. The development of the military balance between the USSR and the United States will be briefly reviewed in order to accord the military background its proper significance.

At the end of the Second World War, the chances seemed poor for the Soviet Union to match the United States in military power in the next quarter century. First, the United States had enlarged its already superior industrial base during the war, and the Soviet Union had suffered great destruction. Second, the United States had a lead in nuclear weapons, air power, and naval forces which made it hopeless for the Soviet Union to hope to win a race in the accumulation of any of these arms. Therefore, the Soviet Union prepared a firm technological base for a decade or two hence and procured the forces required in the interim. Until the middle fifties the Soviet Union did not have the weapons which could strike directly at the United States; its military forces could fight with the United States in Europe and Asia, but the damage each of the major contestants might expect to suffer on its home grounds was markedly unequal.

Although the United States had a monopoly of nuclear weapons for part of the period, and overwhelming preponderance for most of it, the political struggle between the two major powers did not reflect this great difference in military potentials. For most of this period the United States had only small numbers of nuclear weapons. Stockpiles did not grow significantly until after the outbreak of the Korean War. Second, the US ability to deliver nuclear weapons to the Soviet Union was in varying stages of readiness and completion. This circumstance meant that a Soviet provocation of the United States, even on a vital matter, could not be followed by the immediate nuclear devastation of the Soviet Union. It was a foregone conclusion, however, that sometime after the initiation of hostilities, when the United States should have been able to procure adequate numbers of nuclear weapons and delivery vehicles, the Soviet Union could be totally destroyed with only negligible damage to the United States. Europe, of course, would have to bear the brunt of an attacking superior Soviet ground force, and this reflection deterred whatever little impulse existed in the Western camp to roll back communism in Europe. The time required for the United States to mobilize completely, then, made it possible for the Soviet Union to retreat, or make peace, if, by some gross miscalculation, it had provoked the United States to strike out. The actual risks taken by the Soviet Union, however, were well within the margin of safety permitted by the military balance.

Although it is difficult to set precise dates in such matters, it seems clear that when President Eisenhower took office and concluded the Korean War, the United States was capable of instantaneous and massive reaction to any Soviet probe. No longer was there a cushion of time within which it was possible to retreat from an offensive which had provoked an unexpected response. It was much more dangerous to follow the old policy of pushing until the opponent resisted. Now probes had to be more tentative.

From that time until the recent past, Soviet and Chinese Communists have hardly advanced. Even when the necessary qualifications are made, the period 1944-49 can be described as one of major advance and the period 1949-61 can be characterized as a period of geographical stability. The entry of Soviet forces into the Caribbean in 1962 probably marks the beginning of a new period.

It would certainly be an oversimplification to explain this periodization solely by the change in the military balance. The death of Stalin, Soviet troubles in Eastern Europe, the increasing realization of the consequences of nuclear war have all played a role, but I would argue that American ability to retaliate rapidly and massively has been of critical importance.

Stalin's successors realized the restrictions placed upon their ambitions by the military imbalance and sought to improve the Soviet military posture. At the risk of oversimplification, the changes they effected will be briefly described with emphasis on the features relevant to a program of political advance.

The Soviet Union has been able to develop nuclear weapons rather rapidly and has boasted recently that it possesses larger warheads than the United States. The Soviet Union also developed aircraft with intercontinental range, but never entered on what would have been a hopeless attempt to equal the United States in numbers.

The long Soviet head start in the development of ballistic missiles has not been converted into a Soviet superiority for reasons which are not quite clear, but apparently derive from a combination of technical difficulties and economic constraints. The Soviet leaders were certainly aware of the great political value of superiority in ICBM's because they tried to convey the impression that they had such a superiority and sought to exploit it. The Soviet Union still has very much larger forces on the European continent than NATO and these are equipped with the most modern weapons. Apart from submarine forces, the Soviet naval arm has been reduced.

Thus the Soviet Union has not been able to reverse the situation existing at the end of the Korean War and make the United States vulnerable at short notice to a massive nuclear attack and the Soviet Union invulnerable. But if a Soviet probe provoked the United States, the latter's calculations must now be different. Europe would be even more grievously damaged than before, and the United States would suffer nuclear damage; how much would depend on the tactics and circumstances of the outbreak of the war. Although at present the United States would probably suffer much less than the Soviet Union, the results would nevertheless be appalling. It is idle to talk of negligible nuclear damage.

Hence the theoretical possibility arises that Communist advance can proceed on the "pounce and snatch" principle. The Communists seize a position and then say, "This is surely not worth a nuclear war." This theoretical tactic has the best chance of success when (1) the area is not one of major importance, and (2) no conventional weapons are available to repulse the advance. Since the United States now, in contrast to the post-Korean situation, would suffer on its own soil, the chances are even greater that if the United States decided to resist, it would invite the Soviet Union to retreat before attacking. Obviously aggression has hardly become riskless for the

Soviet Union but the present balance represents an improvement over the post-Korean situation.

## Communist Expansion: Pressure For and Against

The long period of relative Communist quiescence between 1949 and 1961, internal changes in the Soviet Union, Soviet appreciation of the destructiveness of nuclear weapons, the Sino-Soviet controversy in which the Soviet Union advocated a more cautious policy of expansion than did the Chinese—have all raised the legitimate question of whether the Soviet Union has modified its objectives. The simple assertion that communism never changes is not very useful, because everything changes. The simple assertion that industrialization and a rising standard of living predetermine abandonment of œcumenical goals is equally useless. One need only draw attention to the Nazis who made war *after* carrying German industrialization forward further and very considerably improving the standard of living.

It is probably more useful, although more difficult, to view the formation of Communist objectives as a process constantly undergoing modifications and adjustments. Instead of asking the question, "Have the Communists given up the objective of getting X?," it is better to ask the question, "What resources are the Communists willing to invest and what risks are they willing to take to gain object X?" But world communism is not a single object; many goals must be attained and often they compete with each other. In the following pages we shall seek to isolate the main strands in the complex of Communist objectives, attempt to assess their interrelationship, and then offer some judgment on how Western policies can influence the general direction of Communist goals.

A vulgar and wishful oversimplification will be dealt with at the outset. The argument runs that the Soviet Union is weary of strife, is essentially interested in tilling its own garden, and that all the statements about the inevitability of world communism and the necessity to strive for it represent lip service to a formalistic religion. This interpretation enjoys a certain currency partly because some Soviet people, predominantly those uninvolved in political affairs, have such views and are often chosen to represent the Soviet Union abroad in scientific and disarmament meetings.

A personal anecdote may serve to illustrate the point. On one occasion the author of this paper was lunching with a prominent Soviet scientist, an exponent of general and complete disarmament. When the point was made that the Soviet Union could not really be interested in complete disarmament because then it would be unable in the future "to give assistance to a Hungarian government threatened by a Fascist uprising," the Russian responded with great emotion that he did not give a damn about those foreign Communists. The author of this paper replied that he believed that personal statement, but wondered if the Soviet government shared that view. The Russian could only mutter, disconsolately, that the scientists had to teach the government.

The point of the anecdote is that although many Soviet citizens are prepared to have their government modify its objectives, it would be wishful to believe that they represent the effective policy of their government. The Soviet leaders take a long historical view; as they never tire of reminding themselves and others, communism has come a long way since 1917. In less than a half-century, their success has been enormous and the necessity for periods of consolidation and the failure of some attempts at expansion hardly demonstrate that communism has reached the high-water mark. It will take more than one rebuff, or some years of failure to advance to cause the Communists to abandon their objective of making communism a world system. If and when Communist objectives are radically modified, there probably will be no formal notice of the abandonment of old objectives. More probably some objectives will be postponed so often that they will have been effectively abandoned; in other cases the objectives may be maintained, but reluctance to take risks will constitute effective abandonment.

This is the best we can hope for. On the other hand, the Chinese and/or the Soviet Communists may make the kind of gains which will encourage them to continue. In the pages that follow, the factors encouraging Communist advance and those deterring it will be examined. The question will be treated in the following categories:

1) Communist military policy

2) Communist domestic policy

3) Policy toward the advanced industrial states

4) Policy toward underdeveloped countries

## Communist Military Policy

If military technology had not advanced beyond World War II levels, the Soviet Union could never have hoped to catch up with the United States, because military potential was so direct a function of economic potential. But the appearance of new weapons, each in itself terribly destructive, gave the Soviet Union the opportunity to catch up in the newest and most critical technology and thus achieve over-all parity, if not superiority. But when military systems started to be planned and procured, Soviet inferiority in economic resources constituted a genuine constraint. This is probably *one* of the reasons why the Soviet Union has not converted its priority in the *development* of missiles into a superior weapons system.

The Soviet military problem is indeed difficult and we can see evidences, in their press and in their actions, of the hard choices they have to make. The major unresolved military problem for the Soviet Union is American military strength. The Soviet Union has never denied the official statements made since the fall of 1961 that the United States has a great superiority in intercontinental nuclear missiles. This great American lead in numbers would make it very difficult for the Soviet Union to enter and win a race with the United States for superiority in numbers.

The Soviet Union still maintains very large and well-equipped land armies. Since the Soviet Union neither possesses nor plans a large surface navy, and since its airlift capability is modest, these forces must be earmarked for the campaign against NATO forces in Europe. One suspects considerable reluctance to surrender long-term superiority in Europe in the probably illusory hope of trying to gain superiority over the United States in intercontinental means of attack.

Essentially the Soviet Union, if it wants superiority or even parity is driven to a strategy of "end runs," technological and geographical. Although it is probably unlikely, one cannot exclude Soviet technological breakthroughs in fields such as anti-missiles or perhaps bacteriological warfare. Giving up hope in such fields is tantamount to giving up hope of drawing even with the United States, because the Soviet Union cannot hope to win in a straight production race without jeopardizing some other vital goals.

The Cuban adventure is a good example of the geographical end run. In addition to the enormous political advantages which could have reasonably been expected, the positioning of Soviet missiles capable of reaching the United States would have improved the Soviet military position vis-à-vis the United States.

This improvement is worth considering, even briefly, because it illustrates the importance of strategic power as a platform for political advance. It would be an oversimplification to argue that if the Soviet Union had clear strategic superiority she could take what she willed and that if she had parity she could follow "pounce and snatch" tactics without much risk. But, nevertheless, strategic parity or superiority greatly influences events, particularly when employed to advance a forward strategy. The aggressor uses this military strength to change the political balance; the defender is, or at least has been, reluctant to use strategic superiority to push the aggressor back. Without trying to refine that generalization further, one can safely say that both the United States and the Soviet Union agree that Soviet strategic superiority or parity would open up many political opportunities for the Soviet Union.

Improvement of the Soviet Union's ability to wage war is only part of the reason for the Cuban attempt. The Soviet Union would probably have no genuine interest in starting a war, even from a military position improved by emplacing missiles in Cuba. American military strength is too extensive to make this anything but a mad scheme. But, nevertheless, the Soviet Union is eager to move off dead center, in Europe at least, where its progress has been halted. When the Soviet Union revived the Berlin question once more in an ominous way, the US President made it clear in an interview that in case of a major Soviet threat, the United States might take the nuclear initiative. This reasserted the traditional policy of freedom to choose an appropriate response when vital American interests were threatened. The possibility of a massive American response to such provocation is greater when Soviet ICBM strength is inferior as Soviet leaders have tacitly admitted. Such considerations have a relevance beyond the hypothetical case of a direct Soviet attack on Western Europe. The strategic balance influences the whole range of possible Soviet attempts to advance.

Soviet inferiority in intercontinental missiles is a relative, not an absolute, matter. Improvements, which fall short of parity, not to speak of superiority, may still yield important political benefits. Such improvements would give the Soviet Union "a pre-emptive capability." By this term is meant an ability to strike first in a period of crisis, with the minimum aim of making losses on both sides roughly equal, and with the outside chance of winning the war by sheer shock effect. The Soviet Union would hardly want to precipitate a war and risk everything on such expectations, but Soviet possession of such a capability would presumably give the United States pause and impel it to accept a sudden limited Soviet gain without precipitating a dangerous crisis. Such considerations probably explain the Soviet return to prominence in October 1961 after many years' lapse, of the theme of pre-emption. A Soviet success in Cuba, among other things, would have measurably enhanced the Soviet pre-emptive capability.

Enough has been said on this large subject to make the point that Soviet expectations of political gains depend in part on Soviet military posture and that, consequently only minimal gains can be expected from minimal posture. Hence Soviet military policies furnish an important clue as to how vigorously the Soviet Union intends to pursue its policy of political advance. When, as in the recent past, the Soviet Union refuses an opportunity to cease nuclear tests and concentrates on large warheads, the indications are that it means to continue the struggle for supremacy with the United States. Conversely, if and when the Soviet Union is prepared to make the kind of arms-control agreements which put a term to Soviet efforts at military superiority, an important step in the limitation of Soviet goals will have been made. But Soviet attention to military improvements is not simply a function of the intensity of their attachment to their ultimate political objectives. Technological opportunities and constraints, US military policy, and competing demands for economic resources enter into the equation.

### Communist Domestic Policy

In the Soviet vision of the future, as the world at large enters upon the path to communism, the Soviet Union will be reaching a perfect stage of communism—which translated into simple terms means that Soviet people will be able to enjoy minimally decent standards of housing and a generally satisfactory standard of living. The projected Soviet plans for such an improved state depend very heavily on increased investments in agriculture and on increased productivity of labor. Increased productivity of labor, in turn, is very sensitive to improvements in the standard of living. As long as Soviet standards are markedly below those of Western Europe, it is difficult for Soviet leaders to believe that their system has fulfilled its purpose. Thus demands for internal improvements make strong claims on resource allocation. It is noteworthy that in the recent reduction of the living standards for urban workers, Khrushchev, speaking for the Communist Party, clearly stated that military necessities limited the funds available for the needs of the population. Internal Soviet needs, which grow, limit resources available for military and foreign policy needs.

### Policy Toward The Advanced Industrial States

As the years pass, Soviet expectations about making progress toward communism in the advanced industrial states diminishes. The success of the Marshall Plan reduced the chances of new Czechoslovakias. The Soviet Union had to accept the more modest goal of neutralizing parts of Western Europe on the Finnish model if possible. Neutralization on the Austrian, Swedish, or Swiss model did not promise as many opportunities for Soviet policies, but it represented an improvement over a Europe, politically linked within itself and to the United States through the NATO Treaty. The Soviet policy of neutralizing Europe counted on three major opportunities, which could be exploited concurrently.

The first was the program of nuclear terror. The Soviet Union sought to exploit the strength of its ground and missile forces in Europe to, either frighten the Western European nations out of NATO, or to reduce the extent of their participation in that Alliance. From the Soviet point of view, the best than can be said of that policy is that it prevented some countries from stationing nuclear weapons on their territories. But no reductions in existing commitments can be pointed to.

France appeared to offer a second major opportunity. The Soviet Union hoped that the political polarization produced by the Algerian War would at best lead to civil war in France and at the very least produce strains in NATO by focusing French interests on her own problems and reducing her interest and participation in any European schemes, military or economic. To this end, the Soviet Union made the minimal complaints about French independent development of nuclear weapons, believing it to constitute a disruptive influence within NATO.

The Soviet Union also encouraged the Algerians with military supplies and urged them not to make peace with France on any terms except complete surrender of France's few remaining conditions. But the settlement of the Algerian question has dashed the Soviet hope for the temporary elimination of France from the European equation.

The third area offering opportunities to Soviet policies in Europe has been West Germany. The outstanding political problem in West Germany is its separation from East Germany. Although West Germany has enjoyed very great political and economic progress, no West German nationality exists, and the German problem is as far from solution as ever. The loss of West Berlin and the recognition of the East German regime by the NATO Powers would provoke a searching political self-examination in West Germany. The alternatives would be either some kind of disengagement from NATO and a degree of political and military neutralization which would make possible Soviet agreement to German reunification, or the abandonment of the idea of reunification and the acceptance of a future West German "nation" within a large West European framework. Fear of causing the latter rather than the former development has been one of the sources of Soviet hesitation in forcing the Berlin question after repeated announcements of intent to do so. The Soviet policy would have the greatest chances of success if West Germany had been "abandoned" by her allies, but thus far the Soviet Union has not been certain that this would be the result of a West Berlin crisis.

Although the West Berlin question has been a major political preoccupation of the West because of its limited strength in this exposed salient, it has also been a major problem for the Soviet Union. The continued existence of West Berlin has thrown into relief the economic and political failure of East Germany. After all, the wall was built to keep Germans in East Germany, not to keep them out of it. Moreover, with each year that passes, the shock of the loss of West Berlin will probably be less for West Germany. Continued progress toward West European integration, economic and political, will make the hard loss of West Berlin, if it comes to that, easier to assimilate. Thus, with every year that West Berlin remains free, the Soviet Union, in measuring the risks and gains of an assault on West Berlin, must reduce its expectations of political changes favorable to itself in West Germany—if West Berlin should be lost.

The Soviet attitude toward the Common Market negotiations is consistent with the analysis just offered. The Soviet Union could have appraised them as a symptom of the disintegration of "American hegemony" in Western Europe, but it has chosen to view them, correctly in my opinion, as a harbinger of a stronger Western Europe, as the creation of two capitalist centers still operating in broad harmony although making the adjustments suitable to Western Europe's passage from dependence to relative independence.

## Policy Toward Underdeveloped Countries

Perhaps the greatest successes of Soviet policy since 1953 have been in the so-called underdeveloped areas of the world. The poor outlook for Soviet progress in Western Europe has directed Soviet attention elsewhere. One of the salient features of the postwar international situation was the speedy termination of imperial rule. The Soviet leaders hoped that the colonial revolution might fuse with the socialist revolutions. Even if this great goal could not be attained immediately, the Soviet Union wanted to play a role in countries beyond the periphery of the Soviet Union.

In 1955, therefore, the Soviet Union embarked on a course of seeking political influence in areas which had separated or were being separated from the West. The first such attempt was made in the Mediterranean when the Soviet Union supported Egypt in its quarrels with Great Britain over the Suez Canal. This diplomatic support was followed by economic support in the building of the Aswan Dam. The Egyptian case was a model for the new Soviet policy toward colonial areas. Any colonial country which had a quarrel with a member of the West European or American alliance system could expect both military and economic aid from the Soviet Union.

The Soviet Union has followed this policy in Egypt, in Indonesia, in the Congo, and in Afghanistan and Laos with varying degrees of success. In many cases the recipients of aid have been ungrateful, have harried the local Communist Parties, and have used the Soviet assistance as a lever to extract assistance from the United States and its allies. Egypt furnishes a good example. In the Indonesian case, the Communist Party has been allowed to lead a protected political life. In Cuba, the Communist Party plays a dominant role in the state and the leader of the state has himself become a Communist.

Although this program has been costly for the Soviet Union and disappointing in some respects, it must be accounted a success on the whole. Neither Imperial Russia nor the Soviet Union ever had a position in the Mediterranean, in Southeast Asia, or in Latin America. A Communist nucleus in the Caribbean is no small gain.

The Soviet policy toward these new areas is not yet fixed. On the one hand Soviet policy concentrates on proximate objectives, namely, the exacerbation of the hostility between the new country and its former imperial connection. To maximize the results of such a policy the Soviet government is prepared to deal with whatever social class is in power and to accord them the label of "progressive." The Soviet Union has even been willing to give these countries economic aid in order to build up the state sector of their economy in the hope that in the long run the small ruling classes may become converted to communism on the Cuban model. On the other hand, it is feared that Soviet aid may stabilize capitalism in these areas. These dangers and opportunities have been the subject of a recent Soviet policy debate. This Soviet division of opinion on the best policy toward underdeveloped countries is a sign of increasing Soviet flexibility in making policy choices. The world from Latin America to Southeast Asia is so complex and varied that Soviet interests will best be served by differentiated policies. In some places it is the better part of wisdom to support an anti-Communist ruling group; in other places the opposite course promises better results.

At this point it is useful to consider the Sino-Soviet controversy because one of the major differences is over policy in the underdeveloped areas. At first glance the dissensions within the Communist Bloc seem greatly to Western advantage. If Communists are disputing, this can only redound to our benefit. This is probably true in the very long run, but some possible disadvantages for the West can be discerned in the near future.

The chief difference between the Chinese and the Russians is over resource allocation. The Chinese Communists are very bitter about Soviet aid to non-Communist leaders. The Chinese Communists feel that if the Soviet Union has any funds to expend abroad, they have a better claim than bourgeois states. The Soviet Union, on the other hand, takes the traditional position of the strongest power in an alliance. They prefer to allocate whatever resources can be spared for the support of foreign policy to try to break off members of the opponent's camp or to keep neutrals neutral, although it is sometimes necessary to employ them to prevent disintegration of one's own system. Such was the situation in Eastern Europe in 1956 and 1957. But the very intensity of Chinese Communist hostility to the United States is reassuring to the Soviet Union. Thus one of the causes and consequences of the Sino-Soviet conflict is that the Soviet Union has been able to invest resources in Cuba, Indonesia, and Egypt. Does this feature of the Sino-Soviet conflict help or harm communism in the long run?

This paper has argued that the problems of policy choice in the Soviet Union are difficult because so many competing objectives have to be served. The general conclusion, largely on historical grounds, is that the Soviet leaders have not abandoned their large goals of making the world Communist, but it is possible that a long series of disappointments will cause a modification of their objectives. And it must be the object of Western policy to cause the modification and finally abandonment of the Communist conviction that the expansion of their dominion is historically fated. What are the opportunities to influence Soviet policy from the outside?

One obvious, but nevertheless central, point is that Soviet leaders will hardly abandon the ambitious goals of communism as long as they continue to succeed. Why should they give up a successful policy? In this central area, the opponents of communism have employed their resources effectively, especially since the end of the Korean War. By making Communist expansion dangerous, they have deterred the Soviet Union. But as people weary of tension and conflict, the question: "What have the Communists taken lately?" is put with increasing frequency. But it seems quite clear that Western, and especially American, military power had restrained the Soviet appetite until the Cuban attempt. Furthermore, a necessary, although not sufficient, condition for the progressive modification of Communist objectives is the maintenance of superiority over the Soviet Union in the economic and military spheres.

If it is believed that the Soviet Union may modify her objectives piecemeal, then it must be our object to make Soviet choices difficult rather than easy. Let them choose between domestic improvements and the arms effort. If Communist China needs economic aid desperately, let the Soviet Union choose between aggravating relations between the countries and other needs. It would be unwise for us to make Soviet choices easier by helping Communist China. Unfortunately, there is no dearth of other needy and deserving claimants for aid.

But a policy of making Soviet choices more difficult must not be confused with a policy of automatic opposition to any Soviet initiative. Since the purpose of the policy of making Soviet choices difficult is to modify Soviet objectives, we must be alert to Soviet initiatives which may indicate that our policy has borne fruit and that Soviet leaders are modifying one objective or another. By this time we have had enough experience to distinguish between a Soviet desire to change the atmospherics of a situation with a genuine decision to alter a position. In the pursuit of such a policy, disappointments will be frequent and the evidence of success hard to discern. Only persistence and steadiness over a long period will succeed.

# Soviet Strengths and Weaknesses

*—KURT LONDON*

*Summary*

*1) Ideology still is, and probably will remain for years to come, a source of strength for the Soviet state, particularly because a merger has been achieved between the symbols of the Soviet system and the Soviet state. Ideology is more than merely a state religion: it has become the "soul" of the state. Were ideology in fact eroding, as the adherents of the "national interest" school claim, the fabric of beliefs and the system of implementation would break up and weaken the USSR.*

*2) At present conditions do not seem to exist in the USSR that would lead to a prolonged succession struggle. Khrushchev's successor probably will be in his fifties, a technocrat yet also an* apparatchik, *more sophisticated in his reasoning but still hostile to "imperialism." Except in minor details, such a man is unlikely to abandon prevailing policies. We cannot rule out the possibility, however, that a leader of more fanatic fiber might succeed whose aggressiveness may force the Free World to further increase its defense posture.*

*3) The Party's position has been strengthened ever since Khrushchev came to power. It now has been given virtual command of Soviet economy. It is a prime strategic target since it directs the Soviet state as well as international communism. It is an element of singular importance and one of unique concentration of power. But the Party must be presumed noninfluenceable ideologically, and has enormous vested interests which it is unlikely to sacrifice for any reason. For the CPSU there is no compromise; it must either rule or die.*

41

*4) It cannot be too strongly emphasized that in Communist states the military is but an arm of the Party. Although the army forms the power base upon which Soviet foreign policy is formulated and is also the vertebra of the organizational skeleton of the Soviet state, the Party has been its master since the inception of the Bolshevik regime. An attempt to split the army from the Party appears to be most unlikely even though the possibility should not altogether be dismissed. The armed forces of the USSR have a highly privileged status, and their leading officers most probably act as expert advisers in the Presidium's decisions on matters of high policy. The Soviet armed forces constitute a decided asset of strength for the USSR and world communism. We have no evidence of weakness or even restiveness which would indicate the contrary.*

*5) The Western belief in resentment by the nationalities other than Great Russian is highly exaggerated, with the exception of the Baltic states and perhaps the recently acquired Polish and Rumanian territories. If resistance exists at all, it is weak and poorly organized. The experience of World War II, Hitler's cruel treatment of the minorities, and the subsequent improvement of living conditions following Stalin's death—not to forget the recovery of the USSR and its technological advances— have submerged national feelings of opposition. We should avoid policies that would rely on a possible uprising of Soviet nationalities in case of conflict. Even in the event of war and defeat of the Soviet forces, and even if a wise and humane occupation policy were established, it would be difficult to arouse much sympathy from these groups. Whether more than sympathy can be expected cannot be predicted because the fires under the Soviet melting pot are still burning. As cohesion becomes stronger, it is doubtful that Western principles and practices would effectively appeal to these minorities.*

*6) The USSR at present is making a tremendous effort to bolster its industry and heal the ills of its agriculture. It has created a new control system, shifting from a limited decentralization to a more centralized economy. Whether or not this will work remains to be seen, but in any event, the industrial establishment of the USSR still is vigorous enough to produce the tools of national power and to concentrate on technological progress. Agriculture remains the Achilles heel of the Soviet Union, but it has not so far cut down Soviet strategic power to an extent where a new US strategic appraisal is indicated. It is also important to keep in mind that the quest for an improved economy has much to do with Khrushchev's desire to begin the "transition to communism." Although the goal of "overtaking America" seems to have been abandoned for the time being, chances are that—as before—the losses will be made up. It is not advisable to compare Communist with Western economies; such comparisons are meaningless and serve no purpose. It is necessary for the United States and the West to understand that the present regression does not constitute grounds for jubilation because the USSR, if required to, would undoubtedly be able to produce the necessary tools for waging war.*

*7) Tales of unrest and "ferment" among the intellectuals and youth should be put in proper perspective. If any restlessness exists, it is not directed against the Soviet system but against the interpretation of doctrine in matters of intellectual and artistic expression. Recently, some of the limited freedom that had developed since the "Thaw" was curtailed again. This demonstrates that the Kremlin is well able to cope with the problem, and it would be a mistake to assume that intellectuals or a few restless students constitute a serious vulnerability.*

*8) The East European Satellite Bloc, while not immune to outside influences, remains politically and economically dependent upon the USSR. Soviet military control and a common border rule out successful uprisings; since Moscow regards these areas as its security sphere, it will permit no outside interference even at the risk of war. A successful revolt would probably upset the entire satellite organization. Vestiges of nationalism may gradually fade with new generations, and if the USSR succeeds in coping with its problems and takes the satellites with it on the road to communism, there may be no more resistance. However, in the unlikely event of war, the loyalty of the satellites may be questionable and an occupation of Western troops almost certainly would lead to an end of fealty to Moscow. Since this contingency will hardly occur during the next ten years, Kremlin control remains firm and does not permit a weakening of its cordon sanitaire.*

*9) Yugoslavia, at present, does not constitute a Soviet weakness. Its sympathies, particularly in foreign affairs, tend toward Moscow even though it insists upon independence of action. So long as Yugoslavia remains generally in the "Socialist camp" and its basic ideology Marxist, differences of practical application will fade as the Khrushchevite reformist movement allows for modifications of Marxism-Leninism by adjusting its interpretations to prevailing conditions.*

*10) While Sino-Soviet arguments have produced a weakness by fostering divergency rather than unity of the Bloc, the conflict should not be overrated in terms of Western security. It is probable that, unless there is a change in leadership, the Sino-Soviet dispute may continue over an extended period of time. But a complete break between Moscow and Peking, on both party and state levels, while possible, is not likely unless Communist leaders are reconciled to a split in the Communist Movement. In spite of the harsh words between Moscow and Peking, there is no evidence now that they are willing to risk the consequences. The notion of some Westerners that the United States might combine with the USSR to tackle Red China is too absurd to deserve serious consideration. Nor would a break be necessarily advantageous to the West.*

*11) The Albanian rebellion is perhaps, to a very limited extent, a chink in the Soviet armor. The elimination of the Soviet naval bases is a loss, especially so long as Yugoslav bases are not at the Kremlin's disposal. But the significance of such bases will diminish as military technology advances. Chances are that Moscow, believing in the changes of war techniques, is not overly concerned over the loss of Albanian bases. Finally, it is doubtful that Albania can continue for ten more years with no support from the USSR or the West; Red China will hardly be able to send more than token aid. However, to a limited extent, Albania's deflection from the Kremlin line constitutes an element of embarrassment.*

*12) In sum, the USSR possesses power second only to the United States. Its weaknesses will be compensated for by its strong points. We must assume that, during the coming decade, Soviet strength will increase rather than decrease despite the fact that Bloc infighting may deflect Soviet courses of action and throw its policies somewhat out of gear. The optimism displayed in certain US and Western circles concerning the expected "erosion" of communism and the hope for a reversion of the USSR from a Communist to a national (traditionalist) power is highly dangerous and, if applied to Western policy, suicidal. Polycentric communism or even a Sino-Soviet split do not eliminate our problems and may not even alleviate them. Indeed, they might exacerbate them.*

*Therefore, in order to cope with Soviet-Communist power, the United States and its allies must maintain a strong, modern military establishment of nuclear and conventional forces, a sound economy, an unmatched advancement of science and technology, a high degree of social consciousness, and a first-rate educational system which offers a higher education for all intellectually endowed, regardless of their financial status.*

---

## Ideology

It is no exaggeration to say that the USSR could not have become what it is today and would not constitute a mortal danger to the West were it not for its secular religion, the Marxist-Leninist ideology. This socio-political philosophy which has shaped Soviet strategy in all fields of endeavor, and which has determined its tactical maneuvers was not conceived to remain forever unchanged. Since Marx and Engels outlined its fundamentals, since Lenin began to implement their theses in his characteristic way, since Stalin almost wrecked the Party by concentrating power in his hands, and since Khrushchev introduced a large-scale "reformist" movement restoring the influence of the Party and adapting Leninism to the new conditions—the ideology has undergone considerable modification. However, the Marxist-Leninist concept of the world has remained basically intact; what has changed are the methods by which the Communist goal of world victory is to be accomplished. The three post-Stalinist textbooks of Marxism-Leninism (*Fundamentals of Marxism-Leninism, Problems of Marxist-Leninist Philosophy,* and *Political Economy*) have been revised here and there, but in perusing these books, the student of Communist ideology cannot but reach the conclusion that the basic tenets of communism are unshaken. Indeed, one might say that, in the Soviet Union at least, it has been strengthened by its realistic adaption to prevailing conditions. In other words, it has been modernized.

Does modernization constitute an "erosion" of doctrine? Is it necessary to maintain the original revolutionary fervor such as still appears to exist in the Red Chinese Party? Not in this writer's opinion. After four and a half decades of Communist rule, new generations have grown up under the Soviet system, and the old Bolsheviks are dying out. Consequently, the *élan* of 1917 and the twenties obviously no longer exists. Instead, constant propaganda—or rather agitation—and scientifically organized indoctrination have made ideology part of Soviet life, and Soviet thinking is filtered through these concepts. In a Christian country, only a minority consists of fervent church-goers, but Christian ethics has become part and parcel of individual and social behavior for most who would regard themselves as good Christians, even if they do neglect religious participation. In the USSR, the "man in the street" may not have much appreciation for the subtleties of dialectical materialism, but he nevertheless looks upon himself as a good Communist even if he is not a Party member. At least he would believe in being a socialist, and his feelings toward the "imperialists" would be dictated by the prevailing theses of his party and government. It is quite possible that intellectual isolation from the West has perpetuated his one-sided and uncritical attitude. This is one of the reasons why the Soviet government will continue, for a long time to come, to limit the import of such information rather stringently. If it succeeds in keeping its people isolated for a few more decades, the Soviet citizen, after generations of Bolshevik traditions, probably will be well-insulated against unwelcome influences. For, as we know now, human beings *can* be conditioned. The great Pavlov's lessons were not lost on the Kremlin, and the Pavlovian methods of conditioning, in much modernized form, dominate the principles of training, indoctrination, and education.

Thus I submit that ideology still is, and probably will remain for years to come, a source of strength for the Soviet state, particularly inasmuch *as a merger has been achieved between the symbols of the ideology and the Soviet state.* In other words, the ideology is more than merely a state "religion;" it has become the "soul" of the state. The Soviets distinguish between forms and types of states. The form is not decisive because it can be filled with different contents. The type is what matters, it being determined by ideological factors. The Soviet state is, in a perverted sense, a theocracy; its form is as immaterial as are the "elections" for the Supreme Soviet, that docile forum of rubber-stamping "delegates." Soviet diplomats appear in shiny, gold-embroidered uniforms, yet they are not diplomats but *apparatchiki*, propagandists, saboteurs, and spies. The form means little, the type all.

Were ideology in fact eroding (as the adherents of the "national interest" school claim), the fabric of beliefs and the system of implementation which now gives strength to the Kremlin leadership, and is part of what is called Soviet patriotism, would weaken and break up the USSR. If ever Russia were to slip back into the traditional posture of a national power minus its secular religion, its objectives would no longer be unlimited as are the aims of revolutionary totalitarian states, but would become more reasonable, national aspirations.[1] It is difficult to foresee such development in our time.

## Succession

Khrushchev now is 68. His health is neither bad nor good; he is reported to suffer from high blood pressure. Whether, during the coming decade, he will remain in power is questionable though possible. If he should be compelled, for reasons of health or politics, to retire, or if he should die, who would succeed him? More important, would the succession strengthen or weaken the USSR—or would it substantially remain the same?

In a totalitarian regime, the demise of the supreme leader almost always creates elements of weakness though not necessarily for an extended period of time. Certainly not long enough, if we consider the Stalin succession, to create conditions that would lead to a serious deterioration of Soviet power.

At present there do not seem to exist conditions that would lead to a *prolonged* succession struggle, nor are there good chances of an infight which would be advantageous for the West. The men from whose circle Khrushchev's successor may be picked are in their fifties. Many of them are technocrats, having graduated from technical colleges. They are not only politicians and *apparatchiki;* they are also men of substantive knowledge. They have been reared in the Marxist-Leninist faith since childhood, and whatever reservations they may have regarding the finer points of its ideology, their world concept is bound to reflect their political beliefs. They are not pure technologues such as might shrug off politics, or they would not be where they are now. They are more sophisticated in their reasoning but their distrust and contempt of "imperialism" is a factor to be reckoned with. Under no circumstances should it be assumed that they will be unfaithful to their secular religion. Even if there were an unbeliever among them, he hardly would dare to jeopardize his position in the Soviet hierarchy.

Khrushchev, it will be remembered, has one abiding objective which has become his obsession: to initiate the "transition to communism" during his lifetime. The picture painted by such men as Strumylin, published in articles for the Party elite and audiences abroad, may sound fantastic to us, but much of it

almost certainly is taken at face value in the Kremlin. It fulfills
the double function of stimulating age-old human hopes for a
utopia, and provides a rationale for demanding that the "material-technical" premises for the classless utopia be created post-
haste. Khrushchev's successors could scarcely renege on this
goal, even though it is conceivable that they might either sharpen
or soften some external policies. The Cuba affair has proved to
what length Khrushchev will go to prevent complications which
could jeopardize his schemes and dreams; his successor almost
certainly could not deviate unless he wishes to undertake the
hopeless and outdated task of reintroducing Stalinist methods to
please Peking and Tirana.

In sum, it seems unlikely that Khrushchev's successor will
materially change prevailing conditions except in minor details of
a predominantly internal nature. For the Free World in general
and the United States in particular, no expectations of improvement in relations with Moscow should be expected. There is, on
the other hand, a danger that a man may succeed who is of more
fanatic fiber, agrees more than Khrushchev with the Red Chinese,
and whose aggressiveness may force the Free World to
strengthen further its defense posture.

In this writer's opinion, Khrushchev's demise cannot be expected to produce a strategic bonus for the West unless the
Marxist-Leninist faith is eroding. It can at best result in the
maintenance of the status quo.


## The Party

To a very great extent, the internal strength or weakness of
the USSR will depend upon the Communist Party of the Soviet
Union (CPSU). If the Party should weaken, either in substance
or in organization, it could become the Achilles heel of the USSR.

What are the dangers that may impair the position of the
Party? Doctrinally, it is the leading element, the "vanguard," of
the Soviet state. In actual fact, it rules the state. The government is a mere executive, carrying out the Party's *ukasi*. Under
Lenin, the Party was unquestionably the dominant factor of
Soviet rule. Under Stalin, it gradually lost its standing and became a manipulating organ of the dictator. After Stalin's death,
and particularly under Khrushchev, it was restored to influence
which it has been able to increase steadily. In one of the most
drastic organizational shake-ups in the Soviet Union, the recent

Plenum of the Central Committee, in November 1962, gave the Party the reins over the nation's economic life. Abolishing the District Committees, about 1,500 Party Committees (called Agricultural Production Directorates) are to be set up to lead and supervise agricultural activities in collective and state farms. Similar Directorates will be set up in the industrial areas. Inasmuch as these Party units remain responsible to the Moscow center, one might say that Khrushchev's decentralization drive has been halted, that Party centralization has been reinvigorated and that local government for all practical purposes has been sidetracked. This puts a heavy responsibility upon the Party and, if it is unsuccessful, might damage its standing considerably. It is not possible to blame individuals forever; failures eventually will reflect on the Party as a whole.

This reorganization emphasizes Khrushchev's intent of combining theory and practice which has been propagated since Lenin but which Khrushchev has implemented in earnest. The Party leaders thus must fulfill the double function of preserving and stimulating ideology while carrying out practical tasks to be fulfilled by an industrial society. It remains to be seen whether the Party will succeed in combining these two activities.* Moreover, the Party has been chosen to lead the people towards communism once the state has "withered away." It would thereby assume all duties of the legislature, judiciary, and executive. Thus successes and failures can be laid at its door since it *is* the state or, if you will, the successor to the state.

It is hard to judge the height of the Party's standing at present. Since conditions have generally improved and a limited but noticeable degree of freedom of movement has replaced constraining terror, it probably enjoys a reasonably high reputation; besides, it still is looked upon as the hierarchy destined to carry the torch of world revolution. Most likely it is at present impervious to outside deprecations. The Party leadership constitutes, of course, the key element, and one that is all-important to US strategy. It must be presumed to be non-influentiable ideologically, and has enormous vested interests which it is unlikely to sacrifice for any reason. Thus, for the CPSU, as for all Parties in the Communist Bloc, there is no compromise; it must either

---

* In a lecture for the AAASS (American Association for the Advancement of Slavic Studies) in Washington on November 14, 1962, Wolfgang Leonhard pointed out that there is a conflict between the ideological aims and the economic realities.

rule or die. Since it does not want to die, it will defend its rule to the last.

Nevertheless, from the point of view of Western strategy, the CPSU remains the primary target. It is more important than any military or economic target because the Party leaders are in command of the apparatus that sets the Soviet wheels in motion—in peace, cold war, or hot war. It is thus an element of singular importance and one of unique concentration of power. What remains of its organizational decentralization is not really a problem because all Party organizations outside Moscow are dependent upon the Kremlin's direction, and now more so than ever. The Party Presidium, the Central Committee, its secretariats, and its functional bureaus are in Moscow. And even though some of its units outside the capital are permitted a limited amount of autonomy, they are still subject to the general line which is determined by the Presidium and Central Committee.

## The Military Establishment

If there was ever any hope that the Soviet army, if dissatisfied with the Party leadership, might stage a *thermidor*, the ouster of Marshal Zhukov should have effectively destroyed such idle dreams. It cannot be too strongly emphasized that in Communist states, the military is but an arm of the Party. If there is an *esprit de corps* in the Soviet army, it is characterized not by political ambitions, but by that combination of national sentiment and adherence to Marxism-Leninism which may be called "Soviet patriotism." Besides, the Soviet military command has no reason to be dissatisfied with the efforts of industry and science to furnish most of the materiel it desires, nor with the favored status granted to its officers.

There have been instances where individual Soviet marshals acquired more power than the Party could permit. Tukhashevsky was one; Stalin liquidated him. Zhukov was another; Khrushchev demoted him. In the latter's case, the somewhat troubled and confused period following Stalin's death contributed to army restlessness; Malenkov's increase of consumer goods production worried the military. When Khrushchev assumed power, he had the support of some prominent marshals, of whom Zhukov was the most important. This support may have saved Khrushchev in June 1957 when the Malenkov-Molotov-Kaganovich trio sought to unseat him. The Presidium's majority had voted against him, but Khrushchev did not accept the verdict and appealed to the Central Committee which he had packed with his own men. Zhukov then claimed that the army supported Khrushchev, a statement which was illegal: Zhukov could not commit the army politically.[2] When he was elevated to full membership in the Presidium, his ambitions should have stopped. Since they did not, it was not surprising that in the same year, 1957, he was ousted. The precise reasons are unknown, but it may be surmised that, in the first place, Zhukov's popularity had surpassed the limits acceptable to the Party, and secondly, that the position of the army had to be redefined as being under, and not separate from, the Party.

This affair was a reminder to the marshals, political and otherwise, that the Party was the master. Obviously, the military establishment forms the power basis upon which Soviet foreign policy is conceived, and is also the vertebra of the organizational skeleton of the Soviet state. This has been so since the inception of the Soviet regime, when the army was regarded as the military vanguard of the revolution, just as the Party was the political vanguard. But so long as the Party continues to be the all-powerful leader group of the USSR and the guiding force of the international Communist movement, the military will be its tool. Let us not forget that most ranking officers are members of the Party and subject to its discipline.

If this relationship should ever change, it would indicate a complete reversal in the system. Is it possible to promote such a change and drive a wedge between the Party and the army? Perhaps one should not dismiss this possibility altogether but it seems, for the time being, quite unrealistic. The armed forces of the USSR have a highly privileged status, and their leaders most probably act as expert advisers in the Presidium's decisions on matters of high policy. Altogether, their position must appear to them highly satisfactory, and many of them are, no doubt, loyal and believing Communists, especially since to them the interests of the Soviet state and the objectives of Soviet ideology coincide.

Therefore, we must come to the conclusion that the Soviet armed forces constitute a decided asset of strength for the USSR and world communism. We have no present evidence of weakness or even restiveness which would indicate the contrary.

## The Nationality Question in the USSR

Lenin's view of nationalism was characterized by his belief that it might impede revolutionary action. Self-determination also must be subordinated to the interests of socialism. The Red Army was employed to prevent secession from the new Soviet state. Stalin, who became Commissar for Nationalities, generally followed Lenin's theses. During the prewar Stalin era, lip service was given to autonomy of the national components of the USSR. It was to be a "cultural" autonomy. National languages, no longer banned, could be spoken and taught, side by side with Russian. Although this policy vaccillated—particularly during and after World War II when sanctions were carried out against unreliable national minorities—the idea of a voluntaristic *sodruzhestvo,* a commonwealth of nationalities constituting the Soviet Union, was furthered by Stalin and his successors. Nevertheless, cultural autonomy could not be equated with political or economic autonomy. Most Union Republics and autonomous regions are ruled by a mixed administration, the highest officials usually being Russians or trusted Party members who no longer feel and act as members of these nationalities but as Soviet citizens and Party officials.

Does this forcible incorporation of minorities into the Soviet state produce resentment? Are there elements of vulnerability in the nationalities of the USSR? Excepting the Baltic states, and perhaps the recently acquired former Polish and Rumanian territories, resistance against the Moscow regime should not be overestimated. If it exists at all, it is weak and poorly organized. For many years, we have taken for granted that Soviet nationalities were opposed to central control in Russia, that they were not satisfied with cultural autonomy but also wanted political self-determination. Such sentiments were attributed not only to the larger European nationalities, e.g., the Ukrainians and the Georgians, but also to the Central Asian minorities. The West was persuaded by émigré representatives of national minorities that unrest existed and, no doubt, flare-ups did occur. The defection of the Vlassov forces in World War II and the dubious loyalty of such small minorities as the Volga Germans or some Crimean and Central Asian nationalities seemed to indicate disillusionment; the unstable conditions during the war, especially at the time of the German progress, stimulated defection. However, the brutalities of the Hitler armies and SS as well as the eventual rallying of the Soviet forces, which finally stopped the invaders and began their victorious advance, changed the situation. I submit that during the final years of the war, the common experience welded the Great Russians and the Soviet minorities together. The improvement of living conditions after 1953 and the relaxation of the terror further contributed to appease the nationalities. As the USSR gained power and prestige, they wanted to share the glory of Soviet successes. The infighting receded further as new generations grew up, thoroughly indoctrinated in the Soviet system and the Marxist-Leninist ideology.

I do not mean to claim that all antagonism has disappeared, but I suggest that what remains has become chiefly "non-antagonistic." One might therefore conclude that the USSR no longer is as vulnerable to minority unrest or defection as before and during the first war years. There may be islands of opposition; there may still be a modicum of indigenous nationalism; but we may question whether it should be counted a serious vulnerability by Western strategists. The Nazi experience has left vivid memories, and any successive invasion, different though it may be, would suffer from the prejudices the Nazis left in their wake. (This would not be true for Balts, who in general seem to remain opposed to Soviet domination. But, as they become increasingly outnumbered by Russians, the time may come when even their resistance will fade.)

It is hard to say whether sentiments for national independence are merely submerged and ready to reappear when circumstances permit, or whether they will gradually disappear as Soviet indoctrination takes hold of the young generations, isolates children from their traditionalist elders in time to prevent their influence, and finally produces Soviet citizens who are just that. Since the loyalties to the country and the Soviet system have become amalgamated to the point where they can no longer be separated, an eventual merger between the nationalities and the dominating Great Russians cannot be altogether ruled out. This would also be doctrinally defensible because, after all, Marxism-Leninism militates against nationalism except when it furthers "national liberation."

For these reasons, I would be inclined to disagree with any policy which relies overly on a possible uprising of Soviet nationalities in case of conflict. Apart from the fact that they are well controlled and fitted into Soviet political, social, and economic patterns, they may not see much gain in renouncing

their present masters. I would consider it unrealistic to plan
on the basis of such upheavals. Only if, in case of war, Western
forces actually penetrated Soviet territory and were able to
occupy areas inhabited by national minorities, only if a wise
and humane occupation policy were then established, would it
be possible to arouse the sympathy of these groups. Whether
more than sympathy can be expected cannot be foreseen. One
must not forget that the USSR is in fact a melting pot; the
results of such a process in the USA may not yet be fully applicable to the USSR, but there is a lesson to be learned from it.

## The Economy

This is not the place to present a statement on the Soviet
economy and engage in the battle of economists who are divided
roughly into two schools of thought: one believes that the Soviet
economy is weak and overestimated, the other claims that it is
strong and underestimated. Without being an economist, I
would submit that the picture is not at all clear even though
the recent measures to strengthen the industrial and agricultural
sectors of the Soviet economy seem to point to serious shortcomings. But it should be emphasized that Soviet power cannot
be assumed to be impeded because of this. What is important
from Khrushchev's point of view is the delay in reaching the
stage of "transition to communism" which requires a strong
"material-technical basis." At present, the budding prosperity of
the country is in recess and the transition stage probably postponed.

Is the doctrinal commitment to economic planning at the
bottom of the difficulties as has so often been claimed by the
adherents of free enterprise?

The bureaucracy in charge of planning and implementation
has always been cumbersome. It has wasted capital and manpower. But still it has succeeded—on the backs of suffering
people—in creating within four decades an industrial establishment second only to that of the United States. Since planning became a basic policy and since the introduction of the first Five-
Year Plan in 1928, the method of planning has changed often and
veered between extreme centralization and moderate decentralization. For example, a few years ago, Khrushchev created the
*Sovnarkhozi* to be in charge of local economies. (He took a leaf
from Tito's book; Yugoslavia's economy was decentralized along

such lines quite some time ago.) Apparently, this did not work. Industrial production limped and agriculture ailed. Therefore, Khrushchev, never tired of introducing new methods, had the November 1962 Plenum of the Party's Central Committee vote for a far more centralized and strictly controlled system of Party supervision in the industrial and agricultural sectors. Indeed, the Party is now responsible for nursing Soviet economy back to health. If it does not succeed, it, rather than the managers, will be held responsible. The supposed "managerial revolution," which allegedly had been gaining strength, should be on its way out—if it ever really existed.

It is important to keep in mind that the present shortcomings of Soviet industry probably are not much worse than before but, from Khrushchev's point of view, alarming in that not nearly enough progress is being made toward the achievement of the "material-technical basis" which is necessary to push the USSR toward the road to communism. Furthermore, the achievement of this goal probably is considered vital for the position of the USSR vis-à-vis the countries of the "world socialist system," especially Red China, and, of course, for successful competition with the United States. (In the CPSU's slogans for the first of May 1962, the exhortation to "overtake the United States" was significantly missing.) But, lest we indulge in optimism: a Harvard forecast of 1956 that there will be an inevitable decrease in the rate of growth of the steel industry has since been refuted. Furthermore, American geologists have claimed that Soviet iron and other mineral resources probably are the richest in the world and will permit the Kremlin autarky at least in this field. Add to this that the export capacity of the USSR is considerable, thereby securing the import of such raw materials as may not be available in Soviet territories; what cannot be bartered can be bought with gold of which there is plenty.

There can be no question that agriculture is and remains a weak spot of the Soviet economy. There is enough food for a monotonous fare, and the Soviet people are used to getting along without delicacies. But agricultural production is too backward to guarantee the economy of plenty which would be considered necessary for a "transition to communism."

Whether or not Soviet manpower is adequate for the development of both industry and agriculture—particularly highly trained manpower—is hard to say. During the second half of the fifties labor-force shortages occurred as a result of the declining birth rate during the war years. This crisis probably has ended, but there remain other problems such as the most advantageous distribution of manpower and the fact that "polytechnical" education, i.e., the integration of intellectual and manual training and experience, has complicated, rather than alleviated, the issues. A decrease in labor productivity, which often occurs in maturing economies, has troubled Soviet leaders, all exhortations to "overtake America" notwithstanding. However, as automation progresses, this difficulty will be remedied to a considerable extent and the Soviet government will not have to worry about unemployment, but will simply transfer surplus labor where it is needed.

It has often been claimed that the satellite economies constitute a source of weakness for Soviet economy. Certainly, Moscow has had to help some of them, especially East Germany, but such help must be regarded as an investment. The better off these dependent states are, the easier it is for the Kremlin to exploit them. Therefore, on balance, the USSR probably has gained more than it lost by bolstering satellite economies. Morever, the intensification of the activities of the Council of Mutual Economic Assistance (CEMA, also called COMECON) most likely is geared to the needs of the East European Bloc as a whole, and the Kremlin is striving to organize the various economies in a manner that would create an economic division of labor in accordance with the strength and weaknesses of the individual countries. If this can be achieved, the USSR will be the chief gainer while the satellites, in losing a balanced economic production, would become even more dependent on Moscow.

To sum up, I believe it to be a mistake, made on both sides, to compare the free economy of the West with the controlled one of the East. Except in wartime, the "success" of one or the other can be gauged only by the over-all goals to be attained. In peacetime, there seem to be distinct advantages for consumers in the West and for political strategy in the East. In the last analysis it matters little whether or not the Soviet people have a monotonous diet and cannot get enough meat. The main strategic question is whether the industrial establishment of the USSR remains strong enough to produce the tools of national power, and whether, in these times of mutual deterrence, they can continue to concentrate on technological developments which would keep them abreast of the West.

To answer this question: there is no reason to assume that economic weakness per se will cut down Soviet power to the extent where a new US strategic appraisal is indicated. The present cautious attitude of the Kremlin toward the United States may be an indication that it does not feel altogether secure of its economic base. It is also possible, perhaps even probable, that the lack of progress in the game of "peaceful competition," and particularly the greater demands of the Soviet people for higher living standards, as well as the delay in creating the "material-technical" premises for a "transition to communism" have combined to press for changes of internal and external policies. However, I should like to point out emphatically that this does not constitute a retreat, and that the USSR, if required, would undoubtedly be fully able to produce the necessary tools for waging a war.

### Youth and Intellectuals

There have been many tales of unrest among these groups. They are mentioned here because they are important in every Communist state: youth symbolizes future generations of "new Communist men" and the intellectuals, especially the writers, exert a far greater influence upon the intellectual life, both politically and artistically, than they do in a society such as ours.

Even since 1956, with the onset of the "thaw," Soviet youth and intellectuals have been quite vociferous in their desire for free expression, although it must be emphasized that they have never, to my knowledge, attacked the Soviet system, the Party, or the government. They have opposed certain policies, methods, and personalities; they have shown anger against Stalinism and its consequences, as demonstrated by the poems of Yevtushenko, Tvardovsky, and their fellow poets and writers. Much older men also have rebelled: the frankness of Ilya Ehrenburg only underlines the general desire of the intelligentsia to give vent to their feelings.

However, the oft-cited wish to know more about the outside world does not imply a desire to do away with a system under which both youth and intellectuals live. The West is always eager to explain ferment as an indication of opposition to communism. I cannot share this view. Apart from the fact that generations which have grown up under the Soviet system are used to it and look upon it as their own, and apart from the fact that intellectuals, even if they don't like all the regime is doing or saying, have an enormous vested interest in a state which has elevated them to a new kind of aristocracy—apart from such

considerations, one must also remember that young people as
well as artistic temperaments are easily inclined to be opposition-
ist. This is true all over the world.

In sum, I do not believe that the much-discussed ferment of
youth and intellectuals makes the USSR vulnerable in any sense
of this term.*

## The East European Satellites

There are weaknesses in the satellite system which may
produce vulnerability. But claims that such weaknesses are of
major, strategic proportions, especially during a period of
non-war coexistence, are almost certainly mistaken and even
dangerous. A policy based upon the concept of a priori rebellious satellites, in some mysterious ways "allied" to the
West, a legend which former nationals of these states are fond
of promoting, can only lead to disillusion, disappointment, and
even disaster.

All present "people's democracies" except Albania are contiguous to Soviet territory; it cannot be assumed that these
states will be permitted to move away from Moscow. What
happens if they try has been clearly demonstrated by the
Hungarian massacre of 1956. When Imre Nagy attempted to
remove Hungary from the Warsaw Pact, Moscow risked the ill
will of the entire civilized world rather than let Hungary drop
out of what it regards as its sphere of interest and security.
Had Hungary succeeded, the entire satellite system might have
collapsed. Yugoslavia and Poland were bad enough examples
for the Kremlin's taste; Hungary in addition would have undermined the remaining loyalties and alienated the Communist
stooges of Moscow from their masters.

There is no denying that local nationalism still exists in these
countries although its intensity varies. Moreover, the Communist governments probably are looked upon as what they are:
Moscow's *gauleiters*. Here one should except Poland mainly
because Gomulka is regarded, rightly or wrongly, as a Pole
rather than a Communist, was imprisoned by Stalin, and stood
up to Khrushchev. Opposition is directed against other leaders

---

* In early December 1962, the Party began to exert renewed pressure on
artists who were trying to shed "socialist realism" for more experimental
expressions in their art forms. In March 1963, following Khrushchev's attack against "angry" Soviet writers, Yevtushenko and others had to recant,
just as in the good old times of Stalin.

not so much because they are Communists but because they submit to foreign—Soviet—domination. On the other hand, there is little love lost for the West (again, Poland excepted). Capitalism is unpopular. There are, however, tendencies toward Titoism and social-democratism. The idea of achieving "socialism" along different, "national" roads rather than the Soviet way probably captivates the imagination of many satellite citizens and possibly also of men in influential positions who, in order to protect their safety and position, cannot but follow the official line. "Revisionism" will remain a danger to Moscow, but a danger that can be controlled.

During the years when the USSR exploited satellite economies more severely than now, the reliability of average citizens of the rank and file of the armed forces remained an open question. But even before the 20th CPSU Congress resulted in the development of polycentric communism, as terror abated and living conditions began to improve, opposition probably has more and more given way to resignation and conformity.

At the same time, CEMA has been given a shot in the arm. This economic organization of the East European states, designed to achieve a division of labor, strives to make them an integral part of Soviet Bloc economy, gradually depriving them of their economic freedom of movement. In fact, in my view, the satellite economies would cease to be national if CEMA's objectives were reached.

The Kremlin is certainly well aware of the weaknesses of the Communist regimes it set up after World War II. If there was any doubt in their minds, the events in Poland and Hungary in 1956—following the 20th CPSU Congress and the Stalin denigration—have taught them an effective lesson. Khrushchev ever since has taken steps to strengthen the Soviet *cordon sanitaire,* but in a manner which differs greatly from that of Stalinist tyranny. Following the 1956 upheavals, several measures were taken to stabilize the East European Bloc. These were partly of institutional and partly of "diplomatic" or persuasive character.

Institutionally, two organizations already were in being: the Warsaw Pact (1949) and CEMA (1955). Both serve political purposes, although the Warsaw Pact is military, and CEMA economic, in nature. The political element in the Warsaw Pact is indicated by the establishment of its Political Consultative Committee even though there is little evidence that it ever has played an important role. CEMA probably is a much more important organization for promotion of Bloc unity, and as such has increased its activities during the past few years after a period of relative inactivity.

Apart from such specialized intra-Bloc cooperation as the Institute for Nuclear Research there are no other statutory organs designed to hold together the Soviet Bloc. There exists, however, a vast system of bilateral treaties which grew out of innumerable meetings between Party and government representatives of both East European and Far Eastern Communist regimes with the Kremlin leaders.[3] These "diplomatic" activities, which began immediately after the unrest in Poland and the uprising in Hungary, petered out toward the end of 1957 when the stabilization of the Bloc had been completed. Subsequently, several conclaves served to enhance the Bloc's cohesion: the meeting of the Communist and Workers' Parties at the occasion of the fortieth anniversary of the October Revolution (November 1957), the 21st Party Congress of the CPSU in early 1960, the Rumanian CP Congress in June of the same year, and the 22nd CPSU Congress in 1961. There are strong indications that, in 1957, the creation of a new Comintern was suggested, especially by East Germany, Czechoslovakia, and Albania. The Kremlin was not opposed to the idea, but neither Red China nor Poland favored such an organization.

To summarize: the Eastern-Central European Bloc is not immune to outside influences but remains politically and economically completely dependent upon the USSR. Soviet military control and a common border line rule out any important, not to say successful, uprising; besides, the police and armed forces in the satellite states must be regarded as generally reliable in view of their vested interest in the regime.* As time progresses and old traditions gradually dim in the minds of new generations, the vestiges of nationalism may well be whittled away by Communist teachings and the Soviet example—provided, of course, that the Soviet Union remains successful in coping with its economic and political problems. Since an outbreak of full-scale war between the United States and the USSR is unlikely, due to the nuclear stalemate, it is hard to envisage a situation wherein Western troops could liberate the Satellites. If they did, loyalty to the USSR would vanish without, however, necessarily shifting toward the West.

* East Germany is and will remain an exception for an indefinite period of time.

## Yugoslavia

Since Tito broke away from the Soviet Union, relations between Moscow and Belgrade have been fluctuating. Stalin's mistake in judging Tito's staying power was clearly recognized by his successors, and Khrushchev took the initiative to bring him back into the fold. This did not succeed. Since then, Soviet-Yugoslav relations have been characterized by Soviet caution and Belgrade's determination to choose its own "road to socialism." But in one respect the Yugoslav policy line has more or less followed the Kremlin's, namely, in the field of foreign policy. There have been no basic differences between the foreign policy of Khrushchev and Tito, and the latter's attempt to appear before the world as "non-aligned" is ludicrous.

Stalin's effort to isolate Yugoslavia was not successful. Tito has never become the forgotten man of socialism; on the contrary, he has gained friends and influence among the neutralists. However, I do not believe that the Kremlin regards him as a source of danger to the "true religion" as do the Chinese Communists and their followers, the Albanians. Titoism remains essentially a variant of orthodoxy, not a repudiation of it. While Tito will maintain, as much as possible, his Western economic ties, there can be no doubt that he is a Marxist and a Communist. He is not much of a Leninist but, in some respects, not far from Khrushchev's basic beliefs. Above all, he is a proud, vain, and stubborn man who cannot be swayed either by Chinese invectives or by Soviet pressures. From the Soviet point of view, the existence of Titoist Yugoslavia is not necessarily a weakness for the "socialist camp" though his joining the fold would undoubtedly strengthen it. The unknown factor is the question of Tito's successor, and this is where the Kremlin's lack of control over Yugoslavia creates certain hazards.

In my opinion, Yugoslavia does not constitute a Soviet weakness. Its sympathies tend toward Moscow even though it insists upon independence of action. So long as Yugoslavia remains, in a general way, in the "socialist camp" and its basic ideology Marxist, differences of practical application will fade as the Khrushchevite reformist trend allows for modifications of Marxism-Leninism by adjusting its interpretations to prevailing conditions. The results of this development already are noticeable—there has been a considerable *rapprochement* between Moscow and Belgrade.

**Sino-Soviet Relations**

We now come to a crucial problem: the serious strain in the relations between Moscow and Pekıng. It is a problem which concerns not only the USSR but the entire international Communist movement. The controversy already has done harm to some segments of communism, but may not be irreparable if the argument can be stalemated without impairing the basic alliance. Should it go farther than a continuation of "non-antagonistic contradictions," should there occur an open break such as that between Moscow and Tirana, world communism would have to face up to a split of the secular religion which can only be compared with that between Rome and Byzanz.

The ramifications of this problem are so multitudinous that it is impossible to do them justice in a few pages. Thus for the purposes of this essay, it is not the whys and wherefores that are to be examined but the question as to what extent the Sino-Soviet squabble may or may not constitute a Soviet weakness or could develop into one.

The political and social histories of Russia and China have made their peoples different. It must be hard for them to understand each other. Only the language of Marxism-Leninism, as spoken by Party leaders and cadres, has made the alliance possible. Aggravating are two aspects: the national and racial characteristics lead to differing interpretations of world politics and political methods; and the level of economic development differs greatly, the USSR being far ahead and, in comparison with China, a "have" nation. Yet I have always believed that neither side wants to break with the other, since both must realize what this would mean for communism—internally and externally. Nor do I doubt that the basic objectives of Moscow and Peking remain identical as both are believers in the Communist gospel. Contradictory views have developed regarding the methods for obtaining these objectives. Methodology pertains to interpretation of the doctrine; the interpretation is influenced by the difference in socio-economic and political conditions of the two countries. Thus arguments are bound to arise. So long as they remain in the realm of dialetics, no serious harm is done; only if they attack the heart of the relationship does the danger of a break arise.

There have been indications, ever since the twenties, that the Kremlin was not anxious to see China become prematurely a great "socialist" power. The quick victory of Mao was unexpected in Soviet circles, and so was the self-reliance with which Mao went to work to create his own brand of "socialism." However, as long as Stalin lived, his monumental image overshadowed the arguments on methods, though Mao probably never forgot that the 1927 massacre of Chinese Communists was the consequence of Stalin's orders to create a united front with the Kuomintang. Mao's independence of action increased after Stalin's death, and particularly after the 20th CPSU Congress, which promoted a new Soviet trend, Khrushchevian reformism, and created a dilemma for the Mao regime. If I may be permitted to quote myself: "On the one hand, Mao is a Stalinist in that he advocates the necessity for central leadership of the Bloc. As a result, Red China has often extolled and supported Soviet leadership. On the other hand, the Stalinist concept of a dominant USSR prevents Mao from being as independent as he wishes to be, either in the execution of domestic policies or in his effort to establish a preeminent position in Asia." [4]

This dilemma raises a very fundamental question. If the members of the "Socialist commonwealth" follow "different roads to socialism" and believe in Khrushchev's statement of January 6, 1961 that "in the Communist movement, just as in the socialist camp, there has existed and exists complete equality of rights and solidarity of all Communist and Workers' Parties and socialist countries," that "the CPSU in reality does not exercise leadership over other Parties" and that "all Communist Parties are equal and independent," then Red China is only a part of the polycentric "commonwealth" and the right to follow its own direction is uncontested so long as its methods do not bring harm to communism. What may cause harm, what methods should be used to further Communist objectives, are the main issues of disagreement between Moscow and Peking. The views of the two Communist giants differ for reasons of historic development, economic level, geography, national character, and the undeniable fact that the USSR is far ahead on the road toward the "transition of communism." One may add that the personal antagonism between Mao and Khrushchev contributes not a little to the tensions.

The aforementioned points should serve only to sketch some of the major aspects of the Sino-Soviet controversy in order to estimate whether or not the crisis constitutes a weakness of the USSR and the Bloc. Although I maintain that a complete break between Moscow and Peking on both Party and state levels, while possible, is not likely unless the Communist leaders are reconciled to a permanent split of the movement with all the consequences this would entail, I do suggest that the state of present Sino-Soviet relations constitutes a weakness in that it tends to fragmentize the "world socialist system" and the Parties all over the world.

But in the unlikely event of an East-West war, China would hardly stand aside, nor does it seem likely that a major Chinese military involvement, which might lead to the demise of its system, would be tolerated by the USSR. We therefore must not exaggerate the consequences of the Moscow-Peking squabble, and must view it in its proper perspective. It is not a mortal weakness by any means; it merely creates difficulties for the Bloc, holding over it the threat of a Chinese secession which would be a great blow and would have psychological as well as practical consequences. However, the basic objective of Moscow and Peking, Communist world conquest, remains identical. In the Soviet view, the China problem may delay, but will not prevent, this objective from being reached when the time is ripe. Major conflicts between Communist and non-Communist groups may end intra-Bloc squabbles or put them on ice; besides, a change of leadership in either country might possibly cause a sudden about-face and a new *rapprochement*.

Therefore, while Sino-Soviet arguments have produced a weakness by fostering divergency rather than unity, the conflict should not be overestimated in terms of Western security. We cannot be at all certain that a major war or a change of leadership or policy would not automatically bring the two large Communist countries together again. The notion of some naive Westerners that the West might combine with the USSR to tackle Red China is too absurd to deserve any serious consideration.

## Albania

A brief word on this small, excommunicated Stalinist satellite which has become Red China's only friend in Europe. Albania is not only little and poor; it is also friendless since the break with Moscow. It is isolated, surrounded on all sides by countries that covet slices of its territory and hate its leaders and everything they stand for.

Objectively, Albania is an interesting phenomenon, but, I submit, not nearly so important an issue as a great many distinguished specialists have made it appear. It is perhaps a symbol of the changes that have occurred in the Bloc since its stubborn adherence to Stalinism has driven Albania from Khrushchevian reformism into the wide open arms of Mao. The effect of Albania's disobedience to Kremlin policies, together with its siding with Red China in the Sino-Soviet controversy, cannot be compared with the impact upon the satellites of Tito's break with the Cominform. Albania, whether under royal or Communist rule, has never had the respect of other nations, which look upon it as a kind of operetta country. Rightly or wrongly, Albania has never been taken seriously, and the implication of its break with Moscow is more symbolic than substantive.

For the Soviet leaders, I believe, Hoxha's rebellion is annoying and troublesome but not a crucial issue. Albania is isolated; its friendship with Red China is, so to speak, platonic, because China is too far away and too troubled with its own problems; Yugoslavia and Greece have never ceased to look at Albanian territory with covetous eyes; the Bloc nations no longer extend help, and so Albania is stewing in its own juice. Unless non-Communist help is forthcoming or Communist China should miraculously be in a position to extend more than its present token assistance, there is little chance that Albania can develop a viable economy sufficient to keep itself going.

Is the Albanian rebellion a weakness in the Soviet armor? Perhaps to a limited extent it is, but not enough to matter seriously. Strategically, the elimination of Soviet naval bases is a loss. The Soviet Bloc's Black Sea bases cannot replace them in wartime due to the Turkish barrier. So long as Yugoslav bases are not at the disposal of the USSR, access to the Mediterranean would unquestionably be hazardous. However, the significance of such bases in any future war of greater dimensions, should it ever occur, would decrease in proportion to the new technology. Since the Kremlin apparently believes in this change of technique, chances are that it is not overly concerned at the loss of Albanian bases.

## The Future

The heyday of the nation state in the 19th century produced a fascinating political game called the balance of power. The statesmen of that era, if checkmated, relied on that notorious Clausewitz maxim that, *in extremis,* war would merely continue the game in a rougher manner and enforce an end to the dead-lock. If this was a risky way to conduct foreign affairs then, it is far too dangerous in the nuclear age, for there can be no more victors.

Moreover, the world today is divided roughly into three camps: the West, the East, and the so-called non-aligned na-tions. This may seem to be an oversimplification, but in spite of the pluralism within all three camps, East and West are poised against each other, unwilling to compromise, and the neutrals have no real power: they are pawns in the East-West struggle. Compromise is possible among leaders whose cultural and ethical backgrounds are similar; it therefore is possible among the components of the West as well as those of the East. It is impos-sible between the Eastern and Western camps simply because neither feels that it can afford to relinquish principles which constitute its ideological rationale; thus all that can be hoped for are day-to-day working agreements.

In this essay, we are concerned, of course, with the Eastern Bloc. The leading power in that Bloc still is, and will continue to be for many years, the USSR. Communist China, with all its potential cannot hope even to approximate the present-day strength of the Soviet Union for decades to come. Therefore, the posture of Moscow is of prime importance for American strategy, political and otherwise, and a clarification of Soviet strengths and weaknesses, which may develop during the coming decade, must be a major object of investigation.

In the previous pages, an attempt has been made to assess sketchily the more significant items of Soviet strengths and weaknesses both internally and externally, as they appear today. An attempt will now be made to submit a preview of things to come during a period of roughly ten years. This is a desperate undertaking because, obviously, those future developments and conditions which could influence Soviet approaches cannot now be foreseen. But an understanding of Soviet theory and practice, within the framework of world communism, permits certain points of departure.

1) Let us begin by estimating the development of the Com-munist faith. We can expect changes in methodology and pos-sibly even modifications of doctrine should conditions require. There is much that is outdated in Marxism-Leninism; if the Khrushchev reforms continue, even if Nikita Sergeievitch should retire or die before the end of the sixties, gradual and careful doctrinal adjustments to changed situations may be foreseen.

However, such modification would not necessarily lead to what is frequently termed "erosion of communism." The ideology of Marxism-Leninism has undergone modifications ever since Stalin died; it has adapted itself to the nuclear age. This is what Lenin himself would have endorsed, for he was not only a doctrinaire, but also a realist: when he recognized that developments were not proceeding along predetermined lines, he changed his course. In this sense, Khrushchev is a far better Leninist than Mao, who still firmly holds to outdated concepts,* perhaps because he believes he needs them internally just as Stalin made use of the slogan of "capitalist encirclement." That there have been and will be further changes in Communist theory and practice, no one can doubt. That these changes will lead away from revolution to evolution is highly unlikely during the next decade.

2) This leads us to the decisive question as to whether polycentric communism might foreshadow a deterioration of world communism. Since 1945, we have been used to looking at the Communist Bloc as a monolith which it no doubt was during Stalin's lifetime. When the tyrant died, it became clear to his successors that it would be impossible to rule the entire "socialist camp" from Moscow, and that the time had come when the CPSU would play the role of a guiding vanguard rather than a domineering force that brooked no interference with its views. The 20th Party Congress of the CPSU established the principle of "different roads to socialism" together with that of the "non-inevitability" of war. According to Khrushchev, "capitalist encirclement" no longer existed, and consequently the need for warlike intolerance of even the smallest deviation had lost its rationale. Polycentrism was on its way and the Communist orbit became somewhat decentralized in so far as its internal policies were concerned. In matters of foreign policy, adherence to the Kremlin line was expected. In addition to this loosening of Moscow's reins, there occurred growing disagreements between Moscow and Peking which led to unprecedented quarrels, resulting in a strain between the two large Communist powers and Albania's split with the USSR. Such events had never happened before; they were considered impossible until 1956. Was this the beginning of the end of the "socialist commonwealth"?

* The December 31, 1962, declaration of Chinese Communist principles is based upon outdated Leninist theses and refuses to recognize the need for adjustment to new and unprecedented conditions.

Decidedly not. I cannot agree with those who believe that
the present changes will lead to dissolution. At least not in our
lifetime. Ideology and organization are too strong and common
hatreds of the Bloc toward the West too deep to be discounted.
There may not be a monolithic cohesion, but a cohesion exists,
the Moscow-Peking controversy notwithstanding. Even if an
outright split occurred between the Soviet Union and Red China
such as that between Moscow and Tirana, we should not count
on Communist erosion. Two world centers of communism would
increase rather than decrease our troubles. When the Eastern
and Western branches of the Christian churches separated in
1054, Christianity remained very much alive. Since communism
can be regarded as secular religion, some degree of fractionaliza-
tion would not necessarily destroy it.

In any event, during the next ten years, we should not anticipate radical changes in the application of Marxism-Leninism,
except that they will be handled by the Kremlin in a more
sophisticated manner. The basic thinking and behavior of Soviet
leaders, however, will continue to be strained through the filter
of doctrine, and although modifications will occur, they should
not be taken as signs of deterioration. Rather are they emana-
tions of Communist dialectics.

3) The primary policy objective of Khrushchev is and remains
the achievement of the "material-technical basis" needed for a
"transition to communism." Within this ideological and political framework, some startling innovations may be expected by
the end of the coming decade (e.g., the distribution of free meals,
or at least one free meal per day, to all Soviet citizens). Such
measures would not necessarily indicate that the classless society
had arrived, but the Kremlin might wish to advertise *urbi et
orbi* that the realization of communism was impending. Since
doctrine by itself, while still being fed to adults and children,
might not be sufficient to stimulate persistent fervor, material
achievements and technological advances will help to promote
communism by paying a tangible dividend of the revolution.
The tactics of incentives, now frequently used in the Soviet
Bloc, are still "socialist" (everyone gets as much as he deserves);
to open the portals to the kingdom of heaven on earth, a change
in human desires must have taken place and no one should ask
for more than he needs. We do not know whether this can ever
be achieved. But certainly it cannot be done within a decade
or two.

Whether Khrushchev still will be at the helm at the end of the coming decade is questionable. We know him as a formidable opponent but also as a man who realized that war no longer pays and that it could be the undoing of the Soviet system together with that of Western democracy. So long as he is in a dominant position, he will want to proceed toward the door that opens into the never-never land of communism. His "peaceful coexistence" campaign is undoubtedly geared to promote the "transition to communism" and to prevent it from being harmed. Moreover, there is still much work to be done in the USSR to make such a transition possible, and the present economic problems are not conducive to its early realization.

We do not know whether his successor will follow his policies, possibly even outpace them, or, on the contrary, revert to a much tougher, more Stalinist-Maoist line. In this connection, the succession to Mao is also an issue of prime importance. As noted above, the demise of either man could bring about a decisive change in Sino-Soviet relations and thereby affect "peaceful coexistence." Khrushchev's successor is likely to be a man who is both technocrat and *apparatchik*, a generation removed from the old Bolsheviks, realistic and calculating, but not necessarily devoid of fanaticism. Whether his rule will be better or worse than Khrushchev's remains to be seen. Whether the demise of Mao will bring about an easing of tensions and a decrease of Chinese aggressive policies is uncertain. In any event, a disruptive, protracted succession struggle in either Moscow or Peking is unlikely to occur, given the prevailing trends, and the change of personalities might strengthen rather than weaken world communism.

4) Has there been or is there now a "power struggle" in the Kremlin? Khrushchev's position at present is stronger than ever; there is no evidence to the contrary except in the speculating minds of Kremlinologists. He has packed the Central Committee with his creatures; he has no equal among his colleagues of the Presidium; he is, in Orwell's words, more equal than the others. His ouster of Zhukov has demonstrated that he will tolerate no military "Thermidor," and he controls both the armed and police forces. Speculation that, in his now famous anti-Stalin poem, Yevtushenko meant Kozlov when he referred to an alleged Stalinist who had a heart attack, is idle. Kozlov's influence goes only so far as Khrushchev will permit, and it would be folly to assume that Khrushchev does not know all there is to know about Kozlov. We should finally lay to rest the

idea that a power struggle in the Kremlin is preordained. Even
if it occurred, it would not necessarily create a chink in the
Soviet armor. This applies even more in Peking; the cohesion
of the ruling group through the years has been astonishing even
though it is reasonable to assume that not all leaders agree with
Mao's irrational policies. But no power struggle seems to be
in sight and succession to Mao probably will proceed in an
orderly manner.

5) The Kremlin will continue to probe political weak spots
throughout the world, and whenever an apparent vacuum appears, will try to fill it. However, experiences in Guinea and
Cuba have taught it a lesson and it will proceed more carefully
than before—but proceed it will, without risking major involvement with the United States. The Soviets will be quite prepared
to retreat if they find resistance hard and determined as the case
of Cuba has demonstrated in October 1962. At the same time,
they will ensure that Soviet armed forces remain in a high
state of readiness and will continue to invest a considerable part
of their national resources in research and development of new
weapons, with emphasis on missiles and nuclear power.

The Kremlin will persist in prohibiting foreign policy deviations by the Eastern European Satellites. It regards these areas
as a Soviet security zone whose manpower and economic resources require supervision. Moreover, the concept of the "world
Socialist system" or "Socialist commonwealth" of which Eastern
Europe is to be the center, will not be permitted to get out of
line with Soviet strategy and tactics. No change in this policy
can be anticipated; on the contrary, measures will be taken to
strengthen Eastern European cohesion both politically and economically. Outside interference in this system would most likely
be regarded as a *casus belli*.*

In this connection it might be well to reiterate that satellite
weaknesses will be given little opportunity for Western exploitation. For the time being all we can do is to maintain the image
of the West, particularly the United States, and hope for the best.
But within the next decade, barring a sudden decline of the
Soviet Union or a collapse of international communism, no significant changes can be expected.

6) We should anticipate startling developments in Soviet
space efforts. Khrushchev will continue to channel considerable

* This writer is convinced that Western military interference in the
Hungarian revolution almost certainly would have led to war.

assets into this undertaking in order to further enhance Soviet prestige abroad, stimulate pride in the Soviet system at home, and strengthen confidence in his military might. There can be no doubt that Soviet space achievements should be looked upon not only as scientific achievements, but largely as demonstrations of military power. Every satellite shot into space is supposed to testify to the ingeniousness and resourcefulness of Soviet science and technology in order that the entire world may take note of such power. It should not be assumed that, due to any economic difficulty, space efforts might decrease. This is one area which has greatly aided Khrushchev to advertise Soviet power; furthermore, aware of US efforts, he will continue the space race even to the detriment of less important branches of industry, especially consumer goods. A Soviet landing on the moon during the next ten years is well within the realm of the possible, and it would have ominous political and military significance.

7) Experimentation in the Soviet economy and its organization will continue until solutions have been found. Various systems of control may be tested. It will soon become apparent whether or not the recent reorganization of industry and agriculture under centralized Party control are more successful than the decentralization experiments. If not, something else will be attempted. It is also possible that, under some high-sounding disguise, collectivized agriculture will be granted a reprieve in the form of a new kind of NEP, as the now famous Lieberman plan suggests.

It would be unwise to expect the Soviet economy to deteriorate dangerously. During the next ten years, enormous efforts will be made to bolster it so that the "material-technical bases" for a "transition to communism" can be built. Even if this does not succeed—and probably it will not materialize—the Soviet economy will be strong enough for its own purposes. Comparisons with Western economies mean little; just as we should be cautious not to expect the Soviet economy to falter, so we should also exercise care not to exaggerate the very bad conditions of the Red Chinese economy. They are indeed deplorable and have caused untold suffering, but suffering is not new in China, and it would be a dangerous mistake to believe that the Chinese economy will collapse altogether. On the contrary, a slow but gradual improvement already is evident, since the Mao regime has reversed itself on the "Great Leap Forward" and modified the communes.

8) To what extent the Sino-Soviet, the Sino-Yugoslav, and the Soviet-Albanian controversies can be regarded as weaknesses depends upon the time factor. At present they undoubtedly do not contribute to the strength of the Bloc nations even though they do not deflect significantly from Soviet power per se. However, the cohesion of the "socialist camp" is impaired, and it remains to be seen whether this will turn out to be a short- or long-range impediment. It is possible that a splintering trend in the Communist movement, greatly weakening international communism, might constrain Soviet actions internally and externally. However, we must not forget that the basic elements of cohesion still exist and probably will continue to exist during the period of this forecast. There has been unrest and upheaval in the past and it was mended. It would be short-sighted to exclude a repetition of, say, the 1956-57 stabilization move on an even grander scale.

It seems rather safe to predict that during the next ten years arguments between Peking and Moscow will continue in a more or less exacerbated manner unless a sudden change in the top leadership reverses the present trend toward schismatic methodology. However, if China were attacked by large-scale forces, or were embroiled in a struggle against a combination of forces with which it could not cope, Moscow probably would come to her aid in accordance with the 1950 Mutual Assistance Treaty. Similarly, Peking probably would assist Moscow if the USSR were involved in large-scale war.

The West's position in the Moscow-Peking struggle—in which Albania and Yugoslavia are *not* major factors—should be one of discernment and detachment. Despite the great differences in racial, historic and social experience, in present economic levels, and the resulting arguments concerning interpretation and implementation of Marxism-Leninism, Peking is still far closer to Moscow than Moscow is to Washington. The time for a major undertaking in psychological warfare designed to widen the rift between Moscow and Peking has not yet come; if carried out now, it might boomerang by bringing the opponents together again. Only if a genuine break occurred, and the two centers of world communism were to fight for the leadership of the Communist movement, could a well-thought-out propaganda campaign be effective.

Should Yugoslavia indeed be ready to renew Party ties with the CPSU and agree to a broad *rapprochement* with the USSR, the West, particularly the United States, would have to review its policies, especially those concerning economic aid. As for Albania, it merits watching only as an indicator of Sino-Soviet arguments. It is neither viable nor of major strategic importance. In my view, its significance as a nation has been exaggerated.

9) Altogether, the Soviet Union possesses power second only to that of the United States. Its weaknesses will be compensated by its strong points. We must assume that, during the coming decade, Soviet strength will increase rather than decrease despite the fact that Bloc infighting may deflect Soviet courses of action and throw its policies somewhat out of gear. The optimism displayed in certain US circles concerning the expected "erosion" of communism and a reversion of the USSR from a Communist to a national power is highly dangerous, and, if applied to Western policy, might be suicidal. Also, the belief that Red China is about to fall apart, that the Chinese people will revolt against their regime, and that the Sino-Soviet conflict indicates the beginning of the end of the "world socialist system" belongs in the realm of daydreaming by analysts who are unfamiliar with the history, doctrine, and organization of international communism. At least during the next ten years, such development should not be expected, and our planning should not be based upon such a contingency.

Therefore, in order to cope with Soviet Communist power, the United States and its allies must maintain a strong, modern military establishment of nuclear *and* conventional forces, a sound economy, an unmatched advancement of science and technology, a high degree of social consciousness, and a first-rate educational system offering opportunities for higher education to all intellectually endowed, regardless of their financial status.

Furthermore, there is great need for more understanding of those principles and practices of international communism which affect the actions and behavior of Communist-ruled states and for the realization that, with the demise of traditional diplomacy, propaganda has become its substitute. Indeed, under communism, policy and propaganda have merged into one— which has been very confusing to the Western mind that basically detests propaganda.[5]

Last, but not least, we should never again lose the initiative to act instead of reacting. Our Cuba policy is not necessarily applicable to other areas, but it has demonstrated that we succeed in reaching working agreements only if we are strong and let the Communists and the world know we will not be bullied.

74      KURT LONDON

It is my belief, that, in the next ten years, the East-West struggle will be predominantly a battle of brains. We have the brains; we need only permit them to function.


FOOTNOTES


¹ See Kurt London, *The Permanent Crisis* (New York: Walker & Co., 1962), pp. 15-16.
² See Raymond L. Garthoff, *Soviet Strategy in the Nuclear Age* (New York: Frederick A. Praeger, 1962), chap. 2.
³ For a detailed account of intra-Bloc activities see Zbigniew Brzezinski, *The Soviet Bloc* (New York: Praeger, 1961), Appendix 1, pp. 445 ff.
⁴ See K. London, ed., *Unity and Contradiction* (New York: Praeger, 1962), Epilogue, p. 415.
⁵ See London, *The Permanent Crisis, op. cit.*, pp. 283 ff.

# The Sino-Soviet Alliance

—*RICHARD L. WALKER*

## Summary

Since it was cemented in 1950, the alliance between Communist China and the Soviet Union has not escaped from the
great changes which have swept the world. Despite continuing
incantations of fraternal solidarity, the relationship between the
two partners has changed so that the term "Sino-Soviet Bloc,"
which was a legitimate characterization at the time of the
Korean War, is no longer apt for describing a relationship which
has neither the solidity nor the homogeneous unity implied
by the word "bloc." Mao's China has drawn upon many traditional despotic institutions to fashion a political system which
is more totalitarian, more dogmatic, and more uncompromising
in its hostility toward the West than is the Soviet Union.

A survey of developments over the first thirteen years of the
alliance indicates that from an attitude of enthusiasm with
which the two partners first embraced each other they have
turned away toward different world views. The Soviet Union
of Khrushchev has faced toward the West where it has been
concerned about the revival of Germany and the resurgence
and growing unity of Western Europe. An industrialized and
technically sophisticated Russia has more to gain in direct competition with the West than by the almost exclusive concentration on the underdeveloped areas as do the Chinese. Europe's
prosperity has done much to undercut the Chinese contention
that the colonies and former colonies are the front line in the
world struggle. As the Chinese Communists have moved away
from dependence on to an interdependence with the Soviet
Union, traditional factors as well as their inability to accept

*status-quo policies on their borders have given them a different world outlook. They have turned away from the Soviet Union toward a preponderant concern in East and South Asia.*

*Within the framework of increasingly different cultural and intellectual approaches toward their struggle to create a Communist world, there are five areas in which stress and tension between the alliance partners are likely to increase:*

*1) Peking's great power aspirations will create problems for Moscow. Two items are particularly worthy of attention: Chinese Communist claims to leadership of the revolution in the underdeveloped lands and their drive toward nuclear great-power status. Given historic distrust between the two peoples, this latter will prove exceptionally troublesome for the Soviets.*

*2) Chinese Communist insistence on exporting their own type of revolutionary violence around the world and their dogmatic position that war is not only necessary but desirable.*

*3) Peking's bid for regional hegemony in East Asia which brings it into rivalry and disagreement with Moscow whose support is less than wholehearted.*

*4) The great problems of the China scene such as agrarian failure and overpopulation. The impending death of Mao is likely to provoke a power struggle in which the Soviets could become involved in order to preserve the alliance.*

*5) The self-reinforcing isolation of the Chinese Communist regime from the realities of the space-age world.*

*The prospect of continuing stresses and strains in the alliance offers little occasion for comfort in the outside world. Both partners agree that we are the enemy. Their competition to prove that each has the superior strategy for burying the West makes the situation more, not less, dangerous.*

*Current diverging strategies and world outlook point toward an eventual break in the alliance, but, in the decade of the 1960's, the penalties of a rupture outweigh any advantages. Western strategy must be designed to intensify the continuing distrust and tension in the alliance without the direct interference that would encourage renewed solidarity. A key method is to insist that the Soviets speak for and be responsible for their Chinese allies.*

**Part One**

It has become commonplace to comment that we live in a world where there is not only change but change at an ever-accelerating pace. Events which were compressed into a decade at the beginning of the century would seem to be proceeding at a leisurely pace today if they extend more than a year. This means that ideas, analytical frameworks, and particularly the clichés and stereotypes which may have been valid yesterday simply do not apply today—and we hardly dare to project them into tomorrow. There are, of course, factors and forces which will persist, but the different milieus in which they operate change their impact. Some come to the surface with renewed vigor while others fade toward insignificance.

Certainly since October 4, 1957, when *sputnik* was added as a standard word to our vocabulary, the changes have been grandiose enough to raise signs of caution as regards the use of outworn terms and frameworks for analysis. The age of commercial jet travel, of world-wide television, of thermonuclear missiles, of proliferating new states, and of the resurgence and growing unity of Western Europe—to mention just a few developments in diverse fields—has wrought transformations in international affairs which none of the great powers can escape. The Western Alliance system, the Communist states, and even the nature of the Cold War have been profoundly affected.

Despite the incantations of "eternal and unshakable friendship," "fraternal solidarity," and "monolithic unity," the Sino-Soviet Alliance has not been able to evade the impact of our revolutionary age, or the changes within its own area of control. Communist China and its relations with the Soviet Union are far different now than when Mao Tse-tung cemented his alliance with Stalin in Moscow on February 14, 1950. After almost fourteen years in power the Chinese Communist leadership has felt itself subject to entirely different forces than were operative at the time of their first flush of victory. Responsibility for the staggering problems of the China scene, for example, has become a factor of increasing weight in determining the approach of the top leadership in Communist China toward both internal and external policies.

The Sino-Soviet Alliance operates today in a world environment which has been profoundly altered. The great anti-Western sentiment, which affected leadership in most of the colonies and former colonies when the Sino-Soviet Alliance was formed

and to which it appealed, is mostly over. Europe's retreat from
empire and its concomitant economic resurgence have brought a
realization in many former colonies that much can be gained
by continuing close association with the metropoles. The Sino-
Soviet Alliance of 1950 reflected the force of such factors as a
history of the subordination of the Chinese Communist Party
to the interests of the Comintern, the personalities of Stalin
and Mao and their interrelationship, the economic dependence
of China upon its Soviet big brother, and an agreement on
Moscow's doctrinal leadership. It still reflects such factors but
they have been radically transformed.

The simple fact is, therefore, that whereas in the first few
years of the alliance, and particularly during the period of
the Korean War, it was legitimate and accurate to speak of the
"Sino-Soviet Bloc." This term is grossly misleading in 1963.
It is an example of the type of phrase which can lead us unwittingly into inaccurate lines of reasoning. The word "bloc"
implies a solid and homogeneous unity which is not characteristic
of the alliance today.

Another example of an equally misleading term is the phrase
"Bamboo Curtain," frequently used by journalists to describe
Communist China's totalitarian isolation from the realities of
the outside world and presumably the Chinese counterpart of
the Soviet "Iron Curtain." But "bamboo" suggests a less
formidable barrier with some flexibility, and surely this is not
descriptive of Mao's China today. The Stalinesque structure
of the present Chinese Communist regime is such that if we
refer to an "Iron Curtain" between the Soviet Union and the
West we should probably refer to Communist China's new
"Great Iron Wall."

The China of 1963 is comparable in many ways with the
Soviet Union of the latter-day Stalin, but it also bears comparison with and undoubtedly draws form and inspiration from
its own despotic past. Indeed, there is an historical resonance
in the voice of Mao's China which increasingly sets it apart
from its Soviet ally. With the passage of time this factor has
tended to give a different direction to the manner in which the
Chinese partner of the alliance has viewed and dealt with
prodigious world changes.

Imperial China maintained a splendid and haughty isolation
from the outer barbarians. Its Confucian gentry, like today's
Communist cadres, maintained a monopoly of learning of a
dogma with which the benighted outside world was expected

eventually to concur. Inside the Middle Kingdom, foreigners were managed and isolated, controlled and supervised. Over many extended periods Chinese were forbidden to travel abroad, and the imperial rulers took great pains to prevent their subjects from being contaminated by alien ideas and people. Much of Imperial China's difficulty in adjusting to the world in the eighteenth and nineteenth centuries stemmed from the intellectual and political wall of isolation which prevented comparison between internal achievements of the Chinese state and developments outside the area of control, an attitude of superiority which projected the Chinese pattern as the basis for the pacification of the whole world.

Impressive construction and achievements, the greatness of the land, the power of the mass population, and the authoritarian political structure all operated in Imperial China, as they do in Communist China, to reinforce the isolation of the Wall. Perhaps this is nowhere better illustrated than in the despotic inability to admit mistakes or failure and in the sycophancy and adulation which reach ludicrous extremes in the worship of the supreme ruler. Documents which flowed to the Chinese emperor during the Opium War (1839-42) reported victory after victory for the forces representing his august might just as the documents flowing to the Chinese Communist capital during Mao Tse-tung's "Great Leap Forward" (1958-60) proclaimed equally false victories on the production front. The arrival of a giraffe in Peking in 1414 was regarded as a sign which justified the following outburst to the Yung Lo Emperor by one of the court sycophants:

> Our Emperor plans his government by modeling himself on his Heaven; the fame of his teaching has spread; the East is impregnated with it and the West has received it. There is no darkness but is brightened, there is no distance but is illuminated. From where the waters gather and the clouds assemble, bowing their heads all bear gifts. Thus many auspicious signs are collected arriving one after another in pairs. How comes this? Only through the perfect virtue of our Emperor which brings harmony in the eight corners of the world; beyond the horizon and to the ends of the earth there are none but are respectful and loving.

This is hardly more extreme than some of the paeans to Mao

Tse-tung, such as the following by the Communist writer Hu
Feng, who was later purged for being anti-Mao:

> Mao Tse-tung
> Standing erect on the mountain's topmost peak
> Looks like one turning to himself
> And to the world, announcing:
>
> . . .
> High over the sea
> Would I be magnified—
> Magnified that I may be able to embrace the whole world
> Magnified that I may be able to flow into eternity.

Such cultural and historical resonance has increasingly formed
a basis on which the Chinese Communist leadership conducts its
internal affairs as well as its policies toward friends, neutrals,
and enemies abroad. The Chinese language has been geared
through centuries to provide a reinforcing vigor to the Leninist
two-camp view which the current rulers accept. Outsiders, including Communist allies, are judged in terms of the extent to
which they fall in with the pattern of truth as proclaimed by
the new emperor from on high. Authoritarian institutions and
patterns have brought to Mao's China an intellectual quarantine
from outside reality and have affected the whole world view of
the Chinese People's Republic.

**Part Two**

It is probably desirable to summarize briefly how the world
views of the two Communist allies have changed since they signed
their Alliance in Moscow in 1950. This will afford at least some
basis for projecting future trends and developments.

Mao joined with a Stalin who had withdrawn the Soviet Union
both culturally and spiritually from the West. Stalin had completed the Russian "Asiatic restoration" Lenin had once feared.
He looked toward the East. The Five-Year Plans focused attention on Asiatic Russia and the development of the Asian heartland; from 1949 until 1953 the Russian people were made China-
conscious as never before; China became the Soviet Union's
greatest trading partner; great efforts were expended in aid of
Chinese development; even Stalin's foray into the field of linguis-
tics was an effort to prove by decree from on high that Russian
did not belong to the Indo-European family of languages. The
Iron Curtain itself symbolized the despotic mysticism and secrecy
of a Russia that had turned its back on Western Europe and
had cast its lot with the China of Mao Tse-tung.

But, following Stalin's death and beginning with the travels of Khrushchev and Bulganin in 1955, the Soviet Union has gradually faced again toward the West. In an industrializing and atomic age, Russia obviously has more to glean from the West. The remarkable vitality and viability of Western Europe has made it a formidable competitor as well as a more significant and attractive target for Communist expansion. With the passage of time, the Soviet leaders and intellectuals have found their Chinese comrades dogmatic and dull, have noted that they tend to be clannish and humorless, and have commented that they are difficult to understand. Undoubtedly the enormity of China's problems has also made itself felt inside the Soviet Union and in Eastern Europe. Khrushchev must deal with the Chinese Communist Party, numbering 17 million, and with a nation whose gargantuan population and ambitions are sobering. A high Polish Communist official commented to Western diplomats, "Before in Eastern Europe we used to say that an optimist studies Russian and a pessimist studies Chinese. Now we know we have no choice. We'll all have to learn to eat caviar with chopsticks."

Though obviously never expressed openly, perhaps Western Europe's increasing prosperity and moves toward unity pushed the Soviet leadership under Khrushchev to the conclusion that the future of world communism depended primarily upon the USSR's ability to confront, compete with, and outdistance the Western powers. The road to Rio and New Delhi now lay through Rome and Paris. The almost step-by-step correlation of Europe's retreat from empire with its economic growth has tended to undermine much of the propaganda appeal of Lenin's theory of imperialism which had been a major weapon in the Communist arsenal for world revolution. Nationalist leaders in the newly independent lands are less likely to be convinced by Communist arguments that their own underdevelopment as well as European prosperity were a result of colonial status. The European experience has indicated that in many cases, far from contributing to the wealth of the mother country, the colonies were a net drain.

Russia's turning toward the West, undoubtedly reinforced by a preponderant concern over the phenomenal recovery of West Germany, expressed itself in forms which would obviously cause misgivings and distrust on the part of the Chinese Communists. In their view, Khrushchev's travels, including his tour of the United States in 1959, exposed him to the risk of contamination.

Increasing cultural contacts with the camp of the enemy, including such extremes as the successful visit in the Soviet Union of Benny Goodman, probably gave the impression that in turning toward the West, Khrushchev had turned his back on his Communist allies. Such an impression was undoubtedly reinforced by the Chinese exclusion from the Council for Mutual Economic Assistance (COMECON) when Mongolia was admitted in June 1962.

This is not to say that renewed contact with the West was making the Soviet leadership any less committed to the victory of world communism. The power play in Cuba in 1962 demonstrated only too clearly continuing Soviet ambitions. After all, the policies of Peter the Great and Catherine II in opening a window to the West had hardly made Imperial Russia a less formidable opponent in world affairs. What was only too obviously clear by the time of the thirteenth anniversary of the Sino-Soviet Alliance in 1963 was that the Soviet world outlook had changed appreciably. The Soviet leaders in the space age seemed disillusioned with their Oriental allies and even a bit apprehensive. It is conceivable that, in the disputes on doctrine and strategy, Moscow's leadership was preparing to disassociate itself and the future of world communism from a possible Chinese economic failure and from the increasingly unattractive expressions of Chinese Stalinism and chauvinism.

If the Soviet Union under Khrushchev has faced increasingly to the West, since the death of Stalin the China of Mao Tse-tung has turned toward the east and south. During the early years of the alliance, the Chinese people were given a steady diet of "great Stalin," "learn from the great Soviet Union," and Russian language training. No foreigner had ever been given the worship and adulation accorded Stalin in China. The Sino-Soviet Friendship Association, which had been formed only a few days after Mao's regime had been proclaimed, boasted a membership of more than 68 million Chinese members by January 1953. The Soviet state was hailed as a beacon illuminating the road for the progress of all mankind. Chinese scholars were urged to abandon their own learning and those who had studied abroad to discard the "pseudo-science of the West" in favor of advanced Soviet experience.

But if there was enthusiastic leaning to one side in favor of everything Soviet and Russian in the initial years of the Mao regime, there was an undercurrent which placed emphasis on the "exploited people and oppressed nations of the entire world," and within this framework the Chinese Communists made sweeping claims about the significance of their own victory for the future of world communism. In terms of promoting the world revolution, Mao's China pressed toward a far more rigid adherence to Lenin's theory of imperialism and an uncompromising hostility toward the "imperialist West." Peking insisted on a one-for-one identification of the future of world communism with the "national emancipatory struggle" and Communist victories in the underdeveloped world. From the outset, the Chinese Communists maintained a dogmatic attachment to the view that the fall of the West was imminent and could be culminated by pushing the great world struggle against imperialism, even if it meant war. On June 25, 1962, Chinese Communist Foreign Minister Ch'en Yi opined, "No matter how vicious and insidious the strategic plan of the Kennedy Administration is, everyone can see that the trend of the imperialist camp toward disintegration is inevitable, that the raging flames of the national liberation movement can in no way be stamped out, and that no force on earth can disrupt the great socialist camp."

Within a short time after the death of Stalin, forces were operating to change the Chinese outlook on the world. As the Soviets turned away from Stalinism and toward more direct challenges to the West, Mao's China turned intellectually and culturally back to its own areas of interest in the East. Peking maintained its profound suspicion and distrust of the West. The regime's internal measures as well as its position in foreign affairs were those associated with the name of Stalin in the USSR and characterized by secrecy, suspicion, and growing concern for national prestige. The Chinese leadership was obviously dismayed by Khrushchev's February 1956 denunciation of Stalin with whom so many had identified themselves. In Mao's domain there was a period of hesitation during which Peking admitted some of Stalin's shortcomings but praised his measures for centralizing and building state power. But this was followed by the full-flown development of the cult of Mao Tse-tung.

There were many developments which indicated a gradual fading of the initial enthusiasm with which the Chinese "little brothers" embraced everything Soviet. By 1956, intensified study of Russian as a second language was quietly dropped, and the regime began to stress China's own "superior traditions." That year large-scale Soviet aid ceased, and the Chinese began to export more goods to the Soviets than they received. Terms of trade showed that the USSR was not the most generous of trading partners—and this was at the very time when Moscow was moving actively into direct-grant aid programs abroad, as contrasted with a policy of loans to China. The Chinese were probably not pleased with Soviet attempts to compete with the United States and Western Powers in aid programs to prop up "bourgeois nationalists" in Asia and Africa if this meant a cut in assistance to the fraternal Chinese People's Republic. Their own approach favored promotion of violence such as in the case of Algeria, where they assisted with far more enthusiasm than the Soviets. Although the Sino-Soviet Friendship Association continued its ritual of fraternal greetings and congratulations, it obviously lacked its former support and vigor in China.

After a relatively successful First Five-Year Plan, the ambitions of the regime soared. Its basis for comparison was not the outside world, but its own seemingly magical transformation of the Chinese landscape. The measures of 1958 reflected a leadership increasingly lost from the stream of world reality, more than ever convinced of its infallibility and inevitable success, beset with a Stalin-like paranoia, and directed by the chauvinism which had once characterized Imperial China. In 1958, the frenzy of the "Great Leap Forward," of the back-yard iron furnaces, of the people's communes, of the everyone-a-soldier movement, of the grandiose production claims, of the crisis in the Taiwan Straits, and of the sudden rupture of trade relations with Japan, reflected a world view which was obviously out of line with Moscow. Proud and sensitive Chinese leaders could hardly have enjoyed comments in Eastern Europe and in the USSR itself that their measures were stupid. A "culted" Mao Tse-tung probably did not relish the Soviet rejection of his thesis that the Communist camp was now stronger than the "camp of imperialism." Moscow failed to take up or even to repeat Mao's own post-Sputnik expression that "The East Wind prevails over the West Wind."

Events in 1959 led to a further Chinese turning away from the line of Khrushchev. The Soviet leader was touring the United States, talking status quo and evincing his primary concern for Europe. The economic reckoning in the wake of the "Great Leap Forward" and the insecurities occasioned by the revolt in Tibet led to an even further concentration by the Chinese on their own problems and to a reinforcement of secrecy. In November, Peking stopped export of all but a very few publications to the outside world, including even Eastern Europe. Soviet advisors returning from China the following year confessed that the

Chinese were so secretive it was impossible to know what was going on at the national level. Since 1959, Peking has published no significant production or trade figures, although the Soviets revealed that in 1961 China's share in Soviet trade had shrunk from 20 per cent to only 8 per cent.

The growth of Stalinist suspicion and secrecy was reflected even in the policies toward members of the Chinese Communist Party and other officials inside China. The National People's Congress which finally met, after an illegal year's hiatus, in the spring of 1962 carried on its deliberations in absolute secrecy. For the first time no foreign Communists, including the Soviet big brothers, were present, no budget figures were given, and no production statistics published. Faced with a crisis of major proportions at home, Mao and his colleagues maintained the stance of being engaged in a life and death struggle with the outside forces of imperialism, and this was used to justify secrecy. On October 14, 1962, Party members were advised:

> Some comrades in order to satisfy their own curiosity like to find out things they are not supposed to know. Such a practice is incompatible with security requirements. Steps must be taken to limit dissemination of state secrets because the greater the number of people who know about them the greater the possibility of leakage. We must therefore treasure the interests of the Party and state and do away with this bad habit of finding out about things we are not supposed to know. Some people are not security-conscious enough; they are frequently discussing state secrets in public places. This practice must be rooted out forthwith. As the saying goes: "This wall has ears." By indulging in loose talk, these comrades without knowing it have often given important state secrets away to the enemy.

By 1963, it was manifestly clear that the Chinese Communist outlook on the world and the strategic approach of Mao and his fellow leaders in Peking were quite different from those of the Kremlin, despite their obvious sharing of a Marxist-Leninist faith. The Chinese Communist political creation is more total in its control, and partly for this reason as well as because of the continuing existence of the alternate Nationalist regime on Taiwan, more insecure, more uncompromising. As Peking turns toward the problems of China and the surrounding areas in Asia, its great power ambitions and its determination to reassert Chinese prerogatives in that area seem to be undermined, rather than aided, by a Russia more concerned with the power of the West. Such seemed to be the Chinese point of view on the Soviet

policy regarding the Sino-Indian border dispute and the outbreak of fighting between the two great Asian countries in
October, 1962.

Just as Russia's major concern has been Germany, so, since
World War II, the Chinese Communists have been sensitive about
the miraculous new productive capacity of Japan. Perhaps the
following exchange between Kenzo Matsumura, who had just
returned from a visit to Communist China as a representative of
the ruling Liberal-Democratic Party in Japan, and the editor
of the *Asahi Journal* as published on October 7, 1962, symbolizes
the extent to which Mao's China has turned away from the Soviet
embrace toward traditional areas of Chinese concern:

> Editor:        What about the so-called antagonism be-
>                tween China and the Soviet Union?
> Matsumura:     Officially there was no reference to that
>                problem. In his Table speech the Prime
>                Minister [Chou En-lai] emphasized "liai-
>                son in the East" for coexistence and co-
>                prosperity. He also talked about the "two
>                countries in the East." I do not think that
>                one of the "two countries" was the Soviet
>                Union. He never used such expressions
>                three years ago.

What should be apparent from this brief survey of the manner
in which the Chinese Communists and their Soviet axis partners
have abandoned their initial enthusiasm and agreement is that
each has a somewhat different world view. As the Chinese moved
from a state of dependence upon, to one of interdependence with,
the leadership in Moscow, their outlook has been determined by
a number of considerations which have been working their way
to the surface and now disturb the smooth features of the common cause of a world-wide Communist victory. Such considerations include the depth and background of Chinese history,
traditional Chinese xenophobia, Chinese experience with Western
(including Russian) imperialism, and, most important, differences in the nature of the problems faced by the two regimes. It
is such considerations which must be projected into the rapidly
changing future and which suggest that the difference in *Weltanschauung* of these two great powers may be the single most
important factor in their alliance in the next five to ten years.

**Part Three**

Within the framework of the changing nature of the general
approaches of the two alliance partners discussed above, it is

possible to single out at least five general areas where we may
expect continuing strains and disruptions as well as resultant
differences in their strategic projections for a world-wide Communist victory.

## Area One

A first such area lies in the great-power aspirations of Peking.
These include not only Chinese Communist attempts to make
their views and national greatness felt in far-off Africa or Latin
America but involve Chinese determination to play the role of
co-equal partner in setting world Communist strategy. Many of
Mao's policies and actions, which of course have other motivations, may be viewed in terms of Chinese ambitions within the
Communist camp. These would include, for example, Chinese
support for and assistance to Albania, the Chinese Communist
attempts to take over active leadership of the Afro-Asian Solidarity Conference, and the claims advanced for Mao Tse-tung's
position as the "outstanding living theoretician of Marxism-
Leninism." The Chinese have insisted that the Sino-Soviet
Alliance is now the foundation of the Communist camp and in
so stating are asserting their great power status.

There are two aspects of the Chinese Communist drive for
great power status which will cause special problems for the
Soviet Union. The first is Peking's determination to be spokesman
for the revolutionary forces in the underdeveloped lands and
here the Chinese appeals to racialism and solidarity among the
colored people are unlikely to be received enthusiastically by
the Russians.

The second aspect is far more sensitive and troublesome for
the Soviets—the Chinese Communist drive to become a nuclear
power of first magnitude. Here the Soviets are caught up in a
dilemma somewhat analogous to that confronting the United
States in coping with de Gaulle's attempt to restore some of the
grandeur of France by building an independent nuclear force.
Foreign Minister Ch'en Yi told Kenzo Matsumura in the fall of
1962 that the Chinese Reds were "developing nuclear weapons on
a grand scale." Since the Chinese leaders are investing heavily
toward an independent nuclear strike capability, the Soviets
must decide whether to resist this to the end, as they now seem
to be doing, or to renew assistance at some point or in some
manner which will provide them at least monitoring if not control. Soviet attempts to hinder China's entrance into the nuclear

club are likely to reinforce impressions in Peking that Russia is Western after all and not committed to the solidarity of the Communist camp, especially if the Soviet leaders continue negotiations pointing toward some sort of nuclear balance based upon a two-great-powers concept of the world. Here, too, the traditional Chinese xenophobia and the historical district of the Russians can influence the Chinese Communist assessment.

### Area Two

A second area in which the past performance of Mao and his colleagues points toward disagreements and disruption in future relations with the Soviets is the Chinese insistence on exporting its own type of revolution around the world. Chinese views on a number of issues are reinforced by the bureaucratic sycophancy of the Mao cult which proclaims his path to power as an eternal and world-shaking truth. Peking has not hesitated to encourage guerrilla violence or to stress the desirability of warfare around the world. The uncompromising Chinese hostility to the West has in the past seemed to be asserted stridently enough to interfere with different Soviet approaches. In Africa, Chinese Communist representatives have at times embarrassed their Soviet big brothers by encouraging violence and subversion of governments toward which Moscow has taken an entirely different approach. The large-scale attack on the Indian border on October 20, 1962, was hardly calculated to help the position of international communism or the Soviet Union in a land where the Soviets have been attempting to win victories for their cause by other means.

It is likely to be many years before the leaders in Peking abandon their view that their formulas for Communist success— organization, mass movements, anti-imperialism, violence, and war—are classic for underdeveloped areas. Mao, who has written their scriptures maintains, "War can only be abolished through war; in order to get rid of the gun we must first take it in hand." Following his formulations the Chinese insist on the necessity of turning the anti-imperialist movement into the major battleground for the winning of the world Communist victory, and toward this end, war is not only necessary but desirable. Although the Soviets can also support some "wars of national liberation," as a nuclear power they cannot do so with impunity or with seeming unconcern about escalation like the Chinese who have far less to lose. Serious misgivings about the Chinese approach to war were expressed by Eduard Kardelj in his August 1960 book, *Socialism and War*. In his view, which the Soviets now indicate that they share, it is only necessary to read:

> The Chinese authors who, rehashing sentences torn out of Lenin's speeches or articles, written in view of specific political junctures, draw conclusions about the inevitability of war, to see what little and poor use these Chinese authors make of Marxism and Leninism. This is, of course, no accidental feature. Their theories, no matter how much they flaunt a Marxist phraseology, serve quite definite socio-political tendencies. That is why Marxism has been specifically "modified" in Chinese circumstances.

If Mao's aggression on the Indian border embarrassed his alliance partner, Khrushchev, the Soviet policy indicated that the Chinese approach to violence did not have the solid backing of the Communist camp.

### Area Three

The Chinese Communists and their alliance partners are not likely to share the same views on Chinese regional goals. Peking is obviously determined to be the sole arbiter of developments in the Far East in the pattern of Imperial China. Until the surrounding areas, including Japan, are respectfully bearing tribute to the Chinese capital and attempting to participate in the new Communist ritual, the Chinese mainland regime is not likely to press for acceptance of a status quo in the manner in which the Soviet Union seeks to legitimize its control of Eastern Europe. In Korea, in Taiwan, and in Southeast Asia, the Chinese see the need for "liberation" from "US imperialism." As an anti-status-quo power in its own area the Chinese regime is prepared, especially given Mao's doctrines, to run greater risks. Moscow will probably be repeatedly in the position of having to restrain its ally, and Khrushchev's less-than-enthusiastic backing for "liberation" around China's borders is hardly likely to convince Mao that the Soviets truly support wars of national liberation.

There has been Sino-Soviet rivalry along their common border. The new occupant of the dragon throne may possibly not accept with continuing grace the Soviet victory in Mongolia which was cemented with Mongolia's entrance into COMECON in June 1962. Mao has squeezed Soviet influence out of Manchuria, and Chinese pressure brought Kim Il Sung down on the

side of Peking in the doctrinal dispute in 1962. In his speech to
the Supreme People's Assembly on October 23, 1962, the Korean
leader noted, "Despite all sorts of calumny and slander by the
imperialists and world reaction, the Chinese People's Republic
stands firm in the heart of Asia as a great socialist power and
its international influence is further growing." Kim went on to
say, "No struggle for peace can be mentioned apart from the
fight against imperialism, U.S. imperialism in particular. . . .
Peace must not be begged for, but must be won through the
struggle of the popular masses."

### Area Four

A fourth area which will provide for tension and disruption
within the Sino-Soviet Alliance involves some of the great problems of the Chinese scene. The world and regional ambitions of
the Chinese Communist leadership are likely to make them dissatisfied with Soviet performance. There is serious question
whether in the 1960's Khrushchev's Russia can supply, or will
supply, the wherewithal for the grand-scale economic development the Chinese still want. China's population problem (six
times as many people per square kilometer of arable land as the
Soviet Union) is such as to lend little encouragement for development. The Soviet Union claimed full credit for the political asset
which Mao's victory in China gave to international communism,
but it is not impossible that Moscow would now like to rid itself
of an economic liability.

As was the case in the Soviet Union, a major power struggle
is to be expected at the death of the "great leader Mao Tse-tung."
Given the thorough nature of the political structure he has built
and the complete Party monopoly over and control of communications and transport, it is unlikely that revolts in mainland
China can be anything but isolated and sporadic in nature. But
the contention for Mao's throne after his death could bring anti-
Soviet resentment into open expression as a political force. Contending forces could conceivably appeal to the Chinese Nationalists in terms of anti-Soviet national unity or to the Soviets in
the name of preserving the "Socialist victory." The Soviets
must consider the real possibility that they may have to become
directly involved in Chinese politics to preserve the alliance.
Mao's death will bring more immediate and pressing problems
within the Communist camp than for the outside world. The
problems of the China scene are not small ones. Since many of

them stem from China's overwhelming agricultural difficulties, the Soviet Union will not find them easy to deal with at a time when its own agricultural shortcomings have yet to be remedied.

### Area Five

The fifth area of concern for Mao Tse-tung's alliance partners is China's self-reinforcing isolation from the realities of the outside world. As noted above, today's occupants of the Imperial. City in Peking cling to the formulations of pre-atomic age Marxism-Leninism-Maoism as the Chinese gentry of old clung to their vested interest in Confucianism. They are far more out of touch with today's great changes than the more industrially and technologically sophisticated Russians. This is probably best symbolized by Mao's almost mystical faith in the mobilized masses. For a leadership which watches disciplined millions of Chinese parade to its commands, Mao's 1958 statement that the liberation of the forces of the masses is the equivalent of smashing the atom, may seem real. At a Peking rally on September 15, 1962, Liu Ning-i, president of the All-China Federation of Trade Unions opined:

> The masses of the people are the decisive factor in defending world peace. As long as the powerful socialist camp, the surging national democratic revolutionary movement of the peoples of Asia, Africa, and Latin America, and the working people and all the other peace-loving people of the world close their ranks still more tightly, form a broad anti-imperialist united front, keep their vigilance high, and persist in their struggle, the vicious claws of the US aggressors will not doubt be clipped by the peoples of the world, and the forces of war headed by US imperialism will be crushed to pieces by the masses of people.

The Chinese Communist position at the time of the Cuban crisis in October and November, 1962 indicated little understanding of the awesome nature of nuclear missiles. Editorials in the *People's Daily* noted that the Cuban revolution began with seven rifles and that now the mobilized Cuban people were "the most powerful and reliable military weapon." Peking made its display of power by mass demonstrations throughout the length and breadth of the land.

The static and doctrinaire position of the Chinese allies will probably not be quickly modified even were Khrushchev to invite them to witness the testing of a thermonuclear weapon. Their oversimplified view of imperialism, their failure to grasp the meaning of the economic revolution in Japan and in the West, and intellectual isolation from the new ideas and forces of the space age will make the Chinese Communists increasingly intractable allies.

**Part Four**

With the prospect of continuing and even intensifying stresses and strains between Moscow and Peking, however, there is little reason for the outside world to rejoice. Both alliance partners share a faith in which there is complete agreement that we are the enemy. That their power struggles and strategic disagreements are argued so spiritedly in ideological guise is at once an indication of how seriously they take their Marxist-Leninist beliefs. There are numerous reasons which would tend to preclude either the Soviet Union or its Chinese allies from allowing the five areas of future strain mentioned above from developing into a complete rupture. Within each of these areas the Chinese will attempt to maneuver to gain their point, but they, like the Soviets, recognize the near-fatal blow that an open schism would have for the shared faith.

Chinese leaders have invested personal loyalties and long years in a commitment to the Communist camp. Although Peking has seemed at times to be "protesting too much" over the past few years as it insisted that the unity of the Socialist camp was sacred and unshakeable, there was more than empty verbiage. When Chou En-lai chided Khrushchev for washing dirty linen in public by his criticisms of Albania at the 22nd Congress of the CPSU on October 19, 1961, the Chinese Premier was expressing worry over damage to the unity of the camp. The same Chou En-lai had spoken to the 21st Congress in Moscow on January 28, 1959, asserting:

> Our international Communist ranks are united by a common ideal. The most sacred international duty for us Communists in all countries at any time is to strengthen the unity of the countries in the socialist camp headed by the Soviet Union, to strengthen the unity of the ranks of the international Communist movement, with the Soviet Communist Party as its center. No force in the world can impair our great international unity.

At the fortieth anniversary celebrations in Moscow on November 6, 1957, Mao himself had noted:

> We share the same destiny and the same life-spring with the Soviet Union and the entire socialist camp. We regard it as the

sacred international obligation of all the socialist countries to strengthen the solidarity of the socialist countries headed by the Soviet Union.

Although in 1962 Chinese and Soviet leaders were openly castigating each other for threatening the "sacred unity," the Chinese were still in no position to wrest control of the world Communist movement from Moscow or to resist full Soviet pressure. The Chinese economy and military machine is geared to Soviet standards, and Peking is dependent upon the Soviet Union for critical supplies, particularly petroleum. Mao's China depends on Soviet missiles and atomic weapons for ultimate deterrence and requires Soviet logistical support for a long conventional-type war.

Obviously a major fracture in the Sino-Soviet Alliance would be to the long-run interest of the outside world. It would be a deadly blow to the appeals of communism on the world scene; it would cause reinterpretation of an outworn dogma that cannot bear honest intellectual scrutiny; it would make the Communist power centers concentrate on their own conflict; it could encourage adjustment and accommodation to the West; and it would strengthen the bargaining position of the Western Alliance system. These are, of course, the very reasons why the alliance partners cannot allow the open break.

Short of a breakup of the alliance, the competition between Khrushchev and Mao as to who has the most effective strategy for the burial of the United States and the West hardly offers pleasant prospects in the 1960's. Those who find a basis for optimism or derive comfort from current Sino-Soviet differences usually fail to note that ultimate Communist world victory remains the major goal of both disputants. In the years immediately ahead, differences between Communist China and the Soviet Union are likely to result in increasing variety and more unpredictable strategems with which the outside world will have to contend. Each alliance partner intends to prove that his is the most effective formula for the defeat of the West, and while Moscow and Peking may at times frustrate and counteract each other's policies, the necessity for our own sacrifices and risks will not be diminished. Therefore, we must anticipate that continued Sino-Soviet disagreement will result in more crises and problems rather than less. A soft line of peaceful coexistence from Khrushchev is infinitely more dangerous and convincing and is likely to evoke many more concessions if it contrasts with war threats from Mao.

Our survey of the course of the first thirteen years of the
alliance and the developing differences in world view as two
great civilizations and world powers have turned away from
their first embrace suggests that there are several areas where
tensions and disruptions will increase. If the United States and
its allies can persist through the coming years of increased
danger they may yet see, or even assist, the cultural and institutional forces to bring about the desired break. In any event,
their strategy must be designed to intensify the current causes
of distrust and disruption within the alliance. This would suggest such policies as the following:

1) Insistence that Moscow speaks for the whole Communist
camp;

2) Continuing discussions and negotiations with the Soviets
on issues where the Chinese Communists feel they should have
equal voice;

3) Cultural and other contacts with the Soviet Union which
can heighten traditional Chinese xenophobia and distrust of the
Russians as Westerners;

4) Policies which place Chinese economic problems as a
burden on the Soviet Union;

5) Calculated leaks to indicate that Soviet representatives
have been discussing China's problems in the absence of delegates from Peking;

6) Avoidance of any direct attempts to interfere in the relations of the alliance partners.

Obviously there are no easy solutions or panaceas for the
West. The despotic structure and nature of both the Soviet
Union and Communist China remain a commanding feature
built into their whole societies and their approach to the outside
world. Whether quarreling or working in harmony, they constitute a challenge which will call upon us for the strength which
makes concessions or compromises unnecessary.

# Sino-Soviet Trade and Aid

—*GEORGE E. TAYLOR*

*Summary*

Communist theory on the relation between strategy and economics stems directly from the writings of Marx and Lenin. Marx and Engels provided the basic analysis of historical development. Lenin took the general theory of capitalism a step further in his analysis of imperialism. From the assumption that capitalism depended for its survival on the exploitation of colonial peoples, it followed that the strategy to be followed against the capitalist powers was that of depriving them of their colonies. These assumptions still lie at the core of Communist thinking about the nature of capitalism and of the world. Although most of the important colonies of Asia have been independent for some years, it is still possible for the Communists to speak of economic imperialism and thus keep alive the fear of exploitation and the return of political control. The facts, to put it mildly, have hardly borne out their theories. But the 22nd Party Congress still held that the deepening of the general crisis of capitalism was inevitable because the basic contradictions of imperialism have become even sharper. The Communist Chinese are particularly insistent upon the Marxist-Leninist view of the relationship between capitalism and war: the danger of war still lies in the imperialist system, which is by nature predatory. According to Mao, the contradiction between colonies and imperialism is to be resolved by national revolutionary war. An early example of Lenin's strategy was the Soviet assistance to the Chinese national revolution in the 1920's. Another was Stalin's efforts to encourage another war by increasing Soviet exports in order to increase the competition between the capitalist countries.

*Since this time there has been a tremendous increase in Bloc trade with the rest of the world, much of it directly to the underdeveloped countries. In spite of some indications to the contrary, there seems to be no reason to suppose that the Communist world has given up the grand strategy of Marx and Lenin, or feels that there is any reason to doubt the analysis. It is clear that the principle of peaceful coexistence is not intended to deny the struggle of classes or of the socialist revolution; it is a special form of struggle, just as war and peace are different forms of class struggle. The present balance of nuclear forces and the differing stages of Chinese Communist and Soviet development make it both possible and necessary for the two powers to play different roles in world affairs. The Soviets, having nuclear capacity, can stress the importance of maintaining nuclear peace while insisting that wars of national liberation are "just" wars. The Chinese, who have no nuclear capacity, can provoke and support wars of national liberation without taking into account the need to assure the United States that they wish to avoid nuclear war. Peking stresses its role in the overthrow of imperialism and brooks no compromises, even criticizing the Soviet Union when it seems to compromise with imperialism. The Soviet Union keeps alive the horrors of nuclear war, emphasises its technological achievements and economic might, and tries to neutralize the West while Peking carries out Lenin's objective of denying to the Western Powers access to the resources of the former colonial world. The antagonism between Moscow and Peking, we have to assume, is not antagonistic.*

*The Bloc economic offensive toward the uncommitted nations of Asia began in 1954. There is very little evidence to suggest that the Soviet Union is using its economic relationship with Western Europe mainly to disrupt that area and create havoc, at least on the short run. Most of the economic relationship can be explained in terms of the need of the Bloc to buy from Western Europe and to get the currency to do this. On the other hand, the special economic activity toward the underdeveloped world seems to be motivated more by political than by strict economic considerations. It was part of a large-scale shift in political tactics. The new economic policy was merely one part of the total policy that included efforts to exploit legal, diplomatic relations with non-Communist states. The economic offensive can thus be understood only if it is clear that Moscow and Peking use diplomatic, economic, and cultural missions;*

*trade agreements; technical training; international organizations; and programs for cultural exchanges as instruments for agitation from above; while the local Communist Party uses national fronts and covert organizations, schools, literature, newspapers, and para-military bodies as instruments for agitation from below. Economic penetration is an essential element in this scheme of subversion.*

*What is the extent of Sino-Soviet aid? In the middle of 1962 it involved relations with 29 extra-Bloc countries which had received a total of $7.2 billion in credit and grants. There seems to be a rough division of labor. The Soviet Union is the source of most of the Bloc credits, the East European Satellites provide many of the technicians, while Communist China uses the much-abused device of giving grants. Credits have the advantage of tying up the foreign exchange resources of the countries concerned, thus making them unavailable for purchasing goods from the West. The real costs of Soviet aid are much higher than they appear to be on the surface.*

*The Bloc apparently seeks first to secure acceptance and then to undermine the whole basis of trade in the non-Communist world. By offering credits without discussing the advisability of the projects for which they are to be used, the Communists accomplish the double objective of pleasing the national "bourgeoisie" by seeming not to attach strings while helping to bring about an imbalance in the development of the economy. Considerable political advantage is derived from the technical assistance program. Trade between the Sino-Soviet Bloc and the Free World is quantitatively not impressive. The general pattern is marked by the exchange of Soviet and East European manufactured goods in exchange for the raw materials and agricultural commodities of the less-developed countries. Communist China exports textiles, light industrial products, and a few heavy industrial items. It imports food and rubber. Most of the trade is on a barter basis. For many countries this has been an unprofitable experience. In addition to the unsatisfactory Soviet performance, it is clear that the Bloc is more interested in using the promise of trade as a propaganda weapon than for the actual exchange of goods.*

*Particular attention has been paid to India, which has received nearly $100 million in Bloc credits. Many of the projects planned are undertaken as an integral part of the Indian Five-Year Plans. This gives some control over the growth of the state sector, along non-capitalist lines. It seems reasonable to ex-*

*pect that here, as in other places, the intent is to speed up social and institutional change and to make it as uneven as possible.*

*There seems to be every reason to expect that the Sino-Soviet Bloc has a capacity for considerable expansion of trade and aid if it wishes to divert its resources for these purposes. It can be assumed that the economic offensive is also geared into the Bloc program of military aid. The Bloc Council for Mutual Economic Assistance appears to be more and more in control of foreign economic policy.*

*Although Communist China goes along with the general policy of the Soviet Bloc, its economic activities deserve special study. Grants made by Communist China to Cambodia and Nepal are of particular interest. It is quite clear that Communist China is less interested in the economic development of those countries than in softening them up for subversion. While the Soviet Union is highly involved in Southeast Asia, on the very borders of Communist China, so Communist China has been very much involved in Cuba on the borders of the United States. In April 1962 Peking agreed to export to Cuba, Chinese rice, soybeans, canned meats, and other items in exchange for sugar, tobacco, and mineral oil. There was famine in China at the time.*

*The economic offensive cannot be isolated from the whole range of Bloc policy, but some results can be traced to the use of economic power. Large numbers of nationals from less-developed countries have been trained in the Soviet Union. The economic offensive must have borne considerable fruit in the way of intelligence. Something has been done to break the economic ties between some of the less-developed countries and the West, although the results have not been overly impressive. The strength of the Indonesian Communist Party may be due in part to extended Bloc help to Indonesia. The emphasis upon heavy industrialization has put the systematic approach to economic development of the Free World to some extent on the defensive. Considerable success was achieved in persuading Indian leaders that heavy industrialization was a necessary political and economic goal. There have been some negative factors, but in the main, the Bloc economic offensive has secured more gains than losses.*

## One Strategy—Two Roles?

The two major Communist parties of the world today are now engaged in an organizational struggle which has put severe strains on the common strategy that both seemed to have been following up to 1957. While there is no evidence to suggest that the intra-Bloc conflict has brought about any change in the over-all purposes of Communist policy towards the rest of the world, the Chinese and the Russian Parties seem now to be following parallel and occasionally competitive roads. But both still share a general theory on the relation between strategy and economics that stems directly from the writings of Marx and Lenin. It is Lenin's theory of monopoly capitalism and of the relation between imperial powers and colonies that still lies at the core of Communist thinking about the nature of capitalism and of the world. In spite of the fact that most of the important colonies of Asia have been politically independent for several years, this theory makes it possible for the Communists to speak of economic imperialism and thus keep alive the fear of exploitation and the return of political control. Curiously enough, Lenin's theory of imperialism failed to explain why the United States, admittedly one of the great capitalist powers, was, to use his own words, "without colonies." And even Communists must have noted that in spite of the withdrawal of the empires from most of their colonies, Western Europe is more prosperous today than it has been at any time in its long history. But the theory still stands. In its report on the present stage of the national liberation movement, the 22nd Party Congress of the CPSU stated that the development of the young sovereign states is hindered by the fact that the majority of them "have not yet torn themselves away from the system of the world capitalist economy even though they occupy a special place in it. They constitute that part of the world which is still being exploited by the capitalist monopolies. As long as they do not put an end to their economic dependence on imperialism, they will be playing the role of 'world countryside,' and will remain objects of semi-colonial exploitation." The 22nd Party Congress also complimented the 20th Congress on its conclusion that the deepening of the general crisis of capitalism was inevitable, for the basic contradictions of imperialism have become even sharper.

One of the earliest examples of the application of Lenin's general strategy was, of course, the economic, military, and political aid given to Sun Yat-sen in 1924 in the hope that the Chinese nationalist revolution would drive the imperial powers out of China and bring that country in line with the Soviet Union. Another tactical application of the same general strategy is evident in the efforts made by Stalin in his last years to encourage another war between competing capitalist states by increasing Soviet exports. It was Stalin's expectation that increased Soviet exports would cut into Western markets and thus increase competition in the free countries, damage their export industries, and bring about unemployment. At that time, Soviet Bloc exports to the Free World, thanks largely to Stalin's own policies, amounted to less than two per cent of the total Free World imports. There was not a great deal of influence that he could bring to bear. But since that time, Stalin's successors have increased Bloc trade with the Free World and added to it other features such as credit and technical assistance, and have directed it mainly to the uncommitted nations while broadening the scope of the whole operation. Stalin would hardly recognize what has happened since his death. Between 1954 and 1962, the Sino-Soviet Bloc spent a total of $7.2 billion in credits and grants to 29 countries. Trade between the Bloc and these countries increased from $860 million in 1954 to $3.4 billion in 1960, an increase of 295 per cent. The significance of this development is that it is concentrated on certain countries, the underdeveloped part of the world.

The tactics have changed, but there seems to be little evidence that the grand strategy of Marx and Lenin has changed or that the Communists see any reason to doubt the basic analysis. This is true in spite of the fact that Mr. Khrushchev stated in 1960 that it is wrong to repeat mechanically now what Lenin said about imperialism many decades ago and to keep on saying that imperialist wars are inevitable until socialism will be victorious throughout the world. This famous statement has been followed by others from the Soviet Union to the effect that Lenin could hardly be expected to anticipate everything that happened since his death and that there are changed circumstances. Taken literally, Mr. Khrushchev's famous statement, "Let us prove to each other the advantages of one system, not with fists, not by war, but by peaceful economic competition," seems a long way away from Lenin's analysis of imperialism and of the coming struggles between the Socialist and capitalist worlds. It is very dangerous, however, to take literally the Aesopian language of the Communist world. Nor is there any need to do so. Pravda and the other journals have pointed out that the principle of peaceful coexistence did not deny the struggle of classes or of the socialist revolution. It is a special form of struggle just as war and peace are different forms of class struggle. In Communist jargon "peace" is not the opposite of "war." War and peace in Communist theory transform themselves into each other. War is the constant companion of capitalism, whereas peace is equated with socialism and is in harmony with revolution. Both Moscow and Peking claim that they are utterly devoted to peace, but if the imperialist powers try to disturb it, they will be swept off the face of the earth. There are differences of emphasis on this level, but there seem to be few differences in strategy between Moscow and Peking.

The Soviet Union, which is in a different stage of development from China, has sufficient nuclear power to discourage the deliberate provocation of a full-scale nuclear conflict by either side in the Cold War. Taking advantage of this, it can stress the importance of maintaining nuclear peace, knowing how welcome this will be in the Free World, at the same time insisting there are wars that are "just," such as wars of national liberation. The Chinese, who have no nuclear capacity and are in an excellent position to provoke and support wars of national liberation, naturally emphasize their interest in such "just" wars. In this way, they hope that the West, horrified at the thought of nuclear war, will be paralyzed in the face of aggressively promoted wars of national liberation, as in Vietnam and Cuba. Peking stresses the overthrow of imperialism and brooks no compromise, even criticizing openly the Soviet Union when it seems to compromise with imperialism. The Soviet Union keeps alive the horrors of nuclear war while emphasizing its technological achievements and economic might. If Moscow can neutralize the West, Peking can carry out Lenin's objective of denying to the Western Powers access to resources in the colonial world, now referred to as the underdeveloped countries. Given the Communist concept of peace and of "just" wars of national liberation, it is easy to agree with the Pravda statement that the peaceful coexistence of countries with different sorts of systems does not mean conciliation of socialism and capitalism. On the contrary, it implies intensification of the class struggle for the triumph of socialist ideas and the total victory of socialism. As Khrushchev put the matter in January, 1961, "The policy of peaceful coexistence promotes the growth of the forces of progress, or the forces fighting for socialism; in capitalist countries it facilitates the work of the Communist Parties and the other progressive organizations of the working class, makes it easier for the people to combat the aggressive war blocs on military bases, and contributes to the success of national liberation."

It is wise to proceed, therefore, on the assumption that the antagonism between Moscow and Peking, has not completely shattered Bloc strategy. The organizational struggle may cause the two parties to act at cross-purposes, but not necessarily to our advantage. Whether or not they are acting in concert or not, it is thoroughly in keeping with the Communist ideology for Peking to assume an intransigent and war-like role in the struggle against imperialism while issuing firm statements advocating peace, at the same time that the Soviet Union stresses the gambit of peaceful coexistence while actually cooperating with China in "just" wars of national liberation—for example, in Cuba and Vietnam.

### The Pattern of Sino-Soviet Trade and Aid

What is usually known as the Bloc's economic offensive began in 1954 and was directed toward the "uncommitted" nations of Asia. While it can be described as the latest phase of a general strategy for capturing the underdeveloped part of the world, it has several specific features. In a very general sense, it is true that the Sino-Soviet Bloc uses trade and aid and other foreign economic policies as the instruments for the furtherance of political objectives. But the nature of the Bloc economic organization does not make an economic offensive the most powerful of the instruments available. The Soviets have always had an autarkic approach to their economy; they supply themselves first and they plan in quantitative terms. The planning process is done by the leaders of the Communist Party in the various countries of the Sino-Soviet Bloc, and there are no cross-references on the lower levels from one country to another. The absence of a comparative basis for estimating costs is so obvious that the Bloc uses capitalist prices as a control. There is not even a convertible currency within the Bloc. Before 1956, the Bloc countries did not coordinate their economic activities, and there was no joint planning. After 1956, Moscow permitted a greater degree of freedom to plan among its satellites and reactivated COMECON partly as a result, perhaps, of the arguments advanced by the Hungarian economists, Liska and Marias.

These economists attacked the autarkic position while advancing the case for an international division of labor on the grounds that the small countries cannot develop every branch of production and that foreign trade does not rest on absolute advantage, and its purpose is not simply to secure essential raw materials. In 1956 the 20th Party Congress of the CPSU primly announced that the European Satellites would be permitted to specialize in those branches of industries or in production of those commodities in which natural and economic conditions were most favorable. The rapid increase in trade and aid that followed after 1954, modest as it is compared to the Free World, would hardly have been possible without the structural changes within the Bloc that began in 1954. At the same time, there seems to be little evidence that the Soviet Union is yet in a position to use its economic relations with Western Europe to disrupt that area and create havoc. Most of the economic relationship can be explained in terms of the need of the Bloc to buy from Western Europe and to get the currency to do this. Fear of the Common Market may give rise to the use of such economic powers as the Bloc possesses to engage in disruptive tactics, and there is evidence of this in Soviet petroleum activities. On the other hand, there has been special economic activity in the rest of the world, and this seems to have been motivated more by political than by strictly economic considerations. In general, the new approach made by the Sino-Soviet Bloc to Asia was an adjustment to the strength rather than to the weakness of the Free World. It was part of a large-scale shift in political tactics.

There were several reasons for this. One thing, it had become clear during the Korean conflict that direct aggression for the time being had been stopped and adjustments were in order. More important, it became clear that the efforts to take over the newly independent countries of Asia, which had started in 1948, in most places had failed to achieve success. Most of these countries withstood the challenge from within. Since 1954, therefore, the Asian Communist parties, while not giving up completely their para-military organizations, have put much more emphasis on the overt and, where possible, legitimate aspects of the movement. The corollary of accepting the failure to subvert the independent former colonies of Asia was to support neutralism, a commodity for export, but not for internal consumption. Furthermore, it has become clear that the survival of the new Asian governments as independent political entities, the stabilization of their economies, the healing of the wounds of war, the beginning of a new period of dignified cooperation between former imperial powers and former colonies, and the rising volume of world trade, were due not only to the courage and skill of Asian leaders but also to the flexibility, understanding, and economic assistance of the Free World. In order to compete, the Bloc had to accept the competition on Free World terms. Hence, the Bloc economic aid programs, technical assistance, and extension of credit to those members of the Free World that were willing to accept it. For the time being, the Soviet Bloc was compelled to accept competition of ideas and political and economic models in Asia in order to recover from the mistakes of the period of armed struggle.

Under these circumstances, it made sense to give encouragement to neutralist foreign policies among non-Communist countries in order to reduce the military and diplomatic effectiveness of the Free World. Communist Parties were instructed to stir up their political following, make coalitions near the political center, and when possible, get a parliamentary majority by legal means. In order to facilitate this strategy, it was necessary for Moscow and Peking to have open and friendly relations with those new governments which they had both been so actively engaged in attempting to subvert. Both Peking and Moscow went out of their way, therefore, to establish diplomatic relations with all Asian states and to assure them of their goodwill, friendship, and desire for peaceful coexistence. The Chinese did their part in the soon-to-be Bandung Conference of Afro-Asian states. Agitation from above requires the respectability of legitimacy, and occasionally the correctness of official Communist relations with non-Communist states had to take priority over direct help to local Communist organizations. The new policy was marked by world-wide journeys by Premier Khrushchev, cultural missions, invitations to Asian heads of state to visit Moscow and Peking, and an intense program of cultural exchange. Together with this went the new economic policy of trade, aid, and technical assistance to Asian countries. It seems clear that this policy was an instrument for the achievement of the same political objective that had been attempted by other means and had not succeeded. The Sino-Soviet Bloc had to adjust itself to the mood of the Afro-Asian countries, the nationalist aspirations of these states, to the sentiments of war-weary Asia against armed revolution, and to the desperate desire of many countries to be neutral in the world conflict. The economic offensive can thus be understood only if it is clear that Moscow and Peking use diplomatic, economic, and cultural missions, trade agreements, technical training, international organizations, and programs for cultural exchange as instruments for agitation from above, while the local Communist Party uses national fronts and covert organizations, schools, literature, newspapers, and para-military bodies as instruments for agitation from below. Economic penetration is an essential element in this scheme of subversion. Startling as may have been the increase of Bloc economic efforts in 1954, in a sense the new policies that were given approval at the 20th Congress of the CPSU, February, 1956, were a return to the earlier policy of supporting the "national bourgeoisie" in their struggle to establish national independence, while at the same time helping the local Communists. This is what was attempted in China between 1923 and 1927, and after 1935. It must be clearly understood, therefore, that the so-called economic offensive is only one aspect of a strategic approach to the less developed countries; in fact, it could hardly have been pressed without the political, cultural, and military programs that went with it.

What is the extent of Sino-Soviet aid? In the middle of 1962 it involved relations with 29 extra-Bloc countries which had received a total of $7.2 billion in credits and grants. This sum has to be broken down into several categories. Some $2.4 billion was credit extended for the purchase of Soviet Bloc arms, the main purchasers being Egypt, Syria, Indonesia, Iraq, Cuba, and Afghanistan, and now India. The rest was used for economic purposes and of this the Soviet Union provided by far the largest amount. Communist China made grants and loans totaling $263.93 million to Cambodia, Ceylon, Nepal, Egypt, Yemen, Indonesia, Burma, Ghana, and Guinea; and the East European Satellites were responsible for $920 million worth of economic aid. To Communist countries China has extended loans and grants worth $1,282 million. According to figures provided by the Bureau of Intelligence and Research of the Department of State (RSD-145, September 18, 1962), the Soviet Union is concentrating on major lines of credit for general economic development. "Thus, agreements involving $100 million or more account for nearly 60 per cent of all Bloc economic assistance. These include: credits of $500 million to Afghanistan; $100 million to Argentina and Ethiopia; $100 million to Cuba for the expansion of the nickel industry in addition to $200 million for general economic development; three credits to India of $135 million for a steel mill, $125 million for

industrial enterprises under India's Second Five-Year Plan and
$500 million under its Third Five-Year Plan; $325 million to
Egypt for the Aswan Dam in addition to $175 million for in-
dustrial development; $150 million to the Syrian Arab Republic;
$138 million to Iraq; and two credits to Indonesia of $100 million
and $250 million respectively."

The other Bloc countries, as might be expected, undertake
smaller projects. There seems, however, to be a rough division
of labor. The Soviet Union is the source for most of the Bloc
credits, accounting, with Czechoslovakia and East Germany, for
over 90 per cent of the total. The East European Satellites
provide many of the technicians mainly, perhaps, because they
are more acceptable than those of the Soviet. Communist China
is the member of the Bloc which has used the much-abused
device of giving grants, and these have gone significantly to
Cambodia and Nepal among others. Peking is in a very different
position from Moscow, which has given billions of dollars worth
of credits to its European Satellites and therefore cannot very
well give substantial grants to non-Communist countries. Communist China also plays a special role within the Bloc and in
Southeast Asia.

Credits offered by the Bloc are either interest free or at an
interest rate of 2.5 per cent, which seems to compare well with
the international bank rate of 4.75 per cent and is large enough
to give the transaction a business-like flavor. The figures are
deceptive, however. The credits tie up the foreign exchange
producing exports of the countries concerned. The chances are
that the Soviet type of credit arrangement will result in the
uncommitted countries having less foreign exchange with which
to buy goods in the West, obviously a part of the design. Credits
are usually extended over a number of years. A recent Soviet
credit to Indonesia of $250 million, for example, has a seven-
year term. Most credits and grants are ear-marked for specific
purchases or projects. Some 57 per cent of the total credits
is spent on manufacturing projects; mineral surveys, transportation and communication, multi-purpose projects in agriculture
share most of the rest. Among the large-scale undertakings,
the Aswan Dam on the Nile is among the best known. The
Bhilai steel mill in India was finished in 1961, and an oil refinery
at Gauhati began operation by the middle of 1962. One quarter
of the total of credits extended by the Bloc has been used. It has
been suggested that one of the reasons for the use of credits
rather than grants is to keep down the number of requests and

to maximize the contact with the recipient country over a long period. There are annual negotiations to establish lists, prices, and quantities of goods to be delivered in repayment because the Soviet Union decides which commodities it wishes to receive and sets its own evaluation on the goods that it sends in return. Many countries have discovered that the real costs of Soviet aid are much higher than they appear to be on the surface. The imposition of an interest rate is designed plainly for political purposes, for the charging of interest on investment is not a Soviet custom. The fact that a large-scale loan has been made to Afghanistan without interest and for repayment over 50 years, the first payment not beginning until 25 years after the aid is used, shows that serious exceptions can also be made for political purposes.

Is the Soviet Union really interested in the development of sound economies in the underdeveloped countries, upon which it is concentrating its aid, if these economies are not under Communist control? The evidence is that the Bloc is attempting first to secure acceptance, and then to undermine the whole basis of trade and aid in the non-Communist world. The emphasis upon credits for manufacturing goes along with the propaganda emphasis on industrialization as the basis for independence. The granting of credits without careful adjustment to sound economic plans is obviously quite deliberate. To offer credits without discussing the advisability of the projects for which they are to be used accomplishes the double objective of pleasing the national "bourgeoisie" by seeming not to attach strings and of helping to bring about imbalance in the development of the economy.

The Bloc also squeezes every political advantage it can out of the technical assistance program that goes together with the extension of credits. The Soviet Union has had considerable experience in the field of technical assistance with its own satellites and with Communist China, but until 1953 it boycotted and denounced the United Nations' Technical Assistance Fund. When it began to contribute to the Fund, the contribution was given in rubles, and all technical training takes place in Bloc countries. This is contrary to the established pattern. The Bloc has a sizeable number of technicians available. In 1961, to take an example, there were some 1200 Soviet Bloc technicians in the West African state of Guinea alone. In the first half of 1962, it has been estimated that about 12,000 Bloc technicians spent some part of the year in 29 less-developed countries. Even more impressive, nearly 22,000 nationals from these countries have gone to the Bloc, mainly the Soviet Union, for study and technical training during the last five to six years. During 1962, about 9,600 Bloc technicians were employed on economic projects. About one-half of the Bloc non-military technicians were in the Middle East, 25 per cent in Africa, about 15 per cent in Asia, and the rest in Latin America. Communist China, which provides about 10 per cent of the technicians, has sent them to Burma, Ceylon, Yemen, Guinea, Cambodia, Nepal, and Cuba. The political advantages of these efforts are quite obvious assuming that the technicians conduct themselves with skill, and the projects with which they are associated are successful. The Bloc technicians have, on the whole, avoided overt propaganda—a wise precaution in situations where the Communist Party is not in control. In spite of a good many claims to the contrary, there is little evidence to show that Bloc technicians have any more knowledge of the languages and customs of the countries to which they are assigned than do their counterparts from the Free World. They may very well have less.

The rapid increase in the amount of trade between the Sino-Soviet Bloc and the Free World is quantitatively impressive only because there was so little trade before 1954. In order to keep the figures in perspective, it is important to realize that even today the total Soviet trade with non-Bloc countries is only around $3 billion, about the same as that of Denmark. In spite of all the noise and commotion with which the trade drive has been accomplished, trade between the Bloc countries is still very much greater than with non-Bloc countries. Between 1954-60, the total trade turnover of the Bloc with the less developed countries increased from $860 million to $3.4 billion, of which the Soviet Union in 1961 accounted for $1,376 million, the East European satellites for $1,479 million, and Communist China $547 million. These figures do not represent a very large share of the total trade of the less developed countries, but as the trade is selective, the percentage of their total exports that some countries send to the Bloc is quite high. Afghanistan, the UAR, Iceland, Yugoslavia, Greece, Cuba, Syria, Iran, and Guinea exported more than 20 per cent of the total value of their exports to the Bloc. For Finland, Iceland, Yugoslavia, Egypt, Cuba, and Afghanistan, the figure is 15 per cent for the same year, 1960.

The general pattern of trade is characterized by the exchange of Soviet and East European manufactured goods in exchange for the raw materials and agricultural commodities of the less-developed countries. Communist China, which has not recently been able to maintain her level of export to the less developed countries because of economic set-backs at home, exports textiles, light industrial products, and a few heavy industrial items. It imports food and rubber, in fact much of its trade outside the Bloc is designed to pay for imports of food.

Most of the trade between the Soviet Bloc and less developed countries is on a barter basis and, by and large, this is not a satisfactory arrangement. By the middle of 1961, there were 252 bilateral trade agreements between the Bloc and 35 other countries. These agreements set up official arrangements for the trade, indicate the quantity to be exchanged, and in some cases, set trade targets and specify the means of payment. The targets are not very often met. These arrangements are comparatively simple when, for example, Ceylonese rubber is exchanged for Chinese rice. It is worth noting that Peking settled its debts rather slowly with the earlier regime, but quite quickly with the new one that was politically inclined much more toward the Bloc. But there have been many disagreements over prices. It is much more difficult when one country, such as Burma, is exchanging one commodity, rice, for many different commodities. Taking advantage of the inability of the Burmese to sell their rice at the price they wanted, the Bloc moved quickly to offer a barter agreement. Agreements were signed with Communist China in April 1954 and December 1955 for 15,000 long-tons of rice to be paid for almost entirely in goods. When one Bloc country has made an inroad, the others follow rapidly. Burma made an agreement with Czechoslovakia for an annual level of trade of three million pounds sterling, and other agreements were made with Hungary, East Germany, Poland, Rumania, and Bulgaria, all for rice in exchange for goods. Between 1953 and 1955, Burma's trade with Eastern Europe alone grew from one million to seven million dollars, and with Communist China from 2 to 17 million. In 1955, Burma signed an agreement with the Soviet Union on a three-year basis. The Soviet Union was to take 150,000 to 200,000 pounds of rice in exchange for 20 per cent sterling and 80 per cent goods. This was extended six months later to a five-year agreement. As a result of all these agreements, Burma's total commitments came to 80,000 tons of rice, or half her annual average rice exports. The rice was used up, cash customers came on the scene, the Soviet Union did not have the goods that Burma wanted, and much less rice was shipped than the agreement called for. But at the end of 1956, Burma had a credit of $11 million with the Soviet Bloc. In May of that year, U Nu said, "Our experts have laid before us the implications of the barter trade. The prices are manipulated so as to place us at a disadvantage by 10 per cent to 30 per cent on the goods exchanged." So much Burmese rice was resold in Burma's traditional markets that the later agreements contained provisions that this practice should stop. Most of the other difficulties connected with the Communist barter trade have also arisen in Burma. The Burmese have lost heavily on unacceptable goods. There has been a great deal of publicity and propaganda about the trade agreements, but many remain unfulfilled. In addition to poor quality goods, unfamiliar specifications, poor sales service, slow delivery, uncertain supply of spare parts, there is the problem of the political activities of large Soviet diplomatic staffs who use the trade arrangements for activities among the local businessmen, especially the overseas Chinese.

In the case of Japan, it is also clear that the Chinese Communists are more interested in using the promise of trade as a propaganda weapon than in the actual exchange of goods. The agreement of 1955, for example, was used to bring pressure on Japan by offering commodities Japan badly needed—iron ore, coal, and soybeans—but only in exchange for goods on the embargo list. The Bloc has also taken advantage of the problems of Egypt in the disposal of cotton, of Uruguay in selling wool, and Iceland in disposing of its fish. Trade with Yugoslavia goes up and down according to the political climate, the Soviets using the threat to cut off trade as a political weapon.

While it is tempting to explain Bloc moves to take advantage of the disposal problems of the less developed countries as political opportunism, it should also be pointed out that the disadvantages of trading with the Soviet Union are becoming so generally well known that it is only when countries have such economic problems on their hands that they are willing to turn to the Bloc for barter arrangements. Compared with the advantages of trading with the Free World, the disadvantages of trading with the Soviet Bloc are very considerable. The less developed countries cannot usually use a trade balance accumulated in one Bloc country with another one within the Bloc and, as there is little choice of the goods and services the Bloc will export, the less developed country often ends up with inferior goods at high prices. It is reported that Uruguay had to accept Poland's coal at prices higher than those in the world market in order to use up its balance with that country. Bloc products are generally of antiquated design, and, where the Bloc is unable or unwilling to provide the things that the less developed country requires, large balances in their favor accumulate in the Bloc. It has been pointed out that this, in effect, constitutes a credit from the less developed countries to the Bloc.

What is of greater importance is that an examination of the plans of the Bloc countries gives no indication that there is going to be any change in the pattern of trade. For political purposes and immediate economic need, the Bloc will make large purchases of primary commodities, but it would be dangerous to count on the growth of an expanding market for the products of the less developed countries in the Sino-Soviet Bloc. As Roger Hilsman points out, "One of the outstanding features of such trade to date has been its sporadic nature, in some cases reflecting internal economic developments in the Bloc and in other instances clearly indicating political pressure on a trade partner.[1]"

In view of the Indian-Chinese dispute it might be interesting to use India as an example of Bloc policy. India has accepted more economic aid from the Bloc than any other country in the Free World. The Soviet Union has extended to India credits amounting to almost $811.1 million. Credits from some of the European Satellites, particularly Czechoslovakia, bring the total Bloc credits up to $950 million. In addition to the Bhilai Steel Mill, the Bloc has also committed itself to the building of an oil refinery, several sugar refineries, cement plants, and hydroelectric installations at Neyveli on which quite a bit of progress has been made. The important thing is that many of the projects which were being planned or undertaken were an integral part of the next Indian Five-Year Plan, thus giving the Bloc a considerable influence over Indian economic development. For the year 1961, India exported to the Bloc $115.3 million worth of goods and imported $124.6 million. These figures are higher than those for any other country in the Free World except Cuba, after the Castro revolution, and Malaya. A very small percentage of this trade was with Communist China although Peking concluded its first barter trade agreement with India early in January, 1951, during the Korean War when Chinese assets were frozen and the United Nations declared Communist China an aggressor.

Why the special attention to India? One reason may be that the Soviet Union was trying to involve itself in India's Five-Year

Plans in such a way as to capture the planning process. It is also a clearly stated Communist policy to increase the role of the state sector.[2]

The national liberation revolutions, as the Communists call them, give rise to new social and economic phenomena, one of which is the formation of the state sector, but the state sector can be strengthened in the interest of developing a country along a capitalist or a non-capitalist path. The Soviet Union makes an investment in the strengthening of the state sector—whoever controls it—with a view to using political influence with the "progessive strata of society" to have the state sector become the material base for the transition of the country to a socialist path. Communists prefer to take over a going concern, but we can be sure that what they cannot ultimately control, they will attempt to destroy. The attack by Communist China on India's northern frontier may very well be an expression of the fact that the Chinese most certainly, and the Russians in all probability, have come to the conclusion that it is necessary to increase the importance of the state sector by creating political and economic problems that are bound to demand radical solutions. In this way, the polarization of Indian politics can be speeded up.

The Bloc is not so much interested in ordered or balanced economic development outside the Bloc as in reaping the whirlwind of social and political dislocation. The first move, therefore, is to wreck the ordered economic and political development of the less developed countries of the Free World by undermining their institutions and speeding up their industrialization in order to unbalance their economies. Hence, we have the reckless encouragement of industrialization which can be found in any speech by Bloc leaders. The Bloc's economic drive is certainly not to be measured by quantitative standards. It is political in purpose and by quantitative standards the effort is small and well within the economic capacity of the Bloc. Nor should we be too complacent about the unsatisfactory experiences that many countries have had with barter agreements and all the other disadvantages that go with the bureaucratic management of economic affairs. Late deliveries, unsuitable and shoddy goods, and broken promises have to be weighed against the real objectives which are not trade for the sake of trade or assistance in the economic development for the sake of the country concerned. The purpose is to establish a base for agitation, not to make a record in honest trading. The Communists are well aware that industrialization involves great changes in the countries where it takes place. It brings labor to factories and away from the countryside, it means urbanization and the breakdown of old patterns of kinship and village relationships, it leads to a concentration of power when social and political conflicts deepen, as they must, in the hands of those who want to press for change. By the time these changes develop, it is obviously expected that the process of Communist subversion and infiltration will have gone far enough to make it possible for the Bloc to take political advantage of a situation that it has helped to produce.

**Appraisal of Sino-Soviet Development Efforts**

An evaluation of the way in which economic strength is used for political purposes depends to some extent upon estimates of how much economic strength the Bloc will have at its disposal. As both the Soviet Union and Communist China have shown that they are willing and able to sell food abroad when the people are starving at home, it is wise not to underestimate the capacity of these countries to divert economic strength to political purposes under the most distressful conditions. It is quite clear that the Sino-Soviet Bloc is able to export impressive numbers of civilian technicians, a capital resource that it did not have two or three decades ago. It can be expected that the quality of the technicians to be sent abroad will probably increase as a result of large-scale efforts that are being made to train people in foreign languages and cultures. Special schools have been set up and other measures taken to achieve this purpose. As for the economic resources of the Soviet Union, it is quite clear that there has been economic growth, certainly of the power economy, and that the Sino-Soviet Bloc, by and large, has the capacity for considerable expansion of trade and aid if it wishes to divert its resources to these purposes.

Excluding its nuclear and military power the general standard of living in the Soviet Union can be roughly compared to that of Japan, with Japan being slightly ahead. It is not likely that the Soviet Union will be willing to cut down its military expenses or its military aid. These expenditures certainly limit the amount that can be spent on other things, but it must be realized that the military and the economic policies are geared to each other. Military aid is given in such a way as to increase the possibilities of conflicts in the Free World, especially in the less developed countries, and to promote, when ready, national liberation revolutions. It is hardly likely that the economic offensive is designed to be antagonistic to the purposes of military aid. As we have seen, the latter complements the former, for the long-range purpose of economic credits, trade, and technical assistance is to further the political objectives of the Bloc. War is still the breeding ground of communism.

Expert opinion suggests that the Bloc is able on the whole to take care of its commitments and that, as for the heavy industrial equipment, these can be integrated into future Bloc economic planning. It is suggested that "areas of particular Soviet capability are illustrated by recent initiatives in the field of petroleum exploration and production, development of civil aviation, construction of hydroelectric facilities, offers to provide standardized machine tools in agreement to construct small or medium-sized, fully-equipped manufacturing plants." [3] At the same time, the forced industrialization of Eastern Europe combined with the long traditions of the countries of Eastern Europe has increased the capacity of the Bloc to conduct an economic offensive that in turn has increased the need for expanded markets, for the export of industrial goods, and for sources of raw materials and food. Some of the prime commodities that the Bloc imports from the less developed countries it definitely needs, others it takes merely because there is no alternative and uses them to disturb markets in the Free World. There would appear to be a definite trend in the Bloc to coordinate its foreign economic policy more effectively by giving more power to the Bloc COMECON and by improving cooperation between the Soviet Union and its Satellites.

Although Communist China goes along with the general policy of the Soviet Bloc, its economic activities deserve special study. While Communist China has played a special role within the Bloc and in Southeast Asia, it is not alone in the field of Communist economic aid to Southeast Asia. The Soviet Union and the East European Satellites are very active in Burma and Indonesia. Soviet technicians have turned up on the borders of China and Cambodia. Southeast Asia is clearly an important target for the whole Bloc. For Communist China there is a mixture of political and economic motives. There seems to be a definite need for foreign exchange for use in trading with other members of the Communist Bloc, for the Chinese Communists conducted at least 80 per cent of their trade within the Bloc as recently as 1959. By 1962 trade with the Soviet Union had fallen by over 50%. This is often blamed on the Sino-Soviet dispute, but it is also explicable as a consequence of the Chinese need to import food from the West. Having decided to emphasize industrialization, the Chinese need capital goods. To get the foreign exchange China has to export consumer goods and some of the simpler machines. Communist China does not need most of the great agricultural products of Southeast Asia, except for rubber. As might be expected Peking trades where it must, but manipulates this trade in such a way as to secure the maximum political advantages. In spite of its difficulties with shortages at home, Peking, unlike Moscow, has extended a few modest grants to countries it wishes to impress and where it hopes to gain a foothold for subversion. The grants made by Communist China to Cambodia and Nepal are of particular interest. In June 1956 Peking announced a grant of $22.4 million to Cambodia for two years to be spent on materials for the construction of textile mills, cement, paper, plywood plants, universities, hospitals, youth and sports centers, railroads, bridges, and power plants. Soviet experts arrived to survey the possibilities of industrial and agricultural investment. This was followed by a trade and payment agreement with Czechoslovakia by which manufactured goods were to be exchanged for Cambodian rubber, corn, rice, pepper, and leather.

Czechoslovakia also promised scientific and technical equipment and technicians. On the basis of the promised aid the Chinese began stepped-up propaganda activities in Cambodia. It is quite clear that the Communist interest in the economic development of Cambodia and Laos has all been secondary to the general strategy of softening them up for subversion. In October 1956 Communist China made a grant of $12.6 million to Nepal, one-third in money, which was paid on time, and two-thirds in capital goods. Here again it is not the amount of money involved that is important but the fact that the Soviet Bloc entered this strategic area. Although the efforts which Communist China can make are small, they are used with some effect.

In a very real sense it is very difficult to answer the question of the economic capacity of the Bloc to enlarge, if it so desires, its economic trade offensive. This is so because the offensive does not stand alone. It is only part of an integrated operation that includes the cost of maintaining a massive military establishment and an expensive outer-space program, military aid to selected countries in the Free World, vast propaganda efforts— including the movement of large numbers of people in so-called cultural exchanges—trade fairs, and big investments in the training of foreign nationals in the Soviet Union. Bloc imports from Cuba, for example, were 60.5 million in 1959 and 478 million in 1961. The Bloc exports to Cuba increased from 1.5 million in 1959 to 395 million in 1961. The military investment must have been quite high. While the Soviet Union was the chief supporter of Cuba, Communist China also cooperated enthusiastically with the Castro regime. On the last day of 1959, Communist China and the revolutionary government of Cuba concluded its first trade agreement which stipulated that Peking would purchase 50,000 pounds of Cuban sugar at 2.98¢ per pound. Some months later an additional 80,000 pounds of sugar was added to the agreement. In July 1960 Peking and Havana concluded the first trade and payments agreement valid for a five-year period. Peking now agreed to purchase 500,000 metric tons of sugar a year and to pay for it 80 per cent in goods and 20 per cent in transferrable pound sterling for the first year, and in goods only in the following four. In November 1960 Peking signed an agreement on economic cooperation with Cuba agreeing to advance a loan of $60 million without interest which Cuba was to use for purchase of equipment and for technical aid. In April 1962 Peking agreed to export rice, soybeans, canned meat, and other items in exchange for Cuban sugar, tobacco, and mineral ores. There was famine in China at the time. Communist China cannot purchase as much sugar or provide as many technicians as the Soviet Union, but it has been holding its own in a fraternal manner and probably been much more of a model for the Cuban Communists in economic planning, mass organizations, and military training than has the senior partner. Peking quite clearly is using its limited resources to build up its prestige and to further the cause of national liberation.

Impossible as it is to isolate the economic offensive from its whole range of Bloc policy, it may be possible to point to some results which can be traced, in some measure, to the use of economic power. On the positive side there is no doubt that large numbers of nationals from less developed countries have been trained in the Soviet Union as part of official agreements and in connection with definite projects. There is no way of knowing to what extent the Indians being trained as engineers or pilots in the Soviet Union are favorable to communism, but it would be rash to assume that all of them were politically unaffected by this experience. The economic offensive must have borne considerable fruit in the way of intelligence as Bloc technicians have joined in the national planning effort of many countries and have necessarily been permitted to travel in large areas and have contact with the people. In strictly economic terms something has been done to break the economic ties between some of the less developed countries and the West although the results have not been overly impressive. It is probably true to say that the strength of the Indonesian Communist Party is due in part to the investments in trade, aid, and technical help that the Bloc has extended in that country. The emphasis upon giving heavy industrialization a high priority has met with a favorable response in some quarters, and this has tended to put the efforts of the Free World to some extent on the defensive. Prime Minister Nehru said recently, "We are convinced that the industrialization of the country must rest on heavy industry, and I understand this industry to mean machine building, not to mention ferrous metallurgy." The reality of India, says *Kommunist*, disproves the dogma of the imperialists that economically backward countries can develop only light industry.

The impressions that the Soviet wishes to create can be judged by a statement made by the same writer:

> Soviet aid has many features by which it differs fundamentally from the aid of the imperialist powers. It is granted without any political or other shackling conditions and therefore corresponds to the aspirations of the young states, which object to any binding conditions. It is exceptionally favorable (low interest rates, long term payment through delivery of the traditional goods of the given country) and is therefore not burdensome for the newly liberated countries' economy, which had been weakened by the imperialist domination. It promotes the advance of the branches of the economy that are most important for the given country (heavy industry in India, irrigation and power engineering in the U.A.R., roads in Afghanistan). Therefore Soviet aid produces maximum economic effect. In addition to contributing directly to the economic progress of the newly liberated countries, the aid of the socialist states helps indirectly also by compelling the imperialist powers to increase their financial aid to the underdeveloped countries and to grant the aid on more favorable conditions.
>
> In the near future the socialist states will produce more than one-half of world output. Their capacity for granting economic assistance is growing immeasurably, and this means that the opportunities of the young states for utilizing the experience of the countries of socialism will grow too.[5]

On the negative side, many less developed countries have had bad experiences with Soviet credits and barter agreements, and there have been troubles with Bloc technicians. But if the main objective of committing the less developed country, even for a short period, to the diversion of 20 per cent of its trade to the Soviet Bloc, to commitments for the building of sport stadiums and theaters that it does not need, or heavy industrial complexes for which it is not ready, and if official contacts have been firmly established so that espionage can proceed, then the positive factors far outweigh the negative.

Of one thing we can be certain. The economic power of the Soviet Bloc will not be used in a popularity contest for the goodwill of the uncommitted nations to see which system can provide the best living conditions for its people. It will be used whenever possible to further the political ambitions of the Bloc. These ambitions appear presently to have no limits.

FOOTNOTES

[1] *US Department of State Research Bulletin, RSB-145.*
[2] *The Current Digest of the Soviet Press,* XIV, No. 41, November 7, 1962, p. 9.
[3] *US Department of State Research Bulletin, RSB-145.*
[4] Peter S. H. Tang and Joan Maloney, *Chinese Communist Effect on Cuba,* Research Institute on the Sino-Soviet Bloc, Monograph Series No. 12.
[5] *The Current Digest . . . .,* p. 13.

# The Role of Economic Growth

—MORRIS BORNSTEIN

## Summary

An analysis of the role of economic growth in Sino-Soviet strategy over the next five to ten years is undertaken by examining trends and patterns of economic growth in the Bloc and assessing their implications for various strategic objectives of the Bloc. Attention is focused primarily on the two principal members of the Bloc, the USSR and Communist China. Although it is recognized that policies and actions of the United States and its allies will influence both the rate and pattern of Sino-Soviet growth and its relationship to Sino-Soviet strategy, possible strategies for the United States to meet the challenges posed by Sino-Soviet growth are not discussed.

Measured in terms of national product and industrial production as the indicators most relevant to Bloc strategic objectives, the economic growth of the Bloc in the 1950's was more rapid than that of the United States and its principal allies. The most important single reason was the emphasis in Bloc resource allocation upon a high rate of investment, concentrated in the producer goods industries, at the expense of consumption. Other factors contributing to rapid economic growth in the Bloc were intersectoral shifts in the labor force from agriculture to industry, rising skill levels, and technological progress. As a result of its more rapid growth, the Bloc's comparative economic strength relative to the Western Alliance increased from 1950 to 1960.

119

*A continuation of these trends and patterns of economic growth is to be anticipated in the 1960's. Bloc growth rates in the 1960's may be expected, for various reasons, to be somewhat lower than in the 1950's—particularly in Communist China— but they may still on the whole exceed those likely to be attained in the United States and Western Europe. However, it is not simply the over-all pace of Bloc economic growth which is the economic foundation of the Bloc's threat to the Free World. Equally, and perhaps more, important are the composition of this growth and its use in military, scientific, and economic competition with the West.*

*The most immediate threat of the Bloc to the Free World is its military capability, particularly Soviet missile and nuclear capabilities. Soviet economic growth, together with the progress of Soviet military technology, will increase Soviet strength in both conventional and advanced weapons. It will also make possible additional support of Communist subversion abroad and additional military aid to non-aligned countries.*

*Soviet scientific and technical progress will strengthen the Soviet position in economic competition with the West by stimulating economic growth, by enabling the Bloc to compete more effectively in furnishing capital goods and technical assistance to the less developed countries, and by reducing the vulnerability of the Bloc to NATO strategic trade controls.*

*The Bloc leadership's estimate of possible political benefits will be more important than the limitations of its economic capacity in determining the size and distribution of the Bloc's trade and aid program in the less developed countries. The threat of Bloc competition with the West will come not from an all-out aid and trade offensive, but rather from selective, timely, and often relatively modest deals with individual countries. In addition, the "demonstration" effect of Bloc growth will contribute to its influence in the less developed countries.*

*Because trade with Western Europe is important to Bloc development programs, the Bloc will endeavor to weaken the NATO strategic trade control system and will oppose in various ways the unification of Western Europe in the Common Market. Bloc competition in Western markets will increase, but the motivation is more likely to be the economic one of earning foreign exchange to pay for imports than the political one of waging economic warfare. The effects of Bloc sales may, nevertheless, still be disruptive.*

*Finally, economic development in the Bloc during the 1960's will be marked by the increasing economic integration of the USSR and the European Satellites, which will contribute to the cohesion of the Bloc. Political and ideological differences, however, impede closer integration of Communist China with the USSR and Eastern European members of the Bloc.*

———————

This paper analyzes the role of economic growth in Sino-Soviet strategy over the next five to ten years by examining trends and patterns of economic growth in the Bloc and assessing their implications for various strategic objectives of the Bloc. Although the discussion concerns the Communist Bloc as a whole, attention is focused primarily on its two principal members, the Soviet Union and Communist China, whose foreign and domestic policies and actions are of greatest concern to the United States and its allies. Some attention is devoted to the Eastern European Satellites, but none to the less important Asian Satellites: Mongolia, North Vietnam, and North Korea.

To be sure, the policies and actions of the United States and its allies will influence both the rate and pattern of Sino-Soviet economic growth and its relationship to Sino-Soviet strategy. However, this paper does not attempt to analyze in any detail possible strategies for the United States to meet the challenges posed by Sino-Soviet economic growth, inasmuch as these questions are the subject of other papers prepared for this conference.

The first section of the paper analyzes recent and probable future trends and patterns of economic growth in the Sino-Soviet Bloc. The second section examines the relationship of economic growth to each of several objectives of the Bloc, including military power, scientific and technical progress, influence in the less developed countries, weakening the NATO Alliance, and the internal cohesion of the Bloc itself. The final section summarizes the conclusions of the paper.

## Economic Growth in the Sino-Soviet Bloc

There are, of course, various possible indicators or measures of economic growth. For example, one could measure (for all or part of a nation's economy) output, employment, capital stock, etc. As far as output is concerned, one could measure actual output or potential output, that is, capacity, under various assumptions. Finally, one could measure total output, output per capita or per consuming unit, or some aspect of productivity, such as output per worker, per man-hour, or per unit of capital. All of these, in some sense or other, are measures of economic growth, and a truly complete discussion of economic growth would consider carefully all of them, as well as others.

For the purpose of this paper—the relationship of economic growth to Bloc strategy—the most significant indicators of economic growth appear to be gross national product (or the total output of final goods and services) and one of its components, industrial production. GNP is the most comprehensive measure of economic performance, while industrial production is the economic sector most relevant for the pursuit of the economic, military, scientific, and political goals of the Bloc. The discussion of Bloc growth that follows, therefore, focuses on the rate of growth, composition, and relative size (in comparison with other countries) of the national product and industrial production of the Bloc.

Tables 1 and 2 show the average annual rates of growth of national product and industrial production, respectively, of the Sino-Soviet Bloc, the United States, principal West European countries, Japan, and India during the 1950's. Although the figures for the various countries are not completely comparable, for various conceptual and statistical reasons, they do depict the differences in rates of growth with sufficient reliability for the purposes of this paper.[1]

The decade of the 1950's is chosen as the period most representative of the conditions of economic, political, military, and scientific competition between East and West which may be anticipated in the decade of the 1960's. In this respect it is more suitable than a longer period, such as that from 1913, 1928, or 1945 to the present. By 1950 the Soviet economy was already well along the path of industrialization, and most of the world had largely recovered from the effects of the Second World War. During the 1950's, the Soviet Union and the European Satellites pursued the twin goals of rapid economic development and a strong military posture, and embarked on a foreign aid program in the less developed countries. Communist China began the drastic transformation of her economy from a backward agricultural country into a modern industrial state. The Western European countries and Japan, with moderate defense burdens, were able to achieve relatively high and steady growth with both high employment and rising standards of living. The United States experienced moderate growth of both national product and consumption, in the face of cyclical fluctuations in output and employment, while maintaining large military and foreign aid programs. By and large, essentially the same conditions appear likely to characterize the economies of these countries in the 1960's.

The data in Tables 1 and 2 show that growth rates in the Bloc in the 1950's were on the whole higher than in the United States, most of Western Europe, and—for purposes of comparison with Communist China—India. (It should be noted that the figures for the Communist countries are not their official statistics or claims, but instead are the more conservative estimates of Western experts, which correspond more closely in both coverage and methodology to the figures for the Free World countries than do the official Communist statistics.) Growth rates in the Soviet Union and the European Satellites were roughly about double those in the United States and higher than those in most of the Western European countries, but lower than those in Japan. In the case of Communist China, the picture is not so clear. It seems generally agreed, however, that the growth of national product, and especially of industry, was quite high from 1950—or 1952, if the period of reconstruction from 1950 to 1952 is excluded—to 1958. Following the agricultural crisis caused by communization and the failure of the "Great Leap Forward," growth has been negligible, or modest at best. Nevertheless, the data in Tables 1 and 2 indicate that during the 1950's national product and industrial production grew in Communist China at rates double to triple those in India.

A comparison of Tables 1 and 2 shows that in all of the countries the rate of growth of industrial production was faster than that for national product. In part, this reflects the role of industry as the leading sector furnishing the capital goods which traditionally are the principal means of economic growth. In part, it reflects the slower growth of other sectors of the economy, such as agriculture, in both the Communist countries and the West, and services, in the case of the Communist countries. The reasons for the slower growth of agriculture, compared to industry, in the Communist countries and in the United States are, of course, almost directly opposite.

A detailed analysis of the many factors responsible for the rapid growth of the various economies of the Sino-Soviet Bloc

Table 1*—Average Annual Rates of Growth of Real Gross Domestic
Product of Selected Countries and Areas, Selected Periods

| Country or Area | Period | Rate (per cent) |
|---|---|---|
| USSR | 1950-60 | 6.8 |
| | 1950-55 | 7.0 |
| | 1955-60 | 6.5 |
| Communist China | 1952-57 | 6.0-8.6 |
| | 1952-59 | 8.4 |
| | 1950-59 | 9 |
| | 1952-61 | 5-6 |
| European Satellites | 1950-59 | 6.5 |
| United States | 1950-60 | 3.3 |
| France | 1950-60 | 4.3 |
| (West) German Federal Republic | 1950-60 | 7.6 |
| Italy | 1950-60 | 5.9 |
| United Kingdom | 1950-60 | 2.7 |
| Japan | 1950-60 | 9.5 |
| India | 1950-60 | 3.4 |

Table 2*—Average Annual Rates of Growth of Industrial Production in
Selected Countries and Areas, Selected Periods

| Country or Area | Period | Rate (per cent) |
|---|---|---|
| USSR | 1950-61 | 9.3 |
| | 1955-61 | 8.7 |
| | 1959-61 | 6.6 |
| Communist China | 1952-57 | 14.4 |
| | 1952-59 | 20.6 |
| | 1950-59 | 23.0 |
| European Satellites | 1950-59 | 9 |
| United States | 1950-60 | 3.6 |
| France | 1950-60 | 7.2 |
| (West) German Federal Republic | 1950-60 | 9.6 |
| Italy | 1950-60 | 8.7 |
| United Kingdom | 1950-60 | 3.1 |
| Japan | 1950-60 | 16.9 |
| India | 1950-60 | 6.9 |

in the last decade is beyond the scope of the present discussion.[2]
Probably the most important single reason was a high rate of
investment, a high proportion of which, in turn, was devoted
to investment in capital goods industries, rather than consumer
goods industries—in order to provide the sinews of industrial

*Sources and notes follow footnotes at end of paper.

development and economic growth, as well as military and scientific capabilities. On the one hand, despite low consumption levels (especially in Communist China), totalitarian Communist governments suppressed consumption in favor of investment and military programs. On the other hand, they directed this investment to the metallurgical, fuel, electric power, chemical, and machine-building industries, rather than to agriculture, textile and consumer durables production, and housing and consumer services. Other factors of importance, in addition to the rate and direction of investment, were intersectoral shifts of labor from agriculture to industry; an increase in participation rates through the entry of more women into the labor force; an increase in the skill level of the labor force; technological progress (in part adopted from the West); and, in the case of Communist China and some of the European Satellites, capital and technical assistance from the Soviet Union.

The emphasis on investment at the expense of consumption in the Communist resource allocation pattern is indicated by the figures in Table 3, in which the most recent data available on the distribution of national product by end use in the USSR, Communist China, the United States, major Western European countries, Japan, and India are assembled. Unfortunately, the figures for Communist China and India in the table are shares of the total at market prices rather than at factor cost. At factor cost, the shares of investment and defense would be somewhat higher, and the share of consumption somewhat lower, than the figures shown in the table.*

Nevertheless, the data in Table 3 do indicate, if only approximately, the higher rates of investment in the more rapidly growing countries (both inside and outside the Sino-Soviet Bloc), the higher shares of national resources devoted to mili-

---

* Factor cost data reflect resource allocation patterns better than market price data because they exclude indirect taxes (which are not payments for resources but which are included in market prices) and include subsidies (which are payments for resources but which are not included in market prices). Because the adjustment for indirect taxes is the more important one, and because they ordinarily fall proportionately more heavily on consumption than on investment and defense, adjustment from a market price to a factor cost basis tends to raise the shares of investment and defense at the expense of consumption. While the difference in results is small for a country like the United States where indirect taxes are much less important than direct taxes, it is larger for countries like Communist China and India where indirect taxes on consumption are a much more important source of government revenue.

### Table 3*—Distribution by End Use of Gross National Product of Selected Countries and Areas, Selected Years
#### (Per cent of total)

| Country or Area | Year | End Use | | | | |
| --- | --- | --- | --- | --- | --- | --- |
| | | Personal Consumption | Govern-ment Civil Con-sumption | De-fense | Invest-ment | Total |
| USSR | 1960 | 47.1 | 10.1 | 10.2 | 32.6 | 100.0 |
| Communist China | 1957 | 63.6 | 11.3 | | 25.1 | 100.0 |
| European Satellites | n.a. | | | | | |
| United States | 1960 | 60.4 | 9.8 | 10.1 | 19.7 | 100.0 |
| France | 1960 | 58.3 | 10.7 | 6.6 | 24.3 | 100.0 |
| (West) German Federal Republic | 1960 | 50.4 | 11.9 | 3.9 | 33.8 | 100.0 |
| Italy | 1960 | 58.7 | 13.7 | | 27.4 | 100.0 |
| United Kingdom | 1960 | 61.3 | 11.8 | 7.1 | 19.8 | 100.0 |
| Japan | 1960 | 48.9 | 9.6 | | 41.5 | 100.0 |
| India | 1959 | 77.1 | 5.3 | 2.0 | 15.6 | 100.0 |

tary programs in the USSR and the United States, and the greater degree to which Communist China, in comparison with India, has suppressed consumption in favor of investment and military strength.

This pattern of resource allocation, emphasizing investment and the preferential development of heavy industry, has been responsible for the rapid rates of growth in the Sino-Soviet Bloc during the 1950's and for the improvement in its comparative economic position relative to the United States and its allies. According to a US Government comparison of the Sino-Soviet Bloc (the USSR, European Satellites, and Communist China) and the Western Alliance (United States and its NATO, SEATO, OAS, and bilateral allies), the combined GNP of the Bloc increased from about 30 per cent of the combined GNP of the Western Alliance in 1950 to about 40 per cent in 1959. In industrial production, the Bloc's relative position improved from about 22 per cent of the Western level in 1950 to about 33 per cent in 1959.[3] While the precision of these comparisons is limited by both conceptual and data problems, they do convey reasonably

*Sources and notes follow footnotes at end of paper.

well the change in relative economic strength of East and West which has resulted from the rate and character of Communist economic growth.

What will be the rate and character of Sino-Soviet Bloc economic growth in the 1960's? Long-range economic forecasting is hazardous, as many practitioners have discovered to their embarrassment. This is certainly true so far as any effort to forecast growth trends and patterns in the Sino-Soviet Bloc is concerned, and it would be presumptuous and misleading to attempt to offer precise forecasts on these questions. Nevertheless, it is possible to indicate in broad outlines, at least for the Soviet Union and the European Satellites if not also for Communist China, what seems to be the consensus of expert opinion in the West regarding prospects for economic growth in the 1960's.[4] On balance, it appears that Bloc growth rates in the 1960's will, for a variety of reasons, be somewhat lower than those in the 1950's but may still exceed those likely to occur in the United States, most of Western Europe, and India.

In the case of the Soviet Union, there are a number of factors tending to depress growth rates in the 1960's compared with the 1950's. In fact, their retarding effect is visible in the decline in Soviet growth rates in the last few years shown in Tables 1 and 2. First, there is the increased pressure to divert resources from investment, for future economic growth, to military and space programs, improvements in living standards, and foreign aid. Other retarding factors are the likelihood of a slower growth of agricultural output than the sharp increase obtained in 1953-58 (in large part by expanding the cultivated area by almost 25 per cent); a lower rate of increase in the non-agricultural labor force in 1960-70 than 1950-60, accompanied by a reduction in the length of the work week; and a possible increase in the real costs of raw material exploitation.

On the other hand, there is the determination of the Soviet leadership to maintain rapid economic growth as part of the pursuit of its goal of world domination. This may involve an increase in the rate of investment, in order to maintain or even increase the rate of growth of the capital stock, in the face of rising capital-output ratios. This would reduce somewhat the share of consumption as a fraction of national product—assuming that investment were not increased at the expense of military programs instead. But it could still permit a modest continued increase both in aggregate consumption and in per capita living standards, so long as the rate of growth of the national product outstrips population growth by a sufficient margin. Other growth-promoting factors are the intensified search for improvements in the planning and administration of the economy, emphasis on the widespread application of new technology, and the steady improvement in the quality of the labor force.

The economic plans of the European Satellites for the 1960's call for a continuation of the pattern of economic development followed in the 1950's. As in the case of the Soviet Union, their industrial goals are more likely to be attained than their agricultural targets, particularly since all of them except Poland have recently socialized their agriculture and now face the problems—already experienced in both the Soviet Union and Communist China—of increasing output in collectivized agriculture. For this reason, as well as others, including smaller rates of increase in the industrial labor force during the 1960's than the 1950's, growth rates in the 1960's are likely to be lower than in the 1950's.

It is especially difficult to make a useful estimate for Communist China during the 1960's, in view of the lack of reliable statistical information on economic developments since 1958, the severity of its current agricultural crisis, and the drastic structural changes yet to be accomplished in the course of its industrialization. Despite the radical changes made in the commune system and the current emphasis on agriculture, at the expense of industrial expansion, the basic Communist Chinese goal remains rapid industrialization with minimum regard to the human costs. Thus, the steps taken to deal with the food crisis and the cutback in new industrial investment should be regarded as transitory measures to meet a serious crisis, rather than as a reversal of basic policy. However, it is not possible (even, surely, for the Communist Chinese leaders themselves) to predict how successful these measures will be and how soon the industrialization drive can be resumed with at least some of its former vigor.

In summary, it appears that the rates of growth of both national product and industrial production in the Sino-Soviet Bloc will be lower in the 1960's than in the 1950's. However, because these lower percentage growth rates will be applied to higher absolute bases, as a result of the growth achieved during the 1950's, the absolute annual increments resulting from growth are likely to be higher in the key industries than they were in the 1950's. For example, an 8 per cent increase in Soviet steel production over the 1961 level represents more steel than a 12 per cent increase over the 1951 level did ten years earlier. The same is true for machine tools, electric power, electronics, etc.

However, it is not simply the over-all pace of Sino-Soviet Bloc economic growth that is the economic foundation of the Bloc's threat to the Free World. Equally, and perhaps more, important in this threat are the composition of this growth (its "anatomy") and its use in the pursuit of the Bloc's strategic objectives. The mobilization and concentration of its resources for strategic purposes have enabled the Bloc to become a formidable rival in military, scientific, and economic competition with the West, despite the Bloc's still relatively much smaller total and industrial output. The relationship of Bloc growth and Bloc strategic objectives is the subject of the next section.

## Economic Growth and Sino-Soviet Strategy

Both the rate and the anatomy of economic growth play an important role in the pursuit of the Sino-Soviet Bloc's strategic objectives. This section examines the relationship of economic growth to the following Bloc objectives: (1) military power, (2) scientific and technical advance, (3) influence in the non-aligned and less developed countries, (4) weakening the NATO Alliance, and (5) internal cohesion of the Bloc itself.

### Military Power

The most immediate threat of the Sino-Soviet Bloc to the Free World is the military capability of the Soviet Union, particularly in missile and nuclear weapons. Although the Soviet economy as a whole is still much smaller than the United States economy—to consider the problem in terms of the two leading powers—as a result of past concentration of human and material resources on the military effort and related scientific and industrial programs (such as machine-building, electronics, and chemicals), the Soviets now present a challenge to the United States in both conventional and nonconventional military strength. In the past, the military position of the United States benefited from our geographic isolation and our superior mobilization base. Unhappily, the former has disappeared with the advent of intercontinental aircraft and missiles, while the latter requires time after the initiation of hostilities and is thus not decisive in case of nuclear war. In the case of smaller wars, inventories of military equipment are more important than mobilization capacity. Finally, the US margin in mobilization capacity is being reduced by the more rapid expansion of Soviet industry, especially in such key areas as machine-building.[5]

The Soviets believe in diversified forces, flexibility, and capabilities for both nuclear and non-nuclear warfare, including speedy commitment of forces in a geographically limited ("local" or "peripheral") war. Thus, they consider important both the possession of intercontinental striking power, and its corollary of home defense against the enemy's long-range attack, on the one hand, and the maintenance of large, modern "theatre" land armies, with supporting air, missile, and naval forces, on the other.[6] In this light, demobilization of some two million men from the armed forces in the late 1950's is seen to represent not an over-all reduction in Soviet military capabilities but rather a shift in the balance between manpower and more advanced weapons.

The maintenance, equipment, and further development of this large and diversified military establishment involves large real costs to the economy in terms both of smaller consumption and of smaller growth than would otherwise be possible. The failure of the Soviets to expand their ICBM stockpile in the late 1950's as fast as was expected in the West may be explained at least in part by the Soviet leadership's reluctance to allocate additional resources to missile production, at the expense of civilian investment and consumption. Although in aggregate terms the Soviet leadership is clearly more disposed to sacrifice consumption than civilian investment in order to advance military programs, the specific resources needed for missile and space programs—high grade scientific, engineering, and technical manpower; machine-building facilities; and special alloys and chemicals—must be diverted from the producer goods industries, rather than the consumer goods industries. However, the Soviet leadership has shown itself willing to accept such sacrifices of consumption and/or growth in the past, and it may be expected to do so in the future if it decides that additional resources should be allocated to military programs. There is evidence that this in fact has happened to some extent in the last few years. Since 1958, armaments production has been growing more rapidly than civilian machinery production, reversing an earlier trend.[7] In 1961, scheduled demobilizations from the armed forces were halted, and the announced military budget was sharply increased. A more modest investment program was announced for 1962, compared with 1960-61; and retail prices were increased and scheduled cuts in income taxes were suspended in 1962.

Soviet economic, and especially industrial, growth in the 1960's will therefore provide the means for the development of greater capabilities in ballistic, submarine-launched, and air defense missiles, nuclear-propelled aircraft and rockets, and weapons (including nuclear weapons) for the land forces. It will also make possible additional support of Communist subversion in areas like Laos, as well as additional military aid to non-aligned countries like Egypt and Indonesia. This assistance, moreover, may conveniently include weapons and equipment which have become obsolete as far as the Soviet armed forces themselves are concerned, as a result of the advance of Soviet military technology.

In the case of Communist China, the military threat to the Free World rests primarily on large conventional forces, with Soviet equipment. This reflects the decision of the Communist Chinese leadership in 1956 to allocate resources to investment in the expansion of heavy industry, in order to create the foundation for an enhanced military posture in the future, rather than to emphasize military output immediately, at the expense of economic growth.[8] In terms of the categories in Table 3, resources were allocated to "investment," rather than to "defense." It is impossible to say, on the basis of available information, how the present economic crisis in Communist China has affected the allocation of resources to military purposes. However, despite severe economic problems in the past few years, the Communist Chinese government has been willing not only to support actively Communist military activity in Vietnam and Laos but also even to undertake its own recent military action against India. The poor outlook for China's economic growth in the next few years therefore by no means implies a corresponding moderation in its aggressive intentions, or a weakening of its military capabilities or even a corresponding reduction in the rate of improvement in these capabilities.

### Scientific and Technical Progress

Scientific and technical advance may be regarded both as a product of economic growth and as a means to it. As the economy grows, more human and material resources can be devoted to research and development (R&D). In this sense, scientific and technical programs are a form of investment—investment in knowledge, rather than in plant, equipment, or inventories. The fruits of this investment can in turn contribute to economic growth, and as industry expands there are more opportunities to apply the results of R&D programs.

Sino-Soviet Bloc scientific and technical progress presents a challenge to the United States in several respects. Foremost is the enhancement of Soviet military capabilities resulting from the success of Soviet R&D programs in missile and space technology. In addition, scientific and technical progress strengthens the Bloc's position in economic competition with the West, by stimulating the rate of growth, by enabling the Bloc to compete more effectively with the West in furnishing capital goods and technical assistance to less developed countries, and by reducing the Bloc's vulnerability to the strategic trade controls of NATO. Finally, Soviet scientific and technical advances— especially dramatic achievements in space exploration—help Soviet propaganda in creating the image of the Soviet Union as a dynamic, progressive, technically advanced society. In science, as elsewhere, the Soviets are careful to define the terms of "peaceful competition" to their advantage, stressing the fields in which they lead and ignoring those in which they lag.

The present level of Soviet science and technology varies markedly from area to area, according to the priority assigned by the Soviet leadership.[9] In the space sciences, aeronautical sciences, applied mathematics and mathematical theory, geological sciences, meteorology, oceanography, and certain branches of metallurgy, Soviet science is quite advanced. On the other hand, in medicine, biology, chemistry, and physics (except high-energy physics) the Soviets lag, in comparison with Western science.

In industrial technology, the picture also is varied. On the whole, the technological level in the producer goods industries is far superior to that in the consumer goods industries. The best of Soviet technology compares favorably with US technology in such industries as steel, iron ore, electric power, machine building, aircraft, and electronics. However, there is a wide disparity in some of these industries between the technological levels of the leading and the typical enterprises. Technology in the chemical industry as a whole is clearly behind the United States level, apparently because of difficulty in applying research results to production, attributable in large part to a shortage of chemical engineers. Nevertheless, the Soviet chemical industry is able to produce the plastics and fuels needed for intercontinental ballistic missiles, spacecraft, and jet aircraft.

Steady scientific and technical advance in the Soviet Union in the 1960's is to be anticipated for several reasons. First, the Soviet leadership will continue to emphasize both basic and applied research as a source of economic growth and military power. The Soviet Union is now turning out large numbers of highly trained scientists and engineers and building well-equipped research establishments, including the "science city" at Novosibirsk. Second, in addition to developing its own technology, the Soviet Union will continue its extensive effort to acquire Western technology, both through the translation, abstracting, and widespread dissemination of foreign scientific and technical journals and through the importation of foreign machinery and equipment for study and copying in Soviet plants. Finally, because of the wide disparity in technological levels both among branches of industry and among different enterprises within a given branch, there are still many opportunities in the Soviet economy to apply more widely the more advanced technologies now used only in selected priority activities or in the newest plants.

Communist China also is emphasizing scientific and technical progress, as a means of modernizing its backward economy and as a means of securing an independent nuclear capability. At present, the Chinese are stressing the instruction of cadres and improvement in the level of applied technology, rather than basic research, with the ambitious goal of reaching Western levels of technology in various parts of the economy by the end of the 1960's.[10] They hope, however, to achieve a nuclear capability even sooner, by detonating their first nuclear device by 1963 and achieving a limited nuclear stockpile a few years later.[11] Even the detonation of an experimental nuclear device would be of great significance, signaling Communist China's entry into the "Nuclear Club" and modifying the balance of power between the Sino-Soviet Bloc and the Western Alliance, as well as within the Bloc between the Soviet Union and Communist China. It would in addition enhance China's influence and prestige as a model for economic development in Asia.

### Influence in the Less Developed Countries

The Sino-Soviet Bloc's strategic objectives in the less developed countries include the creation of good will toward the Bloc,

the weakening of economic and political ties with the Western
Alliance, and the orientation of these countries toward the Bloc.
If it is not able to draw countries into the Bloc, it hopes at least
to keep them non-aligned, rather than leaning toward the West.
Bloc economic relations with these countries—in the form of
trade, economic and military credits, and technical assistance—
are used to pursue these objectives. In addition, the Bloc expects that its own rate of economic growth will have a powerful
"exemplary" or "demonstration" effect on the less developed
countries.

Bloc trade with the less developed countries increased from
about $860 million in 1954 to about $3.4 billion in 1961.[12] This
trade consists primarily of the exchange of machinery and
equipment, petroleum, ferrous metals, and food from the Bloc
for foodstuffs and raw materials, particularly raw cotton, wool,
and natural rubber, from the less developed countries. In 1961,
the European Satellites conducted about 43 per cent of this
trade, the Soviet Union about 40 per cent, and Communist China
17 per cent. About 10 per cent of total Bloc foreign trade was
directed to the less developed countries, accounting for about 6
per cent of the total trade of these areas. However, the Bloc's
share in the total trade of various individual less developed
countries is much higher. In 1960, for example, the Bloc took
45 per cent of Egypt's exports and supplied over 25 per cent of
its imports, while the corresponding figures for Guinea were
23 and 44 per cent. In many cases, the Bloc has been able to
make a strong impact on less developed countries as a buyer of
last resort, willing to absorb primary products which less developed countries have difficulty selling on the world market.

As in the case of trade, the Bloc's aid program has made a
strong impression not because of its total magnitude but rather
because of its recent emergence and rapid increase, and its concentration in a few key countries. From January 1, 1954, to
June 30, 1962, the Bloc made economic assistance commitments
to less developed countries amounting to $4.9 billion, of which
over 96 per cent consisted of repayable credits and less than
4 per cent grants. The bulk of the assistance (75 per cent)
was extended to a few countries—Indonesia, Egypt, India, Iraq,
Afghanistan, Cuba, and Syria. The USSR was the principal
source, providing about 70 per cent, the European Satellites 20
per cent, and Communist China 10 per cent. In connection with
this aid, the Bloc had some 9,600 economic technicians in 29
less developed countries during the first half of 1962. In addition

to economic assistance, credits amounting to $2.3 billion were extended for the purchase of arms from the Bloc, mainly by Egypt, Syria, Indonesia, Iraq, Cuba, and Afghanistan. During the first half of 1962, about 2,500 Bloc military technicians were working in 10 less developed countries.[13]

The Bloc economic aid program is much smaller than that of the US Government alone—and even still smaller than total Western assistance, including assistance by other governments, private capital, and capital from Western-supported international organizations such as the International Bank. Nevertheless, the Bloc program has had a strong impact because of the novelty of a new source of capital, low rates of interest, willingness to accept repayment in traditional exports, emphasis on industrial projects which identify the Soviets in a conspicuous way with the industrialization of the recipient country, and the Bloc's heavily advertised claims of non-intervention in national economic development programs and of attaching no political "strings" to its assistance.

The "burden" of this assistance to less developed countries upon the Bloc has not been very great. For example, annual aid commitments by the USSR during the past few years represent less than half of 1 per cent of Soviet GNP, and actual deliveries less than half of that. Moreover, these figures are for credits, rather than grants, and some repayment of past credits apparently has already begun, to judge by export surpluses of various "aid" recipients with the Bloc. Deliveries of machinery and equipment for particular projects may, it is true, strain Soviet production capacity at certain times. But this would appear to be more a question of scheduling deliveries under aid programs, or scheduling the expansion of production facilities for certain kinds of output, than a question of general economic growth and the over-all ability to provide foreign aid. At the same time, it should be recognized that Soviet credits to non-Bloc countries do mean a diversion of scarce resources, including technical personnel, which could be used instead in the Soviet economy, for investment, military programs, or consumption, or in Soviet assistance to other members of the Bloc. Thus, there is clearly some "opportunity cost" to Soviet aid to the less developed countries (except in the provision of obsolete military equipment).

The evidence suggests, however, that the amount of Bloc aid to the less developed countries does not depend primarily on the size or rate of growth of the economies of the Bloc. Rather, the amount, as well as the geographic distribution and composition, of Bloc aid appears to depend as much or more on a judgment of the political gains to be expected from such aid. Moreover, the amount of Bloc aid is determined also by the desire of less developed countries to seek it. And this in turn depends on various factors, including their ability to finance their development programs from exports of their primary products on the world market, the availability of Western aid on attractive terms, and their evaluation of Bloc performance under previous aid agreements.

All of these factors have played a part in the decline in new economic credits by the Bloc from $1,190 million in 1960 to $970 million in 1961 and $310 million in the first half of 1962. It appears, however, that advantageous opportunities, rather than limitations of economic capacity, are more likely to be the principal determinant of the level and distribution of Bloc aid in the 1960's. And the extent (and terms and timeliness) of Western aid offers will significantly affect the emergence of these opportunities.

As for Bloc trade with the less developed countries, it appears likely to grow at a slower rate during the 1960's than it did during the late 1950's, when it increased rapidly starting from very low levels. It is true that as the industrialization of the Bloc countries progresses, their economies will need more primary products and will produce more manufactured goods which could be exported. However, most of the expansion of trade which will accompany Bloc economic growth is likely to take the form of intra-Bloc trade. The Soviet Bloc is still committed to a policy of autarky which avoids undue dependence on non-Bloc sources. In addition, the Bloc's pattern of economic development emphasizes the importation (whether from Bloc or non-Bloc sources) of machinery and industrial raw materials, rather than foodstuffs, manufactured consumer goods, or raw materials for the consumer goods industries. Moreover, the less developed members of the Bloc will need to export foodstuffs, raw materials, and manufactured consumer goods to the more developed members in order to obtain the machinery and fuels needed for their industrialization. For all of these reasons, a large expansion in Bloc imports from the less developed countries seems unlikely.

Bloc exports to the less developed countries in turn are limited by the high priority assigned to the internal development of the individual Bloc countries and to the economic integration of the Bloc. These objectives will receive preference, over a general expansion of trade with the less developed countries, in the allocation of resources in general and of machinery and other producer goods in particular. Also, the Bloc countries need to export to Western Europe to obtain machinery and materials not available either in the Bloc or in the less developed countries. And at least one of these exports, Soviet petroleum, will compete for European markets with exports from less developed countries in the Middle East.

In summary, the prospects for the growth of Bloc trade with the less developed non-Bloc countries are limited by the Bloc's autarkic policies, its interest in imports which the less developed countries are unable to supply, and the presence in the Bloc of several less developed countries, including Communist China. As a result, a very large global increase in Bloc trade with the less developed countries seems unlikely. At the same time, the Bloc may be expected to take advantage of selected opportunities to increase trade where there are significant political advantages to be gained from the Bloc's willingness to take primary products which countries have difficulty selling on the world market. Thus, in Sino-Soviet Bloc competition with the West in the less developed countries in the 1960's, the threat is likely to come not from an all-out aid and trade offensive, but rather from selective, timely, and often relatively modest deals with individual countries—which need not involve significant economic costs to the Bloc.

In addition to these "direct" economic methods, however, the Bloc hopes to gain influence in the less developed countries by the "exemplary" or "demonstration" effect of its own internal economic development. By pointing to its rapid rate of economic growth, the Bloc attempts to convince the leaders and élites of the less developed countries (1) that it will win in economic competition with the Western Alliance and that they should therefore align themselves with the Bloc, and (2) that they should follow the Soviet model in their own economic development.

The ruling elites of many of the less developed countries find the Soviet model of interest because they want rapid development with drastic changes in both economic structure and social institutions.[14] To them it appears that the Soviets have a successful formula for rapid industrialization and the expansion of national power and prestige—a formula offering both a strategy of development and an institutional apparatus for accomplishing it. The strategy involves high rates of capital formation, priority for heavy industry, emphasis on modern technology, etc., while the institutions include public ownership and entrepreneurship, comprehensive planning, and the collectivization of agriculture. To many leaders in the less developed countries, this combination appears a much more promising path for their economic development than the experience and methods of the United States and the Western European countries.

This is true in part because these leaders often fail to appreciate other aspects of Soviet experience. They tend to overlook the already relatively developed state of the Soviet economy on the eve of the Five Year Plans; the absence of population pressures; the size and resource endowment of the Soviet economy, which made autarkic development possible; the real nature and poor results of agricultural collectivization; and, most important, the enormous human cost, in lives, in the loss of freedom, and in the sacrifice of living standards.

However, even when they are aware of the coercion underlying the Communist approach to economic development, some of these leaders still conclude that the sacrifices are worth the results in economic growth and change, given the backward political, economic, and social conditions in their countries. Thus, while they may not become Communists, or support the Sino-Soviet Bloc in international politics, they nevertheless turn to the Bloc for advice and assistance in their development programs.

### Weakening the NATO Alliance

Sino-Soviet Bloc objectives in regard to the NATO Alliance include weakening the ties between the United States and its European allies and impeding the economic integration and political and military unification of Western Europe in the Common Market.

Trade with Western Europe is important to the Bloc as a source of machinery and equipment and the technology which they incorporate, as well as raw materials and semimanufactures such as iron and steel products, chemicals, and fertilizer. In return for these commodities the Bloc sells primarily raw materials, fuels, and foodstuffs. The Bloc would like to continue this pattern of trade in the 1960's in order to advance its industrialization—and thereby also to reduce its vulnerability to the West's strategic trade control system. Moreover, the Bloc hopes that offers of trade will lead businessmen in Western Europe to exert pressure on their governments for a more favorable attitude toward the Bloc, including not only the relaxation of strategic trade controls but even the extension of credits to finance exports to the Bloc.

In this light, the Sino-Soviet Bloc's opposition to the European Economic Community (EEC) is seen to have economic as well as political foundations. The Bloc opposes the EEC because it contributes to the political unification of Western Europe and the economic growth of the capitalist world. More immediately and concretely, however, the Bloc, particularly the European Satellites, is concerned about losing markets in Western Europe and thus the foreign exchange with which to acquire needed imports. The Bloc fears that it will be excluded from foodstuff sales to the EEC countries as a result of a common agricultural policy of self-sufficiency, and that its other exports will suffer as a result of the reduction of trade barriers inside the Common Market. The Bloc is responding to these implications of the Common Market in various ways. It appeals to other countries with similar fears about being excluded from the Common Market—such as Yugoslavia and various less developed raw material and foodstuff exporting nations—to unite to combat the "discrimination" of the EEC. It warns neutrals like Austria not to adhere to the Market. It encourages Italy to resist a common fuel policy in the EEC which would restrict the importation of Soviet petroleum. And it endeavors to build up its own rival customs union in Eastern Europe under the Council for Economic Mutual Assistance (CEMA).

It is sometimes suggested that Bloc economic growth represents a threat to NATO because it increases the Bloc's potential for economic warfare, such as the disruption of world markets through "dumping." While this is of course a possibility, it does not appear to be the motivation behind the expansion of Bloc exports in the 1950's nor the expansion likely to take place in the 1960's. Rather, Bloc exports have been increased in order to earn the foreign exchange to pay for imports needed in the Bloc development programs. This expansion does mean increased competition by the Bloc in world markets, and the experiences with tin and aluminum in 1958 and petroleum at present show that the Bloc is willing to cut prices and disregard established marketing arrangements in order to make sales. (In the case of industrial diamonds, on the other hand, the USSR is selling through the diamond cartel.) Although the effect of Bloc sales may still be disruptive, the motivation seems to be primarily economic, rather than political. Moreover, the economic benefits may be offset by political disadvantages, inasmuch as Bloc exports of oil and tin compete with exports from less developed countries whose good will the Bloc seeks to cultivate.

### Cohesion of the Bloc

An important Soviet strategic objective is the further political, ideological, military, and economic unification of the Bloc.

It appears likely that the economic growth of the Bloc in the 1960's will be characterized by the increasing integration of the economies of the USSR and the European Satellites under CEMA. (Communist China is not a member of CEMA.) Although CEMA was founded in 1949, serious efforts at economic integration did not begin until 1958, and even since then progress toward Bloc-wide coordination of investment, production, and trade has been slow, for a number of reasons.[15] These include irrational internal price structures and arbitrary exchange rates which make it difficult to devise a rational pattern of specialization; emphasis on bilateralism rather than multilateralism; and the greater independence of the European Satellites since 1956. Although a number of important decisions were taken in June 1962 to speed up the economic integration of the CEMA countries, quick results cannot be expected, given the complexity of the problems to be solved. Rather, the benefits are more likely to be observed in the late 1960's, after yet-to-be-chosen investment projects are brought to completion. Nevertheless, greater exploitation of the opportunities for specialization, economies of scale, multilateral trade, etc., which do exist in the CEMA countries will contribute to their growth in this decade. Moreover, because this pattern of specialization and trade will, by and large, be acceptable to the European Satellites, not simply imposed by Soviet fiat, it will help create a more unified Eastern Europe more closely tied to the Soviet Union.

In regard to Communist China, the situation is by no means so clear. Economic logic suggests a pattern of intra-Bloc trade in which Communist China exports raw materials and unfinished goods to the more developed members of the Bloc in return for machinery and semimanufactures, as was the case in the 1950's. However, political and ideological differences between Communist China and the USSR have led to the suspension of Soviet aid, and there has been a sharp drop in Chinese trade with the USSR and the European Satellites, reflecting China's inability to pay in exports for her imports, as a result of her severe economic difficulties. Thus, while economic growth in the USSR and Eastern Europe does provide the means for more trade with Communist China, and more aid to her, political considerations so far stand in the way of increased economic ties between China and the European members of the Bloc.

## Conclusions

The conclusions of the preceding analysis of Bloc economic growth and its relationship to Bloc strategy may be summarized as follows.

Measured in terms of national product and industrial production as the indicators most relevant to Bloc strategic objectives, the economic growth of the Sino-Soviet Bloc was more rapid than that of the United States and its principal allies during the 1950's. The most important single reason was the emphasis in Bloc resource allocation upon a high rate of investment, concentrated in the producer goods industries, at the expense of consumption. Other factors contributing to rapid economic growth in the Bloc were intersectoral shifts in the labor force from agriculture to industry, rising skill levels, and technological progress. As a result of its more rapid growth, the Bloc's comparative economic strength relative to the Western Alliance increased from 1950 to 1960.

A continuation of these trends and patterns is to be anticipated in the 1960's. Bloc growth rates in the 1960's may be expected, for various reasons, to be somewhat lower than in the 1950's, but they may still exceed those likely to be attained in the United States and Western Europe. However, it is not simply the overall pace of Bloc economic growth which is the economic foundation of the Bloc's threat to the Free World. Equally, and perhaps more, important are the composition of this growth and its use in military, scientific, and economic competition with the West.

The most immediate threat of the Bloc to the Free World is its military capability, particularly Soviet missile and nuclear capabilities. The expansion of the Soviet economy in the 1960's, together with the progress of Soviet military technology, will provide the means for enhancing Soviet military strength in both conventional and advanced weapons. It will also make possible additional support of Communist subversion in areas like Laos, as well as additional military aid to non-aligned countries like Egypt and Indonesia.

In addition to its contribution to weapons technology, Soviet scientific and technical progress strengthens the Soviet position in economic competition with the West by stimulating economic growth, by enabling the Bloc to compete more effectively in furnishing capital goods and technical assistance to the less developed countries, and by reducing the vulnerability of the Bloc to NATO strategic trade controls. Steady scientific and technical advance is to be expected in the Soviet Union in the 1960's.

The Bloc's program of trade, credits, and technical assistance in the less developed countries has had a strong impact not primarily because of its total size, but because of its novelty, rapid increase, and geographic concentration. Advantageous opportunities are likely to be more important than the limitations of economic capacity in determining the level and distribution of Bloc aid in the 1960's. The threat of Bloc competition with the West in the less developed countries will come not from an all-out aid and trade offensive, but rather from selective, timely, and often relatively modest deals with individual countries. In addition, the "demonstration" effect of Bloc growth will enhance its image in the less developed countries.

Because continued trade with Western Europe is important to Bloc development programs in the 1960's, the Bloc endeavors to weaken the NATO strategic trade control system and opposes the unification of Western Europe in the Common Market. Bloc competition in Western markets, such as Soviet petroleum sales to Western Europe, will increase, but the motivation is more likely to be an economic one of earning foreign exchange to pay for imports than a political one of waging economic warfare by disrupting capitalist markets. The effects of Bloc sales may, however, still be disruptive.

Finally, economic development in the Bloc during the 1960's will be marked by the increasing economic integration of the USSR and the European Satellites, which will contribute to the cohesion of the Bloc. Political and ideological differences, however, impede closer integration of Communist China with the European members of the Bloc.

## FOOTNOTES

\* The author is Associate Professor of Economics at the University of Michigan. This paper was written while he was an Associate of the Russian Research Center, Harvard University, on leave from the University of Michigan on a Ford Foundation fellowship. The assistance of the Center and the Foundation is gratefully acknowledged. The author is grateful to Abram Bergson, Holland Hunter, and other colleagues at the Center, and to Gregory Grossman, for helpful comments.

[1] Even a brief discussion of the various conceptual and statistical problems involved in such international comparisons is outside the scope of this paper. Recent sources on these problems, in which additional references are cited, include the following:

On the measurement of national product, see George Jaszi, "The Measurement of Aggregate Economic Growth: A Review of Key Conceptual and Statistical Issues as Suggested by United States Experience," *Review of Economics and Statistics*, Vol. XLIII, No. 4 (November, 1961), pp. 317-32; and Abram Bergson, *The Real National Income of Soviet Russia Since 1928* (Cambridge, Mass.: Harvard University Press, 1961), Chs. 3 and 12. On the measurement of industrial production, see G. Warren Nutter, assisted by Israel Borenstein and Adam Kaufman, *Growth of Industrial Production in the Soviet Union* (Princeton: Princeton University Press, 1962); and Richard Moorsteen, *Prices and Production of Machinery in the Soviet Union, 1928-1958* (Cambridge, Mass.: Harvard University Press, 1962).

On the construction of national income accounts for Soviet-type economies, see Bergson, *op. cit.;* Alexander Eckstein, *The National Income of Communist China* (New York: The Free Press of Glencoe, Inc., 1961), ch. II; and "A Note on Some Aspects of National Accounting Methodology in Eastern Europe and the Soviet Union," United Nations, Economic Commission for Europe (ECE), *Economic Bulletin for Europe*, Vol. 11, No. 3, 1959, pp. 52-68.

On interspatial comparisons of national product, see Milton Gilbert and Irving B. Kravis, *An International Comparison of National Products and the Purchasing Power of Currencies* (Paris: Organization for European Economic Cooperation, 1954); Morris Bornstein, "A Comparison of Soviet and United States National Product," US Congress, Joint Economic Committee, Subcommittee on Economic Statistics, *Comparisons of the United States and Soviet Economies*, 86th Cong., 1st Sess., 1959, pp. 377-95; and Abraham S. Becker, "Comparisons of United States and USSR National Output: Some Rules of the Game," *World Politics*, Vol. XIII, No. 1 (October, 1960), pp. 99-111.

On Communist economic statistics, see Gregory Grossman, *Soviet Statistics of Physical Output of Industrial Commodities: Their Compilation and Quality* (Princeton: Princeton University Press, 1960); Choh-ming Li, *The Statistical System of Communist China* (Berkeley: University of California Press, 1962); and Kang Chao, "On the Reliability of Industrial Output Data of Communist China," *Journal of Asian Studies*, Vol. XXII, No. 1 (November, 1962), pp. 47-65.

[2] The source and characteristics of their past growth, and prospects for their future growth, are analyzed in a number of recent studies, including Alec Nove, *Communist Economic Strategy: Soviet Growth and Capabilities* (Washington: National Planning Association, 1959); Bergson, *op. cit.;*

Stanley H. Cohn, "The Gross National Product in the Soviet Union: Comparative Growth Rates," US Congress, Joint Economic Committee, *Dimensions of Soviet Economic Power*, 87th Cong., 2nd Sess., 1962, pp. 67-89; John P. Hardt, "Strategic Alternatives in Soviet Resource Allocation Policy," *ibid.*, pp. 1-31; ECE, *Economic Survey of Europe in 1961* (Geneva: 1962), Part 1, Ch. II; Comments by Abram Bergson and Gregory Grossman, *Survey*, No. 47 (April, 1963); Choh-ming Li, *Economic Development of Communist China* (Berkeley: University of California Press, 1959); United Nations, Economic Commission for Asia and the Far East, *Economic Survey of Asia and the Far East 1961* (Bangkok: 1962), pp. 90-98; and Peter Schran, "Some Reflections on Chinese Communist Economic Policy," *The China Quarterly*, No. 11 (July-September, 1962), pp. 58-77.

[3] US Congress, Joint Economic Committee, Subcommittee on Economic Statistics, *Comparisons of the United States and Soviet Economies, Supplemental Statement on Costs and Benefits to the Soviet Union of Its Bloc and Pact System: Comparisons with the Western Alliance System*, 86th Cong., 2nd Sess., 1960, pp. 48-49.

[4] See sources cited in footnote 2.

[5] John P. Hardt, with C. Darwin Stolzenbach and Martin J. Kohn, *The Cold War Economic Gap* (New York: Frederick A. Praeger, Inc., 1961), p. 43.

[6] Institute for Strategic Studies, *The Communist Bloc and the Western Alliance: The Military Balance, 1962-63* (London: 1962), p. 2.

[7] Rush V. Greenslade and Phyllis Wallace, "Industrial Production in the U.S.S.R.," US Congress, Joint Economic Committee, *Dimensions of Soviet Economic Power*, 87th Cong., 2nd Sess., 1962, p. 122.

[8] Alice Langley Hsieh, *Communist China's Strategy in the Nuclear Era* (Englewood Cliffs, N. J.: Prentice-Hall, Inc., 1962), pp. 167-68.

[9] The following discussion of Soviet science and technology is based on the conclusions of a symposium of specialists reported in Institute of International Education (IIE), *Report on the IIE Seminar on Industrial Technology in the Soviet Union, March 24-25, 1960* (New York: IIE, 1960). For a review of the various areas of potential competition between the Soviet Bloc and the West in science and technology in the 1960's, see US Senate, Committee on Foreign Relations, *United States Foreign Policy: Possible Nonmilitary Scientific Developments and Their Potential Impact on Foreign Policy Problems of the United States*, prepared by the Stanford Research Institute, 86th Cong., 1st Sess., 1959.

[10] Sidney H. Gould (editor), *Sciences in Communist China* (Washington: American Association for the Advancement of Science, 1961), p. vii.

[11] Hsieh, *op. cit.*, pp. 170-71.

[12] Sino-Soviet Bloc economic relations with the less devloped countries are analyzed in Joseph S. Berliner, *Soviet Economic Aid* (New York: Frederick A. Praeger, Inc., 1958); Henry G. Aubrey, with the assistance of Joel Darmstadter, *Coexistence: Economic Challenge and Response* (Washington: National Planning Association, 1961); EEC, *Economic Survey of Europe in 1960* (Geneva: 1961), Ch. V, pp. 10-19; Milton Kovner, "Trade and Aid," *Survey*, No. 43 (August, 1962), pp. 44-54; US Department of State, *The Sino-Soviet Economic Offensive Through June 30, 1962*, Research Memorandum RSB-145, September 18, 1962; and Marshall I. Goldman, "Soviet Foreign Aid: Has the Giving Hurt?," *Challenge*, Vol. XI, No. 4 (January, 1963), pp. 7-11.

[13] US Department of State, *op. cit.*

[14] On the appeal and the applicability of the Soviet model of economic development to the less developed countries, see John Michael Montias, "The Soviet Model and the Underdeveloped Nations," Nicolas Spulber (editor), *Study of the Soviet Economy* (Bloomington, Ind.: Indiana University Publications, 1961), pp. 56-80; W. Donald Bowles, "Soviet Russia as a Model for Underdeveloped Areas," *World Politics*, Vol. XIV, No. 3 (April, 1962), pp. 483-504; and A. Nove, "The Soviet Model and Under-developed Countries," *International Affairs* (London), Vol. 37, No. 1 (January, 1961), pp. 29-38. See also Peter S. H. Tang, *Communist China as a Developmental Model for Underdeveloped Countries* (Washington: Research Institute on the Sino-Soviet Bloc, 1960).

[15] CEMA is discussed in Nicolas Spulber, "The Soviet-Bloc Foreign Trade System," *Law and Contemporary Problems*, Vol. XXIV, No. 3 (Summer, 1959), pp. 420-34; Frederic L. Pryor, "Forms of Economic Co-operation in the European Communist Bloc," *Soviet Studies*, Vol. XI, No. 2 (October, 1959), pp. 173-94; and Robert S. Jaster, "CEMA's Influence on Soviet Policies in Eastern Europe," *World Politics*, Vol. XIV, No. 3 (April, 1962), pp. 505-18.

## SOURCES AND NOTES, TABLES 1-3

*Table 1.*

All figures are for gross domestic product at market prices, unless otherwise noted. Gross domestic product = gross national product minus net factor incomes received from abroad.

USSR: Gross domestic product at factor cost. (Gross domestic product at factor cost = gross domestic product at market prices − indirect taxes + subsidies.) From Stanley H. Cohn, "The Gross National Product in the Soviet Union: Comparative Growth Rates," US Congress, Joint Economic Committee, *Dimensions of Soviet Economic Power*, 87th Cong., 2nd Sess., 1962, p. 75.

Communist China: Ta-chung Liu and Kung-chia Yeh, "Preliminary Estimate of the National Income of the Chinese Mainland, 1952-59," *American Economic Review*, Vol. LI, No. 2 (May, 1961), p. 490, estimate 6.0 per cent for net domestic product at market prices. (Net domestic product = gross domestic product − capital consumption allowances.) William W. Hollister, *China's Gross National Product and Social Accounts, 1950-57* (Glencoe, Illinois: The Free Press, 1958), p. 2, estimates 8.6 per cent for GNP at market prices for 1952-57. The difference in estimates appears to be due more to differences in the data and methodology used than simply to the difference in coverage between the two concepts of national product, however. Liu and Yeh estimate 8.4 per cent for 1952-59, but they describe their "conjectural" estimates of 14 per cent for 1958 and 15 per cent for 1959 as follows (*op. cit.*, p. 498): "Though much lower than the corresponding Communist figures (35 per cent and 22 per cent, respectively), they still appear extraordinarily and unpersuasively high." The 9 per cent figure for 1950-59, based on preliminary data for 1959, is a US Government estimate in US Congress, Joint Economic Committee, Subcommittee on Economic Statistics, *Comparisons of the United States and Soviet Economies, Supplemental Statement on Costs and Benefits to the Soviet Union of Its Bloc and Pact System: Comparisons with the Western Alliance Sys-*

146     MORRIS BORNSTEIN

*tem*, 86th Cong., 2nd Sess., 1960, p. 48. (This publication is cited below as US Congress, *Comparisons . . . Supplemental Statement . . .*) The range for 1952-61 is from United Nations, Economic Commission for Asia and the Far East (ECAFE), *Economic Survey of Asia and the Far East 1961* (Bangkok: 1962), p. 92. It is a rough estimate for net material product which combines alternative estimates of ECAFE for 1958-61 with the official Communist Chinese figure of 9 per cent for 1952-57. (The "net material product" concept excludes most services.)

European Satellites: Based on preliminary data for 1959. From US Congress, *Comparisons . . . Supplemental Statement . . .*, p. 48.

United States, France, (West) German Federal Republic, Italy, United Kingdom, and Japan: United Nations, Department of Economic and Social Affairs, *World Economic Survey 1961* (New York: 1962), p. 63.

India: Gross national product at factor cost, fiscal year 1950/51 to fiscal year 1960/61 (fiscal year, April 1 - March 31), according to official statistics cited in ECAFE, *op. cit.*, p. 82. (Gross national product at factor cost = gross national product at market prices − indirect taxes + subsidies.)

*Table 2.*

USSR: Index for civilian industrial production in Rush V. Greenslade and Phyllis Wallace, "Industrial Production in the U.S.S.R.," US Congress, Joint Economic Committee, *Dimensions of Soviet Economic Power*, 87th Cong., 2nd Sess., 1962, p. 120. The principal other Western estimates are compared in G. Warren Nutter, assisted by Israel Borenstein and Adam Kaufman, *Growth of Industrial Production in the Soviet Union* (Princeton: Princeton University Press, 1962), pp. 157-61 and 328-40.

Communist China: Index for factory production in Kang Chao, *Indexes of Industrial Production of Communist China, 1949-1959* (Ann Arbor: University Microfilms, Inc., 1962), p. 174. Chao considers his estimates for 1958 and 1959 less reliable than those for earlier years (*ibid.*, p. 171).

European Satellites: Based on preliminary data for 1959, from US Congress, *Comparisons . . . Supplemental Statement . . .*, p. 49. Some comparative data for East Germany, Hungary, Poland, and Czechoslovakia are presented in George J. Staller, "Czechoslovak Industrial Growth: 1948-1959," *American Economic Review*, Vol. LII, No. 3 (June, 1962), p. 396.

United States, France, (West) German Federal Republic, Italy, United Kingdom, and Japan: United Nations, Statistical Office, *Monthly Bulletin of Statistics*, Vol. XI, No. 12 (December, 1957), pp. 23-26, and Vol. XVI, No. 9 (September, 1962), pp. 18-22.

India: Fiscal year 1950/51 to fiscal year 1960/61 (fiscal year, April 1 - March 31), in ECAFE, *op. cit.*, p. 82.

*Table 3.*

USSR, United States, France, (West) German Federal Republic, Italy, United Kingdom, and Japan: From Cohn, *op. cit.*, p. 72. All figures are shares of gross national product at current factor cost. Components may not add to total because of rounding. For all except USSR, "investment" is the sum of Cohn's figures for gross capital investment, inventory investment, and foreign balance. Cohn's estimate for the USSR excludes the foreign balance and thus differs slightly in coverage from his estimates for the other countries.

Communist China: Net domestic product at 1952 market prices. From Ta-chung Liu, "Structural Changes in the Economy of the Chinese Mainland, 1933 to 1952-57," *American Economic Review*, Vol. XLIX, No. 2 (May, 1959), p. 93. Hollister (*op. cit.*, pp. 12-13) estimates the percentage distribution of gross national product in current market prices in 1957 as follows: personal consumption expenditures, 69.8; government current purchases of goods and services, 9.8; gross domestic investment, 20.0; and net foreign investment, 0.4.

European Satellites: n.a. = not available.

India: Gross domestic product at current market prices. From ECAFE, *op. cit.*, p. 172, and United Nations, Statistical Office, *Yearbook of National Accounts Statistics 1961* (New York: 1962), p. 129.

# The Effects of Economic Growth on Sino-Soviet Strategy

—*G. WARREN NUTTER*

## Summary

*This paper focuses on the record of economic growth in the Soviet Union and the implications that record may hold for future strategic developments. Performance of the economies of Communist China and the European Satellites is discussed only very briefly and generally, not for lack of relevance and importance, but for lack of competence on my part.*

*In the case of Communist China, developments over the last three or four years suggest that earlier progress in industrialization has been effectively nullified, at least temporarily. The leaders face a grave crisis in which the survival of communism in China is at stake. The course of events will depend on critical decisions yet to be made—such as whether to reinstitute private farming—and fortuitous circumstances—such as whether last fall's harvest was relatively bountiful. If the leaders continue to follow the "tough line," there is a good chance either that the Communist system will fall in China or that the Communist Bloc will be split permanently into two camps.*

*While the European Satellites have encountered a number of economic and political difficulties in recent years, their economies continue to develop roughly apace with the Soviet economy. Interdependence has grown and probably will continue to grow. At the same time, considerable latitude is being allowed to individual countries in organizing their economic systems, so that several variants of the Communist economic order are arising.*

149

*The Soviet economy has continued to grow at a rapid pace in the postwar period, but growth has also continued to retard in most sectors of the economy. The slowing down was particularly marked in 1960 and 1961. Serious concern is now being shown by Soviet leaders over the need for fundamental reforms in the economic system to improve its efficiency in allocating resources and in generating innovation. The leaders have perhaps become aware of this need by noting that Soviet economic growth in recent years has been slower than in a number of other rapidly developing countries in the West, and by realizing that Soviet growth over the long run has not been exceptionally rapid. The latter may be particularly disturbing because recent growth rates are approaching long-run trends as they continue to retard.*

*By my estimates, the Soviet national product measured in current US prices was between a fourth and a third of the US level in 1960. Total expenditures on the military-space program were, on the other hand, around half of the US level, and production of military-space products around four-fifths. The heavy burden of the military-space program is probably an important factor influencing the marked slowing down in growth over the last couple of years.*

*Over the future, Soviet leaders face mounting difficulty in reconciling three interrelated but conflicting goals: short-run strengthening of power, long-run strengthening of power, and raising of living standards. No one goal can any longer be considered as wholly subservient to the other two. Efforts to meet growing problems may lead in any combination of three general directions: toward extensive reforms in the structure of the economic system involving decentralization and "liberalization"; toward increasingly bold and adventurous use of power politics in external affairs, that is, toward intensification of the Cold War; or toward renewed campaigns of "conciliation" and "negotiation" to induce unilateral concessions by the West, including disarmament.*

––––––––––

The subject assigned to this paper ranges far beyond matters I am qualified to discuss. I hardly know what is going on in the economy of the Soviet Union, let alone the economies of the European Satellites and Communist China. In any case, not having made a serious study of the latter and hence not being able to do any more than repeat what others have said, I shall concentrate my remarks on the Soviet Union, trying to assess its economic growth up to the present and some implications for the future, particularly as they bear on strategic issues.

Developments in Communist China and the Satellites cannot, however, be ignored, for they clearly will affect future policies of the Sino-Soviet Bloc. While specific figures could be cited as measures of economic growth in these countries, they are not sufficiently reliable to warrant serious attention, being at best crudely adjusted official indexes. Western scholars have not, for a variety of reasons, yet made the same careful audit of basic data and recomputation of indexes for these countries as they have for the Soviet Union. My remarks will therefore be essentially qualitative in character.

Let us consider Communist China first. Through 1957, industrialization apparently proceeded at a very rapid pace, reminiscent in important respects of developments in the Soviet Union during the first two Five-Year Plans. As is normal for a period of this kind, actual industrial growth can be fully assessed only if one knows what happened to workshops as well as factories. Official statistics are limited to factory production, and they reflect diversion of output from the small-scale to the large-scale sector as well as net increases in output. The question of what happened to the small-scale sector is particularly important in the Chinese case because hand trades must have accounted for a very large fraction—perhaps half to three-quarters—of industrial production at the beginning of the Communist era. This means that, if nothing had happened except a shift of resources from hand trades to factories (statistically if not "really"), recorded output could have doubled or tripled. In fact, more seems to have happened than this: there was a real expansion in the industrial sector. But the magnitude of the expansion was undoubtedly significantly less than the statistics show, the question of their reliability aside.[1]

Whatever actually happened in the years up to 1958, there is little doubt that progress has since been largely undone. Joseph Alsop characterizes developments over the last three or four years as "China's descending spiral,"[2] and this phrase seems to be apt. Although problems had already accumulated under collectivization of agriculture, the turning point came with the drive to communize, which was mainly carried out in late 1958 and early 1959 as a major element in the "Great Leap Forward." Bad harvests followed in three successive years: 1959, 1960, and 1961. The entire economic situation has progressively deteriorated. It is too weak to say that industrialization has slowed down; the program has actually been put in reverse. People are being forcibly removed from the cities and sent to rural areas. According to Chou En-lai, 30 per cent of the urban population is to be relocated.[3]

Under these circumstances and in the absence of comprehensive and reliable statistics for the last few years, it is impossible to say whether current production in the Communist Chinese economy is, in any meaningful sense, larger than it was in 1950. Famine has been widespread for three years running. Industrial production may be no higher than 30 per cent of capacity,[4] which would mean that the growth during 1950-1957 has vanished. Indeed, Joseph Alsop considers the present situation to be so desperate that he sees a massive uprising in prospect unless there was a good harvest last fall.[5]

Conditions may not be so desperate as Alsop believes, but they are bad enough to create a serious crisis. If an immediate uprising is averted, if the communal system of agriculture is completely abandoned, and if the current ideological breach within the Sino-Soviet Bloc is narrowed, there could be a rapid recovery of the Chinese economy and a re-establishment of the earlier pace of growth. The foundation for such a recovery is there in the form of modern industrial plants and a trained industrial workforce, two undoubted contributions of the earlier industrialization drive.

On the other hand, there are no signs so far that events will take this course. The alternative route is for the leaders of Communist China to become increasingly obstinate about internal policy and to try to channel their internal difficulties into external conflicts with Communist as well as non-Communist countries, simultaneously attempting to maintain internal order through terror. If recent events suggest anything, it is that the latter route is being followed. The situation cannot be comforting to the Communist world. If the Chinese policies do not succeed, communism will be overthrown there. If they do succeed, the Communist camp will probably be split in two, perhaps irreparably.

While the European Satellites have experienced their own critical times, the climax occurring around 1956, nothing resembling the Chinese debacle has taken place. On the contrary, as far as one can tell, the average pace and the general directions of economic growth have been roughly the same in the Satellites as in the Soviet Union. Even the recent slowdown in Soviet economic growth, which we shall discuss at a later point, has been mirrored in the Satellites. On the matter of economic policies, the Satellites have become considerably more independent since 1956, and Soviet doctrine speaks now of the "many paths to socialism and communism." In some respects the Satellites may be viewed as proving grounds for experiments with the Communist economic system.

As already indicated, the economic fortunes of the Soviet Union and the Satellites seem to be closely interwoven. This will probably become increasingly true as the European Common Market develops and the Bloc countries come to rely more and more on trade among themselves.

Turning now to the Soviet Union itself, we may open discussion, as seems to have become customary, by noting that the Soviet economy has been growing at a rapid rate. Over the decade of the 1950's, Soviet national product apparently grew at an annual compound rate of around 6 per cent, industrial production at around 8 per cent, agricultural production at around 3 per cent, and freight transportation at almost 10 per cent. These estimates, all subject to sizeable margins of error, are derived from official Soviet data on physical output of individual products combined together into production indexes by procedures normally followed in the West. The only resulting index to be adjusted is the one for agriculture, whose values for recent years have been reduced substantially in an effort to eliminate the exaggeration of output that has once again crept into these statistics.[6]

The rapid pace of growth in output was maintained with a relatively small expansion in employment. Hence output per man-year of labor advanced at an annual compound rate of around 3.5 per cent in the case of national product, around 5 per cent in the case of industry and transportation, and around 3.5 per cent in the case of agriculture. Since average hours of work apparently declined in several sectors of the economy, growth in labor productivity on an hourly basis was even faster.

On the face of it, this performance looks creditable enough, and one might wonder why all the fuss is being kicked up in the Soviet Union over economic problems. A deeper examination of growth trends suggests two reasons. First, even though Soviet economic growth has been rapid by normal standards, it has been overshadowed in many important respects by happenings outside the Soviet Bloc, particularly in the European Common Market, South America, and the Far East. Second, the Soviet economy has shown signs of running out of steam. Growth in production has slowed down not only in the postwar as compared with the prewar period, but also within the postwar period itself.

During the first two Five-Year Plans (1928-1937), growth was faster than over the decade of the 1950's for the economy as a whole and for every major sector except agriculture (see Table 1). Even if the prewar period of comparison is extended through 1940, thus covering three additional years in which economic stagnation was the rule if gains from territorial expansion are excluded from consideration, the picture does not change as far as the non-agricultural sectors of the economy are concerned. Only in agricultural production has there been an acceleration in rate of growth between 1928-1940 and 1950-1960, and this is not likely to continue. It is the unusual development in agriculture that accounts for a somewhat faster rate of growth in national product over 1950-1960 than over 1928-1940.

Table 1—Average Annual Growth Rates [a] of Composite National Product, by Sector: Soviet Union, Benchmark Periods, 1913-1960
(per cent)

| | Composite National Product | | Industry | Agricul- ture | Trans- portation | Other Sectors [b] |
|---|---|---|---|---|---|---|
| | Total | "Material" | | | | |
| 1913-60 | 2.9 | 3.1 | 4.5 | 0.9 | 5.9 | 2.3 |
| 1913-28 | −0.0 | 0.5 | 0.1 | 0.6 | 0.4 | −1.6 |
| 1928-60 | 4.3 | 4.3 | 6.5 | 1.0 | 8.6 | 4.2 |
| 1928-40 | 5.2 | 4.7 | 9.0 | 0.4 | 12.0 | 7.0 |
| 1940-50 | 1.5 | 1.4 | 2.2 | −0.3 | 3.5 | 1.6 |
| 1950-60 | 6.0 | 6.9 | 8.1 | 3.1 | 9.6 | 3.8 |
| 1928-37 | 7.0 | 6.3 | 12.1 | 1.1 | 15.0 | 9.4 |
| 1950-55 | 6.0 | 7.6 | 9.6 | 2.7 | 9.9 | 2.3 |
| 1955-60 | 6.0 | 6.3 | 6.7 | 3.5 | 9.3 | 5.4 |
| 1959-60 | 4.3 | 3.5 | 4.9 | −1.2 | 5.7 | 6.5 |
| 1960-61 | 4.6 | 4.5 | 5.3 | 2.7 | 4.5 | 5.1 |

Source: Table A-1, *infra*. Adjusted to eliminate gains from territorial expansion and estimated overstatement of agricultural production in official Soviet data for recent years.

[a] Calculated from data for terminal years by compound interest formula.
[b] Measured by employment in man-years (Table A-4, *infra*).

A similar slowing down in growth rate may be observed in industry and transportation within the postwar decade. Growth in industrial production fell from an annual compound rate of 9.6 per cent for 1950-1955 to 6.7 per cent for 1955-1960. In both 1960 and 1961 production grew by around 5 per cent, the smallest annual percentage increase within the postwar years and a rate close to the annual average for the entire period 1913-1960. While the retardation in growth of freight transportation is not so marked on the average, the annual compound rate having declined from 9.9 per cent for the first five years to 9.3 per cent for the second, once again the drop was sharp in 1960 and 1961: the increase in these two years was 5.7 per cent and 4.5 per cent, respectively. With the exception of 1933, these are the lowest annual percentage increases in freight traffic on record in Soviet statistics since institution of the Five-Year Plans. Similarly, although agricultural production grew at an annual compound rate of about 3 per cent over the postwar decade, output has been essentially stable since 1958.

Why has growth been slowing down? In part because this is normal as an expanding economy matures. But there is more to it than that as far as the most recent years are concerned. The growing burden of the military-space program and agricultural failures have been important depressants since 1958. Through indirect calculations based on the divergence between growth of civilian and total industrial production, the output of military and space products can be estimated as having grown at an average annual rate of 10 per cent over 1955-1960, accounted for almost entirely by a sharp increase of more than 40 per cent in 1958 and more than 30 per cent in 1959 following sizeable declines in the preceding two years. In the last few years military-space products have probably accounted for around a third of total industrial production, a heavy burden on the economy (see Table 4). There is every reason to believe that the accelerated military effort has imposed a large part of its cost on investment and thereby on the pace of growth. Complex machines are being shot into space instead of being put to work in the economy.

It is interesting that civilian employment in man-years, after a turning point of no change in 1958, grew more percentagewise in 1959 and 1960 than in 1956 and 1957 (see Table A-4). Similar patterns emerge in the specific cases of industry and transportation. Higher growth rates for employment combined with lower growth rates for output mean that percentage growth in output per man-year was generally slower in 1959 and 1960 than it was on the average in the postwar decade under review (see Table 2). While this may reflect shorter hours of work to some extent, the evidence indicates that recent difficulties in generating growth in production are not attributable to the perennial "shortage" of labor.

Nor does the recent program of foreign loans seem to be a critical factor in explaining the slowdown in growth. It is doubtful that the net flow of resources under this program from the Soviet Union to countries outside the Soviet Bloc has exceeded $200 million in any recent year,[7] or an insignificant fraction of Soviet industrial production. The unilateral flow of goods to Communist China may have been on a larger scale in some recent years, but this is not evident from Soviet trade statistics. In the last year or two, Soviet exports to Communist China have dropped precipitously.

As seems clear from the most recent public discussions in the Soviet Union, one important reason for economic difficulties is that the complexity of the economy is outgrowing traditional Soviet techniques of centralized planning and control. Khrushchev's recent speeches are replete with examples of managerial

Table 2—Average Annual Growth Rates [a] of Output Per Man-Year of Labor, for the Economy and Major Sectors: Soviet Union, Benchmark Periods, 1913-1960
(per cent)

|         | Composite National Product | | | | |
|---------|-------|------------|----------|-------------|----------------|
|         | Total | "Material" | Industry | Agriculture | Transportation |
| 1913-60 | 1.3   | 1.9        | 1.7      | 0.5         | 1.9            |
| 1913-28 | −0.3  | −0.1       | 0.6      | −0.2        | −1.4           |
| 1928-60 | 2.2   | 2.8        | 2.1      | 0.9         | 3.5            |
| 1928-40 | 1.3   | 1.3        | 1.4      | −1.2        | 3.5            |
| 1940-50 | 1.3   | 1.6        | 0.3      | 1.1         | 1.7            |
| 1950-60 | 3.9   | 5.6        | 5.1      | 3.3         | 5.0            |
| 1928-37 | 1.8   | 2.0        | 1.9      | −1.3        | 6.0            |
| 1950-55 | 4.2   | 5.9        | 5.3      | 2.9         | 5.5            |
| 1955-60 | 3.5   | 5.2        | 4.7      | 3.2         | 4.5            |
| 1959-60 | 0.5   | −0.9       | 1.4      | −1.5        | 0.4            |
| 1960-61 | 1.1   | 2.2        | 0.4      | 1.6         | 0.0            |

Source: Tables A-1 and A-4, *infra.* Production indexes have been adjusted to eliminate estimated overstatement of agricultural production in official Soviet data for recent years.

[a] Calculated from data for terminal years by compound interest formula.

inefficiency at the highest levels and proposals to "modernize" the organizational structure of the economy. Schemes for greater reliance on a price system and profit motives are being seriously discussed, and planners are being told to look to capitalist economies for good as well as bad examples. The need for a system that will automatically generate innovation over broad areas— the primary engine of growth in Western economies—is becoming increasingly apparent. Whether important changes are in the wind or not, all this grumbling must have some basis in fact. There is sound reason to believe that the economy is being badly run and that this is being revealed, among other ways, in a faltering growth rate.

The Soviet leaders may well have been alerted to their problems by rapid progress being made, particularly in industrialization, in other parts of the world. The percentage growth of Soviet industrial production between 1953 and 1961 has been outdistanced by a large number of countries outside the Soviet Bloc (see Table 3), and there are few signs that the situation will change in the near future. The argument that the Soviet Union is outperforming the United States in the percentage rate of growth of industrial production loses its force when the same thing is found to be true for almost every other country. It is not

Table 3—Comparison of Trends in Industrial Production in
Twenty-Four Countries: 1961 as Per Cent of 1953

| | | | |
|---|---|---|---|
| Japan | 316 | Soviet Union | 175 |
| Pakistan | 275 | India | 170 |
| Venezuela [a] | 225 | Finland | 170 |
| Brazil | 215 | Norway | 162 |
| Taiwan | 214 | Netherlands | 160 |
| Italy | 200 | Sweden | 142 |
| Greece | 194 | Ireland | 141 |
| West Germany | 190 | Belgium | 135 |
| Portugal | 189 | Canada | 134 |
| Austria | 187 | United Kingdom | 130 |
| European Economic | | Argentina | 129 |
| Community | 182 | Chile [a] | 126 |
| Mexico | 178 | United States | 120 |
| France | 175 | | |

Source: Table A-1, *infra* and United Nations, *Statistical Yearbook, 1961,* and OECD, *General Statistics,* November, 1962.

[a] Manufacturing only.

the fast pace in the Soviet Union but the slow pace in the United States that takes the center of the stage, insofar as such matters command attention.

Perhaps even more disturbing to Soviet leaders is the suggestion in recent events that growth is accelerating in other important economies while it retards in the Soviet Union. They also cannot be heartened by the miserable record of the major cohabitant of the Communist camp, China, a record that may lead to a gradual redressing of the power balance away from Communist areas and toward non-Communist areas in Europe and Asia, a vision likely to bring some sleepless nights to the Kremlin.

It is often asserted by Western commentators that our eyes should focus solely on the unfolding performance of the Soviet economy, not on the broad historical record, if we wish to assess the future. The past, it is said, is of no more than academic interest, particularly anything that happened before 1928. This view, which I have never accepted, is perhaps not so strongly voiced today, though it may be only in temporary eclipse. But the interesting thing is that it makes little difference whether we look at performance over the last two or three years or over the long run, the picture of growth is roughly the same (see Table 1).

Over the period 1913-1960, Soviet "material" product (adjusted to eliminate gains from territorial expansion) grew at an annual compound rate of about 3.1 per cent as compared with about 3.5 per cent for 1960 and 4.5 per cent for 1961; industrial production, at about 4.5 per cent as compared with about 4.9 per cent and 5.3 per cent; agricultural production, at less than 1 per cent as compared with almost no growth; and freight traffic, at about 5.9 per cent as compared with about 5.7 per cent and 4.5 per cent.

It would be asking a lot to demand that these figures be as reliable as those for Western countries. Some would definitely argue that the rates for industrial production in recent years are too low.[8] But suppose the figures are correct. What do they tell us about the future? Not much. A wiggle does not make a trend; it is far too early to know whether the happenings over the last two or three years have long-run significance. All we can say is this: so far, nothing has happened to challenge the conclusion that the percentage growth rate for industrial production and freight traffic is steadily retarding, and that the postwar spurt in agriculture is transitory. As long as this conclusion continues to hold, long-run growth trends are the best guide of what lies before us beyond the immediate future.

To the extent this is so, the Soviet future is not particularly rosy, since the long-term Soviet growth rates are not exceptionally high. The implications for the Soviet power position, as far as it rests on an economic base, are reasonably clear and have undoubtedly not escaped the notice of Soviet leaders. We may, therefore, expect them to undertake whatever reforms they find feasible and effective to avoid the consequences of a rather ordinary growth rate. Before considering what those reforms might be, let us briefly review the current economic position of the Soviet Union.

By my estimates (see Table 4), Soviet industrial production measured in current US prices was about 29 per cent of the US level in 1960, while Soviet agriculture was about 70 per cent and freight traffic about 60 per cent. Combined production of these sectors, again measured in US prices, amounted to about 36 per cent of the US level. There is no way of directly measuring relative production in the remainder of the economy, essentially the service sectors, but an indirect estimate can be made on the basis of employment data and assumed relative labor productivity. If Soviet output per man-year in the service sectors is taken as 22 per cent of the US level, the fraction applying to industry, Soviet output would be 15 per cent of the US level. If, on the other hand, the former is taken as 40 per cent, a larger fraction than applies to any other major sector where direct measurement is possible, Soviet output would be 28 per cent of the US level. Using this range, we find Soviet national product to be between 24 and 31 per cent of the US level. By contrast, the national product of European members of OECD was about 83 per cent of the US level in 1955 [9] and is even higher now.

I am bound to say that my estimate for relative total production is much lower than the figures usually derived from aggregative data by Western specialists. For example, in a recent report to the Joint Economic Committee,[10] Stanley Cohn gives Soviet GNP as 47 per cent of the US level in 1960, and this is said to be an average of calculations in US and Soviet prices. In US prices, the fraction would have been higher, probably around 60 per cent.[11] The difficulty is that such high fractions can scarcely be reconciled with data on relative output for economic sectors,[12] which are in turn consistent with relative growth trends of those sectors.

Table 4—Estimated Comparative Production, Population, and
Employment: Soviet Union and United States, 1960

|  | US (1) | USSR (2) | USSR as % of US (3) |
|---|---|---|---|
|  | (Billion Dollars) |  | (Per Cent) |
| Gross national product ....... | 503.4 | 120-158 | 24-31 |
| Industry ................ | 166.2 | 48 | 29 |
| Agriculture .............. | 20.9 | 15 | 70 |
| Transportation ........... | 22.4 | 13 | 60 |
| Other sectors ............ | 293.9 | 44-82 | 15-28 |
| Military-space expenditures .. | 46 | 22 | 48 |
| Products ................ | 21 | 17 | 81 |
| Support of troops, etc. ..... | 25 | 5 | 20 |
|  | (Millions) |  | (Per Cent) |
| Population ................ | 180.7 | 214 | 118 |
| 14 years and over ........ | 125.4 | 142 | 113 |
| Males ................... | 61 | 61 | 100 |
| Labor force ............... | 73.1 | 100 | 137 |
| Employment in man-years ... | 67.3 | 93.0 | 138 |

*General Note:* Soviet figures on population and employment are derived
from official statistics (see also Table A-4). Those on gross products are
derived from cols. 1 and 3. Percentages in col. 3 are derived as follows:
for industry, projection of calculation for 1955 (Nutter, *Growth of Industrial Production in the Soviet Union*, 1962, p. 238) by ratio of my
production index for Soviet Union (Table A-1) to FRB index for US; for
agriculture, based on work in progress of Gale Johnson and Arcadius
Kahan; for transportation, ratio of commercial freight traffic in ton-miles
in the two countries adjusted downward by 10 per cent to allow (inadequately) for upward bias in data and poorer quality of service in the Soviet
case; for other sectors, see text.

The figure for Soviet production of military-space products is my estimate for 1955 (*ibid.*, p. 255) projected by my index of Soviet military production. For other defense expenditures, an outlay of 5 billion (new)
rubles is assumed (*ibid.*, pp. 327f.) and a ruble-dollar exchange rate of
unity.

US data are from *Survey of Current Business* (October, 1962), pp. 1 ff.


But wealth does not imply power, nor power wealth. Whatever
may be the case for the economy as a whole, there is no doubt
that productive activity in the Soviet Union relative to the
United States is larger for the defense sector than for the
economy as a whole. My estimates, undoubtedly subject to large
margins of error, are given in Table 4 and need be only briefly
summarized here. Measured in current US prices, the Soviet
Union spent about 48 per cent as much as the United States

in the entire military and space program and about 80 per cent as much on production of military and space products. The difference between these two fractions is caused by the relatively much smaller Soviet expenditure on support of troops, in turn explained by the low pay and subsistence of the Russian soldier relative to the American level. Total expenditures on the military program amounted to between 14 and 18 per cent of GNP in the Soviet Union (as compared with 9 per cent in the United States); expenditures on military-space products amounted to about 35 per cent of industrial production (as compared with about 11 per cent in the United States). The military program imposes a heavy burden on the Soviet economy.

The Soviet Union enjoys a considerable advantage over the United States in population and an even larger one in labor force and employment (see Table 4). Since both populations are growing at about the same percentage rate, relative sizes are likely to remain the same over the more immediate future, though the United States made a considerable gain in the past. From the military point of view, it is interesting to note that the Soviet Union probably now has no more males over thirteen years of age than the United States, but she should gradually pull away in this regard over the future. Despite the parity of available men, the Soviet Union maintains significantly larger armed forces.

If the Soviet Union can count on favorable economic development over the current decade, its economic position will improve relative to the United States but not dramatically. For example, if industrial production were to grow at 6.7 per cent in the Soviet Union and 2.2 per cent in the United States—the respective rates for 1955-60—Soviet production in this sector would reach 45 per cent of the US level in 1970. And it seems doubtful that even with the most successful and feasible Soviet policies, such a favorable growth differential can be maintained throughout this period. We should not anticipate an even more favorable differential, unless we feel that the American economy will fall to pieces. To attain anything like the suggested improvement, substantial changes will have to take place in the organizational structure of the Soviet economy.

What possibilities may we look forward to? In some respects, the Soviet economy stands at a critical crossroads, and some ways seem to be barred. The old formula used to be: when in trouble, squeeze the consumer. As long as the system could follow this path with impunity, it could at least partially resolve conflicting demands on resources in other areas and it could stand a large amount of wasteful activity generally. But the man in the street is a more reluctant whipping boy these days, and there seem to be definite restrictive limits to what he will stand for in the absence of a reign of terror. Promises of future glory and paradise are much poorer substitutes for "more now" than they used to be.

The major goal of Soviet leaders has always been to enhance Soviet power, and the rate and directions of economic growth, along with the current allocation of resources, have been planned accordingly. Even with such an overriding goal, serious conflicts of interest are bound to arise. To achieve power in a hurry, strategically important kinds of economic growth must be achieved in a hurry. But this may lead, as it has in the Soviet Union, to distortions inhibiting longer-range growth. Similarly, the desire for military strength-in-being conflicts with the desire for rapid growth: armaments and investments compete with each other. In the Soviet Union as elsewhere, you can't have your cake and eat it. Finally, sustained rapid growth is important not only for what it means directly in terms of future power, but also for what it means indirectly in terms of immediate power by virtue of its propaganda value, by impressing outsiders with the alleged superiority of the Communist system.

In brief, Soviet leaders must be concerned with accommodating conflicts among three interrelated goals: short-run strengthening of power, long-run strengthening of power, and raising of living standards. While one may dominate depending on tactical decisions, none can any longer be neglected. Being caught in this position, the leaders must give increasing attention to improving the organizational efficiency of the economy, which they clearly recognize to be in critical need of improvement, and to relieving international tensions, which impose such a heavy burden on the economy.

The reason little decisive action has yet been taken on internal reforms seems plain: the leaders are not convinced that they can decentralize decisions on the operating level of the economy without losing control over fundamental allocation of resources. From a short-run point of view, it is difficult to see why they are so worried. By budgetary powers a government can effectively control productive activity even in a full-fledged market economy. The real dilemma seems to be more deeply seated and to apply to the longer run, namely, whether autocratic rule can survive indefinitely within the atmosphere of a highly decentralized economy run by educated people. The Soviet leaders have good reason to believe that it cannot, as the history of their own country up to the Bolshevik revolution cogently argues.

No doubt, ideology also plays a role. Turning Marxist economics upside down, as must be done if a workable decentralized economy is to be devised, is bound to be a painful process. It surely cannot be done overnight without introducing serious political disruptions.

The disturbing question is whether the Soviet Union may not already be embarked on a dangerous race between erosion of the internal Communist system and fulfillment of the Communist design of world domination. Such a race becomes more and more dangerous as Soviet leaders become increasingly aware of it, for they may be induced to take reckless gambles in order to forestall the steady march of internal events so distasteful to them. The accelerating tempo of armaments production, the intensive effort to dominate space science and technology, the resumption and continuation of nuclear tests, the Cuban adventure—all these recent developments are disturbing signs of a concerted effort to achieve world domination "before it is too late." This conclusion seems to force itself upon one in spite—or, perhaps, because—of Khrushchev's continuing protests that the Communist world, renouncing war as a normal instrument of policy, has taken on the rest of the world in a race of "peaceful economic competition."

Of course, Soviet leaders would prefer to achieve world domination through relaxation of Western effort rather than through intensification of Soviet effort. The ideal solution from their point of view would be unilateral disarmament by the West, and we should expect mounting enticements in this direction if Western policy encourages them to expect unilateral concessions.

The moral is that we must be on guard against the classic Communist seesaw of alternating "conciliation" and "negotiation" on the one hand, and bold power politics on the other, which Soviet leaders will employ; not because they are confident of winning the economic race, but because they are not. Developments within the next few years will indicate to what extent internal problems will be externalized. Movement in the opposite direction would be signaled by significant decentralization of the economic system, by a relative reduction in the military and space program, by steps to increase the standard of living, by agricultural reforms leading to more rather than less private family farming, by a revival of the residential construction program, and so on. These things may all happen—and indeed ultimately will, in my firm opinion, if the world is not blown up in the meantime and if we follow a firm policy of our own that turns Soviet weaknesses to our benefit instead of harm. They will not happen if we actively appease or passively wait and see.

FOOTNOTES

*Note:* The views expressed in this paper are my own, and neither they nor the data given in their support should be attributed to the National Bureau of Economic Research, which has not reviewed the contents of this paper.

[1] For some comments on reliability of official data, see Kang Chao, "The Reliability of Industrial Output Data in Communist China," *Journal of Asian Studies* (November, 1962), pp. 47-66 and the book review in the same issue by Sidney Klein, pp. 100-01.

[2] Joseph Alsop, "China's Descending Spiral," *The China Quarterly* (July-September, 1962), pp. 21-37. For a thoughtful and revealing discussion of the agrarian crisis and its origins, see Karl A. Wittfogel, "Agrarian Problems and the Moscow-Peking Axis," *Slavic Review* (December, 1962), pp. 678-98.

[3] Alsop, *op. cit.*, p. 25.

[4] *Ibid.*, p. 23.

[5] *Ibid.*, pp. 33 ff.

[6] See Table A-1, *Infra.*

[7] US Congress, House, Committee on Foreign Affairs, *Hearings, Foreign Assistance Act of 1962*, 87th Cong., 2nd Sess., 1962, Part II, p. 334.

[8] See Table A-3, *Infra.*

[9] Milton Gilbert and Associates, *Comparative National Products and Price Levels*, OEEC, 1958, p. 85.

[10] US Congress, Joint Economic Committee, *Dimensions of Soviet Economic Power*, 87th Cong., 2nd Sess., 1962, p. 76.

[11] See the estimates by Morris Bornstein in US Congress, Joint Economic Committee, *Comparisons of the United States and Soviet Economies*, 86th Cong., 1st Sess., 1959, Part II, p. 385.

[12] In a recent article ["U.S. and Soviet Industrial Output," *American Economic Review* (September, 1962)], Alexander Tarn and Robert W. Campbell argue that Soviet industrial production measured in US prices was 75 per cent of the US level in 1960. As I hope to explain in a forthcoming article, this conclusion derives from an estimating procedure that is bound to exaggerate the relative size of Soviet production.

Table A-1—Production Indexes of Composite National Product,
by Sector: Soviet Union, 1913-1960
(1913 = 100)

| | Composite National Product | | Industry | Agriculture | Transportation |
|---|---|---|---|---|---|
| | Total | "Material" | | | |
| 1913 | 100 | 100 | 100 | 100 | 100 |
| 1920 | | 50 | 20 | 67 | 22 |
| 1928 | 99 | 107 | 102 | 110 | 106 |
| 1932 | | 111 | 144 | 87 | 192 |
| 1937 | 183 | 186 | 285 | 120 | 373 |
| 1940A | 183 | 186 | 286 | 116 | 413 |
| 1940B | 216 | 210 | 318 | 135 | 435 |
| 1945 | | 152 | 264 | 81 | 315 |
| 1950 | 249 | 241 | 393 | 131 | 615 |
| 1951 | | 260 | 448 | 128 | 690 |
| 1952 | | 282 | 488 | 136 | 758 |
| 1953 | | 297 | 516 | 141 | 814 |
| 1954 | | 325 (320) | 563 | 148 (141) | 973 |
| 1955 | 341 (333) | 356 (345) | 620 | 167 (150) | 987 |
| 1956 | 370 (361) | 391 (377) | 664 | 191 (170) | 1,096 |
| 1957 | 390 (379) | 412 (398) | 711 | 190 (167) | 1,229 |
| 1958 | 422 (409) | 451 (432) | 762 | 217 (187) | 1,325 |
| 1959 | 446 (429) | 475 (452) | 818 | 217 (180) | 1,456 |
| 1960 | 467 (448) | 496 (468) | 858 | 222 (178) | 1,538 |
| 1961 | 488 (468) | 518 (489) | 903 | 228 (182) | 1,607 |

Source: Work in progress, National Bureau of Economic Research.

Note: Current territory except 1913 and 1940A, which cover interwar territory. Figures in parentheses are adjusted to remove estimated over-statement of agricultural production in official Soviet data. Index for composite "material" product formed from production indexes for industry, agriculture, and transportation combined by 1937 weights. Index for total composite product formed from index for material product and employment index for other sectors (Table A-4) combined by 1937 weights. Income originating is used as weight, with percentage distribution as follows: industry (including construction), 35.8; agriculture, 29.7; transportation (including communication), 7.9; and other sectors, 26.6. Latter data from A. Bergson et al., Soviet National Income and Product, 1928-48, (RAND, 1960), p. 33.

Table A-2—Comparison of Bergson and Nutter Indexes of
Over-all Production: Soviet Union, 1928-1955

| Gross National Product, Bergson [a] | Composite National Product | | |
|---|---|---|---|
| | Bergson [b] | Nutter [c] | |
| | | Total | "Material" |
| Index (1928 = 100) | | | |
| 1928 | 100 | 100 | 100 | 100 |
| 1937 | 162 | 168 | 185 | 174 |
| 1940A | 178 | 178 | 185 | 174 |
| 1940B | 197 | 196 | 217 | 195 |
| 1944 | 196 | | | |
| 1945 | | | | 142 |
| 1950 | 243 | 241 | 251 | 224 |
| 1955 | 350 | 342 | 343 (336) | 331 (322) |
| Average Annual Growth Rate (Per Cent) | | | |
| 1928-55 | 4.7 | 4.7 | 4.7 (4.6) | 4.6 (4.4) |
| 1928-40B | 5.8 | 5.8 | 6.7 | 5.7 |
| 1940B-50 | 2.1 | 2.1 | 1.5 | 1.4 |
| 1950-55 | 7.6 | 7.2 | 6.3 (5.9) | 8.2 (7.6) |
| 1928-37 | 5.5 | 5.9 | 7.0 | 6.3 |
| 1937-40A | 3.5 | 2.1 | 0.0 | 0.0 |
| 1940A-40B | 10.0 | 10.0 | 17.7 | 12.5 |

*Note:* Current territory except 1940A, which covers interwar Soviet territory. Figures in parentheses are adjusted to remove estimated overstatement of agricultural production in official Soviet data.

[a] A. Bergson, *Real National Income of Soviet Russia* (Cambridge, Mass.:
Harvard Press), pp. 177, 217f. (1937 prices).

[b] *Ibid.*, p. 128. (1937 weights).

[c] Table A-1.

Table A-3—Comparison of Nutter, Kaplan-Moorsteen, and Greenslade-
Wallace Industrial Production Indexes: Soviet Union, 1950-1961
(1950 = 100)

| | *All Products, Nutter* [a] | *Civilian Products* | | |
|---|---|---|---|---|
| | | *Nutter* [a] | *Kaplan-Moorsteen* [b] | *Greenslade-Wallace* [c] |
| 1951 | 114 | 107 | 112 | 112 |
| 1952 | 124 | 111 | 119 | 119 |
| 1953 | 131 | 119 | 130 | 131 |
| 1954 | 143 | 133 | 144 | 146 |
| 1955 | 158 | 145 | 158 | 162 |
| 1956 | 169 | 157 | 172 | 179 |
| 1957 | 181 | 173 | 188 | 199 |
| 1958 | 194 | 180 | 202 | 217 |
| 1959 | 208 | 188 | | 235 |
| 1960 | 218 | 197 | | 250 |
| 1961 | 230 | | | 267 |

[a] G. W. Nutter, *Growth of Industrial Production in the Soviet Union* (Princeton: 1962), p. 196, as extended from 1958.

[b] N. M. Kaplan and R. H. Moorsteen, *Indexes of Soviet Industrial Output* (RAND, 1960), II, p. 234.

[c] US Congress, Joint Economic Committee, *Dimensions of Soviet Economic Power*, 87th Cong., 2nd Sess., 1962, p. 120.

**Table A-4—Persons Engaged in the Economy, by Sector:
Soviet Union, 1913-1960**
(million full-time equivalents)

| | Total Economy | "Material" Sector | | | | Other Sectors |
|---|---|---|---|---|---|---|
| | | Total | Industry | Agriculture | Trans-portation | |
| 1913 | 38.6 | 31.1 | 5.9 | 24.2 | 0.98 | 7.5 |
| 1928 | 40.1 | 34.2 | 5.5 | 27.4 | 1.3 | 5.9 |
| 1937 | 62.8 | 49.6 | 12.9 | 34.0 | 2.7 | 13.2 |
| 1940B | 74.4 | 57.0 | 14.6 | 39.0 | 3.4 | 17.4 |
| 1950 | 75.8 | 55.6 | 17.6 | 33.9 | 4.1 | 20.6 |
| 1955 | 82.7 | 60.0 | 21.5 | 33.5 | 5.0 | 22.7 |
| 1956 | 84.5 | 60.8 | 22.0 | 33.6 | 5.2 | 23.7 |
| 1957 | 86.5 | 61.7 | 22.1 | 34.2 | 5.4 | 24.8 |
| 1958 | 86.9 | 60.8 | 22.2 | 33.0 | 5.6 | 26.1 |
| 1959 | 89.7 | 61.1 | 22.7 | 33.4 | 6.0 | 27.6 |
| 1960 | 93.0 | 63.6 | 23.6 | 33.7 | 6.3 | 29.4 |
| 1961 | 96.0 | 65.1 | 24.7 | 33.8 | 6.6 | 30.9 |

Source: G. W. Nutter, "Employment in the Soviet Union: An Interim Solution to a Puzzle," *Soviet Studies* (April, 1961). For 1960, derived from *Narodnoe Khoziaistvo v 1960 g.*, pp. 260 and 636; for 1961, from *SSSR v Tsifrakh v 1961 g.*, pp. 310 ff.

*Note:* Current territory.

**Table A-5—Indexes of Persons Engaged (Measured in Full-Time
Equivalents) in the Economy, by Sector: Soviet Union, 1913-1960**
(1913 = 100)

| | Total Economy | "Material" Sectors | | | | Other Sectors |
|---|---|---|---|---|---|---|
| | | Total | Industry | Agriculture | Trans-portation | |
| 1913 | 100 | 100 | 100 | 100 | 100 | 100 |
| 1928 | 104 | 110 | 93 | 113 | 130 | 79 |
| 1937 | 163 | 159 | 219 | 140 | 272 | 176 |
| 1940B | 193 | 183 | 247 | 161 | 351 | 232 |
| 1950 | 196 | 179 | 298 | 140 | 419 | 271 |
| 1955 | 214 | 193 | 364 | 138 | 517 | 303 |
| 1956 | 219 | 195 | 373 | 139 | 531 | 316 |
| 1957 | 224 | 198 | 375 | 141 | 551 | 331 |
| 1958 | 225 | 195 | 376 | 136 | 571 | 348 |
| 1959 | 232 | 196 | 385 | 138 | 612 | 368 |
| 1960 | 241 | 204 | 400 | 139 | 644 | 392 |
| 1961 | 249 | 209 | 419 | 140 | 672 | 412 |

Source: Table A-4.

# Discussion—Part I

*Cerny*\*: As the title of this panel suggests, there is no formal intention to discuss Sino-Soviet objectives. Indirectly, of course, these objectives are bound to be considered. But our intention is to move directly to an assessment and consideration of likely or possible Sino-Soviet strategies over the next five to ten years. Such assessments are generally based upon certain assumptions related to future Cold War developments.

In order to give some broad, over-all picture of the various possible developments with which the United States may have to cope in the next few years, an abbreviated portion of Professor Niemeyer's paper is most helpful. This also may illustrate the range of assumptions which may be made in regard to future contingencies. Our apologies to Professor Niemeyer if the abbreviation has done some violence to his more careful statements of the various possibilities. For our purposes, however, they provide in fairly understandable form a broad framework within which our discussion can proceed.

POSSIBLE FUTURE DEVELOPMENTS OF THE COLD WAR
    a)  Showdown
    b)  Shift in favor of East
    c)  Shift in favor of West
    d)  Protracted contest
    e)  Settlement

In the papers submitted by our panelists it became rather evident that there are certain key problems, certain key issues, the answers to which have an important bearing on the likely outcome of one or another of the possible future developments of the Cold War. Accordingly, we have selected four such issues for our immediate discussion: Polycentrism; Economic constraints on strategy; Erosion; Unlimited, limited, and sub-limited wars; Capabilities and attitudes.

Let us turn now to the first of these issues.

\* Dr. Karl H. Cerny, Associate Professor of Government, Georgetown University, and Research Associate of the Center for Strategic Studies. Dr. Cerny was chairman of the discussions in Part I and Part II.

169

## Polycentrism

The most significant aspect of this issue is undoubtedly the relationship between the Soviet Union and Communist China. We have selected three statements that appeared in the panel papers submitted by Professors Taylor, Dinerstein, and Walker. It will be noted that the statements of Professors Taylor and Walker seem to be going in opposite directions.

> There is a Bloc strategy being carried out, in their different ways, by Moscow and Peking. The antagonism between Moscow and Peking, we have to assume, is non-antagonistic. It is thoroughly in keeping with the Communist ideology for Peking to assume an intransigent and warlike role in the struggle against imperialism while issuing firm statements advocating peace, at the same time that the Soviet Union stresses the gambit of peaceful coexistence while actively cooperating with China in "just" wars of national liberation—for example, in Cuba and Vietnam.
>
> George Taylor

> Whereas in the first few years of the alliance, and particularly during the period of the Korean War, it was legitimate and accurate to speak of the "Sino-Soviet Bloc," this term is grossly misleading in 1963. It is an example of the type of phrase which can lead us unwittingly into inaccurate lines of reasoning. The word "bloc" implies a solid and homogeneous unity which is not characteristic of the alliance today.
>
> Richard Walker

> The chief difference between the Chinese and the Russians is over resource allocation. The Chinese Communists are very bitter about Soviet aid to non-Communist leaders. The Chinese Communists feel that if the Soviet Union has any funds to expend abroad, they have a better claim than bourgeois states. The Soviet Union, on the other hand, takes the traditional position of the strongest power in an alliance. They prefer to allocate whatever resources can be spared for the support of foreign policy to try to break off members of the opponent's camp or to keep neutrals neutral, although it is sometimes necessary to employ them to prevent disintegration of one's own system.
>
> Herbert Dinerstein

Professor Taylor, would you care to expand on the point made in your paper?

*Taylor:* Mr. Chairman, I cannot see immediately any reason to disagree with this statement on anybody's part. I will try to anticipate possible disagreement by taking off on Mr. Walker's interesting statement.

My feeling is that it's hardly worth quarreling over the word "bloc." We have here a situation that brings two very important

Communist Parties in conflict with each other over certain issues. I would like to say immediately that behind my statement there is another assumption, and this is that it is very dangerous to speak of China and Russia; it is more appropriate to speak of the Chinese Communist Party and the Soviet Communist Party. They may be struggling as parties between each other or there may be some Russians plus some Chinese struggling against other Russians plus other Chinese. It is in this sense a very complicated struggle.

The other assumption that lies behind my statement is that these struggles could go on for a long time. They are an expression of the normal behavior of societies very different from our own. You can have a tremendous amount of internal commotion within a Communist Party or between Communist Parties and still have the impact on the rest of the world be an expression of the general ideology of the Communist movement.

I would not exclude, obviously, possibilities of a break. One cannot anticipate exactly the forces within either Communist China or the Soviet Union. But I would draw the same conclusion from what is happening in the so-called Bloc today as the Communists properly should have drawn from the conflict in the Free World over the Suez crisis.

Although we differed very much on that, I don't think there was any intention on the part of the British to assist the other side.

*Walker:* The point which I think needs to be made very forcefully today is that after a great number of years in power the Chinese Communist Government is committed to a different set of conditions for its goals than is the Soviet Union. It can't escape some of these conditions.

The Chinese Communists, for example, still face the situation where they are challenged by an alternate Chinese government that is in power. One of the important aspects is one's world outlook. In a way they have turned their backs on their Soviet big brothers whom they were almost fervently embracing during the first few years of the alliance.

The Soviets, on the other hand, have found that they have much more to gain in an attempt at a victory over a resurgent Western Europe; they are very conscious of the vitality and viability of Western Europe today, and there are all too many indications that the Soviets find their Chinese little brothers a pain in the neck at times.

So, one finds more and more different expressions of national flavor coming out within the alliance.

Let me hasten to add that there is absolutely no reason why we should attempt to draw any comfort from this. I think Professor Taylor is absolutely right in pointing out that there is a general over-all agreement on the world stance, on the necessity to eliminate what they call the imperialists. Certainly there is some disagreement on the tactics to be used for this.

The Chinese are also far more wedded now to the concept of the imperial camp and to the necessity for fighting with violence what they call wars of national liberation. In many respects, with Europe's retreat from empire, Western Europe has not been hurt by the loss of the colonies. In fact, as many economists pointed out before, and we found it difficult to believe, the colonies actually were a drain on some of the European powers. The result, therefore, is that much of the Leninist theory of imperialism has been undercut. The Soviets are possibly more acutely aware of this than are the Chinese. In terms of national interest, in terms of the immediate problems faced at home, which are entirely different in China and in the Soviet Union, there is a solid basis for some disagreement in addition to the ideological dispute which has erupted.

Therefore, we must consider the possibility that this is not a homogeneous grand conspiracy always working so effectively, that it can play a very covert game, and that the whole procedure that went on in East Berlin, for example, is just a farce or an attempt to fool the West. I don't think this follows at all.

Within this framework I think we therefore must consider that perhaps we are dealing with rival morticians who have different theories of burial.

*Dinerstein:* I find myself in unexpected agreement with two other people close by me, so I should like to amplify rather than contest.

I think if we look at the Sino-Soviet dispute from the point of view of a Communist, we can come to no other conclusion but that it is a great disappointment and that it borders on tragedy. But I think if you look at the same facts from our point of view and from the point of view of the next ten years, you could make out a pretty fair case that the Sino-Soviet conflict is a positive development from the Communist point of view.

Let me give two reasons. Actually, they are arguing about different ways of getting to the same place. And I dare say that if the Soviet Union had been willing to adhere to the Chinese request that both countries enter the stage of communism at the same time—which means that the Soviet Union would have had to make very, very large investments of resources into China— if this had happened and the Soviet Union had chosen to do this, the differences which exist today would exist in much more muted form. They would still exist, but they wouldn't be so obvious. The Chinese would be getting massive economic aid. But I think that the Soviet refusal to do so was wise from their point of view and rather unfortunate from our point of view.

If you consider that the resources of one kind or another which could have gone to China have gone to Cuba and to Indonesia, and may go to Africa, I would say on the whole, the Russians have chosen a better place to invest their resources.

Another very positive consequence of this conflict, for them, was referred to by Dr. Taylor. He said that it was a complex situation; that there were different groupings within Chinese ruling circles and within Russian ruling circles. I think it's a very great advantage for communism when, instead of having to agree on a single strategy, there are automatically two-plus strategies. As soon as you have different strategies, different positions within a single camp, you get this multiplication of strategies. This gives communism much greater flexibility. It makes it possible for Communist Parties in different countries to have different policies. This really means that in many parts of the world, Communist Parties can be as good as their leaders.

With a single, more or less inflexible Communist world-wide policy, very often a Communist Party has to pursue a policy which its leaders feel is not the optimum policy. So this great conflict has meant that some smart national Communist Party leader has a menu of policies to choose from and he isn't bound by a single one.

While I would not by any means minimize the problem that the Sino-Soviet conflict creates for both the Chinese and the Soviet Communist Parties, I think that for them in the long run it is a positive, rather than a negative, development.

*Taylor:* I think what they probably argue about most is the organizational problem. This is a real contest to see who is going to run the show. These conflicts are expressed in ideological terms.

I think if you look around the world you can see that we have to modify Mr. Walker's statement that it is not a solid and homogeneous unit. In some things they are extremely homogeneous and very solid, indeed. In other things they do not seem to be.

One could suggest that the Bloc is suffering to some extent under the pressures that we have put on it: the pressure of American nuclear power which obviously restrains them in many ways; the pressure of the economic revival of the West since World War II, which has shocked and surprised many of the dogmatists and is something that had to be faced and dealt with particularly by the Soviet Union; and the pressures that have come about through the political adjustment—flexible, imaginative, and rapid political adjustment—of the Free World to the new nations of Asia and Africa. But on the whole it's been a tremendous political adjustment.

*London:* There seems to be a very lively competition between the Soviet Union and Communist China in some of the so-called non-aligned countries. We don't know exactly how this is going to turn out: whether it is a competition to eliminate the other one or whether the competition is simply one of two good friends who want to achieve the same goal. Our evidence is still not quite clear about the subject. We only know that they use different tactics. For instance, in Africa the Chinese direct themselves to individuals, to groups, rather than to government. Of course they do the latter one, too, but not to the extent the Soviets do. The Soviets mainly deal with governments. They have become much more cautious since Touré threw out the Russian Ambassador.

There is another point I'd like to bring up: a very strong difference of opinion exists concerning the effects of nuclear warfare. The Chinese declaration of a little while ago, which is a rather old-fashioned Leninist declaration based on documents originating roughly between 1905 and 1920, has only paid lip service to the effects of nuclear war, and has to all practical purposes stated, "So what?"

The Russians, of course, have a very different view on that. This seems to me one of the strongest bones of contention between the two.

*Walker:* The Chinese position within an alliance—and I realize parallels are very dangerous—does bear some parallel to our current problem with the French. There is the insistence by the Chinese that they do want to become a nuclear power. With regard to the point you raise, Professor London, I think this is a key item as far as the Chinese are concerned. Given the insistence of Mao and his colleagues on the efficacy of war and the importance of military power, I'm sure it nettles them that they do not have nuclear weapons.

Furthermore, it nettles them even more because the Chinese do have a chauvinism. They do have the determination to prove that they are one of the two or three or four great powers in the world who have to be consulted about everything. And this, I suspect, is a large part of their motivation for getting involved in Africa and in Latin America. This is a part of an assertion on their part that China is the land that has to be reckoned with as one of the great determining powers in the world.

### Impact of Split on West

*Cerny:* I would suggest that we might turn to the next series of statements which will be still in keeping with the problem of polycentrism. As has already been suggested, the problem is not only what is the nature of the split, the degree of the split, but also what is the impact of that split on possible American strategy.

> Short of a breakup of the alliance, the competition between Khrushchev and Mao as to who has the most effective strategy for the burial of the United States and the West hardly offers pleasant prospects in the 1960's. Those who find a basis for optimism or derive comfort from current Sino-Soviet differences usually fail to note that ultimate Communist world victory remains the major goal of both disputants.
>
> Richard Walker

> Even if an outright split occurred between the Soviet Union and Red China such as that between Moscow and Tirana, we should not count on Communist erosion. Two world centers of communism would increase rather than decrease our troubles. When the Eastern and Western branches of the Christian churches separated in 1054, Christianity remained very much alive.
>
> Kurt London

Professor Walker, perhaps you would care to comment on the reasons for your qualifying phrase, "short of a breakup of the alliance."

*Walker:* What I mean essentially by saying "short of a breakup of the alliance . . ." is that, given the traditional Chinese antagonism toward Russians, given the Chinese ambitions even to assert a Japanese-like co-prosperity sphere in East Asia, a breakup in the alliance could lead to a whole spectrum of conflicts between the Chinese and Soviets. One end of that spectrum of conflict—namely, an overt military conflict between the Chinese and Soviets—it occurs to me might not be entirely to our disadvantage.

*London:* I've been rather disturbed lately by the, in my opinion, unwarranted optimism concerning the erosion of communism as a result of polycentrism. I regard communism as a kind of a secular religion. It may change, it will change, it will have to change in order not to stagnate. But there is no reason to assume that, because some of the Communist states have differences of opinion, this secular religion will suddenly disappear.

I've been intrigued by the question as to what would occur if there is a real break between Moscow and Peking. I don't really believe that it will occur to the extent that there is a break even between the states. There may be alienation of affection between the Parties, but I'm not so sure that is going to be the case between the states. If we do have two world centers of communism, which would be the effect of such a break, I think that our difficulties would multiply.

I cannot help thinking of the fabled old Greek animal, the Hydra. When Hercules chopped off one head, two grew in its stead, and so it went. In addition to our own relations with Peking and Moscow, there would be trouble in the world because Moscow would have lost the last vestige of influence on Peking. And if the Chinese should succeed in obtaining nuclear weapons, then the situation would be extremely dangerous, indeed. But I don't believe for a moment that any major split between these two large Communist countries would lead to an erosion of communism.

*Nutter:* It's a little bit puzzling to me to hear comments that we are worse off to have the Communist Bloc members fighting among themselves than to have them solidified in some way and not fighting. It would seem that the counterpart would be that the Communists would be worse off if the Western Alliance fights among itself, and maybe this is true.

But on the other hand, surely the situation of a group of nations that now is trying to seek one or two or split itself between two leaders is quite different from a group of nations that is following one. And I would think that the whole set of strategic problems for the West would be quite different. I don't see why we should characterize them as more difficult. I think they are different. I think we need to exploit different kinds of policies.

I think we need to take account, perhaps more than has been taken account so far, of the vastly different internal conditions of these two countries, which I think, in and of themselves would lead these two countries to want to pursue different kinds of policies. Whether we call them Communist or something else really doesn't matter. And I'm just wondering whether it really is correct to say we're worse off to split the Bloc than to have it more unified.

*London:* I didn't mean to imply that one situation is worse than the other. I thought that one might be more complicated than the other from the point of view of the policy-maker and the strategist. Both have to look into the crystal ball.

If we have a monolithic Bloc, I think the predictability is somewhat easier than if we have a split movement in which we don't know who is going to do what.

*Dinerstein:* I'm going to use the year 1962 to try to disagree with my colleague, Mr. Nutter. I think that most of us would agree that 1962 marked the height of the Sino-Soviet conflict. Which were the two main events in international life in 1962? I'll start with the one that was more important—the most important event for Asia. The most important event in Asia in 1962 was a demonstration that the Chinese are a great military power by their successful invasion of India. So, this was one major event and a great change in Chinese policy after two years of relative quiescence.

The major event in the Western Hemisphere was a very bold Soviet attempt in Cuba, one which probably came closer to succeeding than we now like to think since it has failed, but nevertheless has left as a residue, a Soviet base in the Caribbean.

I think that these two facts somehow are so large that they overshadow the very just remarks that Mr. Nutter made. Of course we derive some benefits from their difficulties. Difficulties cause them trouble. But the result of the difficulties seems to have been to spur each one of the members to try to demonstrate that he is more successful in gaining his ends.

It may be, if you want to look at the bright side of things, that in the long run these Communist initiatives will fail. It may be that the Communist initiative in India will be an important stage in making India a unified country. But it is very hard for me to put the same construction on the Communist success in the Caribbean.

We have accepted as a normal feature of life that there can be non-strategic Soviet military installations in Latin America. They are there now.

It's very hard for me to minimize the tremendous significance of that fact for the political life of Latin America. So, if we look not at the structure of the conflict between the two, but at the events that transpired during the conflict, I think that we should be more pessimistic than optimistic.

*Wittfogel**: Actually, since 1949, the Communist world has indeed differentiated itself into two parts. A new axis has emerged because a second major Communist country has come into being which is not subordinated to Russia. It was not created by the Russian Red Army, but by its own army, although with considerable Soviet help. And therefore, we have had since 1949 a double-centered situation with the possibilities for inner rifts and divergencies.

Russia was the senior partner in this axis, but in terms of personal leadership, Mao, as the elder statesman of world communism, had a higher position than Malenkov or Khrushchev, who were relative newcomers. Naturally, Moscow has wanted to regain its strength and its original level of leadership.

Things did not reach an open conflict until the Great Leap Forward and the establishment of the communes, which in my opinion were very irrational attempts to resolve the agrarian crisis. I think that any effort to evaluate what will happen in the next ten years is rather pointless, if we are not able to identify the character and depth of this crisis.

You may ask, "Will China collapse?" I do not think so, and on this, I believe, all of us are agreed. Certainly the Russians do not want China to collapse. But Khrushchev can let Mao stew in his own juice and this he has been doing. The situation is such that Mao can no longer blackmail him for economic aid.

I also believe that if Mao said, "I'll go to war against Taiwan," Khrushchev would say, "Help yourself; go ahead." In the Chinese rural areas, to use Herman Kahn's term, in the "B-country," Mao has the most hostile peasantry in the world, and I think he is unable, for economic and psychological reasons, to wage a major war.

---

* Dr. Karl A. Wittfogel of Columbia University and the University of Washington, and author of *Oriental Despotism*. Dr. Wittfogel graciously consented to participate in the discussion of issues in Part I of the Conference.

The Indian situation offered a wonderful opportunity to make a big noise without getting into a really serious war, because the geo-military situation prevents the possibility of such a war. I think if anything would help to weaken the Communist Bloc, it would be to have Mao himself in a war he cannot afford.

When we talk about polycentrism, let us not forget that there are really only two centers. When we talk about the relation between these two centers, let us not forget that the Chinese Communists are in a crisis which I think is bound to last for a number of years, certainly for the next ten years. As long as they do not take the only step that would restore the economy— the return to private family farming—in my opinion, China is bound to be agriculturally very weak and also very weak industrially and militarily.

*Walker:* I would like to suggest a question for Professor Wittfogel. Given the crisis in China which——I share his opinion—— is very real, I wonder if there is a possibility that the Soviets might be preparing a position to disembarrass themselves for failure in China. We have tended always to assume the continuous success in power building, economic build-up, and so forth, for the Chinese Communist regime. I wonder if it is entirely possible that Mr. Khrushchev sees himself with a Chinese partner which, if he gave continued aid, would end up being a long-term drain on Soviet goals in the world and on the Soviet economy itself. And perhaps much of the initiative in the dispute could have come from the Soviet side.

*Wittfogel:* I think that Mr. Walker is certainly correct in what he implies. And I think in fact the whole invisible struggle between the two leaders, the two centers, Moscow and Peking, has had this background.

*London:* It is well known that Khrushchev and Mao dislike each other heartily. This point has not come up. I think it is a very important point, and I would like to have some reaction to it from my colleagues.

*Taylor:* I think there is no question that Mao has every reason to dislike Khrushchev. When the commune system began, you remember the loud introduction of it in August; and by December, Chairman Mao was no longer even head of state. I have a feeling that Mr. Khrushchev had something to do with Mr. Mao's decision to give up one of his positions.

There is no question that he has every reason to dislike him. I think also that the Russians do not understand the Chinese agrarian crisis any more than the Chinese do. There is something to Mr. Walker's point that they would like to be disassociated from it.

I'm just wondering as a hypothesis, if I may go back to India, why Mr. Mao started the border war. Quite obviously it takes quite a while to mount an invasion over the Himalayas; it takes quite a while to mount an enterprise such as the Cuban enterprise. I don't know how long the preparation took, but it must have been at least a year.

The extraordinary thing to me is the timing of these two events. We are so fascinated with the fight between Moscow and Peking that I haven't seen publicly examined very carefully the hypothesis that these two events were carefully timed to happen about the same period. Imagine what would have happened if the Cuban thing had succeeded. I wonder whether China would now be withdrawing or stopping the fighting. It would be extremely difficult for American or British supplies to be going to India if Cuba had succeeded. It's not impossible, surely, that there was a certain amount of coordination in these efforts.

The other point I wanted to make, and I didn't want Mr. London to get away with it completely, is that in his paper he suggests that the time has not yet arisen for a well-thought-out propaganda campaign to be effective. We have to wait until there is a genuine break between the two centers of world communism. I wonder whether he really believes this statement.

I agree that we did very little to turn Tito away from Stalin. Stalin did that. I just wonder whether the time isn't long since past when we should be engaging in psychological warfare against the Bloc with a view toward making their problems as great as possible.

This raises a very, very deep problem. What is our general attitude toward Communist China and the Soviet Union? Are we out to destroy the power of Communist Parties, or are we out to try to live with them?

If we are, as I believe we should be, engaged in a long-range effort to get rid of them—which is not our present policy as far as I can make out—then, of course, our propaganda and psychological warfare would be a very different matter. We should be engaged in it now.

*London:* In the first place, I think that they are fighting each other so well now that we can add very little to it. If we do it now, I would not do it overtly. What we can do covertly is a different story, and I don't think any subject of our discussion. But overtly, I don't think that the time has come right now. I feel that it's a good thing to let them stew in their own juice at present.

## Economic Constraints on Strategy

*Cerny:* Let us turn to our second issue, economic constraints on strategy. This involves a number of things. It involves an assessment of the economic potential of the Soviet Union on the one hand, and of Communist China on the other. There seems to be little disagreement that the economy of Communist China is in bad straits. With regard to the Soviet Union, however, two statements by Professors Nutter and Bornstein seem to point in opposite directions.

> By my estimates, the Soviet national product measured in current US prices was between a fourth and a third of the US level in 1960. Total expenditures on the military-space program were, on the other hand, around half of the US level, and production of military-space products around four-fifths. The heavy burden of the military-space program is probably an important factor influencing the marked slowing down in growth over the last couple of years.
>
> Over the future, Soviet leaders face mounting difficulty in reconciling three interrelated but conflicting goals: short-run strengthening of power, long-run strengthening of power, and raising of living standards.
>
> G. Warren Nutter

> The expansion of the Soviet economy in the 1960's, together with the progress of Soviet military technology, will provide the means for enhancing Soviet military strength in both conventional and advanced weapons. It will also make possible additional support of Communist subversion in areas like Laos, as well as additional military aid to non-aligned countries like Egypt and Indonesia.
>
> Morris Bornstein

Professor Nutter, would you care to elaborate first?

*Nutter:* I think that the isolated statement is not one that I would want to stand behind completely in all its details. The question as to how big the Soviet economy is, relative to ours, depends so much on how you measure it that the precise figures are not important. The emphasis here is, I think, on the relative burden of the armaments program of the two economies. In the Soviet economy there is no question but that keeping up with the armaments race imposes a much heavier cost on the Soviet Union than it does on us, and so heavy that I think it has without doubt reduced their gross national product considerably, particularly in the last couple of years. There are other factors involved, too, but I think this is a very important one.

I think it would be a very great mistake to think that the growth of military power in the Soviet Union can be automatically projected ahead by supposing that they have the power to expand the economy roughly at the same pace as in the past and, hence, they will continue to have the possibility of increasing their military strength.

One thing that the Soviet Union could do is to press for maximum effective use of the power it now has; that is, attempt to make great gains through power politics based on strength in being at the present moment. This would involve a great many bold ventures such as they have engaged in, in rocketry and in the Cuban adventure. It would involve attempts to get unilateral disarmament on the other side so that the gap in military strength will increase.

Another sort of policy they could follow would be to attempt to improve their own economy so that the difficult choices among these three goals could be lessened. This involves considerable internal reform. There have been very serious discussions of this in the Soviet Union. These reforms, if followed, would lead to a quite different kind of economy than we have seen in the past, and there would be other international repercussions. There would probably be temporary disengagements or efforts to disengage, and so on . . . the view being essentially, I think, that of the leaders to work toward future power.

A variant of this second course of action is to seek some kind of an accommodation with the West, a *détente* or something of the sort. During this period there could be disarmament on both sides and this, at the same time, would provide possibly greater investment, greater growth in the Soviet Union . . . the hope again being that in the future the situation would improve.

**Bornstein:** I don't see any basic disagreement between the quotation from Mr. Nutter's paper and the one from mine. Certainly both of them are compatible with the idea that Soviet leaders are encountering difficult choices, and specifically choices between economic growth and improvement in consumption levels and strengthening of their military power.

On the other hand, I think, as I pointed out in my statement, to the extent that the Soviet economy does expand, this together with progress in Soviet military technology will provide the means for the kind of improvement in the Soviet military posture that I think we can all reasonably expect.

Now, in regard to my reaction to the statement that was quoted from Professor Nutter, I find myself in really very strong agreement with the last two parts and would tend to question the first part.

I think I'm among the group who would question the specific estimates that were stated here. Without getting into a very long, complicated discussion, I would only point out that alternative estimates on these very questions tend to differ quite a bit from Professor Nutter's, being considerably higher.

For example, he estimates Soviet GNP measured in dollars as about a fourth to a third of the US level in 1960. There are other estimates by reputable scholars also that put the figure closer to 55 or 60 per cent. Similarly, although it's not mentioned here, in Professor Nutter's detailed book on Soviet industrial production he estimates that in 1955 Soviet industrial output was about 24 per cent of ours. There is another also very detailed estimate which appeared in the *American Economic Review* a few months ago that has a figure of 46 per cent compared to his 24 per cent for 1955.

These estimates of relative size aren't the most important thing for the point under discussion, namely, that there is a conflict between a stronger military program and economic growth and the improvement of consumption standards in the Soviet Union, and that it seems that this is going to increase in intensity in the Soviet Union.

This suggests some intriguing questions, and I would just like to pose these.

One could argue that if this strain exists, and the Soviet leadership is really interested in long-run economic growth and power, and is seriously committed to some improvements of living standards, then the Soviets could conceivably have some interest in reducing the demands on their economy of their military program. This is the kind of argument that would be cited in saying that the Soviets could and indeed, might, have a sincere interest in some kind of disarmament.

On the other hand, one could argue just the other way by saying, "If the military program strains the Soviet economy more than it does the US economy, does this suggest a tactic for managing the arms race? If we were to maintain and widen our military superiority and the Soviets had to continue to strain their economy in an effort to reduce the gap, try to catch up, possibly try to overtake us, would this be an indirect way, but a very effective one, of further straining the Soviet economy?"

### Growth and Aggression

*Cerny:* The following series of statements are related to the impact of economic constraints on Sino-Soviet strategy.

Professor Bornstein, would you want to elaborate on the first statement?

> The poor outlook for China's economic growth in the next few years therefore by no means implies a corresponding moderation in its aggressive intentions, or a weakening of its military capabilities, or even a corresponding reduction in the rate of improvement in these capabilities.
>
> Morris Bornstein

*Bornstein:* What I had in mind is that even though China has had severe economic crises, the Chinese certainly have not reduced their aggressive intentions. In fact, they have undertaken aggressive activities in India, continued subversion in Southeast Asia, and seem very determined to pursue a nuclear-energy program, which I think on economic grounds, we would argue, they surely can't afford. Therefore, what I tried to argue in this sentence is that we shouldn't translate economic crisis into military retreat.

*Wittfogel:* I think it would be important here to distinguish between two types of action, namely the gun that shoots and the hand that gestures. At present, the Chinese ability to make wild military threats is unimpaired. I doubt whether their military striking power is at all comparable with it.

I do think that their military potential is weakened along several lines. One is their weakened army morale; and the second, their weakened industrial situation. A third factor, their military aggressiveness, and I refer here to the Indian situation, depends largely on the Russians providing the Chinese with oil. One of the threats that Khrushchev quite likely has made is "I'll cut off the oil supply if you go on wasting it there over in the Himalayas."

*Walker:* I think it is worth considering that while the Chinese economy promises to continue to be in somewhat desperate straits, it was in an utterly hopeless state in 1949 and early 1950. By 1952 one of the members of the Central Committee stated that the anti-"American Aid to Korea" campaign had been a necessary campaign which drove the economy on in all phases. So that given the belief of the Chinese Communists in war, I would like to underscore Professor Bornstein's comment here. We cannot necessarily expect that an economic breakdown is going to preclude overt aggression or further overt warlike moves on the part of the Chinese Communists, even to the point of stupidity.

There is an almost benign conviction. Mao says, "Political power grows out of the barrel of a gun." I suspect he would also say that economic power grows out of a barrel of a gun.

*Cerny:* I would like to turn to a statement by Professor Dinerstein, which suggests that Soviet inferiority in economic resources does constitute a genuine constraint, certainly with regard to the actual procurement of a superior weapons system.

> The appearance of new weapons, each in itself terribly destructive, gave the Soviet Union the opportunity to catch up in the newest and most critical technology and thus achieve over-all parity, if not superiority. But when military systems started to be planned and procured, Soviet inferiority in economic resources constituted a genuine constraint. This is probably *one* of the reasons why the Soviet Union has not converted its priority in the *development* of missiles into a superior weapons system.
>
> Herbert Dinerstein

*Dinerstein:* I would like to amplify in the light of some things that have been said, and give what I think is the new strategic background for arms races.

I think there is a very great contrast between the Soviet and the Chinese military problem. We haven't realized sufficiently how much the Soviet military problem has changed. We have had our sights correctly fixed so closely on the Soviet entry into the nuclear league, the Soviet progress toward parity, and we have been so justly sensible of the advantages this has brought to the Soviet Union, that we haven't looked at some of the problems that this has created for them.

I think that the best analogy is from the period before World War I. In the period before World War I, both French and German military establishments were very intimately connected. A major change in the German railroad system introduced major problems for the French planners. There couldn't have been any really large change in one military system without at least creating a problem for the other military system.

Until the Soviet Union had come into the same class in long-range weapons as we have, it didn't have these problems of an intimate military relationship. So the old animal analogies about the military power were quite appropriate. I think the British used to be represented as the shark and whatever land power in Europe was dominant at that time was represented as a land animal. For a long time the American and the Soviet military establishments were different animals.

This meant that the Soviet Union did not have to be so immediately responsive to big changes in the American military establishment. I think the situation has become altered. Thus, if the United States has a very large Air Force, the Soviet Union has no choice but to try to meet this with some kind of a defensive system. If the United States promises to have a very large missile system, the Soviet Union has considered it necessary to try and get some type of anti-missile system.

So we have a kind of symbiosis between these military establishments of two powers that are many thousands of miles away, making many military problems urgent which fifteen years ago could have been deferred.

One of the big differences between the Soviet and the Chinese attitudes towards military problems grows out of this. It does not make much difference to the Chinese whether the United States has two hundred missiles or six hundred missiles. They can't do anything about it anyway. It's not a real problem for them. It is a real problem for the Soviet Union. And when the Soviet Union undertakes certain political actions, one of its calculations should be—and I suspect it probably is—that an increase in international tension will create new military problems of the kind I've been describing, which are economic problems. The Chinese don't worry about that. The United States is so far away from them militarily that it doesn't make any difference if the United States is angrier or if the United States has a larger strategic force. The Chinese are so far behind that it's irrelevant to them.

So the Chinese can pursue irritating policies without this consideration in mind. This brings me back to the point of Mr. Bornstein which stimulated this. The weapons race is not simply a military race, but is also an economic and political race, and has its political and economic opportunities and costs on both sides. I think that it is incorrect to view this weapons balance only in terms of the weapons themselves and not of all the concomitants that are produced.

## A New US Strategic Appraisal?

*Cerny:* We might now consider another statement on the second issue, economic restraints on strategy.

> In the last analysis it matters little whether or not the Soviet people have a monotonous diet and cannot get enough meat. The main strategic question is whether the industrial establishment of the USSR remains strong enough to produce the tools of national strength and whether, in these times of mutual deterrence, they can continue to concentrate on technological developments which would keep them abreast of the West.
>
> To answer the question: there is no reason to assume that economic weakness per se will cut down Soviet power to the extent where a new US strategic appraisal is indicated.
>
> Kurt London

*London:* Let me begin by recalling first that in the old days when Marx was still alive, economics dominated politics. This is no longer the case. Politics dominate economics. Politics also determines questions of priority, no matter what the deprivations for the people. In other words, if a military build-up is required, it will be done and, as we have seen in World War II, it can be done, no matter what the deprivations are.

From our point of view, and from our point of view only, a point I intend to bring out is that we hear very much about weaknesses in the Soviet economy. They are not that bad . . . certainly not for our strategic consideration. There might be a dilemma however, in Khrushchev's mind. Khrushchev, I think, is obsessed by the idea to live and see the transition to communism, which requires the "material-technical base" on which it can proceed. For that purpose he needs a stronger economy, a very strong development in both industry and agriculture. And I suspect that the new organization in the Soviet Union through which the Party is taking charge of both industry and agriculture has something to do with that.

But so far as military equipment is concerned, it seems to me that there is plenty of reason to assume that whatever they need, they will produce. All they have to do is determine priorities. They did determine priorities, for instance, in the matter of space, and they achieved their purposes. This is what they can do. They neglect certain areas and compensate on others.

*Bornstein:* I have two or three comments. One of them is that some people might question whether the transition to communism is Khrushchev's main goal or whether he has at least corresponding goals about communism and world power. We don't want to underestimate the role of ideology, and the political and military strategy that springs from it, or is based on it. In this specifically ideological connection, however, we should keep in mind that in the Communist Party program in which the transition to communism is discussed at great length, there is a specific reservation that the need to carry on a defense program to meet capitalist-imperialist aggression may delay the achievement of this.

There is certainly an "out" in ideological terms for the reallocation or diversion of resources from the peaceful programs to military programs.

On a lower plane, I might challenge Professor London's remarks that we shouldn't assume that economic weakness would cut power down to the extent that a new US strategic appraisal is indicated. He may not really disagree with me if I suggest we want to keep reappraising Soviet power and corresponding US strategy. And I don't think he meant to suggest by that that we have the answer for a long time to come.

*Taylor:* We are discussing, of course, mainly Soviet economic power, and I think Mr. Bornstein in his paper made it clear that he was not going to discuss Communist China. Professor Wittfogel has drawn our attention to Communist China. He didn't have to draw mine, but I think it's quite clear to everyone that this is the key economic problem in the Soviet Bloc at the present time.

I would challenge the statement, that has been made several times, that economic difficulties may lead to even more aggressive policies.

There was a time in the growth of the Soviet Union when economic difficulties led to a very radical shift in strategy during the NEP period. We may possibly have to postulate the possibility of a NEP period for Communist China, which is in true distress. And because she is in distress, it's not impossible that there may be a semi-withdrawal from the apparent purpose of the Bloc. It's just a hypothesis that, unable to get the economic succor from the rest of the Bloc which she needs to survive, she may be compelled to look for some sort of *détente* with the West.

This would put us into a very difficult position. It is my belief that, last March, American and Canadian wheat saved the Communist regime. We fed the armies and thus enabled the Chinese Communist regime to weather what, every observer who was in Peking at the time reports, was a very critical situation indeed. I say American wheat. I stand to be corrected if I'm wrong. It's my understanding that we sold much more wheat to West Germany than we had before and West Germany sold much more to Communist China.

But this is a possibility. I think it's quite possible that the situation is so serious in Communist China (I see very little hope of their getting out of it very quickly) that they may have to do this. At the present time, 50 per cent of their trade is with the West. This is largely because of the wheat, I believe, but it shows that they are not adverse to eating our food if they have to.

This, of course, raises a relationship between the economic situation and strategy that has happened before. It may happen again. We may even find the Soviet Union forced to do the same thing. Unable to turn our flank by a brilliantly conceived and almost-successful move in Cuba, realizing that she doesn't have to put very much more money into her military establishment in order to keep ours going at full blast, she may take advantage of this, give us five or six listening posts in the Soviet Union, and I think we would have great difficulty restraining a lot of people from rushing in with loans, help, and so on to the Soviet and Chinese economies.

I feel that this possibly is the sort of thing that we should be looking for, if the facts are correct that the Chinese are in real distress, if Khrushchev is unable to bring them to heel, or if he's unable to help them. This seems to me the real issue in the Bloc today. It's the only possibility I see of a temporary relaxation in the apparent unity of the Bloc, and I think it would be a Tito-type situation. I would very much like the comments of my economist colleagues on this possibility.

## Politics or Economics?

*Nutter:* I'm not going to comment directly on that immediately. I think I agree almost completely with Professor Taylor's analysis of how the economic affairs in China might impinge on their political decisions. But I'd like to address myself to the point that Dr. London made that political matters now dominate economic matters in Russia.

I think it's a mistake to speak of either as dominating the other. If I may speak tritely, they're both very closely inter-related. The nature of the political system determines how successfully the economy can function on the one hand, and certainly there are great difficulties in this regard in Russia at the present; and, secondly, the success with which the economy functions determines to a large extent the popular support of the government and political rulers. And we certainly can't disregard this question, nor can the Communist Party leaders.

It seems to me that the Russians face two alternatives. If they wish to plow ahead, as Professor London suggests they might, in pursuing their military program willy-nilly and squeezing the consumer, and so on, then I think they have to turn to a program of terror much worse than during the Stalinist period because I think the population now is much less ac-quiescent than it was then. That's one alternative—simple brute power.

The other alternative is substantial reform, a kind of NEP withdrawal inside, and a substantial economic and political reform. I don't think that the present expedient of supposedly putting the Party in charge of the economy follows either of these paths. It's a very curious thing; it doesn't seem to change much of anything except who bosses whom and so on, but nothing fundamental.

The real dilemma that they face, I think, on the question of internal reform is the dilemma of whether or not it's possible to decentralize an economy and still maintain an autocratic government. This is again a very trite point, but obviously the primary concern of the Communists is to maintain the Com-munist Party in power. And this, I think, becomes much more difficult if you change the economic structure in the direction that it would have to change in order to make substantial improvements.

Which way they will move, I think, is very much up in the air. I think it depends a great deal on a lot of internal develop-ments that are going to take place inside of Russia in the next few years which we can't possibly at this moment predict. I think there's a great deal of unrest in all groups in the system, and how this will work itself out is hard to say.

Now, just a concluding remark on China. I think Professor Taylor is quite correct in saying that an alternative to an aggressive policy is a kind of NEP. The only question is who the leaders are to be and what they're going to try to do and what their assessment of the ability to stay in power under the different systems is. It seems to me that if Mao, or whoever his immediate successors might be, try to maintain their present policy, the only course they can follow is that of increasing the aggressive policy and increasing internal terror, and so on, in order to maintain their rule. Now, this could very easily turn the other way, and we just can't tell.

*Wittfogel:* I suggest that in analyzing both the Communists and ourselves, we look at the economy systems in two ways. One part we may call the power economy and the other we may call the subsistence economy. The correlation between them is not a simple one. There may be a very modest subsistence economy and a very dangerous power economy. There is no doubt that the Russians have over the years improved their power economy while keeping production in their subsistence sector very low.

May I repeat what I once said about Genghis Khan. His subsistence economy did not amount to much, but combined with this miserable subsistence economy, there was a military potential that made it possible for the Mongol hordes to overrun half the world.

We Americans have a wonderful subsistence economy. But we don't shoot with refrigerators and TV sets; and a population long accustomed to an affluent subsistence may be soft. We have a very serious problem here, and I think a fundamental one for our side of the Iron Curtain. Not only must we keep our military power strong, but we must also keep our population from going soft.

*London:* Just a brief word. I have great doubts about popular support in Communist countries—to answer some of Professor Nutter's statements. In a totalitarian country the use of military forces and communications can easily control the people; they can turn it on and off as propaganda is concerned. I've heard people saying that there is something developing like public opinion, referring particularly to the intellectuals. I don't think that we should overestimate it at all. I don't believe it plays a decisive role in the formulation of policy in the Soviet Union.

I'm sorry I can't agree with Professor Nutter. In my view the political aims decide what should be done in all other fields. I don't deny that there is a dovetailing between politics and economics, but still it seems to me that the political objectives are first.

I also would like to say that it is hard to compare the present with the era of Stalin. During Stalin's time the industrial establishment of the USSR was not nearly as developed as today. Today, in a limited way, I think Soviet industry is able to take care of at least some of the basic needs of the consumers. I don't believe for that reason that they'll stand up and attack the government.

### Erosion

*Cerny:* I should like to turn now to a discussion of the third issue on our agenda: erosion. We have in mind here the discussion of the possibility that various internal developments within the Soviet system, or developments in the present international climate may lead to a lessening of Communist ideological fervor, a weakening of the Communist Party's monolithic power, and a consequent lessening of aggressive foreign-policy objectives.

The following quotation of Dr. Dinerstein suggests that the process of erosion is not yet in sight.

> In less than a half-century, Communist success has been enormous, and the necessity for periods of consolidation and the failure of some attempts at expansion hardly demonstrate that communism has reached the high-water mark. It will take more than one rebuff, or some years of failure to advance to cause the Communists to abandon their objective of making communism a world system. If and when Communist objectives are radically modified, there probably will be no formal notice of the abandonment of old objectives.
>
> Herbert Dinerstein

Dr. Dinerstein, would you care to comment on this statement?

*Dinerstein:* I would like to just put it a little more in context. I want to make clear that I don't think that the changes within the Soviet system, whether toward a modification of objectives or toward greater attachment to them, go on behind the Iron Curtain without any reference to what happens abroad. I think a main factor in what will happen to Soviet objectives is American behavior.

*Cerny:* Any other comments from the panel?

*Taylor:* I would like an interpretation of the concept of erosion from anybody.

*London:* Gradual deterioration of the Communist system—the whole system and its components.

*Taylor:* Would you know when they're eroding?

*London:* Not immediately.

*Taylor:* What sort of evidence? Would you see a change in the system, might it collapse as it becomes less confident?

*London:* It's not only a question of confidence; it's a question also, it seems to me, of changing Party statutes, constitutions, activating some provisions in the constitution that sound very democratic and have never been carried out and practiced.

*Taylor:* Would you say when they began to practice their constitution that they are eroding?

*London:* To some extent this might be a symptom.

*Taylor:* So they could erode and become stronger?

*Dinerstein:* I think Professor Taylor has raised a very important point and really has outlined what the main task of diplomacy and analysis is—how do you know when you're winning? This is a very important question.

I think that if changes do come in the Soviet Union—and by changes I mean changes favorable to us—the most favorable change I could conceive of is if the Soviet Union should decide operationally, but maybe not verbally, not in Party Congresses, that we're just too tough for them and they had better be satisfied with what they have. I would say that would be a major change from our point of view, one which has not come yet.

The difficult thing to determine is the steps in such a process. I think it's quite possible that the Soviet Union might in the next year or two agree to some kind of a test ban on nuclear weapons because they would think that they would have more to gain than to lose from it, just as they decided when they resumed weapons tests that they had more to gain than to lose. And I could very well conceive of such an agreement being made by the Soviet Union with the intention of letting it run for a few years and then reviewing the situation.

But it might be quite possible that such an agreement made with only temporary objectives in mind might stretch out, and the result would be that the Soviet Union would have accepted

—although I don't think it has accepted yet—a position of strategic inferiority.

Mr. Taylor's question is a very good one. If this kind of thing takes place—I think it's possible although not the most likely—when do you know that it has happened? It's a very difficult problem, and it requires the rejection of wishful thinking. It requires a kind of sobriety and patience that usually doesn't characterize political thinking in most countries.

*London:* Just one basic point raised by a political scientist. We have two types of empire, so to speak. One is a totalitarian; one is the traditional. It would seem to me that the ultimate objectives of a traditional empire are, by its very nature, limited, while the totalitarian empire has unlimited aims. And it would also seem to me that if there is any indication that the final objectives of the Communist area are no longer unlimited, this would certainly be an indication that they have changed, that they have eroded.

### Succession in the Communist World

*Cerny:* Might I suggest that perhaps from the general statement of Professor Dinerstein we move to some specific examples of possible breakdown of Communist power as suggested by a series of statements. One aspect certainly that is often raised is the possible impact of succession crises within the various Communist regimes.

Two statements by Professor Walker and Professor London suggest that the succession problem may take a different turn, depending on whether we speak of Communist China or the Soviet Union.

> As was the case in the Soviet Union, a major power struggle is to be expected at the death of the "great leader" Mao Tse-tung.
>
> Richard Walker

> At present, conditions do not seem to exist in the USSR that would lead to a prolonged succession struggle. Khrushchev's successor probably will be in his fifties, a technocrat yet also an *apparatchik*, more sophisticated in his reasoning but still hostile to "imperialism." Except in minor details, such a man is unlikely to abandon prevailing policies.
>
> Kurt London

*Walker:* I go on the assumption that, within a totalitarian political structure where the power and position goes to those who seek power, the death of the leader at the apex of this pyramid is almost of necessity going to lead to a struggle for power.

In the case of Mao Tse-tung and his impending death, the Chinese are dealing with the Soviets, and the Soviets are attempting to have some say-so in the direction of China. The cult of Mao, which is developed and is in many ways as intensive or more intense than the cult of Stalin, is also a reflection of certain Chinese characteristics, certain institutional characteristics, too. The cult of Mao reflects a sensitiveness on the part of the Chinese, their determination that one of their great leaders can speak for the Communist movement. It bespeaks some of their chauvinism, their nationalism, if you will. Indeed, the cult of Mao is partly a reflection of Chinese xenophobia.

Now, given the differences that have come along, and particularly the Chinese approach to agriculture that has been discussed here, about which Khrushchev actually used the word "stupid," it seems that the Soviets have little choice but to get involved in a power struggle which would follow the death of Mao. They naturally want to find some successor who is going to be more amenable to their own direction.

The very fact that the Soviets in all likelihood will be involved, means in effect that certain nationalistic elements in the struggle will possibly assert themselves against the Soviets. Within this framework, I don't think we should rule out the possibility of political action, political warfare on our part. If I may harken back to something that was said earlier; in many respects the economic crisis and chaos in China today is something which I think we should adopt every possible way to put on the backs of the Soviets. They claim the credit for the political plum they got; they found out they ended up with an economic lemon.

In many respects, if we keep these two giants pushed tightly together, if we insist that the Soviets do speak for Communist China, that they are responsible, and if we call attention to the failure of the Soviet system in China, the Communist system, we are making greater headway toward exacerbating the tensions and disagreements within the Bloc.

I cannot see that the death of Mao, who has been "culted" far beyond Stalin, unbelievable though it is, can lead to anything but a very serious power struggle. Within this framework, one has to consider the fact that there is an alternate Chinese government. It is very nationalistic. It has some of the same policies toward the Indian border that the Communists do. I suspect these leaders of the Chinese Nationalist Government see this possibility as an opportunity for them to exert leverage.

*London:* In the first place, as far as China is concerned, the leadership group in China has been uniquely cohesive, particularly if compared with the Soviet leadership. Let me speculate. When Mao dies, couldn't it be assumed that Liu would follow him without much, if any, change in the leadership? If both of these men are out, there may be some kind of a struggle in which Chou En-lai might possibly be involved. But I'm not so sure that the struggle would be so hard, inasmuch as there is a very strong cohesion which apparently embraces also the somewhat younger people.

*Walker:* I don't think we should underestimate the extent to which Mao Tse-tung himself supplies the cement within that leadership group.

*London:* When I wrote this paper, which is an estimate, really, I polished my crystal ball very hard, and at that time I didn't see any particular succession struggle in the USSR. I'm quite sure that in that respect I may well be in the minority; most people assume that there will be one. There is coming a new generation of people who are no longer only Party people. They are also educated men. They are technocrats. I don't know whether this diminishes the chances of the succession struggle, but if Khrushchev manages to keep alive for several more years, I think that he will probably solidify the situation more. This is, I think, different from the Stalin time when the group was held together by sheer terror, as you remember from Khrushchev's secret speech. In my opinion, at least at the present time, we should not figure on such a struggle, although in any kind of policy paper this ought to be kept in mind.

*Wittfogel:* I think it is possible, as Dr. Walker has said, that, after the death of Mao, extremists might take leadership. But I consider it more likely that there would be a concerted effort for reconciliation with Moscow. I consider it much more likely, since Mao thinks of himself as personally superior to the newcomers in the Kremlin, that, once the elder statesman idea was eliminated by his death, young leaders might say, "Let's forget about this adventurism; let's make our peace. We'll get more economic aid; the Russians will talk with us in a different way."

And I'm sure that the Russians might, under such circumstances, be more ready to help. So I think it is more likely that a situation which, through the peculiar personality of the autocratic leader, Mao, has been enormously strained, might ease up. The death of Mao will probably create a power struggle among China's top-ranking Communists, but the Bloc as a whole might reconsolidate.

## Role of the Military

*Cerny:* I should like to turn now to another statement that poses another aspect of our issue—the possibility of a split between the military and the Communist Party in the Soviet system.

> It cannot be too strongly emphasized that in Communist states the military is but an arm of the Party. An attempt to split the army from the Party appears to be most unlikely even though the possibility should not altogether be dismissed. The Soviet armed forces constitute a decided asset of strength for the USSR and world communism. We have no evidence of weakness or even restiveness which would indicate the contrary.
>
> Kurt London

*London:* I want to recall the Zhukov affair where quite a few people thought a Thermidor had arrived and the armed forces in the Soviet Union might take over, which was not the case.

I feel very strongly that the army is entirely under the thumb of the Party and that we should not assume that it will take action by itself, particularly now, because it really has everything it wants. And what it wants it gets, apparently, from Khrushchev.

*Bornstein:* While I would like to agree with Kurt London on the general principle of the pre-eminence of the Party, I would like to take issue with the statement that the army gets everything it wants. I never knew an army that got everything it wanted. And in a way that's a political problem in the Soviet Union. And I think one of the interesting things that has been happening in the Soviet Union, a sign of their increased flexibility and range of opinion, is that the political leaders cannot impose military strategy upon the army in the easy way in which Stalin did.

The military in the Soviet Union have an area of maneuver, and if Khrushchev wants to impose his views against theirs, he has to at least stimulate discussion among them so he can say "somebody agrees with me." He can't just dismiss them.

I don't want to suggest for a moment that the army is for the hard policy and Khrushchev is for a soft policy. I've seen very little evidence of that besides the statement itself. But I do want

to suggest that the situation is more complicated and more interesting than it was ten years ago. The lines are not so clearly
drawn. It is a political situation in which each side has some
power and makes some points.

*Nutter:* There certainly have been occasions in recent history
in the Soviet Union in which factions have developed in the
Party. There is no such thing as a complete monolith here,
obviously. And the army has certainly been a decisive influence
in deciding which faction was to win. Most recent, of course,
was the struggle between Khrushchev and the anti-Party group,
as they were labeled, in which, apparently, Zhukov sided with
Khrushchev and got his temporary reward. But earlier than
that, of course, was the struggle after Stalin's death. The army
did put itself on one side against the secret police.

I am not suggesting that this is a fundamental question.
Obviously it is a question of the army operating as something of
an independent force ready to be used by different groups in
power. It doesn't destroy the fact that it will not put itself at
the control of somebody outside the Party, but just what "the
Party" is may sometimes be in serious question.

*Taylor:* It seems to me in the early days that cooperation between the army, between those Party members who carried out
military functions and those who carried out purely political ones
——this again is a false distinction——was not too difficult.
In the earlier days military technology was not very highly advanced in the acquisition of power. And there are certain areas
in the acquisition of power today in certain parts of the world
where military technology is not very high-level.

I wonder if we shouldn't be looking at the role of the scientist
and the relation between the Party member and the scientist
and the army leadership and the scientist? Presumably most
military Communists today still read the great books on military
strategy, but not all of them are going to be scientists. I wonder whether anybody could give us any guidance on the possible
relationship between the Party and the military and the top
scientists?

*London:* I can only talk a little about the relationship of the
Party to the scientists, which is a very simple one because the
Academy of Sciences, the Academy of Social Sciences, the Academy of Pedagogics, the Academy of Psychology—all these organizations are arms of the Party, just as the army is an arm
of the Party.

If there is any particular project to be dealt with scientifically, the army will determine it and the academies take it up. This is so particularly in the production of the "New Soviet Man," where all the resources of the social and physical sciences are combined as a matter of priority to produce whatever can be done to achieve such a specimen. There is no question, and there is plenty of evidence to that effect, that the scientific academies which direct individual sciences are directed by the Party in what to do.

*Cerny:* We will now turn to another statement on this third issue of our panel.

> The disturbing question is whether the Soviet Union may not already be embarked on a dangerous race between erosion of the Communist system and fulfillment of the Communist design of world domination. Such a race becomes more and more dangerous as Soviet leaders become increasingly aware of it, for they may be induced to take reckless gambles in order to forestall the steady march of internal events so distasteful to them.
>
> G. Warren Nutter

*Nutter:* What I mean by the erosion of the Communist system is something very specific. I mean a fundamental change in the nature of the political-economic structure of the Soviet Union taking form in such things as a withdrawal from the highly comprehensive material-type planning system, direct allocation of resources, to a system more involved with use of prices, more decentralized decisions, and so forth. I think this is an erosion and a useful meaning of the term. I think that it is happening to some extent already, and I think that it is going to continue although unevenly. To this extent I'll certainly stick my neck out. I believe that there are many signs of unrest, of deep-seated unrest, in the Soviet Union among the intellectuals, among the population, among the Communist leaders themselves. I think this is reflected in a lot of the very serious and far-reaching discussions that have come out into the open and have been carried on for a long time before that in private.

I think that there is a feeling which is gradually becoming more and more prevalent that the system as it exists will not be able to cope with the problems it faces, that it will have to be changed, and that, even if it is changed, perhaps the future is not as rosy as might have been thought before. And on this basis, it seems to me we ought to be prepared for more moves of the nature of Cuba and the like.

*Walker:* I think we ought to turn right back to the question Professor Taylor raised—one of definition. What is erosion? If in terms of the open expression of some dissatisfaction with the system, this means a real weakening of the whole Soviet political system and commitment to world domination, this might be termed erosion. But I'm sure there were dissatisfactions under Stalin even though they weren't expressed openly. I just cannot see erosion meaning anything else than a retreat from advanced positions, necessitated by internal changes.

If the demands internally eventuate in the retreat of the Soviet forces from Cuba, this might possibly be termed an erosion. But I think the way in which they link internal and external policies make it absolutely impossible to consider this subject of erosion outside the linking of the two fields, internal and external.

*Dinerstein:* I don't think we're going to settle the question of erosion, so I'll raise another question that we won't be able to settle either. I think I disagree with Mr. Nutter about reckless gambles.

I would not characterize the Cuban attempt by the Soviet Union as a reckless gamble. I would, if I were writing about it, I think, five years from now, give them very high marks for good sense. After all, the problem for the Soviet Union is how to advance communism. That is still their problem. It may not be ten years from now, or twenty-five years from now, but it's very much their problem now. And I think that in assessing the Cuban situation, the question for them was not: am I sure of succeeding? The question for them was: if I don't succeed, what will it cost me? If I do succeed, what will I gain? And how do these balance out? There is a tendency to think that whatever happened had to happen. I think we shouldn't fall into the comforting belief that they were bound to fail in Cuba, that the only possible policy the United States could have pursued was a policy it in fact did pursue.

I think it's possible that there might have been enough hesitation and enough temporizing so that the Soviet Union could have gotten its missiles in place and then said, "Let's start talking from this basis."

The gains they would have acquired from such a success would have been enormous politically and not negligible militarily. What have they lost? Well, they've lost a lot of prestige; they didn't get quite what they wanted, but they haven't had to retreat from anything they had before.

So when you're playing this game that they're playing with a non-aggressive set of powers, such as the United States and its allies, the price of failure is not giving up what you've already gotten; it's desisting from what you're attempting. If that is a true characterization of the Cuban situation. I don't think it was a reckless gamble. I think it was a very sensible risk.

I would agree very much with Mr. Nutter that we might expect more of this kind of thing if they continue to be worried about the future of internal developments, but I wouldn't characterize them as unwise.

*Cerny:* I would like to turn to the final statement on the issue of erosion, a statement that is made by Professor London in which the issue is: to what extent the problem of the intellectuals and the students may pose an issue for the Communist system?

> Recently, some of the limited freedom that had developed since the "thaw" was curtailed again. This demonstrates that the Kremlin is well able to cope with the problem and it would be a mistake to assume that intellectuals or a few restless students constitute a serious vulnerability.
>
> Kurt London

*London:* The situation in the Soviet Union is very different from that in the Satellites. We know, for instance, that the intellectuals in Hungary were quite instrumental in producing the events of 1956. I think generally speaking, young people are inclined to rebel against something. That's perfectly all right; they wouldn't be young if they didn't. I have, however, yet to hear from reliable observers that any of the young people, students particularly, in the Soviet Union are actually rebelling against the system as such. They rebel against certain matters, against perhaps certain personalities, they would like to know more of the West, of course, but I don't believe they are anti-Soviet per se.

As to the artists, pressure can be turned on and off, and this has happened several times since the "Thaw." You all remember Khrushchev's statement about abstract paintings being painted with the tail of a jackass. Well, I suppose some of us think so, too. I don't see any particular reason to think that this would harm the Soviet Government. Even if they give up socialist realism as the prevailing style, I don't think it would harm them, but they won't give it up.

**War Capabilities**

*Cerny:* To open discussion on the fourth issue of Part I, we have chosen a statement by Professor Dinerstein. It suggests Soviet inferiority in intercontinental missiles may not at all lead to any moderation in Soviet capabilities or attitudes.

> Soviet inferiority in intercontinental missiles is a relative, not an absolute, matter. Improvements, which fall short of parity, not to speak of superiority, may still yield important political benefits. Such improvements would give the Soviet Union a "pre-emptive capability." By this term is meant an ability to strike first in a period of crisis, with the minimum aim of making losses on both sides roughly equal, and with the outside chance of winning the war by sheer shock effect.
>
> Herbert Dinerstein

Professor Dinerstein, would you care to elaborate on your concept of a pre-emptive capability?

*Dinerstein:* I think the main emphasis of my remarks, which may not come out completely in this paragraph, is that this pre-emptive capability is essentially a political one. Almost by definition, nobody wants to be in a situation where he is forced to strike a pre-emptive blow in a war since a definition of pre-emptive means that the other man starts the war because he thinks he's going to win and then you try to do the best you can in a bad situation by striking first. So no one seeks that kind of a solution.

But a pre-emptive capability, although it's not the most desirable military posture, does have considerable political power over a mere retaliatory capability, and I think the Cuban situation illustrates this.

If you have the kind of situation that we have had in the last years, and which has been clearly recognized on both sides since the fall of 1961, when you have a situation in which the defensive power has clear military superiority in intercontinental means, and the aggressive power has inferiority, then pre-emptive capability begins to have important political advantages for the inferior power.

The Soviet Union was committed to a situation of political advance when it was militarily inferior. In such a situation it was very important for the Soviet Union to be able to present the United States with this kind of a dilemma: true enough, we are weaker than you, but look at the small value of what we have just taken—let's say the missile placement in Cuba. If you raise the level of tension, we have announced publicly that we might strike first and thereby equalize the military balance. This is not something we want to do, but this is a possibility you must reckon with.

For the aggressive power which is weaker, it's important to put a doubt into the mind of the defensive power about how the military situation could be equalized if the aggressive power had priority and seized it. And I think, therefore, that if the Soviet Union had emplaced its missiles in Cuba, it wouldn't have very successfully increased its ability to strike back after being hit. But it would have greatly increased its capability to strike a pre-emptive blow. I think then it would have had a great deal more political leverage.

I don't want to suggest—because I think it's absurd—that the Soviet Union is looking for a situation where it can start a war with inferior military capability. But I do want to suggest that there are many gradations between inferior and superior and that these gradations have important political consequences.

*Cerny:* We have given Professor Dinerstein an opportunity to comment and expand on his remarks, and I have been told by the staff that Dr. Raymond Garthoff* is in the audience and might be willing to comment with regard to this statement.

*Garthoff:* This is an unsolicited comment and, as a matter of fact, will not be addressed to this particular statement, which I thought was very helpful and useful. But I would suggest one additional point and would like to see what the attitudes of members of the panel and others might be to it: that is, the proposition that the Soviets have, in fact, made a significant decision that while they're still ready to use any means they deem expedient to advance their interests and communism, they no longer see war between states, above all general war but also really limited war, as expedient; that they no longer see war as an expedient instrument in the foreseeable future or at the present time; and that this view has been expressed, refined, restated at the cost of contributing still more to the debilitating controversy within the Communist camp, and therefore is a serious proposition. It does not, I think, mean that we can afford to let down our military guard in any respect. But it is a proposition which would lead us to put particular emphasis on methods or policies short of war, including the political manip-

* Raymond L. Garthoff, Office of Politico-Military Affairs, Department of State, and author of *Soviet Strategy in the Nuclear Age*.

ulation and political use of military power short of hostilities, as the main areas in which we will have to concentrate in the future.

## Chinese Nuclear Capability

*Cerny:* I would like to turn to the next statement, taken from the paper of Professor Bornstein, which suggests that China's joining the nuclear group is not too far off.

> They (the Chinese Communists) hope, however, to achieve a nuclear capability even sooner, by detonating their first nuclear device by 1963 and achieving a limited nuclear stockpile a few years later. Even the detonation of an experimental nuclear device would be of great significance, signaling Communist China's entry into the "Nuclear Club" and modifying the balance of power between the Sino-Soviet Bloc and the Western Alliance, as well as within the Bloc between the Soviet Union and Communist China. It would, in addition, enhance China's influence and prestige as a model for economic development in Asia.
>
> Morris Bornstein

*Bornstein:* I find myself supported by the just-announced US Government estimates that it is indeed a possibility that the Communist Chinese will detonate their first experimental device in 1963 or 1964 and achieve possibly a limited number of nuclear weapons perhaps by 1970. I think it's clear that this would have an influence in changing power relationships not only between East and West but certainly within the Sino-Soviet grouping.

I might make a slightly qualifying comment about the last sentence of the quotation. There is no doubt that China's economic crisis has severely damaged or tarnished whatever kind of model or image China could hope to present to other less developed countries, particularly the Asian ones. On the other hand, it seems to me, the detonation of a nuclear device would, to some extent, help partly to refurbish this image, showing that the Chinese are able to make this kind of scientific and technical progress.

*Walker:* The detonation of a nuclear device by Communist China, it seems to me, in all likelihood would increase the prestige of the Chinese Communists, particularly in Eastern Asia. We sometimes tend to overrate the idea of a model for economic development and tend to underrate, in talking about such countries as China, the importance of building national power. The very fact that the Chinese Communist regime has been able to shove its weight around the areas of Eastern Asia is the item which enhances the Chinese path, I suspect, far more than economic development.

The current controversy over nuclear weapons, it seems to me, between the Chinese Communists and their Soviet partners in our own discussion of the Chinese attitude toward nuclear weapons, has tended to give any threats that the Chinese Communists may make when they do acquire nuclear capability, far more credibility than they would otherwise have.

The Soviets, in other words, in the current controversy, may well have given credibility to Chinese Communist threats in the nuclear field when they do get that capability; and I think we must be very realistic in talking about it not in terms of if they get the capability, but when.

**Teller:** I would like to say a word about the Chinese bomb. I have no inside information, and will give you none. I think it is entirely possible that they will detonate one. The main fact is that in connection with nuclear weapons, a myth has grown up which has practically no relation to reality, and that is that it is very difficult to make nuclear explosives. This is just not so.

One possible consequence of the Chinese experience, if they indeed detonate a bomb in the near future, may be to end this myth. To that extent it might even be helpful because it might introduce into international relations a small amount of realism where none has existed so far.

Another consequence, or rather another consequence that will not appear, is that the big strategic picture certainly will not change. A few atomic weapons without the much more difficult and expensive, sophisticated delivery capabilities are not likely to make a great change. However, an atomic explosive is, after all, something that is powerful, that is dangerous, and in the hands of, let us say, more adventurous people, this could lead to almost any consequences, not because of its power but because of the unusual combination.

**Cerny:** I should like to turn now to a statement that has been chosen from the paper of Professor Strausz-Hupé. It is a rather forceful statement of a point of view, namely, that during the next ten years the danger of war is likely to increase rather than decrease.

More likely than not, during the next ten years the danger of war will increase rather than decrease. Totalitarian regimes are most dangerous when they have passed the peak of their ideological vigor and expansionist *élan* and met with growing external resistance. It will be precisely when the effectiveness of Communist psychological-political strategies decreases and the economic bankruptcy of the Communist system becomes apparent, that Communist leadership will be most tempted to forestall the slow erosion of its power by a quick military gamble. Paradoxically, this danger increases in direct ratio to the growth of Western strength.

Robert Strausz-Hupé

There are actually two points here; there is an estimate of what is likely to happen and a reason given for the estimate.

*Dinerstein:* I would much prefer if Mr. Strausz-Hupé were here because I am going to disagree with him sharply.*

I just think that unless the character of the Soviet leadership changes very radically, the one thing they have learned in the last fifteen years is that a war with the United States with nuclear weapons would be disastrous for them, no matter what it would be for the United States. I think this has really been burned in on their consciousness. I can't see what kind of situation would lead them to abandon that, and, therefore, I agree very much with the remarks that Mr. Garthoff made a few minutes ago, that the Russians simply can't see that a nuclear war with us, given the present balance of power or something roughly like it, is a useful strategy.

But their attitude could change if the military balance changes. The reason they don't think war is a paying proposition is because they think they would lose, not because they think that war in itself is an evil instrument that must never be used.

But I think that even with reasonable inefficiency on our part, and just ordinary stumbling along, we still will probably have the kind of military strength which I think makes this quotation unduly pessimistic.

*Kintner:* I would like to suggest that the Communist leadership still is committed to the continuation of their system. If certain eventualities take place, namely, the build-up of NATO power and the continued political growth and unification of Western Europe, the ideological bankruptcy of communism may be very difficult for them to withstand. The leadership would have one or two choices, perhaps. One would be to make a

---

* Although Dr. Strausz-Hupé contributed an advance study paper, he was unable to attend the panel discussions of the Conference.

genuine accommodation of the West, which would mean the termination of their ambitions; or, secondly, to play with a military situation that might be in their favor.

One such situation is the exploitation of the advantage they now possess and may continue to possess in the short-range, surface-to-surface missiles which might perhaps permit a clean disarming strike of Western Europe, which if accompanied by the political neutralization of the United States and its unwillingness to risk its all for the defense of that area, might perhaps give them a decisive advantage on the world scene.*

*Cerny:* Let us turn to a statement that we have drawn from the paper of Dr. Dinerstein.

> Essentially the Soviet Union, if it wants superiority or even parity, is driven to a strategy of "end runs," technological and geographical. Although it is probably unlikely, one cannot exclude Soviet technological breakthroughs in fields such as anti-missiles or perhaps bacteriological warfare. Giving up hope in such fields is tantamount to giving up hope of drawing even with the United States, because the Soviet Union cannot hope to win in a straight production race without jeopardizing some other vital goals.
>
> Herbert Dinerstein

Could you perhaps elaborate on what you mean by "strategy of end runs"?

*Dinerstein:* If I had to make a guess, I would say that the Soviet strategy would fail. I'm essentially optimistic. I think that they are going to lose and we're going to win. But I don't think they're going to lose easily. I don't think they're going to give up without a great deal of opposition.

Because they've tried and they haven't done it, I think it's very difficult for them, given the kinds of problems of economic choice which have been so well described in the two economic papers here, to have larger military forces than the United States, in bulk. They just can't out-build us. I think the history of missiles and the history of aircraft is indicative in this regard. But does this mean they have to give up?

I think what has happened is that US production superiority has forced the Soviet Union into a strategy, which we may regret at some time, of trying to be original, of trying to be novel, of trying to make technological innovations which might help to counterbalance our economic and industrial strength.

---

* Dr. Possony also discusses in Part II, *infra*, the issue raised by Dr. Strausz-Hupé's paper.

Whether or not they succeed is not a self-contained question. It depends almost completely on what we do. After all, in anti-missile missiles, which is one of the things that the Soviets are interested in, the effectiveness of such instruments depends on what we do with our missiles. It's not a simple one-sided problem.

So I think that the Soviet Union will try very hard to pull ahead technologically. It may try again if it thinks the signs are auspicious to make geographical short cuts like the one in Cuba. But the success of the Soviet strategy of end runs will depend very much on the environment, partly created by us, in which these end runs have to be made. It will depend very much on the kind of military and economic and political policies that the United States is pursuing. This is a case where the Soviet Union only has a part of the future in its own hands. We have at least half of it.

*Cerny:* Many of these points will be taken up again at greater length in Part III.

# Part II

# Political Requirements for U.S. Strategy

Part II

Political Requirements for CBS Strategy

# Objectives and Priorities

—*STEPHEN KERTESZ*

## Summary

*Aggressive and subversive Communist actions will remain major factors in international politics in the decade to come. Eventually communism will change but substantial change may take a considerable time. For the foreseeable future there is little hope of settling basic political issues with Communist states. In view of Communist hostility, the most crucial problem is preservation of American military and technological superiority. I use the word "technology" in the broadest sense, and imply leadership in the physical sciences and specifically in basic research. Superiority in military might and combat readiness, and leadership in the physical sciences and technology are not questions of domination or even of power per se for the United States. They are only the first steps on the long and arduous road which Americans will have to travel for preservation of a way of life worth living according to the standards of free men. Since totalitarian leaders have little moral restraint, the ultimate deterrent for them is American superiority in strategic weapons and means of delivery and American control of strategic bases.*

*Unilateral American concessions to the Communist government of China or the USSR would be foolish, because it would not improve their attitude toward the United States. On the contrary, friendly gestures toward them would vindicate their hostile policies and prove that the United States is a "paper tiger."*

*American diplomacy should sharply distinguish between the Communist regimes and the people dominated by them. We*

211

*should try to reach the people and influence long-range developments within Communist societies through cultural diplomacy. The principle of self-determination must not be abandoned for nations in Soviet captivity. Preservation of the national cultures of East Central European peoples and maintenance of their ties with the West should be important objectives of Western diplomacy.*

*The United States and Western Europe should combine military, political, and economic forces because separately they might not be able to counterbalance aggressive Communist powers. Events since the Second World War prove that the interests of the United States and the entire non-Communist world require the strengthening of the North Atlantic area from which freedom and economic well-being can expand. Coordination of Western economic diplomacy is most important.*

*The United States will have to persuade her European allies to assume a considerably larger share of defense burdens and economic aid. The European states should accept international obligations in proportion to their growing economic strength and should increase purchases from the United States to help offset the gold outflow caused in part by US military spending in Europe. Mutually satisfactory cooperation between the United States and the Common Market through tariff and other concessions is important. In this area the new Trade Act gives to American diplomacy an important leverage.*

*NATO should be transformed in the spirit of fair partnership. This would involve for the European states a more equitable sharing of military expenditures as well. The United States, in turn, should increasingly strengthen NATO with atomic weapons so as eventually to achieve a Western Alliance with independent atomic capability. Of course, the primary condition for such a policy is the establishment of a unified political authority in Western Europe and possibly in the North Atlantic area.*

*Military and economic aid and technical assistance should continue, but the underlying political philosophy must change. False emotionalism must be overcome. The United States cannot help everybody. We should, therefore, help primarily those countries which are threatened by Communist aggression and subversion. Moreover, we should help those states which side clearly with the West in fundamental matters. This does not suggest servility, but a long-range compatibility should be an absolute requirement. Foreign policy is not a game in which one can win by putting some money on most of the numbers. Neither is it a global popularity contest to be won by indiscriminate handouts of foreign aid and technical assistance. We should not throw good money after bad solely for reasons of propaganda. Since American resources are limited, long-range planning and control is necessary, and strict priorities must be established.*

*Western states should fight communism in the sphere of ideas. Even poor people are sensitive about their dignity, and the new nations are hungry for ideas. The great advantage of communism is that in a world filled with desire for change, communism offers not only almost unlimited and often unscrupulous promises, but also presents the ideal of a system in which man's wants will eventually be satisfied and human dignity will prevail. What is more, communism gives an organizational pattern and a timetable for action, while democracies offer mainly economic help and possibly some general advice. Western information activity should call the bluff of communism in the theoretical sphere as well as in the realm of politics. Some fundamental changes in society are greater in the West than in Communist states. Even in the economic sphere, despite substantial Communist gains, the West has clearly demonstrated a superior ability to provide the material needs for man. The contemporary revolutionary process—the idea of equality, large-scale production of material goods, and application of science to the economic field—started in the North Atlantic area.*

*Western resources are sufficient to support a reasonable development of the new nations. The West probably would be able to solve their economic and related organizational problems. But this is not sufficient. Man does not live by bread alone. Between the Western and Communist states a fundamental question is: which society will concentrate on higher purposes and work for the common good of mankind in a way understood by the multitude on all continents?*

*The United Nations is an important new theater for diplomacy. Tactical moves in the United Nations as elsewhere should be directed within the framework of clearly established and defined national foreign policy. Achievement of concordant attitudes in the United Nations, NATO, and other regional and functional international organizations, and in our bilateral diplomacy, is necessary for effective foreign policy. Harmony in diplomatic procedures and government actions is almost as important as a right policy. For settlement of important foreign policy problems, bilateral diplomacy and ad hoc conferences with select participants remain the normal diplomatic channels.*

*The United Nations may perform several useful functions and facilitate a "cooling off."*

*The UN General Assembly is an arena in which the game of parliamentary diplomacy is played out. In the future, public diplomacy in the United Nations should be used whenever practicable, together with other UN channels, though we should be aware that the UN is not an independent agency. Ultimately, policies of the superpowers—to act or not, in specific cases— remain decisive.*

*Since success or failure of American foreign policy depends to a large extent upon general developments within the United States, the paper refers to some areas where domestic reforms would be desirable for strengthening American influence abroad and thus facilitating the effectiveness of American foreign policy.*

## Some Basic Objectives

In the contemporary world an unusual burden has fallen on the American nation. Many oppressed peoples and nations threatened by aggressive totalitarian dictatorships regard the United States as their natural ally and partner in a struggle between two ways of life. Even without specific American statements and promises they rightly consider the United States a beacon of liberty. A powerful North American tradition, originating with the Declaration of Independence and continuing to our time, affirms universal political principles. The American creed is a belief in the fundamental rights and liberties of all men, in the equality of all men, and despite glaring difficulties, in the universal validity of democracy—the principle that people can rule themselves and define their own goals for a better future. As Abraham Lincoln stated, "Our Declaration of Independence meant liberty not alone for the people of this country but hope for all the world for all future time. It means in due course the weight should be lifted from the shoulders of all men."

The primary objectives of American foreign policy are self-preservation, security, and continued existence under the best possible social, political, and economic conditions. These objectives are not in conflict with the real interests of other nations and can be pursued best as part of a cooperative endeavor. In fact, the trend toward closer interdependence in the non-Communist world and the tasks thrust upon the United States by the

Communist threat make such a collective endeavor not merely an obligation for Americans but a condition for our survival. Moreover, the exploitation of the desire for social justice by international communism has probably served a deep historical and moral purpose by directing the attention of thoughtful citizens in all free countries to their responsibilities for eliminating poverty and oppression from their own environments. The Communist menace may also have impressed upon those citizens their obligations to seek liberty and dignity for all persons, regardless of where they live. It is in line with this increase in awareness of a need for social progress for all men that American foreign policy now stresses our determination to promote freedom and social justice and to raise living standards in the underdeveloped countries.

The world-wide demands for economic advancement and for the curbing of Communist aggression and subversion constitute an unprecedented challenge to American foreign policy. And there is also a special responsibility not only to our own people, but to our allies, the newly established neutral states, and the captive nations. American psychological warfare against the Communist Bloc should not use tactics which will mislead our allies or the captive peoples.

Let me say in particular that American statements should not create hopes which cannot be fulfilled in foreign aid or general political support. The American propensity to be a "good fellow" in the eyes of everyone is not useful in world affairs. Identification of international politics with a popularity contest can have disastrous effects indeed. No serious problem can be settled in international politics with popularity alone. Requisites for long-range effectiveness of American foreign policy would include a more reserved attitude and less sloganeering. For a world power it is, of course, more important to be respected than to be loved.

In policy planning we must be aware of the fundamental changes which have occurred in world environment.

One of the superpowers is consolidating its role as the center of an international revolutionary movement, on a scale which has changed the former system of national states and has involved in a global Cold War every free nation, including those asserting their neutrality.

International society has at the same time become more complicated through the emergence of many new states and the growth of many new regional, global, and functional organs for international cooperation.

Acute social evils have developed in some economically advanced countries, whose populations are becoming stationary and will soon begin to age. On the other hand, the populations of certain underdeveloped areas are growing rapidly. Population explosion is complicated in some cases by unrealistic economic expectations and extreme nationalism.

Meanwhile unprecedented advances in weapons technology has given each of the superpowers adequate capabilities for the destruction of the whole human race, and similar capabilities are gradually being acquired by a few smaller powers. The arms race might extend into outer space with the orbiting of thermonuclear weapons. Yet at the same time science has developed other great potentialities which, under conditions of international peace and good will, could provide vast material and social advances in the service of mankind. Boundary lines between politics, economics, and science have changed, and in some respects have disappeared.

**The Tasks of American Foreign Policy**

These broad developments must be in our minds when we scrutinize specific trends and tasks that challenge American foreign policy:

1) In Europe the Soviet Union is apparently developing a new strategy to thwart NATO and the progress of the European Economic Community (EEC); but serious internal tensions are weakening the unity of the Communist Bloc, and the long-term stability of several Communist regimes is uncertain.

2) Strengthening defense capabilities and cooperation in the North Atlantic area remains one of the major tasks of American diplomacy. Atlantic partnership or even some form of Atlantic union and the creation of a united political authority in Western Europe must be considered. Economic opportunities are drawing the United States into closer cooperation with the EEC, but at the same time the United States is being compelled to look for closer association with other groups of countries outside Europe.

3) While the balance of terror persists between the United States and the Soviet Union, Communist efforts to gain power in the underdeveloped countries are being intensified. The Soviet

Union is placing great emphasis on economic assistance to these countries as a means of popularizing and spreading communism, whereas the Chinese are urging the Communist movements in these countries to concentrate on preparing for armed revolts. Foreign aid and technical assistance remain major means of Western and Communist foreign policies. The United Nations remains as well an important forum to measure the interplay of Western and Soviet policies and their impact on the emerging nations.

4) Since in our age foreign and domestic political and economic problems are closely interwoven, success or failure of American foreign policy is greatly influenced by internal developments in the United States.

What with all these problems it is unnerving to confront the rapidity of change in world politics. Recently the pace of history has greatly accelerated. Since whimsically irrational changes push the movement of history into unknown areas, unexpected change in international politics has itself become a major factor for statesmen to consider. The lack of stability and the swiftness and unpredictability of our times characterize the world environment within which American foreign policy will function during the next decade.

In years to come foreign policy will be similar to navigation on an uncharted sea. Historical experiences may be of little value and it will be necessary to adjust our thinking constantly to changing conditions and new possibilities. This is a general problem in contemporary human relations, but foreign affairs present special difficulties. Although well-established international institutions function differently today than in the past, diplomacy is still using traditional concepts and methods developed in bygone times. With Communist countries participating in international politics, several time-honored diplomatic practices have become outdated. Some even confuse and hinder the intelligent appraisal and handling of contemporary problems.

Western political leaders have often only partly accepted or completely disregarded the intrusion of totalitarian ideology into international politics. This shortsightedness has constituted one of the major sources of Western weakness in international affairs. The complacent Western attitude is all the more remarkable since Soviet leaders from Lenin to Khrushchev have not been secretive about Soviet objectives, but from the outset have practiced diplomacy by propaganda, invective, and subversion.

American policy-makers and diplomats are influenced by Western traditions and concepts which were developed during the past few centuries in a homogeneous society of Christian states. It is often overlooked that conditions in international politics have changed fundamentally with the consolidation of the Communist Party's hegemony in Russia and the admission of the USSR into the society of states. This was indeed a momentous change, since the Communist conception of the community of mankind differs greatly from that prevailing in a society of national states.

The Cold War is a consequence of Communist doctrine. It is a natural situation for Communists as long as non-Communist states exist. In a cooperative state system in which countries pursue limited national goals, the role of diplomacy is entirely different from the role it plays between two groups of states, one of which has unlimited ideological objectives and intends to destroy the other. Despite the changes after Stalin's death, the basic doctrine, party guidance, and control have remained stable in the Communist Bloc, and the Communist parties have manipulated power across national boundaries in addition to, and irrespective of, diplomatic relations.

Although Marxism-Leninism is based on a fallacious interpretation of history and constitutes an anachronism in the atomic age, it is still the official doctrine of the Communist leaders who impose their system on more than a billion people. Antagonism and implacable hostility toward Western states remain the most permanent characteristics of their policy. Communism within the Sino-Soviet Bloc means an implicit declaration of war upon the strongest Western state, the United States. Communist countries recognize one set of rules in their mutual relations, and another set for dealing with the outside world.

It is true that a great deal of built-in conflict of interest and mistrust exists in Sino-Soviet relations. Both the Chinese and the Russians are suspicious toward foreigners, and both China and Russia interpret Communist doctrine according to the requirements of their national policies. The Chinese have challenged Soviet hegemony in the Bloc mainly, it appears, on the ground that Moscow seeks to advance primarily Russian interests. In a new phase beginning with the Cuban crisis they have attacked Khrushchev personally, suggesting that there cannot be reconciliation with him. Since China has been treated as a junior partner, differences and disputes might further develop within the Communist Bloc. Such phenomena are almost normal between two large states with conflicting national expectations. Still, overriding common interests and ideology determine the form and dimension of their alliance and demand periodic accommodation between the major partners. Although American diplomacy should take advantage of the cleavage between China and the USSR, we should not forget that without changes of basic Communist doctrines, the hostility of the Communist states toward the West is more important than their internal quarrels. In their behavior toward most other powers China and the Soviet Union are on the whole continuing to act in concert. The Chinese attack on India is a major exception. Sometimes more attention is given in the West to disputes within the Communist orbit rather than emphasizing Communist hostility toward the Western world. This inclination has become the source of some deceptive and dangerous illusions.

Mao Tse-tung rephrased Clausewitz's dictum: "Politics is a war without bloodshed, and war is politics with bloodshed." Only in a tactical sense has Khrushchev modified the bellicose Communist doctrines, and the new interpretations accepted by the Party congresses since 1956 are entirely of a tactical nature. In Khrushchev's terminology a war without bloodshed is peaceful coexistence. Although for many decades no foreign country helped the Chinese people as much as did the United States, the "hate America" campaign has been one of the central themes of the Communist regime in China. In that respect there is little prospect of change. Unilateral American concessions to the Communist governments of China or the USSR would be foolish, because they would not improve China's and the Soviet Union's attitude toward the United States. On the contrary, friendly gestures would vindicate their hostile policies and prove that the United States is a "paper tiger."

In the USSR the situation is different in so far as Americans are warmly received even during times of tension and crisis. Given the nature of the Soviet system, however, superficial cordiality between individual Americans and Russians does not change or influence the ideological hostility of the Soviet regime toward the United States. Cordiality of Soviet citizens toward Americans does not mean lack of support for, let alone opposition to, the official Soviet line. Hostility toward the United States remains the basic characteristic of Communist foreign policy.

In view of Communist hostility, the most crucial problem is the preservation of American military and technological superiority. I use the word "technology" in the broadest sense, and imply leadership in the physical sciences and specifically in basic research. Superiority in military might, and leadership in the physical sciences and technology, are not questions of American domination or even of power per se. They are only the first steps on the long and arduous road which Americans will have to travel for preservation of a way of life worth living according to the standards of free men.

While it may well be that the Communist leaders do not plan military aggression, the expansive thrust of their doctrines and reckless Communist practices could create an acute conflict. Moreover, a Soviet breakthrough in the field of long-range missiles or even newer weapons development could have fatal consequences for democracies. Since totalitarian leaders have little moral restraint, the ultimate deterrent for them is American superiority in strategic weapons and means of delivery, and American control of strategic bases. In view of the conditions of our time, there is no substitute for power.

Diplomacy geared to orderly international intercourse will not suffice in relations with Communist states, but open debate and increasing communication with them may bring a gradual change in their societies. Cultural exchanges are desirable, as well as other means of cultural diplomacy. As the Western nations have the ability to provide a better future for mankind, they certainly have no reason to fear an intellectual debate or economic competition. Intellectual developments could eventually influence the nature of the regime, but this is a slow and uncertain process for which no timetable can be suggested.

Meanwhile, the Communist governments should be recognized for what they are, according to their own doctrines and practices, and should be handled in international politics on this basis. The ugly features and contradictions of Communist policies should be pointed out through public diplomacy. Existence of the six-thousand-mile-long Iron Curtain along Soviet and Satellite boundaries, and the ugly Wall in the heart of a divided metropolis cannot be emphasized frequently or loudly enough. Although the new states in Asia and Africa have concentrated on their own problems, the Curtain and the Wall cannot escape their eyes. Communist jamming and propaganda do not change the fact that the Curtain and the Wall are necessary to keep the "happy people" from getting out of the Communist paradise.

Force remains the major instrument of Communist domination and expansion; American public diplomacy should point this out. In its manifestoes the USSR does not question the principle of national self-determination and the right of all people to freedom. Stalin signed the Atlantic Charter and the Yalta Declaration on liberated Europe, and Khrushchev propagandizes against imperialism and colonialism. Soviet spokesmen repeatedly declare that every people has the right to live as it wants, and no state has the right to impose its way of life on other peoples. Despite such remarks, the Baltic States were annexed by the USSR, and Communist governments were imposed on East Central Europe. After 1948 the Soviet regime and its supporters resorted to ruthless political propaganda and economic warfare against Yugoslavia for asserting its right to pursue a local brand of communism. Having installed a Communist regime in North Korea, Moscow supported that country's aggression against South Korea. Soviet tanks quelled the uprising in East Germany in June 1953. Khrushchev threatened to use the Soviet Army against the Poles in October 1956, and a few days later did use it to suppress Hungarian freedom. Cuba's position in international relations has demonstrated that cooperation with the USSR may rapidly lead to the loss of independence. During the October 1962 crisis Washington dealt directly with Moscow, and the decision for the withdrawal of offensive weapons was made in the Kremlin without prior consultation with Castro. This record should be recounted whenever Soviet leaders decry imperialism and colonialism while limiting application of their principle of national self-determination or "liberation" to countries outside their own Bloc. To Africans and Asians the Soviet Union presents itself as a benevolent and progressive power advocating national independence and "revolutionary" social change— change which it hopes under Muscovite direction will lead to the establishment of Communist regimes.

Although communism claims to be the best political and social system, a free intellectual give-and-take between Communist-dominated countries and the rest of the world is still prohibited. Promises of high living standards and the failures of agricultural production from the Yellow Sea to the Austrian boundary are other cases of Communist double talk. Numerous examples can and should be used to expose the double standards which characterize Communist policy.

In the ups and downs of foreign politics it will be necessary to give a higher priority to nations in Soviet captivity than has been the case in the past. For them the principles of self-determination must not be abandoned. The increase of cultural contacts with them seems a desirable first step. There are about

100 million people in East Central Europe who belong to Western and Mediterranean culture. In few areas of the globe are people more pro-American than in the Eastern European Satellite countries, although their pro-Americanism is seasoned with the bitterness of disappointment.

Under the Gomulka regime Polish intellectuals maintain a lively cultural intercourse with the West. Western diplomacy should seek to foster similar opportunities in the other Satellite states in order to nurture their Western spiritual and intellectual heritage. Were most Western states to follow a purposeful policy in this respect, freer communication of ideas between East Central Europe and the West might follow. In the general area of cultural diplomacy, the high standards and reliability of Western broadcasting to Soviet Bloc countries are of utmost importance. The oppressed peoples are fed a diet of lies, and they are interested in facts and in Western achievements.

Cultural diplomacy may also have some short-range effects. Khrushchev offered a free competition of ideas during his memorable debate with Vice President Nixon in Moscow. Although his proposal did not change the Soviet system of thought control, cultural exchange between the West on the one hand, and the USSR and some Satellites, on the other, increased. The West, of course, should consider the potentialities of cultural diplomacy without illusion, for the possibilities of influencing public opinion in totalitarian states with their elaborate system of thought control are limited. Moreover, Western precautions are necessary because true reciprocity in cultural contacts is not welcome in Communist states. The Soviet Union supports mainly those cultural exchanges which inflate its prestige or promote specific interests in its own scientific, technical, and industrial advancement.

American diplomacy should sharply distinguish between the Communist regimes and the people dominated by them. We should try to reach the people and influence long-range developments within Communist societies through cultural diplomacy. But American policy toward the Communist governments must be tough and prepared for a showdown any time. This is the only language they understand. In political relations with the Communist Bloc, policy statements and notes of protest do not impress the Chinese and Soviet governments—unless they realize that the United States is prepared to do something, as in the case of northern Iran (1946), Korea (1950), the Formosa Straits and Lebanon (1958), and Cuba (1962). Military strength cannot serve as an asset unless there is a willingness to use it when vital American national interests are involved. In some instances, it would be advisable to use economic diplomacy to show our determination to resist Communist encroachments. If the Communist states continue their efforts to contract the positions of the West by methods of indirect aggression and by threats of limited war, further trade restrictions should be considered against the entire Bloc, even including a complete embargo.

Disarmament negotiations have demonstrated that progress cannot come in world politics without some substantive agreements between the superpowers on the general structure of world power relations and security. A meaningful disarmament —within or outside the framework of the UN—cannot result unless there is a minimum of confidence between the two major power centers. In view of Communist doctrines and practices, uncontrolled disarmament should not be considered at all. What then should be our attitude toward disarmament? We must recognize that the applications of Communist doctrines would make it impossible for a Communist state—as long as capitalist states exist—to espouse seriously any kind of genuine disarmament in spite of Communist propaganda statements and the flexible stand taken by Soviet diplomatic representatives.

Without major changes in Communist doctrine, the Communist attitude will be characterized by aggression and subversion. Eventually, communism will change, but change may take a considerable time. The high cost of modern arms as well as the danger connected with their spread and use may eventually make some controlled reduction in armaments desirable and feasible. For the present there is little hope of settling basic political issues, including disarmament.

Such are the problems which the United States and its allies confront.

In the past, great powers usually accumulated their strength and acquired skill in foreign affairs over a period of several centuries. Such gradual development did not take place in the United States. Although Alexis de Tocqueville, A. T. Mahan, Theodore Roosevelt, and other statesmen visualized America's world leadership, the United States after the Second World War was suddenly catapulted into an unwanted position of world leadership on the ruins of the Western state system. It is a truism that the United States was not prepared for this role. It is equally true that, in view of radically changed world conditions and the suddenly unbalanced power relations, no nation could have been prepared.

At first the spirit of wartime cooperation with the USSR influenced American postwar foreign policy. As Soviet intentions for further expansion became obvious, the policy of containment was formulated in the Truman Doctrine of 1947, which proclaimed that "it must be a policy of the United States to support free peoples who are resisting attempted subjugation by armed minorities or by outside pressure." Since 1947 the Truman, Eisenhower, and Kennedy Administrations have implemented this doctrine on a world scale: the United States is now committed to the defense of more than forty nations. Moreover, since proclamation of the Point Four Program in 1949, the underdeveloped countries, particularly the new states, expect American economic aid and technical assistance as a matter of course.

Since the balance of terror limits political maneuvers in many regions, the importance of economic diplomacy has greatly increased. Since 1955 the Communist Bloc has been able to support its policy in some critical areas of the world with effective economic diplomacy. Although Communist economic activity outside the Bloc is small, it is effective because it is centrally directed and concentrates on strategic countries to earn maximum political dividends.

**The Atlantic Alliance**

Although the economic strength of the Western states in the North Atlantic area has increased much faster than that of the Communist Bloc, Western economic diplomacy remains handicapped by a lack of coordination. A major task will be purposeful organization of their immense strength. The machinery of the Organization for Economic Cooperation and Development (OECD) can be most useful. The United States and Western Europe should cooperate closely against Soviet economic strategy not only in so far as this is directed against themselves, but also in respect to its threat to the underdeveloped countries. The OECD should respond to the needs of selected underdeveloped countries by establishing effective machinery for the stabilization of prices of their primary products. The Western nations should not promote economic developments in Communist states, because the Soviet doctrine of victory through peaceful competition with the West includes economic weapons in the underdeveloped countries, and the increased economic power of Communist states would only strengthen these weapons at the expense of the West. This policy would not exclude aid to some Communist countries for humanitarian reasons or for specific political purposes. But this is a delicate matter, because such aid should not include material which could strengthen the Communist Bloc as a whole.

The United States will have to persuade the European members of NATO to assume a considerably larger share of defense burdens and economic aid. The European states have fallen considerably behind on their NATO commitments. They should accept international obligations in proportion to their growing economic strength. They should urgently increase modern conventional weapon and manpower contributions to their own defense and should increase purchases from the United States to help offset the gold outflow caused in part by US military spending in Europe. It is important to establish mutually satisfactory cooperation between the United States and the Common Market through tariff and other economic concessions. In this field the Trade Expansion Act gives to American diplomacy an important leverage.

NATO should be transformed in the spirit of a fair partnership. This would involve for the European states a more equitable sharing of manpower contribution and military expenditures. The United States should increasingly strengthen NATO with atomic weapons so as eventually to achieve a Western Alliance with independent atomic capability. Of course the primary condition for such a policy should be the establishment of a unified political authority of the North Atlantic area.

Though it would be desirable to have a reliable partner as an atomic power on the European shores of the North Atlantic, some doubts persist. Since unified political authority in Western Europe does not yet exist, it remains an open question: who would command the generals? As of today, only the national governments would be entitled to make decisions, and in a serious crisis the usual diplomatic procedures might not be practicable.

The lack of central authority in a democratic alliance system is a source of many difficulties. If countries in the North Atlantic area could cooperate effectively, they would become easily the strongest power center in the world. A basic understanding can be achieved more easily within NATO than in other political groups because some important human values are the same or similar in most member countries. But on the procedural level, fifteen governments control the resources of NATO and their affirmative decisions are necessary for action. This politically unintegrated NATO structure confronts the monolithic Soviet empire in which decisions are made most of the time at a single center, the Kremlin. Since free nations cannot be forced to cooperate through methods contrary to Western principles, a united policy can emerge only through consultation.

While cooperation and unity are highly desirable, the great disparity between the power of the United States and other NATO members is a situation that cannot be eliminated through a fiction of equality. Most NATO members recognize and even expect American leadership, but in some cases members resent its display or even its discreet exercise. Although a democratic alliance depends on the voluntary cooperation of its members, NATO cooperation cannot become in all respects a two-way street because of the disproportion in power and in willingness to contribute to the common cause. Since the Communist Bloc operates as a unit in international relations, it is highly desirable that cooperation and particularly the decision-making process in NATO and in Western Europe be brought into harmony with contemporary realities. The Atlantic partnership must develop in the political sphere into a new form of political union. This union eventually would include a North Atlantic Parliament with power in carefully limited fields and an Atlantic system of international courts.

A united Europe, Canada, and the United States should cooperate in world affairs, while at the same time remaining open societies. The establishment of close cooperation between the two shores of the North Atlantic is not solely in the interest of the West. It does not imply antagonism toward other regions but would foster freedom everywhere. Without Western strength it would be difficult for countries in Africa and Asia to follow a neutralist policy.

Developments in the North Atlantic area should give some hope for the future. Politically and economically, the United States and her Western allies are entitled to be optimistic, and history may be favorable to them if they keep their powder dry. In the world in which we live there is no substitute for overwhelming military might and the willingness to use it when vital interests are involved. But, because of the changed weapons system, a military showdown would be entirely different than it was in the past. The likelihood is great that in the shadow of Armageddon the Cold War will go on primarily in the areas of ideas, political competition, economic aid, and technical assistance. Military and economic strength only provides a respite during which American foreign policy may prepare answers to the fundamental challenges of contemporary world society. The battle for men's minds is easy to lose if fought with yesterday's weapons.

### Aid: Its Implications and Criteria

In our time one of the most important trends in world politics is a general desire for social change. Societies, which have been static for many centuries, desire a better fate. Longing for change has become a basic political motive, particularly in the developing countries. American policies toward these nations have been influenced mainly by trends which could be called roughly: anti-colonialism, anti-communism, and an enlarged Point Four Program.

The principle of anti-colonialism is embedded in American thinking as part of the American heritage. It is often overlooked that the revolution of discontented Englishmen in politically well-developed communities had a different meaning at the end of the eighteenth century from the wholesale recognition of the independence of former colonies today. For this reason the stressing of our anti-colonialism is not necessarily the key to successful policy in Asia and Africa. To them we are not, and do not act like, an anti-colonial nation. Quite the contrary.

The rapid multiplication of states in recent years has become a source of confusion in international politics. Some fictions in the contemporary world are connected with this process. The European idea of national states, self-determination, and the high living standard in Western countries created the myth that similar results can be achieved almost anywhere. This view overlooks the fact that, in other areas of the world, conditions of life are different. Some of the former colonies do not possess solid prerequisites of statehood. The ideas of the nation-state and self-determination simply are not applicable in numerous cases. The chance factors of colonial conquest and the arbitrarily established boundaries of the colonial powers can hardly be considered as solid foundations for statehood. The viability of the contemporary setting thus created in some parts of Africa and Asia is open to serious doubts. Leaders of new states have one common characteristic: all want to develop their countries overnight. They realize that political independence is meaningless unless they can fight poverty, ignorance, and various social plights. They affirm peremptorily that "Africa won't wait," that "Asia won't wait."

The pace of history, of course, has greatly accelerated and the new nations are worthy of support as long as their citizens are willing to contribute the sweat of their brows. The ambitions and emotions of the developing nations are most respectable, but policy-makers of a world power must consider the cold facts of life. It is probable that the population explosion will make a rising living standard difficult in several countries—no matter how much economic aid they receive. Irrespective of population increase, many undeveloped countries will always be poor for want of natural resources, favorable climatic conditions, or other factors; and even those with substantial resources may move haltingly. We should give opportunity to these countries to benefit from our technological experience. But they must be taught realistically. The less fortunate nations cannot be expected to follow the same path Western nations have pursued. Their conditions of life, natural resources, historical and social backgrounds are different. They must follow the path marked by their tradition, incorporating into this tradition new features which will benefit their societies. American economic and industrial methods and the American forms of social justice cannot always be transplanted to the other parts of the world, whatever the attractions of the American way of life and potentials inherent in the American system. The universal character of the American creed does not imply transplanting American standards, methods, and values to other countries.

There is an American inclination to help anyone anywhere on the globe. It is a fallacious assumption that such an obligation really exists—with the exception of strictly humanitarian aid. We should help people wherever we can, in a reasonable way, but some facts of life need not be overlooked. It is necessary to make a distinction between charity and policy. To squander resources might lead to the undoing of beautiful dreams. Many states expect American support. Once the American Uncle started to deliver packages, discontinuation or even limitation of these activities caused resentment.

Economic aid and technical assistance should continue, but the underlying political philosophy must change. Foreign policy is not a game in which one can win by putting some money on most of the numbers. Neither is it a world popularity contest to be won by indiscriminate handouts of foreign aid and technical assistance. The United States should aid the poor nations, but should not throw good money after bad solely for reasons of propaganda. Since American resources are limited, the United States cannot help everybody. Long-range planning is necessary and strict priorities must be established.

One of the requirements of the policy of containment is that we should first strengthen all nations fighting for survival along the perimeter of the Communist Bloc.

Second, we should everywhere help the politically reliable states. Reliability does not mean blind obedience to the United States—those states need not follow American policy through thick and thin—but long-range political compatability should be an absolute requirement.

It is not a good policy to become a benefactor of any country without considering its political attitude. Experience indicates that a "no strings attached" policy might not ultimately prove wise. Without a minimum of social and economic foresight, economic aid and even technical assistance can become a waste of money and resources. Economic aid under such untoward circumstances will have a negative effect because of general disappointment. America should only give aid where there is a reasonable chance for institutional development taking place within the receiving country. In the long run technical assistance is better than economic support and of course much better than handouts.

Latin America is an area of special interest to the United States. As far as economic aid can secure balanced social and political conditions, it is necessary to give more effective aid to most Latin American countries. The Alliance for Progress is a step in the right direction, but its effectiveness depends to a large extent on the strength of constructive political forces south of the Rio Grande. The stabilization of prices for their essential export products would be perhaps more beneficial to most Latin American states than outright economic aid. Brazilian diplomats have pointed out time and again that their country has lost more through the fall in coffee prices than it has gained by foreign assistance. Stabilization agreements, similar to that worked out by the EEC with the eighteen Associated African States, would be needed in Latin American relations as well. But commodity support programs must be contingent upon internal measures, so that added revenue will not increase only the wealth of a small segment of the population, but will make possible the development of national resources and facilitate wide distribution of an increased per capita income. These internal measures would depend on special conditions in individual countries and would probably include modification of the tax structure, agrarian reform, and the integration of particular projects into the wider context of national development plans. This is, of course, the essence of the Alliance for Progress. The tough decisions come when a state does *not* fulfill these conditions, and yet has a generally cooperative government that needs economic help.

Another matter for consideration is our frequent attitude of impatience with political regimes of other countries. American diplomacy should support governments able to carry out social reforms, raise living standards, and promote democratic institutions. But we should accept political realities as they appear in history. The British and continental types of democracy differ from American democracy, and we should not expect the establishment of Western types of democracy overnight in countries with entirely different socio-political backgrounds. The important criterion of American support should be social justice in a political framework which would eventually allow people to rule themselves in harmony with their own traditions.

Most Americans agree that the United States should support democratic regimes, but in practice there are numerous difficulties. In many countries there are no reliable democratic elements. The choices are not between good and evil but between greater and lesser evil. If democratic elements do not exist in a society, democracy is not an alternative.

While in some countries possessing genuine democratic forces the social and economic conditions are balanced and make possible development toward a democratic system, many times this is not the case. It is unrealistic to expect democratic developments in countries which lack balanced economic and social conditions as well as democratic political leadership. In such situations introduction of a democratic system of government should be a long-range proposition and a gradual process. Of course, the United States should help democratic forces whenever possible. But development toward democracy is slow. Truly democratic governments have always been a minority. Corrupt and inefficient governments are most dangerous. In some countries an honest authoritarian or military rule—for a limited time only—is better than a corrupt system which, behind the façade of a democracy, merely offers freedom for a few to exploit the many. The latter system may lead to chaos. Countries which are frustrated socially and economically cannot be trusted. Reliability and honesty of a regime is most important.

The great advantage of Communist propaganda is that, in a world filled with desire for change, communism offers not only almost unlimited and often unscrupulous promises, but also presents the ideal of a system in which man's wants will eventually be satisfied and human dignity will prevail. What is more, communism gives an organizational pattern and a timetable for action, while democracies offer mainly economic help and possibly some general advice.

Western states should fight communism in the sphere of ideas. Even poor people are sensitive about their dignity, and the new nations are yearning for ideas. Many individuals in the new nations, faced with the breakdown of their traditional cultures, are searching for a sense of identity. The Western nations should recognize this critical situation and call the bluff of communism in the philosophical sphere as well as in the realm of politics.

Forceful American opposition to communism has created the false impression abroad that contemporary Americanism is essentially a self-defensive attitude of a selfish and highly materialistic society. Nothing could be farther from the truth. Few men despise well-being, physical comfort, and other material advantages of life, but the basic characteristic of American society is not materialism. Americans feel deeply the situation of others, are not indifferent to human suffering anywhere on the globe, and respond generously to the outcry of those in distress. Not selfishness, but humanitarian action and the principle of helping one's fellow man, particularly the underdog, are characteristic features of the American society.

Western resources concentrated in the North Atlantic area are sufficient to support a reasonable development of Latin America and of the new nations of Africa and Asia. The West probably would be able to solve their economic and related organizational problems.

The task of the West is that of all mankind, to build a world civilization. To this end we must realize a higher purpose than mere material comfort. Between the Western and Communist states, a fundamental question is: which society will concentrate on higher purposes and work for the common good of mankind in a way understood by the multitude on all continents? The

Communists can show spectacular success in military technology and in certain industrial and economic fields. They have presented to the downtrodden of the world a model—tarnished but nonetheless a model—for social and economic development. But man is seldom motivated solely by economic gain. Human dignity is more important. If the Western ideal should become only the affluent society, one affluent in nonessentials, we may lose. If Western man is but a tool-making animal of high order looking only for material comfort, the Communist may win. If in Western societies the individual promotes only his own selfish interests in the name of freedom, world conditions will not improve.

We should recognize and make it clear to the developing nations that some fundamental changes in society are greater in the West than in Communist states. General conditions of life for the workingman improved far more significantly in the United States than in the Soviet Union during the last four decades. Even in the economic sphere, despite substantial Communist gain, the West has clearly demonstrated a superior ability to provide the material needs for man. The real "workers' paradise" came into being in the North American Republic. The contemporary revolutionary process—the idea of equality, large-scale production of material goods, and application of science to the economic field—started and developed rapidly in the North Atlantic area.

## The United Nations

Public confrontation of Western, Communist, and noncommitted nations is taking place in the United Nations before a world audience. The UN represents the contemporary world with all its political divisions and complexities. The General Assembly and other UN meetings constitute a convenient forum where achievements of the West and the negative sides of the Soviet system should be brought up again and again. The force of repetition is great and can be used for Western purposes.

The United Nations has caused many disappointments in the United States, primarily because it was oversold to the American public. Expectations developed which had no basis in the Charter or political conditions of our age. Many official statements since 1945 emphasized that the UN was the cornerstone of American foreign policy. Such statements helped to foster the myth that it was enough to "support" the UN and the big problems of the world could somehow be solved. Victories in General Assembly voting were taken to mean that the United States was winning in international politics. Consequently, the American public has overestimated the effects of UN resolutions and publicity, and even the opinions expressed in UN corridors.

In reality the UN is a meeting place of a divided world; it is one of the theaters where the national interests of many states confront one another. The UN has policy only in a limited sense —if the Secretary-General is a forceful person. Most of the time, the UN is an instrument for the policy of member countries. Its organs and forums are used by national governments for specific political purposes, within the limits of world realities.

The "Uniting for Peace" resolution of November 1950 brought a shift in the structure of the world organization. Although, according to the Charter, the Security Council was supposed to be the "government" of the United Nations, the Soviet abuse of the veto power made the exercise of this function impossible, and the General Assembly became the center of UN diplomacy. The "Uniting for Peace" resolution has made possible the transfer of cases from the Council to the General Assembly whenever a deadlock situation developed in the Security Council. This change has had several important consequences. The change from the traditional unanimity of diplomatic conferences to a two-thirds majority system in the Assembly, combined with equality of voting power of each member state, has created a strange situation. The joint voting power of a small fraction of the world's population could dominate the Assembly through a two-thirds majority. Although the likelihood of such a domination by minority is not great, since most small states depend on some support from the great powers, on some occasions unrealistic political trends may prevail in the General Assembly. Practices amounting to a double standard would dig the grave of the world organization.

One consequence of parliamentary procedures in the UN is that delegations of member states form blocs according to geography, tradition, national background, special interests, and *Weltanschauung*. Even so, with the exception of the Communist states, members of the same bloc may take different positions on issues. In concrete cases much depends on American leadership. Numerically the Afro-Asians dominate the General Assembly, but they form a bloc only on colonialism; otherwise, they are divided on most issues. The Russians have been frustrated in several instances because they could not use the Afro-Asians for their purposes. The Congo and Ruanda-Urundi resolutions are cases in point.

The UN is particularly important to the new nations. It provides a school for diplomacy and parliamentary method in the rough-and-tumble of world politics. It is a place to engage in parliamentary tactics; it teaches the parliamentary ropes. Democracies are for free exchanges, and the UN is an excellent forum for such purposes.

The UN introduced some elements of orderly process into the maze of political changes. While the Communists advocate revolutionary transformation, American interests require a slower pace and a measure of stability. Communists support the greatest possible acceleration of changes—in many cases the direction of change is immaterial to them—because rapid changes lead to upheaval, revolution, and chaos, which, in turn, can be dominated by trained Communist organizers.

Although some of the Western states carry the crippling legacy of colonialism, and divide on important issues, the appeal of economic development in an atmosphere of freedom is greater than the attraction of totalitarian communism. Parliamentary diplomacy offers a new stage where democracies can operate in a familiar environment, where they can compete with Soviet diplomacy. No country is better fitted for open diplomacy than the United States because foreign political questions have been debated in this country since its establishment. Now the debate includes the whole world, where it is also true that "you can't fool all the people all the time." The United States may have much appeal to other nations, but such an appeal should not be taken for granted. Ideas should be promoted by public diplomacy through UN organs in the competition for support of the uncommitted millions.

In the UN, contacts can be made with a greater number of states more easily, and possibly more successfully, than through ordinary diplomatic channels. A great power can ascertain the range of support for a particular policy. The hurly-burly of open meetings need not exclude simultaneous confidential negotiations and consultations. Sometimes gaining time can be the objective of UN debates. Where national emotions are turbulent, pressure can be channeled through debate, while the "quiet diplomacy" advocated and practiced by Dag Hammarskjöld and U Thant may work out reasonable solutions.

All told, parliamentary diplomacy in the UN and action of an energetic Secretary-General provide opportunities and channels for diplomacy that did not exist a few years ago. While the UN is unable to force cooperation between states, it can facilitate it. This new theater for world affairs necessitates blending diplomatic skill with the flair of a politician and mobility of a newspaperman. Immediate rebuttal of Soviet accusations by Ambassadors Lodge and Stevenson in recent years is an example of how publicity in the General Assembly and Security Council supports American policies. In some cases, of course, silence is wisdom.

In many cases it is impossible to ascertain the effects of a UN resolution, but the composition of voters supporting the resolution is important. In the case of cooperation between the two superpowers, a resolution will become effective policy. In many instances there is no showdown between the superpowers, and the case apparently can be settled, as far as the UN is concerned, through a resolution. If one of the superpowers manifests strong opposition, a resolution of the Assembly, even if accepted by a massive majority, is ineffective. Suez and Hungary serve as dramatic illustrations of these alternatives.

Activities of the American delegation in the UN should form part of the essential means for carrying out our policy consistently, and supplement bilateral and multilateral diplomatic actions. Tactical moves in the UN as elsewhere should be directed within the framework of clearly established and defined national foreign policy. Achievement of concordant attitudes in the UN, NATO, and other regional and functional international organizations, and in our bilateral diplomacy, is necessary for effective foreign policy. Harmony in diplomatic procedures and government actions is almost as important as a right policy.

For settlement of important foreign policy problems, bilateral diplomacy and ad hoc congresses, with select participants, remain the normal diplomatic channels. The UN may perform useful functions in several stages of negotiation and facilitate a "cooling off." Agreement must be reached by the states themselves for the UN seldom has power to impose a decision.

The UN does not change the power realities of the contemporary world, nor does it hinder strengthening of the Western Alliance system and, particularly, integration in the North Atlantic area. Most of our difficulties would exist without the UN. The Suez blunder occurred because American policy in effect made common cause with the USSR and turned against the British and the French, who, having lost confidence in American leadership, decided to act independently and without consultation of the American Government. Solution of the Suez conflict was facilitated by the tranquilizing effect of UN action. The Russians have accepted certain arrangements—like occupation of the Gaza strip by UN troops—which otherwise would have been much less acceptable to them. In several other cases a cease-fire and a stand-still was possible through UN channels. These are lessons to keep in mind for the future.

### Some Domestic Considerations

The success or failure of American foreign policy depends to a large extent upon general developments within the United States. A favorable American image in the world cannot be created by speeches not followed by political action. Solution of important domestic problems is one of the conditions for success of American foreign policy. American pronouncements must be in harmony with domestic political realities.

The American system is an attractive form of democratic government, but the attractiveness of democracy can make itself felt effectively only over an extended period of time. Unless the US maintains a leading power-position in the world, the attraction of democracy will not have a chance to prevail. Clear determination in foreign policy, more progress in social affairs and other aspects of domestic policy, and, above all, more up-to-date solutions of social conflicts will be necessary.

The best qualities of the American people are not adequately known in foreign lands and often do not come through in newspaper reports, movies, and in brief contacts with Americans.

Our friends may lose confidence in American policies, and this would have untoward effects in many regions. This is not an academic matter. The fate of many nations depends on American wisdom in international and domestic affairs. Trust in American judgment and ability to contribute to the solution of the problems of the contemporary world is important. Friendly countries realize their future is deeply affected by US political and economic decisions.

A stagnant and aging country could not give an example to a world rapidly developing in social and economic fields. The anomaly would be all the more striking because many foreign countries make progress with the help of American economic aid and technical assistance.

Some domestic reforms would strengthen the power position of the United States and influence the effectiveness of American foreign policy. For example:

1) *Human problems arising from automation and other massive technological changes.* The continuous expansion and diversification of our economy imposes stronger social obligations on all of us and specifically on the Government as well as management and labor. New systems for the solution of labor-management conflicts are needed. Many rules dealing with labor-management relations are obsolete in an atomic age aggravated by the Cold War. Strikes and even inter-union disputes of small groups can paralyze national industries, including industries important for the security of the country. Strikes in missile plants and disputes between the Union of Flight Engineers and the Pilots' Union are cases in point. A new system should provide for a more reasonable and a faster solution of strikes and eliminate them from strategically important industries.

2) *A proper rate of economic growth* in the United States will be important not only from a domestic point of view, but it would greatly increase the strength and flexibility of American foreign policy in world affairs.

3) *A better social security system.* The social security system should expand, but some features of the related legislation should be modified to avoid abuse. Certain requirements for relief should be tightened. But there is an overwhelming case for the extension of medical care provisions and establishment of a reasonable public health system. While the United States is a benefactor all over the globe, social legislation for Americans has been blocked in Congress in such an important field as health. It is ludicrous that legislation less progressive than measures enacted by the German Empire in the 1880's is called socialism. The American social security system, however, should avoid the vast bureaucracies established in European states for similar programs.

4) *Suppression of organized crime in the US.* The situation in some major American cities has few parallels abroad and is extremely harmful to the prestige of the United States.

5) *Civil rights legislation* would strengthen the American moral and political position in world affairs. Still, we should consider this problem in realistic perspective. No matter what the American Government does, criticism of conditions in the United States will continue because the social side of the Negro

question will remain unsolved for the foreseeable future. In these matters there is no feeling of, let alone agreement for, justice in many countries. Some of our African and Asian critics practice racial, class, or caste discrimination in their own countries, but this does not detract from the truth of some of their indictments of our society. Every positive step taken by the American Government in the civil rights field should be publicized as part of a consistent effort to solve the problem of a multi-racial society. It would be particularly important to inform foreign countries of the general progress of the Negro population in the United States in the last decades.

6) *Reform to improve the decision-making process.* There are built-in delaying and complicating factors in the foreign-policy-making machinery of the United States. Over-research and over-administration often replace decisions. People afraid of responsibility postpone decisions, and the complex machinery of a modern government offers many opportunities. There is a point when analysis must end and action follow. In reality, action often gives way to further research, consultation, and conference. Such delays can be tolerated as long as time works for the United States, but the latter situation is not always the case.

Measures should be taken for the elimination of other shortcomings of the American political process which may influence decisions on the highest level in crucial periods. Presidential decisions are prepared by Government agencies. Handling of the U-2 incident and the failure of the 1961 Cuban venture in the Bay of Pigs demonstrated mismanagement and breakdown of executive authority in the first case, and malfunction of the Executive in the second. Malfunctions may occur particularly in the early stage of a new administration. A great power can afford some failures and inadequacies, but there is always a straw which breaks the camel's back.

7) *Congress.* The American nation is fortunate because the flexible American political system has every chance to prevail in an era of world-wide revolutionary change. Congress has on occasion given spectacular examples of the dynamism and flexibililty of the American system in foreign policy. Although in 1939 neutrality legislation was in force, in less than ten years Congress was to accept presidential recommendations which revolutionized American foreign policy. Ratification of the Charter of the United Nations was the first important step. Subsequently, without full Congressional support the Truman

Doctrine, the Marshall Plan, and NATO and the other alliance systems would not have been possible.

But without some overhauling of the Congressional political system it is doubtful if the United States will maintain its leading position in world affairs. Some difficulties originate from the fact that Congress and Congressional committees have many rights without corresponding responsibilities. Archaic Congressional rules and procedures make the situation worse. One example suffices. In the summer of 1962, the Chairmen of the Senate and House Appropriation Committees refused to meet, and so managed to block passage of the annual appropriation bills for several weeks. In light of such episodes, the United States sometimes appears as a huge operetta land where anything can happen.

In some cases, Congressional handling of questions connected with foreign policy has not been in harmony with contemporary requirements and has been harmful to American interests. It is enough to mention the contradiction between bellicose anti-Communist attitudes in Congress and the Congressional refusal to accept effective civil defense legislation. Congressmen who advocate a bold foreign policy which might lead to war, are reluctant to vote measures for the defense of the American people. This attitude manifests serious irresponsibility. The ignorance and complacency connected with civil defense is frightening. The thalidomide scandal forced Congress to strengthen regulations of the drug industry, but it would be too late to prepare civil defense when thermonuclear bombs have begun to fall.

Although most specialists in Soviet affairs agree that the Soviet Union does not want a war, the methods of expansive and subversive Communist policy may lead to an explosion. Soviet installation of missiles in Cuba is a recent example of Communist recklessness. Khrushchev may be a cautious gambler, but he is also a totalitarian ruler who does not understand the strength of a free society, and he may go too far. Once an armed conflict breaks out between the superpowers, the degree of escalation is unpredictable. Things might get out of human control. A full-scale atomic war, though utter madness, is within the range of possibilities. It therefore is a primary obligation of a responsible government to do everything to insure the safety and survival of the largest number of its citizens. It is well known that even primitive shelters saved the lives of many millions in major cities during the Second World War.

Though thermonuclear bombs represent a greater and different danger than conventional weapons, the survival problems are similar.

8) *Reconsideration of the public relations mania in the American political system* would be useful because the United States is threatened by totalitarian dictatorships. Of course, in a democracy even foreign policy, like all major policies, must be decided in harmony with public opinion. But many dangers arise from abuses of publicity in the conduct of foreign affairs.

The worship of public relations is typical of many US institutions which favor making news-gathering by the press as easy as possible. One of the results of this attitude is that it is easier to collect intelligence about strategic planning and military capabilities in America than in most other leading countries. Easy access to important data is harmful to the American national interest. Foreign agents find substantial information in the publications of Congressional Committees, periodicals, and newspapers. Sensitive information is often leaked to newspapermen on purpose, and such abuses are tolerated.

Unnecessary publicity is not part of a thoughtful political process. The Madison Avenue approach to foreign affairs can have grave consequences. It is mistakenly believed that this kind of publicity is a useful part of a democratic system. Publicity did not create pressure for the improvement of our space endeavors. Many newspapers emphasized that we had many more gadgets in the air than the Russians. The public relations approach added tranquilizers to failures, and failures became natural parts of a success story.

To comfort and help the enemy and to discourage America's friends through publicity is not necessary. Secrets can be kept in the American system of government. There was the Manhattan Project, and the landings in North Africa and Western Europe. It is true that it was more natural to keep such secrets during the Second World War than in peacetime, but we are not at peace today. The Kennedy Administration's discreet handling of the Cuban affair in October 1962 was a model of proper conduct in the Cold War. Adverse reactions in the press were characteristic of the worship of publicity.

Undoubtedly, public opinion is of great importance in a democratic system, and in no other country does public opinion have such importance as in the United States. But publicity for publicity's sake can have adverse effects in this dangerous world of ours.

The average man is preoccupied with the daily chores of life, and has little time, interest, or background for forming detailed judgments on complicated foreign political problems. Moreover, there is a tendency in the United States to transfer domestic political experiences to international politics. Americans incline to believe that what is just and reasonable will prevail in international as well as in domestic politics. In the realm of foreign policy *vox populi, vox Dei* is not always true, and this identification can be dangerous. Politicians sometimes expect an uninformed public to give advice to policy-makers even in foreign policy questions. A physician asks the patient to describe his symptoms but not to prescribe the best cure in case of illness.

People elect representatives to study and take a stand on important political questions. It is the Congressmen's duty to transmit essential information to the people. Otherwise, how could the man in the street make prudential judgments? The reply addressed to President Kennedy by the Chairman of the House Armed Services Committee on August 1962 is a revealing document in this respect. He replied to the President's call for Congressional action on the proposed civil defense program. According to press reports, the Chairman explained he did not believe the country was ready for a shelter incentive program. It seems a sorry situation that an uninformed public is used as a scapegoat for Congressional apathy and inaction in a vitally important question.

9) Unless we can overcome our complacency in fundamental political matters and develop a *higher degree of public responsibility*, the American political system cannot act in harmony with the requirements of our age.

When interest groups and public relations men organize a campaign for a specific "cause," Congressmen do not like to fight back; many of them submit to an artificially created public opinion and often vote accordingly. So it may happen that uninformed and misinformed public opinion can mold Congressional attitudes.

The dwindling sense of public responsibility in politics is sometimes disconcerting. Manipulation of public opinion by skilled politicians before elections often creates an unreal political atmosphere. Moreover, creation of an optimistic attitude is the purpose of many communications between the National

Government and the people. If people are told only facts they like to hear, how can a realistic political attitude develop?

Unpopular issues are avoided by politicians in much the same fashion as in Britain and France during the 1930's. The harsh realities of the world in which we live are seldom discussed. This is a poor state of affairs. Irresponsibility of many politicians, newpapermen, and intellectuals is great, not to speak of interest groups and lobbyists. In the formation of Congressional policies, special interest groups frequently prevail over national interests. These groups can hinder such long overdue reforms as establishment of a comprehensive tax system which should facilitate a balanced budget and provide for more defense expenditures, if needed.

One of the subconscious reasons for the somewhat complacent American attitude may be a residue from experience in world conflagrations. Protection of the two oceans, the slow-acting pre-1945 weapons systems, and general political conditions of the world allowed the American nation to have from two to three years for preparation in both World Wars. Although most people realize that in the next conflict this would no longer be the case, their attitude has not changed sufficiently to be in harmony with the requirements of a new situation.

\*     \*     \*

Let me say by way of conclusion that vital foreign policy objectives and commitments should have support of determined political actions and, if necessary, military means. Cuba was a warning and the not-too-distant future might bring the moment of truth in several areas.

The supreme question remains: when and where should American armed forces be used? This can be and should be decided solely by the President not merely for constitutional reasons, but because he is the only man who possesses all factual information necessary for responsible judgments in concrete cases. It is important to make clear that under certain conditions the United States will fight. This is what President Kennedy did in his address to the nation on Cuba on October 22, 1962. Otherwise, armed might, no matter how strong, can be a burden and a liability, not an asset.

Although military strength is important, to have only military superiority would be insufficient. Intellectual, social, political, and economic developments in the United States should remain in harmony with the historic processes of our time.

For the longer run, the battle in the realm of ideas will be decisive. A revolution is taking place all over the world in the minds of the young generation which will direct the affairs of the world in the decades to come. They look for ideas for the solution of their problems, and the West can provide them. The Common Market's association with African states is an example. Active US participation in the OECD and GATT can be useful to the entire non-Communist world. The newly emerged countries have not embraced communism and the Communist system has not subjugated the national genius of the Satellite peoples. Most Satellite nations belong to the West culturally, and even Russia is a partly Western state. What does Khrushchev promise the Russian people? To "overtake" American standards in the 1970's or 1980's. His Twenty-Year Plan aims at catching up with the United States. Today the Common Market alone far outproduces the Soviet Union in most fields, and Common Market policies might influence developments in East Central Europe. The strength of a united North Atlantic area staggers the imagination. And North Atlantic partnership does not imply antagonism toward other regions; it can foster freedom and economic well-being everywhere.

The main aspiration of the developing nations is to attain Western standards of life. Perhaps some contemporary writers are not far from the truth when they claim that we are witnessing a world-wide expansion of the West, possibly the triumph of the West. On the long and arduous road ahead the spirit and courage of brave men ought to prevail.

# Political Requirements

—*GERHART NIEMEYER*

## Summary

*The most probable assumption for future developments of the Cold War is that it will both continue as a protracted conflict and take the form of a series of contests for political objectives, neither of which will be considered decisive. On this assumption, one can base certain general expectations, to wit:*

*a) The Cold War will be conducted aggressively by the Communist forces and defensively by the West, since the West aims at the preservation of the status quo, but the Communists at the destruction of Western society.*

*b) The Cold War will take on the form of a number of concrete conflicts, each of which seems capable of settlement, so that the potential settlement of such conflicts will tend to be confused with an over-all settlement of the Cold War.*

*c) The basic conflict between aggressive communism on the one side and the social order of the Free World on the other will be soft-pedaled by both sides, for different reasons; and both sides will therefore emphasize the possibility of peace with militant communism.*

*d) Disarmament will be continuously negotiated, but the negotiations will not be allowed to succeed, since the Communists need the Western fear of war and the West needs armed strength. But repeated hopes and disappointments regarding disarmament will redound to the disadvantage of the West.*

*e) The favor of colonial and ex-colonial "public opinion" will be courted by both sides, but the result will be that this contest takes the form of a discussion of the West in the colonial and ex-colonial areas.*

*f) Superior strength will be considered very important, in its form of prestige.*

*g) Political operations will aim at political, military, diplomatic, and economic control of key areas in Asia, Africa, and Latin America. In these contests, the United States will directly encounter, not the Soviet Union, but rather local Communists.*

*These expectations can be summed up in two still more general conclusions:*

*As long as the West conducts the Cold War mainly as a defensive operation against what is believed to be Russian power, and mainly with the chief objective of avoiding a new World War, the result will probably be a series of defeats of the United States rather than the Soviets.*

*On the other hand, because the Communists are likely to make blunders and suffer from internal setbacks, the development of the Cold War cannot be predicted, as it were, like a timetable of Communist world conquest. The Cold War will continue to offer open possibilities for a number of years.*

*The Cold War is an unprecedented kind of conflict which we so far have conducted with the wrong kind of conflict theory. Our theories of international conflict have been drawn from nineteenth-century power diplomacy as well as from the twentieth-century pattern of League-of-Nations collective security. The enemy we are facing is, however, not a country but an ideological group in control of a country, or countries.*

*The Cold War requires a new theory of conflict that is applicable to it. A theory of conflict should furnish concepts regarding the opponents, the cause, ends, and means involved in the conflict, and the limits of the conflict. Derived from these basic notions should be such secondary ones as objectives, interests, and termination of the conflict. On this kind of theory one can base principles of strategy.*

*In the Cold War, the opponents are not entities of the same class. On the one side there is the West—a going society defending its existence; on the other side there are the Communists, an ideologically united group with irrational motivations which act destructively as long as they are allowed to exist. Peace in this case means the dissolution of the Communist enterprise as an organization holding any kind of power. The limitation of the conflict—which will be conducted all over the world, wherever there are Communists—is one constituted by the principle of non-intervention in the internal affairs of other countries. The objective is only partially a defense against military aggression. In addition, and chiefly, it is the wresting of political power from the hands of Communists.*

*Our strategy requires the establishment of a list of strategic, political objectives. Tactically, we should equip ourselves with capabilities for political warfare in various parts of the world, including the Free World. The role of Western military strength should be considered as a political as much as a military one. Weaknesses in the enemy's camp offer opportunities which must be exploited. For this purpose, we must have both plans and means available.*

---

## Part One

An investigation into the political requirements of American strategy calls for some assumptions to be made within the range of possible future developments of the Cold War. Theoretically, one can envisage that the Cold War may:

a) culminate in an all-out military showdown between Russia and the United States;

b) take a dramatic turn through a sudden shift in the balance of forces in favor of the East;

c) take a dramatic turn through a sudden shift in the balance of forces in favor of the West;

d) continue for an indefinite time as a slow, protracted contest for territories and other power positions;

e) end through a "settlement" between the United States and the Soviet Union.

Of these possibilities, the first and the last can be eliminated offhand as too improbable. One can and must assume that a military showdown with the Soviet Union will not be brought about by deliberate decision of any US Government. On the other hand, it is unlikely to come as a deliberate decision of the Soviet Union, inasmuch as the outcome of a military contest between the two countries must appear to the Soviet leaders too unpredictable to stake everything on it. Besides, the Communists have been trained to look upon any war as primarily a political process and thus will not attribute to sheer force by itself a predictable political effect, so that a military showdown must be doubly unpredictable in their eyes. The entire pattern of Communist operations has been one of delaying the decisive stroke of violence until its political success is virtually guaranteed on the basis of careful preparations. Thus the Communists, unlike the Nazis, are unlikely to gamble on war as such.

As for a "settlement," one can think of a good many arrangements between the United States and the Soviet Union which might be called by this name but none that would remove the basic cause of hostility. Any "settlement" is likely to be couched in terms of international power politics, whereas the cause of the conflict is the Communist determination to destroy and dismantle the society of the West and subject the peoples of the earth to Communist control. To the West, this hostility may appear in the form of the threat of a foreign national power, but no settlement in terms of the national power interests of Russia and the United States will remove the underlying hostile intent of world communism. Its conflict with the society it has set out to remove cannot conceivably be "settled."

As for a dramatic shift in the balance of forces, it could come as the result either of a technical breakthrough favoring one side over the other, or else of a political breakup either of governments or alliances, again favoring one side over the other. While such developments are possible, they are not so clearly predictable as to warrant the basing of the main assumptions of American strategy on them, although it would certainly be advisable to have emergency strategies in store for such occasions.

Having eliminated four of the above theoretical possibilities, we are left with the one that assumes the probability of a continuing protracted conflict, studded with a series of contests for political objectives, none of which would be considered decisive. In other words, the Cold War must be considered as likely to go on in the same form in which it has for the past fifteen years. Its battles and skirmishes are meant to add up to the victory of one side and defeat of the other, but in a cumulative way. This kind of conflict is an invention of the Communists. The West is inclined to think in terms of either peace or war, and of the present kind of tension as an anomaly that is bound to pass and is capable of being "settled." Thus the Communists are likely to look upon the Cold War with the aim of total victory, and the West with the aim of world peace. One may add the qualification that in the conduct of the Cold War, both sides will seek to avoid all kinds of direct military conflicts. Their basic decision not to seek an all-out military showdown will probably deter them even from limited fighting, since neither side can be sure that any direct military engagement of US and USSR forces can possibly be kept limited. Thus military force is likely to play a marginal role in the Cold War. It is likely to be used as a potency for purposes of intimidation, or directly between powers other than the USSR and the United States. In addition, it is likely to play a decisive role in the final stages of the Cold War, when other measures and maneuvers have prepared its political success.

On the basis of this main assumption, one can essay certain generalizations about the probable conduct of the Cold War:

a) *The Cold War will be conducted aggressively on the part of the Communist forces and defensively on the part of the Western nations.* This follows from the difference of the concept which the two sides have of the conflict. For the Communists, the conflict is that decisive process of human history in which the last class society will be destroyed and a truly human existence will become possible in the emerging new Socialist society. For the West, the conflict is a somewhat exacerbated collision between a nation's power expansion and the order of the status quo. The Communists are likely to look, beyond any partial gains, to the total subversion of the society of Western countries. The West has no idea of destroying the Communist regimes, but simply wants to prevent their expansion, and above all wants to prevent the Communist drive from kindling a world war. The Communists will conduct Cold War operations not primarily as attacks on boundaries, but as flanking and undermining movements against the spiritual, political, legal, psychological, and economic foundations of Western society. The West will not direct any comparable operations against Communist regimes but rather will seek to strengthen its positions by branding the Communists as international aggressors, mobilizing military defensive strength, protecting Western boundaries, and maintaining the unity of a formidable defensive alliance.

b) *The Cold War will tend to consist of a number of concrete conflicts, each of which might conceivably be settled.* The West will tend to identify the Cold War with particular issues since it assumes that such issues represent the power interests of the Soviet Union and of Red China and that the pursuit of these power interests is the true cause of the Cold War. The Soviets will cooperate with the West in focusing attention on particular conflicts since this will enable them to arouse Western hopes that an end to the Cold War is possible and even imminent on certain occasions, thereby reducing Western combative stamina. The West will incline to identify the Cold War with concrete issues because it finds the assumption of an underlying Communist ideological aim of total victory unbelievable, and thus tends to ignore the ideological motivation of Communist policies. The Soviets, by contrast, do emphasize their own ideological motivation but have always known how to convince their opponents that they were at any given stage really interested in some limited objective, the attainment of which would satisfy and appease them. They have always moved from step to step, using concrete issues both as smoke screens and as power bases for further advances. Both sides cooperating in the emphasis on concrete conflicts, the Cold War will appear to the public as consisting of a series of Berlins, Vietnams, Congos, Cubas, Laos', plus such concrete but drawn-out issues as disarmament, nuclear test bans, organization of the United Nations, and world trade.

c) *As a part of the Cold War, both sides will tend to behave toward each other as if no major conflict existed.* The Communists are interested in creating and maintaining the impression that there is no basic conflict because this will induce their opponents to lower their guard and put away their arms, physically and psychologically speaking. The West is interested in pretending that there is no conflict because the West desires above all the return to normalcy and the aversion of war, and believes that these aims can be furthered by the cultivation of mutual "confidence." Both attitudes root in policy patterns of more than forty years standing. The Communists have again and again lulled their enemies into the false hope of a common order of peace, only to avoid an open clash of arms and undo their victims under the cover of a common "legality." The West during the same period has cherished the widespread hope that a world order of peace is about to be realized and can be brought into existence by behaving as if it already were a reality. Thus both sides will from time to time cooperate in pretending that the "tensions have been lessened," that "peoples have learned to understand one another," that "trust and confidence are growing," and that "war is unthinkable." Both sides will also cooperate in concealing an underlying basic hostility and stress the crucial importance of "concessions" for the attainment of world peace.

d) *Disarmament negotiations will continue, but will* not *be allowed to succeed.* Again both sides will cooperate in keeping up this enterprise as well as assuring its futility. In view of the West's predominant interest in avoiding a world war, one of Moscow's major weapons is the repeated war scare. The war scare can have its full effect only if disarmament talks fail again and again, each time painting the effect of failure in more and more horrifying colors. Only if disarmament talks continue can the West be led into the illusory hope that modern warfare could actually be banned by agreement between East and West, and only if they continually fail can parts of the Western public be maneuvered out of their will to use arms in self-defense.

On the part of the West, the prospect of disarmament constitutes a genuine hope based on a spurious expectation, so that Western leaders could not bring themselves to abandon disarmament talks as long as the other side is willing to join in them. But the West, too, will not allow them to succeed, since it cannot find in its heart that degree of political trust in the Soviet government which would warrant the risk of reducing, rather than maximizing, its defenses.

The effects of continued but repeatedly unsuccessful disarmament talks are likely to be corrosive for the West rather than for the East. The hope of disarmament represents the Western idea of a millenium—enduring peace between nations with different forms of government and ways of life. The longer disarmament persists as a millenarian political hope that can be again and again frustrated, the more psychopathic are Western reactions likely to become. Unilateralism, gradualism, and other disarmament-isms will grow into political causes considered to represent the "last and only hope" for mankind. In the Communist world, the millenium is linked with a vision not of peace by agreement, but rather of total victory of the Communist Party. With class war as the dominant assumption and motivation, the Soviets will look on disarmament not as a hope but as a stratagem in the protracted struggle for total power.

e) *The Cold War will be conducted to a large extent as a contest for the favor of public opinion in Asia, Africa, and Latin America.* Both sides hold a concept of these areas as constituting something equivalent to "the people" as distinct from the "ruling classes," on a world scale. The Communists entertain this notion because it is the main thesis of Lenin's *Imperialism, the Highest Stage of Capitalism,* which now dominates Communist strategic thinking. The West derives the same idea from the assumption that there is such a thing as "world public opinion," to which the West tends to concede the ultimate

authority in passing judgment on governments and their conduct, an idea most strongly formulated by Woodrow Wilson.
The Communists thus believe that they can mortally wound the
West if they can win over to their side the areas of the West's
former colonial rule. The West feels that it is under moral and
political criticism from the nations of these areas and feels the
need to rehabilitate and justify itself as part of its Cold War
defense. The contest for the favor of what Toynbee would call
the West's "external proletariat" is likely to take place on the
moral ground of the West, because the Communists aim to
arouse the masses of these people to hostility against the West
rather than to allegiance to the East, but the West does not
similarly aim to arouse hostility against the Communists while
desiring to create an opinion favorable to itself. The contest
is thus one which could be characterized by the formula, "For
or Against the West?" with the result that the West and only
the West is under discussion in the battle for "world public
opinion." Under these circumstances, the Communists are likely
to win more propaganda battles than the West, since the West
is the target of resentment and rebellion in the areas of former
rule.

f) *In other respects, the Cold War is likely to be conducted
as a rivalry for the appearances of superior strength.* As both
sides are interested in avoiding a direct and all-out military
showdown, the prestige of strength is bound to play a great
role in the Cold War. On the part of the Communists, there
is the hope, now explicitly formulated, that the impression of
invincible strength of the Communist camp will be sufficient to
bring about a "peaceful transition to socialism" in a number of
countries. No corresponding hope is entertained in the West,
where the reputation for undefeatable strength is treasured
mainly as a deterrent of a direct Soviet attack and thus as a
means to preserve world peace. Thus again, the attitude of the
West is defensive while that of the Communists is offensive,
although both sides will cooperate in making the rivalry for
prestige of strength an important Cold War operation. The
operation will be conducted through various means, among
which spectacular feats of rocketry and space exploration,
production statistics and other demonstrations of economic
prowess, and displays of political unity will be the most important. Since the Soviets were "behind" and maintain that
they are now catching up to the West, the contest is likely to be
more often successful for them than for the West.

g) *In still another respect, the Cold War is likely to be con-*
*ducted as a series of contests for the political control of various*
*countries in Asia, Africa, and Latin America, between local*
*Communists on the one side and the United States on the other.*
While the political control of the countries of the West, particularly the United States, is the ultimate objective of Communist strategy, the control over countries in the former colonial
areas has been accepted by both sides as probably a decisive,
intermediate step. Here again, the Communists are on the
offensive, and the West is trying to hold its own. There is no
terrain corresponding to the former colonial areas where the
West is seeking to extend its political control at the expense
of the Communists. Thus the contests for territory take place
in the domain of the West. Moreover, they are being conducted
with different weapons. The West has no equivalent of the
Communist Party. There is nothing that could be called a
party of the West, with the possible exception of the free trade
union movement. To the local political organizations of the
Communists, the West can oppose only its own governmental
means of influence, such as economic and military foreign aid,
the deployment and engagement of troops, and trade. Until
recently, these means of power were handled by a number of
different Western governments. The United States has used its
policy to oust from the area of contest the power structures of
Britain, France, Belgium, Holland, and to some extent Portugal.
The task of opposing local Communists in their bid for power
thus has come to rest on the US Government practically alone.
The US Government has sought to put itself in the role of the
champion of local freedom movements. These are often the
same movements which the Communists use. The contest is thus
one between the attractiveness of US help and support and the
organized power of local Communist movements. In these contests, there can be successes only for the Communists since the
United States might be able to prevent Communist advances for
a while but cannot destroy the Communist forces. Where the
Communists do gain decisive influence, they will appear as the
David that has conquered the Goliath. Where the United States
prevails for a while, it will appear as the exponent of militarism
and wealth trying to compel or buy political favor. Permanent
gains for the West would require the permanent presence of
Western military forces in order to discharge the same function
as the Communist Party on the other side.

As a general formula about the probable development of the

Cold War one may essay the following: *As long as the United States conducts the Cold War mainly as a defensive operation against the expansion of Russian power, with the overriding desire to avoid a World War, the result is likely to be a series of defeats for the United States rather than for the Soviets.*

By "defeat" we understand events like the establishment of Communist control in countries such as Laos, Algeria, the Congo, Brazil, Mexico, Iran; the isolation of Western power positions such as Berlin, Formosa, Turkey; the ousting of Western influence from countries such as Saudi Arabia, Thailand; the ousting of governments which were firmly on the Western side; the admission of Communists to coalition governments in countries where Communists were previously beyond the pale; or the joining of non-Communist mass movements with Communist groups under Communist leadership. One cannot assume, of course, that the Communists will be able to attain every one of these objectives whenever they so desire. Quite frequently, they will try and fail. But as long as the United States aims at "successes" consisting in nothing more than keeping the Communists from gaining such objectives, our defensive "successes" are bound to be partial as well as temporary and can never be booked as genuine defeats of Communist forces. Communist achievement of such objectives, on the other hand, must be considered real defeats for the United States in the sense that the Communists can count on maintaining the positions they have thus won, and need not fear any US effort to undo them. In this sense, it is reasonable to expect in the Cold War a series of US defeats rather than defeats of the Communist enterprise.

The question arises whether (and, possibly, when) the cumulative effect of a series of US defeats will add up to something like a final victory of the Communists in the Cold War. If one US defeat were to follow another, and if each reinforced the political and psychological effects of the previous defeat, one would have to predict the total surrender of the United States within not more than fifteen or twenty years. But such an assumption cannot be realistically entertained, for a series of Western defeats is likely to be interrupted by countervailing effects of Communist blunders or Communist political calamities. One other theoretical alternative to the thesis of eventual total defeat of the West should be dismissed entirely, however—the wistful hope that the mere passage of time as such is likely to transform communism from an enterprise of destruction and subversion into one of construction and cooperation. There are those who manage to believe that even though the Communists would reap success after success, a long duration of the Cold War would sap them of their revolutionary energy so that at the end of their series of successes they would no longer entertain the desire for conquest of the West, but only the will for the good life at home. There is no historical evidence to give even a shred of support to such a notion. Time, of course, does in a sense affect all human goals. *But it may be a very, very long period of time before communism ceases to be what it is now.* The aggressiveness of Islam, after all, was maintained for about a thousand years. As far as communism is concerned, the third generation of Communists is coming to power in Russia with a spirit no less aggressive and expansive than that of the first, while in China, communism has established a second power center of its enterprise in which the first generation is also ready to hand the gun to its successor, and in Cuba and Africa, new centers of Communist militancy have sprouted. The total record since 1917 is one of increasing and spreading, rather than of ebbing, revolutionary *élan*.

Communist blunders, however, are indeed bound to interfere with the cumulative effect of Communist successes. The most significant Communist blunders in the past have consisted in moves which have hardened rather than softened Western determination to resist. Such blunders occurred in Berlin in 1948, Korea in 1950, and Cuba in 1962. Increased Western unity, Western determination, and Western armed preparedness has been the result in each case. The Communists will not be able to avoid repetitions of such blunders, because their very successes will tempt them to overestimate their own strength. They can always be counted upon to overreach themselves from time to time, and each time will undo the effect of some previous successes. Nor will the Communists escape political calamities in their own camp. Death of their leaders will always throw them into a deep crisis. Political rebellion will rear its head. Khrushchev and Tito will die before long. A political crisis in China is not unlikely. Another explosion may occur in East Germany.

Such events will set the Communist offensive back. But the setbacks will not be turned into Western successes. The immediate reason is that the United States is never ready with a plan to capitalize on suddenly-occurring enemy weaknesses. Nor will it do to attribute this unpreparedness to ineptitude. The United

States has its full share of talent and even genius among planners of policy and strategy. If we have no plans to take advantage of the enemy's moments of weakness, it is because we have inhibited ourselves from advancing at the enemy's expense. In other words, we have limited ourselves to the defense, and are not contemplating the enemy's defeat in the same sense in which the enemy aims at our defeat. We rather incline to stand back when the enemy suffers from internal difficulties, possibly in the hope that by this kind of conduct we can reassure him of our basically peaceful intentions. Thus there will be opportunities for Western successes over the Communists, but, with the presently prevailing attitude toward the Cold War, the United States will continue to miss them. All the same, the opportunities for Western advances will interrupt the series of Communist successes again and again and introduce the quality of open possibilities into the Cold War.

To the above-stated general formula about the Cold War one should therefore add the following qualification: *The long-range development of the Cold War cannot be logically predicted. To the series of Western defeats one cannot impute a timetable for the Communist conquest of the West. The development will continue to offer open possibilities, if not forever, for a period that cannot be limited to just a few years.*

**Part Two**

The analysis adds up to the judgment that the United States has had the wrong approach to the situation. If we desire security, we have not obtained it. If we are interested in peace, we have not secured it. If we are committed to defending our friends and certain territories, we have not been able to do so effectively. If we intend to dissuade the enemy from his hostility toward us, we have singularly failed.

The Communists approach problems of policy through a hierarchy of concepts which they call Theory—Strategy—Tactics. It is submitted that, in a formal sense, this is a valid approach, and that there can be no strategy unless there is an underlying theory, and no tactics unless there is a strategy. Our national strategic concepts have not been devoid of a theory. But we have not given any attention to the theory on which we have been operating, with the result that we are relying on theoretical concepts derived from past ages and befitting different situations. Actually, our theoretical concepts of international politics have been derived from two theories which, though opposed to each other, are combined in our thinking and planning about policy.

The first of these is the theory of international power politics which was elaborated during the 19th century, has found literary expression in the leading 19th century textbooks on international law, particularly Oppenheim, and was articulated in the United States particularly by President Theodore Roosevelt. It looks on the world scene in terms of power rivalries focusing on boundaries, spheres of influence, armaments, prestige, and relative shares of trade.

The second is the theory of a world order of peace through collective security and the orderly peaceful settlement of international disputes which was elaborated early in this century, and which has found institutional expression in the League of Nations and the United Nations. In the United States it was articulated above all by President Wilson, but was echoed strongly by President Franklin D. Roosevelt and his Secretary of State, Cordell Hull. This theory causes policy to focus on the problem of aggression, conceived on the analogy of a disease that can be overcome by isolating (or "quarantining") the aggressor and curing him of his "abnormal" intent.

While these two are the theories underlying our view of international conflicts, we also have theories guiding our policy apart from conflict. One pictures the development of the world in the direction of a growing equality of all nations in cultural progress. Another one looks upon the present time as one destined to "liquidate imperialism." A third one postulates the real existence of a world public opinion before which the governments of the world must justify themselves. The critical exposition of these underlying theories is a task that cannot be undertaken within the framework of a short paper of this kind. Moreover, we are referring here only to the theory of conflict as applying to the US conduct of the Cold War.

The prevailing theories of conflict, whatever their merits or demerits may be intrinsically, have to do with the problem of national power in its relation to other national powers and to the entire pattern of international relations in the world. It is submitted that the prevailing theories do not fit the conflict in which we find ourselves at present, for this conflict is caused by a political movement attacking not merely the power of nations, but the entire social order of these nations. It is a conflict that cannot be understood and conducted through theories concerning merely international conflict.

A theory of conflict furnishes concepts regarding the opponents, the nature of the conflict (causes, ends, means, losses to be feared, and gains to be desired), and limits of the conflict (distinction of areas of life involved in the conflict from others which are not). Derived from concepts regarding the nature of the conflict are concepts regarding one's own conduct in the conflict, such as objectives, interests, and termination of the conflict. Again derived from these are concepts of strategy.

The peculiar difficulty about the Cold War is that, unlike most conflicts, it does not involve two sides of the same class. On the one side is an ideological movement considering itself engaged in a protracted and irreconcilable struggle with the forces of "capitalism" which it considers concentrated in the United States. This movement is in itself an historical curiosity, for it is both an ideological group competing with others through methods of domestic politics (although not within the traditional limitation of these methods) and also an entity using the power resources and policies of nations. Thus it partakes of the characteristics of nations and of those of parties but cannot be described as either. It resembles, if anything, the movement of the Taborites (Hussites) in the 15th century who were a religious sect with a fixed territory, a standing army, and an irresoluble quarrel with the rest of the world.

The Communist movement cannot and must not be identified with Russia, even though it uses Russia as its chief instrument of power. What confronts us in the present conflict is not the nation Russia with its power interests, but rather a militant enterprise with a revolutionary design of destruction. This design creates a political interest of its own, an interest not merely in the reduction of the power of other nations, in the change of boundaries and spheres of influence, but beyond this in the disintegration and destruction of Western society as an order of life. This is not merely the ultimate objective, but also an operational objective of Communist conflict management. The conflict thus is not between interests of national power, but between a totalitarian subversive movement of a number of extant societies, with national armaments and national foreign relations figuring as prominent, but nevertheless only partial, means and ends. The use of national power on both sides creates the deceptive impression that the opponents are entities of the same class. In truth, they belong to different classes and cannot be compared with each other.

This conflict does not resemble anything that we have experienced in our national history and does not fit the categories of our established theories of international conflict. The difference can best be grasped when one considers the conceivable end of the conflict. In the 19th-century theory of international relations, the end to a conflict was envisaged as a treaty of peace that would be concluded between both sides, both remaining in existence as entities, although their relative rank as powers might be modified by the contest. The treaty of peace would once again initiate normal relations and, in due course, mutual respect between the contestants.

The 20th-century theory of collective security looked for an end to a conflict to some kind of situation through which the aggressor had been frustrated and taught a lesson in international rational behavior, and the other nations of the world gained an increment of confidence in collective security as an instrument of peace. Again, all participants would still exist at the end of the conflict, even though the system of their interrelationship might have undergone a progressive development.

In the present conflict, the Communists do not envisage the continued existence of their opponents after the conflict has ended. Nor is their vision an equivalent of the age-old concept of conquest: the dominion over a foreign people which, as such, would continue to exist, even though in subservience. What the Communists envisage instead is the complete dissolution of the social entities they attack. At the end, there would only be the total power of the Communist Party engaged in cleaning up the last remnants of traditions, and changing people and their relations into something completely different from their present existence.

The term "peace" as a terminating point of conflict in our sense thus simply has no meaning for the Communist enterprise. For them, the conflict must continue (as a "protracted struggle") beyond the point where Communist power is established over a society, until the (improbable) day when man's nature supposedly will have been changed. In view of this Communist determination to maintain their hostile intent ad infinitum, it does not make sense for the defending societies to envisage a traditional peace as a terminating point at which the former relations of combat will turn into normal relations of live-and-let-live. It takes only one party to make a war, but two to make peace. A movement with the kind of ideological attitude toward the world that the Communists have, however, cannot ever be at peace with people it does not control. Against such a movement, one must continue the struggle until it is dispersed, or thoroughly demoralized, or isolated to the point of political impotence.

## Part Three

After identifying the two dissimilar opponents—the Communist enterprise on the one side, and the Western societies as going concerns on the other—one can begin to re-examine the theories underlying our strategies, and recast our thinking to fit a conflict with the movement of destruction which also employs military and foreign policy means of national power.

Present strategic thinking in the West clearly reflects the underlying idea that the conflict is over extension of national power and its most catastrophical development would be the outbreak of all-out nuclear war. Our national courses of action envisage the ultimate danger of a Soviet military attack on the West and are conceived as means to dissuade the Kremlin from attempting such an attack. If successful, they will indeed prevent nuclear war. Since Communists have not been in the habit of destroying other societies mainly by means of war, such strategies obviously do not address themselves to the conflict with communism but only to the total-war possibility which is one of its aspects. It is true that deterrence strategies are passed off as methods of dealing with the Communist threat in its entirety. If one looks closer, though, one finds that the strategies are spelled out only to the point where our power is adequate to the purpose of deterrence, and merely add as a kind of wishful afterthought the hope that from then on, the Communist threat will begin to fade.* The causal link between the full achievement

---

* Thus it is said that, if we can prevent an all-out attack long enough, communism is bound to lose its revolutionary *élan*, an assumption based on a single precedent, that of the French Revolution. Even there, however, what happened was not that revolutionary leaders regained their sanity but that they rather lost their heads at the hands of non-revolutionary elements which, after only two years of terror, still happened to be around and capable of concerted action. Again, those who demand that we positively out-arm the Soviets put their hope in subsequent "negotiations for peace," without telling us how one can negotiate peace with a totalitarian enterprise. Still others want us to "put our own house in order" so that the Communists, discouraged, finally will "give up their goal." Communists, in this sense, do not have a "goal" but rather a world view in the light of which they claim their enterprise as the only one that can possibly make sense out of history. A world view, however, is not given up merely from practical disappointment.

of our strategic purposes and the end of the Communist threat has never been argued in practical and realistic terms. It is clear that our thinking has focused on the military thrust of the Soviet Union as if that were the gist of the danger threatening us and has neglected the full dimensions of the real conflict which include the danger of a non-military victory of the Communist enterprise.

A more appropriate view comprehends that we are in conflict with Communists rather than with nations or a nation, that is, with an enterprise now including about thirty-five million people who, obsessed by political irrationality, manage to keep the entire world in fear and disorder. As Communists, they maintain an implacably hostile attitude toward the rest of the world by means of intra-Party ideological discipline and a combination of persuasion with force. Communists in possession of organized power thus are always a threat. They cease to menace others only as they cease to be Communists. This should be the fundamental concept of our assessment of the conflict.

Possibly the most difficult theoretical problem is that of the limits of this kind of conflict. Every human conflict has its limits; some areas or aspects of human life always remain unabsorbed by the necessities of the struggle. Where, in this case, is the line to be drawn? The traditional theory of power conflict between nations circumscribed the area of struggle in terms of military requirements, beyond which it assumed a realm of relative peace. In the Cold War, this concept can no longer apply. The enemy is a militant ideological movement spread over the entire world and perverting all aspects of human life to its power strategies. Thus we can hardly recognize any geographical limitation of the conflict, since we shall have to fight Communists everywhere in the world. Nor can we except any areas of life (such as trade, science, art, sports, tourism) from the realm of struggle, since a totalitarian enemy uses all of them as means of power. Nevertheless, a limitation of the conflict is possible and imperative. The struggle against the Communist enterprise does not require that we busy ourselves with the correction of other peoples' political, legal, or economic systems. The struggle against communism may be world-wide and cover all areas of human life, but precisely because of this total extension it must not be handled as a crusade to establish everywhere democracy, free enterprise, or the Western way of life. It should be limited by confining it to a negative purpose: the ousting of Communists from seats of power.

An appropriate theory of the conflict also requires a re-thinking of the notion of peace. Traditionally, we have thought of peace as an aspect of politics among nations. That concept has no meaning in the present situation, as we have seen. Never-theless, every fight must aim at peace in some sense. Peace with Communists is unthinkable, as Communists are people whose ideological obsessions prevent them from living at peace with anyone, even each other. In this respect, our peace can consist only in total victory. Total victory over a destructive element *within* nations should not be morally equated with total victory *over* nations, which is an evil design. But the destruction of communism as an effective political power can and must be achieved for the sake of peace, that peace within and among na-tions which organized communism is bound again and again to disturb. As we fight communism, we must strongly emphasize our commitment to peace with all nations, even those now subject to Communist rule, as well as our peaceful disposition to one another in the societies of our own traditions. We cannot pro-claim that notion of peace and friendship among citizens and nations if we also assure the Communists of our good will—the Communists who conduct even the office of government as a process of perpetual warfare against their own subjects. The commitment to the kind of peace that is the alternative to the present struggle requires uncompromising hostility to those who are fundamentally peaceless and hostile, the Communists.

### Part Four

If the above remarks on a theory of the conflict are sketchy and tentative, the following observations on strategy must be even more provisional. They serve to raise questions rather than to provide answers.

We have seen that our present strategies are deterrence strate-gies rather than Cold War strategies. Deterrence is certainly an indispensable element in any Cold War strategy, but it can be no more than a part. Beyond that part, which has been very well elaborated, we have no strategies addressed to the problem of dealing with the Communist threat as such. The vague hopes that, having achieved deterrence, the Communist threat will somehow go away cannot be called strategies or even part of strategies. This is not the same as saying that those hopes neces-sarily must be false. It is, of course, possible that the Communist danger will wane of its own accord. But as long as it has not done so, we cannot excuse ourselves from the task of figuring out what our Government should do about it.

In a true Cold War strategy, the holding of certain lines as geographical boundaries can be considered only as a part of the entire operation. In addition, there are institutional and psychological power positions that must be conceded comparable importance. Similarly, military force should not be considered a decisive instrument of policy. An act of force, even if wholly successful, will do no more than open a breach. Against an opponent that is not a nation but an armed ideological enterprise, force alone cannot win permanent gains. The action of arms must always be considered in combination with political, educational, and organizational measures aiming at the isolation and total political discreditation of the enemy, a goal that can very well be approached in piecemeal fashion.

If we develop a more appropriate theory of the conflict in which we are engaged, and if we accordingly focus on the thirty-five million organized Communists as the enemy whom we should defeat, our strategy would shift from a defensive to an offensive one. The defensive function of deterrence would become a mere part of a wider plan to evict Communists from all kinds of positions of power. The strategy would be based on two axioms: (a) the Communists are entrenched in formidable positions of total power in Russia and China; (b) Communists are a small minority of the population everywhere, and, apart from some non-Communist countries, are not supported by widespread allegiance to their Party or to their ideology. The eviction of Communists from all positions of power is therefore not an impossible objective, but the attainment of the objective requires a long, drawn-out process of loosening the reins of power which are now firmly in Communist hands.

Power is the ability to command people and obtain their obedience, and the majority of people even in Communist-ruled countries are not Communists. The new strategy concept would thus no longer center exclusively on the problem of military aggression but rather on that of political power. It would inspire a concept of method that aims at the roots of such political power as the Communists possess in different countries and different situations. The method would necessarily consist in a combination of force, organization, legislation, and education. Intermediate objectives would consist not merely in pushing

Communists out of some position of power now held by them, but also in making that position impervious to any new Communist attempt to reoccupy it.

The theater of the struggle would be global, and the Western countries would not be excluded. While the ultimate goal is to disorganize, discredit, and disestablish the Communist Party, the pursuit of this goal must be governed by considerations of feasibility, and the greatest advances are obviously possible where Communists are politically weakest. There it is possible to infiltrate and to disband their organizations, to deny them the legal status of a bona fide party, and to promote campaigns of anti-Communist mass education. In countries where this is politically not possible and where Communists enjoy the advantages of organizational influence and mass sympathies, anti-Communist organizations must be created and equipped with effective instruments of propaganda. Their aim must be to get the governmental means of power committed to their side and to render any Communist political activity as difficult as possible. No advance of this kind can be considered permanent unless it culminates in thorough education, above all of the intelligentsia, about communism and its evils. The discrediting of the Communists is the sole blow that can be called ultimate.

The United States as a nation can promote such political processes by committing its support to any anti-Communist party of another country, regardless of political program. Among several anti-Communist parties, US support should be given to the most influential and effective one. It should be made clear that the United States does not identify itself with any domestic program of the parties it thus supports, and that it considers the domestic policies of foreign countries the responsibility of those countries' citizens. US national interests in these matters should be confined to the cause of evicting Communists from power. The indifference of the United States about domestic political affairs of other nations should go to the point where the United States refuses even to object to the retaining of the economic and social system introduced by Communist rulers, provided that the Communist Party is ousted from power.

The principle of non-intervention in the political choices of other peoples is so important that it would be worthwhile to undertake action against some Communist regime for the main purpose of demonstrating that the Communists as such, and not a political or economic idea, constitute the target of US strategy. Once the Communist rulers of, for instance, Albania or Cuba are ousted by appropriate action, including force, the United States should allow these countries to retain whatever amount of socialism they please. Against the background of such a demonstration, US support of anti-Communist parties would be less likely to be misinterpreted. Another aspect of the same strategy would be to give official recognition only to anti-Communist organizations. This would involve a recognition policy which would on principle recognize only anti-Communist governments of any country, even if such governments exist only in exile. A corresponding labor policy would instruct labor attachés to deal only with anti-Communist free trade unions.

As a part of the same attempt clearly to pinpoint the target as the peaceless Communist enterprise, the United States should define Communists, not only in terms of their ideas, but also in terms of their loyalty to the enterprise begun by Lenin and centered in Lenin as its chief authority. As it is not inconceivable that something like a "polycentric" communism might develop, all loyalties to centers of Communist power and leadership should be treated alike, even though we may also attempt to play off the various parts of the Communist enterprise against one another.

There should be a list of partial US objectives in various parts of the world, ranked in terms of their attainability, adding up to a complete strategy. The objectives may range all the way from free passage throughout Berlin to the eviction of the Communist Party from the Kremlin. It should distinguish key positions from others which have mainly propagandistic significance. Distinctions should also be established regarding the parts of population in various countries and their significance in the struggle. Obviously, greater strategic significance should be accorded to the population behind the Iron Curtain. More efforts should be made to counteract Communist penetration of the intelligentsia, particularly in Japan, India, and Latin America. Populations of strong religious beliefs should be considered our natural allies, as should rural populations with private property holdings.

At this point, a word may be in order about tactics. While a few of these strategic concepts have already gained currency in our policy, their tactical supplementation is almost invariably inadequate. Our propaganda uses mostly the grapeshot rather than the rifleshot, spraying the shot as it leaves the barrel. What is more, it is believed that propaganda alone will have significant political effects. All the masters of propaganda insist, however, that propaganda is effective only if followed up by organization which in turn provides a basis for further propaganda. Perhaps ugly parallels to totalitarian rule would be avoided if one puts the sequence in this form: propaganda—organization—education.

Another tactical device of which we seem never to have heard may be called that of political pursuit. Pursuit of a beaten enemy force is part of the military primer. In political warfare, we have repeatedly beaten off a Communist attack or inflicted setbacks on the Communist forces, only to see the enemy return at a different time, in different ways, but with the same intent, and this time with success. Great care should be given to the task of making any partial gain politically as secure as possible. In the field of guerrilla warfare, we seem to be learning this lesson in Vietnam. In political warfare, we have yet to become aware of the problem. Curiously enough, it is a part of the struggle in which the Communists are at a distinct disadvantage. Communist rulers can never be secure, as they themselves know very well. By contrast, a government rooted in its people's traditions, and sharing with its citizens the most important values, can be made secure against Communist infiltration for an indefinite time, particularly when military and diplomatic devices are added to the domestic power arrangements of security.

In view of these strategic and tactical tasks, new types of forces should be developed by the United States. The Peace Corps was a good idea, but its members should, in addition to their present training, also receive thorough education in the ideology and methods of, and possible counteraction to, communism. The bill concerning the Freedom Academy should be passed, and the Freedom Academy should train students from foreign countries for anti-Communist propaganda, organization, and legislation. One may think of a corps of highly dedicated, highly trained specialists who would infiltrate the satellite countries and there form sleeping cadres for purposes of intelligence, sabotage, and eventual leadership. In addition to the unconventional warfare units of the armed forces, we need equally well-trained volunteer groups, consisting of both US citizens and citizens of captive nations. West Germany is putting its high school teachers, public attorneys, administrators, labor leaders, and journalists through a program of education about communism which is administered by highly qualified professors, and which produces a knowledgeable body of intermediary civic leaders. The German example should be imitated, under our prodding, in as many free countries as possible. The experience of the American trade unions in fighting Communists has been utilized far too little for training purposes. There is need for a kind of Interpol regarding Communists and their activities. There is similar need for interparliamentary discussions about anti-Communist legislative devices.

One should not pretend that such operations as are possible with these means and methods would suffice to oust the Communists from their power positions in Russia and China. For the impatient, force is the only method which will accomplish that. We should, however, allow our enemies, the Communists, to teach us the lesson that military strength is a function of political power, and that political power rests on spiritual, psychological, and intellectual foundations.

As long as the Communists have missiles and nuclear weapons, it would be folly to precipitate a military showdown with them. But is it quite possible to gnaw away at the cement of allegiance and loyalty which permits the Communists to issue commands to those who handle such weapons? In other words, it is possible progressively to isolate the Communists in the world to the point where they have nothing but brute force left to compel obedience? Again, the Communists have themselves greatly facilitated this undertaking, as they regard themselves as a "vanguard" that cannot entertain any common values with non-Communist populations. The self-willed alienation between the Communists and the rest of the world until now, has not been politically exploited by our side. It is conceivable that this alienation may be pushed and intensified to the point where the Communists find it increasingly difficult to contemplate the use of military force that would require the sustained support of wide masses.

The power of communism will end when factions within the Communist Party begin to fall out openly with one another. Past experience suggests that this is more likely to happen when the Communists face crucial but difficult choices in which either alternative seems equally fraught with danger. In other words, it is under pressure of events or outside forces that Communist disunity is most likely to develop. Western preference for one of the contending sides would not only make no difference, but might lead to a slackening of the outside pressure and then to a reconsolidation of Party unit. At most, the West can hope to influence events within the Communist Party through infiltrated agents. One should expect that the very fact of disunity in leading Party circles will set in motion popular forces of rebellion which would in all probability produce their own political leadership. At that point, but only at that point, Western help is decisive. It would matter little whether it is massive or token help. In either form it would encourage the upsurge of anti-Communist oppositional forces against which the small band of Communists could not hold out very long. In this kind of situation, Western military power is bound to play an auxiliary but nevertheless indispensable political role.

# Vehicles of Political Strategy

—*ARNOLD WOLFERS*

## Summary

*Nations can attain their objectives in foreign policy only if they possess means or vehicles that permit them to threaten and inflict punishment or to promise and grant benefits. The former inevitably dominate in the direct confrontation with enemies and can be called instruments of power politics; the latter, the means of influence politics, are almost exclusively used in dealings with allies and non-aligned nations where they become means in the indirect confrontation or competition with enemies. Military force and alliances constitute the chief coercive vehicles, but they are supplemented by the means of adversary diplomacy, hostile propaganda, subversion, and economic pressure, all potentially capable of imposing considerable constraints.*

*In view of the present position of the United States it is not surprising that most of its means of policy, military and non-military, coercive and non-coercive, are monopolized by the demands of the Cold War.*

*How much the United States and its allies need in the way of coercive means depends on the objective they pursue in the Cold War. As of today, it can be assumed that their goal is to deter further Communist expansion and to this end to establish and preserve an East-West balance of power. Even those who advocate going beyond this defensive goal do not call for an offensive* **military** *policy.*

*The objective of equilibrium on all levels of military confrontation—though far more modest than the goal of supremacy necessary to destroy the opponent—turns out to make formidable*

269

*demands on the United States. While the US strategic deterrent gives security against a direct attack on the American homeland, its value for the protection of Europe and America's other overseas allies and friends is declining as the credibility of the US threat to intervene with nuclear force for the defense of its allies recedes. Yet, the irony is that America's vital interest in protecting itself against the indirect threat of a Communist takeover of Eurasia was the original cause of the massive rearmament and alliance policies pursued by the United States since the late forties; the American homeland became vulnerable to direct attack only at a later date.*

*How to remedy the growing deficiency of a predominantly nuclear defense posture as a means of "extended deterrence" and defense is a matter of grave controversy especially among the members of NATO, with some European countries plugging for a supplementary European nuclear deterrent capability, the United States urging a build-up of conventional forces coupled with an increase in the counterforce capacity of its strategic force. Barring the early emergence of a highly centralized single European political authority capable of placing a single finger on the nuclear button, the best solution may lie in American accommodation to the idea of moderate national European deterrents in return for substantial European efforts in the conventional field.*

*In Asia the US strategic deterrent will be caught in the same process of erosion unless a break occurs between Red China and the Soviet Union which would deprive the former, for a long time to come, of an effective nuclear umbrella. The non-nuclear military imbalance in favor of the Communists is most serious along the southern borders of the Soviet Union but will also continue in the areas adjoining Red China until the non-Communist nations there achieve more unity and do more in the conventional and subconventional field to supplement the power the United States can project into the area, chiefly by means of its naval and air forces.*

*In the field of non-military vehicles of constraint the non-Communist camp, despite its initial handicaps, should at least be able to match its opponent. Communist propaganda has been strikingly ineffective when addressed to the "capitalist" countries and has not succeeded, so far, in the important struggle for the amity or non-enmity of the underdeveloped countries—the indirect East-West confrontation—in drawing any country except Cuba into the "Socialist camp." With respect to economic com-*

*petition the West has striking potential advantages, including the advantage of being able to step up its expenditures for armaments and foreign aid to a point at which the Communists may find it impossible to stay in line.*

*Looking toward the future, the tenuous East-West balance of today could conceivably give way either to Western or to Communist supremacy. If this should not happen and the trend toward a more stable nuclear stalemate persists, the Communists, still facing the threats of escalation, of technological breakthroughs in favor of their opponents and of exhaustion in a stepped-up arms race, might in time recognize the hopelessness of their ambitions to make the world over in the Communist image. After losing their expansionist dynamism they might open the way for a tolerable East-West modus vivendi that would permit the United States, with reasonable security for itself and its overseas allies, to wait patiently until the superiority of its values and institutions—measured in terms of the essential demands of human nature—could assert itself.*

In line with the general subject of the Conference and the specific topic of discussion of the panel for which this paper is designed, chief attention will be focused on the vehicles of *American* political strategy. However, by way of introduction I propose to say something about policy vehicles in general, hoping thereby to prevent subsequent misunderstandings about the terms I shall use and about the conceptual framework within which my arguments will be placed.

The term "vehicles," which was suggested to me, will be taken to be synonymous with means of policy, in contradistinction to policy goals or objectives. This distinction is indispensable for the analyst although it can be treacherously misleading if taken to mirror reality. What are means in one situation are likely to be objectives or proximate goals in another; moreover, means and ends are interdependent. Nothing is more deceptive than the idea that policy goals can be chosen without regard to the means that are—or can be made to be—available to attain them; means, in return, cannot be evaluated except with an eye to the specific purposes they are intended to serve. Because of this fundamental interdependence it will be impossible in this

The vehicles of policy at the disposal of nations or govern-
paper to avoid transgressing into the field of objectives, which
form the subject of another paper. I would hope that in return
the paper dealing with American objectives, actual or desirable,
will not pass lightly over the question of whether they are within
the means with which the United States can pursue them.

ments form a most heterogeneous assortment of instrumentalities, ranging from massive military forces to such means of
soft pressure or sheer enticement as economic aid and the skills
of diplomatic negotiators. So different are they from one another
that it may be asked whether they have enough in common to
merit being included under the same label; the answer is in
the affirmative. All foreign policy depends on the ability to get
other nations to do what one wants them to do or to desist from
doing what one does not want them to do. A vehicle of policy is
anything, then, that gives a nation some element of such ability.
A naval blockade, a nuclear threat, a grant of aid, a summit
meeting are or are not vehicles of policy depending on whether
they offer a reasonable chance of affecting the behavior of others
in line with one's own goals. Their value as vehicles depends,
however, not merely on the benefit they promise but also on the
sacrifices their use demands relative to the costs of alternate
means.

The reason why some vehicles appear so far removed from
others, if not incongruous with them, lies in the fact that nations
can be moved in principle both by the threat or infliction of
deprivations and by the promise or grant of gratifications. The
contrast between these two modes of affecting behavior justifies
a distinction between power politics and influence politics, the
former to mean the use predominantly of constraint, the latter
the use predominantly of persuasion. The inclusion of the word
"predominantly" in these definitions is necessary because some
degree of both constraint and persuasion is present in practically
all policies. No strings need be attached explicitly to grants of
foreign aid in order to put the recipient under some pressure,
especially if he wishes to qualify for more aid in the future, and
nuclear weapons, coercive as they can be, would have little value
as means of policy if they did not also have a highly persuasive
deterrent influence.

As a rule, where relations are inimical, primary reliance must
be placed on means that are capable of hurting the opponent.
Negotiations, e.g., are likely to produce advantageous results

only if the opponent is made to fear the effects of not making concessions. Among friends, on the contrary, the mere hint of a threat of penalties may destroy the existing amity and thus produce negative results. Because enmity calls for constraint, it pushes both parties to a conflict toward much reliance on such highly coercive means as armaments and military alliances, and toward a concentration of effort and resources on them.

The interdependence between means and objectives of policy, which was mentioned earlier, raises some ticklish problems. It is tempting to indulge in visions of the kind of a world one would like to see emerge—a world free of tyranny, for instance—and to conclude, without further investigation into the means, that such visions should be translated into policy goals. The trouble is that they may be beyond the reach of practical policy or not be worth the sacrifices their attainment would demand. One can, of course, criticize or may seek to influence the prevailing value patterns of a society that decide what is or is not worth the costs of any specific action; but no government, not even the most dictatorial, can ignore them and yet hope to succeed. Any isolated consideration of the goals, then, tends to cloud the issue of restraints imposed by the lack of the means indispensable for success. The statement that some specific objective is an absolute "must" is worthless, if meant literally, for the policy-maker who has to remain within actual possibilities.

To discuss the means separately from the goals, or to devote primary attention to them, can be a source of grave error too. Some means, such as nuclear weapons systems, look exceedingly impressive and, considered in isolation from the specific services they are expected to render under specific circumstances, prepare one little for the frustrations a government equipped with large nuclear forces may encounter. The question of the specific suitability of a vehicle of policy, and of the credibility of a threat to use it, cannot be judged without consideration of the goals it is intended to help attain.

There is also the danger of exaggerating the restraints imposed by the inescapable scarcity of the means. While none of them are available in unlimited amounts and are often, as in the case of relatively small and poor countries, pitifully inadequate to meet even the most vital national needs, the elasticity of the supply of means has been a cause of many startling surprises, some agreeable, some disagreeable. "Where there is a will there is a way," though clearly an overstatement, points

nevertheless to the defeatist sin of concluding too easily that
objectives are beyond one's reach. How often have we been told
that the United States would go bankrupt if X billions of dollars
were added to the expenditures of the Government, only to discover later that much larger financial burdens prove compatible
even with rising prosperity. If some have to be told, then, that
the sky is not the limit of what even the most powerful country
can achieve in its foreign policy, others need to be reminded that
when high value is attached to goals—and when they are pursued with wisdom, dedication, and courage—unsuspected potentialities of power and influence may disclose themselves.

Descending now to a less abstract level of discourse and taking
up the American vehicles of foreign policy, it should not be
surprising that the objectives of the Cold War presently hold
a near-monopoly of these vehicles. There are people who are
deeply chagrined, if not shocked, when they discover this fact
and see how meager are the means that are reserved for goals as
dear to Americans, for instance, as sheer humanitarian assistance to others or as the spread of democracy in the world.
Everywhere they detect what appears to them as the corrupting
impact of Cold War considerations and the resulting employment
even of instruments of amical influence, such as economic aid or
cultural exchanges, for purposes of "cold warfare." However, if
one considers how recent has been the transformation of the US
peacetime arsenal of means into an arsenal of cold and hot war
instrumentalities, such regrets and complaints of some are less
astonishing than the speed and broad consensus with which the
transformation has been accomplished. While it would be an exaggeration to say that no expenditure of effort is currently undertaken that has no pay-off in terms of the Cold War, it is a
bitter fact that little room is left under present conditions for
anything but the security exertions dictated by the struggle with
the Sino-Soviet opponent.

The transformation of the US peacetime arsenal of means did
not start with what at the time was regarded as the break with
isolationism. When this "break" occurred in the closing years
of World War II, it was assumed that all the United States would
have to do after ceasing to "go it alone" was to help establish
and join the United Nations and to participate with the other
great powers in the task of what was called the policing of the
peace. It was perfectly reasonable, given that assumption, to
expect that the United States could carry its share of such a
policing burden while simultaneously dismantling most of its

military establishment and avoiding military alliances. If all the great powers except the disarmed enemies of World War II were going to form part of one and the same peace-loving and peace-enforcing camp, not much demand for coercive power would be made on any one of them.

This noble Utopia collapsed when, shortly after the close of the War, the old antagonism between major powers, now in the form of a formidable antagonism between two new superpowers and their friends, came to dominate the world scene. In this new conflict situation the United States found itself at first almost unaided while forced to stand up to the hostility of an ascending, expansive, and ideologically aggressive power bloc operating out of the heartland of Eurasia. As the task now cut out for the United States came to be understood in its many dimensions, the process of "retooling" the American arsenal got underway.

The beginning of the Cold War, then, marked the actual American break with its isolationist past, now no longer for the alluring specter of a Utopian world but under the impact of drastic changes in the real conditions of the world. Threatened, if indirectly at first, in its own security and even in its chance for survival as a free and independent nation, the United States was led to pursue a course its spokesmen had often condemned in the past as alien to American values and ideals—it came to place primary reliance on the "power-political" means of armaments and alliances, soon to be engaged in an arms race of unprecedented costliness and in the build-up of an alliance system equally unprecedented in scope. Other vehicles of policy with considerable potentialities, such as propaganda and foreign aid, were added in time to the American arsenal and more and more consciously fitted to meet the demands of the Cold War.

What the United States requires under the new dispensation in both national and allied armed might and in non-military power-political instruments depends, as mentioned earlier, on the objectives it sets for itself in the Cold War. It is one thing to want to destroy the power of an enemy, another to be satisfied with preventing him from gaining the upper hand. To accomplish the former requires military supremacy; for the latter the minimum need is a military balance of power.

I cannot undertake to discuss here what is meant by such a balance and what it takes to establish and to maintain it. Suffice it to say that a reasonable balance or equilibrium can be said to exist when both sides are deterred from attacking their opponent, which presupposes that on the ground of their respective estimates they consider his countervailing power sufficient to defeat them if they attacked. That the existence or non-existence of such a balance of power (and influence) cannot be gathered from a sheer comparison of the tangible power assets of East and West need hardly be mentioned. While material vehicles of policy, adequate armaments especially, are a major and indispensable ingredient, the respective ability of the two sides to move each other depends on a large composite of human qualities and capabilities that have to be mustered in any inimical confrontation. I shall not attempt to deal with them in this paper because one can hardly speak of such intangibles as determination, good nerves, public morale, or wisdom as "vehicles" of American or Soviet policy. But neither side can hope to prevail over the other or even to balance the power of the other if it is relatively deficient in those human assets that are essential to any conflict policy.

I shall leave it to those who are charged with presenting the problem of American objectives to discuss the merits of more or less ambitious goals. Here it may suffice to inquire what the chief American objective is, as of this time, and what consequences follow from it with respect to the demands on America's means of policy. I see no reason to doubt that, as far as the military means are concerned, the United States is firmly committed to the objective of balancing the power of the Sino-Soviet Bloc and not of destroying it. Its policy has gone under the name of containment, though if the Communists succeeded in leap-frogging, militarily, beyond the Eurasian containment barriers—as they attempted to do in Cuba—a new term would have to be found to characterize the military goal of equilibrium, described earlier as a goal of deterrence of hostile military expansion.

There are not a few advocates of a more ambitious, or less defensive, course of US policy. Yet, only a few among them call for a militarily dynamic policy which would mean a policy of offensive or preventive war to crush the Communist opponent. Instead they content themselves with suggestions for an offensive use of economic, psycho-political, and subversive vehicles of policy, which is not incompatible with a military equilibrium or deterrence policy.

The present broad consensus with which the official military containment policy is being backed might break down: either if, in a despondent or defeatist mood, it came to be held that the balancing process is running inexorably in favor of the Communist camp—which has not been the case so far and need not happen in the future—or if, in a buoyant mood, it came to be widely believed that the United States was capable, perhaps for a passing moment of history, virtually to disarm the Soviet nuclear forces by a first-strike counterforce blow and thereby to win the Cold War at tolerable sacrifices. If there are those who believe this to be the present capability of the United States, they may still agree that, barring an unforeseeable technological breakthrough in favor of the West, the trend toward increasingly secure retaliatory forces on both sides will tend to harden the stalemate. So far there is no evidence that the Administration, the Congress, a large body of the American people, or either of the political parties is contemplating or urging a military policy aimed beyond the deterrence of Sino-Soviet aggression.

One may wonder why a mere balancing of power policy should place exceptionally heavy strains on a group of countries with the rich resources and potentialities of the United States and its many allies. It is the peculiar situation in which they find themselves that makes the task a formidable one. This was true already in the early years when the United States was still enjoying the privileged position of not being exposed to the danger of an attack on its homeland because the Soviets had nothing with which to strike at it directly. If this had meant that there was no threat to American security, rearmament—not to speak of alliances with insecure overseas countries—would have been hard to justify in terms of the national interest. However, the United States was facing the same indirect threat to its security that had drawn it into World Wars I and II. From both wars it could have steered clear had it not been for the danger that inimical powers on the other side of the great oceans might gain control of Europe and Asia, thereby isolating the United States in a hostile world, later to subdue it. This time the danger was even greater because a single power bloc—one, moreover, in control of a world-wide anti-Western and revolutionary Communist movement—might succeed in subjugating the whole of the Eurasian land mass and the adjoining islands.

In the period of invulnerability of North America the need was for enough military power to protect the rimlands of Eurasia, a need that, given the military technology and nuclear scarcity of the period, could not be satisfied except by the projection of American power into the endangered areas and its support by local forces. It is doubtful whether it could be otherwise satisfied today. The purpose of the alliances, then, was not the usual one of mutual assistance in defense of one another's territory. Because the United States needed no such assistance, the purpose was to protect the overseas members of the alliances by common effort and in the common interest. While most of these countries were not in a position to make substantial contributions in the form of armed forces, they did hold the key to real estate without access to which American deployment in the danger zones is impossible.

When, in the fifties, the United States itself became vulnerable to attack, a second task had to be assumed by the American military forces and one to which overseas allies could at best make marginal contributions—the task of deterring a nuclear attack on the American homeland. An actual defense against such an attack remained technologically a remote possibility at best. The question was whether the same military forces would suffice to carry out both tasks. For a short period of time the answer was taken to be in the affirmative, at least as far as deterrence of massive attack was concerned. The US strategic bomber force and the American nuclear stockpiles had reached proportions that appeared to assure American nuclear supremacy. Chief reliance was placed, therefore, in accordance with the doctrine of massive retaliation, on the Grand Deterrent, which in NATO was referred to as the Sword, while the conventional forces, American and allied, deployed overseas and making up the Shield, were relegated to a supporting role. As long as the doctrine prevailed, there appeared no reason to be concerned about particular military requirements to meet the overseas task of deterrence and defense which called for trip-wire and brush-fire forces that made relatively modest demands.

It was not long, however, before doubts arose, particularly in Europe, about the adequacy of the protection to be derived from US double-purpose strategic forces. Would they be able to cope with the overseas problem of deterrence in the face of greatly increased US vulnerability to Soviet nuclear attack? Would the US threat to intervene with its strategic nuclear force on behalf of allies that became victims of a local, and especially a conventional, attack remain credible to the Soviet Union and therefore suffice to deter it? While these questions came to be uppermost in the minds of Allied statesmen, American policy-makers were asking themselves whether there was no way of lessening the danger to the United States of the risk of finding itself some day with no means of honoring its commitment to its allies other than by a self-destructive, if not suicidal, strategic nuclear strike against the Soviet Union. An intense search for alternative means got under way and is under way today. It has caused a controversy within NATO that might undermine allied solidarity and disrupt NATO itself. The alliances in Asia are less affected, both because there has been less reliance in Asia, all along, on the US nuclear umbrella and because the threat of US nuclear intervention remains more credible in those parts of Asia where the chief opponent is Red China, a country that does not yet possess nuclear retaliatory capabilities of its own.

Within NATO two views of how best to strengthen the deterrent and give Europe more protection are in conflict with each other, the first held chiefly in the United States, the other chiefly in Europe. According to the prevalent American view two major efforts are required to meet the new dangers, one on the part of the United States itself, the other on the part chiefly, though not exclusively, of the Europeans. Speaking of American efforts first, one way of adding credibility to the US threat of nuclear intervention is, it is held, to equip the United States with a counterforce capability sufficiently impressive to make the Soviets fear future American willingness to accept as tolerable the expected effects of Soviet retaliation. How long it will take the Soviets to raise the invulnerability of their retaliatory forces to a point where it will destroy the credibility of the US threat, despite efforts at greater counterforce capability, is a matter of speculation. In any case, more emphasis is being placed on a second effort urged by the United States, which would consist of raising NATO's conventional forces to a level at which they can become an important, if not the decisive, means of deterrence and defense in Europe. The idea is to supplement a balance of forces on the strategic and tactical nuclear levels—which is to remain the minimum objective of the nuclear effort—by as close an approximation to equilibrium on the conventional level of forces as conditions permit. Such an equilibrium does not presuppose matching the Soviet forces, both because the defensive side, it is assumed, can get along with inferior forces and because the risk of escalation, which no approximation to stalemate can completely eliminate, will continue to place a ceiling on the scope of engagements the Soviets might risk to undertake.

The American call for larger conventional forces is evoking at best a lukewarm response in Europe; it is even regarded as a threat to European security by those who believe that it will further undermine the credibility of the Grand Deterrent. Those Europeans who do conceive of a substitute for the sole reliance on US nuclear protection are advocating European nuclear forces instead, which would operate side by side with the US Grand Deterrent. There are three variants of this proposal, the first calling for individual national nuclear forces, the second for a collective European force, the third for a NATO deterrent. While doubting the military value of any of the three variants— or even fearing their adverse military effects—the United States has become willing to make concessions to the European point of view for political and psychological reasons. It favors variant three, a NATO deterrent, rejects variant one, national deterrents, and may be ready to compromise on variant two, a European collective deterrent.

I must leave it to Panel Three to discuss in detail the military value and implications of these American and European proposals. What is important here is that, failing some agreement within NATO, neither any substantial conventional build-up nor the establishment of more than token nuclear forces in Europe is likely to occur, leaving means to deter attacks on Europe and to defend Europe in a state of inadequacy. In my opinion, the increase in conventional forces is of such vital importance that almost any concession to our European Allies would be justified that would induce them, in return, to make a substantial effort in the conventional field. It is hard to see how a NATO deterrent could satisfy them because the American veto on the use of a NATO force would rob it of any credibility not already possessed by the US force. A purely European collective deterrent, though far preferable from a European viewpoint to a NATO deterrent, is not practical today. There is not within reach, and there may not come into being even over a decade, the kind of centralized political authority in Western Europe that could meet the requirements of a credible and workable nuclear deterrent. One cannot compromise with pluralism when it comes to the authority of releasing a nuclear striking force on which hinges the survival of whole nations.

Failing agreement on or the practicality of some form of collective deterrent, should not the United States consent to European national deterrents which it cannot prevent anyway and support them in return for a greater European effort on the conventional level? I don't believe that either of the two American objections to national deterrents are justified, which does not, however, dispose of the argument that no European

nation alone can afford to pay for a strategic force of any consequence. First, I don't see how one can dismiss as militarily
senseless the desire of countries to have some strategic nuclear
power of their own, when there is at least a chance that the
threat of nuclear retaliation, even if suicidal, by a country
directly attacked will prove more credible to the Soviet leaders
than an American threat of intervention on behalf of its allies,
which, if not literally suicidal, would still be extremely self-
destructive. Second, the prevailing fear of abuse by a European
ally—by West Germany, for instance—of a modest nuclear force
which it may acquire, appears to me greatly exaggerated. Rather
than to fear the trigger-happiness of countries to whom nuclear
war spells extermination, one must fear their lack of willingness
to participate in the risks of nuclear brinkmanship in cases in
which there is no direct threat to their national territory. European unity is still far from the point of any complete self-identification of every country with all of its European partners in
NATO.

It is necessary to say something about Asia here. Even if the
United States and its NATO allies should succeed in attaining
and preserving a reasonable equilibrium of forces in the North
Atlantic area, they will not, thereby, make themselves secure.
They must also be able to prevent a Communist take over of
Asia which would open the way for a flanking movement through
Africa and into Latin America. Yet, in the areas adjoining the
Soviet Union and Red China from Iran to Japan and South
Korea, indigenous forces on which the West can rely, though
not negligible, are, and are likely to remain, greatly inferior
to what the Communists can put into the field. Everything
hinges, then, on the naval, air, and land power the United States
is able and willing to project into the areas in question.

Speaking first of the countries adjoining Red China, the question arises whether the American nuclear umbrella does not protect them and cannot be counted upon to do so into the foreseeable future. After all, for years to come the credibility of the
US threat of nuclear intervention is not likely to be eroded by
a threat of Chinese nuclear retaliation against the American
homeland. But, so far at least, Red China has enjoyed the protection of a Soviet nuclear umbrella, with the Soviet threat of
nuclear intervention on behalf of Red China no less credible
than the American threat to come to the assistance of its weak
Asian allies with nuclear force. Therefore, only an open rift
between the Soviet Union and Red China would permit the

United States to discount the risk of escalation of a Sino-American war to the level of two-way Soviet-American strategic warfare, and to rely on its strategic nuclear force for the balance of power in the Far East and Southern Asia. One can gather from this hypothetical contingency the far-reaching potential military implications of the Sino-Soviet feud.

When it comes to conventional forces the superiority of the Red Chinese is usually taken for granted because of the advantage of numbers which they enjoy everywhere except with respect to India. But numbers are not the only factor that counts, and not necessarily the decisive factor. In the fields of logistics, weaponry, and economic resources the non-Communist nations, Asian and North American, are potentially far superior in many parts of Asia and only moderately handicapped in others. The ability to balance Red Chinese power depends, therefore, primarily on the determination of the neighbors of Red China to defend themselves and to regard a threat to one as a threat to all. The deficiencies of the alliances, and specifically of allied solidarity among the countries in the Far East, are the chief obstacle to equilibrium.

India is a special case. While, as things stand today, it is at a stark disadvantage in the early phases of any Red Chinese southward drive, an attempt by Red China to defeat India—if it should ever materialize—might lead to a reversal of the roles of the two opponents. Even if, at the outset, India lost much of her territory to the invader, as Germany's and Japan's neighbors did in World War II, the resources she could mobilize at home and the assistance the outside non-Communist world could give to her far exceed what China could move across the Himalayas, even assuming the Soviet Union threw all its weight to her side.

The outlook is much bleaker if one turns to the Asian area adjoining the Soviet Union, particularly to Iran and the Arab areas south of her borders. Here the US nuclear deterrent is threatened with an even more rapid erosion of its credibility than in Europe and local forces for use for defense against the Soviet Union are virtually absent outside of Turkey. As a consequence, the task falling to US conventional land, sea, and air forces is extremely exacting.

Nothing has been said so far about subconventional forces. Yet, in some areas of Asia the military balance rests, in part at least, on their relative strength and effectiveness. The United States has only recently begun to develop a serious capability in this field, but as demonstrated by Britain in Malaya and by France in Algeria, the West, though handicapped here in a struggle with a revolutionary opponent, is far from impotent and may succeed in matching him in time wherever it becomes necessary.

So far the discussion of US means to conduct policy toward its chief adversaries has been limited to military forces and military alliances which, as mentioned earlier, excel over other means because no others, except on rare occasions, can threaten or inflict equally painful and effective punishment. Moreover, the course of the Cold War has shown not only that both sides place prime reliance on military means but also that they owe their respective successes chiefly to these means. Continental China would not have fallen to the Communists except for their military victory over Chiang's armies, and Chiang would not today hold Taiwan and the off-shore islands if he had not been able, with American aid, to assert his military supremacy there. The line that separates the areas controlled, respectively, by the Communist camp and its adversaries reflects the relative military pressures the two sides have been able to exert in such contested areas, as Eastern Europe—Czechoslovakia and Yugoslavia included—Southeast Asia, Korea, the Congo, and Cuba.

Yet, it would be a great mistake to overlook or minimize in the context of the East-West struggle the role of non-military means of constraint. While Khrushchev did not turn his back on military means to concentrate instead on ideological and economic competition, he did not fail to appreciate, more than Stalin had done, the advantages he could gain from utilizing more fully such instrumentalities as subversion, propaganda, blackmail, and foreign aid. No territory has been conquered by the sole use of these means, but the military outcome might have been different if Mao had not enjoyed the dynamic support of Communist propaganda; the fate of North Korea was finally decided by psychological and political forces rather than by military means; and in the Cuban crisis, the United States experienced the leverage it could gain from successfully mobilizing the political support of allies in both hemispheres.

The value people in the West place on means of non-military constraint tends to go to extremes. In the days of the Hungarian crisis many insisted that the West could protect the revolution by meting out such "punishments" on the Soviet Union as a break in diplomatic relations or as the supply of small arms to the revolutionaries. Such "pinpricks" will usually not only fail, however, to move a mighty country, but backfire as demonstrations of impotence. At other times one hears it said that the West is incapable of standing up to the propaganda barrages or the economic dumping policy of the Communists, measures supposedly capable of pushing the West out of important positions it seeks to hold.

The fact is that in the direct confrontation between the Sino-Soviet Bloc and the US alliance system—which must be distinguished from the indirect confrontation in the non-aligned areas—inimical diplomacy, espionage, subversion, propaganda, and hostile economic competition have not, so far, gained major victories and are unlikely to do so in the future.

Communist propaganda has enjoyed the advantage of being able, until recently at least, to speak with a single voice, and the other means of non-military constraint are far more congenial to Communist views than to Western tradition. Yet when addressed to the "capitalist world," Soviet propaganda has either failed or made headway only where it was able to parade as the champion of indigenous ideological causes. While the West has far more allies beyond the Iron Curtain—as revealed in Hungary, Poland, and East Germany—than the Soviet Union can call its own in Western countries, the Communists are able to embarrass the West by their propagandistic support of deeply rooted pacifistic proclivities in the West which antedate communism, a phenomenon similar to the Communist support of anticolonialism and nationalism in non-Western countries. Whether the West could reciprocate effectively by appealing to nationalist, religious, or pacifist forces inside the Soviet Union only experts could judge. I doubt the wisdom, however, of writing off the Russian people as supposedly lost to communism or enamored with it. There is an inclination to do so in the United States which is not only self-defeating but grossly unfair to the majority of the population of the Soviet Union.

When it comes to economic weaponry neither side can expect startling results when using it against highly autarkic opponents. Whether the American embargo on strategic materials has had more of a restraining and delaying effect or more of a stimulating effect on Communist economic development remains an open question. And while a total naval blockade of Red China —never a practical option so far—would severely punish the Red Chinese regime, the fact that Mao was able to launch an assault on far-away India at a time of unmistakable economic strains at home shows the difficulty of placing economic restraints on the military power of countries prepared to shift the pressure onto the consumers.

Probably the strongest vehicle of economic constraint, one of which the West enjoys a monopoly as long as it maintains its economic superiority, is its ability to step up the arms race and the competition in foreign aid to a point that will force its opponents to make painful choices. While no early effects on the balance of power can be expected whether the Soviets choose to cut back on armaments or to forego giving more satisfaction to the consumer, in the longer run the effects might prove decisive.

Despite the inevitable predominance of power-political means in the conduct of policy aimed directly at an opponent, even a total struggle does not rob the instruments of influence policy or persuasion of all value. Diplomacy ranks highest among these instruments. Not that diplomatic negotiations per se, however ably conducted, could push the Soviet Union out of a "Hungary," any more than they could push the West out of its positions in West Berlin. But Western diplomacy is not doomed to failure in dealing with the Communists and has, in fact, proved unwarranted the suspicion that it is incapable of learning the unpleasant art of adversary diplomacy. There is always room for efforts to open the eyes of an adversary to the danger of the course he is pursuing or to probe his intentions with a view to discovering whether his hostility is receding or to negotiating an exchange of concessions with him that will leave the distribution of power untouched. Moreover, since the Communists contend, quite realistically I suggest, that the result of negotiations among adversaries merely reflects the existing distribution of power, our statesmen and diplomats, if backed by the appropriate demonstrations of power, may often be able to make the opponent see this distribution as they would want him to see it.

However, if the vehicles of influence policy, such as persuasion or financial grants, are of relatively little avail when employed for the purpose of settling East-West disputes or of obtaining concessions from the Soviet Union or Red China, their role is preponderant in the struggle for the amity—or at least the non-enmity—of the unaligned countries. The terms amity and enmity are used here in a diplomatic, not in a sentimental, sense. The struggle for the unaligned nations represents an indirect confrontation between East and West. How important it is in the context of the Cold War is controversial. Its importance is being exaggerated by those who in international affairs think primarily in terms of numbers of people or in terms of votes in the United Nations, both only of marginal impact on the world balance of power. The importance is being underestimated by others who believe that the decisive military balance is unaffected by changes in the attitudes of the peoples of entire continents. It is surely no accident that both the Sino-Soviet Bloc and the members of the American alliance system are putting increasing effort into the competition for favorable attitudes of the unaligned nations with the minimum goal of preventing them from going over to the opposite camp.

It stands to reason that power political means, though not as counterproductive here as when employed against allies, can play only a subordinate role in US policies toward neutrals and neutralists. On occasion economic pressure and other even more stringent punitive actions may be in order to unsaddle a regime that, on the model of Castro, threatens to take a nation over into the Soviet camp or that, in oppressing its own people, threatens to provoke a rebellion and a Communist take over in its own country. Military assistance, including anti-guerrilla support employed in favor of friendly but unaligned nations, either to stabilize them internally or to protect them against external attack and incursions is not power political in character as far as the assisted countries are concerned. When neutralists accuse the United States of militarism, they forget how dependent they may become some day on the benevolent or protective exercise and availability of US military power. Recent experience may have taught India and some of the Latin American republics a lesson in this respect. American power may also be necessary if violence not of Communist making erupts in one of the unaligned countries, as it did in the Congo, because disorder or anarchy in themselves tend to play into Communist hands, adversely affecting the position of the non-Communist camp.

The instruments of influence policy available to the United States and its Western Allies in their relations with the unaligned and predominantly underdeveloped countries are manifold and potentially superior to what the Communist Bloc can muster. This holds particularly true for foreign economic aid. The Sino-Soviet Bloc cannot provide the equivalent in markets and capital resources that the West can offer if only it chooses to do so. The problem is not whether the United States and its allies can afford to beat their opponents in a competition directed at superior material grants-in-aid, but whether and up to what point such aid actually serves the objectives of US foreign policy, among which the objective of preventing a rise in Communist power and influence, though not the sole objective, ranks first. The United States would have reason to extend aid even if there were no Cold War. Yet it would be sheer hypocrisy to deny that the Cold War is the most potent motivating force behind an aid program of the present dimensions. No one is more aware of this than the unaligned nations themselves who cash in, often quite shamelessly, on the advantages they can gain from being courted by two competing power groups. The only drawback the East-West struggle has from their point of view is that it may compel those who give aid to concentrate on the types of assistance most immediately effective in their struggle with each other and to economize on projects for economic development that would be most useful to the recipient countries. Economic aid by the Western countries is not limited as much by what they can afford to spend as by what the under-developed countries are capable of absorbing. Funds that go down the drain, cause run-away inflations, or merely serve to corrupt and enrich the élites of the recipient nations cannot qualify as effective vehicles of either the Cold War or of humanitarian assistance to others and should, as a rule, not be made available even to countries that threaten—as skillful black-mailers—to switch to the Communist camp if their demands are not met. Only in exceptional cases will any particular unaligned country have so much strategic value that the United States could not afford to lose whatever favors it might otherwise hope to obtain from it.

Propaganda and diplomacy, two other instruments for the conduct of amical relations, are being used by both camps to lure the unaligned countries to their respective side or to draw them away from the other. Supposedly the advantages in this competition by means of words and ideas lie unalterably with the Communists, who indeed, by posing as the champions of revolutionary change, of anti-imperialism, and anti-capitalism can exert much pull in post-colonial and unstable areas. The tendency is, however, to overestimate the effects of Communist propaganda in those areas. If one looks at the record to this date one is struck by the fact that not one of the new states, with the exception of Cuba, has joined the "Socialist camp" of its own, or of its rulers' volition. Nationalism and the passionate drive toward sovereign independence have proved stronger than Communist and even anti-capitalist sentiment and the attraction of the Communist model has not been able to silence the fear of totalitarian excesses. The West should find it easier as time goes on, not perhaps to sell its own values and institutions but to help unmask the Communist myths and deceptions that are revealing themselves anyway in economic failures, in intra-Communist feuds and in mass dissatisfaction. Already, one after the other of the countries the West was just about to write off as Communist satellites—Egypt, Guinea, Syria, Iraq, Indonesia—proved ready and able to remain, at worst, on the radical wing of the neutralist camp, and not beyond the reach of Western influence. While it would be extremely dangerous to be complacent about the adequacy of the vehicles of propaganda with which the United States conducts the "indirect struggle," it is encouraging, nonetheless, that the Communists have proved so little effective in profiting from the explosion of exceptionally fanatical postwar sentiment against Western colonial rule and from the social unrest in non-Communist countries at the close of World War II.

One further instrument of US influence policy which bears foremost on American relations with the new states deserves to be mentioned here, namely the United Nations. Despite the embarrassments collective diplomacy—diplomacy by means of quasi-parliamentary voting procedures—can cause to a United States that is seeking to protect the security of the non-Communist world, the West should be able on balance to gain much advantage from the new instrumentality when it comes to winning the favors of the unaligned nations. It can do so by backing the one institution in which they are able to play a role and in which their leaders can gain prestige, and in demonstrating American respect for the principle of sovereign equality and independence even where its impact on American interests is not favorable. The Sino-Soviet Bloc is handicapped when trying to use the UN because the voting "number game" of the UN runs counter to Communist ideology and the quasi-parliamentary rules of the game are derived from Western practice and experience. While it is debatable whether within the UN the United States or the neutralists have proved more apt in avoiding entanglement in the special interests of the other, there is no evidence that the Communists are coming out as the winners in the arena of UN diplomacy.

From what has been said so far certain conclusions can be drawn concerning the US vehicles of policy and their adequacy for the tasks they may be called upon to perform in the years ahead:

Two assumptions were made, first, that the Cold War will continue and absorb most of the means of policy available to the United States and its allies, and second, that the chief American objectives in the Cold War for which adequate means are required are the preservation and, where necessary, the restoration of a reasonable East-West balance of power. Whether the second assumption will hold true as far into the future as, say, ten years must remain a matter of speculation. A change might occur either for the better or the worse.

To start with the better, there is the possibility of a break-up of the Sino-Soviet Bloc or even of a collapse of one or both of the major Bolshevik regimes. In the case of either of these contingencies, the world distribution of power would be radically changed and might give the United States and its allies a comfortable superiority of power without military action on their part being required to bring it about. While it is grossly premature to seek to imagine the environment that the United States would face if such were to happen, it is necessary to warn of false expectations. It cannot be taken for granted that communism as a revolutionary international force would disappear as a result of a shift in the scales of world power in favor of the non-Communist camp. There is even less reason to assume that the new situation would spell the dawn of a disarmed and warless world in which the United States could shed its power political armor. The chances are that such a radical change— accompanied probably by the appearance of a power vacuum in some areas—would, as so often in the past, open the door to new ambitions, conflicts, and resorts to violence, requiring the United States to put a considerable part of its power political vehicles to new uses in accordance with its continuing world responsibilities.

Turning to the worse hypothesis, it is conceivable that a change no less radical might occur at the expense of non-Communist power, thereby, for opposite reasons, destroying the chance of a balance of world power. Such a change might come as a result of a new consolidation of the Sino-Soviet Bloc followed by the expansion of Communist control into the Southern Hemisphere whether through revolutionary, subconventional, or conventional means. It might occur, instead, as the result of a Soviet technological breakthrough in the field of nuclear armaments; or be brought about by the collapse of the NATO Alliance.

The consideration of such unpleasant contingencies points up some of the chief tasks with which the United States must be able to cope in the future: it must be in a position to contain the military forces of the Soviet Union and Red China as well as the revolutionary and subversive forces that serve or play into the hands of Communist expansion; it must keep up with the Soviets in nuclear weaponry and strategy—though not necessarily in the "space olympics" of beating them to the moon, a space activity chosen by a peace-minded United States because it promises to have the least military implications! It must finally strive to cement solidarity with and among its allies and to induce the neutralist countries to become as nearly neutral in the traditional sense of the term as possible.

Barring all of the hypothetical changes suggested above and assuming, instead, a period of ten more years of successful American effort to balance Sino-Soviet power, one can then imagine the occurrence of significant modifications in the character of the East-West struggle. If the nuclear balance continues to move in the direction of a relatively stable stalemate—as increased invulnerability and size of nuclear retaliatory forces on both sides makes probable—the decreasing risk of escalation to the strategic nuclear level will increase the premium on less than total forms of violence. The outlook would then be for more rather than less conventional and subconventional hostilities and, consequently, for more rather than less need of other than nuclear vehicles of inimical policy.

However, in the course of the same development, countervailing influences may come into play to improve the prospects for peace and a genuine relaxation of East-West tensions. A prolonged state of close approximation to nuclear stalemate, while reducing the chances of any deliberate initiation of nuclear war, would not eliminate the danger to both sides of unforeseen escalation, technological breakthroughs by the opponent, and sheer exhaustion resulting from a stepped-up arms race. Conceivably, therefore, the Communist leaders might gradually realize the hopelessness of their ambition to make the world over in the Communist image and lose the expansionist dynamism that started the Cold War in the first place. If that were to happen, the sting might be taken out of the balancing process which would begin to generate growing mutual restraints. Such a development would improve the chances for at least a tolerable *modus vivendi*. Once the United States acquired, thereby, a reasonable measure of security for itself and the rest of the non-

Communist world it could afford to wait with patience until the superiority of its values and its institutions, measured in terms of the essential demands of human nature, could assert itself, an outcome greatly to be desired in the interest of all the peoples of the world.

# NATO's Nuclear Dilemma*

—*HENRY A. KISSINGER*

## Summary

*Our new strategic doctrine confronts our allies with serious dilemmas. Few Europeans agree with our judgment about the feasibility of a purely conventional defense. Even the acceptance of our goal of non-nuclear defense would not remove all pressures for development of European nuclear strength, nor answer all questions. What if the Soviets use nuclear weapons in Europe only, and perhaps in a controlled, flexible way? Furthermore, Europeans are more concerned with deterrence than with defense.*

*There are many intermediate stages where a country's bargaining position depends on the risks to which it can expose an aggressor. To some of our European allies it appears that even a small nuclear force is more effective for this bargaining purpose than a few more divisions. Our frequently expressed outrage at the seeming European doubt about the reliability of our nuclear guarantee has blinded us to the fact that we have, in effect, accused our allies of being too irresponsible to be entrusted with the ultimate means for their protection.*

*The real basis of our opposition to national nuclear forces is not so much their ineffectiveness as the fact that we do not want to be drawn into a nuclear war against our will.*

*The heart of the issue raised by European nuclear forces is this: does the interdependence of the Atlantic area have to be vindicated by a structure in which only one ally possesses the physical ability to engage in nuclear war? Is the test of Atlantic partnership really a "single strategic force?" Or is it possible to have several centers of decision coordinated politically so that their power serves a common end?*

*So far, we have indicated a preference for continued hegemony. Terms like "multilateralism" and "interdependence" have hidden the reality of an attempt to maintain undivided US physical control.*

*We have repeatedly hinted at our willingness to consider that the proposed NATO force could in time be transformed into a European force if our allies request it. The major obstacles to this, however—our strategic doctrine, our insistence on a unified command, a single target system, and the need for instant response—are as inconsistent with a separate European force as with national forces. Moreover, as long as France is not part of a NATO force and Britain's contribution is token only, an attempt to turn it into a European force will raise the specter of German denunciation.*

*Nothing is more likely to promote Third Force tendencies in Europe than for us to engage our prestige in pressing for a force which on our own showing makes no sense militarily, does not alter existing control arrangements significantly, and yet requires a heavy European financial contribution.*

*Instead of being hostile to the French nuclear program and, at best, indifferent to the British effort, we should use our influence to place them in the service of a European conception. This would also be the most reliable road to Atlantic partnership. The emerging European force could then be related to ours through political coordination and joint strategic planning. Such a policy would require a change of attitude on our part; at the very least the technical pressures from the Defense Department would have to be subordinated to an overriding political direction.*

*Remedies are still within our control, and the West is less imperiled by outside pressures than by a tendency to waste its own substance.*

---

### The Case for National Nuclear Forces

The nature of the crisis is underlined by the inability of the two sides to agree on what really is in dispute. We have called national nuclear forces—particularly the French effort—divisive, inimical to the West, based on distrust of the United States, and prone to obsolescence. It has been said that the French nuclear program is based on a rejection of the interdependence of the Atlantic Community.

The French have not helped matters by pressing their own arguments with a kind of Cartesian rationalism that sometimes threatens to turn valid arguments into parodies. It is one thing to argue the undeniable fact that, in the age of nuclear plenty, the old notions of nuclear protection must be modified and that a redistribution of responsibilities on nuclear matters is required. It is quite another to insist that this ends all possibility of one country's coming to the assistance of another. Both sides have had a tendency to set up straw men for debating purposes: the French, the bogy of our complete unreliability; the United States, the futility of the French quest for complete self-sufficiency. In demonstrating that France—or Great Britain—cannot win a nuclear war by itself, we have neglected to examine the more sensible arguments on behalf of European nuclear power. And we have shown little understanding of the political and psychological motives behind the French and British nuclear programs.

Our new strategic doctrine, for all its subtlety, does confront our allies with serious dilemmas. It *is* difficult to decide at what point the effort to develop a tolerable strategy not only enhances the credibility of the response but also lowers the risks of the aggressor to an acceptable level.

Few Europeans agree with our judgment about the feasibility of a purely conventional defense. Most of them believe that a great gap in conventional power exists and that we have adjusted our intelligence estimates to fit our strategic preference. Their judgment may be mistaken, but we must remember that we have no advantage in experience over the Europeans in the analysis of conventional war.

In any event, Europeans have too many memories of the defeat of supposedly adequate conventional forces not to ask what happens if our assessment turns out to be mistaken. Even those who favor as a more modest goal a "pause" before nuclear weapons are used—and they are not in a majority—must be concerned about the options available at the end of that pause.

But the acceptance of our goal of non-nuclear defense and the theory behind it still does not remove all pressures for the development of European nuclear strength. Europeans are bound to want to have a share in determining their fate if the

Soviets do not follow the strategy preferred by the United States. What if the Soviets use nuclear weapons on Europe only? Even more, what if they use them on Europe in the controlled, flexible way recommended by Secretary McNamara? It is a great deal to ask of the Europeans to concentrate all their military efforts on weapons that can be overcome by the introduction of nuclear arms while the United States reserves control over the weapons at any level of conflict that is not purely conventional. Such a situation would be made to order for Soviet "nuclear blackmail."

Words like "nuclear interdependence" should not obscure the fact that there is an inevitable difference of perspective between ourselves and some of our allies. If the NATO area is looked on as a unit, a strategy that exposes a limited territory to the fluctuations of conventional combat may seem eminently sensible. To the allies on whose territory such a war would be fought, however, a Soviet penetration of even a hundred miles might well spell the end of their national existence. They have compelling incentive to strive for a strategy that poses the threat of maximum devastation for the Soviets. Europeans are almost inevitably more concerned with deterrence than with defense. They will prefer a strategy that seems to magnify the risks of the aggressor rather than reduce the losses of the defender.

Of course an improvement in NATO's conventional capability is desirable. But as in the nuclear field, we have pushed valid arguments to such extremes as to defeat our objective. The notion of a purely conventional defense of Europe goes much further than arguing for an improved capability to resist Soviet local pressures. It has the paradoxical consequence of removing the incentive for a conventional build-up as well as raising the nuclear issue in an acute form.

In this context, such statements as Under Secretary Ball's to the NATO parliamentarians last November are extraordinarily double-edged. Secretary Ball argued that the Cuban crisis proved the importance of superiority in conventional weapons. It was fortunate that the Cuban crisis occurred in an area of overwhelming US conventional superiority. But most Europeans are convinced that in Europe the reverse relationship obtains. They tend to draw two lessons from the Cuban episode: that they were faced with nuclear war without being consulted and that a settlement was made by the two nuclear powers without the participation of Cuba—the country which was most concerned but which possessed conventional weapons only.

The incentive for nuclear forces thus cannot be assessed entirely in terms of military operations. The issue of peace and war does not arise in terms of either-or. There are many intermediate stages where a country's bargaining position depends on the risks to which it can expose an aggressor. To some of our European allies it appears that even a small nuclear force is more effective for this bargaining purpose than a few more divisions, whose effectiveness in every case depends entirely on a solid allied front, thus, in effect, giving a veto to the least resolute ally.

During the Berlin crisis it was often said that since the United States has the entire responsibility for nuclear defense, we would reserve the right to negotiate even without the consent of our allies. (President Kennedy made this quite clear, for example, in his press conference of May 9, 1962.) And last October, McGeorge Bundy wrote: "Outside the nuclear field, in which mutual understanding must include the present fact of our special responsibility, our claims upon our allies can be entrusted to the formula of reciprocity." In these terms, our allies have an incentive to develop national nuclear forces not only to bargain with the Soviet Union but also to gain a greater influence over *our* actions.

Since the chief impetus for the European nuclear programs derives from intangibles of political and psychological influence, it is immature to turn the issue into a personal debate about the integrity of the assurances of a particular President. For the Europeans to forego national nuclear programs would be to resign forever from a realm of technology on which their future security and indeed their economic welfare will depend to a greater or lesser extent. It would mean entrusting their fate not to this President but to all future Presidents, and not only on clear-cut issues of war and peace but with respect to every nuance of policy. In effect, this would transform Europe from a partner into a satellite.

Apart from the moral issue this raises, Europe has had too many recent proofs of the inability of one President to commit another not to want some means of determining its own fate. The change in emphasis in US strategic thinking over the past two years, the peremptory way in which we canceled Skybolt, withdrew the Jupiter bases, and altered the strategic doctrine of NATO, indicates that no President can possibly predict the judgments of his successors in an age of extraordinarily volatile technology.

But the problem goes deeper still. Europeans, living on a continent covered with ruins testifying to the fallibility of human foresight, feel in their bones that history is more complicated than systems analysis. They have had too much experience with the nuances of interpretation that are possible with all formal commitments. They know that in this century no person, however wise, could have predicted at the beginning of any decade what the world would be like at its end. They do not believe that they must be able to describe the exact circumstances in which they might have to rely on their nuclear forces in order to wish to reserve some degree of control over their destiny.

Our frequently expressed outrage at the seeming European doubt about the reliability of our nuclear guarantee has blinded us to the fact that we have, in effect, accused our allies of being too irresponsible to be entrusted with the ultimate means for their protection. The asymmetry—to use a favorite word of the new strategic analysis—between the two kinds of distrust is pronounced. For if the Europeans are wrong, the chief penalty is a certain duplication of effort; while if they are right, our policy would seal their fate.

Our arguments that we oppose European nuclear efforts because they are useless tend to be overdone even on the purely technical plane. A few hundred British and a few score French delivery vehicles cannot be without some impact on Soviet calculations. The Soviets cannot launch a pre-emptive attack against these forces even if their bases are vulnerable. As long as the NATO guarantee retains any validity, such an attack would involve an immense risk of US retaliation—as the President pointed out with respect to the NATO nuclear force in his press conference of March 6, 1963. And in launching other forms of attack the Soviets must surely consider whether the objective is worth the very large—even if not decisive—casualties that could be inflicted by the British and French retaliatory forces. The real basis of our opposition to national nuclear forces, then, is not so much their ineffectiveness as the fact that we do not want to be drawn into nuclear war against our will.

Of course this concern casts a curious light on our frequently repeated assertions that no difference in the conceptions of vital interests between us and Europe is possible. Above all, the fear that France and Great Britain may prove more reckless than we can only be based on a misunderstanding. They must know —perhaps better than we—that using their forces independently would be a desperate last resort, though we can hardly expect them to advertise this fact. Whatever they may say now, they will learn that they must think of their nuclear forces much as Sweden and Switzerland think of their armies. Neither country is able to withstand a full-scale attack by a major power. Both would prefer allies in such a case. Their military forces do give them the possibility of posing risks that an aggressor may consider out of proportion to the objectives to be achieved. And they may gain time for allied assistance to be effective.

The frequent insinuations that those of our allies developing nuclear programs *prefer* to do without the Alliance are the result of a grave misapprehension. Taking out fire insurance does not indicate a liking for fires. On the contrary, it may prevent a remote contingency from turning into an obsession and thus free energies for more constructive tasks.

We thus reach the heart of the issue raised by European nuclear forces. Does the interdependence of the Atlantic area have to be vindicated by a structure in which only one ally possesses the physical ability to engage in nuclear war? Is the test of Atlantic partnership really a "single strategic force" integrated into a "single chain of command," as Secretary McNamara asserts? Or is it possible to have several centers of decision coordinated politically so that their power serves a common end?

After all, one of two things is likely to happen with respect to European nuclear power: either our allies will realize the importance of coordinating their forces with ours, or they will assume the major burden of their own defense, which is what we have always said we wanted. All considerations of technology, strategy, and policy indicate that the former is by far the more likely outcome. Our allies—if they understand their own interests—will always prefer the assistance of our enormous nuclear arsenal. This has been our experience with Great Britain. It is likely to be our experience with France, if we ever get away from scholastic arguments over the relative merits of "integration" and "coordination" and face practical issues of how to relate a French nuclear force to the common defense.

A policy of confidence in our European allies is all the more necessary because the range of our control over events is extremely limited. A British strategic force exists. A French nuclear program has been in operation for nearly a decade. Attempts to atrophy them are liable to lead to the most extreme formulations of strategic doctrine and to the most dangerous, because vulnerable, strategic design. Or else, if we succeed, we may well discredit not a particular defense policy but *all* attempts to assume responsibility for national defense. Then we will have brought about the kind of Third Force that should really worry us: one based on the resentments of the impotent and relying on the manipulations of the irresponsible. Not everyone who gives us no trouble will give us support. This is illustrated by the contrasting behavior of President de Gaulle and Premier Fanfani during the Cuban crisis. The former backed us without reservation; the latter adopted an essentially noncommittal policy.

To be sure, many of the formulations on behalf of European nuclear forces have been extreme and one-sided. A rudimentary technology has produced an often crude strategic doctrine. But these theories are subject to the same evolutionary process as they have been in the United States. We should not judge a mature European program by its beginnings—which, moreover, are needlessly protracted by our opposition.

The real problem is whether we are ready to face an independent European center for decision on nuclear matters, and rely on political consultations to relate European purposes to ours.

So far, we have indicated a preference for continued hegemony. Terms like "multilateralism" and "interdependence" have hidden the reality of an attempt to maintain undivided physical control—which in terms of our strategic doctrine has to mean US control. Given European pressures in the opposite direction, this policy has forced us to adopt remedies more dangerous than the ill they have sought to cure. We have purchased brief respites in Allied disputes by mortgaging the future. Almost every program that we have advanced in the name of our notion of multilateralism has had the practical consequence of accentuating rather than ameliorating NATO's nuclear dilemma, and therefore it has undermined the long-term political stability of the Atlantic Alliance.

### Proposed US Remedies: The Creation of a Multilateral Force

The Administration has adopted three policies in pursuit of its goal of a single, centrally controlled nuclear force for the Alliance.

a) It has indicated increasing willingness to permit Europeans to share in the targeting of our strategic forces, which remain almost entirely under our exclusive control.

b) It has "assigned" nuclear submarines to NATO subject to agreed NATO guidelines.

c) It has pushed—ambivalently and with various degrees of intensity—the creation of a NATO multilateral force.

Of these steps, the first is constructive even if it does not go to the heart of the problem. It is no doubt highly desirable for Europeans to know of the targeting of our strategic forces and to participate in planning. Joint targeting does not, however, alter the US monopoly position. To some extent, it meets the interests of all allies in a common war plan. It does not solve the far more important problem of political control, specifically the decision to enter nuclear war.

As for the assignment of Polaris submarines to NATO, this measure was first announced by President Kennedy in Ottawa in May 1961. It was then repeated with considerable dramatic effect by Secretary McNamara at the NATO ministerial meeting in Athens last year. At that time, it was stated that five Polaris submarines had been "assigned" to NATO, with more to come. In his report to the House Armed Services Committee on January 30, 1963, Secretary McNamara pointed out that we had "earmarked a fully operational Polaris force to the NATO Command."

However, it is important to understand what this "earmarking" consists of. All forces in NATO are national forces. The line of command of US forces runs from Washington through the appropriate US headquarters. NATO headquarters are planning outfits that control forces "assigned" to them only during specified maneuvers or in war. Each ally, of course, retains the right to go to war according to its own constitutional processes.

With respect to Polaris forces, the line of command runs from Washington to the US Commander-in-Chief, Atlantic. The same admiral is also NATO Supreme Allied Commander, Atlantic.

The practical effect of the "assignment" of Polaris to NATO is that the admiral involved can give orders in his capacity as NATO commander to himself in his capacity as United States commander. Whatever hat the admiral wears, the President continues in ultimate control of our Polaris force. Our veto remains absolute. The influence of our allies over the targeting and planning of this force is not noticeably greater than over those strategic forces which remain under exclusive US control—particularly if Europeans can participate in the targeting of the latter. In other words, the "assignment" of the Polaris force to NATO is largely symbolic.

In fact, the influence of our European allies on nuclear strategy has actually diminished with respect to the three Polaris submarines "assigned" to the Mediterranean to replace the Jupiter missiles in Italy and Turkey. The Jupiter missiles were subject to the double-veto system; that is to say, Italy and Turkey had to agree before the Jupiters could be fired. The only influence Italy and Turkey will have over the Polaris submarines in the Mediterranean is through NATO guidelines, if these can be agreed upon.

The notion of guidelines presents serious problems of its own. Are they to be conceived as a kind of contingency plan for the employment of nuclear weapons, *provided* the governments concerned agree to implement these plans? Or are they to be considered a delegation of authority to use nuclear weapons in certain specified contingencies without further reference to political authority?

If guidelines are to be interpreted in the former sense—as a form of contingency war plan—they are another version of the joint targeting previously described. But in that case it is not clear why a formal assignment to NATO was necessary or how the NATO-committed Polaris forces are to be distinguished from our other strategic forces.

If, on the other hand, the guidelines are to determine not the targets but the circumstances in which nuclear weapons are to be used, serious problems would arise. A guideline so conceived not only includes; it also excludes. It defines not only when nuclear weapons are to be employed but also the circumstances when they will not be used. It is possible that the only contingency in which all the Allies would agree in advance is a massive Soviet nuclear attack on Europe—the circumstances about which there is likely to be least doubt and where the seeming need for prior specification may only magnify uncertainties. In short, if the guidelines are too vague, they may multiply concerns; if an attempt is made to be too specific, they will magnify divisions.

Whatever else the guidelines may accomplish, they will not affect the US veto or, for that matter, the right of any of the other allies to determine whether the circumstances to which the guideline refers have in fact arisen. At the same time, pre-delegation of authority to use nuclear weapons either to the Secretary-General of NATO or to some Allied commander or to both acting in concert—as has sometimes been suggested— would represent an unprecedented abdication of Constitutional responsibilities. It is difficult to see any President or Prime Minister agreeing to this step. If it were taken, it is certain that the pre-delegation of authority would be confined to the most obvious and unambiguous cases of nuclear aggression, raising uncertainties about the ambiguous cases that have caused much greater worries. In short, guidelines have the uses and limitations of joint targeting; they are only a small step in the direction of solving NATO's nuclear dilemma.

These considerations come to a particular focus with respect to the keystone of our NATO nuclear policy: the NATO multilateral force composed of mixed crews. This proposal has had a checkered history. It was first advanced for study by former Secretary of State Christian Herter in December 1960. It was then cold-shouldered in the first few months of the Kennedy Administration. Then in May 1961, at Ottawa, President Kennedy announced a willingness to consider "a NATO sea-borne missile force, which would be truly multilateral in ownership and control . . ." Our European allies were invited to make proposals to this end.

Given the fact that none of our allies possessed sea-borne nuclear systems and that a command and control system even for a national force is not a simple matter, the probability that our allies would come up with a meaningful control system was not great. Indeed, many believed that the problem would be recognized as insoluble. Our allies were then expected to ask the President to act as executive agent of the Alliance with respect to nuclear weapons.

When this did not happen, the United States a year later again offered to consider a NATO nuclear force, provided our allies first built up their conventional forces and came up with an acceptable control system. Since the control problem had not become any easier and since most of our allies were dubious about the need for the kind of conventional build-up we were proposing, it was not clear whether our proposal was put forward in order to be accepted or to be rejected.

Three months later, in September 1962, McGeorge Bundy spoke in terms of a multilateral *European* force: "It . . . would be wrong to suppose that the reluctance which we feel with respect to individual, ineffective, and antiquated forces would be extended automatically to a European force, genuinely unified and multilateral, and effectively integrated with our own necessarily predominant strength in the whole nuclear defense of the

Alliance." This speech said nothing about what we understood by "multilateral," "integrated," or "unified."

Two months later, Under Secretary of State George Ball returned to the theme of a NATO force. He argued that we thought "a European nuclear contribution" to NATO militarily unnecessary. However, "should other NATO nations so desire, we are ready to give serious consideration to the creation of a genuinely multilateral Medium-Range Ballistic Missile force fully coordinated with the other deterrent forces in the North Atlantic Treaty Organization."

At the regular NATO ministerial conference in December 1962, nothing was done about the creation of a NATO multilateral force. A week later, on December 21, President Kennedy and Prime Minister Macmillan signed the Nassau Agreement, which provided for two multilateral forces: one that would absorb the strategic forces of Great Britain and France together with a US contribution of nationally owned submarines; another in which the non-nuclear countries of NATO would create a truly multilateral Polaris force, which was later explained to mean that it would be jointly financed, owned, planned, manned, and operated.

Nothing was said about how either multilateral force was to be controlled, deployed, or targeted. On January 10, prior to President de Gaulle's press conference. Under Secretary Ball was back in Paris to explain to the NATO Council that the multilateral NATO force that he had declared militarily unnecessary in November was now a high-priority goal of the Kennedy Administration. Indeed, he was reported to have suggested that the United States was ready to begin training submarine crews of mixed national composition immediately.

This sequence of events is important to keep in mind because it might well have led even political leaders less suspicious of US motives than President de Gaulle to doubt whether we really had a "grand design" or whether we were not simply offering palliatives to perpetuate our hegemony.

In any event, after President de Gaulle's press conference, the multilateral force composed of the presently non-nuclear powers was pushed energetically. "Informed sources" were quoted as having said that we would create a force so strong that the Federal Republic of Germany in particular would see that the advantages of our notion of multilateralism far exceeded any benefits to be gained by association with France.

In order to thwart French nuclear pretensions, we proposed to create a counterweight by bringing some of the non-nuclear European countries into the nuclear field. The already difficult issue of multilateral control has thus become further complicated because we have made membership in the "mixed" force a test of Atlantic solidarity. Livingston Merchant was appointed to carry out the negotiations to bring this force into being.

Since then, the US position has continued to shift. We have recently indicated that surface ships are a better solution than submarines. Secretary McNamara and President Kennedy have spoken of both a European and a NATO multilateral force. But the practical requirements they impose make the distinction elusive. They agree that any NATO force must be "integrated" with our strategic forces; there must be a single chain of command and a single finger on the trigger. In the light of Secretary McNamara's strategic theories, this must mean that either a European or a NATO nuclear force has to be under ultimate US command. "The American representatives also will make it clear," the *New York Times* reported on February 27, "that there will be only one finger on the trigger of any nuclear force established by NATO. It will be that of the President of the United States."

In giving multilateralism this definition, we are trying to defend Atlantic solidarity on an issue and with a solution certain to magnify Allied disagreements in the long run. The valid and important concept of interdependence can only be discredited by association with schemes that deprive our allies of the physical possibility of independent action while we reserve this right for ourselves. US dominance in the nuclear field may be a desirable solution from our point of view—though it is apt to prove shortsighted. But we should not call such an arrangement a partnership, and we must recognize that it will generate rather than alleviate pressures for change.

At the moment, the political constellation of Europe prohibits an articulation of this problem, perhaps even its clear recognition. Great Britain, though in practice striving to retain a nuclear independence very similar to France's, cannot afford any further controversy. Nevertheless, the much-heralded "assignment" of the British V-bomber force to NATO has had the same significance as our previous "earmarking" of Polaris submarines. It was a symbolic act that did not diminish British control. It is not clear whether the assignment of national forces represents the total British contribution to NATO's nuclear arsenal. But Britain's national program can leave resources for only a token contribution to the multilateral force composed of mixed crews.

As for the other Allies, West Germany has seen in agreement to a multilateral NATO force of mixed crews an opportunity to reassure us about Atlantic solidarity and to enter the nuclear field. The other European countries that have agreed to participate—at last report, Italy, Belgium, and perhaps the Netherlands—are more likely to do so to keep an eye on Germany than because of strategic convictions.

Indeed, any reflection about the structure of the multilateral force composed of mixed crews gives us as much reason to worry about the allies that agree to join as about those who refuse. For one thing, the requirement of mixed manning is a symptom of distrust, since the chief reason is to prevent any national government from withdrawing part of the force. Is every national contingent to receive separate instructions before the missiles can be fired? No wonder nearly all the military commanders, US as well as Allied, regard mixed manning with extreme distaste.

Apart from the problem of what may be termed control by the threat of mutiny, it is difficult to see just what would be achieved by the proposed force. According to Secretary Mc-Namara's testimony, it cannot be used independently of our much larger forces. In any event, we would presumably keep control over the nuclear warheads of the NATO multilateral force—according to the McMahon Act, we would have no other choice. Even if the law were changed with respect to the physical control over warheads, the problem of the veto would remain.

If we retain the veto, one of two things would happen. If we decided to engage in nuclear war and our allies refused, we would use the Strategic Air Command and our entire Polaris force, including that part of it "assigned" to NATO. If the situation were reversed—that is, if our allies wished to use nuclear weapons and we disagreed—neither the NATO force nor SAC could operate.

Can we give up the veto? It is not easy to see how a country can abdicate so fateful a decision to a majority vote of allies, no matter how close. The Constitutional issue would surely be formidable.

Moreover, what would giving up the veto commit us to? Does it mean that we would not obstruct the utilization of the NATO force in which we participate? In terms of Secretary McNamara's testimony, this partial employment of nuclear power is what must in all circumstances be avoided. In any event, it is difficult to imagine making a commitment to go to nuclear war indirectly and with only the smallest part of our forces.

But if we agree to go to war with our entire nuclear arsenal, what is the point of creating a NATO force? Then it would be wiser to create a political control body for the Alliance as a whole and agree to go to war on the basis of whatever majority vote seems indicated. (Such a commitment would probably still not meet the need. Even under existing arrangements, we could refuse to aid our allies if we are reluctant to honor our NATO commitments, and that situation would not change under the new scheme.)

It has also been reported that the United States is willing to accept a European commander for the proposed multilateral force. But this is either a palliative or a source of concern. If political control is effective, the veto will remain regardless of the nationality of the commander. If political control is not reliable, we would be in a position of showing more confidence in a European military man than in the Constitutionally established leadership. Unauthorized use is likely to be a particular problem in an organization deliberately constructed so that its members can have no primary allegiance to any of the established political entities.

What of the argument that the proposed NATO force could in time be transformed into a European force if our allies request it? We have repeatedly hinted at our willingness to consider this prospect. However, there are two major obstacles. The first is our strategic doctrine. Our insistence on a unified command, a single target system, and the need for instant response is as inconsistent with a separate European force as with national forces.

Even if we are prepared to change our strategic doctrine, serious problems would remain. The only way a NATO force as now conceived could be transformed into a European one would be for our allies to ask us to withdraw from it. This would defeat the prime purpose of many of the smaller countries in joining the force: to demonstrate Atlantic solidarity. Such a step, even if it were politically feasible, is much more likely to accentuate Allied divisions than beginning with an explicitly European program. Moreover, as long as France is not part of a NATO force and Britain's contribution is token only, any attempt to turn it into a European force will raise the specter of German domination and thus create powerful antagonisms in other European countries.

It can be argued, of course, that the fear of German domination will make Britain and France more eager to join the multilateral force. This is doubtful. But even if it were correct, such a process of arriving at a European force would be extremely worrisome. It would be better for the long-term stability and cohesiveness of Europe if West Germany joined a Franco-British program than for Britain and France to be obliged to seek membership in a grouping of which Germany is the senior European partner. History has been altered by smaller nuances.

This suggests the need to re-examine another of the assumptions behind our advocacy of the NATO force. The NATO force is often said to be a device to avoid the issue of nuclear weapons in German hands. The contrary is likely to be the case. The multilateral force as now conceived may wind up by frustrating every member. If West Germany is seriously interested in acquiring strategic weapons, the multilateral force is apt to prove only an interim step and may turn out to be the easiest way of getting Germany into the nuclear business. The danger in the multilateral force is that those who want effective control over their nuclear destiny will not long remain content with the projected arrangements, while those who go along for such motives as pleasing us, defying France, or keeping an eye on Germany will soon grow tired of the expense and will search for other options.

This becomes apparent when the financial implications of our proposals are examined. The number of missiles most frequently mentioned for the NATO nuclear force is three hundred. It is interesting that this represents four times the delivery vehicles of the French Mirage force and three times that of the projected British Polaris force. We are in the curious position of opposing the existing national nuclear forces, but in order to thwart them we are engaged in diffusing an even larger number of weapons to a group of countries not now in the nuclear business and with no immediate prospect of entering it.

The cost of a fleet of Polaris submarines is estimated at more than $1 billion a year, or an increase of twelve per cent in the defense spending of the participating countries. A fleet of merchant ships has been estimated to cost upwards of $500 million, or an increase of seven per cent. And as the technical problems of placing Polaris missiles on merchant ships is studied and the requirements for assuring invulnerability are analyzed, the costs are liable to mount.

For this heavy expense, the participants would obtain no significant increase in control over nuclear weapons. Can anyone seriously believe that this can be a permanent state of affairs? Is it not infinitely more likely that after a few years we would face repetitions of our current problem with France in relation to some of the projected members of the NATO nuclear force?

Our present proposals grant the need for a separate force, but they do not grant the equality that would give that force meaning. In a few years, after they have gotten into the nuclear business with our assistance, some of the countries now projected as participants will indeed be much better able to raise the nuclear issue than France is today. They will not have to argue about the possession of nuclear technology—since this will have been conceded—but about the control of a force where their influence is patently out of proportion to their contribution. If we resist these pressures, we may bring about a violent swing toward de Gaulle's conceptions. Nothing is more likely to promote Third Force tendencies in Europe than for us to engage our prestige in pressing for a force which on our own showing makes no sense militarily, does not alter existing control arrangements significantly, yet requires a heavy European financial contribution.

The multilateral NATO force is thus likely to combine the disadvantages of every course of action. It will not prevent the diffusion of nuclear weapons; it may well accelerate it. It will neither stop the acquisition of nuclear arms by West Germany nor satisfy over any extended period whatever demands may exist there for a greater voice on nuclear matters. It *will* stop the building up of conventional forces, for none of the countries reported ready to join the NATO nuclear force is likely to increase its defense budget beyond the expenditures required for the multilateral force. Among the many inconsistencies of our present position is the simultaneous pressure for the NATO multilateral force and an increase in European conventional strength. The two policies are incompatible.

Finally, the NATO nuclear force will not represent any significant burden-sharing. Since some of the European countries will possess some kind of veto, our strategic planning could not count on the NATO force. The strategy envisaged by Mr. McNamara would then require us to maintain whatever strategic forces are thought necessary for a US counterforce response—as if the NATO force did not exist.

As for other political effects often advertised as the chief, if not the sole, purpose of the NATO nuclear force, Allied cohesion is unlikely to be strengthened. On the contrary, Europe will be fragmented even further. France will be isolated, but at a heavy price. We will have shifted the relative weight in Europe toward countries which, while more pliable in the short term, may prove more unstable in the long run. If the influence of West Germany in the multilateral force becomes too great, neutralism may grow in Britain, Scandinavia, and the Low Countries. (The *New York Times* of March 9 reported that the Federal Republic would contribute about two-thirds of the European share of the NATO force, or about forty per cent of the total costs, and that influence in manning and operational control would be proportionate to the financial contribution.)

The effort to isolate France by developing in the nuclear field a structure in which West Germany would be the key European member may in fact overstrain the fabric of European cohesion and Atlantic solidarity, and also undermine the domestic stability of West Germany. It is in nobody's interest—least of all West Germany's—to set in motion events that can only end with suspicion and concern in most of the countries of the West about Germany's nuclear role. This is bound to aid the Soviet thrust to divide the West through the fear of Germany. A divided country, which in the space of fifty years has lost two wars, experienced three revolutions, suffered two periods of extreme inflation and the trauma of the Nazi era, should not—in its own interest—be placed in a position where, in addition to its inevitable exposure to Soviet pressure, it becomes the balance wheel of our Atlantic policy. We are encouraging tendencies that we may later regret. There must be better ways for West Germany to demonstrate its devotion to the Atlantic Alliance than to become the largest European contributor to a multilateral nuclear force.

The danger of our present course thus goes far beyond disputes about strategic theory. An issue as complicated as the control of nuclear weapons within the Alliance cannot be expected to have a quick or a neat solution. Nevertheless, the frequent and rapid changes of our position undermine our reputation for reliability—whatever the merit of particular proposals.

How can the most well-disposed governments follow our lead when our proposals are in a constant state of flux, moving from indifference to eager advocacy of a NATO force and from submarines to merchant ships all within two months?

Even so staunch a friend as Great Britain must be bewildered. First we abruptly canceled Skybolt. Then Prime Minister Macmillan loyally supported the Nassau Agreement with the argument that the acquisition of Polaris submarines would align Great Britain with our strategic thinking and our NATO conceptions. A month later we proposed that the multilateral NATO force of mixed crews be composed of merchant ships. This leaves Prime Minister Macmillan exposed to the criticism of having purchased an unnecessarily expensive system for Great Britain. It makes us vulnerable to the charge of foisting a second-best system on the Europeans. And the situation is made the more poignant by the fact that Britain has been asked to join *both* forces.

Our friends do not know what to support. Our opponents are encouraged to exert pressure or at least to procrastinate in order to elicit other offers. Open-mindedness is often a virtue. But we must remember that the leader of a great coalition simply cannot afford to do all of its thinking in public.

To be sure, we are still able to obtain support, partly because we remain the strongest ally and our good will continues vital; partly because many of the smaller European countries have developed a habit of dependence. Our influence is still sufficient to generate domestic pressures in many European countries. But all this is to no avail if the basic direction is mistaken. Then, the domestic forces we encourage may well produce long-term instabilities.

One of the major achievements of American postwar policy has been the growth of a moderate, self-confident Europe that is willing to assume a degree of responsibility for its destiny. We take this so much for granted that we tend to forget how difficult the process has been and how precarious the balance still is in many European countries. In our eagerness to advance our new strategic theories, we have failed to perceive that ultimately success or failure depends on the political forces associated with us.

In this respect, there is reason for serious concern. In too many countries, governments that painfully obtained a commitment to the existing defense programs and to the very concept of NATO find themselves charged with undermining US relationships by those who opposed every step along that road. In several countries, our policies are supported by groups who see in the slogan of Atlantic solidarity a convenient tool to discredit the existing European structure. The Nenni Socialists in Italy have not become converts to our concept of nuclear defense; they half-heartedly support us because they want to retain an option for their favorite schemes of nuclear disengagement. Britain, if it abandons its nuclear program, will not introduce conscription. Conventional defense may be invoked to wreck the nuclear program; the result is much more likely to be a form of neutralism than a conventional build-up. Undermining the major program of an ally must produce upheavals that cannot be measured by purely technical standards.

Our present course may thus encourage simultaneously neutralism and rabid nationalism, a sense of impotence and frustration. In another five years we may be confronted by a Europe that can truly be described by many of the epithets presently applied to President de Gaulle. The fact that many of our actions are taken with the seeming agreement of much of our press and some of our allies is no consolation. The test of leadership is not tomorrow's editorial but what history will say of us five years from now.

### Where Do We Go From Here?

It is always difficult to reverse course. The longer a given policy is maintained, the more vested interests—in dedication, in conception, and in bureaucratic persistence—it is bound to create. Yet sometimes the wisest policy is to resist the temptation to rely on momentum, and to step back and take stock.

Perhaps the best way to begin a reappraisal would be to ask ourselves what our real interests in Europe are. We should examine what kind of structure we desire in the long term rather than seek for devices to head off immediate pressures.

The goal of a strong, unified, and self-sufficient Europe, which American policy has consistently pursued for a decade and a half, is as valid today as it was when first developed in 1947. We may not have fully understood then that an economically powerful Europe would be more self-assertive in the political and military field as well. We may have believed subconsciously that our policy would relieve us of economic burdens without requiring a redefinition of Atlantic relationships. But whether or not we fully realized the implications of what we were doing, the Europe of today stands as a testimony to our foresight and our ability to subordinate short-term advantage to long-term benefits.

However, in the past few years there has been a tendency to recoil before the inevitable implications of our policy. It was always in the cards—indeed, it was our stated purpose—that as Europe regained its economic health it would also seek to develop its own specific policies. It never occurred to us originally that the relations of the European states to each other should not be closer than each of them was to the United States. On the contrary, the original conception was that a cohesive Europe would be a more effective partner for the United States. Atlantic partnership was then thought of in terms of establishing a relationship with a Europe whose internal structure would be firmer than the Atlantic bonds.

This great conception can be reversed today only by undermining the structures that have been laboriously developed over the past fifteen years. Fifteen years ago it might have been possible to try to construct an Atlantic Community on the most favored nation principle; that is, that no nation have closer relations to any other than to the United States. Today this attempt jeopardizes all that has been achieved.

Yet stripped to its essentials, this is the course we have been pursuing with Europe in the nuclear field. Our definition of interdependence has the practical consequence of discouraging the emergence of any European identity in nuclear matters. We are fostering a concept of multilateralism that will add new divisions to the existing rifts in Europe. A multilateral force in which France does not participate and to which Britain makes only a token contribution will lead to a structure in the nuclear field inconsistent with all our postwar policies. The result is likely to be either competing European groupings or the ultimate emergence of a European unity in which the leadership roles have been drastically altered with our assistance.

It is still possible—though it is getting late—to prevent these developments by fostering a European nuclear identity growing out of the British and French programs. It is often said that such a course would divide the Alliance. But surely we are not going to maintain that partnership is possible only with nations incapable of independent action. Moreover, if we cut through the phrases to the facts, a separate European entity need be no more divisive in the military than in the economic field. In both instances it calls attention to the need for a political effort to devise common objectives.

It would be idle to claim that conceding European nuclear autonomy would by itself solve NATO's nuclear dilemma. The problem of relationships in the nuclear field is sufficiently complex to resist simple remedies. But encouraging a separate European center of decision-making is a vital first step.

We have had two choices with respect to Europe's nuclear future. We could accept the British and French national efforts and encourage first a common Franco-British and ultimately a European program. Or else we could group the non-nuclear countries into a multilateral force more responsive to our notions of a single chain of command and an indivisible target system.

We have chosen the second course. The first is preferable by far. It is hard to conceive a stable Europe that does not include France as well as Britain. Any genuine nuclear policy must grow out of existing programs that will continue whatever the fate of the multilateral force. A policy that cannot relate us to the existing nuclear powers—our traditional allies—is not likely to be more effective when the present non-nuclear powers have become members of the nuclear club with our help.

Thus, instead of being hostile to the French nuclear program and, at best, indifferent to the British effort, we should use our influence to place them in the service of a European conception. This would also be the most reliable road to Atlantic partnership. The emerging European force could then be related to ours through political coordination and joint strategic planning. Such a policy would require a change of attitude on our part; at the very least the technical pressures from the Defense Department would have to be subordinated to an overriding political direction.

This is not to say that the United States should support every strategic theory developed in Britain or France. It is plain that we have certain interests in any European nuclear development which we are bound to foster:

a) The European forces should be well protected so that they do not invite pre-emptive attack or have to be used precipitately because of their vulnerability.

b) These forces should possess an effective command and control system so that they are at all times responsive to political direction.

c) They should be a part of a strategy that includes the possibility of flexible response.

d) They should become an instrument to foster European integration.

e) They should be coordinated with our forces.

All these objectives are more likely to be achieved by offering assistance to Great Britain and France in enhancing the invulnerability of their forces and improving their command and control than by the so-called NATO multilateralism. We could make the scale of our assistance depend on the British and French ability to develop common programs and a common strategy. We could encourage Britain and France to put their nuclear forces into the service of Europe, perhaps by associating other countries in the control mechanism. We could strongly urge that the savings accomplished by our assistance in the nuclear field be devoted to a build-up of conventional power.

Such a program would maintain the principle of flexible response (though not perhaps of counterforce general war). It would grow organically out of existing European nuclear programs. It would avoid the necessity of organizing the presently non-nuclear powers into their own separate nuclear force and thus in the long run represent a smaller diffusion of nuclear power. It would make Britain's entry into Europe inevitable. And it would lay the basis for a more natural association between Europe and the United States than the so-called multilateralism.

It may be argued that once we help Britain and France, every European country will want its own national nuclear force. The President has mentioned even a Belgian nuclear force as a possibility. We must distinguish, however, between the possession of some nuclear weapons and the development of an indigenous nuclear program. The latter is beyond the present capability of any European country, for either political or economic reasons or for both.

West Germany is prohibited by the Paris treaties from manufacturing nuclear weapons. While treaties have been broken before, in this particular instance the international repercussions are apt to be so serious as to give any German government pause. At the moment and for at least the next legislative period—that is, until about 1969—there are in any event no signs of any domestic pressures in Germany for a national nuclear-weapons program. This may change, however, after the multilateral force has whetted appetites.

Italy has neither the resources nor the domestic support for a national nuclear program. As for Belgium and other smaller countries, it can hardly be argued that the French program exceeds France's resources but that we must gear our NATO nuclear policy to preventing the development of similar programs by much poorer countries.

To be sure, a joint Franco-British program would probably lead to efforts by West Germany and perhaps other European countries for a degree of participation in at least the control mechanism. But in this way the Franco-British effort could become a spur to European political integration. France and Britain would have a high incentive to foster European unity before the issue of nuclear weapons under German national control becomes acute.

Whatever is done in the military field, the current crisis underlines the urgent need for greater political cohesion in the Western Alliance. We are now in the curious position of pressing for military integration while practicing political bilateralism. On a variety of issues from Berlin to the test ban, we have claimed the right for independent approaches to the Soviets.

However, unity in the security field is bound to be ephemeral without a common diplomacy. We cannot have different conceptions of a possible *casus belli*—which is at least one implication of different negotiating positions—and insist at the same time that the resulting strategy must be unified. If we want to spur integration, the political field would seem much more promising than the military. If the nations of the Atlantic Community follow common policies, the existence of different centers of military decision would present primarily a problem of technical coordination, not a challenge to allied unity.

The Atlantic Alliance requires urgently a political body to define common objectives and the means to achieve them. It might be useful to begin by developing a common position on such issues as Berlin, disarmament, or the test ban. If it should be argued that this is impossible, the emptiness of nuclear multilateralism is patent. Nations that cannot agree on common negotiating positions on such matters are not likely to be able to devise a common strategy for an apocalypse.

Withal, it is important to keep the difficulties of the Western Alliance in proper perspective. Deep as the divisions are, they are the result of the success of previous policies. They testify to the emergence of a strong and self-confident Europe—a consistent goal of US policy in the last three Administrations. Few of the recent fissures in the West have been produced by Soviet actions. This is another way of saying that the West is less imperiled by outside pressures than by a tendency to waste its own substance. It also means that the remedies are still within our own control.

# The Middle East and North Africa

—ALBERT J. MEYER

## Summary

To sum up, the longer-term economic trends in the Middle East point toward a growing intimacy between the area and the United States and united Europe. So far the Soviet Union has done little but prove that its strategy, its export of human beings, and its intellectual arsenal of advice are less adaptable than ours, and less acceptable, to the nations of the Middle East. The West still leads in this lap of the race. In the arms race, however, we are all (the United States, the nations of the area, Western European countries, the Soviet Union) in a mess, and we all bear blame.

The strategic task facing the West for the next fifteen years is obviously to play those hands where it is strongest—trade and investment, promotion of educational opportunities of all kinds for Middle Easterners, in the area and in the West, maintenance and improvement of technical and economic aid programs, and promotion of "free trade" in human beings. And with it all we must find ways to moderate the arms race, and above all maintain the embargo on nuclear weapons available to local leaders.

No discussion of strategy and economics in the Middle East and North Africa can overlook a series of longer-term developments which influence today's decisions and problems. I shall begin by treating several of these, and shall then turn to assessing recent occurrences and hazarding a series of guesses about future Western policy.

317

## Longer-Term Developments

First, we now have enough evidence to conclude that the decade and a half since World War II has been punctuated in the Middle East by impressive economic growth. Disregarding such economic museum pieces as Kuwait and Qatar, whose rise from $50 a head in 1945 to more than $2000 today is irrelevant for our purposes, one may point to substantial growth elsewhere. Cyprus, Israel, Iraq, and Lebanon have all gone ahead at 3-5% net (after adjustment for population increase and inflation) for the decade of the 1950's; Syria did about the same between 1946 and 1956; Turkey's rates have been lower, but well above 2%, since World War II; Iran, Jordan, and Egypt claim net advances in excess of 1% for most of the past ten years. The economic performance has been impressive.

It has also been accompanied by, and has probably helped create, rapid political change, with frequent interruptions of tranquility. We have seen dramatic changes of government in Turkey, Iraq, Egypt, Cyprus, Syria, and more recently Yemen; the Arab-Israeli War, the Sinai campaign, Iraq's threats toward Kuwait, Lebanon's troubles in 1958, and now the quadrangular joust between Jordan, Egypt, Saudi Arabia, and Yemen have at least one lesson in common—the countries where economic growth has been most rapid seem just as unstable politically, or just as prone to international altercations, as those where there has been little growth—or none. So far the Middle East has performed not unlike the West over time in this respect —to the disappointment of many post-World War II idealists, who have tended to link higher incomes to political tranquility.

Next, one can point to an enormous growth in economic interdependence between the Middle East and the governments and people of Western nations since 1945. A few examples will suffice: from a mere trickle at the end of World War II, the flow of oil westward from five Middle Eastern nations has grown to over 6 million barrels daily, and revenue payments to producing governments now exceed $1.5 billion yearly; shipping through the Suez Canal has increased enormously since nationalization; Western economic aid and military support programs have transferred more than $100 million yearly to Middle Eastern nations since 1950; Cyprus has sustained itself for fifteen years on UK treasury transfers for military base expenditures, mineral exports, emigrant remittances, and tourism; American and European tourists each year play an increasingly important role in Middle Eastern foreign exchange earnings; for almost 15 years Israel has relied on gifts, reparations, and additions to its national debt, all originating in the West, to cover its import deficit in amount of almost a third of national income.

Despite many unsolved problems—such as those of cotton and other "problem crops" produced in the Middle East—the record of growth of economic interdependence has been remarkable. Private investors from America and Europe have put more than $4 billion to work in the Middle East in recent years, most of it in oil and in Israel. Middle Eastern public and private investors, meanwhile, have put easily half as much —probably more than $2 billion—into European, British, and US securities. A major part of the total public and private investment in the Middle East, which has averaged a respectable 10-20 per cent of national income yearly in many nations, is directly traceable to trade or investment between the Middle East and the West since World War II.

Third, we now have, after six years of observation in the Middle East, a better idea of what the Soviets are up to—and their successes and failures. But briefly, they have, since 1955, abandoned their earlier policies of merely tweaking the tail of the West in the Middle East and have themselves promoted programs of various kinds—economic and technical aid, military assistance, educational exchanges, and the like. The result, supportable with many examples, so far has been that the Soviets have met the same frustrations, suffer from the same shortages of "exportable" nationals, and are just as mollified as we Westerners at the results obtained and at the magnitude of the problem. Instead of capitalizing on what looked, in 1955-56, to be a made-to-order climate for the practice of subversion, they have in reality done little but join us on our own shaky limb of confusion on the whole subject of aid, propaganda, and military assistance—contrary to predictions of the "Ugly American" school of foreign aid interpretation.

Abundant evidence supports the above conclusion. Despite the tries of recent years, no Middle Eastern government today can be said to be influenced substantially by practicing Communists—indeed, throughout the area no more than a handful are in positions of real authority; the Communist Party is either outlawed or harrassed mercilessly by CID's in most Middle Eastern nations, such as Egypt; Soviet Bloc technicians and advisors, usually speaking only their own national tongues,

live in segregated housing and mingle rarely with local popu-
laces; the Soviet loan credits, estimated to total over $1 billion,
have not in most cases been taken up and have failed to play
the demonstrable roles hoped for by Soviet planners—Syria
is a case at point; Soviet advisors and technicians still work
on projects designed largely by Westerners (such as the many
undertakings in Egypt and Syria) and not on new, dramatic
projects contrived by them; the much-discussed reorientation
of trade toward the Soviet Union has been much less significant
than many forecast (Egypt indeed has reorientated its trade
back to more than 50% with Western nations); Soviet economic
theory has proved less exportable than our own; relatively few
young Middle Easterners go East for education; oil still goes
West.

In contrast, Soviet efforts so far would seem to have been
most successful in Cyprus, where a well organized labor movement with leftist leadership offered a convenient vehicle—and
the far right of the autocephalous Greek church of Cyprus
an enticing target. Here, Eastern Bloc nations have concentrated on aiding dissent movements and have cannily avoided
offering independent Cyprus the chance to place its aid demands
on the escalator to the stratosphere.

Fourth, the most persistently disturbing element on the Middle Eastern scene has been the steady growth in arms expenditures. Since World War II almost every nation in the area,
beginning from negligible outlays, has pushed its arms budget
upward. The present area-wide average, in percentage terms,
now equals that of the civilized nations of the West—50% of
most government budgets, amounting to 10% of total national
income—now goes to military expenditure. In round numbers,
more than $1 billion *of local money* now goes toward "defense"
—as Arabs and Israelis gird against one another, Arab against
Arab, Turk against Arab, Iranian against Arab, and so on. Even
Cyprus seems intent on mounting an army.

Early national military expenditures in the Middle East undeniably served useful purposes, through promoting internal
order and augmenting public efforts at education. But since
1955—when the Russians joined us at the game of providing
weapons and advice to Middle Eastern armies—the situation
has become increasingly untenable. A new jet or rocket launcher
in one country leads inexorably to the same across its neighbor's frontier. The competition between funds for development
and those for military hardware is bad enough, but the creation

of a climate for another Cuba-like adventure is downright horrifying.

So much for the longer-term developments of the past fifteen years which underlie any discussion of Western strategy toward the Middle East. Let me now turn to a list of possible points of friction.

## Possible Points of Friction

The first of these concerns the dual polarization which now seems under way in matters of Eastern Hemisphere oil. Put briefly and superficially, Western Europe appears now to be moving to accelerate its abandonment of coal as a major supplier of energy (coal and oil now provide roughly 50% each of Europe's total energy requirements). The many influential supporters of this policy feel that Europe can now, for the first time, undertake development using imported energy because of diversified supplies (such as those in the Soviet Union, North Africa, and Holland), Europe's capacity to absorb excess coal workers in other jobs, and the need for Europe to cut production costs in an increasingly competitive world. But these same advocates would, with few exceptions, link the sped-up "flight from coal" with regulations of many kinds—import quotas, excise-tax rates, guarantees protecting "European" owned oil companies and sources of supply, rules about standby capacity, to mention a few. Enforcement of such regulations, enormously complex in fact and implication, could well lead toward broad-spectrum Common Market energy boards, wielding considerable economic power.

This trend, which is very much under discussion at the moment, is accompanied by, and indeed has encouraged, a corresponding polarization at the other end of the spectrum. I refer to the movement within the oil-producing countries of the Middle East, North Africa, and South America to form organizations to protect themselves against drops in earnings such as those which came with the cuts in price postings in the autumn of 1960. At the moment, the champion of the producing countries is the Organization of Petroleum Exporting Countries (OPEC). Contrary to many early forecasts, OPEC seems to be gaining strength (Libya recently joined, Algeria will probably come in soon). Today many informed observers would forecast that OPEC (or its successor) will be an inevitable accompaniment to Europe's accelerated "flight from coal" and the continued incapacity of the international oil industry to itself control capacity and police prices.

The interaction between the energy boards of United Europe and OPEC (or its successor) poses an enormously complicated set of problems, which can only be alluded to in a paper of this sort. Which oil-producer countries will get the lion's share of the enormous increases in petroleum demand certain to come if Western Europe continues to step up abandonment of coal? What role will United Europe permit Soviet oil to play in its future growth? What will be the long-term attitudes of the "consumers club" and the "producers club" to the international oil companies—which up to now have performed most of the functions now envisioned by many for the clubs? What action —economic or military—might United Europe take should threats to its energy life-blood occur from nationalization, or severance of pipeline or canal transit? One might point to a dozen other problems, and points of friction, but these will suffice. The polarization deserves watching.

The second strategic problem which merits speculation is that which might evolve should Communist China step up its petroleum imports markedly and become a really large-scale buyer of Middle Eastern and North African oil. At the moment most-observers discount this possibility heavily, pointing to the massive reserves of Ural oil in the Soviet Union, sources on the Chinese mainland itself, and the ability of the government of Red China to control fuel usage. Yet others reason that Russia's own "flight from coal" (now under way along with Eastern Europe's), the enormous cost of pipelines from Russia to the Far East (don't forget that much of the pipe for the new lines to Europe came from Europe!), and the evidence of disenchantment between the Soviet Union and the Red Chinese might join to make the economists and geologists as wrong on this forecast as they have been on so many others—over time and very recently!

Should Red China become a large-scale buyer of Middle Eastern and North African oil—from, for example, national oil companies now operating in almost every Middle Eastern nation, or from the international companies—closer political collaboration might well ensue. Revolutionary governments in several Middle Eastern and North African countries might well seek Chinese planners and Chinese advice—having seen already that the equivalents from the West and the Soviet Union had so far failed to work miracles. Admittedly this is still wildly speculative, but one might even contemplate formation of some global alignments quite different from today's.

A third possible point of friction would be that accompanying emergence of a revolutionary government friendly to the Soviet Union *and* owning a contiguous frontier with it—Iran or Turkey, for example. One might guess that should friendly, or even strongly neutralist, governments emerge in Iran or Turkey, the Soviet Union might well abandon its customary penury on matters of foreign aid and make an all-out, and, for it, unbelievably generous try. The nearby availability of the Soviet army would interject another new, and equally disquieting element. Under such circumstances, chances of another confrontation between East and West would rise sharply.

Let me remind you that the above is, like my earlier point, highly speculative. Iran and Turkey have made real economic strides since World War II; US economic and military aid to both has been generous and continuing; consortia of other Western nations are now rallying to the task; Iranian oil needs a market in the West; Western private firms—such as the Consortium now building, with Turkish partners, the steel mill near Eregli—have shown enormous imagination in their tasks. But Turkey and Iran still face tremendous economic and political obstacles, and recent developments indicate that elements of instability are decidedly present in both countries.

Finally, no forecast of points of tension can omit the dreary matter of Arab-Israeli strife. There is *no* evidence that the two warring camps have, in fifteen years, moderated their mutual animosities one particle. All governments concerned are currently rejecting categorically Mr. Joseph Johnson's proposals for Arab refugee settlement; budgets for "defense" against each other rise yearly; Arab fears rise as immigration into Israel rises and falls with crises throughout the world (as in Algeria) and in consonance with Zionist urgings to Jews of the Diaspora (as in Tunisia and Morocco, most recently) to ingather; some forecast that a flood of Jews from Russia might soon seek entry to Israel; restraint on both sides and the UN force in Gaza have, happily, kept border incidents recently at a minimum. But both sides have rockets, and the Soviet Union has shown increasing willingness, as did Western nations earlier, to tamper with the military balance. In this context, one may nervously recall the early chapters in Neville Shute's *On The Beach*.

**What Should the West Do?**

Prescriptions for therapy and preventative treatment at the same time reduce to the following:

First, it is stressing the obvious to say that Western nations should do all possible, individually and collectively, to promote trade with, and through, the Middle East. With some exceptions—such as the problems attendant upon Egyptian and Syrian cotton—the record in this respect since World War II has been impressive. Oil tax royalties, Suez Canal tolls, and earnings from primary commodity sales (and a few manufactured goods) play an enormous role in the area's economy and account for much of its recent expansion. But much more flexibility and intelligent decision-making will be needed in the next ten years on many matters—surplus agricultural commodity disposal, petroleum import quotas for the United States, antitrust policies toward integration in the international oil industry, and as yet unpredictable energy developments in Western Europe affecting, and affected by, US firms. More imaginatively conceived private ventures such as the Eregli Steel Consortium in Turkey, RCA's venture in Egypt, the Cyprus Mines Corporation's new development of low-grade ore bodies in Cyprus, and many US private investments in Israel will be needed. The record of the past fifteen years suggests that the task *can* be done.

Next, the United States would do well to continue the policies begun by the present Administration in Washington to abandon post-World War II aid program strategies based on the "good guys" and "bad guys" approach. From 1948 to 1960 the Democratic and Republican Administrations seemed, in dealing with the Middle East, to draw much of their intellectual sustenance from Hollywood's cowboy thrillers of a decade earlier. Pressures at election time furthered the trend. But now we seem, fortunately, to be realizing that flirtations with the Soviet Union have led to little, that we indeed have many interests in common with the so-called "bad guys," and that peace and prosperity in the area might best be enhanced by our taking sides less strongly. Examples of this sort of thing are too many and too obvious to mention.

Third, in this same connection, and again to stress the obvious, our aid programs need to continue the trend already under way —but with an immense distance still to go—to attract better people to the staffs in Washington and abroad. The Peace

Corps seems a new and vigorous element. But the fact still remains that we send too many very inferior Americans abroad, their costs per man-year ($30,000 to $60,000 including overhead charges) preclude serious thoughts of continuation with local financing by any underdeveloped country, and the arsenals of economic theory and export technology on which they base their advice too often contains faulty ammunition—or is empty.

Fourth, and on a somewhat different subject, the United States and its Western allies would do well, over the next ten years, to promote free trade in human beings, *in and out* of the Middle East and North Africa. Since 1945, the three countries of the Middle East which have made the rapid economic strides have been Lebanon, Cyprus, and Israel—all have experienced crucial movements of populations. All three, and other countries, such as Algeria, will probably have surplus *employable* citizens to export during the coming decade. Western Europe's burgeoning economy might well take them—as the French economy has sopped up much of the recent Algerian exodus. Anathema to doctrinaire Zionists, some feel that should Russian Jews flock to Israel, a useful safety valve (for strategic and economic reasons) might well be movement of skilled and well-trained Israelis to Europe and the United States. Fraught with emotion, the subject merits consideration by those shaping Western strategy toward the Middle East and North Africa.

# The Far East

—*FRANK N. TRAGER*

## SUMMARY

*Since the beginning of World War II, the United States has been forced to make drastic reappraisals of its national security policy. Pearl Harbor signified the effective end of American isolationism. During the war and throughout the immediate postwar period, ideas and ideals of "One World"—including our wartime Soviet allies—still flourished. The United Nations gave expression to such aspirations.*

*However, the Communists, led by Stalin, were determined to take advantage of war-weariness and the rapid American demobilization. Soviet aggression in Europe was finally halted by the policy of containment and by the economic and military measures which led up to NATO. In the interim, that is from 1945-49, disengagement and limited or no involvement (not containment) were the policies applied to Asia, and with disastrous results. The Communist advance in Asia, though challenged from 1950 on, continued unabated until 1954, by which time North Korea, China, Tibet, and North Vietnam were added to the Communist World. Since 1955 the Sino-Soviet Bloc has renewed or reinvigorated its Asian campaigns by an economic offensive directed toward the neutralist countries in Asia. Since 1959 stepped-up Communist guerrilla and military challenges have been directed at Laos, Vietnam, and India.*

*Despite the Manila Treaty of 1954 (SEATO), which presumably afforded protection to Laos, the United States was forced to disengage in that country following the conclusion of the 1962 Geneva Agreement. It has, since 1961, committed its power—independent of SEATO—to Vietnam and Thailand;*

*and in 1962 has responded affirmatively to Indian requests for military assistance. Thus, since World War II, it can be said that three major US policy alternatives and their concomitant political, economic, and military strategies, have been considered for Asia: disengagement, containment, and roll-back. The first two have been, at different times and places and to different degrees, actualized.*

*The free Asian countries have sought their security in the framework of competing concepts of neutralism, regional collective security, and bilateral security arrangements. With notable exceptions, domestic instability and underdeveloped economies have inhibited their efforts at nation-building following the attainment of independence. They have also been pervious to Communist pressures to exploit their instability and to affect the outcome of their efforts at modernization.*

*The continuing undeclared war in Asia (and elsewhere) will not be quickly or cheaply won by the Free World. The dangers of further loss will be increased over the next decade, if this war is fought, as the Communists intend, only within the territory of the Free World in Asia and elsewhere. Hence, even to make the policy of containment effective, and to defend the so-called receding defensive perimeter, it is necessary to adopt the third policy alternative, roll-back, based upon a forward military strategy. To defend Saigon, it will, in other words, be necessary to penetrate, undermine, threaten, and, if necessary, attack Hanoi.*

*The past weakness of indigenous and imposed regional approaches for this task strongly suggest that in the immediate period ahead it will be necessary to extend and deepen US-Asian bilateral relationships, as well as to encourage other Free World bilateral relationships with the Asian countries. Perhaps in time new concepts of regionalism—a Pacific-Indian Ocean Alliance—may find widespread support in the area. But until they do, and however much they may be quietly encouraged, the United States must gear itself, as its Free World allies must gear themselves, for intensive cultivation and support of bilateral economic, political, and military policies and programs in free Asia. Only in this way can stability, security, and an improved standard of living be brought to the area. And in good time we may then expect democracy to become rooted in the area.*

## Introduction

Basic national goals, aims, or objectives, and the broad national strategy for attaining them generally rise above partisan politics, and generally represent a predominant national consensus which usually is voiced by the President as the Chief Executive and Commander-in-Chief. The speaker and the words vary, but especially since the close of World War II and the slowly growing recognition of "the global civil war [which] has divided and tormented mankind . . . our basic goal remains the same: a peaceful world community of free and independent states—free to choose their own future and their own system, so long as it does not threaten the freedom of others. Some may choose forms and ways that we would not choose for ourselves— but it is not for us that they are choosing. We can welcome diversity—the Communists cannot. For we can offer a world of choice—they offer the world of coercion." [1] Our broad national strategy, built on unity, freedom, and strength at home, is "to preserve the peace . . . by deterring the start of wars of all kinds and dimensions, by providing backing for diplomatic settlement of disputes, and by insuring adequate bargaining power bring about an end to the arms race." We must have adequate armed forces, sufficiently flexible "to meet national commitments and to insure national security." Our military posture should help to lessen tensions and to obtain peaceful solutions. "Diplomacy and defense are no longer distinct alternatives, one to be used where the other fails—both must complement each other." [2]

The difficulty is not in stating such goals and broad strategy; the difficulty lies in carrying out the strategy to achieve the goals. The global civil war which has divided and tormented mankind did not begin, as President Kennedy suggested, with the "close of the Second World War." It was merely interrupted by that war. It began in earnest—if a date is desired—with Lenin's "Theses on the National and Colonial Questions," presented to the Second Congress of the Comintern in 1920. From then on, Russian and other European Communists were actively assigned to working with Asian followers from India, China, Indonesia, and Indochina. Ho Chi Minh, Mao Tse-tung, Chou En-lai, and Semaun are among the leading survivors of these early efforts.[3] And their efforts in Asia have not been unsuccessful.

## A Backward Glance

In order to look forward to the next decade—which is the task of this paper—it is necessary to sum up briefly just where we are now, since we do not enjoy the luxury of a Lockean *tabula rasa*. In doing this it is useful to begin with the end of World War II. At this war's end there was to be no return to the presumed security of the two oceans, or to a Western Hemisphere defense posture. Residual American impulses toward withdrawal, toward some kind of American isolationism, may remain in the diversified political stream of American life, but these had become, and continue to be, recessive strains in the body politic. What William James once called "the rivalry of the patterns" polarized the world into two blocs led by the United States and the USSR respectively. We no longer suffer, however much we may have cherished, the illusion of "One World." * We learned painfully after the days of World War II that we were inexorably entwined in the affairs of this split world.

In February 1946, Stalin announced a series of Soviet policies, constituting a new shift to the left, which in time evoked the US policy of containment. This came to represent our central conception of foreign policy—in Europe. The Truman Doctrine for Greece and Turkey announced on March 12, 1947; the Marshall Plan, spoken at Harvard the following June; peacetime conscription in March 1948; the decision to use the airlift to Berlin from June 1948 to April 1949; the North Atlantic Treaty, signed in the same month; these are among the well-known and deservedly commendable steps taken to carry out the policy of containment in Europe.

But during the same period in Asia we did not follow that policy. There we closed the book on the fall of China after the failure of the Marshall and Wedemeyer missions. We were un-

* Perhaps the last official statement of such One-World views was President Harry S. Truman's "Restatement of Foreign Policy of the United States" speech at a Navy Day Celebration in New York City, October 27, 1945. Department of State *Bulletin*, XIII (October 28, 1945), pp. 653-656. President Truman restated twelve "fundamental principles of righteousness and justice" on which "US Foreign policy is based." These are conventional US expressions for peace, security, well-being, and freedom; opposition to armed force, coercion, and territorial aggrandizement. The United Nations was supported "to insure peace." Hope was expressed that the wartime alliance would be maintained. Communism was not included among the dangers. Russian cooperation was invited.

willing to participate in or otherwise help to organize a "Pacific Defense Pact" [4] or "collective defense arrangements" in Asia. We were willing to play a role secondary to that of our European allies, England, France and Holland, whose Asian empires were being transformed into newly independent states. Almost simultaneously these new nations came under a series of Communist revolutionary attacks which were signaled in the main by a sequence of meetings following the organization of the Cominform in 1947. These meetings were held in India in late 1947 and early 1948. Revolutionary activity had already begun in Indochina and the Philippines. After the Bombay and Calcutta Communist meetings, revolutions broke out in Burma (March 1948), Malaya (May-June 1948), and Indonesia (September 1948). Perhaps no better exposition of this negative policy of relative non-involvement in Asian affairs can be found than Secretary Acheson's "defensive perimeter" speech of January 12, 1950, which he made at the National Press Club, Washington, D.C.[5] This is a masterful lawyer's effort, able and evasive. Our allies, the British, the French, and the Dutch, were "making progress" and "discharging their responsibilities harmoniously." Otherwise the "responsibility is not ours," except for the island chain from the Aleutians to Japan, the Ryukyus, and the Philippines, which we will defend as the "defensive perimeter." The remaining Asians, newly independent or otherwise, can be helped "only when conditions are right for help to be effective."

In many ways the Acheson speech defined a past policy. It was backward looking and apologetic. For within weeks of its occurrence Washington dispatched to Asia a series of missions (Griffin, Jessup, Melby, McGhee, Bangkok Ambassadorial Conference, etc.) designed to see what could be done in South, Southeast, and East Asia. Then the Korean War broke out in June.

From 1950 to 1954, we recast our Asian policy. We had previously rejected strategies of collective defense and mutual security; now we sought to apply them everywhere in Asia. Bilateral defense treaties were signed with the Philippines (August 30, 1951), Japan (December 8, 1951), Republic of Korea (October 1, 1953), and Republic of China (December 7, 1954). A trilateral treaty was signed with Australia and New Zealand, the ANZUS Pact, (September 1, 1951); and all these were capped by the Southeast Asia Treaty Organization (SEATO, September 8, 1954). SEATO included the United Kingdom, France, the United States, Australia, New Zealand, Thailand, the Philippines, and Pakistan; and its Protocol

covered the new nations of Laos, Cambodia, and the Republic
of Vietnam. In addition, bilateral defense assistance and/or
economic aid agreements were signed with all other free Asian
nations. During the remainder of the decade of the 1950's we
pursued policies resulting from these strategic agreements.

## A Strategic Assessment of US and Communist Policies in Asia

More than one-third of all the free people of the world live in
the borderlands and islands of Asia. These countries, especially
those of Southeast Asia, contain extensive natural resources.
Although most of the area is underdeveloped, the industries of
Japan overwhelmingly surpass those of Communist China and
make it the fourth largest industrial complex in the world. The
free countries of Asia, most of them newly and sensitively independent, screen important air, sea, and land routes. They
half-surround Communist China and the area provides key
strategic and logistical bases crucial to the Free World. The
island chain running through Japan, the Ryukyus, and the
Philippines also serves as a Western first line of defense for the
Americas. Conversely, the free countries of the Far East lie on
the borders of expansionist Red China and the Soviet Union.
The Communists have interior, even if inadequate, lines of
communications, while the Free World must defend, if it so
resolves, an extremely long and diversified periphery.

Politically, this arc of free Asia has not yet produced—perhaps
it could not yet have been expected to produce—unifying international institutions such as those we have in the Atlantic Community and in the Western Hemisphere. Concepts of neutralism
have competed with those of collective security. Each has attracted more or less determined country followers while a strong
current of nationalist pride and concern has accompanied whatever the choice. SEATO includes only three states of the region,
and one of these, Pakistan, is also a member of the Central
Treaty Organization (CENTO). The future of SEATO has been
somewhat clouded by recent events in Laos. The defense of the
area is further complicated by a lack of consensus both at home
and among our allies.

The United States assists in maintaining large armed forces in
South Korea, Nationalist China, Pakistan, and Vietnam as well
as less sizeable but not inconsiderable forces in some other Asian
countries. We also maintain several bases whose futures require

careful consideration. However, no free Asian country alone could defend itself against a major attack by Communist China, still less one from the USSR.

Since the end of World War II, the era of Western colonialism, except for Hong Kong, Portuguese Timor, and Macao has passed from Asia. But since these countries of Free Asia have achieved independence, revolution and international armed conflict have been instigated by the Communists in India, Burma, Laos, Vietnam, Malaya, Indonesia, the Philippines, Korea, and the offshore islands of the Formosa Strait. However successful these countries may have been in meeting such attacks, the Communist threat remains as a continuing inhibition to the achievement of internal and external stability. The Communists, through the use of "hard" or "soft" strategy, have succeeded in retaining North Korea (after a costly war), winning North Vietnam and some minor offshore islands, and procuring an international agreement on, and recognition of, Communist participation in the coalition government of Laos. As a result, Laos, more than any other Asian country, is currently endangered by subversion. The "defensive perimeter" of which Secretary of State Acheson spoke in January 1950 has been pushed back in each of the US national Administrations since then. Currently there is a contest of arms in the Himalayan border areas of India which, for the first time since Indian independence, has forced that country to breach its own concepts of neutralist policy. Communist China, heralded by India until 1959 as a "brother" country, has once again become an aggressor. The USSR has indicated to India by its slow-down in military aircraft deliveries that, contrary to India's expectation, it will support its "ally" Peking. In South Vietnam Communist forces, reinforced from the north, are pressing to hold previous gains. US armed forces are being drawn into action, if for no other reason than to protect themselves, while supporting the Republic of Vietnam. And in Indonesia, the Communist Party, a part of President Sukarno's government, has built up the largest membership of any Communist Party outside the Bloc itself.

Even if there were no Communist threat, the domestic troubles of most of the states of Free Asia would present the United States and the West with serious problems. The political institution-building inexperience of the nationalist elites, the shortage of technical skills, the problems of expanding populations and economic development, and the gaps between democratic aspirations and fulfullment have contributed to domestic instability in the several countries. These conditions, in combination with relatively weak national loyalties, widespread illiteracy, and low levels of living and of productivity, have provided a fertile field for Communist infiltration and potential subversion.

The objectives or aims of the Sino-Soviet Bloc during the past decade have been relatively clear. Where and when they could not gain control by revolutionary means they have attempted to extend the area of Asian neutralism, in part to weaken Free World alliances, in part as an intermediate step toward accommodation with some of these states, now called "national democracies," while seeking by political, economic, and cultural means to gain ascendancy over their manpower and resources. The Sino-Soviet Bloc's "economic offensive" has been a successful weapon to the extent that it has redirected patterns of trade and increasingly created a dependency on Sino-Soviet credits and grants among the Asian producers of primary products. Though there is no definite indication of the reasons for the current Chinese attack on India, one major line of speculation suggests that Communist China is motivated by a desire to thwart or inhibit India's economic gains under her third Five-Year Plan, thereby making it more difficult for India to succeed in furnishing a democratic, economic, and political model for the other underdeveloped Asian nations. That Communist China may also be inclined to use external adventure in the form of pursuing traditional Chinese expansionist claims in order to relieve domestic tension over the failure of the "Great Leap Forward" may also be a factor in this situation.

Since World War II Communist strategy has alternated between the "hard," "left" line of revolutionary, paramilitary, and military advance; and the perhaps even more dangerous "soft," "right" line of courting the governments and peoples of Asia by exploiting anti-colonial nationalist and neutralist issues, and, since 1954, by granting credits and grants for economic development. At certain times during these years Communists have simultaneously utilized both strategies where, in their estimation, "objective conditions" in different situations warranted them. The Sino-Soviet ideological debate has not interdicted the Communist application of either strategy in Asia. It established, or seeks to establish, the policies and the order of international Communist leadership in the realities of promoting the Communist road to power in Asian (and other) countries.

A comparative examination of Sino-Soviet Bloc and US economic aid to Asian countries reveals the extent of the Communist offensive with its necessary concomitant of Communist penetration and influence. The magnitude of American aid has been and is greater than Bloc aid. However, sheer magnitude is not the determining factor in the reactions to an aid policy. Bloc credits and grants have been extended with considerable skill in developing the large-scale visible projects which are considered desirable by recipient countries. These include the inevitable steel mills (in India and Indonesia), hospitals, schools, hotels, and stadia (in Burma and Indonesia), street paving (in Kabul) and a 470 mile road from Kandahar to the Soviet-Afghan border, various factories in Cambodia, Ceylon, Nepal, and oil exploration in Pakistan.

Bloc credits have been advanced on low (2 to 2½ per cent) or no interest terms, frequently repayable by the export commodities of the recipient countries. Since 1959 such credits have averaged approximately $1 billion per year. These transactions have been accompanied by large numbers of Bloc technicians estimated at about 3000 per annum for the Asian countries in 1960-61 and almost 4000 for the first six months of 1962. Calculated by-products of the aid relationship are the extraordinary increase in the number of cultural exchanges between Bloc and

Comparison Between Sino-Soviet and US Economic Aid to
the Same Countries in Asia, January 1, 1954—June 30, 1962 [a]
*(Millions of Dollars)*

|             | BLOC      | US        |
| ----------- | --------- | --------- |
| Afghanistan | 515       | 193       |
| Burma       | 93        | 72        |
| Cambodia    | 65        | 249       |
| Ceylon      | 58        | 80        |
| India       | 950       | 3,618     |
| Indonesia   | 641       | 383       |
| Nepal       | 55        | 48        |
| Pakistan    | 33        | 1,769     |
|             | 2,410 [b] | 6,412 [b] |

[a] Does not include military grants and credits.

[b] Includes Bloc credits and grants and US grants, loans, PL 480 arrangements.

Sources: "The Sino-Soviet Economic Offensive through June 30, 1960," US Department of State, Statistics and Reports Division, Agency for International Development, *Research Memorandum, RSB-145* (September 18, 1962); U.S. Foreign Assistance . . . July 1, 1945-June 30, 1961 (Revised), and *Ibid.*, July, 1945-June 30, 1962 (Preliminary).

recipient countries and in the redirection of the patterns of trade. Total trade between the Bloc and underdeveloped countries between 1954 and 1960 advanced from $860 million to $3.4 billion. Total trade with the Asian countries in 1960 amounted to approximately $800 million. Afghanistan, India, Indonesia, and Malaya share the bulk of this rapidly expanding trade relationship.

If there were to remain any doubt about the purposes and effectiveness of Sino-Soviet Bloc strategy and its never-deviating, always-contesting, two-camp analysis of the world, the mere listing of its gains in Asia since World War II should dispel it.*

Though an accounting could also be made of their failures during these years, it seems to me that such an accounting, however important these failures may have been, is irrelevant to the inescapable conclusion. The Communists have made, (and at this writing are still making) significant advances in Free Asia. Thus far they have neither been "contained" nor "rolled back."

Certainly, after the failure of the Marshall and Wedemeyer missions to China, the gains registered by the Communists in Asia must be counted as setbacks for US (and Western) goals and strategic policy. Our policies and the consequent political, economic, and military programs have helped to sustain what is left of Free Asia—and this is a considerable majority of its peoples, governments, and resources. But the evolutionary process in which our policies and programs were planned and executed, policies and programs to strengthen, help modernize, win, and hold the friendship of the states of Asia, did not suit the revolutionary situation promoted by Moscow and later also by Peking and Hanoi. Our strategies to advance Asian security, stability,

---

* The Communists have gained control of mainland China and Tibet; they retained North Korea after a full-scale conventional war with the United States; they gained control over North Vietnam after successfully defeating the French in a colonial struggle; they have acquired without contest some minor offshore islands; they have received international sanction for an official place in the coalition government of Laos—a situation which will lead to further success for them unless there is Western counter-intervention at some crisis. They are presently engaged in a stepped-up insurgency campaign in Vietnam, the outcome of which may well be decided only after further US intervention in Vietnam and possibly in Northern Vietnam; they are engaged in a trans-Himalayan venture which appears to seek a slice of the "top of the world" from India's northwest frontier through Ladakh. Elsewhere in this border area, notably in the fifteen provinces of northeast Thailand, they are engaged in an operation which has been aptly called "aggression by seepage."

and improvement in the conditions of living were complicated at times by differences and difficulties with our Western allies whose aims and interests were, at important junctions, in conflict with our own. The failure of SEATO to honor its own words in the case of Laos is adequate illustration of this difficulty.

Our difficulties were not wholly "abroad." They were compounded by domestic attitudes toward foreign aid and toward the political stance of Asian neutralists, who were content during the 1950's to abide by the policies which we had supported in the late 1940's. The majority of the US public has been willing to approve of generous assistance given to underdeveloped countries, especially those which have joined us in a common defense effort. Impartial neutralism, neutrality, or non-alignment had gradually acquired some understanding and even sympathy. However, the growing awareness of the need to keep the uncommitted or neutralist states out of the Communist orbit was clouded by popular, and at times official, suspicion of those neutralists who received aid but whose leaders seemed to be, and frequently were, less critical of international Communist policies than they were of those of the Free World. The mild response of some of the neutralists to the Soviet atomic tests just before and during the September 1961 Belgrade Conference underlined this US attitude. Other domestic factors contribute to the uneasy feeling over the US aid programs. These included the continuing unfavorable balance of payments, the softness in our economy, the burden of tax rates necessary to sustain our security, and other related programs. In 1961 the Senate Foreign Relations Committee, in reporting on the Foreign Assistance Act of 1961, said:

> The Committee believes, no less than the President, that the United States must plan for and contribute generously toward a decade of development. Foreign aid is both an unavoidable responsibility and a central instrument of our foreign policy. It is dictated by the hard logic of the Cold War and by a moral responsibility resulting from poverty, hunger, disease, ignorance, feudalism, strife, revolution, chronic instability and life without hope.[6]

No such language accompanied the Act for 1962.

As we now turn to the future the following conclusions seem to me to be justified; and these in turn form the basis of projections on which policy must be based:

First. Though single isolated issues may be negotiated, such as the 1962 Geneva Declaration on Laos, based mainly on the

Kennedy-Khrushchev meeting of June 1961 in Vienna or the Cuban Crisis of October 1962, over-all tension and conflict have persisted and will continue. Sino-Soviet two-camp analysis and consequent hostility to the United States may fluctuate in intensity, but so long as that analysis is held by the Bloc, the global civil war does not admit resolution.

Second. Optimistic calculations based upon a presumed Sino-Soviet split because of the Khrushchev-Mao debate on ideology and leadership represented an erroneous estimate of the strength of the powerful sinews which bind the Communist world. These are stronger than those which divide Communist debaters. A careful analysis of the Soviet response to the Sino-Indian border war indicated what Communist organizations will say and do despite the genuine conflict between the leaders of the two major Communist parties.

Third. Vital statistics based upon the ages of leading actors in the Sino-Soviet world and in Asia require attention at the policy and personnel levels. For legitimate succession has been a difficult problem in all states where leadership has been confined and held by a few, or where *de facto* dictatorship exists. This is as true in allied Thailand or friendly India as it is in hostile China. Who and what after Mao, Nehru, and Sarit are not merely questions of personality—though they are that too, since each leader has a style of politics which colors his involvement in politics— they are also political questions of moment affecting policy both at the time of inevitable succession and during the not infrequently uncertain period of consolidation which the new leaders, whoever they are, will face. Contingency political planning for these eventualities is obviously indicated, though it is far less common in the United States than is contingency military planning.

## Aims and Consequent Actions in the Next Decade

The choice of US strategies for Asia short of general atomic war during the next decade depend, in the final analysis, on the choice among three, and only three, possible constellations of national goals, aims, or objectives. These are: (1) the decision to withdraw or disengage from Asia, thus consigning it to whatever accomodation it can make with communism; (2) acceptance in some definable sense of a defensive perimeter which will maintain the status quo in Asia; and (3) the decision not only to help maintain the security and domestic stability of what remains of free Asia at this time but also to take the action necessary to defeat the Communist enemy within his own territory.

Deliberate, over-all withdrawal or disengagement from Asia is an improbable choice today. It is questionable whether, even in the most Europe-centered diplomacy of some US diplomats, it was ever fully advocated. However, piecemeal disengagement was seriously proposed at various times during the late 1940's and 1950's. It was accepted however reluctantly for North Korea, Mainland China, Tibet, and North Vietnam. In 1949-51 it was advocated for Burma by highly placed Washington officials. And I would here argue that acceptance of the 1962 Geneva policy for coalition in Laos amounts to *de facto* piecemeal withdrawal in that remote country. But the potential loss of Laos and the consequent deflation of SEATO have apparently heightened US resolve on a bilateral basis to raise its political and material concern for friendly Asian governments and peoples. This has been dramatically exhibited in the cases of support for Vietnam, new bilateral assurances for Thailand, and military aid to India. Less spectacular but still significant are such illustrations as the appropriation settlement of Philippine World War II claims and the successful diplomatic involvement and resolution of the long-festering Dutch-Indonesian New Guinea conflict. Short, therefore, of a colossal failure of nerve or a deep depression improbably confined only to the United States, withdrawal or disengagement is an unlikely choice for the next period.

The choice of objectives, then, is reduced to the two remaining. Neither is simple, though each may be summarized in the not inaccurate, single, fulsome words of recent policy debates: "containment" and "roll-back." By and large, since the Korean War the over-all aim of containment has been pursued albeit with less than uniform success. Containment, to be successful as an objective for the next decade, requires either a genuinely acceptable and accepted *détente* with the Sino-Soviet world; or a considerable strategic nuclear and conventional mobile defense system so extensive and so used as to be immediately able to hold the defended perimeter or bring about an almost immediate restoration if it were to be breached.

Is containment possible within the ranges of these two alternatives, that is, either on the basis of a negotiated settlement of conflict issues which would allow the rest of the world, including Asia, to pursue its diverse paths freely and in peace; or on the basis of such deterrent strength that the Sino-Soviet Bloc will avoid adventurism beyond its borders? On any logical basis one must admit that containment is possible as a *détente* and as a state of defensive equilibrium (achieved either by nuclear superiority or by parity). Is it probable on either of these bases during the next decade?

This is the type of question which transforms political and military science into the "art of action under the pressure of the most difficult conditions," or strategy. If one's estimate of the future situation expects the Sino-Soviet Bloc to evolve and so mature at home as to satisfy the ambitions, aspirations, and ideological goals of its leaders and its people, and if what we do and say can assist them in that process, then containment as a species of legitimate peaceful coexistence of different systems is probable. If one's estimate of the future situation expects that nuclear superiority (or parity) and conventional strength will in fact deter, will put an end to Communist adventurism—called by whatever name—then containment is possible. If, finally, one's estimate of the situation forsees a genuine split—not, as I have here implied, a conventional, bitter, factional, but typical Communist debate between passing leaders—in the Sino-Soviet world then containment is probable at least for a short run for the Soviet world in Europe but only possible for the Chinese Communist world in Asia.

In my view the Leninist—not just the Stalinist, Khrushchevian, or Maoist—tradition deeply, though not necessarily irrevocably, imbedded throughout the Communist world for the past six decades makes all three above estimates unreliable. Only when there appears some evidence—and none has ever survived if it has appeared in the Communist Bloc—that this Communist world is prepared to relinquish the Leninist view of reality as composed of two hostile camps in which the Communist camp inexorably and inevitably, according to history, aided by all kinds of struggle, must survive and triumph, then and only then is containment by *détente* or by deterrence probable.

If the past fifteen years, that is, since George Kennan first advocated a policy of containment for Europe (he was and is generally indifferent to, or has a low assessment of, any involvement in Asia), have demonstrated any one fact, it is that Communist ideology, power policy, and advancing strategy have not been contained, even when we had nuclear monopoly. It should be evident in terms of the above-noted past and recent East, South, and Southeast Asian experience that even to maintain the *current* defensive perimeter we shall sooner or later have to make an effort at penetrating, undermining, threatening, and possibly attacking the enemy at his bases on his terrain. Americans will not be willing to suffer casualties over a long period in Vietnam for want of stopping Viet Minh at the source. Sooner or later we shall have to face up to the strategy of defending "Saigon" by seriously threatening or attacking "Hanoi." In a slight adaptation of Cicero's words to Cataline, "How long, O pray, will we continue to let you abuse our patience?"

The use of the present participles as in "penetrating," "undermining," "threatening," "attacking" arouses at least two negative reactions to the spectrum of actions intended by these words. The first two participles contravene popularly held American notions of peacetime non-interventionism and international morality. Although there is tacit acceptance of such interventionism when it is modestly successful as in the case of Guatemala, there is an outcry when it fails, as in the case of the Bay of Pigs; and there is indifference or ignorance when it is half-heartedly tolerated as in the case of early support for the Chinese Nationalist (KMT) troops in Burma. But these variations in attitude disappear rapidly when war becomes overt and declared.

The second two call forth visions of the unloved "big stick" of earlier years in the twentieth century, and the feared "big bomb" associated with the narrowly conceived strategy of "massive retaliation." What we as a nation have not yet assimilated is that there are many varieties of "little sticks" and means other than the big bomb. As General Taylor pointed out, the ability to deter the general atomic war for which we are preparing effectively does not relieve us of the necessity of considering "cold-war requirements." And in this arena he found that "there is a relatively unexplored field of possibilities in relating military strategy and armament to the reaction of allies, neutrals, and potential enemies."[7]

Our exploration of this field of possibilities has been less than imaginative, and certainly not bold. The difficulty in these matters, I believe, stems from an illusion which we have nurtured unduly. This illusion assumes that the Cold War is cold, i.e., not a "true" war; it is an unpleasant activity which merely endangers the peace. The truth of the matter is somewhat different. The Cold War is war though it is undeclared and hence does not conform to the historical pattern. It has various degrees of heat in different parts of the world, and especially in Asia. It is planned warfare at the lower end of the spectrum, and this gulls us into accepting it, especially in far-off places of Asia, as "cold" war. It is in fact organized violence, sustained by an enemy, and prosecuted relentlessly with many forms of ammunition, verbal and lethal. It uses the means appropriate to the occasion to secure Communist objectives. Its strategy is a "combination of individual engagements to attain the goal of the campaign or war."

The folly in these matters is to conform to the stereotype of the ostrich or, in other words, to outworn concepts of international discourse and action. The Cold War is a form of undeclared war against every people and every government where the Communists have found what they call suitable "objective conditions" for the pursuit of their goal. It is a variation in degree upward in the spectrum from conventional Communist class war to wars of national liberation, war-by-proxy, brush-fire war, insurgency, guerrilla war, civil war, sub-limited war, limited, non-nuclear war, and on this issue there is no debate in principle even between Khrushchev and Mao Tse-tung. Both are committed to a systematic strategy of conflict by attrition. Khrushchev has emphasized the dangers of mutual nuclear destruction while pursuing more determinedly the politico-economic offensive with military aid. Mao Tse-tung, in apparent tacit acceptance of nuclear stalemate or in indifference to nuclear conflict, has opted for the risk of protracted campaigns and protracted warfare. Mao has made clear that "to annihilate the enemy means to disarm him or to deprive him of his power of resistance and not to annihilate him completely in a physical sense." Their joint objective, as so often has been said, is global Communist predominance by piecemeal expansion and by isolating the United States and making it morally incapable of action by nuclear blackmail.* Certainly they have given substantial documentation to these views; there has been no peace

---

* Note should be taken of a widely received article, Zbignew Brzezinski, "Peaceful Engagement, How We Can Profit from Communist Disunity," *The New Republic*, March 26, 1962, pp. 13-16. Professor Brzezinski denies the relevance either of a policy of containment or roll-back because both "were based on the premise that there is a united Soviet bloc." However, he gives away half of his argument by admitting that the "bloc" is a bloc at least "from the defense point of view"; he also admits that "from the standpoint of Western policy, it is dangerous to assume that the internal conflicts of the Communist World will necessarily lead to a relaxation in international tensions." The Sino-Indian conflict and the Soviet response have already damaged the remainder of his argument. His tactical suggestions for exploiting Communist debates on the basis of a "policy of differentiated amity and hostility" seem to me to require the assumption that serious Communist leadership would be taken in by such tomfoolery.

since World War II and there is, short of an unexpected, un-assisted domestic overturn of the Communist dictatorship, little prospect for peace in the decade ahead.

The recognition of this past and present truth and its probable projection requires, in my view, the adoption of the third US national objective indicated above: the decision not only to help maintain the security and domestic stability of what remains of Free Asia but also to take action to help interdict and defeat the enemy within his own territory. Such an objective should begin to be operational during the so-called "Cold" War. In more concrete illustration, to make possible the "defense" of Saigon by seriously "threatening" and if necessary by "attacking" Hanoi might then contribute to a potential roll-back. Instead of further erosion of the area of Free Asia there may thus come about an erosion of the area of communism. At the very least, such a national objective would more likely establish and sustain a defensible defensive perimeter.

In Asia, Communist China is the primary threat to, and dis-turber of, the peace, followed by the Soviet Union and their two Asian satellites. Communist China's adherence to Leninist formulations, to classical Communist ideology on the "war question," as it is called in Communist debates, may from time to time be tactically at variance with the USSR, but strate-gically Moscow and Peking are still one. Faced by unmanageable problems of food shortages, overpopulation (cheap manpower), an overburdened economy, a seemingly desperate need for self-glorification and self-justification, Communist leadership in China today constitutes a dogmatic, implacable, and dangerously irrational enemy, seemingly indifferent to the nuclear power which it does not yet have and may for some years to come be unable to afford in significant quantity. Though the nature of China's irrationality makes countering national strategy and contingency planning more difficult, the weakness of Communist China now and for some years to come make it more vulnerable. On the other hand, the weaknesses and instability which char-acterize so many of the countries on China's periphery offer tempting external opportunities for her domestic physical and psychological difficulties. Herein is the danger in Asia.

A strong, resolved US political and multifaceted military presence—"pre-positioned," in the current military jargon—in or near the vulnerable areas peripheral to China is the sole insurance—I do not say deterrent—against the evident dangers of Chinese risk-taking. The years of violent hostility directed against the United States by the present generation of Chinese Communist leadership is not likely to be stilled even after they join their ancestors. There are no discernible prospects ahead for any easing of tensions. So long, therefore, as we refrain from taking overt (and other steps) to inhibit Chinese Communist action, and refrain in similar fashion from inhibiting the Viet Minh and North Koreans *in situ*, we are endangering the present wobbly perimeters in Asia, inviting further blackmail, rapacity, and warfare by whatever means the Communists elect to use at the moment of their "truth."

Similar reasoning applies to the Soviet Union in the three major and profitable areas of its present Asian activity: [8] neutralist Afghanistan, Laos, and Indonesia. But otherwise, as indicated above, Khrushchev, advancing on the nuclear base provided to him in the Stalin era, has perhaps a keener appreciation of the risks of nuclear war. He has openly, but not exclusively, assessed the next two decades as ones in which there will be a "transition from capitalism to socialism," that is from, in the main, free and open societies to Communist dictatorships. He "will bury us" by "peaceful competition" in the arena of the uncommitted underdeveloped world, if in no other arena. And he will not hesitate to advance his cause by supporting "wars of national liberation" and by all the tactics of international Communist warfare short of the big war involving the big bomb or the conventional war which might use tactical nuclear weapons and thereby escalate. Nuclear fears may deter the big war between the USSR and the United States. But such fear is, in the Soviet guidebook to world revolution, no deterrent to Soviet non-nuclear machinations in Asia and elsewhere. Communist programs of, and emphasis on, subversion and insurgency have in fact increased.

Thus a projection of strategy for the next decade not only presents the United States with a limited range of choice of aims, but it also clearly divides the world, like Caesar's Gaul, in three parts: the advancing Communist Bloc; the Allied defending Bloc (since it includes Japan, Pakistan, Thailand, South Korea, Taiwan, the Philippines, Vietnam, and Oceania, it should no longer be called the "West") ; and the uncommitted, more or less, Neutralist Bloc, whose members make up at least half of the United Nations and who are the immediate targets of the Sino-Soviet enemy.

In the choice of aims I have not only rejected disengagement in Asia; I have in effect argued that containment, essentially a negative, short-run policy, is an immediate necessity but cannot any longer be regarded as an exclusive or even sufficient aim. It would be useful to have a clear defensive perimeter sustained by an immediate or early political, economic, and flexible military capability. But over the years, unless the Sino-Soviet world were to become non-Leninist or non-Communist, its dynamism will impose on us the task not only of containing its aggressiveness, of defending the status quo, but also contesting it aggressively at the source even to sustain the status quo. To hold off and merely to defend is to believe in physical and ideological Maginot Lines. Rather, we shall have to place the Communist drive for power in the perspective of other earlier attempts at world power hegemony. To oppose it we shall have to give substance and currency to a world delivered from this protracted threat. This is the task of pushing forward the frontiers of freedom. It has been called roll-back based on military conceptions of a forward strategy. It could be called by any other name. But whatever name this aim acquires, its denotation is not the aim of status quo "peace," or in other words, containing the Cold War, but rather of present and advancing freedom and welfare at appropriate and responsible levels of individual and social life, of national and international institutions. Short-run containment only when coupled with long-run advancing freedom seems to me to be the only aim which can enkindle and support the requirements to bring security, peace, and freedom.

What strategy—using the political, economic, and psychological powers of the nation, together with its armed forces—shall we adopt to secure this national objective in Asia?

## Political and Military Strategy in the Next Decade

### On Bilateralism

It is not possible in this paper to discuss in detail the political and military strategies and policies appropriate to each of the sixteen countries included in the title of this paper. The following guidelines for the area as a whole and for the regions within the area should be rounded out in accordance with the specific conditions of and findings on each country. Geographical propinquity in the area and cartographical area designations are relevant to strategic planning but these represent the beginning of the exercise. They should not be allowed to obscure the necessity for treating each country in its own terms and in relation to the United States. The excessive haste which led to the creation of a Southeast Asia Treaty Organization containing only two Southeast Asian countries among its eight members— Pakistan is in South Asia and the other five are non-Asian— perhaps points up this particular lesson. The failure of SEATO since 1954 to add to its Asian membership, reinforced by its fatal weakness with respect to Laos, should be a warning that regionalism as an approach to Asian problems, no matter how desirable or convenient it may be, when imposed from the outside, is not an appropriate response to the issues which stare at one out of the conventional flat map.

On the other hand, US bilateral relations with each free Asian country have now weathered the past period with its large elements of doubt, confusion, error, and ignorance. They have demonstrably never been as good as they are now. In no small measure, the growing Asian awareness of Communist subversive and imperialist intent—to us painfully slow-growing—has contributed to the present good state of bilateral affairs. This is not to say that each US-Asian country relationship is free from two-way difficulty. But the number and the intensity of such difficulties have declined.

*Hence the major strategic approach to US-Asian relationships here proposed for the next decade is to use the present occasion as the basis for an intensive re-examination of each such relation so as to extend and deepen it at every possible level.* Let no one be beguiled by the fact of existing US diplomatic relations with, and "country teams" in, each of the sixteen Asian nations. The content of such diplomatic relations has been largely set in the mold of the early 1950's. There has been little, if any, profound, sustained, official "new look" or "New Frontier" analysis since then,* except when and where crises, such as the off-shore islands, the remaining Kuomintang "irregulars" in Burma, end-

---

* One might cite the 1955-56 effort made by the US Army—over the intense opposition of the US Department of State—to commission a series of "country studies" designed to provide the military with handbook country data comparable to the United Kingdom's prewar "Blue Books" and wartime Naval Intelligence "Handbooks"; and the 1958 Senate resolution (*S. Res. 336*, 85th Cong., 2nd Sess.) which authorized a "full and complete study of US foreign policy" as attempts to meet the above requirements. However, though the country handbooks were produced for the Army and the Senate studies published, there is little evidence that these have been cranked into the basic knowledge and instrumentation of US-Asian bilateral relations.

ing the shooting between the Dutch and the Indonesians over West New Guinea, or facing up in 1961 to the heightened Communist offensive begun in 1959 against Vietnam, etc., bring about bustling activity.

A crisis approach does not fulfill the requirements of fully developing bilateral relations though it may trigger a mechanism to bring about improvements. The high level "task force" assigned to the current crisis in Vietnam has apparently led to a more comprehensively-charged "task force" to consider the over-all problems of (mainland?) Southeast Asia. If the latter can take a clean, fresh look at Southeast Asia and be free from the obligation of defending or continuing the past just because it is past; if it can avoid the mistake of imposing US regional and other conceptions on the countries of the region; and finally, if it can quietly explore its findings with responsible people in the countries of Southeast Asia (not all of whom will be the "capital city" leadership) then we may expect good results from such enterprise.

Bilateralism to be successful does require knowledge—two-way knowledge—at every important level of individual and social behavior. With the possible exception of the Philippines, every free Asian culture pattern is essentially alien to ours. This is not only a matter of diverse histories and languages; but it is also, perhaps more profoundly, a matter of religion, individual, family, and societal patterns, philosophy, politics and the arts, and racial color. We can no longer afford to be content with a surface relationship with the "Western-educated" or "Westernized" élites who frequently lead their countries. For this is indeed a thin layer in each Asian country and it, too, is permeated by the indigenous culture no matter how much Western education its members have acquired. It is sometimes said that US-Asian military relations are more easily established and maintained than other kinds because of the pervasive doctrinal character of the military profession. This is certainly true on a "nuts and bolts" or "hardware" basis. However, assumptions beyond this point should be tested before being dogmatically retained. Precisely because successful bilateralism requires two-way knowledge in depth, it is not infrequently downgraded by regional enthusiasts and diplomatic and strategic generalists. Expertise on a country or area gets to be referred to as "apologetics" for that country or area. Yet, without such expertise, we shall surely make more difficult whatever policy or strategy we are to follow in Asia.

Bilateralism does not exclude present and emergent forms of desirable regionalism in Asia. When these come about invariably they must have wide indigenous support if not immediate inspiration. For otherwise they will not root. Malaysia is a prospective example on a small scale. Asian talk of a "common market" in the United Nations Economic Commission of Asia and the Far East (ECAFE) region is at least Asian talk and, thereby, has a greater chance of being heard. ECAFE itself has, in small but not insignificant ways, contributed toward Asian consideration of various economic problems in ad hoc regional terms.

## On Bilateralism and Economic Development in Free Asia

Free Asian countries, just as their counterparts in Africa and Latin America, are in the midst of the economic revolution, the aim of which is modernization. In comparative terms only Japan in the area is a highly organized, competitive industrial society with actual and potential high growth rates (an average of 9.1 per cent per annum for the decade 1950-59) and increasing per capita income (about $400 per year). The protectorate of Brunei, "the floating oil well," which may be included in Malaysia is also excepted. For the rest, the economic communities of Free Asia, exhibiting most of the varieties of public and private institutional arrangements for development, range from the relative stagnation and subsistence levels, as in Laos, to some kind of growth everywhere else. But the real growth of the last decade has been uneven; it has not yet repaired the low levels of living (per capita income well under $100 per year); it is running a close race with population increases in some countries; and, as one consequence of improving conditions of education and health without the related ability of utilizing these skills, it is contributing to the difficult task of maintaining domestic stability.

Economic development or modernization depends on the capabilities of the human and material resources for efficient productivity, and on political stability. Both are possible, as the Russians and European Satellites have shown, at the expense of democracy. On the other hand, we have assumed because of our own experience that sustained economic progress makes possible the conditions for social mobility and for more open or democratic systems of polity. Obviously economic development is not to be necessarily and causally identified with either "closed" Communist or "open" democratic political systems. If we wish to help Asians and others establish the connection between development and democracy we shall have to work harder at the problems of development, for that is what the Asian leaders want before they want democracy. They also want to avoid some of the destabilizing and demoralizing aspects of modernization when it proceeds too slowly or inefficiently. In sum, we and our Asian friends must turn to the complicated problem of finding or maintaining political stability, pursuing modernization, and attaining an open, democratic, self-sustaining society, most probably in that order.

The main economic development problem in the area (Japan excepted) is still the problem of economic growth. This in turn requires investment, efficient allocation of human and material resources, and above all, the nurture of the skills required to handle so complicated a problem. Each country in the area requires these, at the same time each must begin to rationalize its investment effort in terms of the possible complementarity of the economies in the area. This, if wisely understood and handled, can have a multiplier effect on investment and utilization of scarce resources.

Where does bilateralism fit into this picture in the years ahead? In my view, bilateralism should not be thought of exclusively as a US-Asian country policy. Where our Allies in Europe and in Asia have the will and means to pursue bilateral Asian policies they should be vigorously encouraged to do so. Even small nations such as Norway have been able to initiate projects (e.g., with India).

One promising device which has gained Asian appreciation and at the same time brought about some sharing of the burden of preserving freedom is the use of the consortium in aid matters. Among the best examples of this are the consortium of the United States, Canada, France, Japan, the United Kingdom, and West Germany pooling resources for certain aspects of Pakistan's current development plans; and a similar effort involving Australia and New Zealand but excluding Japan among those just mentioned for the Indus River Valley project. In both of these the International Bank for Reconstruction and Development (IBRD) acted, in effect, as the other half of the bilateral relationship with the recipient country. A second related device—though in my view somewhat obscured and perhaps handicapped by its generic name—is the Colombo Plan begun in 1950. Essentially, this, too, is a bilateral program carried out under the framework of internationally shared economic data. It has been useful in making British Commonwealth resources, especially those of Australia, Canada, and New Zealand, available in Asia. A third illustration which may serve as a desirable springboard for what I called above the "complementarity" of Asian economies, may result from the approximately $1 billion of Japanese reparations and investment capital assigned to Burma, Indonesia, and the Philippines.

As bilateralism is extended among the nations of the Free World, that is as numerous long-range and ad hoc "partnerships" are multiplied, mutual Free World relations so engendered will acquire depth; they will tend to diminish fears of what is called neo-colonial, especially economic, dependency. They will also tend to avoid the fears of Asian small nations that their needs will be lost in the shuffle of attending to the needs of big Asian nations. This was the fatal defect in Stassen's FOA attempt to regionalize aid at the Simla Conference in the early 1950's. There should develop consequently a desirable kind of international economic division of labor. For with the exception of Japan all other nations of Free Asia require in varying degree the same kinds of assistance in considerable magnitudes. Not even the rich resources of the United States are equal to the need; and even if they were, it would not be desirable for the United States to become the sole source of assistance in the area.

Multiple Free World bilateral relationships, as here proposed, offer special advantages in all matters affecting the socio-economic development of the Asian countries requiring such assistance. They permit proper establishment of program and project criteria, efficient phasing of infrastructure and productive capacity development, and progressive diversification of the economy so as to diminish reliance upon the excessively fluctuating market character of typical Asian primary products. Such bilateral programs should be financed by a limited number of "hard" currency IBRD-type loans and the far larger number of "soft" loans and credits. Grants should be limited to welfare and education projects, to other non-direct, non-profit-making infrastructural projects, and to surplus commodities. (The "sale" character of PL 480 commodities is basically a fiction the value of which—if it ever had any, has long since disappeared.)

It will be noted that no reference has thus far been made to the United Nations. This is deliberate at least for two reasons: The UN is here regarded primarily as a forum for international discourse. Secondly, the UN aid program is necessarily limited among other reasons by the nature of the Cold War struggle.

Since the UN Expanded Program began in 1950-51 it has disbursed yearly sums from $6.4 million in that year to $81.4 million in 1961-62. In the latter year, Asia and the Far East received $19.4 million.[9] These miniscule multilateral aid figures speak for themselves.

In a number of respects this next decade of bilateral aid relationships should prove less difficult than the past one. The Asian emphasis on rapid industrialization at the expense of agriculture, the so-called "steel mill complex," has to a large extent been downgraded in Asia. Whereas many Asians at the time of gaining independence regarded their extractive economies as among the stigmata of the colonial past and advocated rapid industrialization as the cure, they are now more concerned with problems of improving and marketing what they have while more gently easing into a diversified or balanced economy. This hard-won growth in economic experience coupled with greater appreciation of the interdependence of the public and indigenous private sectors of the economy make it more possible to find temperate solutions to the problems of development. Throughout the recent past and certainly for the decade ahead in Asia the problem of finding capital for development is and should be less difficult to solve than finding solutions to the human problems created by the noneconomic factors in economic development. The approaches to legitimate national and individual pride and to the acquisition and development of necessary skills at every level require more intelligence and imagination than they have thus far been accorded. We can make our contribution by focusing our aid relationship: first, on the task of finding and maintaining the institutional arrangements for political stability; second, on assisting in the solution of the economic problems of development without insisting that ours is the best or only model. In helping to close the gap between economic aspiration and performance we will thereby decrease the vulnerability of our Asian friends to Communist appeals. The long-range nation-building outcome of both of these, that is of political integration and economic performance, will then make possible the emergence of a free and open modernized society.

### On Bilateralism and Law and Order

Thus far I have dealt mainly with the easiest element in the bilateral relationship—though it is not itself easy. Far more difficult is the already mentioned problem of political stability, of law and order, of free institutions in Free Asia. Political stability or integration both feeds and is fed by economic development wisely handled. At independence the countries of Free Asia in the main adopted and adapted Western-type democratic constitutions and political institutions. Whether they were in fact or in name one-party (e.g., India, Burma) or multi-party (e.g., Pakistan, Indonesia) states they were so committed. The search for democratic law and order and for domestic stability has not been too successful since independence. Thailand has remained virtually since the coup in 1932 a more or less benign military dictatorship. Afghanistan has remained and Nepal has become a more or less royal autocracy. Taiwan has remained and Indonesia and Vietnam have become more or less benign republican autocracies. Korea, Burma, and Pakistan have become more or less benign military dictatorships. Ceylon is a multi-party democracy in a state of almost chronic emergency. We do not yet know what Laos is or is to become. That leaves Japan, the Philippines, Malaya, India, and, in its own unique way, Cambodia the remaining and on the whole stable political democracies of Free Asia.

Obviously the internal conditions which led to the above changes cannot in the first instance be appropriately changed by US or other bilateral assistance. Nor should the United States insist or otherwise advocate that Western-style democracy is a necessary condition for bilateral friendly relations and aid. There is much in the argument which holds that the cultural lag between the nationalist Asian élites, who helped to bring about independence, and the majority rural population, who in the main supported them, has to be lessened before any but the indigenous village democracy can in fact work.

In connection with law and order the first lien on US bilateral assistance is to provide the recognized government with whatever is required to maintain stability where it is threatened by Communist subversion and insurgency. At the same time, US assistance cannot afford to be politically tied to the kind of military dictatorship and corruption characteristic of US-Cuba relations before Castro. To seek out alternative leadership possibilities wherever and whenever these are necessary requires a degree of sustained political art and continuous knowledge of local conditions. These usually cannot be had by the absurd US practice—absurd as applied to the relatively less well-known Asian countries—of biennial diplomatic and almost annual military turnover in these countries. The remedy for the situation is not only longer tours of duty; it is also better preparation and backstopping for such duty.

In the short run our task is to help preserve domestic order because that is what is largely under Communist attack in Asia. In the long run our task is to help responsible Asian leadership, *on hand or to be discovered*, find its way toward an indigenous Asian solution to the age-old problem of coupling and maintaining freedom, welfare, and order. There is no blueprint for the delicate factor of timing as to when and where short- and long-run policies merge. Each instant case requires continuing intelligent attention and intelligent concomitant action. It also requires that we let our present friends know of our interests in both the short- and long-run objective. To impart such views may make for momentary and inescapable unpopularity, but that perhaps cannot be avoided.

What we must not lose sight of is that within the rural 85 per cent of Asian societies there are deeply imbedded traditions of village cooperation, compromise, search for consensus, and other elements of what has not improperly been called "village democracy." That there are also anti-democratic elements of caste (as in South Asia), authority, landlordism, and feudal concepts pertaining to one's station and one's duty, is also true. The presence of both of these traditions even within one country, is also an inescapable aspect of the human condition. Obviously, our task, given the nature of our goal in society, is to assist in the indigenous nurture of the former at the expense of the latter. To do this in Asian terms gives us the positive content to and the reason for our already determined anti-Communist posture.

To sustain that posture I now turn to the task of first priority. Without military security the rest falters.

### Bilateralism and Security

As a matter of policy our security program should require an annual review of the overseas bases and a defense of their continued necessity by the Joint Chiefs of Staff. As our long-range missiles based in the United States and at sea achieve reliability, the need for overseas bases for bombers and missiles tends to disappear. Likewise, when we have limited war forces properly trained and equipped for rapid strategic movement, the purely military need for overseas garrisons at present strengths will also diminish. Our policy on this subject should be clearly and openly

stated, and the withdrawal of forces should be undertaken
voluntarily well in advance of the development of local pressures.[10]

It would be hazardous and perhaps unnecessary to argue
against the just quoted statement on security policy. It is increasingly clear that the need for foreign bases for strategic
deterrence, that is for intercontinental ballistic missiles; Polaris-
equipped, nuclear-powered submarines; air-refueled, nuclear-
weapon-carrying bombers; etc., has been rapidly declining and
may before the end of this decade no longer be needed. The
process of hardening missile sites and dispersing missile capabilities, the advent of increased strategic mobility, diverse
weapon systems and fire-power, the planned increments in rapid
air- and sea-lift give body to such policy. We know that the
ten-year forecast of the defense budget by the last Administration, amounting to $47 billion per year at the end of the 1960's
was in fact surpassed during the first full year of the present
Administration. We are presently spending for defense at a
rate slightly in excess of nine per cent of GNP. But strategic
capability and deterrence is not enough of a policy for Asia.
Its application to Asia leaves virtually unassailable the continuing need for conventional forces, materiel, and some bases suitable for the types of limited, sub-limited, and guerrilla warfare
which has been Asia's lot since the end of World War II.

The new crisis in Vietnam which began in 1959 served to
persuade, in 1961, incoming President Kennedy and General
Taylor to prepare for the Asian-type conflict. Doctrine and
budget were retooled for conventional warfare and counter-
insurgency. Roles and missions, command and control, forces
and materiel were redefined and deployed partly to meet the
situation in mainland Southeast Asia but also to face the protracted Communist conflict of which it was but one illustration.

The task for the next decade is to convert this solution to the
"crisis" in Vietnam to a continuing defense readiness in Asia.
Our substantial on-site position in Korea is in effect tied to
Korea. The needs in mainland Southeast Asia will not decline,
they will probably grow as the situation in Laos deteriorates.
And they have begun to grow in South Asia. Flexible, deployed
strength in Asia will inevitably cost more in the decade ahead
than in the past one. Conceivably there may come about com-
pensatory over-all defense savings as a result of greater Allied
expenditures in Europe and a slow down in outlays because of
earlier investment in nuclear defense. Those who think in such
terms are inclined to stabilize within a fixed range the quantum

of the US annual defense budget. On the basis of the foregoing analysis of "objective conditions" it seems to me that prudence would require us to plan our defense as a minimum in terms of the present percentage ratio of GNP. There is no question that we can afford it. This would allow for the modernization and flexibility of our ground, tactical air and naval forces deployed in the Pacific. Nuclear deterrence did not succeed in preventing Korea, Laos, or Vietnam. Aggression in Asia to be stopped— not just deterred—requires credible US, Allied, and indigenous conventional strength which is prepared to act and which is back-stopped if it is required by tactical and strategic nuclear power. The short-run probability is that such strength will be required in Vietnam where we are committed; and may be required for re-entry into the Laos situation as it slides down the Communist-coalition drain.

It is in this Asian context that we need to examine our Asian bases for the next decade. We know that our bases in Japan and in Okinawa have been the occasion for the kind of friction which has worried General Taylor (and others) and led him in January 1961 to express his concern over bases on foreign soil. These and our other Asian bases in Korea, the Philippines, Taiwan, and on our own soil in the Pacific serve to guard vital sea-air lines, ease the lines of communications and intelligence, affect the control and distribution of the food and natural resources, especially of Southeast Asia, and otherwise serve as staging areas close to the Sino-Soviet Asian perimeter. They also, in no small way, contribute to the economy and psychological reassurance of nearby allies and friends. Asian and Pacific Ocean bases are necessary parts of the forward strategy required for flexible maneuver and operations in the current and prospective phases of the ongoing war. Those on our own territory, Hawaii, Guam, and other Pacific Islands pose no difficult problems; those in Korea, Taiwan, the Philippines, and Australia, no unresolvable problems. However, those in Japan and the Ryukyus require careful consideration.

Japan will have to face up to the problem of her defense. In the July 1962 elections for half of the 250 seats in the Upper House of the Japanese Diet, the Liberal Democratic Party again gave a convincing demonstration of its hold on the electorate. It pursued a cautious policy with respect to amending the constitution so as to provide for defense, pledged loyalty to the United Nations, cooperation with the free nations and amity with the Afro-Asian nations. The leading opposition, the Japa-

nese Socialist Party, committed to neutralism, abrogation of the
US-Japan Security Treaty, and diplomatic ties with Communist
China was not able to improve its position—it still controls about
30 per cent of the national vote and seats in the Diet. (A
Buddhist, quasi-pacifist, clean government party, the Soka Gak-
kai has become the third party in the Upper House.) But this
took place before the current increase in Sino-Indian hostilities
which according to some reports has caused some soul-searching
even in Socialist ranks.

The issue of the Japanese and Ryukyuan bases will continue,
however, to be debated not only when incidents occur but because
foreign policy in Japan is a political issue, much as the Common
Market has become one in the United Kingdom. It may well be
the case that the annual review called for by General Taylor
may lead to the phased elimination of the bases in Japan, especially if the latter decides to spend more than the less than two
per cent of her GNP now assigned to defense. Perhaps the
most critical issue in these East Asian bases is that of Okinawa.
Here in momentary aberration we committed ourselves to
residual Japanese sovereignty. It would seem prudent to decide
this question as part of a settlement of the Japanese defense
posture, and, in any event, to come to a conclusion as to when
and under what conditions residual sovereignty is to be reas-
sumed by Japan. A proper Japanese defense effort as well as
possible alternative locations for the Okinawa base are preferable to political friction with Japan. Despite the increase in
Sino-Japanese trade there is little chance for a long-range accommodation between Tokyo and Peking. Japan in her own
interests will be forced to find a solution for her constitutional
defense provisions and concomitant defense attitudes.

I do not believe that we need to pressure Japan towards this
development. Quite the contrary, our pressure could be politically "counter-productive." Perhaps the surest way to assist
Japan in adopting an effective defense posture is through consideration of her problems of Free World trade. For without
the latter, Japan would surely lose the growth and stability she
now enjoys, the fruits of which she now begins to share with
other free Asian countries. Our interests in Free Asia are
strengthened to the extent that Japan democratically accepts
some of the burdens of defending Free Asia. In any estimate of
the next decade, Japan and Australia are the key partners in
the East Asian and Pacific security arrangements.

At the other end of the area, in the South Asian sub-continent, it is clear that India has been forced by Communist China to reassess her defense posture. Prime Minister Nehru at long last openly accuses Peking of waging "war" and of being an "imperialist" power. No graver charges could be made by an Asian leader. India's neutralism and reliance on Moscow's friendship have not provided Indian security. This in turn could lead to reassessment of the problems of the sub-continent as a whole. India not only has accepted US and other Western military assistance, she also recognizes that her third Five-Year-Plan has been knocked out of gear by new and continuing defense needs. Pakistan's Second Five-Year-Plan has not yet reached any self-sustaining stage and without US military assistance her defense posture would rapidly decline. Ceylon is in a dangerous situation arising from her inability to feed herself and find forms of productive employment and social solutions to the corresponding problems of her growing and divisive population. Afghanistan is the fish on the Russian economic aid and military assistance hook.

Obviously, one cannot return to the pre-independence days when the sub-continent could be and was treated as a political, economic, and security entity. But a *détente* might now be possible and should certainly be sought. "Kashmir," "Pushtoonistan," "Singhalese versus Tamil," Nepal's chafing at the Indian bit—these are real problems, not to be whisked away by any sudden sub-continental unity of purpose and outlook in face of the Chinese threat. But, though there may be some short-sighted South Asian and other satisfaction in India's plight, the latter makes possible a new approach to South Asian problems as part of the attention given to the new aspect of the continuing Communist threat. Since South Asia's security now and for some years to come can be provided only by the United States and other Free World sources, these latter are in position to apply some quiet diplomacy to the resolution of these problems as the price for security. To make such diplomacy palatable a large Free World effort, using among others the device of the already, mentioned consortia, to help the 20 per cent of the world's population who inhabit the area, is in order. Its target over the next decade would be to help the South Asians on a national and regional basis reach a level of self-sustaining independence.

The key to the problem of South Asia is the resolution probably by some form of partition of the Pakistan-Indian conflict over Kashmir. The latter is more difficult than the related conflict over the waters of the Indus River valley but a solution was found for it by means of an equitable distribution of the flow of the six rivers. In international circles, Krishna Menon was the chief spokesman and defender of Nehru's views of Kashmir. With his eclipse at this time the issue may prove less recalcitrant to compromise. And that is what should be sought in an attempt to build up the Pakistan and Indian defense of the sub-continent. In this situation the US-Pakistan defense relationship and the US-Indian aid relationship on the one hand, and the UK-India-Pakistan-Commonwealth relationship on the other, may provide the lead elements in a new diplomatic and security equation for South Asia.

The course of politico-military strategy and action with respect to providing security in East Asia and in South Asia during the next decade hinges to a large extent on the US ability to work out cooperative arrangements with Japan and Australia, with India and Pakistan. It would be simple to suggest that the defense of the Pacific and Indian Oceans could be readily solved by enlarging SEATO or by scrapping SEATO and creating a new Pacific and Indian Oceans Alliance having the character of NATO. In such an alliance the four countries named would then serve as the anchors of the defense plan. But what is simple—despite Occam's razor—is not always practicable. SEATO, I believe, remains at best a name for intended US action. Its vitality is gone. It would be easier to scrap it and start afresh. Any new proposal now for a grand Asian-Pacific Alliance would in my view be premature and self-defeating. The Burmese proposed it in 1949. No one then would listen to them. Since then we have witnessed the costly competition between concepts of collective security and neutralism. Neither of these have been particularly successful in Asia. However desirable such an alliance might be conceptually, there is a long road ahead in which the United States and the Asian countries must build mutual confidence, understanding, and appreciation before it can be essayed.

Perhaps the most telling argument against such an alliance at this time and against exclusive reliance on these pairs of East and South Asian security anchors is the predictable response of the nations of Southeast Asia and the other smaller Asian nations. For two of the basic facts of Asian life partly as a consequence of the colonial past, partly because of pre-colonial Asian history, is the weakness of inter-Asian relationships and the fear and suspicion of the smaller Asian countries for the big Asian countries. Intercourse between the Asian states in the pre-colonial days was largely a matter of dynastic rivalries and frequent wars. With the arrival of colonial power, intercourse between the Asian states, except in the border areas, largely disappeared. The relationship was between the metropole and the colony. The effect of this past has not yet been worn away by independence.

On any social distance scale in Southeast Asia the resident Indians and the "overseas" Chinese would be at the bottom of the list, closely followed by the Japanese since World War II. The first two are the unloved competitors and feared minorities; the Japanese wartime treatment of the indigenes accounts for their presence on the low end of the scale. In addition, Burmese-Thai relations are improving slightly after a joint effort to eradicate the unpleasant memories of 14 previous wars. Cambodian-Thai and Cambodian-Vietnamese relations are usually at a low level primarily because of their past wars and respective "irredentist" claims. Malayan-Indonesian relations, despite common ethnic, religious, and language backgrounds are less than fulsome, because Malaya suspects that Indonesia would like to thwart the idea of Malaysia. And so it goes, not only in Southeast Asia, but also in South and East Asia.

In sum, inter-Asian relations are not such as to be now ready for a Pacific-Indian Ocean Alliance; and more particularly Southeast Asian nations as comparatively small ones (Indonesia of course is large in population and in ambition) do not take kindly to the possibility that they may be swallowed up in the big nation's arrangements. These are among the additional reasons for supporting a strong US bilateral policy in the area as a whole and with each free Asian country.

The above references to some inter-Asian difficulties should not be allowed to distract us from the main issue. These difficulties will be ameliorated in time for they are not fundamental in any political or economic sense to the future of the several countries involved. What is fundamental is the fact that Southeast Asia is the most vulnerable sector in Free Asia and therefore all the more requires US attention. For, even on the best possible schedule of building up the defense of East Asia and South Asia by proposals indicated above, the countries in those parts of Asia are unable now and for some time to come to contribute more than a token to the security of the eight Southeast Asian states. Mainland Southeast Asia is certainly *a*—I believe it is *the*—target of Communist China. If China were to get control of this peninsula she could dominate, short of a global war, the strategic connections between all of South Asia and the Pacific. Peking has done well in mainland Southeast Asia. After playing a cat-and-mouse game with Burma she finally gave the latter a good border solution and a $84 million credit. The possible USSR-Finland analogy of Sino-Burmese relationships should not be overlooked. She has come to the assistance of the Cambodians in their quarrels with the Thais and the Vietnamese. The neutralization of Laos places trusted Communists at the northeast border of Thailand and the northern border of Cambodia. Since 1954 her influence has been extended to the 17th parallel in Vietnam. That leaves Thailand and Vietnam.

The United States is presently honoring commitments made to these two countries and is trying to reduce the effect of Peking's gains elsewhere in mainland Southeast Asia. At this time, however, what we do in Vietnam—after the fiasco in Laos—is the key to the situation. There, with our Vietnamese ally, we are engaged in a bloody war with the Communists. The British and the Malays took ten years to liquidate that kind of war in Malaya where the Communists did not have the advantage of a contiguous sanctuary and support as they do in Vietnam. Even so, the British estimated that defense against insurgency demanded a force proportion of 15 to 1—a high cost affair. Now in Vietnam we shall have to decide how long the battle will last, how many casualties we are willing to suffer, and at what cost? This is the decision which should be made—to defend Saigon by threatening and probing the vulnerabilities of Hanoi and if necessary Peking. This would not only shorten the war, reduce the costs in blood and treasure; it would also have an effect on the rest of Southeast Asia. It would persuade these countries that we mean what we say and that we have the power to back it up.

It may be argued that the same end can be achieved by defending Saigon in Vietnam. My guess is that if we allow the battle to go on for a long time (even for the most optimistic estimate of three years, made by Admiral Felt) we make our task more difficult with the Vietnamese people and lose the confidence of other Southeast Asians. We also further endanger the security of the rest of the peninsula. Speed and firmness in reestablishing the internal security of Vietnam avoid these risks and carry with it dividends outside of Vietnam. For example, it may inhibit Hanoi in any attempt at using the 9960 Viet Minh which it presumably left behind in Laos after the 40 Viet Minh were counted by the International Control Commission at their check-point departure!

Twenty-twenty hindsight will not be necessary to predict the outcome of the 1962 Geneva Agreement on Laos. Neutralization of that country under its terms meant, as I pointed out in January of that year (*Asian Survey, op. cit.*), that we must and can trust the bona fides of Moscow and Peking, and of its troika-like government and International Control Commission (ICC). Such trust was misplaced and the *Troika* coalition merely provided the Communist Pathet Lao-Viet Minh forces the opportunity for "the pause that refreshes." During the months after Geneva 1962 the ICC was denied access to Pathet Lao held areas. In the spring of 1963 the Communists, completing a phase of their classical "united front from below" tactic succeeded in wooing a portion of the Laotian neutralist forces under General Kong Le and then attacked him, ignoring while so doing the Premier's powerless pleas for peaceful restoration for the *status quo ante*. Now, they have added more territory to that which they already controlled in North and Northeast Laos. They have advanced down from the Plateau Du Tran Ninh to the plains above and about Xieng Khouang, across from the town and province of that name, almost to Vang Vieng on the direct road and water-way (the river, Nam Ngum) about 100 miles north of Vientiane.

Even if new cease-fires are arranged, they will be temporary phases for Communist regroupment. No coalition with Com-munists in such a politically underdeveloped country as Laos can be sustained. Laos clearly represents the futility and mor-tality rate inherent in such agreements as those of 1954 and 1962. And it presents the clear and present danger outlined in the policy alternatives of this chapter. If we disengage from Laos it will certainly succumb, and early, thereby accelerating the timetable for Communist conquest of mainland Southeast Asia. If we temporize after another round of misbegotten negotiations with Moscow, more of Laos will slip behind en-croaching Communist force, only postponing the lethal end. If we alone or preferably with allied Asian and other forces *now* make a stand, we can save something of a free Laos and add a measure of defense to the rest of Southeast Asia.

It must be remembered that beginning in 1963 Kunming and the Nanning-Tsungshan complex of South China, unlike their condition in World War II, are both connected by rail and road to the industrial Chinese north and to each other. And from there, descending into Burma, Thailand, Laos, and North Vietnam via Szemao, Koiku-Mengtsz, and Hanoi, there comes an ever-increasing supply of better-equipped and trained replacements for the current Communist forces in Laos and South Vietnam. The longer we take to stop this build-up and advance, the more rapidly we approach the point of no return.

A victory, complete and swift is intrinsically necessary in Vietnam. It will also increase confidence in us throughout Southeast Asia. But above all, it will demonstrate to Peking that we intend to deny them their Southeast Asian target by whatever means may be necessary. At this moment in history the advantage is ours. Peking is in difficulty at home and is extended on long lines to India and on her southern coast line. We should press the advantage as quickly as we can maneuver in position to do so. If we are unable to use this advantage, another will come at the time of Mao's death and the probable confusion over succession. This is a ghoulish thing to think and write about. But since the event is inevitable we should be prepared to follow on its consequences.

For, in the final analysis, as this paper has tried to make clear, the Sino-Soviet enemy will give us no quarter in this war. The defense of mainland Southeast Asia requires that China's "march to the tropics" be stopped. No Southeast Asian country has ever welcomed the Chinese marchers. They have had the historical will to contest it at various times in the past, sometimes successfully. Our task is to instrumentalize Southeast Asian will with US power.

While this is being done and especially during the next decade there is a further task. We, together with our East, South, and Southeast Asian friends must acquire a relatively new skill. We must be able to utilize in a dual capacity the disproportionately large military establishments in the Asian countries, called forth by the Communist threat. These security forces must, of course, be appropriately trained and equipped to defend their country. But they must also be trained and equipped to help bring about internal law and order, to counter subversion, and otherwise to assist in the many necessary tasks of nation-building. In this sense, military skills are transferable to peaceful activity even when there is no peace for the forseeable decade ahead. And only on the secure foundations of domestic stability and improved living conditions can we expect democracy to emerge as a sturdy growth in this nation-building process.

FOOTNOTES

[1] President John F. Kennedy, *State of the Union Message*, January 11, 1962.

[2] President John F. Kennedy, "Budget Message To Congress," March 28, 1961, *Congressional Record*, March 28, 1961, pp. 4717-18. See also the valuable annual—since 1957—series of *U.S. Defense Policies*, prepared by Charles H. Donnelly, The Library of Congress, Legislative Reference Series, (Washington: U.S. Government Printing Office, 1957, *et. seq.* 1961).

[3] Xenia U. Eudin and Robert C. North, *Soviet Russia and the East, 1920-1927, A Documentary Survey* (Stanford: Stanford University Press, 1957).

[4] See statement by Secretary of State Acheson of May 18, 1949, in Department of State, *Bulletin*, XX (May 29, 1949), p. 696.

[5] Dean Acheson, "Crisis in Asia—An Examination of U.S. Policy," Department of State *Bulletin* January 23, 1950, pp. 111-18.

[6] *S. Report 612*, 87th Cong., 1st Sess.

[7] Maxwell D. Taylor, "Security Will Not Wait," *Foreign Affairs* (January, 1961), p. 176.

[8] See Chester Bowles, "A Balance Sheet on Asia," US Department of State, *Bulletin* XLVI (April 23, 1962), p. 675, for a gloomy appraisal of the "effective" Soviet advance in Afghanistan; and the author's "Never Negotiate Freedom: The Case of Laos and Vietnam," *Asia Survey*, I (January, 1962), pp. 3-11.

[9] *UN Technical Assistance Newsletter*, II (August-September, 1962), p. 2.

[10] Maxwell D. Taylor, *op. cit.*, p. 180.

# Alliance in the Western Hemisphere

*—WILLIAM S. STOKES*

## Summary

*I. One option for the United States to consider in the Western Hemisphere is to recognize: (1) the* nuestra América *or two Americas concept—one Anglo, the other Latin; (2)* Hispano-americanismo—*the amorphous cultural union which in fact is in existence; (3) cultural, economic, and political anti-American-ism as expressed in the literature of many of the* pensadores *(leading intellectuals) of Latin America; (4) the attempts to form Latin American confederations in the nineteenth century and the present-day efforts of the Institutes of Hispanic Culture to establish a "Community of Iberoamerican Nations." The im-plications of the recognition of the above factors might lead to the conclusion that it would be in the interests of the United States to encourage the Latin American countries to form a separate organization in the Western Hemisphere. Such an or-ganization might enhance their feelings of dignity and im-portance in dealing with the United States and might mitigate or even eliminate the antagonisms that the disparate situation of one rich, united, and powerful country dealing with twenty weak, underdeveloped, and disunited countries now permits.*

*II. If the United States and the Latin American countries prefer to continue to attempt to solve common problems through the alliance system which now prevails, concern should be given to the structural and procedural weaknesses of the OAS with a view to the achievement of strength through reform. In order to employ the sanctions provided by the Inter-American Treaty of Reciprocal Assistance (Rio de Janeiro, 1947), a two-thirds vote of all members is required. This provision constitutes an* *obstacle so great that it becomes difficult, if not impossible, to meet threats to the security of the Hemisphere. However, the Organization of Consultation of the OAS approved President Kennedy's interdiction order on October 23, 1962, by a vote of 19-0. The Latin American countries have long opposed United States intervention in their internal and external affairs and have managed to obtain Article 15 of the Charter of the Organization of American States (1948) which reads: "No State or group of States has the right to intervene directly or indirectly, for any reason whatever, in the internal or external affairs of any other State. The foregoing principle prohibits not only armed force but also any other form of interference or attempted threat against the personality of the State or against its political, economic and cultural elements." Under the Alliance for Progress, the United States promised to allocate $1 billion within twelve months and ". . . a major part of the minimum of $20 billion . . . which Latin America will require over the next ten years . . ." The expenditure of billions of dollars through the Alliance for Progress inevitably involves some degree of interference or intervention in the affairs of the Latin American countries. Since Premier Khrushchev has said (speech of January 6, 1961) that the Communists "fully and unreservedly support wars of national liberation" or "popular uprisings," it must be assumed that subversion or covert aggression will be attempted in the Latin American countries. For the above reasons, one option the United States might consider is the "mobilization concept"—the proposal that all available personnel in the Latin American field be mobilized in support of US and Latin American objectives in the Western Hemisphere. This would involve making an inventory of professionally qualified specialists in Latin American affairs from journalism, business, religion, and the academic world; and issuing invitations to them to make their talent available to the Latin Americanists in the United States Government and in the OAS.*

---

### Nuestra América

There is a vast literature of ancient as well as contemporary origin which argues that there are two Americas in the Western Hemisphere—the Latin and the Anglo-Saxon. When the Latin American author uses the phrase *"nuestra América,"* he almost always has in mind the America with a common language, common religion, and a common historical experience, all of which have contributed to the development of common values. More than a half-dozen distinguished thinkers of the colonial period conceived of unions or confederations of the Latin American states. Bolívar's conceptions come immediately to mind, but one must not overlook the views of José Cecilio del Valle, Bernardo de Monteagudo, Bernardo O'Higgins, Juan Martínez de Rosas, Juan Egaña, Bernardino Rivadavia, Francisco Miranda, and others. Following the failure of Bolívar's "Union, Alliance, and Perpetual Confederation" (1826), efforts were made in 1831, 1834, 1840, 1847-48, 1856, 1858, and 1864 to form political unions which would in varying degree resist the influence of the United States in the Western Hemisphere. With the development of the Pan American system, beginning with the Washington Conference of 1889-90, official pressure for a Latin or Hispanic alliance system subsided. However, the idea persisted in the literature and one great political movement—*Aprismo*—continues to call for formal union.

### Hispanoamericanismo

Upon achieving independence, the Latin American countries adopted in their first constitutions various of the values of individualism, liberalism, and representative democracy characteristic in a general way of the United States, Great Britain, and the Western European countries. However, the Latin American countries would not, or could not, make the revisions and modifications in their social, economic, and political institutions which would make such values meaningful in their practical affairs. Noting the discrepancy between law and fact (*el derecho y el hecho*), the intellectuals or *pensadores* so severely criticized their societies as to contribute to a national psychology of melancholy or even inferiority. The works of such men as Sarmiento, Bulnes, González Prada, Agustín García, Colmo, Octavio Bunge, Ingenieros, and Argüedas amply demonstrate the validity of this generalization. This situation was reversed beginning with the publication in 1900 of the classic, *Ariel,* by José Enrique Rodó. Rodó argued that the values of utilitarianism, materialism, positivism, and individualism of US culture were in theory and in fact inferior to the values of human solidarity, social aesthetics, and individual integrity of Hispanic culture. Rodó's defense of Greco-Latin humanism, with its emphasis on intellectual, romantic, and aesthetic idealism, provided the foundations for an intense nationalism which swept Latin America then and which largely prevails today. A very large number of Latin American *pensadores* have come to argue that the values of Hispanic and US culture are in conflict and that their own values are superior and must be protected at all costs from the "cultural imperialism" of the United States. Some of the *pensadores* whose works illustrate this point of view include Altamira y Crevea, Araquistaín Quevedo, Pereyra, Vasconcelos, Vargas Vilá, Blanco Fombona, Martí, de Hostos y Bonilla, Ugarte, García Calderón, Gálvez, Zurano Múñoz, Oliveira Lima, Palacios, Rojas, Saenz Peña, Jackson de Figueiredo, Henríquez Ureña, Pinochet, Henríquez y Carvajal, de Maeztú, Enamorado Cuesta, Elgüero, Suárez Somoano, González Arrili, Fernández y Medina, Moreno Quintana, Travesi, Osorio, Silva, Fabela, Caraballo y Sotolongo, Roldán, Saenz, Wagner de Reyna, Ibarguren, Díez de Medina, and many others.

The great majority of modern-day *pensadores* agree that there should be a cultural union of the Spanish-speaking peoples of the Western Hemisphere. The term that is used most frequently at this time and for the recent past to describe such a union is *hispanoamericanismo*. Other terms which have been used which refer at least to union of the Spanish-speaking peoples but which perhaps include Spain or Portugal or both are: *Panhispanismo* (by Fernando Ortiz in 1911 and J. Francisco V. Silva in 1918); *unión latino americana* (by José Ingenieros in 1922); *alianza hispanoamericana* (by Emilio Zurano Múñoz in 1931); *paniberismo* (by Francisco García Calderón in 1913); *Mundo Hispánico* (by J. Enamorado Cuesta in 1936); and *iberoamericanismo* (by José Suárez Somoano in 1930, José Luis Bustamante y Rivero in 1951, and Alfredo Sánchez Bella in 1957). An additional term, used more frequently by writers of Spain than of the Latin American countries, is *hispanidad*.

*Hispanoamericanismo* proceeds by publication of books and articles which proclaim and defend the values of Hispanic culture, both past and present; by the organization of literary and professional clubs and societies; through sponsorship of student and teacher exchange programs and lecture series; by holding expositions of an artistic or cultural nature; and by honoring the cultural origin of the Latin American countries through such ceremonial observances as the *día de la raza* (Columbus Day). The specific system for the present period centers in the

Institute of Hispanic Culture, organized in Madrid in 1946 as the parent body for 45 member Institutes of Hispanic Culture, all of which seek a "Community of Iberoamerican Nations." From 1946-56, the Institute published 300 books and sent to Latin America the following: 550,000 volumes, 4,000,000 copies of magazines, 80,000 booklets, thousands of records, hundreds of thousands of sheets and short publications, and hundreds of films. It organized 22 congresses on a wide range of cultural, economic, and governmental activities, bringing 3,000 specialists and *pensadores* to Spain. More than 12,000 university students from Latin America studied in Spain in the period 1946-56. The Institute's library of 100,000 volumes all deal with contemporary problems of Latin America. Although the Institute originally sought a "spiritual community," after ten years of operation, it began to embrace a "material community" as well.

### Political and Economic Anti-Americanism

Enough has been said to suggest that cultural differences and even conflicts exist in the Western Hemisphere between the United States and the Latin American countries. Differences can also be shown in the political and economic areas.

As one reviews the very recent literature of thoughtful writers, such as Pierre Maxime Schuhl and Alberto Wagner de Reyna, and that of more aggressive, even violent, critics of political liberalism, such as Julio Ycaza Tigerino, it becomes clear that, according to their conception of the nature of man and society, it should be the function of the state to establish and protect human solidarity, moral and spiritual ends, nationalism, and a "living together" (*convivencia*) of the classes. They propose a governmental structure characterized by order, discipline, and hierarchy under the guidance of strong, virtuous, moral, executive leadership, and disciplined parties or political organizations with functional rather than numerical representation. The amorphous congeries of "rightist" thinkers agree on one position—that the values of Hispanic culture cannot be achieved under either capitalism and individualistic democracy or under communism and totalitarian dictatorship. They, therefore, advance theories of the state which are "equidistant" between the "monsters that would waylay us," as Miguel Angel Ponce de León puts it. They propose a Third Position or Third Force, some writers openly using these terms and others not, although all support in general the same idea.

Among the supporters of the Third Force must be included many "Christian Democrats" and other Catholic thinkers who advocate either the cooperative movement or the corporative state. Both *Integralismo*, which never acquired power in Brazil, and the *Estado Novo*, which did, were opposed to individualism, democracy, and liberalism. In Colombia, an organization called *Movimiento de Acción Nacional* (MAN) was created in January 1955 which was clearly a Third Force effort. The eminent Chilean Catholic thinker, Alejandro Silva Bascuñán, expresses the conviction that "materialism," and "liberalism" are "dehumanizing" and impede the achievement of "social justice." Although he admits that "liberal individualism" is not as evil as communism, both must be rejected and a corporate state established. The *peronista* dictatorship in Argentina (1943-55), with its ideology of *justicialismo*, the Third Force, *Doctrina Nacional*, or *Filosofía Peronista*, as it has been called, is the best known, most dramatic, and undoubtedly most influential "rightwing" deviation from the principles of individualism, democracy, and liberalism ever to occur in Latin America. What *peronismo* and other Third Force ideologies in general have sought—moral, spiritual ends, human solidarity, nationalism, abolition of the class struggle, economic planning, the welfare state, strong, centralized, executive government, responsible or disciplined political parties, and order and authority in society in general—are values that have had serious support from serious intellectuals and men in public life in periods much earlier than the last decade and a half in Argentina. Finally, it should be noted that Fascist and Nazi ideology had significant impact and direct political influence in a number of Latin American countries in the 1920's and 1930's. It diminished in most countries in the 1940's and disappeared almost entirely with the defeat of the Fascist and Nazi forces in Europe.

Left-wing deviations from liberalism include: The Mexican Revolution; the Cuban Revolution under President Ramón Grau San Martín, 1944-48, and President Carlos Prío Socarrás, 1948-52; the Guatemalan Revolution, 1944-54; the *Movimiento Nacionalista Revolucionario* (MNR) of Bolivia, which acquired power with the military lodges by force in 1943, lost it in the same way in 1946, but came back by violence in 1952 and which continues to govern today; the *Alianza Popular Revolucionaria Americana* (APRA); the *Aprista* movement, or *Aprismo; Acción Democrática* in Venezuela; *Liberación Nacional* in Costa Rica, and other similar movements. Communism is best represented by Cuba from 1959 to the present. These political theories or ideologies tend to restrict in varying degree the initiative and participation of the individual in economic life, expand the functions of government, and centralize political authority, sometimes in an institution such as a party, or a combination of institutions, such as party, army, and labor unions, and sometimes, less frequently, in a single individual. Historical tradition, social mores, customs, the influence of family or church, accidental or emotional factors, and the effect of personalities all explain, in varying circumstances, why some individuals are "leftists" and others are "rightists." In the area of ideas, however, the insistence on moral and spiritual ends which have a religious origin and which, therefore, are based primarily on faith and only secondarily on reason, is what separates most sharply and most positively the ideologies of "left" and "right" in modern-day Latin American political theory. Programmatically, both "left" and "right" are similar, as one can easily discover by making comparisons, such as a case study of the "leftist" government of Arbenz of Guatemala and the "rightist" government of Perón of Argentina.

The heart of all the great political ideologies in Latin America of recent decades—"left" or "right"—is the insistence that government can better provide, through nationalization of the means of production or by direction, regulation, control, and planning of the economy, material standards of living significantly higher than those to which the masses of the people have been accustomed in the past. The modern-day constitutions, beginning with the Constitution of Querétaro of Mexico of 1917, reflect such points of view. Most of them contain statements on the social functions of property, state ownership of subsoil rights, rights of expropriation, planning, social security, many kinds of material welfare for everyone from the unborn to the aged, regulation and direction of the economy by the state, and governmental assistance to labor. Much state interventionism is to be found in the volumes of recent laws expressing economic nationalism. In trade and commerce, the following procedures have been characteristic from the 1930's to the present: centralized executive control over raising and lowering tariffs; foreign-exchange control supplemented by clearing agreements, payments agreements, compensation agreements, and regulatory procedures; import quotas; national monopolies; government corporations; export subsidies; price fixing; barter agreements; and cartels. Under such circumstances, it is only natural that the *pensadores,* especially those who specialize in economic matters, should be antagonistic toward private initiative and enterprise and sympathetic toward state interventionism or collectivism. It would follow almost certainly that US companies operating in Latin America would be subject to criticism, and this has been the case, especially since the end of World War II.

## Latin American Imperatives

So far in this essay I have dealt with ideas as they appear in the literature of the Latin American *pensadores.* It should be quite clear that there is a considerable body of literature which can only be described as anti-American in the cultural, political, and economic areas. Although no one has made a study of the quantity of anti-American literature which has appeared in Latin America since Rodó's *Ariel* in 1900, sample studies for selected periods have led me to the hypothesis that the amount of such literature has been increasing, even during the period of the Good Neighbor Policy. If the *pensadores* of Latin America lacked influence in public affairs, it might be possible to describe this effort as a literary exercise. However, the "doctor" from the *aula* (university lecture hall) has long exercised great power and influence in Hispanic culture. The works of such men constitute one source for understanding the nature of Latin American problems, objectives, and policies.

The literature of the *pensadores* makes crystal clear that the Latin American countries seek rapid, even revolutionary, change. The pressure of the lower classes for social and economic improvement is so great that even in the more developed areas, such as southern Brazil, Argentina, and Uruguay, reform is the keynote of every political movement. It is not only the insistent demands of the lower classes for social justice that explains revolutionary ferment in Latin America, however. The élite groups of educated, cultured, and talented leaders in the Latin American countries are, in the very great majority, determined to achieve modernity in their several states. But, saying this, one should remember that the Latin American countries are not "emergent" states. Their independent existence dates almost from that of the United States, and their prior affiliations were with states which achieved world leadership. They have a long and, in many ways, distinguished cultural tradition and economic and political history which influences the thinking of those who conduct their affairs at the present time. The Latin

American oligarchies generally seek change, but they desire solutions to their social and economic difficulties which will not alter fundamentally the basic values of their culture.

Many studies by individual scholars, foundations, governments, and international organizations have suggested that dramatic economic development is theoretically possible. About 70% of the total land area of Latin America is suitable for some form of agricultural, pastoral, or extractive purpose, but only about 3% is in use. The problem is to select a method of combining capital, human, and physical resources so as to produce goods and services efficiently and economically. The mercantilism of the colonial period was not replaced in fact by economic liberalism in the independence period, and the Latin Americans permitted a far greater degree of state interventionism in their economic systems than ever was the case in the United States. The conditioning impact of their historical experience has rendered modern-day theories of "right"- and "left"-wing collectivism understandable. In addition, such collectivism promises rapid, easy economic development, creating the illusion that traditional Hispanic values can be preserved.

But, the application of both "left"- and "right"-wing solutions to economic development has to a large extent proved *contra-producente* (the reverse of expectations). Sovereignty guarantees to governments the power to nationalize the means of production, whether locally or foreign owned. Whether Latin American governments, through the *fomento* corporation or other entities, are equipped to produce goods and services efficiently and economically, constitutes a much more serious and difficult problem. Mechanical or technical activities never enjoyed high prestige in Hispanic culture, as contrasted to achievement in the arts and humanities. It was traditional for the universities to produce far more graduates for the professions and the bureaucracy than for scientific pursuits, agronomy, or business. Studies of enrollment figures in major universities in eleven Latin American countries for the period preceding and following World War II reveal that the great majority of students almost invariably selected law, medicine, and engineering (almost always taught with strong theoretical emphasis).

In Chile, a country of known mineral resources, the University of Chile conferred 1,700 law degrees in the period from 1898 to 1918 but only 22 degrees in mining engineering. In order to bring enrollment figures up to date, I wrote to 80 institutions of higher learning in Latin America in 1957. I asked for total enrollment by fields for the most recent year for which such figures were available. In general, the more recent figures substantiate the pattern of choice Latin American students have traditionally made in institutions of higher learning. The figures indicate that training to become farmers, veterinaries, specialists in animal husbandry, miners, or businessmen is almost always far down on the list of preferences. The figures for Brazil showed that Brazilians apparently believe that they need about ten times as many lawyers as specialists in agriculture and approximately twenty-one times as many lawyers as veterinaries. For these and other reasons, state owned and operated enterprises almost always are inefficient and deficit-ridden in Latin America. Far from providing the rapid rate of economic development which is desired, they become a drain on the economy.

There are other problems. The seizure of private property and redistribution of wealth and income or both has the effect of reducing the rate of foreign investment. Local capital often takes flight, unemployment results, and governments are encouraged to engage in deficit financing and inflationary schemes. Since the rate of population increase in Latin America as a whole is higher than in any other major area of the world, it becomes difficult to maintain standards of living and even more difficult to achieve significant per capita increases.

## US Interests and Options: A "Community of Iberoamerican Nations"

It does not have to be demonstrated that the United States has vital military, economic, political, and cultural interests in the Western Hemisphere. The Founding Fathers recognized such interests, and it would be difficult to discover a single study by any scholar or responsible figure in public life from that time to the present who would advance a contrary position. During most of the history of the United States, the Monroe Doctrine was a policy of the first magnitude. There has been virtually unanimous recognition of the essentiality of prohibiting Communist encroachment in the Hemisphere in recent years. There was much public and official concern with Communist efforts to seize control of Guatemala (1944-54), and Castro's Cuba, the first Soviet satellite in the Americas, continues to command intense attention.

In theory, one option for the United States to consider in seeking to achieve stated ends as enunciated in policies would be that of encouraging a separate Latin American bloc—the "Community of Iberoamerican Nations" of the Institutes of Hispanic Culture. The *nuestra América* concept, efforts to achieve formal union in the past, *Hispanoamericanismo*, and the anti-American literature of the *pensadores* in economic and political areas suggest such a course. There are other reasons. Although the inter-American system has been operative since 1889-90, only a tiny percentage of all the treaties, conventions, protocols, and other agreements which have been negotiated have been ratified and the ratifications deposited. The principal objective of the Latin American countries has been to achieve guarantees that the United States will not intervene in their internal or external affairs. They succeeded in this objective beginning in 1933, and Article 15 of the Charter of the Organization of American States (1948) reads: "No State or group of States has the right to intervene directly or indirectly, for any reason whatever, in the internal or external affairs of any other State. The foregoing principle prohibits not only armed force but also any other form of interference or attempted threat against the personality of the State or against its political, economic and cultural elements." The United States has been called upon to pay about two-thirds of the total expenses of operating the inter-American system.

The collective power of the Latin American countries in a "Community of Iberoamerican Nations" would enhance their feelings of dignity and importance in dealing with the United States and might mitigate or even eliminate the antagonisms that the disparate situation of one rich, united, and powerful country dealing with twenty weak, underdeveloped, and dis-united countries now permits. This is not to say that the Latin American countries would find it easy to agree among themselves; for nationalism, boundary disputes, uneven rates of growth, and historical rivalries have periodically resulted in discord which on occasion has resulted in wars. However, a similar situation prevailed in Europe for centuries, yet in a short period of time the European Economic Community has come into being with demonstrable economic benefits to the member states. So successful has been the effort at European economic integration that many responsible leaders see the early possibility of political union. It has been, and is now, the official policy of the United States Government to encourage the development of European union. The Latin American states have already taken certain steps in the direction of economic cooperation, which, if successful, could lead to integration. The Latin American Free Trade Association (LAFTA) is designed to reduce tariff barriers over a 12-year period beginning in 1961. In November 1962 Brazil, Mexico, Colombia, Venezuela, and Argentina contemplated an air consortium to integrate the commercial air transportation industry in order to advance the Latin American common market. The General Treaty of Central American Economic Integration became effective June 3, 1961. There is a Central American Bank of Economic Integration, and other cooperative steps are contemplated within the Organization of Central American States, which now includes membership of all five Central American republics.

## US Interests and Options: The Mobilization Concept

Despite all difficulties and dissatisfactions, the Latin American countries have valued the inter-American system and might not favor a "Community of Iberoamerican Nations," even if the United States were to encourage its formation. It was the Latin American republics which took the initiative at Mexico in drafting the Act of Chapultepec (1945) which proposed the establishment of a Western Hemisphere security system. The Inter-American Treaty of Reciprocal Assistance (Rio de Janeiro, 1947) provided that if there is an attack against an American state, each state is bound "to assist in meeting the attack in the exercise of the inherent right of individual or collective self-defense recognized by Article 51 of the Charter of the United Nations." In the event of any other threat that "might endanger the peace of America, the Organ of Consultation shall meet immediately in order to agree on the measures which must be taken." The sanctions which may be imposed by the Organ of Consultation range from "recall of diplomatic missions" to "use of armed force," but to employ sanctions a two-thirds vote of all members is required. This did not constitute an impediment in the case of surreptitious installation of Soviet missiles and other offensive weapons in Cuba. The Organ of Consultation of the OAS approved President Kennedy's interdiction order on October 23, 1962, by a vote of 19-0 (Uruguay abstained when unable to secure instructions from Montevideo).

The United States is well aware of the priority which the Latin American states place on economic development. President

Kennedy described the Inter-American Economic and Social Conference (Punta del Este, Uruguay, August 5-17, 1961) as ". . . one of the most significant meetings in the history of the Western Hemisphere in this century." The conference concluded with a 26-page Charter of the Alliance for Progress (and 14 appended resolutions), signed by the United States and all the Latin American countries except Cuba. The Punta del Este Charter set the goal of an average annual cumulative growth in per capita income of 2.5 per cent in the next ten years. The social goals included six years of free schooling for all children, literacy for 50 million persons who are now illiterate, eradication of malaria, large-scale public housing, and potable water for more than half the population of Latin America. The United States promised to allocate $1 billion within twelve months and ". . . a major part of the minimum of $20 billion . . . which Latin America will require over the next ten years . . ." In return for the financial assistance, the Latin American countries were required to prepare development plans which include both agrarian and tax reform. The United States made available to the Latin American countries a total of $1,029,576,000 in the period from March 3, 1961, to February 28, 1962.

Since the United States has undertaken security, economic, and social responsibilities in the Western Hemisphere through the OAS, the success of the Alliance might be enhanced by mobilizing all available personnel in the Latin American field. This would involve making an inventory of professionally qualified specialists in Latin American affairs from journalism, business, religion, and the academy, and inviting them to make their talent available to the Latin Americanists in the Government. There are probably more individuals in the United States who are technically trained in Latin American affairs or who have had long-time experience in the area than for any other major region in the world. The problems are very great indeed, and it seems reasonable to assume that their solution might be facilitated by enlisting the services of the best qualified personnel in the entire country.

A majority and perhaps all Latin Americanists would agree that internal instability is likely to characterize a number of Latin American countries in the foreseeable future. President Kennedy has said that the economic aid programs "cannot succeed without peace and order." In his January 6, 1961, speech, Premier Khrushchev declared that the Communists are opposed to world wars and local wars, but he also said that they "fully and unreservedly support wars of national liberation" or "popular uprisings." This type of subversion or covert aggression undoubtedly will be attempted in the Latin American area and must be coped with by the United States and the Latin American countries.

The United States has a most important interest in the success of the Latin American programs to achieve rapid economic development. In the event of general war, the initial nuclear exchange probably will destroy or seriously impair the producing and distributing system in the United States. The transportation network may be immobilized for an indeterminate period of time. On the other hand, it is unlikely that the Latin American countries will be hit. If it were possible for the United States to establish food, medicine, fuel, and perhaps even industrial-parts depots in various parts of Latin America, a nucleus of basic materials would be available to restore US power for resumption of the conflict. The supremacy of US naval power would provide transport for such materials. However, Latin America could not expect to continue to supply food and industrial equipment for even an interim period unless viable economies existed with potentiality for some degree of surplus over local needs.

If a mobilization of talent were undertaken, it seems probable that arrangements could be made with the Latin American countries in advance for economic aid and assistance to the United States. It would also seem possible, to me at least, that antipathy to the use of United States technical aid through private companies could be overcome. As has already been demonstrated, the Latin American countries lack the technically-trained manpower at the upper and intermediate levels of management which is required to achieve rapid industrialization. It should be made known to the Latin Americans that private enterprise in the United States spends several times as much for education of its employees than is spent by the federal, state, and local governments, foundations, and all private educational systems combined. Not all of this education is in the scientific and industrial field. Indeed, private enterprise spends more money on education in the arts, humanities, and social sciences than the total amount expended by all governmental and private education in the entire United States. It is entirely possible that the educational breakthrough which

Latin America needs might be achieved through private corporations, both US and Latin American.

### Political Instability: The Permanent Problem

Political instability has long been a characteristic of Hispanic culture and is likely to constitute a serious problem in Latin America in the foreseeable future. The primary function of the armed forces, of course, is to protect the homeland from attack, implement foreign policy decisions, and guarantee person and property in accordance with constitution and law. In addition, however, the armed forces in Latin America have seen fit from time to time to question civilian control of the state.

There are reasons for the relative primacy of the armed forces in Hispanic culture. The invasion of the Iberian Peninsula by the Moors in the eighth century led to armed resistance by the Spanish and Portuguese. In the eleventh century the sporadic resistance of earlier years culminated in the *reconquista* or reconquest of the Moorish lands leading to the final surrender of Boabdil on January 2, 1492. About 700 years of intermittent fighting against the Moors enhanced the role of organized violence and helped to create the cult of the hero. The conquest of the New World served to maintain the prestige of the armed forces. The long struggle for independence (roughly 1810-26 for most of the Spanish-speaking colonies; different dates for Brazil, Haiti, Panama, Cuba) further strengthened the role of the military in Latin America. The military man on horseback dominated politics everywhere in Latin America after independence was achieved. However, frequently the generals fought among themselves for supreme power in the state. (The situation in Spain was little different, where there were 43 *pronunciamientos* in the period 1812-1923—32 failures, 11 successes.) Honor and *dignidad* (dignity) are among the most cherished values of Hispanic culture, and the armed forces consider it their function to protect the sacred honor (*pundonor*) of the *patria*. National disgrace or dishonor due to civilian corruption or ineptitude must be corrected at all costs, even if it means violent overthrow of the existing government.

The problem of the armed forces in Latin American politics is complicated by the fact that the services often are in conflict with each other for reasons which need not be explored here. In addition, in recent decades there has been a discernible trend for the armed forces to affiliate with, or at least to support, ideological movements dedicated to achieving rapid economic development and social improvement for the masses through state interventionism, direction, and control of the economy. In some instances, "people's militias," "armed proletarian militias," and other politically-oriented forces have been created for the specific purpose of protecting the interests of an existing regime. Examples are Guatemala (1944-54), Bolivia (1952 to the present), and Cuba (1959 to the present).

In addition to the historical tradition of armed forces intervention in internal politics and the use of violence for organizing and changing governments, the authoritarian nature of most of the social and economic institutions of Hispanic culture has contributed strongly to a concept of personal domination of affairs (*personalismo*) in which a well-defined principle of leadership in politics (*caudillismo*) has emerged. When authority is concentrated, the *caudillo* assumes personal credit for all favorable developments in the state but must also suffer responsibility for adverse events. Intolerance—a "for" or "against" attitude—prevails. *"Quien no está conmigo, contra mi está."* Competing leaders or groups find it easy to blame their disappointment or frustration on the *caudillo* in power and, concomitantly, to believe that the *patria* can be saved only by ousting the government from power by force.

Thus, in classifying the kinds of violence which are used in Latin American politics, elements other than the armed forces play an important role. *Machetismo*—the process of mobilizing violence at the local, regional, and sometimes national level, symbolically represented by the *machete* or all-purpose knife but actually involving light weapons, explosives, and combustibles—leads to the creation of *caudillos* who may or may not be military men. The single or multiple *cuartelazo* or barracks uprising places a premium on military skills, but this is not necessarily the case with the *golpe de estado* or *coup d'état* in which a direct assault is made on the person of the *caudillo supremo* or president. Revolution, defined as mass employment of violence for the purpose of effecting fundamental change, may involve both military and civilian leaders (the "doctor" and the "general"). These classifications, which I first developed formally for publication in 1952, do not include individual and group action, mainly in urban areas, involving arson, assassination, bombing, the general and partial strike, and the like, which are designed to achieve limited objectives rather than to oust the general government by force. If such violent methods continue, as I suspect will be the case, a new classification may have to be devised.

The peaceful methods of mobilizing political power all too frequently involve techniques violative of the representative republic. Such methods include *imposición* or the rigged election, *candidato único* or single candidate election, and *continuismo*, the extension of tenure of the president beyond the period set by the constitution or law. When rival claimants to power discover that they have been gulled, they frequently react by organizing violent assaults upon the government. All the Latin American countries have established political power by means of free, fair election from time to time, but the political parties still tend to be *personalista*, ephemeral, and generally lacking in ideology and program. *Personalismo* and multiple constituencies combined with various forms of proportional representation, where used, encourage fragmentation of the parties. Thus, coalitions in the legislatures are required to provide the majorities needed for governing. Such coalitions have been notoriously unstable in Latin America. The legislature finds itself incapable of either formulating policy or of checking the executive. The president is encouraged to act unconstitutionally, thus inviting charges of dictatorship or tyranny. Crises may then result which may lead to localized or general violence.

Although local and regional violence have long characterized Latin American politics, modern-day insurgency provides the possibility of a new dimension. Eudocio Ravines, in his important book, *The Yenan Way*, long ago made clear that international communism intended to employ subversion or covert aggression ("wars of national liberation," and "popular uprisings," to use Premier Khrushchev's expressions) in Latin America. The famous Prestes column in Brazil as well as the case studies of Guatemala (1944-54) and Cuba (1959—) are worthy of detailed study. The guerrilla activity in Colombia has probably resulted in the loss of 200,000 lives since the *Bogotazo* of 1948. The Soviet specialist on Latin America, V. G. Sprin, has stated that the Mao strategy, the Four Class Alliance of workers, peasants, middle classes, and the nationalist bourgeoisie under the leadership of the Communist Party, is to be used in Latin America. The "Institute of Latin American Affairs of the Chinese Communist Party" maintains a school for training Party and Trade Union officials for Latin America. In 1959-60, the Institute convened three Latin American Summit Conferences at which the General Secretaries of the most important Communist Parties of Latin America and the leaders of the Chinese Communist Party led by Mao Tse-tung took part.

If we assume that the Soviet and Chinese Communists mean what they say with respect to indirect political aggression in Latin America, the problem of insurgency will continue to command the attention of the United States in the foreseeable future. Guerrilla warfare depends upon civilian support and an external source of supply for arms. It seems probable that President Kennedy will achieve all of his stated ends with respect to the issue of Soviet missiles and other offensive weapons in Cuba, but the government of Castro will remain in power. The Castro government can therefore be used as a Communist base for supplying insurgents in Latin America with political propaganda and perhaps arms as well. In addition, Latin Americans have traditionally found it possible to acquire arms from the United States and Europe. One option of the United States is to employ air and sea supremacy to prohibit arms deliveries to insurgents in the Latin American countries. Since successful insurgency depends in part on tactics based upon mobility, surprise, flexibility, and deception, the US Government can aid friendly Latin American governments through providing training, light weapons, communications equipment, chemical agents and explosives, and propaganda and psychological materials. The possibility of considering active and open support on request of Latin American governments might legitimately be considered. Although it is clear that political instability based on violence in politics inhibits the development of free governments as described by Presidents Eisenhower and Kennedy, the ability of the Latin Americans to change governments rapidly by force is not always contrary to US interests. One must remember that the government of Arbenz of Guatemala, demonstrably anti-US, was removed by force in 1954. Other illustrations could readily be cited from the recent past.

Historical, political, and, as Segundo V. Linares Quintana, distinguished Argentine scholar, adds, "ethnic, social, and economic factors" explain the use of violence in Latin American politics. The use of violence is complex and sophisticated. It will not be eradicated by simple formulas. The solution to political instability (which has resulted in more than three dozen governments being ousted by force since the end of World War II) is, of course, primarily a task for the Latin Americans themselves. However, the mobilization concept, developed earlier in this paper, offers possibilities of US assistance. Sometimes even relatively small mechanical changes in governmental procedure can be productive of important results. It would be difficult to discover a government more unstable than that of Germany under the Weimar Constitution, or, indeed, that of France under the Fourth Republic. Both governments employed multiple constituencies and proportional representation which had the effect of creating a multi-party system, coalition government, and legislative ineffectiveness. When the single-member constituency was adopted in the Bonn Basic Law of 1949 (in part) and in the Fifth Republic in France in 1958, profound changes leading to a reduction in the number of splinter parties began to appear at once. The more fundamental changes in social and economic institutions are susceptible of solution, as President Kennedy has made clear, through the Alliance for Progress.

# The Politicalization of Strategy

—*WILLIAM R. KINTNER*

## Summary

*A purely military strategy is no longer possible. The failure to recognize the nature of modern strategy and to plan and conduct our affairs accordingly is largely responsible for an inadequate American response to a direct and deadly challenge.*

*Among the factors which contribute to the changing nature of strategy are: nuclear warfare, the American policy of collective security (entangling alliances, foreign aid, and foreign bases), the development of modern electronic communications systems, and Soviet reliance on political warfare.*

*The main thrust of Communist Cold War strategy is to downgrade the power of the US armed forces by non-military means. The Soviet Union's operational code has always reflected intimate marriage of political and military and all other factors. Communist leadership thoroughly grasps the significance of Clausewitz's aphorism, "War is a continuation of politics by other means." Communist policy and strategy in the broad sense have always been determined at the top level of the Communist hierarchy. At the same time, it should be noted that many of the senior generals in the Soviet Army are Communists and a few of them participate as high-level Communists in the formulation of over-all Soviet strategy.*

*Detailed political guidelines for conducting US strategy and comparable comprehensive political restraints imposed by the Presidium on Soviet military operations are likely to dominate the pattern for the future planning of conflict operations.*

*National strategy must be far broader and far more comprehensive than customary strategic and military planning. In the realm of high strategy, there is no clear-cut line of demarcation between military and political matters. Political direction must be firmly based on military power realities. National strategy can be formulated only by the closest integration of political, military, and economic information and technological considerations. It should be a consensus of the best thinking of all departments and agencies with a capacity to implement this strategy.*

*The fact that the United States has not as yet regarded its conflict with communism as an organic whole, explains, in part, the circumstances in which this country now finds itself. In the United States, national security requirements and decisions to take any action outside American frontiers invariably cut across the traditional responsibilities of existing departments and agencies. Nevertheless, except for the White House, it is difficult to locate a single focus in the US Government for the viewing of strategy problems as a whole.*

*It seems that we are not yet sufficiently organized at the national level to conceive, direct, and implement the kind of positive integrated strategy required by the radical challenges confronting this nation. With some notable exceptions, the United States continues to take refuge in ad hoc expedients rather than in policies which anticipate and avoid problems that grow into crisis proportions.*

*US strategy-making machinery has undergone many gyrations during the course of the Cold War. The Kennedy Administration, shortly after coming into office, discarded both the National Security Council Planning Board and the Operations Coordinating Board in favor of a highly personalized and centralized control over policy. At the same time, the present Administration has brought into being an informal community of policy-making operators. This influential group has shown some willingness to consider strategy in its broadest and most extended forms.*

*It is still too early to tell whether the pattern employed in the October 1962 crisis will become a model for the future development and execution of strategy. In the Cuban embargo, policy, strategy, and operations were conceived and conducted at different levels. The entire undertaking was extremely sensitive to international, Allied, and domestic political considerations. The Cuban crisis, an integrated part of the total world confrontation, could be dealt with by a small Executive Committee of the National Security Council. In the opinion of this writer, however, the strategy group in the trilogy of policy-strategy-operations utilized in the October 1962 Cuban crisis is far too small to cope with the wider vista of global conflict. Its representation was not weighted in proper correlation with the importance of the various factors which must be considered in devising a comprehensive long-term national strategy for the United States.*

*As a nation, we are limited in the course of action open to us by the size, character, and capabilities of our military forces. Despite the politicalization of strategy, military power is still a dominant reality in the present conflict and the key underpinning of American policy. During the past several years, however, professional military men have had less and less to say as to how such decisions on military posture are made and have had less and less influence on the actual choices.*

*President Kennedy introduced some major modifications into US military doctrine, in a statement given to Congress in March 1961: "Our arms must be subject to ultimate civilian control and command at all times, in war, as well as peace." Such increased emphasis has led to civilian design and even to detailed operational direction of the strategy employed in almost every American Cold War confrontation with Communist aggression.*

*A crucial aspect of strategy, the provisions of flexible means for tomorrow's policy-makers to employ, is increasingly taken out of the hands of professional military planners. Apparently, we face a situation in which the American military are becoming technicians—technicians who have less and less to do with the formulation of strategy which they may be subsequently called upon to implement. Over time, this trend will undermine the military pillar of American security. To reverse it the United States needs a more orderly, integrated strategy to allow the professional military people to play a more active role in the formulation and design of strategy.*

*The ancient ghost of civilian control over the American military is not at issue. What is needed is a clarification of the military role with respect to the formulation of national policy, national strategy, and military operations in order that the military professional's function, in an age when conflict and warfare have become so irreversibly politicalized, might be understood.*

*Strategy, national in scope, must be devised by the President in his dual role as Chief of State and Commander-In-Chief of the armed forces. National strategy for today and for tomorrow must, however, be a broad, grand, or extended strategy which embraces the full spectrum of political, military, economic, psychological, and other actions.*

*It seems logical that the military should be represented in whatever organizational mechanism that may be set up to formulate and supervise the execution of national strategy. Two steps should be taken: the military should be given adequate representation on whatever government-wide group—a national general staff or expanded EXCOM—that might be established to devise the kind of integrated strategy which the circumstances of today and tomorrow demand. Simultaneously, the planning and conduct of military operations should be restored to the military as its primary province. In this way, our armed forces would effectively support US policy with the coordinated power of every material resource placed at their disposal.*

Many forces have converged to change fundamentally the nature of national strategy. A purely military strategy is no longer possible. Yet despite the recognition that national strategy has been transformed, the prevalent system for the design of American strategy still has not advanced adequately from the techniques used when political, economic, and military matters could be dealt with in isolated compartments.

The United States has come under direct and deadly challenge. The American response to this challenge during the many dreary battles of the Cold War has been less than adequate. While many reasons can be given for what has been at best a humdrum performance, the failure to recognize the nature of modern strategy and to plan and conduct our affairs accordingly is the most crucial.

### The New Elements of Strategy

The ultimate paradox of this age is that while military power is more important as a backstop of policy than ever before, it is perhaps less important as an operational instrument. The advent of the almost unimaginable power of nuclear weapons, which led President Eisenhower to say once that there was "no substitute for peace," is the chief source of this paradox. But there are factors other than nuclear weapons which also helped shape the substance of the new strategy. One of these is the Communist reliance on political warfare in adroit combination with other types of Soviet power. Another is the American policy of collective security. The fact that the United States has entangling alliances with over forty nations dispersed throughout the globe has placed severe political restrictions on both the deployment and potential employment of US armed forces. A related aspect of the US collective security policy is the inescapable dependence on American bases abroad. The influence of the United States military assistance program on the force structure of many of our allies has led to an intertwining of military, political, and economic decisions at the seat of our government in Washington.

Finally, the development of modern electronic communications systems has made possible the control of forces deployed in combat from the Pentagon command post, ten thousand miles away from the scene of action. During the Korean War, battalion-size actions were monitored by the JCS. This degree of control is now commonplace. However, forty years ago it would have been regarded as both impossible and ridiculous. Now it is at most only ridiculous.

In 1945, two primitive atomic bombs were dropped on Japan at the close of World War II. Regardless of whether or not nuclear weapons are ever employed in any future conflict, the efforts to achieve large and diversified stockpiles of nuclear weapons and warheads, highly complex delivery systems, and sophisticated means of defense against intruding aircraft and missiles have preoccupied the defense establishments of both the United States and the Soviet Union. Soviet technology, although lagging behind that of the United States in many areas, as of 1960, had challenged the dominance the United States once enjoyed in the area of intercontinental strategic exchange. A basic shift in the technological balance and the attendant military-force posture cannot be ruled out. Consequently, technology itself has become an indispensable element in all strategic calculations.

Even as the technological race see-saws back and forth, other actions—political and economic in nature, or aggression conducted under the rubric of "wars of national liberation"—may change the strategic balance of power through capturing strategic geographic areas. A possible result is that "the most important battles may not be fought by exchange of nuclear firepower, but, like the conflicts of the sixteenth and seventeenth centuries, will consist of maneuvers or diversions designed to achieve a decisive advantage by one side or the other."[1]

In Communist hands, political warfare has become a primary instrument within a closely-knit total weapons system for waging the protracted conflict against the United States and its Free World allies. Political warfare includes diplomatic, economic, and psychological warfare, and a host of other activities conducted by governments, by disciplined political parties operating under governmental direction, or by private groups. Military action in the unconventional band of the conflict spectrum takes place within this context in the form of guerrilla warfare and counter-insurgency operations. All of these activities are conditioned and motivated by political considerations. Political warfare may be just a preliminary move to secure favorable political positions which could enhance the success of offensive military operations if they should take place. But beyond that, it now offers a means of expansion that may not involve the overt employment of military force.

Countermeasures against Communist political warfare involve the closest cooperation between political and military leadership. At the core of political warfare is the ideological struggle—the battle for the ascendant idea which moves people to seek social change or to battle aggression in all of its disguises. Political and military policies and strategies draw their strength from the power and persuasiveness of the fundamental ideas and values which shape a nation's objectives in relation to the rest of the world.

A main thrust of Communist Cold War strategy has been the attempt to destroy or downgrade the power of the US armed forces by non-military means, particularly by campaigning for the elimination of the US overseas base system. Already the United States has felt it necessary to give up bases in locations of considerable utility. One by-product of the Cuban missile crisis is the possibility that the United States will match the Soviet withdrawal of missiles from Cuba by some kind of negotiated pull-back of US atomic weapons from the NATO area. There will, of course, be changes in desirability of this or that base location because of changes in technology and shifting patterns of weapons systems. Nonetheless, the strategic importance of logistics is such that no major power can successfully fight without having available large, complex, and consequently vulnerable, bases. But again, the problem of access to bases has many political, psychological, and even economic overtones. Because of the asymmetries and the respective geopolitical positions of the Soviet Union and the United States, a comprehensive overseas base structure is far more valuable to the United States than it is to the Soviet Union. Bases are absolutely essential in stopping local wars or "wars of national liberation." Furthermore, the space race also requires a complex and widely distributed geographical tracking and guidance system. In a broad context, the problems inherent in acquiring and disposing of bases will be of ever-growing importance to any US national strategy.

All these factors taken together prompted President Kennedy to introduce some major modifications into US military doctrine. In a message submitted to the Congress in March 1961, the President spelled out his new military policy. The principle that is most pertinent to this analysis follows:

> *Our arms must be subject to ultimate civilian control and command at all times, in war, as well as peace.* The basic decisions on our participation in any conflict and our response to any threat— including all decisions relating to the use of nuclear weapons, or the escalation of a small war into a large one—will be made by the regularly constituted civilian authorities. This requires effective and protected organization, procedures, facilities and communication in the event of attack directed toward this objective, as well as defensive measures designed to insure thoughtful and selective decisions by the civilian authorities.*

Subsequently, this emphasis on civilian control of the military—the established American principle since the foundation of the Republic—has led to civilian design, and even to detailed operational direction of the strategy employed in almost every American Cold War confrontation with communism. Examples are legion. US military assistance advisory personnel in Laos came under the direct and personal supervision of the American ambassador to that country. The ill-fated Bay of Pigs invasion of Cuba in April 1961, seems to have been inspired and directed by an assorted group of civilian officials and guerrilla warfare experts with intermittent responsible participation of the military chieftains in the Pentagon.

The details of military preparations, alerts, and counters in Berlin appear to be carefully monitored, if not actually directed, by a civilian-dominated Berlin task force in Washington. Considerable authority on contingency operations, however, has been delegated to military authorities in SHAPE, CINCEUR, and

* Italics added.

Berlin to carry out contingency plans approved in Washington. Of course, in any major crisis, the contingency responses are carefully directed from Washington. Assistant Secretary of Defense (ISA) Nitze and his British, French, and German colleagues in Washington are always accompanied by military representatives when Four-Power meetings take place on military problems. The JCS also have a permanent representative on the US Berlin Task Force who often attends instead of Mr. Nitze.

The partial blockade imposed on Cuba in October 1962, was executed within carefully circumscribed political parameters. The Chairman of the JCS participated in the small executive committee of the National Security Council appointed to supervise this action. But other than General Taylor, the remainder of the US professional military establishment appears to have contributed little to the design of the strategy pursued.

One may agree or disagree with the political parameters established for the Cuban quarantine. Far more important is the fact that detailed political guidelines for conducting US strategy and comparable comprehensive political restraints imposed by the Presidium on the Soviet military operations are likely to dominate the pattern for the future planning of conflict operations. If this statement is true, it is important to explore its implications.

## Communist Conflict Operations

Because Communist strategy is one of the new elements confronting US policy-makers, a brief survey of its characteristics is in order.

The Soviet Union's operational code has always reflected the intimate marriage of political, military, and all other power factors available to the Communist movement. The Communist Party of the Soviet Union and its world-wide offshoots are quasi-military in their organizational structure. In the planning and conduct of a wide range of operations, Communist leadership from Engels and Lenin on has thoroughly grasped the significance of Clausewitz's aphorism, "war is a continuation of policy by other means." Communist leaders have gone farther, and have made peace a continuation of war by other means. In addition, because of their revolutionary tradition and their reliance on propaganda and agitation as a means of inciting the masses to action, the Communist leaders readily visualize conflict opportunities in the areas outside the boundaries imposed by orthodox Western thinking.

Every Communist operates according to a clear-cut, well understood policy that if he does anything to destroy non-Communist social orders and works toward world domination, he does well. Within this clear-cut policy the considerable organizational skill which the Communists have displayed in meshing together the many strands of their conflict operations has been one of their greatest sources of strength. They appear to regard their relationship with the non-Communist world as one of continuous conflict. Communist leaders have developed a machinery for conflict organization comparable to that which democracies achieve only during participation in a recognized shooting war. In short, the Communists have learned to develop and coordinate many forms of activity as instruments of conflict.

Because they seek ultimately to erode their opponent's will to resist the Communist advance, they have recognized, far better than we have, the significance of *time* as a strategic, fourth dimension. In fact, the Communist protracted conflict operates almost entirely on a time axis, since it requires time for the impact of a series of events to change the attitudes of people toward a certain conflict issue. Believing that time is on their side, the Communists are willing to temporize and to play for small advantages, each of which is calculated to erode the will to resist.

Consequently, Communist strategy is multi-dimensional. Pursuits which Western peoples look upon as those of peace are regularly employed by the Communists as tools of war. Under cover of the umbrella of Soviet military power, the Communists probe into troubled areas of the non-Communist world, seeking to create situations which are difficult to check militarily. If such situations can be met only by military means, they will require a far greater investment of Western treasure and blood than the Communists employ to instigate them.

The many-sided Communist assault on the Free World is conducted by a professional group of conflict managers. The Soviet leaders adhere to an ideology which provides them with a uniform set of basic objectives. *There is no need to argue out underlying assumptions,* as often must be done in the West, before leaders are agreed on either the nature of problems they face

394     William R. Kintner

or on the policies to be pursued in dealing with them. Furthermore, the Communist leadership group is, on the whole, power-motivated. In climbing their way up the Communist ladder, members of the Presidium tested all the tricks of infighting and political manipulation. Consequently, when they reach the inner group directing the Communist strategy, they instinctively apply the conflict techniques which are second nature to them. Their basic world plan stems from these basic motivations: to become more powerful militarily, economically, psychologically, and politically than their opponents. To their historically varied weapons arsenal, the Communists have added in recent years an appreciation of, as well as a capability for, the development of an advanced technology. They have skillfully blended their technological achievements into political programs as well as into their military posture.

The Communist power base of the Soviet Union, and to a lesser degree that of Communist China, is reinforced by the existence in many countries outside the Bloc of the disciplined Communist Parties subordinated to the political direction of either Moscow or Peking. The Communists thus dispose of a world-wide network of Communist-sponsored organizations. This enables them to wage the fight against the West by proxies and "independent" forces, thus making it very difficult for the West to strike back against the real instigators of its difficulties.

In the framing of their long-range strategic objectives, the Soviet military operates at two levels. They first function at the technical level, seeking to design and, if necessary, employ military forces in a professional military manner. It might be well to point out that since the coming to power of the Communists in Russia, the Soviet military per se has very little to do with the formulation of high Communist strategy. Many of the original officers of the Red Army had served the Czar. These were retained by the Communists because of their military skills, but they were treated as technicians. The same observation can be made concerning many of the diplomats initially employed by the Soviet Union. Communist policy and strategy in the broad sense have always been determined at the top level of the Communist hierarchy, whether by the Politiburo or by the Presidium.

At the same time, it should be noted that *many of the senior generals in the Soviet Army are Communists and a few of them participate as high-level Communists in the formulation of over-*

*all Soviet strategy.** Such a man is Marshal Malinovsky, Minister of Defense of the Soviet Union. A notable speech which he gave to the Twenty-second Congress of the CPSU in October 1961 illustrated the manner in which the Soviets harmonize policy, strategy, and the posture of the Soviet military forces.

Under the Soviet system the over-all strategy, guiding Soviet military deployment and operations, is conceived politically to advance Soviet political objectives.

### Policy, Strategy, and the Planning of Military Operations

A frequent criticism leveled at the US Government's conduct of its security affairs is that basic national security policies are so broad and general in character that they provide inadequate guidelines for the development of forces and resources, and almost no direction for the employment of these means should the need ever arise to use them. Another criticism is that policy is, in fact, formed not by statements of purpose but rather by the budgetary allocation of resources between competing governmental claimants, military or otherwise. Frequently, there is a gap between policy and budgetary commitments.

Some of these difficulties could be overcome if we would clearly distinguish between the functions of policy and the role of strategy, and thus identify an appropriate place for professional military planning and operations in the total scheme of things. The relation of policy to strategy can be seen in Clausewitz's precepts. "None of the principal plans (strategy) which are necessary for a war can be made without insight into the political conditions. When people speak, as they often do, of the harmful influence of policy on the conduct of war, they really say something very different from what they intend. It is not this influence, *but the policy itself*, which should be found fault with. If the policy is right, that is, directed toward the proper end, it can only affect the war favorably. Where this influence deviates from the proper end, the cause is to be sought only in a mistaken policy."

* The case for participation of US military personnel in national policy formulation should not be patterned on the Soviet system. Obviously, the real case for military participation must lie in an analysis of what comprises national strategy, the military role therein, the interdependence of the military and political input, and the further recognition that the military can implement the strategy far more effectively if they have participated in its development—or at least understand it.

In this context, policy means two things. First, it is a statement of intended actions calculated to safeguard national interest with regard to international issues. The statement of intended action should be specific enough to provide the basis of national strategy and thus determine the character of political guidance, military forces, and economic and psychological actions through which strategy will ultimately be expressed. Second, policy should provide some indication of the degree of commitment that the country places on a given policy objective. Commitment is reflected in the kinds and extent of resources allocated to make the policy operative.

For the most part, the United States has been deficient in enunciating American policies which can provide a concise foundation for effective global or regional strategic planning. Too much flexibility—desirable in itself—can lead to inchoate policy without proper focus.

Effective policies should satisfy these requirements:

1) Permit maximum favorable utilization of the existing critical and favorable factors in a given situation.
2) Conversely mitigate the influence of adverse critical factors.
3) Lead so far as possible to actions acceptable to both the United States and to its allies even though the motivations leading to the action may often be dissimilar.
4) Be realistic within available resources.

Since strategy is the expression of policy, it will invariably reflect the character of its origin. If a given policy is loose and indeterminate, the strategy devised to attain it will either be so weak as to be incapable of attaining its ends, or, on the contrary, may achieve ends other than those sought.

Strategy might be defined as the orderly marshalling of resources and their efficient application to obtain an objective within time limits imposed by the problem involved. Because of the many factors already discussed, national strategy must be far broader and far more comprehensive than customary strategic-military planning. In the realm of high strategy there is no clear-cut line of demarcation between military and political matters. Political directions must be firmly based on military power realities. What we do in the military field must be in complete accord with the political guidelines established by policy. The nature of our military forces is an indispensable element of the total national posture which supports US policy and the conduct of US diplomacy.

In this day and age, strategy is no longer the province of the soldier with the diplomat occasionally looking over his shoulder. Instead, national strategy can be formulated only by the closest integration of political, military, and economic information and technological considerations. Although too often ignored in practice, the concept of an integrated national strategy has long been recognized. When General Bradley was Chairman of the JCS, he called on civilians and soldiers to work out together the measures required to protect US world interests and responsibilities. As General Bradley stated it:

> The conduct of foreign affairs is a civilian responsibility. Military policy in our democratic America must always remain the servant of national aims.
>
> But today, amid new global dangers, neither the diplomat nor the soldier alone can lead the American people to wise international action. Both voices must be heard if the course pursued is to be realistic and effective.
>
> The soldier can see strategic perils that the civilian might readily overlook. The soldier must not direct the civilian policy, but the civilian must never overcommit the soldier. *We must never have a foreign policy that sends our armed forces to world tasks beyond their capabilities.*\*

At the national strategic level some decisions have been made in a sometimes haphazard fashion without due regard for military considerations available to the DOD or to the JCS. There has been a tendency to keep senior military men working strictly on military problems. If a sound national strategy is to be devised, however, military personnel must participate in its formulation.

From an integrated national strategy should emerge guidelines from which the JCS and their military planners can design and deploy forces. The design of these military forces is a professional task and one for which the military should assume full responsibility. This does not mean, however, that the military professionals cannot turn to other groups, including scientists, research analysts, and others, for advice and assistance to carry out their responsibilities. As military planners and operators, the soldier, the sailor, and the airman are true military instruments of the state. They should be given the political directions upon which to act, and they know professionally how to put their power into action. National strategy should be a consensus of the best thinking of all departments and agencies with a capacity

---

\* Italics added.

to implement this strategy. The Government as a whole must comprehend the military components of strategy as well as the other factors that shape the grand strategy of the nation. In this sense national strategy provides the frame within which the total picture of the US foreign policy is painted.

The organization and process for developing and executing the national strategy must be able to plan for and provide resources for meeting emerging contingencies and long-term requirements. Furthermore, it must be able to coordinate tactical operations designed to deal with "normal" Cold War conditions as well as to function effectively in times of "high crisis" as exemplified by the Cuban missile affair. The National Security Council Executive Committee, with some modifications, appears to be a useful device for dealing with "high crisis" situations, but it is not the most appropriate instrument for monitoring the series of interrelated actions which comprise the "normal" Cold War confrontations nor for systematic long-range planning.

## An Organic Whole

The fact that the United States has not as yet regarded its conflict with communism as an organic whole explains, in part, the circumstances in which this country now finds itself. By contrast, the leaders of the Soviet Union, because of their ideology and because their conflict management is based on cold-blooded analyses, have pursued a bolder strategy.

In the United States, national security requirements and decisions to take any action outside American frontiers invariably cut across the traditional responsibilities of existing departments and agencies. Nevertheless, except for the White House, it is difficult to locate a single focus in the US Government for the viewing of strategic problems as a whole. The subject matter of national strategy is varied—the impact of transportation and rapid communications, the development of nuclear weapons, the many-pronged Communist offensive, the increasing reliance of the American economy on imported raw materials. The base problem and other factors must be considered. No matter what the subject, it is increasingly impossible to deal with any one matter in isolation from other factors. Consequently, to treat problems in separate airtight compartments runs counter to both logic and to the nature of the present world environment.

Strategy must be planned as a whole and developed by minds which are capable of seeing the interrelated ramifications of a variety of economic, military, and political forces. The political guidance which is necessary to make military power an integral instrument of an over-all national strategy has already been mentioned. Geography continues to remain the most important underpinning of strategy, even though technology may modify its importance. Yet, there is still a chance that under present conditions the significance of a technological "breakthrough" might prove to be decisive. Technological advances, such as the race for space, can alter the world psychological climate with a direct bearing on national prestige and influence. Information and propaganda to influence the psychological attitudes of other people regarding technological triumphs or other issues must be disseminated and implemented within a framework of over-all strategy. Propaganda cannot be a mere auxiliary used in a detached or independent manner, or in a political or military vacuum. Simultaneously, propaganda and information must convey the ideology of a free and open society.

Arms control discussions and proposals for general and complete disarmament, which have preoccupied statesmen as well as won much public interest and support in many countries, introduce another important force operating on the formulation of strategy. Until recent years the tendency has been to separate the design of arms control measures from strategic considerations. There may be some unilateral arms control measures which the United States or other countries might take which would, in fact, enhance their security in the thermonuclear age. If this possibility is to be realized, however, arms control proposals must be developed and, if need be, implemented within the framework of a total strategy. Otherwise, the haphazard choice of a particular arms control measure might prove damaging to US national security.

Khrushchev's January 6, 1961, statement that it was "the sacred duty" of communism to support wars of national liberation is a firm promise that the United States and its allies will be confronted with Communist-supported guerrilla wars in many parts of the world over the next decade. By its very nature, guerrilla warfare is intimately entwined with political and psychological activity. Guerrilla warfare in a given country is but a manipulation of the over-all Communist plan, which is a global guerrilla war of systematic erosion against Western strength and positions. In both the global campaign and its local manifestations, motivation spurred by politically attractive objectives is the most potent means of marshalling the population's support either to overthrow a government by guerrilla action, or to defend a government against an insurrection supported by outside forces.

Finally, we must recognize the reciprocal relation of military actions to national political decisions. No better example of that can be found than the handling of the October, 1962 Cuban crisis engendered by Soviet deployment of offensive missiles into Castro-dominated Cuba. At every step in the sequence of this confrontation domestic and foreign political considerations were intertwined with the military actions either taken or contemplated.

## The New Strategy Process

What would a strategy which consciously incorporates political considerations be like? The strategy would systematically employ the power and resources of the United States to help frame and evolve an over-all international environment compatible with the interests of the United States and its Free World allies. In short, it would aim consciously at the establishment of a more harmonious political order. To achieve this objective, national strategy would be planned on the scale of decades, not of years. An individual problem or conflict issue would not be viewed as an isolated phenomenon, but as a phase of a total endeavor, a part of a multiple series of integral actions both offensive and defensive in character needed to transform the world from a pattern of international anarchy to some more cooperative structure. In sum, the new strategy would do the following: it would provide a comprehensive design intertwining all the interrelated measures the United States should adopt and implement consistent with the national policy of defending and extending the frontiers of freedom. It would provide a program package of over-all long-term requirements for foreign policy, national defense, economic activities, and domestic programs (such as an increase in scientific and technological education) affecting our world position.

It would set forth in an orderly series of priorities, a long-term projection of the resources needed to meet requirements in various categories listed above. Finally, it would relate requirements of needed resources to the present and future economic capacities of the nation.

A dominant feature of the new strategy would be continuity of policies and programs. Essential to the implementation of this strategy would be the development and sustaining of a momentum which would permit a steady application of pressure on our enemies and of influence on our allies toward constant ends with maximum continuity of effort. Fluctuation and inability to set a line of policy and hold to it, particularly as regards military preparedness in the support of political action, is both wasteful and unproductive.

There will be no endeavor here to spell out the detailed applications of a strategy designed to steer the global balance of power in a direction favorable to our interests. It must be stated clearly, however, that the strategy pursued should relate the underlying spiritual and political values of this nation to the power that assures their protection and extension. This means that the strategy would favor limited rather than unlimited use of power, and would eschew a global strategy of annihilation. Furthermore, the United States would not attempt to go it alone. The strength of our allies must be nurtured and marshalled in our quest for order and freedom.

Recognizing, however, that we and the Communists are seeking conflicting types of order, it seems self-evident that the Communists will seek to prevent the attainment of our objectives. Consequently, there will be circumstances in which we may have to use force. This we must always be prepared to do. We must realize also that a defensive policy, which ignores the methods of warfare practiced by our opponents, has little chance in the long run of stopping a dynamic enemy who is willing and able to use all methods in the pursuit of his goals. The American people must make settlement of the twentieth-century conflict their mission, a settlement consistent with both freedom and justice.

Out of the contemporary struggle which now rends the world, the United States must endeavor to create an order which assures the survival of American society and other societies committed to the belief that man's destiny can best be realized in freedom and not in the conditioned beehive of Communist totalitarianism. This goal requires the pursuit of an increasing variety of initiatives of our own to which the Communist leaders will have to react, and to which one day they will have to accommodate. The most important of these initiatives is the creation of an Atlantic union of free nations. As this community grows, others will join and back a single policy to expand freedom and order.

The order we seek cannot be achieved until we have convinced the Communists that they cannot win. Consequently, such a policy and its derivative strategy will involve risk, as do all great enterprises. It will require a supreme effort of will and wisdom, and a commitment far greater than the peoples of the West have so far accepted. In this strategy, non-military action will occupy the foreground of the scene, but it must be supported at every turn by the backstop of a competent and rationally-designed military power.

## Organizational Innovation

It seems that we are not yet sufficiently organized at the national level to conceive, direct, and implement the kind of positive integrated strategy required by the radical challenges confronting this nation. With some notable exceptions the United States continues to take refuge in ad hoc expedients rather than in policies which anticipate and avoid problems that grow into crisis proportions.

The failure of orthodox statesmanship to deal with novel forms of aggression has frequently been recorded in history; the Greek submission to the Macedonians, the Carthaginian defeat at the hands of the Romans, and the collapse of European resistance against Napoleon. The initial success which Hitler enjoyed against most of the nations of Europe parallels the generally inadequate performance of the Western Allies in the face of Communist protracted conflict strategy. Clausewitz' description of the European reaction to the aggression following the French Revolution stands as a warning for us today. Clausewitz castigated the blundering policy of the allies against Napoleon because "they endeavored with their ordinary means to hold their own against forces of a novel kind and overwhelming strength."

The United States also has found that the traditional means of diplomacy and orthodox military operations are not effective in dealing with the kinds of problems continually posed for us by Moscow. The problem is both substantive and organizational. Whatever strategy-making machine we choose to employ, it will be manned by human beings whose judgment, skill, determination, and cooperation will weight heavily the solutions reached. The problems they will face are staggering. As Dean Rusk has expressed it: "The problems of negotiating within the shadow of a nuclear exchange, the problems of really identifying the vital interests for which you must be prepared to use whatever force is necessary . . . these are things which make pygmies of us all."

Furthermore, these problems must frequently be handled within a limited period of time without a chance for considering expert political and military advice—even when it is available. This means that the principal participants in the national strategy field should have first-hand knowledge of, and long experience in dealing with, the complex issues of international conflict situations.

US strategy-making machinery has undergone many gyrations during the course of the Cold War. The Kennedy Administration, shortly after coming into office, discarded both the National Security Council Planning Board and the Operations Coordinating Board in favor of a highly personalized and centralized control over policy. It has set up individual task forces to deal with the information, military, economic, and political aspects of a given problem; but it has not devised a comparable strategy group for the purpose of dealing with the total world confrontation between freedom and totalitarianism from an over-all perspective.

At the same time, the present Administration has brought into being an informal community of policy-making operators. This influential group has shown some willingness to consider strategy in its broadest and most extended forms.

It is still too early to tell whether the pattern employed in the Cuban-missile crisis of October 1962 will become a model for the future development and execution of strategy. In this instance, policy and strategy were determined by an extremely small group, in which General Taylor was the only uniformed member. The President established an Executive Committee of the National Security Council both to supervise and to monitor the total US operation. This group consisted of the Vice President, the Secretaries of State, Treasury, and Defense, the President's Assistant for National Security Affairs, and the Chairman of the JCS, plus the Undersecretary of State, the Deputy Secretary of Defense, the Attorney General, and the Director of the CIA. The Chairman of the State Department Policy Planning Council and the Assistant Secretary of Defense (ISA) also regularly attended NSC EXCOM meetings. Hence the EXCOM was actually larger than the statutory NSC. It should be noted that the EXCOM continues to exist and meets regularly.

The Cuban operation, conducted under the aegis of the EXCOM, presumably, achieved the limited goal set, namely, the elimination of missile bases from Cuba. The attendant limited aspects of a world-wide confrontation between US and Soviet power and influence appear to have been well-coordinated and executed. Diplomatic negotiations, the military blockade, and the back-up of all US military power was closely supervised and regulated.

It was noteworthy, however, that *the basic policy and major decisions* of this operation, involving the risk of a much wider conflict, appear to have been formulated with limited participation of senior military representatives except for that of the Chairman of the JCS himself. It also appears that there was considerable detailed *operational* direction by both the President and the Secretary of Defense of those military forces actually employed in establishing the blockade around Cuba. In short, the broad mission-type orders by which major military commands normally operate were not always used in this particular situation. Since this may set a precedent for the future, it might be well to examine the implications of this particular solution.

In the Cuban embargo, policy, strategy, and operations were conceived and conducted at different levels. The entire undertaking was extremely sensitive to international, Allied, and domestic political reactions. To all intents and purposes, Ambassador Stevenson at UN Headquarters in New York and Admiral Dennison in the Atlantic approaches to Cuba were both instruments of a single integrated strategy.

The Cuban crisis was not a one-shot affair. In reality it was part of a world-wide pattern of upheaval and combat. One need only recall the concurrent Indian-Chinese conflict, the unsettled and almost pre-revolutionary atmosphere of Brazil, the war in South Vietnam, the smoldering fires in the Congo, Laos, and Algeria, and the recurrent pressures against Berlin, to see that the crisis in Cuba was but one scene of a global panorama. Furthermore, the Cuban crisis had its antecedents in the past, as did the events unfolding in the other trouble spots throughout the world. Moreover, the Cuban crisis of October 1962, was but one chapter in a book yet to be completed. From the parallel crises, other threats, disputes, and possible wars will emerge to confront the United States with serious threats to its own security and the security of its Free World allies.

The Cuban crisis, an integral part of the total world confrontation, could be dealt with by a limited EXCOM of the NSC. It is reasonable to ask, however, whether any such committee could simultaneously keep track of the myriad forces, hostile, friendly, and neutral, that were simultaneously in operation elsewhere and could at the same time determine how US resources should be developed and deployed to deal with the other problems.

In the opinion of this writer, the strategy group in the trilogy of policy-strategy-operations utilized in the October 1962 Cuban crisis is far too limited to cope with the wider vista of global conflict. Furthermore, its representation was not weighted in proper correlation with the importance of the various factors which must be considered in devising a comprehensive long-term national strategy for the United States. The group dealt effectively with the ad hoc problem of the single crisis—Cuba, but it is questionable that it would be adequate in its present form to deal with multiple problems on a long-term basis.*

## The Military Role in National Strategy Formulation

As a nation, we are limited in the course of action open to us by the size, character, and capabilities of our military forces. Despite the politicalization of strategy, military power is still a dominant reality in the present conflict and the key underpinning of American policy. In the long run, the choices we make in the realm of military posture and weapons systems may prove to be decisive. If these choices prove faulty, the strategic balance can be upset in such a way that the aggressor may one day be able to dictate his political terms.

Critical choices regarding the present and future US military posture confront the current US Government leadership. They must decide, for example, whether we share our nuclear weapons with our European allies, whether or not we will build up our military forces for dealing with limited and guerrilla warfare, and whether we will invest adequately in the air and sea lift. The avowed aim of the Kennedy Administration is to open up greater flexibility of policy choice by providing more flexible military means. Flexibility requires that we have a wide array of forces. Modern military forces cannot be improvised in a tactical response to a given situation.

During the past several years, professional military men have had less and less to say as to how such decisions on military posture are made and have had less and less influence on the actual

* See previous discussion of "normal" vs. "high crisis" situations.

choices. Thus, a crucial aspect of strategy, the provisions of flexible means for tomorrow's policy-makers to employ, is increasingly taken out of the hands of professional military planners. What has been left to the military is the actual conduct of operations within minutely circumscribed directives. Furthermore, the other element of strategy, namely, the coordination of military plans and projected actions with political objectives is one in which few of our senior military men play much of a role. This too has largely become the problem of civilian theorists who have acquired their military expertise through operations research backgrounds or through defense-strategy institutes at well-known universities. The background, experience, and diplomatic "feel" which military men have acquired through their varied and responsible assignments during the many years of the Cold War in many countries has too frequently been ignored.

Apparently, we face a situation in which the American military are becoming technicians—technicians who have less and less to do with the formulation of strategy which they may be subsequently called upon to implement. Even when they carry out a particular operation, be it in the waters around Cuba or in the rice paddies of South Vietnam, they are often told not just to do a job, but how to do it.

Over time this trend will undermine the military pillar of American security. To reverse it, the United States needs to allow the professional military people to play a more active role in the formulation of a more integrated strategy. More important, for the moment, they should join in the design of the strategy as it is now being formulated. It would have been difficult to conceive a few years ago, that the professional military would find itself relegated to such a non-policy-making, strictly executory, operational kind of role as it has today.

The blunt fact of the matter is that civilians in both State and Defense have usurped the formulation of what used to be called military policy or strategy. It has been alleged, with some justification, that the professional military are partially responsible for the situation in which they now find themselves. The structure of the JCS, as legally established by Congress, has tended to nurture inter-service rivalries and has frustrated the development of integrated military policies. Civilian leadership in the Pentagon faces a continuous requirement to make decisions, and it needs advice and help in many fields in which joint professional military expertise is rarely made quickly available. Furthermore, JCS procedure is such that it is almost impossible for a JCS representative to participate effectively in the birth of a new policy for the simple reason that there is not collective JCS opinion on a particular issue until the Chiefs themselves have reached a collective judgment concerning it. Consequently, there is, within the Defense Department, a steadily increasing civilian influence in areas which are principally the proper responsibility of the military professionals.

One might well ask whether trends tending to downgrade military participation in policy-making reflect the political administration in power. In others words, would a change in administration reverse these present trends or would they continue to assert themselves?

Among the claims and attacks which the "outs" were making on the Eisenhower Administration during its later years, particularly during the campaign of 1960, was that the Eisenhower Administration had over-bureaucratized the policy machinery. The "outs" were asserting that the bureaucratic process resulted in "bloodless" policy in that strong dissenting viewpoints did not receive an adequate hearing. One could expect that the Kennedy Administration would organize itself in one way or another so as to give play to the expression of sharply contrasting policy recommendations. But this has not been the case. The highly personalized operation which so characterizes the New Frontier tends to have much the same result as the over-bureaucratized organization of the previous Administration— i.e., the persons in this present Administration tend to think so much alike that dissenting views at top level are even rarer than they were several years ago.

## The Professional Military Role

It has long been recognized that it is impossible for the professional military to give "purely" military advice in the formulation of national strategy, for even the conduct of military operations is severely circumscribed by, and in turn sets a framework for, political considerations. In fact, nowadays there are very few actions which can be regarded as purely military, i.e., actions which have no political side effects or which do not spill over to affect the civilian population in the area of combat. Only on the lower end of the operational spectrum does purely military confrontation now seem conceivable—two ships engaged in solitary combat at sea, two aircraft in a dog-fight in the sky, or two infantrymen slugging it out with each other in hand-to-hand combat. On the other end of the scale, the exploding of a thermonuclear weapon over a large metropolitan area is both a military and a political action.

Not too long ago, it was commonplace to assert that the military was responsible for strategic planning designed to prepare for various contingencies and for training, equipping, and appropriately deploying national forces consistent with the strategic plans. They were and are responsible for conducting operations involving the application of military force against other nations. Except for the actual training of forces, political decisions and influences now enter into what was once the realm of accepted military responsibility.

Much of the politicalization of strategy and even of military operations that has been sketched in this paper is an inevitable reflection of the new circumstances in which the world finds itself. Part of it, however, is the result of a US tendency toward detailed civilian control, verging on domination, of the armed forces. The necessary civilian function of budgetary control inevitably involves decisions between competing demands for funds by various military elements to meet stated political objectives, but it is questionable whether these decisions must get into detailed examination of weapons which in themselves have relatively no political impact on whether the decisions should be limited to setting priorities for forces to perform specified tasks.

The precedent for the detailed supervision of our military forces was established with the creation of the Atomic Energy Commission. As Hanson Baldwin wrote in 1946:

> Today (1946) atomic energy is military power and nothing more, and to bar the military from representation on a policy-making control commission, as the scientists would do, is to set up virtually an entirely new department of war, separate from, and outside of, the War and Navy Departments. It makes no sense. As long as atomic energy is to be used for military purposes in the world, our military must have a hand in it or our own national defense will be hopelessly crippled. Of course, in any atomic energy control legislation that is passed the principle of civilian preeminence and civilian control over the military—fundamental to our type of Government—must be upheld, and the secrecy restrictions must be liberalized as much as possible. Otherwise we shall defeat our own purposes—the preservation of democracy and the fostering of scientific research.

Prior to 1916, civilian control of the military was largely exercised by Congress legislating detailed administrative laws for almost every aspect for our military forces. Congress no longer establishes the detailed policy for the operation of the Defense Department. Increasingly, however, decisions as to weapons to be developed, the character of forces to be raised, trained, and the areas of their deployment are primarily determined by civilian officials of the Defense Department—often without the advice or consent of professional military men who presumably will command these forces in actual operations.

The ancient ghost of civilian control over the American military is not at issue. The military in the United States has always accepted a subordinate role as an instrument of the nation. The few instances where there has been any questioning of civilian authority over the military only served to confirm the conclusion that supremacy of civilian direction in the armed forces is well established. But the deeper issue of the proper role of the military professional in the present era remains.

A clarification of the military role with respect to the formulation of national policy, national strategy, and military operations would be most helpful in clarifying the military professional's function in an age when conflict and warfare have become so irreversibly politicalized. In this perspective, the following is suggested: policy has been, is, and will continue to remain the problem of the President as civilian Chief of State. Strategy national in scope must be devised for the President in his dual role as Chief of State and Commander-In-Chief of the armed forces. National strategy for today and for tomorrow must, however, be a broad, grand, or extended strategy which embraces the full spectrum of political, military, economic, psychological, and other actions. National strategy should assign priorities to the development of appropriate resources, and should deploy and utilize these resources to implement comprehensive and integrated plans. National strategy thus defined must be developed by men who are intimately aware through experience of one or another important capability available to the United States, whether the capability be political, technological, or military.

With this in mind, it seems logical that the military should be represented in whatever organizational mechanism that may be set up to formulate and supervise the execution of national strategy. Only a broad national strategy can allocate effort between the military, political, economic, and other arms of the US Government. National strategy would thus determine the kind of military posture most appropriate to present and future execution of policy. The national strategy should also relate military posture and the possible employment of military force to the national values which the strategy is to support and defend.

As things stand now, the kind of national strategy that world circumstances require is not being developed consciously in a rational, consistent, and comprehensive fashion. A critical missing factor is a clearly defined role for the military in its development. Instead, elements of a national strategy are occasionally imposed upon the military, but in a haphazard, random, and often contradictory fashion.

Haphazard and partial US response to the threats of war and conflict has left the US military in a peculiar and somewhat isolated position. The JCS and the individual military services may believe that they are devising strategy. In reality, they are making military plans for elements of a potential strategy—not comprehensive and unclearly defined—which may or may not be utilized. Simultaneously, the military has been largely excluded from the sporadic efforts that have been made to formulate a genuine national strategy. Likewise the military has found that the problems of military planning, in the broad sense of the word (force levels, choices as to weapons systems, logistic support, etc.) have been invaded by civilian staffs (as opposed to the Secretary of Defense and the President) with relatively little military experience and no responsibility for the conduct of military operations if such operations should ever ensue.

Is there a way out of this confusion? There is, provided two steps are taken: The military should be given adequate representation on whatever government-wide group—a national general staff or expanded EXCOM—that might be established to devise the kind of integrated strategy which the circumstances of today and tomorrow demand. Simultaneously, the planning and conduct of military operations should be restored to the military as its primary province. Military plans should be made, and operations conducted, within the framework of an explicit and comprehensive national strategy which will provide ample political and related budgetary and technological guidance for sound and responsive military planning and/or action. In this way, our armed forces would effectively support US policy with the coordinated power of every material resource placed at their disposal.

In a revealing post Cuba-missile crisis column, Joseph Alsop described Khrushchev's personal participation in the elaborate Soviet deception and cover plan "of strictly military character" which was "an integral part of the larger scheme to upset the nuclear balance." In conclusion Alsop stated, "The sum is a grave and terrible warning that Soviet methods of waging the Cold War are coming very close to hot-war methods." [2] Under these circumstances, it should be apparent that war—to extend Clemenceau's observation—is far too serious a business to be left either to generals or to civilians. The authority of the one and the responsibility of the other must be preserved and respected. Both must work together to devise and execute the integrated national strategy which these times demand.

FOOTNOTES

[1] R. Strausz-Hupé, W. R. Kintner, and S. T. Possony, *A Forward Strategy For America* (New York: Harper & Brothers, 1961).

[2] *Washington Post,* November 5, 1962, p. A-17.

# Address to the Conference on January 23, 1963

*—SENATOR HENRY M. JACKSON*

We are all aware of the fact that the United States has come a long way since the end of World War II. Then we were wondering whether we could afford 14 billion dollars for a defense program. Today we are supporting a defense program that involves a 50-billion-dollar-plus budget.

Only a few years ago our problem was to create strength out of weakness. As we look to the decade ahead, we find that our essential problem is to use our strength wisely. It is well for us to keep in mind at all times that it is much easier to build strength than to use it wisely.

Now recently we have had an example (at least as far as we have gone) in the wise use of strength and military power. I refer, of course, to Cuba. Those of us who are involved in the practical side of this problem every day can certainly point with pride to the enormous impact that has come from that decision— to manage military power to achieve sensible foreign policy objectives. The impact is not applicable just to Cuba, but it has been world-wide  It is one of the rare times that we have been able to make the Soviets back down, I believe, since 1946, when President Truman in his usual understandable language indicated to Mr. Stalin that either they get out of Iran (Persia) or big things would happen. The Soviets understood, and started moving.

The effect of Cuba — as far as we have gone, and I emphasize that because we still have a problem of dismantling sooner or later what I think is the real missile, Castro—has been enormous on our allies, our friends, and the soft neutrals around the world. As a matter of fact, it is much like the experience that those who have run for office have gone through— that is, nothing succeeds like success. If you are running for office and losing, you don't have many friends, and the going is pretty rough. Yet as you make progress, and it looks like you're going to win, supporters start coming over to your side. A day or two before election they are all coming over on your side, and if they are not there a day or two before election, you can be sure they will be there a day after to explain how they have been for you from the beginning. Some of our allies and good friends have gone through that particular experience as a result of Cuba. It is a form, I suppose, of retroactive righteousness. But if it helps, so much the better.

The second point I would like to make is that there has been a splitting in the monolithic structure that the Communist world has been endeavoring to build. This at least complicates their situation, but it also leaves them with problems. I think we have to keep in mind that the mere fact there is a schism does not mean that we can relax. I spent eight days out in the field in Vietnam in December. I found that whatever ideological split there may be between the Moscow Communists and the Chinese, there is a meeting of the minds on the value of supporting "wars of national liberation" that Mr. Khrushchev referred to in his speech at the 22nd Party Congress last year. But, nevertheless, the schism can be considered a plus on our side.

The third development, of course, is India. In planning and looking ahead, we have to include at all times the obvious mistakes that the enemy will make. Who would have thought that China would help us do a job that we have been most unsuccessful in putting over, especially with India and other so-called non-aligned nations? That is, the necessity of their becoming (if they are neutrals) at least "hard" neutrals. We failed, but certainly the recent Chinese pressure has worked to our advantage in this regard. This has not been an easy task for the United States because we have had significant policy differences with India. If the United States had followed Mr. Nehru's policy and philosophy, we would not have had the arms to give him when he came so hurriedly to us for help. I am sure Mr. Nehru does not relish this on-the-job training program, but it may save others from a similar schooling.

At the same time this does not mean that we should ignore India, because the preservation of the territorial integrity of India—with 400 million people—is essential to the national security of the United States of America. It is in our own national interest to help preserve the integrity of that country.

Now these are some of the pulses, and there are many others. But I would like to look ahead a decade or so and pose some of the problems that come to mind, and that we need as a society to be thinking about.

First of all, the United States has military alliances with more than forty countries and provides military aid to more than sixty countries. But we were brought up on George Washington's Farewell Address, and we have had little experience in the management of alliances in periods short of open warfare.

It is clear, I think, that the next decade will see some heavy strains on our system of alliances. But if it is true, and I believe it is, that we must remain united in the Free World if the Communists are not to have success with a strategy of "divide and conquer," we must overcome these strains. This may be very difficult for us—and for our allies.

Possible questions for this group might be: how can we preserve and strengthen our alliances in a period when other states are gaining economic and military strength and are increasingly tempted to act independently? What means of influence are available to us? How best can they be used? Is there need for new political, economic, and military structures in the West?

Secondly, it would be well to consider the fact that we are providing economic assistance in a variety of forms to many countries. There is much dissatisfaction in this country with the results of economic aid. Yet it seems increasingly likely that the outcome of the world struggle will be decided by what happens within societies in the rest of the world, provided, of course, that we and our major allies remain militarily strong. The United States will probably have to continue many types of non-military programs and perhaps (and I hesitate to say this because it's not good news) increase certain types in the years ahead.

Therefore, questions that merit serious study are how can we make economic aid a more effective tool of foreign policy? What are the proper goals of economic aid? What are reasonable tests of success or failure? How can we develop a public opinion that will support the wise use of our economic strength as a tool of foreign policy, bearing in mind that this is a tool in which the United States has an enormous advantage.

A third observation. In every major country but our own, legislative bodies have been losing influence in relation to executive power in recent years. When you think about it, the reason is clear enough. The need to concentrate power of command in one man varies with the powers of others to inflict sudden damage. As questions of foreign policy become more complex and more delicate, the need for a strong executive obviously increases. This has been the universal experience in time of war, and we are living, indeed, in a Cold War, when the pressures for executive leadership—or for what Hamilton called "an energetic executive"—are very great, though less intense than in a hot war.

Therefore, questions of fundamental interest and concern to me are what adjustments will enable us to preserve a strong, effective Congress as a necessary check on the Executive? What changes in the way Congress handles its job can contribute to the development of clear, purposeful, national policy adequate to the challenges of our time?

And fourth. Wise national policies require both good organizations and good people. The people are indeed the critical factor in all of this, as Admiral Burke pointed out. And I might add you can have a very fine organization with inadequate people in it and the organization is not going to mean very much. But good people can even survive a poor organization.

More often than not, poor policy decisions are, in fact, traceable to inadequate people, to their inexperience, to their bad judgment, to their failure to comprehend the significance of information crossing their desks. Our Government does have, in fact, many first-rate people in it, but the number of critical jobs is far larger than the number of able and experienced people available to fill them.

The heart of the problem of national security is this: how are we going to use to the fullest the good people now in government? And how are we going to recruit our best people for key foreign policy and defense posts in the future?

I know that many things will be accomplished by this Conference. I do hope that one of the primary accomplishments will be to help bring better people into the area of national security. And secondly, if I may be so presumptuous as to observe, I hope your proceedings will be such as to be useful and meaningful to those people who will, in fact, make the decisions in the national security area of your Federal Government.

In that connection, to be realistic about it, (and I say this half in jest), I do trust that you will think long enough about your papers and hard enough so that you may be able to limit them to twenty pages. Not to one page, but twenty pages. In my experience, if an idea takes more than twenty pages to explain, I feel that the people you want to look at it are not going to do so, and it probably isn't a very good idea anyway.

You have to ask yourselves: what are you here for? Well, you add to the great dialogue that is very important in the national security area. You make information available to your colleagues, and this gets printed and gets to the scholars. But in the last analysis, you really *do* have to ask the question: what can you do here to (a) get better people into the national security posts and (b) when they are there, what can you do to help them do a better job? This is really the heart of the problem and, I would trust, one of your top objectives.

Let me conclude by merely making this observation. As we look ahead ten years, or a decade, I think it is well for us to remember that the future that we are talking about is in fact the history that we are making day by day. And the page that we are working on, my friends, is bright with promise.

# Address to the Conference on January 24, 1963

## —THE HONORABLE WALT W. ROSTOW

Perhaps the best way to begin is for me to sketch out, roughly speaking, what the Government's task in military and foreign policy is like; to sketch out the main headings as they appear to me. This should permit you to probe in terms either of the framework itself or in terms of the specific aspects of policy that must move forward effectively if anything like this framework is to be fulfilled.

I start with the assumption that the job of the United States in the world is, at a minimum, to maintain the precarious military and ideological balance of power which emerged from the Second World War and its immediate aftermath; and, at the maximum, to achieve what I would call an ideological victory in the Cold War, if possible by non-military means.

Within that broad framework our job has a series of major dimensions, all of which I think are quite familiar to you.

In military affairs we have articulated and tried to execute a policy which, contrary to much discussion in the press, is not new. It is not the product of a new group of intellectuals who descended upon this town. The way this nation has behaved in the period 1945-61 in the face of Communist thrusts was systematically somewhat at variance with articulated policy. In earlier postwar administrations articulated policy relied overwhelmingly on the deterrent power of our nuclear weapons, which, of course, remains the backbone of our military position. But when we were faced with limited thrusts (in northern Azerbaijan, in Greece, in the Berlin blockade of 1948-49, in Korea, and elsewhere) this nation did not, in fact, invoke its nuclear power. We generated some form of force, at about the same level as the thrust, trying to preserve, with minimum use of force, the major interests of the Free World community.

419

What we have now done is to articulate a policy and to build the forces necessary to maintain it, which meets our actual behavior, as a nation in the Free World community, rather than articulated doctrines we never applied. One of the reasons we believe this is a wise policy is because our perception of planning in the Kremlin is that they have systematically looked for gaps in the spectrum of deterrence, whether regional or technical, and probed at them. Our hope is that if we build this full range of capabilities—which will provide to the President in a nuclear age the widest possible range of military choice—we will minimize the number of thrusts against us.

We're going forward with that policy, the wisdom of which I think has been confirmed in our minds not only by the cumulative history since 1945 but the experiences of responsibility since January 1961.

Now in January of 1961 we came to responsibility at a particular phase in what might be called Khrushchev's post-Sputnik offensive. In the period roughly between Sputnik and January '61, a number of holes were punched into the Free World, each of which had the potentiality of endangering the balance of military and ideological power in major regions of the world.

In 1958 Khrushchev laid down his threat on Berlin. I suspect the Kremlin believed that a mixture of three factors would lead, in the end, to a Western cave-in on Berlin: first, the nuclear capability they mounted against Western Europe; second, differences of view about Berlin and Germany that existed within the Alliance; Third—with this mixture of nuclear threat and political ambiguity—they hoped that a tactic which would force us to initiate military action would be incapable of being sustained by the Alliance. Many times Khrushchev has said that the West would have to initiate a war over Berlin—meaning, presumably, we would have to shoot our way through a blockade. In Laos they had moved down from the two provinces that were granted in the 1954 treaty: from Sam Neua and Phong Saly into Xieng Khouang.

In 1958 the Communist Party conference in Hanoi quite explicitly announced it would mount a new guerrilla war in South Vietnam, and this war was at a very dangerous point in 1961. In the Congo there was an extremely precarious situation which the Soviets were actively exploiting. And from the point of view of guerrilla strategy, one can understand easily how a base in the Congo would look enormously attractive to the Communists, given the overlapping of tribes over the arbitrary colonial frontiers.

Finally there was Cuba where Castro came to power on the first of January of 1959.

Our first duty, therefore, was to try to seal off and control these probes into the Free World and avoid the regional loss of the balance of power that might flow. Southeast Asia was in jeopardy and still is in jeopardy all the way down to Djakarta. Central Africa was in jeopardy. The Caribbean and Latin America were in jeopardy and remain to a degree in jeopardy. Meanwhile the Berlin crisis posed for us the viability of collective security and of NATO and the balance of power in Western Europe.

I won't go through the history of those crises. You may wish to question me about them. Our view would be that none of them is yet finally solved. At the maximum, what has been done has been painful and difficult uphill work, involving in all cases potential or actual confrontation with Communist power, which has to a substantial degree sealed off these crises. The momentum has been drained out of them. They all remain dangerous and none of us is throwing his hat into the air about that series of crises. They remain our first-priority consideration. Nevertheless, the status of each of those crises is somewhat better than it was a while back.

But it would have been, I think, a great failure if this Administration, so absorbed with this series of urgent crises that we had to face—that it was our duty to face—had failed to develop a positive policy within the Free World.

You all know the main contours of the military policy that has developed. It has involved large increases in the military budget; an expansion of invulnerable missiles; expanded conventional forces with radically increased mobility; and the allocation of first rate men and high priority attention to the problem of dealing with or deterring guerrilla war and subversion.

But, as I say, dealing with the crises and expanding our military capacity would have been an insufficient performance. While dealing with these first priority matters, the President set in motion a set of constructive policies. First, we began to move off the stagnation in our relationship with Europe in the 1950's, where a number of critical issues remained under the rug, into an active effort to move toward a long-run partnership with this part of the world. Europe had gone through the most remarkable decade of growth in its history. It obviously could not for long remain in the position of relatively pure dependence on the United States which had existed from roughly 1945 down to the late fifties.

We're in the midst of an extremely interesting, difficult, and important phase of the transition to partnership. It will take time to work out. It has many dimensions: joint work in the underdeveloped areas under the Development Assistance Committee; problems of trade relations, economic growth, and monetary reserves. It involves above all the nuclear relationship which Europe will develop with us over this decade and the methods of political control and decision-making that obviously must come if we are to have a partnership which embraces serious European participation in the nuclear business.

I might add that, in the face of recent headlines, none of us is dismayed by the evident difficulties ahead. We all have a sense that this piece of international architecture we're in the midst of working out with the European nations is, perhaps, the most remarkable effort ever undertaken among nations at a time of peace.

Deep memories and conflicts between historical impulses and hard contemporary realities are involved for every country. Great interests are involved. None of us thinks the Atlantic partnership and the movement of Europe towards unity will come cheaply, or easily, or quickly. It will take a long perspective on our part and everyone else's to see this piece of architecture through.

With respect to the underdeveloped areas our view is simple: it is our major military and ideological interest that these nations retain their independence and develop as national units, increasingly recognizing the responsibilities of interdependence, avoiding the tragedy of a Communist takeover.

The kinds of policies needed to help them maintain their independence depend greatly on the stage of development these countries are in: underdeveloped countries are not all of a single type. They represent a wide spectrum. Policy also depends on the kinds and intensity of pressure they confront from the Communists. Some of them are right up against the Communist borders and face, as in Korea, major armies across their frontiers. We have a major guerrilla war going on in Vietnam. Others are more distant, and the problem of maintaining their independence lies rather more in preventing takeover from within. But the problem of preventing domestic takeover is not merely a problem of countering Communist moves. It is that. But it is also a problem of helping generate the positive forces in the community needed to see it through the precarious transition to modernization in ways that will provide a firm long-run basis for independent nationhood.

The more we have learned in the postwar period about the problem of underdeveloped areas, the more we have seen that the military and the civil problems are part of a spectrum of policy-making in which there is a lucid, common objective: namely, the maintenance, under a variety of threats (depending on the stage of their development and the nature of the thrust into them from the Communist side)—the maintenance of their independence and integrity.

With respect to the Communist Bloc our objective, as I suggested earlier, is to maintain at the minimum the political and the ideological balance of power which still lies with the West and with free men, and at the maximum to work with the forces of history, if possible peacefully, to see the community of free men and independent nations extended beyond their present frontiers.

The ways in which you move toward that objective are various, but the minimum condition for moving towards it is to maintain the balance of power and to make it lucid to Moscow and Peking—and to the various other chaps who are associated with them—that aggression will not pay.

We are doing our job with an increasing sense that the underlying forces of history are very much working with us and what we stand for, if we have the wit and the will to work with them. Obviously the Cold War is not going to be resolved by someone doing the job for us or by anonymous forces of history. We are the only true world power within the Free World. We're bearing heavy burdens which, I'm sure, the economists among you will discuss tomorrow. These burdens come to rest heavily on our balance of payments and on the allocation of our research and development talent and our intellectual resources. We hope that, in time, these burdens will be increasingly shared by our partners who have come through this remarkable phase of postwar reconstruction and development. But as far ahead as we can see, the fate of these large objectives—which embrace the fate of freedom everywhere—rests with us.

As we see it in the Administration we are very much in mid-passage both with respect to our crises and our constructive enterprises; but, as I say, we work at these precarious and difficult tasks with a conviction that the underlying forces of history, both within the Bloc and in the Free World, are moving with us.

To be specific, I think that the tide of history in Europe and in the Atlantic Community is towards a united Europe linked with North America in partnership.

I believe in the underdeveloped areas—despite all the perfectly evident temptations that communism must represent to people at that stage in their development with that kind of history—that men are increasingly conscious of the dangers that communism represents and increasingly clear about the kinds of policies they must pursue, within their countries and in relationship to the West, if their independence is to be maintained.

Within the Bloc itself—the claim of communism as an international system for organizing on a modern basis different types of nations and societies; the claim of communism as an efficient way for developing an underdeveloped area; the claim of communism as a unique and satisfactory solution for the social and economic problems of advanced societies—all of these claims are increasingly empty.

The President said in his State of the Union message that we're on the side of a steep hill. But we're climbing upward in good heart.

# Discussion—Part II

## Cold War Policy Objectives

*Cerny:* In Part I Dr. Taylor as well as Dr. Dinerstein noted that in a number of instances the problem always was one of: "What is the game about? What does the United States intend to do ultimately vis-à-vis the Soviet system?" * A fundamental problem regarding Cold War policy objectives is that of the chief objective of the United States vis-à-vis the Communist system.

These statements have been chosen from the papers of Professors Wolfers and Niemeyer:

> The chief American objective in the Cold War for which adequate means are required is the preservation and, where necessary, the restoration of a reasonable East-West balance of power . . . The objective of equilibrium on all levels of confrontation—though far more modest than the goal of supremacy necessary to destroy the opponent—turns out to make formidable demands on the United States.
>
> Arnold Wolfers
>
> A movement of such irrational hostility toward the rest of the world cannot ever live in peace with its environment. One can only struggle against it until it is dispersed, or thoroughly demoralized, or isolated to the point of political impotence . . . The struggle can come to a halt only when the enemy has disappeared as an organized entity, or has been deprived of the decisive means of political power, or has been maneuvered into hopeless isolation.
>
> Gerhart Niemeyer

*Wolfers:* I was not asked to write about objectives, but about means, and merely introduced in the beginning of my paper a

---

* In previous discussion, Dr. Dinerstein had said:
*Dinerstein:* If the purpose of American policy is to cause the destruction of communism, then it is out of the question. If the purpose of American policy is to make the Communists behave reasonably—because that's what they really want, and you just have to show them the way to what they want—if that's the purpose, well, then that's obviously the end of the road.

But I believe neither is the purpose. I believe the problem is much more difficult. I think the problem is to behave in such a way that they have suggestion that one cannot talk about means if one doesn't know what the ends are. So I had to make an assumption about the existing objectives of our foreign policy, and I said that I thought as a matter of fact, not of desire, that we are committed to a policy of deterrence in the military field, which, in fact, is a policy of equilibrium and not of supremacy. I go a step further and say I think this is a wise objective, the only one that seems to me to be reasonable. We could do less or we could do more, in theory. We could try to obtain military supremacy, but in the nuclear situation supremacy means that one can disarm the other side and not merely do a great deal of harm, because doing a great deal of harm means doing a great deal of harm to oneself too, which is not a rational goal of policy. We could do less. And I think some people, maybe Mr. Niemeyer, too, imply by much of what they say that the military balance is not really so important any more, that the Soviets have shifted almost entirely now to the non-military confrontation, and that, rather than concentrate on the conflict with the great powers of China and Russia, which are military powers, we should concentrate on the Communists as kind of a religious sect, with whom one

---

to abandon their goals because we force them to abandon their goals. Now, the great difficulty with that kind of policy is that there will never be a day in which the Soviet Union rents a page in the *New York Times* and says: "We've given up our goals; now make a settlement with us."

But there will be, if we succeed, all kinds of fluctuations, all kinds of ups and downs. There may be arms controls measures which the Soviet Union will agree to because they despair of winning the arms race with us. That would be a partial reduction of their objectives.

If they do reduce their long-term objectives, it will be a very mixed picture; there will be ups and downs, and I think the great difficulty in pursuing that policy from our point of view is that very often we're going to mistake the first swallow not only for spring, but for summer, too.

This requires a kind of a steadiness and a kind of a long-range policy which is very difficult to achieve in a democracy, where public expectations and public hopes play such a large, and I think proper, part in the formation of policy.

I think the answer one gives to people who say, "Well, won't we get a settlement after all because they're also human beings and they want to be like us?" is a very complex one, and, I'm afraid, very unsatisfactory. You have to say to them, "Well, maybe fifty years from now we will realize that for the last ten years no matter what the Soviet Union has tried it has not been able to succeed; then we'll realize that we've won the game." And, of course, this is not a very satisfactory answer to this kind of question, but I think it's the only kind of answer that one can give—at least the only one I can give.

cannot fight wars, but with whom one has a different type of struggle. I think we need, as a minimum, a military balance that deters the other side. It seems to me if we could obtain that, then I would be more optimistic than Mr. Niemeyer and say that I would not be so frightened of the crusading quasi-religion of communism which is going to be with us for a very long time.

Let me explain briefly what I mean. If we were sure that we had the military means to keep the Russians and the Chinese from trying to expand by means of military power, if containment were a certainty, then I believe we could handle the struggle with the Communist quasi-religion quite effectively, and I would be much less defeatist about that than Mr. Niemeyer is. I think we've done much better and I think we could do even more than we have done in the struggle with communism as an ideology.

One often compares it to Islam. But Islam, of course, was dangerous when it was a militant force that swept across Africa and into Europe. From a Christian point of view, it would have been desirable if it had died completely as a religion, but it was able to maintain itself. I would suggest that the difference between Islam in the post-militant stage and communism is quite considerable. I'm not sure whether we're not giving the Communists much too much credit by saying that they have a kind of religion like Islam. There is one fundamental difference which I think would make them very much weaker, and that is that they are promising paradise on earth, which is something that can be disproved. I don't think the paradise the religions offer can be so easily disproved.

I am not so worried about the crusading spirit of communism, which might die anyway. But I am very much more worried than some of the speakers seem to be, about the military balance. True, we have nuclear superiority, whatever that may mean. It's not enough even in the minds of the most counterforce-minded of my colleagues to disarm the nuclear force of the Soviets. We don't have to worry, I would say, in the long run— maybe at the moment not at all—about a nuclear confrontation. The Russians won't dare, as many have said. But the more we get into a situation of established nuclear stalemate—which seems to me to be inescapable, due to the possibility of securing one's retaliatory forces—the more we come to a stabilized stalemate, the more the non-nuclear forces are going to be decisive. They are going to be decisive for our ability to protect the Free World overseas. We can protect ourselves with nuclear weapons, but we can't protect others with nuclear weapons once there is stalemate. We can't even deter any more with nuclear weapons once there is seriously a condition of stalemate. Then we will find how weak we are, compared with the Russians and the Chinese.

We are inferior because of the imbalance on the non-nuclear level. And this, as you all know, is extremely difficult to correct and it would be extremely difficult to maintain a balance on these other levels of military confrontation.

*Niemeyer:* I do think that the balance of power in a military sense is important. I think that it is needed as a minimum, but when Mr. Wolfers ascribes to me a policy or an objective of supremacy, in the sense in which he means it, I have to disclaim that. It seems to me that Professor Wolfers is talking of this conflict as if it were a conflict between nations. In this sense I would not claim an objective of supremacy. First of all, this is not exactly within our reach. Secondly, before we ever get there we will have brought about a war. So, in the sense of a national policy of defense—military preparedness—vis-à-vis the Russian military power, I fully agree with Professor Wolfers.

The objective which I suggested in my paper and of which in the quoted statement is indeed quite out of context and looks much sharper than is really meant, is based on an estimate of the Communist mentality and the militant movement of communism and what it means for the world.

And I should like to take my departure here from some remarks which were made during the discussion of Part I, with all of which I would take issue. There was repeated mention of the purpose of world conquest and that the Communists could be made to give up their purpose or their goal of world conquest. There was repeated mention here of the Communist system, and if the Communists had to do this and that, it meant that they would have to change their entire system, which again was described as a kind of defeat of the Communist enterprise.

The Communists are not people who have a purpose of world conquest. They have an expectation. The expectation is that our system, the system of bourgeois society—a capitalist society—is doomed, and history is going to pass over it. The other part of the expectation is that our society will be followed by a socialist society, sooner or later—the time is unessential—and that the Communists are the people of the future. In this sense they are not entertaining a goal. They are entertaining an attitude which increases this expectation. The expectation in a sense is deeply rooted in a world view.

There are those who don't believe that people in government entertain world views, that people in government are hard-boiled men who simply calculate interests and move *from* practical sources *to* practical sources. I would submit that this is a mistaken view of men in general, and of people in government in particular, and most especially of people in government who display such drive, such enthusiasm, such unmitigated hope, as the Communists have maintained. These are people who are driven by a world view and their world view is precisely the one which I have just now given.

In view of this, the Communists have maintained a militant enterprise to accumulate power, in order to be ready for all kinds of situations in different parts of the world. And what we have called the Communist system, namely the particular order which is maintained in the Soviet Union, is not in all its features essential to that militant enterprise. It does happen to be the way in which the Communists govern Russia. But there can be variations from that, as we have seen in the case of Poland and in the case of China, and as we have seen even in the case of Russia itself where the system has been changed from time to time. So, a change of the system itself would by no means be equivalent to a defeat of the Communist militant enterprise.

Communists stop being Communist to the extent to which they give up their world view and some of their expectations, their thinking in terms of two camps.

This kind of change is something that comes extremely hard to any individual and ten times as hard to an individual who is a member of that society in which this kind of expectation is authoritatively maintained and socially rewarded. I would say, that this is not the very nicest thing to happen to Communists. We must expect Communists to be people who live among us with an irrational world view—an irrational attitude toward the world and towards men. They are people who are incapable, by virtue of this world view, of keeping peace with other men and keeping peace with the means of power which they have in hand. So the Communists are going to be people who disturb world peace, who disturb the peace in their own land, and, as a matter of fact, disturb the peace in their own party. What I said is that there can be no peace in the world until the Communists as a power have been reduced to impotence.

I do not expect Communists to change their view. But I think it is within the feasibility of the world to separate such people from the means and the organization of power and have them run around, if they will, with their dogma. As long as they don't carry their activism into the policy of nations or into the politics of the world, I don't think we need lose any sleep over Communists.

I would agree with Professor Wolfers in saying that communism must not be compared with Islam. This is a completely different matter. Islam is a religion, after all, entertaining views about reality, whereas communism constitutes an ideology that is a system of thought based from the beginning on an arbitrary position, and is therefore irrational.

But, I do believe that if we focus the objectives of the Cold War on measures against Communists anywhere in the world, rather than on warfare against Russia or China or other countries, the chances of isolating the Communists from their followers, of rendering them impotent to handle the weapons which are now placed in their hands, are not bad at all. And I'm not being a defeatist, but quite optimistic that this kind of objective can be attained with skill and with God's help.

**Kintner:** These two poles which we have just heard do have some serious differences between them. I believe that the choices which we make toward our over-all goal are perhaps fundamental in the determination of any strategy, because as anyone who has been exposed to military training knows, the objective is that which determines all other actions leading toward obtainment of that objective.

I read recently the President's State of the Union Message, in which there is a statement of our goals which I think is appropriate to relate today. I can't quote him exactly, but I believe the substance of his thoughts was that our objective is not the victory of one system over another, but the victory of humanity. This is a type of articulation of the objective which has become rather prevalent in the last several years.

I would like to suggest that we might raise a few questions about it. If we take a look at the world we are in, I believe that most of us would recognize that, because of modern technology, for the first time in history a world order is technologically possible. Perhaps we are moving toward such a world order.

The fundamental question is, what will be the character of that order? And, if the values of the Western world are suppressed or eliminated in the process of achieving that order, will this in fact be a victory for humanity or will it in fact be a victory of one system over another? I personally believe, and it may be parochial, that the values of the West—the inheritance that we have received from our past, our total tradition—correspond more to true humanity than the rather archaic formulation which we witness in the Communist teleology, and that these values themselves are the fundamental issues at stake. Consequently, whether the world order as it emerges will be more or less ordained as it has been in the Communist grip, or whether it will follow the forces which have built the civilization of which we are members, is a very important matter. In short, I suggest that the objective over time must be the defense and enlargement of these values in spheres throughout the world.

The techniques and tactics and strategy to be pursued to achieve this is a very difficult and complex problem. I don't think the world order will be resolved in this generation and perhaps not in the next. But I think eventually we will look forward to a world order where the open values of the West are permanently imbedded in human institutions and the relations of human beings with one other. I believe that this must be the determining factor in the choice of our strategy.

There have been several discussions raised on at least the military posture that one should pursue or maintain with respect to whatever objectives are selected. The thought has been suggested not only just recently but in Part I that a military stalemate of one sort or another either already exists or is just over the horizon. I am sure this matter will be debated by others in the military panel. But I don't think we can apply to military problems any more static an attitude than we can apply to others. From what I have been able to read, the Soviets have been spending a great deal of time and energy trying to upset whatever imbalance may exist against them now, and that part of our problem will be, as Dr. Wolfers suggested, to maintain an adequate posture. I question whether we can find a posture that will stay at a state of beautiful equilibrium indefinitely, and it may be that the imperatives of the problem will force us to achieve something that perhaps borders on at least a degree of superiority. Perhaps then we will be able to do the other things that have been suggested, leading toward a future world where Western values will have a chance not only of surviving, but of inspiring future generations of the human race.

*Trager:* I'm not quite sure whether Professor Wolfers is giving us a descriptive analysis of what he calls the American objective as it is or as he thinks it ought to be. Let us assume that it is not what he thinks it ought to be, and that it is what he thinks it is.

I will submit that, if it is supposed to be a descriptive analysis of the current American objective, it is an insufficient analysis of that objective, or I find no such single consistency with the expression of either the objective or the way to obtain it. I would submit that whether you look at the Executive, the Congress, the military, public opinion or what have you, or even academies, if you attempt to find objectives stated, they will appear within a spectrum that goes from one extreme of disengagement to a middle point of perhaps accommodation or equilibrium or *détente* or to another extreme—which I will defend later—of pushing back the enemy. Within the American society today the absence of a clear-cut objective does not yet make it possible for us to achieve the means necessary to obtain that objective if we could agree upon it.

My second point would be that I doubt very much that the description of a restoration of an East-West balance is an adequate description of the current state of affairs. That would imply that at the moment the balance is in favor of the East or of the Sino-Soviet Bloc. If the balance were in favor of the Sino-Soviet Bloc, I would submit that Cuba of October 1962 would not have happened. I would also submit that they would take more liberties with their superiority than they are presently able to take.

## Roll-Back

*Cerny:* Let us consider the next statement chosen from the paper of Professor Trager.

> The dangers of further loss (in Southeast Asia) will be increased over the next decade, if this war if fought, as the Communists intend, only within the territory of the Free World in Asia and elsewhere. Hence, even to make the policy of containment effective, and to defend the so-called receding defensive perimeter, it is necessary to adopt the third policy alternative, roll-back, based upon a forward military strategy. To defend Saigon, it will, in other words, be necessary to penetrate, undermine, threaten, and, if necessary, attack Hanoi.
>
> Frank Trager

*Wolfers:* I have to spell out what I had in mind, because I agree with some of the things Professor Trager said and disagree with others. I did not suggest, and I would not suggest, that the East has a superiority today. It is distinctly inferior on what we have regarded as a most important military level, namely on the nuclear. I think that may last for quite a long time. But my contention is that this is not decisive, although it is important and vital. It does more for the security of the United States than anything one could imagine, because they can't attack us as long as we have nuclear superiority. So nobody, I should expect, would want to give up that superiority.

The trouble is that this is not the whole issue. All our troubles with our allies today stem from the fact that this nuclear superiority does not give them sufficient protection. They are beginning to realize it, because in order to be able to protect them, or for what one calls extended deterrents to be effective, means not only superiority, but a degree of supremacy that permits one practically to knock out the nuclear opponent. And this I say, if we have it today, is a fading asset. I doubt whether we have it today. But as time goes on, and as the retaliatory power of the Soviets becomes more secure, no amount of counterforce in our hands is going to change this very dangerous situation for the entire Free World overseas, which is after all most of the Free World. And here we have not got a balanced situation. We are facing a future in which this imbalance will become more and more striking.* I mentioned in my paper that the weakest of all points is the Near East, where there is practically nothing on our side, in Iran and south of Iran. It is weak enough in the Far East. It is amazing that we have been able to hold as much as we have held there with the weak rimlands around Red China.

* Professor Wolfers subsequently answered this question from the floor by Mr. Boudinot P. Atterbury: "If supremacy is not to be our objective, but equilibrium, do you agree with Kenneth Boulding that, whenever we do become superior, we must build up our enemy to restore equilibrium? In other words, do you subscribe to Boulding's doctrine of enemy-supported behavior?"

*Wolfers:* I am afraid the answer is simply "no." This concept seems fantastic to me. If we can have supremacy, let's have it and let's not be afraid of it. But, I don't think we can have it; that is the problem. It is not that this is something which would be so undesirable; "Oh do beware us of our domination of the world." I think we can handle that when we get it. But, I don't think we are going to have it. I would be the last to want to build up my enemy. I am even a little afraid of building up our friends too much sometimes.

What I heard this morning has given me some explanation, namely the weakness of China. But is there no remedy for this Asian situation but to "roll back," whatever that may mean in terms of Mr. Trager? I can only imagine a roll-back in which you win the war—a military roll-back. And if we can't hope to win a war now or wouldn't dare to start one because of the consequences, then the word roll-back to me doesn't suggest any clear-cut policy alternative.

*Kissinger:* Professor Wolfers said that all of our troubles with our allies derived from the fact that they are beginning to learn that we no longer have nuclear superiority. I would say most of the troubles with our allies derive from the fact that we (a) assert we have nuclear superiority, but (b) insist that they develop some other arms that they do not consider of equal priority, and that we insist on retaining exclusive control over the weapon in which we insist we do have nuclear superiority but that we don't choose to use in their defense.

*Kertesz:* Before I make a general statement on the issues under discussion, I would like to ask a clarification of Professor Trager.

You mentioned roll-back, as far as would be necessary, based upon a forward military strategy, in order that we shouldn't defend only Saigon, but that we should penetrate North Vietnam directly and, if necessary, attack Hanoi.

I think that it is a very good idea. But frankly I do not know how to do it. Who will do the job? Do we have local people there whom we could organize, even though we have difficulty in keeping our head above water, even in Southern Indo-China? I don't think that you meant by the general roll-back policy that we should attack the Soviet Union everywhere. But you had in mind specifically the situation in Indo-China. I must confess my utter ignorance as to how this job could be done, and I would like to ask you for a clarification of this particular point.

## Southeast Asia

*Trager:* Actually this statement comes at the end of a fairly long argument in which I have attempted to examine three possible postures in the difficult area of Southeast Asia.

I believe that the three possible postures, which I have already alluded to, are: disengagement, which we have in effect accepted under the disastrous July 1962 Geneva Agreement for Laos; containment, which we presently hold as the limited policy in Vietnam, where we have now committed some 12,000 men, among whom there have already been more than 200 casualties; and what I am calling for want of a better word, roll-back, which I shall now attempt to make clear.

It seems to me that, if we accept Mao's own description of strategy and tactics, amply made clear now for twenty years, and recently restated by Giap in North Vietnam, we know that the Chinese Communists and the Viet Minh are perfectly prepared.to continue protracted war on soil other than their own. They are willing to ignore space and consume time while they win people.

I submit that in the case of Vietnam and generally in Southeast Asia, so long as we fight on their terms by giving advice and materiel and suffer the attrition which will continue, we will find ourselves at that kind of disadvantage in which the American public will in time—and sooner rather than later— come to a conclusion of "what for?" "Why suffer more, why not accept a kind of disengagement for the whole Indo-Chinese peninsula which we've already accepted in Laos?" That would be a defeat for a stated American objective, which has been to preserve the integrity of Vietnam. Therefore, some other kind of objective and strategy has to be adopted, if we are at least to fulfill our own stated objective under the previous and present Administrations.

What can that be? It seemed to me that there is no inability on the part of Americans, Thai, Vietnamese, Philippines, and others who have been associated with the SEATO organization in Asia to fight if trained, if encadred, if supplied, if given a motivation. There is no special fighting ability that the Viet Minh have which either the Laotians or the Vietnamese do not have.

We have to find the way to martialize—to make a bad coinage —the forces there with our participation. We had pledged that participation in SEATO. We welshed on that participation when the time came in Laos, or we failed to fulfill our commitment there.

If we continue in Vietnam, we suffer the possibility of a war of attrition, which I submit is in the interest of Peking; or we interdict, close off, stop the supply line down the Ho Chi Minh Trail in Laos, across the border at the 17th Parallel and down the Eastern seacoast at the China Sea. We interdict, and we stop supply support, and we do that publicly. We announce to Hanoi—and Peking will hear it—that the supply route will be stopped. We announce that our policy is to stop the supply, stop the infiltration, and give them a limited time as we did in Cuba. And if there is no stoppage, we then take the appropriate steps. The first step could be a token step, say, at Haiphong, and a second announcement. The "we" in this context would be Americans, SEATO allies such as there are, or Americans and Vietnamese certainly.

This is what we threatened to do in Cuba—we Americans alone. One might argue that Cuba is next door and Vietnam is 8,000 or 9,000 miles away. But we've committed ourselves to Vietnam and I don't see how we can withdraw that commitment and still remain a first-class dominant power.

I won't develop this further, but I would assert here that even in Laos there were Laotians who were willing to fight, as illustrated when Phoumi marched up from Savannakhet to Vientiane; that even in Laos our supply lines were better—that is, more economically handled—than the Chinese supply lines. We had at least a road head to Vientiane out of the port of Bangkok. I am anticipating arguments that may be made against the difficulties by pointing out that not the whole story has been exposed here, or elsewhere. Under the circumstances I say that the way to defend Saigon is by undermining, threatening, penetrating covertly and otherwise, and if necessary attacking, announcing in advance that we are defending Saigon and will preserve, as we have already promised, the integrity of Vietnam.*

---

* At a subsequent stage of the panel discussion, Dr. Trager pointed out: I do not believe that my outline would be sufficiently correct if I left you with the notion that I am satisfied merely to defend the 17th Parallel. In the actual operation of such a contingency, if it were to come to pass, then the difficulties that we have heard about in China and difficulties that we have not yet heard about, but are equally real in North Vietnam, become factors which make possible the enlarging of one's viewpoint.

I am not talking only about South Vietnam. I am talking about mainland Southeast Asia. The rice-bowl of the world is Burma and Thailand, number one and number two respectively among the rice-exporting nations of the world, with density of about 75 to 85 persons per square mile, an obvious target area for Peking for all kinds of reasons. What I am suggesting, therefore, is that looking at Vietnam has to become one of the pluralized objectives which the United States must have for different parts of the world. Different strategies and tactics would have to be applied to each of the pluralized objectives.

*Kintner:* I am in accord with Dr. Trager's point of view. I would like to point out that in this instance as well as in many other developments that have taken place in the Cold War, the argument inside the Government is essentially between taking this kind of action, the countering action, or trying to find the easiest settlement, sometimes by developing a strategic posture that is not employed, sometimes by fighting on terrain which, in the case of South Vietnam, is pretty much against us if our objective is to hold the line against someone else who is trying to send in gasoline and light it.

The argument generally is won by the side which chooses to take the least risky alternative, for the very reason that we discussed in the beginning. Our presumed objective is not necessarily over time to undermine the opposing value system, undermine the opposing political order, but hopefully that, if we are able to hold the line indefinitely, the type of erosion that was suggested earlier will take place automatically. The real issue strategically is, what kind of pressures or inducements will bring about these fundamental changes in the other side. On this issue there has been debate throughout the entire Cold War, but there has rarely been action taken.

*Cerny:* I would like to ask Professor Meyer and also Professor Stokes to what extent the underlying reasoning of Professor Trager's statement may be applicable to other areas of United States concern—for example, the Middle East or Latin America?

*Meyer:* It seems to me that the situation in the Middle East is so far different from that in South Asia that any comparison becomes very difficult. After all, we are dealing here with a series of quite independent countries which have not yet gone under. It is not a question of roll-back but rather a question of, it seems to me, maintaining economic aid and assistance and developing a point of view in those nations which will permit them to make their own decisions and act as members of the civilized community of nations. We are not faced with the same sort of situation as the West faced against the Soviet Union in Korea, for example, or in Vietnam and elsewhere. Now, I would be prepared to agree with the statement that the Middle East perhaps is potentially a very weak place and a place where the Soviets well may step up their offensive, particularly in Iran and perhaps in the not-too-distant future in Turkey, both of which have contiguous frontiers with the Soviet Union. But it seems to me that the rest of the Middle East differs widely in so many respects that comparison is highly difficult.

**Stokes:** I also find that comparisons usually at best are bad. For Latin America the only current case study that we have which would involve the test of the value of the concept of roll-back would be in connection with Cuba. There we have, I think, by all accounts achieved an outstanding and resounding success. Very great praise has been heaped upon all of those who have participated in the planning and the execution of the plans which resulted in the removal of the missiles.

But, on the other hand, Castro still does remain. He still retains a system—a political and economic system, and in terms of international relations, a Communist system as a part of, so far at least, the Soviet Bloc, but with some influence from the Chinese side—which does constitute a continuing problem for us in the Western Hemisphere. As to whether there was any conceivable possibility in October or at any other time of removing this particular threat, which I would assume to be more or less or in a general way at least consistent with a concept of roll-back, I am simply not competent to say.

On the other hand, one does not have to go much beyond the reading of the Latin American media of communication or listening to the radio broadcasts or examining the internal operations of various governments to perceive that the task of the United States and the fulfillment of its stated objectives in the Western Hemisphere is enormously complicated by the fact that Castro is still there. If one examines the literature of the last fifty years which deals with United States-Cuban relations, either from the Cuban point of view or from ours, I think I'm speaking correctly when I say that not a single responsible observer or scholar ever conceived of a situation in which there would be ninety miles away from us a threat of this sort to the security of the United States and to the security of the Western Hemisphere. This was something that no one ever deemed possible in any way whatever. We are paying for this, for whatever reasons it came about. If I interpret roll-back correctly and properly, I certainly express a sympathy for the possibility of getting this out as rapidly as possible, consistent with all of the problems that are involved there.

We had the other little episode in connection with Guatemala, which began in 1944 with the establishment of a leftist revolution; which was incidentally very, very similar in its initial aspects to what took place, at least ideologically, in Cuba. Power was seized in a different way. But when you began to examine the people who had power in Guatemala, it became evident very early that this was a highly dangerous situation, if your objective was to keep the Communists out. When the situation in Guatemala was finally recognized, it was necessary to roll it back. That was at least indirectly US policy. To be sure, it was done by Guatemalans themselves, operating through a haven in Honduras. But, I felt at that time that it was indispensable to get rid of that system, to roll it back if you like, if the term can be used there; but the situation with Cuba creates a problem infinitely more difficult to handle throughout the whole Western Hemisphere.

*Meyer:* Those of us who deal with the Middle East and who think about it and work in it may be wrong in our judgments as those who deal with Latin America have been wrong. But I believe that nobody who is well-informed on the Middle East at the moment would feel that the Soviet Union has established any sort of a foothold which would indicate that we might be confronted with a roll-back in anything resembling the immediate future.

There has been a lot of irresponsible talk, I think, for example, about Egypt being a place where the Soviets have made a play and are making a play. But I believe that anybody who knows anything about Egypt would be the first to feel that Egypt is a far cry from being a Soviet satellite or from taking orders or commands from inside the Iron Curtain; and probably Egypt comes the closest to having been in some form of alliance with the Soviet Union in the Middle East.

*Wolfers:* I am not in conflict with Mr. Trager in principle. What he calls roll-back is the restoration of a *status quo ante* where the Communists have made advances. They haven't made them in many places, but they have made them in Vietnam. They have made them in Cuba. If we can drive them out, surely it's something we want to do. The reason, however, why we are not doing it, is not in my opinion the cowardice of the Government or the desire not to get into trouble. The Government has to look at it not from the local point of view. From a local point of view every situation seems easy to handle. But we are threatened at so many points, and there I come back to my feeling of still a very serious imbalance in many places.

The Cuban thing is so serious, because for the first time the Soviets leap-frogged our containment front and established a position outside. They threatened to do it elsewhere—in Iraq. They might do it in Indonesia. They might do it in several places. Moreover, we have this one lone position in Berlin to worry about and we have the difficulties of our allies to worry about.

If we do not do what seems within our power, it is because we have to look in terms of the total power that is involved. I am not sure whether we can conquer North Vietnam today at reasonable risk. These are matters partly of military strategy and logistics. Surely those in the military establishment who decide on these matters are not held back by any kind of philosophy that tells them it would be a wrong thing to do, but it's because in the total calculation of power today we are not in that position, which proves again that the issue is fundamentally military.

**Kissinger:** The debate about containment or roll-back does not seem to me to be the most acute issue that we face right now in the Free World.

The deeper problem we have is a psychological one, rather than the military one of how we deal with guerrillas in South Vietnam, whether by offensive actions or by purely defensive actions.

We have a notion that the normal pattern of relations among states is peaceful. The Communists, for example, can put bases into Cuba and four weeks later, when they begin a peace offensive, we immediately assume that fundamental changes must have taken place, because it is after all reasonable that people be peaceful and engage in peace offensives.

We talk about settlement as if we knew what we meant by a settlement. If the Russians came to us today and offered to sign a settlement, I have the impression that there wouldn't be five people in the Government who could describe what our notion of the settlement would be. When high-ranking officials write that our goal is decency and a good human life, one is not overwhelmed by the precision of that description as a view of the world. It is not necessarily easy for foreign governments, trying to predict what we are going to do, to guide their actions on the basis of such assertions.

Because we really do not know what we would consider a settlement or a fair arrangement or a possible solution, as soon as the immediate pressure ends, we then go on to the next fire. One of the problems that people have around the world is that the impression is created, either that we respond only when there are immediate pressures, or that we are so tactically oriented that we are completely unreliable, and that we respond in every situation to the exigencies of that situation. We do not know what it is that we are really after four or five years from now. This, I would think, is a more fundamental problem—important as these issues are—than the problem of whether we now want to have roll-back or not, because we're too far from even being able to face that question when there are so many troubled spots within the Free World. The question of what kind of a world we want is really the one that we haven't sufficiently addressed.

**Kertesz:** We cannot act now according to traditional principles. For example, one of the sources of our difficulty with General de Gaulle is that he considers Russia both as a somewhat mischievous enemy, and yet a national state. I don't think that he really understands what communism means in the contemporary world. Professor Niemeyer proposed the destruction of the Communist Parties as a solution of our problem. I think that this is a very good suggestion, but the real problem is how can you destroy the Communist Parties when they are at the same time based in one of the most important territorial states.

How do you destroy communism if at the same time Communists are the government in one of the most important territorial states? In the final analysis we need military might, and we need an entirely different strategy which is unprecedented when compared with all past situations. I wonder what Professor Niemeyer would suggest?

**Niemeyer:** I do agree that the question of what to do about the Communist Party is indeed a problem, but I would like to suggest that so far the best minds of the nation have not addressed themselves to that problem and to the substance of Professor Kissinger's statement, with which I wholeheartedly agree. We are incapable of setting up a list of desirable priorities as our national objective.

I do believe that the trouble in the world at present, that trouble about which we are all talking, comes from the presence of an activist movement with the irrational ideology of communism.

The Communists themselves are fully aware of our power and,

as has been brought out by the discussion so far, are not trying to destroy our power by a frontal military assault. They are trying to erode our power, to destroy our power by destroying the social fiber that makes our military power possible.

I would submit that a similar strategy is possible against the Communists with far more chances of success than the Communists have against us. Between the Communists and the populations ruled by them there is no natural link, there is no confidence, there are no shared values. There is indeed a formidable totalitarian organization; but it is possible to drive in wedges between the population and the Communists.

We have not made an attempt, we haven't even addressed ourselves to that problem; and confronted with the formidable might of Soviet Russia and also of China in the future, we might at least attempt to paralyze the Communist might, by making it impossible or very difficult for them to command their followers to handle those weapons in those countries.*

---

* At a later point in the Conference, Dr. Niemeyer and Dr. Dinerstein expressed their contrasting views on attitudes toward the struggle with communism.

*Niemeyer:* There is a strategy that is geared to the danger of military tack and the problems of deterrence and survival, should they come. This strategy, however, should be distinguished from a Cold War policy. And it seems to me that during this Conference, as indeed during the past fifteen or seventeen years, we have tended to confuse this kind of strategy with the Cold War policy. The results have been that we have built up strategic concepts and have tucked in at the end an expectation, a hope of victory, which had very little, if anything, to do with our strategy. Let me just give you a few examples in terms of strategies here proposed, during this Conference.

We heard about a strategy of a balance of power, or containment. The hope of victory which it contained is that with the passage of time the nature of communism would change and the threat would disappear.

We heard about another strategy here, with which I am personally very sympathetic, namely the one which would concentrate on the development of technological superiority. The hope of victory which is implied is that eventually one could negotiate a peace on this basis, which also assumes that one can negotiate with people like Communists for something like peace.

There were elements of a strategy which dwelled particularly on unity in the Allied camp and on the kind of Free World as a going concern which would be so satisfactory that it would leave very little room for the Communists to appeal to it and to penetrate into its fissures. The hope of victory which this implies was that the Communists, aware of this fact, would eventually give up.

Now, all of these strategies envisage an eventual peace with Communists, with a Communist-ruled empire. They look forward to a kind of Communist

## Strategy Options in Areas of Indirect Confrontation

*Cerny:* I would like to turn now to a discussion of our second issue of Part II, entitled "Strategy Options in Areas of Indirect Confrontation."

Here we are actually concerned with specific areas and problems of United States strategy.

---

Party that somehow has ceased to be the threat that it is now and has somehow become manageable, reasonable, and capable of partnership with other forces and powers in the world. This, of course, is quite a logical assumption, given our view of the conflict. If one looks at this conflict as something that is going on between nations, one looks forward to an eventual peace with the same powers with which one is in conflict.

I should like to submit that the view of the conflict underlying all of these strategies thus mistakes the notion of communism and the notion of Communists. Communists themselves are people who do not look forward to an eventual peace with us. They do look forward to an eventual dissolution of our society, a total destruction of our society, a *tabula rasa* on which they can build their own rule and change man and the world as they see fit. They do not look forward to anything like coexistence in the long run.

With people who hold this kind of attitude towards others and towards the world, one cannot make peace, and any kind of hope which looks forward to peace with Communists is simply an unrealistic hope. One cannot make peace because they do not change. And may I just insert here a very brief historical note. The hope for change in the Communist camp is almost invariably based on the event of the Thermidor in the French Revolution. May I just remind all of us that what took place in Thermidor was not a change of heart or of mind, but the removal and execution of the ideological totalitarian activists who were then in power, and the coming to power of other people who indeed were capable of living in peace with their environment.

We have to make it our business to counter the Communists with a notion which looks forward to solution of the conflict in terms of an eviction of Communists from the seat of power or the total discreditation of the Communist Party with the public. There is no other possibility of peace with Communists. We cannot have peace with Communists in power. We can only have peace when Communists have been driven from the seats of power.

I should like to submit that the one big question that was not considered by this Conference was the question or the problem of methods of strategy which aimed not so much at military power—that, too, is important of course—but which aimed at change in political power in countries now dominated by Communists and even in countries in which the Communists are in strong opposition, a strategy which aimed at reducing, destroying, and ultimately annihilating the political power in the hands of Communists. This kind of strategy has not been considered at this Conference and I do hope that at a follow-up conference or maybe in future treatment and revision of the papers of this Conference, there will be an opportunity to give attention to this problem.

*Dinerstein:* I'd like to disassociate myself from the pessimism that I thought I detected in Professor Niemeyer's remarks, and after disassociating

## Latin America

### The first statements are from Professor Stokes' paper:

A Soviet specialist on Latin America has stated that the Mao strategy, the Four Class Alliance of workers, peasants, middle classes, and the nationalist bourgeoisie under the leadership of the Communist Party, is to be used in Latin America . . . If we assume that the Soviet and Chinese Communists mean what they say with respect to indirect political aggression in Latin America, the problem of insurgency will continue to command the attention of the United States in the foreseeable future. Guerrilla warfare depends upon civilian support and external source of supply for arms.

\* \* \* \*

It seems probable that President Kennedy will achieve all of his stated ends with respect to the issue of Soviet missiles and other offensive weapons in Cuba, but the government of Castro will remain in power. The Castro government can therefore be used as a Communist base for supplying insurgents in Latin America with political propaganda and perhaps arms as well. In addition, Latin Americans have traditionally found it possible to acquire arms from the United States and Europe.

\* \* \* \*

One option of the United States is to employ air and sea supremacy to prohibit arms deliveries to insurgents in the Latin American countries. Since successful insurgency depends in part on tactics based upon mobility, surprise, flexibility, and deception, the US Government can aid friendly Latin American governments through providing training, light weapons, communications equipment, chemical agents and explosives, and propaganda and psychological materials. The possibility of considering active and open support on request of Latin American governments might legitimately be considered.

William Stokes

---

myself from that pessimism, I'd like to point to some of the costs of such pessimism.

I agree completely with Professor Niemeyer that the leaders of the Soviet Union don't want to make peace with us now, and that they want to get what we have. That's their policy. And I think they're malevolent. But I do disagree with him in his appraisal of their ability. I've been professionally occupied with studying the Soviet Union for about twenty years, and I'm not impressed with their ability. I'm more impressed with their inability and very often their stupidity.

I would like to point out that I don't think that it's impossible for them to change their minds. I think that's up to us. We can make them change their minds. They will never change their minds about what they want willingly, but I think it's within our power to force them to do so. They expect that we will deteriorate, but I think we can turn it the other way

*Stokes:* I think from the ideological point of view there is almost overwhelming evidence from the Soviet theoreticians, as well as from the Latin American ones—and also from our own scholars who have the ability to use the Hemisphere languages and also to use Russian—that this is indeed the objective which is in mind and it goes back a long time. It goes back in the 1930's to the Prestes Column in Brazil, which was a very great effort made through the use of tactics of this sort. One perceives it in a book by Ravines called *The Yenan Way.* We perceive it in the intervening period in a number of areas in Latin America.

I don't want to take time to distinguish between two conceptions: the traditional orthodox Marxist-Leninist conception of achieving a dictatorship of the proletariat and the contention that prior to that, you may have to obtain *"revolución nacional"* —a national revolution in which an *alianza de clases*—an alliance of the middle classes, the intelligentsia, the proletariat, and the peasants—will be utilized. Sometimes the theoreticians point out that if they can get that far, then at a suitable stage in the

---

and hope that they will deteriorate if we are active. I don't associate myself with easy optimism. If we sit back and just wait and say: "They will fade away as all flowers do," we shall fail. I think that some of the things that have been pointed to in this Conference would be effective in helping them decline and making them give up their objectives. Mr. Schelling talked the other day about the arms race as an instrument in this. I think the changes in our economy could help. I think there are many things that we could have done and didn't do that would have pushed them further along the line. I think it is possible to force the Soviet Union to give up its objectives if we are vigorous and imaginative.

The second point concerns the costs of pessimism. I, like most of us, have done a lot of public speaking to various groups, and I have noticed that if you emphasize very heavily the great skill of the Communists, if you emphasize very heavily their great unbroken successes, and if you're very pessimistic about the outlook, the reaction of most people is, "Well, I suppose you're right—there's no use trying." And if you leave the implication that the only way of dealing with communism is by war and that there aren't any other alternatives, then the reaction you usually get is, "Well, it's too bad—there's nothing we can do about it." So I think we have to be very careful because I've suffered from this kind of reaction when I have over-emphasized my point. We have to be very careful not to frighten people into believing that there's nothing they can do and they may as well enjoy the world while it's the way it has been for the last years.

*Niemeyer:* Dr. Dinerstein attributed to me the statement about Soviet ability and also pessimism. I would like to point out that I did not say anything about an unbroken string of successes, nor anything about the ability of the Communists, nor am I pessimistic.

Cold War—preferably when the United States is defeated—they can have the class revolution and liquidate their former allies, or at least eliminate them from consideration.

There is a considerable amount of evidence to demonstrate that ideologically there is such an expectation. A considerable amount of effort is being made along these lines.

I think the evidence is quite clear that the Castro system constitutes a tremendously valuable gain, from the standpoint of the Marxist-Leninist effort, in the Western Hemisphere. This is something that we must continue to cope with one way or the other.

I have suggested that certain things might be done. The difficulty, however, is that this suggestion is predicated on prior achievements of certain things. In particular, it is predicated on the assumption that we reform, revise, modernize, beef up—whatever terminology you want to use—the Western Hemisphere alliance system.

Here we encounter very formidable problems for the purpose of taking any kind of action at all in the Western Hemisphere. The United States, beginning in 1933, gradually deprived itself of the right—within the Hemisphere system—of utilizing various types of activities on a unilateral basis. This culminated in Article 15 of the Charter of Bogotá, which set up the Organization of American States, and which constitutes a complete denial of any type of unilateral action on our part in any of these areas: cultural, economic, political, or military. The Rio Treaty of 1947 makes clear that, if force is ever to be used for the purpose of repelling any kind of aggressive activity or a threat to Hemispheric security, there must be a two-thirds vote of the total membership. In parliamentary terms, this is virtually impossible to achieve. Consequently, in order for this kind of an option to be implemented, it seems to me, it is necessary for certain prior developments to take place.

I certainly was not here proposing that the United States embark upon some kind of activity which would alienate those elements in the Latins which share our own ideals, our own values, and in many respects even the same kinds of machinery which seem important to us in an institutional sense. These elements exist in Latin America, in all of the countries. Here I couldn't share more the idea expressed by Professor Niemeyer, Professor Kissinger, and perhaps others, that we ought to be concerned not only with what it is we are against, that is with prohibiting further encroachments with roll-back in connection with Cuba and prohibiting further encroachments of Marxism-Leninism, but also we must be concerned with what we are for —with the alternative attitudes and values, with the alternative economic concepts and ideas, and with alternative political methods and forms of organization and procedures. This, to me, is absolutely essential if we expect to achieve victory within this Hemisphere.

*Kintner:* With respect to Latin America, the particular tactics outlined here are sort of last-ditch tactics. In other words, there may be sufficient arms already in a country like Brazil to carry on a revolution along the lines of the Yenan Way.

The problem down there is very complicated. But essentially the ideological penetration which the Communists have made over the past twenty or thirty years in the activist leadership group is the most complicated obstacle we have to try to overcome. In Brazil we find now a situation bordering on fiscal and economic chaos and political ineptitude of the greatest sort, whereby the very strong Communist Party—about a half a million members—may be the only solution that is regarded as having any feasibility.

Now our problem is to find out who might be left down there who would be ideologically willing to cooperate with us in bringing about the new design for Brazilian society and to back these people all the way. Many times in the past ten or fifteen years we've had difficulty in discovering whom we wish to back. Often when we find that the backing of a certain individual becomes unpopular or ineffective, for one reason or another, we abandon him. And consequently, there may be fewer and fewer candidates who wish to identify themselves with our side. But unless we approach the problem of selecting from the leadership élite of Latin America people that we can work with and energetically support, we may not, by these prophylactic methods suggested here, save that continent from future Communist inroads.

*Stokes:* I would like to call attention to what in my paper is referred to as the "mobilization concept." What my distinguished colleague is suggesting is not at all beyond the realm of possibility, and this has been the case for a long period of time in the past.

Latin American societies are oriented very strongly in the direction of intellectual élites, who make very clear what their attitudes and values are in the public word. They do this in oral communication as well. But, there are literally thousands of publications, which reveal very clearly what a man like Frondizi, of Argentina for example, has in mind, or in an existing government, what Victor Paz Estenssoro believes. And they are not speaking in an idle way, because in Latin America the written word and the spoken word are honored very greatly, and over a period of time it is possible for specialists to find out who are those individuals and groups who share attitudes and values similar to our own. This is not by any means impossible.

But it is impossible, when you have people attempting to do this job who do not know the languages, who do not read the books, who do not read the manuscripts presented at their learned institutions, and who do not equip themselves with what is already available for reaching solutions in connection with these problems.

Probably we know more about the Latin American area than any other major region in the world. There are people who really know in almost every area in which you can investigate. If we are interested, as we have said, in the *Alianza Para el Progreso* and certain types of reforms—of which two have been mentioned over and over again: tax reform and land reform, in each of the countries, beginning in Mexico—we know men in this country who have dedicated their entire lifetimes to an analysis of Latin American problems. The Latin Americans also know it. Bring these two together and you have got some information which is of some value.

If we do not mobilize the talent and ability we have available in the United States for finding out who are those individuals and groups who share similar attitudes and ideals to our own, then we cannot achieve the most important objective, which is to discover what it is we are for, and to support those ideas, those policies, those individuals, those groups. Unless this is done, then, I am in entire agreement: we have pretty well lost the struggle before we begin, because the other side is doing and has done this for a long time.

**Kertesz:** Professor Stokes, I think you defined very well the kind of people whom we should support. However, in many areas of the globe and even in some Latin American countries there are no reliable democratic elements. Would you agree that under certain circumstances it would be preferable to support a reliable regime, which has perhaps from the long-range point of view similar expectations, but in practice would be a kind of military rule for a limited time, because there are simply no democratic elements who would be able to create order in that particular state? I think that well-meaning idealists who are unable to govern can be much more dangerous than even gangsters in a particular country. I think this is a choice which we have to make. For, as Professor Niemeyer suggested, we should primarily profit from and support those who are anti-Communist leaders.

*Stokes:* I would not be willing to concede, for the twentieth century at least, and certainly not for the period of recent decades, that the situation described by my colleague prevails or has prevailed in connection with Latin America. Among the educated, cultured, travelled, virtuous, wise groups that one can find in Latin America, a very large percentage of them reflect the traditional values of Western Civilization in a general sense, and those of the Mediterranean cultures in particular. They have also been influenced in considerable degree by Anglo-American conceptions of the rule of law and the supremacy of law.

I recall the case study of one of my colleagues which argued that, after all, there was no alternative to Dr. Castro; that all one had was a society beset by corruption of the worst sort, in which there were no leaders to whom we might appeal or with whom we might cooperate. The specialists on Cuba never said this, because they can go down the list in everything from science, education, to the military, to politics, and produce as large a percentage of dignified, cultured, wise, just, decent men as you would possibly want.

There are circumstances under which the armed forces, usually the army, might participate effectively. I cite one illustration, one that has, I think, been quite widely misunderstood, at least by the press. This is the election in Peru. Now, they happen to be saddled by a system under which the Constitution requires that the successful candidate receive at least a plurality of one-third of the popular vote. And if no candidate receives one-third of the popular vote, then the legislature selects the supreme *mandatorios*. Among the four candidates and among the three who got the largest number of votes, no man got thirty-three per cent. In several weeks of intense negotiations the Congress was unable to make any selection, for the very good and solid reason that it was divided in about the same way the electorate was divided. The political scientists might well have told them that they should have had a method of election which involved something different from the one that they had; for example, the single-member constituency. Consequently, under those circumstances, in a situation in which turmoil was not only possible but was actually prevailing in certain areas, the armed forces did take a certain stand.

They came in for very considerable criticism at the official level. We withdrew recognition and withdrew aid. We even withdrew the basketball coaches who had been sent to that country. And this is something that hurt their feelings, because they think that they are great basketball players. This decision later was reversed. But it would seem to me that in that particular kind of circumstance one would have to accept the political realities of the moment and then apply other criteria for a future political development. I would not want to be put in the position of categorically condemning any one separate element in Latin American politics.

In many ways I would argue that of all the institutions in Latin American society the armed forces come closest to being the most democratic. They constitute the maximum opportunity for people in the lower social classes to achieve distinction, to rise in a process of vertical mobility, and to exert influence in society.

If we merely support an existing regime because it happens to be there, but foresee that they are embarking upon economic policy, for example, which Western Europeans and we ourselves have found does not function; then it might not be inappropriate for us to say that some ideas are better than others, and that in this instance we do not propose to subsidize an idea that does not seem to lead to anything other than economic collectivism, or to something that is pretty closely associated with what our enemies want to achieve in Latin America. This is but one illustration of the complicated kind of problem, but one that can be solved if we mobilize at this end the talent and ability that we have to seek out and support cooperatively those elements which do share values that are in common with our own.

*The Middle East*

**Cerny:** I would like to shift to a few other areas of strategy options of indirect confrontation. The statement that we will now consider has been chosen from the paper of Professor Meyer.

Early national military expenditures in the Middle East undeniably served useful purposes . . . Since 1955—when the Russians joined us at the game of providing weapons and advice to Middle Eastern armies—the situation has become increasingly untenable. A new jet or rocket launcher in one country leads inexorably to the same across its neighbor's frontier. The competition between funds for development and those for military hardware is bad enough, but the creation of a climate for another Cuba-like adventure is downright horrifying.

Albert Meyer

*Meyer:* I feel strongly that one can say that the early national military expenditures in the Middle East did serve a useful purpose after World War II. I think that the armies which were created there served an educational purpose in many instances. They certainly did contribute to internal security, and they certainly contributed to building up some attitudes of confidence which many of the new countries of the area did require as part of their consolidation effort.

I think it is also worthwhile mentioning that in the early years after World War II the British did have a lot to say with regard to the nature and shape of those military efforts, and this imparted an aspect of responsibility to it all. One can point as evidence of all this to Turkey, Iraq, Iran, Israel, which most certainly through building up her army did gain confidence in the face of threats from outside. Many of these military expenditures were certainly a reasonable thing and were to be expected.

About 1955, however, the matter began to change. By then the Arabs began to put wholesale expenditures into armaments. In the early years before 1955, they had contented themselves largely with making offensive noises while the Israelis were arming, and meanwhile we had helped Turkey and Iran build up their armies as part of our Cold War strategy. The balance began to swing after 1955 as the Arabs, too, joined the arms race in a really serious way. And in recent years, the amount of money spent on armaments in these nations is now running between 800 million and a billion dollars a year. This is just about the amount of money which is necessary to put a good two-thirds of the development programs which are now on the boards into effect. So, it is a very dreary sort of thing, one which we have seen elsewhere in the world.

The competition between the funds for military hardware and for funds which might go into development is an increasingly pointed thing throughout the Middle East. Each outlay for rockets or whatever on one side of a frontier creates a similar outlay on the other side of the frontier, as the neighbor arms against his neighbor. The nations of the Middle East, with few exceptions, are not concerned at all in their military build-up with playing a role in the Cold War between the West and the Soviet Union. Their principal interest is to protect themselves against their nearby neighbors. In view of this situation, one can imagine all kinds of circumstances, where, in an act of haste, the balance might be thrown way off, and any one of several outside nations, among them Western nations or the Soviet Union, might well provide some sort of armament to a Middle Eastern nation, which would trigger similar outlays across the frontier, which could lead us into something really dangerous.

*Kintner:* I would just like to ask a question for clarification. As I understand the present situation, the two countries that we are giving the major support to, I believe, are Turkey and Iran. And I don't think we are doing much with the Arab countries, which you seemed to focus your remarks on. In the first place, is that correct? Secondly, do you think that our aid to Turkey and Iran is contributing to this type of situation you were discussing?

*Meyer:* It seems to me that what our aid to Turkey and Iran did really was to establish a precedent in the area for a substantial military build-up within the states of the region. The Arabs and Israel is, of course, had really nothing in terms of armaments prior to 1952 or 1953. We established this precedent, and it was an easy thing then to be picked up. The Arabs and Israelis, of course, have not had much from us in terms of actual military equipment. They have managed to buy a lot of surplus.

*Kintner:* That is what I was trying to find out.

*Meyer:* I am not sure what we do about it.

*Kintner:* What can we do about it if they are not getting their arms from us? That is my question. Neither Israel, nor Egypt, nor Iraq, I believe, is getting very much from us at the present time.

*Meyer:* Probably what we can do at this point is to attempt to discourage them, when they will listen to us, from this sort of thing. We can also do as we have, give indications to them that we in the West will not permit a wholesale outbreak to go on in which one or several states might well be destroyed. I don't think we can go much further than this.

*Wolfers:* Mr. Meyer seems to believe that these countries some-how slipped into this unfortunate arms race. They had conflict there. They had conflict with Israel. Where in the world have nations who get into conflict not tried to arm themselves? It is unfortunate that poor nations should be spending their money on armaments. They know that, too. But, they are in the same position we are in. If they have enemies, the enemy tends to arm, they tend to arm. Nobody wants to be the late-comer.

Unless we can solve their problems, their conflicts, unless we can pacify the area, we won't get anywhere in trying to prevent them from getting arms. They will get them from somewhere. I think the question as to whether we can pacify the area is a very serious one. At the moment things are getting worse probably. We have the Yemen situation. We have still another very serious one, the Kuwait situation. Iraq is still playing with the possibility of getting Soviet jets. Therefore, the problem of the Middle East is not how we can prevent these people from getting arms, but how we can help them solve conflicts that make it unnecessary for them to spend their money on arms.

## A Pan-African Coalition?

*Cerny:* The next statement we will consider is one that we have drawn from a letter that Herbert Dinerstein sent us. Our panelists were all asked to tell us what kinds of issues they them-selves would like to see considered.

> I should like to suggest a focal point on which domestic political and international problems might converge. We must think particu-larly about the probability of a severe crisis in Africa within the next 5 or 10 years in which the United States and the Soviet Union will be participants, namely a Pan-African coalition war against the Union of South Africa.
>
> Herbert Dinerstein

*Kertesz:* Frankly, I am not afraid of a Pan-African coalition war against the South African Union within the next 5 or 10 years. I am much more afraid of a general breakdown of public order in several African states. Unfortunately, we have com-pletely abandoned sound criteria of recognition in the course of establishment of an African state system. Whether conditions in a former African colony corresponded at all to the criteria of statehood became immaterial; they were recognized as states and admitted to the United Nations almost automatically. Most of the former French colonies receive substantial support from

France; others from the United States, the Soviet Union and other sources. Despite a lack of some elementary conditions of statehood, they are considered as members of the contemporary state system. I think that this has been a foolhardy policy which might have untoward consequences. A more cautious procedure would have served the long-range interests of the newly created African states as well. Several areas in Africa might become centers of turmoil which will give chances to the Communists for intervention. What we have seen in Togo might be repeated in some other African states as well. The general principles of the European state system developed under entirely different political, social, and cultural conditions, and cannot be simply transferred and applied to African conditions as some people had hoped a few years ago.

*Trager:* I would like to take a crack at this issue of Pan-African coalition. Since Ghana has achieved its independence, there have been at least four major efforts at some kind of African coalition: the Casablanca powers, the Monrovia powers, the former French colonies that formed the twelve in a kind of loose alliance, and most recently the twenty that met at Lagos.

Actually, notions of Pan-Africanism, which have been part of what Professor Wittfogel called Homeric shouting, have not been much more than shouting. I would say that certainly in the time span that Mr. Dinerstein has called our attention to—in five or ten years—the likelihood of a Pan-African coalition is not very great with respect to South Africa. Perhaps more closely on the agenda would be an attitude toward Angola, and it seems to me there are very real opportunities not for a Pan-African approach to Angola, but for certain of the African countries, such as Algeria or the Congo, serving as jump-off places for an African attack on Portuguese hegemony in the area.

On the whole, though I am not an African expert, I would say most Africanists with whom I have consulted in recent years would tend to put far down on the timetable possibilities for Pan-Africanism in the next five- or ten-year period.

*Kintner:* I would agree that the political organization of Africa under anybody's aegis is going to be very difficult in this period of time. But I do think that the strategic problem Professor Dinerstein presented is a very critical one. If you take a look at the consequences of the developments in the Congo, there are several pictures that can be drawn. The first is that the man there who sided somewhat with European interests has been pretty well eliminated politically. Concurrently, the Angolan rebellion against the Portuguese interests is actually being mounted around the Leopoldville area. The impact of the settlement in the Congo will probably have disastrous effects on the Federation of Rhodesia, and this may take three, four, or five years for it all to wind out, with, of course, the settlement in Kenya taking place in the next six months or so.

The goal on which African nationalists are all united is the elimination of South Africa. There is also evidence that inside South Africa the dissident elements there have already established some communication links with the Communist Bloc. This, if it could be maneuvered and manipulated, would be, from the Communist point of view, one of the great prizes of the Cold War, because it could feed also on many of our unsolved domestic problems. I think we should not dismiss this as a final conjecture. I think it is politically feasible that some such coalition can be developed. Because of the policies now being pursued in South Africa, it is a natural, from the Communist point of view and, I believe, we have to keep our eyes focused on this possibility.

*Wolfers:* I would like to add that our difficulties may be even greater, because, instead of an African coalition, what is possible is a new African attempt to use the UN and to build up an African-controlled UN force to fight the remaining colonialist, racist, and other governments in South Africa; in which case we would be again in the difficult position we were in Katanga. If we don't go in with them, if we don't back the UN, this is an opportunity for the Soviets. If we go in, then we play into the hands of the black racialists in Africa, and the consequences may be very serious too.

*Meyer:* It doesn't require political confederation to mount a substantial guerrilla warfare effort, which might well play quite a role in South Africa. The Algerians have proved that they are quite successful at this sort of operation. Nor does it require confederation to mount some sort of a subversion effort, and the Egyptians have proved that they are quite good at this.*

---

* Dr. Trager later pointed to two additional areas which could involve indirect confrontation:

*Trager:* The most recent investigation of the Finnish situation indicates that Kekkonen, the President, and his heir apparent, his son, are playing a fairly close Soviet game. His son is already identified with the left group in the dominant party. Kekkonen believes he can handle the Soviets. The

## Foreign Aid

*Cerny:* I would like to consider now the last set of statements for the second issue of our panel. We haven't discussed the problem of our various aid programs, and the two statements which we will discuss have been chosen from the papers of Professors Kertesz and Meyer. They point, I believe, to different aspects of our aid program.

> We should help first of all nations fighting for survival along the perimeter of the Communist Bloc. Second, we should help politically reliable states. Reliability does not mean blind obedience to the US—these states need not follow American policy through thick and thin—but a long-range political reliability should be an absolute requirement.
>
> It is not a good policy to become a benefactor of any country without considering its political attitude. Experience indicates that a "no-strings-attached" policy might not be ultimate wisdom.
>
> Stephen Kertesz

> The United States would do well to continue the policies begun by the present Administration in Washington to abandon post-World War II aid program strategies based on the "good guys" and "bad guys" approach.
>
> Albert Meyer

*Kertesz:* I believe that one of the American characteristics in foreign policy is that we are inclined to transfer domestic political experiences to the international sphere; and I think Americans like to help each other. This is one of the old frontier traditions.

There is a general American inclination to help all needy people anywhere on the globe. This kind of inclination belongs

---

Soviets have actually formulated a purge list of those Social Democrats and Agrarians whom they will not have in the Finnish Government, and by and large there is a kind of absorption by seepage in Finland.

In Afghanistan some $515 million of Soviet aid has gone to that country, including the rather unusual item of at least a hundred million dollars of that $515 million in grants, direct grants. It is the case that in Afghanistan today American machinery is being used and demonstrated by Soviet technicians. Afghanistan is a country in which we have already invested about $183 million as against the $515 million of the Soviets; and the ruling family believes that they, too, can handle the Soviet incursion in this area.

Although I have no pat solution, I suggest that unless we seriously consider these kinds of confrontation, where there will be the possibility of seepage behind the Iron Curtain, Soviet gains will loom even larger than they already appear.

to the category of Christian charity. We should give humanitarian help wherever we can; however, this is not part of our
national policy. This quotation refers to economic aid and technical assistance which is something else, and in this category
I think consideration of national interests should prevail.

First of all, we should help the countries on the edge of the
Communist Bloc. This is part of the containment policy. We
have to create balanced social and economic conditions in order
to contain communism. Such policy was more successful in
Western Europe—the European Recovery Program and similar
programs. In other areas of the globe the difficulties are of
much greater magnitude. For example, in Southeast Asia, Laos
is a prize example of our difficulties in this matter. However,
here geography determines our policy, and we have to deal with
the difficulties, whatever their nature might be.

Communist expansion, however, is of global nature. Communist subversion can easily leap-frog any geographic boundaries. Therefore, we should help reliable governments everywhere. "Reliable" in this context would mean two things. We
should help governments in countries whose foreign policy is
compatible with long-range Western expectations and goals.
Now, these will be the "good guys," if I understand Professor
Meyer correctly.

But, this "good-guy business" also contains a domestic requirement: that we should help governments which are able to use
American aid in a purposeful way; that the institutional development in certain countries, in the receiving countries, should
give promise for the future. This might involve domestic reforms in the tax system, agrarian reforms, long-range planning,
and so on. These are questions which will be dealt with, I believe,
by the subsequent panel.

*Meyer:* I made the point in my paper that the two preceding
administrations in Washington—one Democratic, one Republican—seemed, to me, to have drawn their intellectual sustenance
for their basic economic policy toward the Middle East from
the Hollywood cowboy movies of the 1920's and 1930's, namely
they had tended to divide the Middle East into the "good guys"
and the "bad guys," and to help out those countries who were
made up essentially of "good guys." In other words, anything
that the Turks and Israelis did during the immediate postwar
years seemed to have been worthy of our support, and anything
the Arabs did was probably wrong. And I believe that the new

Administration has, with the passage of time and with a fresh look at it, taken a different view toward this. The new aid program to Egypt, I believe, is a case in point. This represents, I believe, an effort to come to terms with the new facts of life as they are now developing in the Middle East.

I don't really believe that there is any difference between my approach to this and that of Professor Kertesz, despite the seem- ing disagreement in the quotes as made.

*Wolfers:* I merely suggest that what the two gentlemen have said does contradict—they contradict each other. I am confused. Are we giving aid to anybody who needs help, or are we giving aid only to the "good guys?" I think neither of the two state- ments is quite correct. But, the two gentlemen seem to take different views on the subject.

*Kertesz:* I think that the aid policy is changing to some extent. From time to time we take into consideration the need of certain areas on the globe, and the different administrations, I think, determine in a different way the qualifications of the "good guy" —who is a "good guy" from the American point of view. So, certainly it is true that there is a changing pattern.

What is our national interest? Should we help the Arab countries, or should we help Israel? This is, I think, a question of opinion, as the national interest is determined differently. It depends on governmental policy which kind of country should be really strengthened and what would be our major interest.

*Meyer:* I think we are coming belatedly to the recognition that perhaps our national interest could be served by helping both sides, under these circumstances, in the Middle East.

*Kintner:* One of the fine differences between our aid program and that of the opposition is that they have established some kind of priority in their effort. We need to do much the same thing.

For example, the Soviets have concentrated about 800 million dollars of aid in Indonesia, the third largest resource area in the world, which they regard as a prime target. We cannot, in my opinion, follow a scatter approach—either "good guys" or "bad guys"—but we have to relate it to some sort of comprehensive strategy. Unless we do that, we will be subject to the type of blackmail we have been subjected to all over the world. I feel that we have not yet found the formula for using aid in support of our national interest, which was presumably the goal of this and prior administrations. Unless we do so, foreign aid will continue to be ineffective in many areas of the globe, and the US effort will do very little to contribute toward the creation of a type of world which we would like to live in.

## Western Unity

*Cerny:* I would like now to turn to the third issue of our second panel, the issue of "Western Unity," with a quote from Professor Kissinger:

> The creation of the Atlantic Community, which should be the next step forward in Western policy, depends to a considerable extent on the ability to define what Atlantic relationships should be like five or ten years from now. Many technical questions which now divide the Alliance can be dealt with only in a larger framework . . . (But) to base policy on the expectation that historical evolution will do our job for us is to abdicate statesmanship. A policy which sees in two great national leaders an obstacle rather than an opportunity runs the risk of making us prisoners of events. The time for creative action is at a moment when old patterns are disintegrating, not some time in a future which is problematical and when the challenges may prove quite different.*
>
> Henry Kissinger

*Kissinger:* Let me begin first with the end of the statement. I read quite frequently that we are led by dynamic, young, forward-looking people, while the Europeans are led by old men, and that, therefore, the problem we have is to be able to outlive these short-sighted old men who live in the past in order to give us a chance to vindicate the vision of the future of our leadership. I disagree with these notions. I disagree with the mentality that it reveals. I disagree with it for the following reasons.

First, we have to ask ourselves, what is it that we really want from Europe? What do we mean by "Atlantic Community?" Do we mean by Atlantic Community that we want governments in Europe that will carry out any policy devised in Washington? Or do we mean that we want a Europe which is a partner, which may not necessarily agree, and in which we are willing to admit at least the theoretical possibility of our fallibility, so that, perhaps it is not always foreordained that the policies as devised by us are the correct policies?

It is in our interest to have a powerful and united Europe, because its natural interests are likely to run parallel to ours.

---

\* The statement is taken from Mr. Kissinger's article, "Strains on the Alliance," *Foreign Affairs*, January, 1963.

If it is true that the interests of the Atlantic Community are as indivisible as we never tire of asserting, then I fail to understand why we are so excited about the assertions of independence in Europe. If the interests are really so indivisible, we ought to be able to give practical expression to this in policies, so that the right they claim to independent action will not be exercised. If, on the other hand, there does in fact appear a difference of interest between us and Europe, then our attempt to deprive them of the physical ability of independent action is not only going to produce a sense of impotence, but will lead to various forms of neutralist policies.

We are now in the very curious position in Europe where there are many people who loudly affirm Atlantic unity and in the name of Atlantic unity conduct a very soft policy. We have others who are accused of dividing the Atlantic Community, and who in times of crisis nevertheless have turned out to be rather staunch allies.

General de Gaulle has a rather irritating way of stating his propositions, particularly irritating to people who are used to producing policy documents in committees. But, if I look at the behavior of the European governments during the Cuban crisis, I am not sure that say General de Gaulle was more inimical to Atlantic unity when the chips were down, even though he reserves the right not to maintain Atlantic unity, than, say, Prime Minister Fanfani, who loudly protests his devotion to Atlantic unity, but who, when the chips were down, expressed himself with an ambiguity which gave him the possibility at least of not being on the losing side.

We have to separate agreement with every assertion that comes from Washington from the long-term trends. What worries me very much is the policy of out-waiting those in Europe —and this is particularly true of Chancellor Adenauer—who have painfully, practically single-handedly, over thirteen years moved the Federal Republic into Western relationships, and of suddenly asserting that these are the people that are really blocking progress. What worries me is that, in order to have our way on what are essentially technical questions related to propositions of command and control, we have tended to ally ourselves with all those forces in Europe who have opposed Atlantic relationships, who have opposed defense policies, and many of whom support us now, not because they agree with us, not because they are in favor of Atlantic partnership, but because this is the most convenient way to attack the governments that established the Atlantic partnership. This is not without irony. The question of common control of nuclear weapons is a technical thing that could be solved. But it is simply not true to say that there can be no differences in opinion between us and Europe, if we look at the events over the past years, not only outside of Europe, not only in Suez and the Congo and many other places, but even inside Europe.

In a recent article a very high official said that we are in favor of full partnership, except in nuclear matters, where we happen to have the preponderance, and where our views had to prevail; and, of course, the European views will be taken very seriously, except, of course in disarmament, since we happen to be the country that will bear the brunt of a nuclear war. We said last year that, regardless of what the French and the Germans thought, we would proceed in negotiations on Berlin, because we had the full responsibility. If this is our political policy, then we cannot blame the Europeans for wanting to assert some of their responsibility.

The methods that have been chosen in individual cases have been sometimes equally unfortunate on both sides. One doesn't have to subscribe to everything that President de Gaulle or Chancellor Adenauer is saying or doing in order to address oneself to that fundamental question: what kind of a Europe do we want?

If we are really serious about phrases like the "Dumbbell Theory" and "a strong, united Europe," we have to accept the fact that such an entity must have the right to reserve its own independent judgment. It would be disquieting in the extreme if we asserted as a postulate of American policy that the only countries we can be allied with and that can be true partners are those that are too weak to vindicate their own point of view.

*Kertesz:* What worries me is that diplomatic methods and procedures used in inter-Atlantic relations, irrespective of the issues involved, have been greatly deteriorating in the last few years, and particularly in the last few months.

The Cuban affair in October 1962 was handled extremely well by the present Administration. But I am wondering whether we should use similar methods with our allies. I was amused to listen to the discussion about the open conflicts and debates between China and Russia as a fine thing from our point of view. But, is it useful to apply similar methods in our relations with

Britain, France, and Germany? This is what we have been doing lately.

For example, in the Skybolt decision was it necessary to make a unilateral statement in the United States on this matter? Would it not have been better to agree with the British *in camera caritatis* according to the methods of bilateral diplomacy, and to present the whole issue as a great triumph for Western diplomacy, as a much better military defense, thus allowing Macmillan to return with a diplomatic triumph, instead of that which caused him, in my mind, absolutely unnecessary difficulties? This is just one example. But we could multiply the examples in Franco-American or in American-German relations.

*Kissinger:* I think that the method of procedure with Britain was brutal and had the consequence of bringing home to the British a sense of their impotence. This is apart now from the technical validity of the judgments that were made about Skybolt and Polaris. If we had such a good case about Skybolt and Polaris, and if the interests of the Allies are as indivisible as we claim them to be, and if we assume that our allies are not less intelligent than we, then it ought not to be beyond the wit of man to convince reasonable allies that the course we are trying to pursue is the wise course and is in the common interest. And it should not be necessary for us to proceed through a series of accomplished facts, and, what is worse, sometimes through a series of subterfuges in which we pretend to meet Allied demands by means of technical devices which, if they don't see through them now, they must see through within a year or two.

*Trager:* Since Western unity seems to be the last item on the agenda for Part II, I want to suggest something in addition.

If I were an Asian or an African or a Latin American friend of the United States, I think I would wince many times when subjected to discussions of the Atlantic Community, not because I am not in favor of the Atlantic Community, but because, it seems to me, that in our interest in that rather consuming subject, we tend to continue to neglect any additional short- and long-range policies for the Pacific area, or for the South Atlantic area, or for the South Pacific area.

For example, between 1950 and 1954 we consummated a series of bilateral and multilateral security treaties with the chain going down from Korea, around to Thailand, and Australia, and New Zealand—the bilaterals with Korea, Philippines, Taiwan, Japan, the multilateral of ANZUS and the multilateral of

SEATO. One additional understanding has been established with Thailand after the fiasco in Laos. Since then I find very little constructive exploration with Pacific powers—to say nothing of African states—on what may be intended for that area.

It would seem to me that, in looking ahead for the next decade, it is high time we oriented ourselves toward regarding the Pacific Basin, or the Pacific and Indian Ocean Basins, as areas for important diplomatic and strategic arrangements leading toward some kind of security policy in that area.

*Kissinger:* I would not think that policy toward other areas of the world ought to be in competition with policy toward the Atlantic area. I believe that the region where the possibility for the greatest constructive action exists is in relation to Western Europe. Here we are associated with countries of a similar state of economic development and a similar cultural background with whom we are united by history, by tradition, and by overwhelming common interests. And, if we fail in this area to establish a true community of interests, it is difficult for me to see how we will be more understanding in relation to countries about which we know so much less and where the community of interests is not nearly so obvious.

I would not, however, say that these two efforts are competitive with each other. I would argue that if we are very successful in the Atlantic area, this could serve as a magnet and as an example, particularly if it is an outgoing structure to other areas of the world.

**Atlantic or European Community?**

*Wolfers:* I think that there is another kind of competition, another kind of conflict within our policy that deserves to be emphasized at this time. We have been talking Atlantic Community very strongly in the last few months. It is growing—so to peak—the new enthusiasm for the Atlantic Community. Before that the emphasis was all on European unity, and this I don't think is accidental.

I have not shared that enthusiasm for a strong and powerful united Europe that prevailed in our official policy and in public opinion, because I thought I foresaw the danger that if Europe became really strong and united, as a United States of Europe, for instance—that we would not find that "Dumbbell" situation a very comfortable one.

If one has dealings with people who are rather obstinate and who have their own interests, the last thing one wants is that they become a bloc. The idea that it is more natural and easy to deal with a great bloc than it is to deal with two or three friends is, I think, a mistaken view. But this was our policy. We convinced Europe that we were behind them in their effort toward European integration, and this was a time when Britain was not a part of that growing bloc. Now, when the bloc was almost in sight, we push Britain to demand admission at the worst moment for the Six, at the most delicate moment of their consolidation, without any regard for what the effects would be on European integration. Then, after this was beginning to go sour, we have now decided to fight a fierce battle against one of the pillars of this Europe of the Six, or possibly against two, against de Gaulle certainly, and possibly against Adenauer, which can only have the effect of destroying what there is in the way of European unity. And we are beginning to talk quite openly and in a way in which the Europeans can't help hear it. We are speaking of: "Maybe it is better to substitute some broader union for this beginning unity of Europe." We can't have it both ways, in my opinion.

If we today begin to emphasize the Atlantic Community, as Mr. Kissinger himself does, without asking the Europeans whether on their time schedule this is what has to come now, we may destroy what we have been trying to do in Europe. De Gaulle said so the other day. But many Europeans told me last summer that this is a very bad moment to emphasize Atlantic Community with a capital "C" as a kind of substitute or alternative to the European Community, which has features of real community. This means that the British begin to be torn between the two communities, and begin to wonder whether they are wise to go into the European Community wholeheartedly. After all, there is also this other bigger community in which they can find a place; and the Germans find themselves torn between military policy connected with France versus military policy connected with the United States. This has a disintegrating effect.

I should have thought that if we want to stick by our policy of European integration, this would have been the time to tone down the need for trans-Atlantic ties and let them have their way and recognize their right to develop their own policy, always, of course, maintaining NATO as the great link between the two, and then, in the economic field, trying to see how one can manage to get along with this European economic unit, rather than trying to destroy it right away with some kind of ideal of free trade between the United States and the European Community. After all, in the economic field, the community of the Six, which we did everything to promote and to bolster, with its European institutions was built clearly on an economic compromise among the Six. The compromise, as de Gaulle has spelled it out, was based on the concept that there must be room in this economic union for all the products of French agriculture. They must have a privilege over all outsiders. Well, this was obviously harmful to American agriculture, as it was perfectly destructive for the rights of Commonwealth countries to have preference in England. The British gave in to this. They knew this was the price they had to pay.

For the sake of our Europe, for the Europe we were trying to build, have we at any time shown an inclination to sacrifice the interests of our poultry farmers in order to give France what she demanded of her associates? Certainly not. This shows that there are very profound conflicts of interest, and they exist also in the nuclear field, between, as we now call it, a "very narrow parochial European view" and an American view. But, this "parochial European view" is the view that we have been fostering, because European self-identification, as a community of its own, as a separate entity to which nations would be willing even to sacrifice their sovereignty, this new unit had to produce its own nationalism, if you like—Europeanism—and was bound to turn somewhat against the United States in order to be able to identify itself with itself.

Now we have to choose. Are we going to make the necessary sacrifices and adjustments to allow this Europe to develop, or are we going to go back on our European policy and say: "Well, this doesn't seem to work; it runs against our own interests; it is harmful to the British."? Let us change over to the Atlantic Community, to an Atlantic free-trade area, to a nuclear deterrent for the Atlantic Community, rather than for Europe. If we do that, we are going to be in a very serious struggle, particularly with the French, but probably also with the Germans. We'll have all the small countries probably on our side. This is a break with the policy we have pursued consistently for the last fifteen years, which was beginning to bear fruit, and I wonder whether we are aware of the possible consequences of such a reversal of our policy.

**Kissinger:** I substantially agree with Professor Wolfers. But, I think, as far as my own personal views are concerned, I do not feel that the Atlantic Community needs to be pushed simultaneously with European integration. I agree with Professor Wolfers that the process of European integration, now that it has reached this point, should be encouraged to proceed.

I am afraid that at the present the assertions of Atlantic Community will lead to a Balkanization of Europe. The only way we can now have our way is to encourage the very European rivalries that we have been trying to combat for the first fifteen years; and I must moreover say, as I said in my paper, that I don't agree with what we are trying to accomplish. Perhaps my view is somewhat jaundiced. I don't consider it a disaster if the Europeans assume a responsibility for their nuclear defense. I would say that we have to be very careful that we do not use the banner of Atlantic Community to wreck whatever has been accomplished in the way of European integration, a new slogan around which all the people in Europe that have fought all the battles of the last fifteen years against our policies can rally.

**Kintner:** I believe that the Atlantic Community concept is the one which we must use all of our energies to bring into realization. I think that the issues have been well expressed by Dr. Wolfers and Dr. Kissinger, that the current policies we are pursuing to achieve that goal are actually counter-productive and may turn out to be divisive. I believe that our policies, however, are shaped by other factors, by our vision of the future, and particularly by our vision of our future relations with the Soviet Union. If ever a genuine *détente* is to be achieved with the Soviet Union, in my opinion it will take a long time. But, there seems to be a school of thought that *détente* is feasible and possible in the near future. Many of our policies toward Europe, in my opinion, seem to be influenced by this desire. I am referring specifically to the endeavors to neutralize Europe, which, I think, can be read between the lines in various agreements that have been discussed or various policies we have advocated, leading, as the next phase, to a possibility of some nuclear stabilization or denuclearization of the European defenses, on the assumption that we can, in the very near future, achieve a general *détente* in the area of arms control. If that is the objective, and if the great gamble does not pay off, then over the course of the next ten years I can see the European Community either neutralized or fractured, and the United States in a very lonely and isolated nuclear Fortress America.

*Kertesz:* I am not sure whether European integration and the realization of Atlantic Community necessarily contradict each other. I think this is mainly a question of timing.

Western European unity, should be achieved, and then, with a united Europe we might be able to establish gradually an Atlantic Community. But, this is a very long affair. I am not sure whether the American Congress would be very cooperative, for example, if we would try to establish an Atlantic Parliament or something like that. This is a very long affair, which, I think, will be one of the targets of Western European and American diplomacy for decades to come, not only for the next ten years. I think that our diplomacy should support integration in Western Europe, but the over-all establishment of an Atlantic Community should linger in our minds as a simultaneous goal. I think that this does not contradict our policies in any other part of the globe, because if there is a strong community around the shores of the North Atlantic, this will be a center which will foster freedom and economic well-being in other regions of the world as well.

## A Question on Berlin

*Cerny:* A question from a guest is addressed to Dr. Kissinger:

"How can we deal with the Berlin problem once we enter into an age of nuclear parity with invulnerable nuclear deterrents? Will we have the military capability to protect Berlin?"

*Kissinger:* It depends what you mean by nuclear parity. In part the question of nuclear parity isn't only a physical problem, but also a psychological problem. In other words, is the other side ready to pay whatever price you are prepared to exact for the loss of Berlin?

I don't believe that there are absolutely symmetrical situations in this strategic equation. But, most importantly, I think that what protects Berlin today and what will have to protect Berlin in the future is the fear of a substantial degree of escalation. The more we get the impression that we are absolutely calculable, rational, careful, measuring our response absolutely precisely, the more we will encourage adventures in this particular area. The way to protect Berlin, it seems to me, is to convince the Soviets that this is such a neuralgic nerve for the West, that, if they touch it, there is no telling what we will do, even if what we will do is not absolutely rational by their previous calculation, and that therefore the risk is not worth it to them. If they should nevertheless start a crisis, I believe that it is very important that we take a step which is sufficiently large, that they will have to face the problem of whether they dare to defeat it, even if they have the physical ability to defeat it at that point. Therefore, I think, it is extremely unwise constantly to insist publicly on the vulnerability of Berlin. It is true, Berlin is vulnerable. But in a way it isn't much more vulnerable than Hamburg. If they want to take Berlin with conventional forces, they can do it. And regardless of what is said at NATO Council meetings, if they want to take Hamburg with conventional forces, they can do it, if they want to pay the price for it. Protection for the foreseeable future in both of these cases is not whether we can win an over-all war, or whether there is a theoretical parity. I would think that the protection is that we are facing the Soviets with risks they are unprepared to run; that problem is a little more difficult in Berlin than in other areas; but the principle is the same, and, therefore, the danger of escalation and of potentially irrational action on our part has to be one of the elements in the protection of Berlin.

*Kintner:* I would like to suggest that one of the major safeguards of Berlin is the fact that Mr. Khrushchev or his successor may not wish to liquidate the situation. It is a very useful one for him for many reasons, and if we just have steady nerves and take into account that he is going to play on this particular strength from time to time, there will not, in my opinion, be a crisis in which he will seek to liquidate Berlin, unless he wishes at the same time to engage the entire Western Alliance, which will not take place, if we follow Dr. Kissinger's advice.

*Dinerstein:* I am in agreement with the position suggested by Mr. Kissinger that we shouldn't talk publicly what we will do and won't do about the defense of Berlin. Vagueness is our best policy in public statements.

But as the years pass, and West Germany becomes more integrated with Western Europe, the Soviet Union must reduce its expectations of political gain in West Germany as a result of an assault on West Berlin. Thus, with every year that we retain West Berlin, we make it a less lucrative target for the Soviet Union.

*Kissinger:* Judgments about the political situation of any country are very risky. My judgment would be that there is no way to lose Berlin which will not have the catastrophic effect on the domestic situation of Germany, regardless of how it is integrated into Western Europe at that time. And I would add that even the people who may demand of us, when there is a crisis, that we give up Berlin and Germany, will, six months later, when it is safe, use that as a demonstration of American unreliability. I would, therefore, think that in terms of national policy, we have to make up our mind that there is no way to lose Berlin without catastrophic effects on the whole political future of Germany, regardless of where it is, in the Atlantic Community.

## A Question on Vietnam

*Cerny:* A question from a guest has been addressed to Dr. Trager:

"Isn't support of Viet Cong by China very limited; hence, does not merit major operations?" The second part: "By attacking North Vietnam, won't we actually be inviting a major war with the Chinese?"

*Trager:* In each case one has to make an estimate of how much, how far, how long. As far as we know, and our intelligence is not very profound for the Viet Cong, Peking is supporting the Viet Cong. There are Chinese armed forces just over the line of North Vietnam, which serve as supply and other kinds of aid to the Viet Cong. The rail head at Tsungchan, just over the border, is probably one of the main areas of supply from China to the Viet Cong. How much goes to the armies of Giap, I am not sure. I do know that the encadrement in Viet Minh forces is strongly supported by Chinese elements. The answer, therefore, to the first question is that there are supplies and man-power coming from China to Viet Minh and then into the Viet Cong. 28,000-30,000 members of the Viet Cong are among the estimates that we now have of its size. Also, some of the materiel that has been captured, and some of the materiel that has been used to shoot down our helicopters, is of Chinese and Russian make, and they are not the kinds of weapons that could have been captured from American supplies in Vietnam.

The second part of the question is: would we not risk a war with Peking if we attacked Hanoi or Viet Minh? I think not. In many ways I agree with what Professor Taylor was pointing to yesterday on several occasions. China, as we have heard, is in a serious crisis. It is perhaps less badly off today than it was a year ago. Pre-emptive buying of wheat in 1961-62 would have cost about $330 million. It would seem to me that it would have been worth our while to have tried to do some pre-emptive buying on wheat to further the crisis at that time in China. I believe that there are risks involved, but I was rather careful in saying that we would announce limited objectives in the first instance, and that having announced such objectives, we would diminish, I believe, the elements of a major war with Peking. I do not think that the desirability of acquiring Vietnam and possibly the south of Laos is worth the risk to Peking.

If I might take another moment on the Laotian question. Even as late as May 1962, when Viet Minh, Pathet Lao, Chinese forces, got down as far as Nam Tha, that is, on the southwestern anchor of Phong Saly Province, within a few miles of the Thai border, even at that time, when Nam Tha was taken, and thereby insured Phong Saly to the North, there was an opportunity, it seems to me, despite the bad handling of the Royal Lao forces by the Lao generals, there was an opportunity at least to save a portion of Laos, going from Luang Prabang down over to the south of Xieng Khouang and over to the seventeenth parallel. Partition, in that instance, would at least have saved most of Laos and also perhaps even more effectively, closed off the Ho Chi Minh trail. Blackmail, I say again, coming from the danger and the fear of escalation, can inhibit necessary action.

### A Question on the Formulation of Strategy

*Cerny:* Up until now we have been concerned with problems of objectives and strategy and a weighing of alternatives. There is, of course, also the problem of whether our government is properly organized to formulate strategy. Dr. Kintner has some remarks to make on this subject.

*Kinter:* May I look at the broad problem a minute? I would like to make the suggestion that apparently our strategic approach is being influenced in a way which tends to give a tremendous domination to political considerations. I'm not against that in principle because I believe that policy must always set the framework of strategy. But the peculiar problems of the present, the threat and fear of thermonuclear war,— escalation, the requirement of collective security, have made strategy almost excessively political in its content. I think our problem is complicated by the fact that our enemy has an organically related strategy whereas we in the West and in the

United States have not yet been able to develop an objective as to what our strategy should be. The three general alternatives are the roll-back—for example, the Trager thesis on Southeast Asia—active containment, or passive containment verging on accommodation. I believe that we are quivering around the latter at the present, though there are other instances, such as Berlin or the effort in Vietnam which suggest that we have still an element of active containment in our strategy. But whether we take the roll-back or active containment, both strategies are conflict strategies and they involve many of the aspects of a military war even though they may be waged with non-military methods.

Both conflict strategies have two major elements—the power on the military-technological side and the non-military. And in the United States we run into the situation that our society, particularly in the Government, divides into two groups. One is the military itself, which is essentially the conflict-oriented group and yet a group which up to the present time has paid only lip service to non-military aspects of conflict. The civilian element which is in charge of the actual active conflict sectors, either fails to recognize that we are in a conflict and hence does not wage it with great will, or often fails to see the relation between power and the non-military aspect of the conflict.

I think the first point is that national strategy requires a better integration of power in the non-military aspects, and that implementation requires a far better operational sense than we have shown. For example, in a given country we are not very good at picking the right horse or backing him when we pick him, or discarding him if he proves to be the wrong horse. Now the determination of this strategy, whatever it be, requires the fullest exploitation of experience and knowledge, the deepest examination of alternatives, and a constant reappraisal.

I would like to make two criticisms of the present trend. First, there is currently an inadequate examination of alternatives for the total strategy, as well for particular elements. I merely cite the question of whether we go into a test ban moratorium or whether we do not. I doubt very much if the alternative which Dr. Teller so persuasively suggests, namely that we must continue the tests in order to take advantage of the constantly changing, dynamically changing technology, has been examined as fully and as deeply as the possible advantages of a test moratorium.

The next issue, which I think is even more important, is the down-grading of professional military people in the determination of the national strategy. I would say that now they are about at the third or fourth level on the totem pole when it comes to making up choices—choices as to weapons, choices as to level of forces, choices as to the desirability or non-desirability of employing military force passively or actually in a given situation. I would further contend it is mostly their own fault. Service parochialism still prevents the military from forming a genuine consensus as to the nature of the strategic problems confronting them. Another aspect of the problem, however, is the advent of the distinguished civilian analysts we have here who have gained tremendous influence for one simple reason. They have done their homework on the complicated and difficult issues of defense far better than many of the professional military have. I doubt if you could find in certain areas the competence at the staff or senior command level on the intricacies of these problems which are now being decided by default in the upper echelons of the Defense Department. I think this trend is a disastrous one, because if it continues, if the professional military are euchred out of full participation in national strategy, over a time the services will not attract the caliber of men that we need to maintain the power advantage which we must have over not just ten years, but perhaps over a generation or more in order to come out victorious in the conflict between the free, open societies of the West and the totalitarian system on the other side.

# Part III

# U.S. Military Strategies

# Escalation and its Strategic Context[1]

—*HERMAN KAHN*

## Summary

*This paper analyzes some kinds of international crises and a selection of mechanisms for dealing with them. The focus is on escalation and the escalation ladder, a methodological device which provides a convenient list of the many options facing the strategist in a two-sided confrontation and facilitates the examination of the dynamics of the growth and retardation of crises.*

*In a typical escalation situation there is likely to be "a competition in risk-taking" or at least resolve. There are two basic sets of elements in the escalation situation to be considered: those related to the particular region of the ladder, and those related to the dynamics of escalation up the ladder. Accordingly, there are two basic classes of strategies that each side can use. One class of strategies makes use of features of particular rungs or regions of the escalation ladder in order to gain an advantage. The other class of strategies uses the risks or threat of escalation and eruption.*

*Studying the ladder should prod the imagination, not confine it. Most important of all, it indicates that there are many relatively continuous paths between a low-level crisis and an all-out war—a path that is not inexorable at any particular time or place, and yet one that might be traversed.*

---

## Introduction

This paper will analyze some kinds of international crises and some mechanisms for dealing with such crises. The focus will be on escalation and much of the discussion will revolve around a methodological device which will be referred to as an escalation ladder.

In the typical escalation situation there is some form of limited conflict between two sides; either side could win by increasing its efforts in some way, *provided that the other side did not match the increase.* Furthermore, in many situations it will be clear that, if the increase in effort were not matched and thus resulted in victory, the costs of the increased effort would be low in relation to the benefits of victory. It is, therefore, precisely the fear that the other side may react, indeed over-react, that is most likely to deter escalation, rather than the undesirability or cost of the escalation by itself. That is, in an escalation situation there is likely to be "a competition in risk-taking"* or at least resolve.

Two basic sets of elements are in constant interplay in the typical two-sided escalation situation. One set of elements is composed of the political, diplomatic, and military issues around the particular conflict and the level of violence and provocation at which it is fought. The other set of elements comprises the considerations raised by the possibility of escalation to various higher levels of violence and provocation or of eruptions directly to central war.

Very roughly, the degree of escalation in a crisis or war could be measured by such things as: (1) closeness to all-out war, (2) provocation, (3) precedent-breaking, (4) committal (resolve and/or recklessness) demonstrated by each antagonist, (5) damage done or being done, (6) scale, scope, or intensity of violence if the crisis includes violence, (7) threat intended or per-ceived, and so on. In practice, the correlation between the various criteria will not be unity, but it will be reasonably high. There-fore, in general, the exact criteria being used to determine the degree of escalation will not be specified. In most situations the context or the correlation between the possible criteria will be clear enough to avoid confusion.

There are many reasons why a nation might deliberately seek to escalate a crisis. Each of the criteria given above to measure the degree of escalation might also be a means or objective which one side or the other seeks. That is, one side might wish to escalate specifically to threaten the other side with all-out

* Thomas C. Schelling's phrase.

war, to provoke it, to demonstrate committal or recklessness, and so on. A nation may also escalate for prudential as well as coercive reasons: to prevent something worse from happening, to meet a problem, to prepare for likely escalations on the other side, and so on. Thus a nation might evacuate its cities simply because it wished to protect its people without necessarily thinking through or even facing the thought that by making its people less vulnerable it increases its bargaining and military power perhaps to such an extent that the other side may feel under pressure either to pre-empt or to back down. Sometimes the reasons for escalation—prudential or pressure producing—will affect the technique and consequences of the escalation, and other times they will not.

## A—A Useful Metaphor

A metaphorical tool which has been found useful in preliminary studies of escalation is the physical analogue known as an escalation ladder. The escalation ladder is a metaphor and not a theory of international relations, though it may be a fragment of such a theory. Its utility derives partly from its providing a convenient list of the many options that are available and partly from its ordering of escalatory activity in a way that facilitates examination and discussion. The escalation ladder also may be used to set a context for the discussion of escalations in terms of regions of the ladders, steps up and down the ladder, rungs of the ladder, and so forth. The ladder is particularly useful when one attempts to examine the interrelations between two basic sets of elements in any escalation situation, i.e., those related to a particular region on the ladder and those related to the dynamics of moving up and down the ladder.

Just as there are two basic sets of elements in the escalation situation—those related to the particular region of the ladder and those related to the dynamics of escalation up the ladder— so there are two basic classes of strategies that each side can use. One class of strategies makes use of features of particular rungs or regions of the escalation ladder in order to gain an advantage. The other class of strategies uses the risks or threat of escalation and eruption.*

Some mixture of the elements of both classes of strategies are combined in almost any move on either side's escalation ladder.

---

* Eruption is defined as large, sudden escalation to the top rungs of the ladder.

The first class of strategies could include strategies which deliberately try to eschew the eruption threat by having a fixed limit on how high that side will go. This limit could be kept secret—in which case one side may run some risk of a full-scale preemptive eruption by the other side—or it can be announced in advance with varying degrees of credibility and solemnity.

The second class of strategy is associated with the term "brinkmanship." (We will sometimes use the term game of "chicken" when the brinkmanship is overtly two-sided.) It includes strategies which use the risks of escalation to induce an opponent to let one keep an advantage that could be wiped out.

These preliminary remarks on two-sided escalation situations can be summarized as follows:

1) Either side can usually put enough into the particular battle to win if the other side does not respond.

2) The value of victory is usually great enough so that it would pay either side to raise its commitment enough to win the escalation *if it were certain that the other side would not counter the raise.*

3) Upper rungs of the escalation ladder are unpleasant and each side wishes to avoid them. Therefore, the risks of escalation to undetermined heights and the risks of direct "eruption" to general war are a major element in almost all decisions about escalation or de-escalation.

4) There are two basic types of strategy that each side can follow:

   a) strategies based on factors relating to particular regions of the escalation ladder or the specific situation; and

   b) strategies based on manipulation of the risks of escalation or eruption.

## B—Description of an Escalation Ladder

An "escalation ladder" is a linear arrangement of roughly increasing levels of intensity of crisis. Such a ladder exhibits a progression of steps in what amounts to, roughly speaking, an ascending order of intensity through which a given crisis may go. Any particular ladder is intended as an archetype which can serve as a pattern and context for the study of a certain class of international crisis. Specific crises in this class do not necessarily follow any step-by-step progression and they may never escalate very far, but the escalation ladder provides a useful framework for the systematic study of the possibilities—both realized and unrealized.

We will defer the detailed discussion of the value of this methodological tool and some of its pitfalls until we have defined a particular ladder and discussed each rung, merely noting here that the particular ladder described should not be taken too literally. The order of the rungs is not sacred; many people would interchange some. There is also no implication that one must inexorably go *up* the ladder. One could go down as well as up or skip steps. In short, the ladder is intended to describe only a class of situations and is useful only for the situations which are appropriate.

Specifically, the ladder is not a complete model or theory of international relations but only serves to bring to our attention possibilities and alternatives that could occur, and to present some plausible structural relations that could hold between these possibilities and alternatives. It is suggestive of the range of possibilities and alternatives rather than predictive. Studying the ladder should prod the imagination, not confine it. Most important of all, it indicates that there are many relatively continuous paths between a low-level crisis and an all-out war—a path that is not inexorable at any particular time or place and yet one that might be traversed.

The particular ladder we will use has thirty-seven rungs, and it is bordered by a pre-escalation stage labelled "Disagreement—Cold War," and a post-escalation stage called "Aftermaths." The ladder can be considered as being a scenario generator which converts subcrisis disagreements or incidents of the Cold War into some kind of aftermath—and this is indeed a fruitful way to view a crisis escalation or war.

The thirty-seven rungs of the escalation ladder we are considering have been divided into seven groups with varying numbers of rungs. These seven groups are separated from each other on the diagram by six spaces which represent (mixing metaphors) a sort of firebreak or threshold in which there is a very sharp change in the character of the escalation. A metaphor as useful as the escalation ladder would be that of an elevator with various floors. We can think of the escalation ladder, in terms of the elevators, as having seven floors, each offering a number of op-

**Table 1—AN ESCALATION LADDER**

A Generalized (or Abstract) Scenario

———————————— Aftermaths ————————————

| | |
|---|---|
| Civilian Central Wars | 37. Some Other Kind of General War<br>36. Spasm War<br>35. Countervalue Salvo<br>34. Slow-Motion Countervalue War |

(City Destruction Threshold)

| | |
|---|---|
| Military Central Wars | 33. Counterforce-with-Avoidance Attack<br>32. Constrained Disarming Attack<br>31. Slow-Motion Counterforce War<br>30. Force Reduction Salvo<br>29. Formal Declaration of War |

(Central War Threshold)

| | |
|---|---|
| Nuclear "Gunboat Diplomacy" | 28. Reciprocal Reprisals<br>27. Complete Evacuation (~95%)<br>26. Exemplary Attacks on Population<br>25. Exemplary Attacks Against Property<br>24. Exemplary Attack on Military<br>23. Demonstration Attack on Zone of Interior |

(Central Sanctuary Threshold)

| | |
|---|---|
| Bizarre Crises | 22. Evacuation (~70%)<br>21. Unusual, Provocative, and Significant Counter-measures<br>20. Local Nuclear War—Military<br>19. Declaration of Limited Nuclear War<br>18. Local Nuclear War—Exemplary |

(No-Nuclear-Use Threshold)

| | |
|---|---|
| Intense Crises | 17. "Justifiable" Counterforce Attack<br>16. Spectacular Show (Demonstration) of Force<br>15. Limited Evacuation (~20%)<br>14. Nuclear "Ultimatums"<br>13. Barely Nuclear War<br>12. Declaration of Limited Conventional War<br>11. Conventional Warlike Acts<br>10. Super-ready Status |

(Nuclear War is Unthinkable Threshold)

| | |
|---|---|
| Traditional Crises | 9. Dramatic Military Confrontations<br>8. Harassing Acts of Violence<br>7. "Legal" Harassment<br>6. Significant Mobilization<br>5. Show of Force<br>4. Hardening of Positions—Confrontation of Wills |

(Don't Rock the Boat Threshold)

| | |
|---|---|
| Subcrisis Maneuvering | 3. Congressional Resolution or Solemn Declaration<br>2. Political, Economic, and Diplomatic Gestures<br>1. Ostensible Crisis |

———————————— Disagreement—Cold War ————————————

tions of varying intensity, but still appropriate to that floor, from which the decision-makers on one side or the other may choose. This report will also discuss to some extent the threshold or firebreak phenomena.

It will be useful to start by considering a hypothetical escalation that goes through each rung in turn, though we warn again that there is nothing sacred about either the order or number of rungs, and that between rungs great efforts will be made to settle or compromise any given issue or to leave it unresolved but less threatening. In other words, there will be attempts—which may be partially or completely successful—to de-escalate. The situations summarized in the following discussion provide a great deal of the background and environment for our relations with the Soviet Union.

### Disagreement—Cold War

There is, of course, no necessity for a dispute to lead to a crisis or even bad relations: the antagonists can either have the dispute resolved by some mutually satisfactory technique, or can leave it unresolved, hoping that time will bring some sort of a decision. In fact it is perfectly possible for two nations to disagree sharply and still be polite, even friendly, to each other. However, if the disagreement takes place against the background tension that exists between the American and Soviet populations and governments, then it is more likely to escalate than if the disagreement occurred between friendly nations. There are many people in both countries who believe even without getting "on the ladder" that there is essentially nothing wrong with the world in the present situation except that the other side exists and has goals that interfere with "peace" and with legitimate acts or aspirations. There is almost a consensus on both sides that so long as the other side does not make major internal changes, regardless of what its leaders do or say, there is at least a subcrisis disagreement or even an ostensible crisis (discussed next). In such an environment, any new disagreement can result in a slow or rapid climb up the ladder. However, it is also possible that the rivalry between the USSR and the United States will reach the "agree to disagree" stage, and each side will maneuver and conspire without using the language or techniques of escalation, though these will always be in the background.

### Rung 1—Ostensible Crisis

In the ostensible crisis stage, one or both sides assert—more or less openly and explicitly—that unless the dispute is resolved in the immediate future, more rungs of the escalation ladder will be climbed. Vague or explicit threats may be made that one will go to extreme measures rather than back down. These threats are made credible by various hints as to how important the government considers the issues. There may be officially inspired newspaper stories to the effect that the chief of state takes a serious view of the matter. There may be explicit announcements or speeches by other important officials—but none of them of the bridge-burning variety, none deliberately designed to make it difficult for these same officials to back down later.

Extremist groups may be urging firm, decisive action, and there may even be newspaper headlines, but most people will not be worried. The "crisis" looks more like a "play" to them than a serious endeavor to put real pressure on the opposition. Neutrals and hysterical groups will become concerned, however. There may be pressures put on either or both sides to meet, to moderate their demands, or at least to have them mediated.

One might conjecture, for example, that, since Khrushchev's speech in 1958, the Berlin crisis has vacillated back and forth from an ostensible crisis to a real one, and that currently with the building of the Berlin Wall and the subsequent lack of serious reaction, the Berlin situation has declined again to the state of ostensible crisis, though it may not remain there.

### Rung 2—Political, Diplomatic, and Economic Gestures

If the other side does not look as though it were going to be reasonable, one can do more than drop vague hints of trouble to come; one can perform legal but unfair, unfriendly, discourteous, inequitable, or threatening acts to put pressure on an opponent —to carry unmistakable (or at least relatively clear) messages. Acts by one government to seek redress for, or prevent recurrence of, an undesired act by another government are called retortions. For example one can: (1) recall an ambassador for lengthly consultation; (2) refuse to facilitate negotiations on other issues; (3) make overtures to the other side's enemies; (4) denounce a treaty; (5) make some kind of legal or economic reprisal; (6) push resolutions in the UN against the other side; (7) replace an official in a key spot by one who is known to be "hard" or "tough"; (8) start a violent publicity campaign, indulge in mass meetings, spontaneous public demonstrations, and so on. The public may become involved—in this case the tone of castigating the "enemy" will tend to be shriller than before—or most of the accompanying communications can be made privately. The private threat creates less pressure because the side making it has revealed an unwillingness to make a public commitment. However, if the other side yields to the threat or accepts some face-saving compromise, then it hasn't lost as much prestige as it would otherwise have lost.

Political and military gestures can be part of an escalation process and still be justifiable independently of the process of escalation. The creation of the NATO Alliance, an alliance clearly designed to fight a defensive (or possibly a preventive) battle against the Soviets if need be, was a military (as well as a political and diplomatic) gesture *par excellence* to counter the Berlin blockade and the Communist *coup* in Czechoslovakia. Yet it could also be justified as a reaction to postwar technology and the existence of two superpowers.

### Rung 3—Congressional Resolution or Solemn Declaration

A political action which in some way goes further towards demonstrating one's resolve, although it may not be directly hostile, is a formal resolution passed by Congress or a solemn declaration by the President, Premier, or other high authority. Such a resolution or proclamation may be a simple notice to other nations of one's policy in a certain geographical area, such as the Monroe Doctrine, or it may deliberately avoid precise geographical limitations to deter enemy action in a wider area. An example of the second type is the Congressional Resolution of January 28, 1955, authorizing in advance any military measures the President might take outside Formosa proper and the Pescadores, in order to defend Formosa.

Such proclamations or resolutions can be used as a warning to the enemy not to climb further up the escalation ladder, at least in that area. They may be thought of as a pre-emptive or preventive escalation which tries to forestall escalation by the opponent.

### Threshold I—(Don't Rock the Boat)

In a thermonuclear balance of terror, both nations will be reluctant to start a crisis which could escalate, perhaps inadvertently, possibly even going beyond control and erupting into an all-out war. This is particularly true if each nation feels that the other has a large degree of commitment to the issue. In that case, both nations will be willing to escalate to some extent before backing down and it is more than possible that even if one nation or the other finally wins, it will have risked too much or too little. This victory may even be Pyrrhic in comparison to the costs incurred. There is therefore a tendency not to let crises start—a pressure not to rock the nuclear boat.

### Rung 4—Hardening of Positions—Confrontation of Wills

The real crisis is characterized by the fact that the antagonists attempt to increase the credibility of their demands by "bridge-burning" acts. There may even be a deliberate increase of the stakes, a joining together of other issues—again with the deliberate purpose of making it harder for the other side to believe that it can make one back down. Often, concomitant with this hardening of positions, there are angry outbursts in the press against the other side, bellicose speeches by prominent men, including the chief of state, and speculation on possible military measures that will be implemented—if necessary—to make the other side desist from its aims or regret its acts.

### Rung 5—Show of Force

As a crisis intensifies one side or the other may hint or even make clear that violence is not unthinkable. Airplanes or ships may be moved around, reserves mobilized, provocative exercises held. By indicating that one not only has the means with which to indulge in violence, but is also preparing to do so, an attempt is made to frighten the enemy while simultaneously mobilizing one's moral and physical resources. There are various ways of showing force: direct or indirect, silent or noisy. A direct show of force might consist of massing troops in a certain area, placing naval units in a certain sea, evicting diplomatic representatives, etc. An indirect show of force might be an increase in the draft call, the test firing of missiles, or the conduct of maneuvers. All these shows of force may be silent; or they may be accompanied by a press campaign and official speeches in which it is specifically stressed that the "enemy's" behavior or the need to rectify injustice has "forced us to do what we are doing."

As part of a show of force, practice evacuations for either cadres or population can be ordered, or a limited evacuation for particular cities can be tested. Each side can accompany its demonstrations with public statements about the strategic balance of terror. These can be designed to influence one's own side, one's allies, neutrals, or the opposition. Khrushchev, for example, often points out the totally disastrous effects of all-out war and the impossibility of limited war. Lately he has even emphasized the notion of mutual annihilation, though this emphasis may not be very good internal political propaganda. We, on our side, point out the enormous superiority we have in weapons. We might amplify these remarks by making public relatively detailed calculations on how the United States could conduct a controlled counterforce campaign.

### Rung 6—Significant Mobilization

The accompaniment of a show of force by a modest mobilization not only increases one's strength, but also indicates a willingness to call on more force or even to accelerate the arms race, if necessary. This phase of the escalation would begin with the traditional cancellation of leaves and discharges of military personnel and the calling in of special forces. If these moves are followed by a general mobilization they may be accompanied by a governmental explanation why such measures are needed. It will be shown that one's own security or vital national interests are threatened by the enemy to such a point that only a show of fighting strength—or preparations for actual fighting can save the situation. Generally speaking, the present and the past mood of the "public" in both the Soviet Union and the United States is such that these measures, if ordered, would not need long-winded explanations or preconditioning of the population. It is likely to be taken for granted that such steps are needed. In addition to calling on military manpower reserves, one might fail to phase out obsolete equipment, cancel previously announced cuts in arms, announce increases in the budget, increase conscription, or deploy one's forces on a wartime footing.

The next step might be to have cadres and transportation agencies take modest but serious preparatory measures to move people, and to make further preparations in rural areas to feed, receive, and protect evacuees from cities. These last measures can be made to appear threatening or they can be presented as routine safety measures taken without much thought about their use as a pressure tactic. It is hard to decide in advance which image would be more frightening to the opponent. All such measures could be accompanied by publicity, official statements, and speeches, varying according to how bellicose or reasonable one wishes to appear. As always, private communications— either direct or through intermediaries—can play an important role. One might also arrange deliberate leaks.

### Rung 7—"Legal" Harassment

In addition to perpetrating "internal" acts whose major purpose is to show committal, anger or preparation, one can harass the opponent's prestige, property, or nationals "legally." For example, one can embargo the shipment of goods to a certain country, or one could even actuate a "peaceful" blockade. This could be done outright or under the guise of being something else. For example, the Soviets can deny access by rail transportation to West Berlin under the pretext that the railroads are out of order. One could also interfere with shipping, claiming that public health or safety measures require it. One could put vessels in port and force them to stay there, perhaps, by enforcing arbitrary health or safety regulations. One might confiscate bank deposits or other property of the opposing government or its nationals. One can arrest or expel on trumped-up charges some of the other side's nationals who are within one's own borders.

If done on any scale at all, such acts would be described as legal harassment rather than as economic or political gestures since they are very hostile and will be regarded as being more provocative than a gesture.

### Rung 8—Harassing Acts of Violence

If the crisis is still not resolved, acts of violence or other incidents designed to harass, confuse, exhaust, violate, discredit, frighten, and otherwise harm, weaken, or demoralize the opponent or his allies and friends may be manufactured. Bombs may be dropped by unauthorized or anonymous planes; enemy nationals within one's border can be arrested and charged with real or fancied crimes; embassies may be stoned or raided; soldiers guarding the border may be shot. There may be kidnapping or assassination of important, or (more likely) unimportant personalities, or the limited use of para-military actions such as guerrilla warfare, piracy, sabotage, terror, ambushes, border raids, and other terror tactics. Reconnaissance probing operations or other intelligence activities may be increased. There may even be overflights or other invasions of sovereignty. Harassing acts can also be verbal—either abusive or threatening in nature.

### Rung 9—Dramatic Military Confrontations

Tension can build up further, and there may be limited but dramatic military confrontations, either local (as, for example, at the Brandenburg Gate) or global. Such confrontations are direct tests of nerve, committal, resolve, and recklessness. They are also dramatic enough to make all the participants and observers take note of what has happened. Because it seems so obvious that they can blow up and because such incidents have traditionally caused wars, many people think of them as being closer to the edge of all-out war than, in fact, they are. Under contemporary conditions of a relatively firm balance of terror, it is hard to believe that a war will erupt directly from a frontier incident, though the uncertainties are such that the possibility cannot be completely disregarded. However, the main purpose of such confrontations, in addition to showing the resolve mentioned above, is indeed to indicate clearly that reasonably large acts of violence are possible, that the unthinkable all-out war is becoming thinkable—even possible.

The existing permanent alert is an almost continual global confrontation; therefore, a case may be made that this is pre-escalation (i.e., subcrisis disagreement—Cold War). Generally, this is so. However, if an increase occurs the situation changes. For example, American bases overseas and American targets on the American mainland are at all times zeroed in by Soviet missiles, and vice versa, but this activity can be increased and made more visible. Moreover, the military confrontation can be conspicuously accompanied by various forms of political warfare. In particular, under modern conditions either side could vividly point out to the other side's population or to its allies the totally destructive character of thermonuclear war. It can now be stressed that nobody will survive and that there is no alternative to peace, with the clear implication that, unless the madmen on the other side come to their senses, all will be lost. Alternatively, one can reassure one's own side by pointing out that the other side is not mad, and will therefore back down.

## Threshold II—(Nuclear War is Unthinkable)

Exactly where this threshold would occur is somewhat arbitrary and probably very dependent on the specific course of events, but at some point the "nuclear incredulity"* that all of us share may be sharply decreased, if not eliminated. The feeling of safety may seem less sure, and the unreal and hypothetical nuclear stockpiles may suddenly become more real and less hypothetical. This change will not come all at once, and may not be extreme, but it may occur to a large enough degree so that a certain percentage of the population and most of the decision-makers seriously begin to envisage the possibility of a nuclear war actually occurring.

### Rung 10—Super-ready Status

A ready status may be partial or total. The present handling of SAC is an instance of a partial-ready status. It may be regarded more as a routine precaution than as the highest point that escalation has reached in the tension between the US and the USSR. However, this tension is a necessary political background for partial-ready status; it has come about by accumulation—ten years or so ago a great deal of criticism would have been leveled against the idea of keeping forces with ready triggers, but now there is hardly any (at least in the United States). However, even our routine-ready status creates problems with allies and in the United Nations. A *complete* super-ready status would, of course, involve very much more. In particular, it would automatically involve dangerous or costly actions. If it did not, we would be doing these things normally. Strategic forces may be dispersed, leaves cancelled, preventive and routine maintenance halted, training deferred, every possible piece of equipment and unit put in a ready status, and limited war forces deployed. All these measures are expensive to carry out, involve an increase in the probability of inadvertent war, interfere with normal training, and possibly produce other political and military repercussions. One is now saying clearly, "I would not do all of these dangerous and expensive things unless I were willing

* Raymond Aron's phrase.

to go pretty far, perhaps to the limit. Clearly you had better reconsider your estimate of my resolve." The super-ready status might be accompanied by limited spoofing or jamming or other acts which tend to degrade the opponent's defensive capability so that he will be less able to retaliate after a surprise attack. While at this stage these acts may not be carried so far as to make a great difference, they still demonstrate one's own resolve and also tend to weaken the resolve of the other side precisely because they are so dangerous. Such preliminary spoofing and jamming are methods of bluntly asking the other side to make a choice among compromise, a dangerous continuation of the crisis, or immediate escalation to an all-out war.

### Rung 11—Conventional Warlike Acts

The stage has now been set for some kind of organized military violence. It may simply be large-scale border raids such as occurred between the Japanese and the Soviets in 1939 (involving thousands of soldiers), a Trieste-type occupation of disputed territory, or a large-scale "police action" as in Korea. If such a war is fought with any intensity, both sides will kill each other's soldiers at great effort but will not use their more "efficient" or "quality" weapons—the nuclear, bacteriological, or chemical weapons. Paradoxically, the more "useful"—in the narrow military sense—these weapons are, the less likely they are to be used.

### Rung 12—Declaration of Limited Conventional War

As will be discussed later, most Western strategists currently favor waging limited wars with conventional weapons, believing that the use of nuclear weapons is likely either to result in escalation into all-out war or, almost as bad, to set precedents that would both accelerate the USSR-US arms race and make escalation into all-out war from a limited nuclear war more likely. Moreover, even the limited use in nuclear weapons is likely to create pressures either for unsafeguarded disarmament or for the acquisition of nuclear weapons by many nations—both situations to be guarded against.

More important yet, if it were possible to limit a war to conventional weapons, our superior industrial capacity and probably superior logistic capability would be likely to give us a decisive advantage in the long run.

It might therefore be in our interest to reply to major Soviet provocations and hostile acts with a declaration of limited conventional war. This would be an attempt to achieve one or both of the following objectives:

　　a) It would be a clear-cut, unilateral announcement of "no first use," giving the enemy an incentive to reciprocate.

　　b) It could be used to try to limit the conventional war geographically in a manner considered most favorable by us.

In addition such a declaration would have the characteristics and results enumerated under Rung 29 (Formal Declaration of War).

One important effect of the conventional war could be a large-scale mobilization, major increase in military budget, and various kinds of crash programs—particularly in the area of civil defense and ground troops.

### Rung 13—Barely Nuclear War

It may occur during the conventional warlike act (Rung 11) or the super-ready status (Rung 10) that a small number of nuclear weapons are used unintentionally; i.e., accidentally or unauthorizedly, or that one of the antagonists tries to give the impression that the use was clearly unintentional. There are at least two possible reasons for such a deception. (1) The mere fact that an accident might occur indicates clearly to the other side that the situation is dangerous, while the fact that the event was considered to be unauthorized or accidental decreases the likelihood of retaliation or further escalation. (This, of course, is a two-edged sword that might frighten one's own side, but this depends on details of the balance of military power and the relative control that each side has over its internal decision-making and political structures.) (2) One side may have some particularly important and vulnerable installations which the other side would like to destroy: for example, centralized command and control headquarters, a particularly important strategic base, a warning center, or the like. The second side might go ahead and destroy these important installations with some weapons that were "accidentally," or "unauthorizedly," launched. The offending side could offer to punish the guilty individuals, give some sort of indemnification, or permit an apposite reprisal by the other side. In this second kind of barely nuclear war the purpose of using weapons is exactly the opposite of the symbolic or communications use. Here one side is actually using the weapons as a source of blast and thermal energy to destroy something on the other side but attempts to disguise this act as accidental or inadvertent so that the other side will not consider this a true escalation to nuclear conflict.

### Rung 14—Nuclear "Ultimatums"

Whether or not there is a conventional or barely nuclear war, the crisis could enter a stage of such increased intensity that the state of what Raymond Aron called "nuclear incredulity" is not weakened but vanishes. Such a crisis might be termed "intense." It could occur when one side or the other is seriously considering the possibility of a central war and has communicated this fact convincingly to its opponent. Presumably most crises will have been settled before this stage, since every rung of the ladder climbed so far has increased the pressure on both sides to settle. But it is also possible that the exertion of pressure will simply provoke counterpressures. In any case, we wish to illustrate how such a situation might escalate.

At this point, the decision-makers are no longer thinking, "Neither side wants war, so the other side must back down," or even, "The current tense situation is obviously accident-prone. The other side must feel this pressure and is therefore likely to back down." Now they are *announcing*, "Unless *you* back down, *we* will go to war"—a quite different position, or sometimes, "One of us has to be reasonable before this crisis blows up, and it won't be me." Hopefully, no crisis will ever reach this stage.

One outstanding element of the intense crisis stage is the ultimatum (or quasi-ultimatum) which may be explicit or implicit. This ultimatum forces the side to which it is addressed to think in terms of real nuclear war. It shatters the illusion that unthinkable means impossible. In any case, with or without a quasi-ultimatum, the populations of both sides now fear war as an actuality and not as a hypothetical and unreal nightmare. Accordingly, people begin to leave target areas. One might define an intense crisis operationally as that time when 10 or 20 per cent of the population of New York City or Moscow has left the city because of fear of war.

The Berlin situation has not come close to this rung of the escalation ladder because the "ultimatums" which Khrushchev made were too vague and cautious to generate a feeling of intensity.

### Rung 15—Limited Evacuation (Approximately 20%)

Either the Soviet Union or the United States or both may actually carry out a partial official evacuation of their cities. There is no doubt that, barring an intense crisis, evacuation would meet with very great resistance from part of the population. However, the evacuation order itself might generate this sense of crisis. The effect of the evacuation on the resolve of the people and the decision-makers might be very different. Even if the decision-makers have ordered the evacuation for prudential rather than bargaining reasons, they may still feel they can play a stronger hand if most of the population is, or soon can be moved to a place of relative safety. The people, on the other hand, may become both frightened and resentful. Depending on the details of the crisis, the success of the evacuation, and the appearance of the protective arrangements, the people may very likely be an influence for moderation, accommodation, or even appeasement. Of course, during the most intense moments of crisis, the public will have little influence on national actions. However, later popular reaction, if there is a de-escalation, may be an all-important influence on the ability of the country to meet future crises or even the threat of future crises.

### Rung 16—Spectacular Show (Demonstration) of Force

A spectacular show or demonstration of force would involve actually using major weapons in a way that does little or no damage or destruction but does look menacing, reckless, and determined. Its purpose is either to punish the enemy for a previous or anticipated act (with the intention of establishing a precedent that would deter later provocations), or to intensify the fear of war to the point where the enemy will become so frightened that he must back down. The relatively harmless detonation of a big weapon high over enemy territory or the delivery of leaflets by ICBM's would fall in this category. Demonstration of force is intended to be as harmless, yet as arresting, as a guard's shooting into the air and shouting, "Halt, or I'll shoot," or a naval patrol's shot across the bow of a suspicious vessel. Such a dramatic and publicly provocative gesture would undoubtedly bring about mixed reactions both in decision-makers and various publics. In the initiating country large numbers of people would be violently opposed to this type of action regardless of who had manufactured or escalated the underlying crisis—and the resulting disunity might be dangerous. In the threatened nation some would equally strongly demand concessions, others reprisals, regardless of all other factors. There are obvious asymmetries among the United States, Soviet Union, China, France, and so on, both in their ability to initiate and carry through and to resist this tactic.

### Rung 17—"Justifiable" Counterforce Attacks

There are many situations which allow "legal" or extralegal local counterforce attacks in peacetime. In such cases the concept of legality is irrelevant, or enough of a case has been made for committing a given act so that the question of legality or illegality is controversial, or at least is made to seem controversial. For example, it is often possible for one side actually to attack, harm, or otherwise forcibly degrade the capabilities of the other side in a significant or dramatic fashion without actually crossing clear-cut jurisdictional lines. One might shoot down a plane outside one's borders but claim that the plane was within one's borders. Or one could destroy a submarine and claim that it had made threatening maneuvers. Clandestine or covert acts of sabotage by unacknowledged agents could make a significant difference in the performance of the opponent's defensive system and could also be extralegal attacks.

The Soviets could launch a missile against an isolated Allied or US base or aircraft carrier, claiming that a U-2 had flown from it. They might bomb the radar we are said to have in Turkey on the grounds that it was used for spying. The Soviets could even arrange to have a US missile stationed in Europe shot at themselves, and then proceed to destroy some of our missiles in return, on the grounds that though these missiles were dangerous, we refused to operate them safely and insisted on keeping them on accident-prone alert status.

A "justifiable" attack would be sufficiently specialized and have sufficient cause to look like a limited reasonable response to an intolerable provocation, and yet it might significantly or even disastrously degrade the military capability, prestige, or morale of the defender.

### Threshold III—(No-Nuclear-Use Convention)

Up to this point, while the illusion of nuclear incredulity may have been shattered, nuclear weapons have not really been used in a serious way, i.e., we are assuming that even if the barely nuclear war had occurred, it would have been accepted as an accident and even a nuclear show of force would be thought of as nuclear sword-rattling rather than nuclear use. In some ways the nuclear-nonnuclear threshold is the most widely recognized threshold of all. Many in the United States feel that we are unnecessarily hampering ourselves by denying our forces the right to use these weapons as a normal part of the arsenal. Others feel that the use of such weapons may cause so great a revulsion against the United States or so great an acceptance of the nuclear weapon as "conventional" that either the subsequent political problems or arms race will likely more than negate any military advantages unless these are very great indeed. Still others maintain that while we may be able to fight "progress" for a time, eventually nuclear weapons will spread, and if we divert a spread to a time when a very large number of nations can obtain nuclear weapons easily and quickly, we are likely to have an explosive diffusion to many nations within a very short period of time rather than a slow diffusion which gives the national society a chance to adjust to the new weapons. Whatever one's attitudes towards this question, they are likely to be firm and emotional. In any case everybody recognizes that, for practical purposes, this threshold exists and as a matter of actual policy is not likely to be crossed by the United States at least except in the most dire circumstances.

### Rung 18—Local Nuclear War—Exemplary

Because of the above threshold, the actual open use of nuclear weapons to destroy or damage, even if done on a very small scale, is very likely to escalate.

As has already been mentioned, most analysts who have seriously studied these problems are firmly against the US initiating the use of nuclear weapons under almost any circumstances. They believe that since the weapons exist, we should procure, deploy, and maintain them, unless and until better arrangements can be worked out; but these analysts do not believe that they should be used except as a last resort in a vital situation. However, it is important to inquire, "How would we use nuclear weapons if they are going to be used?" or even more important, "How would we react to someone else's use of nuclear weapons?" Almost every analyst is now agreed that the first use of nuclear weapons—even if used against military targets—is likely to be less for the purpose of destroying the other side's military forces or to handicap its operations physically than for redress, warning, bargaining, punitive, fining, or deterrence purposes. For example, one side can drop a nuclear bomb or two in order to show the other side that, unless it backs down or accepts a reasonable compromise, more bombs are likely to follow. Such a use could easily occur in the following limited war situation:

One side is losing conventionally and decides to use nuclear weapons. It doesn't use them to damage the other side in a way that really hurts, because that could easily cause escalation to get out of control. But it might drop two bombs on two bridges the other side is using. This may not kill a large number of soldiers. It may not even hurt the logistics very much, but it unmistakably tells the enemy something such as, "Look, I've dropped two bombs; having dropped two I may be willing to drop twenty. In other words, I'm crazy or determined, or both. I've demonstrated it. Don't you want to listen to reason?" Such an act might cause escalation. It might produce the desired results. Or the other side might reply in a tit-for-tat reaction to show that it has not been deterred and then (since it actually is deterred) consider compromising the conventional war rather than fully exploiting its earlier advantage.

The basic reason for not using nuclear weapons may not be the one that most people assume: that such action would immediately and inevitably erupt into an all-out war. Under many circumstances this would be unlikely. After all, both sides are very fearful of all-out nuclear war, and if one side uses a nuclear weapon, both sides are likely to be frightened and relatively anxious to back down. However, a major problem that results from the use of a nuclear weapon is that precedents are set. Particularly if the use of nuclear weapons works in the first war, somebody will try it in a second war. By the third war it may escalate to a large or all-out nuclear exchange. Another objection is that even one use of a nuclear weapon might stimulate the arms race. If anyone uses nuclear weapons, every country may feel it has to get them. Thus such an action would set precedents that are very important.

Or the opposite effect might be produced. Even the single use of a nuclear weapon could cause an almost hysterical reaction that could lead to a unilateral or even multilateral partial disarmament—a disarmament which, because of its precipitousness and lack of safeguards and control, might be more dangerous than losing the battle that the use of nuclear weapons was supposed to win.

The use of nuclear weapons could probably be made even more frightening if, instead of being launched locally, the weapons were launched strategically, though against local targets. By using the same weapons systems that would be used in a general war, one would communicate to the enemy a willingness to disregard precedents, and a likely willingness to go further. It also makes it more difficult to see how the local conflict can be terminated or stalemated without excessive destruction. Conversely, if one wished to diminish somewhat the possibility of escalation, one would be careful to use only local launchers of nuclear weapons, such as the relatively short-range missiles owned by the army.

### Rung 19—Declaration of Limited Nuclear War

At this point the decision-makers would have the option of a formal declaration of limited nuclear war. Such a formal step might have several advantages. For one, the declaration itself could set exact limits on the type of nuclear action that the declarer intends to initiate and that he is prepared to countenance from the enemy without escalating further himself. In this way eruption to all-out war might be made less likely.

For another, it gives some legal form and sanction to acts of war that are regarded with abhorrence by many people at home, in the enemy country, and (perhaps even more) in some neutral and allied countries. The declaration could be used to explain the enemy acts which had forced one to take such a weighty step and might at the same time announce the conditions under which the declarer would be prepared to de-escalate.

In addition, the declaration would have the ten characteristics and results enumerated in the discussion of Rung 29 (Formal Declaration of War).

### Rung 20—Local Nuclear War—Military

It is also possible that nuclear weapons will be used in a local situation for traditional military purposes—for defense, denial, destruction of opponent's capability, and so on—and that the scale and targeting would be dictated by such military considerations. Indeed, past NATO planning has envisaged the immediate use of hundreds of nuclear weapons even in reply to a conventional attack by the Soviets. Such wars seem to many military strategists to be less desirable than either compromise or immediate escalation to a higher rung of the ladder. However, we detect among analysts an almost dogmatic unwillingness to consider this possibility seriously; and while we will go along with the current fashion and treat the possibility very cursorily, the increasing actual or potential availability of a varied inventory of small, inexpensive, nuclear weapons (including such esoteric devices as Davy Crockett and neutron bombs) is likely to raise the discussion again.

### Rung 21—Unusual, Provocative, and Significant Countermeasures

One side can stage threatening maneuvers that also have the effect of shifting the balance of power by sharply increasing the other side's vulnerability to surprise attack. For example, our warning system has not been built to deal with peacetime spoofing and jamming if the Soviets institute these practices on a scale so large that we could no longer tell the difference between small training missions and actual attacks. Thus by making the possibility of a successful surprise attack much greater, one might succeed in looking much more threatening. One is, in fact, more threatening. It is quite possible that such spoofing and jamming will take the place of the classical ultimatum or quasi-ultimatum. However, one can make the spoofing and jamming even more frightening by delivering a quasi-ultimatum or full-fledged ultimatum with it. What can be done about these tactics? For example, if the Soviets used aerial jamming against our early warning lines or BMEWS system, there is little we could do to shoot their planes down, even if we wished. It is currently impossible for us to defend these lines actively. Moreover, the Soviets might even be willing to use shipboard jammers since this would be somewhat less expensive and in some ways more satisfactory. They could even become very aggressive and station a half-dozen ships 50 to 180 miles off our shores and jam our contiguous radar cover. In this case even our hard missile bases might suddenly become vulnerable to surprise attack, since this jamming might put the radars out of commission, and Soviet bombers could sneak through.

The Soviets could also increase the pressure on us by stationing missile-launching submarines or ships off the coasts at the same time, by sabotaging communications, command and control or

other warning systems, or by staging additional threatening or
confusing maneuvers.

### Rung 22—Evacuation (Approximately 70%)

At this point the situation is getting very close to large-scale
war. It may now seem advisable to evacuate the maximum convenient number of people from the cities. This would probably
be between two-thirds and three-fourths of the population.
By leaving one-quarter to one-third behind, all the important industries, communications, transportation facilities, and
other things that the government might want to continue could
be operated. There would be, of course, an enormous loss of GNP,
but most of it would be in industries or businesses which are
ultimately expendable. In other words, we would have a loss
in the rate of accumulation of wealth and in our current standard
of living, but the evacuation might not affect national defense
preparations very severely.

### Threshold IV—(Central Sanctuary)

The chosen firebreak for the present Administration has been
far lower on the ladder—the nuclear threshold. As one Administration spokesman has said,* "In efforts to limit violence there
is and will remain an important distinction, a 'firebreak' if you
like . . . a recognizable, qualitative distinction that both com-
batants can recognize and agree upon if they want to. Beyond
the nuclear threshold there is no other obvious 'firebreak'—all
the way up the destructive spectrum of large-scale thermonuclear
war." The key word in this argument is "obvious." Attacks
which avoid the zone of interior of the enemy also have a
salient threshold: one sanctified by convention, and ratified by
emotion, one which may reasonably be considered at least one of
the most important of the transnuclear thresholds—because the
world, for any combatant, may be divided unequivocally into
categories of "Homeland" and "not-Homeland." To recognize
the distinction does not deny the important nexus of relations
between a major power and its allies and dependencies, still more
its overseas forces. But the distinction between the homeland of
a nation and its allies, or even its overseas bases and forces, is
perhaps as salient as "nuclear"-"non-nuclear." Indeed the line
between "H" and "not-H," between the external world and a

* A. C. Enthoven, Deputy Assistant Secretary of Defense (Comptroller).

nation itself, is the legal *frontier*—a concept strongly delineated, salient, and sanctified by convention. Indeed as a firebreak it may even be stronger than the threshold between conventional and nuclear war, since it is older and invested far more with emotion and prestige. Of course, as in the case of nuclear-non-nuclear, one can blur the difference, and many in the West are urging this to obliterate distinction between Natonians and Americans. The very awkwardness of the word reveals how far it is from being sanctified. It is reasonably apparent that in the next decade the credibility of a nation inviting certain annihilation for the sake of an alliance will tend to diminish to the vanishing point—however repugnant and dishonorable this development may now seem. But the credibility of a nation running the risk of the various restrained attacks we have suggested in this paper may or may not so diminish—depending on how likely the decision-maker is to consider the observance of "rules." All of the above remarks hold true with even greater force for the Soviet Union.

### Rung 23—Demonstration Attack on Zone of Interior

We have already discussed the very limited use of nuclear weapons in a local war or in a demonstration of force to warn the enemy to consider backing down. The same kind of warning might be delivered even more effectively—and dangerously—by a "harmless" attack on the other side's country which, however, did do recognizable and unmistakable physical damage. For example, the Soviets could explode a small weapon in an uninhabited part of the Rocky Mountains or in the great American desert. Or they could explode a weapon over one or more American cities high enough to break windows, but not to do much real damage. Or they could do a relatively small amount of damage to military, industrial, or agrarian targets (small as compared to an all-out war or to the three attacks considered below).

### Rung 24—Exemplary Counterforce Attack

The next step might be to begin actually destroying portions of the other side's weapons systems, but in a relatively careful way so as not to cause much collateral damage. The simplest thing, of course, is to start shooting down equipment which is outside the opponent's borders as has already been discussed. The ideal objects are airplanes, ships, and submarines. One can imagine this going on for quite a while without actually touching off an all-out war. But it might touch off an immediate escalation. One could also attack warning stations much more openly than was considered in the previous rung, or even destroy isolated SAC bomber bases or missile bases. These attacks could be made purely to exert psychological pressure, or to reduce the defender's military capability significantly by finding leverage targets. We could, for example, attack the Soviet staging bases in the far north. This would seriously degrade their ability to use medium bombers although it would be a small attack compared to other possibilities. Whether or not we could get away with this would depend a great deal upon the strategic equation, but there are circumstances when this kind of attack might appear safer than all-out war or compromise and accommodation.

### Rung 25—Exemplary Attacks Against Property

The next step would obviously be to increase the level of these limited strategic attacks. It is hard to decide at this point what the next rung would really be. One possibility might be a limited attack on cities, presumably after warning had been delivered and the cities evacuated. The purpose here would be to destroy property, not people.

In a modern, wealthy, industrial society, the destruction of material wealth does not jeopardize the survival of the community. It is more like a fine. If no one is killed, "it is only money." In fact, it is conceivable that the controlled reprisal concept could reach the point where, rather than actually launching the missiles, one simply insisted that the other side donate a fixed sum of money to the UN or pay some other kind of ransom. In the controlled reprisal, the objective is less to gain the advantage from the ransom than it is to punish the side being coerced.

Rather than cities, the controlled reprisal could involve the destruction of relatively "sanitary-looking" targets such as expensive industrial installations—particularly ones which have a semi-military character, such as gaseous diffusion plants, and which, therefore, are legitimate military objectives. Alternatively, it could involve attacks with bacteriological or chemical weapons against food or crops. It could even involve incapacitating, but not overwhelming, attacks against population.

## Rung 26—Exemplary Attacks on Population

This used to be the highest rung short of all-out war on early versions of the ladder, and indeed, in any crisis of the early sixties it would probably be much higher than we put it here, but as the balance of terror becomes more stable, this kind of attack becomes more plausible. Such an attack could take the much-discussed form of city-trading, fallout attacks on population, or even biological or bacteriological attacks (possibly partially disguised or anonymous in order to limit the provocation to some extent). It is difficult to believe that such attacks could occur without touching off some kind of all-out war; but if the balance of terror is sufficiently stable, and governments are in control of themselves, even this could occur without the eruption to spasm or other central war.

## Rung 27—Complete Evacuation (Approximately 95%)

At this point, one is on the verge of, or actually in, a large war. If at all possible, each side is likely to evacuate its cities almost completely, leaving five or ten per cent of the population behind to operate essential facilities. This, of course, would cause enormous political, social, economic, and psychological problems. It is possible that in the United States some form of martial law would have to be declared, and some rights under the Constitution suspended.

A great danger in complete evacuation is that it might touch off an attack by the other side. One must therefore have some confidence in one's Type I Deterrence or in the prudence of the opponent before carrying through such an operation. However, with all its dangers, evacuation may be safer than an all-out attack and the almost certain reprisal that such an attack would bring. The main advantage of evacuation as a deterrent (threat) is that it is more credible than the mere threat of attack without evacuation and, at the same time, it mitigates the effects of the war which has now become likely. Although there might have been a relatively large-scale evacuation before this in which the majority of the people had been evacuated, even if we left only 30 per cent of the population in a city, the Soviets would still have in the neighborhood of 20 million obvious hostages. If we reduced these 20 million hostages to two, three, or four million, then we might be able to put our potential losses into the classic arenas of World War I and World War II. This might indicate quite convincingly that we are willing to go to war if the other side is unwilling to compromise. We are, of course, still not eager to go to war. Nobody wants to lose three or four million people, and nobody likes to lose so many empty cities.

## Rung 28—Reciprocal Reprisals

If there should be a more or less continual tit-for-tat exchange—whether of the symbolic, exemplary, or more destructive kind—we are in a war of almost pure resolve. As discussed later, this situation has many analogies with a labor strike situation or the game of "chicken" played by juvenile delinquents. Many strategists believe that reciprocal reprisal wars of resolve against resolve may be one of the standard tactics of the future when the balance of terror has become firm and absolute. Such wars, depending on their length, are at or across the next threshold.

## Threshold V—(Central War)

In a certain sense, this is the traditional threshold between war and peace. The fact that there are many thresholds beneath this in which violence could be initiated changes the situation only partly. These new thresholds have been created by the new conditions of the balance of terror (though such things have occurred in past history). To some extent the old "all-out war" or peace threshold still remains (the term "all-out," of course, should have the connotation of all-out effort rather than indiscriminate and unrestrained).

There are, of course, many different kinds of central wars and there are thresholds between the different kinds. For example, there is an important firebreak between city-sparing and city-destroying types of campaigns. It is quite possible that, if a nation were engaged in a city-sparing campaign, it would never find the threshold to a city-targeting campaign very hard to cross. On the other hand, unless the decision-makers had been doing a good deal of strategic thinking they might not have the same sense of there being a firebreak between the two kinds of campaigns. This could be true even though the McNamara no-city doctrine has made this notion relatively well known.

## Rung 29—Formal Declaration of War

A possibility almost completely overlooked in modern defense planning, but one which is perhaps less improbable than many, is that we will respond to some provocation with explicit rather than implicit or quasi-ultimatums, involving timetables, or even with a formal declaration of war. Such an ultimatum or declaration of war might not be followed immediately by a strategic strike, but, as in World War II, it might be followed by a "phony-war" period, in which there is some limited tactical or strategic harassment but no all-out actions. The reason for this possibility is, of course, quite clear. During the tense period described by the medium rungs on the ladder, both sides presumably put their forces into a state of super-preparation for defense and reprisal. For example, both the United States and the Soviet Union might deploy their missile-carrying submarines, disperse their strategic bomber forces to the approximately 500 airfields that are available, and tighten up the alert status of their ground-based missiles. An effective disarming attack would then become very difficult. Just how difficult depends on details which cannot be discussed here. However, given the strength of the balance of terror and the general fear on both sides, it would not be at all unlikely that both nations would be so cautious at this point that, even though they had been provoked to the limit, they would not wish to attack. In many circumstances a formal declaration of war might be an acceptable substitute.

The formal declaration of war could cause either escalation or de-escalation. In both cases it makes clear that the side issuing the declaration has no immediate intentions of attacking (since if it had such intentions, it would simply attack and not alert its opponent*) but would like some time to talk, consider, prepare, or just wait, intending to keep open the issue being argued during that time. Such a declaration would have the following characteristics and results:

1) It is a solemn, formal announcement that will look very significant.

2) The declaration gives information—both symbolically and through content and interpretation.

3) It prevents de-escalation to an ordinary crisis, threatens further (eventual) escalation, and therefore keeps the

---

* Unless it is a double-double-cross as in the Minsk-Pinsk joke.

issue that was the *casus belli* open. It therefore prevents even implicit "ratification" or acceptance of any *fait accompli*.

4) It may, however, look temporizing—i.e., it may have some aspects of de-escalation, but not much in most situations (usual alternative in ordinary crisis is talk—not missile launchings).

5) It removes inhibition against the use of force and coercion (controlled reprisals and ultimatums), such as described on later (and also earlier) rungs of the ladder.

6) It puts pressures on allies and some neutrals to cooperate.

7) It has many legal effects (blockade, internment, confiscation, control of travel, etc.).

8) It releases energies. One could easily envisage the United States increasing its defense budget to $250 billion a year.

9) It mobilizes people and prevents internal opposition.

10) It forces the other side to recognize explicitly that it is going to have to write a formal peace treaty, etc.

Actually the Declaration of War is just one of a whole series of legal and quasi-legal measures (such as a congressional resolution) useful in escalation situations. The exact escalating character of these measures, including the declaration of war, depends, very sensitively, on specific conditions and tactics.

### Rung 30—Force Reduction Salvo

This is an attack, constrained or not, in which the attacker attempts to destroy a significant but small portion of the defender's force in a single strike. It is especially likely to be used against weak links or high-leverage targets. If the attacker destroys enough of the defender's force we call it a disarming attack (see Rungs 32 and 33).

It is common now to predict that at some point in the late sixties or the early seventies the United States and the Soviet Union will have such adequately protected strategic forces that it will be physically impossible to destroy them or degrade their operation very much by any conceivable attack. It is important to keep in mind that this is "invulnerability by assumption." Many a seemingly invulnerable system (e.g., Singapore) has proved under test to be startlingly weak. An intelligent attacker will study the defender's system for weak points and may be able to find them even though the defender is unaware of these weak spots. In fact, the more confident the defender is, the more likely that such weak spots will remain undetected or develop through apathy or incompetence.

### Rung 31—Slow-Motion Counterforce War

This is a campaign (which might follow a Force Reduction Salvo) in which each side attempts attrition of the other side's weapons systems over time. One can conceive of a slow-motion counterforce war lasting for weeks or months in which Polaris submarines are hunted down, hidden missiles found, land bases dug up, and so on. While this possibility is almost unstudied, as forces become less vulnerable it would seem to become most important. One would expect most wars in the future to start with a series of force reduction salvos which may or may not be constrained by various requirements for reducing (or increasing) collateral damage to civilians.

### Rung 32—Constrained Disarming Attack

Once one has opened up the possibility of trans-attack and post-attack deterrence, many types of attacks may be considered. One of the most important (under current conditions) could be called the constrained disarming attack. One of the major arguments for the counterforce-with-avoidance attack (discussed next) is that not much is lost in the narrow military calculations and, the possibility that post-attack blackmail would work is increased enormously. In the constrained disarming attack one may follow the same path even farther. Tremendous military disadvantages might be accepted in order to improve the possibilities of successful negotiation to terminate the war on an acceptable basis. In a constrained disarming attack the attacker would try to destroy a significant portion of the defender's first-strike forces and even some of his second-strike forces but would carefully avoid civilian targets as much as possible. This would make it very disadvantageous for the defender to launch a counter-strike since the defender's damaged forces might be able to do only a limited amount of damage even with a countervalue strike, while the attacker might be able to deliver an annihilating blow in reprisal with his withheld and regrouped forces. The defender is also under pressure to negotiate since it is now probable that the attacker would continue with an all-out strike on the rest of the second- and first-strike forces if the defender were not reasonable. If one side had the kind of strategic superiority that some have claimed for the United States, then it could make its case more convincing by giving the other side very detailed calculations about what the war would look like simultaneously with the attack, rather than the kind of vague, general hints of strategic superiority that are appropriate for the lower rungs. It is difficult to believe that the opposing side would not be willing to look at these calculations. Of course, the other side might launch some missiles out of reflex or anger or because this is what its war plans call for, and the attacking side might have to be willing to accept such damage if it wanted to avoid further escalation. Thus, it might turn out that if things were settled at this point, the initiating side might suffer many more casualties than the defending side, even though the initiating side both seized and kept a military advantage. It is also possible that the initiating side would insist on a final counter-reprisal before agreeing to a cease-fire. In fact, the tit-tat-tit sequence may be as stable as a tit-tat sequence.[2]

A scenario for such a constrained disarming attack might go as follows: because of some incident or crisis, or as part of a planned aggression, the Soviets might threaten a massive attack on Europe and refuse to back down, even though we went through the temporizing measures of evacuating our cities, alerting SAC, and augmenting our air defense. The Soviets might believe we would be deterred from attacking them. They might have calculated that even if we launched an all-out attack against their strategic forces, they could still destroy 50 to 100 of our partially emptied cities in a retaliatory blow. Suppose the Soviets then launched a large conventional attack on Europe and we fought back with augmented conventional forces. There would then be two reasonable possibilities: (1) we hold, or (2) we impede the Soviet advance but do not halt it. Assume the latter possibility and carry the scenario to the point at which a military debacle for the United States and its allies seems imminent. At this point we would have a number of choices: we could use nuclear weapons in the combat zone and hope that the resulting bomb damage to civilians (either from the enemy's weapons or our own) would not be too great and that it would weapons or our own) would not be too great, and that it would not escalate into all-out war or strategic bombing in Europe; accept defeat. Suppose now that we are not deterred by the

Soviet threat to destroy 50 to 100 of our empty cities. We might believe the studies indicating that we could recover from such a debacle in about ten years. Perhaps we would argue that, if the Soviets are going to behave this way now, their behavior will be much worse after they have added Europe's resources to their own, and that this is as good a time as any to stop them—delay will only make them stronger and us weaker. Perhaps we would not stop to read studies and make calculations, but simply act out of a sense of obligation and outrage. Whatever the reason, suppose we decide to attack the Soviet Union.

While we would be reluctantly forced to risk those "empty" cities, we would in no sense be eager to lose them. In such circumstances we might most sensibly limit our actions in a very careful and controlled fashion. We might strike missile bases in Siberia, Soviet bomber bases away from cities, identified submarines at sea, and in general any target that does not involve the destruction of important non-military assets. We could take particular care to avoid civilian targets. If the Soviets happened to have a bomber base in a city such as Leningrad or Moscow, we might deliberately refrain from attacking it, even though this self-restraint might result in our suffering more damage in the long run. Alternatively, if we did attack such a base, we would probably use low-yield kiloton bombs rather than multi-megaton bombs, and thus greatly limit the collateral damage to the neighboring city. We might simultaneously point out to the Soviets * that since we had damaged their strategic forces in our strike, there were now no possible ways in which they could win the war. We could then point out that our only war aim was the removal of their threat against Europe. We would ask, "Do you really prefer to start a city exchange rather than accept our peace terms? Is it the right time for you to start trading cities when we have such a large military superiority?"

Under the conditions of the early sixties,** even if our first strike were only moderately successful, it would very likely be successful enough in these hypothetical circumstances for

* More likely this would have been pointed out as part of a previous ultimatum while we were still lower down on the ladder, or "unofficially" in inspired stories about US strategy, or by deliberate private leaks and conversations.

**This does not imply that conditions in the late sixties or early seventies will necessarily be startlingly different, only that it is an open question. It seems possible but not inevitable that much of the current advantage in a USSR-US confrontation of having the first strike may be eliminated or greatly decreased in the next decade.

the Soviets to have little rational choice. If they were to continue the war, they would be beaten. The only rational thing for them to do at this point would be to sign a truce. It is, of course, implausible that human beings would be this rational, even in the case of the relatively self-controlled (one step backward, two steps forward) Soviets. But, even if they struck back and hostilities continued for a short time, they might be willing to limit their counterblow to counterforce targets. They might do this because it would be clear that if the war ended in stalemate, it would be much less costly to both sides if each were careful about how it had used its strategic forces. Care on their part would be made more probable by our own care and the limited objectives which we had proclaimed. Moreover, even if events should go wrong and the war should degenerate into a city-busting phase after 10 or 20 hours, the reluctant attacker might have gone a great distance in achieving his "limited-damage" objective. After 10 or 20 hours of war much of the defender's forces would have been destroyed, used up in the controlled phase of the war, or degraded in effectiveness because of impairment of important parts of his system.

The pressures upon our European allies to limit a general war would be even stronger than the pressure upon the United States. In most wars, because of proximity, it would be much easier for the Soviets to destroy Europe than to destroy the United States. It might even be sensible in some cases for us to encourage the Europeans to declare some degree of armed or even unarmed neutrality, depending on our tactics and strategy and their capabilities. Because of the development of the ICBM and the Polaris submarine, and because of vulnerability and warning considerations and the difficulty of maintaining secrecy in operations, European-based forces will not be as valuable military assets to the NATO Alliance as they were in the past. For this reason, a European declaration of neutrality or military disengagement on the open-city * model might in some circumstances be militarily acceptable even though costly. There is also a possible bonus in some degree of European "abstention." To the extent that the Europeans can preserve some independent military or political bargaining power, they may represent a third force which, after the United States and Soviets have attacked each other's military forces, may be able to exert an arbitration-type pressure on both sides to be reasonable

---

* In international law, it is not legal to attack a city which is not being defended locally and not being used to aid the military forces directly.

in their negotiations. In a curious way the existence of an armed China might have the same result. Neither the Soviet Union nor the United States is likely to relish the thought that, if they knock each other out, the Chinese Communists will reap the benefits.

### Rung 33—Counterforce-With-Avoidance Attack

This attack differs from the constrained disarming attack by being less scrupulous about completely avoiding any possible collateral damage to cities, and about possibly even deliberately sparing a certain amount of second-strike force. Here one mounts a much larger counterforce attack, trying to pick up everything that doesn't involve major collateral damage to civilian targets. In the case of a Soviet attack on the United States, this would include such things as hitting Tucson (a city of 250,000 population) which is completely ringed with Titans, but it would probably mean avoiding Brooklyn Navy Yard, Norfolk Navy Yard, and the Pentagon in Washington. If they did hit these targets or any SAC bases near very large cities, they could drop 20 kilotons, rather than 20 megatons on these military targets in order to keep down the collateral destruction. After such an attack one can almost assume a counterattack, but one can still try to use threats of further escalation into countervalue wars to limit the defender's response.

One possible attraction of counterforce warfare at either Rung 30 or 31 is that it looks like traditional warfare. It is the military fighting against the military, rather than the military destroying helpless civilians. It fits in with the "just war" doctrine.[3]

This analogy can be stretched too far because, if one side wins the counterforce warfare, it will not necessarily be true that the defeated side will allow itself to be occupied by military forces or even that the victor will have the military forces to occupy the defeated country. It is possible that the victor will have to threaten or actually destroy some of the defeated side's cities in order to force acknowledgement of defeat. Therefore, the counterforce attack is, in a sense, a preliminary to the bombardment of cities. In addition, the possibility of controlled reprisal is always present. However, it is also true that, as in previous wars, one might expect the defeated side to surrender when it can no longer protect itself, or if it still has some ability to inflict damage on the superior side, to accept a compromise peace.

### Threshold VI—(City Destruction)

At this point the warring nations would find themselves at another threshold. In a speech at Ann Arbor on June 16, 1962, Defense Secretary Robert McNamara said that "principal military objectives, in the event of a nuclear war stemming from a major attack on the Alliance should be the destruction of the enemy's military forces, not of his civilian population."

While there is a lot to be said for this principle, both on strictly military and on humanitarian grounds, in actual practice the boundaries are a little fuzzy. We have seen under Rung 33 how it may be necessary to destroy some cities in a counterforce action, if major counterforce targets are practically inseparable from those cities.

Nevertheless, if the escalation proceeded slowly up the ladder without skipping too many of the central war rungs up to this point, it would seem a momentous step to give the order to destroy cities, whether for their military potential, or to intimidate the enemy so that he backs down at last, or to increase his recuperation problems.

However, if eruption to the top rungs occurred rapidly from some lower rungs, this threshold would be less easy to perceive. Khrushchev has repeatedly declared that he does not perceive it. This could be true, or else it could be a useful posture feigned to discourage disarming attacks on the Soviet Union.

Partly because of such difficulties, McNamara modified his earlier statement somewhat in giving evidence before the Senate Armed Services Committee on the Defense Budget for Fiscal 1964:

> In talking about global nuclear war, the Soviet leaders always say that they would strike at the entire complex of our military power including government and production centers, meaning our cities. If they were to do so, we would, of course, have no alternative but to retaliate in kind. But we have no way of knowing whether they would actually do so. It would certainly be in their interest as well as ours to try to limit the terrible consequences of a nuclear exchange. By building into our forces a flexible capability, we at least eliminate the prospect that we could strike back in only one way, namely, against the entire Soviet target system including their cities. Such a prospect would give

the Soviet Union no incentive to withhold attack against our cities in a first strike. We want to give them a better alternative. Whether they would accept it in the crisis of a global nuclear war, no one can say. Considering what is at stake, we believe it is worth the additional effort on our part to have this option.

In planning our second-strike force, we have provided—a capability to destroy virtually all of the "soft" and "semi-hard" military targets in the Soviet Union and a large number of their fully hardened missile sites, with an additional capability in the form of a protected force to be employed or held in reserve for use against urban and industrial areas.

There is still a strong implication that this reserve force would only be used against urban and industrial areas if the Soviet Union went beyond this threshold first.

### Rung 34—Slow-Motion Countervalue War

In this attack (which could accompany or follow a slow-motion counterforce war), each side destroys something other than military targets on the other side (presumably cities or property), in a tit-for-tat fashion. We sometimes refer to this as a War of Resolve because each side is attempting to force the other side to back down and there is a naked matching of resolve against resolve. If the exchanges are few in number we call them reciprocal reprisals (see Rung 28).

### Rung 35—Countervalue Salvo

It is, of course, always possible if one is fighting a slow-motion counterforce or slow-motion countervalue war or other kind of war, that one side will fire a large number of missiles at targets other than military systems, either because of inadvertent or deliberate eruption.

### Rung 36—Spasm War

The figurative word, spasm, is deliberately chosen to describe the usual image of central war in which there is only a "go-ahead" order; all the buttons are pressed, and the decision-makers and their staffs go home—they have done their job. The attitude is typified by Dulles's remark that the State Department will be closed down as soon as a central war starts; i.e., there is no possibility of any negotiation or settlement until one side

is completely destroyed or both sides have used up all their
weapons. A spasm war may, of course, occur, but to the extent
that there is any art of war possible in the thermonuclear age,
the attempt must be to try to get the losing side to cease fire
before he has used up his weapons.

## Rung 37—Some Other Kind of General War

It is also possible to have many other kinds of "all-out" but
controlled as well as all-out uncontrolled wars. (The term "all-
out" is put in quotes to emphasize that this is not necessarily
a spasm war in which each side would strike indiscriminately
against the other's cities and military bases. The "all-out" refers
to the level of effort and not to whether or not there is discrimination in targeting or negotiation.) In a "rational," "all-out"
but controlled war, military action would be accompanied by
threats and promises, and military operations themselves would
be restricted to those that contribute to attaining victory (an
acceptable or desirable peace treaty) or to limiting the damage
the enemy can do. The situation is more or less summarized by
the following table:

### Table 2—Various Thermonuclear Attacks

| | |
|---|---|
| 1. Countervalue Devastation | |
| 2. Mixed Counterforce-Countervalue | Classical |
| 3. Augmented Counterforce | |
| 4. Unmodified Counterforce | |
| 5. Counterforce with Avoidance | Current Doctrine |
| 6. Constrained Disarming | |
| 7. Countervalue Salvo | |
| 8. Slow-Motion Countervalue | |
| 9. Slow-Motion Counterforce | Avant Garde |
| 10. Force Reduction Salvo | |
| 11. Exemplary or Reprisal | |
| 12. Show of Force or Demonstration | |
| 13. Covert or Anonymous | |
| 14. Special Instrumental | |
| 15. Environmental Counterforce | Also to be |
| 16. Environmental Countervalue | Considered |
| 17. Anti-Recuperation | |
| 18. Blackmail Enhancing | |

Until the late fifties only attacks 1-3 were considered in "responsible" public discussion. Today there is much discussion of attacks 4-5. If the balance of terror gets more stable we can expect the discussion to shift to attacks 6-12. It is, however, important also to keep in mind the possibility of attacks 13-18. We discuss these latter attacks briefly, since attacks 1-12 have already been considered in the discussion of the previous rungs.

### Covert or Anonymous Attack

There are many reasons why a nation might want to launch covert or anonymous attacks. We have already referred to one possibility in the discussion of Symbolic Attacks. Another possibility would be a relatively safe way of carrying out any of the first three Special Instrumental Attacks. In addition the known possessor of a covert capability is likely to find his ability to deter provocation enhanced since it is obvious that he can be more reckless with his attacks. Indeed, the possessor of a covert attack capability has a rather effective reprisal against being covertly attacked himself. He can launch a covert reprisal attack on mere suspicion. If he is right in his choice of victims, the original attacker will have been punished and will assume that he has been found out. If the victim is innocent, he is as likely as not to assume that he is simply the second victim of the original attacker.

### Special Instrumental

This category is supposed to denote a situation in which some special problem is being presented to the potential attacker who feels that he can solve this problem by destroying people or objects with strategic weapons—or at least that this "solution" is his best or least undesirable alternative. One far-fetched but simple example would be the extinction of a mad leader who has access to strategic capabilities and whom one wanted to kill before he could do irrevocable harm. More generally one might wish to launch special attacks whose purpose was to change the character of or overthrow the opposing regime. For example, one could attack the administrative centers, troops and police used to keep order, key decision-makers, warehouses, communications, transportation, and so on. Some of the symbolic attacks already described could also be used to create pressures that might change the regime, and these pressures might be enhanced by the destruction of selected targets. Or one could imagine the existence of a political opposition to the regime (perhaps created or strengthened by the pressures resulting from previous escalations or even by the current escalation) and a very limited attack being launched to help this opposition group carry through a coup d'état by eliminating or weakening selected parts of the existing regime and its organs of government and internal coercion. This could be done with or without the cooperation of the rebels. It might even be done to influence the outcome of an ongoing rebellion or civil war.

**Environmental Counterforce**

The next attack is the environmental counterforce. Megaton weapons are comparable to gross forces of nature such as earthquakes and hurricanes and, paradoxically, the effects of the use of such weapons, beyond being extremely violent and widespread, can also be very subtle and hard to predict. The effects of nuclear weapons include blast, thermal and electromagnetic radiation, ground shock, debris, dust, and ionization—any one of which may affect people and equipment. Indeed, the effects of multimegaton weapons are so powerful and complex that even if they do not destroy a system by blast, they may damage it by more subtle effects or change the environment in such fashion that the system will be temporarily or permanently inoperable.

For the first time in the history of war we face what might be called the *problem of the post-attack environment*—the real danger that both the short- and long-range environment in which we operate our weapons systems and conduct our recuperation will be adversely affected both in expected and unexpected ways.

Following is an example of how an effect which has not been predicted and thus not adequately prepared for could cause an unexpected operational failure. A black-out of high-frequency communications occurred once during the testing of some high-altitude weapons over the Pacific Ocean. News stories mentioned that about three thousand square miles were blacked out. Any system that depended on high-frequency communication which was not corrected for this effect, might well run into serious and possibly disabling trouble in the first few minutes of war.*

## Environmental Countervalue

The next attack we might wish to study would be environmental attacks against people and property. Such attacks could be made to enhance such effects as long-term radiation (cobalt bombs), short-term radiation, area fires, tidal waves, the covering of large areas by blast by a pattern bombing technique, and so on. There has been much discussion of such attacks in popular and semi-popular literature, and many people think of them as either the most likely or the only form of attack.

At first sight, such environmental countervalue attacks do not seem to make too much sense. It is expensive to be prepared to deliver such an attack; furthermore, such attacks typically use very large weapons and the missiles that are required are also large and, therefore, difficult to protect. In other words, such preparations tend to go in a direction exactly opposite to that followed by the United States (towards smaller weapons such as in the Polaris or Minuteman systems). We are turning to these smaller weapons for a reason—they are easier to protect. This means that a force designed for an environmental countervalue attack may not be a very reliable second-strike force. On the other hand, an environmental countervalue attack is a very poor first-strike tactic; even though it can destroy an enemy's civilians and property, it is not likely to harm his properly protected

---

* In *On Thermonuclear War* (Princeton: Princeton University Press, 1960), pp. 428-33, I gave other examples and further discussion of such possibly unexpected weapons effects. Because of this possibility it would not surprise any sophisticated observer too much if even a seemingly well-designed system manned by adequately trained and indoctrinated personnel failed to operate because of some unexpected human or physical failure.

There are many known examples of systems which almost everybody agreed should be quite workable when they were designed but which subsequently revealed vulnerability to subtle effects that had been over-looked. Such effects are now taken seriously, as was made clear in a recent speech by President Kennedy in which he said: "We are spending great sums of money on radar to alert our defenses and to develop possible anti-missile systems—on the communications which enable our command and control centers to direct a response—on hardening our missile sites, shielding our missiles and their warheads from defensive action, and providing them with electronic guidance systems to find their targets. But we cannot be useless—blacked out, paralyzed, or destroyed by the complex effects of a nuclear explosion."

strategic force very much. Even when combined with an environmental counterforce attack, the countervalue portion of the attack would represent a large, needless diversion of resources.

However, further examination indicates that the case against being prepared to deliver an environmental countervalue attack is not quite as strong as the above would imply. Such attacks are so horrible and destructive that even a very small probability of such an attack—either first or second strike—may indeed contribute either to the balance of terror or to nuclear blackmail. For example, if the Soviet Union possessed twenty or thirty ICBM's, each carrying 100-megaton warheads, even though these ICBM's might be vulnerable, the United States could not be certain of destroying them; the United States might not even know exactly where they were. Under such circumstances, the Soviets would have a pretty good deterrent to attacks by the United States, and many in the United States—particularly those who were willing to believe in the possible irrationality of Soviet decision-makers—might even be fearful of provoking the possessor of such fearful weapons into a first strike against countervalue targets.

### Anti-Recuperation

One should also consider attacks against recuperation. There are many reasons why a country might wish to be able to deliver such an attack. First, its opponent might have been able to put his civilians under pretty good protection. Indeed, studies have shown that it is relatively inexpensive, particularly if there is one or two weeks' notice, to defend civilians (by a combination of movement and improvised shelters). However, it is much more difficult to protect concentrated wealth in the cities, or such natural resources as forests or the fertility of the soil, if an attacker has the capability to destroy them. Therefore, to maintain its deterrent in the face of countermeasures, a country may wish to be able to concentrate on destroying its opponent's ability to recuperate.

There is another reason why a nation might be interested in an attack on recuperation. To the extent that there is no conflict with other war aims (particularly the possibility of having a controlled war and an early peace treaty), a nation may be interested in the long-term competition between the two societies, and, to the degree that one side could handicap the other, it might wish to attack the other side's ability to recuperate.

### Blackmail-Enhancing

We will terminate this discussion of various attacks with a few comments on what may be called "blackmail-enhancing" attacks. Under this name is grouped a large variety of attacks specially designed to attack morale or resolve.

Each side is likely to attack morale or resolve in addition to inflicting physical damage, because, with relatively invulnerable forces, resolve may be more vulnerable than weapons. Attacks against resolve could use communication, persuasion techniques, misinformation, sabotage, espionage, and tactics designed to frighten and deter while minimizing provocation that might lead to the "wrong" kind of emotional or irrational acts. Or one might want so much to maximize apprehension that worries about provocation would be secondary.

As a hypothetical example, imagine that the attacker spares the ten largest cities on the defender's side while destroying as many of the other cities as he is capable of hitting. If successful, the side with only ten cities surviving might easily be intimidated by the prospect of losing them. Having lost so much, it might feel, possibly correctly, that these last assets—the largest ten cities—would be essential to its recuperation. In this way the attacker could both shock the defender and dramatize his vulnerability to further attack. It would be crystal clear that the attacker has more than enough capability left to destroy these last ten cities. Thus, by creating a situation in which all of the defender's eggs are in a small number of baskets, the attacker might achieve a stronger bargaining position than he would have had, had he concentrated on destroying strategic forces and ignored cities. In other words, the importance of the assets visualized as being at risk greatly influences the effectiveness of threats.

Another blackmail-enhancing attack could result from the attacker's wish to negotiate with a dissident part of the defender's nation by deliberately directing his attack to remove political personalities, decision-makers, and organizations with whom he did not wish to negotiate, or who might interfere in his negotiations. The many "moments of truth" encountered on the way up the escalation ladder may be very effective in creating such groups—indeed, the escalation may be conducted in such a way as to encourage dissidence in the opponent's camp. The negotiation, or, at least, contacts with the dissidents may also be started on the lower rungs of the escalation ladder or even pre-escalation. Another example of a blackmail-enhancing attack is one side's deliberately attacking in an uncontrolled way, either feigning ignorance of the "rules of the game," or making, in effect, a specific announcement that it did not intend to follow any rules, thus trying to deter the opponent from further reliance, in his calculations or acts, on any constraints being observed.

It should be clear from the above that a great variety of attacks and wars is possible. We have stressed here only the target system chosen by the attacker on his first strike. Wars are also, of course, affected by the objectives desired by the participants (i.e., the peace treaty they wish their opponent to sign), and the other circumstances in which the war was initiated (for example, whether or not there was a previous tense period). It turns out that this is a very useful way to look at a war in trying to work out strategy and tactics. One tries to think about the kind of peace treaty each side wants or would accept, how the war started, and, in terms of these two variables, one can then usually put together a plausible or rational version of the proper tactics to be used by each side. In a more general sense one can look at an escalation ladder in the same way: one considers how the escalation started, the kind of aftermath each side desires or would accept, and, given these two variables, one can determine, to some extent, what kind of tactics and strategy each side should follow.

We feel that it is useful to study escalation ladders partly because each rung is important by itself as an alternative or possibility, and partly because every action must be considered in the context of what may have preceded it and what may follow it in the form of military or political actions, as well as in terms of morale. With respect to a given limited military action, it is necessary to consider whether this might interfere with the potential effectiveness of the strategic forces in handling other crises which may occur, such as all-out war. In considering each rung, we must also ask ourselves not only how the enemy will react to our actions, but how neutrals, allies, and even our own people will react. For example, we might wish to choose our tactics so as to increase the level of tension among the American people or our allies without trying to affect the Soviet Union (e.g., we might wish to mobilize or increase our strength or resolve without seeming bellicose or threatening to our opponent). On the other hand it is possible that we might wish to make moves which appear relatively innocuous to our own side and to neutrals but very threatening to the Soviets. Finally, we wish to consider the long-run effects of each move on the arms race, on our ability to cope with future crises, on the resolve and morale of our opponents, and so on.

It is because each tactic must be considered in a broad context that rather detailed decisions must often be made at the national level. This goes completely counter to the American tradition of giving the man on the spot the utmost flexibility and responsibility. Under current conditions, however, a less detailed and accurate knowledge of things on the spot can often be more than made up for by greater and more informed consideration of the broader issues. Therefore, it is useful to make more decisions from a national or international point of view even if this means that local factors and details are inadequately considered. However, to the extent that decision-making is hampered because the upper level decision-makers do not have the requisite information and the lower level decision-makers do not have sufficient authority, decisions are likely not to be made at all—or more accurately, are likely to be made by default.

**Aftermaths of Escalation**

We should also study de-escalation—how to climb down, and even off, the ladder. Normally this could be done by the forced or negotiated settlement of the dispute, but sometimes unilateral initiatives can be helpful. Such measures may relax tension to the point where it is easier to settle the dispute or leave it unresolved, but less dangerous. Typical de-escalation gestures might include: a reversal of a previous escalation move, the settling of an extraneous dispute, the freeing of prisoners, conciliatory statements, the replacement of a "hard" key official by a "softer" or more flexible individual, etc.

It is worth considering small as well as large de-escalations. For example, a Soviet provocation followed by a controlled reprisal might occur in such a way that, while neither side backs down, fear overtakes both sides and the situation de-escalates to a lower rung, such as local war. In fact this possibility is used as a tactic on Rung 13 (Barely Nuclear War). In general, one judges that in many situations de-escalation in several steps down the ladder will be as likely as de-escalation in one large step.

In any case, having gotten on the escalation ladder in a particular situation, one must eventually get off it. We may get off

Table 3—Aftermaths of De-Escalation from Lower Rungs

1. Fear and relief
2. Anger, tension, and hostility
3. Rigidity, soberness, and demoralization
4. Education for innovation
5. Preparations, reorganization, mobilization
6. Arms race, competition, *détente*, entente, agreement, alliance, or condominium
7. New alignments

after Rung 2 or we may not get off until the last rung. In any case, there will be an aftermath. As used here, the term includes not only the aftermath of an upper rung thermonuclear war, but also the aftermath of de-escalation from lower rungs which do not involve the highest level of violence.

Some possible characteristics of the aftermath of de-escalation from lower rungs are shown in Table 3. First there will be both fear and relief: fear because the crisis could have been worse and relief because it was not. There is likely to be anger, tension, and hostility. After all, the two countries have been threatening to destroy each other. As a result, some people will become more rigid in their determination not to give in, others will be sobered by the close brush with more dangerous situations, and, finally, still others will be demoralized and anxious to avoid such strain in the future at all costs.

In any case, almost everybody will be looking for ways to improve the situation, and "non-conservative" behavior may become possible. People may be interested in innovation. Unless the escalation has been spectacularly successful, the policy of inertia, of doing the same thing in the future that was done in the past, will now be obviously less attractive. As a result there will be preparations for new policies, there will be reorganizations, there may even be mobilization. The relationship between the two opponents is also likely to be very different. As nations they may have an arms race and they may compete more fiercely. Or both sides may become intensely aware of the great threat posed by nuclear weapons, their previous feeling of "nuclear incredulity" may be shattered, and they may negotiate agreements, alliances, or condominiums. Or, less dramatically, the result of a crisis might be increased cooperation in solving international problems.

It would be advisable to be in a position to take full advantage of any of these possibilities, exploiting a *détente* to achieve arms control or real stability, or an accelerated arms race to achieve "superiority." The aftermaths to be prepared for include not only relations between the two opponents but also other internal and external relations. As we know from experience, serious crises can disrupt alliances or destroy their morale to such an extent as to render ineffective seemingly adequate capabilities. On the other hand, the cohesiveness of alliances may increase rather than decrease; or there may be accretions rather than desertions. And morale, or at least determination and resolve, can go up as well as down—depending on the course of events and the national character.*

The effects of de-escalation from the upper rungs will evidently be much greater than from the lower rungs. There will have been death and destruction. As a result, de-escalation is likely to involve formal cease-fires and peace treaties. As a result of both the death and destruction and the formal character of the de-escalation, lower-rung aftermaths may be intensified. They will be more intense because death and destruction have a great emotional impact, and formal cease-fires and peace treaties can make tremendous changes in the international system. Outside of the formally negotiated changes there may be additional drastic social and political changes, both internal and external, as a result of the bizarre and frightening character of the events and the reaction to them.

Finally, there may be disjunctive solutions to the conflict which precipitated the crisis, solutions which could not have been arrived at or which would have been unlikely to occur through evolution from the current system, solutions which represent a sharp break with the past. Such solutions may not, of course, be desirable, and they may lead only to new troubles,

Table 4—Aftermaths of De-Escalation from Upper Rungs

---

1. Death and destruction
2. Formal cease-fires and peace treaties
3. All lower-rung aftermaths intensified
4. Drastic social and political changes
5. Disjunctive "solutions"

---

* For additional comments on the consequences of crisis aftermaths for policy-making see HI-180 Crisis Report.

but they may also represent at least a temporary resolution to the particular crisis and even lead to a more or less permanent improvement in the international order.

## C—Analysis of the Escalation Ladder

There are two interesting analogies which one can apply to the escalation ladder: the strike in labor disputes and the game of "chicken." Neither of these analogies is entirely accurate, but each of them is useful in explicating the concept of escalation and in conveying a feel for the nuances and tactics of the escalation ladder.

The strike analogy operates primarily on the lower and middle rungs of the ladder. In a strike situation, labor and management threaten and then inflict harm on each other, and, under pressure from the continuation of this harm, they seek agreement. It is usually assumed that events will not escalate to the limit. We do not expect workers to starve to death or businesses to go bankrupt. In a strike each side is expected to hurt or threaten to hurt, but not to kill or even permanently injure the other side. Under pressure of continuing threats of harm, it is assumed that some compromise will be arrived at before permanent or excessive damage is incurred. Occasionally these expectations are not fulfilled. The business does go bankrupt or the workers do look for work elsewhere. But this is rare. Usually the strike is settled long before such limits are approached. In this context, the question immediately comes up, "Why go through this expensive, dangerous, and uncomfortable route to settle disputes? Why have a strike at all? Why not settle it?"

The answer is obvious. In the absence of enforceable or acceptable adjudication, the side most afraid of a strike will tend to get the short end of the bargain. A "no-strike" policy— the analogy in labor disputes of non-violence—rarely works for any length of time. And even when it seems to work for some years and disputes are settled without strikes, a strike situation or a serious strike threat may arise eventually. The threat of a strike or a lockout is ever present as a last-resort pressure for compromise.

Our escalation ladder has one major feature which is not present in most strike situations—the possibility of eruptions. In the strike the maximum punishment that the workers can inflict on the management is to deny it one day's production at a time. The maximum punishment that management can ordinarily inflict on the workers is to deny them one day's wages at a time. There is, therefore, a natural limit to the rate of punishment—a spasm of anger is not likely to force either side over the brink. An escalation ladder for international relations is quite different since each side decides at what rate it wishes to inflict harm on the other side. This makes the escalation ladder incomparably less stable than the strike situation. A moment of anger, a surge of emotion, a seemingly innocuous miscalculation or accident, or a "wrong" decision can have catastrophic consequences.

Another useful—if misleading—analogy which brings this aspect to the fore is the game of "chicken." It illustrates the basic implication of the escalation ladder that the higher rungs on the ladder are closer to some kind of general war than the lower rungs. The game of "chicken," however, greatly oversimplifies international conflicts. It is played by two drivers on a road with a white line down the middle. Both cars straddle the white line and drive toward each other at top speed. The first driver to lose his nerve and swerve into his own lane is "chicken" —an object of contempt and scorn. He loses the game. The game is played among juvenile delinquents for prestige, for girls, for leadership of a gang, etc.

The escalation ladder is much more complicated than this game. Still, the game is a useful analogy because it brings out *some* aspects of international relations that are important and should be emphasized—for example, the symmetrical character of many escalation situations. Some juvenile delinquents utilize interesting tactics in playing the game of "chicken." The skillful player gets into the car quite drunk, throwing whisky bottles out the window to make it clear to everybody just how drunk he is. He wears very dark glasses so that it is obvious that he cannot see anything. As soon as the car reaches high speed, he takes the steering wheel and throws it out the window. If his opponent is watching, he has won. If his opponent is not watching, he has a problem; likewise if both players try this strategy.

One of the reasons why people do not like to use the game of "chicken" analogy is that the phrase emphasizes the fact that two sides can play it in the same way. It seems to us that some people who object to this label want to play the game of "chicken" a little, but do not like to concede that that is what they are doing. We feel that it is a good thing to label the tactics, and we also think that, under current conditions, we may have to be willing to play the international version of this game whether we like it or not.

It is clear from the above why many people would like to conduct international relations the way a juvenile delinquent plays "chicken." They seem to believe that if our decision-makers can only give the appearance of being drunk, blind, and out of control, they will "win" in negotiations with the Soviets on crucial issues. We do not believe that this is a useful or responsible policy. We may be willing to run some risks, and we do not want to hem ourselves in tactically by being completely sober, clear-visioned, and in full control of ourselves, but we will obviously benefit by having a reasonable degree of sobriety, a reasonable degree of clear vision, and a reasonable degree of self-control. It is also clear that the Soviets are likely to pursue a similar policy.

But the escalation ladder is descriptive of a bargaining and risk-taking situation, with a crucial point of similarity to the game of "chicken"—how can one side convey the impression to the other side that he must be the one to give way or at least be willing to accept a reasonable compromise?

Thus the escalation ladder has analogies to both the strike and the game of "chicken," and both of these analogies are illuminating. However, almost any analogy can be misleading, and these cases are not exceptions. Therefore, although we will use both analogies we must now consider the points at which these analogies break down.

In the case of the strike in labor disputes both sides are likely to recognize their absolute need for each other, and this basic community of interest will tend to dominate the negotiations. There will be no attempt by one side to eliminate the other. In fact, no strategy which envisages a great possibility of grievous harm to the other side is likely to be acceptable. Thus the strike analogy probably overestimates the recognized sense of community of interests.

In the game of "chicken" analogy, the difficulty is the exact opposite. In this game, there is no give-and-take bargaining. There are no natural pauses or stops or even partial damage, but only all-out collisions. Even more important, the primary objective of the game is the total humiliation of the opponent. If one side wins, the other side has lost everything.

In international relations, escalation is used to facilitate negotiations or to put pressure on one side or both to settle a dispute without war. If either side wanted a war, it would simply go to war and not bother to negotiate. For this reason the common observation that "neither side wants war" is not particularly startling even though it is often delivered with an air of presenting revealed truth. Neither side is willing to back down, precisely because it believes or hopes it can achieve its objectives without war. It may be willing to run some risk of war to achieve its objective, but it feels that the other side will back down or compromise before the risk becomes very large.

In addition to the difference in objectives, there is also a fundamental difference between escalation and the *playing* of the game of "chicken." This game would be a better analogy if it were played with two cars starting an unknown distance apart, traveling toward each other at unknown speeds, and on roads with several forks so that the opposing sides are not certain that they are even on the same road. In addition, each driver should be giving and receiving threats and promises. Finally, tearful mothers and stern fathers line the sides of the road urging, respectively, caution and manliness. In all these respects the analogy with the strike is much better than the analogy with "chicken."

In addition, in the escalation situation both sides understand that they are likely to play repeatedly. Therefore, they do not wish to create a psychological or political situation in which there will probably be a blowup on the next play. Indeed, both sides may become anxious to work out some acceptable methods of adjudicating the game, or to adopt general rules embodying some principles of equity or fairness. In fact, both sides may become so interested in getting such rules of procedure or rules of adjudication accepted that either side might be willing to lose a particular issue occasionally simply because trying to win that issue would set a precedent that would reduce the applicability of the basic rules.

It is clear that there may be a basic disagreement on what adjudicatory principles are acceptable, but such disagreement is likely to be less agonizing than disagreements about the division of spoils. It is often easier to agree on tentative and informal principles of adjudication than to agree directly on the adjudication of a particular issue. Both sides may, in fact, be so fearful of being locked in by a set of rules that it may be impractical for the time being to agree on a permanent system of formal adjudication, but this kind of agreement is not essential to alleviating significantly some of the risks of uncontrolled escalation.

In any case, the balance of terror is likely to work well enough to induce some degree of restraint and prudent behavior on each side. Precisely because both sides recognize that deterrence strategies are unstable, they are likely to refrain from going to the upper rungs of the ladder or from indulging in the kind of behavior which might provoke such a response from the other side. Both sides will understand that a strategy of deterrence requires the support of precedents and widely understood and observed thresholds if it is to last for any length of time.

One may still ask the question, what are we buying this time for? Why don't we settle these matters now, without running such great risks? Unfortunately, in this respect the situation is much like the "chicken" or "strike" analogies. There is no obvious reason why the manufacturer and workers should not be able to reach a settlement without threatening or undergoing the great mutual harm of the strike, but, unfortunately, if either side desperately desires to make the settlement without harm or risk of harm, it is likely to get a very bad bargain. In fact, if one side does this repeatedly it is possible that both sides might suffer harm: the manufacturer might go bankrupt or the workers might receive such low wages that they become incompetent or are forced to leave the industry. In the absence of formal methods of adjudication both sides must be willing to escalate.

While it is important for us to have a greater understanding of national goals and objectives, we may decide to run great risks in order to prevent disaster rather than to accommodate ourselves to it meekly. That is, we may be able to agree on what we are against, even if we cannot agree on what we are for. But we need alternatives other than all-out spasm war or all-out peace at any price, if we wish to avoid the simple dilemma: war or surrender. However, conceding all this, the probability of war as a result of playing "chicken" once too often might be very high. In any long period of peace, there may be a tendency for governments to become more intransigent as the thought of war becomes unreal. This may be particularly true if there is a background of experiences in which those who stand firm do well, while those who are reasonable seem to do poorly. After a while the hypothetical danger of war may look less real than the tangible gains and prestige that are being won and lost. It may turn out that governments learn that it is not feasible to stand firm on incompatible positions only when peace fails. Today there is reason to hope that we can reduce the dangers of the game of "chicken" by considering carefully how wars might start and how they might be fought. Therefore, our serious study of escalation. However, unless workable arrangements are made for effective adjudication, someone may play the international analogue of this game once too often. Hence, to rely even on slow, rung-by-rung escalation in international crises is a dangerous strategy.

We do not wish to play the game of "chicken" in the same spirit as the juveniles play it. One major alternative is to have sufficient capabilities on the lower rungs of the escalation ladder so that the opponent is not tempted to play a limited game of "chicken." He must not be given reason to believe that he can outdo us on lower rungs since this might tempt him to risk low-level escalation in the belief that neither side will escalate to higher rungs. The alternative to having significant capabilities for the lower rungs of the ladder is to make reliable threats of going directly to the higher rungs. However, there is a temptation to rely on this tactic too heavily, and it may be well to remind ourselves that in dealing with violence there is a tendency in the United States to take strong moral stands, and then, because we have defined the issue as a moral one, to make excessive threats and take excessive risks.

It is because of this tendency that we have been so blunt about referring to the use of threat of escalation as playing or intending to play some version of the game of "chicken." To the extent that we are serious, or to the extent that our pretense creates seriousness, we will have to face the consequences of being on the escalation ladder. And when one competes in risk-taking, one is taking risks. If one takes risks one may be unlucky and lose the gamble. It may, in fact, be that, unilaterally or bilaterally, we should agree not to play the game of "chicken." This could be done by decreasing the possibility of reaching the upper rungs and thus converting the escalation ladder into something more like a labor strike or by reducing the role of escalation threats in settling international disputes.

## D—Problems of the "Escalation Ladder" Concept

The escalation ladder is a simplified model or metaphor that is designed as an aid in the study of a class of situations which are very complex in reality. Such simplification inevitably leads to gaps between real situations and the model employed to discuss them. In this section we consider some of the problems of this type which arise in using the escalation ladder concept.

### Discontinuities in and Importance of Distance Between Rungs

In our discussion of the escalation ladder, we treated all rungs as being basically equivalent. There was almost an implicit assumption that each rung is separated from the preceding and succeeding rung by the same amount of importance. Indeed, to some extent the escalation ladder was drawn up with this end in view. However, we did not quite succeed—partly because there are many natural discontinuities on the ladder. While in almost every case these discontinuities can be blurred by any participant who wishes to blur them, the fact that discontinuities exist may be very useful to both parties, who may wish to preserve these discontinuities. Let us consider as an example the question of using nuclear weapons to coerce the opponent by means of a spectacular show of force. In this case it is clear that there is an almost continuous spectrum of alternatives available which can be ranked as follows: (1) testing a very large weapon for purely technical reasons, (2) testing a very large weapon on a day which has particular political significance, (3) testing a weapon off the coast of the antagonist so that his people can observe it, (4) testing a weapon high in outer space more or less over the antagonist's country, (5) testing lower in outer space directly over the opponent's country, and finally, (6) testing so low that the shock wave is heard by everybody, and perhaps a few windows are broken. In spite of the fact that the alternative ways of carrying out a spectacular show of force vary in a continuous fashion from very innocuous to very provocative, we tend to think of a spectacular show of force as being high on the escalation ladder since it would be so in most cases.

To take another example, it is possible to blur the distinction between the use and non-use of nuclear weapons in tactical situations. One could, for example, simply increase the probability that nuclear weapons will be used by bringing them up to the front lines and decentralizing decision-making in such a way that the possibility of unauthorized or inadvertent use of nuclear weapons is increased. Further, it is possible to use nuclear weapons that are equivalent to no more than a few tons of TNT. In such cases it might be difficult for an opponent to know whether or not nuclear weapons have been used. It is hard to believe that upward escalation would be seriously considered simply because one side dropped a nuclear weapon equivalent to 100 pounds of high explosives. This would be particularly true if the same side dropped 10,000 pounds of high explosives right next to it. If one could then move by degrees to larger and larger nuclear weapons, the process might become so automatic and gradual that the use of large nuclear weapons would not evoke discontinuous responses.

### Twilight Zones (Ambiguous Actions)

To the extent that the protagonists are anxious to maintain precedents, both may be very careful not to move into a twilight zone. From the viewpoint of bargaining, twilight zones may be the worst of all places in which to use nuclear weapons. Such action may be so careful that it is neither provocative nor pressure-building and yet it may tend to destroy precedents. The main purpose of indulging in twilight zone behavior is less likely to be to increase bargaining strength than the desire to break a precedent in order to make some technique more acceptable, or to bring a rung on the escalation ladder lower down deliberately so that it will be more usable in the future, or to gain a tactical advantage (as in Rung 13, the Barely Nuclear War).

### Criteria for Evaluating Position of Rungs

There are other objections to the escalation ladder as a model, as there must be to any attempt to describe a complicated sequence of acts on the international scene by a linear progression. In general such actions simply do not form a unique, one-dimensional array. Depending on previous history and special circumstances, some rungs of the escalation ladder ought to have higher or lower positions.

We have already suggested that there are also many possible criteria for their order, such as degree of: (1) closeness to all-out war, (2) provocation, (3) precedence-breaking, (4) committal demonstrated, (5) damage done, (6) violence, or (7) threat perceived. We also mentioned that the correlation between these criteria is not 1, although it is reasonably high. Since the correlation is less than 1, the escalation ladder must be looked

upon as a very rough approximation to real structural relationships. Nevertheless, these structural relationships seem important enough to warrant prominent display and thorough
discussion.

## Objections to the Upper Rungs

In addition to these general problems of the "escalation ladder" concept, there are some specific objections to the upper
rungs of the ladder. Let us turn now to a short discussion of
some of these objections.

The objections listed in this table are the most significant
ones that have come to our attention. They are listed here in
order of increasing importance. The first objection is that the
escalation ladder presents an excessively rational sequence of
events. Can it be assumed that people will actually do this kind
of thing, that they will think clearly or that they will be calm
and collected? These worries are, in fact, based on an important
phenomenon: in normal circumstances as well as under stress
and strain, decision-makers may not be entirely rational. However, researchers who study these problems do not really assume
that decision-makers are wholly rational. To the extent that they
assume anything of this sort, they assume that the decision-
makers are not totally irrational. This assumption is quite different from the assumption of rationality.

The next objection which we have encountered is that the
discussion underestimates the effects of ambiguities and uncertainties. Consider the city-trading notion. Are any two cities
equal for trading? Is a trade based on population, on wealth, or
on per cent of GNP? This is a very real objection, and, in general, it is correct. Moreover, the ambiguity problem is actually
more complicated than this example indicates. In addition to
the question of what constitutes equitable tit-for-tat exchange,
there is also the question of whether or not each side understands the other's intentions in taking any particular step on
the escalation ladder. For example, one side might mobilize

**Table 5—Three Objections to the Upper Rungs of the Escalation Ladder**

1. Assumption of Rationality
2. Failure to Deal with Ambiguities and Uncertainties
3. Existence of Acceptable Alternatives

simply to signal to the opposing side that it is tough, but the opposing side might read this move as a real intention to go to war, and, therefore, it may be tempted to pre-empt. It may be so tempted, not because it thinks that the first side will go to war in weeks, months, or years, but because it believes war will start immediately. The possibility that such misunderstandings will occur is great, and in certain circumstances this possibility might be useful in deterring escalation. For example, given the great size of the stakes in international crises, there will be a tendency for each side to act conservatively—to overestimate the resolve and rigidity of its opponent. In such cases, the pressure for compromise will increase. Moreover, the chances of deterring frivolous escalations up the ladder will also increase.

The problems of communication of intent in escalating can be interestingly contrasted with the problems of diplomatic communication in the eighteenth and nineteenth centuries. In those days there was a very precise format for communication which went more or less like this:

1) His Majesty's Government is not uninterested in this problem. (There is a vague implication that the country might go to war—e.g., 0.01 probability.)

2) His Majesty's Government is interested in this problem. (There now exists 0.05 probability of recourse to war.)

3) His Majesty's Government is concerned. (0.1 probability of war.)

4) His Majesty's Government is vitally interested. (0.25 probability of war.)

5) His Majesty's Government will not be responsible for the consequences. (There is 0.5 probability of war—the statement may be regarded as an actual ultimatum.)

There are two reasons for the effectiveness of such precise language and communications during the eighteenth and nineteenth centuries. First, when such statements were made all sides recognized that war was actually possible. Second, such language had been followed by war in the past—there were enough precedents to make clear the implications of the language. However, we have no such precedents today. The probability of deliberate war is low, and no nation has taken steps on the escalation ladder and then followed through with the use of nuclear weapons. Therefore the meaning of a given move on the escalation ladder is not clear.

There are other kinds of ambiguities and uncertainties. Let us consider an example: Assume that P has blown up a bridge on Q's territory. Q might interpret this in several ways: (1) it was simply an accidental firing; (2) P actually intended to hit something much more important, but the plan went astray; (3) it was the first missile of a large attack, but somebody did not obey firing discipline and fired early; (4) P really wanted to destroy the bridge because he was trying to degrade Q's logistics; (5) P really wanted to destroy the bridge as a symbol that he might be willing to do more damage later.

Now, Q's response will depend on the way in which he interprets the act. P may or may not wish Q to interpret it accurately. For example, P may intend the bombing partly as a symbol of resolve, but he may also want Q to interpret it as an indication of nervousness or irrationality. Thus P leaves it to Q to decide whether to pre-empt or to back down. In this context, it must always be remembered that the basic purpose of climbing the escalation ladder is to be able to say to the opposing side: "You really don't want to escalate further because it's too dangerous; in fact, it is even dangerous to stay where we are; therefore, you'd better back down."

This brings us to the third important objection to the upper rungs of the ladder, that "there ought to be acceptable alternatives." Let us, therefore, consider some alternatives to escalation. We have already mentioned that situations can occur in which appeasement, accommodation, or compromise might be desirable. There are many cases in history where accommodation and flexibility have not only prevented war, but have also led to *détente*, entente, and friendliness. On the other hand, there are also cases in which the exact opposite has occurred. In such cases, appeasement, by making weakness clear, has provoked the expansive side to make greater demands. Appeasement may also cause the appeasing side to become unnecessarily rigid. This would happen if the appeaser comes to the conclusion that appeasement does not pay or develops moral objections to all further appeasement or even compromise. This possibility should not be startling. Extreme policies often evoke extreme reactions. However, the outcome in any specific case will depend on the nature and degree of the appeasement and the nature of the two opponents. The slogan "appeasement never pays" is clearly a misleading summary of history (there are many examples of successful appeasement), but it is an understandable legacy of the unsuccessful appeasement of Hitler and, to a lesser extent, Stalin.

The statement that "there is no alternative to peace" is also misleading. If it means anything, it must be a call for "peace at any price." However, a very undesirable peace may have consequences that are worse than those of many wars—even thermonuclear wars. Moreover, an attempt to impose a very undesirable peace on a nation may stir reactions that produce a major war because of popular revulsion or refusal to surrender under dishonorable conditions. A bad peace might be accepted to avoid a war that would be worse, but the choices may not always be so simple. In any case, mutual destruction cannot be avoided by slogans or even by good intentions.

## FOOTNOTES

[1] This paper expands and revises some ideas that were considered in Herman Kahn, *Thinking About the Unthinkable* (New York: Horizon Press, 1962). The material was further elaborated in the Hudson Institute's report to the Deputy Assistant Secretary of Defense for Disarmament (International Security Affairs), under ARPA Contract No. SD-105: A. J. Wiener & H. Kahn, Editors, *Crises & Arms Control*, HI-180-RR, Oct. 9, 1962; and Herman Kahn *et al.*, ed., *The Use of Force in Peace and War*, HI-205-PR, March 18, 1963, prepared under AF Contract 49 (638)-1180. The author would like to thank Felix Kaufmann, Anthony J. Wiener, and Max Singer for their comments and suggestions.

[2] See Hudson Institute Report, H.I. 180—*Crisis and Arms Control*, p. 158.

[3] See Paul Ramsey, *War and the Christian Conscience* (Raleigh: Duke University Press, 1961).

# Toward a Strategy of Supremacy

*—STEFAN T. POSSONY*

## Summary

*The threat arising from the Soviet Union and its advancing technology is the most dangerous of the many threats confronting American and Free World security. With superior technology, the Soviet Union can "bury" us at an instant's notice. We must overcome and end this threat.*

*The Soviet threat,* inter alia, *is increasing in terms of firepower, but the United States is holding back the development of high-yield weapons. Also, the United States is phasing out bomber aircraft in favor of low-yield missiles, thus reducing even our present firepower capabilities. Superiority in firepower could be decisive. As a result of continuing Soviet military growth, the United States may be losing its capability to deter aggression.*

*The victor in the technological race will win the world struggle. Consequently, a genuine Free World strategy would aim at winning the technological contest with the Soviet Union, while maintaining sufficient force levels.*

*Given the rapid obsolescence of military equipment, a country which stops modernizing will soon be disarmed* ipso facto. *Unfortunately, we have embarked on a policy of deliberately delaying arms modernization. This policy, which constitutes unilateral nuclear disarmament by omission, tends to perpetuate and deepen the world crisis. Abandonment of this policy and adoption of a strategy of supremacy is necessary if we want to deter conflict, to fight it—should it occur—without excessive casualties, and ultimately to win the struggle for freedom.*

535

*The program of winning the technological race and providing adequate defense systems, while at the same time maintaining a high standard of living, poses enormous economic problems for the United States. To lighten the burden, the United States and its allies must achieve a common integrated and technologically up-to-date defense. To accomplish this objective, nuclear weapons must be made available to our NATO allies who, in their own and in the US interest, must acquire effective capabilities for self-defense.*

*For the time being, US strategy, in many ways, reflects the untenable assumption that the clock of history can be turned back. The Free World's best hope lies in a strategy through which we would capitalize on our strongest capabilities— economic power and technological competence.*

Among the many threats to American and Free World security, the threat arising from the Soviet Union and its advancing technology is by far the most dangerous: it is the only threat which can kill us instantly. Additional dangers are posed by limited nuclear war by proxy, conventional limited war, guerrilla warfare, Communist China, uprisings within the Bloc, upheavals in the underdeveloped areas, subversion, etc. Though these threats are dangerous too, they are not of the "sudden-death" variety, and even in their acute phases allow us time for counteraction. I shall devote this discussion to analyzing some of the broad concepts of Free World strategy through which the challenge of total nuclear war may be neutralized.

Our strategy must be designed to overcome and end the threat without sacrificing our free institutions or the conditions wherein free institutions can flourish. In the nuclear age, moreover, the protection of life in conflict has become one of the strategist's foremost obligations. Hence, if war should eventuate, we must fight and win without "unacceptably" high loss of life.

Let us start by asking ourselves how these objectives *cannot* be attained.

### Surrender

It has been suggested that we forget about preserving free institutions and, to prevent war, minimize human loss by surrendering to the Communists. The contention that, though we would suspend freedom, temporarily for 200 or 300 years, we would survive physically, is strengthened by the unwarranted assumption that nuclear conflict would exterminate the human race altogether. Yet such a prospect would seem to preclude aggression in the first place; and indeed, the Soviets repeatedly stated their belief that nuclear war, though costly all around, would not destroy civilization but merely put an end to "capitalism."

A strategy of surrender hardly would save casualties. Militarily speaking, surrender means the turning over of weapons by the vanquished to the victor. But at distances of 6,000 miles or more, there is no practical way of surrendering effectively. Our weapons can be put out of action only by the Soviets' dropping nuclear weapons on our strategic bases. In theory, to be sure, Soviet military teams could travel to the United States and remove or destroy our carriers and our nuclear stockpiles. In practice, however, this operation would require full occupation or, in any event, would last for many months. The Soviets could not risk that, before the arrival of their emissaries, many death-dealing weapons would be abducted, or that, in the midst of this process of surrendering, the as yet armed United States would not resume hostilities. The Soviets would have no choice but to resort to destructive military attack.

Furthermore, the establishment and preservation of a Communist state always has been a violent affair, usually costing the lives of 10 to 20 per cent of the population. In the United States, with its predominantly "middle-class" population (which, according to Communist prescription, would have to be "liquidated"), the implantation of communism would be far more lethal. Actually, the take-over of the United States which, because of the surrender, would remain intact, is hardly feasible: the American people are too indomitable. Hence, resistance is bound to occur in many places inside the United States. Naturally, other nations also would resist the Communists, who therefore would be required to deploy considerable forces across the world to institute bloody repressions. This type of conflict would be protracted and costly, and the outcome would be uncertain. Even after victory-through-surrender, the take-over of the world would require nuclear mass attacks to decimate populations and demoralize potential aggressors.

After the Communists are installed in every country, the Communist states would quarrel and, sooner or later, fight each other by military means including, naturally, nuclear weapons.

Whether the blood toll resulting from surrender is viewed optimistically or pessimistically, the ultimate cost of this strategy in human lives is *not* calculable. Those who advocate surrender on humane grounds would be highly disappointed to find that the human cost of their strategy, whether through nuclear attack, reprisals, repression of resistance movements, liquidations, or terror, would be of the same order of magnitude as that of a very devastating nuclear conflict. Actually, surrender may cost considerably more lives than nuclear war. There are no tricks and gimmicks to ensure that surrender would be "cheap." Hence surrender can be ruled out as a genuine choice confronting the American Government.

I should add that a strategy of surrender has no chance of being politically acceptable; it would not work, even on a Fabian installment plan. Surrender propaganda merely confuses and weakens the Free World.


**Preventive War**

The obverse strategy, deliberate nuclear attack by the United States upon the Soviet Union, might eliminate the Communist threat and ensure Free World survival. However, it is difficult for an open society to mount nuclear surprise attacks with the utmost secrecy. For example, we probably would be unable to evacuate populations prior to striking and find it difficult to conceal pre-strike mobilization. Missiles and aircraft would get off, presumably, according to schedule, but the country as a whole would be unprotected and highly vulnerable. Since a hostile counterstrike cannot be averted even through a most successful surprise attack, success of the operation would be jeopardized. (It is important to remember that, other things being equal, a Soviet first-strike strategy could be mounted with a greater chance of success.)

Hence, the aggressive solution hardly meets the criteria for an effective American strategy. Politically, the notion of an offensive American war of liberation is as unrealistic as surrender.

Propaganda for aggressive war tends to create frustrations and to divide the Free World. For that matter, such a strategy can be rationally proposed only on the basis of three question-able assumptions: that communism cannot be stopped and super-seded by means short of all-out war; that there is absolutely no hope that the Communists can be induced to forswear their aggressive designs; and that the United States is incapable of devising effective second-strike forces as well as defenses which even a strong-willed aggressor would consider imprudent to test.

I believe that the opposite assumptions happen to be correct, but I must stress one point which makes this outlook somewhat less comfortable: the decision to forego nuclear attack has *as its corollary* a decision to develop and employ, to the fullest extent needed, those strategies-short-of-offensive-war which might allow the Free World to reach its objectives. If we are unwilling to pay the admittedly high price of *a winning defensive strategy* or *a strategy of peacefare*, we probably will not elect preventive war either; but we might stumble into war from panic.

Is there a case for preventive war? We never can be sure, weeks or months before the putative attack, that the enemy will take the plunge. If we were reliably informed that the enemy plans to strike, we should try by rapid countermoves to prevent war rather than make it inevitable. On the assumption that the aggressor would attack only if he felt that he had the strength to win, the most promising solution would be for us to demon-strate that he cannot count on strategic or tactical surprise.

We also must be prepared, however, for an "irrational" strategy by the enemy. A rational offensive strategy, in my nomenclature, would be one in which the would-be aggressor attacks only if he possesses substantial superiority of force, benefits from a high chance of obtaining surprise, and has ade-quate military and other means to fend off and absorb residual retaliatory strikes. An irrational strategy, by contrast, is one in which the aggressor attacks without possessing substantial superiority, including one which predicates success almost en-tirely on the surprise element.

But irrational strategies are *not* impossible strategies. In fact, many aggressions which have occurred in history were highly irrational. An irrational Communist attack may occur because the Kremlin miscalculates the world-wide "relationship of forces;" because a war is provoked by uncontrolled elements; because there is no chance of ever attaining a sufficient measure of superiority, and the militant Communists deliberately adopt a high-risk strategy; and because the power position of the Communist dictatorship is threatened by erosion, intra-Party power struggles, and upheavals within the Bloc compelling the Kremlin to adopt a "rationale of political survival" and to strike in the expectation that they can survive war with a greater probability than inaction.

If the evidence shows that the Soviets are about to strike the United States within the next few hours, we would be morally obligated to "pre-empt" this blow by all means at our disposal. Only in this fashion can we optimize our own chances of success and survival. The justification of pre-emption is implicitly recognized by the US Constitution, Article I, Section 10, No. 3: "No state shall . . . engage in war, unless actually invaded, or in such imminent danger as will not admit of delay."

On the other hand, when intelligence about an imminent strike does become conclusive, which usually is very late, we may no longer have time to fend off the attack. Hence we might be placed before the dilemma to strike early, on the basis of inconclusive evidence, or take the risk of inaction—both choices could be deadly. Hence, as in the previous case, when it was a matter not of preventive war but of preventing war, it would be preferable if, instead of trying pre-emption by firepower, we could induce the Soviets to reverse an earlier attack decision. Pre-emption through firepower may deny victory to the Soviets, but the odds are that our bombs and warheads would explode too late to protect ourselves. Instead of relying on pre-emptive attack as an expedient *in extremis,* it is obviously a more effective— and moral—course to maintain armaments which even in an acute international crisis might dissuade the opponent from considering attack as a preferred course of action.

There is obviously very little we can do to influence directly those intra-Bloc developments which may culminate in an "irrational" decision to attack. But if we maintain clearly superior armaments, we would lessen the danger of miscalculation which tends to become maximal in "stalemate" situations. We also would strengthen the hands of those elements within the Soviet Union which, in a situation where the militant Communists are desperate enough to seek political survival in war, would oppose such an irrational and anti-national-interest course of action; in other words, we would, through the mere existence of our superior posture, pit the "opportunists"—and possibly the military*—against the fanatics.

In short, strategies of prevention or pre-emption may be imposed on us. Yet they are clearly hazardous, uncertain, and destructive, and should be considered inadmissible except as a last resort. In general, therefore, Free World strategy, for sound moral, military, and survival reasons, excludes surrender as well as nuclear aggression in any shape or form.

It is an entirely different question whether, in order to help allies who are under attack, the United States should turn to a "first-strike" strategy. If the Soviets initiate war in Europe or Asia, there would be no virtue in not striking them immediately, especially since, should we honor our obligations ultimately, a nuclear attack upon the United States would follow as a matter of course. If war is upon us and the United States is given the "benefit" of the first strike, it would be foolish *not* to use that option. This sort of strategy is envisaged by the NATO Treaty. But the success of this strategy is a function of the force with which it is implemented. If our force be superior to that of the opponent, and if there are no illusions about our resolve, the contingency probably will not arise.

## Technological Strategy

Solutions of "expediency" or despair, whether surrender or preventive war, are not strategies, but the consequences of lack of strategy; they are nothing but reactions to enemy initiatives. Strategy, whether offensive or defensive, is primarily a set of *initiative* actions executed through a protracted span of time.

What, then, would be a genuine strategy for the Free World?

Incessant and accelerating progress of technology is the foremost fact of the military environment. Since in many ways technology develops as though it were an impersonal force, it is impossible to decelerate technological change, let alone to stop it. If one side deliberately retards its technological programs, the other side, almost inevitably, will win the technological race, perhaps even without strenuous effort. Other things being equal,

---

* Soviet military leaders usually are Party members, but the significance of this fact in life-or-death situations should not be exaggerated. History has shown repeatedly that the rationality of the military profession often primes political convictions; professional soldiers, at any rate, are rarely genuine political fanatics.

the winner of the technological race can impose his law upon the loser.

At the present pace, weapons systems must be replaced every five to ten years by new "generations" of equivalent weapons. Compare, for example, the progression of Soviet jet interceptors from the Mig-15 through the Mig-17 and the Mig-19 to the Mig-21. Similarly, our bombers advanced from the B-17 via the B-29 and B-36 to the B-52, perhaps to the RS-70 and an operational version of the Dyna-Soar. This advance was paralleled by the development of ballistic missiles from Thor and Jupiter via Atlas and Titan to Polaris and Minuteman, and beyond. Within each of these "generations" there are subsidiary progressions, e.g., from a B-52A to B-52H, and from Atlas A to Atlas D, and from Titan I to Titan II.

According to the standards of weapons under development or in the blueprint stage, the weapons that are deployed in battle order are always obsolescent or obsolete. Thus, irrespective of the size of the military budget and the number of soldiers and weapons, a country that stops modernizing will be disarmed within one or two weapons cycles. If its modernization rate is slower than that of the competitor, that country will fall behind in military capability. By contrast, the country which modernizes faster and pulls ahead of the opponent by one or more generations of key weapons systems, will "outarm" the adversary, possibly to the point of impotence. The continuous acceleration of technological change tends to bring about the "unilateral disarmament" of the nation that falls behind. The defeat of France in 1940 gave a foretaste of this military "law" which controls modern strategy.

The military purpose of war is to disarm the opponent or render his forces harmless. In the past, this objective could be attained only through battle. Today, this same objective is potentially attainable, more or less without bloodshed, through winning the technological arms race.

"Victory" achieved by technical means only would not be durable, nor always conclusive. Superiority can be preserved only by regaining "technological victory" several times in succession. To recreate this "victory" repeatedly and continue winning the race until the threat abates is a formidable task. The modernization of weapons would have to be accomplished, albeit at a slower pace, even if there were no acute threat. Moreover, this type of military contest is less risky and destructive than ordeal through battle; and it allows more satisfactory options for peace-making. The very fact that we now are able to choose a strategy-short-of-catastrophe surely constitutes progress about which we should rejoice.

Does it follow that the Free World's struggle against the Communists can be waged exclusively as a technological contest? There is little doubt in my mind that the Soviets have grasped the essence of technology and presently are trying to win the technological arms race for communism. At the same time, their propaganda and political warfare is aimed at bringing about a slow-down of Free World military technology. If we allow the Soviets to win but one or two rounds of the technological contest decisively, the United States might be lost; at best, it would be in serious trouble. If the race remains inconclusive, war probably will be avoided (unless "irrationality" takes over), but the balance will be so delicate that an unexpected "breakthrough" in Soviet technology might allow the Kremlin to overtake us in a sudden spurt.

Consequently, the only safe course of action is to ensure that the United States will stay technologically ahead of the Soviet Union and to lengthen this lead through successive weapons cycles; a broad margin of superiority must be maintained until peace is assured. This is a technological-industrial challenge. But the contest must also be won in the psycho-political arena. This task is partly defensive: we must prevent being deflected from our course. But there also is the offensive task: we must see to it that the Communist dictatorship exits from the scene, hopefully through gradual internal reform. It is important to understand that negotiation cannot end the conflict unless and until the Communist regime either is transformed in orientation and structure, or is replaced by another regime which is peaceful in intent.

The challenge, thus, is total along a broadening spectrum of conflict techniques. The technological struggle is the "infrastructure" of the over-all conflict, while the other techniques compose the supra-structure—if I may be allowed this transgression into Marxian terminology. Only if we prove conclusively successful in the technological contest can we hope for the internal evolution within the Bloc which would pave the way toward a stable settlement.

Technological victory, by itself, does not permit a drastic reduction of force levels. Nor can the funds required for accelerating technology be procured by reducing forces-in-being. Such reductions, however, may be feasible *after* a substantial qualitative lead has been gained. In most cases, security can be bought more cheaply and with smaller numbers if technological superiority is preserved throughout the contest. A technological program that is systematic and fast, in the end is far cheaper— and safer—than a program in which development decisions are delayed and accelerations and "stretch-outs" follow each other in erratic progression.

In passing: a mutual agreement to reduce force levels would save money but hardly would help the defender's security. On the contrary, the lowering of nuclear force levels would enhance the feasibility of surprise attack. Under pre-nuclear conditions, low force levels made it practically impossible for the aggressor to execute a successful blitzkrieg attack; hence, in the past, controlled force reductions would have been in the defender's interest. Under nuclear conditions, the situation is reversed: since severe devastation can be achieved through a relatively small number of high-yield weapons, it is not necessary to use large numbers against a weakly armed opponent. Moreover, it is far simpler to plan and execute a small-scale attack involving tens or hundreds instead of thousands of weapons and targets. If the attack fails, the risk of retaliation is less in a small-force than in a big-force war. *Under nuclear high-yield conditions, therefore, the defender is safer with a regime of high force levels.*

Thus, in the midst of a permanent revolution of technology, the safest method of deterring nuclear attack is to maintain, within a regime of high force levels, a military force which, at all times, enjoys qualitative and quantitative superiority over the putative aggressor. The broader the margins of the defender's superiority, the more dependably peace can be maintained.

But here an economic dilemma arises. The United States presumably has the capability to win the technological and the arms race, but it would have to pay a high price in terms of economic "stability" and progress. Up to the present, the US economy was able to support our armaments without serious dislocation, but the growth curve of our military expenditures often was negative, and never was as steep as the advance of technology—and the growth of the threat magnitude—would have required. As a result, our margins of safety have tended to become too narrow.

The Soviet Union labors under economic handicaps that are more severe than ours, but the dictatorial regime prefers the growth of military power to the growth of social security, and does not hesitate to sacrifice living standards for arms. The Soviets also possess specific advantages: they are able and willing to make faster decisions; with their subversion and intelligence capabilities, they are parasitic on Western science and technology; they exploit the substantial scientific resources of Eastern Europe; and they finance their enormous military effort by manipulating the currency and putting much of the burden upon the peasants and the Satellites. In addition, Iron Curtain secrecy and the political capability to strike first whenever the military situation may be optimal are worth billions of rubles (or dollars), and these "free commodities" must not be paid for. Since they underpay their soldiers and sustain them on an austere basis, and since they pay low civilian wages, the "military ruble" goes a longer way than the "military dollar." We do not always recognize the economic magnitude of the Soviet challenge. The fact is that with their narrow resource base, the Soviets produce almost as much military hardware as we do, perhaps as much as 80 per cent, and their expenditures for military R&D may equal or surpass ours.

One need not assume that the Soviet economy will make quantum jumps forward, nor must entire series of revolutionary technical breakthroughs in Soviet weapons be anticipated. (Contingencies of this type, however, are not to be ruled out.) Adjustment to the high energy weapons that exist or will exist soon; the problems posed by global ranges and the near-astronomical speeds of delivery systems; the high rate of discovery and invention; and many additional factors are driving the costs of defense upward automatically. Yet practical politics determine the Government's tax income, and unfortunately even a healthy economic growth rate tends to be lower than a moderate technological growth rate. Hence the decisive winning of the technological race does pose a most difficult resource problem.

### The Promise of Alliance

Fortunately, a solution to this difficulty is available.* The United States does not stand by itself and, therefore, does not need to carry the whole burden of the technological race alone. Our main allies, the United Kingdom, France, Germany, Belgium,

* This paper does not discuss problems of resources reallocation within the United States.

Holland, Italy, Canada, Australia, and Japan, are among the industrially and technologically most advanced nations. This bloc represents a combined GNP of 750 to 800 billion dollars. The Common Market is accelerating the economic growth of continental NATO. Yet, so far the extraordinary potential resources of our European allies have not been used effectively for the purposes of *mutual modern* defense.

The European nations have been reluctant to move into modern military technology, partly because they were busy reconstructing their war-torn economies, partly because of political complications, and partly because of public confusion about nuclear weapons. On our part, we still are attempting to keep an American or Anglo-American nuclear weapons monopoly within the Free World. Due to backwardness in our own strategic thinking and, in some measure, because of unconscious technological isolationism, we have not insisted on advanced technical contributions from and to Europe.

Hence, much of Europe's military expenditure has failed to buy genuine security. The time now has come to put an end to this state of affairs and advance NATO one enormous—and potentially decisive—step forward. We must decide to achieve a common, integrated, and technologically up-to-date defense system.

To make the NATO Alliance prosper, we must progress beyond the generalities of deterrence and retaliation. *First*, in line with what I said before, we must achieve genuine deterrent strength, i.e., *substantial superiority*, and we must not assume that the deterrence we have achieved will last unless the deterrent-weapons systems are constantly recreated in modern technical configurations and unless our deterrent strength grows more rapidly than Communist military power. *Second*, we must ensure that in addition to retaliating (which is little more than taking revenge or exacting a price), we possess capabilities suitable to *win* military conflict and to avoid "unacceptable" damages and losses. These two tasks require a dynamic program to keep *ahead* both of the growing armaments of the Soviet Union and of the challenges posed by technological change. Without programs of a type that would bespeak of our resolve to prevail, the Alliance will not keep together. We should have no illusions about its present cohesion.*

---

* This sentence was written long before January 1963, when many of the American illusions about NATO were shattered.

But we must go beyond these rock-bottom requirements. We must ensure dependable deterrence in specific theaters, notably in Europe and the Far East. We must see to it that the territories of our allies cannot be overrun and be transformed into bases and suppliers of the Communist war machine. We must prevent that friendly nations be placed under Communist dictatorship and become hostages, be it only for a short period. We must enable our friends to prevent their own physical destruction. It is painfully obvious that we have been ignoring many of these problems, an oversight which is the root cause of the NATO disarray.

There is another vast problem which so far has not attracted much attention. If we believe in our own political philosophy, we must operate on the assumption that most of the people enslaved behind the Iron Curtain are our friends. Some of them will be more on our side, and some less, but we do enjoy a strong measure of silent support not only in the Satellites but also among the Ukrainians, the Caucasians, and even the Great Russians within the Soviet Union. It would be a tragic mistake to plan for a strategy which needlessly entails killing many of these allies. I realize that military operations cannot be cut too finely, and I understand the compulsions which may be generated by an all-out enemy attack. But we must *plan* for weapons systems and strategies which allow us *options* of fighting war without causing unnecessary casualties even in the enemy country. We also need weapons to fight effectively in friendly territories, without killing citizens of nations who are fighting on our side.

In the nuclear age, these are challenges to the designer of nuclear weapons; and they also are challenges to the designer of defensive arms as well as to the pioneers of space operations— if a substantial part of the conflict could be removed into space as a decisive theater, surely the earthlings would have nothing to complain about. A design philosophy which, like the strategy of Krishna Menon, is preparing for past wars, is *not* the way to reach these objectives. On the contrary, a war patterned after World Wars I and II that suddenly "escalates" into nuclear exchanges really would be the bloodiest conflict in history. The next war must be designed as a truly modern conflict—then, and only then, will it be "manageable." Sustained scientific progress, technological inventiveness, managerial competence, productive skills, economic power, and forward-looking military planning, combined, have been, and remain, our strongest asset in the fight for freedom.

But just like the lawn in the yard which must be trimmed and watered every day, and be fertilized quite often, so technology must be helped and nurtured, and not mistreated and suppressed. The concept that it would be in our interest to slow down technology is faulty from the point of view of the many unsatisfied military requirements. Since technological change is occurring "naturally," the notion is irrelevant. An invitation to go slow or "stabilize" technology is, implicitly, a proposal to accept defeat piecemeal; at best it is a proposal to fight war the hardest, the costliest, and the bloodiest way.

But even if technological slowdown were a valuable theoretical idea—how can this concept be applied in practice? Certainly, we can cut our own technological programs; and we have already slowed them down. But will the opponent do the same? Of course he will do the very opposite, despite the assertions of our perennial hopefuls. Even if he promised to behave in line with the slowdown scheme, there is no way to make him conform to this promise. And this is not at all a matter of agreements, inspection, bad will, or good will. Science and technology, if only because of the "serendipity" phenomenon, are really uncontrollable. Irrespective of what any government does or does not do, the obsolescence of weapons systems is essentially a function of time: after dozens and hundreds of little improvements, qualitative changes will have occurred even in the absence of fundamental new inventions. As we move forward, weapons obsolesce automatically.

This fact is often forgotten. There is the related illusion that until an international "arms-control" agreement has been signed, sealed, and delivered, disarmament is just a verbal exercise. Not so. Disarmament is taking place all around us, despite the fact that no disarmament agreement has been signed. With respect to the major defense challenges, there exists a system of *de facto* disarmament within the Free World. Britain has arms but no armament systems, and France is barely getting a few initial arms.

Armaments restricted to non-nuclear weapons are not suited to prevent or win World War III. They are in the nature of automobiles for which only water is available as fuel. It does not matter whether you acquire a Volkswagen, a Cadillac, or even a Rolls-Royce; the car will not move. European NATO spends about $15 billion, and Japan, Australia, New Zealand, South Korea, and Taiwan another $4 billion on conventional arms, except for the UK and French nuclear programs, which are included in these sums. The United States, too, is spending large amounts on conventional weapons. My estimate is that, in round figures, of a Free World military outlay of about 75 billion dollars, perhaps 25 and not more than 30 billion are genuinely devoted to preparedness against nuclear war. NATO armaments are costly; but unless there is the proper firepower, even the most costly weapons will remain "in the garage."

Only two world powers, the United States and the USSR, are armed, but neither is presently capable of fighting an all-out nuclear war *defensively*. The "fit" between intentions, strategy, and armaments is presently best in the Soviet Union. The sphere of disarmament is widening because the United States presently is delaying or foregoing the modernization of its armaments. The unilateral nuclear disarmament,* which in effect is taking place gradually in the Free World, largely in the form of disarmament by omission rather than commission, perpetuates and deepens the world crisis.

### Disarmament by Omission

This gradual approach to our unilateral disarmament deserves an illustration. In 1961, the Soviet Union announced that they would develop 100-MT (megaton) weapons, and proceeded to test super-yield devices. We failed to adopt a parallel program. By March 1962 the Soviets had tested half again as many high-yield devices as the United States, and by January 1963 they had tested twice as many high-yield weapons. Hence, their technical proficiency in this area should exceed ours.

During 1962, the American Secretary of Defense announced that henceforth the United States would pursue, whenever possible, a counterforce rather than a counter-value strategy. Yet in January 1963 the same official explained to Congress that due to expected hardening of Soviet missile sites, attacks on such targets may become infeasible. He failed to discuss the point that hardening and increases in yield are in a see-saw race: we must counter Soviet hardening by increasing our

---

* The point is *not* that non-nuclear systems are superfluous, but that modern armaments require a mix between nuclear and non-nuclear systems. The two types of weapons are supplementary.

yields, just as the Soviets have been countering the hardening of our missile sites. The fact of the matter is that even with an accuracy of 1,000 feet (a daydream in intercontinental war), a 10-MT shot could take out only a moderately hardened site; a site hardened to 100 psi (pounds-per-square-inch pressure), even with this fantastic accuracy, would require a 20-MT warhead. Obviously, if we forego increasing our yields, we allow the Soviets to build up an invulnerable missile force. By contrast, Soviet high-yield weapons really could engage in a counterforce strategy against us, with the result that this single omission on our part may tip the balance against us.

Despite the fact that, in terms of firepower and, hence, risk to our forces and people, the Soviet threat is increasing, we are holding back development of both ground and space-based anti-ICBM's. More specifically, we are slow in pushing new designs for suitable weapons systems, we are slow in testing the models we have, we are holding back deployment, we carry out only insufficient high-altitude nuclear-effects tests, and we practically refuse to develop the new nuclear technology, i.e., neutron devices, which hold the greatest promise for providing the most effective anti-ICBM firepower.

As a next step, we are phasing out bomber-aircraft which can deliver heavier firepower than missiles, and we are building mostly those ICBM's which have a low yield. Thus, we are reducing the firepower capability we possessed during the Cuban crisis of 1962 by about 90 per cent; if in the fall of 1962 our bombers had been equipped with bombs of very large yields (i.e., yields technically attainable without new "breakthroughs"), the reduction in firepower resulting from a phase-out of bombers would be about 98 per cent.

The contention is not that firepower is the single military element to which everything else must be subordinated, nor that firepower must necessarily be maximized. The contention is rather this: by restricting ourselves, in the main, to low-yield weapons and by drastically curtailing the "salvo-power" of our strategic forces, we (a) rule out even the possibility of effective US attacks on targets of the highest priority, (b) allow the opponent gigantic superiority in firepower, which could be decisive in war, and (c) essentially destroy our capability to deter aggression, for the would-be aggressor has little to fear from a retaliatory attack carried out by a residual force of missiles with small warheads. This should be enough for one illustration.

## Strategic Concept

Is there a better way to take care of our security?

Adoption of the following strategic principles would ensure that Soviet nuclear aggression will be prevented:

1) To maintain a technological lead over the Soviet Union of one or preferably two generations of weapons and firepower cycles;

2) To acquire weapons systems suitable to neutralize every specific threat posed by Soviet weaponry and to pose potential technical threats which they will find hard to counterbalance;

3) To develop technologies and strategies designed to reduce casualties and material damage;

4) To maintain quantitative strength superiority over the Soviet Union such that a Soviet first strike cannot, under any circumstances, preclude a retaliatory blow of *unacceptable* dimensions;

5) To arm the Free World alliance as an integrated entity;

6) To wage and win the Free World's struggle against the Communists as a technological contest, preferably in lieu of war.*

Under these headings, there are many weapons programs which need rebirth or stimulation.** There is no time to go into details. Let me just illustrate the problem through a concrete example, that of anti-missile defense. I am selecting this example because it illustrates US-European "interdependence" better than other systems. I am not talking about the Nike-Zeus. I am just talking about the mandatory requirement for this *sort* of weapon, irrespective of how the solution of the technical problem is attempted. Nevertheless, a question is in order: if Nike-Zeus does not fill the bill, where, pray, is the system which does? If there is no effective anti-missile program, why isn't there?

---

* The struggle cannot be restricted to technology but also involves political, economic, psychological, ideological, etc., operations.

** Our blindness or our nuclear trauma is evidenced by the negative attitude we take toward clean weapons, nuclear propulsion, radiation medicine, food pasteurization through radiation, etc. It is notable that Communist military dictionaries talk about radiological weapons (RW) as though Soviet forces possessed them, but we have decided such weapons make no sense. Yet an alliance which at the beginning of a conflict may have to trade space for time surely would fare better if the enemy were prevented from using abandoned installations which are made temporarily inoperative by RW agents rather than by physical destruction.

The Soviets claim they solved the problem of intercepting ICBM's. We therefore must expect them to deploy a defense system soon. Incidentally, even a rudimentary Soviet defensive system might force us to explode our warheads at high altitudes; if so, our low yields would be quite ineffective. High-yield weapons permit a partial neutralization of anti-ICBM defenses. How, then, can we survive if we allow the enemy to acquire both high yields *and* defenses, and deprive ourselves of both elements of strength?

I am afraid our anti-ICBM program has been stretched out or headed for limbo, and Euro-American interrelations have been ignored, because strategic planners got mixed up on a few essential points.

1) The Free World does not want to attack. Hence, to facilitate the enormous task of surviving under aggression and preserving military capability to continue fighting successfully, anti-ICBM capabilities are mandatory. Cliches about the supremacy of the offensive over the defensive do not negate the need for defensive arms.

2) A "100 per cent defense" is unattainable, but this does not prove defense is useless. Defense serves:

(a) To force the aggressor to increase his attack force, thus imposing heavy economic and time penalties on preparations for aggression. Time penalties may be even tactical in nature, which would help the defense. But the most important time penalty would be strategic and would constitute a gain in time for the Free World. If we are serious in anticipating an evolution of the Soviet system, we should buy systems that provide us with additional time.

(b) To complicate the tactics of aggression and force the attacker into multiple offensive and back-up systems.

(c) To reduce the probability of successful attack, hopefully, to below 50 per cent and, at the very least, render the calculus of success more difficult and uncertain.

3) The attacker has, or will have, global-range missiles. Soviet missile-carrying submarines will be operating on the high seas; sooner or later we will have to try to blow them out of the water. Hence, defensive missile bases should be geographically dispersed on a supranational and possibly global basis. (The need for a global defense deployment will grow as space becomes militarily more important.) To express this differently: anti-missile defenses cannot be set up to defend individual

countries within the alliance, but require at least *continental* basing in Europe and North America, and probably intercontinental basing to link, through the world oceans, Europe, America, and Japan. (In case of global-range missile or space attack, Latin America would have to be drawn into the defense structure.) A broadly-based defense system has the added advantage that it improves warning, complicates the attacker's timing tactics, and dilutes fall-out. The anti-ICBM (and antispace) systems could be partly ship-based and partly land-based. If there were no ship-based systems, the attacker might find it easy to utilize the over-water approaches to some advantage; moreover, ship-based systems are mobile, which would be another complicating factor for the aggressor. Such ship-based defense systems are yet to be developed. Yet it is predictable that possession of such systems would spare us many political headaches.

4) Individual parts of the alliance cannot be left unprotected lest they be exposed to nuclear blackmail and their surrender jeopardize the alliance in its entirety.

5) The development of an effective anti-missile system requires considerably more R&D work.

6) The establishment of a properly based anti-missile system will cost, in over-all orders of magnitude, 30 to 40 billion dollars.* The United States cannot by itself finance such an intercontinental system. If it were to assume exclusive responsibility for anti-missile R&D, the program would be stretched out, as it has been, and many new approaches would be overlooked.

7) The system can be effective only if it incorporates nuclear warheads (though not necessarily to the complete exclusion of other destructive agents). There is a good chance that for interception above the sensible atmosphere, radiation and notably neutron weapons will prove to be most satisfactory. Interception within the atmosphere should probably be accomplished by clean devices. To achieve the requisite nuclear capabilities, our atomic programs must be stepped up and testing must be resumed in a serious manner.

8) The United States certainly cannot man an intercontinental defense system exclusively with American hands. Yet for

---

* The cost of our abortive Cuban strategy, by early 1963, has been estimated at about $5 billion, including losses to nationalization. If Cuba remains a Communist base, US defenses must be extended to cover the southern approaches against low flying aircraft and missiles. Nothing is more wasteful than a strategy of half-measures.

obvious reasons of tactical timing, the concept that warheads must remain in American custody until the President releases them, is unworkable for a rapid, anti-missile defense system.

For all these reasons, it seems to me, a properly conceived anti-missile system presupposes a world-wide defense net, plus technological, nuclear, and financial sharing. To put it more sharply: effective defenses in missile war presuppose an adequately working alliance structure.

It is in the nuclear area where most of the resistance has arisen. It has been argued that Europe does not need its own deterrent or retaliatory force and that, at any rate, a decision can be delayed until the negotiations about the Common Market have been concluded and Europe has been integrated. The US policy of monopolizing the deterrent has brought NATO to the brink of break-up. At the same time, while much ink has been spilled about the "credibility" of our deterrent, the point was overlooked that there is only *one* way to ensure this credibility: the ability of each victim of aggression to defend himself with nuclear weapons instantly, and before allies come to his rescue.

Furthermore, I believe that the arguments against the nuclear arming of NATO ground forces, especially those that are stationed on the lines of contact, are specious and mistaken, but I do not have the space to go into this problem except to state that the continued neglect of tactical nuclear weapons in Europe will destroy the Alliance for good.

Whatever the theoretical validity of the opposition against the sharing of strategic and tactical weapons, no reasonable arguments against the sharing of anti-ICBM warheads have been advanced. Even the fear that design secrets would be compromised can be alleviated. The discussion was side-stepped as a result of the allegation that anti-missile defenses so far are not feasible. To make this defeatist allegation stick—the allegation also served to buttress the argument against bombers—anti-missile development has been slowed down.

Thus, we are confronted by a vicious circle: first, by not developing defenses we fail to reduce our vulnerability and jeopardize our capability to strike back. Second, by claiming the practical invulnerability of missiles, we justify the elimination of bombers and the massive reduction of yield. Third, by allowing the Soviets to forge ahead with their anti-missile systems, we allow them to reduce *their* vulnerability. Fourth, we are compounding the resultant danger by using low-yield missiles and placing increasing reliance on Polaris missiles which, whatever the great advantages of the submarine system, are relatively speaking more easily interceptible than ICBM's. Fifth, by not acquiring defenses, we allow the Soviets to gain maximum advantage from their high-yield weapons: in the absence of defenses which would compel the attacker to explode his warheads at high altitude, the aggressor is free to select optimal heights of burst. Sixth, by not pushing proper defenses, we undermine the military usefulness of Free World alliances. Seventh, we are enhancing, by our do-nothing strategy, Soviet capabilities for launching surprise attacks.

Among the many specious arguments adduced against even an exclusively American development of anti-ICBM defenses, the allegation of excessive cost looms high. Actually, the costs of the anti-missile system would be in the same order of magnitude as those of other large weapons systems. But granting that the cost would be additive to existing outlays, if there were a well-planned NATO-wide effort, this economic difficulty could be overcome more easily. Unfortunately, the sensible alliance-wide approach is blocked because we do not want to open the nuclear Pandora's box. Is it not self-evident that this strategy of postponement, illusion, and nuclear trauma in a really frightening manner, pushes us gradually to the brink of the *real* abyss?

**The Crisis of the Alliance**

Up to 1956, American policy was intent upon bringing about the military integration of Europe in the literal sense of the word. It was hoped that the European Defense Community treaty would accomplish a rapid upgrading of Western Europe's military capabilities. When this treaty failed to obtain ratification, the push toward integration lost its momentum. American strategy continued to be based upon NATO as one of its cornerstones, but the development of NATO became a routine task, to be accomplished through SHAPE in a thousand and one little steps. It remained axiomatic that an American presence in Europe was indispensable if deterrence was to be secured permanently and if Western Europe were to be held politically and economically. But this was more or less a political arrangement, essentially a guarantee like Britain gave to Poland and Rumania in 1939. The difference was merely that this current political guarantee was strengthened by military means, i.e., coordination and the American presence in Europe. Due to their atomic armaments, the US contingents in Europe continued to be the main local force able to oppose a full-fledged Soviet attack. But so far NATO has not functioned as a military arrangement designed to help the Allies acquire effective self-defense capabilities.

The decline in American interest was connected with a technological change: strategic delivery means had grown to be long-legged, and, consequently, the need for overseas bases seemed to have abated. This was an erroneous or oversimplified assessment, even with respect to "strategic warfare," but it strengthened the conviction that while Europe would continue to remain an American obligation, it would not become an element of genuine strength. In addition, the basing of main American strengths in the Zone of the Interior was deemed to reduce vulnerability. And how many political headaches could be avoided by keeping our strategic systems at home!

Another development has been exerting considerable impact. After the United States originally had staked the defense of NATO upon nuclear weapons, gradually American leaders had second thoughts about the destructiveness of nuclear armament. Nuclear war was described as "unthinkable," but it was not explained how, in this case, Europe or the United States was to be defended should the "unthinkable" attack come after all. The Soviets, stopped in their quest for world conquest by the American nuclear arsenal, turned their propaganda guns against these very weapons. Simultaneously, they made haste to acquire a nuclear arsenal themselves, to achieve nuclear superiority, and to assert (which should have been self-evident to US decision-makers, too) that a major future war would inevitably be nuclear in nature. It was specified, for example, in Marshal V. D. Sokolovsky's book, *Military Strategy*, that the advent of nuclear weapons has not changed the function of war, i.e., war remains an instrument of policy.

An enormous propaganda barrage, in part stimulated by the Soviets but in part self-inflicted, persuaded American leaders that the "image" of the United States was suffering because of our nuclear armaments. After a desultory effort to "sell" atomic energy through the Atoms for Peace Program, Washington decided that the "image" needed refurbishing through initiatives toward nuclear disarmament. There is no need to recount the dreary sequence of disarmament and test-ban conferences.

Yet this exercise in futility had a profound influence upon the NATO Alliance. By constantly offering new ways to achieve an uncertain and unenforceable test ban; by displaying an ever greater willingness to risk Soviet cheating and to chance the resultant loss of technological superiority; by denying and disregarding well-founded suspicions about actual test-ban evasions; by acquiescing, except in propaganda, in the terroristic resumption of nuclear testing by the Soviets; and by meekly and belatedly acknowledging Soviet technological gains in the nuclear competition—by all this eagerness to get roped and raped, the United States was suffering an eclipse in leadership.

Moreover, the United States was bartering away its capability to defend Europe. By not testing the reliability of the weapons on which we are basing our defenses; by not checking in actual target practice entire missile assemblies with their warheads; and by not even trying to find out through actual shots whether our hardened missile silos can do the job for which they are designed, we are playing with our capability to defend ourselves. The American folly was quietly and fearfully noted. Europe heaved a sigh of relief when the missile gap did not materialize, partly because the incipient danger was in time loudly advertised. The gaps which may be emerging presently in nuclear strength and space capabilities are developing more silently, which may preclude timely prophylactic action. The trends are everywhere watched with great attention.

The situation has been aggravated by the fact that the test-ban negotiations included as one of their proclaimed objectives the closing of the "nuclear club" to the present members. Thus, the "superpowers" jointly are intent upon preventing any additional nation from acquiring nuclear capabilities, be it strictly defensive in character; as a result, the "superpowers" would remain on top and everybody else at the bottom. It was intimated that this stratagem aimed at precluding the nuclear arming of China and thus would reduce the danger of war. But so long as China does not possess an industrial capability to build adequate means of delivery, this argument remains fanciful; besides, nothing can be done to stop Chinese nuclear programs, if any, even supposing that the Soviets have not, or will not, in the future, rig up some sort of proxy arrangements with their hostile friends in Peking. The invalidity of this type of wishful reasoning was shown when the Soviets attempted to place nuclear weapons into Cuba—but this argument is Phoenix-like and will be reiterated in different forms.

There was, to be sure, an honest hope of securing world peace more effectively. But in practice, arms negotiations have become an instrument through which, on a seemingly functional level, the "Anglo-Saxons" and the "Russians" may be working out a *modus vivendi*. This may not be the intent, but an agreement would have the effect of keeping the "nuclear club" closed. This effort will not succeed because other nations will not tolerate such disregard of their national interests, and because they will resent the notion that they are too immature to possess weapons which the world can leave trustingly in the hands of Americans, Englishmen, and Russians. But, while it lasts, the maneuver could eliminate NATO as an element of Free World security. All that is necessary for the NATO collapse to eventuate is a general belief that disarmament negotiations are truly taken seriously by the United States, that America is willing to buy "peace" through an agreement with the disturber of that peace, that the United States is not a reliable ally, and that Washington remains immature enough not to see through the Soviet stratagem.

Indeed, the *de facto* abolition of NATO has been the asking price that the Kremlin wants the United States to pay for any "arms-control" agreements, including the phony ones the Soviets are really interested in.

It has proved impractical for the United States to throw Europe into the bargain, and naturally, there was no intent to do so. But the test ban did offer an opportunity to mask the nature of the US-USSR "negotiation," especially in the minds of those US proponents who only were interested in the nuclear deal, and did not bother much about its political implications. Indeed, if the United States (together with a small British capability) and the Soviet Union were to perform as nuclear duopolists, the world would be divided into two "orbits," just like China and Rome were the twin masters of the ancient world. Shorn of verbiage and illusions, a nuclear test ban between the United States and the Soviet Union would constitute a *modus vivendi* and possibly an implicit quasi-alliance. But duopolistic arrangements are notoriously unstable. This particular arrangement would last only until Strategic Judgment Day, when the Soviet Union, through clandestine testing, will have achieved clear-cut superiority to stand up the United States before the wailing wall of history.

The contention is *not* that Washington wrote off NATO for the purpose of achieving an agreement with Moscow. Washington's mass production of arms-limitation projects is partly psychological warfare. As Khrushchev allegedly was producing missiles "like sausages," we were trying to counteract our real or fancied unpopularity by constantly inventing new "plans" and increasing the share of illusion and delusion in our own strategic thinking. To a large extent, this has been amateurishness in propaganda. But there also is a sincere conviction, not entirely unfounded, that *some* conversations with the Soviets are necessary. Yet what is there to talk about except schemes of unreality?

The contention *is*, however, that precisely because the American Government is not staffed by cynics but strongly influenced by wishful thinkers and naive technicians, our insistence on disarmament has been genuine and honest. As a by-product of this delusionary effort, the development of NATO was allowed to lapse. (Note that the term "development" is used here with the same meaning that we apply to the economy of under-developed countries.) Since NATO was taken for granted, the tasks, which still must be solved, were not seen; and the building is showing signs of cracking up.

For a while, we were the power monopolist among the democratic nations, but the fact is that this country cannot by itself, like Atlas, carry alone the main burdens of the Free World. The more we must be doing ourselves, the more urgent it becomes to share the burden.

After the war and long after NATO had come into being, the European nations possessed neither the resources to acquire nuclear weapons, nor the motivation to ask for them. Having just emerged from a murderous war, they were entirely content to have the United States defend Europe. The United States formulated the main strategies; it provided the main leadership within SHAPE where it achieved some sort of common outline planning, according to American guidelines; and, by and large, the European forces were developed and deployed to function as supplements to the decisive weapons systems which were kept in US hands. It would be a grievous mistake to underrate the military progress which was made in many areas of integration, but it is unwise, in things military, to count the distance which one has walked and to ignore the magnitude of the tasks still ahead.

In the meantime, the main European states recovered economic and political strength. Unfortunately, military progress did not keep pace with the political recovery, let alone with the stupendous economic advance. This European failure is partly rooted in doubts as to whether the United States, if and when the call comes, will be true to its word. These doubts are un-

justified, but they are a reflection of vacillating US leadership in
NATO—vacillation which, under the guise of "flexibility," frequently is considered a useful approach among American politicians. In any event, the present system has many glaring
defects: (1) It places too much responsibility on the United
States; (2) it provides merely for partial and weakening deterrence; (3) it opens the way for Soviet miscalculation; (4) it
does not provide an effective physical defense of our allies; and
(5) it does not supply the psychological cohesion without which
an alliance cannot endure.

Countries which possess no self-defense capability lose their
sovereignty. Since duopoly is unsafe, it is in the interest of
America to restore the sovereignty of our European allies in a
genuine sense. But the vitalization of NATO is not merely a
matter of political wisdom, let alone of American altruism. It
is, above all, a matter of mutual self-interest. If our allies
remain disarmed, every Soviet nuclear bomb and warhead will
hit American targets; let us share *that* wealth. If Europe falls
and we fight on, we shall have the costly job of liberating the
moribund continent. But if Europe were armed properly, casualties and damage both in North America and Europe would be
reduced, the war would be shorter and easier, and the probability of a major conflagration would be reduced substantially.

**Whose Initiative?**

The United States, which is at lesser jeopardy than its allies,
has not risen to the occasion. This is bad enough. But our
European friends, with one or two exceptions, do not seem to
care. This is worse. Let me illustrate.

An offer by a Republican administration to put Polaris submarines at the disposal of NATO was followed by the offer of a
Democratic administration to assign these ships, with American
crews, to the NATO Supreme Commander. This maneuver was
a somewhat transparent attempt to reconcile military facts of
life with the announced US policy against national deterrents:
the NATO Commander happens to be an American officer, and
the American President's exclusive authority over the nuclear
arms of these ships would have remained unchanged despite this
formal transfer.

Nevertheless, the introduction of Polaris submarines into the
NATO system would be a gigantic step forward. Moreover,
Washington did suggest, albeit obliquely, that its opposition did

*not* mean the United States was closing the door to the nuclear arming of NATO: whereas the United States did not want any national deterrent forces, it would not necessarily object to multi-national arrangements. By hitching the nuclear conversation to the prior success of political arrangements in Europe, we were hoping, perhaps, to help the Common Market negotiation. Rightly or wrongly, it was put up to the Europeans to make the proper suggestions concerning the organization of a multi-national or supranational force. But the European politicians do not quite understand the strategic problem, and hence this attempt to hurry them along did not work. In the end, this detour maneuver allowed everybody to postpone hard decisions, but invaluable "strategic time" was lost.

Thereupon, late in 1962, there followed a second round. It started with the US cancellation of Skybolt which had been promised to Britain. Irrespective of whether technical reasons really were overriding, which is doubtful, the US broke a commitment and forced the British to accept a new Polaris offer. The proposed arrangement, although hedged with escape clauses, did in effect deprive the United Kingdom of its independent deterrent. The Polaris offer was extended to France; had it been accepted, it would have disorganized the French armament program and delayed by five to six years the acquisition of a French deterrent. Neither to the United Kingdom nor to France did the United States offer the warheads, nor were the offers accompanied by a Presidential message to Congress requesting amendment of the McMahon Act.

The Skybolt breach of promise in 1962, of course, made it virtually impossible for a realistic government to realign its efforts in the expectation that the United States can be relied upon, with absolute certainty, to redeem its promise on Polaris in 1970. In addition, the United States still was pursuing the test-ban agreement with the Soviet Union. The French, who do not have a warhead suitable for Polaris, must develop one, and this would require testing. If there were a test ban, we would expect the French not to test, but at the same time we won't give them the warhead, a major objective of the test-ban agreement being to prevent "proliferation" of nuclear arms.

This mess has been, almost exclusively, an American contribution toward the destruction of NATO. But thereupon the British and French did their share——the British because they have no policy and did not stand up for their rights, in the somewhat obsolete hope that they could carve out for themselves a special relationship with the United States; and the French because they overreacted to what they considered, quite rightly, American unilateralism and because they found the British, again, unreliable.

Also, early in 1963, a storm broke with Canada. The United States had argued against proliferation of nuclear weapons among our European allies, and had done virtually nothing to help Europe acquire a defense system. But when the Canadians, claiming they, too, were against proliferation, dragged their feet in accepting our warheads for their defense system, we castigated them and through an undiplomatic note toppled the Canadian Government. It appeared as though we wanted to insure effective defenses on the approach routes to our own country but showed no similar concern for the security of our European allies. Surely, this is not the way to build an alliance.

But beyond these enormous political blunders, there remains the vast unsolved question: how NATO should be equipped with nuclear arms. The fact is that the Europeans proved incapable —and even unwilling—to present a workable plan. If, on its part, the United States had had a positive concept of a NATO atomic structure, it was not disclosed. According to inspired leaks, no suitable concept has yet been discovered. This *carence* of thinking and planning appears to be the fault of practically everybody within the Alliance. The Europeans cannot possibly be as misinformed as they pretend to be, and many of their policies are either bluff or attempts to pass the buck to the United States. But the greatest blame attaches to ourselves. We have not been interested in feeding the requisite information to our allies—and we could have done so without compromising legitimate security.

The real issue, however, is this: the thankless task of providing the leadership to revitalize NATO *cannot* be lifted from American shoulders. No one but the United States is capable of achieving worthwhile results. The procedure used to initiate the Marshall Plan indicates the pattern which we will have to follow.

Naturally, the spreading of nuclear weapons poses risks, but the hazards in not defending Europe properly and in not basing our strategy upon the principle of mutuality are greater. These risks include shortening the life expectancy of NATO as well as the possibility that an atomically disarmed Europe may tempt the aggressor, with the result that the United States may be forced to retaliate in full strength.

There are dozens of devices through which the legitimate fears about abuse of shared weapons can be allayed. For the time being, we can minimize the risks inherent in nuclear sharing by concentrating first, as we are trying to do in the Canadian case, on air and missile, and perhaps ground, defenses. Obviously, the problem of effective defense will not go away if we just continue to sleep over it. It is up to Washington to give NATO a second start.

## Conclusions

We can wage the conflict with the Soviet Union as a technological contest; and we can gain decisive technological and arms superiority by combining the capacities of the main industrial nations within the Free World.

The wisdom of a strategy of supremacy is grasped readily if we ask ourselves whether we could survive in case the Soviets acquired supremacy over us. Obviously we could not, and therefore our minimum goal must be to avert the contingency of Soviet superiority. It is also reasonably self-evident that we shall not be able to dissuade the enemy from continuing with his plans for revolutionary world conquest unless and until he becomes convinced that he has no chance of victory, now or ever. Moreover, the strategic situation of both camps is not symmetrical: since we won't attack, and therefore cannot pick the time, the weapons, and the type of the ultimate conflict, we need stronger and technically more capable forces.

If these premises are granted, the question arises whether we should aim at moderate or massive superiority. The answer is that, due to the unpredictability of technological change, a "balance" based upon moderate superiority might be easily upset; hence, the hazards of such a strategy are very high. Also, if we allow the Soviets to continue the game in a somewhat leisurely fashion, the Cold War will be continued indefinitely, and our ability to talk them into adopting a new policy will remain very weak.

But is a NATO strategy of supremacy feasible? Economically, it certainly is, although considerable sacrifices would become necessary. My main contention is that we possess a massive (though still only potential) superiority in technical resources, above all in inventiveness and know-how. It is *this* capability which should allow us to achieve the required military supremacy. Specifically, this capability, notably our nuclear potential, should allow us to revitalize the powers of the defensive, and thus satisfy one of the chief military requirements of a second-strike strategy; and it should also allow us to put to excellent use the new dimension of space which should benefit us more than the opponent if only because the Iron Curtain cannot survive in the face of sustained space operations. Through technology, the Alliance should be able to keep the conflict manageable and ultimately to bring about its liquidation.

The pooling of the entire Alliance's technological, industrial, and financial strengths, and the establishment of a North American-European defense community embracing well over 400 million people, therefore, has become the paramount strategic task of the current decade.

But just as the United States has been holding back technology, so the European members of NATO and Canada have refused to increase their defense expenditures in terms of percentages of GNP to a level corresponding to US outlays. If military and technological complementarity were achieved, defense costs would become more bearable for everybody, and broad, safe margins of security, i.e., supremacy, could be achieved. In this case, even with the utmost effort, the Soviet Union could not "reach and overtake" the Atlantic defense "colossus."

In the interim, unfortunately, the United States is compelled to continue bearing the brunt of Free World security. Therefore, it must accelerate rather than decelerate its technological programs. The creation of a genuine defense community necessarily will be time-consuming. Yet if the United States were to push this effort with the same vigor it has devoted to other international undertakings, this community can be created long before Soviet power might become intractable.

If we are successful in these undertakings, *we can win without waging total war.* Should war occur, our possession of better and more arms, together with an improved ability to protect friendly people, would allow us to minimize losses without reducing our military effectiveness.

This assessment is admittedly hopeful. Still, it is based on the undisputed fact that the Free World's resources are considerably larger than those of the Soviet Union. There is a high probability that throughout the foreseeable future, our economic and technological strengths will remain preponderant. Perhaps, due to the Common Market and an American economic upswing, coupled by economic difficulties within the Bloc, and notably in China, our relative advantages will increase rather than decrease.

If reasonably successful, a strategy aiming to outarm the opponent holds out the hope that the Communist leaders will find it increasingly difficult and unprofitable to prepare themselves for aggression. In the long run, if it is demonstrated that aggressive strategy does not and will not work and that the world revolution has become a myth as well as a moloch, the population of the Soviet Union may be able to assert stronger claims for its pursuit of happiness. More is at stake than just gaining time: the Free World must become stronger, but while it is strengthening its muscles it need not just sit by passively waiting for the erosion of the Communist ideology. It also can and should strive for "ideological victory," to use a telling phrase by W. W. Rostow.

No strategy is infallible. Consequently, there is no gaurantee that this particular strategy will work in the quadruple sense that it will prove to be politically and materially feasible, deter Communist aggression and eliminate Communist aggressiveness, maintain free institutions, and allow us to fight and win an unavoided war with "acceptable" losses. But the chances that this ambitious strategy *can* work are infinitely greater than the prospects of alternate strategies proposed so far. Notably, this strategy is preferable to the unstable "balance of terror," which results not only in a most undesirable political situation, but involves a *deliberate choice not* to drive the Free World's technological effort to the limits of our capacity.

We need friends and we need arms, and our friends need us and need arms which we have been withholding from them and, through inaction, from ourselves. If we acquire and share the proper arms, we will preserve friends and strengthen friendship; and if we cooperate with our friends, we—and they—will create ever stronger and more reliable defenses. If we succeed in starting upon this *circulus virtuosus*, we shall have seized the initiative and *without* provocation, crisis, and preventive war, turned the wheel of history to roll toward peace and freedom. We are able to play this game more smartly than we have in the past. There is no overriding reason for democracies, as Shakespeare put it in King Lear, to act like "fools by heavenly compulsion."

# An Approach to Military Strategy

—*JAMES D. ATKINSON*

## Summary

*The recurring crises in Berlin, the shadowy war in Southeast Asia, the conventional warfare tactics in Communist China's aggression in India, and the growing Communist penetration in Africa and in Latin America (viewing Cuban events as initial skirmishes in a many-faceted Western Hemisphere campaign) indicate how difficult it is to make politico-diplomatic decisions except as integrated with a military strategic frame of reference. Force may be masked at times, but it is ever-present in the realities of world politics. Military power has a wide range of applications. In the area of low-intensity conflict (Cold War and "peaceful coexistence") or in sub-limited warfare it can be coordinated with the exercise of other forms of power, and be developed, organized, and employed in varied situations without the often-feared risk of escalation. The many capabilities of military means can be applied most effectively to situations that range from those relatively peaceful, to those characterized by subversion and insurgency or by limited warfare.*

*It is suggested that a spatial-maritime strategy is best structured to provide the mix of non-forcible, semi-forcible, and forcible measures from which our constitutional officials can choose in initiating national security actions. This would appear to be so because the variety of our possible choices of action (for example, ranging from interrupting an opponent's communications to the delivery of nuclear weapons on his key targets) and an enemy's complications in responding to our initiative, can be heightened by a strategy which exploits spatial-maritime possibilities.*

*The psycho-political advantages accruing from a nation's ability to exercise power in and through the space environment are immense. The propaganda advantage alone would constitute a valid reason for giving consideration to space strategy. But it is historically correct that military control of an environment permits psycho-political exploitation. In the past, nations enjoyed vast psycho-political advantages from their ability to exercise control in the sea environment and later in the air environment. It would appear obvious, therefore, that space can be used by us or against us. To state that this is obvious does not mean that it is accepted as such. Despite much evidence that the Soviets treat the scientific side of space as quite incidental to the military, many Americans continue in the belief that we can treat space as a peaceful arena.*

*There are unique relationships as regards the maritime position of the United States and the pervasive possibilities of space operations. Additionally, the rather loose coalition we call the "Free World" is a sea-oriented complex, highly dependent on the oceans in terms of natural resources and practical geography. Who controls the seas can control the land, and the space far above the whole planet. Indeed, the oceans and the vast spaces above and below them may provide the key to integrating the baffling prospects of space with the reality of our being an earth-born race.*

---

In modern times American statesmen and the American people have generally understood the supreme importance of military power and military strategy in a situation of open war. They have been less cognizant of the role of military power and military strategy in the successful conduct of national policy in time of ostensible peace. Our thought processes and our governmental apparatus are structured in such a way that we are often unable either to plan or to act vigorously until the line between peace and war is crossed. Prior to the Second World War, this—while at times hampering our military strategy—was not a major defect. But in the US-Soviet Bloc confrontation in the aftermath of World War II, this peace-war line distinction has had a continuing (if not always apparent) role in inhibiting the adoption of a viable American military strategy.

The arguments and counter-arguments about the military strategies of "massive retaliation," "finite deterrence," "counter-force," and "controlled response" are the shadows which obscure the substance of the problem.* These strategies have been advanced largely on the concept that the mission of the armed forces is "to be prepared for war and to fight and win if war should come." This is a traditional view. But is it a proper guide for the strategy of the 1960's and 1970's in face of non-traditional Marxist-Leninist strategy? Admirable as certain aspects of these traditional strategies are, they are all posited on the premise "if war should come." They preclude the hard question: is the real and present struggle, now and in the future, taking place in the area of neither war nor peace, but in the intermixture of the two? These shadows—argued also on the basis of how best to deter general thermonuclear war—have obscured the basic issue confronting American national policy: the adoption of a *strategy*—not organizational improvisations—permitting the projection and use of the national power for rendering harmless the new kind of warfare actually being waged by the Communists.

What are the dimensions of this new and continuing struggle? Why did it blur the distinction between war and peace and thus create a semantic as well as a strategic problem? Bernard Baruch used the term "cold war" to designate the uneasy truce that followed the Second World War. Said he: "Let us not be deceived—we are today in the midst of a cold war. Our enemies are to be found abroad and at home . . ." General William J. Donovan, World War II Chief of the Office of Strategic Services, believed that a more all-embracing term should be used rather than "cold war." Hence he began using the term "unconventional warfare" in order to describe the new pattern of neither peace nor war. In other writings,[1] I constructed the term *polyreconic warfare* in an attempt to describle this phenomenon of using warlike methods operating in the context of peace, without a sharp breaking-line between war and peace.

This mixing of war and peace embraces a broad spectrum of struggle. It involves forcible, semi-forcible, and non-forcible techniques. It includes propaganda, economic warfare, sabotage, espionage, subversion, the fomentation of strikes, civil disturbances, terrorism, psycho-political attack (in the form, for example, of threats of nuclear obliteration), diplomatic pressures,

* Although these terms mean different things to different people, they have come to be quite influential whether properly so or not.

guerrilla warfare, and limited, conventional, "undeclared" war. In this non-traditional struggle, 2000 demonstrators in London chanting "Hands off Cuba" and "Kennedy to Hell"[2] may be more significant than a dozen ICBM's in planning the strategy of the next decade. The military strategies of the post-World War II period have been grafted onto traditional thinking. They have not fully taken account of the psycho-political revolution occasioned both by the mixing of war and peace techniques and the development of nuclear weapons. With reference to nuclear weapons, the West in general and the United States in particular have been so obsessed with the military fact of nuclear weapons and the idea of "escalation" that they have tended to underestimate the much greater psychical impact of the atom and hence its supreme psycho-political role. In fine, "Ban the Bomb" demonstrations and "peace marches" (of the 1960's and 1970's) need to be evaluated just as thoroughly as physical military equipment (the "sticks and stones"), and the strictly military effects of nuclear weapons to determine the national strategy.

The construction of a sound military strategy must take into account certain inhibiting factors which have influenced US strategy during the immediate past and some or all of which may be expected to do so in future. As a prelude to a proposal for a military strategy for the future, it is necessary to dissect these factors, though such dissection is painful, since some of them enter areas in which emotion is apt to be stronger than reason. It is suggested that these factors include: (1) The nature of the new warfare, the seeming failure fully to comprehend it, and the interrelated role of national power in non-traditional struggle. (2) The United Nations as an inhibiting factor in US national security policy. (3) The amorphous and elusive concept of "world opinion" as an inhibiting factor in US national security policy. (4) Public opinion in the United States as a possible future inhibiting factor.

### The Nature of the New Warfare

In his courageous speech on the Berlin crisis in September 1961, President Kennedy pointed out that the Soviet formula for non-traditional warfare was "what's mine is mine and what's yours is negotiable." Yet, though the President cogently summarized Soviet psycho-political diplomacy in such clear terms, it may well be asked whether we Americans have—even after all these years—taken cognizance of the new warfare which masquerades as peace. A striking feature of the present world crisis is that not only do most citizens not recognize and relate the polyreconic operations which make up the current conduct of "war," but that some of our most influential and prestigious writers and publicists seemingly fail to grasp its true nature. Mr. Walter Lippmann, for example, has written with reference to the Soviet exploitation of Cuba that "we are able to spot anything like an expeditionary force against Cuba's neighbors in the islands and in the Caribbean."[3] He then went on to say that US policy should be "to wait and see whether Castro and his Soviet helpers do any overt act against the United States or its neighbors."[4] Now this is to misread the lessons of history of the polyreconic warfare which the Communists have been waging these past many years. Where was the "expeditionary force" that made Cuba an advanced Soviet base? What overt, declared act of war has been committed in Vietnam? In Laos? Is any open expeditionary force to be seen in the current struggles in Venezuela, in Guatemala, in Brazil, in Chile? What overt act of war accompanied the building of the Berlin wall? In the shadowy area of no war, no peace, the Communist legions move forward with muted trumpets and muffled drums. Past conquerors with designs for world hegemony have sought primarily to explode their ideas and their forces against the outer shell of the peoples or countries they were attacking. The overt, even the declared war, they did not avoid. The Communists, even when they cross a frontier, prefer to operate in the twilight zone of no war, no peace. Concurrently with the seizure of territory, as in India, they call for "negotiations." They do not disdain the hardware of war, the missiles, the nuclear weapons, but they much prefer to exploit these as blackmail to attempt to force compliance with their will. What is significant about Cuba as a Communist *point d'appui* is not so much that it can be used as a base for directing missiles, or aircraft, or submarines against the United States. More, perhaps, is the fact that it is the intelligence and operations center for the conduct of unorthodox warfare against the United States and all of Latin America and the islands of the Caribbean. It is the base for para-military and for cold warfare which does not send out expeditionary forces with flags flying and telegraphed warnings to all the world. Its real significance was underscored by Mr. Adlai Stevenson when he said: "The crucial fact is that Cuba . . . has made itself an accomplice in the Communist enterprise of world domination."

It would be well not to speak of "victory" in the recent Cuban affair. Rather, this was but a skirmish in the new warfare which extends into a future whose end no man can see.*

A lesson that perhaps can be learned from Cuba, however, is the role of power in the non-traditional struggle. If military strategy and force are to be held back on the "if war should come" premise, then the great potential of power is precluded. The highest success of the military art is to accomplish the objective without firing a shot in anger. Power thus has a potential far beyond the actual engagement of an enemy in fighting. This highest potential has been well stated by former Army Chief of Staff General George H. Decker: "We *can* develop and apply power as subtly and persistently as the Communists. We can do this without automatically causing escalation. *Military power has great potential beyond its evident combat application.*"**

A military strategy which will project this "great potential beyond its evident combat application" will be based on the idea that power is not evil *in se* and, equally, that power used purposively will lower, not raise, the so-feared threshold of "escalation."

### The UN and US National Security Policy

In the new warfare in which we are engaged, the United Nations constitutes, unhappily, an inhibiting factor. For this new warfare demands what *The Federalist Papers* so cogently called "secrecy and dispatch." The United Nations, admirable as a forum for discussion of world politics, is particularly ill-suited to move with the speed, and without the advance warning which are the requirements either for the minimal checkmating of the Communists or the optimum of seizing and keeping the initiative in the world arena.

A further difficulty is posed by the proliferation of member states of the United Nations*** with their highly disparate inter-

---

* Perhaps the significance of Cuba was foreshadowed in July of 1960 when S. M. Kudriavtsev was appointed Soviet Ambassador to that country. He had been First Secretary of the Soviet Embassy in Ottawa in 1946 and a key figure in espionage and subversion operations directed against Canada.

** Italics added.

*** As of January 1, 1963, there were 110 member states with many more pressing for admission.

ests and their greatly varied concepts of man and of man's role in society. Lord Cherwell outlined this difficulty when he said:

> The governing body, the Assembly, consists of a heterogeneous collection of so-called sovereign states, some of which are thousands of times more numerous than others, and tens of thousands of times more powerful and wealthy. Some of them are highly civilized; others are all but illiterate. Yet they all have an equal vote. Their decisions are given with no attempt at impartiality. They act on no known laws and have no rules of evidence. . . . In these circumstances, nations, especially those dependent upon the sanctity of treaties and contracts for their survival cannot be expected to entrust their fate unconditionally to U. N.[5]

Of course this does not mean that the United States should fail to use the United Nations and its agencies as a part of its diplomacy. It does mean that the United Nations is simply one facet of diplomacy and by no means—in all cases—the most important one. It does mean that a national strategy denied the initiative because of supposed inhibitions about the nature of the United Nations is apt to be sterile. Senator Henry M. Jackson stated the case precisely when he pointed out: "The test of the national security policy process is this: Does it identify our vital interests and does it develop foreign and defense policies which will defend and promote these interests? . . . The United Nations is not, and was never intended to be, a substitute for our own leaders as makers and movers of American policy. The shoulders of the Secretary-General were never expected to carry the burdens of the President or the Secretary of State." [6]

### "World Opinion" and US National Security Policy

It is paradoxical that the United States—in which the puff of the public relations man has so long resounded—should be fearful of being unable to influence "world opinion." By contrast, the Communists, inherently contemptuous of individual opinion, believe that they can influence "world opinion," especially by taking the psycho-political offensive. Thus China's Number Two Communist, Chou En-lai has said: "The leaders of imperialist nations are low types. We must constantly attack them, scold them and threaten them with confusion."

One can hardly fail to be impressed with Chou En-lai's recipe for the psycho-political offensive when one recalls the U–2 incident of May 1960. We all remember the alarm and the apologies of many of the molders of public opinion in the United States, in Great Britain, and in some of the other Western democracies over the U-2 affair. Yet the U-2 project—successfully flying high over the Soviet Union for more than four years—was one of the most brilliant strategic conceptions in the intelligence and technological fields of recent times. Rather than an occasion for exclaiming *mea culpa* one would expect it to have been a cause for rejoicing that Americans could act rather than merely react in the world arena.

It is of more than passing interest that the Soviets did not publicize nor did they use diplomatic channels in an attempt to stop the "invasion" of their air space by U-2's until they could do so from a position of relative strength. They wished to show proof of military power by bringing down a U-2. The psychological position of strength as a persuader of world opinion was considered more important by the Soviet leadership than enemy intelligence gains permitted in the interim.

If the United States should develop and employ a more sophisticated type of aerial reconnaissance device we may expect from the opposing mentalities two things: first, secrecy by the United States and concealment of its successful scientific and military exploits; second, silence from the Soviets despite their distaste for constantly prying surveillance. The evidence suggests that they would pursue this course rather than expose their inability to defend against or to match the military and scientific position of strength demonstrated by such an advanced system of aerial reconnaissance. By contrast, if the Soviets are in future caught in the act of penetrating the air space of the United States, they will most certainly attempt to capitalize on it as a "scientific" achievement.

The U-2 incident is revealing with reference to the way it illustrates the attitude of many in the Western democracies toward the area which has been designated as "world opinion." One recalls that some American public figures, writers, and commentators were fearful that the U-2 had harmed America in the eyes of world opinion. What is "world opinion?" It would seem to be a rather nebulous, amorphous thing—so much so that one may seriously question how real it is. Yet too frequently the hand of the United States has been stayed by fears that "world opinion" might disapprove a contemplated course of action. And the impact of "world opinion" may be an inhibiting factor on the adoption of a military strategy. It has been reported, for example, that as long ago as 1954 the United States hesitated to go ahead with the development of a military rocket-powered space vehicle because of the fear of irritating "world opinion." Even so outspoken an American as the late Secretary of Defense Wilson testified before a Congressional committee that *"too big a military force on our part might convince most of the people in the world that we were going to start trouble.*\* They might be afraid we are going to start a war." One may ask whether fears of "world opinion" have acted as a brake on our efforts to exploit space for military purposes.

Despite President Kennedy's success in facing down Soviet belligerence over Cuba in October 1962, some timid counsellors apparently believed the President should weaken his stand. For a reporter noted that "US diplomats are concerned that *world opinion*\*\* will tire of the whole affair and perhaps even turn against the US once the fanfare over the missiles' departure subsides." [7]

What then is "world opinion?" On close examination "world opinion" has often turned out to be simply the expression of some particularly well-organized propaganda operation. It may be the result of "demonstrations" in the important cities of a few countries. Or it may be the statements of some self-appointed seer. Again it may be the views of some small but highly articulate pressure group. Sometimes, too, "world opinion" consists of the published utterances of celebrated scientists, philosophers, and other notabilities of particular countries. Prominent members of the Western intelligentsia, for example, are assured of a world-wide audience for their statements as a result of the quest of the mass media for news. Lord Bertrand Russell received a vast hearing for his condemnation of the resumption of nuclear testing by the West when he spoke in Trafalgar Square on February 25, 1962. To quote the *New York Times*: "Bertrand Russell accused the British Government today of preparing 'global butchery.' He also questioned the sanity of United States military leaders."\*\*\*

---

\* Italics added.

\*\* Italics added.

\*\*\* The *New York Times*, February 26, 1962; some might argue that the noble Lord's true position was better understood in a review of his book, *Has Man a Future?* Writing in *The Spectator*, December 1, 1961, Constantine Fitzgibbon stated that Lord Russell's "determination to equate America with Russia has led to such a loathing of the United States that we find him accepting every point of the current Communist offensive, from the Rapacki Plan and recognition of Red China to expulsion of German troops from Welsh training grounds."

It is not suggested that "world opinion" is confined to pressures with an impact on the policy of the United States. Rather it is suggested that this is an area that must be given consideration with reference to increased pressures on policy considerations in the next decade. Somewhat more than two years ago, for example, the French Government set off a very small nuclear device in the Sahara desert. "World opinion" was outraged. Pacifists and neutralists expressed alarm. But especially interesting was the action of the Communist Bloc. The entire salivating apparatus of the Bloc as well as its camp followers throughout the world poured forth a torrent of denunciation upon France that was supposedly indicative of world opinion. The Bloc furor apparently impressed other countries, for the new state of Ghana went so far as to break diplomatic relations with France. In the fall of 1961, as is well known, the Soviet Union—as part of a series of 50 or more tests—exploded a nuclear bomb of vast size, apparently in the range of 50 megatons. The result: "world opinion" has thus far been relatively placid as regards the Soviet action. Needless to report, no state has terminated diplomatic relations with the USSR because of this action. One is reminded of the same lack of display of effective "world opinion" after the Soviet Union crushed the Hungarian people's uprising of 1956; or against Communist China after the liquidation of the once-independent government of Tibet.

An analysis of "world opinion" with reference to its possible inhibitions on US military strategy for the next decade is, therefore, very much in order. We might do well to follow the advice of former Assistant Secretary of State A. A. Berle, Jr. Said he: "The 'Cold War'—if it can still be called 'cold'—is said to be a test of ideologies. So it is; but I urge that, in dealing with it, we discard at once a lot of sanctified false myths. It is time we dealt with realities—anything else is dangerous. First to be discarded is the myth of 'world opinion.' God forgive us, devotion to the myth is supposed to be 'liberal' doctrine. I think liberals are not as softheaded as that."[8]

## US Public Opinion

Of all of the aspects of the polyreconic warfare of the times in which we are fated to live, a study of the technique of inducing nuclear fear may be most rewarding. More and more this would seem to be the psycho-political technique that the Communists will employ in attempting to prevent America from acting in the world arena. Linking all of the techniques of political warfare and serving as the negative pole for the positive pole of "peaceful coexistence" is the psycho-political technique of nuclear psychical suggestion. Communist psycho-political campaigns on the horrors of nuclear war, on the power and deadliness of Soviet weapons of mass destruction, on the supremacy of Soviet space vehicles, and on the danger of "war by accident" can be expected to rise to a crescendo during the next decade. The general objective is the creation of a climate of fear and futility in American public opinion. The ultimate objective is —through the vehicle of public opinion—to paralyze the will of the constitutional leaders of America, the Chief Executive and the Congress, to make and to carry out a strategy which would resist and overcome the Communist offensive.

The constant outpouring of nuclear gloom and doom from the Soviet Bloc has been reported widely in the mass media of the Western democracies. In fact, we Americans tend to expand on and perhaps increase the fearful stories about the dangers involved in nuclear testing, and especially the nuclear war which supposedly must result if we take any positive actions. It has been reported that Dr. Milton Dushkin of Chicago has been so impressed with the exhibition of neurotic symptoms related to atomic fears that he has coined a new term to describe this phenomenon. This is "nucleomitophobia"—fear of the atom. He has used it to describe the phobia of people who are disturbed by the outpouring of material on nuclear hazards and the danger of nuclear war in the mass media. That Soviet strategy takes account of "nucleomitophobia" and that it aims at our moral posture in order to blunt and deflect our military power is indicated by an interesting statement by Khrushchev. Said the Soviet *vozhd*: "The peoples must seek replacement of leaders who oppose disarmament and nominate people who really understand [sic] . . . a policy of peace . . . The key to peace is in the resolute action of the masses." [9] Soviet Bloc leadership seems to understand only too well that the memory of the American public is short.* When, therefore, the Kremlin changes its frowns to smiles, many segments of American public opinion quickly respond. When there seems to be a diminution of direct threats against our national security, we Americans are prone to consider that we can best show proof of our own good faith by reducing our military strength. Then too, we frequently fail to press our advantages during the ebb of the

* One critic has said 48 hours as regards foreign policy.

Communist tide and realize too late that the Communists have eroded our position during the period of "friendship." This is powerfully reinforced by the belief of many of our citizens that even the possession (much less the use) of force is somehow immoral *in se* and to be avoided, if at all possible. Hence disarmament schemes are often viewed as a positive good quite apart from any intrinsic merit they may possess. Rarely are they subjected to critical analysis in our newspapers and magazines or on radio and television.

The founders of our government were well aware that in world politics we should have to deal not with angels but with men, and often men who were ruthless in the extreme. Wisely they understood that only power can check power, that force has a necessary and licit use in an imperfect world. Can we expect this heritage of reason to have a lasting influence? Certainly it was terribly diminished during the sleep-walking of the Munich era. Has the American public learned from the Second World War that aggressors are encouraged by signs of weakness but checked by power? Tellingly we were reminded of this during the Cuban crisis. Speaking to a nation-wide radio and television audience on October 22, 1962, President Kennedy recalled that 'the nineteen-thirties taught us a clear lesson: aggressive conduct, if allowed to grow unchecked and unchallenged, ultimately leads to war."

The President's speech was calm and courageous. The actions he outlined in his speech were certainly not excessive. Yet the Student Peace Union called on its 15,000 members for a march on Washington in protest against President Kennedy's announcement of a quarantine on all offensive military equipment being shipped to Cuba.* Elsewhere across the nation "peace" marchers turned out in protests in many cities; a Mr. Carl May headed a newly formed "Veterans for Peace"; and the press stated that Professor H. Stuart Hughes, a candidate for the US Senate, cut short personal appearances in order "to assume the task of spearheading a national peace movement."[10]

In the aftermath of the Cuban crisis, there was a tendency to dismiss such protests and demonstrations as being insignificant. So, perhaps, they were. But is their significance not of the passing moment, but for the next decade? When one com-

* The *New York Times*, October 25, 1962; the national secretary of the group, whose name just happened to be Miss Paradise, stated that "the group was growing at the rate of 200 members a week and predicted that the present crisis would increase this rate."

pares the decision of President Truman to intervene in Korea with President Kennedy's action on Cuba, one is struck by the almost complete absence of "peace" demonstrators in the June 1950 crisis. And the cloud no larger than a man's hand of 1962 may well grow to large proportions in the coming years. It has been pointed out that the various "peace" organizations are, under the impact of the Cuban crisis, giving indications of national unity.* Who would be so bold as to predict that a future Chief Executive and a future Congress might not be swayed from the adoption or the execution of a "hard" military strategy by such expressions of public opinion? President Kennedy has warned that "if the self-discipline of the free cannot match the iron discipline of the mailed fist—in economic, political, scientific and all other kinds of struggle as well as the military—then the peril to freedom will continue to rise." [11]

Nowhere is our self-discipline likely to be put more to the task than in the area of public opinion. Increasingly those who chart military strategy for the future must take into consideration the pressures generated by those ardent, articulate, and often high-minded persons in our society who abjure the role of power and who are seemingly more concerned about "our unborn children" and a remote nuclear "holocaust" than a terribly immediate future for all.

## Strategy for the Future: A Proposal

The armed forces of a nation are not something apart from the life of the nation. Rather, they mirror the national personality, the national character, the particular national genius. So it is with military strategy. Even assuming its desirability, it would probably have been out of character for America to have adopted a Schlieffen Plan. In our governmental system specific plans may be closely held, but the outline of broad military strategy is and should be approved by the proper constitutional authorities—the Chief Executive and the Congress—and should be understood in general terms by the public. Certainly the press

* The *Wall Street Journal*, October 29, 1962; the *Journal* noted that the New England Committee for Political Action for Peace had begun publication of a "Peace-Politics Newsletter" earlier in 1962 as a clearing-house organ for peace candidates. It quoted Marshall Kaplan, executive director of the committee, as stating that: "Two years ago there were only a few peace candidates, not enough to try to keep up with, but this year there are peace candidates all over the country."

will insure that any proposed strategy will be subjected to public discussion. One need not agree or disagree as to the ideal. Our system tends to function in this way. A good example is the now-abandoned strategy of "massive retaliation." Whether or not "massive retaliation" was an adequate strategy or represented a workable policy will long be argued. The fact is that from the moment it was announced * it became the subject of such vigorous debate that Secretary of State Dulles felt compelled to issue supplementary statements from time to time to modify the strategy to such an extent that little remained of the original concept.

If any lesson can be drawn from the experience with "massive retaliation," it would seem to be that an enduring military strategy must do more than get minimal Congressional and public approval. Understanding and consensus from Congress, the press, and the public is of continuing importance. It was also not unimportant that "massive retaliation" met with considerable opposition from some of our allies, especially the British. The NATO powers, for example, seem to have come around from their earlier position on retaliation. At one time they were afraid that the United States would be too quick on the trigger. Now, with the rise of Soviet nuclear capability, they appear to be afraid that our trigger finger will freeze. A solution to the difficulty might be to have informal strategic consultation and idea exchange among the highest NATO political as well as military figures in the process of policy formation.

This paper does not attempt to advance solutions to the many problems of NATO. It is relevant to suggest, however, that in thinking about national strategy options, consideration needs to be given to a strategy as compatible with the interests of NATO member-nations as possible. The NATO grouping is that of a coalition with a predominant maritime base ** as compared to the continental-based Soviet Bloc. As the leader of such a coalition, the United States is maritime-oriented. Additionally, America's geographical position and the trading thrust of its

* January 12, 1954. "Massive retaliation" was never fully spelled out in terms of national purpose or military application, but Mr. Dulles' statement that "local defenses must be reinforced by the further deterrent of massive retaliatory power" and his point that "the basic decision was to depend primarily upon a great capacity to retaliate instantly, by means and at places of our own choosing" was generally understood.

** ANZUS, SEATO, and even CENTO are manifestations of the same checkmating process of the maritime-oriented as against the continental-oriented.

private sector economy would impel it toward a maritime orientation and grand strategy. A global maritime view of the coming decade would also seem advantageous in that it lends itself to a linkage with the unfolding space horizon.

## A Spatial-Maritime Strategy?

The recurring crises in Berlin, the shadowy war in Southeast Asia, the conventional warfare tactics in Communist China's aggression in India, the growing Communist penetration in Africa and in Latin America (viewing Cuban events as initial skirmishes in a many-faceted Western Hemisphere campaign) indicate how difficult it is to make politico-diplomatic decisions except as integrated with a military strategic frame of reference. Force may be masked at times but it is ever present in the realities of world politics. Military power has a wide range of applications. In the area of low-intensity conflict (Cold War and "peaceful coexistence") or in sub-limited warfare it can be coordinated with the exercise of other forms of power, and be developed, organized, and employed in varied situations without the often-feared risk of escalation. The many capabilities of military means can be applied most effectively to situations that range from those relatively peaceful, to those characterized by subversion and insurgency or by limited warfare. The object of a sound military strategy ought to be the most timely and efficient projection of military power into each place where the advancement of US national policies can be served. Beyond this, military strategy must meet the test of acceptability. It needs the support of Congress, and at least the tacit approval of the public, the latter sometimes meaning the mass media. As previously noted, some support from allied states is not a negligible factor. Since Congress, the Chief Executive, the public, and allied states are susceptible to considerations arising from the inhibiting factors cited earlier in this paper, these, too, should be given some weight. Finally, a military strategy most in consonance with the national character is one that should be opted for. Indeed, one might well give this factor a much higher place. The restless, questing nature of the American character is epitomized by the Wright Brothers and Henry Ford. The Wright Brothers telescoped distance and time. Henry Ford viewed the machine and machine-systems as necessities which freed men from the drudgery—and hence from the waste and inefficiency—of manual operations. Together they represent a main American thrust: the maximization of mobility. Hence it would seem that the military strategy most in accord with the American national character would be that which avoids the reflexive, reactive posture and stresses the initiative-seeking, mobility-flexibility posture.

It is suggested that a spatial-maritime strategy is best structured to provide the mix of non-forcible, semi-forcible, and forcible measures from which our constitutional officials can choose in initiating national security actions. This would appear to be so because the variety of our possible choices of action (for example, from interrupting an opponent's communications to the delivery of nuclear weapons on his key targets) and an enemy's complications in responding to our initiative can be heightened by a strategy which exploits spatial-maritime possibilities.

## Spatial

The psycho-political advantages accruing from a nation's ability to exercise power in and through the space environment are immense. The propaganda advantage alone would constitute a valid reason for giving consideration to space strategy. But it is historically correct that military control of an environment permits psycho-political exploitation. In the past, nations enjoyed vast psycho-political advantages from their ability to exercise control in the sea environment and later in the air environment. It would appear obvious, therefore, that space can be used by us or against us. To state that this is obvious does not mean that it is accepted as such. Despite much evidence that the Soviets treat the scientific side of space as quite incidental to the military, many Americans continue in the naive belief that we can treat space as a peaceful arena.

Space military capabilities would broadly appear to be: (1) intelligence operations: observing, recording, detecting; (2) direction: of land, sea, air, or combined operations; (3) offensive actions: against land, sea, or air targets; against other space vehicles; (4) defensive actions: neutralizing attacking missiles, counteracting other space vehicles; (5) psycho-political operations in advance of or in support of military actions.

The transference of classical military operational concepts to space remains to be accomplished and the next decade will see this taking place apart from the obvious projections of well-understood military operations. Space offers intriguing new possibilities for the exercise of power at low intensity levels, but with enormous strategic import.

The following is suggested as an exploratory concept for the United States to adopt in space/earth control.

1) The creation of a global intelligence system for detecting. observing, tracking, recording, and analyzing movements in space. This system would follow and report all satellites in orbit, spacecraft, and space stations. It would be initiated through the use of existing space surveillance nets, and would be followed up by measures to bring about a space-global communications-control network based on land stations, ships on all the world's seas, satellites, and manned space platforms. The state-of-the-art in space exploitation is such that we undoubtedly plan on the launching of manned space platforms during the coming decade. Such manned space platforms* would form a significant part of a space/earth control system. The nation-state which develops such a control structure will enjoy unique advantages in the exercise of power.

2) If we were to follow such a course of action with vigor, a control system could be operative at about the time when much of the world would be increasingly dependent on communications satellites, possibly around the turn of the decade. By having such a control device, the United States would be able to inform a trouble-inciting or trouble-making nation that unless it abandoned its untoward activities, we would find it necessary to disrupt the offender's communication and command systems nets, thus severely obstructing both at-home control and external communications. The possibilities for the non-violent exercise of power accruing from a program of this nature are vast.**

3) Although much of the world would be reliant on communications relayed by space vehicles, there would still be countries willing to risk communications breakdowns. Hence the suggested control of communications would be a low-intensity action which would be employed to signal our willingness to employ, if necessary, appropriate weapons from space against the trouble-inciting or trouble-making nation. If the United States has effectively pre-empted her enemies from controlling their space-based communications, surveillance, and target-location means, then the United States should be able to neutralize weapons-

---

* Current designs envision space platforms having working room for 20 or more persons with electronic and other equipment.

** Another possibility in the exercise of power at less intensity than that of employing weapons would be the use of space to affect the weather over an enemy's homeland.

carrying satellites or spacecraft. By controlling both the communications utility and the military threat of attack from space, one nation-state could preclude another from effective functioning on earth and from operating (such as delivering an attack) in and from space.

Such a space/earth control system is technologically feasible. It would require, of course, heavy expenditures. The cost of the DEW line and of BMEWS, for example, has been in excess of two billion dollars. A projection from this figure suggests six billion dollars as the cost for the initial stages of a space/earth control system.* More importantly, it would require much vision and a deep appreciation of the psycho-political realities of world politics. In thinking about these possibilities we might consider them in terms of a cogent observation of David Sarnoff. Said he, "Years before any Western nation, the Kremlin grasped the values of space probes [and realized] that breakthroughs in . . . technology would have direct political repercussions."

Spatial proposals may also serve a useful purpose if they suggest not only the control of communications and the exploitation of manned and of remotely-controlled spacecraft, but also a rethinking of the entire question of manned aircraft. The next decade will see many new possibilities for the employment of aircraft in total-war prevention and in limited and sublimited warfare. V/STOL's, convertiplanes, air-cushion vehicles, vastly improved helicopters—all indicate the expansion of ideas and the development of tactics in support of strategy that can be applied to the new modes of conflict facing us. Research and development on the unconventional, the conventional, and the general war capabilities of very low-level aircraft flying at very high speeds should also be pressed.**

---

* A review of budget allocations with reference to the idea of the "peaceful" use of space is in order. It has been reported, for example, that NASA will request $5.7 billion from the Congress for fiscal 1964 and that about 73% of this amount will be toward putting a man on the moon by 1968. While putting a man on the moon may be related to the national security, more portentous for the survival of our national ethos will be the development of military capabilities in and from space. An analysis of Soviet space efforts, for example, indicates that the entire Soviet space program is directed toward *military* objectives even though there is a heavy psycho-political spin-off.

** Developments in metals and the knowledge acquired from metal fatigue and other studies offer the promise of speeds even in excess of Mach 3 for very low-flying (dense air) aircraft. Also on the horizon are advances in low-altitude penetration equipment of the greatest relevance to the utility of low-level aircraft.

In the decade of the 1970's the ICBM and IRBM may well become neutralized by advanced generation systems. It would be well, accordingly, to rethink the strategic role of ultra-fast, ultra-high altitude manned aircraft. Projected a decade hence, such aircraft (or aerospace or "low-space"* craft) can be envisioned as having significant capabilities. Some of these are: (1) unpredictable flight pattern; (2) enhanced versatility, notably stand-off capability; (3) the operation of foxing devices more sophisticated than those which could be employed from missiles; (4) propulsion systems based on nuclear fuel or, perhaps, on fuel cells; (5) being in human hands all the way; that is, under the direct control of man, who, with all his imperfections, can respond to unpredictables in a way in which no machine ever can.

A special case may be the operation of manned aircraft (or aerospacecraft) in what might be termed "low space." The X-15 rocket research aircraft has, for example, flown at 314,750 feet.** Manned air or "low-space" craft will be operational at altitudes well in excess of this figure in the coming decade. The advantages in the operation of recording and sensory devices by manned vehicles to a critical and continuing strategic problem—intelligence—will be considerable.***

Whether one envisions manned vehicles near the surface of the earth or well out in space, it is hardly conceivable that they can be wholly replaced in any environment. The uncertainties of the universe (in future not less than presently) require respect for the operational factor that governs all multivariable operations, the proper "mix" of men and materiel for the optimization of an acceptable set of outcomes. The arguments in support of the "mix" would alone justify man in air and spacecraft.

**Maritime**

Alfred Thayer Mahan has rightly been assigned a place among the greatest of the military theorists of all time. He is one of

* I use this in preference to the term "space equivalence."

** Legal arguments have been advanced that operations above 100,000 feet do not violate the airspace of the country concerned. Since operations 300,000 feet and above are entering "low space" or space equivalence, jurists will probably wish to re-examine the entire question of airspace violation.

*** Manned "low-space" craft can be envisioned as possessing greater potentials than surveillance or sensing satellites such as Samos and Midas.

the very few Americans so ranked. Yet today it is in some ways paradoxical that Mahan's writings were so effective. For they stressed "sea power." Mahan, of course, was conscious of the broader implications of his ideas. But now and in the future, emphasis needs to be placed on a global "maritime" * rather than "sea" strategy. It is vastly more than a cliché to insist on emphasizing that three-fourths of the surface of the earth is water.

Strategy has by no means yet caught up with technology in many areas. The application of nuclear power to the submersible vessel so that the underwater craft has become a true "submarine" has been reflected in our current strategy as evidenced by the deployment of the Polaris weapons system. But strategy and technology have yet to be interdeveloped with reference to the role of the true submersible in the grand strategy of the space age.** There are unique relationships as regards the maritime position of the United States and the pervasive possibilities of space operations. Additionally, the rather loose coalition we call the "Free World" is a sea-oriented complex, highly dependent on the oceans in terms of natural resources and practical geography. Who controls the seas can control the land, and the space far above the whole planet. Indeed, the oceans and the vast spaces above and below them may provide the key to integrating the baffling prospects of space with the reality of our being an earth-born race.

At another echelon of significant effect on strategy are the changes resulting from present—and projected future—developments in hydrofoils, water-jets, near-surface vehicles, and VTOL-craft with a capability of taking off and landing on water surfaces. Flying amphibians capable also of travelling beneath the seas are not out of the question, even though presently we might not contemplate missions for such vehicles. The emerging prospects for the next decade and beyond, in fact, are such that we might well use the term maritime-riparian strategy since even "maritime" may seem too narrow to embrace the possibilities for the controlled use of power, almost, one might say, where the ground is slightly damp. As often in the past, strategy today

---

* In the broad sense, maritime would include the seas, littoral areas, and sea-river interconnections.

** To cite two instances: the submarine's role in Arctic operation; the possibilities to be derived from (operational) deep-depth submarines. For example, within the next decade it is not infeasible to envisage combatant submarines capable of operating at depths of 4,000 feet.

tends to lag behind the development of weapons, vehicles, and propulsion systems; especially, the almost bewildering (yet salutary if exploited) possibilities inherent in new vehicle concepts, systems, and propulsion methods.

It should be noted that the use of the term "maritime" avoids the parochial connotation sometimes associated with the term "sea" strategy or "sea" power. A spatial-maritime or spatial-maritime-riparian strategy avoids a single-weapons-system or "single-service" strategy. A sophisticated strategy in keeping with the coming times will demand the most diverse (hence all-service) talents.

Obviously these ideas but scratch the surface of the possibilities of a spatial-maritime strategy. The desideratum is the projection of the power of the United States not merely in the known environments of land, sea, and air. Rather it is the projection of that power through linking those natural elements as a maritime entity with the all-embracing dimensions of space. This concept, inarticulate and inchoate as it may be at this stage, does embody the potentiality of crucial new dimensions for military strategy and beyond that, for grand strategy for the United States in an era in which the traditional concepts of "war" and "peace" are no longer meaningful.

### FOOTNOTES

[1] *The Edge Of War* (Chicago: Regnery, 1962).

[2] The New York *Herald Tribune*, October 24, 1962, reported that the mob was "organized by the 'Committee of 100,' which urges complete nuclear disarmament and is headed by Bertrand Russell."

[3] *Ibid.*, September 18, 1962.

[4] *Ibid.*

[5] Address in the House of Lords, December 11, 1956.

[6] Address before the National Press Club, Washington, D. C., March 20, 1962.

[7] The *Wall Street Journal*, November 9, 1962.

[8] Address, New York City, October 6, 1961.

[9] Moscow speech of March 16, 1962.

[10] *Ibid.*; see also the Washington *Evening Star*, October 25, 1962, and the New York *Herald Tribune*, October 24-25, 1962.

[11] Address to the American Society of Newspaper Editors, April 20, 1961.

# Nuclear Explosives And
# The Atlantic Community

—*EDWARD TELLER*

"*A nation does not gain the confidence of another nation on demand. Nor does one nation have faith in the competence of another because the other loudly proclaims its competence.*"

*From remarks by Admiral Arleigh Burke at the Center for Strategic Studies' Conference, January 1963.*

## Summary

*Disagreements concerning nuclear weapons have brought about a crisis in NATO. To resolve this crisis we should initiate exhaustive and free discussions within the Alliance on a number of difficult questions. These should include nuclear defense, nuclear research, and application of nuclear explosives in limited and all-out conflicts. Such discussions could and should lead to evolution in the Atlantic Community toward true interdependence and eventually toward federal union.*

---

**Crisis of the Alliance**

In historic perspective the change of alliances in the 1960's may turn out to have great importance. We may see favorable signs in the deterioration of the Sino-Soviet relationship, and even more in the successful progress of the Common Market nations. But the French barred the entry of Great Britain into the Common Market. We are engaged in a controversy about nuclear weapons with de Gaulle. The cancellation of Skybolt has caused worries in Britain, and there is friction even between the United States and Canada in connection with nuclear preparedness.

Science has made the world smaller and more closely interrelated. Nuclear arms and intercontinental rockets have made the world more dangerous. Both the well-being and the safety of the United States are tied today irrevocably to the rest of the world and particularly to the free and advanced democracies. Both the President of the United States (in his speech in Philadelphia on July 4, 1962) and Governor Rockefeller (in his third Godkin lecture at Harvard in March 1962) have stressed the matter of interdependence. In Nelson Rockefeller's opinion we should actually establish a federal union of the free. Yet a few months after these wonderful statements we find ourselves divided from some of our allies more severely than at any time since 1945.

The fact of nuclear explosives has exposed us to the danger of surprise attack. This fact perhaps more than any other one has convinced the American people that our alliances are of paramount importance to us and that we must not stand alone in a dangerous world. Our strength in nuclear weapons served as a foundation of the NATO Alliance in its early years. This strength has been gladly accepted by our European friends as an insurance against Russian imperialism as brutally demonstrated in Czechoslovakia. Yet, in the recent past, questions connected with nuclear bombs have become a dangerously divisive influence in the Atlantic Community.

This question has to be resolved, and, as the events of 1962 show, we have to apply ourselves to the problem with determination and speed. The problem has two aspects. One can approach it from the point of view of the object of the debate, or one can attack it by considering the different parties that are involved. The latter question is probably the more basic. The former is the one on which I have more competence. It is, therefore, this former one which will be in the foreground in the following considerations.

### The Question of Secrecy

It appears to be axiomatic in US policy that the secrets of nuclear weapons must be kept. In this endeavor we have been successful as far as the American public is concerned. We may have been partially successful with respect to Allied countries. But we have failed completely to impede Russian preparations for nuclear warfare. Sometimes, I fear that the Russians are in possession not merely of all the secrets known to us, but they are informed at present of those secrets which we are going to discover in the next two years.

One simple remedy should be strongly recommended. Retaining our present procedures of secrecy with respect to the general public and to some other nations, we should remove all barriers between ourselves and the responsible governments and representatives of our NATO allies in order to initiate a complete and frank discussion.

Our own civilization sprang by tradition and sometimes by contradiction from Western Europe. In the technical field we have forged ahead. Unquestionably the younger American culture has advanced beyond the technical accomplishments of the European countries. In the development of nuclear energy this is more obviously true than in any other field. Here the traditional roles were reversed, and in all realism we had to consider ourselves as advanced while regarding, in this particular respect, the old countries of Europe as mere children. This figure of speech, which of course can be used in no rigorously valid sense, is nevertheless appropriate to illuminate the difficulties in which we are now involved. Children cannot be kept in a dependent state for an indefinite period. The time has come when more and more of the European countries want a substantive voice and independent strength. The problem of French atomic arms will not be the last problem of this kind. If we persevere in the belief that nuclear power should be concentrated in our hands and that the decision to use this power should be our exclusive responsibility, our troubles will multiply and the Atlantic Alliance will be disrupted. We cannot continue to act on the discredited educational principle that the right behavior of teenagers can be insured by attempting to keep them in ignorance of the facts of life.

It is painful to consider the eventuality of an armed conflict, particularly that of a nuclear conflict. According to our present plans we can state our conclusions concerning the best defense of Western Europe, but we do not explain our reasoning. We formerly argued that little reliance should be placed on conventional weapons and that the main defense lay in the strategic nuclear striking power of the United States. This possibility was not attractive to our allies because it left them without power and without a strong and effective voice. We now tell them that conventional weapons must be built up. This is painful, and our allies strongly suspect that in the end it is useless. Our change of approach has weakened their confidence. But even the most reasonable proposal by the United States could hardly find wholehearted support since actually any proposal concerning military preparation and military planning is painful. The determination made by another party will automatically evoke resistance; its undesirable features will be glaring while the reasons —which our nuclear policy compels us to keep secret—cannot be explained. The only constructive procedure is the same as that successfully employed by enlightened parents in facing the problems of their teen-age children. We must take the growing generation into our full confidence.

And indeed our European allies are growing in strength, in confidence, and in their desire for responsibility. A full and frank discussion of all strategies, in which all information is made available about our existing nuclear weapons and the potentialities for new nuclear explosives, could change the situation. The discussion itself would have a beneficial effect, and its results might lead to new approaches. At any rate, solutions obtained in such discussions, even though they be temporary, will be supported by our allies in a greater measure because they will feel that they have been given a fair chance to participate in these decisions.

What are the questions, and what are the alternatives?

## Civil Defense

Of all problems connected with nuclear warfare, civil defense is the simplest, at least from one significant point of view. Such defense can and should be undertaken by each nation separately. In fact, even within one nation some local control of civil defense measures might turn out to be preferable.

Some writers have represented civil defense as another turn in the spiraling arms race. They have represented it as a militaristic measure. If so, Switzerland and Sweden are the prime examples of this militaristic procedure in Europe. These are the very countries which, through preparedness, managed to stay out of the devastating wars of our century.

Much of civil defense depends on the construction of shelters and on the maintenance of order and coordinated action following a nuclear attack. These are tasks best undertaken on the local level. But there are other tasks which call for joint action.

One of the most important links in the preparation for civil defense is appropriate early warning. On this the NATO Alliance could cooperate with great profit. The cooperation should extend not only to a common radar system (already in existence in the Canada-United States community), but it should also embrace surveillance satellites which so far have been the sole responsibility of the United States. This need not remain so. The economic and technical difficulties could be shared by the advanced industrial countries in the NATO community. Ambitions of some of our partners could be usefully channeled into this discussion.

The next step in defense is to develop an anti-missile system. Here again our interests and objectives coincide. But such defense requires nuclear warheads of a sophisticated kind. To share these with our allies would obviously be to the greatest mutual advantage. The defensive nature of the system would practically eliminate any misuse. The protection offered by such a system, even though it is not complete, will decrease the feeling of helplessness that has paralyzed many phases of the necessary planning.

If ever a nuclear strike should hit some or all of the NATO countries, the recovery phase will be of utmost importance. This recovery depends on stockpiles. It may be best to distribute these stockpiles and to locate them in safe places within each territory. That calls for early action and could be carried out at the present time. The great and growing agricultural surpluses of the United States could be used in part to supply the necessities, not only for the United States but for some of its allies, that would arise in the critical weeks and months following a heavy atomic attack. Such supplies would not enter the commercial channels and would not unsettle national economies. Instead, these supplies will increase our confidence and our chance of recuperation throughout the whole Alliance.

Nobody can expect that stockpiling alone will be sufficient to supply the needs of recovery. When some or each of us has suffered heavy blows, mutual help on a short-term basis will be badly needed. An approach to working out the system of transportation and the channels of decision-making by which such exchange of goods could be expedited, should be considered in the near future.

All this is predicated on the idea that a nuclear conflict is not necessarily the end of the human race, and, in fact, not even the end of Western civilization. I do believe that survival and recovery after a nuclear attack are possible and that the speed of recovery may be decisive in shaping the future world. This I state realizing to the fullest extent that an all-out nuclear conflict will be a catastrophic occurrence. But being prepared for this occurrence is better than not being prepared for it. In fact, adequate and obvious preparations may well discourage the Russians from starting a fight. It is their belief that the capitalistic countries cannot survive another war that makes war itself more probable. Showing our ability to survive is the most peaceful and perhaps the most effective way of deterring a nuclear war.

**Joint Research**

If we grant the premise that secrets should be shared among the NATO Allies, we obtain a possibility which could well become decisive in the conduct of the Cold War. Decade by decade new scientific discoveries and developments shape and shift the balance of power. The contest of the future depends to an increasing extent on brain power. In this respect our European allies must certainly not be underestimated.

It is an incredible waste of effort for the British and French scientists to retrace the same steps and undergo the same labors which we have left behind some years ago. Our nuclear secrecy makes such duplication inevitable.

By pooling our scientific resources we can probably outdo the Russian research teams by a very considerable margin. This need not mean abandonment of secrecy. It means only extending the area of inclusion in our classified research.

It is clear that if this proposal is accepted, all our allies will be at least conceptually on the same level on which we find ourselves. Those who recoil from the "proliferation of nuclear weapons" will necessarily object, but those who have understood that scientific and technical progress cannot long be kept a secret will look at the proposal with a more open mind. I believe that the necessary restraints should not be imposed on our allies by ignorance. Rather do I believe that both we and our friends abroad should be restrained by reason and by the practice of common responsible decisions.

This has relevance to research in all fields—peaceful, abstract, applied, and military. It is not necessary, nor is it desirable, that we should strive for a monopoly in space among Western nations. In some fields like meteorology and oceanography the necessity of cooperation is particularly obvious. But there is no field in which we have impeded international cooperation in a manner more determined (and in my opinion more damaging) than in the field of nuclear explosives. Not only have we erected artificial barriers in connection with the military applications of these explosives, but we have not placed even the important peaceful uses (which we call Project Plowshare) on a completely broad basis in which our NATO allies can join to a full extent.

The language of science and technology is inherently international. When this language is spoken by people who live in similar and friendly societies, there is no inherent barrier to effective cooperation. The American-British-Canadian enterprise on nuclear explosives during World War II is an outstanding example. Nuclear weapons helped to terminate the last giant conflict in a sudden manner. But even before the use of nuclear explosives our victory had been assured. Today the issue of the Cold War hangs in the balance. It seems obvious and necessary that the well-tried methods of scientific cooperation be extended to the NATO community within the shortest time in order that the purpose of common survival be served.

### Escalation

Wars must be avoided. But if they occur, they should at any rate be limited. Our present doctrine is that limitation can be achieved only if we avoid the use of nuclear explosives. The first atomic bomb dropped in a wartime operation will—so it is stated—necessarily lead to a holocaust.

It is not my purpose to try to settle the difficult questions connected with this topic. I should limit myself to a statement which will show that escalation might be avoided or at least slowed down by other means than elimination of nuclear explosives. I also want to raise the question of whether indeed the elimination of nuclear explosives on our side may not stimulate escalation. If we and our allies can consider alternatives, we have a better chance in a joint and free discussion to come to a practical solution.

There is great danger of escalation in a massive conventional war. The first danger is that such a conventional conflict may be lost by our side. So far our preparations give no reason to hope that we indeed could match a Russian conventional onslaught. If we lose Europe in this manner, our allies will surely press for the use of nuclear weapons on the biggest scale. And we, standing alone against the military might of the Soviets, may well be tempted to use this ultimate horrible alternative.

But even if our conventional forces should prevail, the situation may not be much better. It is of the essence in conventional warfare that manpower be concentrated. A great number of soldiers must be supplied with food and ammunition, thus raising the necessity of a massive supply line. Both the concentrated armies and the pipe lines feeding them are highly vulnerable to nuclear attack. If the Russians should be defeated by conventional means in a Európean conflict, their answer may well be to use nuclear weapons to wipe out our gains in Europe. In doing so, they may limit themselves to the military objectives mentioned above. This, then, would almost certainly result in a military collapse of our side. The Russians having chosen the time of the transition to nuclear weapons, will probably catch us in a vulnerable position while they will have taken precautions to guard themselves against retaliation on or near the battlefield. If the allied armies are killed by the millions and if our own losses amount to hundreds of thousands, would this not be the strongest psychological provocation to let the war turn into an all-out nuclear conflict?

Let us compare the plan of conventional warfare with the plan to limit the conflict with respect to the area of the conflict and the aims of the war. This limitation is the classical one. Even as recently as Korea it has worked. In an answer to a Russian attack the whole NATO Alliance could and should react. But we should also declare that we are not going to enlarge the area or aims of the conflict unless the Russians take the initiative toward a bigger war. At the same time we should firmly declare that, in the area of fighting, the most appropriate weapons including nuclear weapons will be used if needed. This would mean that, if the Berlin crisis leads to actual fighting, we may try to confine the military operations to East and West Germany. If, on the other hand, Turkey is attacked, Turkey will be defended by our joint power without involving the territory of any of the other NATO countries. For the one country involved, this will of course be highly undesirable. But this plan might appeal to our allies because it will lead to a lesser chance of direct involvement for each nation.

Recent events make it clear, most unfortunately, that even the United States could not feel assured that its own territory will escape the first ravages of war. It might be the right psychological move to include in the agreement the situations that may arise as a consequence of our strained relations with Cuba. At the present time it is no longer completely fanciful to state that fighting may occur in Cuba, Panama, and the Gulf Coast without an involvement of our friends in Europe. In this situation we should be able to call on the active help of the NATO Allies without risking the extension of the war to Europe unless this should be done on Russian initiative. Such an agreement would emphasize in the most appropriate manner that our dangers are common and our response to the dangers must be joint.

To limit the territory and aims of the conflict rather than the type of weapons to be used is actually a more hopeful way to prevent escalation. In a conflict the losing side will always look for more effective weapons and will be tempted to have a more violent war rather than a lost war. On the other hand, in the case of territorial limitations, the defeated party will not be tempted to increase the area of conflict and thereby to expose himself to even more catastrophic losses. This will be particularly true if we limit the aims of the war and thereby furnish assurance that a defeat in a limited area will not be pressed home by ourselves and that additional territories dominated by the Communists will not be automatically endangered.

Thus the justified fear of escalation does not necessarily rule out the use of nuclear weapons in a limited conflict. But we cannot abandon this subject without dealing briefly with another deeply ingrained objection to the use of nuclear weapons. It has been accepted in a somewhat uncritical manner that nuclear weapons are instruments of mass destruction which can be used only for the indiscriminate devastation of populated centers. The developments and refinements of the last seventeen years make it possible, however, to use nuclear explosives in other and much more justifiable ways. Nuclear explosives could be used to prevent concentration of enemy forces, to impose utmost dispersion on both warring parties and thereby to create a situation in which the local population will be in a better position to deal with the invaders, who can no longer appear in massed formations. Nuclear explosions can even be used for harmless purposes such as the rapid blasting of new harbors which might make it possible to supply our side after the regular harbors had been occupied or destroyed.

Much has been written on this topic.[1] It is impossible to arrive at a completely convincing solution, and we should be satisfied if the NATO Alliance could come up with any acceptable answer. But this is possible only if full information is available on nuclear weapons, both existing and in prospect. The above statements have been made on the side of the use of nuclear weapons, not because of a complete conviction that this is the right way to proceed, but because of the fact that insistence on the opposite conclusion has unbalanced the discussion.

## The Strategic Strike

It is obvious that a strategic nuclear strike by either the United States or the USSR will start an all-out nuclear conflict or at least will come exceedingly close to such a conflict. Some have entertained hopes that we may destroy Russian striking capacity without hurting Russian cities. Considering Russian secrecy, considering the relative ease with which missile sites can be hardened, and also considering that the Russians have or will have nuclear missiles on ships, it is hardly credible that we can deprive the Russians of the relatively little power which they need to strike at our cities. In any case, a strategic nuclear strike is a possibility from which I personally recoil as both immoral and impractical.

This point of view may or may not be accepted by a comprehensive NATO conference. If it is accepted, one has to spell out clearly under what conditions we will use a second-strike force.

There can be little doubt that a massive nuclear strike on the United States will bring about massive retaliation on our part. It may well be that the same should and will be the case if strategic nuclear bombardment is aimed against another NATO nation. A third possibility is that each of the NATO Allies have under its direct control some strategic nuclear warheads so that strategic bombardment on any country will bring about retaliation by that country and only that one. This possibility looks quite frightening to us in the United States. It might be more reassuring to our friends on the other side of the Atlantic.

It is my belief that this is actually the most difficult question which we have to resolve. A logical and desirable resolution would be to bring about a close enough union so that the Atlantic Community would act as a single nation. Determinations of vital questions would be made on a clearly understood, democratic basis with no one retaining a veto or dictatorial powers, and with all nations making a contribution to the common decision on the basis of some appropriate procedure, distributing the influence according to some of the many criteria which have been justly considered in organizing big communities. In this case as in other essential and critical areas, evolution may be more appropriate than a finished solution. We might agree to a procedure that does not differ much from the present American predominance, but we may envisage that, in a planned manner during the course of years, the distribution of voting power will be changed in accordance with the population or the contributions of the participant nations.

The crucial provision in this discussion is that enough time be given to the evolution so that during the evolutionary process common loyalties will gain time to arise. Today we know intellectually that the European nations and ourselves will not survive without each other. But this knowledge has not yet been accepted by our sentiments and by our reflexes. The new realities will demand a readjustment in the area of decision-making. This readjustment cannot be too rapid, but will have to be expeditious. Only a determined and well-planned effort can lead to a favorable outcome. At the present time even the wisest among us could not give the details of such a plan. But in another decade the ship of our Alliance must be shaken down. The Atlantic Community must mature into a federal union. The threat of nuclear war should serve as a catalyst in this inevitable process.

## FOOTNOTE

[1] Henry A. Kissinger, *Nuclear Weapons and Foreign Policy* (New York: Harper & Brothers, 1957). Henry A. Kissinger, *The Necessity for Choice* (New York:Harper & Brothers, 1961). Edward Teller and Allen Brown, *The Legacy of Hiroshima* (Garden City, N.Y.:Doubleday & Co., 1962), pp. 267-89.

# Managing The Arms Race

—*THOMAS C. SCHELLING*

## Summary

*Military policy is concerned with enemy intentions, not just capabilities. Deterrence depends on our ability to influence an enemy by making him take our likely reactions into account. We try to be explicit about the consequences of Soviet adventures beyond their borders, and we commit ourselves to action in various ways intended to be persuasive.*

*Do we also influence the military build-up that takes place within Soviet borders? Should we not take more account of our own influence in setting our goals, making our plans, and projecting our budgets? Is there any possibility that we can deter or otherwise influence Soviet participation in the arms race? If we commit ourselves to an attempt to influence the Soviet arms build-up, do we successfully communicate what we want to communicate?*

*We certainly influence each other. The influence may be indirect, sluggish, haphazard, and unintended, but it is there. Beliefs about Sputnik and the "missile gap" influenced American decisions in much the same way as did the Korean War and the Berlin crisis of 1961.*

*In the long run, if not in the short, there must be feedback from our own military plans: today's Soviet strategic-force programs to some extent must be a reaction to the American reaction to the "missile gap." The fact that the missile gap was misjudged reminds us that one reacts to what he thinks he sees, not to what is actually there. It also reminds us that the "inspection" problem is as relevant to armament plans as to disarmament; keeping track of what the Soviets are doing, through whatever intelligence is available, is no less essential without disarmament than with it.*

*If we increase our awareness of the interaction between Soviet and Western military programs and want to influence this interaction, we have to consider more explicitly what we want the Soviets to do and what we want them not to do. We think in this context all the time with respect to their moves outside their borders. But with respect to their arms preparations, we seem to treat their behavior more as something to estimate than as something to influence. In the short run this is probably right, in the longer run probably not.*

*Actually, though we do not make it a conscious policy we do engage in arms build-up bargaining with the Soviets. Some decisions and many public arguments about decisions appear to be oriented towards expected Soviet reactions.*

*Much of our foreign policy is concerned with proving to the Russians how we shall react to what they do, and committing ourselves visibly to the reaction we want them to expect. The Formosa Resolution of 1955, for example, was a ceremonial act intended not only to persuade the Russians that we were committed to defend the off-shore islands, but to enhance the commitment itself. Is there some scope for taking the same attitude towards the arms build-up?*

---

In earlier eras, American armed forces in peacetime were just on stand-by. Except for minor interventions, as in Cuba and Nicaragua, the peacetime function of the armed forces was to stay alive. Their purpose was to maintain a capacity for mobilization in the event of war. The enemy was the budget. The participation of our armed forces in foreign policy was modest until war broke out or was imminent at which point war policy virtually dominated foreign policy.

The present is different. American armed forces are the principal instrument for diplomacy with an important set of countries—the countries we recognize as potential enemies. Military deployment, the defense budget, and weapon decisions are not just preparations for war; they are a means of communication to the Soviet Bloc. The stationing of troops in Europe, the pre-emptive landing of troops in Lebanon, the call-up of reserves, the alert status of the Strategic Air Command, the dispatch of a battle group to Berlin, and even the blockade of Cuba are at least as important in what they do to Soviet expectations as in what they do to Western capabilities.

In other words, military policy in this era is concerned with enemy intentions, not just capabilities. The idea of "deterrence" assumes that we not only can estimate enemy intentions but can influence them. And we do it by conveying to the Soviets an appreciation of how the Western nations will react. Our military policy is continually concerned with manipulating enemy expectations. For that purpose, we confront potential enemies with threats of resistance and punishment for misbehavior and with assurances that they will not receive gratuitous punishment if they stay within bounds.

Much of our policy is concerned with making believable to the Russians a pattern of American response. In cases where they might doubt we are sufficiently resolute (or foolhardy) to react violently to their intrusions, we often try to get ourselves into a position that leaves no doubt—a position where the choice is made for us, or where the costs in leadership, reputation, and prestige in failing to respond as promised would be so intolerably high that we could not but react as we had threatened.

The Soviets engage in the same process of military diplomacy. Each of us, furthermore, tries to erode or to undermine the other's threats and to detach each other's military force from political commitments, in order that the other's threatened response, not being obligatory, may not be forthcoming. This is a continuous bargaining process between potential enemies, each having substantial capacity to damage the other but only at substantial cost to itself. Each continually tests and probes; each tries to burn its bridges to show that it cannot be expected to back down. Each tries at times to help the other to discover a bridge by which it can gracefully retreat in the hope that, if graceful retreat by the other is possible, graceful retreat may occur.[1]

With respect to what we call "aggression"—overt penetration of political boundaries with military force—this process of deterrence and brinkmanship is taken for granted. But the bargaining process is less explicit and less self-conscious where domestic arms preparations are concerned. We threaten the Soviets that if they seek strategic advantage by invading Turkey or Iran we shall react with military violence. We do not so explicitly threaten that we shall react with military violence if the Soviets seek military advantage through procurement of a large missile and bomber force or if they seek to deny us an effective force by building missile and bomber defenses. On the whole, we consider war, even a very limited war, an overt act calling for a military response; we do not consider arms preparations, even when directed against us, an overt provocation requiring or justifying hostilities.

Nevertheless, in principle, an arms build-up with hostile intent might be met with a military response. The concept of preemption suggests that "hostilities" can be initiated by an enemy country within its own borders, entailing quick military response. Mobilization of armed forces has typically been considered nearly equivalent to a declaration of war. At the outbreak of World War I "deterrent threats," unfortunately unsuccessful, were aimed at domestic acts of mobilization as well as against overt aggression. And preventive war against an arming opponent has been a lurking possibility at least since the early Greek city-states.*

More recently, the United States has engaged in directly coercive military threats to deny the Soviets the military advantage of advance deployment of missiles. While Cuba is probably best viewed as a political and geographical Soviet move, it can also usefully be viewed as a Soviet effort to achieve quickly and cheaply an offensive military advantage. An interesting question is whether a comparable crash program within the Soviet Union to acquire a first-strike offensive force might be eligible for comparable sanctions.

As a matter of fact, arms-build-up bargaining does seem to take place, though in a less explicit fashion than the overt territorial bargaining that takes the form of alliances, declarations of commitment, and expressions of retaliatory policy.

---

* The Corinthian delegates:

" 'You Spartans are the only people in Hellas who wait calmly on events relying for your defense not on action but on making people think that you will act. You alone do nothing in the early stages to prevent an enemy's expansion; you wait until your enemy has doubled his strength. Certainly you used to have the reputation of being safe and sure enough; now one wonders whether this reputation was deserved. The Persians, as we know ourselves, came from the ends of the earth and got as far as the Peloponnese before you were able to put a proper force into the field to meet them. The Athenians, unlike the Persians, live close to you, yet still you do not appear to notice them; instead of going out to meet them, you prefer to stand still and wait till you are attacked, thus hazarding everything by fighting with opponents who have grown far stronger than they were originally.' "

Thucydides, *The Peloponnesian War*, tr. Rex Warner (Penguin Books, 1954), p. 50.

During most of the Eisenhower Administration the American defense budget was a self-imposed restraint on the Western arms build-up. The motivation may well have been mainly economic, but it is a fair judgment that part of the motivation was a desire not to aggravate an arms race. Even when the assumed "missile gap" created grave concern about the vulnerability of American retaliatory forces in 1959 and the Strategic Air Command displayed a lively interest in the rapid enlargement of an airborne alert, the Administration was reluctant to embark on crash military programs, and there was some evidence that its reluctance was a preference not suddenly to rock the arms-race boat. Moreover, among the many inhibitions on civil defense in this country over the last several years, one was a desire not to add a dimension to the arms race, not to appear frantically concerned about general war, and not to destabilize the defense budget.

There have also been direct efforts to negotiate understandings about the relation of armed forces on both sides. With the exception of the test ban, these have come to nothing; and the test ban, whatever combination of good and harm it may have done so far, pertinently illustrates the combination of threats and reassurances that, at least implicitly, go with any bargaining process. In addition to the argument, "We won't if you don't," there has been the argument, "And we will if you do."

But the bargaining goes further than that. In the early summer of 1961, in response to provocative Soviet statements about Berlin, President Kennedy deliberately called up reserves and raised the defense budget. The evident purpose was not only to increase quickly our preparation for a military emergency in Berlin, but also to impress on the Soviets the costs and dangers of aggravating the arms race by provocative action, an arms race that was not yet nearly as furious as it might be. Khrushchev's "retaliatory" announcement of Soviet increases is surely better interpreted as "negotiation" than as just military preparation.

And when the summit conference in Paris collapsed in May 1960 in the wake of the U-2 incident, Khrushchev showed his sensitivity to this bargaining process. In response to a reporter's question why American forces had gone on some kind of alert the night before, he remarked that it was probably the American Administration's attempt to soften up American taxpayers for a defense budget increase. In that remark, he showed himself perceptive of the arms-build-up bargaining that goes on between us and alert to the early symptoms of an aggravated arms race.

In a less articulate way, we surely do relate our arms programs to Soviet programs, and they relate theirs to ours. Our estimated "requirements" for bombers, missiles, submarines, and ground forces are related to what we believe will be the forces opposing them. Our bomber build-up in the 1950's was a reflection of the expected Soviet bomber forces and air defenses. The "missile gap" of the late 1950's spurred not only our research and development but also our weapon procurement. The most recent appropriations for Minuteman, Polaris, and other strategic forces must relate to US intelligence on what the Soviets may confront us with in the years to come.

Presumably the Soviets, too, have to make their long-range military plans with a view to the expected capabilities of the United States and other countries in future years. Whether the Soviets aim at superiority, equality, or some acceptable ratio of inferiority, they have to have some idea of whether American missiles year by year throughout this decade will be numbered in the scores, hundreds, or thousands.

Implicitly, then, if not explicitly, each of us in his own program must influence the other in some fashion. The influence is surely complicated and uneven, indirect and occasionally irrational, and undoubtedly based often on inaccurate projections of each other's programs. But the influence is there. The Soviets may not have realized when they lofted their first Sputnik into orbit that they were doing for American strategic forces what the Korean invasion had done earlier to Western military programs. They might have guessed it; and even if they did not, in retrospect they must be aware that their early achievements in rocketry were a shot in the arm to American strategic weapon development. Whether the Soviets got a net gain from making the West believe in the missile gap in the late 1950's may be questionable, but it is beyond question that both our bomber and our missile forces were enhanced in qualitative performance, and some of them in quantity, by our beliefs.

The Korean War was undoubtedly the most dramatic postwar demonstration of how much Western military programs are a response to a perceived threat. The Greek Civil War and the more recent Berlin crises had a similar effect. Overt aggression appears to be more provocative than domestic military programs in this respect, but some interaction between both sides' long-term military programs is always evident. Recently, Soviet boasts about an anti-ICBM capability have probably spurred greater American interest in problems of penetration and interception. Boasts, of course, are different from the real thing. But the same principle is involved; the difference is only one of evidence.

Here it becomes clear that the so-called "inspection" problem, widely argued in relation to disarmament, is really no more relevant to disarmament than to armament. We always have our "inspection" problem. With or without disarmament agreements we have a serious and urgent need to know as accurately as possible what military preparations the other side is making. Not only for overt political and military responses around the world, but even for our own military programming, we have to know something about the quantity or quality of military forces that oppose us. In deciding whether to plan for 20 or 200 Polaris submarines, for 500 or 5000 Minutemen, in deciding whether the RS–70 will have special capabilities against particular targets, in reaching decisions on the value and the performance of defenses against ICBM's, in deciding what to include in the payload of a missile we build and how to configure our missile sites, we have to estimate the likely military forces that will confront us year after year throughout the planning period.

We have to use what information we can get, whether from unilateral intelligence or from other sources. If we decide unilaterally to be just as strong, twice as strong, or ten times as strong as the Soviet Union over the next decade, our need to know what the Soviets are doing is as important as if we had a negotiated agreement with them that we should be just as strong, twice as strong, or ten times as strong over the decade.

The difference is apparently that under disarmament agreements it is acknowledged (at least in the West) that each side needs information about what the other is doing. It is even acknowledged that each ought to have an interest in displaying its program to the other in the interest of maintaining the agreement. But this should be equally true without any agreement: the Soviets in the end may actually have suffered from our belief in the missile gap, much in the way they would suffer under a disarmament agreement that provided us insufficient assurance about the pace of their own program. If we insist on a given ratio of superiority and drastically overestimate what the Soviets have, not only do we spend more money but *they* must, too. They have to try to keep up with us; and in so doing may "justify" *ex post facto* the program that we had set afoot on the basis of our original exaggerated estimates.

Once this interaction between armed forces of both sides is recognized and acknowledged, it is hard to see that "arms control" adds anything new in principle. Acknowledging "arms control" as a legitimate and almost inevitable part of the interaction process may help to increase both sides' consciousness of the bargaining relation between them. It may help to improve communications between both sides (although it may, as it often seems to at Geneva, just add noise to the channel). The role of information in the arms race may become better understood, and we may become more aware of the possibility of "deterring" Soviet military preparations as well as deterring overt military acts.

But, at least unconsciously, each side surely is aware of the "feedback" of its program on the other's future program, both qualitative and quantitative. It is doubtful that a country as hard pressed economically as the Soviet Union would maintain, year after year, a military program without regard to the size and character of Western military programs. They could undoubtedly do more; they unquestionably would save valuable resources by doing less. In the short run there is great inertia in defense budgets, probably in the Soviet Union as well as here; in the longer run it can hardly be supposed that Soviet military forces, both in the aggregate and in detailed composition, will be derived from Marxist-Leninist principles that do not take enemy strength and intentions into account.

In the short run, we can presumably base our military plans on decisions the Soviets have already taken and programs they have already set afoot. There is substantial lead time in the procurement and deployment of weapons, and for some period, measured in years rather than months, it is probably safe to *estimate* enemy programs rather than to think about *influencing* them. At least, it is probably safe to estimate them rather than to try to influence them in the downward direction. We could probably boost Soviet military production within a year or two, just as they could boost ours by their actions; it is unlikely that either of us would slack off drastically on account of any short-run events—short of a change in regime or the discovery that one's information has been wholly wrong for several years. (The fading of the "missile gap" did not nearly reverse the decisions it had earlier provoked.)

But in thinking about the whole decade ahead—in viewing "the arms race" as an interaction between two sides (actually, among several sides)—we have to take some account of the "feedback" in our military planning. That is, we must suppose that over an appreciable period of years Soviet programs respond to what they perceive to be the "threat" to them, and in turn our programs reflect what we perceive to be that "threat" to us. Then, by the end of the decade, we may be reacting to Soviet decisions that in turn were reactions to our decisions early in the decade; and vice versa. The Soviets should have realized in 1957 that their military requirements in the middle 1960's would be, to an appreciable extent, a result of their own military programs and military public relations in the late 1950's.

This is the feedback process in principle, but its operation depends on the fidelity of perception and information, biases in the estimating process, lead time in military procurement decisions, and all of the political and bureaucratic influences that are brought to bear by inter-service disputes, budgetary disputes, alliance negotiations, and so forth.

An important question is just how sensitive either of us actually is to the other's program. To approach that question, we ought to inquire into the processes by which either of us reacts to the other. These reactions are surely not just the result of a coolly calculated and shrewd projection of the other side's behavior and a coolly calculated response. Nor do the military decisions of either side result simply from rational calculations of an appropriate strategy based on some agreed evaluation of the enemy. Partly they do, but partly they reflect other things.

First, there may be a certain amount of pure imitation and power of suggestion. There is usually a widespread notion that, to excel over an enemy, one has to excel in every dimension. There seems to be a presumption that, if the enemy makes progress in a particular direction, he must know what he is doing; we should make at least equal progress in that direction. This seems to be the case whether in economic warfare, nuclear-powered aircraft, foreign aid, ballistic missile defenses, or disarmament proposals. This particular reaction seems to be based on hunch; it may be a good one, but it is a hunch.

Second, enemy actions may simply remind us of things we have overlooked, or emphasize developments to which we have given too little attention.

Third, enemy performance may have some genuine "intelligence value" in providing information about what can be done. The Soviet Sputnik and some other Soviet space performances may have had some genuine value in persuading Americans that certain capabilities were winthin reach. The US detonation of nuclear weapons in 1945 must have been comparably important in making clear to the Soviets, as to everyone else, that nuclear weapons were more than a theoretical possibility and that it was perfectly feasible to build a weapon that could be transported by airplane.

Fourth, many decisions in government result from bargaining among services or among commands. Soviet performance or Soviet emphasis on a particular development may provide a powerful argument to one party or another in a dispute over weapons or budget allocations.

Fifth, many military decisions are politically motivated, inspired by the interests of particular congressmen or provoked by press comment. Soviet achievements that appear to be a challenge or that put American performance in a poor light may have, beneficially or not, some influence on the political-decision process.

And in all of these influential processes, it is not the true fact but beliefs and opinions based on incomplete evidence that provide the motivating force.

I see no reason to suppose that the Soviets react in a more rational, more coolly deliberate way, than the West. They surely suffer from budgetary inertia, interservice disputes, ideological touchstones, and the intellectual limitations of a political bureaucracy, as well as from plain bad information. Furthermore, both we and the Soviets play to an audience of third countries. Prestige of some sort is often at stake in weapon-development competition; and a third-area public exercises some unorganized influence in determining the particular lines of development that we and the Soviets are motivated to pursue.

On the whole, the evidence does not show that the Soviets understand this interaction process and manipulate it shrewdly. The Korean War, in retrospect, can hardly have served the Soviet interest; it did more than anything else to get the United States engaged in the arms race and to get NATO taken seriously. The Soviets may have been under strong temptation to get short-run prestige gains out of their initial space successes; perhaps they lamented the necessity to appeal to a public audience in a fashion that was bound to stimulate the United States. Whatever political gains they got out of the short-lived missile gap which they either created or acquiesced in, it not only stimulated Western strategic programs but possibly gave rise to a reaction that causes the Soviets to be viewed more skeptically at the present time than their accomplishments may actually warrant. Maybe the Soviets were just slow to appreciate the way Americans react; or maybe they, too, are subject to internal pressures that keep them from pursuing an optimal strategy in the arms race. But if on their own they do not understand the extent to which Western programs are a reaction to theirs, perhaps we can teach them. Do we want to teach them? How would we go about teaching them?

### Implications of Interaction Process

One possibility is that we do not want to teach them. We are economically superior to the Soviets and will hold that advantage for some time if not indefinitely. Perhaps we want to maximize the strain on the Soviet economy by our influence on the Soviet defense budget. Making them try to keep up with us in an expensive arms race may be a way to retard them economically. Alternatively, making them try to keep up with us in some other expensive race—for the moon or for the underdeveloped countries—may be a way to limit what they can channel into the arms race. In a sense, those who want to maximize the tempo of the arms race to strain the Soviet economy and those who would like to divert resources to a "peace race," with emphasis on economic aid and all that, are both proposing that we use our economic advantage to strain the Soviets' defense budget.

A quite different policy would be to persuade the Soviets that the arms race is something they just cannot win. This would involve two parts: first, to persuade them that *if* we choose to outmatch them in military assets, we have the economic strength to do so; second, to persuade them that we have determined to pursue that goal, outdoing whatever they do.

Historically, this kind of thing has happened. Samuel P. Huntington examined a number of qualitative and quantitative arms races during the century since about 1840, and he does find instances in which one power eventually gave up challenging the supremacy of another. "Thus, a twenty-five year sporadic naval race between France and England ended in the middle 1860's when France gave up any serious effort to challenge the 3:2 ratio which England had demonstrated the will and the capacity to maintain. Similarly, the Anglo-German naval race slackened after 1912, when, despite failure to reach formal agreement, relations improved between the two countries and even Tirpitz acquiesced in the British 16:10 ratio in capital ships." He points out, though, that "in nine out of ten races the slogan of the challenging state is either 'parity' or 'superiority.' Only in rare cases does the challenger aim for less than this, for unless equality or superiority is achieved, the arms race is hardly likely to be worthwhile."[2] The latter statement might, however, be more relevant to a pre-nuclear period in which military force was for active defense rather than for a deterrent based on retaliation potential. "Minimum deterrence" or something like it may not have had a good counterpart in the 19th century.

Our question, then, is whether it might be possible and worthwhile to attempt to make clear to the Soviets that any effort to achieve strategic superiority over the United States—or even any substantial parity—is too unlikely of success to be worth the cost.

Consider a missile race for purposes of illustration. Suppose that we have solved the complex problem of comparing Soviet forces in the aggregate with our own and that one can speak in very crude terms of a numerical ratio. Suppose that we design and present to Congress our long-term defense-budget plans not in terms of a given size of force to confront a foreseeable threat, but as a functional relationship between the Soviet force expected at any given point in time and the appropriate US force.* Suppose, just for illustration, that we decide to have a force equal to three times the Soviet force, no matter what. Then, the defense budget is presented only as an estimate of what would be required by this ratio, with the understanding that we would actually do whatever the facts determined under this ratio. Suppose this policy were bolstered with congressional resolutions or with new defense-budget legislation prescribing that some specified ratio vis-à-vis the Soviets be maintained. Could this be done and communicated in such a way as to leave the Soviets under no doubt about American resolution to main-

---

* Relative, not absolute, force goals were not uncommonly legislated by the British and German Governments prior to World War I. Cf. Winston S. Churchill, *The World Crisis: 1911-18* (London: 1943), pp. 75-81.

tain a stipulated ratio of superiority? And what might be the Soviet response, once they appreciated it?

Alternatively, without being quite so arrogant or patronizing as to legislate some specified superiority in perpetuity, we might just use our behavior or private and subtle communications to inform the Soviets that we had every intention of staying ahead in the arms race—that we would continually glance back to see how they were doing and would accommodate our speed accordingly. What alternatives would then confront them?

It is hard to believe that the Soviets could openly acknowledge that they were reconciled to perpetual inferiority. It may even be extremely difficult for them to acknowledge it to themselves. It might, however, be possible to discourage very substantially their genuine expectations about what they could accomplish in the arms race. In particular, we might demonstrate to them— if in fact it is demonstrable—that a good first-strike capability was just not in the cards for them, at least not sufficiently likely to make it a wise gamble of the resources invested in the attempt. It might be possible to ease them into some kind of "minimum-deterrence" posture.

It still has to be decided whether we want to discourage them in this way. It may be wiser to let them spend futilely on a losing race rather than to show them where it will all end so they can cut back and use the money elsewhere. It might be even wiser, if we can get away with it, to tantalize them with the prospect of strategic parity, so that they continually slight their ground forces, their foreign aid programs, and domestic investment in the vain hope of overtaking us strategically.

Essentially, this process of discouraging the Soviets in the arms race is no different from trying to persuade them that they are getting nowhere by pushing us around in Berlin. In Berlin, as in Cuba, we are trying to teach them a lesson about what might have been called "peaceful coexistence," if the term had not been discredited by Soviet use already. We did, in the Cuba event, engage in a process intended to teach the Soviets something about what to expect of us and to discourage them from making future miscalculations that might be costly for both of us. In the vicinity of Berlin we have been trying, not without success, to persuade them that certain courses of action are doomed to futility.

I am suggesting that we might want to consider teaching them similar lessons with respect to the arms build-up itself.

We might not use the same techniques of education—direct military confrontation and threats of military hostilities—but the principle is much the same. We would instead seek an equivalent of a "Formosa Resolution" in the arms-race arena.

It does seem worthwhile to have some design for managing the arms race over the next decade or two. It is prematurely defeatist to suppose that we could never persuade the Soviets, at least tentatively, that this was a race they could not win. The principle of "containment" ought to be applicable to Soviet military preparation. However constrained they are by an ideology that makes it difficult for them to acknowledge that they are bested or contained, they must have some capacity for acceptance of the facts of life. But it would be up to us to make our response appear to be a fact of life.

I cannot suggest that the Soviets could be taught, once and for all, that crime does not pay. To tame a beast so that it no longer has any interest in consuming its keeper is an ambitious prospect; to teach it that a vigilant keeper cannot be overcome, and will make the attempt painful, may be feasible. And while one may hope that sustained discouragement may eventually lead to tameness, the urge to relax vigilance would have to be resisted.

This is a kind of "arms control" objective. But it differs from the usual formulation of arms control in several respects. First, it does not begin with the premise that arms agreements with potential enemies are intrinsically obliged to acknowlege some kind of parity. (But since there are many different ways of measuring military potency, it might be possible to permit an inferior power to claim—possibly even to believe in—parity according to certain measures.) Second, it explicitly rests on the notion that arms bargaining involves threats as well as offers.

It may be impolite in disarmament negotiations explicitly to threaten an aggravated arms race as the cost of disagreement. But, of course, the inducement to agree to any reciprocated modification of armaments must be some implicit threat of the consequences of failure to agree. The first step towards inducing a potential enemy to moderate his arms build-up is to persuade him that he has more to lose than to gain by failing to take our reaction into account. Perhaps it is not altogether unwise deliberately to plan and to communicate a somewhat excessive military build-up ratio relative to the Soviet force in order to enhance their inducements to moderate their own program. (This sort of thing is not unknown in tariff bargaining.)

Finally, this discussion has raised the question whether we might not profitably be more explicit about the kind of arms build-up bargaining that takes place in any case between the Soviets and ourselves. We always have an implicit threat, whether we intend it or not, that an intensified Soviet arms build-up will lead to an intensification here. We might make the explicit threat stronger, and we might articulate the kind of power relationship that we would demand and settle for.

This discussion has for the most part assumed that the arms race is a matter of "more" or "less," a matter of quantity. Of course, it is not. There is a difference between a first-strike force and a second-strike force, even though it is not as clear-cut as theoretical discussions assume. There is a difference between weapons systems designed for counterforce tasks and systems mainly designed for the destruction of cities. There is a difference between good and poor facilities for command and control. There is a difference between weapons so co-located with cities as to oblige the destruction of cities in a counterforce war and weapons substantially separated from cities.

Some dimensions of the arms build-up are not of the character suggested by the term "arms race." There are facilities that are not competitive: facilities to minimize false alarm, facilities to prevent accidental and unauthorized acts that might lead to war, and many other improvements in reliability. That is to say, it may be no disadvantage to one side that the other make progress on those particular capabilities. Furthermore, some developments are more purely defensive or deterrent than others, some more offensive or pre-emptive. A missile-hardening race is not the same as a missile-numbers race. Getting across to the Soviets the kind of reaction they can expect from us therefore involves more than quantitative plan; it may involve getting across the kinds of weapons programs that would appear less provocative and those that would appear more so. The Cuban affair is a reminder that there can be a difference.

If, in our attempts to plan a decade or more ahead, we take seriously the problem of arms-race management and consider the interaction between our programs and the Soviets', we have to engage in quite a new exercise: thinking about the kind of military-force posture that we would like the Soviets to adopt. Typically in discussions of military policy we treat the Soviet posture either as given or as something to be determined by factors outside our control, to which we must respond in some adequate way. As a result, nothing appears to be gained by thinking about *our* preferences among alternative *Soviet* postures, doctrines, and programs. But if we begin to examine how we might influence the Soviet posture, we have to consider which alternative Soviet developments we prefer and which we would deplore.

Quantitatively, this requires us to decide whether we want a maximal or a minimal Soviet effort. Qualitatively, it requires us to consider alternative Soviet weapons systems and force configurations. The kinds of arguments we occasionally have in this country about first-strike versus second-strike forces, the merits of active and passive defenses of the homeland, a counterforce or a city-busting general-war doctrine, and a mix of forces between intercontinental and limited-war capability— all of these arguments we can also imagine taking place within the Soviet Union, too. If we are to have any influence on the outcome of those arguments, diffuse and indirect though it may be, we have to decide in what direction we want to exert it.

A main difference, then, between military policy for the longer run and military policy for the shorter run is this: the longer the run considered, the more the arms race takes on the character of a two-sided adaptive system rather than a pair of unilateral programs. Actually, of course, there are more than two sides; neither the Western Alliance nor the Soviet Bloc is single-minded in its interests and policies. If we look a decade or more ahead, the world may become less polarized than it is now. By the time that we have learned to think of the process as a two-sided interaction, rather than as a pair of unilateral programs, it may have ceased to be just two-sided.

## FOOTNOTES

[1] Alfred Vagts' discussion of European "armed demonstrations," though less inclusive than the arms-race phenomena discussed here, is highly suggestive. "Since the seventeenth century, governments have not maintained armies and navies merely for the purposes of making war and maintaining order at home. The existence of armed forces in peacetime was also designed to have a continuous or occasional diplomatic effect. . . . As bodies charged with potential violence, a number of their actions could be made highly demonstrative, pointing to an application of the force presented, with more to come if necessary." *Defense and Diplomacy* (New York: 1956), p. 231.

[2] Samuel P. Huntington, "Arms Races: Prerequisites and Results," *Public Policy*, ed. Carl J. Friedrich and Seymour E. Harris (Cambridge, Mass.: Harvard University Press, 1958), pp. 57, 64.

# Discussion—Part III

## NUCLEAR WEAPONS AND THE NATO ALLIANCE

*Armstrong*\*: We will begin discussion with two statements from Dr. Kissinger's paper.\*\*

> Central control of nuclear weapons, which we correctly considered crucial, can become a device by which to tie the Atlantic nations together politically.
>
> \* \* \* \*
>
> . . . we have stressed a technical solution for the composition of the crews at the expense of the political problem of control. And we have created the wrong psychological climate by implying that we would support only one particular solution.
>
> Henry Kissinger

*Kissinger:* I have the impression that our basic approach to the nuclear problem within NATO has been a device, sometimes disguised, sometimes stated explicitly, by which we retain control over the nuclear strategy of the Alliance, and by which we maintain physical control over the ability to conduct nuclear war.

Theoretically, this is not an undesirable situation for us. Practically, politically, and psychologically, it is bound to be unacceptable to the Europeans. Or, to put it another way, it can be effectuated in Europe only by strengthening all those forces which are not only opposed to nuclear strategy, but are opposed to any kind of strategy, and which would like to put the whole responsibility for the defense of the Free World into our hands. If we are successful in this attempt, we are not going to get a conventional build-up, as some of our people believe; rather, we are going to get a neutralist Europe with a sense of impotence. This is a political judgment I make.

Therefore, if we are serious about the notion of partnership, we can afford to have Europeans participate as equal partners

---

\* Brig. Gen. Donald Armstrong, USA (Ret.), chairman of this panel.
\*\* These statements were taken from Dr. Kissinger's article, "Strains on the Alliance," *Foreign Affairs*, January, 1963.

in the development of a NATO nuclear strategy. If it is true that our interests are indivisible, we ought to be able to give political expression to this.

I would think also that, if the Europeans have some nuclear weapons under their own control, we must have enough confidence in their sense of responsibility and in their understanding of the realities of the strategic situation to assume that they would want to coordinate with us.

The other day I read an article by one of our more learned commentators, who said: "There cannot be any policy by which the Europeans distrust us. Such a world can never be." Well, such a world has been for a number of years. We are saying that the Europeans are not to be trusted with nuclear weapons under their own control, because they may use them in a way that is unacceptable to us, and that they will not understand their own interests sufficiently well to realize the overriding need of coordination. The proposals we have made have had the practical consequence of making unnecessary coordination on their part, and enabling us to control the nuclear policy of the Alliance. The basic decision we have to make is whether we are willing to have a real partnership, which includes the theoretical possibility of independent action on the part of the Europeans. This, in my judgment, would have the practical consequence that in all foreseeable circumstances they would coordinate with us, because their self-interest would bring them in this direction.

The second quotation is addressed to the proposal which we have been advancing in various forms for several years, and which is now again being written about in the newspapers— although there are so many American proposals before NATO right now that it isn't easy to tell what it is that we are most urgently demanding at a given moment—that a NATO nuclear force be created, composed of submarines, which in turn are composed of crews of mixed nationalities. These crews of mixed nationalities are designed to give a multilateral character to the NATO force. My conviction is that this proposal answers none of the problems. I cannot imagine a form of nuclear control by which control is exercised through the threat of mutiny. I do not know whether the idea is that each national contingent establishes its own communications system with its home government. The only use I can see in these multi-national crews is the argument that it will occur to no one that this is a national force, and therefore it cannot be withdrawn from NATO. Even that I would question, because presumably the captain of the submarine will determine what is going to be done, and unless we insist that all the captains are Americans, I think even that problem isn't going to be solved.

If we talk about multilateral, multi-national forces with greatly detailed schemes for the technical composition of crews, doesn't this miss the central point, which is the political control of that force? The political control of that force is a much more complicated problem. Secondly, those who have accepted the NATO force have accepted it for negative reasons. The Germans accept it because it gives them a chance to get into the nuclear business; the Belgians and Italians, because it prevents the Germans from being the only nuclear country. I know no one in Europe, and in fact I know no one in the United States, who believes that this force has a positive mission. Everyone who wants it, wants it because he wants to prevent something worse. And this seems to me to be a very poor basis for NATO strategy.

I think the nuclear forces in NATO ought to have a clear mission, and if we cannot devise a strategy in which we are willing to have some degree of confidence in political coordination, I don't believe that these technical gimmicks are going to solve what is a very deep problem, a very deep psychological and political problem within the Alliance.

*Possony:* We must recognize what the legal situation is. The NATO Pact is based on the clear-cut recognition that every member of NATO is a sovereign nation. There is no such thing as an integrated state system or federation. These are states in their own right, and they have joined an alliance and nothing else. The Alliance is perhaps a little bit more advanced than the classical forms of alliance were. Still, it is an alliance.

The NATO Treaty specifically does not stipulate automaticity. There is no obligation, legal or otherwise, that the United States automatically must come to the aid of any country invaded. It would be up to us to decide whether a *casus belli* has occurred. This being the situation, it is perfectly plain that these states must have a capability to defend themselves in case of attack. This is a right which is stipulated, for example, in the United Nations Charter. The right of self-defense is furthermore a perfectly logical natural right that has been in existence since the early days of human history.

This, of course, is not an abstract right, but it has to be implemented by weapons systems that are usable not in 1914, or in 1940, but at the particular time when that war may occur, which may be today or in the future, but not in the past. Consequently, one has to have weapons systems which have the effectiveness of the modern system, and this, today, means basically nuclear weapons. Whether you get rid of them or not is a subject I don't think we can discuss at this moment. But, let us just simply say that, as of today, the decisive military forces in the world are nuclear in character.

The problem of central control has to be split up. It is a long-standing principle that you have to have something like a joint command, or unified command, or a single command, or whatever you might call it. There has to be one strategy, and I think this is the problem of central control in war. But, it is not the problem in peace, and it is not the problem for the individual state, which has to decide, according to treaties and according to historical precedent, whether or not its national interests demand defense or attack. The right to war or peace is the basic element to sovereignty.

In the recent proposal from Nassau, while it proposed a joint force, there was a statement to the effect that the individual members of a multilateral nuclear force would be able to use the Polaris submarines in case of extreme national emergency. So we have now come back and recognized this principle. It is a little bit under the table, but nevertheless it is recognized, and I want to stress that there is no alternative but to recognize this.

With respect to the establishment of the multilateral force, I do not think there is any particular reason to argue that Polaris is the wrong weapon, or that something else is the right weapon. I think you will find that, if you want a multilateral strategic force, you have to have a mixed force of several weapons systems. We were very much surprised, when General de Gaulle, the *bête noire* of modern American politics, turned it down. I think there are three reasons why he turned it down.

One is that the offer of the United States came at a moment when the United States proved to the world its complete unreliability as to a given commitment; I refer to the Skybolt matter.

Number 2: the United States previously had offered to France information on the construction of nuclear submarines. In fact, Congress in 1958 voted a law to the effect that we should give nuclear aid to those of our allies who have demonstrated a nuclear know-how. This, of course, was a subterfuge wording to give aid to Britain and to withhold aid from France on the mistaken assumption that the French would be too stupid or too poor to develop a nuclear weapon. The same type of estimate, incidentally, was made years ago about Russia. Well, as soon as the French demonstrated a nuclear know-how, this particular law was speedily forgotten, and the commitment we had made with respect to the nuclear submarines was also forgotten.

Number 3: When we offered Polaris, we offered the missiles. We did not offer the warheads, which is the crux of the matter. In order for the French to produce this warhead, they would have to reorganize their nuclear program. Presumably they would have to reorganize a great deal more than just their nuclear program, because they are presently set up to develop their force on the Mirage IV model.

Under the best circumstances, in our country, such reorganization would take several years. The effect of this offer, if accepted, could be that the French national deterrent would be delayed by a period of five to six, perhaps ten, years. When we ask the French to accept the Polaris without the warheads, inviting them to develop the warheads themselves, we have simultaneously upped our interest in the test ban.

Just suppose that we sign the test ban. One of the conditions of the test ban would be that the French, and this is a condition specifically laid down by the Soviets, would not test. On the one hand, we don't give them the warheads; on the other hand, we would certainly make every effort, if the test ban were in operation, to prevent them from testing. How can they get the warheads in this case?

If you are surprised that General de Gaulle turned it down, I am not. I think it is the only logical course of action he could take.

**Test Ban**

*Teller:* The question of test cessation has been before the American public for more than six years now. In these very days, due to the generosity of Khrushchev of as many as three inspections per year, this question has become, in the opinion of many of our compatriots, of acute interest.

I have read in the papers of various panels a number of comparisons between the state of the art in the United States and in the USSR. There is nothing more frightening to me than to see such comparisons. We say we are ahead; we are going to keep ahead. Actually, I am not quite sure who is ahead now, but the art of nuclear explosives is rapidly developing, and is unpredictable.

In 1945, at the end of the War, when I was returning to the University of Chicago, Oppenheimer said to me: "We have done an excellent job here in Los Alamos, and it will be many years before anybody will be able to improve on it in the slightest." You know what happened in 1952. In 1958 the majority of the scientific community argued that we had a stalemate, that nothing more could be obtained by testing, that we knew everything there was to be known. Yet, a very few years afterwards we had clear-cut evidence and the Russian statements of developing anti-missile techniques which could easily upset the strategic balance.

Technological surprises are an almost yearly occurrence in this rapidly advancing field. A test moratorium will close to us the avenue of such advances. Nothing can be tested. Predictions are extremely hard, and what cannot be tested rapidly degenerates into meaningless discussion and, eventually, into loss of interest.

We have seen that in the time of a moratorium the Russians can fully and effectively prepare their next test series. Test moratoria in general cannot be policed. Three inspections are ridiculous. Thirty inspections are not enough, and 300 inspections would not quite do the job either. But, even if the Russians kept the agreement to the letter and merely prepared for their next series, we might find ourselves in 1968 outclassed. We might be faced with really reliable missile defenses in the hands of the Russians and no counterpart in our hands. The result might be the same as if they had missiles and we had none. What is the use of a thousand missiles if none of them can hit?

This is the danger that we are up against today. Public opinion has been cleverly manipulated, and is now in turn pushing the Administration into decisions which can become fatal, absolutely and literally fatal, to the United States before another decade has passed.

### The Multilateral Force

*Kahn:* I would like to defend the multilateral proposal with mixed crews for something like the Western European Union or European Political Community. I think Henry Kissinger is absolutely right when he says many US proposals have been fakes; that is, they basically propose giving the Italians a cook or putting the force under one US headquarters. And, to the extent that the multilateral proposal expresses such objectives, I absolutely agree that it is dangerous for the Alliance and for the defense of the NATO area. The fact that it is gimmicky does not impress me as being necessarily a defect. Any concrete proposals will have to be gimmicky in this area, and the multilateral proposal has the defect of being concrete.

It is all right to talk about political control as being central. But, what does political control mean? Are you going to have a committee? Committees don't press buttons under any circumstances. Are you going to turn it over to an executive? It is going to be very tough, unless that executive, that individual, is somehow under very close control. The problem of the control of nuclear weapons is often described as a problem of the trigger and the safety catch; that is, who can press the trigger, or who can prevent the trigger from being pressed? It turns out that each nation wants to have its hands on both the trigger and the safety catch. They want safety catches for all the other weapons systems, because they don't want to be involved in a war which they didn't start, and they want a trigger for their own weapons systems. This, of course, is incompatible.

How do you get some compatibility here? You first have to decide what it is you are trying to do with this force. I think the minimum that the Europeans need is a force under their own control, which would fire nuclear weapons at the Russians, if the Russians fired nuclear weapons at the Europeans. I suspect this is also the maximum of what they really need.

If this is all they need, then the problem can be solved by gimmicks. You can in fact have an executive officer with a firing doctrine; or there may be a whole range of doctrines. I would especially recommend the controlled-response doctrine. You fire the same number of weapons back, but you fire at the Soviet heartland. You might even tell the Soviets what the target lists were. You could publish it. It is clear to me that, for such a system to be reliable in the European area and not to involve very serious defects, it is going to have to be sea-based.

I think that Dr. Possony is absolutely right when he says that de Gaulle had good reasons for turning down our offer of Polaris. In fact, it is a 1970 offer. We could give them Polaris submarines next year if we wanted to.

The multilateralness of the crews, I think, is crucial. A Western European deterrent will infringe on sovereignty, or I don't think it will be acceptable. I think it really has to be multilateral. There are really very major objections to giving reasonably effective deterrents to Germany, to Italy, France, and so on. These may or may not be valid, but they are very effective.

You can have a German captain, and if he tries to take that crew into a German harbor, so to speak, and turn it over, he will have problems. He may succeed or he may not. But it is not a high-confidence measure. There is control. In other words, you can set up regulations for a multilateral crew, where basically you choose people by a kind of efficiency rating, they go to schools, and you tend to mix them. There are details here, but I think we can handle it. You would have to trust individuals, but there is an enormous difference in trusting individuals within this multilateral environment, and trusting nationally manned submarines.

And I would say that this proposal satisfies the arms controllers, it satisfies the people who worry about Germany, it satisfies the people who worry about the|"Nth country" problem, it satisfies the people who worry about the Europeans having a force of their own.

What are the important points? I suspect that, if you take seriously the US controlled-response doctrine, you will find that the European forces are not essential outside that doctrine, for various reasons. You may recall what the doctrine says. If the Russians hit US cities, we will hit Russian cities. This force's only purpose could be, during the war itself, if the Russians hit European cities, to hit Russian cities. In other words, it guarantees that European cities are under the umbrella of intra- or postwar deterrence. Otherwise the force might also be useful in the postwar background situations, or postwar peace treaty situations.

**Kintner:** I would like to talk about the nature of the multilateral force. I think that most people agree that this is desirable, but the level at which you can combine people is a subject of very serious discussion. I think I would hate to be the skipper in a submarine with Turks and Belgians and Germans all thrown together. I did have a little experience in Korea with squads that had Puerto Ricans, Koreans, and American soldiers fighting beside Ethiopians and Columbians. I assure you, it is a very complicated and difficult problem to get out orders for a patrol in three different languages; it is not very efficient, and often creates the type of accidents which, with nuclear weapons, might result in what we all apparently fear—an accidental war.

I think the level of integration can be worked out.* I don't believe it must be at the individual ship or firing unit. The other issue, though, is the fact that the European deterrent must, by the laws of the Medes and the Persians, be a sea-based force. I agree with Dr. Possony that we need to have a spectrum of forces. The sea-based deterrent is a very useful element in it, but I think the people who studied the situation in Europe—I call attention to General Norstad, who spent thirteen years there and who studied strategy very systematically—are strong advocates of a land-based local system in Europe. There are many other analysts in this country, as well as many Europeans, who feel that this is essential, if we are going to have a genuine deterrent, because one of the problems is to pose against the Russians an automatic response in the case of attack. The land-

---

* At a subsequent point in the discussion, Adm. Burke remarked:

**Burke:** Any organization in the world, to be effective, but particularly a ship, is dependent upon the faith and the confidence and the willingness of the people who man that ship to do a job. A ship is controlled by one man, one man who controls not by giving specific orders, but by having trained a ship so that his people do things automatically.

When a submarine, for example, is on the surface, and the captain decides that he wants to submerge, he gives certain specific orders. First, "prepare for diving," and then he gives succeeding orders. He knows that each man in that submarine is going to do a specific job. If any one or most of the crew fail to do their job exactly, the whole submarine may go down and never come back. The captain depends upon the ship, on each man in that ship, to do a job exactly the way it should be done. Now, each man in that ship also depends upon the captain. His faith and confidence in other people is necessary in a ship, and it is also necessary in an alliance or any other organization. If a crew is well trained there is no man who will not obey the captain. If a crew will not obey the captain, it is not an effective ship.

Consequently, one cannot have a multiple manning or mixed manning of a submarine which will serve two purposes: first, as an effective ship, and second, to have the national representatives on that ship control the situation, particularly in this kind of an organization. In this kind of organization the man who has the key, the captain, controls the situation, and everything depends entirely on what the captain wants to do. Either that ship is effective and obeys the orders of the captain, or the ship is not effective, and you can have multiple control.

If there is going to be some way for a multi-national force, it must be at a level which decides when to shoot, and then the orders go out to all ships that now is the time to shoot.

based missile system, which would have to be eliminated by the Soviets if they tried to take Europe by surprise, would be the most direct way of assuring that there would be a response, either national or multilateral in character. I just want to point out that the sea-based deterrent is not the answer for every problem facing NATO, although it makes a very important contribution to solving some of NATO's future security problems.

*Possony:* I do agree that, in addition to national deterrents of some sort, multi-national deterrents would be useful, and I am basically in favor of those. But the whole argument about deterrents at the present moment, when the United States does have a very large deterrent force, is a little bit in the wrong time perspective. What we need to consider is the over-all nuclear problem. We also have to consider the question of the total forces of Europe, the ground forces, and the air and missile defense forces, and those are more urgent problems than the question of the multi-national deterrent. But, on these other items of nuclear sharing, we are moving backwards. In other words, we withdraw, or at least we make noises as though we shall withdraw from Europe our nuclear forces that are suitable for the defense of Europe against a surface and an air attack. Irrespective of the deterrent, that is to say, of the retaliatory measures we would take once the attack has occurred, we must provide nuclear weapons for those other pressing defense tasks.

*Schelling:* William Kintner has brought us back to the ground forces. It seems to me that the discussion about nuclear relations with France, Britain, and Germany involves a number of things. One of these is the question of a NATO deterrent, another is the question of ground forces.

Deterring the Russians from an attack on Western Europe is the one thing we have done best for ten years, the one place where the Alliance is in excellent shape. The more we discuss NATO nuclear strategy in terms of what it takes either to deter or stop a Soviet attack on Western Europe, the less time we have to consider other functions of these weapons and strategies.

I think that the main reason for being interested in what is being called non-nuclear strategy is not a desire to disengage in the hope that disarmament is coming, but rather a recognition that the armed forces which the NATO nations have in Western Europe are not really just defensive forces in a purely tactical sense.

Many kinds of activities that might be considered offensive will require a good deal more flexibility than we would have if all troops of all nationalities have access to nuclear weapons, and more flexibility than we would have if there is a single common strategy. We need more flexibility than we probably have with the numbers of troops presently. I have in mind contingencies of the kind that perhaps are suggested by the Hungarian uprising, or the same kind of thing in East Germany, or relations with Finland, Yugoslavia, Albania, or other places in Eastern Europe in the years to come.

For a number of reasons the United States may want some independence of action in Europe. There may be a number of contingencies that can be responded to only in a non-NATO way, actions that would not invoke the NATO treaty, actions in which the political difficulties of acting as a NATO force would inhibit quick reaction.

If one is interested in the timely use of nuclear weapons in Western Europe, it may be useful to keep very tight US control on nuclear weapons available for tactical use. There is a great tendency in military planning to feel that the more exclusively you plan for a bold reaction, the more likely you are to act boldly. Frequently it is the case that the bolder you are in your planning, the more inhibited you are when the time comes, because you have less graduated ability to act in a non-climactic way.

One reason I am interested in these various NATO strategic deterrent forces, is that I suspect that a splendid way to keep US control of weapons available for so-called tactical use is to divert the European interest to strategic systems, particularly those on the high seas and particularly those that may not be available for several years. I think they can do less trouble to coordinated nuclear control if they have expensive, highly concentrated weapons in possession of the most controllable forces.

My own belief is that we don't need really to talk about what makes a feasible deterrent by way of an independent force. I would guess that even the notion of something not available in 1970 satisfies what the French mainly want, but perhaps not what General de Gaulle wants. If I were a Frenchman, or an Englishman, or a German, I might want a national nuclear weapons program, not because I think that in the 1960's my own forces are more reliable than American forces in an emergency, but because I don't want to be frozen out of nuclear technology in the 1970's, 1980's, or at such other time as NATO ceases to exist, or the Americans have left the Alliance, or one of these countries decides to go its own independent way.

I would think that the critical reason why a major European industrial country, or even an Asian industrial country, wants a nuclear program is for vaguely foreseeable contingencies that it wants to hedge against, rather than a way to patch up deficiencies in a defensive alliance which is one of the most effective and successful bits of American military strategy anywhere around the world.

*Teller:* While we are talking here, the papers say that we are withdrawing our missiles from Turkey and Italy. I think that this will weaken the Alliance and will weaken our ability to deter, which Dr. Schelling has correctly described.

We have been very paternalistic in our approach. "What is good for you is conventional forces. What is good for you is a sea-based nuclear deterrent. You are immature, you can't make your own judgments." The Europeans, whom we treat like teenagers, seem to have been a little rebellious, and I am not quite sure that our parental authority may not, after all, be a little mistaken.

In order to prevent any thought that the 1970's or 1980's will see anything else but solid Atlantic unity, in order to do that, would it not be best, to sit down with our Western allies honestly around the table? We should not have a US position. We should abolish all secrets while talking "in the family," and talk it out clearly. This way we may come to an honest agreement.

*Armstrong:* Mr. Frederick S. Wyle* of the State Department would like to make a comment.

*Wyle:* Thank you, General.

I quite agree with Henry Kissinger's feeling that political control in the multi-national force is, of course, a crucial element. That does not mean that the multilateral force is a gimmick. It does not mean either that it cannot accomplish a great many things now, and that we may not be able to resolve the problem of political control at some time, then, in the reasonably near future, and certainly before any alternative weapons system could be effective.

Now, I think Dr. Schelling put his finger on it when he said that the European desire is not yet articulated and not yet

* Mr. Wyle is a member of the Policy Planning Council, Department of State.

crystalized very accurately in the field of nuclear weapons aspirations. I think they do not want to be "out." The multilateral force is clearly a way in which they will be "in." The precise extent of participation of the various countries is not yet determined. This is something that is very much a matter of discussion among the Allies and with the United States.

In response to Dr. Teller's invitation to sit down and have an open conversation, such invitation has been made . . .

*Teller:* Can we talk with them about everything, or does "daddy know best" because he has the figures?

*Wyle:* Well, we have been trying very hard not to reflect that sort of attitude.

*Teller:* That is a diplomatic answer; can you give me a straight answer?

*Wyle:* Sir, I think I can. I think Dr. Teller himself has participated in enough international conferences, to know that he hasn't taken that attitude, and many other representatives of America have not taken that attitude. In fact, I don't know of any who have.

*Teller:* I have often participated, and I always had to observe the rules of secrecy, and I always will, as long as the secrecy rules apply. It is not a question of attitude. The point is that because I have secrets which they do not have, we are not talking as equal partners, and as long as we are not talking as equal partners, we are not talking effectively.

*Wyle:* As for the multi-national force, to answer two of Henry Kissinger's points, it is, of course, easy to lampoon, because it is unconventional. It is new. It is difficult. And our own people also at first took the attitude that this is a very difficult thing to do. They have, however, decided that it is feasible, if there is a sufficient political will.

Each of the points he has mentioned has been considered, and I think can be resolved in a way perfectly acceptable to the Alliance and to the European nations. These are some of the points now under discussion. Although we can't now predict that it will be the successful means to provide European nuclear participation, the multilateral force is an honest American effort to meet the European desires. It is not a gimmick, and it is not thought of as a gimmick.

## Future US Nuclear Strategies

*Armstrong:* Now, Gentlemen, we'll go on to discuss the second issue, "Future US Nuclear Strategies."

> The military purpose of war is to disarm the opponent or render his forces harmless. In the past, this objective could be attained only through battle. Today, this same objective is attainable more or less without bloodshed, through winning the technological arms race.
>
> \* \* \* \*
>
> The only safe course of action is to insure that the United States will stay technologically ahead of the Soviet Union and to lengthen this lead through successive weapons cycles, until a broad margin of superiority is reached and maintained until peace can be negotiated. This is a technological-industrial challenge.
>
> A mutual agreement to reduce force levels would save money, but hardly would help the defender's security. On the contrary, the lowering of nuclear force levels would enhance the feasibility of surprise attack.
>
> \* \* \* \*
>
> No strategy is infallible. . . . But the chances that this ambitious strategy [of technological superiority] can work, are infinitely greater than the prospects of alternate strategies proposed so far. Notably, this strategy is preferable to the unstable "balance of terror" which involves a deliberate choice not to embark upon an all-out Free World technological effort.
>
> Stefan Possony

*Possony:* Ever since I left Washington and got immersed in academic life, my peace of mind has been growing. I go to these academic gatherings and I find that the problems, which in the good old days worried me most in Washington, have all been solved. They are all gone, specifically the problem of a nuclear attack on the United States, or, to put it differently, the problem of nuclear aggression by the Soviet Union.

Yesterday, for example, Dr. Garthoff said: Maybe the Soviets have decided that they won't launch a nuclear attack. Well, maybe they have. I will put it to you that no state, irrespective of whether this is now a Communist state or not, no state ever can make such a decision. Or, if that is a decision in form of a piece of paper, that is exactly what it is going to remain, a piece of paper. Any attempt to anticipate history, predict history, assumes that there won't be any crises, assumes that peacefulness has settled down after half a million years of human history.

In fact, if this were a correct assumption, then the discussions about strategy are completely purposeless. The object of strategy is certainly to arrange your affairs in such a manner that your objective, which in this case probably is the maintenance of peace, will be secured. This is precisely the task we have to set ourselves. It is not something which an impersonal force will give to us.

We have also listened to a number of discussions about what is going on in the Soviet Union. We found out that there is perhaps such a thing as erosion. I think one interpretation might be that we have a situation in which the symbol of the state, namely the Communist ideology, loses its attraction, and the point simply would be that the ruling élite in the Soviet Union loses its claim for legitimacy. Well, when this happens, that particular élite becomes irrational, just as a matter of historical record, and when its becomes irrational, then it is given to rash acts.

What is irrationality in this particular case? Rationality is a relational term, if I may be academic. It is irrational to go into a nuclear war when you are a "have" nation. I really believe it would be very irrational to destroy your resources for no particular gain you can make. It is entirely different when you realize or fear that your days are numbered, and that you therefore perhaps have the feeling that, well, if you go under, some other people ought to go under too; or, what is not really irrational, that your last chance might be to get out of the fix by a victorious war, quite irrespective of the cost.

The statement by my colleague, Strausz-Hupé, was essentially addressed to this particular problem. It was said to be too pessimistic. It may very well be too pessimistic. But, our job is not here to write the news stories of the next ten or twenty years. Our job is to make sure that Strausz-Hupé is wrong with his assumption. That is a strategic problem.

We also heard about the resource problem in China. Maybe this resource problem is a pretty insoluble situation, given the fact that you have a very large population increase and not much of an economic base, or at any rate, if you have the economic base, you can put it to use only with an enormous investment program, and where will the particular resources come from? I don't quite see how this can be solved by the Bloc. But, suppose the problem can be solved. What is the situation then? Certainly, there is one way to get around some of these resource restrictions, in so far as the Communists are concerned, and that is to make the detour through technological advances. It is probably cheaper in the long run, in the case of technical capability, for the Chinese to solve their problems by moving into nuclear weapons than into anything else.

Now, we assumed that deterrence is assured. There were statements, "Oh well, you have, of course, to maintain a proper military posture." This "Oh well" is not a thing which happens by itself. This is a question for the strategists of this country to solve. For example, we have a very great deterrent force today, and how great it is was proved in the Cuban crisis when we had a superiority which was missile-wise probably double, and airplane-wise probably ten times. But, while we have the great advantage of this superiority, at the same time we are making decisions which, in essence, will reduce our firepower by a very large percentage; that is, we move away from the heavy-yield capabilities of airplanes and move into the low-yield capabilities of missiles.

To carry the contradictions one step further, we announced a counterforce strategy. This is a perfectly good idea, and I am all in favor of it. But, one of the points we have to remember is that when you use a counterforce strategy, the other fellow will guard himself against this particular danger. One of the things he is going to do is to harden his sites and, if you don't counter this hardening process on his part by increasing your nuclear yields, you just won't have any counterforce strategy.

In fact, by now we get all kinds of rumors out of Washington which say that, since the Soviets already have hardened, or are about to harden their sites, well, this whole business of our coming to the rescue of the European Allies by a first strike is water over the dam. Now, how are these things reconcilable? In my judgment they are not.

I believe that the main problem for the United States lies in the strategic area. The main axis of whatever we will do in the foreseeable future is the nuclear problem; that is, the nuclear part and the delivery part and the defense part, and, of course, a protection part. As Professor Teller pointed out, technological change is unpredictable. This is an absolute golden rule in modern strategy.

In Dr. Nutter's paper you find a note to the effect that the Soviets, with a much smaller GNP than ours, nevertheless are able to produce, in terms of military hardware, 80 per cent of what we are doing. If, with a smaller GNP, the Soviets are able to produce 80 per cent of our outlay, then, if they continue to grow, sooner or later they can outproduce us, unless we take the necessary steps to prevent it. At the same time we find that the Soviets' military development program has apparently run itself into a few snags. It is a little surprising to me that the Soviets don't have, at this point, a larger ICBM force. I don't think that there was any particular economic handicap preventing them from getting this force. But, the fact seems to be, and their behavior in the Cuban crisis confirms it, that for one reason or the other, they just don't have it. This is not a lasting situation. When they didn't produce the ICBM's in the late fifties, there must have been a reason, which was perhaps a technical one. But one of the things I believe certain is that in the sixties they will produce another type of ICBM, in order to get the larger number they need for their strategy.

For us to move ahead in a strictly economic race with them is unproductive. The reason why we need military supremacy is to make that deterrent really credible.

The one way to make a deterrent credible is to have a military force which is supreme, which is really superior, in the two ways that (a) you can deliver more firepower on your opponent and (b) you can prevent him from delivering his firepower on you. If that situation exists, you are quite credible.

The way to get this credible deterrent is, of course, to race ahead in the technological area, and we have all the capabilities to beat the Soviets in the technological game. Whenever they made an advance over us, we just let them do it. The Sputnik is a case in point.

Is the United States by itself capable of maintaining this superior or supreme posture? Given various qualifications, yes, but only with extreme efforts, because we are a second-strike force. Consequently, we have to guard against surprise possibilities. We have to have a broader spectrum of technical weapons in order to insure that the other fellow hasn't moved in with an end run and gained a certain advantage which we didn't foresee. So, we have to operate on a slightly broader spectrum, for the defense requirements of a second-strike force are probably more expensive, both in terms of deterrence and actual deployment.

The optimal way to go about it is to join forces with our European allies; if we have the French, the British, the Germans, maybe the Italians, and maybe the Japanese, joining us, not necessarily in all technological programs, but according to a judicious system of divisional labor, we will have concentrated in our hands what I dare say is about 80 to 90 per cent of the world's intellectual and technological resources.

The way to go about this job is to make that alliance a real one, and the way to make it a real one, overriding even the discussion of nuclear sharing, which is a problem of more tactical character, is to make it an alliance in the R&D field.

An alliance is a system, militarily speaking, by which the other fellow adds to your military strength. Presently the Europeans have no military strength because they have a World War II technology. We have to activate the Alliance in a technological sense, and that means that a lot of things have to go—to begin with, the Atomic Energy Act.

*Kissinger:* Mr. Kahn said that a European multi-national force would be desirable, and I am willing to discuss that on its merits. We have never suggested anything of that kind. We have offered a NATO multi-national force, with various vague possibilities later on of increased European participation; a NATO multi-national force seems to me to have very serious problems. If we have a veto, I don't see what we are giving the Europeans. If we don't have a veto, I don't know what we are committing ourselves to. Are we then committing ourselves to use only the part of the force that is assigned to NATO? This raises very serious problems of control.

Secondly, I don't think we should say to the Europeans or to ourselves, we will use nuclear weapons only in contingency A, B, or C. The future is much more problematical. I think responsible statesmen have an obligation to protect themselves against the manifoldness of history, which is much greater than an analyst may be able to project at any moment.

Now, a comment about Mr. Wyle. I didn't say that our proposals weren't fully considered. Our proposals are always fully considered, but that doesn't make them correct. I don't say that our proposals aren't sincere. I am convinced that our proposals are the sincere judgment of serious, dedicated people, who are trying to do the best. Nevertheless, I still believe that the approach we have taken to the NATO nuclear problem essentially has a gadgeteering tendency, and that the multi-national force, which excludes France and Britain, who, after all, have refused to join it, brings together a group of countries that are joining for negative reasons.

The danger in this approach is that we have talked from an American blueprint, that the acceptance or rejection of this is much more significant for the domestic policies of the countries concerned than it is for any strategic thought. The reason I called it a gadget is not because I don't think we can't have our way, but because we should realize that once we have had our way we are at the beginning of a process, and we should think of the end of that process. In my judgment, we are going to magnify the pressures we are trying to stop with this multi-national force. If you have something that is not a genuine answer to a genuine need, you are going to keep having the problem over and over again. This is my objection to it, and it has nothing to do with the sincerity of our offer.

*Wolfers:* This country is really not as free to choose as we pretend. There are going to be national deterrents. The British insist just as much as de Gaulle insists. De Gaulle is going to have his. The British are going to have theirs, and maybe others will.

The NATO deterrent becomes a secondary approach to the deterrent problem. Maybe this can be worked, but, as Mr. Kissinger was just saying, it doesn't meet our main problem. We are antagonizing France. We are trying to isolate France. We may smash the European integration, for the sake of preventing de Gaulle from doing something which he is going to do anyway, and which may not be half as dangerous to us as we are pretending.

Why don't we say: "So what?" We are telling the French that their nuclear force is no good, and yet we are so frightened of it, so frightened that the Germans might have a smaller one of their own, too, although we know that it is of very little military significance. Do we really believe that the Germans or the French are going to be so trigger-happy as to destroy themselves in a situation in which they think we will not march anyway? Are we going to be so feeble that, if they shoot off some of their nuclear weapons, we are bound to go to their assistance? I should think we could make it quite clear to them that, if they want to destroy themselves, "go ahead, boys. If we don't want to go into this war, you are not going to trigger us."

I think the idea of a German nuclear force was what frightened us most, so we didn't want the French to have one. Now the French and the Germans are going to get together and have maybe a common nuclear force. Then we forget about the earlier arguments, because we still don't like anybody else to have nuclear forces. They are going to have them anyway. Why

can't we get together and work out an intelligent NATO
strategy, let them have their reserve of a little supplementary
national force, and go ahead with the problem of how to make
NATO effective. Now, if the nuclear multi-national force is of
any good to NATO, let's have it too, but I doubt whether it is.

### Civil Defense

*Armstrong:* I would like to suggest that we move on to consider
some statements by Dr. Teller concerning civil defense.

> An adequate defense demands that we have early warning of
> attack, shelters, organization, clean-up equipment, and a plan for
> reconstruction.
>
> * * * *
>
> There are, I believe, only two circumstances at all likely to
> prompt the Communists to mount an all-out nuclear attack against
> the United States. They will do it in self-defense, and they might
> do it if they were firmly convinced that only with these terrible
> means could they achieve their end-goal of world domination.
> But as long as the United States is unprepared to absorb and
> survive an all-out attack, the Communists have a temptation that
> might prove irresistible: a quick and easy nuclear victory over
> the nation most effectively thwarting their aspirations for world
> domination.
>
> * * * *
>
> In a sudden nuclear attack upon our nation, there can be no
> doubt that millions of Americans would die. But even the brief
> warning we would have if such an attack came tomorrow would
> be enough to save perhaps ninety per cent of our people—if they
> knew what to do in case of attack and had the means to protect
> themselves.
>
> Edward Teller

*Teller:* We need an early warning. One of the best ways to
have an early warning is to know what is going on in Russia.
The Russians don't like it if we look at what they are doing. I
seem to recall that they were not very happy about the U-2.

We need freedom of space. If we want freedom of space,
we will have to fight for it. We will have to have the right kind
of defensive devices, like appropriate decoys, which will make
it difficult for the Russians to destroy our observational capabilities. We need more. We need the support of the public opinion
across the world. We have made a fetish of keeping observation
of Russia a secret. We have played into the hands of the Russians, because we have made this an intelligence operation, and
therefore a spying operation—which is undignified, but which
in fact serves our own purpose perfectly.

Our surveillance of Russia and China is as important for India as it is for us. In the interest of every free country, in the interest of everyone who does not want to be attacked, we must know what is going on in the Soviet Union. Surveillance should be made a public affair. We should draw into it many of the uncommitted nations, as well as our allies. We should play it openly. Far from apologizing for U-2, we should be proud of these things and we should try to engage in this common defense all free people.

Obviously, I believe in civil defense. I cannot agree with the position which considers civil defense as provocative. I cannot agree with the statement that to have civil defense on our part is more menacing to the Russians than if we have a megaton bomb.

To have civil defense is possible, and Herman Kahn, who has done excellent work in this field, has done a lot to find out that it is more feasible than many believe. It still is a big enterprise. It is still something that will eventually require something like ten per cent of our military expenditures, and it is worth it. We certainly have the wealth with which to do it.

What I want to add to these statements is a modality, how to carry it out. We want to do it in a flexible way. We want to do it so that we adapt ourselves to our effective system of free enterprise. Shelter is one thing. Stockpiling of essentials, so that we can rebuild after an attack, and so that we make it hopeless for an enemy to destroy our national substance, is an even bigger and equally needed phase of civil defense, of passive defense.

We throw away our apparatus, our machines, when we can think of something better. This throwing away the old and making the new is what makes all countries progressive. We are looking now for a tax reduction in order to achieve an economic goal. Why not, instead of an over-all tax reduction, make liberal tax write-offs possible for anyone who will mothball equipment which can be used in the process of recovery?

It has been stated that no matter how we dig in, the Russians can make a bigger bomb, and our shelters will be obsolete. This is true, if we go about it in an unintelligent way. Progress concerning active defense has made it pretty clear that, if we continue to work on the difficult task of anti-missile defense, it will prove Russian missiles can be stopped as low as 30,000 feet. If we can make sure that no nuclear explosion will occur lower than 30,000 feet, then it is easy, for no more than $200 a person, to make shelters even against hundred megaton or thousand megaton explosions. Civil defense is feasible and can contribute a great deal to stability and peace.

## Types of Thermonuclear Attacks

*Armstrong:* I think we can now move on to consider some statements of Herman Kahn which concern various types of thermonuclear attacks.

> Until the late sixties only attacks 1-3 were considered in "responsible" public discussion. Today there is much discussion of attacks 4-5. If the balance of terror gets more stable we can expect the discussion to shift to attacks 6-10. It is however important also to keep in mind the possibility of attacks 11-15.

\* \* \* \*

### Various Thermonuclear Attacks

|  |  |  |
|---|---|---|
| 1. | Countervalue | |
| 2. | Mixed Counterforce-Countervalue | Classical |
| 3. | Counterforce & Bonus | |
| 4. | Straight Counterforce | Current Doctrine |
| 5. | Counterforce & Avoidance | |
| 6. | Partial Disarming | |
| 7. | Controlled Reciprocal Reprisal | |
| 8. | Limited Strategic | Avant Garde |
| 9. | Exemplary | |
| 10. | Show of Force | |
| 11. | Leverage or Weak-Link | |
| 12. | Environmental Counterforce | Also to be |
| 13. | Environmental Countervalue | Considered |
| 14. | Against Recuperation | |
| 15. | Blackmail Enhancing | |

\* \* \* \*

> It is common now to predict that at some point in the late sixties or the early seventies the United States and the Soviet Union will have such adequately protected strategic forces that it will be physically impossible to destroy them or degrade their operation very much by any conceivable attack. It is important to keep in mind that this is "invulnerability by assumption." Many a seemingly invulnerable system (i.e., Singapore) has proved under test to be startlingly weak. An intelligent attacker will study the defender's system for weak points and may be able to find them even though the defender is unaware of these weak spots.

> Herman Kahn

*Kahn:* We are talking at this point about high-level escalations, which are close to the all-out war level, where the word all-out refers to the effort, not to the targeting. In other words, it might be very discriminating in targeting, but still be a major effort, or near all-out, or things you think of as being a major war between the United States and the Soviet Union. These wars come in all different sizes and shapes. Many things influence the course of a war: the size of the force, the objectives, the technology, and things like that.

If you adopt the position that the objective of the military forces is to disarm the enemy, then your range of alternatives is relatively limited. The real objective in war is to impose your will on the enemy or, failing that, to get as good a peace treaty as you can. I am also including, though, the objective of deterring war. So we are talking about two separate things: the deterrence of war and then, if deterrence happens to fail, the attainment of postwar objectives.

The first three attacks are the kinds which I think basically dominated responsible discussion up until about a year or two ago. The countervalue attack is an attack in which the attacker tries to destroy the things which the defender values. It is no problem at all for the Soviet Union, even if we go into rather massive civil-defense preparations with reasonable warning, to launch certain kinds of surprise attacks out of the blue which would kill most of the population in the United States. They couldn't do it today, but they would be able to in the late sixties or early seventies.

The next kind of attack is the mixed counterforce, countervalue, in which you split it about half and half. This attack has somewhat greater rationale than the previous one. It also is historically confirmed by our experience in World War I and World War II, and to·some extent by the Civil War. These wars were long and people and property were legitimate military targets, at least in the sense that they contributed to the other side of the war effort. That is, people got drafted, they became soldiers, their morale was important, they produced war goods.

There is a lot of argument about how long World War III would be. Let me make the following point, that many of the World War III scenarios we have looked at seemed to last, as far as we could tell, somewhere between say thirty minutes and thirty days, and closer to thirty minutes than thirty days. I am not saying you can't have a long World War III. You can. What I am saying is that if you look at the "normal" wars where there is a massive exchange of weapons, bombing cities, and things like this, the wars tend to be short. It is very hard to measure the sequence of events which makes them long. This is particularly true in the bomber era, less true in the missile era, but one can make a plausible guess.

We are doing a study of war termination at the Hudson Institute, in which we are studying how to win and terminate a war and get a peace treaty. We notice that our two most important assets are Leningrad and Moscow. The threat of destroying those two cities in almost any one of our scenarios is absolutely essential. And I wouldn't like to give these valuable assets up early in the war. Otherwise I would be destroying my ability to blackmail the Soviets. So we think of those as contra-productive attacks under most strategic theories.

The current doctrine, if you read McNamara's speeches carefully, seems to be something like numbers 4 and 5.* Four is the straight counterforce. You just ignore collateral damage, don't worry about it. In 5, you say: "I don't want to kill civilians."

The next attack has sometimes been called constrained disarming, and attack which is even more restrained than the avoidance attack. That is, under the avoidance-attack philosophy we avoid civilian targets where it doesn't cost us much militarily. In the constrained disarming attack you avoid civilian targets, even if it costs you a great deal militarily. Let me give you the difference.

Let us assume there was a SAC base in Moscow. In the counterforce plus avoidance, instead of dropping a twenty megaton bomb on that base, you might drop say a hundred kilotons, which is more than adequate under most CEP's (Circular Probable Errors) to take out the base, but will do a fair amount of collateral damage. Under the constrained disarming you might drop only one kiloton or leave the target untouched, simply because you didn't want to hurt Moscow. You wanted to preserve it for various reasons.

The rest of the attacks get into such an esoteric region that I really wouldn't want to discuss them in one or two minutes.

Let me just skip to 11 through 15. Under any strategic

* Referring to table, *supra.*

doctrine, I don't care what it is, one must always worry about these last five attacks. The most important is the leverage or weak-link attack. This is the way it has been referred to by Dr. Possony and Dr. Teller.

It is important to realize that when we talk about the invulnerability of future forces, it is an invulnerability by assumption. People always talk about the theorists. Well, that is true. We are all theorists today though, and nobody in this room has fought a thermonuclear war. Some people were involved in a very small kiloton war, but that is not a thermonuclear war. And the most important part of this theory, typically, is the belief that your forces survive a first attack. That is a theory. You have never tested it.

I have examined, I would say, five to ten weapons systems in the last ten years. Other people have examined equal numbers. It has been uniformly true, when people took a hard look at weapons systems, that they found holes in them which they had not expected to find.

This is likely to be more true in the future, because of the test suspension. Some very important weapons effects which we would like to know simply will not be found out. I am talking about the current suspension against large-yield tests on the surface. Our silos are not tested. The Russians may have tested. We cannot. This is not an overwhelming argument for or against test suspensions. It is an observation on one cost of the test suspension.

The theory that a silo will withstand a hundred pounds per square inch is an architect's theory, an engineer's theory. No architect or engineer in his right mind would really believe those calculations without testing them actually. But these are not tested. There are people who have found mistakes in calculations. They may find more, they may not.

The point I want to make now is that invulnerability by assumption is a different thing than invulnerability by test, and the so-called invulnerable forces of the future which don't allow for counterforce operations and the like are by assumption, and that the greater the confidence you have in these forces, the more likely they are to develop weak spots.

We do not assume the other side is rational. Where I work we fire people for assuming that. We do not use "game theory" for substantive results. I have lost good friends by my almost bitter attacks on "game theory," which I felt were justified, at least to express the point of view. I do want to make clear that we do not assume that either antagonist will necessarily be wildly irrational. That is quite different from assuming that he is going to be rational.

There are many degrees of rationality. Nobody is completely rational. Very few people are completely irrational, and one wishes to be in a position to exploit and encourage certain kinds of rationality and discourage other kinds.

I have found that Americans, both professional and non-professional, find it very difficult to believe that force can be used with any degree of rationality, that there can be any kind of negotiation, bargaining, discussion, goal objectives. Our typical image is the world with the Civil War, World War I, World War II image, where we fight the war to victory, get the other guy's unconditional surrender, and then talk about what we want to do with the surrender.

The typical view which people have of thermonuclear war is the spasm war; that is, where you press every button in sight and then go home—you have done your job.

In so far as I am not in any sense a Soviet expert, but in so far as I have any understanding of these problems, I might add that policies of coercion and threat are probably more likely to work in the Soviet Union. In our society we emphasize self-interest calculation. People are raised from childhood up to calculate: what is good for me, what is bad for me. Communism is too important to be thrown away in a fit of anger. One step backward, two steps forward.

Around an American conference table, the first man who gets up and says: "Give me liberty or give me death" looks pretty good. Around the Russian conference table the man who gets up and says: "Look, it'll hurt us if we do that," is likely to look good. It wouldn't at all surprise me, if, in spite of the usual image of war, incoherence, and irrationality, people were in fact very prudential at the first sign of violence and at the second and third sign, and remained prudential. To give a very recent example, all the writings of the West before World War II talked about the knock-out blow, the tremendous quick attack. But when World War II started, we had a nine-month phony-war period. It wouldn't at all surprise me that that could occur today.

*Morgenstern:* Mr. Kahn makes very frequent and liberal use of the word rationality. It seems as if it is absolutely clear as to what rationality is. Ice-cold rationality I have just heard, and so on. I don't know what hot rationality is.

If what Mr. Kahn has said just now, implying knowledge of game theory leads to the dismissal of people in his office, then I would ask, who would dismiss Mr. Kahn? What he has said shows that he is completely misinformed.

The purpose of game theory is not to start with the idea of rationality, but to discover what rationality possibly can mean and to develop mathematical theory, which would lead to the definition of rationality in precisely such circumstances in which the ordinary, common-sense use of the word fails. This is a very different matter.

The issue is that you are confronted with a situation in which two or more groups are in conflict with each other, where the outcome for all groups depends on a number of variables, with only some of these variables under your own control, with other variables in the control of the others. In addition, there will be a chance factor involved and the problem is precisely to find out what optimal behavior constitutes, and what therefore might be called rational. But, you can't start with the notion of rationality or irrationality before you have analyzed and understood the situation. This is the meaning of it. And, therefore, to combine these matters in this manner, as we have just heard, to my mind is just missing the point completely.

*Kahn:* My friends have just suggested that I should really sit back and enjoy being attacked for not using game theory for a change. I am supposed to be attacked for using it.

We have actually spent a lot of time with the notion of rationality, and let me just explain what I think we mean by it. You talk about a person using rational behavior, when he asks: "Are there alternatives?" when he calculates in some reasonable fashion the consequences of these alternatives, and then, when he cares about these consequences, and when they affect his behavior.

There are degrees of rationality, in the sense that people may not see all the alternatives. They may miscalculate, or they may not care, perhaps because their value systems do not make them care.

## Limited-War Strategies and Other Problems

*Armstrong:* We now want to go on to issue three: "Limited War Strategies," and this is the province of Dr. Teller, whom we shall ask to comment.

Korea gave rise to the popular idea that a war can be limited only if it is non-nuclear. This last idea is not only invalid but dangerous. The misconception that any use of nuclear weapons would expand a conflict and inexorably trigger an all-out global war has been accepted as an unquestioned fact by many of our highest Government officials and has been a prime consideration in our international conduct and military planning. As a result, we have concentrated on preparations for a kind of war that I doubt will ever be fought again.

\* \* \* \*

If a localized, brush-fire war should break out almost anywhere in the world, Communist forces would have the tremendous advantages of concentrated manpower, centralized location, and an initiative devoid of moral considerations. To overcome these dangers, the United States would have to use every means that technology can give us. Among modern weapons, nuclear arms stand out because of their light weight and unmatched power. They would give us the high degree of mobility we would need to stop Communist aggression anywhere.

\* \* \* \*

Our fighting forces in a limited nuclear war would not be measured in battalions and divisions. They would consist of commandos, and in each group there would be as many as fifty or as few as five men. They would be air-dropped, air-suppiled, and if necessary, air-evacuated. American forces fighting a conventional kind of war for the liberation of an ally, on the other hand, would consist of many thousands of men in the front lines of battle, and they would depend upon long lines of supply furnishing them with hundreds of thousands of tons of the materials of war.

Edward Teller

*Teller:* I would like to add to the proposition that limited nuclear war should be seriously considered and planned. A limited nuclear-war situation, though it has been excellently discussed in a book by Henry Kissinger, has by far not been sufficiently explored either in this country or within the NATO Alliance. Our actual keeping of secrets has led to a situation where, in the presence of these secrets, it is almost impossible rationally to discuss the question with our allies, who simply lack information.

*Armstrong:* We would like to move on to issue 4, "New Frontiers of Warfare: Space, Para-military, Arms Bargaining and Control." We will ask Dr. Schelling to comment here.

> This is a kind of "arms control" objective. But it differs from the usual formulation of arms control in several respects. First, it does not begin with the premise that arms agreements with potential enemies are intrinsically obliged to acknowledge some kind of parity. . . . Second, it explicitly rests on the notion that arms bargaining involves threats as well as offers.
>
> \* \* \* \*
>
> A quite different policy would be to persuade the Soviets that the arms race is something they just cannot win. This would involve two parts . . . first, to persuade them that if we choose to outmatch them in military assets we have the economic strength to do so; second, to persuade them that we would set ourselves just such a goal, and stick to it, outdoing whatever they do.
>
> Thomas C. Schelling

*Schelling:* I am skeptical that we shall in fact achieve what Dr. Teller and Dr. Possony exhort us to look foward to, namely, the kind of assured technological superiority which I thought Dr. Teller implied we could not have because of the ineradicable uncertainties of technological progress. No matter what we do in the 1970's, we will be depending on untested weapons. Nuclear testing in the interim will only make a modest change in the fact that we will be dealing with whole weapons systems, ranging from shelters on up to communications and reconnaissance, which have never been tested in war. For that reason I am doubtful whether, in order to face down the Soviets in a crisis, anybody should let us expect that we can quite as confidently have supremacy to wait until we have been attacked, for the moral rightness of it, then win a war successfully and survive at the level at which Dr. Teller says the United States might survive, and at which he didn't tell us whether Europe might survive.

I am inclined to think that the only way we will ever learn to cope with limited-war-type problems is to exploit the risk of general war and learn to acknowledge that brinksmanship is a style of contest that may have to go on between us and the Soviets for quite some time. If we insist on trying to have local military superiority, because anything else makes war too risky, then I think we are conceding to the Soviets a free hand over much of the world. As long as they think that we will only fight in limited territories, where we can win militarily, we have given them appreciable promise that any place else is without risk for them.

I think the reason for engaging the military in most places, and especially in the area of Berlin, is to take advantage of the fact that general war may occur not by any foreseeable process, but by unforeseeable process. I agree with Dr. Teller that some people exaggerate the tendency for the use of nuclear weapons to escalate into general war. I also think some people exaggerate the security with which we and the Soviets could believe that it will not. We don't know because nobody has tested national decisions and command systems yet in a nuclear war.

Until we can manipulate the risk of general war and engage in competitive risk-taking with the Soviets, as long as we insist on waiting until somebody gives us what Henry Kissinger asked for in 1957 and what Dr. Teller is asking for now, namely confident local non-escalatory superiority in all the areas we are willing to defend, I don't think we are going to learn to take care of Berlin, much less to take care of Indonesia and Finland, when the time comes.

As between emphasizing the need for shelters and emphasizing the need for doing what Herman Kahn was saying a little while ago, namely, making the Soviets unwilling to bomb my city of Boston, for the next ten years we ought to get the last message through loud and clear. In terms of emphasis it is much more important to design our own weapons system and our own doctrine and our communication with the Soviets, to render their weapons what Dr. Possony called "harmless," by making them quite unwilling to use them in these ways, rather than to wait until we have dug those shelters and then wonder what it does to the Atlantic partnership if the Western Europeans did not dig theirs, too.

I would like very much to see the United States engage in a civil-defense program, even if it were somewhat provocative, but I doubt whether it is terribly provocative. I wish those for civil defense would get more genuinely interested in it than in winning inflammatory arguments with people on the other side, who are more interested in the arguments than the really essential question of civil defense.

A year ago we went through a kind of plebiscite on who is for war, because civil defense was proposed essentially as a great popular acquiescence in suddenly looking tough to the Russians, and it just turned out that the plebiscite didn't win by a sufficient constitutional majority to get it going. If we ever get civil defense, I think it will be due to the singlehanded efforts of Herman Kahn, and if we don't, it will be because Herman Kahn and some very potent allies killed it. Herman Kahn killed it by making it so much a part of a strategic posture of toughness that he made all kinds of people, probably not including the Soviets, think it was too provocative to be worth going into. The allies he had were the United States Army, Navy, and the Air Force, which, as far as I can tell, have not been adequately interested in civil defense, still aren't, haven't demonstrated an interest, won't give up anything for it, and won't accept it as a military responsibility.

We get what? Just the kind of thing that Herman Kahn proposed five years ago, which I thought was silly then. He put it in the Appendix to his book, and I still think the same. Dr. Teller mentioned it a few hours ago. It is still silly, namely, "tax deduction," "state and local activity," "give people special arrangements if they will build local shelters," and so forth. I think it would make more sense to ask the Massachusetts Legislature to buy its own Polaris submarine, prepare to repel paratroopers, and have the US Army take care of civil- defense, than to say that civil defense is peculiarly civilian, state and local, and only the Federal Government can hire deterrence. If there is anything that gets all messed up, if left to popular state and local activity, it is something as inflammatory and as involving of popular passions as civil defense. If you want civil defense, pay for it through the Federal Government.

I agree, let us not cut taxes. Let us raise the budget, let us not cut taxes for business funds, so that they are going to start stockpiling a few extra materials, as long as it is to their tax advantage. In any case, what I am saying is that when the Army, the Navy, the Air Force, and even Dr. Teller and Herman Kahn will show me what they will give up in favor of civil defense, I'll believe they really want it.

So far, I would say that the main position of the US Army has been that it is for civil defense, as long as it is not an Army responsibility. The National Guard will not accept an overt form of responsibility for civil defense. As far as I know the National Guard hasn't even provided itself with enough fallout shelters to survive long enough to carry on the military function that it would prefer to conduct in time of general war.

Particularly since I despair of the notion that Western Europeans will get the kind of active and passive defense that Dr. Teller has proposed that we should look forward to, this leads me to believe that on the whole we have got to learn to utilize deterrence rather than brute force; active, passive defense, to keep the Soviets from fighting general war, or if they do try to fight it, to keep them from fighting the worst kind, and to meet them in places where limited war is an unpromising tactical operation. I think we have got to learn, to believe in, and to accept the concept of partially controlled escalation—to utilize the genuine risk of the thing getting out of hand to make the Soviets unwilling to pursue advantages that otherwise they will have in many parts of the world.

### The Arms Race and Bargaining

A final word about my own study paper, which was looking forward to the question: are we in an arms race in which we have an influence over the Soviets and they have any over us, or are we both just like two runners on separate tracks, stop-watch in hand, independently running as hard as we can?

My observation is that we react very much to the Soviets, not only in terms of the over-all scale of our efforts, but in the particular kind of effort we make, not just to Sputnik and the Korean War, but even to the particular form that their nuclear weapons take. This creates what I would call fads and fashions in this country, some of which are very valuable because they dramatize the enormous deficiencies in our own planning, and some of which do harm because they suddenly glamorize something that runs through a phase and simply diverts attention. We do react to the Soviets. To a limited extent we recognize our influence on them, in terms of the shape their own internal build-up takes. To some extent we engage in what we might call arms bargaining with them.

One does have to consider though, to what extent we might utilize our own long-term arms program to influence the Soviets. What I have in mind is essentially what I think Dr. Possony has in mind when he says that the only safe course of action is to insure that the United States stay ahead technologically. I would say technology is only one of the fields in which we have to stay ahead of the Soviet Union, and to lengthen these leads until a broad margin of superiority is reached and maintained until a peace can be negotiated.

My question is: how do you negotiate peace? I doubt whether at some point Khrushchev writes to Kennedy, "I am ready to give up, let us talk about it." My guess is that over years at a minimum, possibly decades or generations, one gradually tries to persuade the Soviets that what they may have hoped to do is just riskier, or more expensive, than they can afford. My guess is that this is something, if it ever occurs to them, that would occur to them not all at once and with clarity, but would occur to different Soviet leaders at different times. The question is: how can we be alert to the possibility of persuading them that they aren't going to win? Now we take for granted, in connection with Berlin, that we can persuade them that adventures will be too costly. We tell them, in effect: "If you push us there, we will react in a way that will make you regret it." We may not tell them persuasively all the time, but at least it is acknowledged that foreign policy is mainly concerned with telling the Soviets: "Take our reaction into account and don't do the thing you might otherwise have done."

My question is: can we do something equivalent with respect to their own internal arms build-up? It isn't altogether clear that we want to. Quite possibly the thing to do is to stimulate them into the greatest possible arms build-up, so they can't outspend us in other directions.

It strikes me that one of the things we might try to do more explicitly than we usually do in our arms planning is to see whether we can persuade the Soviets that even in their own military build-up, at some point, they are going to be wasting money, investing in some forces that they are not going to have either the opportunity or the guts to use. And maybe instead of negotiating peace at some point we can teach them that, just as we contain them geographically and make adventures unprofitable, we can make equally unprofitable the most menacing form of arms race.

*Teller:* Let me return to the question of getting ourselves into a superior position. Of course, I know that the future is uncertain and the development of arms is most uncertain. I have heard, and I believe, there are uncertainties. The point is that we are in a very dangerous situation, where, unless we change our ways, we might find ourselves in a greatly inferior position. For this very reason we have to exploit everything that we can, limitation of war, limitation of territory, which Dr. Schelling has attacked.

I don't think that we have a chance here to explore his other ideas. Let me just explain that when one talks about limitation of territory, one does not give the opponent a free chance to attack any territory. You respond by defining the territory yourself. This includes the attacked territory plus as much more as you feel prudent at the moment. But the enemy does not know what your response will be. What I propose is, of course, dangerous; whether my proposal will work I do not know; it can certainly be disproved by misquoting it.

The last point: what is better, what is more possible, deterrence or agreement with natural allies, such as the Europeans? Deterrence may be temporarily successful. But, agreement, the building of unity, can be permanently successful. I understand that Dr. Schelling despairs. I hope that others will go ahead.

*Armstrong:* Perhaps we can now turn to the final statements to be considered under this issue. We will ask Dr. Atkinson to speak on them.

> Space military capabilities would broadly appear to be: (1) Intelligence operations: observing, recording, detecting; (2) Direction: of land, sea, air, or combined operations; (3) Offensive actions: against land, sea, or air targets; against other space vehicles; (4) Defensive actions: neutralizing attacking missiles; counteracting other space vehicles; (5) Psycho-political operations in advance of or in support of military actions.
>
> * * * *
>
> By controlling both the communications utility and the military threat of attack from space, one nation-state could preclude another from effective functioning on earth and from operating (such as delivering an attack) in and from space.
>
> Such a space/earth control system is technologically feasible. It would require, of course, heavy expenditures. The cost of DEW line and of BMEWS, for example, has been in excess of two billion dollars. A projection from this figure suggests six billion dollars as the cost for the initial stages of a space/earth control system.
>
> James D. Atkinson

*Atkinson:* My paper deals with what I call a spatial-maritime strategy. First, three beginning points.

What is the object? The preservation of the greatest good, our Judaeo-Christian Civilization. Not because of any merits on our part, but because we happen to be historically the principal custodians of that civilization. Second, what is to be done? Dissipate the power of the international gangsters, rob control of the apparatus of state power in the Soviet Bloc and in Communist China. In this connection I think it is very necessary to think in non-traditional terms.

The Soviet Union and Communist China cannot profitably be viewed by our policy-makers as true nation states, and the conflict that they are waging, I think, must be viewed as non-traditional warfare.

Thirdly, what policy? Arm, arm to the teeth, but wield the power therefrom wisely. Military power has a wide range of application, far beyond its evident use. That is, it can be projected diplomatically, politically, and psychologically. Especially necessary in this area is an emphasis on the idea that military power is not evil in itself.

What military strategy will we follow for the next decade and beyond? I suggest a spatial-maritime strategy, and let me sketch just a few points. First, space. In the area of low-intensity conflict a space global communications control network would offer, I believe, some decided advantages. Such a space global communications network is technologically feasible. It would be, of course, very expensive. To cite a known figure and then a projection, BMEWS and DEW Line cost slightly over two billion dollars. A projection from those figures into a space global communications control network would be six billion for only the initial stages.

In another area of low-intensity conflict space offers definite possibilities for disrupting weather over an enemy's homeland. In an area for higher intensity conflict, of course, military exploitation of space, I think is self-evident as a necessity.

Three-fourth of our globe is water. In our maritime-oriented system we and our allies have already many possibilities for exploiting military power, and not in its evident use always, from under, from above, and from the surface of the sea.

In the next ten years we ought to think about missiles becoming obsolescent because of advanced generation systems, and I strongly suggest a part of the strategic mix ought to be a hard look at manned aircraft, or manned aircraft and areospace craft.

The first area, converter planes, VTOL's, air-cushion vehicles. In the second, very high speed, very low, that is on the deck, aircraft. I think the French have already given some idea of the breakthroughs we must expect in the next decade in this area. Significant also is what is being done in the area of terrain-avoidance systems, to make this, I think, extremely worthwhile. And, thirdly, in the area of ultra-fast, ultra-high, that is I am using low space which I prefer to space equivalent, that is 300,000 feet in these areas, manned air or perhaps aerospace craft. I think in this last area the possibility in manned aircraft from such things as the ability of men to operate much more sophisticated foxing devices, would alone offer things that we ought seriously to think about, but beyond that, beyond a stand-off capability, which is also, I think, projecting into the next decade, going to be much more significant, beyond that is man himself, so far, then God, much more complex than any computer.

*Teller:* May I try to set a record for brevity. I agree with the paper.

## A Question on Chemical and Bacteriological Warfare

*Armstrong:* I would like to turn now to a question which has come from the floor, and which is addressed to Dr. Kahn: "So far considerations in this conference have been based largely on the power of nuclear weapons and the effects of nuclear stale-mate. Are we overlooking the results which could arise from a breakthrough in the fields of chemical, biological, or radiological weaponry?

*Kahn:* We hear much talk today that bacteriological and chemi-cal warfare are competitive with nuclear weapons. This would imply an increase in efficiency of something over 10 million after World War I.

There are three problems in biological warfare: the problem of picking, maintaining, and procuring a virulent agent, the problem of distributing it, and the problem of actually having it infect the person. People have solved the distribution problem here. That is very impressive. That was a very important breakthrough. If they solved either the first or the third, it is classified. They look like hard problems to solve.

When, however, one looks at the spectrum of conflict notions, escalation notions, specialized uses of things, places where really chemical and bacteriological weapons may be "acceptable," and nuclears unacceptable, then I think it is an open question. In other words, we use tear gas because it is more acceptable than machine-gun bullets. I think there is no question that these must always be taken into consideration. On a cost-effectiveness basis, except for minor strategic wars, I don't think you can make a case for them yet, and I don't ever expect to be able to make a cost-effectiveness case for the chemical but only possibly for the biological.

*Schelling:* "Bugs" especially, but even gas, suffer a little bit from what civil defense suffers from. They aren't sufficiently "military" to appeal to the services. Tear gas we use, but usually we use it by police. I think some of the main inhibitions on the use of these is they just don't go "bang." It is a little like using assassination. My own guess is that there may be a tendency in analyzing biological weapons to think of them as competitors of nuclears. My guess is that they are not, or if they are, they are not terribly good as competitors, rather than as supplementary weapons, for someone who thinks he can't threaten instant destruction on a sufficient scale, and wants to talk about prolonged counter-population attacks. Biological weapons, utilized in the aftermath of a war, or held in reserve to threaten that a long war will be much more destructive of population than nuclear inventories would suggest, may explain why there is some evidence that the Soviets take this more seriously than we do.

*Possony:* We are presently concerned about this counter-insurgency problem, and I think the biological weapons and the chemical weapons, while not in competition by and large with strategic weapons systems, offer a great attraction, especially if you use non-lethal types. It could stand us in good stead, if we go into some of the limited situations without killing people, but debilitating them, paralyzing them temporarily, and then put down the insurrection.

# Part IV
# U.S. Economic Strategies

# An Approach to Economic Strategy

—*VIRGIL SALERA*

## Summary

*The failures of past economic strategies suggest the need to consider novel approaches to the twin problem of weakening the Communist nations economically and reducing their capacity to win over new territory.*

*With respect to the past, the failure to deny the Bloc strategic goods was clearly evident when the United States refused to cut off aid during the Marshall program even though an aid-receiving country knowingly exported tankers to the Soviets. Economic "warfare" since then has been little more than nominal. This is true of so-called embargoes; blockades and more serious measures never had a chance.*

*The West is cutting its throat by supplying the Bloc with three kinds of economic help, much of it on credit terms: (1) strategic commodities, (2) facilities for producing consumer goods in the Bloc, and (3) shipping services for carrying Bloc supplies to areas such as Cuba.*

*The paper takes as given that (1) COCOM controls have been a virtual failure, (2) the US should continue its unilateral policy of denying the Bloc sophisticated goods, (3) the Bloc will continue to have only marginal value to the Free World both as a source of supply and as a market, (4) the multilateral denial of Western sophisticated goods is worth a fairly high gross cost to the West, and (5) the West, largely because of reliance on intergovernmental measures, has not succeeded in consolidating scattered elements of economic strength vis-à-vis the Bloc.*

*Economic defense is too important to be left to governments, which at any rate are too deeply immersed in the many processes of attempting to control or "guide" private domestic economies.*

*A proposal is advanced in which governments would* comple-ment *a thoroughgoing international private business effort to effect trade denial, so as to give primacy to the many-pronged efforts which thousands of the world's businessmen could carry out with surprise, secrecy, and effectiveness to weaken the Bloc's economic position throughout the non-Communist world. Stated generally, this proposal would call for a wholly new government attitude toward business so as to provide maximum freedom for businessmen to effect trade denial in ways which they alone felt would be effective, against reimbursement via deductions against annual tax liabilities to home governments.*

*The net cost to governments probably would be low in relation to benefits cast in terms of a weakened economic position in the Bloc and attenuated trade ties between the Bloc and the West.*

*Such a policy, had it been in effect when Castro achieved power, probably would have delivered a free Cuba long ago.*

*The proposal would enable the West for the first time to deploy its vast business apparatus and know-how in addition to the conventional but limited government activities bearing on East-West trade. We would thus "untie" one of the hands which our ill-considered strategy has kept tied behind our backs.*

*In the process, the West would help create the establishment of a new world-wide cohesive force based on long-tested economic ties among businessmen the world over.*

*The proposal has the added advantage of relatively easy reversibility when the Bloc's threat has been cut down to size.*

---

This essay attempts to discuss a variety of matters having to do with economic strategies related to the Sino-Soviet Bloc. The first parts review certain features of more conventional analysis regarding trade and strategy, while the later portions deal with a relatively new set of ideas which it is hoped will suggest a more effective economic strategy for the Free World.

## Trade As a Vehicle of Strategy

As the world's largest trading nation, the United States cannot avoid trade's being a vehicle of strategy. Some $20 billion of annual exports, plus about $16 billion of imports, give the nation leverage internationally. Because of this leverage, we have doubtless inconvenienced the Bloc (and annoyed some of our allies) through our own trade policy. It is even possible that we enjoy policy leverage, in some potential sense, having great strategic import.

But we must beware of exaggerations in this area of discourse, especially in the context of conventional arrangements—mainly governmental and intergovernmental. First, the history of postwar efforts, chiefly in the framework of the NATO Coordinating Committee (COCOM), shows that a tough US Government position will not make much difference as long as the rest of the NATO countries ship strategic and semi-strategic commodities to the Bloc. And with each passing year, given the growth of Bloc technological capability and GNP, the relative US Government role will decline even more. Second, we should learn a lesson from the early postwar period. If we are candid, we will admit that our NATO partners were right when their assessment during the Marshall-aid period showed that we would not cut off aid (trade) at a time when our position was the strongest, namely, when alternative sources of industrial and other goods were few and inadequate.

The poor experience just mentioned is quite significant, partly or even largely because our undoubted position of (temporary) trade superiority—which we now know was erroneously ascribed to all manner of transient factors by those "selling" the dollar shortage package—had the most lethal backstopping then known to man: a real US non-trade monopoly in the shape of the atomic bomb. Only history will tell, of course, how trade denial and bomb strategy were combined by the administrators of US high policy. Having accomplished little when our hand was relatively very strong, we are unlikely to do much better now that the world finds it all too easy to earn or otherwise obtain dollars and even reminds us that our gold stock trickles away like water from a leaky tap. As a vehicle of strategy, therefore, US trade itself is unlikely to be of more than marginal significance. It will only be in *combination* with the trade of others that ours might play an important role.

## Participation in Economic Warfare

If Western governments have not had signal success in the narrow area of denying the Bloc so-called strategic materials, what hope is there that success will attend a multi-nation effort to blunt or cripple the trade of the Sino-Soviet Bloc, especially now that important Western advisers are also thinking of ways and means of producing or hastening a *real* split between the leading members of the Bloc?

Before considering such a question, let us define a term or two. Economic warfare, *as such*, presumably represents an effort, by a single nation, or several or more, in concert, to "defeat" another power or combination of powers in nothing more than the "economic" sphere. Can we seriously hope, for example, literally to deny another nation or nations access to foreign markets without getting into something hotter than "economic" warfare? Posing the question indicates what we are up against.

I submit that "economic" warfare in a conventional context is likely to represent little more than organized harrassment in the sphere of foreign commerce. If this is a defensible position, and if it be further posited that important Western nations are likely to derive considerable short-term advantages from trade with the Bloc—say, because America's so-called "farm policy" requires this or that Senator to be placated by way of the dumping of the very type of farm surpluses which figure prominently in the exports of friendly nations—how realistic is it to assume that the United States is likely to find other nations in a cooperative frame of mind? If such nations were not sufficiently cooperative in the case of strategic goods at a time when the Bloc's industrial-strategic capability was somewhat in doubt, are they going to pull together to achieve trade harassment when such capability is not in question, and while all else—particularly, concern about the long-term future of the enterprise system at home—remains the same? Who would be so bold as to answer in the affirmative?

It may be no exaggeration to state that government-operated economic warfare worth mentioning is unlikely to be taken seriously by anybody save perhaps the historian writing about, say, the experience of the Board of Economic Warfare (BEW) in World War II.

## Blockades and Embargoes

Is there a place for, and a hope of success in dealing with, formal governmental blockades and embargoes directed to the weakening of the Bloc economically? In the light of the foregoing, it seems safe to say that we would be making a pulp of language if we attempted to offer assurances with respect to such dangerous formal action for the purpose of seeking rather limited economic ends. Even the broad propositions which might be made would be based on little more than shaky foundations, however much they might be trimmed with bright ideas.

In sum, then, we may say that, in the governmental context, notions of trade as a vehicle of US strategy, economic warfare, and blockades and embargoes all eddy and swirl without charting much of a course. This suggests a new question. To what extent is this negative conclusion a function of the governmental and intergovernmental framework within which the topic is conventionally treated? May it not pay us to explore matters along such lines?

## A New Approach

A simple query may suggest a fruitful avenue of attack: after all these years, what are the distinctive features of Western economic strength which have not yet been brought to bear against the trade position of the Sino-Soviet Bloc? Note that the query concerns distinctive features rather than small matters, which are usually overheated with constant pleading.

Before proceeding, let me specify the elements which are treated as given:

First, that COCOM strategic trade controls have not been effective for years, partly because the threat to deny aid under the Battle Act has ceased to operate since the unsuccessful test in 1952 involving the Danish delivery of tankers to the Soviets, and partly because of the new economic independence of Continental Europe and Japan since Korea.

Second, that the United States should continue its virtually unilateral government policy of denying the Bloc sophisticated and highly essential industrial goods, regardless of the views of our allies and friends.

Third, that the Bloc will continue to have only marginal value to the Free World as a source of supply, and only a slightly larger, but easily offsettable, value as an export outlet (the latter proposition, of course, is completely at odds with the oft-repeated Communist charge that the West "needs" Bloc markets to "shore up" economies, some of which have actually been growing at a faster rate than that exaggeratedly claimed by the Soviets).

Fourth, that the multilateral denial of Western sophisticated goods (including plants and equipment for producing consumer products), shipping facilities, and credit is worth any reasonable—meaning fairly substantial—cost to the United States and the West (except some of the confused underdeveloped nations).

Fifth, that the West has tried unsuccessfully, mainly by intergovernmental arrangements, to find a way to consolidate scattered elements of its unquestioned economic bargaining strength with the Bloc. In this connection, we may state in passing, how wide of the mark some pronouncements may be— for example, that of Mr. Pisar in a recent paper for the Joint Economic Committee of the Congress, who asserted that our free economies "are not geared to respond readily to the policy purposes of the State." [1]

As one who participated some years ago in governmental action concerning strategic trade and who has followed the general lines of policy since, I wish to submit that the weakening of the Bloc economically is simply too important to be left to governments. "Economic defense" is not necessarily on a par operationally with military defense, though the contrary has been taken for granted for too long.

There are several reasons why weakening of the Bloc economically must not be left to governments. First of all, governments are usually informed about trade only on a limited basis, however much they employ so-called commodity specialists, keep large files of more or less obsolete information, publish statistics on foreign trade, negotiate internationally regarding tariff and related restrictions, and the like.

In the second place, governments necessarily bring to bear little more than a political interest when dealing with measures to weaken the Bloc economically. This interest is not unimportant, of course. In fact, it is a necessary interest. But it is not a sufficient one if maximum effectiveness is to be achieved in working out the West's economic strategy. This may readily be appreciated if one considers the international business community's concern with the threat of Bloc trade. This community necessarily thinks of the two-sided nature of such trade. One side consists of two sub-elements. First, there is the vicious commercial disruption which often stems from the more or less routine operations of Bloc-state trading monopolies. Second, there is what might be termed the more direct Khrushchevian "burial function" which deploys all the economic, ideological, and diplomatic resources of the Bloc to promote, for example, subsidized nationalized industries in countries in which Western trade ties are strong, but in which the urge to achieve the symbols of "economic development" creates a marked receptivity to Bloc overtures. This is the side of the problem which has suffered too long from unintended neglect by virtue of the excessive reliance on government-to-government methods for dealing with East-West trade.

The other side of the international business community's interest in Bloc trade has to do with the more conventional political interest, namely, the contribution which East-West trade makes to the economic strength of the Bloc as a political force. Now all of us have heard of this interest mainly in the government context: the intelligence estimates, ways and means of reducing the West's contribution to the Bloc's economic build-up by intergovernmental arrangements, use of slow-moving ad hoc "countermeasures" committees, and so forth.

It may come as somewhat of a surprise if I assert that the international business community probably has a stronger interest in the question of Bloc economic build-up than most major Western governments. Unlike many individuals prominent in government policy-making circles, the businessman is not torn by what can only be called a dual loyalty. The businessman, both from his experience and analysis and the theoretical support he gets from the solid core of professional economists, is convinced of the very marked superiority of the enterprise system as the world's best way of getting the economic job done while preserving and fostering freedom. In contrast, there are many in government who either do not share this basic idea or, perhaps more generally, compromise with the world's so-called "democratic left" in the form epitomized, say, by Indian socialism. State trading, thus, is less likely to be opposed in principle by such a group, and in consequence a less aggressive attitude is likely to be held vis-à-vis the Bloc variety than the tough realities warrant.

At this point the objection may be raised that it is meaningless to speak of the international business community inasmuch as the record shows that some international businessmen realize short-term gains from trading with the Bloc. The same record, however, also shows that businessmen have only been allowed to play a passive role in the West's program of trying to weaken the enemy economically. If given an opportunity to play a leading, active, and flexible role, I venture to predict that the international business community, now substantially expanded as the result of recent large-scale foreign investment (much of it American), will astound both the skeptical officials who shape much of present activity in the field of East-West trade policy and all who yearn for a new, more dynamic, and cohesive force in the camp of the Free World.

## The Proposal

What is needed, as the previous remarks may have suggested, is a new system for weakening the Communist Bloc economically—one which reverses the usual government role in this sphere. In a word, governments should *complement* a thoroughgoing private business effort which is truly international in scope. This should be done, only partly because operations to date at the governmental level have not been successful, and only partly because governments in the strictly domestic sphere usually are busy controlling or "guiding" national business in a manner least calculated to inspire millions of businessmen internationally to view the East-West trade problem as a vital one from their viewpoint. These are very serious deficiencies in the governmental approach, to be sure. But there is one really big reason why the government role should be limited to that which complements a great private effort. The reason is simply that Western governments are rank amateurs in the complex field of trade—a field, let it be noted, which is becoming more complicated in its East-West dimensions as the composition of Bloc output grows in variety and technical sophistication.

Now for the proposal. Firms doing an international business would enlarge their activities on a voluntary basis to improve the job of economic defense in the national security interest of Western nations individually and collectively. Such firms should therefore be allowed, with appropriate carry-back and carry-forward provisions and on as generous a basis as is necessary to encourage maximum initiative and minimum uncertainty concerning legal matters, to deduct from each year's tax liabilities all costs and/or losses attributed to a wide variety of international measures taken on an individual company or concerted basis to reduce or deny Bloc access to Western goods, services including shipping, and credit. The arrangement probably should be characterized by the following features, among others: (1) privacy of business operations in the sphere of economic defense, so as to achieve maximum surprise and effectiveness vis-à-vis the Bloc, minimize costs, and maximize the cooperative potential of friendly local business interests world-wide; (2) the lodging of maximum discretion in the hands of American business firms respecting the sharing of economic defense outlays and/or costs with businesses in other countries (as an earnest of intentions, governments should not establish or operate ad hoc agencies to police or supervise the operations, except as mentioned below); (3) Washington's avoidance of all measures, direct and indirect, which in any way threaten the existing position and near-term plans of American subsidiaries and branches operating abroad (among other things, this implies that the US Government should avoid tax and other programs which handicap company operations particularly in so-called "developed" nations whose locus is at the heart of economic defense [2]); and (4) post audits similar to those which apply to the CIA, conducted in such a way and on such a basis as to assure the reversibility of the whole program when the Bloc's position no longer presents a threat to the West.

I am only too mindful of the complexity of the tax and other issues involved in this proposal. The statement thus is set forth only in general form. After all, the spirit with which governments work with their business firms will make or break any such arrangement. This means, of course, that no amount of voluminous legalistic guarantees or so-called safeguards will prove effective unless business firms are treated in a revolutionary new spirit by governments, on a long-term basis. Effectiveness will depend basically on a relationship of sustained confidence, so that business—operating in the national rather than its private interest—can deal early and imaginatively with, say, future Cubas which appear on the globe at the choosing of the Bloc. (The recent unilateral US action in exposing the Soviet military position in Cuba, while praiseworthy, in no wise affects the argument of this paper).

The gross cost is not likely to be small, as is true of nearly all of the West's wide-ranging defense effort. But success could easily produce not only vast net savings to taxpayers the world over, but could yield an international business *esprit* on which the Free World would build both economically and politically more or less as the Common Market countries have built on the new regional *esprit*—and new positive government-industry relations—which pervade Western Europe. Incidentally, it is worth remembering that most so-called experts—including Soviet planners—were rather skeptical about the European Economic Community until events proved them to have seriously misread the potentials of enterprising minds in a region historically noted for its spirit of business enterprise.

### Amplification—and Anticipating the Critics

Since I have been somewhat harsh on officialdom and official East-West trade policy and have suggested a radically new kind of activity for the world's private businessmen, it is perhaps incumbent upon me to amplify my position and perhaps to anticipate some criticisms.

Let me attempt to do this mainly in terms of the still difficult Cuban situation, of which more of the same general kind seem likely to be ahead elsewhere in view of: first, the apparent propensity of Americans to tolerate subtle Communist penetration of less developed countries in the guise of reforming the governmental process in democratic directions; second, the success which the Communists enjoyed in the Caribbean island despite the October 1962 military show-down; and thirdly, the disappointing attitude of most of Latin America in the face of our Cuban dilemma—even since world-wide attention has been focused on the incredibly large Soviet military build-up in Cuba which occurred without apparent detection until late in the game.

Cuba well illustrates the consequences of the West's policy of relying mainly on government-to-government activity of the COCOM variety, coupled with various forms of more or less supporting diplomatic action (including foreign aid) behind the COCOM scenes (COCOM itself represents highly classified activity, though unfortunately not on that account unknown to the enemy). One can demonstrate this without claiming to be fully and currently informed, as if one had the latest official summaries and all of the relevant cables at one's elbow. Consider, for example, just three categories of situations: the early and abortive threat by Esso, admittedly at a time of tanker glut, to blacklist tankers carrying Soviet crude oil to expropriated refineries in Cuba; the substantial measure of success which Castro has had in obtaining US-type products and spare parts from some Canadian and other sources; and the Cubans' success in chartering European dry-cargo vessels to carry arms and materials to the island.

How different would the situation be today if the Free World's businessmen had had the unquestioned and generous tax and administrative support of their governments in the pursuit of subtle, flexible, and business-connected activities directed against the Cuban operations of the world's foremost anti-business movement? "Show me," the skeptic is likely to reply. If this kind of problem could be "explained" by having all the conventional arguments duly stacked into place, we might even expect governments to have a chance of success. Actually, what it takes is the best organizing men of business who, for all their defects (laboriously paraded on the familiar academic lecture platform), translate genius into results. If the Free World had had the system sketched here—and the enormous resources guided flexibly by unmatched brainpower—the Communists from the beginning, I submit, would have had high respect for such a formidable array of information-laden and resourceful opposition. Some academicians, to be sure, would probably still be skeptical. They doubtless would have had their judgment clouded by such standbys as the alleged danger of indirect aid to a possible international cartel movement, the conceivable connection between anti-Bloc trade moves and the reported profits* of firms which were playing a prominent role in every man's defense, the possible concern about the *de facto* delegation of seemingly traditional government functions to private business operating in part under a veil of official secrecy (as would be necessary to keep the enemy guessing), and so forth. More specifically, contemplate if you will the impact on the enemy of the more or less coordinated action of thousands of firms motivated primarily by the combined force of patriotic drive and the satisfaction that comes from efforts to strengthen the position and secure the base world-wide of the system of pro-

---

* One can picture some academicians busily writing papers "showing" that prices which participating firms charged foreigners under the suggested program "proved" the "correctness" of oversimplified domestic oligopoly analysis, and so forth.

duction and trade which not only provides a startling variety of goods and services at unmatched efficiency but also protects the bastions of individual freedom wherever it is allowed to "show its stuff." Economists will appreciate, of course, that the indicated motivation would be powerfully supplemented by every conceivable combination of conventionally classified business results, nationally and internationally.

Clearly, any such complex and only partly specifiable arrangement would involve problems and costs. That goes without saying. Among the problems, for example, are those connected with the international sharing of tax-deductible costs associated with so involved and revolutionary a world-wide undertaking. But the COCOM approach has also had its problems and costs, with little to show in the way of results. In fact, we may well ask ourselves whether we have rigidly stuck with a strategy which maximizes the cost for any given (small) result. At this point, the critic is apt to remark that divisions within Allied ranks have created problems almost from the beginning of COCOM, and that similar divisions probably would attend any concerted effort by the international business community. To what extent would roughly parallel operations by the business community have avoided or minimized the divisions roughly of the type encountered within the COCOM framework? As you may judge from the tenor of my comments, I believe that business would have been incomparably more successful, provided that governments limited themselves to a sensible complementary role rather than the all-too-common direction and control [3] function. The proviso is crucial, as has already been emphasized. In this connection, let us not lose sight of the fundamental fact that the West, if it is truly wise, has the capacity to deploy the immensely powerful and vast apparatus—little understood even by many academic specialists—of the incomparably resourceful and flexible private business system *in addition* to the conventional government arsenal (mainly military), whereas our Communist adversary has only the lumbering apparatus of the state, and thus must work the government-to-government road to the exclusion of all other avenues of action (save, of course, the Communist-controlled ideological and conspiratorial ones).

Vigorous pursuit of the broadly conceived private business interest world-wide in this novel international venture may be advocated in yet another way. Such action is not only completely compatible with the progress of the Western social order but, under the unparalleled Communist threat over the globe, it is a necessary condition thereof. What manner of ideological blinkers do we tolerate, then, as is indicated by the decision to date to fight the *cold* type of war, of all things, with one hand—perhaps our strongest—tied behind our back? Is it possible that our own ideological blinkers have been restricting our vision as much as we are fond of charging the enemy, especially when so many of us seem to feel that we are helpless in the face of the so-called "nuclear stalemate?"

Moreover, if we are candid we probably will agree that, in matters such as these, the US position has been and is of major importance in the Western camp, even now that the European Common Market, though weakened by the French rebuff to Britain, is determined and able to be the master of its own destiny. Indeed, is it not reasonable to believe that, though declining with each passing year, the weighted importance of the US influence alone might yet tip the scales in favor of a successful new kind of international business effort in economic defense? In shaping our thinking on this subject, I would suggest that we be encouraged rather than deterred by the prospect that greater unity in Western Europe will permit an increase of tension between East and West.

There is yet another dimension that is worth exploring. Consider the subtle role which an effective international business effort in economic defense could play in helping to shape economic and social policy in the newly emerging nations, where statist and far-left tendencies in the strictly economic sphere have been all too common for a variety of reasons which need not detain us at this time. Would the Communists have the influence in many such lands that they wield today if they had had to contend with a powerful international business force in being, which gave every assurance that its members were working to maximize the chances that free institutions would take strong root in the newly developing lands? One has only to raise the question, in the relevant context, to suggest the potential of an apparatus with which the West is uniquely endowed but which, perhaps for complex psychological and political reasons, has become rusty from virtual non-use. The apparatus, however, is of sturdy construction and can be made to respond according to reasonable expectations if free men will only awaken to a realization of the tremendous role the apparatus is capable of playing in humanity's name.

FOOTNOTES

[1] US Congress, Joint Economic Committee, *A New Look At Trade Policy Toward the Communist Bloc*, 86th Cong., 2nd Sess., 1960, p. 5.

[2] With respect to relevant tax issues which have been much disputed of late, see especially the espousal—in standard academic fashion—of the reverse of what is called for on economic defense grounds in the Treasury's strained analysis, particularly regarding the relationship between its proposals and the competitiveness of American firms operating abroad. US Congress, Senate, Finance Committee, *Hearings, Revenue Act of 1962*, Part I, Exhibit III, 87th Cong., 2nd Sess., 1962, pp. 200-2.

[3] For the latest example, see the subtle price- and wage-fixing views of the new appointee to the Council of Economic Advisers, Dr. John P. Lewis, *Wall Street Journal*, Dec. 7, 1962. It is strange indeed that the Lewis views were propounded months after Professor G. J. Stigler demolished the idea of administered price inflation in his "Administered Prices and Oligopolistic Inflation," *The Journal of Business of the University of Chicago* (January, 1962).

# Military Alliances and Mutual Security

—*OSKAR MORGENSTERN*

## Summary

A clear understanding of our goals and those of the other side is a prerequisite to discussion of economic strategies in the very deep conflict between East and West. The military character of the conflict gives shape to the economic, diplomatic, and other positions of the two sides. If the military threat is neutralized, the conflict will be intensified in other spheres. A reasonable aim for the United States is to gain more support for the Western cause and to fortify its alliances.

Given the goals, the feasibility of strategies has to be established first. Flexibility then has to be related to costs, not only money but all types of costs. There arises the problem of picking an optimal strategy, a difficult problem even to formulate, especially when we do not know the other sides' strategies. The concrete application of the appropriate theory of games is very difficult. Random elements further complicate the situation. However, one can state that strategies are desirable which impose maximum strain and expense on the other side to counter them.

We are dependent on allies. Alliances, expressing the fundamental aspect of cooperation, are another hard subject to analyze. Distribution of their advantages, burdens, and leadership raises problems. So far, economic cooperation has been less prevalent than political and military cooperation. Alliances are always weaker in peacetime, but now there is scarcely any time to organize or revitalize them when need arises. Keeping them *strong continually is vital. In this aspect we have failed, and indeed have often worked against our allies in the economic sphere which cannot be clearly separated from the military. We have also failed to cooperate in the use of scientific talent.*

*Cooperation needs planning. Without a military-economic opponent, our laissez-faire principles would guide us to act independently, unconstrained by others. However, our aims in the East-West conflict prevent this. In the course of planning, a distribution of the burden among various countries needs to be made, but this cannot be done scientifically. We cannot compare with any exactness the economic positions of the various countries, let alone the effects of following certain policies on them. If we use the very imperfect measures available, it is clear that the burdens of the West are not equally distributed, falling mainly on the United States. However, alliances always have leading members to whom fall special duties, burdens, and privileges. But a fair amount of planning is needed, of which now there is little, e.g., in NATO where there is stagnation relative to the intensity of the development of the Common Market.*

*All persons and organizations have plans. The difficulty is how closely to plan and how much to coerce others. Ours is a "free enterprise" economy only to a limited extent. Its freedom would be perturbed only on the fringes by greater international cooperation. The Western economies have not lost their essential freedom due to the Cold War. Indeed, the burdens of the Cold War have made the Communist countries change, turning towards Western economic systems, marking a demise of their Marxist ideological superstructure. Western interference in the economy is not due to failure to perform, but is conditioned by technology.*

*Cooperation is desirable first of all in arms manufacture, but great problems arise. Civilian goods are produced where they can best be produced. Where military equipment is produced is conditioned by strategic vulnerability, the needs of secrecy, and evaluation of the reliability of allies. We do not get the type of optimality we do with civilian goods. Deliberate political acts could override some of the present failings of the system, both in the location of manufacture and the use of scientific talents.*

*New strategic ideas are needed. One of our prime requirements is flexibility and adaptability to new situations. Graduated response and initiative are needed. Inventions, particularly in the political-economic sphere, are needed and a milieu must be*

*provided where they can occur. The outcome of the present con-*
*flict will depend on how we prepare ourselves for the long run*
*if we succeed in the immediate task of preserving peace.*

---

## The Setting of Goals

In order to form valid ideas and thoughts about the proper economic strategies for the West in general, and the United States in particular, useful in the present world struggle, it is necessary to have a clear understanding of the goals which the West strives to reach and to comprehend the nature of the conflict with the Communist world. Without knowing the answer to the question, "What do we want?" there is no way of designing any strategies whatsoever, military or economic. Obviously we must also know what the goals of the other side are, and try to discover whether and to what extent the goals of the two sides are in conflict with each other, in which areas the conflict is most intense, what the prospects are for it to endure in the future, and what can be done in order to secure and advance the position of the West in this situation.

There is no doubt that the conflict goes very deep. It is an ideological conflict; it is a struggle for power in all its forms. It shows up in the diplomatic and economic areas, and of course it is overshadowed by the fact that both sides possess devastating weapons, of a kind never known to man before, in such numbers that, should they ever be used to their fullest extent, our present civilization would surely be destroyed.

In order to come to the bottom of the matter, it is very important to distinguish between the words used in describing the goals in this conflict and to look at the reality behind them. The two are seldom identical. The Communists have frequently stated that they desire world domination. Yet they also state that they want to live together with the West in peaceful co-existence. All this has to be interpreted, and on the interpretation depends a great deal. As far as the military situation is concerned, very little attention should be given to the words. The *capability* of the two sides is what really matters. The military character of the conflict is clearly circumscribed. However, in this paper, we are not dealing with the military problems except indirectly. The extent and seriousness of the mutual military threat gives shape to the nature of the political, diplomatic, and economic position of the two sides. Each party is committed to maintaining military capabilities of incredibly large, complex, and very expensive nature. This imposes upon the economies of each side a strain of different weight—different because the two sides are structured differently economically and have different economic power; and it is with this question that we shall occupy ourselves in what follows.

The principal point to realize is that, should the military threat of a big thermonuclear exchange have been neutralized for the time being—but the opposition of interest still persists—then this conflict will more actively be carried out in other military areas, and, if compensated there too, finally in non-military spheres; consequently economic warfare is one area in which the two blocs are actively involved with each other, quite apart from the ideological struggle which is also going on but, which, I feel, is not nearly of the importance that is frequently attributed to it. What the West wants first of all is to avoid active war, but certainly not at any price, definitely without receding in vital areas. On the contrary, a reasonable aim is to gain more and more support for the Western cause throughout the world, especially among the non-committed nations, and to fortify the alliance which the West has been able to maintain for the last fifteen years. In general, though the West has been rather passive—has in the main merely adjusted itself to the initiative held by the Communist world—it has nevertheless succeeded in fortifying its position. The most important feature in this phase was undoubtedly that the economies of the Western countries have not been struck by great crises and that the flourishing economies of Western Europe have become integrated and consolidated to an extent unimagined even a few years ago.

The progressing integration of the capitalist countries of Western Europe is probably the single most important economic event of our time. Contrary to the Marxist doctrine that capitalist countries must fight each other in order to try to survive, they are combining peacefully, becoming stronger and raising living standards of the common man in a spectacular manner. The Communist Bloc has nothing to show that could match even remotely the meaning of these events. As this development continues, its significance will impress itself most clearly upon the whole world.

## Feasibility of Strategies

Assuming that our goals are sufficiently clearly established in our minds—unfortunately a far-going assumption—and that they agree with those of our allies—which goes even farther— the question is: "Which are the best strategies to apply?" A strategy is a plan of action. It has to be continously revised in the light of new information, new events in the world, and in view of possible changes in the goals as they become more and more specific as time goes on. A given goal can presumably be reached in different manners. It is obviously desirable to choose that particular course of action which is the most suitable one from among many—each one of which we assume to be feasible; so feasibility has to be established first of all. That is not always a very simple matter—in particular, not in regard to the case when, as it is true for this discussion, not only a single country has to be considered, but a group of countries forming a more or less loosely knit alliance. Among the members of this alliance, a certain degree of cooperation has to take place, but there is also competition, and perhaps even some slight antagonism, varying with the differing development of political and economic fortunes. Yet, everybody is supposed to work in the same direction. Assume then that we have found a list of feasible strategies. Feasibility here must mean that the courses of action are in conformity with our other ideals we live by, such as preservation of freedom of the nation, of its independence, self-determination among our allies, the preservation of an economic system which is essentially based on freedom of enterprise, and on recognition and protection of private property.

The next point is that feasibility has to be related to costs. In other words, the adoption of one strategy compared with another one is that though they both may be suitable otherwise, they may involve different costs. If there is no other difference in effectiveness we would naturally choose the cheaper course of action. It would be convenient if we could express costs solely in money, but costs are not so simply measured in this situation because money does not measure all the efforts which are being made in pursuit of these matters. For example, there is a deliberate, planned, and sometimes only a monetarily induced diversion of talent from one occupation to another, the consequences of which do not express itself in monetary terms. Yet it may be of fundamental importance for the future course of economic or political or military development of a nation to know the costs of each strategy rather precisely. Assume, however, that even this problem has been overcome. Then we are left with nothing else but having to pick the optimal strategy from among all feasible strategies. But what does optimality mean? Clearly if the outcome depended only on ourselves and on chance, the matter would be relatively simple. We would merely pick that strategy which is cheapest and brings us to our goal with the highest probability. However, this would not only be an inadequate, but an outright fallacious description of the situation, because reaching our goal does not depend only on what we do, but also on what the other side does. And the "other side" is not an indifferent nature, but a deliberately acting opponent who is out to win. Therefore, the idea of "what is best" is a very difficult one to formulate; new conceptual ideas are needed. Moreover, we are not well informed or far from fully informed about the strategies the other side will use. Therefore, we have to make our choice without knowing what the other side is doing and will be doing.

It is not entirely impossible to make reasonable decisions even under such circumstances, indeed to form a rigorous concept of "optimality" as has been shown by the theory of games of strategy. But the application to a concrete situation of this kind is a very difficult matter indeed. What we would most like to do, though technically feasible, is not necessarily possible, not possible in a sense of leading securely to the desired result because of the interference of the other side in exactly the same area and situation. To give a trivial illustration: It may be possible for us to build, say, a certain type of airplane, but this will not lead to an increase in our strength if the other side can develop a superior defense against it, thereby nullifying our effort. If, on the other hand, our burden in building the offensive weapon is significantly smaller than his burden to defend himself, this may still be a good operation on our part.

Of course, so far what is true for us is also true for the other side. In other words, the Communist plans also cannot be made according to their wishes alone, but are interfered with by whatever we are doing. Added to this is the chance factor, *viz.*, even if both parties are able to find strategies that appear to be optimal for each, the fact that the world's course is unpredictable, may upset the finest calculations. Clearly, the notion of "stability" is, under these circumstances, a very difficult one and not amenable to analysis by means of the conventional ideas from physics.

Speaking specifically now of economic strategies about which there will be more to say later on, one principle can be announced already at this time: those plans are desirable which, apart from having merits of their own for ourselves, impose upon the other side, in order to be counteracted, a maximum of strain and expense. In other words, we will be well advised to pursue those courses of action which will secure our economic and political position in the world and, at the same time, make it most difficult for the Communists to meet us in our chosen field. This is, of course, a principle which also applies to military matters and it is worth commenting on it in this connection.

## Alliances

The behavior of the United States in the economic war and struggle is not independent of that of our allies. We are fortunate in having alliances, formally, and in many ways informally, with the principal countries of the Western world. Such alliances express a fundamental fact of social behavior—namely cooperation. Although there are many histories of the workings of alliances, we were lacking a workable theory on the basis of which we could learn how to operate alliances better. There must be advantages for forming an alliance and they must accrue to all members—though not necessarily to the same extent. The distribution of these advantages must be agreed upon and have some properties of stability. There is the question of late-comers to an initial alliance and that of its cohesion. All these questions, and many more, are now also amenable to theoretical analysis and the theory of games establishes certain principles that can be made useful for policy purposes. Unfortunately, there are, as yet, hardly any attempts by policy-makers to develop applications to the big issue at hand.

So far there has been more political and military cooperation among the United States and its allies than economic cooperation. For example, our economic assistance programs have not been coordinated; in fact, it has taken a long time to persuade those Western European nations who have emerged from the damage of the War and are now in a very much stronger position than ever, to assume at least some of the responsibilities in this particular area. It is here where modifications are possible and where great progress can be made. The pooling of resources is a most expressive form of cooperation. But when things are going well, cooperation is hard to achieve.

Alliances are always weaker in peacetime; alliances tend to become hard and fast and strong when things are going badly. While this has often proved to be bothersome, the damage done to a political or military alliance during slack times could frequently be repaired when matters became more critical. Though the process took time in past ages (i.e., before the appearance of nuclear weapons and their almost instantaneous deliverability), the possible speeds of reaction to threats corresponded to (slower) speeds with which threats could be made fully effective. Now there is hardly any time to organize new, or revive dormant, alliances when the need arises to cope with an immediate threat. As long as the threats are merely of an economic character, time is perhaps not so precious. Yet the speed with which economic catastrophes develop is always greater than the speed with which countermeasures can be designed. This is seldom realized. Thus it will pay to keep the alliance strong even when it is difficult and seemingly not important. We have failed in this respect. Since the economic affairs of the Western world have been going well over the last decade or so, our efforts toward cooperation were not very strong. We have, therefore, not obtained the maximum advantage which was before us.

Indeed, we have frequently worked against each other. The most noteworthy example is that of forcing France, which was at any rate under great difficulties economically because of the Algerian conflict, to make the tremendous effort of building a nuclear capability of her own without any assistance from the other two Western nuclear powers—the United States and the United Kingdom. Whether it is desirable or not to have nuclear weapons spread among the Allies is a matter which shall not be discussed here, but it is quite clear that France was determined to go ahead. Therefore, since there was no opportunity of stopping her, short of a real break in the Alliance, the proper thing would have been to put our knowledge and our resources at her disposal, as the United States did when Great Britain chose the same course of action. (The knowledge was, at any rate available to the opponent, Soviet Russia, who had developed independently.) This would have freed resources of France for other purposes and the Western world would have made a net gain—at least economically.

This example, incidentally, illustrates a point that also needs to be emphasized strongly, which is that a clear separation of political and economic affairs is impossible and that even economic and military matters are so intertwined these days that it is not feasible to view one without looking at the others. This kind of interaction becomes of increasing importance in the military field, where the question of the "technical" use of weapons is being overshadowed more and more by the political aspects and consequences of any potential weapons application.

Another most serious lack of cooperation shows up in our inadequate use of the *scientific talent* of Europe for purposes of development of new weapons systems in regard to the space effort. It would have been possible and should be possible in the future to pay proper respect to these matters by organizing laboratories which would be run jointly by Europeans and Americans and possibly also Japanese in order to promote the development of technology in all fields, instead of holding the effort within the bounds of the United States which is already so far committed in devoting scientific and management talent to matters of defense. The benefits of such pooling are clearly very great and need only be grasped. Unfortunately, apart from the establishment of a small laboratory on antisubmarine warfare in Italy and a NATO Air Defense Group in Holland, nothing of the sort has happened. A fresh look at these matters is certainly required, and I am convinced that the result would be a move in that indicated direction.

## Planning and Distribution of Burden

Cooperative action of this type and in related fields involves obviously a certain amount of planning. Here is a difficulty which is peculiar to the West which the Eastern Communists do not face. It is the following:

If we had no opponent in the military-economic sphere, we would naturally adhere to our general laissez-faire principle and let each country develop according to its own wishes and capabilities, restrained only by the activities of the others in a generally mild way. In fact, the countries would not be restrained by each other; rather, by their individual increase in wealth and economic activity, they would benefit from each other without formally cooperating. However, we want more than a mere increase in wealth because we must take specific actions in certain areas of the world, such as supporting other countries, developing them—doing this on the basis of general strategic considerations which are not identical with the streams of capital flows which would occur were the capital to migrate only to its otherwise best, i.e., most profitable, employment. Even this amount of planning is not very agreeable, but I believe that there is no choice but to coordinate better.

A specific problem in this connection is the determination of the *burden* carried by the various countries of the West in regard to the maintenance of military power which the West as an entirety represents. In order to plan economic strategies it would at first seem fair to equalize the burden in some measure. But the trouble is that this cannot be done with scientific assurance because we do not know when the burden is equal or even whose burden is greater under what circumstances. Even under normal conditions in a given country, so far it is a political rather than an economic matter to determine whether the tax burden, say of the income tax, is "equally" and "justly" distributed among the different taxpayers. No economic principles applicable to this problem have been developed which are convincing to everyone. The matter is even less certain if entire nations are compared with each other, and these intangibles are put into prominence. The comparison, for example, of the amount of money spent for arms in terms of national income are very rough and certainly do not tell the whole story. Although they are freely used, the expenditures on arms and foreign aid expressed as percentages of national income have a far smaller degree of reliability than they would have to have to be guides for estimating the effort a country makes to the common cause. National income figures for different countries have, at best, a reliability of only ±10 per cent. Thus, a percentage of expenditures for defense computed from such numbers has an even greater unreliability and makes international comparisons doubtful—certainly when they aim to be as precise as their uses would demand. However, it is exactly international comparisons that are wanted, and they are always difficult and of doubtful validity no matter what economic activity is considered. If the statistics for national income of a given country are unreliable, but always have the same bias, e.g., are overstating income by approximately the same percentage, the harm done could be estimated. But the bias is not constant in the first place. Even if it were, in another country the bias may go in the opposite direction (toward understatement), so that the determination of the just share of the burden of different countries for defense is impossible using this method. This appears, indeed, to be the case.[1]

There is, at present, almost an obsession with the measurement and use of GNP. It appears to be most unreasonable to expect that one single number and its changes could adequately express as complex a phenomenon as that of economic growth of an entire country and its economy. That applies even if that measurement were free of error, which is an impossibility. Far more complicated measurements, involving sets of numbers, are needed in order to show the differences in the growth processes of advanced vs. underdeveloped countries, or the differences involved in estimating economic and military power and their changes.[2] To give an illustration of underlying differences: the United States has a burdensome agricultural surplus, while the Soviet Union suffers from a food deficit. What would be the point of growing more food in the United States? Yet, not doing this depresses our weighted "growth" rate while for the Soviet Union the closing of the gap merely means to come up to par.

But even if such imperfect measurements are made, they show plausibly, also using other evidence, that many of the Western countries have not yet been persuaded to devote as much energy to the preservation of the peace by providing the West with the necessary capabilities as the United States has done continuously for so many years. Preoccupied as they were with their own economic rehabilitation at first, they have become used to thinking essentially in non-military terms. They rely fundamentally on the protection offered by the United States and find demands, that they should contribute more, onerous.

A good illustration is offered by the fact that in the US compulsory military service exists for 24 months, while the United Kingdom has no conscription at all, France and Germany only for 18 months, etc. This is a measure of effort that is free of difficulties of comparison.

While much greater efforts by the other members of the Atlantic Community are clearly called for, it is also important to remember a fundamental principle of organizing large alliances of this type. This is that there always is a leading member and that many coalitions have cores. To them fall duties and privileges. These may be unwelcome; the former because they mean that equalization of the burden may prove an unrealistic goal, the latter because the junior members of the alliance dislike the minor role in which they are cast.

Some members of coalitions and alliances are admitted only under less favorable conditions. Even if formal arrangements appear to be symmetrical, the actual behavior of the members may very easily be asymmetrical. The realities of the situation are such that differentiation will appear and has to be accepted if the alliance shall endure.

Whether we try to equalize the burden or acknowledge that some members of the Western Alliance have to carry a greater weight than others, a fair amount of planning is required. Of this there is very little at present. The NATO organization, though elaborate and even cumbersome, does not function nearly as well as it should. NATO has not understood how to mobilize the best talent needed to formulate the proper questions and to solve them. There is intellectual stagnation relative to the intensity with which the economics of the Common Market and other business aspects are explored. It is fortunate, that the latter are not in outright conflict with the needs of the former. But the weight given to the pursuit of economic growth per se appears to be unwarranted when the needs of economic adjustment to the Cold War strategies are considered.

**Cooperation**

It would be absurd to argue that there must be no plan. Every individual, every firm, lays out a more or less considered course of its behavior. We do not and cannot act at random, though the results of many criss-crossing individual plans may appear to be random (or actually produce random behavior on some markets). We insist that our government have a policy, which is precisely the demand for a plan for action. The difficulty is only how far to carry any plan, to which extent to coerce others, how to get voluntary cooperation based on estimation of advantages to the cooperating parties, etc. The idea that our economy is a "free enterprise" economy corresponds to reality at any rate only to a limited degree, considering the regulations imposed by government as well as those worked out by the habits and customs of men. The latter limit our actions not less forcefully than many laws on the statute books. Thus the "free" economies would only be perturbed on the fringes if a greater cooperative effort were made in providing arms and other devices for defense or in advancing our cause in other parts of the world.

The evidence seems to be that, in spite of the demands of the Cold War, the economies of the West have not lost their essential characteristics of freedom of choice for the consumer, or have been hampered in their growth. On the contrary, wealth is increasing rapidly and being not less adequately distributed among the masses of the people, as even a trivial inspection of these countries will show.

Furthermore, rather than the Western nations becoming more planned in violation of their ideals of freedom, in order to carry the economic burden of the Cold War and of preventing a large-scale thermonuclear war, it is the Communist countries who have to change. Not only is there increasingly effective pressure for food and durable consumers' goods, but these nations find that they cannot provide for those needs without turning more definitely toward the economic systems of the West. This is undoubtedly a deeply disturbing development for the Communists. It points toward the demise of a great part of the ideological superstructure built upon the, by now, thoroughly muffy Marxist approach toward society.

The West, having to make no comparable adverse adjustments, is in a far stronger position, practically and ideologically. We may have to interfere in our economies from time to time more than we were used to. But this is not the outgrowth of an inability of the economy to perform; rather it is conditioned by technology. For example, air traffic simply has to be regulated, as well as the handling and safety of drugs, poisons, or fissionable material. But the idea of the free market does not have to be abandoned, and this is the central idea of our economic system.

From all this follows that whatever cooperative regulation is proposed in order to improve our military position does not weaken the roots of our strength.

## Distribution of Defense Effort

It would appear that the first place where cooperation is desirable is in arms manufacture itself, but I would like to point out some of the fundamental difficulties in order to illustrate the magnitude of the task which we face. If we look upon the various Western economies from the point of view of civilian production, we find that goods are being produced where they can best be produced—where it is easiest to make them in view of transportation cost, demand for services, availability of capital and labor, etc. If it is cheaper to make them abroad, this is done; international trade takes care of the proper distribution of effort and the finished goods. In that manner, we achieve an optimum as far as we can describe it, and this is exactly what we would like.

However, when weapons or other military equipment is to be manufactured, there is no market other than what the governments demand. Therefore, a deliberate reaching across borders is necessary, and that is clearly a political decision of the first magnitude. We see very little of that. Theoretically it would probably be best if, say, a rifle for the American army were developed and produced in Belgium, certain radar equipment be manufactured in France for everyone including the United States, nuclear weapons in the US, diesel motors be produced in Denmark to be put into American tanks, etc. If this were all a civilian economy producing goods for civilian use, this would probably develop by itself, given the necessary amount of free trade among these nations. But, when military equipment is considered, the matter immediately assumes very different aspects. Then it is a question of strategic distribution of the vulnerability of the various places of production, of the durability of the Alliance, and other matters of this kind. In addition to this, there is a great deal of instability, or rather quick obsolescence, of weapons systems, a fact which means that the governments have to underwrite a great deal of extra costs which cannot be born by strictly economic operations. Therefore, our utilization of economic resources for military purposes is certainly not "optimal" in the civilian sense. Though it is quite clear that it cannot be made as efficient as production in the civilian sector of the different economies, a great deal more could be accomplished by deliberate political acts which would override the present system. The fundamental dilemma is, of course, that all weapons production and most other expenditures for the military are wasteful if there is no war. Yet a war is even more wasteful, and if none occurs it can never be asserted with confidence whether that was due to having had military strength, or that the enemy did not want to fight in the first place.

Other difficulties that stand in the way of a wide distribution of weapons production according to the specific talents of the members of the Alliance is, of course, that weapons production very often requires secrecy, a flow of strategic information— all of which is very difficult to achieve across national borders—

even among allies. But again, much more than what has been done could be done if only the proper amount of thought and deliberation were given to these problems.

I cannot help but emphasize again that perhaps the greatest omission in mobilizing the resources of the West is the virtual lack of cooperation of a scientific-intellectual nature. The high level of intelligence and education in Europe—and I would certainly add Japan—is well known. But European scientists and engineers are much less involved in problems of defense both in regard to the physical-technical aspects, as well as concerning the development of new concepts of strategy, new ideas on how to stabilize the world and make it secure for a just peace. This is in large part due to the fact that European governments, and especially their military organizations, have only very dim and antiquated ideas as to the help modern science and its representatives can render. As stated above, it is the duty of the leader of the Alliance to remedy such faults. The United States must take the initiative and go beyond the hiring of scientists from Europe and bringing them to this country or organizing subsidiaries in Europe that are, with minute exceptions, concerned with nothing more important than to design a different washing machine. At best they contribute only very indirectly to the common defense; more likely, scarce scientific talent is being tied down to trivia. A solution of this problem is difficult but not impossible. The basic preliminary condition is that its existence must be recognized.

### Graduated Action and Response

I have emphasized specifically the need for developing new strategic ideas. But they are hard to come by. This has to be taken in the widest sense, so as to include other activities than strictly military operations. One of the prime requirements is flexibility and adaptability to novel situations. The latter will always develop. If the West is only poised for massive retaliation when attacked, or when challenged in a minor way, the likelihood of its massive reaction will be small and the familiar piecemeal destruction of our position will take place. Hence the efforts to develop capabilities for limited war. But the matter does not rest there. Graduated response (still better: initiative!) is of the essence. As an example, the United States put only a quarantine around Cuba, not a full blockade. Should a ship have resisted search, it would have been important to be able to halt it without even shooting at it (as can be done), let alone sinking the ship. This is an example of graduation of action. To accomplish it, new devices and new uses of old devices have to be thought of, and it is here where scientific and political imagination can play a big role.

*Inventions*, notably in the politico-economic area, are needed. Examples from earlier times are infiltration, fifth columns, partisan actions, etc., as well as unconventional uses of existing weapons, e.g., dismounted fighters with bows and arrows at Agincourt or the use of the German 88 mm. anti-aircraft gun against fortifications, etc. Since the nature of inventions cannot be predicted—or else they would not be inventions—no preparations can be made to use them. But provision can be made to create a milieu in which they might conceivably be made.

It is one of the remarkable features of the modern age that man has learned how to research and, in a sense, how to make inventions. However, this is limited to the natural sciences. We now need to develop new techniques and to apply these to the social sciences. It is unlikely that reliance on the steady evolution of new social forms is satisfactory. We are dedicated to certain ideals of personal freedom, but it is not clear that this evolution—so strongly influenced by technology—is compatible with their preservation. Hence we may have to decide on alternatives and to make our choice convincing to other nations. Though this observation may appear to be removed from our present problems, we must realize that apart from the short-run issues, the struggle with the Communist Bloc will continue into an indefinite future. The outcome will depend on how we prepare ourselves for the long run if we succeed in the immediate task of the year-to-year preservation of peace.

## FOOTNOTES

[1] This is explored in detail in Oskar Morgenstern, *On the Accuracy of Economic Observations* (2nd rev. ed.; Princeton: Princeton University Press, 1963), chap. XIV.

[2] Cf., Oskar Morgenstern, *The Question of National Defense* (2d ed. rev.; New York: Random House, 1961), chap. 8, pp. 202-4.

# Strategic Leverage from Aid and Trade

—*JAMES R. SCHLESINGER*

*Summary*

*The analysis of this paper rests on the assumption that American policy-makers should not be so concerned with the pursuit of hard-to-obtain ideological objectives that they exhaust the power potential implicit in trade and aid relationships. Rather the trade and aid programs should be managed so as to preserve an environment in which pressures can be brought to bear to serve the national interest at a later, and perhaps more critical, date. This emphasis on power considerations implies both (a) that the assistance program cannot be based primarily on humanitarian or idealistic goals, and (b) that economic ties with other nations should not be severed simply because of our disapproval of other social systems, including those based on communism. Though typically public opinion vastly overstates the strategic leverage that can be gained through economic weapons, this leverage is still not negligible. One can argue that in the past the United States has failed to take advantage of the power potential implicit in aid and trade through its failure to develop concepts and mechanisms of deterrence in ways akin to what has been done in the military field. Much of the difficulty may be ascribed to a failure to develop sanctions, which discourage actions unfavorable to our interests, as well as incentives, which encourage cooperation. No system of deterrence can exclusively stress the carrot and ignore the stick.*

*More is being demanded of the aid program than it can reasonably achieve. Assuming that the primary emphasis of the aid program is to encourage social and economic development rather than to elicit direct support for American foreign policy*

*objectives, it is argued that we should attempt to develop stable
social and political conditions by strengthening the "legitimacy"
of the developing social order in the eyes of the respective
publics—rather than attempting to export the trappings of
American democracy.*

*Technological change, the easy availability of substitutes, and
the lengthy period for adjustment in a prolonged struggle have
all reduced the impact of the "supply effect" which was at one
time the main weapon of economic warfare. If the economic
weapons of strategy are to be at all effective under today's
conditions, the "influence effect" must rise correspondingly in
importance. This implies that we should be in a position to
threaten to do damage to other economies through the curtailment of access to Western markets. In order to keep this threat
an ever-present one, we must, however, continue to trade in
volume with other countries, including Communist ones. Particularly in dealing with the underdeveloped nations the potential
effectiveness of such threats may prove to be considerable.*

---

This paper is based on the twin premises: (a) that American
policies regarding aid and trade may legitimately be employed
as strategic weapons in the Cold War, and (b) that, in such
employment, flexibility is both appropriate and necessary. These
postulates will be resisted in various quarters. They involve,
first of all, rejection of the idealistic-utopian view that aid should
be extended essentially on humanitarian grounds and that
considerations of power should be scrupulously avoided in the
aid program. By contrast, the position taken here is that the
primary intent of both our aid and trade policies should be to
serve the interests of the United States and, also, to assist our
principal allies, whose long-run interests and cultural traditions
are more or less coincident with our own. While it is perfectly
proper to recognize that extension of aid or increase of trade
serves a humanitarian objective of increasing the aggregate income and possibly the standard of life in many nations unaligned in the Cold War, some of which are close to the margin
of starvation, for the present the elimination of poverty cannot
be the *paramount* objective of our policies. In the world in
which we now find ourselves ideal goals must be subordinated

to the more pressing objective of enhancing the security of America and the West.*

A second locus of resistance to the underlying premises of this paper is represented by those who fear that strategic flexibility in the use of these weapons will, for one reason or another, result in the compromising of freedom. Aid and trade policies should reflect the values of freedom. Any compromising on these values, such as would be represented by the conscious adoption of discriminatory trade practices, would weaken the American economy and reduce the moral strength of the society. If we wish to encourage the growth of freedom, aid should either not be extended, or should be extended only with great reluctance, to any nation whose social order departs markedly from our own brand of liberal capitalism. At the outer margin this would, of course, exclude nations which have developed Communist systems and which are to a greater or lesser degree satellites of the Soviet Union. It is contended that any aid to, or even trade with, such nations represents an abetting of the enemy and in some way results in self-contamination.

To accept any of these contentions as guiding principles would be unwise. If we are to be flexible, each situation should be examined on its own merits to assess the net benefits and costs involved. Such an assessment should, of course, take place within the context of a general policy, and policy-makers should be alert to the broader implications of individual decisions. But policies must to some extent be pragmatic and experimental. The public ought not expect perfect consistency between specific decisions and general policies.

Before embarking on a detailed discussion of how the economic weapons of strategy might be used, it seems appropriate to mention a few general considerations that should guide our policy. First, the United States has in the past been accused of lacking a positive policy and of determining its actions negatively and belatedly in response to Soviet actions. There is some justice in such criticism. It ought not be inferred, however, from such comments that it would be advisable for the United States to formulate some kind of positive program and adhere to it in the face of changing developments. If the United States is to em-

---

* Though there is no need to belabor the point, it bears mentioning that there is no necessity to emphasize our security objectives in foreign policy statements directed toward the underdeveloped world. Some window dressing seems advisable. Nevertheless I think that leading figures in the Government should have firmly in mind what the principal objective is.

ploy its power effectively, it must be flexible enough to adjust its policies to take advantage of unforeseen opportunities or to counter a deterioration in its own position with which the over-all program had not been intended to deal. Part of American grand strategy must be to alter its policies and ambitions with alterations in the international posture. Without such flexibility we may be assured that the Soviets will take notice of the character of an unchanging policy, and will design measures which will counter the main thrust of American effort. Power which is spent in attacks on relatively invulnerable points of the Soviet Cold-War battle array or is repeatedly used against the same vulnerable points with diminishing returns is wasted. Whether wasted power is power at all is a question which we may leave to the philosophers. But to design an ideal and permanent policy which is impervious to changing developments and altered Soviet attitudes and actions is a losing venture. One may hope that national policy will not be altered indiscriminately in response to every changing breeze and that the longer-term guidelines and the cost of their abandonment will be taken into consideration in day-to-day control of policy. Nevertheless, there must be tactical and even strategic flexibility. There would be no need to mention this obvious point regarding what might be called the "economy of power" were it not for the fact that many critics of recent policies seem to assume that it is practicable to designate an array of permanent policy objectives and to follow this program willy-nilly.

There is a second consideration which deals with the objectives and, therefore, at one remove, with the guidelines and allocative mechanisms of the program for international assistance. If aid allotments are graduated in accordance with the degree of support provided by the recipient nation of Western strategic objectives, the aid program is unlikely, save by coincidence, to provide a powerful spur to economic progress in the underdeveloped world. On the other hand, if assistance is extended exclusively or primarily to those nations which can most effectively employ those resources in achieving growth, the program may be a weak (or even treacherous) instrument of policy. Elsewhere I have argued, at least tentatively, the advantages to be gained by distributing aid primarily on the basis of the recipient nations' attitudes toward our foreign policy objectives.[1] There is still something to be said for such a procedure. Through it one is in a position to minimize the mutual jealousies that are created by the assistance program—

by creating a relatively objective standard which all potential recipients can understand even if they dislike it. It is relatively riskless in that it seeks to preserve the status quo, but it is riskless in this sense because it lacks daring. It is based on the premise that it is difficult to foretell or significantly to influence long-range changes in the pattern of hostility and alliance among independent states.

Whatever the advantages of a policy of graduating aid in accordance with support of Western objectives, it is plain that the decision in this Administration and in its predecessor has been against it. The primary thrust of the aid program will be, unless a nation is under direct assault, to provide assistance to those that can most profitably employ it to expand aggregate output. Within the context of such a policy, the question is how the aid can be used to serve our own objectives. It may be noted that some of the tensions which exist between an alliance-oriented and a development-oriented aid program have been eliminated by the displacement of SEATO by India as the principal bulwark against Chinese expansionism. These tensions have not been entirely eliminated, as the Pakistani response to American military assistance to India bears witness, yet the sharp conflict between the two patterns of assistance which existed in the late fifties no longer exists.

### Deterrence: Carrots and Sticks

In the past decade considerable ingenuity has been invested in studying the type of force structures which will deter the Soviets from outright military assault. In much of the discussion there was a failure to recognize that the concept of deterrence has a broader applicability than to military matters alone. It is, in fact, relevant to the whole range of foreign policy issues. The Austrian peace treaty provides the Soviets with an excellent device to deter the Austrians from abandoning neutrality and joining forces with the West—a step they might well take were they in a freer position. The risk of Soviet intervention is sufficiently great to preclude such action. The Finns are even more effectively deterred—and the Soviet military presence frustrates the hope for *rapprochement* with the West in at least several of the satellite nations.

On our side we wish to deter the underdeveloped nations from taking steps which are frankly hostile to Western interests. In addition, we should like to have some means of encouraging the satellites to resist Soviet pressures. Conceptually at least, the answer is simple: we must consciously strive to develop mechanisms of deterrence. The very existence of such mechanisms will encourage greater circumspection in dealing with Western interests. They would be most useful if they do not have to be employed, but they may be—in the event of a substantial provocation. Mistakenly in the past we have consciously considered deterrence only in our dealings with the Soviets, and have assumed that it was unnecessary for dealing with the underdeveloped nations and irrelevant for dealing with the Satellites. As a result our responses have been belated and ad hoc.

This failure to think through the nature of deterrent measures that might be applied to areas other than those representing a primary threat may be sheer oversight, but the implicit analysis is faulty. Even where relationships are basically those of coordination rather than rivalry, elements of deterrence are always implicit in the situation.[2] In the past we have not hesitated to threaten our allies with "agonizing reappraisals"— and, in practice, we have made such reappraisals with less advertisement, more subtlety, and perhaps with less agony than we thought might be required. Our policy toward those who are neither wholly with the West nor wholly with the Soviets will be far more effective when a system of deterrence has been constructed—a system of rewards and sanctions which is at least vaguely perceived in advance. In our attitude toward the newly emerging nations we have tended to assume—what it is unwise to assume—that we can be "permissive" and that eventually the new nations will learn to be responsible and reasonable according to our lights.

The implicit analogy to American child-rearing methods, now somewhat out of fashion, is quite relevant, for social attitudes tend to form a complex whole. Where public opinion influences policy, views on child-rearing are likely to be related to those on foreign policy. "Young" nations are supposed to go through the same stages of development as humans. This is, of course, not the case, but even with respect to children, permissiveness is unworkable. Even the most permissive of parents have sneaky ways of obtaining the behavior they desire—ways which children understand even if the parents are themselves deceived. We cannot afford to wait for other nations to acquire a feel for the American temperament; we should instead consciously devise a pattern of techniques for influencing the conduct of others—which combines the values of firmness with independence for others.

During much of the twentieth century the American disposition has been to regard employment of the stick in minor international tensions as immoral. We have instead attempted to achieve our objectives through the overwhelming use of the carrot. But this is hardly an effective method in the long run. Any system that has only reward but no sanctions provides a temptation to those affected to run the minor risk of unfriendly words or adjustment of the reward in order to bring their behavior into conformity with their own ambitions or the expectations of those outside the system.

Even if the primary goal of the assistance program is to promote economic development and social change in the assisted nations, it should be implicit in the program that we look upon our own interests with a little tenderness, and that aid or trade may be curtailed if actions are taken which are provoking as well as provocative. In dealing with the Caribbean nations the existence of the sugar-control system automatically supplied us with an effective mechanism for bringing pressure to bear. Ultimately the Cubans provoked us into taking more forceful steps—on a more or less ad hoc basis. Normally, however, there is no established mechanism for bringing pressure to bear. Before we can expect other nations to be deterred from taking actions hostile to the West we must not only have a carefully designed system of responses, but we must have made it credible to those whom we hope to deter that we might actually put such retaliatory measures into use.

Much of the disappointment we have felt in recent years regarding the behavior of the neutrals may be attributed to our earlier failure to establish an incentive system which would help elicit the type of behavior we desired. Not only was there little risk of punitive action, but on the part of the neutrals there was an awareness, possibly unconscious, that concessions might be obtained from the West by an unsympathetic posture, while nothing could be gained from the Soviets by a similar response. A posture of moral superiority may be disturbing to Anglo-American public opinion, and by generating self-doubt might bring concessions. The Soviet Union was impervious to this sort of pressure. The upshot was that through the absence of firm policies we help to create a situation ripe for Soviet exploitation in which Soviet accomplishments appear large in relation to either their natural advantages or the resources which they were willing to invest in the underdeveloped lands.

We should move toward a posture in which it is recognized by all parties that, while we regard use of military force as only the last possible resort, we have access to a variety of intermediate responses in the event of provocative action. Section 232 of the Trade Expansion Act (originally passed in 1955 as the so-called national security amendment to the Trade Agreements Act) provides for the specification of *commodities* whose importation (allegedly) threatens national security by eliminating domestic sources of supply and provides for limitation of such imports. There is no reason why the law cannot be changed to specify *nations* from which importation can be limited—and to far better purpose.* Access to the American market is something that no underdeveloped nation can lightly surrender. The threat becomes all the stronger, of course, if joint arrangements can be worked out with the Common Market, and to a lesser degree with Britain, Japan, and other industrialized countries. The dependence of the underdeveloped nations taken together on Western markets is very great. Even for a *single* country, like Cuba, the substitution of Bloc markets for Western markets represents a very poor trade—the terms of which would become harsher if any large number of underdeveloped nations tried to "go East" simultaneously.

Making access to American and other Western markets contingent on avoidance of overtly hostile acts, by providing a sanction, would alter the way in which underdeveloped nations perceived the environment. Take a concrete example. Some people have argued that Ghana has been unduly troublesome as the center of anti-Western ferment in sub-Saharan Africa. I do not find the present situation particularly disturbing, but assume, for purposes of discussion, that it were to deteriorate. Suppose

---

* If the authority to restrict application of the law to Communist-dominated or controlled nations, conferred on the President by Section 231 of the Trade Expansion Act, is interpreted broadly enough, the President may already possess the necessary powers. Though the wording is quite general, the plain intent of the section is, however, to prevent or to eliminate tariff concessions which have been or might be extended to Communist nations under the most-favored-nation clause, rather than providing the power to impose more general restrictions on trade. A very generous interpretation of Presidential powers and a very dubious interpretation as to what constitutes a "Communist-dominated" area would be necessary before the present section could be used to put pressure on unfriendly nations in the underdeveloped world.

Ghana were to make use of its solid foreign-exchange position to encourage anti-Western moves in Nigeria. The standard American response would be to augment assistance to Nigeria, but under such circumstances a far more direct approach to the issue would be to bring measured retaliation against Ghana. In this case the policing problems would be relatively simple, for the trade in cacao is sufficiently limited that discovering the source of supply should not be difficult. As heavy a blow against the Ghanian economic position as desired might be struck. To be sure, the Soviets might take advantage of the opening, but the Soviet tendency has been to be niggardly in aid and incompetent in performance. The long-run therapeutic effect on other states of such action might be substantial. And for such a goal the American and possibly the European consumer may be asked to forego chocolate bars—at least temporarily.

I do not believe that the knowledge that sanctions exist need seriously interfere in the long run with our objective of encouraging growth and reform in the underdeveloped areas. In some ways the prospects might be improved, for in the majority of the underdeveloped countries energies that might have been wasted in tilting against the West (with the by-product of discouraging outside investment) may be more productively employed. Nor do I believe that establishing a mechanism of deterrence in this manner needs to imply more than a slight modification of our policy of moving toward liberalized, multilateral trade. The bulk of our trade will continue to be with the industrialized nations of Western Europe, Canada, Japan, etc. At the very most, no more than five per cent of our trade should be very much affected by these restraints.

When the decision is made to apply pressure to a nation for which there is an aid program, the usual assumption might be that aid should be cut first. Under ordinary conditions this may be the case, but there may be circumstances in which it is appropriate to continue with the aid program. Aid implies commitments, and it may be wisest to bring to a successful conclusion projects which have been inaugurated. The maximum psychological effect may be obtained in this way. Also, it may be unwise to sacrifice the personal and informal relationships which have been established by officials of the aid program. Finally, it may be possible to bring pressure to bear more discreetly via the trade route.

One final consideration—it would be unwise to use potential weapons of this sort for niggling purposes. The balance of payments has been troublesome and is properly an object of concern in Washington, but surely it is not a first-order consideration in our relations with the underdeveloped nations. Suggestions have been bruited about that we should make use of the aid program to force recipients to buy from us in ways that go beyond tied aid. Under the best of circumstances, our bargaining power is limited, and shooting away strategic ammunition for so paltry an economic goal would seem to reflect a poor sense of proportion.

### Aid

Within an over-all framework designed to discourage hostile or predatory attitudes toward the West, the aid program may seek to foster the maximum rate of economic and social progress. In the basic policy of AID, the Kennedy Administration has explicitly adopted this goal. As has been indicated there are costs to this decision. Outsiders are not likely to be much liked even under the best of circumstances, which hardly apply to the underdeveloped countries, and their intervention in whatever direction will in the long run excite antagonism based on real or fancied wrongs. Nevertheless, the basic decision has been made. Let us examine in what way we may proceed so that the good effects clearly outweigh the ill effects.

There are two initial postulates: (1) our bargaining power will be limited, and (2) American notions of social reform and of equity are neither necessarily applicable in the underdeveloped lands, nor need we assume that those whose cooperation we must win will find them appealing. These postulates are inter-related. Jointly they imply that we cannot press forward on all fronts to create a society in which a good American democrat will feel at home, but must instead concentrate our energies on those social changes which will spur economic growth even if the immediate results are more consistent with the cultural genius of the peoples involved rather than our own tastes. We ought not expect them to make the same choices as we would, or, if they make the same choices, to achieve in a ten-year period what it took us eighty years to achieve. Finally, in reaching judgments on social processes in other lands, we cannot apply what are our own—or, in reality, higher—standards of purity.

As outsiders, we will be unable to perceive the social function of behavior which is superficially corrupt, and will tend to lump it together with that which is purely parasitical. With respect to our own history, retrospectively we have come to find merit in what once were regarded as the disreputable procedures of an organization like Tammany Hall in that it provided a kind of social security and a welcome for the newly arrived immigrant. We are accustomed to the daily dangling of new post offices, good committee assignments, and bridges over creeks in the outback before wavering Congressmen, and warm approval is given, for its fine sense of political realism, to whatever administration is doing the dangling by those who agree with its goals. Toward similar procedures abroad we are inclined to take a simple muckraking attitude. We look askance at the higgling of the political market—with a naiveté that would do credit both to missionaries and old-style political reformers. If we hope to achieve a fair measure of success, we shall have to sharpen our critical faculties and learn to distinguish between unappetizing social devices which are functional and those which are simple barriers to progress.

The statement of objectives by AID is a very ambitious one. The purposes of the assistance program include stimulation of self-help, encouragement of progressive forces, and achievement of governments based on consent, which recognize the dignity and worth of individuals who are expected to participate in determining the nation's goals. No doubt, a statement of aspirations is in large part window dressing, but the criteria by which self-help is moving toward social and political progress are more specific: a more equitable distribution of income, a more equitable tax system with increased yields, expanded welfare programs, increased political participation and civil liberties, and so on. Several points may be made regarding the objectives: first, there are too many; second, they are to some extent inconsistent; and third, they ignore the real resources available.

There is, in the first place, the long-perceived clash between economic progress, on the one hand, and the combined goals of equitable distribution of income, immediate improvement in living standards, and security on the other. This underlying conflict spills over into a tension between rapid economic progress and the introduction of democratic processes. On this issue there appears to have been a revolution in informed opinion in the United States during the past five years. During the late fifties, it had become almost an axiom that authoritarian, if not totalitarian, governments had innate advantages in guiding economies toward rapid growth. The prevailing view was based, no doubt, on an assessment of the record of the Soviet regime, and an exaggerated notion of how much the Chinese "Great Leap Forward" would accomplish. Perhaps the earlier "pessimism" regarding the relative performance potential of "free" and "controlled" economies was overdone, but have we not gone too far in the now prevailing "optimism" that any clash between economic progress and the democratic institutions which insure the dominance of the *vox populi* is minimal?

The average citizen—particularly when he is ill-housed, ill-clothed, ill-fed, and ill-educated—seems most likely to be interested in the here and now. A government which is responsive to the desires of the public will continually be tempted to mortgage the future for the present. The "abstinence" or "waiting" which classical and neoclassical economics state to be necessary ingredients in economic progress will be hard to require, as will be the incentive schemes (and the accompanying conspicuous consumption) which are likely to strike the average voter as inequitable. We may recall that the Perón regime was (and still may be?) the most popular regime in recent Latin American history. Or we may observe the economic consequences of Brazilian democracy, and have our doubts. The inflow of American resources may be able to make showpieces out of several small, recently-democratized nations like the Dominican Republic, but we ought not assume either that democracy assists in economic development, or that the Dominican example is widely applicable. This is not to say that some judicious prodding in the direction of democracy may not be a wise policy, but it must be *judicious*, and cannot be based on the assumption that democracy necessarily fosters the political stability essential to growth.

One of the criteria by which self-help can be judged as justifying additional aid is an improvement in the savings ratio. Some students of the aid program would put major emphasis on changes in the savings ratio in that it provides a relatively objective standard by which an improvement in economic performance can be judged.* If we apply an objective standard, complaints about the distribution of aid and subjectivity in the

---

* Charles Wolf, Jr. of RAND has been attempting to develop an econometric model which will provide an objective measure of the performance of aid recipients in terms of self-help. The criterion is the savings ratio. In the model the attempt is made to eliminate the influence of other variables, such as per capita income, income distribution, and degree of urbanization, which account for a good deal of the observed variation in the savings ratio as between nations and between different periods of time.

judgment of self-help can be minimized. But such a standard points to the conflict inherent in the wider ambitions of AID. To the extent that a rise in the savings ratio is a primary objective of policy, it will be hindered by movement toward a more equal distribution of income. Achievement of relative income equality either directly or through a progressive income tax may interfere with incentives. Just what the appropriate degree of progressivity is for the tax structure is a delicate question upon which judgments can vary widely. No doubt in most underdeveloped nations there is considerable scope for increasing progressivity without affecting incentives—and without affecting significantly the funds available for investment outlays (even though the savings ratio may be reduced). But this is not universally true, and, even where it is true, there is a danger that enthusiasts will push progressivity too far. The upshot is that for the time being only elimination of the grosser forms of inequality seems to be a reasonable goal. If the goal is to foster growth, we shall very much desire to retain skewness of the income distribution as long as it is related to economic function. American experience is relevant here. Since the Kennedy Administration is now talking about reducing the progressivity of the American income tax and the need for unshackling "initiative," it may be hoped that the urging of greater progressivity abroad and lessened progressivity at home will not be taken as inconsistent. It seems likely, however, that the wrong inferences will be drawn—and the net effect will be to reduce the persuasiveness of the Administration's position.

The emphasis which we have placed upon the paraphernalia of democracy, on income equality, on welfare programs seems to me to be misleading. What we are fundamentally interested in is stable, non-Communist governments which command—and can retain—the support of their peoples. What the aid program should attempt to do is to encourage changes in which currently disillusioned people may perceive a greater degree of legitimacy and effectiveness in their own social systems. Regimes acquire legitimacy in the eyes of their own people, not because of external forms, but because they work. Only ideologues will assume that the average individual can become deeply concerned about forms alone.

The influence of ideology on the ordinary man is quite limited. In the main he will be interested in security and—if he is ambitious—in opportunities for advancement commensurate with his deserts. Ideologies will flourish only where incompetency is dominant and hope disappears. The mission of the aid program should be to enhance acceptance of the legitimacy of society by helping to unblock opportunities. The primary concern should be to provide opportunities for the ambitious, the capable, and the unideological within the existing social framework. If an individual has the capacity and inclination for work, if he can make a contribution, his way to the top should not be blocked by nepotism, incompetency, jobbery, and functionless upper classes. It is the primary goal of the aid program to help remove such barriers—not to reform society as such. We are interested in the redistribution of income, for example, so that it is functional, so that it encourages work, so that it is regarded as justifiable and legitimate—not to arrive at some preconceived distribution. The acquisition of legitimacy by governments in the underdeveloped areas is consistent with a very great variety of social forms—almost all of which should be acceptable to us.

Discussion of the assistance program in the context of enhancing the legitimacy of the social order in the eyes of the people concerned casts some light on the vexing question of "socially disruptive" reforms. Those who are hostile to the assistance program, particularly in its new orientation, have objected to the making of "reforms," which are "socially disruptive," a condition of assistance. Reforms, however, are by definition disruptive. There are short-term costs—and most of those whose interests are adversely affected may be counted on to oppose the changes. The real question is whether the long-term social and economic benefits are sufficiently great to outweigh the costs of short-term disruption. In some societies reform is necessary to preserve social health, to eliminate mechanisms which frustrate progress, even to prevent social disintegration. Under such conditions, it is meaningless to say that reforms are disruptive simply because of the short-term costs. It all depends on the nature of the specific reforms suggested. They may be well-conceived in light of the given circumstances, or they may represent simply the attempt to write American values into other cultures. In the latter case, the reforms may both reduce the hope for social cohesion and the likelihood of a foreign policy orientation not hostile to the West.

Too early insistence on the introduction of the forms of democracy where the spirit of democracy does not exist may provide opportunities, not for the ordinarily ambitious and capable men who are willing to advance by making a productive contribution within a reformed system, but to those who would bring systematic change—to those who would bring revolution. It would be unwise deliberately to bring changes that will probably bring to the top those who, from our point of view, would subvert the society. One of the most successful examples of both economic growth and social change, which we have influenced, has been in Taiwan. At the moment Chiang's regime would probably have popular support if an election were held. Yet, if we had listened to those Americans who urged the introduction of democratic procedures in the early or mid-fifties, the regime would undoubtedly have been swept away—and with it, in all probability, the chances for the substantial social improvements that have taken place. There is a time for the introduction of democratic procedures, and there is a time to avoid such introduction.

I have emphasized this point at some length because I believe a misdirection of our effort is potentially very dangerous. By providing opportunities for the ideologies, we may succeed only in making the existing social order in the underdeveloped areas wholly unworkable, and make probable substantial Soviet gains. Strong leadership is still essential in the underdeveloped world if steady though unspectacular improvement is to be achieved. This implies that we may have to acquiesce in techniques for maintaining the strength of leadership of which we would disapprove under other conditions.

## Trade

Aside from the economic advantages which trade conveys, the expansion of trade under present conditions is useful in that by creating interdependence it provides a medium for non-military deterrence. Some of these possibilities have been suggested in the section on "deterrence," but some amplification is appropriate. Nations which are dependent on trade are reluctant to see the disappearance of substantial markets or cheap sources of supply of essential commodities. Moderate pressures can be brought to bear by great trading entities against their smaller trading partners by threatening to terminate what had been hoped to be permanent trade relationships. The threat to restrict trade has a clear limitation as a strategic weapon in that, like a missile, when it is employed it is gone. When one uses the weapon, one forfeits the threat. Therefore one must consider the costs of employing the weapon. For the United States the economic costs are likely to be slight, but the cost in terms of reduced future influence may be heavy. The cost of using the weapon, however, does not imply that it is inadvisable to build up trade and let it be known that trade may be curtailed under given conditions. In itself, the creation of such a mechanism will give smaller nations pause.

In order to be able to employ the trade weapon, one must be in a position to bargain effectively. Under some circumstances this may imply that a nation should be able to "bilateralize" trade with those it seeks to influence—to ensure that the volume of purchases can be made dependent on political negotiations. The amount of pressure may be too much reduced if sales of foreign producers remain dependent on impersonal multilateral markets. Any movement toward the bilateralization of trade would, of course, require a change in the American perspective on commercial policy. However, one can foresee the continued existence of multilateral trade in our dealings with most nations, especially the principal industrial producers in the Free World. Nevertheless, for the small proportion of total trade carried on with our principal rivals or with smaller nations that might become hostile, the establishment of instrumentalities which can negotiate directly on the terms of volume of trade seems advisable. In the kind of world in which we live, and in which we are reluctant to make use of direct military pressure, it might be unwise to forego use of the trade weapon.

An important step forward would be taken if both the United States and the EEC were to establish trading organizations which had the power to bargain directly with their Soviet counterparts over commercial transactions with the West—and which could exclude from this line of activity firms in these two great economic units. This does not imply that a reduction in trade is desirable. On the contrary, expansion of trade might convey certain advantages. An increase of this type of contract with the Soviet Union would probably be beneficial. The damage that we can do by *refraining* from such trade is slight. We must keep a sense of proportion about these matters. The Battle Act kind of notion that by cutting off trade with the Soviets, we could beat them to their knees in six months is so outlandish it does not deserve comment. When one recalls that the Soviet economy is growing at a rate of six to seven per cent each year, it is clear that the benefits that the Soviets would extract from trade under the best of circumstances are marginal—only a drop in the bucket. However, if trade is built up, the damage that we could do by *curtailing* trade, even though it is slight, might well be the deciding factor between taking some provocative step and avoiding it.

The objections to expanding trade with the Soviets seem unconvincing. Many people would argue that on principle we should not trade with our foes, but why forego the establishment of these connections, if they carry strategic advantages for us?* We must get over this belief that whoever comes into contact with the Soviets is irretrievably lost. The notion that either the United States or the EEC might become strategically dependent on Soviet sources of supply strikes me as ludicrous—although Western producers have been energetically spreading it.** A more interesting argument is that the Soviets would extract undue advantage from such trade because of the difference between their low marginal costs and world prices. Oil is a case in point. Of course, it makes commercial as well as strategic sense to attempt to limit Soviet gains, but this calls for an attempt to bargain prices down toward marginal costs. Presumably two Western trading organizations would possess considerable bargaining power in such matters, and we might well be able to obtain Soviet commodities not only below Western production costs (with the inherent saving of our own resources), but possibly below the full cost of production to the Soviets.

With some modification, the same kind of perspective might govern our trade with the Satellites. In this case the costs of refusing to trade or drastically limiting trade are more impressive. The net effect will be to ease the Soviet strategic problem by forcing the Satellites to integrate their economies more thoroughly into the Bloc than they might otherwise do. The

* The current drive by several right-wing organizations to persuade stores not to stock goods produced in Communist countries is probably something of a strategic boomerang. If we refuse to buy Polish hams (the principal target) or other Polish goods, our influence in Poland will certainly not be strengthened. A potential weapon is being wasted in a petty emotional display. The triviality to which the campaign descends may be illustrated by the exhortation of a Freeport, New York housewife: "I've been told that Russian peat moss is being sold in many nurseries on Long Island. Remember to ask where your peat moss comes from." The whole episode makes an interesting study in frustration.

** One of the three purposes stated for the Trade Expansion Act is "to prevent Communist economic penetration." Whatever relevance the term may have for Iceland or Afghanistan, its relevance for the United States or the EEC is approximately zero. The provisions in the Act have the sole function of protecting American producers; its strategic impact, for the reasons mentioned, is probably negative from our standpoint.

West should hardly cooperate in smoothing the path toward the achievement of Soviet objectives. Moreover, by refraining from trade we forfeit an instrument which potentially could influence the Satellites either to resist Soviet pressures or to avoid provocations against the West. Since one of the assumptions of our foreign policy has been that the Satellites reluctantly accept Soviet dominance because they have no alternative, it would appear desirable that this awareness of various shades of gray existing in the Bloc be reflected in our trade policies— rather than accepting the uncritical notion that trade with Communists is reprehensible under any circumstances, etc.

In controlling trade with the Satellites, it is not necessary, and it might prove to be a disadvantage, for trade to be put on a bilateral basis. The same is true with respect to the under-developed countries, although, if the circumstances arise, it may be advisable to be in a position to shift to bilateral negotiations through a national organization in order to bring maximum pressure to bear. In general, it should be remembered that in this era the "supply effect" has shrunk in importance relative to the "influence effect" in using trade strategically. In order to gain influence, one must put other nations in a position in which they have something to lose, if they are uncooperative. With respect to the supply effect, in light of technological advance and the easy availability of substitutes, no technically sophisticated nation can be significantly hurt by the interdiction of some so-called strategic material. The main exception to this rule is in dealing with underdeveloped countries, where curtailment of deliveries or technical services by the normal suppliers of capital equipment may impose a very sharp increase in costs on the affected nations, because of the difficulty of finding alternative sources of parts, replacements, and advice on maintenance. Investment in capital equipment at any time means the provision of something of a hostage to fortune. It is desirable that the West retain control of this hostage, and consequently, it would seem advantageous to maintain the current dominance of the United States and its major allies in the supply—and the servicing—of capital equipment in the underdeveloped world. Such dependence implies a source of leverage.

The kind of procedures, which have been suggested to exploit the strategic potential implicit in aid and trade, would require the adoption of an attitude toward nations with which we are not at war tougher than has existed in the past. It would require some extension of controls and further departure from the goal of nondiscriminatory trading practices. However, I can see no fundamental objection to having trade with the Soviet Union and China, as well as the Satellites and some of the "neutralists" if necessary, centrally controlled. I do not find the "wedge" argument convincing—i.e., the controls which exist on the five per cent of our trade carried on with hostile nations must inevitably spread to the bulk of our trade which is carried on with friendly nations, thus destroying multilateral trade. If the case for the market or for decentralization in general rests on such a weak basis that it will collapse on account of an occasional deviation from "principle," then it is too weak to survive in any event. My own reading of the situation is different: the area of influence of ideology on economic organization has been very much narrowed since the 1940's, and the argument for decentralization is accepted by most of those who in the earlier period might have been regarded as favoring *dirigisme* in principle. Thus, I would have few hesitations. Without significantly weakening pursuit of its other objectives, I think that the United States can move ahead in designing techniques which will result in greater exploitation of the strategic potential embodied in our aid and trade policies.

## FOOTNOTES

[1] James R. Schlesinger, *The Political Economy of National Security* (New York: 1960), pp. 227-32.

[2] It seems almost sententious to cite the seminal work on the subject, Thomas C. Schelling, *The Strategy of Conflict* (Cambridge, Mass: Harvard University Press, 1960), Part I.

# Developed and Underdeveloped Areas

## Summary

To win its contest with the Soviet powers in the long run the Free World must maintain and strengthen the conviction of the people in the industrially advanced and in the developing countries that the non-coercive, consumer-oriented economy, with its institutions that protect human dignity and freedom, is a basically fair and equitable arrangement. This makes it mandatory to maintain the integrity of the currencies, to keep them freely convertible, and to stay aloof from policies which lead to inflation. Such a strategy puts the special obligation on the United States as the leading power of the West to improve its balance of payments by policies which are compatible with the over-all strategy of economic expansion and optimal exchange of goods, services, and capital within the Free World. Implicit in such orientation are: the avoidance of continual deficit financing of the government household, avoidance of overexpansion of military commitments, drastic curtailment of non-military expenditures that are not vitally needed, and shifting from foreign aid by the Government to private foreign investment and financing.

Among needed changes in policy on behalf of greater strength of the weakening dollar are the return of American agriculture to a competitive market operation, the disengagement from such static farm policy devices as price-fixing, acreage allotments, marketing quotas, government stockpiling of farm surpluses, and subsidization of exports under Public Law 480. Simultaneously the dollar should be fortified by effective efforts of private indus-

*tries as well as of the Federal Government to open foreign mar-
kets to commercial exports of agricultural and industrial goods
inside the EEC, the EFTA, and all other parts of the world.*

*The strategy of US foreign aid toward underdeveloped coun-
tries calls for a hard and clear-cut decision of maximum private
investment and loans, and progressive curtailment of government-to-government grants and loans.*

*The terms of trade for the underdeveloped countries which
are all primary-products exporters have deteriorated during the
last nine years by an aggregate of 20 per cent due to overexpansion of the primary-material-producing capacity. This
overcapacity has been seriously aggravated by output boosting
protection and price-fixing in industrially advanced countries,
including the United States, continental Europe, and Japan. The
change in their terms of trade has cost the underdeveloped countries between $4.5 and $5 billion annual purchasing power for
imports. Moreover, due to a multitude of imprudent and partly
prestige-inspired policies, many of these countries which are
the target for the Soviet infiltration are near insolvency and
will be unable to import similar amounts of industrial goods as
in earlier years.*

*The attempt to solve this serious problem by international com-
modity agreements, i.e., cartels, is not only doomed to failure,
but it destroys in the primary-materials-exporting countries the
possibility of developing a market economy with private property
in means of production—which is the essential position of economic strength of the Free World. The Cold War cannot be won
by borrowing from the enemy his economic philosophy.*

*If the Free World does not want to undermine the foundations
of economic development in underdeveloped countries, it must
refrain from giving support to the socialization of agriculture,
industry, banking, and commerce in those countries. This means
particularly that the US foreign representatives should refrain
from giving support to so-called agrarian reforms which begin
with the destruction of the most productive agricultural enterprises which frequently are the only firms which have at their
command the modern techniques and processes needed for progress. Such "reforms," which involve large-scale confiscation of
private property, lead in the first instance to serious capital flight
from such countries, a process which does immeasurable harm
to such capital-importing countries, and they lead in the second
instance to the preparation for communism.*

*The countries of the Free World must support policies which develop the human resources and skills of the rural small-holder population in underdeveloped countries, and must abstain from policies which confiscate under various subterfuges a substantial part of the income of the farm population.*

*Irrespective of whether this is done under the disguise of commodity price stabilization or via skimming procedures with manipulated multiple foreign-exchange rates, these typical Soviet methods of forced industrialization can only prepare the underdeveloped countries for communism.*

*The remedy must lie in maximum private investment, freer foreign trade, and freer exchange of skills via vocational training.*

*The Free World must not fall into the trap of endorsing or condoning the condemnation of such essential institutions as private leases of land, i.e., farm tenancy, the annual employment of married farm workers against wages in cash and kind, or private-production credit for farmers. The essential strategy must be one of energetic correction of customary defects and abuses of such institutions by legislation which utilizes the accrued capital of experience with successful reforms of the advanced countries of the Free World, including particularly agrarian reforms.*

---

Aside from what is going on in the dimensions of strategy in diplomatic and military affairs with the accompaniment of ideological warfare, the power contest beween the Free World and the Sino-Soviet Bloc will proceed primarily by comparative expansion of strength and performance in the economic realm. What counts in the long run is growth of the potential of an economy, or the development of its human, man-made, and natural resources in their aggregate capacity to produce goods and services, not merely expansion of current output. The gross national product (GNP) of nations can be expanded for many years with serious depletion of the productive assets and resources, including particularly the human resources.

## The Real Issues of Economic Strategy

Sound economic strategy requires first and last of all a clear recognition of the nature of the real issues that are at stake in the world-wide historical contest, and of the economic origin of the inhuman and degrading police-state methods which are inseparable from Communist regimes. The Free World stands and falls with the dedication and uncompromising loyalty of its élite of responsible citizens to the basic values which alone inspire the humane society and separate it from tyranny. The great issue of the historical process in the age of nuclear weapons is not which system of government can produce the greatest amount of steel or concrete or other materials, or which group of states can perform the most spectacular astronautical ventures. On the contrary, the real economic issue in any part of the Free World is the improvement of working and living conditions and of real income for the greatest number of people with due respect for human dignity, integrity of the individual, his responsibility, and his freedom.

What gives the Free World its philosophical and spiritual coherence, its inspiration, and its ideals is the acceptance of the unique spiritual nature of man, endowed by his Creator with the divine spark, with the freedom to choose between good and evil, with a free will and the ability to make decisions, and hence with responsibility and human dignity. This socio-political credo of the Free World lays the foundation for the principles of the limitations of the legitimate power of government, of government by law, and of the purpose of government to serve the pursuit of happiness of the citizens. This credo forbids any attempt of a government to reduce the people to passive parts of a state-directed economy.

Inherent in the Free World's profoundly optimistic and idealistic credo of human nature and of human society is the faith in the extraordinary potential of development of the gifts and talents of the individual, and the enormous increase in creativity within an environment of free enterprise and private initiative. The Free World's greatest economic asset is the fact that free men are incomparably more productive workers than are slaves.

The economic contest between the Free World and the Communist-ruled part of the world affects all human action of any nation. Sound Free World strategy requires, next to its non-coercive economy, that the people have faith in the basic fairness and equity of the national economic system. The government must do its part in maintaining and strengthening that faith. And the public must be aware of and alert to the crucial issues of over-all economic strategy.

## Some Geopolitical Aspects of Economic Strategy

The developed economic heartland of the Free World is the highly industrialized areas of the northern hemisphere on both sides of the Atlantic and the Pacific:  Western Europe, the United States and Canada, and Japan. The greatest geopolitical asset for economic development and foreign trade of this industrial heartland of the Free World is the easy access to the highway of the seas which more than ever before provides transportation at far lower costs than by any other form of transportation. With this asset of natural transport resources, Western Europe and Japan are even far better endowed than the United States and Canada. The heavily indented coastlines of the British and Japanese Isles and of the West European continent, the navigable rivers and canals, and the extraordinary density of population and industries provide far easier access to ocean-cargo shipping than the Sino-Soviet Bloc can ever attain. Particularly in its more industrialized Soviet Russian part, the vast Eurasian land mass has by comparison only scanty access to ocean shipping. The Sino-Soviet Bloc has the other handicap that, due to topography and climate, its so-far utilized agricultural resources are far less favorable than those of the industrial heartland of the Free World. Moreover, the Soviet Union has not yet accomplished in its northern European area what has been achieved in many centuries since the early middle ages by the rural communities, and since the eighteenth century by individual farmers in Western Europe and the United States:  the clearance of the forest on hundreds of millions of acres of fertile, arable land in the temperate humid zones.

## Comparative Advantage of the Free World's Resources

The better geopolitical assets and historical achievements in the development of natural resources give the developed industrial heartland of the Free World a considerable environmental advantage. But the far greater assets concern human resources and social and economic conditions. Their greatest asset for economic development is the freedom of people to use their talents, skills, and drive within the decentralized, decision-making system, and with the incentives of a market economy to participate as consumers in the allocation of resources.

The diversity of national cultures, talents of people and background, and their progessive blending in the more mature and sophisticated society with its alert social conscience, and its political and social respect for the creativity of the free, responsible individual give the West an incomparably greater economic potential than the materialistic state-capitalism of the Soviets with its cynical disregard for the rights of the farm population as well as the urban consumers. There is no evidence that, by its coercion, monolithic planning, and heavily centralized decision-making, the Sino-Soviet Bloc can achieve any greater sustained rate of genuine economic growth than that which has prevailed in the industrially advanced countries of the Free World for the last nine years. Industrial production in Japan has grown during the last five years at a rate of over 26 per cent, and in the six EEC countries by 10 per cent per annum. Moreover, there is no evidence that the growth of the capacity of the Sino-Soviet economy, including all Satellites, will come anywhere near the combined capacity of the economy of the industrialized parts of the Free World.

However, if the values of the Free World shall prevail, the useful measurement of the comparative performances of the industrial economies on both sides of the Iron Curtain do not provide the clues for future policy adjustments and priorities.

The economic strategy of the Free World must be oriented toward strengthening the moral foundations and basic institutions on which the superior creativeness of its economy and the morale of its people stand, and toward mobilization of public opinion for the offensive in the world-wide combat for values of the humane society. This combat demands the recognition that these values are incompatible with the institutional setting of the coercive state-controlled and directed economy, and with manipulation of prices, values of capital, and wages by the state. The struggle for freedom and human dignity may be lost by the resourcefulness of the enemy. It will most definitely be lost by compromising on values and institutions. The Free World cannot prevail by accepting 50 per cent of the economic devices of communism.

## Integrity of the Currency

One of the most vital needs for strategy of the Free World is the protection of the integrity and free convertibility of the currencies of the leading industrial nations, their mutual obligation to guarantee such stability, and the abandonment of fiscal and monetary policies which generate or contribute to inflation. This is for no country more mandatory than for the United States as the strongest military and economic power, and the foremost industrial country. It is inconceivable that the leadership and prestige of this country could remain unimpaired if its currency were to become so weak that its free convertibility would be impeded or that it would have to be devaluated. The US dollar is the standard measure of value of the Free World. Hence, the first strategic necessity today is the improvement of the balance of payments with all appropriate policies. No force is more corrosive to the faith of the people in the fairness and equity of the free-enterprise economy than inflation and insecurity of their currency. Among the conditions which corroded the moral foundations on which the German people, their government, and their economy stood after World War I, and among the causes which spread nihilism and which prepared total disaster, inflation was by far the most destructive one. In some Latin American countries inflation spreads the suspicion among the masses that the state and the economy are a conspiracy of a few against the majority.

In a country whose individual citizens hold the major part of all life insurance written in the world, the automatic and irrevocable change of long-term obligations such as mortgages, savings bonds, and industrial bonds could not but have a profound impact on the fighting morale in the Cold War.

Improvement of the balance-of-payments situation demands a disciplined household of the government at all levels, and, in general, curtailment of the outflow of certain funds and the increase of the inflow of others. The latter could be achieved by a substantial expansion of foreign-trade earnings from exports of industrial goods and of such services as tourist travel and accommodations, patent licenses, and research services. In spite of the concentration of other writers on this subject, reference to this priority requirement of economic strategy seemed justified since many specific suggestions which follow depend on this prerequisite. In the context of improvements in the balance of payments, special reference shall be made to agriculture and food in advanced as well as underdeveloped countries, particularly in view of the fact that, among the remedial actions, some are not yet fully recognized in their importance.

## Disengagement from Price-Fixing for Agriculture

In the United States, as well as in Western Europe, farm income is being supported by price-fixing. This policy amounts to a serious continual drain on the treasuries. The use of acreage allotments as practiced for nearly 30 years in the United States protects high-cost producers, freezes the locations of crop production in high-cost areas, and creates unwanted surpluses which must be exported with subsidies or given away. As a means of improving income of small farmers the policy of price-fixing is ineffective in view of the small volume of their sales. The worst features of the static government manipulation of the prices of major agricultural commodities are: (a) weakening of the otherwise excellent capacity of American agriculture to earn foreign exchange as a commercial competitor in the world market; (b) entrenchment of this sort of protectionist policy in the importing European countries to the detriment of US agricultural exports; (c) further bleeding of the Treasury through the necessity of subsidizing manufacturing industries which use agricultural raw materials, e.g., cotton, at prices above those of the world market; (d) entanglement in more and more embarrassing contradictions in foreign economic policies and weakening the defense of the free-enterprise economy as the greatest asset of the Free World.

A correction of the costly deadlocked farm policy through giving the Federal Government the power to control supply via compulsory commodity cartels would force a deformation of our agriculture from a still relatively free and competitive enterprise economy to a much less flexible, bureaucratically-controlled economy. Such policy would inevitably lend support to the entrenchment of protectionist and autarkic farm policies in other industrial countries. This would throttle the Free World's expansion of production and trade, and thus assist Soviet strategy. Sound strategy demands the return of US agriculture to a competitive-market economy. This would deliver our efficient commercial farm enterprises and the equally efficient food-processing industries from all acreage-allotment and marketing-quota fetters and restrictions. It also would permit all of these enterprises to compete freely without subsidies in the domestic and in the world markets.

It must not be overlooked that in the Free World as well as in the Communist Bloc the roots of the coercive state-managed economy are lodged in the agricultural sphere.

Unfortunately, the unwillingness in the United States and Western Europe to return to the principles of freedom of private initiative and enterprise in domestic agricultural policies has led at this critical juncture to the renewed attempt at extending the fixing of prices and control of supply by government to the world market. The fixing of prices of agricultural commodities by international commodity agreements offers, at best, temporary relief from the results of overproduction, but it cannot provide effective aid to the development of underdeveloped countries. On the contrary. Since international price "stabilization" adopts the monopolistic philosophy and policy of the power state and methods which belong in its arsenal, it weakens the position of the industrially-advanced countries in all underdeveloped countries. International commodity agreements amount to compulsory cartels which try to keep price movements within limits, particularly downward ones. This is done by buying and selling stocks, export quotas, and production controls. All these methods can at best mitigate short-term effects of excess supplies. However, single-commodity cartel policies affect the price relationships to all other commodities in the countries of origin and of destination, and thereby cause unexpected further long-term dislocations and maladjustments which often do irreparable harm to the interest of the producers and the countries which the agreements try to support. For commodities such as wool, cotton, jute, sisal, fibers, or natural rubber, pegging of prices defeats them in their competition with synthetic products. Pegging of prices by international commodity agreements in some signatory countries offers a powerful incentive to outsiders for starting or expanding production in other countries. Pegged prices tend to shift consumption to substitutes and to reduce it.

Since it is inescapable logic that the leading nations of the Free World must adhere to the economic principles which give them the greatest advantage over Sino-Soviet policies, the dubious course of aid to underdeveloped countries via international commodity agreements has one other side effect that is most damaging. The necessity to control production leads inevitably to more government controls on farms in all signatory

countries, to progressive imposition of restraints on the efficient
low-cost producers, and to fettering increases in productivity.

The greatest weakness of Soviet economic policies is the synthetic manufacture of price structures by decree of planning
agencies. The greatest potential asset of the Free World is that
price structures are flexible and in constant flux in response to
changing input-output ratios, to changes in supply and demand,
and to many other factors. The idea of assisting export earnings
of underdeveloped countries by generating artificial price structures is not compatible with the Western strategy of real development aid to the primary-products-exporting countries. Such
strategy requires the removal of trade barriers between advanced
and developing countries, and the opening of a two-way traffic
in the exchange of primary products and manufactured goods.
The advanced countries can attain far more growth by exporting
capital goods than by protecting their primary production
against competition.

### Emergence of a New Foreign Trade Pattern

The reorganization of the foreign trade pattern in the Free
World, which is well on its way within the European Economic
Community (EEC) with the potential entry of Britain as a
member, forces the clarification of the course of foreign economic
policy of the leading industrial countries of the Free World.
These new trade patterns and the enormous economic expansion
in quite a few of those industrial countries is more important
than any of the economic events inside the Sino-Soviet Bloc.

Protected by the nuclear shield of NATO, Western Europe has
made considerable progress toward gradual economic and political
integration. The Treaty of Rome of 1957 and its prompt ratification by France, Germany, Italy, and the Benelux countries has
fortified the strength of the West. The functioning of the three
branches of the supranational preliminary government of the
six federated countries has improved the political solidarity of
these nations in their defense against the Communist menace.
Consolidation of cooperation among the Six has induced Britain
to form under the Treaty of Stockholm a customs union with
the three Scandinavian countries and Austria, Switzerland, and
Portugal.

The EEC is a great asset to the United States, the British
Commonwealth, and Japan in spite of a number of undissolved

conflicting views on specific issues and procedures. The economy of the EEC member states has not only grown enormously, but it also has begun to integrate. Their currencies have become hard and freely convertible, and are today secured by substantially greater gold and foreign-exchange reserves than those of the United States. The greatest impediments to international trade, quantitative controls, have been abolished except for some agricultural products, and internal tariffs have been cut by 50 per cent. Moreover, the progress of the EEC has induced the customs union of the "Outer Seven" to cut their internal tariffs also by 50 per cent. The six EEC countries are equalizing their common outside tariffs and have actually lowered them for a few commodities.

In weighing the implications of the Treaty of Rome from the standpoint of economic strategy, it seems important to notice that—aside from creating a free trade area for 180 million people—it prohibits quantitative restrictions of trade with third countries and any other measures of equivalent effect. The Treaty provides further for the following:

a) Free movement of workers within the Community, the right of establishment of enterprises across the borders of member states, the free exchange of services, and the free movement of capital;

b) A common transport policy;

c) A common energy policy;

d) A common agricultural policy;

e) A common foreign economic policy toward other countries;

f) Common rules concerning competition, harmonization of taxes, and legislation;

g) Coordination of monetary and contra-cyclical policies;

h) Establishment of a European Social Insurance Fund and harmonization of social-security policies;

i) Establishment of a European Investment Bank.

These provisions indicate the determination of the original member nations to actually integrate their economies. Since the Treaty of Rome has no provisions for its renunciation, it seems justified to consider the EEC as having passed the point of no return, the temporary failure of the negotiations for Britain's entry notwithstanding.

For the economic strategy of combatting communism, it is another decisive achievement that the Japanese market economy has gained extraordinary strength. While industrial production of the EEC has reached an index figure of nearly 200 in 1962 (1953 = 100), it reached roughly 350 in Japan.

The great achievements in strengthening the economic position of the Free World's advanced industrial countries have, however, also the inevitable result that in the further expansion of production and trade competition of industrial enterprises in international trade for markets within the Free World will become more exacting and severe.

If Great Britain and her EFTA partners should eventually become members of the EEC, the resulting common market with 325 million people could absorb nearly half of the world's imports. For its own sake as well as that of the Free World, the enormously resourceful economy of the United States should expand its share in foreign trade and negotiate the freest possible access to the EEC market. Any retreat into more protectionism and isolation could only play into the hands of the Soviets. Economic strategy requires therefore that imaginative and resourceful diplomacy use all available leverages in matters of mutual security, foreign relations, foreign trade, and foreign aid to open more foreign markets for American and other Free World exports. Negotiation of mutual tariff concessions across the board by the Government is only one part of the initiative required. To a larger extent the expansion of foreign markets is a challenge to private initiative. It must be achieved by more effective marketing and overseas merchandizing operations of American export industries as a sequence to increased private American investment and banking operations abroad. For unique or new products or for superior qualities of export commodities, a duty of 10 or 12 per cent need not be a real obstacle to much larger exports in a foreign market. Far more serious obstacles are all sorts of hidden protective devices such as packaging or transport regulations, administrative delays at entry, etc. It is the task of export industries to alert their government to such discrimination and to obtain its aid in their removal.

However, it must also be seen in proper perspective that unless all of the leading industrial nations of the West cooperate in the direction of freer exchange of goods and services among themselves and the less developed areas, serious repercussions will emerge. Some of the industrial countries which must export some 20 or 30 per cent of their GNP will be forced to expand trade with the Sino-Soviet Bloc. This holds as much for Japan as it does for the West European countries. It must also be con-

sidered that an optimum expansion of trade among the leading
industrial countries of the West can be attained neither by
bilateral arrangements nor by time-consuming item-for-item
negotiations. Concessions by reduction of tariffs across the board
and multilateral sharing of benefits on the basis of the Most
Favored Nation clause are the more effective methods. Yet, the
more such concessions expose to severe competition industries
which were effectively protected for long periods, the more it
seems advisable to provide for a gradual reduction of tariffs
with a fixed time schedule of several years.

The aggregate economic growth on both sides of the Atlantic
and in Japan will outdistance the results of forced industrialization within the Sino-Soviet Bloc still further if private enterprises are encouraged to invest freely across the national boundaries even more than they have already done. Such initiative of
American firms in different parts of Europe and in Japan, of
European firms in the United States, Canada, and Japan, and
similarly of Japanese firms in Europe and in the United States
promises to expand productivity by blending advanced techniques, procedures, and innovations, and by promoting the
mobility of capital as well as research and skilled personnel
within the industrial heartland.

## The Underdeveloped Part of the Western World

The greatest prospect lies, however, in joint ventures of enterprises from two or more industrially advanced countries in
underdeveloped countries. They are the other part of the Free
World which is particularly subject to world-wide yet intensive
Sino-Soviet economic, military, and ideological offensive. There
the conflict poses much more difficult problems for economic
strategy.

These countries comprise all the geography outside the Sino-
Soviet Bloc and outside the Free World's developed industrial
heartland. Among their population are 850 million persons who
formerly lived under colonial government, and since the end of
World War II have become citizens of independent countries of
Asia and Africa. But the fact that they are all considered as
underdeveloped or retarded in industrial development must not
conceal the even more pertinent fact that there are enormous
differences among these countries in every respect, from old ones
with a long history of independence to even much older ones

with enormously large populations which became independent
only since World War II, and to some where primitive tribal
societies are still under colonial administration. Among these
industrially less developed countries are some with a much
improved per capita income and prosperity while others suffer
from utter poverty and stagnation; there are some with developed
oil resources and big foreign exchange earnings; there are some
others which make great strides in industrialization; and there
are finally quite a few with overwhelmingly agrarian rural
economies. Some of these countries have good government, civil
order, sanitation, and education, while others have corrupt
government, gross injustice, insecurity, and near chaos. To
cover all these diverse conditions with world-wide statistical
averages of dubious conceptual adequacy, it serves only to obscure
the nature of specific problems of economic strategy for positive
action.

Yet there are certain common economic traits. In spite of
varying degrees of industrialization the underdeveloped countries
are all exporters of primary products and importers of industrial
products, including particularly producers' capital goods. In a
substantial number of these countries, particularly in the tropical
and subtropical climates, the major part of the population lives
on small farms, is politically and socially agitated and restless,
and expects and demands the benefits which can flow only from
economic development and social change. These vast areas with
mostly high rates of population growth are particularly exposed
to indigenous political and social unrest, to the voracious appetite
for power of ambitious politicians, and to Communist infiltration.
All of these areas need an increase in the productivity of farm
labor which in turn requires a substantial increase in the output
of food, feed, and fibers per man-year of the labor force employed
in agriculture.

### Ranches, Plantations, and Family Farms

In most of these areas certain commercial crops are produced
with hired labor by highly capitalized and competently managed
large-scale enterprises, the plantations, while some of the plantation crops as well as a multitude of others are also produced by
small family farms. The poverty of masses of small farmers
leads many policy advisers to the conclusion that this poverty
must be overcome by agrarian reform. It is widely asserted that

the underdeveloped part of the Free World cannot begin to attain economic growth unless there is a thorough agrarian reform with distribution of the land among landless farm workers and small holders. It is also widely taken for granted by many policy advisers that on behalf of greater equality for the small farmer the large-scale enterprises must be liquidated, although in the United States there is no such policy for economic development. On the contrary, the merger of the land of two or more operating units into one, and the increasing acreage of the statistical average farm, are a dominant characteristic of increasing agricultural productivity in the United States in recent decades. There is no question that a great deal of reform is necessary in many of those countries. However, instead of social and economic change that amounts to orderly reform, a great many crash programs of agrarian reform turn the countries concerned merely to bloody revolutions which end in dictatorship or communism.

In considering the agrarian policy issues of underdeveloped countries, it is important to realize that in semi-arid climates the main remunerative agricultural land utilization other than irrigated crop farming is extensive grain production or even more extensive grazing of cattle and sheep, or a combination between grain farming and grazing. If the vast expanse of such lands, which in the Free World amount to several times the acreage of all arable land, shall not go entirely to waste, it calls for very large units of ranches or *estancias* with very large capital investment in land, fences, and livestock, and very few hired ranch hands employed. This applies to the western half of the United States and Canada as much as it does to Latin America, Australia, or East and South Africa. To bring the size of such units into comparison with intensive crop farming in humid areas or with irrigation farming in arid areas serves only to confuse the issues of land reform. However, intensive animal husbandry fits very well into small farms with intensive crop production on arable land in humid climates or on irrigated land.

## The Issue of Agrarian Reform

The whole range of problems connected with rural development and agrarian reform is an ideological and economic battleground where the West has a very good chance to lose the battle for freedom and human dignity by confusion about basic principles and by too ready an acceptance of seemingly plausible yet vastly oversimplified and ill-advised solutions, as it was lost on the mainland of China by supporting the supposedly benevolent "agrarian reformers." Latin America is the region where the danger is most acute for unwittingly giving comfort and support to the enemy by advocating crash programs of agrarian reform which lead to revolution.

A few basic observations may serve as guideposts of orientation for constructive agrarian policies toward the underdeveloped countries:

Land as such produces neither income nor is it wealth per se. It offers an opportunity to apply management, labor, and capital. To carve up productive large-scale plantation enterprises which are well managed, are properly capitalized, have a high productivity, and provide steady employment at competitive wages; and to distribute their land in small parcels among people without managerial talents, farming skills, or capital is the opposite of what economic development demands. The destruction of the large and efficiently operating private farm enterprises, and the parceling of their land is precisely the recipe prescribed by Stalin in his book "Lessons in Leninism," namely, the first necessary stage of the Communist revolution which, according to Party doctrine, must precede the second stage of collectivization. Political hostility to plantations has ruined the world's formerly leading cane sugar industry in Java, and it impedes a potentially prosperous agricultural development in the Philippine Islands.

### Symbiosis between Plantations and Small Farmers

Sound economic strategy of the West calls for a more rational solution. Since the plantations are, in many underdeveloped countries, the only enterprises which have full command of up-to-date production techniques and of scientific research, these enterprises should be enabled and induced to share the benefits of their modern farming methods, processing plants, and marketing facilities with small farmers, and to act as their extension service agency. Such symbiosis between a plantation and a large number of small farmers can be organized either on the basis of individual contracts, or it can be set up in the form of a corporation in which the plantation and a cooperative association of small farmers would be equal partners. Such an arrangement would be particularly attractive in all cases where the specialized production of a farm commodity requires a processing factory, or packing houses and elaborate shipping installations, as is the case for sugar cane and sugar beets, oil palms and coconuts, bananas, pineapples, and many tree fruits, nuts, and vegetables.

To provide by legislation for such symbiosis between small farmers and modern large-scale farm enterprises or agricultural corporations seems just as important as legislation passed throughout the world in the latter part of the last century on behalf of the farmers' cooperative association as an additional form of corporative private enterprise.

## Effective Aid to Small Farms

In large areas of the underdeveloped countries it is apparent that even under the most favorable circumstances of industrialization and expansion of non-agricultural employment, a major part of the population will for many decades continue to earn its livelihood on small family farms. To assist these people in their effort to improve their living conditions and real income ought to be a primary concern of economic and social strategy.

Unfortunately, reasonable action is impeded by too many popular but erroneous assumptions.

Many advisers on policies concerning aid to underdeveloped countries take it for granted that:

a)  The income of small farms consists exclusively of products sold in the market;

b)  Small farms are bare of capital;

c)  Small farmers are unable to form capital;

d)  The most generally needed and most effective aid to small farms is the enlargement of their acreage;

e)  Farm tenancy is a destructive form of land tenure, cannot be improved, and must be replaced by ownership.

These assumptions are not only demonstrably false in principle, but they actually obscure the opportunities for genuine improvement. Small family farms yield in terms of real income, aside from cash sales of products, home-consumed food, housing, fuel, and potentially some clothing as well as transportation. How good or how poor the aggregate real income is depends on the skills; work discipline; the art of good husbandry; the existing capital in real estate and improvements; the dead and live inventory; the stores of food, feed, and seed; as well as on the opportunity to earn enough cash to purchase or rent means of production such as tools, implements, or fertilizer. The concept of a farm being totally void of capital is sheer fiction, no matter how small or how poor the farm may be. Equally erroneous is the notion that small family farmers are unable to form capital. Blindness to the opportunities for forming capital on even very primitive farms excludes from development policies one of the great sources of wealth in countries stricken with rural poverty. Raising of draft animals or breeding stock of food-producing animals is the formation of capital. So is the clearance of woodland, the digging of drainage ditches, wells, improving walks and paving roads, the planting of shrubs and trees. In fact, these improvements of productive real estate are considered vital capital investments in most advanced economies. A large part of the early wealth in European countries as well as in the United States was formed by farmers when these countries were still industrially underdeveloped.

From the absurd claim that the rural farm population cannot form capital, many development strategists jump to the non sequitur that therefore the government must form the capital for industrial development by taxing the farmers via foreign exchange controls and multiple exchange rates, or via government purchase of farm commodities at stable prices. Such stable prices then serve the purpose of confiscating a substantial part of the farm income. This kind of strategy for industrial development via the forced-march tour is perfectly aligned with the unchanged Soviet doctrine. It amounts to the abrogation of the entire philosophy of the Free World, it undermines most effectively the economic philosophy of the humane society, and it prepares underdeveloped countries for a materialistic state capitalism. This sort of strategy deprives the rural farm population of the opportunity to improve its real income for the sake of assumed future benefits to others. Besides this immeasurable harm, the squeezing of income from the farm population has the logical result of preventing or crippling the increase in productivity of farm labor which is essential to economic growth. In justification of such coercive confiscation of farm income it is claimed that small farmers will use improved cash income only for senseless consumption or for working less. The evidence in most parts of the world is different. Small farmers acquire bicycles, sewing machines, better work clothes, farm tools, better breeding stock, radios, and a multitude of goods and services which all tend to improve their work capacity as well as their level of living.

By comparison with the interwar period, the present energy-supply situation in the Free World is radically different. The formerly unexpected overabundance of oil and natural gas has led to an enormous expansion of the petrochemical industries, to a decline in transportation costs, continuous price decline of plant nutrients, and an overabundance of their supply. Nitrogenous fertilizers and irrigation water are becoming available to farmers in all parts of the Free World at declining costs in terms of marginal product. The progress in plant breeding, in chemical weed and pest control, combined with lower prices of commercial fertilizer, of small, inexpensive two-cycle combustion engines, and inexpensive centrifugal pumps for irrigation offers the opportunity for intensifying the production of crops, animal feed, and animal products. Since on small farms interest and depreciation of real estate, work stock, and labor must be considered as overhead or fixed costs, the adding of purchased inputs such as seeds, fertilizer, pesticides, and energy for irrigation lowers the costs per unit of product.

Therefore, the greatest aid to family farms is the improvement of their supply with the "small means" for increasing their productivity by making production credit available, and by improvement of their access to urban markets where they can sell their increased output and buy the goods and services they need. Increased efficiency of crop production by use of better seeds, more water, more fertilizer, more pesticides, more weed-killers leads to a higher yield per acre, and this is equivalent to enlarging the farm while lowering costs. The construction of all-weather roads and bus service is the greatest development aid for backward and poor, rural communities.

Since an underdeveloped economy suffers typically from underemployment or seasonal unemployment of farm people, improvement of their income must begin with making constructive use of the idle time of this large part of the labor force. This can be done on the farm as well as in part-time work off the farm. If even in advanced industrial countries the weight of food in the consumer cost-of-living index (including beverages and tobacco) has a range between 29 and 38, while in some fairly progressive underdeveloped countries it exceeds 60 for the non-farm population, then it seems worthy of maximum effort to improve this part of farm family income to its optimum by diversification of food and feed crops and animal products, and by improving home-economic skills. Beyond that family farmers should be assisted in improving their housing, their furniture, and clothing by developing their vocational woodworking and metalworking skills, and by making better tools available to them via effective merchandizing of such imports. Vocational training at the apprentice level in the villages promises almost immediately effective development aid for the greatest number of the rural population. Such training for both sexes will simultaneously make the farm people more adaptable to work off the farm.

Since gaining time is essential, it is faulty strategy for underdeveloped countries to rely in the development of human resources primarily on education and research at the highest level at the expense of building up from the grassroots. All underdeveloped countries have the unique opportunity of utilizing the results of enormously costly agricultural and technical research undertaken in the advanced countries free of charge. The same applies to the importation of farm equipment. However, it would be a wise policy decision not to jump from the draft animal and oxcart level of farm transportation to the immediate abolition of draft animals and motorization of farms with tractors and trucks. Instead, underdeveloped countries should take the step of increasing the effective draft power of their draft animals by better feeding and by adopting wagons built from used truck chassis with roller bearing axles and pneumatic tires. This stage which has preceded the full mechanization of farm transport in all European countries requires far less of the scarce and high-priced capital while it increases the farm efficiency very substantially by making the animal draft power 30 to 40 per cent more effective. It also avoids setting labor free at a rate which is beyond the capacity of the urban markets to absorb. To set unusable labor free at the expense of costly capital equipment raises costs and diminishes income of farm people.

The most important decision for underdeveloped countries concerns the necessity to establish an economic climate that attracts the investment of indigenous as well as foreign capital. Private foreign-investment capital has the enormous advantage, compared with government-to-government loans or grants, that it brings with it the managerial experience and the technical skills that are so essential to economic development. Since such capital investors take the risk of losing if their new enterprises are unable to compete and to yield interest, amortization, and depreciation, the host country has the best assurance for continuity of development and the avoidance of raising white elephants. The national interest of the capital-importing countries can well be satisfied by offering shares in such foreign investment to citizens of the host country and eventual sale of the remaining stock.

### Supplying Land for Settlers and Small Farmers

The necessary confidence of the business community and private investors in the economic stability can easily be undermined by the way in which an agrarian reform is handled. The inadvisability of carving up efficient plantations has already been stressed. The most natural and least controversial procedure for satisfying the land hunger of settlers and internal colonization is the alienation of publicly owned virgin fertile land in the public domain. This may require investment in the construction of roads or the granting of concessions for construction of water dams for power and irrigation use. In wooded areas or areas with mineral deposits it is possible to have even the roads built by private investors in fulfillment of long-term forest or mining concessions.

If no suitable land is available in the public domain and privately owned land shall be provided for settlement of farmers or for enlargement of too small farm units, the best method is the purchase of land by a colonization bank or a settlement agency which buys in the farm real estate market whenever entire landed estates or parts of their acreage are offered. The next alternative is expropriation by condemnation procedures with due process of law. In that case protection of the confidence in the security of private property by all parties concerned requires prompt, fair, and adequate compensation of the former owner in such terms and with such means of payment that the acquisition does not amount to concealed partial or total confiscation. Such confiscatory policies do not deserve the name of agrarian reforms. They are plainly acts of revolution and violence and never fail to do immeasurable harm to the general economic development of the country for prolonged periods.

Fair and adequate compensation has the advantage that the indemnified former owners will have a keen incentive to invest such funds in remunerative enterprises. In that case the funds will tend to accelerate the process of private industrialization which, by decentralized decision-making and risk-bearing, is prone to lead to less business failures than under centralized expansion of public enterprises.

Wise economic strategy of the industrially-advanced countries in their policy of aid to underdeveloped countries calls for the public insurance of a part of the political risk of foreign investment and the exclusion from such insurance of countries which expropriate private foreign property and do not take promptly steps to provide fair and adequate compensation. The provision of the Hickenlooper Amendment to the Foreign Assistance Act which cuts such countries off from US foreign aid should be adopted jointly by the leading industrial countries.

The strategy of wise and successful agrarian reform requires the cautious and gradual amendment of the institutional framework of the underdeveloped economies. This applies first of all to the institution of private property in land which comprises the right to encumber, to divide, to lease, to grant easements, to sell, and the obligation to pay land taxes. Reform requires corrective amendments with due respect for the secondary effects. Instead of condemning farm tenancy, wise reforms of legislation have in many countries not only corrected the defects in the performance of both parties, landlords and tenants, but they have made farm leases one of the socially and economically most progressive arrangements for efficient land utilization. The same applies to the supposed innate evils of farm labor contracts on large-scale enterprises. In a number of underdeveloped countries in several continents, wise reforms have given the hired farm workers and their families more social security and more equitable wage schedules than those enjoyed by industrial workers in urban centers.

What is needed for wise reform is the hard work of resourceful lawyers, economists, sociologists, and bankers who have a full knowledge of the many alternatives which the rich historical experience of the advanced countries of the Free World has yielded.

# Discussion—Part IV

*Johnson:** Four issues that have been raised in most of the papers involve: the economics of our alliances; aid, trade and embargo in relation to Communist Bloc nations; aid and trade policies with the underdeveloped nations; and the Common Market as an ally or third force.

## Economics of Alliance

*Johnson:* I would like to begin issue one by asking Dr. Morgenstern to comment upon the economics of alliance. We will subsequently ask Dr. Possony to comment on the statement from his paper.

Another, most serious, lack of cooperation shows up in our inadequate use of the scientific talent of Europe for purposes of development of new weapons systems in regard to the space effort. It would have been possible and should be possible in the future to pay proper respect to these matters by organizing laboratories which would be jointly run by Europeans and Americans and possibly even Japanese in order to promote the development of technology in all fields, instead of holding the effort within the bounds of the United States which is already so far committed in devoting scientific and management talent to the matters of defense.

\* \* \* \*

Other difficulties that stand in the way of a wide distribution of weapons production according to the specific talents of the members of the Alliance are, of course, that weapons production requires very often secrecy, a flow of strategic information—all of which is very difficult to achieve across national borders.

Oskar Morgenstern

The pooling of the entire Alliance's technological, industrial, and financial strength, and the establishment of a North American-European defense community embracing well over 400 million people, therefore has become the paramount strategic task of the current decade.

Stefan Possony

* Dr. Thomas F. Johnson, Director of Research, the American Enterprise Institute for Public Policy Research, chairman of discussions in Part IV and Part V.

*Morgenstern:* This excerpt from my paper does not constitute the principal point which I have tried to make, but it is important and one which was discussed by coincidence in the previous panel. We are not using the scientific intellectual talent throughout the Western world in the manner in which it would be possible and desirable. I would include also Japan as a source for very high technological and scientific talent. All this should be brought to bear much more on the intellectual, technological, and military output of the Western world. But, of course, in order to do so it would be necessary to educate the NATO governments and the industry in NATO countries much more to understand what science can do for them, and in which way there is an interplay possible of the type we have here in this country between scientific workers and the military, for example.

My second statement deals with weapons production. If we allow production to go on as under a free-trade arrangement, then cars are produced where that is best done and glass and other things elsewhere. But if weapons are considered, then it is obvious we have not yet made the sort of integration which we theoretically could make. For example, let us say we could produce a rifle in Belgium instead of in this country and artillery somewhere else, and perhaps radar sets somewhere else instead of having it done nationally.

Another point I was asked to write on is the question of the distribution of burden to be carried by the members of the Western Alliance. Now, that is a very difficult thing to determine. There exists no absolutely satisfactory and generally accepted economic criterion to compare burdens, especially when these are not expressable only in monetary terms. Even if that is the case, it is difficult to say whether the same amount of money means the same burden and sacrifice in different countries. We have tried to find some measures for it, and one measure which is so frequently used is to take the share in government expenses assumed by military expenses. That is not very reliable, because the budgets are so different, and many defense expenditures are scattered throughout budgets in all countries. Many of ours are hidden somewhere else.

There are means. One of the most popular is to look at the gross national product and also to compare the success of these alliances by comparing the growth rates, which are the rates of change, from year to year, of GNP. Growth rates are extraordinarily shaky things. There is a certain obsession, to my mind, among economists with GNP and with growth rates, and yet not one has taken the trouble to look really at the validity of these rates. The GNP numbers are taken as if they were free from error. That is something which I find very difficult to accept.

We find that growth rates are said to vary from 3.2 to 3.4 or 3.6 to 3.9 per cent, etc., and if a change of this kind occurs, this is considered to be either a success or not a success. However, if you merely make the assumption that GNP is subject to some error, some measurement error, even of one per cent only, in each year, then you are immediately in very grave difficulties, and this applies to comparing burdens.

If anybody has any familiarity with physics, he will know and remember that a 3% measurement, that means 3% accuracy, is a very fine measurement in physics. There are much finer measurements, of course, but that is a very respectable measurement.

Assume you have only a 1% error in GNP in two years. Suppose you have a 3% growth rate, and you measure it when you look at the face value of the figures. If you have a 1% error—a plus 1% in one and a minus 1% in the other, in the successive year—instead of 3%, you get 5%. If you reverse merely the signs of the errors, you get a 1% growth rate. That is only for 1% error. I ask how you measure something as complicated as GNP with only 1% error? It is an incredible measurement and an incredible thing to assume this. In fact, of course, as studies of various kinds dealing with national income and GNP have shown, the error components are vastly greater than that. Therefore, GNP growth rate measures and all the international comparisons of this kind are subject to extraordinary doubt. What I have said now applies to year-to-year measurements or comparisons. GNP figures really aren't useful for making measurements of burden. Therefore, we must look at other things.

If we look at the burdens borne by the different partners of the Alliance again, we find that we have other possibilities of estimating, for example, military service. In the United States twenty-four months is obligatory, in the United Kingdom no obligatory service, in Germany and France eighteen months, and so on. If we apply measures of that kind we do get a difference, a significant difference, and we find what I think inspection would confirm, namely, that the Western European countries aren't pulling their weight. They are obsessed by their prosperity, by the recovery from the damages of war, which is understandable, by the good life which they would like to lead, and they want to leave the burden to the United States.

While that is so, and is unpleasant, there is also a certain justification for it, though it may not sound very correct. The justification is that one feels that in an alliance there is a certain core, and the core has the burden to bear. It has a greater responsibility, while the others are only associated members; and in the comparison of burdens, therefore, this would have to be considered also. While it doesn't lead to numerical measures, if you study this entire picture, it would still come up that the United States should make a much greater effort to impress upon the members of the Alliance the need to raise their input into the entire effort which the Western world is making, or should be making, so that the contribution each makes will be proper.

Another great difficulty is that the present weapons situation —that is to say, the possibility of instantaneous conflict—makes it impossible for the phenomenon which one can otherwise observe in history, namely that one starts out with a small alliance and builds up as the conflict progresses and one sees which way the conflict is progressing. That will not be possible and, therefore, alliances which are valuable at present are more difficult to manage.

## Long-Range Strategy

*Brandt:* Perhaps it might be useful to bring this discussion into the broader perspective of what the long-range strategy on economic affairs in such an alliance ought to be: I would like to indicate some of the apprehensions I have at the moment with reference to this strong Western economy in Western Europe, Japan, and the United States, and simultaneously the weaknesses of the Soviet-Chinese economy.

There is a considerable danger that one is too much carried away by the optimism of this present prevalence. If strategy means anything, it is to prepare for all possible situations in which things may develop not quite so satisfactorily; in other words, to consider the risk that is involved.

What is at the moment a crucial new aspect is that, while this development over the last eight, ten, or twelve years has been all in our favor, since 1958 a change has come about which indicates that we may face, inside the Alliance, quite a few difficulties. One of the first necessities—to make the leading power of the West, with its enormously powerful economy, as strong as possible—would be to see to it that this country is not inadvertently slipping into a situation which creates problems for its closest allies. That is the question of keeping the balance of payments of this country strong enough, so that the leading currency of the world is strong, freely convertible, and hard, and that there are no possibilities that, all of a sudden, developments bring us into a situation as happened in 1933, when suddenly the leading country in the world came to the point that it had to adjust its currency, which immediately led to the Economic Conference in London, and to breaking up the unity of many countries.

From 1933 to 1937, in spite of the coherence of all the ultimate interests, there were so many different policies that it did not do the countries any good. I believe our situation is completely different from the period of 1929 to 1933. But, if I may say so, I believe that there are some signs which indicate that it is not impossible that the Western world, particularly the Allies as I have just named them in their economic position, may face, in the next few years, very serious problems of a similar nature.

I want to refer to what we discussed on the first day: the question that, on the one hand, the Russian economy has this terrific problem of the large underdeveloped part of the world, which is China. The Western countries have something of a similar terrific load to carry. About 850 million people in the former colonial areas have received independence and the West has discharged the immediate responsibility for them. Simultaneously, it is implicit in this struggle that the advanced Western countries have still more responsibility to carry on their backs so that these areas of the world will not just fall into the Soviet orbit by their own deterioration. Here are serious, developing problems which, I would say, should be considered in the long-run strategy.

Even such an enormously strong economy as ours can ultimately drift into a situation in which this country is not as free as it should be in cooperation with its allies. This goes to the point of the competitive situation that exists. Our allies are all in the same position. They all have to export. They have to trade. Each country has still to balance its own payments. It has to maintain its currency, has to keep it freely convertible. If the situation that I see in the underdeveloped countries should continue as it has for the last six or seven years, with the indication that there is an overcapacity for raw materials, which has already created serious problems for quite lot of the these countries, and if there is a situation in which quite a few of the underdeveloped countries are drifting into insolvency, I believe it is highly desirable to see to it that the Western countries tackle these problems jointly.

The six EEC countries now have $16.8 billion of currency reserves. Ours are down to $15.8 billion and are still declining. I cannot conceive of the situation, if this drift goes on, in which we won't have very serious problems and need the closest cooperation with our allies on the other side of the Atlantic, as well as with Japan.

This simply reverts to what was discussed earlier. It requires respect, it requires partnership. We do not want to have any satellites. We want to have allies who stand on their own feet, who are strong, and who are respected. Since we are so much in the same boat it is necessary to join at this time to minimize the difficulties that I foresee.

*Possony:* My statement is more or less self-evident. We would have the greatest resources available and, after all, if you do have superior strength in a material sense, you have always a very good chance to win. Of course, this isn't all. I don't know whether Napoleon was right, measuring morale and materiel three to one, but one does need the materiel.

There was a point raised in the previous discussion: if we move out technologically better than we have, whether or not this wouldn't play into the hands of the Soviets. We have slowed down many of our technological programs deliberately in the hope that the technological race can be moderated. That is a vain hope, in my judgment, because you never know what is happening, because technology in many aspects is an impersonal force which develops.

Suppose that the technological race goes on being run very hard and suddenly the Soviets who, of course, also are using technology for the end-run type of strategy, move ahead. We have a second arrow for our bow here. That is intelligence. If, for example, we were to follow up Dr. Teller's space-system suggestion—Jim Atkinson also suggested it—or intelligence in a general way, we should be able to acquire the requisite knowledge with a reasonable lead-time, so that perhaps we can take countermeasures against what is developing.

It isn't necessarily implied in what I said that you use your R&D and move out automatically into production and deployment. Just because the military situation, from the technological point of view, is very fluid, you may have to cut down on some of the production elements and some of the deployment elements. The main thing is that you are able to move into production with the up-to-date weapons system which your R&D has provided, and also that you have the R&D capability to improvise countermeasures against whatever the enemy throws at you by surprise.

*Schelling:* I want to advert to two dilemmas I think we have in this matter of what Dr. Possony calls pooling the alliance resources. One is that we continually try to get European partners to put more money into defense, as I think we should try, and as I think they should do. But, to do it, just as at home, requires a kind of exhortation that thrives on strategically oversimplified, dramatized threats. That is to say, to get the Europeans to put more into defense, whether it is nuclear weapons programs, or conventional forces, or whatever it may be, we must continually dramatize to them how weak Western Europe is militarily and how imminent is the threat of Soviet attack, how the Soviets can win hands down, and how much, therefore, the West should be afraid of war.

If that weren't necessary for the sake of getting people to put up money, I think it would be very helpful for NATO planning to go on the assumption that the defense problem has been solved, and that there are going to be a lot of problems other than defense. I wouldn't quite call them offense, but they deal with responses to circumstances that do not reflect a premeditated Soviet westward attack. It is politically very difficult to look at these, because the members of the Alliance do not have the same political interests.

We might have to do a little bit what the Chinese and the Russians do, which is to pick a proxy to argue with. Take a contingency in Yugoslavia, for example, because it is embarrassing to plan on comparable things in East Germany. I would like to get NATO planning more oriented toward the contingencies that I think are likely to confront it in the next eight or ten years, for which it really isn't oriented. For some thirteen years, in order to stiffen everybody's back, we and everybody else had to insist that the danger is a deliberate Soviet westward attack. As I said earlier, I think this is the one danger we are reasonably well prepared against, in terms of deterrence.

We have another dilemma, which relates to the pooling question. I don't know how far I would personally go with the active-defense, passive-defense program for the United States that Dr. Teller has described, say, $20 billion for shelters, $10 billion for stockpiling, $20 or $30 billion for ballistic-missile defenses. But, I would like to go a long way.

Is it likely that the Europeans and the Canadians and the Japanese will invest enough in active and passive defense to have anything comparable to what the United States could have at the end of eight to ten years by way of protection against Soviet anti-population attacks? My feeling is that it is unlikely. I imagine that it would be unwise for them to try to, in terms of resource limitations and other things they ought to be doing. The question I raise is: how far can we carry a pretense that we are genuinely a partnership with pooled resources, if the United States is putting, let us say, $50 billion into active and passive defenses over the next eight or ten years, explaining it to the Americans in terms of a high degree of protection that is insisted on as being necessary, which the Europeans and the Japanese and probably the Canadians will have no expectation of accomplishing themselves? I think this is a real dilemma in terms of the appearance of a US go-it-alone active, passive-defense program.

I don't think this is an argument against an active, passive-defense program, but I think it is a genuine potential strain on the Alliance. We do not, and we will not, pool our resources in any such effective sense as would be required to make it look as though we do not discriminate in favor of Massachusetts as against Italy when it comes to ballistic-missile defenses.

*Johnson:* We will now move to a consideration of several statements from Dr. Schlesinger's paper.

### Assistance: Alliance- or Development-Oriented?

It may be noted that some of the tensions which exist between an alliance-oriented and a development-oriented aid program have been eliminated by the displacement of SEATO by India as the principal bulwark against Chinese expansionism. These tensions have not been entirely eliminated, as the Pakistani response to American military assistance to India bears witness, yet the sharp conflict between the two patterns of assistance which existed in the late fifties no longer exists.

James R. Schlesinger

*Schlesinger:* During the 1950's one of the primary objectives of our foreign policy was to establish a ring of alliances around the Sino-Soviet Bloc. In addition to NATO, this included SEATO and, at the time, the Baghdad Pact. It seems to me that there was some tendency during this period to undercut the principal objective of building this alliance system by providing greater assistance to nations which were not only not allies but were, from time to time, actively hostile.

The principal nations excluded from the ring were, of course, India and Burma. At one time Secretary Dulles, shortly after announcing a $500 million assistance program for India, went to Teheran and, at the end of the conference, announced that $30 million would be distributed among the four non-American powers in the Baghdad Pact. I think the message of this particular allocation of resources was quite clear to the participants: that it did not pay, in crude terms, to be allied with the United States.

There were reasons, of course, for the emphasis on aid to India during this period. There were genuine doubts about the appropriateness of the alliance system. As Dr. Possony has observed, we may have believed that we were adding zeroes rather than adding sources of strength. In addition, India could, unlike some of the other nations, absorb aid. There were also two other factors. At the time there was an enthusiasm for India which approached a fad. India was the "awakening giant." India was the voice of the East. This fad, I think, has now passed. At the present time it is Africa which is the "awakening giant," rather than India. Another aspect is that Nehru was more "moral" than we were. This has a certain appeal to Anglo-American opinion. Nehru was able to do what many Americans would have preferred to do, and that was to reject the realities of power.

There are problems which are created by an alliance-oriented assistance program. We could have had an alliance-oriented assistance program which would have graduated aid in accordance with the degree of support for American foreign policy objectives. This would have implied that any nation that was allied with us would have fared no less well than any nation which was on the fence or was hostile. The problem with this kind of program, like the eighteenth-century subsidy system created by Walpole and Pitt, is that it is a system, in the main, of bribery. One accumulates as allies those who are happy to accept bribes during the period that the sun is shining, but who disappear on other occasions.

There are advantages, however, in such a system. It satisfies the need for having a relatively objective standard for distributing aid. It minimizes the mutual jealousies among aid recipients. Recipients may not agree with the objective standard by which aid is allocated; nevertheless, they can understand that standard. Essentially, this kind of aid program is short run. It is based on the premise that in the long run we cannot foretell how the pattern of hostilities and the pattern of international alliances will develop. It is a short-run system, designed to preserve the status quo. It is relatively riskless in the short run, in that it is designed to preserve the status quo.

In the last few years, quite clearly, the American Government has shifted completely away from an aid program based on the objective of encouraging alliances, and toward an aid program designed to assist in development. There are difficulties with this kind of program. For one thing, it may be a weak instrument of foreign policy. It is weak in that it discourages alliances. It may even be a treacherous instrument of foreign policy, in that those who are assisted may in the long run come down on the other side of the fence. Nevertheless, it seems to me that in the last two years we have clearly opted for this development-oriented assistance program, whatever its disadvantages, whatever the advantages of an alliance-oriented program.

One of the things that has become clear, however, is that the tensions between these two types of programs has diminished, because India is now the bulwark against Chinese aggression. Instead of India being the capricious critic of Western policy and the primary recipient of Western aid, it is now in a position where it is clearly not overtly critical of Western policy. It is, partially at least, in the Western camp, by force of necessity and, as a consequence, the jealousies which were developed during the fifties by the tendency to aid India to a greater extent than to aid our allies have tended to depart. They have not departed altogether, as the Pakistani reaction to the military assistance indicates, but many of these tensions have dissolved.

**Trade with Satellites**

*Johnson:* The second issue involves aid, trade, and embargoes with respect to the Communist Bloc nations. Dr. Schlesinger, we would like you to comment on this statement from your paper.

Moreover, by refraining from trade we forfeit an instrument which potentially could influence the Satellites either to resist Soviet pressures or to avoid provocations against the West. Since one of the assumptions of our foreign policy has been that the Satellites reluctantly accept Soviet dominance because they have no alternative, it would appear desirable that this awareness of various shades of gray existing in the Bloc be reflected in our trade policies (rather than accepting the uncritical notion that trade with Communists is reprehensible under any circumstances, etc.).

James R. Schlesinger

*Schlesinger:* This question concerns our fundamental objective in foreign policy. If we are going to have to live with the Satellites and live with the Soviet Union, if we have to accept a condition of peaceful coexistence or if we wish to accept a condition of peaceful coexistence, then we will have to learn to live with the members of the Bloc, and we want to create as favorable an environment in which to live as is possible. We want to establish an instrument by which we can bring low-level pressures to bear on the Satellites.

We would lose something if we eliminated trade entirely with the Satellites, if we reduced it to zero. If we eliminated trade entirely, we would clarify the issues for the Satellite countries. They would recognize that their future associations had to be completely with the Soviet Union. We want to be in a position in which we can influence them, and in order to be in such a position, they must have something to lose if they take action which is overtly hostile to us. If we refrain from trade, we forfeit a club for covertly threatening the Satellites. The club is the threat of curtailment of trade. We cannot threaten to curtail trade if trade is zero.

I am not suggesting that this is an overpowering instrument. It is certainly not one which will move mountains. But, it is a serviceable instrument. In 1948, when Poland and Czechoslovakia wished to join the Marshall Plan, they were forbidden by Stalin. It seems to me that some of those people who argue today that we should eliminate trade with the Satellites are finishing what Stalin wanted to accomplish in 1948, to wit, eliminating entirely the economic contacts between the more restless Satellites and the West.

If we eliminate trade, we will be easing the Soviet strategic problems, because we will be forcing the Satellite nations to integrate their economies into the Bloc more thoroughly than they would otherwise desire. We would be cooperating in smoothing the path for the achievement of Soviet objectives, and I think this would be a mistake.

*Taylor:* I suppose Dr. Schlesinger realizes there are some disadvantages in this too, and I would like very much to hear him give an equally brilliant account of these disadvantages of trading with the Satellites.

*Schlesinger:* The principal advantage is, as I suggested, that we do not anchor them into the Bloc. We have all along emphasized that the Satellites are to some extent unwilling. One of the dangers for the Soviet Union in taking provocative steps around Berlin is that the Satellites might grow restless and the Satellite empire might go up in smoke. This undoubtedly deters to some extent Soviet ambition around Berlin.

Now, what are the disadvantages? It seems clear that if we wish to bring pressure to bear, as Dr. Taylor has suggested, on the food supply in China, that by freely trading with the Satellites we will indirectly be providing food for China. Under normal circumstances the Satellites could purchase wheat in the United States or in Canada and could transship to China. I do not know, however, whether it is possible for us to prevent shipment of wheat to China. We would have to bring pressures to bear on Canada, and there are limits to American power.

There is no doubt that we could seize Canada, or we could cut off the outflow of American capital to Canada, or we could limit trade to Canada, but I do not think this is the appropriate mechanism; and unless we use as powerful a tool as this, I do not think that the Canadian Government is likely to bring to an end the sale of wheat to China. Their surplus problem is even more formidable than our own, and their resources obviously less. Under these circumstances they will welcome buyers wherever they come from.

There is no doubt, also, that international trade provides some expansion of gross national products. In the case of the Soviet Union, if we were to trade on an extensive basis, this would contribute somewhat to Soviet growth and would provide greater resources for the Soviet Union. But I think this is only a drop in the bucket, when you consider that this is an economy which is growing at six or seven per cent a year. This is only a marginal contribution to Soviet growth. I think that the advantages of maintaining contacts, particularly with the Satellites, outweigh any stimulation of growth in the Satellite economies or in the Soviet Union; but these are undoubtedly disadvantages.

*Taylor:* I think there are other disadvantages, perhaps, on the political side—the dangers of the growth of the illusion in the

United States that trade encourages good relations, and that the more we trade together, the more likely we are to get on together. This argument is very often used, but I think history is not very kind to the argument. Countries like the United Kingdom and Germany, for example, traded with each other a great deal, and have also fought each other a great deal. There are these dangers.

It all depends on your objectives in the Satellites, and which Satellites you are talking about. It is very difficult to generalize here. If your political objective is to disassociate them as much as possible from the Bloc, which I believe is what you said, I think you made out a very good case for doing it by trade. You could, of course, suggest another way to try to make the Satellites even more unhappy with their lot than they are now. This is to deny them as many advantages as possible and compel them to suffer all the disadvantages of living under the Soviet Union, on the theory that they are much more likely to revolt under these circumstances than if they are allowed to accept professorships in American universities, have cultural exchanges with the United States, and have trade. We can make out a case both ways, depending upon the Satellite you are talking about. I think Poland, for example, is a very different matter from some of the other European Satellites. You might make a special case for Poland.

I feel that we have tended perhaps in this conference to neglect the political side, which comes up very clearly, I think, in the question we were just discussing—the purposes of our own foreign aid. It seems to me that one of the major purposes, not always clearly stated, is strictly political. One of the greatest gains that we have had out of our foreign aid is the political gain. We have shown that our pluralistic society can adjust to the loss of empires and to a new relationship between former empires and colonies, and that that society can adjust to it rapidly, with dignity, and without the resentment and the desire to get back all the things that the Communists predicted and expected. This has been another nail in the coffin of Marxism-Leninism, and is an extremely important political objective which we have undoubtedly, by and large, achieved.

**Trade Warfare**

*Morgenstern:* One might ask whether it wouldn't be necessary to judge the situation according to specific circumstances, rather than by principles, which is so difficult. Let me give you one illustration.

One of the troublesome situations in Europe at the present is the great penetration of Russian oil into Western Europe. This is accomplished by a very efficient and long pipeline, which was built from Russia right into Czechoslovakia, where the oil is then distributed. Furthermore, a big pipeline has been built through Italy. This was done by the Italians, by Mattei when he was still alive. Where do the pipes come from? They were manufactured by Mannesmann, one of the biggest pipe manufacturers in Germany. The Russians were very eager to get them, of course, several years ago. They were willing to pay not in the normal manner, in fur coats and such things, but in gold or in any other desired commodity which the Germans wished. This trade was effected, and it works counter to all our desires and our own interests, business and political. This is a specific case in which an intervention on our part would have made a lot of sense, in order to stop this. In fact, one can go further.

One could have said: why didn't we build the pipeline in Italy and instead of bringing up Russian oil, use it for a monopolistic manipulation of the Arabian oil which has no other outlet, except to the United States or to Europe? Why could that not be done? Very simple. Because our anti-trust legislation forbids American companies from getting together and working in cooperation.

A similar situation, incidentally, has arisen in Indonesia, where American oil companies wanted to work together, but were stopped by threatened anti-trust proceedings under the anti-trust legislation. At the moment we are out of Indonesia; the oil companies have withdrawn. Everything is gone, and our influence there, our presence, is diminished. Whether these things make sense is very much to be questioned.

*Nutter:* I hesitate a great deal to get into this discussion of trade warfare, because it is a horribly complicated subject. I think some of the aspects are going to be taken up in succeeding statements, but I would like to direct a few remarks to this statement of Mr. Schlesinger's, which I think has good points to it and also has some disadvantages.

What I like to call the dope-addict approach is the approach whereby a country is hooked on your product and it is very painful for him to be cut off. The success with which this kind of approach works depends entirely on timing. It depends on when you are going to cut the country off, because the main pains are the withdrawal pains, after all. Once they are through that and have readjusted, everything goes all right at some cost, and the main cost is an immediate cost.

So this weapon is of only very limited usefulness. It is useful in specific crises, and in those cases it may be very important. The real question is whether you want deliberately to increase the trade initially, in order to be able to exercise this weapon later. That is a very complicated matter, because the increase can provide more benefits than the withdrawal can provide harm. These are questions that are not easily settled. It also depends on the nature of the trade.

I have never been impressed with the notion of general restrictions. I think these work best only in times of crisis. On the other hand, the specific restrictions raise questions as to what should you restrict, what is a strategic commodity and what isn't.

Let me consider another aspect of this. If, to the extent that we trade and we don't have specific policy—we just want them to trade and be dependent on us to some extent—what are they going to buy? If they have any sense, they will buy consumer goods; and to the extent that they buy consumer goods, this, of course, frees the economy to do other things, namely to produce producers' goods or war materiel; and, whether we like it or not, despite all the good sides of unrest in a country like Poland, it is deeply involved in the Russian war effort. There is no question that it is an integral part of the Russian war machine. So these things can't really be separated very completely.

In these questions the real problem that you always come back to is the problem of the Alliance. We don't have an alliance when these questions arise. If the Canadians want dollars, they will sell their wheat, and they don't much care to whom they sell it. They'll trade with Cuba, and they just don't give a darn. The same thing has generally been true of most private traders in most European countries, and the most we have ever been able to accomplish in trade warfare is restricting our own exports or controlling our own exports. We have had virtually no success whatsoever in controlling the trade that other countries in the West carry on.

The West, as we have heard many times, is a big economy and we are only part of it. In fact, we are not much more than half. And I think we had better begin to realize that. We talk about the wealth of the United States, but it isn't all that big. If you lump the European countries together now, even making allowance for the errors in the GNP estimates, their total production is rapidly approaching ours. This is something we have to understand, and either we strengthen the Alliance in some ways, so that it really is an alliance, or we have to abandon hope for the success of this kind of approach.

A final word on the question of oil. This, I think is a straightforward trading venture on the part of the Soviet Union. They have lots of oil, they haven't got much to do with it. They don't have the automobiles and so on. They have been very successful in drilling. I think that there is nothing in the world we could have done to prevent them from selling oil, as much as it might have been attractive to do so. If they hadn't built the pipeline, they would have gotten some ships.

I remember in the Iranian crisis someone said: "Well, don't worry about Mossadegh, all he has to do is hire a German to run the refineries and a Greek to get him some ships, and he is in business." I think this is a very real thing in the world that we live in. We just have to make the best adjustments we can. I think this is a fact of life.

*Schlesinger:* I quite agree with Dr. Taylor that trade does not necessarily make friends for us. I am suggesting that what we want to do is to provide something that the trading partner might lose and might regret losing. Obviously, this is most effective when one is dealing with a small country and there is an asymmetrical relationship between the two. Also, I wonder whether Dr. Taylor would care to turn around this notion that trade cannot be a significant instrument for influencing the policies of nations. That is, would he agree that if the proportion of Soviet trade in Latin America or in some of the Afro-Asian nations were to run up to fifteen or twenty per cent, that we ought not to be unduly alarmed?

Also, I might point out certain inconsistencies in our program. If we are giving $80 or $100 million worth of assistance to Poland during the course of a year, the net effect of ceasing to purchase $30 million worth of Polish ham may be to increase the aid program. I don't see the advantage of this to American foreign policy. I would think that, if we want to cut back, we would be better advised to cut back on aid rather than trade.

*Taylor:* I feel that there would be a great deal to be said for the argument put forward, if we had an alliance and a doctrine for using economic pressures to achieve political purposes.

Secondly, I would say that an increase in Soviet trade with Latin America would be a cause for very great alarm indeed, because their purposes are mainly political and they are reasonably skillful at using economic expansion for political purposes. So I would be very much alarmed.

*Schlesinger:* Consider a nation which trades extensively with the Soviet Union, such as Turkey. One would not regard Turkey as effectively penetrated by the Soviets. One of the advantages of trade with the Soviets is that nations which think of Soviet trade as a horn of plenty gradually learn that there is not that much advantage in dealing with the Soviets. Soviet products have their disadvantages. The Soviets are rather harsh at bargaining.

The underdeveloped nations which do not trade or have no association with the Soviet Bloc tend to assume that over on the other side there is some kind of paradise. A little bit of experience proves that they are as mortal as the West and there are at least as many disadvantages in dealing with the Soviets as with the West.

Brazil has one per cent trade with the Soviet Union and Turkey has twenty per cent trade. One wonders whether a rise of proportion of Brazilian trade carried on with the Soviet Union is that much of a threat. Ninety-nine per cent of its trade continues to be with the West. Thus, once again, the threat to curtail trade is certainly a powerful club that we hold over the heads of the underdeveloped nations. Economic warfare may not be effective in dealing with a nation like the Soviet Union, under present circumstances. It does have measurable effect on dealing with smaller nations, and the underdeveloped nations in particular.*

*Nutter:* There is one area in which I think we ought to be absolutely unrelenting in our trade policy toward the Bloc, and in which we should try to influence our allies as well as businessmen. It is in the area of shipping technology to the Bloc. By this I mean the shipment of prototype goods and factories and

---

* Footnote: In response to a later question, Dr. Schlesinger said: "I would be opposed, under almost all circumstances, to granting credit to the Soviet Union. I would be happy to consider granting credit to the Soviet Union if we could extract an adequate *quid pro quo.* I think that the Soviet Union is probably looking for a free gift. I see no reason to provide them with one. If they are willing to bargain about what they would be willing to exchange for this, I would certainly be happy to negotiate."

things of this sort. We ought to make them pay for their own technological developments, pay in the same way we do, that is, by expenditure of resources in developing the technology. This always has created a very difficult problem for businessmen, particularly when their orders are a little low, or something of this sort.

*Johnson:* In order to pursue this there is a question for Dr. Schlesinger with respect to his argument: "Is it not likely that trade with the Satellites is accomplished only on terms and conditions acceptable to the Soviet Union; that is, Bloc countries may export that which is considered of relatively little value to the Soviet plan, while the imports will be permitted which tend to alleviate the Soviets of the necessity of supply?"

*Schlesinger:* Within limits, I think that that is an appropriate statement. I think we should recognize that Soviet bargaining power, in dealing with the Satellites, is limited. I think that we should also recognize that, if the Bloc sends us relatively worthless goods from the standpoint of strategy, they have the capacity for selling these goods, and that the fact that we are the market gives us, nevertheless, a certain degree of leverage over the Satellite producers.

I would also quite agree with Warren Nutter's comment. We certainly should not ship any material that would ease the problems of the Bloc. I think technological advance is the foremost example of this. The number of strategic materials which now exist is fairly limited.

One of the characteristics of a great industrial nation, like the Soviet Union, is that by bringing pressure to bear in the short run through eliminating certain types of supplies, we force them in the longer run to create their own capacity and in the longer run may put ourselves at a disadvantage.

*Johnson:* We have time for another question. This is in relation to a point made in Dr. Salera's paper: "America's businessmen should be regarded as allies of the Government, rather than objects of suspicion. Restraints and restrictions imposed by the Departments of State, Treasury, Commerce, and Defense, on conducting overseas business ventures stand as daily blocks to reinforcing US interests."

*Salera:* I am not sure that the foreign trade aspects of the Government role are as important, particularly in the case of the United States, as a number of our domestic economic policies, mainly those generally summarized under the heading of anti-trust. To take an extreme case that is roughly parallel to what we discussed in the early phases of price analysis at the undergraduate level: if we were trying to deny wheat to Red China by a vehicle such as I have proposed, I think it is reasonably safe to conclude that the operation wouldn't get off the ground. They have too many tens of thousands of producers that would have to be involved on a strictly private basis. At the other extreme, and concerned with a single supplier, again using the elementary-textbook approach, all you have to do is persuade that supplier. If the proposal that I have in mind has some real possibilities, it seems to me that all manner of adjustments have to be made in what might be called the general government-industry relationship. I think that relationship, as it stands at present, is in about as bad a condition imaginable with respect to the type of idea that I am proposing.

## Aid and Trade Policies: Underdeveloped Areas

*Johnson:* Dr. Schlesinger, in his paper, has some comments concerning possible reorientation, with respect to the underdeveloped nations, that might be utilized in our trade and aid program.

> It would be unwise deliberately to bring changes that will probably bring to the top those who, from our point of view, would subvert the society. One of the most successful examples of both economic growth and social change, which we have influenced, has been in Taiwan. At the moment Chiang's regime would probably have popular support if an election were held. Yet, if we had listened to those Americans who urged the introduction of democratic procedures in the early or mid-fifties, the regime would undoubtedly have been swept away—and with it in all probability the chances for the substantial social improvements that have taken place. There is a time for the introduction of democratic procedures and there is a time to avoid such introduction.
>
> *    *    *    *
>
> The emphasis which we have placed upon the paraphernalia of democracy, on income equality, on welfare programs seems to me to be misleading. What we are fundamentally interested in is stable, non-Communist governments which command—and can retain—the support of their peoples. What the aid program should attempt to do is to encourage changes in which currently disillusioned people may perceive a greater degree of legitimacy and effectiveness in their own social systems. Regimes acquire legitimacy in the eyes of their own people, not because of external forms, but because they work.
>
> James R. Schlesinger

*Schlesinger:* One of the wiser students of trade unionism has suggested that, when Americans think about trade unions, they tend to confuse three kinds of objectives. They confuse clean unionism, democratic unionism, and responsible unionism. The same sort of thing can be said about the underdeveloped nations. Americans tend to assume that a government which is clean will be a democratic and responsible government, that a government which is democratic will become responsible, and so on. This is not necessarily the case. The question is: what is our primary objective? It would seem to me that our primary objective would be to encourage effective and responsible governments, without worrying too much either about the democracy or what strikes us as the cleanliness of the government.

There are many social customs in the United States that we take for granted. We take for granted the dangling of post offices and bridges over creeks in Congressional districts for Congressmen when an important bill is pending. This would strike people from other societies as corruption, but we take it for granted. At the present time we have rationalized the behavior of Tammany Hall in the early 1900's. Whatever the procedures of Tammany Hall, it was a mechanism which helped the immigrants to adjust to American life, and so on. Others might still take a crude, muckraking attitude toward Tammany Hall.

One of our problems is that many of the people who deal with underdeveloped areas tend to take a crude, muckraking attitude toward any of the procedures which may have some kind of social function in a culture with which they are dealing, but which strike them on the surface as simply reprehensible.

My other statement suggests that we need not necessarily push democratic reform at the outset. There is a time for introducing democratic procedures. There is a time to refrain from introducing such procedures. In many societies the immediate introduction of democracy would bring to the top persons who are both hostile to the West and who would probably diminish the chances for progress in the societies which we are interested in helping.

*Salera:* I think I share Dr. Schlesinger's emphasis. However, I would like to see a more pragmatic approach in our programs, with less emphasis on the applicability of the more simple-minded theoretical analyses of the development process. I am afraid that most of us are deceived by treatments that run in terms of half a dozen variables, as allegedly strategic in some meaningful sense.

*Johnson:* I would like to move now to two statements from Dr. Brandt's paper.

> The whole range of problems connected with rural development and agrarian reform is an ideological and economic battleground where the West has a very good chance to lose the battle for freedom and human dignity by confusion about basic principles and by too ready an acceptance of seemingly plausible yet vastly oversimplified and ill-advised solutions, as it was lost in mainland China by supporting the supposedly benevolent "agrarian reformers."

*     *     *     *

> Sound economic strategy of the West requires the finding of a more rational solution. Since the plantations are in many underdeveloped countries the only enterprises which have the full command of up-to-date production techniques and of scientific research, these enterprises should be enabled and induced to share the benefits of their modern farming methods, processing plants, and marketing facilities with small farmers, and to act as their extension service agency.

Karl Brandt

*Brandt:* I would like to discuss the situation that exists in relations with the underdeveloped countries. To my mind, the real issue is the battle for a humane progress of society in which poverty can be diminished. This requires that we see clearly what is actually the situation in all of these large parts of the world where the majority of the people will still for generations live as farmers.

This is true for large areas in the Asiatic circle that goes from Korea all the way to Iran, and this is true for Africa. In some ways this problem exists in Latin America. The question is: is it really the main interest of the West to see that, in a similar fashion as in the Soviet empire, one pushes industrialization and production? I believe we lose the whole battle if we use more trade and more aid to develop systems which ultimately do the same thing that the Soviets do in their area, namely, coerce the people into economic growth for materialistic purposes.

The values on which this Western world stands, are at the bottom of the whole battle. Essentially, it is the conviction of the Western countries, proven by experience, that free men are more productive than slaves. I am not satisfied that the main battle is to have countries remain independent. It cannot be our duty to see to it that economic growth in those countries goes on by methods which ultimately coerce and make the individuals in these countries the slaves of a system that is a materialistic machine which tries to produce more goods. The issue is not whether more concrete or more steel will be produced. The issue is whether this produces human decency in which the people can maintain dignity and freedom.

In so many of the underdeveloped countries, there are policies that begin to say that you cannot form capital in agriculture, and that there is no possibility of improving the lot of the people on the farm unless one has first a huge investment in power plants, in steel factories, and so on.

Naturally, any amount of industrialization that can proceed is fine. But not if it leads to having the people ultimately treated as they are in the Soviet Union, where the whole system economically for forty years squeezes out of its large rural population about half its income to invest under state instructions. I believe the West loses the whole battle if we give assistance to such policies.

The essential aid to these countries, should come primarily in private investment. So long as it comes only in the form of state-to-state transfer of capital, even through international agencies, there is no assurance that it is not ultimately used for the purposes that I believe are those of the enemy.

As to the role of populations, I believe we had better take a careful look at the possibilities, even with the most optimistic assumptions, of what can be done. No matter how much industrialization takes place in underdeveloped countries, no matter how much technical aid and support is given from the industrially developed countries, the large majority of these 850 million people who secured their independence will still live as little farmers. If we exclude the possibility, and it would be absurd to exclude it, that these people can get their living standards improved in such a way that one can see that there is a diminution of poverty, we have given away a large part of the battle, and it will be used by the Soviets on the one hand and on the other by indigenous leaders, who stir the dissatisfaction of the population in those areas. Indigenous communism will emerge. It is not necessary that it come from Russia by agents.

We should take a look at the history of the West. In Western Europe, as well as in the United States, it is absolutely untrue that there was no capital formation in agriculture. A large part of the capital in this country was formed by farmers and, if I may just point out, here are some statistical blind letters in our methodology of looking at the development of economies.

We should, on the one hand, do nothing to undermine the elements of the Western economy. We should not give any assistance to undermining systems that are based on private property. When it comes to reforms, we should not do anything to assist methods of confiscation. We should not assist anything that quells the only advanced enterprises that have technology in agriculture, like the plantations. There is no reason to believe one cannot use the plantation—whether owned and managed by United Fruit or by any other companies—as the extension agency that brings the techniques and the discipline of work to the small farmers.

Take the Japanese economy and how it developed. Japanese industrial development in the last five years, rising at a rate of about 20% per annum, is something that we should study. When it comes to agrarian reform, one has it in Japan. The agrarian reform that was carried out under General Douglas MacArthur was not a reform that advanced all these people. It increased the amount of private property. It also had some aspects to it that were a compromise on the rights of private property. The agrarian reforms in Taiwan and in Japan should be studied. One should not simply say that in Latin America and Asia everybody has to have his own system.

The Western world will lose this struggle altogether if it tries to compromise on the basic values and the main humane issues, and if it has only technical growth in mind.

*Haberler:* I am certainly in complete agreement with Dr. Brandt. He is right when he says that economic aid policies, and not only American economic aid policies, overstress large industries, which are not very suitable for many of these countries. They also stress what the government can do and underestimate what can be done by private initiative.

Let me tell a little story which I heard recently about what happened in Thailand. It illustrates very well what Dr. Brandt has been saying.

The Japanese have tried to stimulate the production of corn, which is a very important agricultural product. They went into Thailand and got the help of the Chinese merchants, and they promised to buy any amount of corn which the farmers in Thailand could produce. They set the price pretty high, and had an excellent response. In two or three years the production export of corn grew very much, and made really a great contribution to the economy of Thailand.

But, now comes the sad part. After a while somebody in the government of Thailand—and mind you, this is not a Communist government, but a staunchly anti-Communist government—found out about it, and declared that this could not be left to private initiative. So, they set up an export monopoly for corn. The farmer had to sell his corn from then on to this new institution, which then sold it to the Japanese. The price for corn which the farmer received was greatly reduced in order to make a big profit for the government monopoly, and after a couple of years production fell.

What you can learn from that is that there is a tremendous response to prices which is something, as Dr. Brandt pointed out, which is very often denied. It is said farmers are stupid and that they have to be told, and that prices have no function, or only a small function. This simply is not true.

In this case of Thailand the United States was entirely innocent. There was no American aid mission which stressed that type of policy. We were bystanders. I think it is true that in some other cases the American influence was not quite on the right side. But even if American aid policy was correct here, we have to be very careful about it, because the tendency in this country is in that direction, to do everything through the Government, and to stress industry; and one has to tread very diplomatically. They don't like to be told: do it this way, or do it that way. The diplomacy of aid is, I think, the most difficult part of diplomacy, but if it is done rightly, I think a lot can be achieved, especially in some Latin American countries.

*Meyer:* Many of the funds available for investment in the Middle East and North Africa initially lie in the hands of governments—incomes from oil, foreign aid of various kinds, and similar sources.

In countries such as Iran, Iraq, Israel, Libya, and Algeria, most of the money for investment will be in the public sector initially. There probably is no alternative but for these governments to undertake to invest these monies under public auspices. The ratio of public and private investment in these nations, at least in the early stages of their development, will look quite different from the ratios of public and private investment that we marked down in the West over time. I think that so far, in the last fifteen years since World War II, the ratios of public and private investment and the general pattern have reflected this odd situation. I think, it is worth emphasizing that that situation is now changing. I think that some of the improvements or changes in the indefinite mix that we would hope for can probably come about now that the infrastructure has been changed, now that there are better systems of highways, now that the public utilities have been installed, now that a better educated labor force and managerial staff is available as a result of investments in health and education, and so on. It seems logical that there may be more private investment. Also, purchasing power has risen markedly in most of these countries since World War II. It now seems logical that perhaps the better climate for private investment in other than extractive industries has been created, and I believe this is borne out by the ventures which I have pointed to here.

The Eregli Steel Consortium in Turkey, an international consortium of private ventures including Westinghouse and a series of other American companies, looks like a very interesting development which is going to have an enormous effect on economic growth in Turkey, and which will have all kinds of collateral effect in creating growth and investment in other spheres of the Turkish economy. This, however, could not have gone on, unless the other investment had first gone on in the preceding years.

I think that RCA's venture in Egypt probably could not go on without some sort of an arrangement between RCA and the Government of Egypt, guaranteeing RCA a substantial share of the market. This, in short, is a somewhat different arrangement, but it is the result of some government activity in earlier years.

The Cyprus Mines Corporation's new development of low-grade ore in Cyprus is still another example. In Israel, obviously, before private investment could be brought in on any sort of a substantial level, development had to go on there publicly. I believe it is worth keeping this in mind when we talk about this matter. Timing, in short, is a major matter.

The second point is that our aid program needs to continue the trend already under way, but with a great deal of improvement. I think this doesn't even need elaboration. I think all of us would subscribe to this thesis, whether or not we are supporters of foreign aid. There is going to be a certain amount of technical assistance at least, and I think we all want to see the best Americans sent abroad. On the basis of my own experience, having watched the aid programs over the last fifteen years in the

Middle East and in North Africa, I have seen enormous improvements in the level of the exportable Americans who are going
abroad. I think this is definitely a healthy sign. Compared to
any of the technicians from Eastern Europe or from the Soviet
Union whom I have seen, I think the Americans are doing a
superb job abroad. There has been a great deal of improvement,
and we are gaining a lot of momentum in this respect.

One area where I don't think we have made much progress is
in the field of a basic export ideology, or economic theory, however you want to label it. To come down to a specific term, I
don't think we really are in a very good position to give—as
part of our advice on how to spend public or private money—
much advice that is of lasting value on the whole subject of
whether investment funds spent on human resources, for example, health and education, provide greater mileage for dollars
invested than funds spent on physical plant and facilities.

Here in the United States we admittedly suffer from a great
deal of ignorance on this subject, but we can probably afford
the waste. In the underdeveloped countries it is doubtful, where
resources are short, whether they can afford these kinds of waste.
I don't think we have really formed an exportable body of economic theory in this respect. Unquestionably, economists have
analytical tools at their fingertips which are of value in assessing
rates of economic growth, doing studies of national income,
balance of payments, and that sort of thing. But once we get
beyond these rough indicators of economic health, our body of
export theory really is lacking, and this is a task which is before
us in the West today to try to shape some concepts of investment which really would be of more value to decision-makers,
at the public and private level, in these underdeveloped countries.

The third point concerns government policy with regard to
our private enterprises operating in the energy field. The problem we are going to see in Western Europe is a rapid change
in the current situation on the heels of Europe's apparent increasing willingness to speed up the flight from coal and to run
its capital plant increasingly on cheap imported energy from
the Middle East, North Africa, possibly Lake Maracaibo, and
probably also from the Soviet Union, as well as from the domestic gas sources that are now becoming available in Holland and
in other parts of Western Europe. This is unquestionably going
to create a whole series of new problems and new developments,
as the energy mix moves from about fifty-fifty, which it is today—
fifty per cent coal and fifty per cent oil and gas, hydrocarbons—

down, probably, to eighty-twenty, which it could well be in the next eight to ten years.

This could mean that Western Europe, instead of having six million daily barrels of oil coming in from outside, could probably have nearer to ten million daily barrels of oil coming in from outside. This will have some effect, certainly, on the over-all cost of production, but it will also have all kinds of other effects on the structure of the industry supplying energy to Western Europe. It is going to have outside effects, in terms of probably giving life to organizations such as the Organization of Petroleum Exporting Countries—OPEC. It could create a polarization at the other end of the energy spectrum.

The oil companies unquestionably are going to be in the middle in all of this. Some are even prepared to predict that they will be in the position of public utilities scampering from one rate board, at one end of the spectrum in Western Europe, to another rate board, at the other end, at the producing end, OPEC. There are interesting possibilities that could come up here, and I would submit that a flexible set of government policies, to keep these petroleum companies in a strong position, and to guarantee that they are able to have the flexibility of action, is going to be needed. This will involve everything from policy with regard to integration in the international petroleum industries to anti-trust legislation, and certainly the import programs.

*Teller:* In the United States we were told in 1945 that once nuclear power can be obtained for seven mills per kilowatt hour, the economic use would be here. We achieved it. In the meantime the price of everything else rose by a factor of two. But the price of electricity per kilowatt hour dropped almost by a factor of two. Therefore, even though we performed with nuclear energy, it is still not economical. I would like to know whether the situation is, or will be, similar in Europe.

Nuclear energy is not very cheap, but at least it has the property that it can be had in any part of the world for the same amount of money, because there is nothing heavy to lug around.

*Meyer:* I have been told by economists who specialize in energy that the possibility of nuclear energy really being competitive with oil at present prices is probably remote for the next five to six years, and perhaps ten years. Now, this is admittedly highly speculative. As you know, there are developments which occur overnight that could change the situation.

People were talking about nuclear energy being a competitor for oil as late as 1958. But, this was at a time when it looked as though the world supplies of oil were going to be exhausted. That situation has changed dramatically in the last four or five years. But, I would guess that nuclear energy probably wouldn't really be a factor in Western Europe short of five to eight years.

*Teller:* There is another use of nuclear energy which some of us have discussed in the last year, and I have tried to use every opportunity to bring it to the attention of people who know more than we.

In spite of some emotional blocks, it turns out that use of nuclear explosives which we have developed has a good chance to pay off in straight economic situations.

We can make an explosion for the purpose of moving great quantities of earth, and we can do it in such a way that the radioactive contamination will be of no importance. What I now said is quite a recent development, and it is not completed yet. But I will say that, given the development of which we now feel certain, with time we can accomplish it. You can make an explosion and walk into the crater minutes afterwards, without exposing yourself to more radiation than we are taking in our laboratories day in and day out, and that have never given rise to any trouble.

You can make these holes big or little. Who wants them? Why should one make them? There are a few very obvious possibilities. We can make a harbor for the kind of cost that we used to pay merely to equip the harbor. A small harbor, in an accessible location, almost anything except the polar regions, will cost a million dollars. A more elaborate thing will take maybe ten million dollars. But they are not exorbitant figures, and you can put the harbor into practically any coastline. I understand that harbors are few on the west coast of either South America or Africa; and that the Australians, for instance, on their Indian Ocean coast, are quite interested in a harbor due to mineral deposits that could become exportable. Another opportunity is the building of canals that can be executed by simultaneous explosions, giving overlapping craters.

A last point, which might be of greater significance than the others, is that massive mineral deposits, down to a depth of at least a thousand feet and probably somewhat deeper, could be made use of: coal deposits, iron deposits, anything else where massive mining is of importance. They could be made available by just blasting off the overburden and exposing these mineral deposits to cheap strip mining. Therefore, in connection with both transportation and mining, very big changes in the economy could be effected by the use of the new instruments.

## Common Market

*Johnson:* The final issue of Part 4 focuses upon the role of the Common Market. We have taken a statement from Dr. Brandt's paper on this, and request that he comment on it.

> The progress made toward gradual economic and political integration of Western Europe under the Treaty of Rome in 1957 has decidedly fortified the strength of the West. The consolidation of the EEC during the first five years of its existence, and the functioning of the three branches of the supranational preliminary government of the six federated countries has cemented the political solidarity of these nations in their defense against the Communist menace. The EEC is a great asset to the United States, the British Commonwealth, and Japan in spite of a number of unresolved conflicting views on specific issues and procedures. The economies of the EEC member states have not only grown rapidly, but have also begun to integrate.
>
> Karl Brandt

*Brandt:* The Common Market, as it has developed, is probably beyond the point of no return. I believe that the system of treaties that exists, particularly the Treaty of Rome—which has no provision for any change or abrogation or termination for any countries—is such a solid system that, to my way of thinking, it is a part of the political geography of the future.

The real question now is to evaluate the impact of this upon the rest of the world, particularly this country, which is, after all, in the leading position in the Free World. The essential strategy of the United States ought to be to see that the world does not shift from a multilateral, maximum economic exchange of goods and services, to something that is regional and protectionist. After the integration that takes place between these countries, the essence of the problem is the creation of something that will eventually become similar to the United States of America, something that approaches a United States of Europe. I cannot work myself into the frame of mind to say that this is dangerous. I probably have a better view than some of my best friends of the power of this country and its resources.

The question now is to see that Western Europe, the EEC, is opening its borders. It has already abolished fifty per cent of the internal trade barriers. It is accelerating the pace. It has eliminated all the quantitative restrictions, which are the most hideous part of impediments to international exchange. It has currencies that are hard, freely exchangeable to the extent that any citizen over there can buy a slab of gold if he wants to forego interest on his money. The question now is to see to it that this ultra-productive system is going to be launched by every means that we can possibly use. If the British join it, we have a great force that will work in that direction. But, even if they don't, we should play the game all around, with military, with diplomatic, and with all the chips that we have. We must see to it, for the benefit of the Europeans, as well as the United States and the rest of the world, that, it opens to allow a maximum of exchange of capital, intelligence, patents, and industrial corporation investment. In that connection I would say that it relates to what we discussed before, namely the question of how one aids the underdeveloped countries.

We have to economize in the capital that can be made available for the development in the world, and this can only be done by going back to the system of a maximum of private enterprise investment in foreign countries, from here to Europe, from Europe to the United States. There is cooperation between corporations of Europe and the United States and Japan, which is all to the good. I have seen it recently working in areas like Malaya in the Far East. There lies the great opportunity.

There is another thing that I believe is very important. The Western world, with all the underdeveloped areas, cannot possibly be developed by going to the extreme of making Western Europe or the United States self-supporting in agricultural commodities and all raw materials. This blocks the whole future development. If the Europeans raise their prices by subsidizing agriculture, they soon will be in the same situation in which we are already by making their whole system less efficient. I, for one, believe that in the past ten years we have sold American agriculture short, because we have here an agriculture that can commercially compete in quite a lot of commodities freely in the world, provided that the prices are not fixed and provided the whole market economy is not upset by making arrangements for cartels that are spread from here over the world.

Some people propose that we help the underdeveloped countries by international commodity agreements. What does this mean? It means establishing international cartels. This is a sedative, and doesn't help. Does anybody want to make a cartel arrangement to fix the price of natural rubber? You thereby ultimately deliver Malaya to the Soviets, because natural rubber will be killed in no time. I believe natural rubber will be with us for twenty years, because it has a marvelous opportunity to lower costs. Does somebody want to establish the coffee agreement by fixing and controlling, in all countries, the movement of coffee beans? We can solve these problems, but it has to be the freest possible exchange, and it has to be by private enterprise.

*Haberler:* I must confess that I am a little less enthusiastic about the Common Market than my friend, Dr. Brandt. Let me make one thing quite clear. There is, of course, no doubt that Europe has developed economically. But, up to now that has very little to do with the Common Market. If you look at the figures, you will find that the rise in output and production in Europe, before the Common Market came into effect in 1958, was faster than it is now. I don't say this is the cause of the Common Market, but it is simply a fact that Europe recovered because France and Germany and some other countries pursued the right policies. In the future the Common Market may have great economic effects, but up to now it probably has had very little to do with it.

On the other hand, Europe also has developed, I think, politically in a very satisfactory way. Germany and France are on very good terms. This, of course, is a tremendous progress, as compared with what happened during the interwar period. But, again, this has nothing to do with the Common Market. It is the other way around. Because France and Germany are on excellent terms, that has made the Common Market possible. Without that the Common Market would have been impossible. I think there is even a probability that the Common Market will split Europe. You all know what Bernard Shaw said. He said the United States and Great Britain are separated by a common language. It almost looks now is if Europe is going to be split by the Common Market.

It is possible that the British will still enter. I think it was perhaps a mistake that they tried to do it. But now that they have tried to do it and that the Macmillan Government has staked its future on that, I think it would be really very serious if they did not go in. If they could go in, I don't see how the rift between the Continent and Britain can be avoided, and also, of course, the rift between France, on the one hand, and the Allies on the other. So, I am afraid that the Common Market is not so constructive as many Americans think it is, and to be quite frank, I think American policy has been a little naive by pushing the Common Market beyond everything else.

But now this is history. It may be true, as Dr. Brandt says, that the Common Market is beyond the point of no return. That is possible. If they can overcome the present difficulties in connection with the British entry, then, of course, they will go on. This is the greatest challenge they have.

But now, assuming that the Common Market is there to stay and that it will go on, what shall we do? Here I think the American response has been extremely constructive. On the one hand, American policy has been naive, by seeing nothing else but the Common Market, and by discouraging it from taking in the neutrals. But, on the other hand, even if the Common Market came about all by itself or through American prodding, American policy on the economic side has been very constructive. By that I mean the Trade Expansion Act, which offers to the Common Market a joint policy of reducing tariffs and trade impediments all around, and which this country aimed at the Common Market. Much will depend on how the Common Market develops. If de Gaulle has his way, it will probably become an inward-looking protectionist enterprise, and then there will be very little we can do. On the other hand, if the other five have their way, especially the Dutch and the Belgians, then there will be a good chance for us to trade with the Common Market.

As far as we are concerned, we have to make tariff concessions, and I hope very energetic use will be made of the Trade Expansion Act, which gives the President tremendous powers, powers which he never had before, to reduce tariffs. But, I am not entirely convinced it will be used very energetically. This is not a good time to reduce tariffs. But still, I think, that can be overcome.

As to the last part of Dr. Brandt's remarks, about commodity agreements and stabilization attempts of individual commodity prices, there I fully agree with him that to set up super-cartels is not the way to do it, as we are now in the process of doing in the case of coffee, and as we have done in the past in the case of sugar. This is not the proper way to expand trade.

## A Response on Economic Warfare

*Clabaugh\**: I suppose it is natural for each of us to think that his particular field of interest suffered in the relative use of the time of the Conference, and I cannot but regret that economic warfare did not receive more attention. The excellent program and syllabus that were prepared gave promise of discussion of economic strategies, including especially economic warfare, but actually we heard more about the role of economic warfare in some *obiter dicta* by Professor Trager, Professor Nutter, and Professor Taylor than we did in that part of the program assigned to the subject.

It has been said of our lack of preparedness in World War I that we had no plans for economic and industrial mobilization; that in World War II we had plans but didn't use them; and that for World War III we have too many plans, literally thousands of them. It has been said that we won't have to wait for Khrushchev to bury us, that we are buried under our own plans. This excess of plans abundantly justifies the inspired creation of this Center for Strategic Studies—formed to "research the researchers." But in all this multitude of plans, I know of no comprehensive plan in the past ten years—in or out of government—that has to do with economic warfare and measures short of force and force short of war. Yet it was exactly in that area that we had to operate in the most serious confrontation we have had since World War II—the Cuban crisis.

That experience affords a revealing case history of a crisis that might have been avoided by the earlier application of effective economic sanctions, either unilaterally by the United States or collectively by our NATO allies and the Organization of American States. The rapid build-up on the island, for example, was made possible by the willingness of our allies to charter shipping to the Soviet Union. It is not necessary here to belabor the successive blunders that have led to Soviet entrenchment in Cuba with a formidable military force. We are concerned here with the lessons in economic strategy that may be learned from the experience. These lessons may be useful in meeting recurring crises in other areas and in resolving the intolerable situation in Cuba without resort to war.

* Col. Samuel F. Clabaugh, USA (ret.), a guest at the Conference, made this response from the floor. During World War II, in the war department, and later in the intelligence community, Col. Clabaugh was in positions dealing with problems of economic warfare, and has contributed to the Encyclopædia Britannica on this subject.

One of these lessons is the importance of advance planning for economic defense and economic warfare. The magnificent military mobilization—land, sea, and air—was the result of years of organization and planning, kept constantly current. There was no such organization or planning for economic strategy. Other lessons include the importance of a proper evaluation of intelligence and the relation of intelligence to operations, of the collaboration of Congress and the Executive, of the prerequisites of bi-partisan support of foreign policy, and of a clear understanding of the applicable principles of international law in contemporary foreign relations. The Cuban case history affords also an opportunity to analyze the events which brought us to the brink of war and of possible alternatives that might have prevented this. It revealed both the discouraging and the hopeful aspects of what may be expected of our allies, and it illustrates how firm and positive action in regaining the initiative can win allies, influence neutrals, and bring a recalcitrant adversary to terms.

Quarantine, blockade—pacific or belligerent—economic warfare by whatever name, may be used in other trouble spots. It can be used effectively in guerrilla warfare—not in the swamps of South Vietnam or on the Plaine des Jarres—but at the port of Hanoi, through which the Communist guerrillas are supplied. There are many who believe that economic sanctions might have been effective in preventing or avenging the rape of Hungary, in bringing down the Berlin wall, and in other major crises.

The Soviet Union, with only a limited economic potential in comparison with the West, has employed economic warfare from the beginning of the Cold War, and with considerable success. In 1948, when the West had a monopoly of atomic weapons, the Soviet Union had the temerity to institute a blockade of Berlin. It was one of those countless probing operations where the probe struck no firm resistance. Since then it has repeatedly waged economic warfare against the West, against the neutrals, against new and underdeveloped nations, and against other Communist nations, including notably Communist China. The U.S. News & World Report in January 1963 quoted American officials as saying that if US allies would impose the same sort of tight embargo against Red China that the Soviet Union was maintaining, the Peking regime would face collapse. The Russians, it was reported, had cut off all arms and technicians and were forcing China to pay the multi-billion-dollar Korean war debt.

In World War II and in the immediate postwar period economic warfare was a glamorous subject in the curricula of our service academies and war colleges. An important factor in all wars, it was a decisive factor in many, and was hailed as a possible preventive of military war. It was the inspiration for Article 16 of the covenant of the League of Nations and Chapter VII of the charter of the United Nations. Now there are none so poor to do it reverence. Why is this so?

A possible explanation lies in two assumptions in some of our postwar planning. One was that any future war would be total and global, that any local or regional or limited war would quickly become world-wide. The other assumption, more or less a corollary of the first, was that in any future war there would be no neutrals, and neutral nations are a major battleground of economic warfare. Proving the dangers inherent in assumptions, the world has since been plagued almost continuously with local, limited, guerrilla, and brush-fire wars, declared and undeclared. And it also has been plagued—plagued is the right word—with so-called neutrals.

Most of the offending nations in the limited wars, and most of the so-called neutrals, are peculiarly vulnerable to economic warfare in any or all of its forms. By the very rationale, therefore, by which economic warfare was denigrated (that is, its implied usefulness against neutrals and in local wars) its role and its potential should now be re-examined.

Part V
Meeting Strategy Requirements
In the Free Economy

# Budget Trends of the 1960's

—*OTTO ECKSTEIN*

## Summary

*This paper reports on a second look at the projections of government expenditures which I prepared for the Committee for Economic Development in 1958. It turns out that except for the space program, which has risen more than anyone could imagine in 1958, things have worked out pretty much according to projections. Despite some years of real economy on the part of the President and the Congress, and a considerable burst of spending thereafter, expenditures are now not far from the levels that the experts estimated back in 1958. On the other hand, the revenue projections have failed to be fulfilled as the economy has developed a substantial gap between its capacity and actual output. This has reduced profits and hence revenues.*

*For the Department of Defense, outlays followed my low projections in the last two years of the last Administration. President Kennedy, partly under the stimulus of outside pressures such as the Berlin crisis, accelerated defense spending greatly; by 1963 he was on the medium, and by 1964 on the high. Looking ahead, the paper projects a continued increase of defense spending, but not at the rate of increase of the last few years. By 1968, defense spending may fall within the range of $57 to $60 billion, assuming that the general international situation does not change much.*

*Total expenditures of the administrative budget by 1968 are projected to fall in the range of $110 to $130 billion. This is a very wide range, but the simple methods used in this review and* *revision of my earlier projections do not warrant a smaller range. It would take a more elaborate study to achieve narrower estimates.*

---

Usually we think of projections as a necessary but inevitably imperfect source of information for reaching decisions involving the future. I need not tell this group that sensible long-term commitments require the best possible judgment about long-term conditions, and hence the task of projection is inescapable. However, we may overlook an equally useful function of projections, namely, a systematic way of learning from our past mistakes. A review of projections lets us ask: why did we think as we did back then? How have actual developments differed from our expectations? And if we were to look ahead once more, how could we learn from experience?

In this paper I shall do a "half-life" study (as opposed to a post-mortem) of a set of projections which I prepared for the Committee for Economic Development (CED) back in 1958. These projections received considerable public attention and have since been followed up by similar projections undertaken by the Federal Government itself.

My CED projections are particularly suitable for this kind of review because they were not mechanical, but rather reflected the best informed opinion of their day. They were based on some 30 interviews with key technicians of the Federal Government, experienced civil servants who had lived through a variety of budget crises and economy and spending waves. Thus the review can tell us to what extent our thinking has changed and how rapidly events are moving. I also hazard some revised figures for 1968, though these are not based on new interviews, and hence reflect less information than my earlier procedure. Perhaps the time is ripe for a completely new investigation, but in any event, the revised figures here presented are no more than an educated guess applied to the 1958 figures. They should be interpreted in this light.

Let me tip off my results to this extent: except for a space program which has risen even more than anyone could imagine in 1958, things have not worked out very differently than expected. Despite some years of real economy on the part of the President and the Congress, and a considerable burst of spending thereafter, expenditures are now not far from where the experts thought they would be. On the other hand, the (rather pessimistic) revenue projections of my study have failed to be fulfilled as the economy has developed a substantial gap between its capacity and actual output; this has reduced profits, and hence revenues.

## Review of Total Expenditure Trends

Expenditures of the 1964 budget are running somewhat above my medium projections, about half way between the medium and the high. On the administrative budget, expenditures are 98.8 actual vs. 94.2 for my medium, and 101.2 for my high. The increase in cash expenditures is even greater, as the trust funds have increased substantially more than I had projected. On the revenue side, after adjustments in tax law including requests for 1964, actual revenues are running $5 billion below my projections. (All my figures quoted are corrected for price.) Without price correction my expenditure figures are further in error, but the revenue figures are almost exactly correct. But my original projections clearly assumed constant prices, not because I believed that prices would remain stable but because I wished to project claims on resources, not future inflation. For the sake of comparison, I also list the projection published by the Bureau of the Budget in 1961, two years after my own, also corrected for price changes. The figures for 1968 and 1970 are given in this table for discussion below (see Table 1).

More can be learned from a review of the details than from the totals. Table 2 gives an agency-by-agency comparison of my projections for 1964 and President Kennedy's budget. It can there be seen that the largest underestimates are in Defense, Space, HEW, and interest, and that these are partly offset by overestimates of Veterans expenditures, Agriculture, AEC, and Housing. Some of the items were estimated very closely, some were not. The 1964 budget is also a projection, of course, and in two of the cases, Agriculture and Housing, I expect the actual 1964 expenditures to correspond closely to my projections.

In subsequent discussion I shall take up each of these fields in turn, analyze the sources of the differences between my projections and the Kennedy budget, and in the light of this analysis review my original projections for 1968. If somewhat tedious, I believe this review should at least give us a few glimmers on the budget outlook in the coming years.

Table 1—Past Projections of the Federal Budget Compared with the
1964 Budget Estimates

(Billions of Dollars)

| | Actual 1959 | Actual 1961 | Budget Request 1964 | CED Proj. 1964 | CED Proj. 1964 * | CED Proj. 1968 | CED Proj. 1968 * |
|---|---|---|---|---|---|---|---|
| Cash Budget Expenditures .... | 94.8 | 99.5 | 122.5 | 106.2 | 113.6 | 117.8 | 130.6 |
| Cash Budget Revenues ........ | 81.7 | 97.2 | 112.2 | 112.3 | 120.2 | 129.1 | 143.3 |
| Administrative Budget Expenditures .... | 80.3 | 81.5 | 98.8 | 88.0 | 94.2 | 97.1 | 107.7 |
| Administrative Budget Revenues ........ | 67.9 | 77.7 | — | 90.5 | 96.8 | 104.6 | 116.1 |
| adjusted for changes in law.. | — | — | 86.9 | 85.3 | 91.3 | — | — |

| | | Budget Bureau Proj. 1965 | | Budget Bureau Proj. 1965 * | | Budget Bureau Proj. 1970 | Budget Bureau Proj. 1970 * |
|---|---|---|---|---|---|---|---|
| Administrative Budget Expenditures ........ | | 88.8 | | 91.7 | | 97.4 | 105.2 |

* Corrected for price changes. All price changes only reflect the rise in
the price level, as measured by the GNP deflators. Relative price changes,
such as the above average increase in Government service costs should
be reflected in the projections. The amounts of the corrections are as
follows: CED 1964—7%, (reflecting the rise in the GNP deflators in
1959-64), Budget Bureau 1965—3.3% (change from 1961-64), CED 1968—
11%, Budget Bureau 1970—8%. I assume that the deflators will rise by
1% a year from now on.

In the last two years of the Eisenhower Administration, defense outlays followed my low projections. President Kennedy,
partly under the stimulus of outside pressures such as the Berlin
crisis, accelerated defense spending greatly. By 1963 he was on
the medium line, and by 1964 on the high.

Political pressures at this time are for higher defense outlays,
as industry push behind weapons systems such as the B-70, is
quite intense, and as local communities are pressing against
closing of old facilities. However, it would be an error to extra-
polate this pattern too far. Our Secretary of Defense has
demonstrated his determination to resist these pressures. Fur-

Table 2—Expenditure Projections by Field

(Billions of Dollars)

|  | Actual 1959 | CED Proj. 1964 | CED Proj. 1964 * | Budget Request 1964 | Differ- ence | CED Proj. 1968 * |
|---|---|---|---|---|---|---|
| Dept. of Defense (military) | 41.2 | 45.8 | 49.0 | 51.0 | +2.0 | 56.6 |
| Foreign Aid | 3.8 | 3.6 | 3.8 | 3.8 | 0 | 4.2 |
| AEC | 2.5 | 3.2 | 3.5 | 2.8 | −0.7 | 3.9 |
| Veterans Admin. | 5.3 | 6.3 | 6.7 | 5.5 | −1.2 | 7.1 |
| NASA | .1 | 1.0 | 1.1 | 4.2 | +3.1 | 1.8 |
| HHFA | 1.1 | 1.1 | 1.2 | .7 | −0.5 [1] | 2.2 |
| Agriculture | 7.3 | 7.0 | 7.5 | 6.6 | −0.9 [2] | 7.8 |
| Interior | .8 | 1.0 | 1.1 | 1.2 | + .1 | 1.2 |
| Dept. of Defense (civil works) | .8 | 1.0 | 1.1 | 1.2 | + .1 | 1.2 |
| HEW | 3.1 | 3.6 | 3.9 | 5.7 | +1.8 | 4.4 |
| Labor | 1.0 | .8 | .8 | .4 | − .5 | .9 |
| Commerce | .4 | .5 | .5 | .9 | + .4 | .6 |
| FAA | .4 | .8 | .8 | .8 | 0 | 1.0 |
| Post Office | .8 | .2 | .3 | .5 | + .2 | .4 |
| Interest | 7.6 | 8.3 | 8.8 | 10.1 | +1.3 | 9.2 |
| Other | 3.8 | 3.6 | 3.8 | 3.5 | −0.3 | 6.0 |
| TOTAL | 80.8 | 88.0 | 94.2 | 98.8 | +4.6 | 107.7 |
| Trust funds | 18.5 | 23.0 | 24.6 | 28.4 | +3.8 | 28.6 |
| Other adjustments | −4.7 | −4.8 | −5.1 | −4.7 | + .4 | −5.7 |
| Cash expenditures | 94.6 | 106.2 | 113.6 | 122.5 | +8.9 | 130.6 |

* See footnote to Table 1.

[1] 1.1 in 1963.

[2] 7.5 in 1963.

ther, despite the responsiveness of the present Administration to our military needs, the President will find that one more year —or at most two—of being so responsive to advocates of more defense spending is going to create an untenable budgetary situation. When that day comes, we shall see a contemporary version of the economy wave, which will dampen the rate of increase of defense expenditures.

In the light of these considerations, I would now project the rate of increase in the coming years at $1.5 to $2.0 billion a year, which would bring defense spending by 1968 to the range of $57 to $60 billion, which corresponds to my earlier medium to high range.

**Table 3—Department of Defense: Military**

(Billions of Dollars)

| | Actual 1959 | Actual 1961 | Budget Request 1964 | CED Proj. 1964 | CED Proj. 1964* | CED Proj. 1968* | Budget Bureau 1965* | Budget Bureau 1970* |
|---|---|---|---|---|---|---|---|---|
| Very High ............ | | | | 52.5 | 56.2 | 71.0 | | |
| High ................ | | | | 47.8 | 51.1 | 59.9 | 45.1 | 48.6 |
| Medium .............. | 41.2 | 41.5 | 51.0 | 45.8 | 49.0 | 56.6 | 42.0 | 43.3 |
| Low ................. | | | | 44.9 | 46.5 | 54.4 | 37.4 | 39.5 |

* Price corrected, see footnote to Table 1.

This discussion assumes that the general international atmosphere will not get much better or much worse. As compared to the 1959 conditions, I would judge the probability of a substantial change in international conditions to be slightly greater. However, I would think the hazard of things getting worse is greater than the possibility of real disarmament.

Table 4—National Aeronautics and Space Agency

(Billions of Dollars)

| | Actual 1959 | Budget Request 1964 | CED 1964 | CED 1964* | CED 1968* | Budget Bureau 1965* | Budget Bureau 1970* |
|---|---|---|---|---|---|---|---|
| Medium..... | 0.15 | 4.2 | 1.0 | 1.1 | 1.8 | 1.6 | 2.0 |

* See footnote to Table 1.

The rate of increase of space expenditures is just fantastic. The bulk of the increase is for the manned flight to the moon to which the country is now very heavily committed. With occasional Russian space successes predictable, the pressure will be kept on us to move ahead forcefully. As Russian space efforts to other planets become larger, the concern already felt by some observers in this country that we have been confining our efforts too exclusively to the moon project will become more widespread and other large scale projects will begin to be phased in.

Without access to inside data, it is very difficult to project space expenditures to the end of this decade. Looking at requests for new obligational authority and recent trends, it seems not unreasonable that space expenditures for 1968 will be $7-9 billion.

Table 5—Foreign Aid

(Billions of Dollars)

| | Actual 1959 | Budget Request 1964 | CED 1964 | CED 1964* | CED 1968* | Budget Bureau 1965* | Budget Bureau 1970* |
|---|---|---|---|---|---|---|---|
| Medium .... | 3.8 | 3.8 | 3.6 | 3.8 | 4.2 | 3.6 | 3.7 |

* See footnote to Table 1.

Foreign aid expenditures have been static for a number of years now. Military assistance expenditures are declining while economic programs are rising. Also, there is some switch from grants to loans which should have favorable budget results later.

I see no reason to revise my earlier projection, with the modest increase partly to be spent for the Alliance for Progress.

### Table 6—Atomic Energy Commission

(Billions of Dollars)

| | Actual 1959 | Budget Request 1964 | CED 1964 | CED 1964* | CED 1968* | Budget Bureau 1965* | Budget Bureau 1970* |
|---|---|---|---|---|---|---|---|
| Medium .... | 2.5 | 2.8 | 3.2 | 3.5 | 3.9 | 2.4 | 2.2 |

* See footnote to Table 1.

Atomic Energy Commission expenditures are running below my projections for two reasons. First, the programs of buying materials, particularly uranium, have been and are being reduced. Second, the Government has moved very cautiously into the field of civilian atomic energy. Even if the Government began to reverse its policy on civilian atomic energy, the resultant costs would rise slowly. I therefore revise my projection for 1958 downward, into the range of $2.5 to $3.5 billion.

### Table 7—Veterans Administration

(Billions of Dollars)

| | Actual 1959 | Budget Request 1964 | CED 1964 | CED 1964* | CED 1968* | Budget Bureau 1965* | Budget Bureau 1970* |
|---|---|---|---|---|---|---|---|
| High ...... | — | — | 8.0 | 8.6 | 9.0 | 7.8 | 7.4 |
| Medium .... | 5.3 | 5.5 | 6.3 | 6.7 | 7.1 | 5.7 | 5.7 |
| Low ....... | — | — | 5.2 | 5.6 | 5.8 | 5.7 | 5.7 |

* See footnote to Table 1.

Veterans expenditures offer one of the real surprises. It had been expected that some sort of limited general pension would be enacted for the veterans of World War I. But so far this has not happened, and the crucial moment for it is rapidly passing as the average age of World War I veterans is now above the age of 65. The political power of the veterans seems to have very much diminished. The present Administration is generally following the recommendations of the Bradley Commission of 1956 which favored good compensation for service-connected disabled veterans, but did not recommend much for other veterans.

The actual figures have corresponded closely to my low projections, which were based on the assumption of no important new legislation. As for the details, compensation and pensions are precisely running along the low figure; medical costs are somewhat higher, chiefly reflecting rising prices; hospital construction is somewhat greater than expected, and readjustment benefits are declining faster. Looking ahead at the 1968 figures, it appears that the low projection is the one coming true. Thus, I would expect the figures to fall in the range of $5.8-6.3 billion.

The decline in the 1964 budget is chiefly due to the planned sale of securities under various programs including mortgages of college dormitories, the special assistance functions fund, etc. These sales may not be feasible in the full amount scheduled.

My CED projections were generally considered too conservative back in 1959. In fact, however, they have been slightly too high, as urban renewal, college housing, and other programs have expanded rather slowly, only somewhat above my "low" figures. In the 1964 budget, a policy of seeking private financing with government guarantee rather than direct use of government

### Table 8—Housing and Home Finance Agency

(Billions of Dollars)

|  | Actual 1959 | Budget 1963 | Budget Request 1964 | CED 1964 | CED 1964* | CED 1968* | Budget Bureau 1965* | Budget Bureau 1970* |
|---|---|---|---|---|---|---|---|---|
| High | — | — | — | 1.2 | 1.3 | 2.4 | 2.7 | 1.6 |
| Medium | 1.1 | 1.1 | 0.7 | 1.1 | 1.2 | 2.2 | 1.2 | 1.6 |
| Low | — | — | — | 0.4 | 0.4 | 1.1 | 0.4 | 0.3 |

* See footnote to Table 1.

Table 9—Agriculture

(Billions of Dollars)

| | Actual 1959 | Budget Estimate 1963 | Budget Request 1964 | CED 1964 | CED 1964* | CED 1968* | Budget Bureau 1965* | Budget Bureau 1970* |
|---|---|---|---|---|---|---|---|---|
| Medium ....... | 7.3 | 7.5 | 6.6 | 7.0 | 7.5 | 7.8 | 6.5 | 6.6 |

* See footnote to Table 1.

funds is announced for various mortgage programs. This policy might cut future costs, if actively pursued.

Although expenditures for urban renewal and other programs will no doubt rise slowly, liquidation of existing assets will offset this, and I now expect expenditures to be closer to the low of my earlier projections, perhaps in the range of $1 to $1.5 billion.

Expenditures for agriculture continue high, above $7 billion. Even in a budget in which the total civilian employment of the Government is kept almost stable, the Department of Agriculture's employees increase from 116,000 to 122,000. Expenditures are to drop, chiefly because of anticipated heavy sales of surplus cotton in 1964, some of which is to be bought in the current fiscal year. Legislation is also to be introduced altering the support programs of dairy products, feed grains, and cotton. Various programs of the Department designed to raise the productivity of agriculture continue to expand at a steady, slow rate.

Given the uncertainties in the price-support field, I would not yet acknowledge my estimate for 1964 to be in error. As for 1968, it does appear that agriculture has hit a budgetary resistance level somewhere near $7 billion and neither Congress nor the President will go along with increases much above that. I would therefore revise my estimate downward, not to my low figure of $5 billion which assumed some real progress in curing the problem of overproduction, but to $7.0 to $7.5 billion. (My over-estimate for 1968 is due to my projection of a level-dollar expenditure; this does not allow for the fact that a rising price level reduces the resultant real outlays.)

In the longer term, say the 1970's, a point will be reached at which the political power of agriculture is going to wane. Rural population is declining steadily, and the Supreme Court decision on reapportionment of legislatures is going to have its effect in the coming years. Some lessons can be drawn here from the experience of veterans expenditures. I think it is unlikely, however, that agriculture's political decline will come in this decade and it would take a better student of political science to determine whether it will be before or after the middle of the next decade.

Table 10—Department of Commerce

(Billions of Dollars)

|  | Actual 1959 | Budget Request 1964 | CED 1964 | CED 1964* | CED 1968* | Budget Bureau 1965* | Budget Bureau 1970* |
|---|---|---|---|---|---|---|---|
| Medium .... | .38 | .90 | .50 | .54 | .57 | .72 | .86 |

* See footnote to Table 1.

Expenditures of the Department of Commerce have risen more rapidly than was expected. This is due to: (1) the area redevelopment program which is making loans on quite a large scale and for which additional authority is requested in the current budget; (2) subsidies to the maritime industry have risen to over $300 million; (3) through some of its traditional activities (e.g., Bureau of Standards, Weather Bureau) as well as proposed new programs, the Department is heavily involved in science and technology. Expenditures of this type are planned in the amount of $275 million, a doubling in two years.

While the maritime subsidies can be expected to slow their increase, the area redevelopment and science programs undoubtedly will rise substantially in the next few years. Consequently, the expenditures in this field have to be revised upward drastically from my earlier projections, perhaps to the range of $1.0 to $1.5 billion.

The rapid rise in the airport program is on schedule with the projections. With over half a billion dollars now spent on operations rather than on investment, these expenditures inevitably will increase, unless the Federal Government applies its philosophy of imposing user charges more meaningfully in this field.

### Table 11—Federal Aviation Agency

#### (Billions of Dollars)

|  | Actual 1959 | Budget 1963 | Budget Request 1964 | CED 1964 | CED 1964* | CED 1968* | Budget Bureau 1965* | Budget Bureau 1970* |
|---|---|---|---|---|---|---|---|---|
| Medium ..... | .44 | .80 | .81 | .75 | .80 | 1.0 | .93 | 1.1 |

\* See footnote to Table 1.

## Other Expenditures

The Department of the Interior and the Department of Defense (Civil Works) are spending in line with the projections, and there is no reason to think that the future trends will differ from the slow up-drift that was expected. Interest is proving more expensive than foreseen, partly because of the minor increase in the debt, but mainly because of the higher interest-rate structure. Total interest cost may fall in the range of $11 to $13 billion. Post Office net expenditures are running at over half a billion dollars even in the year following a rate increase, which is discouraging. It suggests that, instead of vacillating between one-quarter and three-quarter billion dollars between rate increases, the deficits will vacillate between half a billion and a billion dollars. The temporary program of accelerating public works is costing $200 million in 1963 and 1964.

The enormous increase of expenditures in this field, which outruns my projections, is attributable to three causes: first, expenditures for medical research are rising at a terrific rate; total public health expenditures are planned to be $1.5 billion,

### Table 12—Health, Education, and Welfare

#### (Billions of Dollars)

|  | Actual 1959 | Budget Request 1964 | CED 1964 | CED 1964* | CED 1968* | Budget Bureau 1965* | Budget Bureau 1970* |
|---|---|---|---|---|---|---|---|
| Medium .... | 3.1 | 5.7 | 3.6 | 3.9 | 4.4 | 6.8 | 8.7 |

\* See footnote to Table 1.

### Table 13—Department of Labor

(Billions of Dollars)

|  | Actual 1959 | Budget 1963 | Budget Request 1964 | CED 1964 | CED 1964* | CED 1968* | Budget Bureau 1965* | Budget Bureau 1970* |
|---|---|---|---|---|---|---|---|---|
| Medium ...... | 1.0 | .24 | .43 | .77 | .82 | .91 | .72 | .86 |

* See footnote to Table 1.

as compared to my projection of about $.9 billion. Second, public-assistance grants to states were raised from $2 to $3 billion in the last few years, an increase I did not foresee.* Expenditures of the Office of Education so far are following my very conservative projection, as Congress has failed, for the fifteenth year, to enact a general aid-to-education bill; this year the President will request new legislation costing $300 million for an expanded program for federally affected areas, plus a program of limited-purpose school aid.

My projections for 1968 clearly have to be revised for the much greater increase in health research costs and public assistance. These two changes would raise my previous figure of $4.4 billion to the range of $6.5 to $7 billion. Whether to make allowance for a general aid-to-education program is an open question. On the one hand, the record of inaction is providing further historical evidence against Congress' passing such a program in the future. On the other hand, the great concern of the Administration with this program and the experience it is gaining in succeeding squabbles with the Congress and the interest groups, makes it likely that the Administration will succeed in devising a limited program acceptable to everybody. By 1968, such a program might add another $300 to $600 million to the budget, and larger amounts in later years. For a "probable" projection I would use a figure reflecting a moderate, general program.

The decline in expenditures since 1959 is largely due to the consolidation of the unemployment-insurance program into the trust fund, a change which affected revenues and expenditures equally. Actually, expenditures are running somewhat above the projections, mainly due to the new program of manpower

* But should have foreseen in view of the steady trend of transferring more and more of the cost of this program to the Federal Government.

Table 14—Trust Funds (After Expenditures)

(Billions of Dollars)

|  | Actual 1959 | | Budget Estimate 1964 | | CED 1964 | | CED 1964* | | CED 1968* | |
|---|---|---|---|---|---|---|---|---|---|---|
|  | E | R | E | R | E | R | E | R | E | R |
| OASI ......... | 9.5 | 8.2 | 15.3 | 15.6 | 12.2 | 14.1 | 13.0 | 15.1 | 15.3 | 17.8 |
| Disability ..... | 0.4 | 0.9 | 1.3 | 1.2 | 0.8 | 1.2 | 0.9 | 1.3 | 1.1 | 1.4 |
| Highways ..... | 2.7 | 2.2 | 3.4 | 3.3 | 3.9 | 3.9 | 4.2 | 4.2 | 4.7 | 4.7 |
| Unemployment. | 3.0 | 2.0 | 3.8 | 4.2 | 2.3 | 2.4 | 2.5 | 2.6 | 2.9 | 3.0 |
| Other ........ | 2.9 | 3.8 | 4.6 | 5.0 | 3.8 | 4.6 | 4.1 | 4.9 | 4.7 | 5.6 |
| TOTAL ...... | 18.5 | 17.3 | 28.4 | 29.5 | 23.0 | 26.2 | 24.6 | 28.0 | 28.6 | 32.5 |

.* See footnote to Table 1.

E = Expenditures; R = Receipts.

development and training. The rise in expenditures from 1963 to 1964 is chiefly due to a request for a great expansion in this program.

Looking ahead to 1968, it is not unreasonable to expect outlays in the $550 to $650 million range, as the retraining program expands.

Trust fund expenditures have risen more rapidly than anticipated, mainly because of the heavier outlays for unemployment insurance due to (1) high unemployment, (2) recession programs of eligibility extension, and (3) the redefinition of the trust fund to include administrative expenses. Social Security outlays are also somewhat greater than expected due to the lowering of the retirement age for men and the greater use of the program. The highway program has grown less than was expected, although it has kept the projected revenue-expenditure balance.

The total surplus of the trust funds is only $1 billion compared to the expected $3 billion. This is largely due to the slack in the economy. Outlays have been somewhat heavier as people have retired earlier and more have been unemployed. The rise in collections has also been affected adversely.

## Resources

So far my nominal revenue forecasts have come out very well. However, before I take too many bows for them, let me quickly point out that even though I projected the rate of growth

Table 15—Revenues

(Billions of Dollars)

| | Actual 1959 | Budget Est. 1963 | CED 1963 | CED 1963[2] | Budget Est. 1964 | CED 1964 | CED 1964* | CED 1964*[1] | CED 1968*[2] |
|---|---|---|---|---|---|---|---|---|---|
| Individual income tax ......... | 36.7 | 47.3 | 46.4 | 49.1 | 45.8 | 48.5 | 51.9 | 47.9 | 57.8 |
| Corporation income tax ...... | 17.3 | 21.2 | 25.4 | 26.9 | 23.8 | 26.1 | 27.9 | 26.9 | 29.4 |
| Excise taxes .............. | 8.5 | 9.9 | 9.6 | 10.2 | 10.4 | 9.8 | 10.5 | 10.5 | 10.9 |
| All other receipts ........... | 5.6 | 7.1 | 6.0 | 6.4 | 6.8 | 6.1 | 6.5 | 6.5 | 6.5 |
| Total admin. budget ........ | 68.2 | 85.5 | 87.4 | 92.6 | 86.9 | 90.5 | 96.9 | 90.8 | 104.6 |
| Total cash budget .......... | 81.7 | 108.4 | 107.9 | 114.2 | 112.2 | 112.3 | 120.2 | 114.2 | 143.3 |

* See footnote to Table 1.

[1] Corrected for legislative changes and proposals.

[2] Not corrected for legislative changes.

of GNP precisely, at 3.0%, my revenue figures, when corrected —as they should be—for prices, are too high by about $5 billion. There is an important message in the explanation of this error.

Writing before the more sophisticated analyses of the determinants of the growth of potential output by Knowles for the Study of Employment, Growth, and Price Levels of the Joint Economic Committee, and Denison and Solow were available, I assumed that the historical rate of growth of 3% would suffice to keep the economy equidistant from the full employment ceiling. This research makes clear that it takes a rate of growth of at least 3.5% to achieve this goal, and this shortfall of 0.5% for a period of six years has widened the gap between actual and potential output. Corporate profit rates have fallen because they are highly responsive to the utilization rates of industry, which in turn closely reflect the size of the gap between actual and potential output. A shortfall of 3% in GNP will lead to a reduction in profits of 6% to 9%, hence also to a corresponding decline of corporate profit tax collections; a similar effect also applies to individual income-tax collections. These declines account for most of the difference between the actual revenues and the projections. To some extent they are offset by an increase in miscellaneous revenues, which include the advance repayments of loans by foreign governments in the last few years.

The projection of revenues into the future must take account of this relationship between the rate of expansion of the economy and federal revenues. I assume, as a first approximation, that a rate of real expansion of 3.5% a year will keep federal revenues increasing in a strictly proportionate manner to the money value of GNP. Should real growth be 1% greater than the 3.5% rate, that is should the gap be partially closed, I assume the extra per cent of GNP to produce 1.5% of extra revenue. Conversely, should the gap widen, the growth of revenues would be affected adversely in a more than proportionate manner, symmetrical to the above.

Using the official budget estimates of the 1964 budget as a point of departure, I give a series of projections of total federal revenues for 1968, assuming different rates of real growth. The official estimates for 1964 are believed to be conservative both bcause they assume prompt enactment of the President's tax-reduction proposals and because of conservative estimates of revenues that the GNP assumptions yield. On the other hand, the projected GNP for 1963 of $578 billion is on the optimistic side.

### Table 16—Alternative Revenue Projections for Various Rates of Growth of GNP

| Adm. Budget Revenues 1964 Est. (Billions) | Real Growth Rate of GNP (Per Cent) | Revenue Growth Rate (Per Cent) | Revenues 1968 (Billions) | Revenues 1970 (Billions) |
|---|---|---|---|---|
| | 5.5 | 7.5 | $111 | $129 |
| | 5.0 | 6.75 | 108 | 124 |
| | 4.5 | 6.0 | 105 | 118 |
| $86.9 | 4.0 | 5.25 | 102 | 113 |
| | 3.5 | 4.5 | 99 | 108 |
| | 3.0 | 3.75 | 96 | 103 |
| | 2.5 | 3.0 | 93 | 99 |

Assumptions: 1—Static elasticity of federal revenues with respect to output = 1.5.
2—Price rise of GNP = 1.0% a year.
3—Elasticity with respect to price change = 1.0.
4—Complete enactment of the President's tax program, assumed to produce a revenue loss of $5 billion beyond the 1964 figures.

Table 16 shows the relation of economic growth to the growth of Government revenues. The difference between 3% and 4% growth from now to the end of the decade means a difference of $10 billion in administrative budget revenues; between 3% and 5%, $20 billion. This is one crude measure of the stake of defense in economic growth, since, in the long run, revenue growth typically has a major influence on expenditures.

A real growth of about 5% will be necessary to restore full employment between now and 1968. Thus a full-employment revenue projection would correspond to the upper end of the table. Such growth might involve a rise in the GNP deflators of more than 1% a year. This would affect both revenues and expenditures, though the effect on revenues would probably be greater.

These projections assume a fixed-tax program. In fact, the upper end of the table is likely to be achieved only if the tax reduction program is carried out. Thus, two offsetting influences are at work: high growth requires reduction of tax rates; low growth does not require tax-rate reduction, but yields less revenues with the given tax system.

Achievement of a balanced budget requires that the private economy become more expansionary. This is a possibility, as demographic factors underlying consumer demand become more favorable after 1965. If the economy is kept within striking distance of full-capacity utilization, these growth factors may make themselves strongly felt and lift the economy both to full employment and balanced budgets.

### Deficits or Surpluses

Adding up all the revised expenditure projections, a range of expenditures for the administrative budget of $110 to $130 billion is obtained for 1968. This is a rather wide range, perhaps too wide to be useful. But the simple methods used in this review and revision of my earlier projections do not warrant a smaller range. It would take a more elaborate study to achieve a narrower range of estimates.

Nevertheless, even these crude figures make it clear that the budgetary situation confronting the Federal Government in the next few years is not going to be an easy one. The design of a proper fiscal policy under these circumstances is a matter I am happy to leave today to other members of this panel.

# Costs of Alternative Military Strategies

—*MURRAY L. WEIDENBAUM*

## Summary

*This paper examines three alternative military environments during the 1962-72 time period: (1) approximately the current level of military preparedness resulting from continued tensions, (2) continued tensions punctuated by a limited war, and (3) step-by-step disarmament.*

*Within the range of military spending likely in the coming decade, economic constraints do not appear to be an important direct limitation. Indirectly, and essentially through the federal budgetary process, financial constraints may well restrict the portion of our national resources devoted to security programs.*

*Estimates of national security expenditures under Cold War conditions are predicated on an average rate of increase in GNP in real terms of 3½ per cent a year, with federal revenues holding at 19-20 per cent of GNP. Strong pressures for a variety of non-defense programs would help keep total funding for Department of Defense, NASA, and related national security activities at one-half or less of the total federal budget and between 9 and 10 per cent of GNP.*

*In absolute terms, national security outlays are likely to rise from the current level of $52 billion a year to about $68 billion in 1972. The Department of Defense would continue to receive the bulk of national security funding. However, the fastest growth is expected to occur in the space exploration programs of the National Aeronautics and Space Administration, especially during the next five years.*

*The portion of our national output devoted to armaments has tended to diminish in recent years, as have inflationary pres-*

*sures. Also, much unutilized or under-utilized capacity remains in the economy. Hence, analyses of the burden of military expenditures generally conclude that, if necessary, the American economy could handle a higher level of armaments than at present or estimated in this paper. Many such analyses also conclude that the nation's long-term growth and prosperity do not require even the current level of defense spending.*

*Despite the concern over private affluence amid public poverty, our most critical industrial resources—engineers, scientists, and related requirements of research and development work— have been devoted primarily to national security programs.*

*Under a hypothetical case of limited war, it is estimated that national security spending would, in the peak year, rise to a level of about $18-20 billion above the Cold War estimate (up to 11 per cent of the estimated GNP). The mildness of such an increase compared to the Korean experience would result from the fact that the bulk of the resources required to fight a limited war during the coming decade are likely to be in the operational inventory at the start of any such conflict.*

*Under some arms control or disarmament suggestions, the cost of detection and other arms control equipment would at least offset any reduction in direct military outlays. A case is examined in which a net reduction in defense spending does occur. It is based on the gradual step-by-step disarmament program submitted by the US Government to the United Nations in the fall of 1961.*

*It is estimated that, under the US program, defense expenditures would decline from an assumed $56 billion in 1965, the start of the program, to $39 billion in 1968, the end of stage 1; to $27 billion in 1971, the end of the second stage; and would reach a maintenance level of $10 billion by 1977.*

*US contributions to international inspection and police forces, plus reasonable increases in civilian space exploration, would offset only a small fraction of the decline in military outlays. Such a decline would be at a much slower rate than the unilateral disarmament carried out in the United States after World War II.*

*In the absence of major active hostilities, neither Sputniks nor economy drives result in the sharp shifts in military spending which occur in wartime periods. Although we cannot forecast the specific weapons systems which will be funded in the coming decade, the continuation of the underlying threat, and the degradation of any military system over time point to a steady though rising trend of defense spending.*

---

This paper indicates the general range of costs which are likely to be required for the major types of military environments with which the United States will probably be faced in the 1962-72 time period. The paper deals with such questions as:

—What is the likely level of aggregate economic activity in the United States during the coming decade?

—What will the federal budget look like, in terms of both revenues and expenditures?

—What will be the relative pressures for defense and nondefense programs?

—Would the anticipated level of military outlays be a greater or lesser burden on the economy than the present level?

—What are the possibilities for military spending reaching far above or falling far below the contemplated level?

Essentially, this paper examines three alternative military environments: (1) approximately the current level of military preparedness resulting from continued tensions, (2) continued tensions punctuated by a limited war, and (3) step-by-step disarmament.

### Basic Economic Assumptions

This paper is not an exercise in long-term economic forecasting. Depending on the predilection of the analyst, he can choose from a wide array of GNP-type forecasts for 1970 or thereabouts. These generally range from a "pessimistic" 3% average annual increase, in real terms, to a projection of 4½% or 5% based on the "capacity" or "needs" of the economy. The last few years have witnessed the progressive pulling in of horns on the part of the most optimistic and the slight upgrading on the part of the most pessimistic, essentially a tendency toward a group consensus or, at least, an abandonment of what appear to be the most exposed positions.

The present writer has the predilection for an average annual rate of increase in GNP in real terms of 3½%. This is consistent with the reported long-term experience of the American economy and considerably above recent sluggish growth rates. On the basis of the 1962 price level, GNP would rise from $535 billion in the fiscal year ending June 30, 1962, to $770 billion in 1972.

Given the current progressive federal tax structure, the tendency would be for federal revenues to rise somewhat faster than the GNP. It would seem reasonable to estimate that the long-delayed general tax rate reduction would occur prior to the end of the decade. For the purposes of the estimates presented here, it is assumed that tax rate reductions of such magnitude and proper timing are made so as to result in a total level of federal revenues, on a consolidated-cash basis, equal to the current ratio of about 19-20% of GNP (this would be a more gradual tax rate reduction effort than recommended by President Kennedy in his January 1963 tax message).

For simplicity and convenience, an "equilibrium" budget is presented here so that federal expenditures equal federal revenues each year. Essentially, then, we are plotting long-term trend lines of federal receipts and disbursements, and not attempting to forecast the annual surpluses or deficits which will inevitably occur (See table 1).

Within the expenditure total, there will be key areas where pressures for an increased share of the budget will be particularly keen. The largest such area is likely to be the health, education, and social security programs. In the case of the major social insurance programs, the Department of Health, Education, and Welfare has released staff estimates which show that the disbursements of the Old Age and Survivors Insurance system will rise from $12 billion in 1962 to over $20 billion in 1975, assuming no change in the present law. On the quite reasonable assumption that the maximum earnings base will be adjusted

Table 1—GNP and the Federal Budget

| Fiscal Year | GNP | Federal Expenditures (or Receipts) | Federal As % of GNP |
|---|---|---|---|
| | (Billions of 1962 Dollars) | | |
| 1962 | $540 | $108 | 20 |
| 1967 | 630 | 125 | 20 |
| 1972 | 770 | 150 | 19 |

upward in the same proportion as the increase in general earnings levels and that benefits are simultaneously raised, the annual disbursements would rise to almost $32 billion by 1975.[1] Similar projections are available for other social insurance programs, such as the disability insurance trust fund.

The entire field of natural resources is another major example of an area of government spending where program expansions are limited only by budgetary constraints. To cite the potential for increase, the Senate Select Committee on National Water Resources in 1961 presented possible federal programs of water development for navigation, flood control, power generation, irrigation, water supply and waste disposal, recreation, wildlife and fisheries protection, and other similar activities which would require federal expenditures of almost $55 billion through 1980. In other cases, the federal agencies involved have outlined such new programs as those for forest lands ($3.6 billion during a ten-year period), highways through national forests ($2.7 billion by 1971), and range land conservation ($1.2 billion over a ten-year period). The total federal cost of these possible resource programs over a ten-year period has been estimated at about $4 billion a year, almost double the current rate.[2]

Federal aid to education may be in the early stage of a growth cycle. At present, federal programs in this area are essentially fragmentary and special-purpose. Assuming that a political consensus is reached sometime during the coming decade, a program of general aid to education would likely result in a literal tripling or quadrupling of federal expenditures in this field. Health, urban renewal, and local mass transportation are typical of other programs where strong pressures for increase are likely to occur during the coming decade.

Not all federal programs will demonstrate these explosive growth rates. With the essential completion of the World War II GI Bill program, veterans' services and benefits are currently being funded at rates far below those of the early postwar period. Similarly, economic foreign aid is being conducted at lower levels than during the Marshall Plan period. Also, once the bulk of the federal debt is refinanced at the current relatively high interest rates, the annual amount of interest payments will tend to level off. This particularly will be the case under the balanced budget conditions postulated.

Table 2 presents estimates of federal expenditures, by major function, which have been developed by the present writer in

Table 2—Federal Expenditures, by Function

(Fiscal Years, in Billions of 1962 Dollars)

| Function | 1962 | 1967 | 1972 |
|---|---|---|---|
| National security .................... | $ 52.5 | $ 62.0 | $ 68.0 |
| International (non-military) .......... | 2.8 | 3.4 | 4.2 |
| Agriculture ....................... | 5.8 | 6.6 | 7.6 |
| Natural resources .................... | 2.2 | 2.6 | 3.4 |
| Commerce & transportation ............ | 5.3 | 6.4 | 7.9 |
| Housing ............................ | 1.8 | 2.2 | 3.2 |
| Health, labor & welfare ............... | 23.8 | 28.0 | 38.0 |
| Education .......................... | .9 | 1.5 | 3.2 |
| Veterans ........................... | 6.1 | 6.4 | 7.0 |
| Interest ........................... | 6.8 | 7.4 | 7.8 |
| General ........................... | 1.8 | 2.0 | 2.5 |
| Adjustment ......................... | −2.2 | −3.5 | −2.8 |
| Total ........................... | $107.6 | $125.0 | $150.0 |

light of the above influences. National security programs—which will be described in much greater detail below—rise very significantly in absolute terms, from $52 billion in 1962 to $68 billion in 1972. However, when expressed as a percentage of GNP, expenditures for national security will tend to show a slightly declining share. This is consistent with the general historical trend in periods other than "hot war." Alternative projections of national security outlays will be presented subsequently. Certainly, there is no fixed, reserved portion of the federal budget allocated to defense. National security needs will compete continually against pressures to raise non-defense spending above the generous allowances made here.

## Trend of National Security Expenditures

National security expenditures are defined here as consisting of: (1) Department of Defense, exclusive of civilian construction programs and several items cited separately, (2) foreign military assistance, (3) the Atomic Energy Commission, (4) the National Aeronautics and Space Administration, and (5) several smaller activities such as the Selective Service System and stockpiling strategic and critical materials (See Table 3).

At the outset, it may be desirable to focus attention on two of these five elements. The Department of Defense currently spends

Table 3—Composition of National Security Expenditures

| Category | Fiscal Year 1962 in Billions |
| --- | --- |
| Department of Defense | $46.8 |
| Atomic Energy | 2.8 |
| Military assistance | 1.5 |
| NASA | 1.3 |
| Selective Service, etc. | .1 |
| Total | $52.5 |

Source: Federal Budget for 1963.

$47 billion a year, 89% of all national security outlays. NASA is the fastest growing element of national security spending at the present time, having risen from $400 million in 1960 to $1.3 billion in 1962 and scheduled to increase at similar rates for at least the next several years.

Although international comparisons of military spending levels are notoriously poor and misleading, there appears to be a consensus that the most reasonable estimate is to assume that the USSR devotes a roughly equivalent amount of resources to its military establishment. Presumably, the two nations attempt to generally match each other. This may be an assumption of convenience.

Since the end of the Korean fighting, the aggregate total of US military spending has tended to be relatively stable, with a moderately upward tilt in the trend line. Except for the last few years, most of the apparent increase is eliminated when the data are adjusted to exclude the effects of price rises. (It is not generally appreciated that over-all prices on military programs have been rising faster than those for the national economy as a whole. The sizeable shift of research and development (R&D) resources to military programs would be expected to require price incentives.)

Within the relatively stable total, major shifts have occurred in the composition of the outlays: (1) an increased share to research and development, (2) a shift from conventional land warfare equipment to advanced aeronautical weapons systems, (3) a shift from aircraft to missiles and now to space, and (4) a shift from metal working and related fabricating to electrical and chemical sub-systems and similar technologically-advanced components.[3]

In the aggregate, the economic burden of our national security programs has not been particularly overwhelming in recent years. Using the GNP comparison, the portion of our national resources devoted to armaments has tended to diminish rather than increase—a sort of unilateral type of gradual disarmament. In general, much unutilized or under-utilized capacity has remained in the economy, far more than is generally desired, and price inflation has not been particularly noticeable in more recent years. With reference to the concern over the substantial budget deficits which have occurred, it should be recalled that the major increases in federal expenditures in the past five years have occurred in the non-defense area, particularly in the health, education, and welfare programs. To be sure, the balance-of-payments problem continues to be a pressing one. However, the impact of national security programs here is not in terms of its total, but of the allocation between domestic and overseas outlays.

Available analyses of the burden of our military expenditures have generally concluded that, if necessary for military or political reasons, the American economy could handle, with a minimum of dislocation or hardship, a far higher level of armaments than envisioned in this paper. Such studies or statements have been made by such diverse groups as the Committee for Economic Development, the National Planning Association, a panel of the United States Arms Control and Disarmament Agency, and a group of outstanding university economists appearing before the Joint Economic Committee. However, many such analyses also concluded that the long-term prosperity and growth of the United States do not require even the current level of defense spending.

Despite the over-all excess capacity in the economy, there still may be an important opportunity cost involved in some of the highly specialized resources required for the defense program. The most striking case may be that of R&D where at least three-fifths of all the R&D performed in private industry is financed by the Department of Defense, the National Aeronautics and Space Administration, and the Atomic Energy Commission. A corollary of this is that a majority of the scientists and engineers in American industry are devoting their efforts to the defense program. Those who decry private affluence amid public poverty may well reflect as to the allocation of our most vital resources. The national choice has been quite clear—national strength, protection, and survival have been favored over tail fins, electric-powered toothbrushes, and fur-lined bed sheets.

In another fundamental way, the defense program has had a major impact on the industrial and geographic development of the United States. A high proportion of the growth industries and growth regions have been those identified with national security programs. Witness the shift in emphasis from the automobile manufacturing industry of the upper Midwest to the aircraft industry of the West Coast and now to the emerging space complex along the Gulf Coast.

## National Security Spending Under Continued Tension

The projections of national security expenditures shown in Table 4 are predicated on the following assumptions: (1) a continuation of the current state of international tensions, (2) a series of international incidents whose exact timing or nature we cannot forecast (Cuba, Lebanon, Laos), and (3) a continued rise in the economic strength and defense expenditures of the USSR. Likewise, "economy" drives both announced and unannounced are likely to occur from time to time. The net result of these opposing—and essentially unpredictable—forces is a slow, long-term upward trend in defense spending.

During the next five years the program to put a man on the moon and related NASA activities promise to be the fastest-growing portion of the national security budget. The estimates in Table 4 show as a result a larger share of the federal budget being devoted to national security in 1967. With a tapering off in the NASA growth rate in the late 1960's, national security programs receive a smaller portion of the funds in 1972 (45 versus 50 per cent of the total).

No significant increases are assumed here for the Atomic Energy Commission, the military assistance program, or the

Table 4—Comparisons of National Security Expenditures

| Fiscal Year | National Security Expenditures | Dept. of Defense Expenditures | As % of GNP Nat. Sec. | As % of GNP DOD | As % of Fed. Exp. Nat. Sec. | As % of Fed. Exp. DOD |
|---|---|---|---|---|---|---|
| | (Billions of 1962 Dollars) | | | | | |
| 1962 | $52 | $47 | 10% | 9% | 48% | 44% |
| 1967 | 62 | 52 | 10 | 8 | 50 | 42 |
| 1972 | 68 | 57 | 9 | 7 | 45 | 38 |

smaller items in the national security categories. It is anticipated, for example, that the other members of the NATO Alliance will be meeting an increasing part of total NATO defense expenditures during the coming decade. A major civil defense program would raise the military spending level shown here, possibly at the expense of domestic welfare or construction programs.

Within the total of national security spending, important changes will continue to occur in the military product mix. Over-all, aircraft expenditures, after rising briefly on account of the Berlin build-up, are proceeding again on a long-term downward trend. With the initial build-up of our ICBM forces, missile outlays have tended to level off within the last few years (See Table 5). These developments would permit major increases in either military space systems, tactical warfare equipment, or some trade-off between the two.

Without relaxing our assumptions concerning the general nature of the Cold War and of our response to it, variations in the rate of economic growth, federal tax rates, and the allocation of federal budgetary funds could alter significantly the

### Table 5—Trends in Aerospace Programs

*Fiscal Years ending June 30*
*(Dollars in Billions)*

| Expenditures | 1961 Actual | 1962 Estimate | 1963 Estimate |
|---|---|---|---|
| Aircraft | | | |
|   Procurement ........ | $5.9 | $6.4 | $5.6 |
|   R&D ............. | .5 | .6 | .6 |
|     Total ........... | $6.4 | $7.0 | $6.2 |
| Missiles | | | |
|   Procurement ........ | $3.0 | $3.5 | $3.9 |
|   R&D ............. | 3.0 | 2.5 | 2.2 |
|     Total ........... | $6.0 | $6.0 | $6.1 |
| Astronautics | | | |
|   R&D ............. | $ .5 | $ .7 | $1.0 |
|   NASA expenditures .. | .5 | 1.0 | 2.0 |
|     Total ........... | $1.0 | $1.7 | $3.0 |

Source: Federal Budget for 1963.

amounts available for national security. For example, were GNP to grow at 4% rather than 3½% a year, and were federal tax rates to remain constant, and were the allocation of federal expenditures by functional area to remain constant, total outlays for national security programs could reach $84 billion in 1972 rather than the $68 billion shown here.

Likewise, were GNP to grow at the average rate of only 3% a year and were the share of the national security budget to decline at the rate that occurred in 1956 through 1961, national security spending might be only $57 billion instead of $68 billion in 1972. Certainly, the future range of defense spending is a wide one, even under the general conditions postulated here as most likely.

**National Security Spending Under Limited War**

The possibility of the involvement of the United States in a limited war yields various alternative estimates in terms of magnitude and timing of defense spending and resource commitment. For purposes of illustration let us examine the hypothetical case of a limited war beginning in the fiscal year 1965. The assumed conflict occurs in an area somewhat peninsular or restricted in nature geographically. Moreover, an adjacent critical national boundary limits the freedom of action of United States or United Nations forces; any correspondence to recent past limited wars is left to the reader's determination.

The conflict produces inconclusive results and a shaky truce ensues in 1967. The next five years (1968-72) witness a series of international crises culminating in "sub-limited" type war actions, such as Vietnam, the Berlin airlift, and Lebanon— these examples result mainly from the writer's lack of imagination. The net result is the continuation of a high state of limited war readiness by the United States, its allies, and their antagonists. Such an assumed limited war would present a far different situation in terms of national security spending than did the onset of the Korean conflict in 1950.

In the three-year period 1948-50, military expenditures by the United States totaled less than $60 billion. During 1960-62, military expenditures have exceeded $130 billion. In terms of manpower, the three services required a 150% increase in less than three years to reach their Korean peak of 3.5 million men. By comparison, the current level of 2.8 million men would leave a required increase of only 25% to reach a 3.5 million target. In essence, the bulk of the resources required to fight a limited war during the coming decade are likely to be in the operational inventory at the start of any such conflict.

Rough approximations of the cost of additional military expenditures under these assumed limited war conditions would be in the order of $18-20 billion for 1967, the peak year. This would raise the $52 billion here estimated for DOD outlays for Cold War in 1967 to about $72 billion. The latter figure would still represent only 11% of the GNP estimated for 1967 under Cold War conditions (any increase in GNP resulting from the higher level of military spending would reduce the ratio).

The added military costs would occur primarily in selected categories where an increase in operational capability could be accomplished swiftly—tactical aircraft, ordnance, combat vehicles, miscellaneous battlefield "hardware," and military personnel. The R&D, space, and construction categories are not likely to be affected significantly.

After the postulated truce in our hypothetical limited war, procurement of weapons systems would be reduced somewhat from the new wartime peak. However, maintenance and periodic replacement of a force-in-being substantially larger than that prior to the conflict would be required because of the unstable and volatile international situation. This would result in a trend of military expenditures parallel to the Cold War forecast but at a higher level, somewhat similar to the post-Korean trend.[4]

**National Security Spending Under Disarmament**

The available literature contains a great variety of proposals and analyses of arms control and/or disarmament programs. Some of these analyses conclude that, at least for some major period, the cost of detection, monitoring, and related arms-control equipment would at least offset any reduction in direct or conventional military outlays. Such a situation is certainly conceivable. However, from the viewpoint of this paper, such an assumption would conveniently assume away the problem. We will examine the hypothetical case involving a disarmament program which does result in a diminution in federal spending for national security. Specifically, we will examine the United States program for general and complete disarmament which this nation submitted to the United Nations in the fall of 1961 (See Table 6).

#### Table 6—US Disarmament Program

---

*First Stage*

1. Reduce armed forces to 2.1 million.
2. Reduce armaments by balanced steps.
3. Limit or discontinue strategic nuclear weapons.

*Second Stage*

1. Establish UN peace force.
2. Further reduce armed forces and weapon stockpiles.

*Third Stage*

1. Fully functioning UN peace force.
2. Prohibit manufacture of armaments except for internal order or UN peace force.

---

Source: *United States Program for General and Complete Disarmament in a Peaceful World*, September 25, 1961.

Essentially, this was a program for gradual step-by-step disarmament.[5] Table 6 shows the highlights of the proposal. Quite clearly, this would be a more gradual affair than the rapid, unilateral disarmament which occurred in the United States after World War II.

For the purposes of costing out such a disarmament program, this paper relies upon the report of the panel on Economic Impacts of Disarmament on which the present writer served.[6] In a report submitted to the United States Arms Control and Disarmament Agency in January 1962, the panel made its estimates on the assumption that disarmament would begin in 1965 and that, in the absence of disarmament, military spending would be $56 billion in that year. The panel estimated that military spending would decline to about $39 billion by the end of the first stage in 1968, to $27 billion in 1971, which would be at the end of the second stage, and would reach $10 billion in 1977. The latter would be a minimum maintenance level for internal order, and would consist primarily of operating expenditures and a relatively insignificant amount of procurement of new weapons (see Table 7).

Two relatively direct types of offsets were envisioned by the panel: the United States would contribute to United Nations activities in the area of providing inspection and deterrent and police forces; also, a major build-up would occur in the civilian space programs. In good measure, much of the increase in the National Aeronautics and Space Administration budget under disarmament conditions would result from the withdrawal of

## Table 7—Model of General and Complete Disarmament

Expenditures for Security and Associated
Programs (in Billions of 1960 Dollars)

| | 1960 | 1965 | Stage I 1968 | Stage II 1971 | Stage IIIA 1974 | Stage IIIB 1977 |
|---|---|---|---|---|---|---|
| **US Defense** | | | | | | |
| Procurement (inc. R&D) | | | | | | |
| Aircraft ............. | $ 6.9 | $ 6.0 | $ 2.0 | $ 0.5 | $ 0.5 | $ 0.5 |
| Missiles ............. | 5.1 | 5.4 | 0.5 | 0.1 | 0.1 | 0.1 |
| Military space ........ | 0.5 | 2.6 | 4.4 | 2.5 | 2.5 | 0.0 |
| Ships ............... | 1.9 | 2.4 | 1.5 | 0.2 | 0.2 | 0.2 |
| Other ............... | 3.6 | 4.5 | 3.8 | 3.0 | 1.5 | 0.7 |
| Subtotal .......... | $18.0 | $20.9 | $12.2 | $ 6.3 | $ 4.8 | $ 1.5 |
| Personnel ........... | 11.7 | 15.1 | 13.1 | 11.1 | 6.7 | 4.7 |
| Operation and maintenance ........ | 10.2 | 12.6 | 8.9 | 6.0 | 3.9 | 2.1 |
| Construction ......... | 1.6 | 2.0 | 0.5 | 0.2 | 0.2 | 0.2 |
| Military assistance .... | 1.6 | 2.4 | 2.0 | 1.5 | 0.0 | 0.0 |
| Military AEC ........ | 2.1 | 1.4 | 0.5 | 0.2 | 0.0 | 0.0 |
| Civil defense ........ | — | 1.7 | 1.7 | 1.7 | 1.7 | 1.7 |
| US Defense Total ... | $45.2 | $56.1 | $38.9 | $27.0 | $17.3 | $10.2 |
| **U.S. Contribution to International** | | | | | | |
| Inspection ........... | — | — | — | $ 3.2 | $ 2.6 | $ 1.3 |
| Police forces ........ | — | — | — | — | 1.8 | 2.7 |
| Deterrent forces ...... | — | — | — | — | — | 2.6 |
| Juridical & administrative functions ....... | — | — | — | 0.5 | 0.5 | 0.5 |
| US Contributions— Total ........... | — | — | — | $ 3.7 | $ 4.9 | $ 7.1 |
| **TOTAL US EXPENDITURES ON SECURITY PROGRAMS** ........ | $45.2 | $56.1 | $38.9 | $30.7 | $22.2 | $17.3 |
| *Associated Programs* | | | | | | |
| NASA ............... | $ 0.4 | $ 2.7 | $ 4.5 | $ 5.9 | $ 7.4 | $ 8.9 |
| Civilian AEC ......... | 0.5 | 1.4 | 2.0 | 2.0 | 2.0 | 2.0 |
| Assoc. Programs Total ............. | $ 0.9 | $ 4.1 | $ 6.5 | $ 7.9 | $ 9.4 | $10.9 |
| GRAND TOTAL ..... | $46.1 | $60.2 | $45.4 | $38.6 | $31.6 | $28.2 |

supporting research, development, and facilities by the military forces. Even in the absence of any increase in NASA programs, it would be likely that NASA expenditures would have to rise significantly to compensate for this withdrawal.

As can be seen in Table 7, the estimates made for these offsets would not prevent a major, but gradual, reduction in security-related spending—from $60 billion in 1965 to $28 billion in 1977. It is not the purpose of this paper to explore the adjustment problems which would result from disarmament or the potentials for shifting resources to non-defense purposes. Presumably, the problem would not be one of straining the nation's economic capacity, but overcoming the structural problems involved in shifting a major share of the nation's resources to peacetime use.[7]

**Findings and Conclusions**

Figure 1 shows graphically the probable ranges of military spending for the three alternative military environments examined in this paper—cold war, limited war, and step-by-step disarmament.

Essentially, the paper concludes that, within the ranges of military spending likely in the coming decade, economic constraints do not appear to be an important limitation—directly. Indirectly, and essentially through the federal budgetary process, financial constraints will restrict the portion of our national resources devoted to security purposes (this may particularly be the case if a combination of tax reductions and continual increments of new legislation requiring government subsidy and benefit payments results in continuing budget deficits). It certainly is not economic analysis that yields a $100 billion ceiling (or floor) on the federal budget for 1964.

As of the present time, "economic analysis" will be brought to bear on the questions of choice among alternative weapons systems and proposals. Certainly, the increased emphasis on cost-effectiveness and related economic-type comparisons represents a major advance in military programming and budget-making. However, it should be realized that, at least as presently utilized, these are tools for making allocations within a military budget total which in good measure is the result of political rather than economic analysis.

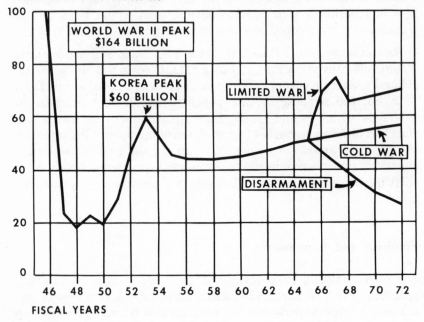

DOD—NASA EXPENDITURES, 1945 — 1972

BILLIONS OF 1962 DOLLARS

Figure 1

## Appendix on Methodology

Economic forecasting was once described as neither an art nor a science, but merely a hazard. Forecasting or projecting defense spending involves more than the usual quota of pitfalls.

The simplest method is to take military expenditures as a constant percentage of GNP. A slightly more sophisticated approach, somewhat in line with recent experience, is to estimate the military expenditure level as a declining percentage of GNP.

However, the realities are certainly more complex than that. Military expenditures have been a major part, but only a part, of the federal budget and certainly an important but smaller proportion of GNP. Within the constraint of a budget which is approximately in balance over the course of a business cycle, the GNP, and its growth, is far more of a limitation on federal revenues than on military spending directly. A model of the federal budget is needed, which is built up from both the revenue side and the expenditure side, which encompasses the various non-defense programs as well as defense programs, and possibly, tax and debt reductions over the period.

In effect, this is the methodology which has been followed in this paper. However, for more detailed purposes, such as industry market research and business planning, resort should be made to what I have termed the "top down versus bottom up" approach. The methodology in this paper is of the "top down" variety, relating, in turn, the GNP to the federal budget to military spending.

The "bottom up" aspect involves arriving at the military budget total by building up from cost estimates of each of the individual weapons systems which are likely to be included in the budget during the forecast period. Often the "bottom up" approach yields a higher total than the "top down" approach during the first few years of a projection. Then, as the analyst tends to "run out" of new systems, the "bottom up" curve tends to show a strong downward trend.

Essentially, the "top down versus bottom up" approach is a series of successive approximations which involves adjustments to the "top line" resulting from phasing of specific key systems as well as adjustments in the "bottom up" items as a result of funding limitations or availability.

Underlying any statistical methodology which may be used, the present writer finds it essential to bring to bear an underlying qualitative analysis of the forces that determine military expenditure levels. Such a budget philosophy shows that, in the absence of major active hostilities, neither sputniks nor economy drives result in the sharp shifts in military spending levels which occur at the beginning or ending of wartime periods. Also, although we cannot forecast necessarily the specific weapon systems which will be funded in the coming decade, the continuation of the underlying threat and the degradation of any military system over time point to a steady though rising trend of defense spending.

Possibly with tongue in cheek, the writer has previously described his approach to military budget analysis and forecasting as resting on an unpatented blend of statistical data, historical relationships, heroic assumptions, and a sufficient mixture of past boners and good guesses usually referred to as experience.

### FOOTNOTES

[1] Moses Lukaczer, *Economic Assumptions Underlying the Medium-Range Estimates of the Federal Old-Age and Survivors Insurance and Disability*

*Insurance Trust Funds, 1966-1975,* US Department of Health, Education, and Welfare, August, 1961.

[2] US Arms Control and Disarmament Agency, *The Economic and Social Consequences of Disarmament,* Reply to the Inquiry of the Secretary General of the United Nations, March, 1962.

[3] Cf. M. L. Weidenbaum, "The Impact of Military Procurement on American Industry," ed. J. A. Stockfisch, *Planning and Forecasting in the Defense Industries* (Belmont, Calif.: Wadsworth Publishing Company, 1962).

[4] The author is indebted to John C. Leeds, Jr., of The Boeing Co., for the estimates and analyses of limited war costs.

[5] *United States Program for General and Complete Disarmament in a Peaceful World,* September 25, 1961.

[6] US Arms Control and Disarmament Agency, *Economic Impacts of Disarmament,* Economic Series 1, January, 1962.

[7] Cf. M. L. Weidenbaum, "Economic Adjustments to Disarmament," *University of Washington Business Review,* February, 1963.

# National Security and Competing Costs

*—ROGER A. FREEMAN*

*Summary*

Economic and fiscal projections in recent years have tended to be slightly more optimistic than the subsequent record justified. Each of the latest six US budgets when submitted to Congress showed a surplus, for a cumulative total of $9 billion. All but one wound up in the red, with a cumulative deficit of $33 billion. The cause: economic growth and governmental revenues had been overestimated, expenditures and the forces demanding them underestimated.

Long-range fiscal projections prepared during the past five years generally expect revenues at existing levels of taxation to meet or exceed prospective expenditures. Current trends make this unlikely to come true. Some of the projections appear to have estimated economic and revenue trends correctly but underrated expenditures; others estimated expenditures correctly but may have overrated economic and revenue growth. If present trends continue—and this, of course, is a big IF—taxes will equal a greater percentage of GNP in 1970 than they did in 1960, and the public debt will be substantially larger.

Long-range (five to ten year) projections of national product, governmental revenues, governmental expenditures for defense and for civilian purposes are needed for national security planning because it is important to know sufficiently in advance:

a) the approximate magnitude of the resources that are likely to become available;

b) the changes that may be required in revenues, or in defense or civilian expenditure programs;

*c) the adjustments that may be called for if defense require-
ments either accelerate or decelerate.*

*The widely-held belief that defense requirements are accorded
a priority over the demands for domestic functions is not borne
out by the postwar record. It appears that budgetary ceilings
(though more sophisticated euphemisms have replaced this
term) for the Defense Department were sometimes substantially
affected by a desired expansion in the domestic activities of
government. Over the past ten years, national defense has declined from 49% of all governmental expenditures in the United
States to 30%, and from 69% of all Federal Government expenditures to 51%.*

*The Federal Government, between 1952 and 1960, increased
spending for defense by 2%, for all other purposes by 123%.
Between 1960 and 1963 defense and civilian expenditures rose
at more nearly equal rates, 22% and 26%, respectively. The
average annual growth of federal non-defense expenditures in
constant dollars may be estimated at 7.5% between 1952 and
1960, at 6.5% between 1960 and 1963 (fiscal years).*

*Projections which used the historical rate of economic growth
of 3% annually for GNP and corresponding revenue estimates
have so far paralleled actual trends. Whether the economy (and
public revenues) will in the future grow at a faster rate, as
several of the projections assume, remains to be seen.*

*Defense costs, which were held steady for some years, started
to turn upward in 1960 and give all signs of continuing up. An
average of some recent projections suggests a decennial rise of
about 32% (constant dollars) which does not appear unreasonable. This would place defense expenditures between 9.5% and
10.0% of GNP throughout the 1960's.*

*Domestic public services have been the country's most ebullient
growth industry, and there is nothing to indicate that this will
not continue. The budgets of the past ten years (as well as of
earlier periods) are a clear warning that no purpose is served
in underestimating the power of the forces that demand a rapid
expansion of the domestic services and benefits of government.
If we project defense costs to rise 32% and non-defense at 63%
(approximately the historical rate) between 1960 and 1970, the
total increase in public expenditures during the 1960's will be
divided: one-fifth to defense, four-fifths to non-defense.*

*Under this projection the expenditures of all governments
(federal, state, local) will, in 1970, equal a greater percentage*

*of GNP than they did in 1960, unless GNP meanwhile rises at an annual average of more than 4%. This will create problems of revenue-raising and of public debt. Much of the financing can be and probably will be done at state and local levels. But pressure on the federal budget for greater support of domestic functions will be heavy and have its impact on appropriations for defense as well as on the future level of federal taxation.*

*Disarmament, if and when, may permit a substantial cut in defense outlays but can come only gradually, with sufficient warning. It could be offset by corresponding tax reductions.*

*A sharp and sudden increase in defense requirements, because of a deterioration in the international or military situation, can be financed, but with difficulty. Experience has proven that public spending for civilian purposes stubbornly and successfully resists efforts at cutting it back and that a slowdown in its growth rate may be the most that can be expected. Income taxes, the mainstay of the federal treasury, are still levied at close to wartime peak rates. They can be made more productive but not by very much. The most productive potential may be a general manufacturers' excise tax. That type of tax is a major revenue producer in other industrial countries but not now used in the United States, where consumption taxation in general is an underdeveloped area of taxation.*

---

The batting average of fiscal and economic forecasts in recent years is nothing to write home about. In fact, somebody who is truly charitable wouldn't even mention them and let them pass from memory without so much as an obituary notice. But then, how are we ever going to do better in the future unless we learn from our past mistakes? If the errors reveal no particular pattern, if they run at random up or down, then we may just have to refine our techniques and use more sophisticated tools. But if they point in one direction—watch out! That may suggest that our emotions or secret hopes or not-so-secret hopes or something else I'd rather not define are getting the better of our knowledge. So, with malice toward none, but with only as much charity as the scholarly spirit will permit, let us look at some predictions or estimates, and see what happened afterwards.

Each of the six most recent federal budgets (1958-63), when submitted to Congress by the President, showed a surplus, for a cumulative total of $9 billion. All but one wound up in the red, for a cumulative deficit of $33 billion. Each of the original budgets had *under*estimated expenditures, for a total of $18 billion. All but one had *over*estimated receipts for a total of $24 billion. This is too consistent a trend to be written off as a coincidence. It shows a built-in bias, not necessarily deliberate, but a bias nevertheless.

We tend to underestimate future expenditures if we underrate the determination and political power of the forces pushing for expansion of governmental activities. Overestimates of receipts are usually due to expectations of economic growth which are not justified under prevailing circumstances. That is the risk of engaging in too much economic growthmanship. Focusing our sights on those high rates can give us tunnel vision, and we may eventually qualify for *The New Yorker's* "infatuation-with-sound-of-own-words department" (unless its editor objects to the slightly mixed metaphors).

Overestimating economic growth rates reaches not only into the future but also back into the past. Speaking to the Economic Club of New York last December 14, the President said: "In the past two years, we have made significant strides. Our GNP has risen 11%, while inflation has been arrested."

This was good news indeed. It's just that I am puzzled why *Economic Indicators* for January 1963, prepared by the President's Council of Economic Advisers, showed the increase in GNP over the past two years (third quarter of 1960 to third quarter of 1962, the most recent period available) at 9.9%, inflation (implicit price deflator for GNP) at 2.6%, and the GNP growth in *constant* dollars at 7.1%. The difference is only 3.9 percentage points which can be defined as 96.1% accuracy. But 3.9% of a GNP that totalled $554 billion in 1962 equals $22 billion. Which reminds me of the legislator who complained: "Sometimes I think we just appropriate a billion here and a billion there, but before I know it, it adds up to a lot of money."

Our economy has shown a bull-headed imperviousness to even the most persuasive pleas for faster growth in spite of rapid expansion of governmental spending, hefty public deficits, and even some tax concessions in 1962. Somehow it seems like pushing on a string. Or, could the true nature and etiology of the ailment have escaped our economic diagnosticians? Could we be using the wrong therapy?

With the one-year estimates of the US budget somewhat off base, we would not expect long-range projections to prove overly accurate. To be sure, most of them, at least those I am going to mention, were carefully prepared by eminently competent scholars. Some of them hit the economic growth rate on the dot, but underrated the dynamism of welfare expenditures. Others plotted expenditures correctly, but overshot the mark on economic growth and tax collections. The net results were the same, and parallel our experience with the US budgets: the expected balance or surplus turned into a deficit.

Despite all the shortcomings and pitfalls of fiscal and economic estimating, however, we cannot afford to quit the business of projecting. Budgets must be prepared. What's more, budgets cannot be intelligently composed in terms of one year without planning for a longer period ahead. Some programs take one or two years to get started, and five to ten years to reach completion. In making choices among innumerable projects, in deciding how many to take on, planners must have a rough idea of the magnitude of the resources that are likely to become available. Without some such structural framework, whatever they are doing can hardly be called planning because it lacks the factual basis without which planning is mere wishful thinking. (Not that planning *with* projections wasn't sometimes wishful thinking. But at least it shouldn't be off the beam quite as much.)

Some people believe that strategic planning really does not require intricate and laborious—and inevitably uncertain and risky—projections of GNP, of governmental revenues, and of non-defense expenditures. Security from foreign aggression, after all, is and must be the nation's first and foremost concern, ahead of all other claims, demands, needs, wants, or amenities. Whatever national defense requires it will get and other public services and consumers just have to do with what's left.

Whoever thinks so may have listened to certain speeches emanating from Washington but has not followed the record of defense budgets and civilian budgets in the period since the end of World War II. Analytical studies by Samuel P. Huntington, Warner R. Schilling, Paul Y. Hammond, Glenn H. Snyder, and others which traced the fate of military requests at the hands of the Presidency and Congress suggest that often the shoe was on the other foot: prospective revenues and the available margin under the debt ceiling were estimated, the cost of the desired domestic programs was deducted, and the balance became the ceiling for the Armed Services.[1] This was, of course, not true during the Korean and Cold War build-up from 1950 to 1952. Nor was it simply a one-way street. If the essential needs of national security had not been so high, domestic programs might have grown at a faster rate. There is a mutual influence between the magnitude of the domestic and military functions: the more is allocated to one, the less is likely to be available for the other, and the emphasis shifts with the situation and prevailing sentiment among policymakers.

Of course there is, as a rule, nothing absolute or sacrosanct about the budgetary requests of the armed services. Military men, as departmental officials generally who know their own field but are not faced with the broad range of demands on the public treasury, tend to estimate their own requirements on the high side. Nor are decisions on weapons systems always clear-cut. Well-informed, reasonable men may disagree on the relationship between investment and probable return on a new project. There is almost no limit as to how much can be done for defense. A safety margin or reserve, a second or third line, are often needed. Several parallel approaches must be pursued in R&D lest we fall behind our opponents. This may also hold true for some operational systems.

Judgment on what programs can be implemented and when, is influenced by the amount of resources that are likely to become available. Only comprehensive projections can give us an approximate idea of what appears to be within the range of probability.

### Fiscal Projections

Probably the best known projections in recent years of GNP, of public revenues, and of public expenditures for national security as well as for other purposes, were prepared by the Rockefeller Brothers Fund "Special Studies Project," [2] by Otto Eckstein for the Committee for Economic Development,[3] by Gerhard Colm and Manuel Helzner,[4] and by the US Bureau of the Budget.[5] All of these projections assume that the Cold War will continue at about the intensity of the mid-and late 1950's, that no revolutionary inventions on either side will radically change the requirements or conditions of modern warfare in a manner that cannot now be foreseen, that there will be no major shift in the balance of power, and that national economies will continue to grow at reasonable rates.

Some authors prepared several sets of projections—high, medium, low, or simply high and low. In those cases I used either the medium projection or an average between high and low. The figures aim to reflect the conditions which the authors deemed most likely to materialize.

Obviously, no strategist can afford to prepare plans for only one course of events though he may feel that it is the most likely one to come true. Several sets of blueprints are required to meet other circumstances that may prevail at some future point. I intend to discuss in the latter part of this paper the adjustments that may be called for:

a) if a genuine and lasting relaxation in international tensions and a multilateral agreement lead to adequately inspected partial disarmament;

b) if our defense expenditures need to be sharply and rapidly expanded because of developments such as these: the Cold War situation deteriorates, brush-fire wars threaten or break out, the Communist countries step up their military preparations, a breakthrough occurs to new and more expensive weapons systems, open war between the major powers becomes a distinct and imminent possibility.

First, however, I shall discuss trends under the most likely set of circumstances.

### Economic Growth Projections

Other members of this panel will deal with problems of economic growth at greater length. I intend only to highlight a few past projections and the experience to date.

In the first decade after World War II, economists generally expected GNP to continue growing at its long-range historical rate of about three per cent annually. Gerhard Colm, in 1952, projected GNP to increase at 2.9% annually and to reach $425 billion (1951 dollars) in 1960.[6] He hit it right on the dot. GNP in 1960 equalled $423 billion (1951 dollars).

Frederic Dewhurst's monumental study, using a 2.6% annual growth rate, placed GNP in 1960 at $415 billion (1953 dollars); this was $18 billion (1953 dollars) low.[7] The staff of the Joint Economic Committee of Congress in 1954 thought that GNP might expand at the rate of 3.2% annually and estimated it at $535 billion (1953 dollars) for 1965. As of 1962, GNP would need to increase an average of 5% annually in each of the three remaining years, 1963, 1964, and 1965 to reach the projected level.[8]

During the second half of the 1950's, economists raised their sights and started projecting GNP at annual rates of 3.5% and 4.0%. Even some five-percenters appeared on the scene but have been less noticeable for the past year or two. Such optimism was encouraged when for two years in succession, 1951 and 1952 (the years of the Korean and Cold War build-up), annual growth ran as high as 8.3% each and yielded some very respectable annual averages for periods that included those years.

It has been suggested that there might be more to the growth in projected growth rates than meets the eye.[9] In the late 1950's, Kenneth Galbraith's *The Affluent Society* attracted wide attention and his advocacy of a more rapid expansion in domestic governmental services gained many disciples. They soon found that budgets could be sharply increased only if either taxes or public debts were substantially boosted or if GNP grew faster. The first two possibilities failed to kindle the general public's imagination but the suggestion of more rapid economic growth caught fire. Unfortunately, sustained economic growth rates of 3.5% annually or more have yet to make their appearance in the United States.

The several studies use different initial and terminal years and various constant dollars. To make them comparable, I extended the data to 1970 as terminal year and converted the amounts to 1960 dollars.[10] Adjusted to a common denominator, the GNP projections of the mentioned four major studies appear as follows:

Table 1—Projected Growth Rates and GNP in 1970

| Author | Growth Rate of GNP | | Estimated GNP in 1970 |
|--------|--------|--------|--------|
| | Annual | Decennial | (1960 Dollars) (Billions) |
| Eckstein (medium) ... | 3% | 34% | $684 |
| Bureau of the Budget (a) ........ | 4% | 48% | 750 |
| Rockefeller Panel (b).. | 4% | 48% | 762 |
| Colm-Helzner (Judgment Model) .. | 5% | 63% | 816 |

(a) Alternative rate suggested: 3%.

(b) Shows projections at 3%, 4%, and 5% and suggests that a rate of 4% appears likely, one of 5% possible.

What has been the experience to date? By straight-line interpolation, with prices adjusted to 1962, the GNP projections for 1962 are:

(Billions)

| | |
|---|---|
| Eckstein ......................... | $554 |
| Bureau of the Budget .............. | 559 |
| Rockefeller Panel .................. | 571 |
| Colm-Helzner ..................... | 576 |

Early in 1962 the Council of Economic Advisers predicted that GNP in that year would total $570 billion. The forecast was gradually scaled down and the present estimate is $554 billion.

The Eckstein projection has so far proven accurate, the others were somewhat high. This does not necessarily mean that the economy will follow the Eckstein projection for the rest of the 1960's. A sustained sharp upturn could still earn this decade the label of the "Soaring Sixties." In fact, the unusually rapid growth in the labor force during the 1960's due to the maturing of the postwar babies, makes this a distinct possibility. Conversely, it is conceivable that the decade might turn into the "Sagging Sixties." But if the long-range historical growth rate of GNP—36% per decade, which approximates the average of the past four years—continues, GNP will total about $700 billion (1962 dollars) by 1970.

**Expenditure Projections**

The Bureau of the Budget projected only the administrative budget of the US Government, which includes all defense costs but excludes certain civilian-type expenditures channeled through trust funds. The other three studies aim to cover all governmental expenditures, including those of state and local governments, but use slightly differing definitions of comprehensiveness. Their totals are not directly comparable with each other without adjustments. Their trend rates, however, can be compared.

The Bureau of the Budget expects defense expenditures to decline during the 1960's. The other studies project them as rising more slowly than GNP, governmental outlays for civilian purposes faster. This continues the trend of the past ten years during which national security gradually slid from 48% of all governmental expenditures to 30%.

Table 2—Projected 10-Year Growth Rates of Governmental Expenditures

|  | All Expenditures | National Security | Other |
|---|---|---|---|
| Eckstein (medium) .......... | 44% | 32% | 51% |
| Colm-Helzner (Judgment Model) ......... | 59% | 23% | 78% |
| Rockefeller Panel (mean between high and low projections) .............. | 64% | 41% | 79% |
| Bureau of the Budget (medium, federal administrative budget only) .............. | | −2% | 71% |

The *actual rates of growth* between the fiscal years 1957 (starting year of the Rockefeller projections) and 1961 (most recent year for which comprehensive fiscal statistics are available from the Bureau of the Census) equalled, if adjusted to constant dollars and to a *decennial* basis:

| All Expenditures | National Security | Other |
|---|---|---|
| 63% | 0% | 74% |

National security expenditures remained stable (in *constant* dollars) between 1957 and 1961, but were significantly boosted in 1962 and 1963. The decennial growth rate during the four-year period 1959 to 1963 amounts to 32%. This equals Eckstein's medium projection for security expenditures as well as the average between the Colm-Helzner and Rockefeller Panel projections (23% and 41%, respectively). Another well-informed study adds weight to a projection at that level. Charles J. Hitch, who has since been appointed Comptroller of the Department of Defense, pointed at the possibility that defense outlays may rise in proportion to GNP, barring unforeseeable changes in the international situation, and that GNP may grow between 2.5% and 3.5% annually.[11] The medium projection according to Hitch thus suggests a decennial growth in defense expenditures of 34%.

The figures cited above show that governmental expenditures for purposes other than national security grew between 1957 and 1961 at approximately the decennial rate projected by the

**Table 3—Governmental Expenditures for Purposes other than National Security, 1902-62**

(as a percentage of GNP)

| | |
|---|---|
| 1902 | 7.2% |
| 1922 | 11.6% |
| 1932 | 17.4% |
| (maximum during the Depression: 20.4% in 1936) | |
| 1942 | 13.5% |
| (low point during World War II: 1944—12.1%) | |
| 1952 | 15.3% |
| 1961 | 22.8% |
| 1962 est. | 23.0% |

Rockefeller Panel and Colm-Helzner, and somewhat faster than suggested by Eckstein. The long-range trend has been for the cost of domestic public services to rise faster than GNP (see Tables 13 and 14 at end of paper).

Since 1902 non-defense, i.e., civilian expenditures of government have been increasing an average of 66% each decade in *constant* dollars, GNP only 36%. The consistency of this secular trend suggests that it could well continue through the 1960's and beyond. Viewing the vast demands in the fields of education, welfare, roads, natural resources, etc., and the many proposals for expansion at federal and state-local levels which barely failed of passage, a decennial increase of about 70% in this decade does not at all seem improbable.

There is even considerable support for a substantial boost in the historical rate of increase in public service expenditures. For example, the National Planning Association, in a policy statement on January 18, 1960, declared that in another decade "non-defense spending by all branches of government—federal, state, local—will have to be doubled if deficiencies and requirements in many fields are to be met."

In summary then, it appears that developments in recent years have tended to confirm the Eckstein projections of defense outlays and GNP, the Rockefeller Panel and Colm-Helzner projections for the civilian expenditures of government.

From the present vantage point it appears likely that governmental expenditures will equal a greater percentage of GNP in 1970 than they did in 1960:

#### Table 4—Projection of Governmental Expenditures to 1970
(1960 Dollars)

| | Fiscal years 1960 (Billions) actual | 1970 estimated | Increase | Fiscal years 1960 (in per cent of GNP) a | 1970 b |
|---|---|---|---|---|---|
| National defense & international relations | $ 47.5 | $ 63.0 | +32% | 9.6% 9.5% | 9.0% |
| Other | 103.8 | 169.2 | +63% | 21.0% 25.5% | 24.3% |
| Total | $151.3 | $232.2 | +53% | 30.6% 35.0% | 33.3% |

Note: 1970a—annual GNP growth 3%.
   b—annual GNP growth 3.5%.

The table above shows a decennial growth in non-defense expenditures of 63% although I mentioned earlier that a 70% rate during the 1960's does not appear improbable. I scaled it down because the increase in defense expenditures of 32% could conceivably exert a restraining influence. However, the record of the postwar period—except for the years 1950-52—suggests that the pressure of the forces behind the welfare functions of government might prove more powerful than military considerations. If so, defense costs may grow less than 32%, civilian spending more than 63%.

It is also conceivable that public attitudes toward governmental spending may turn less favorable and that the civilian expenditure rate may decline. But there is no sign of such a trend at this time.

#### The Record of Federal Spending for Domestic Purposes

That governmental spending for domestic purposes has been rising so steeply may come as a surprise to many who heard oft-repeated statements that the US budget now represents about the same percentage of GNP as it did right after the war and that federal expenditures, particularly during the years 1952 to 1960, declined in relation to the national economy. Both of these statements are literally true but the message they are trying to convey is not. They do not reveal, for example, that between 1952 and 1960 (some prefer to compare the years 1953 and 1961, which yield a similar picture), the administrative budget of the US Government increased 17% but federal payments outside the budget, mostly trust fund and lending operations, increased 568%.

All federal expenditures increased 39% between the fiscal years 1952 and 1960, which is slightly less than the 46% rise in GNP or the 50% rise in personal consumption (*current* dollars). But the significant fact is that national security outlays remained virtually stable while civilian services expanded 123%.

**Table 5—Federal Expenditures, Fiscal Years 1952 and 1960**

(consolidated cash budget)

|  | 1952 | 1960 | *Increase* |
|---|---|---|---|
|  | (Billions) | | |
| Major national security, international affairs, space research & technology ........... | $47.2 | $47.9 | + 2% |
| All other ............... | 20.8 | 46.4 | +123% |
| Total .................. | $68.0 | $94.3 | + 39% |

Source: *The Budget of the US Government for the Fiscal Year Ending June 30, 1962.*

This continues a trend which goes back a long time. M. Slade Kendrick found in a study which traced federal finances back to the inception of the Republic that "over the century and a half as a whole, civil expenditures increased more rapidly than military." [12] He suggested, writing in 1955, that under Cold War conditions "factors are likely to moderate or check previous tendencies toward a relatively greater growth in civil than in military outlays." [13] However, the share of national security in all federal expenditures declined from its Korean War peak of 69% in 1952 and 1953 to 61% in 1955 and to 51% in 1960. It stood at 50% in 1963.

In the last three years federal outlays for national security and for domestic purposes grew at more nearly equal rates:

**Table 6—US Government Expenditures, Fiscal Years 1960 and 1963**
(consolidated cash budget)

|  | 1960 (actual) | 1963 (estimate) | Increase |
|---|---|---|---|
|  | (Billions) | | |
| Major national security, international affairs, space research & technology | $47.9 | $ 58.3 | +22% |
| All other | 46.4 | 58.5 | +26% |
| Total | $94.3 | $116.8 | +24% |

Source: *The Budget of the US Government for the Fiscal Year Ending June 30, 1964.*

Civilian expenditures of the US Government rose an average of 7.5% each year between 1952 and 1960, which is more than twice the rate of growth of GNP or personal consumption (*constant* dollars). Of the total increase in federal spending of $26 billion, about four-fifths, or $20 billion, were channeled to the fields of health, education, and welfare; labor; agriculture; and commerce and housing, which enjoyed by far the sharpest rates of growth.

**Table 7—US Government Expenditures, Fiscal Years 1952 and 1960**
(consolidated cash budget)

|  | 1952 | 1960 | Increase |
|---|---|---|---|
|  | (Billions) | | |
| Health, education, welfare, & labor | $ 5.9 | $18.6 | +214% |
| Agriculture | 1.1 | 4.8 | +328% |
| Commerce & housing | 2.1 | 6.3 | +203% |
| Other non-defense | 11.7 | 16.7 | + 43% |
| National security | 47.2 | 47.9 | + 2% |
| Total | $68.0 | $94.3 | + 39% |

Source: *The Budget of the US Government for the Fiscal Year Ending June 30, 1962.*

Between 1960 and 1963 federal civilian expenditures grew at a slightly lower rate, at an average of 6.5% per year (*constant dollars*). This, the President suggested in his Budget Review Message in October 1961, was related to the simultaneous rise in defense outlays: "In these circumstances it will plainly be necessary to defer or limit increases in many programs which in more normal times would be thoroughly desirable and to shift present staffs and resources to the maximum extent from work of lower to work of higher priority." The 1964 budget shows only a small increase in the combined total of civilian outlays, but that stability is more apparent than real. Some of the expenditure estimates may be no more reliable than those in other recent budgets had proved to be. Also, if several of the proposed new domestic programs for which only token amounts were placed in the 1964 budget are enacted, the cost of civilian functions will continue its upward trend, possibly at an accelerated pace. That trend may be more pronounced if defense allocations remain stable or decline as they did in the mid-1950's; it could moderate if recognized defense needs climb sharply.

**Revenue Prospects**

All of the fiscal studies which I reviewed earlier expect governmental revenues at present levels of taxation to meet or exceed projected expenditures. I do not share such optimism.

The level of taxation has shown a secular upward trend, gradual during peace periods, steep during each war with a modest short-lived decline after the war. Governmental revenues equalled these percentages of GNP:

**Table 8—Governmental Revenues in the United States 1902-62**
(as a percentage of GNP)

| | |
|---|---|
| 1902 | 8.2% |
| 1922 | 12.8% |
| 1932 | 15.3% |
| 1942 | 20.2% |
| (maximum World War II: 32.1% in 1944, postwar low: 25.3% in 1950) | |
| 1952 | 29.6% |
| 1961 | 31.4% |
| 1962 est. | 31.5% |

(Computed from sources cited in Tables 13 and 14 at end of paper).

Governmental revenues in 1962 almost equalled the maximum percentage of GNP they reached during World War II. But in 1944 no less than 78% of all governmental expenditures was allocated to national defense, in 1962, only 30%. The President has recommended sizeable tax cuts to the 88th Congress which, if enacted, will assure large deficits for several more years. Some of the revenue loss, it is hoped, will be offset by a resulting faster growth in the national economy and subsequent increases in tax collections. But, on the whole, the picture gives little encouragement for expecting a lower over-all level of taxation in the years ahead. The chances are that it will be higher if present expenditure trends continue.

If expenditures for national security grow at no faster rate than GNP, as most of the projections and recent trends suggest, they will require no tax boosts. The domestic functions, however, appear likely to expand more steeply than GNP. How will they be financed?

It may be well to analyze expenditures in the latest available fiscal year by sources:

**Table 9—Governmental Expenditures in 1961**
By Type and Source of Funds

|                                      | Total | Federal | State-local |
|--------------------------------------|-------|---------|-------------|
|                                      | *(Billions)* |   |             |
| Total ...................... | $164.9 | $104.9 | $60.0 |
| National defense &                   |       |         |             |
| international relations .... | 49.4 | 49.4 | —— |
| Veterans services &                  |       |         |             |
| benefits ................. | 6.2 | 6.1 | 0.1 |
| Interest on the national debt.. | 7.5 | 7.5 | —— |
| Domestic functions: ........ | 101.8 | 41.9 | 59.9 |
| From trust and                       |       |         |             |
| enterprise funds ....... | 28.9 | 18.1 | 10.8 |
| From general funds ...... | 72.9 | 23.8 | 49.1 |

Computed from: U.S. Bureau of the Census, *Governmental Finances in 1961.*

The table above shows that in 1961 out of a total of $101.8 billion for domestic functions, $28.9 billion came from trust and enterprise funds. Some of these, such as the Social Security Fund (OASDI), have built-in rate increases; others; such as unemployment compensation, may boost rates (and reduce experience ratings) when necessary; enterprises will increase their revenues through fees, charges, etc.

Domestic functions financed from general funds totalled $72.9 billion. One-third of the cost ($23.8 billion) was provided by the Federal Government, two-thirds ($49.1 billion) by state and local governments. The *general* revenues of the Federal Government (not including trust and enterprise funds) increased 100% between 1946 and 1961; in state and local governments they increased 308%. In 1946 state and local governments collected 21% of the *general* revenues of *all* governments (including the federal); by 1961 their share had risen to 35%. The most significant fact may be that during the postwar period, federal general revenues *declined* as a percentage of GNP (i.e., they grew more slowly than GNP) while state and local revenues almost doubled, expressed as a percentage of GNP (i.e., they increased almost twice as fast as GNP):

**Table 10—General Governmental Revenues as a Percentage of GNP, Postwar Period**

|                                | 1946   | 1961   |
|--------------------------------|--------|--------|
| Federal Government ............... | 20.6%  | 17.2%  |
| State and local governments ......... | 5.4    | 9.3    |

Sources: Same as shown in Tables 13 and 14.

The years between World War I and World War II showed a comparable trend. Only during wartime—between 1916 and 1920, 1940 and 1945, 1950 and 1952—did federal receipts increase at a faster rate than state and local.

There is no sign at the present time that the postwar trend of state-local revenues rising faster than federal is weakening or about to end. If it continued through the 1960's, state and local governments could finance much or most of the increased cost of domestic public services from their own sources. The natural increase in federal receipts, arising from economic growth, might provide the balance. This means that: (a) state and local governments will keep boosting taxes as they have been doing throughout the postwar period; (b) general federal taxes (i.e., rates) will slightly decline or stabilize.

There is at least one big IF in this prospect: if the Federal Government significantly expands its role in the domestic field, whether through grants-in-aid or by direct operations, state and local officials will display far less eagerness to accept the political responsibility for raising taxes. In that case the debt ceiling will have to be lifted to a much higher level, and/or federal taxes may have to be boosted.

A deterioration of the national security picture also could call for a substantial increase in federal funds. I shall discuss the alternatives of federal tax boosts in a later section.

## How to Cope with Disarmament

Each of the four studies I reviewed earlier includes a set of "low" projections, but only one, by the Bureau of the Budget, envisages the possibility of a sharp cutback in defense expenditures because of disarmament.

Several authors have concerned themselves in recent years with the "threat of disarmament." They usually start with the proposition that millions of workers and vast amounts of materials and industrial capacity now in defense production or in the armed forces would be released and might become idle. How could we prevent mass unemployment and a deep depression? "Finding desirable ways of spending 40 to 50 billion dollars a year (about 10 per cent of the GNP) requires an orderly planned effort," warned Seymour Melman.[14]

To expect that national security outlays can be reduced to almost nothing—which is what a $40 to $50 billion reduction would amount to—appears unrealistic even if the Communist powers which now constitute the main threat to world peace were to crumble and disappear. That, unfortunately, is not a likely prospect. At this time we may as well assume that those powers will still be in existence and militarily strong by 1970. Disarmament can then at most affect only part of our defense preparations.

Nor is disarmament likely to burst upon a United States that did not expect it. It will come, if at all, only after an extended period of gradually easing tensions, of improving negotiations, and of actions that offer grounds for some, if limited, mutual confidence. In other words, disarmament can, for as long as we can look ahead, comprise only part, and probably a minor part, of our defense preparations, and will be preceded by ample time to get ready.

Moreover, Charles Hitch suggested that "in this nuclear age disarmament sometimes means armament" and may imply "the expenditure of *additional* sums on defense or the purchase of extra conventional armaments." [15] Further, that if an agreement were reached we "would have to prepare for possible revocation of the bargain" and "be prepared to resume the atomic race immediately in order to re-establish an effective deterrent. Otherwise the enemy, facing no deterrent, might dispose of the Free World once and for all." [16]

In any case though, a reduction in the size of the armed forces and sharp cuts in defense production would call for a corresponding rise in the demand for civilian goods and services, both for investment and for consumption. Some believe that the emphasis should be on strengthening the private sector of the economy. Others prefer governmental expansion.

The National Planning Association asked in 1959, "Can the American Economy Adjust to Arms Control?" and prepared *A Five-Year Budget for Peace* which suggested $330 billion in outlays for education, highways, urban renewal, mass transportation, water supply, hospitals, etc., mostly by government.

Gerard Piel, in a widely read article, presented a persuasive plea that any reduction in defense outlays would need to be replaced by other *public* spending and that government will need to expand sharply and rapidly.[17]

Emile Benoit, speaking at the annual meeting of the American Association for the Advancement of Science recently declared massive spending by government to be the only answer to the perils of peace.

The Bureau of the Budget considered the "possible effect of disarmament on budget expenditures" and of a reduction in national security costs of $21.5 billion below its "medium" projection for 1970.[18]

It suggested to apply about one-fourth of the savings ($5.4 billion) to cutting taxes and reducing the national debt, three-fourths ($16.1 billion) to increasing expenditures for welfare and similar purposes. This would present the following total of federal spending for civilian functions in the *administrative budget:*

**Table 11—Non-Defense Expenditures in the Federal Administrative Budget, 1950, 1960, 1970**

| | | |
|---|---|---|
| 1950 | $21.9 billion | (actual) |
| 1960 | 34.4 billion | (actual) |
| 1970 | 65.5 billion | (proposed) |

This suggests that an increase in federal budget expenditures for domestic functions of $12.5 billion in the 1950's, be followed by one of $31.1 billion during the 1960's. The Bureau commented that "these amounts would presumably cover most, if not all, foreseeable domestic needs." It advanced no estimate of the effect which such action would have on state and local governments and on the drastic change it would work in our federal system of government and in our society. Such rapid centralization of fiscal and political power in the National Government may be desirable or detrimental, depending on one's philosophy. But the consequences of such action should at least be referred to and considered when it is proposed as the solution to another problem.

That the President and Congress would apply only one-fourth of a budgetary saving of some $20 billion to tax reduction is very unlikely. Even now, while the budget is running $9 billion in the red, substantial tax cuts have been proposed by the President and the major objection that has so far been heard in Congress is that the action is not accompanied by expenditure reductions. If defense outlays declined by $20 billion, or some such large amount, there would be a rush of big tax cut proposals, which would soon be enacted.

Without some type of action offsetting sizeable defense reductions the budget might show a large surplus, which could be embarrassing. Kenneth Boulding recently advanced the proposition that "the simplest recipe for achieving a smooth transition from a war to a peace economy would be to combine a sizeable budget deficit with temporary price and wage control." [19]

Now, in converting from a peace to a war economy it is not unusual, and often inevitable, that government resort to deficit financing and to wage and price controls. Boulding suggests that we reduce fiscal and economic policy to a simple common formula—whether we go from peace to war or from war to peace: increase federal deficit financing, impose wage and price controls.

Does this not remind us of the doctor who, no matter what the ailment, always prescribes the same medicine? He is, it appears, more interested in selling his patent medicine than in curing the patient.

There must be a better way to meet the "perils of peace." If and when the time comes that we can safely slice $10 or $20 billion off the defense budget, then we should remember how the federal budget reached its tremendous size in the first place: to finance World War II, and later the Korean and Cold Wars, expenditures and taxes were boosted to oppressive levels. If we no longer need to spend some $50 billion to safeguard our security, why not retrace our steps and cut taxes accordingly?

There is now universal agreement that our present tax system, in the words of the President "exerts too heavy a drag on growth in peace time—that it siphons out of the private economy too large a share of personal and business purchasing power— that it reduces the financial incentives and opportunities for private expenditures." [20] Viewed in that context, disarmament may be much less of a "threat" than some authors have chosen to portray it. Public services will continue to expand, and may well grow faster if and when the Cold War ends. But this does not seem to call for a crash program that would radically upset the balance in our system of government.

### How to Increase Funds for National Security

In contrast to the many articles dealing with a possible *reduction* in defense outlays there have been few suggestions on how the financial resources for national security could be rapidly *expanded*. Such reluctance to come to grips with the problem is understandable. Few care to envisage a future that is closer to war than to peace. Who wants to treat war, big or small, or a warlike situation as inevitable? Is not making plans for the possibility like preparing the way for it and increasing the chance of its happening? But then, being strongly opposed to war has kept few from depicting its horrifying and otherwise damaging aspects. Somehow, there seems to be a feeling that if the emergency arises, there will be no difficulty in getting approval for whatever money and resources are needed. So why worry about this now? Why describe in detail how to curtail some of our major public services which we are in the process of expanding?

Unfortunately, the threat of war is likely to hang over us as long as the Communist forces control some of the major countries. They will never *voluntarily* recede from their goal of world domination. Unrest, upheaval, or conflict anywhere in the world is likely to affect the United States, cause its defense or international outlays to increase or constitute the danger of a minor or major war in which we might be involved. Any number of events or developments may require an immediate and large increase in American military manpower or weapons systems. At some point it could become necessary to provide shelters for a major segment of our population and do so in a hurry. Mobilization, when decided upon, would be limited primarily by physical factors—manpower, materials, equipment, and transportation. But the financial methods of meeting emergencies may mean the difference between orderly and chaotic conditions, between a strong and a weakened economy.

Gerhard Colm and Manual Helzner prepared, in 1957, programs for increasing defense outlays by $10, $20, or $30 billion over a three-year period.[21] They concluded that:

a) current and prospective trends in economic growth and in governmental revenues and expenditures will permit a significant tax reduction;

b) a boost of defense outlays by $10 billion would rule out such tax cuts;

c) a boost of defense outlays by $20 billion would require a return to World War II or 1951-53 tax levels and the deferral of planned increases in governmental non-defense programs;

d) short of an imminent threat of a major war and the imposition of direct controls, the economy could not absorb a defense increase of $30 billion over three years.

In World War II federal defense expenditures (and the total of all expenditures) expanded more rapidly than revenues. But the growth rate of revenues also was substantial:

**Table 12—Increase in Federal Revenues and Expenditures, 1914-43**

| Fiscal years | Increase in federal revenues | Increase in defense expenditures |
|---|---|---|
| 1941 to 1942 | +77% | +266% |
| 1942 to 1943 | +75% | +117% |

Source: Annual Report of the Secretary of the Treasury.

Between 1941 and 1943, defense costs multiplied tenfold, all federal expenditures sixfold, federal revenues threefold.

Conditions are now quite different from those prevailing twenty years ago. The military potential then depended on the force that could be mobilized at the outbreak of war or—given the geographic isolation of the United States—some time after. In the nuclear age we have little time left. Most of the resources must have been applied *prior* to armed conflict, the balance very shortly after.

In terms of physical readiness the United States is now far ahead of where it was in 1941. But the revenues of the Federal Government are less expandable and its fiscal reserve capacity narrow. In 1941 federal revenues equalled 8.4% of GNP and gradually climbed to 25.5% in 1944. In 1962 they are already at 20%. One-half of the yield is applied to national defense, one-half channelled into civilian services.

Neither during World War II nor during the Korean conflict did governmental non-defense expenditures decline much, except for agricultural support and civilian construction. Social welfare programs kept on growing. Personal consumption did not contract but merely stabilized. Other goods and services filled the gap when automobile production ceased.

Governmental programs for civilian purposes are now so institutionalized and have become such untouchable vested interests that even a threat of war would not lead to a significant cutback. At most, their growth rate would slow down. The irreversibility of the trend makes the rapid expansion during the postwar period, and demands to accelerate it further, so ominous. Tighter control of these tendencies could help to improve the capacity of the federal treasury to expand its resources if the necessity arises.

The Federal Government has been operating in the red for some years. A sharp increase in defense requirements could push deficits to highly inflationary levels.

Time and again, the question has been raised whether the defense effort which the United States is exerting is equal to the threat it faces. With the grace period eliminated which the United States enjoyed in the pre-atomic age, economic capacity counts largely only to the extent to which it is actually employed for defense purposes prior to open conflict.

The United States is now devoting 10% of its GNP to national security compared with 13% to 15% in the Soviet Union.[22] That does not in itself imply that we ought to spend 15% of GNP just because the Soviets do. But it does suggest some serious thinking of whether our effort is adequate to assure us the "substantive superiority" to which Stefan Possony referred on an earlier panel.

Arthur Smithies, in November 1957, advanced the view to the Joint Economic Committee that defense programs have been held down because they lack the type of lobby which certain other programs enjoy: "Unlike other programs—agriculture for instance—national defense does not have the benefit of organized and continual political support from within the country. The private manufacturers of arms who were the villains of the thirties, are woefully weak in their political influence, compared with veterans, conservationists, and farmers." [23]

More recently defense seems to be back in the role of the villain. Gerald Piel wrote in September 1962: "It is difficult for anyone, including the Secretary of Defense, to resist the demands on the public treasury laid by the armed forces. Those demands are backed by the substantial economic interests of a giant industry exclusively devoted to armament. No such absolute moral sanction supports the claims of education, for example, and no comparable vested interest stands to gain from them." [24]

To appreciate Mr. Piel's comparison it may be well to note from the record that over the past ten years (fiscal years 1953 to 1963) defense outlays increased 6%, expenditures for public education at least 150%. Ten years ago education costs equalled less than 20% of those for national defense, now almost 50%. Mr. Piel, it seems, had the plot correct, but the actors reversed.

Smithies added "that judging by results, something is wrong with our method of budgeting for defense. The root of the trouble is that political democracies have not yet learned to make the sustained defense efforts that are now needed."

Whether our present defense effort is inadequate for its task will be discussed on other panels. But let us assume for heuristic purposes that it should be substantially increased. How could it be financed?

For over twenty years the National Government has been deriving most of its tax revenues from income taxes. Both personal and corporate income tax rates were pushed to levels which seriously retard economic growth. Even under warlike conditions they cannot be driven much higher.

The maximum war-rate scale of 23% to 94% has been eased very little—to 20% to 91% at the present time. Rates in the upper income brackets are now so high that a further boost would yield only insignificant revenue. Most of the additional funds would have to come from an increase in the basic rate. The questions is: how much above 20% could it be raised?

The personal exemption reached its lowest level in 1943 at $500, the equivalent of $870 in 1962 dollars. But we now get only $600 per person. Considering the changed value of the dollar, the federal personal income tax is now, on the whole, about as heavy as it was during World War II.

With all the much talked-about loopholes, the percentage of personal income that is subject to the federal income tax has been rising steadily from 15.2% in 1940 to 31.7% in 1943 and to 43.6% in 1959. Most of the "untaxed income" consists of: personal exemptions, social insurance benefits, imputed income (such as rent on owner-occupied homes), standard deductions, itemized deductions.

Can itemized deductions—for state and local taxes, mortgage interest, charitable and religious contributions, medical expenses, etc.—be materially curtailed? Even the most enthusiastic protagonists of the "Cut the Loopholes" drive, which has been active on the national scene since about 1955, cannot feel particularly encouraged by their progress to date. Experiences during 1962 and the generally hostile reception of the President's "reform" proposals in 1963 must have deprived many of certain illusions. There is, of course, room for reform. But there doesn't seem to be much gold in the hills of loophole closing.

If the yield of income taxes is to be substantially increased under emergency conditions then it will have to be done the hard way: by boosting the basic rate.

I doubt that the additional potential of the income tax is very great (not counting the normal increase from economic growth). Nor should the prospective receipts from an excess profits tax be overrated at a time when corporate taxes are already levied at 52%.

It has repeatedly been suggested that the United States ought to levy a broad-based consumption tax—this being the only industrial country whose national government imposes no such tax as a major revenue producer. A general manufacturers' excise tax could yield between $1 and $1.5 billion for each one-per-cent tax rate, depending on the extent of coverage. To establish such a tax is a time-consuming process which could more easily be accomplished *prior* to an emergency. If levied at a low rate—e.g., 2%—it could possibly serve as a replacement for the various existing manufacturers' excise taxes. When necessary the rate could be raised on short notice without much administrative difficulty and soon bring in substantial sums.

A program to improve the capacity of our fiscal system to allocate larger amounts to national security *if and when needed* without much delay might emphasize the following steps:

1) Governmental policy should encourage economic growth. Without transgressing upon the territory of other speakers I will only suggest that the existing burdens upon industrial expansion as well as disincentives be eased and that governmental action aim to improve rather than to lower the international competitiveness of American producers.

2) The cost of domestic functions of government should not expand at a rate which very substantially exceeds the growth rate of the national economy.

3) Because borrowing from banks may be required if defense preparations need to be sharply and rapidly increased, government should refrain from this type of financing under other than emergency conditions. It should aim to balance its budget over the business cycle, offsetting occasional deficits by succeeding surpluses. It should not pursue a regular deficit policy.

4) In view of the limited expandability of income tax yields the imposition of a broad-based consumption tax should be envisaged.

### TECHNICAL NOTES (See Charts Following)

All revenue and expenditure data, *unless otherwise noted,* are from the Bureau of the Census as published in its annual report *Governmental Finances in* . . . and in the *Historical Summary of Governmental Finances in the United States*, 1957. These census reports are the most comprehensive compilation of governmental finances obtainable. They have been available annually since 1952. Of prior years only those are available which are listed in Tables 13 and 14.

Care should be exercised in making comparisons with statistics from other sources because the Census statistics differ—though not very significantly— from those of the Office of Business Economics and those in the Eckstein, Rockefeller Panel, and Colm-Helzner reports. All financial data are for *fiscal years* which the Federal Government, 46 states, the schools, and some other local governments end on June 30. They are related to GNP and other economic data for the corresponding *fiscal* year. Consequently GNP totals shown in this paper differ from those for calendar year totals.

Opinions are divided on whether GNP is necessarily the best yardstick for measuring the magnitude of fiscal aggregates or other economic items. For some purposes Net National Product, National Income, or Personal Income may be more appropriate measures. But GNP has been so widely used that for reasons of comparability I followed this practice.

*Current* (i.e., actual) dollars were converted into *constant* dollars by the use of the "implicit price deflator for GNP" for the *fiscal* year. Statistics of GNP, price deflators, etc., were taken from the *Survey of Current Business* and its summary volumes such as *U.S. Income and Output* and *National Income,* 1954.

**Table 13—Governmental Revenues and Expenditures in the United States 1902 to 1962**

| Fiscal years ending in: | Revenues | Expenditures | | |
|---|---|---|---|---|
| | | Total | National Security* (Million) | Other |
| 1902 | $  1,694 | $  1,660 | $    165 | $  1,495 |
| 1913 | 2,980 | 3,215 | 250 | 2,965 |
| 1922 | 9,322 | 9,297 | 875 | 8,422 |
| 1927 | 12,191 | 11,220 | 616 | 10,604 |
| 1932 | 10,289 | 12,437 | 721 | 11,716 |
| 1934 | 11,300 | 12,807 | 553 | 12,254 |
| 1936 | 13,588 | 16,758 | 932 | 15,826 |
| 1938 | 17,484 | 17,675 | 1,041 | 16,634 |
| 1940 | 17,804 | 20,417 | 1,590 | 18,827 |
| 1942 | 28,352 | 45,576 | 26,555 | 19,021 |
| 1944 | 64,778 | 109,947 | 85,503 | 24,444 |
| 1946 | 61,532 | 79,707 | 50,461 | 29,246 |
| 1948 | 67,005 | 55,081 | 16,075 | 39,006 |
| 1950 | 66,680 | 70,334 | 18,355 | 51,979 |
| 1952 | 100,245 | 99,847 | 48,187 | 51,660 |
| 1953 | 104,781 | 110,054 | 53,583 | 56,471 |
| 1954 | 108,255 | 111,332 | 49,265 | 62,067 |
| 1955 | 106,404 | 110,717 | 43,472 | 67,245 |
| 1956 | 119,651 | 115,796 | 42,680 | 73,116 |
| 1957 | 129,151 | 125,463 | 45,803 | 79,660 |
| 1958 | 130,403 | 134,931 | 46,127 | 88,804 |
| 1959 | 133,055 | 145,748 | 48,389 | 97,359 |
| 1960 | 153,102 | 151,288 | 47,464 | 103,824 |
| 1961 | 158,741 | 164,875 | 49,387 | 115,488 |
| 1962 est. | 170,000 | 178,000 | 54,000 | 124,000 |

* National Security: National defense and international relations.

Source:  Fiscal data:  US Bureau of the Census, *Historical Summary of Governmental Finances in the US,* (1957). US Bureau of the Census, *Governmental Finances in 1961* (1962). *Survey of Current Business* (November, 1962).

**Table 14—Governmental Revenues and Expenditures 1902 to 1962**
(as a percentage of the Gross National Product)

| Fiscal years ending in: | GNP (Billions) | Revenues as a percentage of GNP | Expenditures as a percentage of GNP Total | National Security * | Other |
|---|---|---|---|---|---|
| 1902 | $ 20.7 | 8.2% | 8.0% | .8% | 7.2% |
| 1913 | 36.7 | 8.1 | 8.8 | .7 | 8.1 |
| 1922 | 72.6 | 12.8 | 12.8 | 1.2 | 11.6 |
| 1927 | 96.2 | 12.7 | 11.7 | .6 | 11.0 |
| 1932 | 67.4 | 15.3 | 18.5 | 1.1 | 17.4 |
| 1934 | 60.5 | 18.7 | 21.2 | .9 | 20.3 |
| 1936 | 77.6 | 17.5 | 21.6 | 1.2 | 20.4 |
| 1938 | 88.0 | 19.9 | 20.1 | 1.2 | 18.9 |
| 1940 | 95.9 | 18.6 | 21.3 | 1.7 | 19.6 |
| 1942 | 140.5 | 20.2 | 32.4 | 18.9 | 13.5 |
| 1944 | 202.8 | 32.1 | 54.4 | 42.3 | 12.1 |
| 1946 | 202.8 | 30.3 | 39.3 | 24.9 | 14.4 |
| 1948 | 246.6 | 27.1 | 22.3 | 6.5 | 15.8 |
| 1950 | 263.8 | 25.3 | 26.6 | 7.0 | 19.6 |
| 1952 | 338.8 | 29.6 | 29.5 | 14.2 | 15.3 |
| 1953 | 359.7 | 29.1 | 30.6 | 14.9 | 15.7 |
| 1954 | 362.0 | 29.9 | 30.8 | 13.6 | 17.2 |
| 1955 | 377.0 | 28.2 | 29.3 | 11.5 | 17.8 |
| 1956 | 408.5 | 29.2 | 28.3 | 10.4 | 17.9 |
| 1957 | 433.0 | 29.8 | 29.0 | 10.6 | 18.4 |
| 1958 | 440.2 | 29.6 | 30.7 | 10.5 | 20.2 |
| 1959 | 466.5 | 28.5 | 31.2 | 10.4 | 20.8 |
| 1960 | 494.8 | 31.0 | 30.6 | 9.6 | 21.0 |
| 1961 | 505.5 | 31.4 | 32.6 | 9.8 | 22.8 |
| 1962 | 539.0 | 31.5 | 33.0 | 10.0 | 23.0 |

* National Security: National defense and international relations.

Source: Table 13 and Department of Commerce, *US Income and Output*, 1957. *Survey of Current Business* (July, 1962). Raymond W. Goldsmith & Assoc., *A Study of Savings in the United States* (Princeton: Princeton University Press, 1956), III. *The Budget in Brief, 1964 Fiscal Year*, p. 63.

## FOOTNOTES

[1] Samuel P. Huntington, *The Common Defense: Strategic Programs in National Politics* (New York: Columbia University Press, 1961). Warner R. Schilling, Paul Y. Hammond, Glenn H. Snyder, *Strategy, Politics and the Defense Budgets* (New York: Columbia University Press, 1962). Maxwell Taylor, *The Uncertain Trumpet* (New York: Harper, 1960).

[2] *The Challenge to America: Its Economic and Social Aspects*, Rockefeller Brothers Fund, Special Studies Project Report IV (Garden City, N.Y.: Doubleday & Co., 1958).

[3] Otto Eckstein, *Trends in Public Expenditures in the Next Decade* (Committee for Economic Development, 1959).

[4] Gerhard Colm and Manuel Helzner, "Financial Needs and Resources over the Next Decade: At All Levels of Government" in *Public Finances: Needs, Sources and Utilization*, a Report of the National Bureau of Economic Research (Princeton: Princeton University Press, 1961), Proceedings.

[5] US Bureau of the Budget, *Ten-Year Projection of Federal Budget Expenditures*, 1961.

[6] Gerhard Colm, *The American Economy* (National Planning Association, 1952).

[7] Frederick Dewhurst & Associates, *America's Needs and Resources* (Twentieth Century Fund, 1955).

[8] *Potential Economic Growth of the United States During the Next Decade*, Materials prepared for the Joint Committee on the Economic Report by the Committee Staff, 83rd Cong., 2nd Sess. (1954).

[9] Max Ways, "A New Mask for Big Government," *Fortune* (April, 1960).

[10] See the appended *Technical Notes*.

[11] Charles J. Hitch and Roland McKean, *The Economics of Defense in the Nuclear Age* (Cambridge, Mass.: Harvard University Press, 1960), pp. 91-96.

[12] M. Slade Kendrick, *A Century and a Half of Federal Expenditures* (National Bureau of Economic Research, 1955), p. 40.

[13] *Ibid.*, p. 54.

[14] Seymour Melman, "Peace without Depression," *Saturday Review*, December 2, 1961.

[15] Hitch, *op cit.*, p. 307.

[16] *Ibid.*, p. 320.

[17] Gerard Piel, "Can our Economy Stand Disarmament?" *The Atlantic Monthly* (September, 1962).

[18] *Ten-Year Projection . . . op. cit.*, pp. 61-64.

[19] Kenneth E. Boulding, "Can We Afford A Warless World?" *Saturday Review*, October 6, 1962.

[20] Speech to the Economic Club of New York, December 14, 1962.

[21] US Congress, Joint Economic Committee, *Hearings, Federal Expenditure Policy for Economic Growth and Stability*, 85th Cong., 1st Sess., 1957, pp. 356 ff., also: *Can We Afford Additional Programs for National Security*, (National Planning Association).

[22] Hitch, *loc. cit.*, pp. 95-96.

[23] *Federal Expenditure Policy . . . op. cit.*, pp. 350-51.

[24] Piel, *op. cit.*

# Economic Growth: Issues and Prospects[1]

—*HENRY W. BRIEFS AND JOSEPH L. TRYON*

## Summary

The main conclusions reached in this paper can be summed up as follows:

First, it appears to us that the economic growth process is much more complicated than a straightforward aggregate demand approach to the analysis of our growth problems tends to imply. From time to time, the shifts taking place in the economy involve structural changes, lagging adjustments, and hesitations which make it very unlikely that a modern private property economy can grow more or less continuously along a full-employment ceiling—with or without a sophisticated policy mix.

Second, in our judgment, strong structural shifts have taken place in the past ten years and particularly since 1955. The most important of these was the shift toward investment in human capital formation and more specifically toward investment in research and development (R&D). It appears that this and other shifts have not yet been sufficiently digested. As a consequence, the economy has been through a period of hesitation and reorganization in its growth patterns.

Third, basic changes which are likely to be strongly stimulating in their economic effects can be expected during the decade ahead. In terms of quantitative importance, these cluster around population growth and changes in its composition. Economic growth is likely to be strong in the areas of housing and related consumer durables, education, and urban area development. Combined with the likelihood of increasing returns on past capital formation in human beings and especially in research and *related work, these developments should produce strong expansions during the next ten years.*

*Finally, we believe that growth and development in the private sector of the economy will be quite sufficient to help produce a conflict between various demands for resources. This conclusion would be strengthened by the enactment of tax rate reductions favoring the lower income brackets. Here the direct stimulus to spending is large and would reinforce the demand increases foreseen in this paper. At the same time, such rate reductions, once made, are very difficult to reverse; offsetting them by shifting the tax burdens involved to higher incomes will also prove hard to accomplish. Obviously, then, substantial tax cuts for lower income recipients are likely to sharpen the competition for available resources and accentuate political struggles about issues such as the allocation of tax burdens, measures to restrict consumption through selective credit restrictions, for example, methods to restrain price increases likely under these conditions, and/or others—all concrete manifestations of resource limitations vis-à-vis our various needs and desires. No doubt, such developments would act as a constraint also on public expenditures, even those directed to national security.*

---

### Growth vs. Development: the National Security Interest

Since there seem to be serious conceptual and statistical objections to the notion that the contribution of US economic strength toward meeting national security requirements is reflected *simpliciter* in the growth rate of national output (GNP), let us first discuss what we believe to be the "true" relationship between these two major variables.

Unquestionably, there is a vital relationship between growth and national security; for policy purposes, however, that association cannot safely be treated as a functional relation only. Questions about economic capabilities in relation to the progress of events, actions, and plans that bear on national security take place in history. Assuming that we will be involved in a sequence of Cold War encounters in the decade ahead, decisions to act will not only have to deal with foreseeable trends, but also with irreversible shifts. Such "breaks" with past developments can have consequences so sweeping as to disorganize the patterns of change that previously could be estimated within tolerable limits. It appears, therefore, that national security decisions must cope not only with more or less stable change but also with structural "breaks" not susceptible to systematic (probabilistic) analysis.* Making decisions at such junctures is like shooting at a target moving on an unknown course that is changing in an unknown way. The premium here is on insight, inventiveness in using the resources at hand, and on the brains-energy combination to learn and adapt patterns of action to the new experience.

Assuming that this premise is correct, the relationship between national security needs and economic growth is not likely to be one of proportionality; the gain in economic muscle, so to speak, is not well measured by the customary growth statistics for the US economy as a whole. Rather, the economic process makes its contribution through the multitude of specific developments in new materials and products, in methods of production and distribution, in efficient administration, and the like. A great deal of privately financed university research also plays an important role here, and the same is true of business R&D induced by public expenditure.** In sum, what counts primarily is the development of new capabilities. The growth in total resources and their shiftability from home use to national security use are not likely to pose problems so severe as to make them matters of overriding concern for security reasons.

In our view, therefore, "development" is the key factor in the relationship between economic performance and national security requirements. The need is for rapid improvement in the range and scope of our economic capabilities. As for the "welfare" objectives, these probably bear a closer relation to over-all economic growth than they do to "development." Unfortunately, maximum gains in total output and employment are more apt to occur when standard demands grow strongly and more or less predictably, when well established methods of

---

* This is equivalent to saying that operational models, capable of dealing with serious structural "break" situations, are not likely to become available in the foreseeable future.

** The restrictive character of this sentence implies nothing other than a desire to distinguish the part played by R&D directly connected with the economic calculus from all the rest.

production are merely extended, and when the rewards for performance in this context are proportioned to that performance. It is a little difficult to think of this as an ideal environment for economic innovating, for "development" in the sense indicated. That requires many independent, vital sources of new ideas along with the opportunities to try them out. Needless to say, "development" also calls for planning, an ordering of priorities, and the specification of development efforts. Both modes of operation are needed: free independent enterprise—in a sense that goes beyond the business connotation of that term to include a wide spectrum of activities, from graduate research to basement fiddling—as well as the organized, integrated, and disciplined efforts of high-powered research and production teams working on well specified problems.

This general view of the relationship between economic development and the demands of national security policy needs elaboration in two respects: first, what does it imply for the problem of US-USSR economic growth and defense burden comparisons; and second, what can we say about possible economic constraints on the scale of our national security effort? Although both of these questions are of primary importance for this conference of strategists and economists, only the latter is central to the present paper. A brief comment will have to suffice in regard to US-USSR comparisons.

### Doubts About US-USSR Comparisons

The widespread practice of measuring Russia's GNP and its growth rate against corresponding US statistics, or of comparing the proportion of GNP which Russia devotes to military and related expenditures with a similar ratio for the United States, is ambiguous in meaning and misleading as to statistical results. In particular, these measures and what they allegedly show do not provide a valid reason for believing that a growth race in these terms is required for national security reasons. Russia's GNP, i.e., the collection of goods and services comprising her total output, has meaning only in terms of her needs, wants, and ambitions on the one hand, and of her particular endowment with scarce resources, human and material, on the other. Were it not for this fact, her GNP would be indistinguishable from a random collection of things. To make a comparison, therefore, between the total of goods and services produced in the USSR, and the collection of goods and services produced for US needs, wants, and desires—which relate to our relative resource scarcities—approaches comparing apples and pogo sticks.

The statistical implications of this point in principle are far from negligible. Comparing Russia's collection of outputs with those in the US requires devising a common unit of measure. This is accomplished either by adding up both collections in terms of their US prices, or by adding both of them in their Russian prices.[2] Unfortunately, US prices have little meaning for the quantities produced in the USSR, and vice versa. This is reflected by the fact that the results one gets making comparisons on one basis or the other vary sharply with the selection of the relative price system used. The same stricture applies to corresponding comparisons of growth rates, since these, too, require using price "weights" that reflect either Russia's or our own preference-resource scarcity pattern.

The statistical difficulties of estimating US GNP—not to mention Russia's—add an entire range of new considerations into which we need not enter here. There seems to be little doubt, however, that they reinforce our reservations about direct US-USSR growth and defense burden comparisons. What really matters for our security is how, and how rapidly, Russia's resources and capabilities are being expanded in relation to (strictly, in interrelation with) her evolving needs, designs, and alternatives of strategy at certain junctures, and, *mutatis mutandis,* the same for the United States. The call is for concrete analyses along these lines, extended, of course, to all relevant countries and areas.

### Economic Growth as a Source of Budget Constraint

The second topic in need of a little more propaedeutic elaboration relates to aggregate economic growth and its logistic implications, so to speak, for national security. Taking the view expressed above, namely, that in the prospective conditions of the next ten years what counts is economic "development," it is clear that we do not attach central importance to statistics measuring the per cent of increase in GNP or similar concepts of over-all activity. Obviously, frequent, wide swings in production and income will hamper development and so will protracted economic depression. But, within the range of variations likely in practice, there seems to be no compelling reason why over-all "growth" and "development" should show significant correlation. Also, over short periods of time, unsatisfactory rates of over-all expansion facilitate the attraction of additional economic resources into national security applications. As incumbent administrations are well aware, increased defense expenditures have an expansionary effect on the economy.[3] Over longer periods such as the decade ahead, economic development and the growth of demand for resources may generally be rapid enough to require that increases in the share of the nation's effort devoted to national security be accompanied by retrenchment in other directions, at least relatively speaking.*

In view of the practical problems attending the determination of defense and related budget items, all of this may seem rather categorical. Many are inclined to believe that, over longer periods of time, the Congress will be reluctant to authorize expenditures that go very much beyond tax receipts. Now, when this assumption is linked with the view that compressing expenditures on major civilian-domestic functions, even relatively, is not only politically difficult but may also be socially and, to an extent, economically undesirable, the conclusion is apt to be that "normally" the ceiling on national security expenditures depends on the rate of economic growth. This view is strengthened if it is believed that without determined policies to promote growth, the rise in output, income, and federal revenues would be quite sluggish. In such a frame of reference, compressing "non-essential" government spending, or raising tax rates to shift resources toward national security uses, tend to be de-emphasized.

This view of the role played by over-all economic growth lends that concept great importance in the present context. It seems worthwhile, therefore, to examine its analytical basis and explore how "development" as defined above fits into the economic process. This will lead to an empirical inquiry concerning the growth and development prospects for the decade ahead. The aim is to form a judgment as to whether or not the enlarged resource demands for national security purposes discussed elsewhere in this volume are likely to collide with private (and other public) demands. The conclusion reached is that such a collision is a distinct possibility, and that hard decisions as to where, when, by

* This is the "compressibility" relation identified in Professor Mason's paper.

how much, and how these other demands are to be restrained will have to be made. It appears that the nation will have to pay a price for greater security. How much of a price and who pays, in relation to how much and what kind of increased security, is apt to become very much of a major policy question. The classical problem of political economy may be more relevant than one might at present assume.

## Two Views of Economic Growth

Economic growth in the usual sense is an enormously complicated, interrelated process. To say that its design and workings are not at all clear, even to close observers, is to state the obvious. Understanding the process requires a basic concept or theory to identify what appear to be the essentials of the process. Since the problem concerns a fairly long period of time, attention must also be given to structural features and their patterns of change.

### *"Potential" Growth of Total Output*

One widely accepted conception of the process of growth can be described as follows. Suppose that over long periods individual economic processes were highly adaptable to changes in "structure" (presently to be defined). Suppose, moreover, that such changes anywhere in the matrix of interrelationships, from buying and selling at various stages, and in the different lines of production, to final production itself, were generally offset by other responses. In a word, assume that the economy were in fact a mechanism capable of more or less continuous self-adjustment, working through substitutions of the factors of production in response to changes in their relative prices, and through process or product substitutions as methods of production and products are improved. Under these conditions, the details of change and the resulting responses within the matrix "wash out," and the focus of analysis can be shifted to the total yield of the matrix, to output as a whole, and to those over-all relationships which determine the level and growth of output in the aggregate.

The next step, logically, is to distinguish between total "potential" output and its growth rate on the one hand, and total actual or likely demand for that supply on the other. The growth in "potential" supply is taken to be a function of the rate of increase in basic economic resources (labor and capital), and of the contribution each makes (per man-hour or per unit of invested capital) to the growth rate of total output. Changes in total man-hours supplied or in the technological properties of the capital stock are taken to be changes in the "basic conditions;" changes in the rate at which each of these factors contributes to growth, i.e., their marginal productivities, are defined as shifts in the "structure" of the relationship. Expressed formally, the "potential" supply function of output growth is

$$\frac{\Delta Y}{Y} = \frac{\Delta L}{L} \cdot a + \frac{\Delta K}{K} (1 - a) + Z .$$

The expression shows the rate of output growth, $\frac{\Delta Y}{Y}$, as the sum of three basic sources. The first source is the growth of the labor input, $\frac{\Delta L}{L}$. Labor's contribution to the total growth rate is its own growth rate times $a$, the share of total output which it contributes. The second is the growth of the stock of capital used in production, $\frac{\Delta K}{K}$. Capital's contribution to the total growth rate is its own growth rate times the share of total output which it contributes $(1 - a)$. Historically, we find that these two contributions do not account for all the growth which has occurred. The remainder, designated Z here, is due to a gain in the productivity of labor and capital, i.e., the rise in the productive efficiency per unit of labor and capital.

Edward Denison [4] has estimated the respective contributions made by labor, the capital stock, and increased productivity to the growth of real output in the United States.[5] His results suggest that the constant-dollar growth rate of GNP for the period 1929-57 (about three per cent per year) can be assigned to the three sources, as follows: Labor* grew at a rate slightly greater than two per cent annually, and contributed about 1½ percentage points to the over-all growth rate of three per cent. Capital** grew at a rate slightly less than two per cent, but because per unit it contributes less to production, the proportion of the

---

* The growth rate of labor was adjusted for such things as the increased education per worker, shorter hours per week, change in the age-sex composition of the labor force, and the like.

** Adjusted in various ways to obtain a measure of the gross stock of capital, exclusive of quality changes.

growth ascribed to enlargements in capital stock was only a little less than half of a percentage point. Thus, capital and labor together accounted for $\frac{2}{3}$ of the three per cent growth rate. The residual, Z in the expression above, accounts for the remaining $\frac{1}{3}$. According to these estimates, therefore, about $\frac{1}{3}$ of the growth in total output is accounted for by gains in the productive efficiency of capital and labor.

Denison's estimates raise certain questions about the imputation of contributions made by labor, capital, and the assortment of factors credited with contributions via the productivity gain. Analytical choices made in this regard are potentially far-reaching in their policy implications. It is probably fair to say that current theorizing is inclined to limit the role of capital (and investment) by classifying capital improvements under a catch-all heading* that emphasizes the scientific and social basis of productivity advances. What matters here, however, is the basic approach, and the fact that it has been made operational by statistical estimation.

### The Analytics of Slack and Gap

In order to avoid misunderstanding, one should keep in mind that the aggregate supply function referred to pertains to "poential" output—i.e., "high" or "full" employment GNP. In concept, this involves the proposition that the economy could grow more or less steadily at a rate sufficient to hold unemployment down to four per cent (and that in due course growth could be faster, given certain changes in basic conditions or "structure"). This provides license for following the practice employed by the Council of Economic Advisers of selecting the low unemployment GNP of mid-1955, passing a trend line through that value which rises at a rate consistent with projections about the contribution to growth that labor, capital, and productivity gain could make, and calling this trend the full-employment growth of GNP. The Council uses this method to estimate full-employment GNP for 1962, say, in order to calculate the shortfall of actual economic performance.[6] The "gap" determined in this way is a

---

* Robert Solow's recent paper on this subject moved in the opposite direction by assuming that technological advances can be introduced only through investment in new plant and equipment. This obviously increases the importance of capital formation in the growth process. Cf. his "Technical Progress, Capital Formation, and Economic Growth," *American Economic Review* (May, 1962), pp. 76-77 and Table 3, p. 85.

measure of the extent to which aggregate demand for output is deficient.

There are a number of theoretical difficulties with this approach. But, for the purpose at hand, only two of these call for comment. Note that estimating "potential" supply turns on the assumption—required by the underlying theory of growth—that economic activity at a time of low unemployment, such as mid-1955, represents a workable approximation to equilibrium. This requirement applies both to the internal adjustment processes and to the over-all relationships between output, income distribution, and the major components of the demand for that output. There is little presumption that mid-1955 can meet these tests. In addition, a "potential" supply estimate along the lines indicated presupposes that the economy is sufficiently self-equilibrating in response to changes currently taking place so that it *could* grow more or less steadily at the full-employment rate, given the right policy mix. For the present there is little evidence that steady growth in this sense would be possible under American conditions.

As already suggested, the concept of "potential" supply is juxtaposed with demand—with aggregate demand and its make-up as required by the concepts of national income theory. Given a determination of demand on that basis, the key question is whether or not demand will be sufficient at any future time to bring "potential" supply* into existence. The answer depends primarily on two relations: first, given the growth in "potential" output and income, some proportion of the rise in income would be saved and the rest returned directly to the flow of spending. This apportionment determines the likely growth of demand for consumer goods and (via business saving and reinvesting) influences the growth in the stock of capital. Secondly, given the rate of saving, demand is also affected by changes in the amount of capital required per unit of output; a reduction in capital requirements, for example, would result in a slower increase in the demand for capital goods. Changed methods of production or an alteration in the type of goods and services preferred might produce such a development. Estimates of these relationships, i.e., of the rise in consumer and capital outlays that are likely under the relevant assumptions, provide a basis for inferring whether demand growth is adequate.[7] If demand growth tends to lag behind the "potential" growth in aggregate

---

* It may be, of course, excessive.

supply, unemployment will result. But unemployment may also result from the substitution of capital for labor.* Needless to say, with additional assumptions quite a number of other possibilities become apparent, possibilities by no means beyond the pale of practical relevance.

Some economists believe that capital (and labor) requirements per unit of output may indeed be declining, and that, for this reason, private investment demand must be supplemented increasingly by public expenditure. To them, business tax reductions or monetary policy encouragement seem too mild a family of medicines. The Council of Economic Advisers recorded a more optimistic view of US economic prospects when it endorsed the fiscal 1962 budget even though it would yield, by Council estimates, a $6 to $7 billion surplus at "potential," full-employment GNP; on the Council's own terms, this is a "restrictive" budget in the sense that private investment (and state and local spending) would have to rise quite strongly in order to power the economy up to full "potential" against the drag effects of such a budget. The 1963 *Economic Report* was somewhat more bearish in its appraisal of underlying tendencies in the private sector of the economy.[8]

The general approach to economic growth just outlined is by no means in sole possession of the field. There are others, and with lineage to match that of the view so far presented. For, while the view outlined counts Alfred Marshall, John Maynard Keynes, and Roy Harrod among its forebears, there are other, legitimate, lines of descent within the house of modern economics. The approach presently to be described and thereafter put to use can make such a claim, descendent as it is from Joseph A. Schumpeter and John R. Hicks, among others. This by way of transition.

### Economic Development as Cyclical Process

The main reasons for favoring an analysis that differs from the basic scheme just described are two: first, the assumption of technical and economic flexibility in substituting factors of production ,production processes, or industrial outputs for each other, along with human skills, industrial locations, and the like,

---

* This result could follow from a rise in the price of labor relative to the price of capital, as well as from a change in the efficiency of capital that is labor saving.

seems too radical. Useful and even indispensable as this assumption may be to get a theory off the ground, application of that theory to policy issues requires careful and specific adjusting through one or more stages of "approximation" to reality. Now it is true, of course, that the longer periods relevant to growth analysis properly so-called provide the time necessary to overcome much of the stickiness, lumpiness, and various other imperfections apparent in many parts of the economic mechanism. Competition can see to that. But if this is all that can be claimed for the adjustment processes that underlie the aggregate interrelationships of the growth theory above, changes in growth rates over periods as short as five, eight, or even ten years cannot safely be approached with nothing more in hand than that growth theory. An effort must also be made to determine what shifts have occurred in the composition of demand, production, and generally in the basic "conditions," and how these are likely to work themselves out in the future.

The second reason is closely related to the first, but its implications are far more encompassing. The flow of investment opportunities ready for economic use may not be steady for many reasons. The application of technological and organizational developments often poses problems requiring considerable entrepreneurial skills. These skills may or may not come into play when and where needed. Also, success or failure may depend on further technological developments or on the availability of complementary knowledge and skills; in other instances, implementation may wait on changes in market organization, changes in collective bargaining agreements, decisions by government at one or more levels, and on similar happenings. If so, the transition from investment opportunity to investment program will involve time lags. Of course, in the aggregate, all of these events may show up as so many random shocks which, by and large, tend to offset each other, and the errors resulting from such a process could then be handled statistically. Unfortunately, innovations and related adjustments are, oftentimes, not random events; frequently, they are interconnected sequences which rearrange the economic terrain (the universe) sufficiently to render inapplicable the statistical method just mentioned. A modern dynamic economy is more than a matrix with fixed or gradually changing coefficients, more than a stochastic process. At times or in certain sectors, coping with new investment opportunities or any decision of major consequences is more like solving an expanding crossword puzzle in which new and old definitions can change without much notice. Allowing for the variability in human ability and for the extent to which individuals and economic groups are given to imitative behavior, it is reasonable to expect that progress should be accomplished at a distinctly uneven pace.

A growth theory that (1) takes account of leads, lags, and interruptions in the underlying adjustment processes, and (2) allows for an uneven pace of investment in response to the opportunities and groups of opportunities that present themselves, differs in a number of ways from the growth theory above. Two of these are crucial for this paper. First, analytically speaking, its focus of attention is on *the specific new developments* taking place through the investment they involve and induce, directly or indirectly via changes in income. In short, the key variable is "autonomous" investment. The primary relationships linking changes in "autonomous" investment to growth in output and in its composition are (1) the usual multiplier effect of investment activity on income via consumer spending, and (2) the "induced" investment expenditures. Secondly, adding the leads and lags associated with the "imperfections" and complementarities mentioned, and allowing for what must surely be a significant amount of inconsistency of expenditure plans—this is, after all, a private economy in which even the Government comes into the market as a private buyer with rights to change plans—we get *cyclical* growth.

This is what all industrialized countries, organized on the market principle, have had for a long time and live with today. In some periods growth is faster and in others it is slower, depending on the character and strength of "autonomous" investment. Bert Hickman of the Brookings Institution examined the empirical evidence bearing on the reasons for these variations at the December 1962 meeting of the American Economic Association.[9]

Cyclical growth obviously calls for policy measures to reduce the fluctuations on welfare grounds and at times also to avoid damage to the economic machinery itself. Expansions strongly propelled by investment activity along major thrust lines of development are likely to evoke a bullish investment response, and this may result in cumulative expansion. Strong booms and sharp recessions cannot be ruled out as a possibility. Also, government spending that marks off lines of more or less definite development has growth and cycle consequences that are of a kind with private investment.

## Doubts About Full-Employment Growth

Taking growth to be a cyclical, uneven process has as a consequence that the economic system does not necessarily oscillate around a "full-employment" growth trend no matter how that is defined. At times, activity will tend to utilize resources less fully, and this may be followed by periods in which demands are excessive on balance. It all depends on the specific developments taking place, their interactions and the leads and lags involved. There is little reason to expect that, with this process, even a sophisticated mix of public policy measures can produce a reasonable approximation to growth along a "full" utilization ceiling. The requirements, in terms of economic forecasting and flexibility as to policy actions, appear to go beyond foreseeable capabilities.

This conclusion does not amount to a rejection of high employment as a policy goal or of the Employment Act of 1946. It merely argues against a literal-minded interpretation of its mandate. If economic growth in the US today conforms in its essentials to the theoretical conception we have urged, fiscal policy, both in regard to tax rates and expenditures, should be primarily longer-term, "development" oriented; to try for continuous "full" employment growth plus a percentage point or two runs the risk of pursuing a creature of logic and statistical contrivance.

## Economic Growth in the 1950's

So much for the exposition of alternative approaches to the problem of growth and our own convictions in the matter. It must now be admitted, however, that the task of working with the concepts we regard as appropriate for an analysis of the prospects for US economic growth and development is forbidding. This is not only because the basic distinction between "autonomous" and induced investment processes are difficult to handle empirically, but also—and perhaps mainly—because the statistical and other factual prerequisites of an analysis along our lines are largely lacking. The basic statistical framework with which economists of all analytical persuasions have to work is primarily designed to serve an aggregate approach to output and growth problems. Progress is being made in providing more detailed information, but for the present the possibilities are quite limited.

As matters stand, the best that can be done is to identify certain major developments that shaped the expansion after World War II, to estimate their trends in the decade ahead, and to arrive at a judgment regarding induced effects and over-all prospects. The relevance of these prospects for national security policy will be indicated along the way.

### Rapid Growth Through 1955

An evaluation of likely future developments begins with the present and recent past. Since 1955-57, economic growth has slowed down, and, according to the prevailing view, this has happened because aggregate demand has failed to rise sufficiently. In turn, the slackening of demand is explained by certain policy actions and the effects of the tax structure on consumer and investment spending. In the end, this part of the diagnosis identifies the very slow growth in private investment spending as focal point of the difficulty.[10]

There is obvious merit in this diagnosis—witness its acceptance to one extent or another by a wide spectrum of competent observers. By the lights guiding this study, however, it should be instructive to penetrate beyond aggregate demand in search of underlying changes. Charts I, II, and III may facilitate the discussion.

A reasoned account of economic developments through 1955 can be very largely expressed in terms of a strong rise in autonomous spending on business capital and residential construction, consumer durables, and state and local government building activity with an emphasis on school construction. There seems to be agreement that deferred wartime demand (aided, to be sure, by wartime accumulations of liquidity and by low interest rates), along with an unusually large supply of current and past advances in technology and organization, provided a large part of the force that powered the economic rise in those years. It is equally clear that the main line of thrust was strongly influenced by the postwar outburst of marriages and births, and by associated demands for family housing, major appliances, automobiles, schools, religious facilities, and so on. The accompanying cultural transformation helped broaden the relevant markets at a very rapid pace. All of this is well-known and needs no elaboration.

**Chart I—PRIVATE INVESTMENT (Billions of 1954 Dollars)**

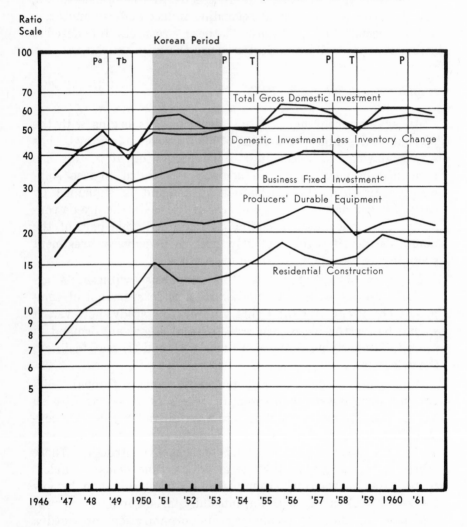

a) *The P's designate busines cycle peaks.*

b) *The T's designate business cycle troughs.*

c) *Series includes producers' durable equipment and industrial, commercial and other nonresi-
dential construction.*

**Chart II—CONSUMPTION EXPENDITURES (Billions of 1954 Dollars)**

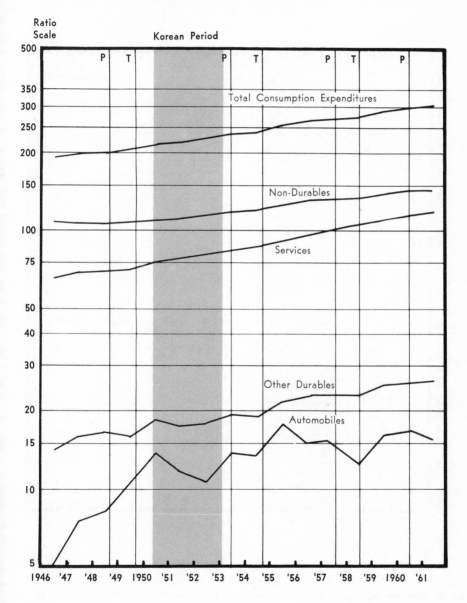

### Chart III—GOVERNMENT PURCHASES OF GOODS AND SERVICES
(In Billions of 1954 Dollars)

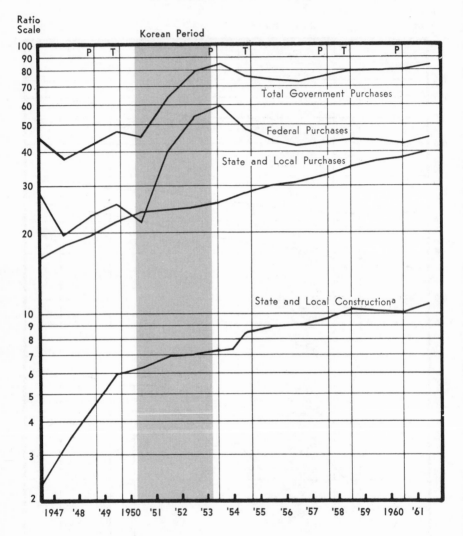

a) The state and local construction series was deflated by the implicit price deflator for new construction other than residential nonfarm.

Sources of Charts I, II, and III: Department of Commerce, *U.S. Income and Output* and *Survey of Current Business.*

## The Economic Consequences of Korea

One feature of US growth through 1955 remains unclear. In examining the expenditure series on Charts I, II, and III (all adjusted for price change) one gains the impression that after early 1951, the rise in Korean defense spending was largely substituted for, rather than superimposed upon, private autonomous demands.[11] This is reflected by the fairly substantial declines in consumer expenditures on automobiles and other durables (even though Regulation W was not very effectively enforced) and also by the fact that our machinery for price stabilization proved, by the time it was fully operational, rather unnecessary. The implication is that in many sectors private demand abated of its own accord [12] during 1951 and 1952; it can be argued, moreover, that a reversal of this shift occurred later on in 1952 at about the time when defense orders were beginning to slacken.[13] The Korean War was fought with conventional means requiring, for the most part, conventional capital equipment, methods of production, and labor force skills. Satisfying the military needs of Korea required comparatively little in the way of reorganizing the processes of production and distribution. These and other circumstances raise serious doubts as to whether so easy a shift between various civilian and military demands can be attributed to the ordinary workings of economic adjustment processes.

If this characterization of the Korean period is correct, the military spending in those years served to sustain and prolong the post-World War II expansion. Certainly it helped to boost profit rates and enlarged liquidity generally. These factors must have contributed substantially to the unexpectedly large investment boom of 1956-57, and to the anticipation that the basic post-World War II demand pattern would continue to show the kind of strength indicated by the expansion of 1955. Depending on the weight given to the influence of the Korean War on developments in 1955 and 1956, the general belief that economic growth through 1955 or 1957 was markedly faster than since that time may have to be revised substantially.

## The Slowdown After 1955

The economic changes since 1955-57 produced considerable shifts between lines of activity. Government policy actions contributed their share to the amount of adjustment required, and it is probably fair to say that the need for reorganizing and redirecting economic activity was for some time not apparent. The period as a whole was characterized by a blurring of basic guidelines for the developments ahead. Nevertheless, these years produced rapid progress in various technologies including those connected with communication, transportation, and administration as well as extensive improvements through the relocation of service and commercial enterprises in suburban and satellite communities.

Certain of the major shifts in the demand for automobiles, housing, and buiness-fixed investment are apparent from Charts I, II, and III above. Professor Charles Schultze has called attention to these diverse movements and has analyzed their implications for costs and prices during the period 1955-57.[14] While it is true that residential construction recovered strongly from its sharp decline after 1955, a close examination of the changes that have been taking place in this group of industries makes it clear that the contribution to economic growth from this quarter has diminished. State and local construction expenditures also lost forward momentum and ceased advancing for a time after 1958. The temporary interruption of the rising trend in school construction outlays partly accounts for this.[15]

The decline in government purchases of goods and services is apparent from Chart III. The effects implied by this and other changes relating to the federal budget for the fiscal year 1960 have rightly been evaluated as having been too restrictive in those economic circumstances. Less appreciated is the fact that the change in composition of these purchases also had an adverse economic impact, quite apart from the dollar magnitudes, and required reorganization on the part of a number of important industries. In the years after 1958, defense spending on major military procurement items underwent a large shift in favor of missiles and against aircraft. Over-all, this substitution did not involve reduced defense expenditures, but the redistribution had adverse indirect effects because the investment called for by missile production has remained relatively low; rapid technological developments and corresponding changes in requirements are partly responsible for this fact.

In contrast, aircraft procurements in the earlier years had induced very large investments in productive capacity. Shifts in the composition of spending can have serious consequences of this sort independently of any change in the *level* of autonomous spending.

Summing up, therefore, we should characterize the period since 1955-57 as one in which a loss of orientation regarding the major lines of development occurred, and in which a great deal of change and adjustment thereto had to be accomplished. Table 1 reflects this in terms of the changed ranking of major industry groups based on their respective growth rates for 1948-57 and 1957-60.*

Judging purely by an aggregate output measure of economic advance, one would believe that a period so marked by shifts, uncertainty, and by comparatively low plant and equipment utilization rates would tend to yield low productivity gains.

In a surprisingly large segment of the economy, the opposite seems to have been the case. An examination of productivity gains in the period 1957-60 covering most of the broad industry groups and some twenty major manufacturing industries ** reveals substantially unchanged or increased gains, as compared with the earlier period, in more than 2⁄3 of the 30 groupings. The industries or industry groups showing strong performance accounted for some 55 per cent of the product originating in all 30 of the industrial divisions taken together. These results are as yet tentative and suffer from difficulties with some of the data. Still, there is confirmation here that the expansion in our potentialities and capabilities, to the extent these find expression in output-per-man-hour statistics, seems not to have been damped by the lower average rates of output increase measured in the GNP accounts.

---

* A test was made to determine whether the dispersion of individual growth rates had diminished as average growth declined. The sample used was a set of 150 three- and four-digit industries. The test showed that dispersion in growth rates did not diminish. This fact suggests that the dispersion may have had a separate effect, increasing uncertainty and adjustment difficulties quite apart from the decline in the average growth rate.

** Together, these accounted for 85 per cent of the GNP originating in the private sectors of the economy.

Table 1—Change in Industry Growth Positions in the Postwar Period *

| Average Annual Growth | Industry Position in | | | |
|---|---|---|---|---|
| | | 1948-57 | | 1957-60 |
| Fast-Growing (5 per cent or better) ...... | 1 | Other transportation equipment | 25 | Apparel |
| | 2 | Public utilities | 2 | Public utilities |
| | 3 | Finance and insurance | 4 | Chemicals |
| | 4 | Chemicals | 18 | Furniture |
| | 5 | Electrical machinery | 6 | Instruments |
| | 6 | Instruments | | |
| | 7 | Communications | | |
| | 8 | Non-rail transportation | | |
| Average Growing (2.0 per cent to 4.9 per cent). | 9 | Paper | 3 | Finance and insurance |
| | 10 | Construction | 7 | Communications |
| | 11 | Motor vehicles and parts | 11 | Motor vehicles and parts |
| | 12 | Retail trade | 21 | Rubber |
| | 13 | Integrated petroleum | 26 | Tobacco |
| | 14 | Miscellaneous manufacturing | 14 | Miscellaneous manufacturing |
| | 15 | Services | 15 | Services |
| | 16 | Fabricated metals | 9 | Paper |
| | 17 | Stone, clay, and glass | 5 | Electrical machinery |
| | 18 | Furniture | 19 | Printing |
| | 19 | Printing | 17 | Stone, clay, and glass |
| | 20 | Wholesale trade | 8 | Non-rail transportation |
| | 21 | Rubber | 24 | Food |
| | 22 | Non-electrical machinery | 31 | Textiles |
| | 23 | Primary metals | 29 | Lumber |
| | 24 | Food | 20 | Wholesale trade |
| | | | 12 | Retail trade |
| | | | 16 | Fabricated metals |
| Slow-Growing (1.9 per cent or less) ..... | 25 | Apparel | 28 | Farming |
| | 26 | Tobacco | 10 | Construction |
| | 27 | Leather | 22 | Non-electrical machinery |
| | 28 | Farming | 27 | Leather |
| | 29 | Lumber | 13 | Integrated petroleum |
| | 30 | Mining | 30 | Mining |
| | 31 | Textiles | 32 | Railroad transportation |
| | 32 | Railroad transportation | 23 | Primary metals |
| | | | 1 | Other transportation equipment |

\* The number preceding each industry is its growth-rate rank in the first period.

Source: Calculated from data compiled by Charles L. Schultze and Joseph L. Tryon for *Study Paper No. 17*, Joint Economic Committee (1960) and by Charles L. Schultze for *Prices, Costs, and Output for the Post War Decade 1947-1957*, Committee for Economic Development (1959). These data have since been brought up to date in unpublished form by the authors.

## The Worry About Business Investment

That leaves an important question at least partially unanswered, namely, what accounts for the low levels of business investment, especially in producers' durable equipment. The following may help to put this in better perspective.

A profound change in the postwar period was the shift in private and public investment from tangible, reproducible goods to non-tangible capital. As a result, the usual statistics tend to understate the growth in capital formation.

Broadly speaking, non-tangible investment covers investment through education, medical care, the dissemination of knowledge about opportunities, etc., as well as investment in research and development, on-the-job training, and the like. Of course, not all expenditures along these lines are investment in an economic sense, and this poses measurement problems. Much of our spending on education, for example, must be classed as consumption since it provides directly only current satisfaction. Such difficulties are insurmountable. It is impossible, therefore, to make accurate estimates of total investment in non-tangible capital. Rough estimates have nevertheless been made and, even making large allowances for error, it is clear that a strong shift from tangible, reproducible wealth accumulation to capital in non-tangible forms has occurred. Table 2 shows some of the

**Table 2—Estimates of Various Stocks of Capital and Annual Rates of Increase Between 1929 and 1957 in the United States in 1956 Dollars**

| | Billions of 1956 Dollars | | Annual Rate of Growth (Per cent) | Per Cent of Total in 1957 |
| | 1929 (1) | 1957 (2) | (3) | (4) |
|---|---|---|---|---|
| 1. Reproducible tangible wealth | 727 | 1,270 | 2.01 | 51.5 |
| 2. Educational capital in population | 317 | 848 | 3.57 | 34.4 |
| Educational capital in labor force | (173) | (535) | (4.09) | (21.7) |
| 3. On-the-job training of males in labor force | 136* | 347 | 5.36 | 14.1 |
| | | 2,465 | | 100.0 |

* For 1939.

Source: Theodore W. Schultz, "Reflections on Investment in Man," *Journal of Political Economy, Supplement* (October, 1962), Table 1.

**Table 3—Research and Development Expenditures**

(Millions of Dollars)

| Year | A—Sources of Funds | | | |
|---|---|---|---|---|
| | Government | Industry | University | Total |
| 1941.... | 370 | 510 | 20 | 900 |
| 1942.... | 490 | 560 | 20 | 1070 |
| 1943.... | 780 | 410 | 20 | 1210 |
| 1944.... | 940 | 420 | 20 | 1380 |
| 1945.... | 1070 | 430 | 20 | 1520 |
| 1946.... | 910 | 840 | 30 | 1780 |
| 1947.... | 1160 | 1050 | 50 | 2260 |
| 1948.... | 1390 | 1150 | 70 | 2610 |
| 1949.... | 1550 | 990 | 80 | 2870 |
| 1950.... | 1610 | 1180 | 80 | 2870 |
| 1951.... | 1980 | 1300 | 80 | 3360 |
| 1952.... | 2240 | 1430 | 80 | 3750 |
| 1953.... | 2490 | 1430 | 80 | 4000 |
| 1954.... | 2460 | 1600 | 80 | 4140 |
| 1955.... | 2720 | 2600 | 80 | 5400 |
| 1956.... | 3170 | 3250 | 80 | 6500 |
| 1957.... | 3750 | 4300 | 150 | 8200 |
| 1958.... | 4430 | 5600 | 200 | 10230 |

| Year | B—Sources of Funds | | | | |
|---|---|---|---|---|---|
| | Government | Industry | University | Other non-profit | Total |
| 1953-54.... | 2740 | 2240 | 130 | 40 | 5150 |
| 1954-55.... | 3070 | 2365 | 140 | 45 | 5620 |
| 1955-56.... | 3670 | 2510 | 155 | 55 | 6390 |
| 1956-57.... | 5095 | 3265 | 180 | 70 | 8610 |
| 1957-58.... | 6380 | 3390 | 190 | 70 | 10030 |
| 1958-59.... | 7170 | 3620 | 190 | 90 | 11070 |
| 1959-60.... | 8290 | 4030 | 200 | 100 | 12620 |
| 1960-61.... | 9220 | 4490 | 210 | 120 | 14040 |

— n.a. —

Sources: Bank A, Department of Defense. (Quoted in Fritz Machlup, *The Production and Distribution of Knowledge in the United States* (Princeton, N. J.: Princeton University Press, 1962), p. 157. Bank B, National Science Foundation. (Quoted in Machlup, *op. cit.*, p. 158.)

estimates made by Professor Theodore Schultz. According to these figures, total human capital was about equal to reproducible tangible wealth by 1957; it also appears that the former has been growing at better than twice the rate of the latter.

### R&D as Private Capital Formation

The concept relevant for our purposes, however, is investment in intangibles connected with economic action, i.e., R&D and on-the-job training. And since the notion of a stock of R&D capital makes little sense conceptually, we confine ourselves to estimates of current expenditures. These expenditures clearly have had and will have a very important effect on the character of output and the methods by which it is produced, and are therefore very much a form of investment.

Until ten years ago, data on R&D spending were very dubious indeed. With this warning, two sets of estimates are given in Table 3. Fritz Machlup's recent book [16] on these questions provides an impression of magnitude in 1920, some $80 million, and shows a rise to $130 and $377 million by 1930 and 1940, respectively. These estimates are shown in Bank A cf Table 3; the B series are based on surveys by the National Science Foundation and are perhaps somewhat more reliable; unfortunately, the data do not extend back beyond 1953.

The showing of these figures—after generous allowances for error—clearly reveals a strong rise in expenditures, including investment in R&D activities and on-the-job training. It is also apparent that over the recent past, this type of investment increased at a much faster rate than investment in tangible wealth. In view of the concern about over-all growth and the lag in business investment, it may well be asked whether nontangible investment is reflected in GNP and the corresponding statistics of private investment. The answer is that the part originating in industry is omitted from these accounts because such expenditures are usually treated as a current expense by the firms involved. Consequently, these items are taken to be "intermediate products" and are excluded from the accounts. If industry R&D and on-the-job training were treated as capital formation, the measure of business investment on the product side of our national accounts would be higher, and so would profits and wages on the income side.

Table 4 presents some illustrative adjustments of conventional GNP figures on the assumption that 50 per cent of on-the-job training costs and 80 per cent of the industry-financed R&D expenditures are business investment in the relevant sense. The results are shown for 1949 and 1958, years for which rough estimates of both expenditure categories are available.

The conclusion to be drawn from the adjusted figures is that on-the-job training and R&D expenditures have increased rapidly enough to make their omission from the national accounts a matter of consequence. In fact, there is some basis for believing that this form of investment may have been large enough to make up for much of the apparent decline in gross business investment as a proportion of GNP which the Council of Economic Advisers has stressed in its diagnosis of economic developments since 1957.[17] By the same token, if the omitted profits were added on the income side (no adjusted income estimates were actually made) the relative decline in profits would probably be smaller than indicated by the income accounts. Both of these aspects suggest interesting new hypotheses about the course of economic development after 1955.

**Table 4—Illustrative Adjustments to GNP for Research and Development, and On-the-job Training**

(Billions of Current Dollars)

| Gross National Product Components | 1949 | 1958 |
|---|---|---|
| 1. Personal consumption expenditures ............... | 181.2 | 293.2 |
| 2. Gross private domestic investment ................ | 33.0 | 56.6 |
| 3. Net exports ..................................... | 3.8 | 1.2 |
| 4. Government purchases ........................... | 40.2 | 93.5 |
| 5. Total .......................................... | 258.1 | 444.5 |
| 6. Industry research and development expenditures x 80 per cent ..................... | .8 | 4.5 |
| 7. On-the-job training costs x 50 per cent ............ | 4.5 | 6.7 |
| 8. Total, human capital investment not reflected in GNP | 5.3 | 11.2 |
| Line 8 as per cent of line 2 ......................... | 16% | 20% |
| Adjusted gross private domestic investment (line 2 + line 8) ............................... | 38.3 | 67.8 |
| Adjusted GNP (line 5 + line 8) ..................... | 263.4 | 455.7 |

Sources: GNP Components, *Survey of Current Business* (July, 1962). R&D Expenditures, Fritz Machlup, *Production and Distribution of Knowledge*, p. 157. On-the-job training, Jacob Mincer, *Journal of Political Economy*, Supplement (October, 1962), p. 57.

These conclusions are fragile; they should not be pressed too far. But it is plain that the nation's output and income accounts seriously distort the picture of a very vital element in the growth process. Moreover, the analogous public expenditures on intangible capital formation of the type under discussion are very large indeed and are growing rapidly. Admittedly, public and private expenditures along this line are not easily fitted into the income and product framework, but that does not excuse us from considering their effect on growth.

### Implications for the Past and Future

What are the consequences of this large shift of investment toward non-tangible forms? One consequence is a rapid change in skill demands made on the labor force. An indication of this appears in Table 5. Since World War II, employment in three of the low-skill occupations—operatives and kindred workers, agricultural workers, and non-farm laborers—declined, while their share in total unemployment remained approximately constant. Apparently, the process of adjusting to higher skill requirements is slow and difficult. The welfare implications of this are obvious. Fritz Machlup has suggested, that ". . . the combination of our social ideas with the continuing technological and economic trends may in fact spell unemployability for certain low-level types of labor . . . and this unemployment is apt to persist even in the face of attempts to create 'effective' demand if wage rates are promptly adjusted to inflated price levels." [18]

The very rapid rise in R&D activities and in similar efforts is directly relevant to the national security interest in growth as we conceive it, and to growth in the conventional sense as well. Investment in human beings generally, and to an extent also in R&D work, has a relationship to future output that differs from investment in ordinary producers' goods. The latter is directly related to more or less definite future goods and is subject to the discipline of cost-revenue calculations. In contrast, non-tangible investment, at the time it is made, tends to have only a tenuous connection with the specific goods and services that will be produced. In addition, non-tangible investment may have little or no immediate effect on productive capacity. For these reasons such investment is not very sensitive to fluctuations in current output. The record of the past half dozen years for the United States appears to bear this out. In a word, we are confronted here by a special kind of "autonomous" investment. Over longer periods,

Table 5 *—Employment, Unemployment Rates, and Per Cent Distribution of the Unemployed for Operatives, Farm Workers, and Non-Farm Laborers—Annual Averages

| Major Occupation Group | 1960 | 1958 | 1956 | 1954 | 1952 | 1950 | 1948 |
|---|---|---|---|---|---|---|---|
| Employment (Thousands): | | | | | | | |
| Operatives and kindred workers | 11,986 | 11,441 | 12,816 | 12,253 | 12,352 | 12,146 | 12,396 |
| Farm laborers and foremen | 2,615 | 2,508 | 2,889 | 2,495 | 2,669 | 3,015 | 3,213 |
| Laborers, except farm and mine | 3,665 | 3,600 | 3,670 | 3,603 | 3,707 | 3,520 | 3,473 |
| All other | 48,415 | 46,417 | 45,553 | 42,809 | 42,261 | 40,967 | 40,225 |
| Total | 66,681 | 63,966 | 64,928 | 61,160 | 60,989 | 59,648 | 59,307 |
| Unemployment Rates: | | | | | | | |
| Operatives and kindred workers | 8.0 | 10.9 | 5.4 | 7.6 | 3.9 | 6.8 | 4.1 |
| Farm laborers and foremen | 5.2 | 6.2 | 3.7 | 4.2 | 2.3 | 5.0 | 2.3 |
| Laborers, except farm and mine | 12.5 | 14.9 | 8.2 | 10.7 | 5.7 | 11.7 | 7.5 |
| All other | 4.4 | 5.1 | 3.0 | 3.9 | 2.7 | 4.5 | 3.0 |
| Unemployment—Per Cent Distribution: | | | | | | | |
| Operatives and kindred workers | 26.5 | 30.0 | 28.5 | 32.1 | 28.8 | 26.9 | 26.0 |
| Farm laborers and foremen | 3.6 | 3.5 | 4.4 | 3.4 | 3.6 | 4.8 | 3.8 |
| Laborers, except farm and mine | 13.3 | 13.5 | 12.8 | 13.7 | 13.1 | 14.2 | 14.0 |
| All other | 56.6 | 53.0 | 54.3 | 50.8 | 54.5 | 54.1 | 56.2 |
| Total | 100.0 | 100.0 | 100.0 | 100.0 | 100.0 | 100.0 | 100.0 |

* For detailed tables showing breakdown of the "All other" classes, and for sources see Appendix Tables 1 and 2, *infra*.

however, the probability of a pay-out in greater capabilities as well as in terms of contributions to economic growth of one kind or another must surely increase quite rapidly. The general presumption is that the outlook for greater productivity gains and an enlarged flow of profitable investment opportunities is promising. Unquestionably this is likely to give a strong impetus to economic development and to growth generally in the decade ahead.

### Three Basic Trends in the Decade Ahead

Trends in total population, family formation, and school age population in the next ten years are obvious guides in an attempt to gauge the direction and strength of certain developments to come. Future levels of demand for housing and related durable goods and for educational services depend in large part upon population changes.

### *The Increase in Two- and Three-Child Families*

What is needed, for the purpose at hand, is a close look at changes in the age and family composition of future populations. To make these estimates, population statistics by single years of age were obtained, and using 1950 and 1960 Census benchmarks along with 1959 mortality and natality rates, all other years through 1972 were calculated.

The resulting projections show a picture that suggest burgeoning demands for housing and related durable goods. Total population and households in the 1960-69 period can be expected to grow at a rate no better than the 1950-59 rate, but their composition is likely to show large, favorable changes. (See Chart IV and Table 6.) From 1950 to 1959, the total number of families having two or three children with the mother between the ages of 19 and 24 declined by six per cent. Given the fact that, typically, the husband in these families is 26 years of age or less, this group is the largest source of apartment demand. Concurrently, the number of families having two or three children with the mother between 25 and 30 declined by nine per cent. This group, with fathers typically in the age bracket from 27 to 32 years, includes the modal class of all families purchasing their first house. Changes in the number of families in this category strongly influence the demand for private dwelling units.

### Chart IV—POPULATION INDEXES

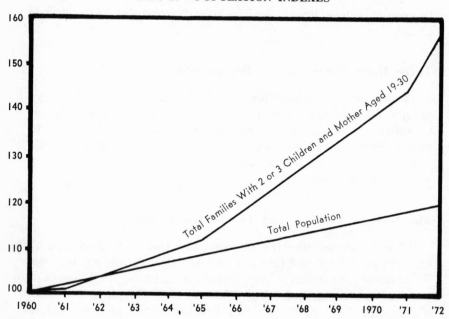

Source: Table 6, columns (1) and (3), base 1960 = 100.

Table 6—Population Projections
Households and 2- or 3-Children Families
(Thousands)

| Year | Total Population (1) | Total Households (2) | Total Families with 2 or 3 Children Mother's Age | | | Indexes of Columns (1) to (5) (1950 = 100) | | | | |
|---|---|---|---|---|---|---|---|---|---|---|
| | | | 19-30 (3) | 19-24 (4) | 24-30 (5) | (6) | (7) | (8) | (9) | (10) |
| 1950 | 151,683 | 43,600 | 1,579 | 878 | 701 | 100.0 | 100.0 | 100.0 | 100.0 | 100.0 |
| 1951 | 154,360 | 44,700 | 1,559 | 863 | 696 | 101.8 | 102.5 | 98.7 | 98.3 | 99.3 |
| 1952 | 157,028 | 45,500 | 1,539 | 846 | 693 | 103.5 | 104.4 | 97.5 | 96.4 | 98.9 |
| 1953 | 159,636 | 46,300 | 1,514 | 828 | 686 | 105.2 | 106.2 | 95.9 | 94.3 | 97.9 |
| 1954 | 162,417 | 46,900 | 1,496 | 814 | 682 | 107.9 | 107.6 | 94.7 | 92.7 | 97.3 |
| 1955 | 165,270 | 47,800 | 1,478 | 807 | 671 | 109.0 | 109.6 | 93.6 | 91.9 | 95.7 |
| 1956 | 168,176 | 48,800 | 1,465 | 806 | 659 | 110.9 | 111.9 | 92.8 | 91.8 | 94.0 |
| 1957 | 171,198 | 49,500 | 1,461 | 808 | 653 | 112.9 | 113.5 | 92.5 | 92.0 | 93.2 |
| 1958 | 174,054 | 50,400 | 1,459 | 816 | 643 | 114.8 | 115.6 | 92.4 | 92.9 | 91.7 |
| 1959 | 177,103 | 51,300 | 1,462 | 827 | 635 | 116.8 | 117.7 | 92.6 | 94.2 | 90.6 |
| 1960 | 179,326 | 51,877 | 1,468 | 840 | 628 | 118.1 | 119.0 | 93.0 | 95.7 | 89.6 |
| 1961 | 182,167 | 52,424 | 1,477 | 858 | 619 | 120.1 | 120.2 | 93.5 | 97.7 | 88.3 |
| 1962 | 184,826 | 53,253 | 1,512 | 901 | 611 | 121.9 | 122.1 | 95.8 | 102.6 | 87.2 |
| 1963 | 187,673 | 54,227 | 1,557 | 947 | 610 | 123.7 | 124.4 | 98.6 | 107.9 | 87.0 |
| 1964 | 190,556 | 55,224 | 1,600 | 988 | 612 | 125.6 | 126.7 | 101.3 | 112.5 | 87.3 |
| 1965 | 193,468 | 56,076 | 1,642 | 1,026 | 615 | 127.6 | 128.6 | 104.0 | 116.9 | 87.7 |
| 1966 | 196,391 | 56,966 | 1,712 | 1,091 | 621 | 129.5 | 130.7 | 108.4 | 124.3 | 88.8 |
| 1967 | 199,416 | 56,960 | 1,801 | 1,163 | 639 | 131.5 | 130.6 | 114.1 | 132.5 | 91.2 |
| 1968 | 202,562 | 59,127 | 1,882 | 1,206 | 675 | 133.5 | 135.6 | 119.2 | 137.4 | 92.3 |
| 1969 | 205,857 | 60,079 | 1,958 | 1,249 | 708 | 135.7 | 137.8 | 124.0 | 142.3 | 101.0 |
| 1970 | 209,412 | 61,094 | 2,033 | 1,294 | 738 | 138.1 | 140.1 | 128.8 | 147.4 | 105.3 |
| 1971 | 212,886 | | 2,113 | 1,350 | 764 | 140.4 | | 133.8 | 153.8 | 109.0 |
| 1972 | 216,507 | | 2,306 | 1,484 | 822 | 142.7 | | 146.0 | 169.0 | 117.3 |

Sources: Projections of total population, total families with 2 or 3 children and the series appearing in Table 7 are by Richard Lurito of the Georgetown University Graduate Program in Public Policy Economics. Population for 1950 and 1960 from *Census of Population* for 1950 and for 1960. Population estimates for 1951-59 and projections for 1961-72 calculated from 1959 fertility and mortality rates from U.S. Department of Health, Education, and Welfare, "Vital Statistics of the United States, 1959." Households for 1950-59, *Statistical Abstract of the United States, 1960*, Table No. 39. Households from 1959-70, Bureau of the Census, *Current Population Reports*, Series P-20, No. 90, December 29, 1958, Table 2.

In contrast with these trends, the years 1960-72 are likely to show that the number of families having two or three children with the mother between 19 and 30 will increase 57 per cent, from 1.5 millions in 1960 to 2.3 millions in 1972. Moreover, the growth rate will accelerate noticeably after 1965. Demand for all types of housing is bound to be strengthened as a result.

This estimate, when divided into the two demand groupings indicated above, suggests that the dominant group among apartment families is likely to increase 77 per cent over the 1960-72 period, while the dominant group among home-owner families will probably increase by 31 per cent. In each case the rate of increase is due to accelerate noticeably after 1965. The change in composition of housing demand likely according to these findings also has a bearing on prospective patterns of community development.

As far as induced demand for durables and construction materials is concerned, what counts is the strong rise in the number of families setting up serious housekeeping, so to speak. Clearly, the prospects in this regard support optimistic expectations.

### Changes in School Populations

These considerations lead directly to the second basic trend likely to exercise a strongly autonomous influence on economic development in the 1960's: the trend in school populations. In the 1950-59 period, the number of children between the ages of six and thirteen, the elementary school population, increased by 46 per cent (see Table 7). This explains much of the strong rise in state and local expenditures during most of those years as shown by Table 8. Not unexpectedly, the 1960-72 increase in the grammer school group may only amount to about 19 per cent. From here on, the big wave will be that of the high school students, with a 41 per cent rise, and even more so of the college age group; the estimates given in Table 7 suggest a 60 per cent rise over the decade ahead. Thus, the outlook is for a decided shift in school construction programs toward high 'school and college facilities. Capital outlays per student at these levels of education tend to be much greater.

Table 7—Population Projections
Elementary, Secondary, and College Age Groups
(Thousands of People)

| Year | Total Population (1) | Age 6-13 a (2) | Age 14-17 (3) | Age 18-22 (4) | Indexes of Columns (1) to (4) (1950 = 100) | | | |
|---|---|---|---|---|---|---|---|---|
| | | | | | Total Population b (5) | Age 6-13 (6) | Age 14-17 (7) | Age 18-22 (8) |
| 1950 | 151,683 | 19,604 | 8,441 | 11,093 | 100.0 | 100.0 | 100.0 | 100.0 |
| 1951 | 154,360 | 20,924 | 8,531 | 10,886 | 101.8 | 106.7 | 101.1 | 98.1 |
| 1952 | 157,028 | 20,919 | 8,743 | 10,678 | 103.5 | 106.7 | 103.6 | 96.3 |
| 1953 | 159,636 | 22,364 | 8,836 | 10,610 | 105.2 | 114.1 | 104.7 | 95.6 |
| 1954 | 162,417 | 23,596 | 9,014 | 10,579 | 107.1 | 120.4 | 106.8 | 95.4 |
| 1955 | 165,270 | 24,725 | 9,169 | 10,578 | 109.0 | 126.1 | 108.6 | 95.4 |
| 1956 | 168,176 | 25,649 | 9,425 | 10,774 | 110.9 | 130.8 | 111.7 | 97.1 |
| 1957 | 171,198 | 26,483 | 10,020 | 10,915 | 112.9 | 135.1 | 118.7 | 98.4 |
| 1958 | 174,054 | 27,496 | 10,467 | 11,098 | 114.8 | 140.3 | 124.0 | 100.0 |
| 1959 | 177,103 | 28,614 | 10,831 | 11,302 | 116.8 | 145.9 | 128.3 | 101.9 |
| 1960 | 179,326 | 28,772 | 11,265 | 11,327 | 118.1 | 146.8 | 133.5 | 102.1 |
| 1961 | 182,167 | 29,200 | 11,900 | 12,027 | 120.1 | 148.9 | 141.0 | 108.4 |
| 1962 | 184,826 | 29,578 | 12,637 | 12,649 | 121.9 | 150.9 | 149.7 | 114.0 |
| 1963 | 187,673 | 30,084 | 13,307 | 13,253 | 123.7 | 153.5 | 157.6 | 119.5 |
| 1964 | 190,556 | 30,669 | 14,039 | 13,712 | 125.6 | 156.4 | 166.3 | 123.6 |
| 1965 | 193,468 | 31,288 | 13,994 | 14,714 | 127.6 | 159.6 | 165.8 | 132.6 |
| 1966 | 196,391 | 31,660 | 14,026 | 15,414 | 129.5 | 161.5 | 166.2 | 139.0 |
| 1967 | 199,416 | 32,086 | 14,306 | 16,047 | 131.5 | 163.7 | 169.5 | 144.7 |
| 1968 | 202,562 | 32,476 | 14,648 | 16,716 | 133.5 | 165.7 | 173.5 | 150.7 |
| 1969 | 205,857 | 32,854 | 15,119 | 17,431 | 135.7 | 167.6 | 179.1 | 157.1 |
| 1970 | 209,412 | 33,292 | 15,464 | 17,503 | 138.1 | 169.8 | 183.2 | 158.0 |
| 1971 | 212,886 | 33,785 | 15,689 | 17,708 | 140.4 | 172.3 | 185.9 | 159.6 |
| 1972 | 216,507 | 34,307 | 15,930 | 18,051 | 142.7 | 175.0 | 188.7 | 162.7 |

a From 1950-59, as of October; from 1960-72, as of April.
b Figures are as of April and exclude immigration.
Sources: Same as Table 6.

**Table 8—Education Expenditures**
(Millions of Dollars)

| | Elementary and Secondary Schools | | | | | | Schools of Higher Education | | |
| | Public Expenditures | | | Private Expenditures | | | Public and Private Expenditures | | |
| Year | Total (1) | Current (2) | Capital (3) | Total (4) | Current (5) | Capital (6) | Total (7) | Current (8) | Capital (9) |
|---|---|---|---|---|---|---|---|---|---|
| 1950 | 5,838 | 4,824 | 1,014 | 786 | 649 | 137 | 2,663 | 417 | 417 |
| 1952 | 7,344 | 5,867 | 1,477 | 1,053 | 835 | 218 | 2,874 | 2,471 | 403 |
| 1954 | 9,092 | 7,037 | 2,055 | 1,368 | 1,059 | 309 | 3,436 | 2,903 | 533 |
| 1956 | 10,955 | 8,608 | 2,387 | 1,656 | 1,295 | 361 | 4,210 | 3,525 | 686 |
| 1958 | 13,569 | 10,716 | 2,853 | 2,079 | 1,642 | 437 | 5,665 | 4,544 | 1,123 |
| 1960 | 15,805 | 13,146 | 2,659 | 2,817 | 2,343 | 474 | 6,948 | 5,628 | 1,320 |

Sources: Col. (1)-(3) *Statistical Abstract of U. S.* (various years).

Col. (4)—Fritz Machlup, *The Production and Distribution of Knowledge* (Princeton, 1962), p. 72.

Col. (5) and (6)—Same ratio as (2) and (3).

Col. (7)-(9) 1950 through 1958, Machlup, *op. cit.*, p. 83; 1960, unpublished figures supplied by U.S. Office of Education.

## Roads and Urban Development

The last of the obvious trends likely to be a source of strong autonomous (and induced) demands is highway construction, especially in and around urban areas. In 1950, one-third of our urban population lived in the suburbs. By 1960, this ratio had risen to one-half.[19] Such statistics bring to mind a whole array of topics, from traffic congestion to urban sprawl and the financial straits of cities. These things more than suggest that transportation problems in and around urban centers may have had a restrictive effect on economic development.

Highway accessibility has become a requirement for the economic health of the metropolitan community—in fact, so much so that freeways are becoming the backbone of the urban transportation system. The American city has been gradually adapting itself to the new mobility provided by motor vehicle transportation. Residential areas, commercial centers, and industrial development are increasingly oriented to automotive accessibility. This orientation, however, comes about only with the development of an adequate highway system.

The realization that urban highways would largely determine the location of future growth and development has caused city planners to evaluate, broadly speaking, three possible outcomes of their highway plans. Urban highway design might especially foster the redevelopment of the metropolitan center or core, it might spur primarily the expansion of the suburbs, or it might help to bring about a population "spin-off," leading to the growth of satellite communities. More realistically, feasible highway programs tend to produce a combination of the above effects. In many places a city's core, suburbs, and satellites have come to be recognized as complementary rather than competitive parts of a developing area.

In the foreseeable future, the highway construction program will be a key factor in the process of adapting urban areas more fully to the automobile and the detached home as items of mass consumption. The highway system is the structural change on which the dynamics of this development hinge. Mass transit may yet come to modify the picture substantially, but it is unlikely that the urban highway system will be dislodged from its pre-eminent position.

What can be expected of the urban highway system in the period ahead? The 41,000 miles of freeways now foreseen as comprising the National System of Interstate and Defense High-

Chart V—PER CENT OF INTERSTATE HIGHWAY SYSTEM COMPLETED

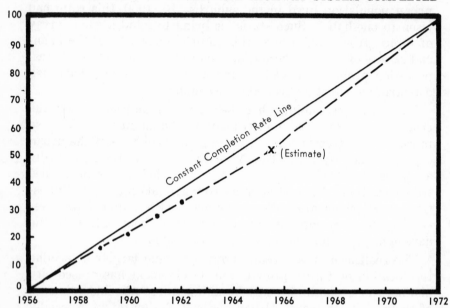

Source: Bureau of Public Roads, U.S. Department of Commerce, *Quarterly Reports on Federal-Aid Highway Program.*

ways will connect most cities of 50,000 population or over by 1972. The beginning plan, drawn when the System was started in 1956, designated some 5,000 miles of the proposed network as "urban" freeways, i.e., roadways designed primarily to serve city populations. But because of the expansion in urban areas taking place, a total of 8,400 Interstate Route miles are expected to be within urban limits[20] when the System is completed.

By now, 30 per cent of the Interstate System is in operation (see Chart V). The estimates are that by late 1965, some 50 per cent will be open to traffic. To reach full completion in 1972, however, the rate of construction will have to be accelerated, so that we can look forward to a growing volume of road building.

Urban areas throughout the United States show various degrees of progress in the planning and completion of freeways. We should also mention that while in some places the Interstate System comprises almost all of the urban freeway mileage, other areas are developing composite systems of Interstate and local freeways. Unfortunately, separate estimates for urban areas are not available; but the indications are that completion rates are broadly in line with the progress made by the System as a whole.

As mentioned before, the route that a freeway follows exerts a strong influence on the location and scope of development. The timing of completions is also important because on that depends the phasing and, to some extent also, the magnitude of development in particular places. Clearly, both location and timing are necessary to "trigger" economic growth along particular lines.[21] An example of good timing and location from the standpoint of maximum effectiveness for economic development is Route 128 in the Boston area.[22]

Needless to say, economic expansion in any one area or part of an area may be competitive with expansion elsewhere. As a result, offsetting disinvestment is bound to be a part of this process. But there seems to be no reason why, on balance, the effects of the highway programs should not amount to a very strong investment stimulus. As the Interstate Highway System approaches the halfway mark, a substantial amount of induced business investment and housing can be expected.

### The Implication for the Next Decade

Since these trends and the impetus they will impart are not systematically considered, one cannot infer from them an answer to the question: What is their likely contribution to the over-all rate of growth? The observed trends do not add up in that sense; they do combine, however, into natural patterns of mutually supporting demands. These have the potential for giving the economic process a good amount of thrust as well as the broad guidelines needed for full-blown expansions in the decade ahead. The likelihood of increasing returns on past investment in human capital, particularly in R&D, should add greatly to the force and scope of development. We conclude that the next ten years are likely to be marked by strong expansions. Conflict between claims on resources for national security purposes, the resource demands made by other public programs, and demands of economic development generally may well become a characteristic feature of the period before us.

## FOOTNOTES

[1] This paper is the result of a cooperative effort by the authors and the members of the Research Seminar on Economic Growth, Graduate Program in Public Policy Economics, Georgetown University. Richard Lurito, James August, and Philip D. Patterson, Jr. carried out the research programs.

[2] Cf. Abraham S. Becker, "Comparisons of United States and USSR National Output: Some Rules of the Game," *The Goal of Economic Growth*, ed. Edmund S. Phelps (New York: W. W. Norton & Co., Inc., 1962), pp. 46-55.

[3] The rise in defense expenditures was a significant factor in the recoveries of 1958-59 and 1961-62. Cf. Wilfred Lewis, Jr., *Federal Fiscal Policy in the Post War Recessions* (Washington: The Brookings Institution, 1962), pp. 213, 255-56, and 260-62.

[4] Edward F. Denison, *The Sources of Economic Growth in the United States and the Alternatives Before Us* (New York: Committee for Economic Development, 1962).

[5] *Ibid.*, pp. 265-66.

[6] *Economic Report of the President* (Washington: U.S. Government Printing Office, January, 1962), pp. 49-53, and *op. cit.*, (January, 1963), p. 27.

[7] For a most instructive exercise along this line, cf. David W. Lusher, "Some Key Economic Variables in the 1960's," *Planning and Forecasting in the Defense Industries*, ed. J. A. Stockfisch (Belmont, California: Wadsworth Publishing Co., Inc., 1962).

[8] *Economic Report of the President* (Washington: US Government Printing Office, January, 1963), pp. 14-18.

[9] Bert G. Hickman, "The Postwar Retardation: Another Long Swing in the Rate of Growth?" To be published in *American Economic Review* (May, 1963).

[10] *Economic Report of the President*, 1963, *op. cit.*, pp. 14-18, 29-30, and 61-63.

[11] Bert G. Hickman, "An Interpretation of Price Movements Since the End of World War II," *Compendium*, Joint Economic Committee, 85th Cong., 2nd Sess., 1958, p. 184.

[12] A paper by John P. Lewis, "The Lull That Came to Stay," *Journal of Political Economy* (February, 1955), is particularly relevant for this point. Cf. pp. 14-19.

[13] *Ibid.*, and Hickman, "An Interpretation of Price Movements," *loc. cit.*

[14] Charles L. Schultze, "Recent Inflation in the United States," *Study Paper No. 1*, Joint Economic Committee, 86th Cong., 1st Sess., 1959.

[15] See Table 8, Column 3, p. 47.

[16] Fritz Machlup, *The Production and Distribution of Knowledge in the United States* (Princeton, N. J.: Princeton University Press, 1962), p. 155.

[17] *Economic Report of the President*, 1963, *loc. cit.*

[18] Machlup, *op. cit.*, p. 397.

[19] Wilbur Smith Associates, *Future Highways, and Urban Growth* (New Haven, Conn.: 1961), p. 7.

[20] *Ibid.*, p. 210.

[21] *Final Report of the Highway Cost Allocation Study*, Part VI, data concerning the Economic and Social Effects of Highway Improvement. House Document No. 72, 87th Cong., 1st Sess., 1961, contains numerous examples of economic effects.

[22] *Economic Impact Study of Massachusetts Route 128*, Transportation Engineering Division, Department of Civil and Sanitary Engineering, (Cambridge, Mass.: Massachusetts Institute of Technology, December 31, 1958).

**Appendix Table 1—Employed Persons, by Major Occupation Group—Annual Average**

(Thousands of Persons 14 Years of Age and Over)

| Major Occupation Group and Sex | 1960 | 1958 | 1956 | 1954 | 1952 | 1950 | 1948 |
|---|---|---|---|---|---|---|---|
| Both Sexes | | | | | | | |
| Total employed | 66,681 | 63,966 | 64,928 | 61,160 | 60,989 | 59,648 | 59,307 |
| Professional, technical, and kindred workers | 7,475 | 6,961 | 6,096 | 5,588 | 5,092 | 4,490 | 3,977 |
| Farmers and farm managers | 2,780 | 3,083 | 3,655 | 3,853 | 3,963 | 4,393 | 4,668 |
| Managers, officials, and proprietors, except farm | 7,067 | 6,785 | 6,552 | 6,201 | 6,182 | 6,429 | 6,344 |
| Clerical and kindred workers | 9,783 | 9,137 | 8,838 | 8,168 | 8,122 | 7,632 | 7,438 |
| Sales workers | 4,401 | 4,173 | 4,111 | 3,934 | 3,674 | 3,822 | 3,641 |
| Craftsmen, foremen, and kindred workers | 8,560 | 8,469 | 8,693 | 8,311 | 8,743 | 7,670 | 8,119 |
| Operatives and kindred workers | 11,986 | 11,441 | 12,816 | 12,253 | 12,352 | 12,146 | 12,396 |
| Private household workers | 2,216 | 2,204 | 2,124 | 1,760 | 1,805 | 1,883 | 1,754 |
| Service workers, except private household | 6,133 | 5,605 | 5,485 | 4,995 | 4,683 | 4,652 | 4,286 |
| Farm laborers and foremen | 2,615 | 2,508 | 2,889 | 2,495 | 2,669 | 3,015 | 3,213 |
| Laborers, except farm and mine | 3,665 | 3,600 | 3,670 | 3,603 | 3,707 | 3,520 | 3,473 |

Source: U.S. Department of Labor, *Labor Force, Employment, and Unemployment Statistics, 1947–61*, Table 10.

**Unemployed by Major Occupation Group—Annual Averages**

| Major Occupation Group | 1960 | 1958 | 1956 | 1954 | 1952 | 1950 | 1948 |
|---|---|---|---|---|---|---|---|
| **Unemployment rate:** | | | | | | | |
| Total | 5.6 | 6.8 | 3.8 | 5.0 | 2.7 | 5.0 | 3.4 |
| Professional, technical, and kindred workers | 1.7 | 2.0 | 1.0 | 1.6 | 1.0 | 2.2 | 1.7 |
| Farmers and farm managers | .3 | .6 | .4 | .4 | .2 | .3 | .2 |
| Managers, officials, and proprietors, except farm | 1.4 | 1.7 | .8 | 1.2 | .7 | 1.6 | 1.0 |
| Clerical and kindred workers | 3.8 | 4.4 | 2.4 | 3.1 | 1.8 | 3.4 | 2.3 |
| Sales workers | 3.7 | 4.0 | 2.7 | 3.7 | 2.5 | 4.0 | 3.4 |
| Craftsmen, foremen, and kindred workers | 5.3 | 6.8 | 3.2 | 4.9 | 2.4 | 5.6 | 2.9 |
| Operatives and kindred workers | 8.0 | 10.9 | 5.4 | 7.6 | 3.9 | 6.8 | 4.1 |
| Private household workers | 4.9 | 5.2 | 4.2 | 5.0 | 3.2 | 5.6 | 3.2 |
| Service workers, except private household | 6.0 | 7.4 | 4.8 | 5.2 | 3.7 | 6.8 | 4.8 |
| Farm laborers and foremen | 5.2 | 6.2 | 3.7 | 4.2 | 2.3 | 5.0 | 2.3 |
| Laborers, except farm and mine | 12.5 | 14.9 | 8.2 | 10.7 | 5.7 | 11.7 | 7.5 |
| *Per Cent Distribution* | | | | | | | |
| Total | 100.0 | 100.0 | 100.0 | 100.0 | 100.0 | 100.0 | 100.0 |
| Professional, technical, and kindred workers | 3.4 | 2.9 | 2.4 | 2.8 | 3.1 | 3.1 | 3.4 |
| Farmers and farm managers | .2 | .4 | .5 | .5 | .5 | .5 | .4 |
| Managers, officials, and proprietors, except farm | 2.5 | 2.6 | 2.0 | 2.5 | 2.4 | 3.2 | 3.3 |
| Clerical and kindred workers | 9.8 | 9.0 | 8.6 | 8.2 | 8.5 | 8.2 | 8.6 |
| Sales workers | 4.2 | 3.7 | 4.5 | 4.8 | 5.4 | 4.9 | 6.3 |
| Craftsmen, foremen, and kindred workers | 12.1 | 13.2 | 11.3 | 13.5 | 12.5 | 13.8 | 12.0 |
| Operatives and kindred workers | 26.5 | 30.0 | 28.5 | 32.1 | 28.8 | 26.9 | 26.0 |
| Private household workers | 2.9 | 2.6 | 3.6 | 2.9 | 3.4 | 3.4 | 2.9 |
| Service workers, except private household | 9.9 | 9.5 | 10.9 | 8.7 | 10.4 | 10.3 | 10.7 |
| Farm laborers and foremen | 3.6 | 3.5 | 4.4 | 3.4 | 3.6 | 4.8 | 3.8 |
| Laborers, except farm and mine | 13.3 | 13.5 | 12.8 | 13.7 | 13.1 | 14.2 | 14.0 |
| No previous work experience | 11.6 | 9.3 | 10.4 | 7.0 | 8.3 | 6.8 | 8.8 |

Source: U.S. Department of Labor, *Labor Force, Employment, and Unemployment Statistics, 1947-61*, Table 13.

# Economic Growth and United States Strategy

—EDWARD S. MASON

## Summary

*All strategies require economic resources in some form or another for their preparation and execution. Conventional warfare imposes huge requirements; other strategies impose requirements on a smaller scale but possibly serious with respect to certain critically scarce factors. The ability to select and implement various strategies depends not only on the availability of resources, but also on the scope and character of the economic requirements involved in alternative strategies.*

*If economic resources were completely interchangeable among different uses, resource availability with respect to various possible strategies would depend, over any substantial time period, on three primary considerations: the total volume of output of which the economy is capable; the compressibility of non-strategic requirements; and the rate of growth of output. Since economic resources, though highly adaptable, are not completely so, some attention needs to be given to the structure of production and how this fits strategic requirements. A comprehensive picture of resource availability would also need to take account of the vulnerability of the production process to attack by military action, economic warfare, sabotage, subversion, and propaganda.*

*With respect to the present resources potentially available for strategic use, the two magnitudes from which the analysis must start are gross national product and the numbers of the population. By the GNP test we are in good shape since our*

*GNP is nearly twice that of any other country. In advanced economies the size of the labor force ranges from 40-50 per cent of the population, but in time of emergency the percentage can be substantially larger than this.*

*The extent to which this potential can be tapped, however, depends very much on the compressibility of non-strategic requirements. The limits here are political rather than economic. In time of great emergency, a high-income economy can devote 50 per cent or more of its output to strategic use. In normal times, however, dictatorial regimes appear to have a substantial advantage over democratic ones in compressing non-strategic requirements.*

*The growth rate comes into consideration if we envisage a fairly long period ahead during which a choice among strategies is maturing. But it does not take a very long period for substantial differences in exponential growth rates to affect very significantly differences in productive capacity. In broad terms, economic growth means a sustained increase in the output of goods and services. Although the concept of economic growth has been used both as an indicator of an increase in social welfare and, in a more limited sense, as an index of change in productive capacity, the second meaning is the only one we need to consider here. Even so, the technical difficulties of measuring economic growth in this limited sense are formidable. In consideration of these difficulties, the conclusion appears to be that, although there is no objectively correct measure of the rate of change, most practitioners appear to agree that it is possible to distinguish between, say, a three per cent and a four per cent rate of growth.*

*The long-term trend in the US growth rate has been about three per cent, and the Soviet growth rate over long periods has been at least double this rate. It would be difficult significantly to increase the US full-employment growth rate without substantial changes in the institutional structure of the economy. On the other hand there is considerable reason for believing that the Soviet growth rate in the 1960's may be substantially less than that attained in the 1950's.*

*If one considers the relation of the structure of production to strategic requirements, it is obvious that a high degree of industrialization is relevant to the requirements of conventional warfare. The problem is much more complicated, however, when the range of strategic alternatives becomes large. With respect to the question of vulnerability, it would seem that the*

*most serious potential vulnerability Western democracies have
to face is a decline in vigilance, an unwillingness to make sacrifices in a period of apparent calm during which, nevertheless,
potential enemies are not so unwilling.*

---

## Strategy and Resource Requirements

All strategies require economic resources in some form or
other for their preparation and execution. Limitations of resource availability in various countries will exclude certain
strategies completely from consideration, and in all countries
these limitations will to some extent shape the choice of possible
courses of action. Presumably, one of the major objectives of
public policy is to assure that these economic limitations on
possible courses of action are reduced to an acceptable minimum.
How serious a drain on economic resources military action can
be is sufficiently indicated by the experience of World War II.
At the height of hostilities, close to fifty per cent of US output
and over fifty per cent of British output was devoted to war
use. Conventional warfare imposes huge requirements on the
economy, both for military manpower and for the production of
goods and services. The demands of nuclear warfare for military
manpower may be less serious, but the drain on production
facilities is enormous. This drain is, of course, accentuated by
the rate of technological change. The requirements imposed by
technological change are so serious that it may be doubted
whether, in considering the "Nth country problem," the value of
"N" can never be very large unless weapons and carrying
mechanisms are supplied from principal development and production centers.

Other strategies also impose economic requirements, presumably on a smaller scale but quite possibly serious with
respect to certain critically scarce factors. In so far as foreign
aid, both military and economic, is to be regarded as an instrument of foreign policy, the resources involved must be considered
to be a strategic requirement. Furthermore, the shape of foreign
aid may be influenced by the scarcity of certain elements. It
might be useful, for example, to enlarge the technical assistance
component in foreign aid programs, but the lack of competently
trained personnel available for overseas service may well impose
limitations. If preclusive purchasing is deemed to be a fruitful

course of action, limitations imposed by balance-of-payments difficulties will have to be considered. Political and informational strategies impose much smaller over-all demands on economic resources, but again, they may impinge heavily on certain resources.

The ability of the United States then to select and implement various strategies depends not only on the availability of resources, but also on the scope and character of the economic requirements involved in alternative strategies. Early in the last war, we were very long on jeeps and very short on most types of firepower. We were in a position to jeep the enemy to death, but unfortunately other things were also needed. Our ability to implement a strategy with one set of requirements may be substantially less at any given moment than our ability to implement another. Presumably, new requirements can call forth new availabilities within fairly broad limits, but, at a minimum, time is required to make this adaptation, and institutional obstacles may be more time-consuming to overcome than technological difficulties. But, having made this obeisance to economic requirements as a factor in US strategy, I now turn to my proper subject which is economic availabilities and in particular, how availabilities are affected by economic growth.

**Resource Availability**

If economic resources were completely interchangeable among different uses, resource availability with respect to various possible strategies would depend, over any substantial time period, on three primary considerations: (1) the total volume of output of which the economy is capable; (2) the compressibility of non-strategic requirements; and (3) the rate of growth of output. Economic resources are, in fact, highly adaptable to changes in requirements; much more adaptable than military experts usually recognize. But there are, after all, limitations both institutional and technological, and in any case, this adaptation takes time. Consequently, some attention should be given to the structure of production in the United States and how this affects the adaptability of output to strategic requirements. Finally, the availability of resources over time will also depend on the vulnerability of the production process to attack by military means, economic warfare, sabotage, subversion, or propaganda. A comprehensive picture of resource availability would need to take these possibilities into account.

It has been a truism that if and when war comes, the war is fought with resources in being and not with a growth rate. Presumably in case of nuclear war, it is only resources in being and not even the compressibility of non-military demands that count. But in the modern world there are various kinds of war, declared and undeclared, all with their economic requirements. And in any case we are here concerned with various strategies designed to deter, and so to prevent war if possible. Consequently a consideration of present output, the compressibility of non-strategic wants, and the growth rate are all relevant.

With respect to the present resources potentially available for strategic use, the two magnitudes from which the analysis must start are some measure of total output—gross national product is, of course, the value of total output of goods and services in any particular time period. If one can assume that resources are completely interchangeable among different uses, GNP would give us a first approximation to our potential resource availability for strategic or any other purpose. GNP makes no allowance for depreciation of capital and this is correct, at least for any short time period. It includes exports and excludes imports, a characteristic that would need consideration in any examination of the vulnerability of US production processes.

By the GNP test we are, of course, in good shape as far as economic availability is concerned. Our GNP is nearly twice that of any other country and still exceeds, though not by much, the total output of the six Common Market countries. If one wants to pursue the GNP analysis further as an indication of economic potential for strategic use, it would be necessary to consider the potential contribution of allies; but this could not usefully be undertaken without considering also the strategic requirements of allies. Such an extension would also raise questions of reliability, vulnerability, etc., that are better considered elsewhere.

The second important magnitude from which the analysis of the relation of present resources to a choice of strategies must start is the size of population. Wars are fought with men—and increasingly, women—as well as materiel. It is a matter of common knowledge that the ratio of men at the front to those behind the lines decreases continually with improvements in military technology and, with current technology, these lines extend throughout the interstices of the economy.

In advanced economies the size of the labor force ranges from 40-50 per cent of total population, but the potential labor force is very much larger than this. Further analysis of the availability of manpower as it bears on the choice of strategies would need to classify the existing stock in terms of experience, competence, and various other qualities deemed to be of potential use.

Ability to supply men and ability to produce output are then the major determinants of current economic potential. The extent to which this potential can be tapped, however, depends very much on the compressibility of non-strategic requirements. The military needs are sufficiently indicated by the experience of the last war. In the United States, the ability to suppress was assisted by the very rapid rate of increase of production as we passed from massive unemployment to full employment. This increase permitted fulfillment of military needs without taking very much away from civilian production, which at the start of the war was abnormally low. But the United Kingdom, which entered the war with its labor force nearly fully employed, succeeded in diverting an even larger percentage of GNP to military use than we did. There is, then, little doubt of the ability of advanced countries, in time of great emergency, to devote a very large percentage of their economic potential to military use.

### The Compressibility of Non-Strategic Wants

This fact, however, seems not to have much bearing on the question in hand, i.e., the compressibility of non-strategic wants as a determinant of the economic resources available to the choice of strategies in advance of, or to forestall, great emergencies. There is no doubt that potential enemies with their dictatorial structures of government have great advantages here, at least for the short run, over the democracies. It is quite possible, by compressing civilian requirements, for a country with a GNP half as large as ours to devote as much or almost as much economic resources as we do to military use.

This contrast between dictatorship and democracy emphasizes a critical fact with respect to the compressibility of civilian requirements: the limitations are socio-political and not economic. Many foolish words are spoken or written on this subject. During the last few years our military expenditures have been running at about ten per cent of GNP. It is said that if we increase this percentage significantly the "United States will go bankrupt," or, if not bankruptcy, then some essential characteristics of a private enterprise economy will be lost forever. Modern states cannot and do not go bankrupt in any meaningful sense of the word. As long as the monetary authority can create money, any conceivable volume of public debt can be serviced. A sharp increase in military expenditures could have serious inflationary consequences but even this is quite unnecessary if adequate measures are taken to increase tax receipts *pari passu* with the increase in expenditures.

Nor is there any serious reason to believe that an increase in military expenditures, if it takes place gradually, would force us into a system of direct controls destructive of the market mechanism or of profit incentives. The priorities, rationing, and price controls of wartime were the products not only of the diversion of a very large fraction of economic resources to military use, but of the rapidity of the build-up. Production for government use rather than private sale does, of course, introduce a set of contracting and compensation procedures within which it is difficult to maintain the impact of normal profit incentives. And, as President Eisenhower and others have emphasized, the growth of a large private business sector working exclusively for government creates dangers of business influence on public policy that are not to be ignored. But neither bankruptcy nor any serious and lasting distortion of the private enterprise system is the inevitable consequence of a substantial increase in military expenditures even above the present high level.

The real difficulty attendant on such an increase is the general unwillingness to pay more taxes, but this is a political rather than an ecomonic limitation. It would be wrong, however, to make too much of this limitation or to stress too strongly the difference between dictatorial and democratic regimes in assessing the compressibility of civilian requirements. Under the pressure of the Cold War, the American people have shown a remarkable willingness to support high military expenditures and there is not much doubt that in the face of deepening emergency even higher expenditures would be accepted. Looking at the other side of the picture, dictatorships do not have a completely free hand in determining the allocation of resources between military and civilian uses. Here also political considerations have to be taken into account as the reaction in the Soviet Union to recent price increases on civilian items suggests. But, while admitting this much, there still remains a difference in the compressibility of civilian requirements as between dictatorial and democratic regimes and this difference favors the former so far as economics set limits on the choice of strategies.

## The Role of Economic Growth

This brings us to a consideration of economic growth as a factor in the choice of strategies. Before considering the meaning and measurement of economic growth, it is necessary to point out certain relationships between compressibility of civilian requirements and growth. To the extent that civilian requirements are not compressible, i.e., if we suppose that defense expenditures can only be a certain percentage of GNP, the only way to increase economic resources available for strategic choice is via economic growth. If defense expenditures can command a constant share of GNP, the resources available will increase the more rapidly the higher the rate of growth. Secondly, there is reason to believe that compressibility, if we understand this to be a declining share of GNP for civilian use, will be facilitated by a high growth rate. The higher the growth rate the easier it tends to be to adjust the interests of various claimants to a share in national income. And military expenditure is one of the claimants. If GNP grows at a rate no faster than population it will be difficult indeed to satisfy wage and other claimants without a reduction in government—including military—expenditure. A growth rate of four or five per cent per annum, on the other hand, can accommodate some increase in military expenditure as a per cent of GNP while still permitting some absolute increase per capita in wage and other earnings. Finally, it should be pointed out that if military expenditures are an efficient claimant to a constant ten per cent of GNP, economic growth at the long-term trend rate of about three per cent will add approximately $2 billion a year in resources available for strategic use.

In broad terms economic growth means a sustained increase in the output of goods and services. A short-term increase that is part of a variation around a constant level cannot properly be called growth. Furthermore, the goods and services produced must have some relevance to social objectives—satisfaction of consumers' wants or planners' preferences, meeting of strategic requirements, or whatever these objectives may be. If all economic resources were concentrated on the production of, say, potatoes, there would no doubt be a sustained increase in the output of potatoes, but this would hardly conform to a sensible notion of economic growth. This adaptation of the production of goods and services to some objective or objectives, characteristically satisfied only through a multiplicity of means, raises the question of valuing the output of various lines of productive activity, and the valuation problems involved create complexities with respect both to the meaning and the measurement of growth.

Undue concentration of economic activity on the production of one good or service will tend to produce a decreasingly useful contribution of additional output to whatever is the social objective. Reflection on this fact suggests that the objective is best served if the available instruments of production (factors) are so distributed among the various lines of production that no rearrangement of factors would improve the attainment of the objective. Under static conditions it is possible to give a fairly precise definition of the requirements of an optimum arrangement. When, however, the character of the objective is changing through time, and there are also changes in the quantities of the factors available and the various ways they can be combined, it is not possible to specify precisely an optimum relationship of the rates of production of the various goods and services involved. It has been pointed out that a set of relationships which is optimum for every moment in time may yield a slower growth rate than another set which would not at any time satisfy the conditions of a static optimum.

Despite these ambiguities and uncertainties, the concept of economic growth relies on an assumption that at any moment of time the distribution of resources among various economic activities is either close to optimal or that over the relevant period of time there is no substantial change in the gap between actual and optimum use. If there is reason to believe that during this period of time there is a marked change in the degree of "rationality of resource use," it would mean that customary measures of growth are more seriously deficient than they are usually judged to be.

This question of the rationality of resource use—whatever the social objective—also bedevils comparisons, at any one time, of the national incomes or per capita incomes of different countries. This difficulty is apart from and in addition to the difficulties of such comparisons between countries having different assortments of consumer wants. For example, it is said that the absence in the Soviet Union of effective market mechanisms imposes great handicaps on the allocation of economic resources in accordance with planners' preferences. This is supposed to produce a greater degree of irrationality of resource use than is customarily encountered in capitalist countries. If this is so, it would mean that national income or per capita income comparisons between the Soviet Union and, say, the United States are unduly favorable to the former. I do not feel competent to offer an opinion on this matter but it should be pointed out that even if this is so it would not necessarily affect comparisons of growth rates over time if we can assume that the "degree of irrationality" in resource use remains about the same in both countries.

Speaking broadly, the concept of economic growth has been used for two different purposes. The first, and broader use, has been as an indicator of an increase in social welfare. The second, and narrower one, is as an index of change in the productive capacity of an economy regardless of purpose. It is the second use that is more relevant to the discussion of the relation of economic growth to US strategy. This is fortunate because, although the difficulties of measuring changes in productive capacity are enormous, they do not embrace the additional difficulty of establishing a relationship between changes in production or productive capacity and social welfare.

Although we are primarily concerned with the second use, it is necessary first to say a word about the relation between production and social welfare since this was the context in which the meaning and measurement of economic growth were first developed. Colin Clark goes so far as to say, "Deprive economics of the concept of welfare and what do you have? Nothing." [1]

To put the matter much too simply, it may be possible to establish some relation between changes in production and changes in welfare over relatively short periods of time, but "When changes in output involve profound changes in social and economic organization, we can no longer plausibly presume that satisfactions from increased output overshadow those that flow from accompanying changes in work and life." [2]

Among the major difficulties in establishing a relation between production and welfare over long periods of time are these: human wants do not remain constant; particular applications of resources lose a welfare connotation; and the assumption that the welfare of individuals is independent of each other's choices tends to lose meaning.

How does one compare the standard of living of a red Indian roaming the plains with that of his successor to the fifteenth generation living, say, in Cedar Rapids, Iowa? The food, clothing, and housing of the Indian could be purchased with a small fraction of the latter's income. But perhaps in the Indian's standard of living the vista of wide prairies and far horizons loomed large. It would take a mint of money to provide this for his successor at the current prices of Iowa real estate.

Consider also the changing relationship between certain types of productive activity and the welfare provided thereby. A familiar and useful example is the provision of commuting services. The factor cost or market price of providing these services is a part of national income. But it is more than doubtful whether the necessity of spending three hours a day getting to and from work adds greatly to anyone's welfare.

Finally, how does the welfare calculus take account of the fact that the satisfactions provided by one person's expenditures are not indepedent of other people's choices. The satisfactions I get from the use of my motor car will be significantly affected by how many other people have motor cars and happen to be using the roads at the same time. In an increasingly congested and urbanized society, changes in the forms of working and living are apt to have as significant an effect on wellbeing as changes in the quantities of goods and services that become available in such a society.

Fortunately, we can brush these difficulties aside and limit our attention to the problem of measuring economic growth conceived as a sustained increase in productive capacity. The question here is what is the average rate of increase (over some period) in the output of our economy at full employment or some constant fraction of full employment? The literature devoted to this problem is extensive and cannot be adequately summarized here. I limit myself to stating what seem to be the relevant conclusions for our purposes and calling attention to some of the principal difficulties. The relevant conclusions would seem to be these: (a) there is no objectively correct measure of the rate of change in the quantum of assorted goods and services provided by a dynamic economy; (b) but despite the difficulties there are ways of devising an index of change that appear to satisfy most practitioners that it is possible to distinguish between, say, a three per cent and a four per cent rate of growth.

The principal difficulties arise out of the facts that apples and oranges can be added only in terms of some value unit; that, over time, the changing quantity relations of various goods and services involves some "weighting" of the relative importance of each and there is no objectively correct set of weights; that new products are continually intruding into the mix; and that certain elements of the mix, notably government services and capital, do not have a determinable market price. There are ways, more or less sensible, of handling all these problems that need not concern us here. We shall have to be content with the conclusion of the "experts" that it is in fact possible to distinguish between a three and a four per cent growth rate and go on from there.

Going on from there presumably involves relating growth rates to current output and the compressibility of non-strategic requirements as elements affecting the choice of strategies, considering | the effect over time of differences in cumulative growth|rates, and speculating on the question of whether current differences in growth rates among countries at different stages of development and with different political structures are likely to persist and must therefore be seriously taken into account.

If we consider current output as a limitation on, or determinant of, the choice among strategies, the United States with twice the volume of output of any other country is, as we have seen, in a favorable position. If, on the other hand, we consider the compressibility of non-strategic requirements, the limitations, which are essentially political, are likely to be more serious in open, democratic societies than in totalitarian dictatorships: the growth rate comes into consideration if we envisage a fairly long period ahead during which a choice among strategies is maturing. But it does not take a very long period for substantial differences in exponential growth rates to affect very significantly differences in productive capacity.

**Long-Term Trends**

The long-term trend of economic growth of American output has been in the neighborhood of three per cent per annum. At this rate national income will double approximately every twenty-five years. For considerable periods of time in the 1930's and since 1950 the Soviet growth rate, conservatively calculated, has been six to seven per cent. A cumulative growth rate of six to seven per cent will double national income in ten years or less. It becomes important, then, for strategic considerations, to ask whether this difference in growth rates is likely to persist.

The long-term trend of American growth has contained substantial periods when the rate was considerably above or below three per cent. Between 1947 and 1957 the constant dollar rate of growth of GNP was at the unusually high level of 3.8 per cent per annum. For the last six years, however, the rate has been substantially less than three per cent. Product per man-hour has shown no significant decline but since the middle of 1957 unemployment has averaged six per cent. The US growth rate has not only been significantly lower than the Soviet rate during the last few years but has been not more than half the growth rates attained by France, Germany, and Italy.

While unemployment in the United States has averaged six per cent during the last six years, unemployment rates in Western Europe have typically ranged between one and three per cent. This failure to attain an output commensurate with a high level of employment plus a relatively slow growth rate obviously imposes serious economic limitations on strategic choice. If we had been able to attain, say, a four per cent level of unemployment during the last six years, GNP would have been $30-40 billion higher per annum than it in fact was, and federal tax yields would have been larger by $9 to $10 billion. It would have to be said, however, that this high marginal yield under present tax structure and rates is probably one of the main reasons why we have not been able to sustain a higher level of employment.

It is clear then that the existence of this considerable amount of slack in our economy, together with a relatively slow rate of growth of output at a given level of employment, constitutes a potentially serious limitation on the quality of resources that might be made available for strategic purposes. The question naturally arises whether these limitations are inevitable or, on the other hand, might, in part at least, be removed by appropriate action. This again breaks down into three sub-questions: (1) Is it possible to sustain a higher level of employment without incurring serious inflation and endangering our balance of payments? (2) If we can sustain a higher level of employment, how would this affect the long-term growth rate? (3) Are there other measures, apart from effective stabilization policy, by which our growth rate could be increased?

Whether we can attain a higher level of employment without running into inflation and balance-of-payments difficulties is a complicated question which I have recently discussed elsewhere and will not recapitulate here.[3] In summary fashion it may be said that there are strong institutional obstacles to effective stabilization policy in the United States and a general unwillingness on the part of business to acquiesce in the assumption by government of the responsibility of managing the economic environment in a manner designed to sustain stabilization objectives. There is, however, reason for believing that these obstacles are not insuperable and that attitudes inimical to effective public policy are in the process of change.

Whether, if we can sustain a higher level of employment, the long-term growth rate would be increased is a question hotly debated by the experts. Those who take the affirmative position stress the effect of a higher level of investment, at full employment, on the introduction of technological improvements made potentially available by recent very large expenditures on research and development. On the other hand, it is said that the existence of a certain amount of slack in the economy makes for a more economical use of resources in the economy forced by this very slackness to become more cost-conscious. The first view is argued effectively by Gerhard Colm and others in a series of National Planning Association publications, the most recent of which projects a long-term growth rate at full employment of four per cent per annum.[4] The second view is cogently argued by Edward Denison, who holds that our growth rate is likely, without extraordinary measures, to be only slightly above the long-term trend of three per cent per annum.[5] It would have to be said that studies of man-hour productivity over long periods of time do not show any marked variation in the rate of increase with changes in the degree of slack in the economy.

There remains the question of whether it would be possible by special effort or unusual measures to increase the full-employment growth rate from whatever level it is projected to attain. A consideration of this possibility would lead us into a discussion of the feasibility and desirability of various changes in policy and in institutional arrangements of varying degrees of novelty. The high growth rate in the Soviet Union depends principally on a ratio of savings and investment to GNP that can be attained only by severe repression of consumption standards, including what we would call the ordinary amenities of life. Presumably, the American people will not and cannot be driven very far in this direction. Denison has given more attention to this question than anyone else, and a consideration of the measures he thinks would be required to raise our long-term growth rate by one percentage point is not particularly reassuring.[6]

What this all adds up to is about as follows. If we can sustain an unemployment level of four per cent as against the six per cent we have experienced over the last six years, our GNP would be from $30-40 billion larger per annum. At a four per cent level of unemployment there is no reason for thinking that we cannot maintain a growth rate at least as high as the long-term trend, and perhaps a little higher. Whether it could be substantially higher, for example four per cent, without the adoption of unusual measures, is a debatable point, but it is certainly not out of the question. To raise the growth rate much above this level, whatever it turns out to be, would require a series of measures of somewhat dubious political feasibility.

How important it might turn out to be to explore those measures depends in part on whether other, much higher, growth rates may be expected to continue indefinitely. Are they a reflection of a stage of development and may they be expected to moderate when this stage is over, or are they the result of a different and, from the narrow point of view of economic growth, a superior form of economic organization that may be expected to continue indefinitely? Writing on the subject of the high rate of growth of Soviet industrial output in the 1930's, Gerschenkron observes:

> The record-breaking result was achieved because a ruthless dictatorial government succeeded in placing the Russian peasants, then the great majority of the Russian people, into the straight jacket of collective farms. Once this was done, it became possible (1) to obtain agricultural produce for the growing population of the cities at a minimum of *quid pro quo* in terms of industrial consumers' goods while at the same time enforcing the transfer of large numbers of peasants to urban occupations; and (2) to dedicate all efforts to the goal of rapid growth of heavy industry, undeterred by the resulting formidable pressures upon the standard of living of the population.[7]

Close students of the process of Soviet industrialization in the 1930's were inclined to stress a number of influences which were thought to be of only temporary effectiveness. The willingness of peasants to continue to produce for small rewards in the form of industrial consumers' goods could not be expected to continue indefinitely. The very large transfer of labor from agriculture to industry must inevitably slacken off. The observers of the 1930's were inclined to stress a number of influences which were thought to be of only temporary effectiveness. The industrialization of the 1930's was heavily dependent on the transfer of Western technology, which is not limitless. Continued large-scale investment in heavy industry must sooner or later bring diminishing returns. And even a dictatorial regime could not indefinitely hold down the standard of living of both the urban and rural working class in order to maintain a high rate of investment.

Many of these students expected, after the postwar restoration of Soviet industry, to see a slackening of the rate of industrial growth. It would have to be said that to date this has not happened. Nevertheless, there are forces at work that may be expected substantially to lessen the Soviet growth rate. The volume of labor migration from agriculture to industry in the second half of the 1950's was half of what it had been in the late 1930's. Agricultural difficulties are finally forcing a sizeable diversion of investment from industry to farming. There is substantial evidence that to sustain a given growth rate will require a continuous increase in the share of GNP devoted to investment. And there are growing indications that the clamor of consumers for a higher standard of living will make such an increase progressively more difficult. What the quantitative effect of these influences will be, it would be extremely hazardous to say, but it does seem unlikely that the rate of growth of Soviet GNP in the 1960's will be as high as it has been in the 1950's.

We have now considered the existing volume of GNP, the compressibility of non-strategic requirements, and the rate of economic growth as possible determinants of, or limitations on, the availability of economic resources for strategic purposes. There remains to be considered briefly the structure of production and how this affects the adaptability of resource use to strategic requirements, and the question of the vulnerability of productive processes to military attack, economic warfare, sabotage, subversion, or propaganda. An adequate consideration of these questions lies beyond the competence of the writer and the following paragraphs are limited to a few observations that may be illustrative.

It has been emphasized that, given time, production activities are in fact highly adaptable to changing requirements. A study of the extent to which Germany, cut off from external sources of raw-material supplies during World War II, was able, by substitution, replacement, innovation, and rationing, to maintain military production is illuminating.[8] Plants designed for civilian production can be extensively adapted to military use. And, under war conditions, the labor force can not only be increased but can acquire added mobility both geographically and among industries. There is, therefore, good reason to start from GNP, regardless of its composition, as a first approximation to an assessment of economic resources available for strategic choice. Nevertheless, there are limits, and time is a desideratum. Under conditions of conventional mass warfare the importance in the economy of iron and steel, non-ferrous metals, and engineering was rightly considered significant. Of two economies with equivalent GNP the more highly industrialized one is probably the one better adapted to the requirements of conventional warfare.

When one considers, however, the current spectrum of strategic choice, it becomes extremely difficult to specify what structure of economic activities is likely to be best suited to probable requirements. The production of large volumes of surplus agricultural crops would presumably be an undesirable use of resources in a more rational world—and also to a large extent is in this very irrational one—but the use of these surpluses serves some purpose in economic assistance programs. The US labor force includes a larger fraction of service personnel, including those rendering professional services, as compared to most economies, but who is to say that this may not be an advantage if strategic considerations favor a sizeable expansion of foreign technical assistance? It is probably important in this period of rapid change in military technology, not only that a sizeable fraction of government resources be devoted to research and development, but that the structure of production and size of industrial enterprises favor research and technical innovation. Beyond this there is, perhaps, not much that is useful to say without a detailed study attempting to match up a complicated set of potential requirements with developing capabilities.

Finally, it should be noted that the vulnerability of production processes to various forms of disruption has a bearing on the relation of economic resources to strategic choice. If we consider vulnerability in time of war, it is obvious that changes in military technology have completely altered the situation during the last twenty years. Before and during World War II it was considered that the vulnerabilities principally to be guarded against were the denial of access to foreign sources of "critical" raw materials, and, of distinctly less significance, sabotage of internal facilities, particularly significant, transportation bottlenecks. The emphasis on stockpiling after the war represented to a large extent an obsolete strategy carried over into a new age. With the advent of the possibility of atomic warfare it is nearly certain that we would lose processing facilities much more rapidly than we would lose the raw materials required by these facilities.

A consideration of the full range of military possibilities, of course, including problems of supplying allies more dependent on overseas sources than we are, may preserve some of the validity of earlier concepts but probably not much.

If we consider the vulnerability of economic processes as it affects the choice of strategy in a period short of war, the possibilities of sabotage, subversion, and political penetration would need to be examined. Sabotage can probably be dismissed as a serious factor unless it is the product of a subversive movement in the hands of a sizeable "fifth column." It would seem that the most serious potential vulnerability Western democracies have to face is a decline in vigilance, an unwillingness to make sacrifices in a period of apparent calm during which, nevertheless, potential enemies are not so unwilling.

## FOOTNOTES

[1] Colin Clark, *Conditions of Economic Progress* (2d ed., London: 1951), p. 16.

[2] Moses Abramovitz, "The Welfare Interpretation of Secular Trends," *National Income and Product in the Allocation of Economic Resources*, Essays in Honor of Bernard Haley (Stanford: 1959), p. 20.

[3] Presidential Address, American Economic Association, December, 1962, "Interests, Ideology, and the Problem of Stability and Growth," *The American Economic Review* (March, 1963).

[4] "Long-Range Projections for Economic Growth," National Planning Association Planning Pamphlet 107, 1959. See also Sidney Sonenblum (Director of Research, National Economic Projections Series), "Potential Economic Growth," *Monthly Report* of the National Planning Association (June, 1962).

[5] Edward Denison, *The Sources of Economic Growth in the United States and the Alternatives Before Us*, Committee for Economic Development (New York: 1962).

[6] *Ibid.* See also an illuminating review of Denison's book by Moses Abramovitz, *American Economic Review* (September, 1962), p. 762.

[7] Alexander Gerschenkron, "Notes on the Rate of Industrial Growth in Soviet Russia," in *Economic Backwardness in Historical Perspective* (Cambridge, Mass.: 1962), p. 260.

[8] Edward S. Mason, "American Security and Access to Raw Materials," *World Politics* (January, 1949), p. 147.

# Monetary and Fiscal Policies in US Strategy

## —GOTTFRIED HABERLER

### Summary

The objectives of over-all economic policies are defined as high rate of growth, high level of employment, and price stability. It is argued that with proper fiscal, monetary, and wage policies the three goals can be simultaneously achieved.

The performance of the US economy since 1945 has been satisfactory—broadly speaking. The over-all rate of growth has been the same or a little better than in previous periods of similar length, and severe depressions, of which there were three during the interwar period, have been conspicuous by their absence. This is due not just to good luck, but to improvements in over-all policies.

There has been a slight slowdown since 1958; the rate of growth has dropped from about 3.5 per cent to about 2.5 per cent, and unemployment has risen from 4 per cent in 1956 and 1957 to a level of between 5.5 and 6.8 per cent (annual averages).

It is asserted that this slowdown is not serious from the point of view of military preparedness. On the contrary, it can be argued that a slack economy is in a better position to adapt itself to an emergency (sudden sharp increase in defense demands) than a fully employed economy. Only if the slack became so large as to impair the maintenance and improvement of industrial capacity would it become a serious problem. This has not been the case, except in isolated instances (railroads) which have nothing to do with the over-all situation and cannot be corrected by over-all policies.

*From the point of view of economic welfare, however, the slack has become unnecessarily large, although it is not nearly as great as it was in the 1930's (not counting the outright depression years of that decade). It should not be assumed, however, that very high employment levels (literally full and overfull employment) are conducive to rapid growth. There is somewhere an optimum. But at present, the level of unemployment is surely higher than that optimum. Expansionary fiscal and monetary policies could reduce the existing slack considerably and thus stimulate growth. There have been, however, two restraining factors in operation—the balance-of-payments restraint and the inflation restraint.*

*The balance-of-payments problem is reviewed, and several policy options for removing the external deficit and thus freeing financial policies from the existing restraint are discussed. These options are: (1) tight money combined with loose budget (deficit) as proposed by European experts, (2) plans for closer cooperation between central banks [including the Federal Reserve System and the International Monetary Fund (IMF)], (3) import restrictions and control of capital exports, (4) a wait and see policy. Options (1), (2), and (4) are deemed to be of uncertain effectiveness. Option (3) is undesirable and clashes with accepted principles of foreign economic policy. This leaves option (5), fundamental correctives of the balance of payments. These are defined as a lowering of our cost and price level relative to that in the competing industrial countries. Three possible methods of bringing that about are available: (a) raising prices and costs abroad, (b) reducing prices and costs at home, and (c) a change in the exchange rate.*

*Before the balance-of-payments restraint became operative in 1958, expansionary monetary and fiscal policies were constrained by fear of inflation, i.e., of rising prices. Over-all price levels have been stable since 1958. Hence the inflation restraint is not operative now.*

*It is argued, however, that if and when the economy resumes more rapid expansion, inflation may, after a while, again become an issue. The crucial role of wages, both for the balance of payments and for internal price stability, is discussed. If it were possible to moderate wage demands, it would be possible by means of monetary and fiscal policies to maintain a higher level of employment, a more rapid rate of growth, equilibrium in the balance of payments, and stable prices. The business cycle would be still with us, but it would play around a more steeply rising trend, and a better job could be made of mitigating recessions by over-all policies if the fear of inflation were removed. For such a policy to be successful, no reduction in* real *wages or a slower rise in* real *wages is required—only* money *wage discipline is necessary.*

*Finally, several other types of policies, not necessarily of over-all nature, in the field of agriculture, labor, taxation, social security, and import restrictions are briefly reviewed—policies that would help to restrain inflation, promote growth, and improve the balance of payments.*

---

### Introduction

The problems which are to be discussed in the present paper have been defined in the program of the whole Conference as follows:

> This paper will discuss the monetary, fiscal, over-all policies for promoting economic growth. Attention will be given to the efficacy of alternative approaches, the policy of strategy mix, the question of limitations, price stability, and the implications of future gold crises for our strategy and for our allies.

It will be assumed that earlier panels have established estimates of peacetime economic and financial defense requirements in the light of the over-all strategic situation. I am convinced and shall take it for granted that the American economy, with proper over-all financial and economic policies, can easily support a defense budget, even if it were substantially greater than the present one of approximately $50 billion, which amounts to a little less than 10 per cent of the gross national product (GNP).

Although the present paper is entirely concerned with peacetime policies and not with policies to be pursued after the outbreak of hostilities, it could be argued that it would be important, for the purposes of the present report, to know what kind of war we have to expect. For certain types of policies—transportation policies, dispersal of industries, stockpiling, provision of stand-by equipment, and others—it would indeed make a great deal of difference whether a long drawn-out conflict, essentially a conventional type of war although with much more destruction through bombing, than the last time, or a short but tremendously destructive nuclear holocaust is in store.

For the purposes of the task assigned to me, I shall not, however, make any specific assumptions with respect to the type of war which is to be expected. I am not competent to make such conjectures and I suspect that nobody can be quite sure. Elementary prudence would seem to suggest that policies should be framed in such a way that the country is prepared for any eventuality. But this applies, in my opinion, to the more specific areas mentioned above—transportation policy, dispersal of industries, stockpiling, provision of stand-by capacities and equipment—and not to the over-all policies which form the subject of the present paper.

### The Objectives of "Over-all" Economic Policies

The task of these over-all policies is to keep the economy in a healthy state. By that I mean rapid growth, a high level of employment, and stable prices. It is one of the contentions of the present paper that these three objectives are compatible with one another—in particular, that with proper policies it is possible to have stable prices, i.e., to avoid inflation and deflation, and at the same time to maintain a satisfactory level of employment and an acceptable rate of growth.

When I speak of high rate of employment, however, I do not mean literally full employment or "overfull employment," that is to say, a situation similar to the one that exists at the present time in several countries of Continental Europe (especially Germany) where the number of unemployed has fallen to one or two per cent of the labor force and the number of vacant jobs greatly exceeds the number of unemployed.

That extremely high levels of employment or overfull employment are hardly compatible with financial stability (stable prices) will probably be granted. But it is also true, although not generally realized or admitted, that extremely high employment levels are not conducive to rapid growth and that in case of war, especially if it were of the long, drawn-out variety, the existence of a reserve of unemployed labor and under-utilized equipment would greatly facilitate the transition from a peacetime to a wartime economy. This is not meant to recommend a state of deep depression (high unemployment), because obviously such a state of affairs would not be compatible with rapid growth. But it is a myth that almost 100 per cent employment would ensure maximum growth. Moreover, some attainable peacetime growth may have to be sacrificed for the purpose of making the economy more flexible and smoothing the transition to a wartime basis by permitting a certain amount of slack.

## Meaning and Types of Over-all Economic Policies

By over-all policies I mean monetary policy (including credit policy), fiscal policy, and some would add over-all wage policy. I shall emphasize monetary and fiscal policy and shall take up the more controversial problem of wage policy later.

Monetary policy is conducted by the Federal Reserve System in close cooperation with the Treasury. It comprises discount policy, open market operations, setting reserve requirements for commercial banks, and debt management. The objective is to contract or to expand the supply of money, thereby changing the interest structure and the flow of expenditures, especially for investment purposes.

Fiscal policy determines the over-all level of government expenditures and revenues (tax policy), thereby creating deficits or surpluses in the Government budget. An excess of expenditures over revenues (deficit) adds to and increases the aggregate stream of expenditures while an excess of revenues over expenditures (surplus) subtracts from and decreases the aggregate stream of expenditures.

Most economists agree that monetary and fiscal policies should be operated in such a way as to counteract inflationary and deflationary pressures, mitigate as far as possible economic fluctuations, the so-called "business cycle," which has plagued the free capitalist economies, and thus assure stability and growth.

## The Performance of the US Economy Since 1945

Broadly speaking, the conduct of these policies has been fairly successful in the postwar period compared with earlier times and especially compared with the interwar period. Economic fluctuations have been much milder since World War II than they were during the interwar period. While between the two World Wars there occurred three deep depressions—1920-21, 1929-33, 1937-38 (in addition to two mild ones)—there have been only four mild recessions since World War II. Considering the truly catastrophic economic and political consequences of

the Great Depression (1929-33), this is not a mean achievement.*

It is true that there has been widespread dissatisfaction with
the performance of the economy since the end of 1957. The
growth rate (average annual rise in real GNP) has been about
3.8 per cent from 1946 or 1947 to 1957, and about 2.5 per cent
from 1957 to 1960, and the unemployment percentage was a
little over 4 per cent in 1956 and 1957, but has since then
hovered between 5.5 per cent and 6.8 per cent (annual averages).
In addition to that, the economy has been plagued since 1958
by large and persistent deficits in its international balance of
payments.

Before I discuss the possible causes and cures of this recent
slowdown and the external deficit, let me emphasize again that
the over-all performance during the postwar period (even including the less satisfactory years 1958-62) has been much better
than during the interwar period. Expansion periods have become
substantially longer and contractions substantially shorter. The
average drop of GNP during the four contractions since 1948
was only 2.2 per cent, while GNP dropped by 19.19 per cent,
49.6 per cent, and 11.9 per cent, respectively, during the three
severe depressions, 1920-21, 1929-33, 1937-38. Other possible
measures of severity of depression—decline in industrial production, personal income, retail sales, etc.—reveal an equally sharp
contrast between the two periods.

Moreover, there are good reasons to believe that the mildness
of the postwar recessions is not simply due to good luck but is
the consequence of a change in structure and of more vigorous
anti-depression policies. Severe depressions are almost certainly
a thing of the past. Most economic experts agree on that. This
conclusion has been corroborated by the fact that the economy
has withstood so well the severe shock of the Stock Exchange
crash last May. It should also be observed that the slight retardation of growth since 1958 and the somewhat higher unemployment percentage is definitely not the consequence of a tendency
of recent recessions to become again more virulent. The last
recession (1960-61) was exceptionally short and mild. The slow-

---

* Technically speaking, the Great Depression lasted 43 months from
August, 1929, to March, 1933. It was followed by a weak upswing which
which was interrupted by a short but precipitous depression (May 1937-
June 1938). The economy was, thus, greatly depressed throughout the
1930's up to the outbreak of the war. In 1939, 17.2 per cent of the labor
force were still unemployed.

down has been due rather to the fact that the last two expansions have been a little shorter and less vigorous than the earlier ones.

## The Slowdown of the Economy Since 1958

Thus, in my opinion, the concern about the recent slowdown has been greatly overdone. From the point of view of military preparedness, there seems to me no cause for worry, at least not as yet. On the contrary, it can be argued with much justification that some slack, that is to say, the existence of reserves of unemployed labor and under-utilized industrial capacity, provides flexibility which will be very handy in an emergency.* The Cuban crisis or a magnified version of it is much easier to deal with and causes much less disruption of the normal working of the economy in a slack than in a fully employed economy. Only if the slack becomes so great as to impair the full maintenance and improvement of industrial capacity would it become a serious matter from the point of view of military preparedness.

I am sure that this dangerous stage has not been reached. There may be certain restricted areas where undermaintenance has gone so far that it has become a serious matter in an emergency. The only important example I can think of is that of the railroads. Especially in the East, the railroads have been allowed to be run down to an extent that cannot be undone at short notice in case of war. But this dangerous development is surely not due to the general slack of the economy (or only to a negligible extent). It is due to structural changes (the rise of road and air transport) and it is greatly intensified by highly restrictive practices (featherbedding) on the part of powerful and well-entrenched labor unions, by wholly antiquated government regulations both federal and local, and by governmental subsidies in various forms to rival modes of transportation. These factors cannot be changed by over-all financial policies.

From the point of view of ordinary peacetime goals of economic policy, any avoidable slack is, of course, undesirable because it implies a loss of output ** and individual hardships

* Furthermore, it will be much easier in a slack economy to get Congress to vote more money for defense than in a fully employed economy. The reason is that if there exists unemployment and excess capacity, it can be argued that larger expenditures will stimulate the economy. In other words it is then possible, within limits, to provide butter and guns at the same time, while in a fully employed economy no such miracles are possible.

** I take it for granted that it will no longer be argued by anyone that we are so affluent that a reduction of output, even if it fell entirely on the private sector, is of no consequence.

(unemployment), in one word, a loss of economic welfare (as it is usually defined). Before I go on, let me repeat that the slack is small compared with the situation in the late thirties—let alone, of course, the years of the Great Depression and the 1937-38 slump. Hardships through unemployment and short time, too, do not really present a serious social problem. To speak of a new case of "secular stagnation" and to conjure up memories of the Great Depression is, in my opinion, entirely unwarranted.

There can be no doubt, it seems to me, that the slack in the economy could be greatly reduced, the economy brought much nearer to its ideal full-employment potential, and output and employment substantially increased by several alternative combinations of easier money and more liberal fiscal policies. There are, however, two constraints—the balance-of-payments constraint, and the inflation constraint. The balance-of-payments constraint is the one actually operating at present. After four and a half years of stable wholesale prices and of only very slowly increasing cost of living, inflation is not a threat at present but could again become one if and when the economy moves into higher gear.

Let me discuss the two constraints in turn and indicate in each case the strategy mix of monetary, fiscal, and wage policies that could be used to overcome it.

## The Balance-of-Payments Constraint

The broad facts about the balance of payments are that since 1958 the United States has been losing gold steadily and has been piling up liquid liabilities. The sum of these two items—loss of gold plus increase in liquid liabilities—is the external deficit as conventionally defined.*

* The substitution of another definition—the so-called "basic balance"—does not change the picture materially and will therefore not be discussed here. Let me add parenthetically that, while piling up short-term and liquid liabilities, the United States has also been a large capital exporter to the rest of the world on a long-term basis. For example, during the 1950's (end of 1949 to the end of 1960) the excess of all foreign assets (public loans plus private investments, not counting Government grants) over all foreign liabilities rose from $38.3 to $44.5 billion. American private direct investment alone rose from $10.7 to $32.7 billion. This last type of investment is especially important because it produces a very considerable backflow of foreign earnings. Income on private American investment abroad has risen from $1.5 billion in 1950 to $3.3 billion in 1961.

The gold stock has fallen from $22.86 billion at the end of 1957 to $16.37 billion on October 31, 1962, and liquid liabilities have increased from $13.64 billion to $22 billion. The deficit has been $3.5 billion in 1958, almost $4 billion in 1959 and 1960, $2.5 billion in 1961 and will probably be only slightly lower in 1962.

There has been a marked improvement in 1961 and 1962 compared with 1959 and 1960, but whether the improvement will continue into 1963 as has been confidently predicted in numerous official statements is, in my opinion, doubtful.

When judging the prospects of the balance of payments, two facts should be kept firmly in mind: First, it is extraordinarily difficult to foresee the future development of the balance of payments, much more difficult than that of the domestic economy for the double reason that the external balance is a small residual in the economy (less than one per cent of GNP) and that it depends on developments at home as well as in foreign countries. Second, there is no area where official announcements have to tread with such extreme caution. If any doubts about the future of the balance were voiced officially, a flood of speculative capital could be loosened which would put the balance into heavy deficit.

The reasons why I am skeptical of the official optimism are the following: The present estimate of the deficit in the Federal budget for the current fiscal year is $7.8 billion. On top of that, a substantial tax cut seems to be in the cards. Hence, the budget deficit is bound to be very large. This is likely to put the economy into higher gear. The recent improvement in the stock exchange is probably in anticipation of these developments. An increase in GNP must lead to an increase in imports and if costs and prices rise, as they always do in a business cycle upswing, exports may well decline. In one word, the balance of goods and services (current balance) is likely to become less favorable. There may come some relief for the over-all balance from the capital account, less American capital going abroad, if the domestic situation improves. But we cannot be sure of that effect and it may be quite small.

Now let us look at the other side of the fence. The improvement in the US balance since 1959-60 has been largely due to a very substantial increase of US exports to Europe. Exports to other parts of the world have not risen much. Two factors have caused the increase in European demand for American products: first, the dismantling of European special import restrictions on imports from the United States. It is true that the coming into operation of the Common Market has meant increasing *tariff* discrimination against US exports. But this was offset and more than offset by the removal of quantitative restrictions which had been imposed on American goods during the period of the dollar shortage for balance-of-payments reasons. This offsetting process has, however, come to an end, because there are no such balance-of-payments restrictions left which could be removed.*

Second, perhaps even more important was the fact that the European economies have grown with amazing rapidity.** This growth was bound to slacken and further retardation must be expected. Moreover, the growth was accompanied by inflationary pressures which, since 1958, were much stronger in Europe than in the United States. Prices and especially wages have risen much faster than in the United States. Wage costs have increased very fast, e.g., German wages have risen by 12 per cent in one year on top of an appreciation of the mark of five per cent, raising dollar wages in Germany by 17 per cent in one year.

The Europeans who, on the whole, are more inflation conscious than Americans, have been forced to take measures to bring their inflation under control. If they are successful—and the chances are good in France, Germany, and the Netherlands because these countries have responsible conservative governments—their prices and costs will cease to rise. There is even a possibility that they may overshoot the mark and bring on a recession, although there is no sign yet that contraction has actually started and the Europeans are confident that they can avoid that.

The upshot is that there is a strong probability that US exports to Europe will cease to rise or may even decline. As a partial offset the attraction of Europe for United States capital may become less. But this is not certain because the further advance of the Common Market towards its goal pulls in the other direction. The Common Market, while reducing trade barriers between the six members, raises them for out-

* There are still special restrictions on agricultural exports from the United States. But they are no longer imposed for balance-of-payments reasons and are much more difficult to remove, partly for the reason that foreign producers have become accustomed to protection, partly because these national protective measures will be merged with protectionist barriers on agricultural products which the Common Market is about to erect.

** This, by the way, has up to now been due only to a minor extent to the coming into operation of the Common Market, contrary to what is often said or implied. The European economies grew faster before the Common Market went into operation.

siders. This makes it more important for US corporations to set up production facilities inside the Common Market area to protect their interests.

Now I have to admit that there are many ifs and buts in this argument. The Europeans may not be able to stop their inflation immediately, or the delayed effects of the inflation they already had may be substantial. Let me repeat, it is a most hazardous undertaking to predict a balance of payments and many economists have burnt their fingers trying to do it.

Elementary prudence demands, however, that we be prepared for balance-of-payments troubles. If the proposed tax cut works and the American economy expands, we ought to know what to do in case the external deficit increases.

What are the options? I list five of them.

## Cures for the Balance of Payments

### Approach One

One answer has been suggested by the Bank for International Settlements, Basel, and European central bankers and has been accepted in some quarters on this side of the Atlantic, viz., to tighten money and raise interest rates and at the same time loosen the budget, i.e., run a large deficit. This would, it is said, attract capital funds to the United States and check the outflow of funds, thus counteracting the deterioration in the current balance which has to be expected to result from the budget deficit.

The success of this type of policy seems to me very doubtful, on two counts. First, it is not at all sure that it will work sufficiently well—in other words, that the improvement in the balance of payments on capital account will, for any length of time, be as great or greater than the deterioration of the current balance (balance of goods and services).

Second, if the policy worked as far as the balance of payments is concerned, higher interest rates and tighter money would also tend to put a damper on domestic private investment. Moreover, the combination of tight money and loose public finance is not the best method to stimulate growth. Many economists have recommended the opposite, viz., easy money and a tight budget, on the ground that low interest rates will stimulate investment and a budget surplus restrains consumption. There is, of course, general agreement that a higher growth rate requires a larger volume of investment.*

A variant of the policy of tight-money-cum-budget-deficits has in fact been applied during the last few years. The Federal Reserve has tried to keep short-term rates relatively high while reducing as much as possible long-term rates on the theory that the former operate on international capital flows while the latter operate on domestic investment. The results of these policies (operation "nudge") have been disappointing.

The upshot is that the balance of payments cannot be substantially improved by clever gadgets. What Under Secretary of the Treasury for Monetary Affairs Robert Roosa said in a remarkable speech before the American Bankers Association (September, 1962)—that the "easier" measures of dealing with the balance of payments have now been taken and cannot be expected to yield substantial results in the future—would seem to apply also to the present one, although he probably was referring to "small measures" such as reducing military expenditures abroad through "buy American" policies, tying loans and grants to foreign countries to purchases in the United States (80 per cent of such grants and loans are now said to be tied), luring foreign tourists to the United States and reducing free import allowance for American tourists from $500 or $200 to $100.**

### Approach Two

Numerous plans of closer cooperation between the central banks of the leading industrial countries and the IMF have been discussed, proposed, and some carried into effect. They are named after their authors—the "Roosa Plan," "Bernstein Plan," "Triffin Plan," etc. They all have this in common: they are not real cures (are not meant to be basic cures, as Mr. R. Roosa and others have made quite clear) but are methods of buying a little more time for fundamental adjustments to work themselves out. Under these plans, the United States (or other deficit countries) could postpone elimination of the deficit a little longer, and in the

* Obviously, for this mechanism to work, the right kind of taxes have to be used. The theory does not mean to contradict the conviction, which is now gaining more and more ground, that excessively progressive income taxes and the high corporate income tax are inimical to capital expenditure (investment) and growth.

** Repayment of Government debt owed us by Germany, France, and some others has helped our balance of payments during the last two years. More important are purchases in the United States of military equipment for NATO forces.

meantime, go on borrowing in one form or the other from other countries. Since the United States started with a huge gold stock which gave it plenty of time to effect a real cure, it would seem that the time has come to think of the basic cures instead of extending the period of grace a little longer.

### Approach Three

There are restrictive and protectionist measures which we should shun like the plague. We could introduce massive restrictions on imports. This would give the lie to our professed policy of liberalizing trade and would impair our leadership in the Free World.* Furthermore, we could control or restrict private capital exports. This policy has been emphatically rejected by Robert Roosa in the above-mentioned speech for excellent reasons. Let me quote:

> This country rejects direct controls on the flow of capital not only because they would be inconsistent with our traditional and fundamental objectives of freeing trade and payments between countries, but for immediate dollars-and-cents reasons—they would cost us more than they could possibly save. Our own money and capital markets are the most highly organized, most efficiently diversified, of any in the world. To try to impose controls over outward capital movements in any one sector of these markets— say bank loans—would only invite a capital flight through many others. And to try instead a comprehensive approach—clamping the cold hand of capital issues controls, or credit rationing, over the entire sweep of the markets—would literally congeal the bloodstream of American capitalism.

Strange to say, control of capital exports has been recommended to the United States by the managing director of the Swiss National Bank, forgetting, evidently, that the situation here is very different than in Switzerland where a telephone call to half-a-dozen bankers would do the trick.

Here is the place to mention the proposal which is again and again being made to double (or triple) the price of gold all round

---

* It should be observed, however, that imports have, in fact, been restricted substantially by putting import quotas on petroleum, so-called "voluntary" restrictions on textile imports, tying foreign aid irrespective of cost, and severely restricting foreign shipping. These latter policies amount to a substantial reduction of real aid provided by a given amount of dollars and is equivalent to the imposition of a high import tariff or substantial export subsidies—measures which stand in glaring contrast to the principles of our liberal trade policy which have been reconfirmed by the Trade Expansion Act of 1962. Tariff increases have been avoided so far with the exception of a sharp increase in the duty on carpets and glass in March 1962.

in terms of all currencies. Doubling the price of gold has this in common with the borrowing schemes just mentioned: it does not by itself constitute a cure of our balance of payments, but buys time, in fact a lot of time, to effect a real cure. It would at one stroke increase international liquidity, that is, international reserves. This would enable deficit countries like the United States and the United Kingdom, which own gold, to run a deficit for several years longer, and through increased gold production would bring large annual additions to international reserves.

The most popular argument against this step has been that it would bestow a great benefit upon the major gold producers— the Union of South Africa and the Soviet Union. In my opinion, this should not be a matter of major consideration. If the Soviets wish to invest heavily in gold digging, it is their business. Only if they started to sell gold in large quantities on the world markets would the problem become serious. So far they have not done this, although they are in a position to do it, for according to all reports, their gold stock is quite substantial.

More important is the objection that a doubling of the gold price would have inflationary effects on a world-wide basis. A situation could arise, however, in which the inflationary effects of an appreciation of gold in terms of all currencies would be welcome—namely, in case of a world-wide recession.

Still another serious objection is that a depreciation of the dollar in terms of gold would penalize those countries which have held a large part of their international reserves in dollars and reward those which did not show the same confidence in the stability of the dollar. A gold guarantee to official dollar holders would overcome this objection but would lead to other difficulties.

All in all, it is understandable that our policy-makers in successive administrations have categorically rejected the idea of tampering with the price of gold.*

---

* A small appreciation of gold of, say, ten per cent would be useless because it would encourage hoarding. Hoarders would hardly believe that a ten per cent appreciation would not be followed sooner or later by further steps in the same direction. Others have suggested that a small, say, two per cent reduction in the official gold price, announced several months before it takes place, would effectively induce gold hoarders to disgorge their hoards. Maybe it would, but would they not then replenish their hoards after the price reduction has gone into effect? Or is the operation to be repeated again and again?

It would seem to me that small-scale tampering with the price of gold is not worth the candle and could do a lot of harm.

*Approach Four*

The fourth option is to sit tight, continue to keep the lid on the price level by not liberalizing money and fiscal policy (forego the tax cut), continue to tolerate a slightly higher volume of unemployment and slightly lower growth rate than otherwise would be necessary and hope for the balance to improve.

From the point of view of military preparedness, this may be an acceptable policy. But the country will probably not stand for it. Moreover, even with no change in policy, the balance of payments may deteriorate if our exports to Europe decline in the wake of a slowdown of European growth or a recession in Europe. In that event, we could not well continue the policy of doing nothing.

**Policies of Fundamental Correction
for the Balance of Payments**

*Approach Five*

This brings me at last to what I would call policies of fundamental correction of the balance of payments. By that I mean a reduction of our cost level, especially wage level and price level, as compared with that in the competing industrial countries in Europe and Japan.*

Such a change in relative cost and price level as between this country and Europe can be brought about in three different ways.

1) Wages and prices rise more rapidly in Europe than here. This is what actually has happened during the last three or four years, but it has as yet not been enough to restore equilibrium in our balance of payments and may have come to an end, if the Europeans are successful in putting the brake on their inflation.

2) If the Europeans do not oblige, our own costs could be reduced. I take it for granted that actual wage reductions are entirely out of the question except in rare cases. If we rule out wage reductions, there still remains a possibility of cost and price adjustment in a progressive economy; if the level of money wages could be kept stable, money costs and prices could slowly

---

* The underdeveloped countries can be ignored, because practically all of them pursue inflationary policies and thus constitute no threat for our balance of payments.

decline, because labor productivity (output per man-hour) rises on the average by about 2.4 per cent a year. It should be stressed that this policy would *not* preclude a gradual rise in *real* wages.* Real wages would, in fact, rise just as fast as they do now, the only difference being that with our present system the rise in real wages takes the form of rising money wages and stable prices (or rising prices and more rapidly rising money wages), while under the other system it would take the form of stable money wages and falling prices. I am under no illusion that, with our methods of collective bargaining and the prevailing mood of labor unions and labor policies in general, it will be easy to stabilize the money wage level or even to reduce the rise in money wages to something less than the average annual rise in labor productivity. But the economics of the matter is really quite simple and straightforward (see below for further remarks on wage policy).

3) If (1) and (2) are not sufficient, if the Europeans do not inflate enough and we cannot control our wage level, there remains only *one* other possibility to change the relative cost and price levels between the United States and other countries; namely, a change in the exchange rate—in other words, an appreciation of foreign currencies or a depreciation of the dollar.

Any change in established exchange rates, that is to say, any depreciation of the dollar or appreciation of other currencies or a change of the gold price, is a most delicate operation. One reason is that any change of that kind cannot be openly and publicly discussed by responsible people because this would lead to a flood of disturbing speculation. It would have to be done quickly without long public debate, but it requires an act of Congress. It is, therefore, quite understandable that all responsible policy-makers reject the idea categorically. But the alternatives must be faced squarely—namely, to sit tight and do nothing, which means accepting an unsatisfactory growth rate and unnecessarily low-employment levels, and which may necessitate a worsening of these conditions; to get other countries to inflate more, which they are reluctant to do; to prevent wages from rising, a nettle which no one wants to grasp; to cut aid and

---

* It must be emphasized that gradual decline of the price level as a consequence of the rise of labor productivity and stable wage levels is not the same thing as a deflation. Deflation is a fall in the price level due to contraction of aggregate demand. In the case under consideration, aggregate demand does not contract. A real deflation creates unemployment (because wages are rigid); the case under consideration does not.

military expenditures abroad and restrict imports and control capital flows, which for the reasons stated earlier would be most unfortunate.

On the other hand, those who advocate a depreciation of the dollar should not forget that after the operation has been performed successfully, it would be more necessary than ever to continue financial discipline and wage moderation. The worst policy would be to follow a depreciation with loose financial policies and wage inflation so that the country would soon again face the same impasse. France was brought, by a period of inflation and several unsuccessful depreciations, to the brink of chaos when the strong government of General de Gaulle imposed financial and wage discipline, and thus made the 1958 depreciation of the franc stick.

### The Inflation Restraint on Expansionary Policies

Before the deficit in the balance of payments became menacingly large and began to be taken seriously in 1959, fear of inflation provided the restraint for expansionary policies. In my opinion, the Administration was right in its policy of restraining inflation on two counts—external and internal monetary equilibrium. The rise in US prices is one of the root causes of the weak balance of payments. This is true despite the fact that the rise in the *over-all* price level has not on the whole been greater in this country than in other industrial countries.* In view of the fact that European and Japanese industries, knocked out by the war, came back into production offering more and more competition to US manufactured products at home and abroad, and in view of the fact that the United States has assumed very large commitments abroad for military expenditures and economic and military aid; the price rise that has occurred, even if moderate by historical standards or compared with that elsewhere, was simply too great for external equilibrium.

Also, from the internal standpoint (apart from the deficit in the external balance) inflation had become a menace. It is true that for each of the postwar business-cycle upswings the price rise was not excessive by historical standards. But the

* Exports prices and prices of manufactured goods, especially steel, however, have risen substantially more in the United States than in competing countries.

new feature is that since 1938 or so there has been no period during which there has been a noticeable price decline. Prices remained stable during recessions and even kept rising (slightly) during the 1958-59 recession. This was something entirely new which has made Americans more inflation-conscious than they were before.

The situation has, however, changed. Since 1958, that is for four-and-one-half years, price levels have been substantially stable. As a consequence, inflationary psychology has disappeared. But I have no doubt that it would reappear, if prices should again begin to creep up. Since prices have been barely stable, it is difficult to believe that they will not rise again if and when unemployment falls substantially below present levels and output rises sharply.

To repeat, there is no immediate danger that this will happen. The price stability over the last four-and-one-half years has provided a breathing spell; inflationary psychology is not likely to be *immediately* revived when prices go up again. It would probably take a year or longer depending, of course, on the speed of the price increase. Thus, if the balance-of-payments barrier to rapid expansion were removed, the chances are that we should, after a while, arrive at an (elastic) inflation barrier to further expansion.

## Wage Push and Wage Policy

It is necessary now to take up the question of the role of wages in the inflationary process and their implications for the balance of payments. Most economists believe that during the postwar period inflation has been greatly intensified by a wage push. It has become customary to distinguish between a "demand-pull" and "cost- or wage-push" inflation. We have a demand-pull inflation when prices and wages are "pulled up" by excessive aggregate demand stemming either from a deficit in the Government budget or excessive credits to private business or in some cases from foreign sources ("imported inflation").* We have wage-push inflation if costs and wages are "pushed up" by union pressure.

Most economists believe that during the postwar period wage push has been an important factor, supported and accompanied, of course (especially during the Korean War period or in 1955-56), by powerful demand pull.

* Inflation in Europe has been, to some extent, of that nature.

Wage push works in the following way. Powerful trade unions force wage increases by threat of strike which then spread (with a lag of varying length) over the whole economy.* It should be observed, however, that even the most powerful unions could not force up the price level if the monetary authorities stood firm and refused to create enough money, since money is required to support the higher level of prices and increased volume of monetary transactions. But if the money supply does not expand and prices cannot rise, or rise only less than cost, the wage push will result in a squeeze of profits, entailing a reduction in output and create unemployment. It is not unreasonable to explain the rise in unemployment since 1958 by a tug of war between the monetary authorities and the unions. Fear of inflation and the deficit in the balance of payments has forced the monetary authorities to adopt a stiffer attitude and to resist the continual demand for more and more money; at the same time, the unions have continued to press for higher wages. This has reduced profits and the inducement to invest. It is true, the wage rise has been slowed down to something like 3-3½ per cent per year, but it required a somewhat larger volume of unemployment to achieve that result.

Most, though not all economists agree with this explanation. Typical of the large measure of agreement is an international report, *The Problem of Rising Prices*,[1] written by a group of leading American and European economists in 1960. After an exhaustive study, the Committee agreed unanimously that wage push has played a decisive role in the inflationary process during the last 10 years or so.** They also link the weakness of the US

---

* The fact that only about 25 per cent of the labor force is unionized does not contradict the theory of the wage push. If the wages of union workers are pushed up, employers find it necessary to raise wages and salaries of non-unionized workers and employees, partly for maintaining morale, partly for the purpose of forestalling unionization of the rest of the labor force. After some time even "fixed incomes" of government officials and teachers have to be brought in line.

** The Committee represented a cross section of experts from right, left, and center. It is interesting that they also agree unanimously that there is no counterpart to the wage push on the business side. They say "there can be a wage-spiral but there cannot be a profit-spiral" (p. 70). That is, the Committee rejected unanimously the theory often advanced in the United States that large corporations in "oligopolistic" industries continuously push up prices in order to amass larger and larger profits in the same manner in which large unions push up wages to provide larger and larger incomes to their members. In other words, there is a wage-push inflation but no such thing as an "administered price" inflation.

balance of payments to the wage-push inflation: "With demand pressures [in the United States in recent years] less intense than in Europe, round after round of wage increases have weakened the competitive position of the American industry . . . Inflation in the US has been an obstacle to economic growth; we believe that moderation in the rate of wage increase is fundamental to avoiding inflation in the future" (pp. 62-63).

If there were no unions or if it were possible somehow to restrain them from pushing up wages faster than productivity (output per man-hour) increases, it would be comparatively easy by monetary and fiscal policy to regulate aggregate demand in such a way that the price level remains stable without creating chronic unemployment. Presumably, there would still be a mild business cycle, but it would play around a more steeply rising trend.

It should be observed that *real* wages would rise in the long run just as much as they do now, because when productivity rises gradually and prices remain stable, competition between employers for labor would raise money wages roughly in proportion to the gradual raise in labor productivity. In reality, real labor income would rise even faster because the waste of unemployment would be greatly reduced.

As was pointed out earlier, if the level of money wages were kept stable, there could be even a gradual decline in the price level. If output per man-hour increased by, say, two per cent a year and the money-wage level remained stable, prices would fall by two per cent. Let me emphasize once more that under this system real wages * would rise just as much as under the present system, the only difference being that it would take the form of stable-money wages and declining prices instead of rising prices and still-faster-rising-money wages. If this policy could be adopted for, say, two years (and assuming that the surplus countries do not let their prices fall) the balance-of-payments deficit would disappear.

Clearly, growth will be promoted and inflationary pressures counteracted if willful restrictions of output, resistance to the introduction of new and more efficient methods of production

---

* It goes without saying that a distinction should be made between the over-all wage *level* and the wages of different groups—*relative* wages as the economist calls them. *Relative* wages should, of course, be flexible and should change so as to reflect relative scarcity and abundance of different skills and types of labor. The argument in the text is couched in terms of wage levels, average wage rates.

(automation, etc.), creation and continuance of unnecessary jobs ("featherbedding"), frequent interruptions of the productive process by strikes and similar practices are suppressed or at least sharply curtailed. It is often alleged that it is impossible to do anything about these abuses without drastic legislation designed to curb union power and change methods of free collective bargaining. In particular, it has been said that public opinion and the Administration are powerless without far-reaching reforms such as compulsory arbitration and government wage fixing.

This issue cannot be further discussed here, but it should be pointed out that on other occasions the Administration found it possible to use very energetic measures, for example in the steel-price episode last year. But the energy evaporates completely when it comes to dealing with the abuses of labor unions.

It would be well to use existing means to curb union power before contemplating radical changes. Platitudinous admonitions to behave, addressed in studiously neutral fashion to everybody, are obviously of no use. Maybe a stern warning to unions that their policies are intolerable will not help either. But then they have never really been told by responsible members of the Government. Before that is done, it is premature to throw in the sponge and to say that public opinion and the Government are powerless, short of radical reforms.

The economics of all this is not very complicated. What is not simple is how to bring about moderation on the part of unions. On this problem in the above-mentioned committee split, the two conservative members recommended dissolution of industry-wide unions. The others recommended what they called a "wage policy," some sort of wage fixing or compulsory arbitration to make sure that excessive wage increases are avoided.

I am not going to make any proposals of my own. Let me simply say that much would be gained if public opinion at large and statesmen, politicians, and union leaders could be made to understand the simple truth: that if average wages rise faster than average labor productivity, we are necessarily faced with the disagreeable dilemma either to tolerate inflation and endanger the balance of payments, or to accept a certain amount of unemployment. If wage demands could be moderated and average money wages rose less than average labor productivity, there would be no inflation, prices could even fall a little, real wages would rise just as much or faster than at present, and we would be spared the recurring embarrassment of our international balance of payments running a deficit.

## Other Measures to Fight Inflation, Accelerate Growth, and Strengthen the Balance of Payments

Let me briefly mention a few other steps that could be taken to combat inflation, stimulate growth, and thereby strengthen the balance of payments, although some of these measures may, strictly speaking, not qualify as "over-all policies."

If farm support prices were gradually reduced (or if they had not been raised in 1961), the cost of living would go down, the tremendous waste of accumulating farm surpluses would be reduced, and more expansionary financial policies could be adopted to speed the transfer of labor and other resources from agriculture into industry.

If minimum wages were not raised, or still better, reduced, the wage push would be dampened with all the beneficial effects mentioned above. Even though most workers receive wages that are higher than the legal minimum, the minimum wage keeps some marginal workers out of employment, and a rise in the minimum wage level tends to push up the whole wage scale because employers find it necessary to maintain wage differentials.

If social security regulations could be changed so as to permit old-age pensioners to work as much as they like without losing their annuities, or if they were permitted, in case they so chose, to work and to earn a greater annuity later on, the supply of labor would be increased and the wage push reduced with all the beneficial consequences mentioned. This reform would also be extremely desirable from the social point of view. Enforced or induced idleness is the worst curse of old age.

The proposed reduction in the legal work week to 35 hours would be equivalent to a sharp wage push. It would stimulate inflation, reduce the rate of growth, weaken the balance of payments, and hence result in a slower rise in real income in general and of real wages in particular.

It is generally agreed that a change in tax policy toward a reduction of the exorbitant marginal rates of the personal income tax (which are higher than in any other country) and of the corporate profit tax is overdue and can be expected to stimulate investment and growth. Mounting Government expenditures and a large budget deficit are not circumstances calculated to make tax cuts easy. For that reason, it is very important to arrest the upward trend in Government expenditures and, wherever possible, to reverse it. A change in agricultural policies, e.g., would save billions of dollars.

Another area where it would be possible to strike a blow against inflation and for growth is tariff policy and import policy in general. If import duties and other import restrictions were reduced, American export industries, which are, in general, more efficient and pay higher wages than protected industries, would be favored, and protected industries which are, in general, less efficient and pay lower wages than the export industries would be exposed to sharper competition. They would either raise their efficiency, or contract and labor and other resources would gradually shift to the more efficient export industries.

It is true that the existence of unemployment and a deficit in the balance of payments does not make the present moment very propitious for a liberalization of trade policy. It should be possible, however, to make the transition smoother by inducing other countries to reduce their tariffs. The Trade Expansion Act of 1962 provides the means for doing that and one can only hope that it will be energetically used. Quantitative import restrictions too (e.g., those on petroleum products) should be negotiable and should be drastically reduced.* Above all, it should be remembered that unemployment and balance-of-payments deficits are not permanent, while liberalization of trade policies and a more rational international division of labor which would result from the liberalization are permanent structural reforms.

Politically, all these reforms—and others that could be mentioned—are, of course, very difficult. But administratively and economically they would be easy to carry out. Some of them would not cost anything, others (e.g., a change in agricultural policy) would even result in large savings to the Government and the taxpayer, and all of them would greatly benefit the economy and speed up growth.

* If the reduction of import restrictions on petroleum products were accompanied by a removal or relaxation of the drastic internal output restrictions which are now in force, especially in Texas, there need be no large increase in imports. Prices of petroleum products would fall; thus, inflationary pressures would be counteracted, which would make it easier to adopt more expansionary monetary and fiscal policies.

FOOTNOTE

[1] OEEC, Paris, 1961.

# Tax Policies, Economic Growth, and Strategy

*—NORMAN B. TURE**

*Summary*

*This discussion focuses on the use of taxation as an instrument of public policy for accelerating economic growth. Whether the degree of success in achieving this goal bears materially on the nation's national security is not an explicit concern in this paper. By the same token, no effort is made herein to develop national security criteria for evaluating the existing tax structure or proposals for tax changes.*

*In the context of this Conference, the relevant concept of economic growth is taken to be an expansion of the nation's production capabilities. As an objective of public policy, growth so defined becomes more meaningful. It increasingly warrants the emphasis it is very widely accorded the closer the economy approaches some optimum rate of utilization of its existing production potential. At full employment, the growth objective becomes one of allocating a larger share of available resources to those activities deemed to contribute to increasing the supply and productivity of factors of production. Insofar as tax policy is to be used for this purpose, we are concerned primarily with changes in the structure of the tax system, rather than with changes in the rate of revenue yield.*

*My discussion, accordingly, is concerned with the effect of changes in the manner in which a given amount of taxes are*

---

* The views expressed herein are my own and are not to be construed as conclusions or recommendations of the National Bureau of Economic Research.

*imposed on some of the components of economic growth. I con-
clude that it would probably require a very large shift of tax
burdens from the returns on capital to the returns of other
factors of production to effect an increase in the capital stock
adequate to increase the rate of expansion of full-employment
Gross National Product by one percentage point. I reach a
similar conclusion concerning the potential of tax changes for
accelerating capital retirement and replacement, i.e., modernizing the capital stock, sufficiently to alter significantly the rate
of expansion of GNP. Acceleration of tax rebates for losses,
and adoption of an averaging device might substantially reduce
the bias in the present tax treatment of business income against
small corporations, new companies, and unincorporated firms
in the assumption of risk, and thereby contribute to innovation
and growth, but these revisions might also serve to prolong
unduly the life of inefficient enterprises.*

*I can offer no firm conclusions concerning the potential of
tax revision for increasing the supply of personal effort, particularly on the part of highly specialized individuals. I am
equally uncertain about the efficiency of tax changes in accelerating the advance of knowledge, upon which, presumably, a
substantial part of the economy's long-run growth potential
depends.*

*These reservations by no means preclude the possibility of
effecting changes in the tax structure which would contribute
to faster economic growth. They do suggest, however, that the
magnitude of the anticipated gains from such tax changes is
often exaggerated and that a realistic appraisal of tax policy
in this regard calls for more modest aspirations than are often
revealed in popular discussions of the nation's economic prospects.*

---

The use of taxation as an instrument of public policy for
accelerating economic growth deserves our attention. The relationship between economic advance and our national security
requirements has been carefully delineated in Professor Mason's
paper and needs no elaboration here. It would be well, however, to emphasize that there is no evidence that inadequate

economic growth in the past has limited today's choice of strategies; in the same vein, no convincing argument has been made that our growth rate in the future is likely to be a decisive factor in the choice of strategy. Many advantages would surely follow from the economy's steadily expanding at an annual rate of, say, four per cent rather than three per cent. It is by no means clear, however, that the difference in total resource availability implied by this difference in growth rates would be meaningful in the choice among alternative strategies since a given rate of expansion of total production capability does not necessarily require an equal rate of increase in the highly specialized resources which may be required by various strategy alternatives. On the other hand, the use of tax policy to stimulate a faster rate of increase in the availability of the highly specialized resources required for defense strategy purposes will not necessarily contribute to and may even retard general economic expansion.

With this caution about the immediacy of the relationship of economic growth and strategy choice in mind, let us turn to the role of tax policy in accelerating economic growth. At the outset, let's be sure of what we mean by "economic growth." There are various concepts of economic growth, the utility of each of which is likely to vary with the purpose to which growth is to be put. In the present context, economic growth is most meaningfully thought of as expansion of production capability, i.e., as increases in the amount of agents of production and in their productivity. The appropriate time dimension of economic growth, so conceived, is quite long; the accretion to the nation's production capabilities which can be achieved in a short period of time, say a year, represents a small fraction of our existing output potential. Only the accumulation of such accretions over a longer period of time is relevant (by the same token, it is only for strategy alternatives which have a similarly long-range focus that economic growth can be a significant factor).

If this is indeed the correct way to conceive the policy objective, it follows that policy instruments should be used to assist the economy in attaining an optimum rate of use of its existing resources, in minimizing fluctuations in the rate of resource utilization around this optimum, and in reallocating resource use toward those activities which will increase the rate of expansion in the amount of resources and in their productivity. I will not dwell on the question of the optimum resource utilization rate, except to say that: (1) the average rate realized over the past 5½ years, as indicated by the rate of seasonally adjusted unemployment, is clearly substantially below the optimum; (2) the notion of an optimum rate is fraught with ambiguities because each of us will differently value the cost which may be involved in any given increment in the rate of resource use; and (3) there is no once and for all optimum rate, i.e., the ratio of expected social gain to expected social cost for any given increment in the rate of resource use is likely to change with considerable frequency in a dynamic environment.

The thrust of the first of these observations is that if this nation is really serious about accelerating growth in productive capability, it should be prepared to demonstrate that it can effectively use what it now has on hand. If the recent estimates of the Council of Economic Advisers are of the right order of magnitude, our current production rate falls about $35 billion short of that which could be attained, without significant changes in the general level of prices, if we more nearly achieved full utilization of our present resources. Moreover, if we assume that the resulting incremental product would be divided in roughly the same proportion as the existing GNP, a reduction in the unemployment rate to four per cent would result in an increase of between $4.5 billion and $5.0 billion in the amount of gross private domestic investment and of about $3.2 billion in the amount of investment in producers' durable equipment and new construction other than residential (in fact, it is more reasonable to assume that the share of this incremental output which would be allocated to capital formation would be significantly greater). While increases in private fixed capital are neither the only nor necessarily the most important components of the increase in productive capability over the long run, they do serve as a partial index of growth. This suggests that the first priority in growth policy should be realizing this one-shot increase in production potential through such changes in fiscal and other policies as may be necessary to bring about a full-employment level of aggregate demand. Indeed, the concern reflected in tax policy developments during 1961-62 with reallocation of resources rather than with increasing the over-all rate of resource utilization appears to many interested observers to be a case of cart before the horse.

But the horse is probably having enough trouble without our belaboring him further at this point. Let's assume, therefore, that the budgetary aspects of tax and fiscal policy will soon be so devised as to permit early attainment of full employment and will thereafter conform, with deviations of inconsequential magnitude and duration, to full-employment requirements. With this assumption, we've disposed of most of the accelerator contribution to increasing one component—the private capital stock —of the increase in productive capability. We must now focus on the use of tax policy to reallocate resources to provide for a more rapid increase in productive capability, hence output, than would otherwise be possible. In short, we want to effect those changes in the tax structure which will contribute to the economy's attaining a larger increase in the supply of factors of production and in their productivity than would otherwise be realized.

Let us note, before proceeding, that this last assertion presupposes that the welfare costs of the necessary shift in the use of fully employed resources have not been ignored in the policy decision to seek a higher rate of economic expansion. Other things being equal, the longer the lag between the change in policy aimed at effecting a shift in resource use and the actual realization of the increment to output resulting from the expanded productive capacity, the greater will be the welfare cost of this policy shift. Unless we assume the lag to be very short and/or unless we discount the future at a very low rate, we cannot blithely assume, as some of us seem to have, that a high growth objective involves no conflict with other welfare aspects of public policy.*

## Tax Policy and the Supply of Capital

One aim of tax policy for faster growth, as I've sketched it above, is to accelerate private capital formation. Since this policy is to be pursued, by hypothesis, in the context of full employment, the realization of this aim presupposes that the proportions of capital and labor in production are not fixed over the period which is encompassed by our growth objectives. Other things being equal, we should expect a relative increase in capital inputs if the nature of technical advance is such as to increase the productivity of capital relative to that of other

* In the following two sections of this discussion, the quantitative illustrations ignore entirely the lag between changes in policy variables and the desired changes in the dependent variable. The illustrations are for this reason, if for no other, quite unrealistic. They are intended only to indicate orders of magnitude under the most favorable assumptions applicable to the case in point.

factors of production. If technical progress is either neutral or results in a more rapid increase in labor productivity, a relative increase in capital inputs will require a reduction in the cost of capital and/or an increase in after-tax returns to capital, i.e., an increase in private returns to capital relative to its social net product. Changes in the tax structure to stimulate investment, therefore, should aim at increasing the rate of saving and/or should operate directly on the after-tax rate of return realizable on capital outlays.

The effectiveness of such tax changes depends in significant part on the assumed shape of the investment demand and saving functions. Assume, for example, that both are highly interest elastic. In this case, a tax change which shifted the saving curve to the right would result in a relatively large increase in capital formation, even if the tax change left the marginal efficiency of investment schedule unchanged. The same would be true if a tax change operated only on investment demand, leaving saving unaltered. On the other hand, suppose the saving—or supply of investible funds—schedule to be highly inelastic. A substantial tax-induced shift in investment demand, of itself, would give rise to relatively small increases in capital formation. By the same token, tax changes which merely increased the supply of funds would be of little consequence if investment demand were highly inelastic.

In a recent paper,[1] I attempted to provide some illustrative magnitudes of the response of outlays for fixed capital to tax changes which both increase net rate of return and enhance cash flow, taking into account varying assumptions about the elasticities of investment demand and the supply of investable funds. With respect to tax changes involving immediate tax savings for business taxpayers of about $2.5 billion a year (at 1962 levels of activity), the indicated increase in such capital expenditures ranged from a low of about $1.7 billion to a high of about $5.6 billion. With more restrictive and presumably more realistic assumptions about the respective elasticities, the estimate of the increase in capital outlays varied over a considerably narrower range, i.e., between $2.2 billion and $3.2 billion (these estimates roughly take into account the feedback effect on capital outlays from the expansion of aggregate demand generated by the initial increase in spending). These calculations point up the significance of the alternative implied assumptions and indicate the hazard in generalizing about the impact of such tax changes on capital formation in the absence of some fairly specific surmises about the shape of investment and saving functions.

A collateral conclusion is that structural tax changes to spur capital formation may require a substantial shift in tax burdens to effect a relatively small (short-run) increase in investment. It may well be that under conditions of high employment and with favorable anticipations about the maintenance of such conditions the elasticity of aggregate investment demand is relatively high, so that the demand response to such tax changes may be relatively large. On the other hand, these are the circumstances in which the elasticity of supply of investable funds is likely to be relatively low. Very tentatively, I suggest that the upper limit on the (short-run) increase in outlays for fixed capital resulting from structural tax changes under these circumstances may be the amount of the shift in taxes (feedback effects needn't be taken into account in the full-employment case, since by hypotheses aggregate demand cannot be permitted to increase significantly in response to the initial increase in capital outlays).

The implications of this conclusion may be seen from an arithmetic example. Suppose the US economy now had realized the favorable conditions specified above. GNP would be of the order of magnitude of $600 billion (using the Council of Economic Advisers' estimate of the gap between full-employment and actual GNP). Suppose further that the policy objective is to increase the growth rate of full-employment GNP by one percentage point. In the first year, this would mean an increase in total output $6 billion more than would otherwise be realized. If this is to be done by accelerating the increase in the fixed capital stock, the necessary increase in the first year would be of the order of magnitude of $40 billion to $45 billion, if Denison's estimates of the relationship between capital inputs and products are used.* If the surmise offered above, that the

* Cf. Edward F. Denison, *The Sources of Economic Growth in the United States and the Alternatives Before Us* (Committee for Economic Development, January, 1962), chap. 12. The relationship estimated here is between gross product and gross capital formation, whereas Denison's measures are of net capital formation and national income. I have used the gross relationship only because popular discussion of economic growth is generally expressed in terms of GNP changes. There are divergent views concerning the effect on potential GNP of a given increase in the capital stock, but even if the most generous of these alternative estimates is used, it would nevertheless require very large shifts in tax burdens to effect a one percentage point increase in the full-employment growth rate, using my assumption about the effectiveness of such tax changes.

amount of the increase in capital formation is not likely to exceed the amount of this shift in taxes, is correct, the amount of such a shift in turn would have to be enormous.* Indeed, it would be impossible at the present time to effect a shift of the order of magnitude of $40-45 billion, since present Federal income tax liabilities on returns to capital fall considerably short of this amount.

These estimates assume that the composition of the additions to the capital stock would be in the same proportion as the existing stock. If, however, the additional capital formation were channeled into fixed business capital, the relationship between the change in potential output and in capital would be somewhat greater. Under my assumption about the effectiveness of a shift in tax liabilities, it might be necessary to shift only $30 billion, instead of $40-45 billion, in Federal taxes from returns on capital to other income.

There are, of course, alternative criteria upon the basis of which more realistic and hence more modest shifts in tax burdens may be sought. In the formation of public policy, however, it might be well to proceed on the assumption, at least as a first approximation, that the changes in *ex ante* saving and investment functions and therefore in the amount of capital formation from such tax revision will also be quite modest.[2]

## Tax Policy and Modernization of Capital

Modernizing capital, as well as increasing the size of the capital stock, has become an important objective of tax policy aimed at accelerating economic growth. Underlying this emphasis is the assumption, which scarcely needs stating, that the newer the physical production facilities, the more productive they will be. The relevance of this premise as a matter of economic policy, however, is not entirely self-evident. Modernization, after all, requires commitment of resources capable of alternative uses. In the context of a fully-employed economy, a policy change which results in allocating a larger proportion of available resources to the production of new production facilities involves the loss of the alternative output of these resources (quite apart from the frictional costs incurred in resource shift-

* This line of argument assumes that the supply of labor is completely inelastic with respect to income. To the extent that this assumption is relaxed, the necessary increase in capital to effect the desired increase in output is greater than indicated above. Cf. Denison, *op. cit.*, p. 130.

ing). Under conditions of perfect competition and a neutral tax system, presumably, the average age of the capital stock should at any time (ignoring lags in adjusting the capital stock) be optimum in the sense that the resource commitment required for a further reduction in the age would involve an opportunity cost greater than the increase in productivity. Since competition is not perfect and the tax system is not neutral, there may well be net social gains to be derived from tax adjustments which impel accelerated retirement and replacement of production facilities, but this does not mean that net gains will continue to be realized as such acceleration is increased.

To a substantial extent, the modernization objective is indistinguishable from the capital stock expansion objective. The assumption herein, which seems reasonable, is that capital additions will almost always incorporate technical advance; a policy of encouraging a higher rate of capital formation, therefore, is simultaneously one of modernizing the stock. But presumably, modernization can occur whether or not the stock expands.

Before discussing tax devices which might spur modernization, let's briefly consider some of the magnitudes involved. Suppose, for example, that the heroic measures required for an increase in capital outlays of the order of magnitude suggested in the preceding section were undertaken and that all of the resulting increase in capital outlays was for fixed capital. Suppose also, in the first instance, that the additional $40 billion to $45 billion were net as well as gross additions, i.e., were not offset by retirements of existing facilities. The effect of these additions would be to lower the mean age of the stock of fixed business capital, as estimated by the Office of Business Economics, by about three-fifths of a year, i.e., from about 10 years to 9.4 years.[3] Next assume that all of the $40-45 billion represented replacement of existing facilities. In this event, the reduction in mean age would obviously be significantly greater than in the former case, but cannot be estimated without some knowledge of the shape of the existing distribution. Merely for illustrative purposes, assume that the average age of the assets retired and replaced is 25 years old. In this case, the mean age of the stock would fall to about 8.4 years.

What would be the effect on the rate of economic growth of reductions in the average age of the capital stock of proportions such as those illustrated above? Denison estimates that each year's reduction in the age of the capital stock would increase the national production by three-eighths of a percentage point.[4] In the first instance, therefore, the *modernization* effect of the $40-45 billion addition would be to increase our full-employment GNP from $600 billion to $601.4 billion. In the second instance, the *modernization* effect would be an increase in production of the order of magnitude of $3.6 billion (taking into account the effect of an increase in the size of the stock as well as the reduction in its age, of course, would mean that the increase in product in the first instance would substantially exceed that in the second; this illustration focuses solely on the age effect).

What kinds of tax changes might impel acceleration of net retirement and replacement of capital facilities? In many respects, the approach incorporated in the 1962 revision of depreciation rules would appear to be effective. In essence, this approach offers the taxpayer a *quid pro quo:* in exchange for the greater cash flow and increased profitability resulting from a reduction in service lives of depreciable facilities for tax purposes, the taxpayer must agree to conform the period during which such facilities are retained in use to the service life he uses in computing depreciation charges for tax purposes. If he fails to do so, service life upon which annual tax depreciation changes are computed will be increased and the taxpayer will forfeit the cash flow and rate of return benefits of faster tax depreciation.[5]

As yet, of course, there is no experience upon which to evaluate the effectiveness of this approach. On a priori grounds, it seems reasonable to assume that some acceleration of retirements and replacements will result. Moreover, if the response is deemed inadequate, the inducements could always be made greater. Nevertheless, the order of magnitude of this acceleration would surely fall far short of that indicated in the illustration above. In other words, tax policy can indeed contribute to faster growth by inducing some reduction in the average age of the capital stock, but this contribution is likely to be very small relative to the increase in the growth rate to which the nation has been asked to aspire.

**Tax Policy and Risk Assumption**

Much of the discussion in the preceding two sections has proceeded along mechanistic lines which ignore risk and tax provisions pertaining thereto in business policies concerning capital formation. If we assume that the income taxation of returns to capital is perfectly proportional and affords perfect loss off-set, this procedure is acceptable.[6] For small corporations, some new corporations, and unincorporated business taxpayers, how-ever, the assumption is not valid. It is conceivable, therefore, that structural tax changes which focused explicitly on more effectively averaging business income fluctuations and on more rapid tax rebates of losses would contribute to expansion of the rate of capital formation. Such tax changes might also enhance the dynamic quality of economic activity which is quite generally regarded as an important impetus for growth.

In the case of large, established corporations, the present tax provisions conform closely to the neutrality conditions indi-cated above. The degree of progression in effective tax rates for such companies is quite limited; quite substantial positive income fluctuations give rise to minor changes in the effective rate of tax. Moreover, the three-year carry-back and five-year carry-forward of losses appear to provide substantial assurance of effective recoupment of losses. A more favorable investment climate for large corporations could, of course, be provided by deliberately biasing the tax provisions to afford a greater par-ticipation by the Treasury in losses relative to its participation in gains.

In the case of small corporations and unincorporated busi-nesses, however, there is substantial effective progression in tax liabilities. The tax is, accordingly, biased against ventures in which relatively large income fluctuations are anticipated. More-over, the loss offset provisions are less than perfect, since the Government's rate of participation in losses is likely to be less than its rate of participation in gains.

For new companies, whether incorporated or unincorporated, the effectiveness of the loss offset provision depends exclusively on the certainty of the loss carry-forward. These companies must rely primarily on profits in the five years succeeding the loss year to recoup the losses popularly supposed to be quite general in the early years of new enterprises. Prospective re-coupment in the five-year carry-forward period may be inade-quate to insure survival even if the company's subsequent income potential is deemed to be relatively great.

Accelerating tax refunds generated by losses, even to the extent of providing negative tax payments in lieu of loss carry-overs, is sometimes recommended as a means of improving the tax climate for risk assumption. There is, however, a hazard in such a change. The more liberal the treatment of losses, the greater is likely to be the tax shelter for inefficient uses of resources. Against the favorable growth effects resulting from greater risk assumption one must weigh the negative effects from impeding the liquidation of unsuccessful enterprises. A priori reasoning, or at least mine, yields no unambiguous predictions of the net effect.

## Tax Policy and Personal Effort

Among the proponents of substantial reductions in the upper-bracket individual income tax rates, an argument advanced with a vigor matched only by its sincerity is that the present rates have a significantly adverse effect on incentives for personal effort. This effect is deemed to be the more pronounced the greater the incremental reward for additional effort, i.e., the higher the bracket rate at which such additional rewards will be taxed. In the context of this argument, increasing incentives for personal effort would significantly contribute to a higher rate of economic growth, implying that a serious gap exists between the actual and potential contribution of upper-bracket individuals to socially valuable production.

In theory, the proposition has merit. An income tax reduces the price of leisure, in the sense that the amount of income available to the taxpayer which is foregone by diverting an hour's time from work is less after the tax than before. If the tax bears differentially on rewards to different kinds of effort, presumably its effect in reducing the total amount of effort will be mitigated to the extent that the taxpayer is able to divert effort to those activities the income from which is taxed less heavily. Such an income tax, accordingly, may very well divert effort from fully taxable to fully or partially tax-sheltered activities. This effect of the tax on the composition of effort may well involve a loss in social product.

Taxes have income as well as price effects, however. The income effect refers to the fact that the taxpayer may seek to offset through greater effort, hence greater income, the reduction in his claims to goods and services, both present and future, effected by the tax. The magnitude of this effect depends on how closely leisure substitutes for the goods and services foregone. If the marginal utility of wealth and income decreases as wealth and income rise, and if the marginal disutility of effort increases as effort increases, it might be assumed that the income effect of a tax on the return to effort would weaken as income and wealth increase. Given these conditions, we should expect to find the income effect of the tax dominant at low levels of income and the substitution effect dominant at high income levels. In other words, the tax should have little effect on the amount of effort when income is low and an increasingly adverse effect as income rises.

This kind of relationship, presumably, should prevail whether the income tax is proportional, regressive, or progressive, although the relative over-all weight of income and price effects would differ. On this line of reasoning, a regressive tax should least deter effort, since it would impose relatively greater burdens at the low end of the income distribution, where income effects are presumed to dominate, and relatively lighter burdens at the upper end of the income distribution where price effects supposedly are significant. A progressive income tax, by the same token, should be most detrimental with respect to personal effort, and its adverse effects should be most pronounced among highly compensated individuals, whose contributions to growth of output are quite widely presumed to be disproportionately great.

Empirical investigations in this area offer few clues for determining either the direction or weight of income taxation on personal effort, let alone what might be expected from reasonable changes in the tax. The research by Clarence Long, dealing with aggregative measures of the labor force and participation rates, shows no trends which may be clearly associated with taxation development.[7] The study by George Break, based on interviews with accountants and solicitors in the United Kingdom, is inconclusive; except for those interviewees at very high bracket rates, about the same number of respondents showed incentive as disincentive effects of taxation.[8]

Thomas Sanders' study of tax effects on executives' efforts showed similar conclusions, i.e., among the executives in his sample, as many worked harder because of taxes as worked less. Sanders also found, however, that some executives refused promotion or attractive offers from other companies when the change meant a substantially greater amount of responsibility and relatively little increase in after-tax compensation. He also found a considerable amount of executive effort devoted to minimizing tax burdens.[9]

Among some who hold to the view that the increase in the level and progression of individual income tax liabilities has not impaired personal effort, a frequently offered explanation is that the progression is more apparent than real. Effort on the part of highly specialized executives and technical personnel, it is alleged, is rewarded to a substantial extent in forms for which differentially lower tax liabilities are provided in the tax law. For many such individuals, presumably, the maximum marginal rate on most of the incremental compensation for additional effort is the capital gains rate.

Differentiating tax liability on the basis of the form of compensation is hotly criticized by those for whom the equity criterion outweighs other standards in evaluating tax policy. But abstracting from this criterion, it is by no means clear that additional encouragement for tax-sheltered compensation arrangements would contribute to greater or more productive effort by highly specialized members of the labor force. There is no reason to assume that all forms of compensation are equally efficient means of rewarding effort, and it is certainly possible that increasing the use of differential tax provisions as a means of alleviating the tax burden on incremental returns for personal effort might result in an excessively complex and inefficient system of personal rewards.

An alternative explanation of the difficulty in discerning any massive impact of the income tax on effort is the familiar "man does not live by bread alone" hypothesis. In this view, the non-pecuniary rewards accruing to positions of responsibility significantly outweigh those which take a taxable form in determining the effort expended in discharging these responsibilities. The individual for whom this is true may very well add his voice to the complaints against the income tax, but his continued devotion to doing his job better than any one else possibly could indicates that he is in fact largely immune to the disincentives of high, graduated income taxes.

If we were weighing these propositions in the context of considerable slack in the economy, it would seem quite reasonable to include substantial upper-bracket rate reduction in a general program of tax reduction to spur a higher rate of resource utilization. In the full-employment context I've assumed to be appropriate for discussion of structural tax change and economic growth, however, the revenue loss, modest though it may be, from such rate cuts must be offset by increases elsewhere. We should acknowledge our uncertainty whether the net effects on growth would be consequential.

## Tax Policy and Technical Advance

The importance for economic growth of the level of attainment in the arts and sciences and of advances in these fields has received increasing emphasis in recent years. A number of quantitative analyses have concluded that technical advance (an ambiguous term which includes a rise in the general level of education and skills as well as extension of exploitable knowledge) accounts for a relatively large proportion of measured economic growth.[10] Such advance contributes to growth because it extends the outside limit on the contribution which may be made by the activities which incorporate better technological practice in production. It also creates new wants and opportunities, important impulses for growth-generating activities. In the context of this discussion, we are concerned with the contribution tax policy might make to accelerating the enlargement of the nation's inventory of knowledge and technological potential, rather than with narrowing the gap between that potential and the average level of its exploitation.

One important aspect of this concern is the extent to which changes in the tax structure might encourage greater and more productive private research and developmental activities. The present law is generally regarded as quite liberal in this respect. Business costs of R&D, apart from outlays for depreciable facilities, may be expensed in the year incurred or may be capitalized and amortized over a five-year period, at the taxpayer's option. Proceeds from the disposition of patents are treated as capital gains, subject to a maximum rate of tax of 25 per cent, rather than as ordinary income. Tax subsidization of the costs of research and development and preferential tax treatment of some of the returns on the capital created by research and development presumably afford significant stimuli for private effort in this area. I have no evidence to offer, however, concerning the significance of these favorable tax provisions for the volume of this activity. By the same token, although I am confident of the direction of the effect of further liberalization of these tax provisions, I can offer no judgment concerning the size of this effect and whether the net effect of the shift in tax burdens would warrant incurring the costs involved.

On the other hand, the very substantial expansion of R&D activity in the federal establishment and of the R&D component in the very large amount of defense, space, and related program contracts would appear to be much weightier influences on the volume and composition of such activity in the private sector of the economy than the tax provision cited above. Similarly, the institutionalizing of research and developmental activity, I should think, has involved substantial economies of scale in this activity.

Another aspect of the relationship of tax policy to technical advance concerns the possibility of raising the level of educational achievement through tax changes. The work of Schultz and Becker,[11] among others, lends substantial support to the appealing a priori view that a relatively modest investment in additional education and training yields a relatively large increase in productivity. Financial considerations, apparently, are the major limitation on the extent of education in the case of a substantial number of young men and women who are otherwise qualified and whose contribution to total output presumably could be materially enhanced by such training. To the extent that lack of personal financial capacity is indeed the important limiting factor, it would seem likely that changes in the income tax could be effected to mitigate this constraint. Goode has suggested, for example, that students be allowed to deduct currently the costs they meet themselves in undertaking advanced education and to capitalize and write off against their subsequent earnings the expenditures on their behalf furnished by parents, relatives, or friends.[12]

This proposal might go far toward eliminating the bias in the present law against this form of intangible investment. On the other hand, other activities which differ from formal education primarily in that they are likely to be less organized or routine may involve the same kind of investment in increasing an individual's productivity, even if on a more limited scale. Extension of the same kind of tax treatment to these other cultural investments would very quickly raise the problem of differentiating consumption intangibles from investment intangibles, a distinction which indeed cannot be sharply drawn in the case of advanced education itself.

A similar problem of fine distinctions arises under the present law, which deals with the question in a highly arbitrary way. If an employer finances a worker's training, the costs are deductible by the employer and are not included in the employee's income, if the training is deemed to be for the employer's benefit. If the employee undertakes to provide the educational training for himself, however, he may deduct the expenses involved if the training is to maintain his present position but cannot deduct the expenses if the training is to advance his position (unless that advance itself is an employer-imposed condition for continued employment).

This arbitrariness is all the more acute since it is invoked in distinguishing among cases in which the individual's advanced training is relatively more closely associated with his future earnings than in the general case of advanced education. It would seem appropriate, in terms of both the equity and growth criteria of tax policy, to permit the capitalization of such expenditures and their amortization over some reasonably short period of time, e.g., five years.

There are, of course, any number of modifications which might be made in the tax structure to encourage activities conducive to advancing knowledge in all fields. For example, raising the ceiling on the deduction of charitable contributions would undoubtedly result in a larger volume of giving to qualified research and educational institutions and in time lead to an expansion of their activities. But any such proposal involves issues in connection with other criteria of tax policy, with respect to which the a priori answers are not unambiguous. Moreover, since our context is full employment, and since the shift in claims over resources involved in any such proposal would not be costless, we would want to be more confident than we can now be of the magnitude of gains and losses involved.

Finally, technical advance is not a matter merely of the amount of resources committed to research and development nor of the number of individuals with a given number of years of educational experience. It is rather a complex of myriad activities involving the organization and channeling of intellectual effort. The basic determinants of each of these activities are probably rooted deeply in the nation's cultural history and, as such, heavily insulated against tax influences. We should not be disappointed, therefore, if acceptable tax revisions to encourage these activities do not produce instant accretions to knowledge.

### Conclusions

This discussion might well leave an impression of complete pessimism concerning the potential of structural tax revision for accelerating the nation's economic development. Actually, my purpose has been rather to show that the expectations often expressed in this regard are likely to be more optimistic than either facts or analysis warrant, particularly if the structural revisions are to be sufficiently limited in magnitude to be realistic for a stable social and political order. This is not to say, however, that such revisions are totally ineffective nor that they should be eschewed because their consequences for the economy's growth rate may be more accurately measured in tenths of a percentage point than in terms of the two, three, or four percentage point increases which enter so readily into popular discussions of our economic prospects.

It must also be emphasized that a severe constraint has been imposed in this discussion, i.e., it is concerned with increasing the growth rate of a fully-employed, highly-developed economy in which relatively little, if any, incremental gain in output potential can be realized by fuller utilization of resources and in which realization of additional economies of scale is likely to be of relatively little consequence for the rate of advance. Achieving and maintaining full employment, or at least significantly reducing the frequency, amplitude, and duration of deviations therefrom, would surely result in a more rapid rate of growth than that emerging from a past characterized by significant instability. This discussion, accordingly, has been concerned only with the additional growth that might be achieved at the margin in a fully-employed economy by relatively limited shifts in the composition of resource use and output.

Structural tax changes can contribute to attaining the latter objective. Indeed, it is unlikely to be attained in the absence of some changes in the tax system. Fundamentally at issue is not whether such tax changes can affect the rate of the nation's economic expansion, but whether the relatively small increments in the growth rate warrant the possible losses with respect to other objectives of tax policy.

## FOOTNOTES

[1] "Tax Reform: Depreciation Problems," presented at the 75th Annual Meeting of the American Economic Association, December 28, 1962.

[2] For a more detailed examination of the possibilities of increasing the national saving rate by structural tax changes, see my "Growth Aspects of Federal Tax Policy," *The Journal of Finance*, XVII, No. 2 (May, 1962), pp. 269-79. For discussions of an alternative route to a higher national saving rate, see Musgrave, "Growth with Equity," presented at the 75th

Annual Meeting of the American Economic Association, December 28, 1962, and Joint Economic Committee, *Staff Report on Employment, Growth, and Price Levels*, 86th Cong., 1st Sess., December 24, 1959, chap. 8, especially pp. 255-74.

[3] U.S. Department of Commerce, Office of Business Economics, "Expansion of Fixed Capital in the United States," *Survey of Current Business* (November, 1962), pp. 9-18.

[4] Cf. Denison, *op. cit.*, chapter 21. James W. Knowles, on the other hand, has attributed a substantially greater increase in output to modernization of the capital stock. See his "The Potential Economic Growth in the United States," Study Paper No. 20, *Study of Employment, Growth, and Price Levels*, Joint Economic Committee, 86th Cong., 2nd Sess., 1960.

[5] Cf. Ture, *op. cit.*, section B-1.

[6] Cf. Richard Musgrave and Evesey Domar, "Proportional Income Taxation and Risk-Taking," *Quarterly Journal of Economics*, LVIII (May, 1944), pp. 387-422, and James E. Tobin, "Liquidity Preference as Behavior Towards Risk," *Review of Economic Studies*, XXV, No. 67 (February, 1958), pp. 65-87.

[7] Clarence D. Long, "Impact of the Federal Income Tax on Labor Force Participation," *Federal Tax Policy for Economic Growth and Stability*, Papers Submitted by Panelists Appearing Before the Subcommittee on Tax Policy, Joint Committee on the Economic Report, Joint Committee Print, 84th Cong., 1st Sess., November 9, 1955, pp. 153-66, and *The Labor Force Under Changing Income and Employment* (Princeton: Princeton University Press, 1958).

[8] George F. Break, "Income Taxes and Incentives to Work: An Empirical Study," *American Economic Review* (September, 1957), pp. 529-49. See also his "Income Tax Rates and Incentives to Work and to Invest," *Tax Revision Compendium*, Committee on Ways and Means, Committee Print, 1959, pp. 2247-55.

[9] Thomas H. Sanders, *Effects of Taxation on Executives* (Boston: 1951).

[10] Cf. Robert M. Solow, "Technical Change and the Aggregate Production Function," *Review of Economics and Statistics*, XXXIX, No. 3 (August, 1957), pp. 312-20; James W. Knowles, *op. cit.*; and Edward F. Denison, *op. cit.*, and "How to Raise the High-Employment Growth Rate by One Percentage Point," *American Economic Review*, LII, No. 2 (May, 1962), pp. 67-75.

[11] Cf. Theodore W. Schultz, "Education and Economic Growth," *Social Forces Influencing American Education, 1961* (Chicago: University of Chicago Press), and Gary S. Becker, "Underinvestment in College Education," *American Economic Review*, I (May, 1960), pp. 346-54.

[12] Richard Goode, "Educational Expenditures and the Income Tax," *Economics of Higher Education*, US Department of Health, Education, and Welfare, Office of Education (1962).

# Industrial and Human Resources in US Strategy*

—*IRVING H. SIEGEL*

## Summary

*Since resources, strategy, and the larger environment are interdependent, something is said about the second and third categories before explicit treatment of the first.*

*Despite a possible calming of surface relationships with the USSR, it is assumed that the policies of so-called "peaceful coexistence" and "wars of liberation" admit no comfortable equilibrium between so-called "capitalism" and so-called "communism." Guerrilla action, sabotage, and subversion will probably spread to the Hemisphere through Cuba. Despite the Sino-Soviet schism, Chinese intransigency may discourage softening of Soviet positions. Disruptive strains will be evident in the Western Alliance as well as in Eastern Europe. Unsponsored neo-imperialist wars conducted by younger nations may also become a feature of the coming decade.*

*Four orders of strategic commitment are briefly described—custodial, managerial, entrepreneurial, and creative—and it is proposed that a shift of the United States toward the latter two is both domestically feasible and internationally desirable. Thus, the United States should go beyond essentially defensive measures and use its resources dynamically to limit Soviet strategic options and, more positively, to improve the world prospect for*

---

* The views expressed in this paper should not be attributed to the organization with which the author is associated.

*our version of peace with justice, diversity, and economic development. Perhaps more appropriate than a race into space would be a race in which we lead for objectives closer to the Soviet citizen's heart—e.g., consumer goods, shorter hours, and more civil liberties.*

*Despite complaints about the sluggishness of our economic performance, the US production base is capable of supporting an impressive array of initiatives. Many features of strength are considered, and certain needed improvements, too—particularly in the realms of research and specialized manpower, because knowledge is a fundamental strategic resource.*

*No country is so richly endowed with resources—and time— that it can afford to wait for putative enemies to mount their varied challenges in different parts of the world. Their military capacity must be degraded by direct external pressure and by the encouragement of internal divisive and centrifugal tendencies. Non-military initiatives must be pushed in the next decade to diminish the military potential of antagonistic nations while the West also strives in positive ways to improve its own posture.*

---

**Interdependent Categories**

A proper development of the theme assigned to this paper requires the recognition of two kinds of interdependence involving resources and strategy. The first kind is bilateral, direct: the volume, varieties, and proportions of the available physical and human resources can, should, and do influence—and, in turn, are in some measure responsive to—the choice of a nation's strategy. The second kind of interdependence is multilateral, contextual: the process of mutual conditioning is not confined to resources and strategy but also embraces the categories of the larger common environment. Thus, resource supplies and strategy decisions tend to shape and accommodate each other; and, in addition, they affect, and are affected by, a great variety of domestic, international, and natural factors, such as the behavior of putative enemies and other nations, the state of technology, and economic and political circumstances at home and abroad. The two kinds of interaction need not be spontaneous, predictably precise, or complete; and unequal weights apply to the forces and constraints that are identified or deemed significant.

Perhaps the concepts of direct and contextual reciprocity seem obvious once they are verbalized.* In any case, they are useful for the organization and exposition of our ideas, and it is for this reason that they are introduced here. By acknowledging the mutual adaptation of resources, strategy, and their larger environment, we are enabled to maintain a dimensionality and perspective that could be lost when the subject of a conference has to be distributed among a number of panels and a still larger number of papers.

Our inquiry into the role of industrial and human resources in shaping and supporting the strategy of the next decade or so accordingly begins with a brief statement on the environmental outlook. We then proceed to a consideration of feasible or preferred strategies and the complementary and compatible contribution of resources.

**Environmental Factors**

The environment offers both challenges and opportunities; and the business of strategy, as a nation like ours must see it, is not simply to guide the use of resources for the containment of current and anticipated challenges. The United States should, in addition, look toward the transformation of many challenges into opportunities and toward even more critical revision of the environment. Thus, our self-declared enemies have exploitable weaknesses, as well as evident or presumed strengths, and the weaknesses offer handles for conceivable initiatives of our own. Furthermore, a leading nation may reasonably look beyond the resolution of conflicts with visible antagonists to establishment in the world of a more "peaceable kingdom" that is consistent with its own values and aspirations.

We should note that the environment also includes many non-material elements of our national life which are not normally reckoned in tallies of resource supplies and deficiencies. For example, popular attitudes and the quality of political leadership, also, will significantly affect our future strategic posture; and, since these are somewhat modifiable, they also offer both challenges and opportunities.

---

* In his speech at West Point, December 5, 1962, Dean Acheson noted that "people often forget . . . in discussing foreign policy the interrelation of ends and means." Specifically, proposals on NATO's future should recognize that military plans, political policy, and economic instruments and decisions "are all interdependent and mutually interacting."

For policy-makers, a bias of pessimism is useful in appraisal of the future international environment. The penalty for a nation's underestimation of the total threat is, after all, much more onerous than the economic "waste" that may be incurred through overestimation. Furthermore, a nation which occupies a position of leadership also has to provide in its contingency planning for failures of friendly nations to respond decisively, on time, and fully to the requirements of common emergency. It should be noted, however, that the redundancies of preparedness tend to be exaggerated. Thus, some of the "waste" incident to provision for the comprehensive defense of an advanced industrial society is actually reclaimable in the form of a positive contribution to the supply of scarce civilian skills and to the level of sophistication of non-military technology.

The West should find a stimulus to strategic innovation, rather than a cause for complacency, in the possibility that certain striking recent developments foretoken a favorable turning point in history. The very recital of these developments—for example, the partial Soviet withdrawal from Cuba under duress, the initial disturbed reaction of neutrals to the voluntarily limited Chinese invasion of India, and the exacerbation of the Sino-Soviet dispute on the most effective anti-Western strategy—highlights their ambiguous significance. If the United States assumes special risks and costs incident to leadership, these and similar events that have attractive potentials but have no absolute meaning might well be turned to good account.

Our self-declared enemies' constantly reiterated goal of "ultimate victory" for so-called "communism" over so-called "capitalism" should be viewed as fixed, while their tactics, timing, and targets are subject to change according to vulnerabilities, resistances, successes, failures, and intra-Bloc pressures. In the first instance, authoritative enemy assertions of aims, antagonisms, and methods should be taken as seriously as Hitler's should have been. They should be appraised in the light of other information and evidence rather than dismissed offhand as "just propaganda." In published Western analyses of Soviet intentions, the considered testimony of Khrushchev and Mao is too often treated as irrelevant, immaterial, and incompetent.

The Soviet shock in Cuba will presumably encourage greater emphasis on low-temperature stratagems that do not invite searing nuclear response. "Wars of liberation," it will be recalled, were candidly promised in Khrushchev's speech of

January 6, 1961, and they also fit into the Chinese program for the future, despite other Sino-Soviet differences. The meaning of "peaceful coexistence," which so many of our journalists and incomplete strategists do not recognize as a term of art, was also spelled out in that speech; and, for some time to come, this avenue toward an offensive peace, toward "capitalist" no-existence, should commend itself to Russian leaders as far safer than direct nuclear confrontation. We may expect new invitations to cliffs disguised as summits; new cynical diplomatic efforts to gull the West into signing the equivalent of the Stockholm Pledge not to take up arms against the Soviet Union in the event of war; new efforts to divide or divert the West with Pavlovian propaganda, blandishments of trade, and offers of limited cooperation on popular projects (e.g., concerning nuclear arms control and space exploration). Meanwhile, stubborn guerrilla warfare, subversion, and sabotage will be promoted in many parts of the world; and fortified Cuba could serve as a base for coordinating Latin American infiltration, as a first resort for defectors, and as a source of future direct threats against the United States. Clearly, despite the assurance given by the Secretary-General of the United Nations in his Johns Hopkins address, it is premature to believe that the shrimp is learning to whistle and that the "Era of the Ruptured Dove" is drawing to a welcome close.

While Moscow peddles its "peaceful coexistence" undiluted with such "bourgeois" connotations as "ideological disarmament," [1] Peking will presumably continue to call for dispatch of the "paper tiger imperialists" without the prior administration of tranquilizers. Attainment of a nuclear capability may be expected to intensify Chinese belligerency, to fortify her demand for greater Sino-Soviet militancy, to encourage her deeper involvement in protracted wars in Asia, and to spur her quest for doctrinal dominance in Cuba and in the revolutionary councils of rural and newly industrializing nations of both hemispheres. Constant open goading by China, furthermore, may oblige the Soviet Union to return toward Stalinist rigidities, to adopt sterner tactics in dealing with the West, and to take occasional rash action.

In looking ahead, it is natural to ignore, or call for inadequate cover against, the storms that will come from clouds not yet visible or not yet larger than a man's hand. Thus, the general preoccupation with danger of a nuclear holocaust may lead to unrealistic neglect of other plausible horrors—those that may result, for example, from the use of chemical and biological agents and powerful directed-energy pulses, or from the control of weather. Similarly, the emphasis on spectacular weapons may lead to an incorrect estimate of the potentials and of the actual future roles of: (a) psychological and economic harassment, and (b) the export of technicians and technical information to less developed lands. Furthermore, the long experience of tension between two large aggregates of nations may discourage forecasts of disassociations, of the proliferation of "third forces," and of the eruption of "unsponsored," localized, neo-imperialist wars involving former "victims" of "classical" imperialism.

A prolonged period of relatively uneventful "coexistence," in which crises are too few, too short, or geographically too remote to be deeply felt by all members of an alliance, is sure to attenuate current cohesive forces. The West should not consider itself more resistant than the Sino-Soviet camp to ideological erosion in the presence of non-ideological irritants. NATO members, as well as Japan, may find—in the general growth of industrial capacity, in the rise of domestic wages and the compression of profits, in the proliferation of common markets in both hemispheres, and in the uncertainties generated by expanding economic competition—ample temptation for the accommodation of self-declared enemies and sufficient non-military outlet for popular energy and enterprise. At this point, it is well to recall Stalin's last testament, with its vision of the disintegration of Western unity in an intense struggle for trade.

The spread of modern technology will create new centers of military decision that may be hard to bring under international or big-power discipline. As nuclear and other weapons of mass destruction become technically and economically available to an increasing number of nations, these *parvenus* may prove no less reluctant than the originators of the lethal instruments to forego establishment of "independent" forces. Countries that newly experience the mutual reinforcement of national pride and industrial power may try, as others before them, to realize their "manifest destiny" in at least small-scale imperialism. We have already witnessed a penchant of new nations, officially still aggrieved by past subjugation, to impose their own design for "progress" on weaker or less adventurous neighbors. The time seems right for the rediscovery of Anatole France's *Penguin Island* (hard by Orwell's *Animal Farm*!). Finally, the Congo affair suggests that the United Nations may become an anomalous instrument of coercion for use especially against minor non-conformists and minor disturbers of the peace.

## Strategic Options

What does this quick survey of the environment imply for future strategic objectives of the United States? A nation with our heritage, ideals, resources, and international responsibilities surely should seek boldly to redesign its surroundings rather than adjust to Procrustean beds of others' devising. It need not smugly proclaim an "American Century" for carrying out this broad aim; but it can, by word and deed, revitalize its image as the "world's best hope," strikingly refute the doctrine of inevitable victory for "communism," and more convincingly lead the world's quest for "peace with justice" and greater general economic abundance.

In the spectrum of conceivable strategies, we may discern four different levels of commitment, two of which are essentially defensive and two of which are more assertive and more likely to lead to desirable resolutions of the troublesome issues of our time. These four are "ideal types," and they are observable only in impure form or in mixture. A fifth level of commitment is ruled out as utterly inappropriate for the United States; it corresponds to defeatist "infra-strategies" compatible, for example, with the proposition that "we are bound to be either 'red' or 'dead' so we might as well select the first alternative." Rejection of this kind of a posture does not mean, of course, that pursuit of more responsible strategies guarantees avoidance of undesirable results. Rather, we may expect better results only as we aim higher; and, even in a world under nuclear arms, it remains prudent to pursue values beyond survival.

The two conservative strategies, which we believe to be less suitable than the two "forward" ones, may be designated as *custodial* and *managerial*. Both accept the environment largely as "given" and look primarily toward adjustments that are consistent with personal and national survival. Both try to maintain the status quo, to "muddle through," to achieve an equilibrium with things as they are rather than the dominance of what ought to be. The custodial posture involves serial response to enemy initiatives and to unanticipated events. It makes virtues of improvisation and the mere act of holding fast. It adapts to siege instead of contemplating remedy through counterattack and seizure of initiative. It seeks no optimum balance of challenge and response in the light of cumulative burdens imposed by serial action on national resources. The managerial posture, on the other hand, is economically and technically more tidy, more efficient. It is characterized by a more rational approach to resource development and allocation for meeting external threats. It involves the assignment of priorities according to asserted "national goals" and "cost-effectiveness" criteria; the blending of research, education, and inventory build-up with the creation of fully ready forces; and the explicit quest for the benefits of standardization, specialization, simplification, and substitution in the production of goods and services.

The remaining two strategies, which are more activist and dynamic, seek in the first instance to reduce, rather than adapt to, menaces in the environment. They reach beyond the minimum goals of personal and national survival, asserting a will "to prevail" in some valid sense—a will to be significantly "ahead" as well as "neither red nor dead." If wars are nowadays too dangerous for the pursuit of "victory," then the United States and her allies should, no less imaginatively than the Soviet Union, design ways "to win" without war.

One of the two forward strategies, the third in our listing, might be called *entrepreneurial*. It is characterized by initiatives, both military and non-military, designed to enhance a nation's own prospects for self-fulfillment and to diminish those of the putative enemies. The non-military initiatives may be diplomatic, political, economic, technological, psychological; and they may be directed toward friendly, unaligned, and unfriendly nations as well as the domestic and natural environments.

The fourth approach, which may be called *creative*, is premised on the growth of a nation's confidence in its own security—a growth partly due, perhaps, to successful entrepreneurial initiatives. In particular, the strengthening of our own nation's position with respect to the Sino-Soviet aggregate would allow more determined pursuit of altruistic, idealistic, and charismatic policies. Projection of our values and aspirations on a grander scale, over a widening area, and into the more distant future would not reflect any new or reawakened imperialist ambition but a theory of advancing self-interest by advancing joint interests. Past and current policies and programs have already defined many directions for creative initiative—e.g., the enlargement of individual and minority rights everywhere (including the United States), foreign assistance for cultural and economic development, international cooperation for the common safety and general well-being, and establishment and reinforcement of supranational agencies really capable of assuming various functions of regional, or even world, government.* But it is essential for our country to avoid participation in group decision-making on a basis that diminishes our leadership, averages down our sovereignty, and blurs our vision of a positive grand design.

Elements of all four postures are discernible in the history of our foreign policy for the period since World War II, but the stage seems to have been set for a major shift in the weighted average toward the entrepreneurial level and for greater experimentation with creative gambits. The dramatic response to the bold Soviet challenge in Cuba and the general public satisfaction with the outcome of the affair, despite the many inconclusive features of the *dénouement*, have contributed to a keener appreciation of the desirability of determined non-military initiatives to support our military posture everywhere. The surer our own security, the more positive can be the leadership we exert for improvement of the common environment of mankind.

If, as seems to be the case, national sentiment is reorienting in the entrepreneurial-creative direction, then a number of advantages in pressing the initiative will appear increasingly plausible. One advantage is to transfer to putative enemies the burdens and hazards of strategic surprise. Military and technological gaps that could prove embarrassing, dangerous, or decisive are difficult or even impossible to close when the lead times involved are long, when specialized and relatively scarce resources have to be developed, and when important adjustments are required in established economic and social patterns. Another advantage of a posture of initiative is the reduction in the variety of contingencies for which a nation must adequately plan. Related to this is the opportunity for generally more rational, economical, and effective use of resources for the achievement of environmental neutralization or control. Thus, a comparatively wealthy and diversified nation like ours may design many supportable challenges that would strain an adversary with strategic redundancy. Indeed, multiple simultaneous initiatives could have a considerable cumulative impact on putative enemies—e.g., the creation of serious resource and capacity bottlenecks, the

* Leading State Department officials set forth these entrepreneurial-creative *Five Goals of National Policy* in a pamphlet of this name based on a television program of September 24, 1962: "security through strength," "progress through partnership," "revolution of freedom," "community under law," and "peace through perseverance."

disruption of timetables for independent action, and the distortion of economic planning. Another benefit of initiative is psychological—the reinforcement of the morale of the activist nation itself, the rallying of allies, the persuasion of neutrals, and the silent rebuttal of the boasts and taunts of blatant antagonists.

A specific implication of the remarks just made is that, if we incline to the Soviet view of two "systems" engaged for some reason in a mortal struggle, we should at least promote "races" which Soviet citizens ought to run and which Soviet leaders are likely to lose. Thus, much more pertinent and much safer for us than a responsive race into space would be an initiated race for consumer amenities, which we have already largely won. These prizes, after all, are closer than the moon to the heart's desire of people in all lands. The output of domestic appliances, housing, automobiles, and meat per capita ultimately means more to the man in the factory or on the farm than the iron, steel, coal, crude oil, and lumber stressed in Soviet-originated international statistical comparisons. The potential for strategic exploitation is evidently large, in view of the numerous and egregious Soviet lags. It is dramatized by a recent news report that, after registering a far greater annual percentage gain than any other nation in the number of telephones, the Soviet Union's total still does not impressively exceed New York City's. Surely, the United States should not concede to others the first strike in non-military competition.

Related non-military initiatives suggest themselves for limiting the Soviet economic surplus available for military uses and for domestic investment. Although the average Soviet citizen may not appreciate many of our freedoms, he should welcome gains in leisure and in civil liberties. In addition to "racing" for greater material comforts, he would doubtless like to enter contests promising curtailment of his hours of work per week and per year and less restraint on his movements and expression. A challenge to the Soviet Union to competition in rendering economic assistance to newly industrializing countries could likewise squeeze the resource share assignable to her military programs and to capital investment.

All of these non-military initiatives illustrate a "principle of equal acts having unequal significance," which Soviet representatives have developed and skillfully employed. Our turn has come to interpret and to apply this principle imaginatively for the achievement of disproportionate or asymmetrical effects that improve the relative position of the United States. Soviet examples include superficially plausible requests for bilateral reduction of military manpower and equipment (especially nuclear weapons) and for equivalent or equidistant withdrawals of forces (from Berlin, Europe, or all extraterritorial bases). Soviet insistence on immediate action by both sides (as in the case of disarmament) precludes negotiation of adequate surveillance machinery. Our applications of the principle should take advantage of our superior wealth, total output, consumer output, and standard of international sharing. We should issue challenges that require comparable demands of those resources that are more abundant to us—demands that we, therefore, can better afford. It will be recalled that the principle can just as well be employed in the military realm to require redundant commitments by the opponent for countering our feints and for matching our multiple threats.

The realm of information and communication offers many opportunities for promoting Western interests. One challenge is to sharpen the ideological awareness of our own citizenry. Press reports on various educational programs designed to enhance appreciation of our own values and to provide a basis for critical understanding of the tenets, aims, and institutions of antagonistic nations reveal needs for greater accuracy, objectivity, and sophistication. Our political leaders themselves could do much to upgrade public opinion regarding the issues of East-West conflict. In particular, they could authoritatively refute dogmatic forecasts of inevitable victory for so-called "communism" and help by their own statements to neutralize the propaganda which our antagonists may introduce at will into our receptive information media. A recent pronouncement by the President, for example,[2] raises a useful standard to which others may repair; he asserts that the doctrine of inevitable victory has already been proved a "myth" and he offers a counterbet to Khrushchev that "the future will be a world community of independent nations, with a diversity of economic, political, and religious systems, united by a common respect for the rights of others."

Initiatives in information and communication that aim at the external environment appear even more necessary than efforts to improve the condition of domestic public understanding and opinion. We have to overcome at last the inhibitions engendered by so colorful and so lingering a phrase as "the Iron Curtain." It is necessary for us to propagate energetically not only our own version of current events but our constructive vision of the future; to encourage agitation within the Soviet Bloc in favor of more consumer goods, more leisure, and more civil liberties; to limit the risks of unilateral idealistic actions that we may take by calls on Soviet scientists and intellectuals to petition their own government for, say, the end of nuclear bomb tests and the conclusion of international agreements that lead to real coexistence; to seek the aggravation of the "internal contradictions" represented by national, ethnic, and class differences within the Sino-Soviet aggregate; to promote our own connotations of "peace," "coexistence," "freedom," and "democracy;" to deny a struggle between two abstractions like "capitalism" and "communism" and emphasize the inadequacy of these labels; and to sponsor the reinterpretation of the phenomena of industrialization and the concept of "imperialism" in accordance with modern conditions and our own values and aspirations.[3] We should promote larger-scale cultural exchanges and tourism to permit correction of the distorted images of the United States reflected by the freak mirrors of our fiction, cinema, and selectively quoted daily press.

Finally, entrepreneurial and creative initiatives will be required in the next decade to achieve favorable relations with friendly and neutral, as well as with hostile, countries. While Western Europe becomes increasingly preoccupied with the new dimensions of its own economic development and with the prospect of political integration, we shall have to prod our NATO allies to remain united in the common defense effort, to assume greater burdens of preparedness and foreign assistance, to regard trade as an explicit instrument of joint policy, and accordingly to exercise discretion in dealings with Russia, Eastern Europe, China, and Cuba. The Cuban threat will remind us of the need for imaginative and vigorous implementation of the Alliance for Progress with Latin America. Appropriate civil and military programs will have to be blended in other parts of the world too—Asia, Africa, and the Middle East—to bolster economic development programs and reduce vulnerability to protracted "wars of liberation." We have had little to say about relations with China itself, which may be difficult to work out compatibly with a vision of constructive and peaceful world development. The challenge is evidently a major one to which we cannot yet have a confident response.

### The Production Base

The preceding discussion of environmental factors and strategic options indicates at least two of the many reasons for desiring an expansive US economy. One is to provide the material foundation for a dynamic—a tiptoe rather than flatfoot—posture. This foundation has to support not merely defensive programs that look toward personal and national survival but also entrepreneurial and creative initiatives that promise reduction of external dangers and the more positive improvement of the world environment. A second reason is that the economic performance of the United States itself is a fact of prime strategic import. This performance vitally affects the morale and outlook of our people and our allies, the attitudes and stability of many neutral and partially dependent nations, and the behavior and effectiveness of our self-declared enemies.

Our survey should make clear that no country, however richly endowed, can afford to wait for multiple antagonists to mount the threats of which they are capable in different parts of the world. Resources that may seem adequate in quantity could prove seriously deficient in kind; and the knowledge and time required to remedy shortage in a given situation (e.g., by substitution or by the exploitation of marginal deposits) may be absolutely scarce. Accordingly, a point already made needs repeated emphasis: the capacity of putative enemies must be degraded by direct external pressure and by the encouragement of internal divisive tendencies, while the United States and friendly nations take military and non-military steps to improve their own entrepreneurial and creative potentials.

Loud and persistently expressed dissatisfaction with our economic performance could easily lead (non-Tocquevillian) foreign observers to underestimate the adequacy of our production base for sustaining an ambitious array of variant strategies. The criticism, however, has a distinctive "American" flavor and meaning, and it comprises an important endemic feature of the domestic environment. It appropriately reflects the spirit of a nation which long and decisively has excelled the others in total output, consumer output, agricultural and manufacturing manhour productivity, and general material well-being—a nation in which "rising expectations" have become ingrained.

A good part of the continual (and now apparently louder) concern and discontent represents the "din of inequity" of a pluralistic, democratic society at work in the presence of open and well-distributed communication channels. It is the din of conversation, signaling, forecasting, exaggeration, distortion, advertising, propaganda, and complaint that accompanies the exertions of individuals and groups possessing wide latitude for economic and political decision-making, seeking to influence the behavior of others and the course of events, and threading with unequal success the accessible mazes and avenues for unequal advancement. It is the din of a high-energy society where there is felt insecurity and the future is largely unpredictable although the predominant temper is optimistic. The sound is amplified by political representatives and information aides; and intellectual hangers-on, who often try to be different in the very same way, tend to accentuate rather than balance or moderate the cycles of opinion.

Foreigners may particularly misjudge—as so many of our own citizens do—the power of government for affecting the material and human resource base and the economic performance of our society. By design, this power has been fractionated—it is federal, state, and local; and it is also executive, legislative, and judicial. At every level of government and in every branch, too, there is opportunity for diversity. Furthermore, the power of government is hemmed in by historical prejudice in favor of private action and decision, the scope of which remains vast despite great and steady inroads. These factors, the diversity of private interests, and the volume and variety of interactions make difficult the pursuit by government of flexible, consistent, closely managed policies and the prediction of the impact of such policies. Indeed, government, like less complex institutions, tends to define and attack problems serially and selectively, rather than simultaneously, in a coordinated manner, and with a fine sense of priority and interrelation; and political factors sometimes dictate sharp and sudden policy reversals. No scientific "marginalism of policy" exists for guiding desired changes to assure intended wholesome results for some without objectionable side effects for others.

It would seem useful to list, in a literal-minded way, a few of the reassuring aspects of the production base that are taken for granted or are simply ignored in the critical commentary on disappointing fringes and on total economic performance. Our society, having reached frontiers of production as yet unfamiliar to others, has no ruts of precedent to follow, and it must solve its problems pragmatically and in context. Other nations that still must determine how to produce food, shelter, and clothing for consumers are not yet fortunate enough to face our special task—how, in addition to meeting security needs and imprinting a favorable pattern on the world environment, to assure routine, adequate, and dignified participation of the whole population in the distribution (not necessarily the mere production) of great abundance.

First, we note that the trend of GNP, adjusted for price changes, continues upward and that actual and potential man-hour productivity (which reflects the contribution of all other factors in addition to labor) is also advancing. The levels attained, as already noted, are not yet matched elsewhere. Accordingly, in references made to our alleged "stagnation," critics often grudgingly—rather than wittily—prefix the adjective "high-level." New investment too remains sizeable, although its volume in recent years has fallen below expectations. No doubt about the resumption of an upward movement can reasonably be entertained and, where inter-industry and international competition has warranted cost-saving investment, as in the case of steel and chemicals, new capacity is being installed despite the existence of under-utilized facilities. Gross stocks of fixed business capital (structures and equipment, measured in constant prices) have meanwhile continued to rise.[4]

Second, the commitment of resources to defense has been growing, and strong efforts are being made to build greater flexibility into our military forces. The Cuban incident has ended talk of a "missile gap," and we are now moving visibly toward a formidable nuclear deterrent based essentially on Polaris and Minuteman. Increasing attention is also being directed toward improvement of our capability for limited warfare, counterinsurgency, and military-civic action; and the need for rationalizing and strengthening the NATO defense structure is being confronted.

Third, military research and development activity is supported annually at multi-billion-dollar levels, and so are foreign-aid programs. These uses of our resources contribute to our potential for undertaking and sustaining entrepreneurial-creative initiatives.

Fourth, the general under-utilization of our industrial capacity permits a relatively rapid production resurgence, especially in established sectors, once sufficiently urgent public or private demands are felt. During World War II and the Korean conflict, the ability of our society to take up the then existing resource slack to achieve and maintain a proper mix of military-civil production was impressively demonstrated. The estimated "gap" between potential and actual gross national products is something like $40 billion on an annual basis;[5] and, although this "scientistic" concept may be suspect and early closure of this "gap" could be only a "technocratic" ambition, the figure does give an idea of the availability of resources for fuller utilization.

Fifth, unemployment may for some years persist at about five or more per cent of the labor force despite ameliorative government measures, but the high rate will partly reflect demographic and socio-economic changes that spell less individual and family hardship than is traditionally associated with the concept of joblessness. Between 1960 and 1976, according to a projection by the National Planning Association, the labor force will expand by about one third. Because of the high postwar birth rates, the demand by youths for jobs and higher schooling could well increase more rapidly during the next few years than our ability to accommodate it.

In a society like ours, the minimum security standard keeps rising with the growth of our productive base. Recently, supplementary employer benefits, distressed-area and rural-area assistance, foreign-trade adjustment pay, and retraining programs have been added to the long list of earlier protective provisions beginning with unemployment compensation, public placement services, and old-age and survivors' insurance. Numerous scholarships, fellowships, and subsistence and loan arrangements nowadays facilitate pursuit of higher education without regard to family circumstances. In short, social invention has been proceeding in the realm of welfare even though the "lag" in social invention is often decried.

The volume of unemployment and its distributions by age group and by duration indicate a smaller "hard core" and far less damage attributable to "technological change" (and its bogeyman variants of "automation" and "cybernation") than would be suggested by political speeches and lurid press accounts. Furthermore, the mechanisms of job erosion and of actual worker "displacement" are complex; and, since causation here is multiple and ambiguous, the occasion for involuntary job separation may give little hint of the manifold underlying reasons. It is easier, of course, to blame idleness on an impersonal and diffused technological force than, say, on a powerful decision-making group or on a price or wage policy. Furthermore, it is not customary to acknowledge that "good" actions and programs can have "bad" incidental effects—like the impairment of labor mobility by home ownership, by the seniority system, by private pension and welfare funds, and by reduction of pressures to take work outside preferred geographic areas and occupations and at less than desired pay.

Sixth, while there may be differences of opinion on the probability and best means of achieving faster growth, the potential for so doing clearly exists, and the topic properly commands great public, academic, and political interest. Population increase, internal migration, and competitiveness in product development and marketing are among the many dynamic nongovernmental forces evidently still at work in our society; and government too exerts considerable influence on the volume and composition of economic activity through its direct demands, its contributions to the supply of productive resources, and its revision of the environment for enterprise.

Studies of explicit routes to faster growth probably give less assurance than the spurts actually experienced in the past that success is at all achievable without heroic effort or without drastic modification of our economic and social institutions. Lists that specify potential sources of acceleration are operationally not very useful; they show eligible targets, rather than indicate needed weapons or offer needed sighting instructions, and the underlying additive models are technically crude and unconvincing. Thus, the productive "gap" of $40 billion mentioned earlier [6] could presumably be closed by a reduction of unemployment, an increase in average hours worked, the employment of persons who have been discouraged from looking for work, and the productivity gain accompanying greater utilization of existing plant and equipment. But this list merely restates the problems of growth in a different way; it does not really give answers. The same is true of a package of 13 possible contributions to a permanent increase in the annual growth rate by a single percentage point: immigration, longer hours, more education, lower structural unemployment and underemployment, higher capital input, less race discrimination, lower trade barriers, end of legal price-fixing, elimination of worker restrictions on output, better wage incentives, consolidation of public service facilities, effective diffusion of advanced business practices, and more cost-reduction research.[7]

The Government, on the other hand, is directly concerned with operations, but the actions it takes are not precisely controllable, nor need they have the short-run and long-run consequences that are predicted for them. Everything that the Federal Government does with respect, say, to research, manpower, education, natural resources, space, or business regulation has some impact—pre-measurable or not and intended or not—on the magnitude, direction, and sustainability of growth. Recently, it has sought especially to stimulate capital investment for economic growth by the liberalization of depreciation rules and provision of an income-tax credit. In general, the present Administration has interpreted the famous policy phrase of the Employment Act of 1946, "to promote maximum production, employment, and purchasing power," as though the qualifying verbiage contained in the remainder of the single Teutonic sentence constituting Section 2 could simply be replaced by dots. Extensive personal and corporate tax reductions are now being proposed with an urgency that was not foreshadowed by Administration pronouncements even half a year ago. Whether or not the advertised growth aims of these tax adjustments are achievable is a matter for conjecture, and the accompanying huge deficits could introduce undesired monetary complications. Furthermore, it might be better to shunt released Federal taxes to state and local uses for improving the supply of teachers, doctors, schools, hospitals, water, urban transportation, and suburban services than to allow an increase in savings or a temporary over-stimulation of cyclical hardware industries (e.g., automobiles, steel, and household appliances). But a methodical or timely massive shift of released funds to state and local governments for accomplishing Galbraithian corrections is most unlikely.

**Natural Resources**

Whichever ingredient of economic production is especially scarce demands special attention for the maintenance of an appropriate strategic posture. Since World War II, the adequacy of our natural resources for defense and other significant needs has been a topic of particular interest; and the Korean conflict gave new impetus to stockpiling of strategic and critical materials. A decade ago, the comprehensive report of the President's Materials Policy Commission, *Resources for Freedom*, added to the sophistication with which problems of conservation have to be viewed. Now, a new report, prepared by the National Academy of Sciences-National Research Council (*Natural Resources*, Publication 1000, 1962) in response to a request by the President, further broadens our horizons. It surveys the prospects for food, fibers, minerals, energy, water, and the physical environment in terms that are appropriate to a nation shifting its strategic sights in the entrepreneurial-creative direction.

The National Academy report recognizes the adequacy of available renewable and non-renewable resources for support of an increasing population at the same or higher living standards for several decades—in a stable world environment. But, even apart from military requirements (which the report does not explicitly treat), there is need to temper optimism, for other nations with huge populations and with ambitions to improve their economic well-being also have pressing requirements. This mission is accordingly proposed in the Academy's publication:

As the largest user of raw materials per capita, the United States as a leader in the world community of nations could and, we believe, should mobilize its unique experience and capability for the benefit of mankind. With its record of exploiting a varied continent more rapidly than any other nation in history, of combining high utilization with large-scale materials production, and of impressive demonstrated competence in agricultural technology and applied research, it has the knowledge and the elements of an organization on which to base an expanded program of great promise.

The report concludes with recommendations for a national program of resources research. With respect to agriculture, basic research is recommended on plant and animal genetics and breeding; and the extension of applied research is proposed for raising productivity in a wider variety of environments. Other proposals relate to low-cost energy sources, water resources, mineral discovery and development, ocean fisheries, systems analysis for international resource planning and management, and establishment of a central natural resources group in the Federal Government (which could, for example, facilitate international cooperation).

Highlighting a study here that focuses on wider horizons should not be misinterpreted as minimizing the need for securing the national base of conventional material resources, both mineral and renewable. As already suggested, progress has been made in alerting our people to this need; and the augmentation of domestic supplies (e.g., of iron ore and petroleum) is a matter of obvious interest to our businessmen and to the officials who make and guide our foreign policy. Oblique testimony to the effectiveness of past measures, erratic as these may otherwise have been, is to be found in complaints about the burden of our agricultural surpluses, the management of our stockpile of strategic and critical materials, and imports of residual fuel oil. We should be able to maintain our conventional material resource base in the next decade of new and shifting challenges.

**Research and Development**

The importance of sufficiently large and varied research and development undertakings for expansion of the range of strategic opportunities is well appreciated, but difficult problems are encountered at numerous levels and interfaces. These problems relate to such matters as the short supply and slow expansibility of technical manpower, the proper allocation of research resources by broad organizational divisions (e.g., national-international, government-private, and inter-agency), rational allocation by broad purposes (e.g., "basic" and "applied" research), the realistic choice of projects in the face of uncertainty and the indefiniteness of priorities, the need for better coordination (e.g., within the Executive Branch and between Congress and the Executive), the dissemination and storage of findings with the aim of reducing unnecessary duplication of research efforts, speed-up of the diffusion and application of findings, civilian utilization of military developments, and the disposition of publicly-financed patents.

In the fiscal year 1963, our total public and private commitment to R&D activity will apparently reach $17 billion (according to the National Science Foundation), as Federal participation, particularly for defense, becomes even more extensive. Efforts to improve the military use of research resources are reflected in, for example, the closer comparison, in the budgetary process, of alternative military forces in terms of cost and anticipated effectiveness; the occasional reduction in the number of more or less equivalent weapon prototypes undergoing development; the concern for compression of lead time from the inception of an idea to operational availability; and the regular solicitation of civilian scientific aid in "invention to specification." Non-functional military expenditure is also evident, however, in the distribution or continuation of contracts with reference to regional economic dependency and the politically desirable participation of small firms. It is also true that much of the activity financed as research is really education, being concerned not with the introduction of genuine novelty but with the acquisition of knowledge already available or with the mastery of established practice. Finally, the rapid increase in space research and the distant horizons of commitment may well interfere with military objectives and atomic energy development, although this diversion could also serve useful purposes in the international competition for prestige and in the encouragement of new domestic industries.

It is already clear that public and private research expenditures do not automatically and alone assure survivability, growth, actual productivity increase, the reduction of cost, and the generation of new industries. Nor do they assure decisive military advantage. But they can help to accomplish vital national purposes that are clearly expressed, advanced by strong leadership, and unambiguously supported.

To improve our military position and to facilitate the conduct of entrepreneurial-creative initiatives, we continually have to upgrade the solutions to persistent problems of the kind stated at the beginning of this section. In particular, it is desirable (1) to assure that military objectives are paramount in decisions on the placement and prosecution of military contracts; (2) to work out a proper balance between military and non-military (especially space) research claims on limited manpower resources; (3) to establish a board for priority rating and allocation among government agencies, to strengthen the technical advisory service available to Congressional committees, and to establish closer coordination between the Executive and Legislative Branches;[8] (4) to give more support to research in behavioral sciences (as recommended by a subpanel of the President's Science Advisory Committee, April 20, 1962); (5) to emphasize the adaptability of research findings to less developed countries;[9] (6) to apply better techniques of dissemination, storage, abstracting, indexing, and retrieval to the handling of research results; (7) to encourage civilian use of convertible military research findings and to promote greater interchange of technical information among the military services; and (8) to pursue liberal policies with regard to corporate rights to publicly-financed patents, since effective private exploitation would mean large tax "takeaways" that more than balance alleged "giveaways" and since antitrust laws (suitably extended, if necessary) could deal with abuses.

### Specialized Manpower

During the past decade, and especially since the shock of the first sputnik launching, the supply of scientific, engineering, and supporting technical manpower has been a matter of intense national concern. The quality of our economy, the nature and effectiveness of our defenses, and our capacity for entrepreneurial-creative initiatives surely depend on this supply. But it is also important to maintain balance in our higher education —not to overemphasize engineering, mathematics, and physical sciences at the expense of all other subjects needed for self-realization and for the fullest performance of social roles. Furthermore, we must avoid establishment of a pattern of rotating shortage due to chronic inadequacy of our technical manpower supply to meet shifting enemy initiatives.

Whatever the fields of academic concentration, it would seem desirable to assure that as many high-school graduates as are intellectually capable proceed to college and that the necessary buildings, equipment, and teachers are available. The postwar baby boom and the trend toward enrollment of larger percentages of the college-age population are greatly increasing the pressures on resources committed to higher education. But the supply of teachers has been adversely affected by the requirements of research and the usually unfavorable salary differential. Furthermore, campus construction tends to lag behind enrollment. Clamor for government assistance, especially Federal, may be expected to increase; and more intensive use will have to be made of existing facilities and the teachers on hand. According to the Department of Health, Education, and Welfare, about twice as many students will be at colleges in 1975 as in 1962. The rise in applications between 1962 and 1965 will be particularly sharp in view of the large increase in the number of youths reaching 18 years of age.

A recent authoritative report [10] on graduate training in engineering, mathematics, and the physical sciences states cogently the many national purposes to be served by scientists and engineers and also proposes several steps for increasing the supply. Eleven national roles are cited—viz., economic progress, military security, space exploration, medical advancement, assistance to developing nations, response to problems attributed to technological change, scientific and technological readiness for new and unforeseen challenges and opportunities, teaching science and engineering, technical enlightenment of the general citizenry, management, and intellectual improvement. Three approaches to obtaining "more manpower of superior ability, with higher training" are offered: (1) increase in the fraction of high-ranking college graduates taking advanced work; (2) improvement in the quality and availability of college courses in science and engineering; and (3) increase in the supply and effective use of qualified technicians.

Traditionally, and even during the postwar period, the United States has benefited from importation of fully trained European scientific personnel. This kind of "piracy" cannot be indefinitely extrapolated without harm. A group of Western educators, researchers, and administrators has recently proposed to the North Atlantic Council the establishment of an advanced International Institute of Science and Technology in Western Europe. This Institute would train 1,000 students annually, making a vital contribution to the West's resource of specialized manpower and to the image of unity.[11] A joint educational endeavor of this sort should be encouraged now, as centrifugal tendencies in the Atlantic Alliance become more assertive.

## FOOTNOTES

[1] Wishful thinkers who consider Soviet "coexistence" a form of disengagement and a condition for symbiosis (see, for example, D. Felix, "The Sense of Coexistence," *American Scholar* [Winter, 1962-63], pp. 76-89) will find illuminating an attack by G. Frantsov (translated in *Current Digest of the Soviet Press*, November 14, 1962, pp. 3-7) on the proposition, advanced by Christopher Mayhew and other Western "bourgeois propagandists," that "ideological coexistence" should be added to the concept of non-military competition.

[2] *Look*, XXVII, January 15, 1963, p. 18.

[3] Much can be learned from informed Marxist critics of "capitalist" literature. See, for example, the review by P. A. Baran and E. J. Hobsbawm of Rostow's "Stages of Economic Growth" in *Kyklos*, 1961, Fasc. 2, pp. 235-42.

[4] *Survey of Current Business* (November, 1962), pp. 10-18.

[5] *Economic Report of the President* (January, 1962), pp. 49-53.

[6] In *Economic Report of the President* (January, 1963), a somewhat smaller gap is shown for 1962 in a chart (p. 27), but no numerical estimate is actually given and acknowledgment is made of "statistical difficulties" (p. 28).

[7] See E. F. Denison, *American Economic Review* (May, 1962), pp. 67-75; and comments by G. Colm, *ibid.*, pp. 87-89, and by M. Abramovitz, *ibid.*, (September, 1962), pp. 762-82.

[8] *Science*, January 4, 1963, pp. 23-27.

[9] *Ibid.*, January 11, 1963, p. 98.

[10] *Meeting Manpower Needs in Science and Technology*, President's Science Advisory Committee, December 12, 1962.

[11] *Department of State Bulletin* (December 10, 1962), p. 896.

# Assuring the Primacy of National Security

*—W. GLENN CAMPBELL*

*Summary*

*The first and foremost priority for national security rests, not on money, but rather on the brains of our top officials— their adequate time for study, for deliberation, and for decision. The multiplication of subject matters with which the national Government now deals places a burden of work upon its top officials with which no human being can cope without neglecting some of them. The scope, knowledge, and insight needed to judge the requirements of national security in the nuclear age are stupendous and overwhelming. They encompass vast areas of science, extensive knowledge of all the countries of the world, and developments in many fields which are hard to comprehend, even by exceptional minds, save through long and arduous study.*

*Part of the problem is that those who make decisions on which hangs the existence of the nation are placed under constant domestic political pressures, not just in awarding weapons contracts, but in giving precedence to non-defense spending. On more than one occasion during the past fifteen years, the resources that could have completed or accelerated defense projects have been used to expand domestic welfare benefits; and yet there is a myth that increased government spending has primarily resulted from national security needs. During the past ten years national defense expenditures expanded only 6% from $50.6 billion to $53.4 billion, whereas federal civilian benefits and services increased 214% from $14.2 billion to $44.6 billion.*

*The charge that has been made so frequently in recent years that there has been poverty and starvation in the provision of public services and affluence in private consumption, turns out on examination to have no basis in fact. We have been going through a period of spectacular expansion of government in the domestic field. The one type of expenditure that has increased out of proportion to anything else has been governmental non-defense benefits and services.*

*" It is also difficult to argue that the Federal Government has to expand non-defense spending because state and local governments are lagging. During the past 10 years state and local governments increased spending from their own sources by 129% from $28.3 to $64.7 billion at a time when population and prices combined increased only 43%. Furthermore, the argument that state and local governments are unable to increase their revenues at a rapid pace is a myth. Since the end of World War II, state and local receipts quadrupled while federal receipts only doubled. The enormous growth in education and health expenditures during the past decade dramatically demonstrates that welfare functions which are provided primarily by state and local or private resources have fared well in recent years.*

*An important first step toward assuring the primacy of national security is to stop the further expansion of federal expenditures for domestic benefits. In order to be able to continue to expand defense expenditures moderately, it is not necessary to engage in an extensive elimination of existing federal outlays for domestic purposes, although this would be necessary if a large increase in national security outlays were deemed advisable. If, however, there is a continued, persistent effort to combine simultaneously, increases in national security outlays and domestic government benefits with a sizeable reduction in income taxes, it is difficult to see how the end result can be other than inflation and balance-of-payments difficulties. Continuation of these policies would, for example, make it highly unlikely that the federal budget could ever be brought back into balance at any time during the rest of the 1960's.*

*The fiscal problem involved in assuring the primacy of national security can be illuminated by looking at the growth of federal expenditures during the last three years. National security expenditures are likely to expand by $10.4 billion from $47.9 billion in fiscal 1960 to an estimated $58.3 billion in fiscal 1963. Other federal expenditures are scheduled to increase by $12.1 billion from $46.4 billion to $58.5 billion. The consolidated cash budget had a surplus of slightly less than $1 billion in fiscal 1960; the deficit is likely to exceed $8 billion in fiscal 1963. In short, if non-defense expenditures had been held at their 1960* *level, it would be possible simultaneously to provide for further expansion in national security expenditures and to reduce income taxes without causing undue inflationary pressures or putting extra strain on our precarious balance-of-payments situation.*

*Both of these objectives are important for our national security. It is now widely agreed that our high income tax rates are a major cause of the disappointing performance record of the American economy during the past five years. The performance of that economy is a vital factor in the ability of this nation to remain the leader of the Free World Alliance.*

---

In this paper it is assumed that, for the foreseeable future, the likelihood is that national security requirements will remain high and that, together with her allies, the United States must indefinitely remain stronger than any possible aggressor or combination of aggressors. In other words, our military power must at all times exceed that of a potential enemy. There must be no room for a gap anywhere, anytime. The magnitude of our effort must be determined by the possible combination of forces that opposes us.

There will, however, be no discussion in this paper of the possibility of limited war or total war during the coming decade and the problems which would arise therefrom, nor of the possibility and conditions under which genuine disarmament might take place and the problems connected with such an event.

Strength in modern warfare calls for a great variety of resources, but, if we aim to express them in terms of national effort, then they must be converted to a common denominator— the dollar. It enables us to measure the effort, past or future, in terms of all resources which the nation produces and as that share of governmental resources which is allocated to safeguarding our security. To a large degree, then, the nation's defense effort finds its concrete expression in the defense budget. The Senate Subcommittee on National Policy Machinery in its report *Organizing for National Security* declared, "The budgetary process—the decisive resource-allocating instrument—lies at the very heart of national security planning and programming. Plans and policies without a dollar sign attached, are mere aspirations. It is the budgetary process which translates them into actual programs." [1]

Of course a country's military strength is not necessarily proportionate to its defense expenditures. Such factors as the intelligence with which over-all strategy is planned and carried out, the effectiveness with which the amounts are spent and resources are mobilized have a major bearing. But, when all is said and done, the military planner knows as well as the economist that all roads lead to the budget. Also, there is never enough money in the budget to do all the things that might be desirable. A tendency for outlays always to exceed the available resources seems to be inherent in the governmental process.

## Priorities: Defense vs. Non-Defense Outlays

In the private sector of the economy, the individual's desire for goods and services is disciplined by the necessity of paying for them. This keeps wants within willingness and ability to pay. There is no such automatic control in the governmental sector, least of all at the national level. Those who demand services know that they will pay only a small share of the price. On the other hand, they frequently have expectations of receiving benefits which far exceed their share of the cost, benefits which accrue either to themselves or to purposes which they value highly. So there is no limit to pleas for a great variety of domestic governmental programs, backed up by briefs which try to prove the existence of vast unmet needs and of the starvation of public services. Inevitably these demands compete with requirements for national defense in the making of the budget.

General principles to guide budgetary decisions are easier to formulate than to apply in specific cases. Pronouncements tend to give defense an overriding priority. The Joint Economic Committee of Congress argued, "National defense requirements should guide rather than depend upon decisions concerning the level and composition of other federal spending programs and the evaluation of revenue prospects and requirements." [2]

Former Budget Director David E. Bell explained in a speech on May 18, 1962: "We give top priority to defense and then argue about what comes second." [3] But he immediately added that this was an oversimplification of the problem, and that only the "rock-bottom" needs of defense get priority over everything else.

There can be—and is—wide disagreement over what constitutes "rock bottom" in defense. The armed services almost always feel that they are not getting enough to meet essential requirements. General Maxwell Taylor—former Army Chief of Staff, now Chairman of the JCS—complained to a senatorial committee, "Each year the services receive rigid guidelines which control the growth, direction, and evolution of the Armed Forces. These guidelines are often set with little knowledge of their strategic implications." [4] Innumerable other military leaders have made similar statements.

This raises some weighty questions: what is an "adequate" defense? How much defense is enough? How far do we have to go to make sure that, with all the inevitable uncertainties, if we do err, we err on the safe side? Can we rely on one weapons system to fill a particular requirement or should we better have two or three overlapping systems—just in case something does not quite work out as we planned it?

A staff report to the Senate Subcommittee on National Policy Machinery expressed well the aim and procedure:

> The task confronting us is harshly plain—to out-think, out-plan, out-perform, and outlast our foes. . . . The key problem of the President is to create such a strategy and to establish an order of national priorities on its behalf. His task is to map a course of action which puts first things first, which separates the necessary from the merely desirable, and which distinguishes between what must be done today and what can wait until tomorrow.[5]

Let us consider some concrete cases. A number of military experts as well as leaders of congressional committees on military affairs hold and have strongly expressed the conviction that development and production of an airplane of supersonic speed as well as the Skybolt missile are essential to our defense. The President has repeatedly refused to advance the B-70 program and only recently made a reluctant concession in the form of a token allocation for the RS-70. It is not that Mach-3 planes are useless but he regarded the cost of producing them as too high in the light of more important demands on the budget. The President also decided to discontinue the Skybolt project because it would require $2.5 billion to complete the system and buy the missiles. Meanwhile he recommended to Congress—and strongly fought for—increased spending for civilian services totaling billions of dollars.

The President holds that the RS-70 and the Skybolt would, when completed, overlap other systems. But a certain amount of duplication and triplication of offensive and defensive strength are undoubtedly needed at a time when technological progress is rapid, when the performance of some of our projects in developmental stage cannot be reliably predicted, when the possibility of some major breakthrough on the Soviet side cannot be excluded and when their strength, present and future, cannot be accurately measured.

At about the time the ending of the Skybolt project was announced, Douglas Aircraft was running large national ads: "Air Force Skybolt is expected to be one of America's most powerful weapons. This air launched ballistic missile will save billions in taxes by extending the useful life of our B-52 and British Vulcan II bombers. . . ."

I do not feel qualified to judge the military value of the RS-70 or the Skybolt. Nor am I an expert on Project Rover which aims to substitute nuclear rocket propulsion for chemically fueled vehicles, for which the President has requested no additional funds in the new budget.

But I would feel a great deal better about such cutbacks or termination of major defense projects contrary to the advice of military experts, if the resources that could have completed or accelerated them or provided the necessary margin for a reduction in income taxes had not been used to expand the range of civilian benefits (it is now widely agreed that our high income tax rates are a major cause of the disappointing performance record of the American economy during the past five years). It appears that RS-70, Skybolt, Rover, and similar projects had to take a back seat to proposals for enlarged welfare benefits and various domestic services which were accorded a higher priority and may have a stronger political appeal. This is not a new development. After a careful study of the postwar record of defense budgeting, Samuel P. Huntington wrote:

> In both the Truman Administration before the Korean War and in the Eisenhower Administration after the war, the tendency was: (1) to estimate the revenues of the government or total expenditures possible within the existing debt limit; (2) to deduct from this figure the estimated cost of domestic programs and foreign aid; and (3) to allocate the remainder to the military.[6]

Huntington attributed the greater pull of the various welfare programs to the organized support by lobbying groups which the Armed Services lack. "Alone the military were no match for the Treasury and the Bureau of the Budget." Disagreement between the three services and "the disunity of the military . . . tended to strengthen the Administration and to increase its ability to limit the defense effort." Huntington found that

> Both administrations were more concerned with finding means of keeping the level of military spending down than with finding

means of pushing it up. For the Administration, a cut in national security spending is easier to achieve than a cut in most domestic programs. . . . The greater power of the Administration over the military budget is the crucial factor limiting that budget. An aggressive, confident, hard-driving Administration can win a struggle with the military while it may face defeat on other fronts. Throughout the period from 1946 to 1960 the ceiling on the military effort was not set by Congress, not by public opinion, and most certainly, not by the economy, but by the deliberate choice of the Administration.[7]

Walter Lippmann, on the other hand, has charged that it was the force of public opinion and the ignorance and shortsighted selfishness of the people that tended to restrict, reduce, and limit the level of military spending and that forced the hands of the leaders of government against their better knowledge.[8] This wholesale indictment of the American people—and in fact of the principle of "government by the people" in a democracy —is without foundation. Numerous public opinion polls by Gallup, Roper, and others throughout the postwar period have consistently shown strong majorities in favor of a stronger military establishment. Huntington summarized the record as follows: "In every case the Administration has been in favor of less military effort and public opinion in favor of more." [9]

Over the past two decades, Congress, in which the Constitution vests the power to raise armies, has increasingly tended to abandon its power to the executive branch, to the President, and to the National Security Council, which, in effect have come to legislate on matters of national defense. Sometimes a tug-of-war developed in which the Executive was trying to keep military expenditures down while pushing expanded welfare programs through a reluctant or recalcitrant Congress.

Congress occasionally tried to strengthen the defense effort beyond presidential recommendations, but the record of the past ten years shows that, as a rule, the Executive prevailed: national defense accounted for 66% of all federal expenditures in 1953, and 58% in 1955 (after the conclusion of the Korean action), and equalled 46% in the President's proposals for the fiscal year 1964. May we conclude from this that our international and defense situations have so decisively improved over the past ten years that our national Government can afford to reduce the share of its resources allocated to defense from two-thirds to less than one-half? The congressional committee which studied *Organizing for National Security* did not think so. It began its chapter on the budgetary process with the categorical statement: "The struggle with communism is broadening, deepening, and quickening." [10]

The "budgetary guidelines," "target figures," "dollar tags," "points of departure," or other euphemisms for dollar ceilings which the Director of the Budget suggests to the Defense Department in advance of the preparation of its budget requests tend to be set so as to leave sufficient space for the increase in welfare programs which the President plans to push through. They can, therefore, force the elimination of some weapons systems and programs which the armed forces deem important, which, if everything works out as planned, they may be able to do without, but, under other conceivable circumstances, could have grave consequences.

It has been said that ten years may be needed nowadays to bring a sophisticated weapons system from the drawing board to the delivery of the hardware. By the time we find out that we do need something that was cut out earlier it may be much too late to produce it. Such a lag could be fatal. We should never forget the experience with the Sputnik and we cannot afford to repeat it.

Neither, of course, can we afford to do *everything* that might someday be useful to national defense. But obviously, the more deeply the Federal Government becomes involved in providing domestic services, the more obligations it assumes and institutionalizes, the more hopes it arouses among special interest groups, the more will defense budgets be affected by political pressures for local benefits.

## The Statistical Record

With all the talk that has been going around, particularly since the appearance of Kenneth Galbraith's *The Affluent Society*, about the starvation of public services and the poverty and stagnation in government, it is not widely known, much less appreciated, that we have been going through a period of spectacular expansion of government in the domestic field. Between the fiscal years 1953 and 1963 the Federal Government increased its expenditures by 52%—which is not out of line with the simultaneous increase in population and prices (combined: 43%), GNP (60%), disposable personal income (60%), personal consumption (62%) (all amounts are in current dollars). But the 52% increase in federal outlays hides the fact that the cost of national defense rose only 6%, civilian benefits and services 214%. In other words the domestic functions of the Federal Government expanded at more than three times the rate of personal consumption and at almost five times the rate of population and prices (see Table at end of chapter).

No less than 76% of the $40 billion increase in federal spending between 1953 and 1963 was allocated to civilian purposes, only 7% to defense. In the last eight years, 1955 to 1963, outlays for civilian purposes went up $26.8 billion, outlays for national defense $12.6 billion (these figures are based on the President's estimates in submitting his budget for 1964).

To be sure, this trend is not new. It goes back a long time but has never been as overwhelming as in the period since the end of World War II, not even during the 1930's. This can be illustrated very dramatically by dividing federal expenditures into two classes: those connected with or primarily caused by national security and past wars (national defense, international affairs, space research and technology, veterans, interest on the national debt) in one class; all other outlays, comprising the civilian functions in the other. It took 160 years—from 1789 to 1948—for federal expenditures for civilian functions to reach the magnitude of $7 billion. It then took only another fifteen years—from 1948 to 1963—to boost them to $45 billion. This increase of $38 billion in a mere fifteen years equals a growth rate of 525% over a period during which personal consumption expanded only 116% (*current* dollars).

It is difficult to argue that the Federal Government had to multiply its spending because state and local governments lagged. Estimates for the fiscal year 1962 show that over the past ten years, while population and prices (combined) increased 43%, state and local governments stepped up spending from their own sources by 129% (from $28.3 to $64.7 billion). This is no mean achievement and suggests no urgent need for federal intervention.

Some authors have for years been casting scorn and derision on the American people for expanding their outlays for frivolous personal consumption while starving government. What has been the rate of increase in some of the major categories of personal consumption for the most recent ten-year period for which this information is presently available—1951 to 1961? Expenditures for new cars (despite tailfins, cerise color, etc.) grew 50%, for clothing 35%, for household operation 54%, for housing 89%, for recreation 76% (this includes an increase of 121% for books). The sharpest increase of 162% was for private education.

From the foregoing it can be seen that when the charge of the rise in conspicuous consumption is examined by the record it turns out to be completely unfounded. The one type of expenditure that increased out of proportion to everything else was governmental non-defense benefits and services.

Governmental employment for non-defense purposes is also a good yardstick for measuring the relative growth of the public and private sectors. Between 1952 and 1962 the civilian labor force grew 14%, the number of public employees—not counting armed forces of Department of Defense—56%. This is an even sharper relative growth for government than occurred during the heyday of the New Deal in the 1930's. Between 1929 and 1940 the civilian labor force increased 13%, governmental non-defense employment 33%. In those eleven years governmental non-defense employment expanded by 1.1 percentage points from 6% to 7.1% of the civilian labor force. In the past ten years it grew 3.1 percentage points (from 8.4% to 11.5%).

Many more statistics could be added but those cited should suffice to show that governmental activities in domestic functions have been expanding at a far faster rate than national production, consumption, or income, and that expenditures sharply outpaced population and prices. This does not suggest that the demands of the Cold War have exerted much restraint upon domestic governmental spending. The restraining force seems to have worked in the opposite direction.

### Necessary Governmental Reorganization to Assure the Primacy of National Security

The methods used to allocate funds for defense have been severely and repeatedly criticized. Particularly well known is Hanson Baldwin's comment that "In the Western World—though not in Russia—costs are a more decisive factor in shaping defense than is military logic." [11] Warner R. Schilling concluded in an incisive study, just published, that "The central fact about the defense budget is that it is a political problem" and that it "is the very stuff of which politics is made." [12] He demonstrated this with the record of the $15 billion defense ceiling in the budget for 1950. Amounts for defense are far higher today but the relationship is unchanged. Nor is it likely to change without a major reform in the methods of determining national security budgets.

In several study papers and in the panel discussions of this Conference, thoughtful proposals have been made for urgent steps in regard to our national security posture—Drs. Teller, Kahn, and Schelling, for example, on civilian defense; and Dr. Possony on maintaining a technological superiority. It is not for me to judge such proposals, but I do feel that decisions against putting more into active or passive defense, or into greater R&D efforts should not stem from the pre-emption of these monies by increased domestic welfare programs.

This tendency might not be too serious or beyond correction if the world were still in the pre-atomic age. In World Wars I and II the United States had a year or two in which to mobilize its forces and economic potential *after* the shooting started. But the next general war (if there is one) is not likely to be conducted in the terms of World War II. Whether there will be a major war and how it will end is more likely to depend on decisions made and actions taken *now*.

Informed observers tend to agree that the most promising way to prevent war is for the free nations to be so strong as to deter any potential aggressors. The Romans' motto *si vis pacem para bellum* is as true today as ever. We must not only be strong but also look strong, capable of destroying an aggressor and surviving any possible blow with sufficient potential to retaliate. Our strength must be ready and operational now, not after the missiles start flying.

The Comptroller of the Department of Defense, Charles J. Hitch, has pointed out some basic principles that bear repeating: "Military power is derived from economic strength, and foreign policy is based on both. Economic strength that is used for national security purposes *in time* is the embodiment of military power." [13] Mr. Hitch stressed the words *"in time."* He added that, "Russia, for example, a much poorer country than the United States, has supported a larger peacetime military program," and emphasized that, *"In an all-out thermonuclear war the superior economic war potential of the United States is important only to the extent that it has been effectively diverted to security purposes before war starts."*

In a "Final Statement" appended to the report *Organizing for National Security* of the Senate Subcommittee on National Policy

Machinery, its chairman, Senator Henry M. Jackson, declared that the shortcomings in our security planning do not lie in insufficient staffing: *"There is a serious overstaffing in the national security departments and agencies."* He found the shortcomings at the top in the Presidency and in Congress:

> *We need a clearer understanding of where our vital national interests lie and what we must do to promote them.* . . . Unless our top officials are in basic agreement about what is paramount for the national interest—what comes first and what comes second— there is bound to be drift and confusion below. This has been so under every Administration.
>
> There is no place in the Congress, short of the floors of the Senate and the House, where the requirements of national security and the resources needed on their behalf are considered in their totality.
>
> The staff report points out that, "The President must grapple with formidable questions: How much of our national substance should be devoted to the requirements of national security? . . ."[14]

A look at the record shows that the President sent dozens of messages covering over 200 proposals for increased spending to the 87th Congress, mostly concerned with civilian services. They cover almost every activity in which government is or could be engaged and run the gamut from public assistance to depressed areas, urban affairs, public housing, sewage treatment, metropolitan transit, schools at every level, adult education, scholarships, a food stamp plan, and many more.

The organized groups interested in these activities assert that the programs are in the national interest and have a bearing on the strength of our defense. It is, of course, true that just about every function of government may contribute in some form or other to economic well-being and may also add to the strength that can be mobilized for defense. But there must be a distinction between direct contributions to our deterrent or defensive strength and those which are only remotely, indirectly, or partially serving that goal.

The special interest groups, however, do not see it that way. They are well organized and can influence large groups of voters—or at least claim that they can. A Chief Executive, or a member of Congress, often can only at his peril refuse to lend them an ear and a willing hand. The shifting of jurisdiction over innumerable domestic and benefit functions of government to the national level means that our top officials in the executive and legislative branches are subjected to greater pressures than many of them are able to resist and politically survive.

If they are to exercise judgment on national security issues free of extraneous pressures, some way must be found to protect them.

Moreover, the multiplication of subject matters with which the national Government now deals places a burden of work upon its top officials with which no human being can cope without neglecting some of them. The scope, knowledge, and insight needed to judge the requirements of national security in the nuclear age are stupendous and overwhelming. They encompass vast areas of science and developments in many fields which are hard to comprehend even by exceptional minds save through long and arduous study. They include detailed information on over a hundred foreign nations, their history, geography, economic resources, finances, military establishment, scientific capacity, political parties and leanings; on alternatives open to them and their potential future course; as well as on a vast array of facts on weapons systems, their strengths and weaknesses; and many more. Even the most gifted who can concentrate all of their time and thinking on these problems cannot fully assimilate them if they must cover too broad a field.

Yet neither the President nor Congress can delegate their thinking to specialized staffs. They must be in a position to evaluate and to judge recommendations—often conflicting, always intricate—of the experts. They cannot let experts who frequently disagree among themselves make the decisions. But how can they make informed decisions if the range of subjects before them is so broad that they cannot devote sufficient time to each for study?

The chairman of the committee that sponsored the above-mentioned inquiry into our national policy machinery, Senator McClellan, warned not long ago: "Senators are no longer able to deal with the workload, either physically or mentally." Inadequate study and deliberation may well have been partially responsible for the debacle at the Bay of Pigs. We can ill afford another such disaster.

As Dean Acheson so well pointed out: "The Chief must from time to time familiarize himself with the whole record." [15] Even a very capable and hard-working President or Senator has only 24 hours a day. Acheson stressed that "one cannot make more time. Isn't the problem, I have wondered, a little different? Doesn't it involve a choice of what the 'very highest echelons,' the President and the Cabinet, spend their time on, and of finding ways of making available to them the right information to think with and about?" Henry Kissinger commented, "There is no substitute for greater insight on the part of our executives, in or out of government. Advice cannot replace knowledge. Neither Churchill nor Lincoln nor Roosevelt was the product of a staff." [16]

The core of the problem is that the President who is called upon to make decisions on which hang the very existence of the nation and the lives of many millions, decisions which require more study than there are hours in the day, must cut short his consideration of foreign policy and national security to deal with aid for sewage treatment plants, to round up an extra five or ten votes for a Department of Urban Affairs or for public works acceleration, to worry in whose district he should place some of the added public works projects, or to figure out how to make some discredited and unpopular aid-to-education bills acceptable to a Congress which has concluded after examining the evidence on innumerable occasions that they are unnecessary, and has rejected them time and again.

A review of the *Congressional Record* shows that most of the time of Congress is spent on approving numerous types of local benefits and not on the most vital and urgent business at hand —national security. There may not have been too much harm in engaging in politically more rewarding pursuits then national security in a simpler world, when the nation was not so gravely threatened. But today it is intolerable to have the President and Congress devote so much of their time to domestic affairs which can as well or better be handled by others.

There are no objective yardsticks, no scientific criteria, and no hard and fast formulae by which anybody can measure the needs of defense and of a hundred other services in order to assign relative priorities. Former Budget Director Bell testified, "It is plain that considering the national security in this broad sense requires the President—and the Congress—to make a difficult series of choices for which we do not have a satisfactory set of criteria." [17] Nor is it possible to solve such choices with an automatic calculus. They require wisdom, and human wisdom of the highest order. If the President and Congress are to concentrate on them we must devise a better division of labor in regard to governmental functions than we have at the present time.

*It would seem, therefore, that the first and foremost priority for national security rests, not on money, but rather on the brains of our top officials—on their adequate time for study, for deliberation, for decision.* They should not be called upon to deal with hundreds of local services and benefits which can be adequately judged by officials who are closer to the scene and can devote their whole time and talents to these tasks.

Why should the national Government decide whether metropolitan rail transit is needed and where, how much it should cost, and how it should be financed? Why not let the residents of an area make up their own minds whether they need it or not and what it is worth to them? The residents of the San Francisco Bay area decided in November 1962 that they wanted, and were willing to pay for, commuter rail service. Likewise, the voters in other areas could decide what they want in the way of public facilities and services of all types, and what they are willing to pay for.

Priorities should be established in regard to subject matters which are to be submitted to and acted upon by the President and the Congress. Officials of the national Government should be free to devote all their time and energies to foreign policy and national security and such other matters that are geographically indivisible, and by their nature cannot be handled other than on the national level. The President and the Congress should decide priorities *among* defense items and not between defense and urban renewal or public housing or adult education or public assistance. In approving or disapproving strategic plans on their merits they should not be influenced by consideration of demands for an unlimited number of local benefits.

The 1962 Census of Governments found 91,236 governments in the United States: 50 states, 3043 counties, 17,997 cities and other municipalities, 17,144 townships, 34,678 school districts, and 18,323 special districts. Why not let the officials of these governments decide what public facilities and services are needed in their area and justify the outlay of tax funds? These officials will take into consideration the weight of the taxes imposed by the national Government for *national* purposes and the ability and willingness of their residents to pay the cost. Whenever they are in doubt, they can refer such questions to their voters who will be both the recipients of the services and the taxpayers who foot the bill—and, furthermore, being closer to the problem will be better informed as to the issues pro and con.

It is absurd to assume that sufficient intelligence to judge the need for and merit of public services is reserved to the President and Congress and cannot be found among the more than 300,000 state and local officials who are elected by their constituents to make those decisions, and that the voters themselves do not know what they need and what is good for them.

## State and Local Government Fiscal Capacity

Sometimes it is claimed that state and local governments lack the fiscal capacity to raise sufficient funds for the support of essential public services and that they must have recourse to the federal treasury whose more powerful machinery is able to gather far larger amounts. The US Treasury has, for the past twenty years, been collecting a greater annual total of taxes from extremely high rates which were imposed for two reasons: (a) to maintain the defense establishment, (b) to finance numerous activities which used to be in the state-local or the private sphere and whose support the Federal Government has assumed in recent years.

To argue that state and local governments are unable to raise sufficient funds and must turn to the federal treasury for aid, because it collects more money, is to confuse cause and effect. The main obstacle to adequate state and local financing is the weight of federal taxes—whose rates were raised (or not sufficiently reduced after World War II and after Korea) in order to support services that were previously provided by states and localities. The more domestic obligations are shifted to the national Government, the less able are states and localities to boost their own revenues.

All income, wealth, or transactions which can be taxed by the Federal Government are located within the borders of the 50 states and subject to their taxing authority. The most significant power which the Federal Government possesses and which the states lack is the power to incur vast deficits by, for all practical purposes, printing the money to cover them. In all but six of the past thirty-three years, federal budget revenues have been insufficient to meet expenditures. Last year's deficit totalled $6 billion, this year's is estimated at $9 billion, and next year's at $12 billion.

That state and local governments are unable to increase their revenues at a rapid pace is a myth. Since the end of World War

II federal receipts have doubled, while state-local receipts quadrupled. Only during shooting wars have federal revenues increased at a faster pace than state-local. In peacetime periods state and local governments have regularly expanded their receipts more rapidly than the national Government.

The true beneficiaries of the shift in the financing of public services to the national Government are certain public officials: local officials whom the grants enable to evade political responsibility for raising the money they want to spend; federal officials, both in the executive and in the legislative branch, who promise their constituents vast benefits "for free" from the inexhaustible federal treasury and who derive much political mileage from appearing as the benefactors who "bring home the bacon." Too often, unfortunately, legislators are evaluated and ranked according to the amount of federal funds they secured for their home districts.

There seems little justification or excuse in today's world for operating about one hundred federal grant programs, each with its own controls and bureaucracy, and adding several new ones each year. If Congress wishes to aid state and local governments it can do so by either channelling back some of the federal taxes, as the Governors' Conference recommended last summer, or by allocating a purely monetary, non-earmarked, unconditional grant. Congress would then not have to concern itself with numerous domestic programs in 50 states and 91,236 local jurisdictions nor need to impose onerous controls upon the recipient governments.

Let us take the case of education expenditures in order to get an idea of how activities, which are still largely state and local, have fared in recent years. The percentage of national income devoted to education has multiplied more than four times since 1890, from 1.4% to over 6%. During the decade of the 1950's the increase was almost 50%—from 4.1% to 6% of national income. Almost every other country in the world, including the Soviet Union, devotes a smaller percentage of its national income to education.

In his Federal Aid to Education Message in early 1961, the President stated that it would be necessary to build 600,000 new classrooms during the next ten years and that this could not be done without federal assistance. Yet, during the period 1958-62 new classroom construction averaged 71,043 classrooms per annum without federal aid for school construction!

About three-fourths of total US health expenditures come from private sources. What has been the performance record here? Currently well over $25 billion or about 5% of the GNP is spent on health—an amount substantially higher than the percentage of GNP spent on health a decade ago and well above the 3.6% of GNP spent on health in 1928-29. It is also well above the 4% to 4.5% of GNP spent on health in Great Britain, a country with governmental provision of health care for all. At the present time, well over half of the aged population has some form of health insurance, which is more than double the percentage a decade ago.

The United States is now at a level of well-being where the individual can lead a much fuller life, both materially and spiritually, than he could at the turn of the century, or even two decades ago for that matter. The income of the average person in this country is now high enough so that he can buy his own health insurance policies, his own life insurance policies, his own retirement policies, not to mention his own cultural and recreational activities. This way he can obtain the combination of goods and services he desires most, which, according to the generally accepted tenets of economic theory, should maximize his satisfaction.

**Concluding Remarks**

Economic growth at the long-term trend rate of 3% will add close to $2 billion per annum in resources for defense purposes if national security expenditures are held at their present 10% of GNP. It is also obvious that adequate resources for national defense can be provided with greater ease if the nation's product and income grow faster. Such faster growth cannot, however, be brought about by simply establishing a high annual-growth-rate goal and pretending that we can reach it by boosting governmental spending and enlarging public deficits. We have already tried boosting governmental spending and enlarging deficits with unsatisfactory results. A set of priorities needs to be established for policies that stimulate economic growth rather than retard it.

In the last few years it has become generally recognized that our tax system is a very serious obstacle in the path of prosperity. Tax rates were pushed up to confiscatory levels during World War II, and again during the Korean conflict. They were only slightly reduced at the conclusion of hostilities. Expansion of domestic benefits required continued high revenues. Government provided both guns and butter. This appears to prove Parkinson's Second Law: Expenditures rise to meet revenues.

There also needs to be tangible recognition that at a time when national security requires 10% or more of GNP, other demands upon the Federal Government ought to be restrained. Cutting taxes without controlling expenditures does not promise sound economic growth. Both actions are essential and should be part of a total program. Whether it ought to be started on one side of the budget or the other is not really so important as long as the connection between the two is recognized. Dissension over the timing should not be permitted to frustrate action.

The weight of our tax system, heavy as it is, may be doing less damage than its structure, which is not designed merely to raise revenue for the Government, but to implement certain ideas of social justice through a redistribution of income. A system of punitive taxation upon those who aim at and succeed in expanding their business activities is effective in discouraging ambition and making leisure more attractive, once a certain minimum level of income and comfort is reached. It helps to weaken the efforts of those elements in our society upon which enterprise and economic expansion depend. High individual and corporate tax rates also soak up the funds which otherwise might go into investment and expansion, and eliminate from consideration many ventures which otherwise would be undertaken.

The importance of controlling or stopping the growth of non-defense federal expenditures, if the primacy of national security is to be assured and if this is to be combined with a much-needed reduction in federal income taxes, can be illuminated by looking at the growth of federal expenditures during the last three years. Unlike the previous Administration which permitted very little growth in national security expenditures during the period from 1955 to 1960, the new Administration has carried through a sizeable expansion in national security expenditures from $47.9 billion in fiscal 1960 to an estimated $58.3 billion in fiscal 1963, an increase of $10.4 billion (expenditures for national defense, international affairs, and space research and technology are included in these totals). However, all other federal expenditures also increased by $12.1 billion from $46.4 billion to $58.5 billion—a lower rate of increase than that of the preceding five years but still a sizeable one.

The consolidated cash budget had a surplus of slightly less than $1 billion in fiscal 1960; the deficit is likely to exceed $8 billion in fiscal 1963. In short, if non-defense expenditures had been held at their 1960 level, it would be possible during the course of the next few years simultaneously to provide for further expansion in national security expenditures and to reduce income taxes without causing undue inflationary pressures or putting extra strain on our precarious balance-of-payments situation.

An important first step toward assuring the primacy of national security, therefore, is to stop the further expansion of federal expenditures for domestic benefits. In order to be able to continue to expand defense expenditures moderately, it is not necessary to engage in an extensive elimination of existing federal outlays for domestic purposes, although this would be necessary if a large increase in national security outlays were deemed advisable.

If, on the other hand, the Administration persists in what seems to be its present intention of simultaneously combining increases in national security outlays and domestic government benefits with a sizeable reduction in income taxes, it is difficult to see how the end result can be anything other than inflation and balance-of-payments difficulties. Continuation of these policies would, for example, make it highly unlikely that the federal budget could ever be brought back into balance at any time during the rest of the 1960's. A possible solution to this dilemma would be the adoption by the Federal Government of broad-based consumption and excise taxes. But, before a federal sales tax is adopted, careful consideration should be given to the fact that excise and sales taxes are important and growing sources of state revenues and that their adoption by the Federal Government would further exacerbate state and local financial problems.

The greatest contribution that could be made to the problem of establishing priorities in resource allocation so as to assure adequate support for national defense would be to insist that the national Government stick to its last. If the President and Congress were enabled to concentrate their thoughts and efforts upon national security and leave the concern for domestic public services largely to state and local officials, if they were freed of the incessant pressures for enlarged local benefits, a natural priority for defense would be established. The military services would receive whatever, in the judgment of a better informed

President and Congress, they need; and that judgment would be based on the merits of the programs and not be influenced by the demands of numerous special-interest groups. The lobbyists would have to fight their battles in state houses, county court houses, and city halls. That might not necessarily make them happier. But it would give the American people greater assurance that their security is adequately safeguarded and not merely a part-time occupation of the President and the Congress.

### Increase in Federal Expenditures Fiscal Years 1953 to 1963

(Consolidated Cash Budget)

| | 1953 | 1955 | 1963 (estimated) (Millions) | Increase 1953-63 | 1955-63 (Per cent) |
|---|---|---|---|---|---|
| TOTAL ............ | $76,769 | $70,537 | $116,774 | 52% | 66% |
| National defense .... | 50,586 | 40,852 | 53,438 | 6 | 31 |
| International affairs & finance ........ | 2,217 | 2,043 | 2,467 | 11 | 21 |
| Space research & technology (civil).. | 79 | 74 | 2,400 | 2938 | 3143 |
| Veterans benefits and services ...... | 4,963 | 5,116 | 6,367 | 28 | 24 |
| Interest on the national debt .... | 4,706 | 4,664 | 7,496 | 59 | 61 |
| *Domestic services* ... | 14,228 | 17,788 | 44,605 | 214 | 151 |
| Health, labor, and welfare ........ | 6,544 | 9,478 | 25,799 | 294 | 172 |
| Education ........ | 321 | 378 | 1,330 | 314 | 252 |
| Housing & community development | 417 | 310 | 874 | 110 | 182 |
| Commerce & transportation .. | 1,857 | 1,148 | 6,233 | 236 | 443 |
| Agriculture ...... | 2,967 | 4,401 | 6,830 | 130 | 55 |
| Natural resources. | 1,513 | 1,259 | 2,479 | 64 | 97 |
| General government | 1,160 | 1,141 | 2,044 | 76 | 79 |
| Deposit funds, etc. ............ | −551 | −327 | − 948 | — | — |

Source: *The Budget of the United States Government for the Fiscal Year Ending June 30, 1963,* p. 282.
  *Ibid., for the Fiscal Year Ending June 30, 1964,* p. 430.

## FOOTNOTES

[1] US Congress, Senate, Subcommittee of the Committee on Government Operations, *Organizing for National Security*, 87th Cong., 1st Sess., 1961, II, pp. 16-17.

[2] US Congress, Subcommittee on Fiscal Policy of the Joint Economic Committee, *Federal Expenditure Policies for Economic Growth and Stability*, 85th Cong., 2nd Sess., 1958, p. 4.

[3] *Congressional Record*, July 3, 1962, p. A 5085.

[4] *Organizing for National Security*, op. cit., I, p. 769.

[5] *Ibid.*, III, p. 93.

[6] *The Common Defense: Strategic Programs in National Politics* (New York: Columbia University Press, 1961), p. 221.

[7] *Ibid.*, pp. 216-20.

[8] Walter Lippmann, *The Public Philosophy* (Boston: Little, Brown, 1955), pp. 19-20.

[9] Huntington, *op. cit.*, p. 235.

[10] *Organizing for National Security*, op. cit., II, p. 93.

[11] Hanson Baldwin, "Arms and the Atom," The *New York Times Magazine*, May 14, 1957.

[12] "The Politics of National Defense: Fiscal 1950" in Warner R. Schilling, Paul Y. Hammond, and Glen H. Snyder, *Strategy, Politics, and Defense Budgets* (New York: Columbia University Press, 1962), p. 214.

[13] Charles J. Hitch and Roland McKean, *The Economics of Defense in the Nuclear Age* (Cambridge, Mass.: Harvard University Press, 1960), pp. 15-16.

[14] *Organizing for National Security*, op. cit., III, p. 93.

[15] The *New York Times Magazine*, October 11, 1959.

[16] "The Policymaker and the Intellectual," *The Reporter*, March 5, 1959.

[17] *Organizing for National Security*, op. cit., I, p. 1135.

# Discussion—Part V

## Strategy Contingencies and Budget Requirements

*Johnson:* We will begin with the first issue of Part V, "Strategy Contingencies and Budget Requirements." Dr. Weidenbaum, will you please comment on these statements from your paper?

> Since the end of the Korean fighting, the aggregate total of US military spending has tended to be relatively stable, with a moderately upward tilt in the trend line. Except for the last few years, most of the apparent increase is eliminated when the data are adjusted to exclude the effects of price rises (it is not generally appreciated that over-all prices on military programs have been rising faster than those for the national economy as a whole).
>
> * * * *
>
> In essence, the bulk of the resources required to fight a limited war during the coming decade is likely to be in the operational inventory at the start of any such conflict.
>
> Rough approximations of the cost of additional military expenditures under these assumed limited-war conditions would be in the order of $18-$20 billion for 1967, the peak year. This would raise the $52 billion here estimated for DOD outlays for "Cold War" in 1967 to about $72 billion. The latter figure would still represent only 11% of the GNP estimated for 1967 under "Cold War" conditions.
>
> Murray Weidenbaum

*Weidenbaum:** In essence I have here a range of alternatives. If you back me into a corner, my defense, of course, is one man's judgment and one man's opinion. However, what I have tried to do is to relate these estimates to some of the suggestions which have been made earlier during this Conference and you can judge to what extent these projections are or are not consistent with some of these earlier recommendations.

For example, yesterday Dr. Atkinson recommended a specific and major military space activity. The projections I have here

* Dr. Weidenbaum reviewed the chart which appears in his study paper, *supra*, p. 800. Further reference to the chart is made by other discussants.

for defense spending in a Cold War do not assume a specific military space system, but in general a rising amount of funds available for a military space mission. This fund availability under the general budgetary assumptions underlying my projections would result from the fact that later in this decade missile expenditures would taper off, aircraft expenditures would either decline or at best taper off and, hence, with an even slightly rising top budget line, there would be an increasing amount for military space.

## Civil Defense

*Johnson:* Dr. Teller and Dr. Kahn have made proposals concerning civil defense. Dr. Teller, would you comment on how your proposal might affect this kind of budget calculation?

*Teller:* Dr. Kahn has said on another occasion, and I agree with him, that if civil defense were decreed today we could not spend much more than $100 million in the first year. However, one can foresee that after plans have been well laid one could, and one probably should, spend something like $5 billion a year for an appropriate mix between shelters and stored resources so as to make recovery possible. Within three or four years this policy could lead to a substantial ability to recover, and in ten years to a satisfactory state, which is about as rapid a change as you can reasonably imagine. This would add to the expense.

Whether we decide on civil defense or not, active defense, so that we can shoot down enemy missiles, has become a necessity. More money will go into that. But, again, we are not yet prepared. I am not arguing for an existing system; I am arguing for the developmental procedure, and I have no doubt something usable will result which will pay off in making a second-strike force harder to hit; and it will also pay off in making our shelters more meaningful.

Dr. Schelling asked a very relevant question yesterday—where do we get this money? What do we give up? I am glad to see from the chart and from the previous statement that we have the flexibility so that we might do it without giving up anything. I, however, believe that probably other requirements also will arise and that we should look for the things to give up. I would look for the things that we ought to give up and instruments which are already obsolete.

We are engaged in an irrational drive to put a lot of money precisely into obsolete weapons over the objections of our allies.

I believe that thousands of tanks, valuable equipment on the surface, and other expensive instruments in the Air Force category should be scrutinized very carefully. In those categories we can make big savings. The Army, the Navy, and the Air Force are finding, and will find, other objects, like the submarine, the nuclear-armed, small, and extremely mobile tactical Army forces, the intercontinental and smaller-range missiles, and various phases of our space effort, which will require the kind of money that is now projected. Whether it will be that or 10% less, or 20% more, is probably even less defined at present than the economic factors. But I am glad to see that, at least from the economic point of view, we are not yet suffering from serious constraints.

*Weidenbaum:* I would like to comment on Dr. Teller's point concerning what we would have to give up. First of all, let me point out that the calculations underlying my middle line, my so-called standard forecast,* assume a modest growth rate in the national economy, midway between the pessimistic three and the optimistic four, a 3½% growth rate. I assume tax reductions in my model, a balanced budget, as one balanced over a period of time, and very substantial increases in non-defense spending. By the end of the decade, non-defense spending is a larger proportion of the Federal budget than it is at the beginning of the decade. Given all that, I still come up with my middle line which is a rising, absolute level of military expenditures in real terms. To some degree this top line makes allowances for the kinds of systems that Dr. Teller mentions, but to some extent it does not.

It does make allowance for increased expenditures on new systems, not just the current generation of ICBM's, not just the current generation of defensive systems, but the estimate makes generous provision for new additional systems, active systems. They do not contain an allowance for any significant increase in the passive civil-defense program. A program of the magnitude of, say, $5 billion a year would mean essentially a movement from the middle line toward the line of limited war, actually somewhere in between. The limited-war line is roughly $10 or $12 billion higher.

My examination of the limited-war line indicated that, given the relatively low rate of utilization of our resources, under-utilized capacity, and high unemployment level, that there are

* Cf. chart, *supra*, p. 800.

ample resources in the economy available so that we can have a significant increase in defense spending.

*Schelling:* If we could get the National Guard to justify its existence by recognizing that it will have higher priority civil-defense activities on this continent than perhaps going overseas to fight the kind of war that both Dr. Teller and I, for quite different reasons, may feel is not going to be their main function, then we would not only pick up a very valuable asset. We would also have a demonstration from the military services of the kind that we have never had, that sheltering people and troops makes sense. I don't believe that the military services have, in the way they take care of their own assets, given the public any reason to believe that defensive structures and stockpiles are really to be taken seriously. The Air Force did not shelter its own strategic weapons for a long time, and it still does not shelter vital personnel during war. And I would think that the best way to start making civil defense look as though it is taken seriously and as though the Government is behind it would be to have the military services do exactly with respect to their own personnel the kinds of things that the rest of us civilian folk ought to do. Then they should admit that quite possibly the personnel requirements of active civil defense under wartime or emergency conditions will require the same kind of disciplined organization that is usually required to fight armies in battle, and that nobody can manage that job except a militarily trained organization once either the bombs begin to fall or begin to be feared by people who don't even have a legal reason to suppose that their function is to stand around on street corners directing traffic in an undeclared emergency.

*Teller:* I express complete and wholehearted agreement.

## Weapons-Systems Procurement

*Possony:* The crucial item from the economic point of view is to figure out what the time span is. If you want to build this in five years, you have one type of budget problem. If you think you can stretch it out for ten years, it's something else. Some thought should go into this problem. Now, in order to make sure, let us say, that you can adopt the ten- or twenty-year figure and that you won't have any war in the meantime, you have to spend on your deterrent perhaps a little bit more than you are spending now. This brings me to my next point, which is that the switch from the airplane to the missile means a very drastic reduction in firepower.

This is simply a form of nuclear disarmament, and I have little doubt that it is deliberate. Furthermore, the implication here is that if you reduce the amount of nuclear firepower that will be available to this country in case of war, you simply reduce the degree of deterrence. This is not a statement, by any means, that you necessarily have to buy the RS-70 or the Skybolt. My main point is not necessarily the specifics of the delivery system, but that to have a delivery system which delivers a great deal of firepower, more than the missiles are presently capable of doing, or to exchange firepower for firepower by going from the airplane system to the missile system, then you have to build the requisite number of missiles.

The military programs dealing with what you might call the heavy systems, the RS-70 and so on, are scaled down or eliminated essentially on budgetary grounds. These are the alleged grounds. And, of course, they are very expensive. The RS-70 program runs, I think, over $10 billion. The Skybolt system was given as $2½ billion.

Depending on various parameters, it is undoubtedly true that the proper anti-missile defense of the United States runs up to an initial cost of $20 billion, or thereabouts. But if you again parcel this out in five-year plans, when you have to go into these systems on the Air Force side alone, you really have to add considerable billions to the budget. Right now, as Dr. Teller pointed out, the additional billions are added to systems which, in my judgment, are certainly obsolete.

*Weidenbaum:* I'd like to make a few comments on Dr. Possony's statements. First of all, I wasn't aware of any insidious plots to reduce our air power by shifting aircraft to missiles. I think in terms of effective bombs on target, so to speak, the idea is that possibly an ICBM would be a harder target to shoot down than the generation of aircraft that it has replaced. I think we need to think in those terms. The question of cost effectiveness needs to be brought in in terms of analyzing proposed new systems such as the RS-70, or any given proposed anti-ICBM system. We need to raise such questions as to the postponement of production of an anti-ICBM not on financial grounds but on technical grounds.

*Possony:* As far as I know, the Air Force is quite convinced that the RS-70 is an effective system, and the Army is quite convinced that the Nike-Zeus is an effective system. Whether this is true or not, obviously in the future you are not going to buy an airplane and not a missile, but you will have to buy a mixed system, which is an entirely different proposition. But suppose the RS–70 is no good and suppose the Nike-Zeus is no good. Is that all we could do? Since when has the security of this country possibly been entrusted to the proverbial "all-the-eggs-in-one-basket?" If the RS–70 is the wrong system, which might well be the case, we should have about three systems under development and pick the right one. The same thing is true, of course, of the anti-missile defenses. Now, there you run into your R&D costs, which have to be upped.

*Freeman:* A country which does not intend a first strike against an opponent, a strike which it may hope may end a war, and a country which plays a foreign policy of brinksmanship which may at some point or other cause the other side to engage in a first strike, must provide sufficient plans and protection to survive the first strike and to continue. This we have not done, and to my mind this is sheer madness.

It seems to me that to provide, as Dr. Teller suggested and several others have suggested, an adequate major protection system so that if the first strike comes we can continue, is of prime importance. It is also of prime importance to do so many other things that have come up at this meeting in the past few days and as Dr. Possony just mentioned.

There has been some reference to who is going to pay for it. I think we are deceiving ourselves if we assume we can get something for nothing. If we want something and we have a sense of value that this is important, then we have to give up something else. The question is—how do you project defense expenditures?

Dr. Weidenbaum followed GNP trends, as most of us do, and defense requirements. Now this is possibly how it ought to be done, but this is not how the defense budget has been determined in the postwar period, with the sole exception of the Korean period. The way the defense budget was determined on the whole was first to estimate revenues, or, to be more accurate, to overestimate revenues, then to make an estimate of how far Congress may be willing to go in raising the debt ceiling, then to determine how much the administration in power or certain strong forces wanted to go in expanding civilian programs, and the balance became the ceiling for defense. Now of course for the last eight or ten years we have become far too sophisticated to use the term "ceiling." We have used certain euphemisms, but they still mean the same thing—that defense received what was left after everybody else got his share.

If you follow the figures over the period since the end of the war or over the last ten years, you will find that defense always was on the losing end. Just over the last ten years defense expenditures have declined in the national picture from 49% to 30%, and in the federal picture, from 69% to 51%. In other words, we have gradually cut the share of total public expenditures of total funds that go into defense. At the present time, as was mentioned, defense is about 10% of GNP, and I think Dr. Weidenbaum projected roughly that this will continue until 1970 or 1972. Another 10% of GNP in Federal funds goes to civilian expenditures. A little more than that, about 11% or 12% of GNP, goes into state and local expenditures.

*Eckstein:* It is true that civilian spending in recent years has risen about as much as military spending in the recent period. Now, of course, if you draw a comparison of ten years ago, that was when we were just winding up the Korean War. Let me also add a footnote to that chart.*

Basically, of course, that chart is correct, but there is a problem of how to measure defense expenditures in constant dollars. Of course, some things have gotten more expensive, but, on the other hand, the productivity of defense expenditures has increased enormously in the sense that every dollar buys far more explosive power. So the adjustment of defense expenditures for price changes is inherently an insoluble problem. It would be my assumption that the best approximation to defense expenditures is the absolute dollar amount, not adjusted for any price range other than a change in the average level of prices in the entire economy. And on that basis they have risen somewhat more.

Let me turn for a moment to this question of the increase in civilian expenditures. Of course they have risen, some for good reasons, some for bad reasons. Basically, of course, the major reasons for the increase in all this upswing is in the school-age population, which has driven up local expenditures, and the beginning of the maturation of our Social Security system. There are a lot of knotty issues in the field of civilian expenditures, and you'll find that in some of these, on a field-by-field basis,

* Dr. Weidenbaum's chart, *supra*, p. 800.

surely economies could be realized in them. But I do think it would be a false economic strategy, so to speak, to suppose that the increase in a military budget is going to come out of a sudden reduction of civilian expenditures, or, for that matter, that if defense expenditures are inadequate, it is because of civilian expenditures.

*Possony:* That was a good old criticism of the theory of "more bang for the buck." Right now we have exactly the opposite doctrine. We buy no bang for more bucks.

*Teller:* I would like to put the figuring slightly differently. I am interested in bangs. I am interested in bucks. I am more interested in the safety of the country. In one respect there can be no doubt. If we compare the situation of today with the situation ten years ago, if we compare what we can do with the power ranged against us, in this really relevant aspect of our power, our safety has declined. This has to be faced. I would rather face it not by decreasing civilian expenditure and increasing our military effort, but by more unity with our allies and by elimination of useless motions. But if that should prove impossible, I think safety should come before the buck.

## Defense Spending

*Johnson:* Dr. Eckstein, we would like to ask you to expand on the projections in these statements.

> Defense costs, which were held steady for some years, started to turn upward in 1960 and give all signs of continuing up. An average of some recent projections suggests a decennial rise of about 32% (*constant* dollars), which does not appear unreasonable. This would place defense expenditures between 9.5% and 10% of GNP throughout the 1960's.
>
> The cost of civilian functions has been pushing up much faster and there is nothing to indicate that this trend will not continue.
>
> Roger Freeman
>
> . . . I would now project the rate of increase in the coming years at 1.5% to 1.8% a year, which would bring defense spending by 1968 to the range of $57 to $59 billion.
>
> \* \* \* \*
>
> Adding up all the revised expenditure projections, a range of expenditures for the administrative budget of $110 to $130 billion is obtained for 1968 . . .
>
> . . . even these [estimates] make it clear that the budgetary situation confronting the Federal Government in the next few years is not going to be an easy one.
>
> Otto Eckstein

A sharp and sudden increase in defense requirements, because of a deterioration in the international or military situation, can be financed, though with difficulty. Experience has proven that public spending for civilian purposes is almost impossible to cut back and that a slowdown in the growth rate may be the most that can be expected. Income taxes, the mainstay of the Federal treasury, are still levied at close to wartime peak rates. They can be made more productive, but not by very much.

Roger Freeman

*Eckstein:* It seems strange to talk about money when our national safety is at stake, and I only do so because in the end it is money which does measure the willingness of the American people to devote resources to this task as opposed to other tasks. As all of you experienced in these fields know, when all the concern about weapons and strategy goes on, at some point a budget number does appear, and this is the total that can be spent.

Let me also make quickly a distinction between a projection and a program. To me, a projection is something close to a conditional forecast of what will happen. You make certain assumptions which you have to make and then you work out the implications as best you can by numerical and judgment methods. And this gives you some notion of where things might be going if certain assumptions come true. It doesn't mean necessarily that the man doing the projecting thinks what is going to happen is good. I am talking only about projections, not about programs. I am not going to pass judgment now on whether we should have shelters or this or that or the other thing. I'm simply trying to get a little bit of a feeling of where defense expenditures might be heading.

It is clear from our experience over many decades that we do not revolutionize our budget pattern in peacetime in the absence of some enormous emergency. And, although particularly Dr. Teller and Dr. Kahn deserve enormous credit in changing the intellectual climate of this country in its attitude toward defense and I would venture to put a billion-dollar price tag on what we have accomplished, surely there has been a clear change in thinking on defense. Nevertheless, basically defense expenditures are a somewhat trend-like thing. The trend can be a little bit high or a little bit low, but all you're really arguing about is the rate of increase. If you really believe in extreme austerity for defense within a sort of realistic context, you are speaking of a rate of increase of a billion dollars a year, and perhaps even level for a year or two during economy waves.

And if you really believe that there is a large impact of intellectual analysis of our defense problem, you will up that number to two or three billion. So the inherent trends, in the absence of something that the outside world does to us, is really not such a complete mystery, although, of course, the pattern of that defense is going to be determined by the very uncertain technological situations.

One does have to worry about these projections. The upshot of my projections, which, incidentally, are very similar to Dr. Weidenbaum's projections—and let me add that I have projected both revenues and expenditures—is that the budget of the American Government is going to be in a most uncomfortable position for at least the next three or four years. And in the absence of some only hazily foreseen favorable event in the private economy, the budget situation is going to remain in a most unpleasant situation for five or six or seven years.

It is possible, of course, that some of the things that Dr. Briefs summarizes in his paper could happen—a favorable development in the private economy could suddenly lead to a burst of growth which would lead to revenues of now unforeseen magnitudes which would make the budget picture brighter. When I say a budget picture is uncomfortable, I mean that the inherent tendency of the budget is to be in deficit and that we continue to have taboos and symbols of our deficit which will make us very reluctant to make those deficits even larger. Thus, the upshot of my findings is that even in thinking of our strategy in defense, one probably has to do it in the context of a somewhat austere budget picture. One might say, "Well, that's too bad, but nevertheless we should make our strategic decisions on strategic grounds." Following the doctrine of the President in his Budget Message, you cannot buy defense at a discount. For example, try to resolve such issues as were discussed here, particularly the ones about a doctrine of superiority and the doctrine of equilibrium, before you get to the budget numbers. Unfortunately, you can't do it.

Suppose that you reach a strategic conclusion that a superiority doctrine is the one you ought to have and now you find you get only a tenth as much money as you would need. It may turn out that a budget package which is eight-tenths of a superiority package is inferior to all of an equilibrium package which in fact you can get the money for. So you cannot impose the economic constraint when all the strategic considerations are done. And it is for this reason that you have to keep both of these things in mind simultaneously as you go along, and even though you can try to influence the political process in the direction of, say, a higher defense budget, nevertheless, even in the strategy side of it, you have to work with some realistic total budget projections.

I know this isn't very cheerful news. Let me add one footnote to it. One of the thoughts that has occurred to a lot of people in various panels in these last few days is this: "All right, I guess they take it for granted that the budget is going to be not too pleasant to deal with, so why don't we give people tax breaks?" I heard about four different proposals on how we could accomplish certain things through tax incentives rather than through budget expenditures. I think these four things include shelters, industry stockpiling, helping business fight economic wars by giving them a tax refund for the resultant losses they suffer, and a tax credit for financing education so that we have more scientists, engineers, and educated people.

It will be my guess that the Treasury is going to be just as worried as the Budget Bureau about its deficit. In fact, I think it is even more worried. And they are going to be just as reluctant to give away tax dollars as the Budget Bureau is going to be reluctant to give away budget dollars. So I don't believe that that strategy is a way out of it.

*Freeman:* I would like to pick up where Dr. Eckstein left off. On the question of tax credits versus direct expenditures, there are certain activities which can be encouraged and can be promoted by reducing taxes rather than by collecting taxes and spending more. This is basically an ideological split. Let us take, for example, the one on educational expenditures. There are many bills which propose tax credit for educational expenditures. The Treasury objects. It objected, in fact, under the Eisenhower Administration. It objects more strongly at the present time because that would give private people the right to spend the money according to their own judgment, while what they would prefer is that the money be spent under public control according to governmental direction. This is an ideological question—whether you would rather have an expansion or a contraction of the area of governmental action.

However, coming back to the question of the budget, I fully agree with Dr. Eckstein that the position of the budget for six or seven years, not just until 1967, is going to be extremely uncomfortable.

Dr. Eckstein also indicated in his paper that defense expenditures may continue to increase for a few years until we have another economy wave. That is a good point because when an economy wave comes about, as it did in 1953-54, the first victim will be the defense budget. The cuts that were made in the 1950's cut defense expenditures by about $10 billion. There weren't any cuts to speak of in the civilian sector. The civilian sector expanded.

Between 1952 and 1960 we heard from Kenneth Galbraith and many others about the starvation of the public services and about private affluence. In that period defense expenditures increased 2% for the whole country over the eight-year period. That means they remained stable. Civilian public expenses increased 123%. They more than doubled, which is almost three times the rate of increase in personal consumption expenditures.

In the paper which I prepared, which was done before the 1964 budget figures were out, I estimated that, since 1960 civilian and defense expenditures increased at the same rate up to 1963. I knew that wouldn't actually happen. But those were the estimates in the President's Budget as it came out a year ago. Three days ago, as you know, the new estimates came out. So I rechecked them and find that what actually happened is that we spent slightly less for defense than had been estimated, but spent about $2½ billion more for civilian expenditures than had been estimated a year ago. I think that trend will continue and I agree in the projections of the likelihood that defense may increase in the 1960's at the decennial rate of about 32%, or roughly not very much different from the rate of growth in the economy, that is in GNP, but that if current trends continue, civilian public expenditures will increase at about twice that rate, if not more. And the value judgment has to be made as to whether this provides in the long run the safety that we need, and whether we discharge in this form the responsibility which we have, for ourselves and for our children.

*Eckstein:* The simple feature of the current budget, that is, the 1964 budget, is a leveling of non-defense, non-space expenditures. In the current budget, everything but defense is kept absolutely under a rigid ceiling, which took a good deal of pulling and hauling to get, while defense expenditure is still rising at well over $2 billion a year. So, certainly the current trend is not "little old defense being eaten up by civil expenditures."

*Freeman:* May I ask Dr. Eckstein or anybody else in the audience whether he is willing to wager that the 1964 civilian expenditures in the fiscal year will be considerably higher than they appear in the present budget, the reason being that a pencil and a computer can be handled any way you please. The last six budgets as presented by the President all showed a surplus, and they all wound up with a considerable deficit. In each of these budgets the revenue had been overestimated and the expenditures had been underestimated. If you analyze the 1964 budget, it indicates only one thing: that it is realized more widely that what is boosting civilian expenditures and holding back defense expenditure is not the mood of the American public. It is realized that the American public wants and demands more attention to defense. We are doing everything for defense. But actually some of the figures in the budget underestimate expenditures, because the actual expenditures, the actual outlay, will be determined by the formulas in the law such as agriculture program, which was cut $900 million and which really doesn't mean a thing, nor does it in public assistance, in Social Security, and several other areas. In other words, one-and-a-half years from now, when we know what actually happened in the fiscal year 1964, I have not the slightest doubt that what actually will happen is that we will have spent less for defense than it now appears, and we will have spent more for civilian purposes than now appears in the current budget.

*Weidenbaum:* I would like to take up Dr. Freeman's bet, although on his side. I strongly feel that on the basis of the information in the present 1964 budget, non-defense spending will rise from 1963 to 1964, and I have two reasons for that.

First of all, despite all of the Administration's emphasis on the so-called cash budget, when they talk about non-defense spending they suddenly shift back to the old-fashioned conventional budget, which conveniently leaves out the Social Security programs, the fastest-rising portion of non-defense expenditures. And if you look at non-defense spending within the traditional conventional budget, you will see that even though the total non-defense spending actually declines a little, there are two opposing categories. All of these straight-appropriated-fund types of operations, such as the Labor Department, Commerce Department, Health, Education, and Welfare Department, show very large annual increases. The business enterprise funds, such as Housing, Agriculture, and Post Office, show forecasted decreases in expenditures, but these are not programs that are primarily dependent on annual appropriations, so that their estimates of expenditures can turn out several billion dollars too low without affecting the amount of money that they will require from Congress in 1964. I think these so-called business enterprise funds and the underestimate in them give us an important key to why Federal Government expenditures are perennially underestimated in the budget document. This is an area of great discretion for forecasters.

## Local or Central Responsibility

*Teller:* I am very glad that it has been emphasized that civil defense will be expensive whether it is done by expenditure or exemption. I agree that we should be guided by one thing only: in which way can the job be done best? I agree that there are strong reasons why it should be done by central expenditure, and I don't combat this position. But I want to point out that there are also factors pushing us in the other direction. Civil defense for instance, or stockpiling, represent an enterprise which has to be adapted to local conditions, geographic locality, or to specialized conditions in special industries. There is, therefore, a possible argument that properly guided local or private initiative might spend more wisely than a central administration. I don't want to take a position. I want only to say that this consideration should be taken carefully into account when making the decision whether we spend by tax exemption or whether we spend by paying out money.

*Ture:* On the question of the proper location of responsibility for civil-defense efforts, one set of observations that have emerged during this discussion is the sort that Dr. Teller has just enunciated. It is suggested that there are some real economies in putting responsibility for such a program to a substantial extent at the state and local levels because they are better suited to adapt these programs expeditiously and efficiently to the needs of those communities.

The other observation is of the sort that Roger Freeman offered: that there is a philosophical element in this. Do we want the Federal Government to assume responsibility which individual states and localities might as well assume, with no difference with respect to efficiency of the activities?

It is very hard to generalize from small samples, but I'd like to suggest a small sample to Dr. Teller. At the announcement of the outbreak of the Cuban crisis, in the suburban community of Washington in which I live, the County Manager and the superintendent of schools decided that something had to be done for the protection of the children in the event that an air raid or an attack occurred during school hours. What they decided should be done was to issue a directive to the principals of each of the schools. The directive said, "Proceed immediately to develop a civil-defense plan with the cooperation of your respective Parent-Teacher Association." I happen to be a president of one of those Parent-Teacher Associations, so this was not an academic matter to me.

We looked around to see what were the resources of our school community for the production of a civil-defense plan. In the school itself there isn't anything that even begins to approach a reasonable radiation shelter area, let alone a blast shelter area. We began to take an inventory of what would be needed on the assumption that by some lucky chance we would not be subjected to an immediate blast peril and that the radiation blast in fact could be overcome by some minor modification of the structure. This involves supplies, sanitation facilities, ventilation facilities, and so forth.

What emerged with crystal clarity was that this was a program that the particular microcosm couldn't even begin to contemplate undertaking. So we then proceeded to put the responsibility back where we thought that it belonged, on the government of this extremely affluent local community.

The response there was, "Well, we set aside some money last year on the contingency that the Federal Government would match the funds that we set aside. By virtue of the fact that the Federal Government did not see fit to move promptly and expeditiously on this, we've allowed this allocation to lapse. Besides which, we couldn't do it anyhow. It's up to the state to do it." And the response at the state level is that is a program that we can't undertake; it's up to the Federal Government to do it.

Whether or not, indeed, there would be some superior gains, some gains in terms of superior efficiency in putting this program at state and local levels, I would submit to you, Dr. Teller, that the more urgently you feel this to be an imperative of our strategy, the greater pressure you ought to put on the Federal Government at least to initiate such a program.

As to the question that Roger Freeman raised, I don't think this is a question of philosophy at all. I think all of us will agree that what private individuals, private companies, state and local units can demonstrably do more efficiently than the Federal Government, they should. I don't believe that the Federal Government really is engaged in a long-run conspiracy to subvert the private-enterprise system. I think what is involved, however, is the technical question of whether or not one can use indirect inducement, tax inducements, effectively to bring about the kind of activity which will contribute to this kind of a defense program. I have yet to see a scientific, empirically based demonstration that the kinds of tax incentives we've been talking about really would be in the least consequential for the kind of thing you are asking us to do. And until that demonstration has been made I would suggest that insofar as we feel these are urgent undertakings, we do them in a way in which we feel fairly confident that the response will be large.

## Impact of Increasing Defense Expenditures

*Johnson:* Professor Mason's* paper dealt with the problem of increasing expenditures for defense, and he has some views that are shared by some members of the panel and not shared by others.

> During the last few years our military expenditures have been running at about ten per cent of GNP. It is said that if we increase this percentage significantly, the "US will go bankrupt" or, if not bankruptcy, then some essential characteristics of a private enterprise economy will be lost forever. Modern states cannot and do not go bankrupt in any meaningful sense of the word.
>
> \*    \*    \*    \*
>
> As long as the monetary authority can create money, any conceivable volume of public debt can be serviced. A sharp increase in military expenditures could have serious inflationary consequences but even this is quite unnecessary if adequate measures are taken to increase tax receipts *pari passu* with the increase in expenditures.
>
> \*    \*    \*    \*
>
> Nor is there any serious reason to believe that an increase in military expenditures, if it takes place gradually, would force us into a system of direct controls destructive of the market mechanism or of profit incentives. The priorities, rationing, and price controls of wartime were the product not only of the diversion of a very large fraction of economic resources to military use, but of the rapidity of the build-up.
>
> Edward Mason

* Dr. Mason, a member of the President's Advisory Committee on Foreign Aid, chaired by General Lucius Clay, was called to a session of that group while this discussion took place.

*Campbell:* First, I wanted to make one or two comments on the previous sections. I believe Mr. Weidenbaum stated that he put agriculture spending in the classification of business operations of government. The agriculture support program of the United States Government in the last ten years, in which budget expenditures have increased from $3 billion to roughly $6 billion, is one of the most interesting business operations I've ever run into in my life. You might say that the taxpayers have been getting the business here.

There's a tendency on all sides to discuss government expenditures almost exclusively in terms of the Federal Government. Somehow or other the state and local sector is the forgotten sector. I would simply like to cite one or two statistics which, in my opinion, cast grave doubts on whether the continuous increase in Federal non-defense expenditures is really necessary or not—and if that increase seems to be what is causing our budgetary problems in recent years. In other words, if we're going to get a cut in income taxes, something is going to have to give somewhere. I doubt that economic growth will take care of everything, economic growth usually being a favorite remedy of the economists whenever we get in serious situations.

We say that by 1970 economic growth will get us out of this predicament and the budget will be balanced again. It is not generally known that, since the end of World War II, state and local tax revenues have quadrupled, while Federal revenues have only doubled. There is one obvious explanation for that. Federal tax revenues were pushed to a fairly high level during World War II, and there was much less leeway left. But there should be a moral in that for us, namely, that there is a limit to the amount of budget expenditures, even with economic growth, that the Federal Government can support.

I agree with Dr. Mason in one part of his paper where he intimated that if we have to increase our national security considerably, we will be able to do it. The American people have always risen to emergencies. The only thing that bothers me is that we seem to have the taxpayer today, at the Federal level, in a state of perpetual emergency which leaves very little leeway for the real emergencies. I would submit that the state and local record, and also the private record, in this country has been good.

There has been much discussion about education expenditures in the last few years and somehow or other we are always given the impression—although education expenditures in total run well over $25 billion—that if we just adopt a Federal program, which initially will only cost $75 or $100 million, that somehow or other that will solve the problem. Well, the actual record of the decade of the 1950's was that as a percentage of the national income, education expenditures went up from roughly 4.1% to 6%. And virtually all of this was done by state and local and private effort. There were some Federal expenditures, particularly the National Defense Education Act of 1958, and also some National Science Foundation expenditures for national security-related purposes. But the overwhelming part of that money came from state and local and private sources. I see no reason why, in the 1960's, the same thing can't happen so that the national Government can concentrate its efforts and its resources on what the national Government should concentrate its efforts on, namely national security and foreign policy.

*Siegel:* I'm not a tax expert but I can't resist reinforcing some of the remarks that Dr. Campbell just made. We seem to be lacking schools, and now we seem to be lacking medical services. We lack teachers. We lack hospitals. We lack all sorts of things, and it would seem desirable to consider, in view of the interest that the Federal Government now has in abandoning various tax revenues, tax sources which it has been exploiting considerably, it would seem desirable at this junction to consider that state and local governments might be able to jump in and take advantage of this relinquishment of tax revenues by the Federal Government to supply many of these needs which the Federal Government also says are still urgent. For example, there is a desire to set up a Department of Urban Affairs, Medicare, and so on. There is a need for another National Education Act. It would seem that at this juncture it would be desirable for all state legislatures to consider taking up the slack and for all suburban communities, like Ture's, to consider taxing themselves a little bit more to supply some of these needs that they urgently feel.

One of the curious aspects of this whole business of Federal diversion or utilization of resources is that there is no symmetry necessarily pursued by the Federal Government in increasing demand and in increasing supply. Much of the Federal Government's activities seem to be directed toward increasing demand rather than necessarily increasing supply. This is particularly the case with respect, say, to medical care.

*Eckstein:* For the sake of completeness, let me just allude to one obvious point. Our national security in the long run is not going to depend only on military expenditures. About the surest way we can guarantee our decline by the 1980's is to have an inadequate educational system. You know, the Russians have been very heavily emphasizing education and science much more heavily in relation to their resources than we have. I don't know what the merits of the aid-to-education bill are. It would depend upon the specific bill. But surely we're robbing the future if we think we can squeeze a few hundred million dollars out of a Federal aid-to-education program.

*Campbell:* Of course, we need healthy citizens. We need well-educated citizens. We even need to clean up water pollution for national security. Fine! We can all agree on this. However, I would submit the proposition that by 1980, to the extent that education contributes to national security, the surest way to weaken it is to have the Federal Government enter the field with a massive program of Federal aid. Just because the Federal Government does something doesn't necessarily mean that we've strengthened the situation.

*Freeman:* We are told that sort of thing every time we are said to have gaps in education and other fields. Now, the story of the gaps goes back quite a way. You all remember there existed a dollar gap outside the United States. Suddenly it seems that the dollar gap is on our side rather than on the side of Europe. Then gradually we developed a missile gap. Now some people wonder where the missile gap went. Then we developed a public service gap, according to Galbraith and Lippmann and several others. In the last two years we have developed another gap, and that is in GNP. This is the number one item in gapsmanship, and I am waiting now for the next gap to develop. Actually, when you check them, they all fall into the same category.

Education has been mentioned time and again. Between 1950 and 1960, enrollment in the schools increased 44%. But school funds increased 171%. So I'm not too sure that is where the gap is. The square footage per pupil in elementary schools now is roughly about twice what it used to be but I don't know of any evidence that reading or that spelling progresses at the same rate as the number of square feet per pupil in the classroom.

*Ture:* Questions of economic policy are primarily questions of priorities, of the relative rankings of objectives and of the cost of their attainment, rather than objectives that are measurable in terms of absolute measures of gaps. I would like to follow that notion a little bit in terms of our present discussion; that is, strategy contingencies and budget requirements.

What Otto Eckstein and Roger Freeman and Murray Weidenbaum were asked to do was something so Herculean that it
staggers the imagination. They were asked to project the
budgetary requirements of defense strategy for some substantial
period into the future. There isn't any such thing as the defense
strategy the cost of which can be so projected. A correct performance of this job would be to take all of the strategy
alternatives, any number of those suggested during the last two-
and-a-half days, and try to cost these out over the periods of
time into the future that are relevant with respect to each of
these strategies.

What I think we have discovered in our discussions so far is
that this group will never arrive at a consensus concerning the
one correct strategy or the one correct strategy complex. There
is a huge array, and the number of such alternative strategies
increases, I think, probably exponentially as we more carefully
delineate the central objective at which these strategies presumably are aimed. So what is, in fact, the policy problem that
is involved in trying to aggregate in quantitative terms the cost
of alternative strategies? It is not to arrive at the one strategy
complex which is superior in some technical sense to all others,
but to evaluate the gains which any one strategy complex will
provide for us in terms of additions to our over-all defense posture, in terms, as well, of the cost of each such strategy complex.

The best strategy complex is not necessarily the one that is
superior in some technical sense. It is the one with respect to
which the ratio of gain to cost, incremental cost, is a maximum.
If that, in fact, is the correct proposition, what we have had in
terms of budget projections really involved an elaborate set of
implicit assumptions that the way in which the benefits and costs
of alternative strategies will be weighed in the future will differ
in no material respect from the way in which they have been
weighed in the past.

The way they have been weighed in the past, of course, has
involved a great number of constraints of a non-economic
character. Most of these constraints, so far as I can see, emerge
from an extraordinarily conservative financial orientation on
the part of both the Legislative and Executive Branches of the
Federal establishment, whether dominated by Republicans or
Democrats, and in terms of what we are likely to do in the future,
I think these are probably still the major constraints.

*Briefs:* We have had, on the one hand, Dr. Eckstein's projection
that for the next four, five, or six years the Federal budget is

going to be in an awkward position. There is an implied statement there, perhaps not by Dr. Eckstein, but by many, that Congress tends to spend in terms of revenues, in other words, that
the expenditures are a function of the revenues and that therefore there is a bind on the things we wish to do or we think we
ought to do. Glenn Campbell and Roger Freeman talk about the
things we ought not to do. And the discussion appears to be a
question of economizing within a budget that is essentially constrained by the fear that the revenues will not match.

On the other hand, Dr. Teller made a very powerful appeal
for the defense needs of the nation. With the economy presently
at less than capacity levels, additional spending for national
security would raise these levels and would not require shifting
resources from some uses to others.

I have myself made some calculations as to what the private
economy may demand in terms of resources over the next ten
years. I am really impressed with the fact that, on the activity
side, on the demand-for-resource side, we are certainly not going
to lack sufficient demand to keep our machinery operating at very
high levels. This does not mean it will be continuous. It doesn't
mean it is going to happen this year or in the coming year. But
looking over the ten years, I think there is more apt to be an
excess demand for resources than there is a constraint of the
kind that seems to be implied.

I think the real problem, therefore, is one of reallocation of
resources according to considerations that Norman Ture has
laid out at levels and at rates of expansion that are more nearly
what the economy and our ingenuity and our capability can produce. I think that if you see the discussion in these terms, then
the arguments about whether we should spend more for one
civilian function or another, or where economies might be
achieved, seem to make a lot more sense.

It seems to me that for the next ten years, and taking into
account both the national security demands on the one hand and
what I think is going to be the expansive character of the private economy, the problem will be one of reallocation.

*Haberler:* I fully agree with Dr. Mason's first passage that it
is possible to extract a few billion more from the American
GNP for defense or for anything else, and it can be done if we
want to by using proper methods without getting into a serious
inflation. And I will also agree it can be done without getting
into direct control. But the real question comes later, in connection with later passages.

But let me say this. There is always room for one more on the back seat even if it's crowded. Even in the New York subway in rush hours you can always squeeze one person in. I will not say that the American economy at the present time is crowded to the same extent as the New York subway in rush hours, but there is always room for more. The question is—how do you finance that "more?"

Prices have now been stable for four-and-a-half years. Therefore, I think it would not be very constructive to dwell on inflationary dangers right now. The balance of payments on the other hand is something which would worry me. But I suggest we consider now the next statement, also from Edward Mason's paper.

> The real difficulty attendant on such an increase is the general unwillingness to pay more taxes, but this is a political rather than an economic limitation.
>
> Edward S. Mason

*Haberler:* This I would subscribe to. I would even go so far as to say that at the present moment we could finance additional expenditure without additional inflation. We surely have more slack than we want to have, though, I take a somewhat less alarmist view of the long-run implication of that slack. But, in the short run, surely we could easily spend three, four, or five billion more without danger of rising prices, without inflationary dangers, and without increasing the tax burden. The only qualification I have here is the balance of payments. That, I think, would feel an impact of increased expenditure very soon.

## Economic Constraints on Strategy

*Johnson:* I think that at this point we can turn our attention to the next issue on our agenda, "Possible Economic Constraints on Strategy Contingencies."

> The US should go beyond essentially defensive measures and use its resources dynamically to limit Soviet strategic options and, more positively, to improve the world prospect for our version of peace with justice, diversity, and economic development. Perhaps more appropriate than a race into space would be a race in which we lead for objectives closer to the Soviet citizen's heart—e.g., consumer goods, shorter hours, and more civil liberties.
>
> Irving Siegel

*Johnson:* Dr. Siegel, will you please elaborate on your statement?

*Siegel:* One of the things that we have to contemplate is the probability that low-temperature warfare will be dominant in the next decade or so. By this I include, among other things, so-called peaceful coexistence, which many people don't sufficiently recognize as a type of warfare.

In this connection there are many opportunities which a country like ours could have for initiative. There are no very serious constraints on our material resources. And, as you know from the other remarks made here, there seems to be even a sort of redundancy of idle or under-utilized capital equipment. Dr. Briefs has already indicated that he felt that there were other sources of growth in our economy to take up certain other options.

Manpower, scientific and technical manpower, will remain in short supply, partly because of long lead times. There are always problems of doing enough research and development at the right time and on time. It is very important to have a posture of initiative because no matter how much you have in the way of resources, if you do not have the initiative and you are in a posture of response, you may never have proper utilization of the superiority of resources which you initially enjoy.

I feel that if we have peaceful coexistence, which I would like to define as the pursuit of war by non-military means, there are certain things you should do to degrade your enemy. One of the most important things you can do, it seems to me, is to tear down our own myth of the Iron Curtain, and through communication and other devices try to get the Russian people to act on their own behalf. I do not mean by ideological values; I mean by consumer goods, the same kinds which invade our own type of society. I think it would be a welcome innovation in Soviet society. Similarly, a shorter work week, I think, would be very much appreciated by people who still work a six-day week, and so on. Similarly, a higher level of civil liberties in terms of more freedom of movement and freedom of expression could be sought.

I do not ask for these simply as human values; I ask for these also as strategic values because the more that is done to degrade the opportunities of the planners who command the resources and to utilize them for their own purposes, the more we are helping ourselves through having the Russian people help themselves. In this connection it is much more appropriate to have a race for consumer goods, something that we ourselves would initiate, a race in which we lead, than a race to the moon.

There seem to be all kinds of strategic options here that ought to be explored. I regret that, as we have conceded in the military realm the first strike and all sorts of other things to the self-declared enemies, but that even in peaceful endeavor we have allowed them to define the first strike and have accepted a responsive posture.

There is a lot to be done here, and we can do it and do it quickly. However, if the feeling is that we are only going to rely on certain strategic and material resources to respond, it is going to be an awfully difficult matter. It seems quite foolish for us to accept the posture of just responding to dangers which we now know to exist and still do not know quite how to handle, and, in addition, allow problems which have not yet presented themselves to emerge. We should structure the future, to the extent that we can, by our own initiatives.

## Priorities in Resource Allocation

*Johnson:* Dr. Campbell's statements dealing with resource allocation bear on our discussion:

> On more than one occasion during the past 15 years the resources that could have completed or accelerated defense projects have been used to expand domestic welfare benefits. During the past 10 years national defense expenditures expanded only 6% from $50.6 billion to $53.4 billion whereas federal civilian benefits and services increased 214% from $14.2 billion to $44.6 billion.
>
> * * * *
>
> The problem of establishing priorities in resource allocation so as to assure adequate support for national defense could be met by having the national Government "stick to its last." If the President and Congress were enabled to concentrate their thoughts and efforts upon national security and leave the concern for domestic public services largely to state and local officials, if they were freed of the incessant pressures for enlarged local benefits, a natural priority for defense would be established. The military services would receive whatever in the judgment of a better-informed President and Congress they need, and that judgment would be based only on the merits of the programs and not be influenced by the demands of numerous special-interest groups.
>
> W. Glenn Campbell

*Campbell:* I think our situation would be helped immeasurably if the national Government were to follow policy along the lines indicated by the statement. It can be illustrated very simply by starting with the 1960 election campaign. For example, foreign policy and defense issues dominated the election, but turn and look at all the various things the President and the Congress must concern themselves with. The President literally sent dozens of messages to the 87th Congress covering over two hundred new spending plans. The same thing pertains to the Congress where a large percentage of its time is taken up with domestic issues.

After the Korean War, expenditures were cut back somewhat. The expenditure cutback, as Mr. Freeman pointed out, was all in the defense field. Actually, non-defense expenditures were in a steadily upward trend. We were able to have a relatively modest tax reduction in 1954 as a result of the cutback in military outlays. From 1955 on, there was some continuous creepage in defense expenditures for the next five years. But in essence the major increase was in non-defense expenditures, and we were able to do that, of course, because of the progressive tax system that we have, along with the growth in the economy. In 1960, however, there was a new Administration and some change in policy. The new Administration, in my opinion, quite correctly has increased defense outlays from 1960 to fiscal 1963 somewhat in excess of $10 billion. However, it has also increased non-defense expenditures.

Now, trying to put this in the broader picture and talk about priorities, it seems to me that we've got to make some choices. In defense of my argument on this, I would take Professor Eckstein's budget projection in which, for fiscal 1968, he projects administrative budget expenditures from a minimum of $110 billion to a maximum of $130 billion. This is at the Federal level, of course. An average of that would be $120 billion. Now, taking a growth rate of 3%, which is approximately the present growth rate, you would only have $100.6 billion in fiscal 1968, or a deficit of $20 billion. This, I would add, is without a reduction in taxes, as I read Professor Eckstein's estimates.

However, if we take larger growth-rate figures, we find that with a growth rate of 4% the yield is still only $106.6 billion in fiscal 1968, or a deficit of over $13 billion. Interestingly enough, even with a 5% growth rate, we still get a deficit in administrative budget expenditures without even taking the tax reduction into account. If we keep on with this present policy we will not get a budget surplus between now and 1968. There are, of course, other alternatives we could adopt. We could pass a general sales tax in this country which would yield considerable revenue. The alternative, of course, which I strongly favor, is that as a minimum, we must stop the growth of non-defense

Federal expenditures because, if we are going to protect our national security properly, there must be some flexibility left in the budget. It is all very well to say that we can afford the security expenditures if we really have to. That is a truism to which I subscribe fully. But I don't think that is the situation that we're talking about.

I would end this discussion with the question addressed to Dr. Weidenbaum. I simply do not see how we can continue to have the growth in both defense and non-defense expenditures that he talked about, plus a tax reduction, and also have a balanced budget, because that is a mighty long cycle.

**Haberler:** I'd like again to confine myself for the moment to the statements here on the screen. There are two opposing theories here. On the one hand we have been told that defense has been starved of appropriations by other types of expenditures. On the other hand, there is Mr. Siegel's theory.

**Siegel:** I said that as a strategy we should direct our efforts to get the Soviet people to demand those same opportunities which we take for granted here in order to dislocate the planner's choice within the Soviet-type economies.

**Haberler:** I'm really grateful you said that because I have seen only that excerpt. I quite agree with Glenn Campbell that the public sector has not been starved. It is simply not true that we have private affluence and public poverty. On the other side, anybody who has been in Russia is tremendously impressed that there the exact opposite is true. There you really see public affluence, compared with their level of private consumption. There the contrast is really tremendous—abject private poverty and ostentatious public consumption and affluence. This simply is not so here. There is no affluence, private affluence, compared with public poverty.

On the other hand, I must say that I do not have the impression that defense has been starved. On the contrary, I have the impression that it is much easier to get money from Congress for defense purposes than for many other things. Of course it is true that in the fifties there was one big cut in defense expenditure in order to get a tax cut. Here was one incident where perhaps economic considerations played some role, but I don't think that Eisenhower would have cut defense if he had not been convinced that it could be done. He may have been mistaken in fact, but surely there were other considerations. But apart from this one incident, my definite impression is that it is much easier to get money from Congress for defense purposes than for anything else.

As to the immediate budgetary situation, I agree that with all the increases in expenditure which are now contemplated for military and non-military purposes, both can be carried out. And if on top of that we did get a tax cut of the approximate magnitude which has been purposed by the President. But then the deficit would become unmanageably large. It is now estimated at something like $8 billion in the current fiscal year. We might get something twice as big if these plans were carried out.

If I have to make a choice between the deficit on the one hand, which is produced by a tax cut, and a deficit which is produced by increased expenditures, I prefer the first one, because that means that private individuals are allowed to do the spending and Government does not do all the spending. And since I do not believe that the Government has been starved, I am all in favor of giving the private individual, the private sector of the economy, a chance to spend a little more.

If there is a large budget deficit, I would not worry about it in the short run. "The short run" means for two years. I would not worry about that from the point of view of internal inflation. If we have a deficit even larger than the one now projected, I don't think this is a serious matter so far as internal inflation is concerned. If wages start to rise again and employment increases, then we may get into inflation again sooner than we think. But at the present I think we need not worry about that.

We do have to worry about the balance of payments. I would not be surprised if the balance of payments would again get worse in the next year. I think there is some reason to worry about it, and I hope that those in the Government who are responsible for dealing with it have some idea what they are going to do if a large deficit in the balance of payments opens again.

***Eckstein:*** The proposition that has been advanced by the quote is this. The defense budget has been limited, presumably below a proper level, by civilian expenditures.

As the statement is presented, the base period is 1953, which is the Korean War. And you couldn't construct the same argument in that extreme form for other years. Second, the definition of mutual security expenditures here includes the narrowest concept and does not include space expenditures which are rising very rapidly, which presumably in the long term have a security justification, at least in part. Third, it includes a definition of Federal expenditures which include Social Security. It includes a number of things.

There are simply some demographic elements which raise civilian expenditures. I would add one other little footnote to that. I think that historical experience has been that governments are either stingy, or they're spenders. And if they're stingy about defense, they're stingy about everything. And if they're spenders about defense, they're spenders about everything. I would say that the historical record suggests that the association between civilian spending and military spending is positive, not negative.

I, for one, happen to think we could save considerable amounts of money in a number of civilian fields, and we should. We start new programs very often without really thinking through the design properly. And given the level of civilian expenditures, I don't think we have as much to show for it in the solution of our major problems in our cities, education, and so on, as we probably should.

Let me look ahead a little bit. What about the future defense budget? As far as I can see, there are two key issues that you have to think about. The first is, how much will the total resources of the Government and of the economy grow? And second, what fraction is going to be available for defense?

A number of the Conference papers say that the relation between growth and our national security is rather tenuous and remote. Let me only point this out to you:

First, taking for granted that projections of the type I am about to mention have a margin error of at least 2% or 3%, if the American economy grows at 3% to 1970, the administrative budget revenues, which are most relevant to defense budget, will be about $108 billion. If the American economy grows at 4.5% —and I'm not taking extreme numbers now—the growth will be $15 billion larger, or $123 billion. Not all of that is going to go to defense, but if defense gets its proportionate share, and it has been doing at least that well under the present Administration, that is a difference in the defense budget of around $6 or $7 billion. That is a very mechanical view, but it's a first approximation of growth and the defense budget. Now $6 or $7 billion will buy quite a bit of defense.

What about this potential growth? Is it really pie in the sky to speak of growth of 4.5% rather than 3%? If you take the last eighty years, the growth rate was about 3.6% the first forty, and about 3% or 3.2% for those last forty years. Growth has been in the 3% range, not in the 4% to 4.5% range. Is 4.5% pie in the sky? I would advance the proposition that it is not. That is, it is within the economic capability of the economy to grow at that rate without any drastic change in the system. I say that for the following reasons.

First, the scientific studies do suggest that the normal rate of growth of the economy under conditions of the contemporary situation, with a rather high labor-force growth, is something on the order of 3.4% to 4%. You will find disputes between that range, but you'll notice you won't find anybody at the three and you won't find anybody at the five among the serious students of the subject. So, you can take as a kind of a baseline of normal growth something on the 3.4% to 4% range. In addition to that, you do have to get into the question of the present gap between actual output and full-employment output. Here again the statisticians have their conceptual differences, they have differences about the meaning of the numbers, and they don't all come up with identical estimates. In fact, you can't come up with the same estimate because to some extent it depends upon the uses to which you put the gap. There are some things in which we have an enormous gap. We could produce far more automobiles than we need or want. You can't get a final number unless you also say what it is that is going to be expanded in this total output. The estimate of gap, as far as I can determine, ranges from the order of $25 to $35 billion.

Take for a moment the lower of these figures, which I think is too low. Suppose it to be $25 billion. From now to 1970, that $25 billion is about five-point-something per cent of the GNP, so the gap is on the order of 5% to 6%. Suppose it to be 6%. If it is spread over sixty years, that would be an extra 1%. If it is spread over more years, then the number goes down. If you estimate the gaps a little smaller, it again cuts the number.

Unless you take a know-nothing point of view, you have to reach some conclusion that the rate of growth of which the economy is capable—that is, the output for 1970 without over-full employment—can involve a rate of growth of, say, 3.4% for the long term plus, say, 0.8% for gap closing, or a total of around 4.2%. Now that 4.2%—and maybe it's 4 and maybe it's 4.5—makes an enormous difference by 1970. The difference in unemployment if you take a 3% growth from now until then would involve an amount which probably would be intolerable, probably more than 7%. On the other hand, the other figure would get you full employment. If you think of it in terms of revenue, you get into numbers like $10 and $15 billion.

We have, in the past really made a mistake in not considering this baseline of a normal rate of growth of the economy. Economic science simply hadn't focused on it. It's a recent concept, a recent development, and we're a little distrustful of it as we should be of all new ideas.

### Strategy Contingencies and Fiscal Policies

*Johnson:* I would like to turn now to the third issue and begin by considering a statement from Dr. Haberler's paper.

> It is asserted that this slowdown is not serious from the point of view of military preparedness. On the contrary, it can be argued that a slack economy is in a better position to adapt itself to an emergency (sudden sharp increase in defense demand) than a fully employed economy.
>
> Gottfried Haberler

*Haberler:* From the point of view of military strategy and military preparedness, I'm quite prepared to argue that the slightly slack economy is better than the literally fully employed economy. If you imagine a new emergency, say, a Cuban crisis or something like that, only on a larger scale, it is much easier to handle in a slightly slack than in a fully employed economy. In a fully employed economy you have to cut down somewhere if you increase defense expenditures. In a slack economy you can have butter and guns at the same time. This is one of the reasons why Hitler was so successful. When he came in, he had a lot of unemployment, so he could give the German people butter and guns at the same time.

Of course, it would be very different if the slack became so large that the maintenance and the build-up of industrial capacity would suffer. But I don't think this has been the case. It has been the case in one particular area. I can really think of one particular area where industrial capacity has deteriorated in recent years, and that's in the area of railroad transportation in the East. But that has nothing to do with the general slack even if our economy went back to full employment.

Full employment is now defined as 4% unemployment. That is probably a reasonable definition, by the way. That would not put the railroads back on the track. That requires something else. This is a structural change that has something to do with specific Government policies. I don't think that the slack which we had in the last few years has in any way deteriorated our industrial plant. In addition, if you have a slightly slack economy and can easily spend without fear of inflation, it is much easier to get money for defense. After all, in 1954, as we were told, Eisenhower cut defense expenditures partly because there was inflation going on, prices were rising and, of course, employment was much higher. Today this is not so. Today it's possible to increase defense expenditure easily and get the bonus on the side. You get more defense and you get a little more employment. So, from the standpoint of giving money to the military, increasing defense expenditures and providing more goods for defense purposes, a slightly slack economy is a boon.

With regard to growth, we should distinguish the two things. We have a little slack, and if we were entirely free, if there were no balance-of-payments problems, we could easily get back to, say, 4% or 4½% unemployment instead of the 6½% we have now, and we could add to our GNP. I think some of the estimates that were made were a little on the large side—$35 billion. Even if it were only $15 billion, that would be quite nice to have. But this is not what we mean by growth. What we mean by growth is that the annual rate over the long period should be, say, 1½% higher. Now that, of course, would be nice to have, but simply by taking out the present slack by more spending we can get one step higher, but we have absolutely no guarantee that the economy will go on growing at a higher rate.

In my paper I've enumerated a number of possible policies which could be undertaken to increase long-run growth, policies partly of commission, but also of omission. We spend billions of dollars a year for unsalable agricultural surpluses. This is anti-growth policy. This money is wasted. If that were cut down some, that would add a couple of billion dollars to the annual real national income.

At the present moment I'm not against increased expenditures and reduced taxes to get some slack out of the economy. But I would insist that, if we do that we ought to be prepared for balance-of-payments troubles that may come pretty soon. Thinking a little further ahead, I think inflation cannot be dismissed; that will depend very much on the wage policy. If the economy goes into higher gears and if unions become bolder and ask for higher wage hikes, then we shall get into an inflationary spiral.

I think an economy like ours simply cannot stand that for long. The lesson of the last few years is really very clear.

You remember that in the last election campaign one of the main economic arguments was that you cannot fight an inflation, such as the creeping inflation we had in which monetary policies of the Federal Reserve were criticized for keeping interest rates too high, and so on. Then came the change in administrations, but nothing changed in monetary and fiscal policies. The present Administration is just as much concerned about inflation as was the previous one. It is in a somewhat better position because there has now been no inflation to speak of for four years, so we can relax a little bit. But if the economy goes into higher gear, if wages are again pushed up in excess of the annual increase of labor productivity and prices go up, I'm certain that the present Administration will react the same way and will again tighten credit and possibly cut expenditures, perhaps even in the defense area if the international situation allows. And then we shall get again a little more slack than we want to have.

## Strategy of Economic Growth

*Johnson:* At this point we would like to consider the next issue, and will begin by asking Mr. Ture to discuss his statement.

> I conclude that it would probably require an extraordinarily large shift of tax burdens from the returns on capital to the returns of other factors of production to effect an increase in the capital stock adequate to increase the rate of expansion of full-employment gross national product by one percentage point. I reach a similarly bearish conclusion concerning the potential of tax changes for accelerating capital retirement and replacement, i.e., modernizing the capital stock sufficiently to alter significantly the rate of expansion of GNP.
>
> Norman Ture

*Ture:* A few moments ago this panel was discussing what is indicated on the board under issue two—"Possible Economic Constraints on Strategy Contingencies." I want to make the observation that, with the exception of a few remarks that Otto Eckstein made, I do not think that I heard one word that pertained to possible economic constraints on strategy contingencies. I heard a great deal about possible budgetary constraints.

Let me point out that that topic we did not talk about is an extremely important one, and I would suggest to the group that it is more important than our discussion of what can or cannot be done within the constraints of a given Federal budget or a trend line of development of that budget.

What is involved in possible economic constraints on strategy contingencies? It seems to me that the kind of strategy contingencies we've been talking about during this Conference are not best described in terms of some broad quantitative generalities of the size of this or that component of the armed forces, or of this and that expenditure for a broad complex of weapons. What we are talking about are technical characteristics of various components in a defense program. I would submit to you that we are therefore talking about variations in defense strategy, each of which involves a high degree of specialization of the inputs that will be required to make it possible to carry out that defense strategy complex.

Any economist knows that, by definition, the quantity of a highly specialized input cannot be changed rapidly. If it could be, it would not by definition be highly specialized. The economic constraint which we could foresee if we had a more precise delineation of the alternative defense strategy complexes would concern itself with possibilities of changing the quantities of the highly specialized inputs required for the implementation of each complex within a period of time short enough for that complex to be useful.

By and large, this is a problem that is independent of the posture that any one of us wishes to assume with respect to Federal budgetary policy. I would submit also that the relationship of such economic constraints to the question of the rate of economic growth is extremely remote, except at the highest level of generalization.

That is a preamble that gets me around to the question of what difference it makes whether you have this, that, or the other form of tax structure. The answer is: only on the context of the presumption, which I regard as poor, that the rate at which the economy expands is relevant to the question of economic constraints on potential for pursuing a flexible defense strategy, but even in the case structural tax changes may not have as large an effect on the growth rate as is popularly supposed.

Essentially, what I have observed in my paper is that if the context in which changes in the tax structure are to be examined is one of a high rate of utilization of our resources, then I am skeptical, on the basis of a lack of empirical demonstration, that any of the popularly advocated changes in that structure will be significantly consequential for the rate at which we see the economy's productive capacity expanded.

For example, I think that many of the changes of the tax treatment of the corporate area are moving in the right direction. But in terms of one limited exercise in quantifying the magnitude of these effects, it suggests that really it doesn't make an awful lot of difference whether or not we adopt such proposals or concentrate on an entirely different criterion for adjusting the tax system in the future.

I come to a similarly uncertain conclusion with respect to what tax changes can do to induce a higher rate of activity with respect to certain other types of behavior that presumably contribute to economic growth. On the whole, it seems to me that, insofar as economic growth really is an important factor in the development of our defense capabilities in the future, that we ought to be concerned more with the broad, more aggregate aspects of fiscal and monetary policy in stimulating rapid growth than with specific structural features, such as those involving modest changes in the Federal tax system.

*Johnson:* I would like now to turn to the statements from Dr. Briefs' paper and ask him to comment on them.

We have tried to make three basic points in this paper. First, it appears to us that the economic growth process is much more complicated than a straight-forward aggregate demand approach to the analysis of our growth problems tends to imply. From time to time, shifts taking place in the economy involve structural changes, lagging adjustments, and hesitation effects which make it very unlikely that a modern private-property economy can grow more or less continuously along a full-employment ceiling— with or without a sophisticated policy mix.

\* \* \* \*

Secondly, in our judgment, strong structural shifts have taken place in the past ten years, and particularly since 1955. The most important of these was the shift toward investment in human capital formation and more specifically in research and development investment. It appears that this and other shifts have not yet been sufficiently digested. As a consequence, the economy has been through a period of hesitation and reorganization in its growth patterns.

\* \* \* \*

Third, basic changes, likely to be strongly stimulating in their economic effects, can be expected during the decade ahead. In terms of quantitative importance, these cluster around population growth and changes in its composition. Economic growth is likely to be strong in the areas of housing and related consumer durables,

education, and urban-satellite community development. Combined
with the likelihood of increasing returns on past capital formation
in human beings and especially in research and related work, these
developments should produce strong expansions during the next
ten years.

Henry Briefs

*Briefs:* I would like to go beyond the statements that are made
here and address myself to Dr. Eckstein's comments. The thrust
of his remarks was, I think, that if we want to get within range
of the defense appropriations called for by some of the con-
ferees, the right way to go about it is to step up the rate of
over-all economic advance. This view is shared by quite a group
of influential economists. Reduced to its barest essentials, the
argument on which it rests goes something like this:

First, it is asserted that we can achieve full-employment and
a substantially higher rate of economic growth than in the past.
New advances in economics have provided policy tools capable
getting us up to such a rate and of sustaining that rate. Tendencies toward inflationary over-full employment on the one hand,
and periodic slow-downs or recessions on the other, can now be
contained.

Secondly, this sustained expansion, from present GNP to its
"full" potential value in 1972, would result in a certain flow of
federal revenues, depending on tax rates. Judging by several
recent attempts to estimate potential economic performance,
and by the work of Dr. Eckstein and others on the relationships
between economic growth and budgetary developments, it is
apparent that federal revenues would make very large gains
as a result of a faster, sustained rate of expansion. National
security appropriations, presumably, could gain in proportion
without difficulty.

Thirdly, since economic growth has been slow and has left
us with under-employed resources, it does not make too much
sense to use recent revenue and expenditure levels as a basis
for evaluating the possibilities for substantially larger national
security appropriations. Such an approach winds up worrying
primarily about the allocation of resources between the private
and the public sector, within the latter, between security related
allocation and the rest. The right approach, so the argument
goes, is to make the pie bigger faster. If the steps are taken that
can assure a high, sustained rate of economic growth, budgetary
limitations on defense and related desiderata are not likely to be
more than a routine problem.

My position in regard to this argument is this: an economy such as ours, characterized by a great deal of decentralized decision-making as it is, can be quite inflexible over shorter periods of time. Some of our major economic and political institutions, for example, strongly work in that direction. In my judgment it is therefore not likely, that we can have continuously sustained, near full-employment growth. Historical experience, certainly, supports skepticism in this regard. Our kind of an economy has sometimes grown faster, at other times slower, but certainly not at a sustained, full-employment rate.

As for the recent efforts to estimate not only *potential* growth, but also the effectiveness of the instrumental variables which the Government could use in various combinations to steer an economic course, this work is very much in its initial, heroic-assumptions stage. One indication of the experimental character of these efforts is the disagreement as to whether it is, or is not, a near-impossible task to raise the long-term full-employment growth rate by one percentage point without significant change in our institutions.

It is possible to argue, of course, that uninterrupted, stepped-up economic growth is so important as to require drastic policy actions, including modification of institutions and values. I do not believe the situation that confronts us calls for such drastic measures. Quite the contrary, the indications are that the economic expansions of the next decade are more apt to be strong than weak and unsatisfactory.

I have done some detailed projections of population changes, isolating those groups of families and children which are likely to originate much of new demand for housing, consumer durables, educational facilities, and related goods and services. Frankly, the picture I got looks explosive. As far as this goes, there is definite reason for believing that much of the private sector and whatever is connected with education is in for much stronger demand growth than in the past few years.

In addition, spending on research and development has increased at an extraordinary pace over the past decade—so rapidly, in fact, that the addition of private expenditures along these lines to the usual statistics on business fixed investment raises serious doubts as to whether private investment over the last few years was actually much of a disappointment as source of growth. I think it is reasonable to expect that the full effect of R&D capital formation during the past 10 years is still ahead, and that this build-up in knowledge capital represents an accumulation of investment opportunities similar to the backlog of opportunities that affected economic activity in the years following World War II so strongly.

Another major configuration in the outlook picture is the un-resolved problem of unscrambling our large population centers. That is where most of the increase in 2- and 3-child families and in high-school and college populations is going to take place. Here is an area in which Government entrepreneurship can have great effect, by removing constraints on investment and economic development generally, by its own direct investment, and in many other ways. All of this will surely give additional impetus to the expansions ahead.

On the basis of these underlying trends—and I concede they provide only a partial fix on what is in prospect—it seems to me that we are in for a period of strong rather than hesitant economic advance. The timing of these changes is difficult to judge, but there is a suggestion in the figures I have examined that the pressures for more rapid economic advance will become stronger after 1965.

By these lights, it appears that drastic expansionary policies—especially actions which may prove difficult to moderate or reverse—should be avoided. I am very much afraid that literal-minded efforts to bring about and sustain more or less continuously the extra rapid economic growth called for on many sides may result in just such policies, leading to unfortunate longer-term consequences. As for the budgetary implications of the prospective developments sketched, it seems that questions about the allocation of Government expenditures may after all turn out to be of great importance. Conflict between claims on resources for national security purposes, the resource demands made by other public programs, and those of economic development generally may well become a characteristic feature of the period before us.

# Notes on Contributors

ARLEIGH BURKE is Director of the Center for Strategic Studies, Georgetown University. During the Korean War he was a member of the United Nations Truce Delegation to negotiate a military armistice in Korea. In 1952 he became Director of the Strategic Plans Division of the Office of the Chief of Naval Operations. In 1955 he was named Chief of Naval Operations, and served in that post until 1961. He is a recipient of the James V. Forrestal Award, a Member of the Atlantic Council, and Member of the Board of Visitors of the Fletcher School of Law and Diplomacy.

DAVID M. ABSHIRE, co-editor of the present volume, is Executive Secretary of the Center for Strategic Studies, Georgetown University. A graduate of the United States Military Academy, he served in command and staff intelligence positions in the Korean War, and has written for professional journals and other publications on military and international affairs. Dr. Abshire is also Program Advisor to the American Enterprise Institute for Public Policy Research.

RICHARD V. ALLEN, co-editor of the present volume, is Research Associate at the Center for Strategic Studies, Georgetown University. He has taught in the University of Maryland's European Division and at Georgia Institute of Technology, has lectured at the University of South Carolina and at American University, and has contributed to various professional journals.

BRIG. GEN. DONALD ARMSTRONG, USA (Ret), was Commandant of the National Strategy Seminars for Reserve Officers at the National War College and Commandant of the Industrial College of the Armed Forces. After serving in the United States Army for thirty-six years, he became Consultant to the United States Information Agency, and was named a Fellow of the American Association for the Advancement of Science. He was a principal contributor to *American Strategy for the Nuclear Age* (1960).

JAMES D. ATKINSON is Associate Professor of Government and Research Associate at the Center for Strategic Studies, Georgetown University. Past President of the American Military Institute, he has contributed to *Soviet Total War* (1956) and *American Strategy for the Nuclear Age* (1960), and is author of *The Edge of War* (1960).

MORRIS BORNSTEIN is Associate Professor of Economics, University of Michigan, and is currently on leave, under a Ford Foundation Faculty Research Fellowship, at Harvard University, where he is an Associate of the Russian Research Center. He has been a consultant to the Fulbright-Smith-Mundt program, and to the Joint Economic Committee of the United States Congress. He is co-editor of *The Soviet Economy: A Book of Readings* (1962).

KARL BRANDT is Director of the Food Research Institute and Professor of Economic Policy, Stanford University. A former member of the President's Council of Economic Advisors, he is the author of *The Reconstruction of World Agriculture* (1945), and *The Management of Food and Agriculture in the German-Occupied and Other Areas of Fortress Europe: A Study in Military Government* (1953).

HENRY W. BRIEFS is Associate Professor of Economics, Director of the Graduate Program in Public Policy Economics, and Research Associate at the Center for Strategic Studies, Georgetown University. Formerly Senior Staff Economist of the Council of Economic Advisors, he is the author of *Three Views of Method in Economics* (1960), and *Pricing Power and "Administrative" Inflation* (1962).

W. GLENN CAMPBELL is Director of the Hoover Institution on War, Revolution, and Peace, Stanford University. Formerly Director of Research at the American Enterprise Institute for Public Policy Research, to which he is now Program Advisor, and former Research Economist with the U.S. Chamber of Commerce, he is co-author of the U.S. Senate Report, *American Competitive Enterprise, Foreign Economic Development and the Aid Programs* (1957), *American Competitive Enterprise Economy* (1953), and *Economics of Mobilization of War* (1952).

KARL H. CERNY is Associate Professor of Government and Research Associate at the Center for Strategic Studies, Georgetown University. During 1958-1959 he was Fulbright Professor of Political Science at the University of Nijmegen. He has contributed to *America* magazine, and is currently working on a text in comparative government.

HERBERT S. DINERSTEIN is Head of the Soviet Section of the Social Science Division, the RAND Corporation. He is author of *Communism and the Russian Peasant* and *Moscow in Crisis* (1955), *War and the Soviet Union* (1955), and co-editor of *Soviet Military Strategy* (1963).

OTTO ECKSTEIN is Professor of Economics at Harvard University. Formerly technical Director of the Congressional Joint Economic Committee study on Employment, Growth, and Price Levels, he is author of *Water Resource Development: The Economics of Project Evaluation* (1958), and *Trends in Public Expenditures in the Next Decade* (1959).

ROGER A. FREEMAN is a Senior Staff Member of the Hoover Institution on War, Revolution, and Peace, Stanford University, and was formerly Special Assistant to the Governor of the State of Washington. In addition to having published numerous articles in professional journals and magazines, he is author of the two-volume study, *Financing the Public Schools* (1958, 1960).

GOTTFRIED HABERLER is Professor of Economics, Harvard University and current President of the American Economic Association. He is a past President of the International Economic Association, and since 1953 has been Honorary President. His *Prosperity and Depression*, originally published in English and French, has undergone four editions, numerous impressions, and translation into Japanese, Swedish, Greek, and German. He is also author of *Inflation: Its Causes and Cures* (1961).

THOMAS F. JOHNSON is Director of Research, The American Enterprise Institute for Public Policy Research, Washington, D.C. Formerly Research Economist with the United States Chamber of Commerce and Assistant Commissioner of the Federal Housing Administration, he is author of *Small Business, Its Prospects and Its Problems* (1951), and *The Price of Price Controls* (1953), and co-author of *The American Competitive Enterprise Economy* (1953), and *Renewing America's Cities* (1962).

HERMAN KAHN is Director of the Hudson Institute, and was previously associated with the RAND Corporation for twelve years. He has lectured at universities throughout the country and has served as a consultant to numerous government agencies and private concerns. He is author of *On Thermonuclear War* (1960), and *Thinking About the Unthinkable* (1962).

STEPHEN D. KERTESZ is Professor of Political Science, University of Notre Dame, and Chairman of the Committee on International Relations. In 1947 he was Hungarian Minister to Italy. He is Advisory Editor of the *Review of Politics*, author of *Diplomacy in a Whirlpool: Hungary Between Nazi Germany and the Soviet Union*, and editor of and contributor to five symposia: *The Fate of East Central Europe* (1956), *Diplomacy in a Changing World* (1959), *What America Stands For* (1959), *American Diplomacy in a New Era* (1961), and *East Central Europe and the World: Developments in the Post-Stalin Era* (1962).

WILLIAM R. KINTNER is Professor of International Relations and Political Science, and Deputy Director of the Foreign Policy Research Institute, University of Pennsylvania. He has served as Special Assistant to President Eisenhower and as Consultant to the Draper Committee. He is author of *The Front is Everywhere* (1950), and co-author of *Forging a New Sword* (1958), *Protracted Conflict* (1959), *The Haphazard Years* (1960), *A Forward Strategy for America* (1961), and *The New Frontier of War* (1962).

HENRY KISSINGER is Associate Professor of Government, faculty member of the Center for International Affairs, and Director of the Defense Studies Program, Harvard University. He is also Director of the Harvard International Seminar. He is author of *A World Restored: Castlereagh, Metternich and the Restoration of Peace, 1812-1822* (1957), *Nuclear Weapons and Foreign Policy* (1957), and *The Necessity For Choice: Prospects of American Foreign Policy* (1962).

KURT L. LONDON is Professor of International Affairs and Director of the Institute for Sino-Soviet Studies, George Washington University. During World War II he was associated with the Office of War Information, and later served with the Department of State and the Department of Defense. He is author of *How Foreign Policy is Made* (1949), and *The Permanent Crisis*

(1962), and editor of *Unity and Contradiction: Major Aspects of Sino-Soviet Relations* (1962), and the forthcoming *New Nations in a Divided World*.

EDWARD S. MASON is Lamont University Professor, Harvard University. During World War II he was Chief Economist of the Office of Strategic Services, and was later Deputy Assistant Secretary of State. He has been a member of numerous Presidential Commissions, including currently the Committee to Strengthen the Security of the Free World. He is author of *The Corporation in Modern Society* (1960), *Promoting Economic Development* (1955), and *Economic Planning in Underdeveloped Areas* (1958).

ALBERT J. MEYER is Associate Professor of Middle Eastern Studies and Associate Director of the Center for Middle Eastern Studies, Harvard University. He was formerly Associate Professor of Economics and Executive Assistant to the President, The American University of Beirut. His publications include *Middle Eastern Capitalism: Nine Essays* (1959), and *The Economy of Cyprus* (1962).

OSKAR MORGENSTERN is Professor of Political Economy and Director of the Econometric Research Program, Princeton University. He is author of *The Question of National Defense* (1959) and *International Financial Transactions* (1959), and co-author of *The Theory of Games and Economic Behavior* (1953).

GERHART NIEMEYER is Professor of Political Science, University of Notre Dame, and is currently Fulbright Professor, University of Munich. He has served with the Policy Planning Staff of the Department of State, and has taught at Princeton, Oglethorpe, Columbia, and Vanderbilt Universities. He is author of *Law Without Force* (1941), *An Inquiry Into Soviet Mentality* (1956), and *Facts on Communism: The Communist Ideology* (1959), and co-editor of the *Handbook On Communism* (1962).

G. WARREN NUTTER is Professor of Economics and Chairman of the Department of Economics, University of Virginia. He is also Associate Director of the University's Thomas Jefferson Center for Studies in Political Economy. His publications include *Extent of Enterprise Monopoly in the United States* (1951), and *The Growth of Industrial Production in the Soviet Union* (1962), and numerous articles in professional journals.

STEFAN POSSONY is Director of the International Studies Program at the Hoover Institution on War, Revolution, and Peace, and is Research Associate at the Center for Strategic Studies and the Foreign Policy Research Institute. Formerly Special Advisor to the United States Air Force, he is author of *Lenin* (1963), and co-author of *A Forward Strategy for America* (1962), *International Relations In the Age of the Conflict Between Democracy and Dictatorship* (1954), and *A Century of Conflict: Communist Techniques of World Revolution, 1848-1950* (1953).

VIRGIL SALERA is Professor of Business and Economics, Alameda State College. Formerly Senior Economist at the American Enterprise Institute for Public Policy Research and member of the Senior Staff of the Council of Economic Advisors, he is co-author of *International Economics* (1947, 1951, 1957), *Elementary Economics* (1950, 1954), and *Government and Politics in Latin America* (1958).

THOMAS C. SCHELLING is Professor of Economics and faculty member of the Center for International Affairs, Harvard University. He is a member of the Scientific Advisory Board of the United States Air Force, and is an editor of the *Quarterly Journal of Economics*, the *Review of Economics and Statistics*, the *Journal of Conflict Resolution*, and *World Politics*. His recent books include *International Economics* (1958), *The Strategy of Conflict* (1960), and *Strategy and Arms Control* (1960).

JAMES R. SCHLESINGER is with the Economics Department of the RAND Corporation, and has taught at the University of Virginia. He is a consultant to the Board of Governors of the Federal Reserve System, and is author of *The Political Economy of National Security* (1960).

IRVING H. SIEGEL is Chief of the Economic and Costing Division, Research Analysis Corporation. He is a former Senior Staff Member of the Council of Economic Advisors, and directed the American Technology Study of the Twentieth Century Fund. He is author of *Soviet Labor Productivity* (1952) and has published numerous articles in professional journals.

WILLIAM S. STOKES is Senior Professor of Comparative Political Institutions, Claremont Men's College, and in 1962-63 was Professor of Foreign Affairs at the National War College. He is author of *Latin American Politics* (1959), *Honduras, An*

*Area Study* (1950), has contributed to more than a dozen symposia on Latin America, and has published numerous articles in English and Spanish.

ROBERT STRAUSZ-HUPÉ is Professor of Political Science and Director of the Foreign Policy Research Institute, University of Pennsylvania. He is Executive Editor of *ORBIS*, author of *The Balance of Tomorrow* (1945), *The Zone of Indifference* (1952), and *Power and Community* (1955), and co-author of *American-Asian Tensions* (1954), *The Idea of Colonialism* (1958), *Protracted Conflict* (1959), and *A Forward Strategy For America* (1961).

GEORGE E. TAYLOR is Executive Officer of the Department of Far Eastern and Slavic Languages and Literature, and Director of the Far Eastern and Russian Institute, University of Washington. He has lectured at the National War College, the Army War College, and the Air University, and is author of *The Struggle for North China* (1940), *America in the New Pacific* (1942), and *The Far East in the Modern World* (1956).

EDWARD TELLER is Professor of Physics at Large and Director of the Lawrence Radiation Laboratory, University of California. One of the developers of the atomic energy effort in the United States, he has made significant contributions to the development of atomic weapons and the hydrogen bomb. He has served as an advisor to the Atomic Energy Commission and as Director, Livermore Laboratory. He is author of *The Legacy of Hiroshima* (1962).

FRANK N. TRAGER is Professor of International Affairs, New York University, and from 1961-63 was Professor of International Affairs at the National War College. Former Director of the Point Four Mission in Burma and Visiting Professor at Yale University, his recent books include *Marxism in Southeast Asia* (1959), *Building a Welfare State in Burma* (1958), and the forthcoming *The Struggle for Mainland Southeast Asia: Laos, A Pivot*.

NORMAN B. TURE is Director of Tax Studies at the National Bureau of Economic Research. He was formerly Staff Economist of the Joint Economic Committee of the United States Congress, and is author of *The Federal Revenue System: Facts and Problems* (1961).

RICHARD L. WALKER is Director of the Institute of International Studies and Head of the Department of International

Studies, University of South Carolina. He has taught at Yale, Taiwan National University, and the National War College. He has published more than a score of articles in various journals and is author of *The Multi-State System of Ancient China* (1954), *China Under Communism: The First Five Years* (1955), *China and the West: Cultural Collision* (1956), and *The Continuing Struggle: Communist China and the Free World* (1958).

MURRY L. WEIDENBAUM is Senior Industrial Economist at Stanford Research Institute, and until recently was Corporate Economist of the Boeing Company and taught at the University of Washington. In recent years he has served as a consultant to the United States Department of Labor and the United States Arms Control and Disarmament Agency. He is author of various monographs and articles on military economics and governmental expenditures.

KARL A. WITTFOGEL is Professor of Chinese History in the Department of Far Eastern and Slavic Languages and History, University of Washington, and has published numerous articles on China and the Far East. He is author of *Mao Tse-tung, Liberator or Destroyer of the Chinese Peasants?* (1955), and *Oriental Despotism: A Comparative Study of Total Power* (1957).

ARNOLD WOLFERS is Director of the Washington Center of Foreign Policy Research, The Johns Hopkins University, and Sterling Professor Emeritus of International Relations, Yale University. Consultant to the Institute for Defense Analyses, the Department of State, and the Army War College, he is co-author of *The Anglo-American Tradition* (1956), *Alliance Policy in the Cold War* (1959), and author of *Discord and Collaboration* (1962).

# INDEX

CEMA (COMECON), 56, 59, 89, 102, 104, 139-40
CENTO, 8, 32
Central American Bank of Economic Integration, 376
Central Committee of the Communist Party, 6, 9, 49-51, 55, 67
Central Intelligence Agency, 665
Cerny, Karl H., 169, 175, 181, 184-85, 187, 192-94, 197, 199, 201-5, 207-8, 425, 432, 437, 443, 450, 453, 456, 459, 467, 469-70
Chapultepec, Act of, 376
Chemical Warfare, 652-53
Ch'en Yi, 83, 87
Chiang Kai-shek, 25, 26, 283
Chile, 571
China, Communist, 39, 44, 48, 60, 62-66, 71, 73, 122, 123, 126, 270, 279-85, 290, 394, 722; and Cuba, 91; capacity to wage war, 178; conquest of, 14, 25; economic plans, 128, 133, 137; economic problems, 90, 181; goals in Southeast Asia, 360; "Great Leap Forward" 71, 79, 84, 152, 178, 334, 696; nuclear capability, 87-88, 133, 174, 176, 184-86, 204-5; population, 90; trade, 114, 115
China, Imperial, 78-79, 89
Chinese Communist Party, 45, 61, 63, 78, 81, 171
Chinese Nationalist Troops (KMT), 341
Chou En-lai, 152, 329, 573
Churchill, Winston S., 23, 612
CINCEUR, 392
Civil Defense Program, 593, 645-48, 736, 794, 986, 988, 998
Civil Rights, 238
Clabaugh, Samuel F., 761-63
Clark, Colin, 884
Clausewitz, 65, 392, 395, 402
Cohn, Stanley, 152
Cold War, 218, 226, 247, 249-50, 269, 274, 275, 283, 285, 287, 289-90, 343, 406, 594, 669, 713
Collective Security, 257, 259, 289, 470
Colm, Gerhard, 888

Colombo Plan, 249
COMECON (See CEMA)
Cominform, 64, 331
Comintern, 60
Committee for Economic Development, 768, 775
Common Market (See European Economic Community)
Communist Aggression in Asia, 333, 336
Communist Bloc (See Sino-Soviet Bloc) 6, 44, 49, 59, 63-67, 72, 73, 286; economic unification, 140; exports, 136; trade, 134, 136-37
Communist Foreign Policy, 219, 428, 429
Communist Movement, 64, 72, 269-70, 277
Communist Party of the Soviet Union (See CPSU)
Communist subversion, 8, 142
Conflict management, 393, 398, 504
Confrontation, direct, 284, 404
Confrontation, indirect, 284, 443-62
Confucianism, 91
Congo, 283, 286, 404, 455, 944
Containment, 12, 23-24, 224, 229, 244-45, 276, 339-40, 427, 435, 440, 442n., 457, 471, 614
Conventional forces, 279-82
Council of Economic Advisors, 806, 841, 843, 858, 921, 925
Counter-insurgency operations, 390
CPSU, 5, 41-42, 45-46, 48-51, 55, 67, 72, 171, 392; 20th Congress of, 59, 67, 103, 105; 21st Congress of, 60, 92; 22nd Congress of, 9, 60, 92, 99
Cuba, 11, 37, 48, 70, 73, 135, 163, 270, 276, 283, 287, 362, 382, 406, 575, 597, 602-4, 613, 615, 665, 667, 685; Crisis of 1962, 177, 200, 255, 296, 376, 400, 403-4, 413, 460, 571-72, 901, 942, 947, 950; embargo of, 404 (See Bay of Pigs Invasion)
Czechoslovakia, 13, 24, 60, 283, 590; coup d'état, 24

1032

Mao Tse-tung, 62-64, 67, 70-71, 90-92, 219, 229, 283-84; alliance with Stalin, 77

Marshall Plan, 24, 29, 35, 239, 330, 457, 657, 659, 772

Marshall, Alfred, 843

Marx, Karl, 45

Marxism-Leninism, 5, 43, 45-46, 50, 53, 61, 66-68, 72, 87, 218, 608

Massive retaliation, 28, 278-79, 298, 580, 591, 598

Materials Policy Commission, 956

Matsumura, Kenzo, 86-87

May, Carl, 578

Melman, Seymour, 820

Menon, Krishna, 358

Merchant, Livingston S., 305

Meyer, Albert J., 752-55

Middle East, 11, 15, 450-53; Arab-Israeli conflict, 323; arms expenditures, 320; economic development, 752; economic growth, 318; oil, 321

Military assistance program, 286, 389, 793

Military doctrine, US, 389

Military training, 731-32

Minimum deterrence, 612-13

"Missile gap," 605-6, 953

Mobilization, 824-25

Molotov, Vyacheslav, 50

Monetary policy, US, 899, 1016

Mongolia, 89

Monroe Doctrine, 374

Morgenstern, Oskar, 643, 730-32, 741-42

Multilateral Force (See NATO, Nuclear Force)

Nagy, Imre, 58

Napoleon, 402

Nassau Agreement, 304, 311, 620

National Academy of Sciences, 956-57

National Aeronautical and Space Agency (NASA), 773, 797, 799

National Guard, 988

National Planning Association, 813, 821, 978

National policy, goals of, 947

National Science Foundation, 857

National Security Council, 392, 398; Executive Committee, 403-04, 410; Planning Board, 403

Nationalism, 15, 944

NATO, 8, 14, 16, 29, 32, 35, 132, 138-39, 216, 225-26, 239, 270, 278-79, 281, 296-97, 315, 392, 483, 496, 555, 558, 619-20, 686; Air Defense Group, 665; Co-ordinating Committee, 659, 661, 666, 668; Council, 304; possible disintegration of, 561; nuclear force, 300ff, 622-29; nuclear weapons, 554, 559, 561-62, 594, 617-18; Polaris submarine offer, 303, 560; political integration, 316; strategic trade, 142; US leadership of, 560, 562

Nazi Party, 30, 53

Nehru, 15, 117, 357

Nenni Socialists, 312

Netherlands, 306, 679

New Economic Policy (NEP), 71, 188

New Frontier, 346, 407

Nicaragua, 602

Niemeyer, Gerhart, 425, 428-30, 441-42, 442n., 443n., 445n.

Nigeria, 695

Nitze, Paul, 392

"No cities" doctrine, 502, 510, 511

North Atlantic Treaty Organization (see NATO)

Norway, 716

Nuclear disengagement, 312

Nuclear energy, peaceful use of, 755-57

Nuclear forces, British, French, German, 294-300, 312-16, 617-21, 622-29

Nuclear stalemate, 427-28

Nuclear test ban, 471, 556-58, 561, 605, 621-22

*Nuestra América*, 366-67, 375

Nutter, G. Warren, 176, 181, 189, 198-99

Nth Country Problem, 554, 594

Old Age and Survivors Insurance, 788

Organization of American States, 375, 446

Organization for Economic Co-operation and Development (OECD), 152, 243, 251

Organization of Petroleum Exporting Countries (OPEC), 321-22, 755

Pacifism, 14

Pakistan, 357

Pathet Lao, 361

Pavlovian conditioning, 46, 943

Peace Corps, 266, 324-25

Peace movements, 570, 578-79

Peaceful coexistence, 8, 93, 101-2, 219, 613, 673, 943, 1007

Perón regime, 370, 698

Peter the Great, 82

Philippine Island, 722

Piel, Gerard, 821, 826

Point Four Program, 224, 227

Poland, 24, 58-60, 284

Polaris weapons system, 301-2, 308, 354, 452, 462, 542, 560-61, 586, 620-21, 623

Politburo, 394

Polycentrism, 38-39, 59, 62, 67-68, 102, 152, 170-81, 218, 265, 338, 414

Population explosion, 216

Possony, Stefan T., 619-21, 630-34, 653, 734-35, 988-89, 992

Power Economy versus Subsistence Economy, 191

Pre-emption, 604

Pre-emptive attack, 298, 540-41

Pre-emptive capability, Soviet, 33

Presidium of the Supreme Soviet, 42, 50-51, 69, 392, 394

Price structure, 716

Productivity, US, 719, 841, 843, 853, 861, 910, 914, 923-24, 953

Project Plowshare, 595

Propaganda, 7, 221, 393, 399; Communist, 231, 284; peace, 14

Qatar, 318

Quarantine, 685

Quintana, Segundo V. Linares, 382

Railroads, 901

Research and Development (R&D), 131-32, 338, 796, 799, 808, 835-38, 855, 857-59, 872, 891, 933, 935, 953, 957-59, 1020

Revisionism, 59

Rockefeller, Nelson, 590

Rodó, José Enrique, 367, 372

Roll-back, 432-443, 471

Roosa, Robert, 906-7

Roosevelt, Franklin D., 257

Roosevelt, Theodore, 223, 257

RS-70 controversy, 968, 989

Rusk, Dean, 402

Russell, Lord Bertrand, 575

Salera, Virgil, 746, 748

Sanctions, trade, 693

Sanders, Thomas, 931

Sarnoff, Gen. David, 10, 584

Schelling, Thomas C., 626-28, 645-49, 652-53, 735-36, 988

Schilling, Warner R., 972

Schlesinger, James R., 737-40, 745-46, 748

Schultz, Theodore, 855, 857, 934

Schultze, Charles, 852

"Science City" at Novosibirsk, 133

SEATO (Southeast Asia Treaty Organization), 8, 331-32, 339, 346, 358, 435-36, 463, 681

Second-strike force, 539, 615-16

Senate Select Committee on National Water Resources, 789

Senate Subcommittee on National Policy Machinery, 967, 973

Shute, Neville, 323

Siegel, Irving H., 1002, 1007, 1010

Sino-Indian conflict (1962), 88-89, 342n.

Sino-Soviet aid, extent of, 105-6, 111-12, 134-36, 335

Sino-Soviet Bloc (See Communist Bloc), 4, 62-63, 78, 126, 132, 138, 276, 284, 286, 288-89, 658, 660-61, 711, 718; economic offensive, 104-7, 112-13, 121; technicians in underdeveloped countries, 107-8

Sino-Soviet Friendship Association, 82, 84

Sino-Soviet trade, 100, 108, 134, 136; barter agreements, 109-12

Skybolt, 16, 297, 311, 462, 561, 591, 620, 968, 989

Smithies, Arthur, 826

Social insurance, 788-89

Sokolovsky, Marshal V. D., 556
Solow, Robert, 841 n.
Sovnarkhoz, 54
Southeast Asia Treaty Organization (see SEATO)
Sprin, V. G., Soviet specialist on Latin America, 371
Sputnik, 77
Stalin, 10, 23, 26, 42, 45-46, 48, 50, 52, 58-59, 63, 67, 80, 83, 283, 330, 944
Stevenson, Adlai, 235, 404, 571
Stock Exchange, 900
Stokes, William S., 339, 438, 444-50
Strategic Air Command, 306, 500, 506, 603, 605
Strategic risk, 296
Strategy, budgetary constraints upon, 395, 923-25, 965-72; Cold War, 101, 169, 247-56, 261, 341-43, 345, 390, 481, 594, 669, 881, 985; Communist trade, 100, 102, 105, 107-11, 114-18; counterforce, 427, 433, 493, 509, 514, 549, 615, 638; custodial, 945-46; definition of, 396, 541, 675, 946-47; economic constraints upon, 39, 42, 56-57, 99, 163-64, 181-84, 272, 399, 544-45, 675-76, 967, 1010; entrepreneurial, 946-47, 950; economic, 662, 709, 718-19; first strike, 541, 551, 990; flexible response, 315, 560; and foreign policy, 690-91; and limited war, 644; managerial, 945-46; Marxist-Leninist, 45-47, 50-51, 68, 393-94; objectives of, 261, 263, 400, 425, 428, 430-32, 433n., 435, 673-74; political constraints upon, 389, 392, 396, 399, 404; psycho-political, 13, 17, 263, 295, 297, 390, 399, 538, 543, 556, 558, 622; requirements of, 536, 546-47, 563; roll-back, 28, 339-41, 432-43; second-strike, 539, 551, 564; of superiority, 13, 32-34, 296, 428, 431, 433n., 442n., 563-65, 633; of surrender, 537-38; of technological superiority, 7, 13, 34, 389, 442n., 543-44, 551, 565

Subconventional forces, 282
Succession in Sino-Soviet Bloc, 47, 194-97, 255
Suez Canal, 37
Sukarno, 343
Summit Conference (1960), 605
Supreme Soviet, 46
Sweden, 299, 592, 716
Switzerland, 299, 592, 716
Syria, 134-35, 288
Taiwan, 89, 283; agrarian reform, 751; economic growth, 701
Tariffs, 718, 758, 760
Taxes, 690, 827, 857-58, 930, 1009-11, 1017-18
Taylor, George E., 170, 173, 179, 188, 193, 198, 740, 741, 744-45
Taylor, Maxwell, 341, 354-56, 392, 403, 967
Technical resources, 563
Technological superiority, 220
Technology, control of, 548; role in strategy, 220, 541-42, 586; strategic requirements of, 536; threat of Soviet, 183, 208, 536; weapons, 216
Teller, Edward, 621-22, 628-29, 636, 644, 649-50, 652, 755-56, 988, 992, 998
Theory of games, 676-77
Thermonuclear attacks, 638-643
Third force movements, 11, 300, 309, 369
Tiflis, 5
Tirpitz, 612
Tito, Josip Broz, 23, 61, 64
de Tocqueville, Alexis, 223
Touré, Sekou, 174
Trade, 324, 659, 661-64, 666-67, 713, 738-41; with the Communist Bloc, 702-5
Trade Expansion Act, 225, 694, 760, 917
Trager, Frank, 432, 434-36, 436 n., 454, 455 n., 456 n., 462-64
Treaty of Rome (1957), 716-17
Treaty of Stockholm, 716
Truman, Harry S., 330; Truman Doctrine, 23-24, 224, 238-39, 330
Ture, Norman, 998, 1003, 1016
Turkey, 16, 282, 437, 596, 603

Underdeveloped countries, 747-57; Soviet policy toward, 37

Unemployment, 954

United Nations (UN), 217, 233, 257, 274, 285, 288, 350, 532, 572, 573, 796-97, 944-45; General Assembly, 233; Security Council, 233

United States, agricultural surplus, 593, 916, 1015; Asian defense policy, 331; equilibrium budget, 788; fiscal policy, 899; foreign aid, 737-38; gross national product, 840-42, 788, 925; cyclical growth, 843-46; inflation, 713, 904, 911-12

United States Berlin task force, 392

U Nu, 110

"Uniting for Peace" resolution, 233

USSR, Army, 52, 394; demobilization, 130; District Committees, 49; economic aid in Asia, 334-36; foreign aid, 111-12, 217; material comforts, 948, 950; military power, 129-30; military program, 608-10; nationalities in, 42; offensive in Middle East, 323; petroleum offensive, 103; standard of living, 113; strategy, 8-10, 15, 399

U Thant, 234, 943

U-2 incident, 238, 493, 573-74, 605

Venezuela, 571

Veterans expenditures (US), 775

"Veterans for Peace," 578

Viet Minh, 344, 361, 435

Vietnam, 332, 336 n., 341, 354-55, 360, 362, 404, 406, 432, 434-37, 439, 469-70, 571, 795

Walker, Richard L., 170-71, 175, 179, 185, 194, 196, 200, 202

War, economic (see warfare, economic); guerrilla, 88, 382, 390, 399, 408, 422, 436; limited, 7, 405, 596-97, 616, 795-96; national liberation, 7-8, 95, 102, 112, 114, 172, 342, 378, 381-82, 389, 399, 414, 538, 942, 950; non-nuclear, 130, 295, 490; nuclear, 9, 130, 674, 879-82; paramilitary, 571; psychological (see warfare, political and psychological); pre-emptive, 202-3; preventive, 539-41, 604; purpose of, 542; unlimited, 598, 616

Warfare, economic, 221, 284, 660-61, 674, 677, 741-47, 761-63; political and psychological, 13, 17, 215, 283-84, 389-90, 487

Warsaw Pact, 58-59

Weidenbaum, Murray L., 985, 987, 989, 997

Western Alliance, 9, 15-16, 126, 459-63

Western military programs, 608-10

Wilson, Charles E., 575

Wilson, Woodrow, 257

Wittfogel, Karl A., 178-79, 184, 191, 196

Wolf, Charles Jr., 698 n.

Wolfers, Arnold, 425-28, 433 n., 434, 439-40, 443, 453, 455, 458, 463-65, 635-36

World Communism, 42, 51, 66-68

World market, 711-15

World War I, 713, 775

World War II, 22, 32, 42, 239, 275, 277, 282, 288, 660, 877

Wyle, Frederick S., 628-29

Yalta, 22-26, 221

Yevtushenko, 57, 69

Yugoslavia, 23, 43-44, 58, 64, 67, 72

Zhukov, 50-51

*National Security: Political, Military, and Economic Strategies In the Decade Ahead* was designed and lithographed by The Hennage Lithograph Company, Inc. of Washington, D. C. The text was set in Century type face and printed on a wove finish offset paper especially made for this book.